May Hill Arbuthnot

Children and Books

Third Edition

CHILDREN AND BOOKS

THIRD EDITION

MAY HILL ARBUTHNOT

SCOTT, FORESMAN AND COMPANY

Preface

To my collaborators, the teachers, children, librarians, parents, and students who have helped make this book . . .

Children and Books grew in the first place out of the tantalizing questions adults are always asking: "What kind of books do children like?" "How can we get our children to read more and better books?" It grew also out of many observations of children choosing or rejecting books in their homes, nursery schools, libraries, and classrooms. It grew from watching artist-teachers using books in such happy and meaningful ways that the children reached new heights of appreciation and taste. It grew from the eager response of college students to the beauty and fun of children's books. It grew from watching parents share their joy in books with their children, making book lovers of them by sheer contagion. And it grew primarily from liking children and books.

Children and Books was planned as a textbook for children's literature courses in English and education departments and in library training schools of colleges and universities. It has been a special source of satisfaction to receive letters from students saying that they have kept their copies and have used them constantly for reference. Parents, camp directors, and Sunday-school teachers also write that *Children and Books* has been helpful, since it covers the reading interests—imaginative and factual—of children from two to fifteen or sixteen. Indeed, the heartwarming letters of appreciation that have continued to pour in over the years have led to the preparation of this third edition.

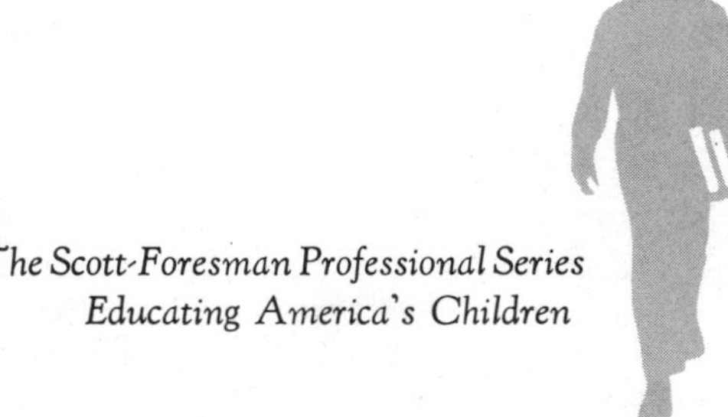

The Scott-Foresman Professional Series
Educating America's Children

THE THIRD EDITION

Anyone who has used the first or second editions of *Children and Books* will be interested in the changes that have been made in this third edition. The general approach and organization of the earlier editions have not been changed. But throughout the book, there have

L. C. Catalog #64-16003

Printed in the United States of America.
Regional offices of Scott, Foresman and Company are located in Atlanta, Dallas, Glenview, Palo Alto, and Oakland, N.J.

been a number of combinations, rearrangements, expansions, and revisions of parts and chapters.

Part One: Children Discover Books includes a new chapter, "The Artist and the Child's Books," which discusses the history of illustrations in children's books and evaluates briefly the work of some of the major artists, past and present. Accompanying this discussion is a sixteen-page color section with examples of the work of thirty-three artists. In *Part Two: Sing It Again,* the traditional poetry, formerly considered in two separate chapters, is presented in Chapter 5, "Mother Goose and the Ballads." And because nonsense verse merges so imperceptibly into light verse about the child's everyday world, these types of poetry are brought together in Chapter 6, "Poetry of the Child's World: Nonsense and Everyday." *Part Three: Once Upon a Time* now closes appropriately with Chapter 13, "Storytelling and Reading Aloud"—a substantial revision and expansion of what was formerly only a section of a chapter. The four chapters in *Part Four: Fiction and Stranger Than Fiction* have been rearranged so that this part now begins with "Animal Stories" and ends with "Biography." *Part Five: Reading Follows Many Paths* has two new chapters—"Reading and Creative Expression" and "Reading in the Family" and two chapters that are extensive revisions and expansions of material from the earlier edition —"Reading for Information" and "Reading and the Mass Media."

In every chapter there are new discussions of authors and books and also new illustrations. The bibliographies have been thoroughly revised and updated, and they have been placed along with the Suggested Readings, Problems, and Projects, immediately after the relevant chapters.

Because splendid anthologies of children's literature and also fine collections of children's books are accessible to most students in children's literature courses, it was thought that the Illustrative Selections could be safely omitted from this edition. But as in the earlier editions, the chapters on poetry provide many complete poems and the chapters on folk tales, animal stories, realistic stories, and biography provide excerpts and detailed evaluations of numerous books.

TO THE TEACHERS OF CHILDREN'S LITERATURE

Children and Books provides a full year's course in children's literature, which means that for courses of only one semester teachers must assign some chapters for detailed study and others for rapid reading or individual reports or possibly omit some. For example, Chapter 1, which is basic to the whole philosophy of guiding children's reading, should be read carefully and thoughtfully, but Chapters 2, 3, and 4 could be skimmed or reserved for later reading. Part Two, the poetry chapters, could be divided—the students who expect to teach younger children being responsible for the section on *Mother Goose* and for certain poets, particularly those in Chapter 6; and the students who expect to teach in the upper grades being responsible for the section on the ballads and for the poets who write at more mature levels. Both groups would, of course, read the chapters on using poetry with children and verse choirs. Through general discussions and reports, everyone in the class would gain some understanding of the total offering.

In Part Three, the sections on history and origins of folk tales could be omitted or skimmed, with primary emphasis being placed on the tales themselves. If your college offers a separate course in storytelling, Chapter 13, "Storytelling and Reading Aloud," need not be assigned. Otherwise divide your class into groups of five or six for practice in telling stories to each other and for discussions in which students can develop standards for both selecting and telling stories.

Part Five may be omitted or used only for reference. Eventually, though, teachers, librarians, and parents should read these chapters carefully. The criteria for evaluating different types of informational books are invaluable as are the suggestions for correlating the mass media and reading, and channeling reading into creative expression. The last chapter, which is concerned with the child's reading in the home and is addressed primarily to parents, will be useful to teachers and librarians who are called upon to advise parents on books for their children's reading or books to buy for them.

TO STUDENTS OF CHILDREN'S LITERATURE

Begin your study of *Children and Books* by scanning the table of contents and this preface to learn what in general the book covers. For your convenience, the guides to study, called "Suggested Reading, Problems, and Projects," and the bibliographies follow each chapter. The "Suggested Reading" usually lists a few children's books to be read along with the discussions in the text. Keep a brief record of each book you read for this course. A 3 x 5 index card should be adequate, but be sure you record the following information:

Author's full name
Title of book
Illustrator's full name
Publisher and year of publication
A very brief synopsis of the book
Your own evaluation of the book

When your judgment is at variance with the text, be sure you can produce valid reasons for the difference.

As you grow in knowledge of authors and illustrators, you will discover that certain names recur in different parts of the text. This repetition occurs because some authors have written both realism and fantasy, for example, and some artists have illustrated the books of others and also have written as well as illustrated their own books. Use the index to find the various discussions and examples of the work of authors and illustrators.

Don't be discouraged by the large numbers of books, authors, and artists in children's literature. You will be surprised by how quickly you become familiar with the outstanding ones and acquire a working knowledge of many others. On the other hand, don't be deceived by the fact that *Children and Books* reads easily. It carries a heavy load of information and principles of critical evaluation, which you must assimilate and learn to use in judging the new books you will encounter.

A NOTE ABOUT THE BIBLIOGRAPHIES

The bibliographies accompanying each chapter of necessity are selective rather than comprehensive. Many of your special favorites may be missing because it was possible to give only samplings of each type of book.

Some of the choice books or editions listed here were out of print when these bibliographies were compiled. They have been retained because of their importance as source material and also because there is always the reasonable hope that they will soon be in circulation again. And, of course, many of them are still available in large libraries. There are so many editions of such children's classics as *Grimm's Fairy Tales* and *Heidi,* that only a few have been listed. If these are not obtainable, others will serve.

The sale or merger of publishing companies is another problem in preparing bibliographies. Generally if a book is in print, we have tried to supply the name of the current publisher. If a book is out of print, we have retained the name of the original publisher.

The bibliographies provide only the first part of the name of a publishing company (for example, Scott for Scott, Foresman and Company). For the full names and addresses of publishers, refer to the alphabetical listing on pages 664-665.

Brief annotations are provided for books not discussed in the text. If a book has been discussed, the bibliography gives only the facts of publication. Age levels have been suggested—with apologies. Children's reading skills, social maturity, backgrounds, and interests are so varied that their taste in books is almost unpredictable. Moreover, a skillful teacher or parent can win enthusiastic support for almost any book he himself enjoys. The suggested age range of a book's appeal is, therefore, only a rough index.

Listings under each author are alphabetical, with the exception of a few series of books where chronological order indicates the order in which the books should be read.

ACKNOWLEDGMENTS

The author is grateful to the many users of *Children and Books* who have from time to time suggested ways in which the text might be made more generally useful to teachers and students. Particularly appreciated are the helpful critiques prepared on the second edition by John E. Brewton, George Peabody College for Teachers; Elizabeth H. Gross, Regional Librarian, Prince George's County Memorial Library, Hyattsville, Maryland; Mary Scott Morris, Arizona State University; Vera D. Petersen, Portland State College; Clarence K. Sandelin, Los Angeles State College of Applied Arts and Sciences; and Sara H. Wheeler, University of Washington.

It is with special gratitude that the author acknowledges the help in the preparation of this edition of Professor Mary Austin, of Western Reserve University. Professor Austin is responsible for the redevelopment and expansion of Chapter 18, "Reading for Information," and of Chapter 20, "Reading and the Mass Media." Her extensive and thorough knowledge of her subjects has made these two chapters a distinguished contribution. The author is also deeply grateful to Miss Margaret M. Clark, head of the Lewis Carroll Room of the Cleveland Public Library, who is responsible for the thoroughgoing revision and updating of the bibliographies for this edition. She also prepares *Keeping Up with Children and Books*. This booklet, published every two years, presents a selective listing of outstanding children's books, and is planned to keep up to date the bibliographies for *Children and Books* as well as those for *The Arbuthnot Anthology*.

Finally, the author is grateful to the many authors, illustrators, and publishers of children's books who have so graciously permitted reproduction of their work. She is hopeful that this reproduction and the discussions will call greater attention to their distinguished contributions to children's literature.

TO ALL ADULTS WHO MAY READ THIS BOOK

Parents or uncles and aunts wishing to buy books for children or to find out something about their reading interests may skip through these pages unhampered by Suggested Reading, Problems, Projects and impending examinations. For you, the books reviewed and the criteria in each chapter should be of special value. Learning of the delightful uses to which children have put their reading ought to be refreshing and helpful for all adults. What a pity that we grownups are no longer so moved by our reading that we must rush to our easels, seize brushes and paint pots, and record our enchantment in gay colors and uninhibited lines! Perhaps in these pages you will catch some hint of the first fine raptures a child feels when he encounters a book he loves. And perhaps from these pages there will emerge some clues to finding more of these treasures for each child—books he takes to bed with him, books he carries along on his summer vacations, books which tickle his risibilities or warm his heart, books to grow on. So, in conclusion, we wish you and your children as always "Happy reading!"

To my mother, Mary Elizabeth Hill, whose faith in her children
and joy in books and people never failed, and
To my husband, Charles Criswell Arbuthnot, whose wise counsel
and gay companionship made this long task possible and worthwhile,
CHILDREN AND BOOKS is dedicated with gratitude and love.

May Hill Arbuthnot

Cleveland, 1964

Contents

part one
Children Discover Books

1 THE CHILD AND HIS BOOKS 2

Competence—the need to achieve 3
Material security—the need for physical well-being 4
Intellectual security—the need to know 4
Emotional security—the need to love and to be loved 5
Acceptance—the need to belong 7
Play—the need for change 8
Aesthetic satisfaction—the need for beauty and order 10
Child guidance through books 10
Suggested reading, problems, and projects 14
References 14

2 THE ADULT AND THE CHILD'S BOOKS 16

Criteria for stories 17
Theme • Plot • Characters • Style
Criteria for other types of books 19
The range of stories for children 20
Picture-stories • Folk tales • Stories of family life • Historical fiction • Biography • Animal stories • Fantasy
Illustrations 23
Format 24
Book care 25
The school library 25
First aids to book selection 26
Suggested reading, problems, and projects 27
References 27

3 CHILDREN'S BOOKS: HISTORY AND TRENDS 30

Books begin 30
For grownups: fables, romances, adventures • For children: hornbooks and battledores • Pedlar's treasury: a tu'penny treat
The Puritans and perdition 33
In England • *Pilgrim's Progress* • In the New World
"Cheerfulness creeps in" 36
Fairy tales in France • John Newbery in England • Adventure at last • A satirical travel fantasy • Poets and children
Didacticism again 41
Rousseau, the apostle of freedom • Didacticism in France and England • Didacticism in the United States
Modern books begin 43
Fairy tales: the Grimms and Andersen • Laughter at last • Illustrations keep pace • Myths: Hawthorne and Kingsley • Realism with characters in place of types • Realism crosses the tracks • Children's literature comes of age
Trends in children's books today 47
Suggested reading, problems, and projects 49
References 49
Newbery Medal books 50
Caldecott Medal books 51

4 THE ARTIST AND THE CHILD'S BOOKS 52

The beginning of texts with pictures? 53
Japanese scroll, twelfth century
Woodcuts and engravings before 1800 54
Comenius and his *Orbis Pictus* • Thomas Bewick • William Blake
The nineteenth century 56
William Mulready • George Cruikshank • Sir John Tenniel • Arthur Hughes • Walter Crane • Kate Greenaway • Randolph Caldecott • Palmer Cox • Arthur Frost • Howard Pyle • Reginald Birch • Leslie Brooke
The twentieth century 60
E. Boyd Smith • Jessie Willcox Smith • Beatrix Potter • Arthur Rackham • Ernest H. Shepard • Newell Wyeth • Kurt Wiese • Wanda Gág • Conrad Buff • Marguerite de Angeli • James Daugherty • Maud and Miska Petersham • Feodor Rojankovsky • Dorothy Lathrop • Robert Lawson • Helen Sewell • Ludwig Bemelmans • Edward Ardizzone • Roger Duvoisin • Dr. Seuss • Ingri and Edgar Parin d'Aulaire • Lynd Ward • Leo Politi • Virginia Burton • Nicolas Mordvinoff • Garth Williams • Robert McCloskey • Leonard Weisgard • Barbara Cooney • Marcia Brown • Maurice Sendak • Irene Haas • Adrienne Adams • Nicolas Sidjakov
Suggested reading, problems, and projects 72
References 72

part two
Sing It Again

5 MOTHER GOOSE AND THE BALLADS 76

Mother Goose 76
Who was Mother Goose? 77

Dame Goose of Boston • *Ma Mère l'Oye* • Dame Goose in England
Early editions of *Mother Goose* 78
Newbery edition • Isaiah Thomas edition • Munroe and Francis editions
Origin of the verses 79
Mother Goose and history • Comparative studies in nursery rhymes
Qualities that charm the children 81
Variety • Musical quality • Action • Story interest • Humor • Illustrations
Popular modern editions 86
Realistic illustrations • Humorous illustrations • Decorative, imaginative illustrations
Variants of *Mother Goose* 89
ABC books
Uses of *Mother Goose* 90
In the home • In the school
Ballads and story-poems 94
Origins of the popular ballads 94
The minstrels • The clergy • Communal composition
Printed sources of the popular ballads 97
Early collectors • Bishop Percy • Francis James Child
Characteristics of the popular ballads 99
Musical quality • Dramatic quality • Abrupt beginnings and endings • Description • Incremental repetition • Anonymity • Subject matter
Using the traditional ballads with children 102
Language difficulty • A ballad program • Children's responses to the ballads • Correlation with school subjects
Folk ballads in the United States 105
American descendants of the popular ballads • Native ballads
Using the native ballads with children 106
Modern narrative poems 107
Poems for children five to nine • Story-poems for older children
Suggested reading, problems, and projects 111
References 112

May 17

6 POETRY OF THE CHILD'S WORLD: NONSENSE AND EVERYDAY *116*

Values of nonsense verse 116
Release from tensions • Relief from reason • Good ear-training • Bait to better poetry
Four poets of nonsense verse 117
Edward Lear • Lewis Carroll • Laura E. Richards • Leslie Brooke
From nonsense to humor 126
A.A. Milne • Rose Fyleman • Vachel Lindsay • Stephen Vincent Benét and Rosemary Carr Benét • James Whitcomb Riley • Eugene Field • Other writers of light verse
Light verse since the fifties 132
David McCord • William Jay Smith • John Ciardi • Ogden Nash, Phyllis McGinley, William Cole
Poetry of the child's everyday world 138
Early poets of manners and morals 138
Isaac Watts • Ann and Jane Taylor • Kate Greenaway
Poets of the child's world 141
Robert Louis Stevenson • Carl Sandburg • Eleanor Farjeon • James S. Tippett • Elizabeth Madox Roberts • Mary Austin • Winifred Welles • Rachel Field • Dorothy Aldis • Harry Behn • Frances Frost
New singers of small songs 158
Suggested reading, problems, and projects 163

7 GROWING UP WITH POETRY *164*

Response to mood and melody 165
Singers of songs 166
William Shakespeare • William Blake • Christina Rossetti
Poets of nature 175
Sara Teasdale • Elizabeth Coatsworth • Hilda Conkling • A book of Eskimo poems
Poets of fairyland 180
William Allingham • Rose Fyleman • Walter de la Mare
"Earth's the best place for love" 186
Robert Frost
Suggested reading, problems, and projects 189

8 USING POETRY WITH CHILDREN *192*

Elements of good poetry 193
Singing quality: melody and movement • Words of poetry • Content of poetry
Why poetry is difficult for children 195
Subject matter • Figures of speech • Long descriptions • Form • Dialogue
To make poetry-lovers of children 197
Know what children like about poetry • Ensure desirable responses • Read poetry to children • Explore poetry books with children • Deepen children's understanding of poems
How to read poetry aloud 205
Creating the mood • Introducing poetry • Anticipating difficulties • Waiting for children's reactions
Poetry in the schoolroom 210
With school subjects • With festivals • Your own collection
Suggested reading, problems, and projects 213
References 214

9 VERSE CHOIRS *220*

Ancient and modern choric speech 221
Laying a foundation for choir work 222
Kindergarten-primary • Middle and upper grades
Beginnings of choir work with children 223

Unison • Grouping children in choirs
Problems in casting a poem 227
Refrains or choruses • Dialogue or antiphonal • Line-a-child or line-a-choir • Solo voices with choirs • Group work • Unison speech
The choir leader: teacher or student 239
A public performance 239
Suitable poems for verse choirs 240
Possible dangers of choral speaking 241
Singsong delivery • Choice of mediocre verse • Overdramatics • Loud voices, increased speed
Standards for judging choir work 243
Speech and voice improvement • Increased enjoyment of poetry • Growing ability to interpret poetry • Better personal adjustments • Ability to lead • Sincerity
Suggested problems and projects 245
References 245
Supplementary list of poems 246

part three

Once Upon a Time

10 OLD MAGIC *252*

Theories of folk tale origin 252
Remnants of myth and ritual • Polygenesis • Origins in dreams and unconscious emotions • Cement of society
Sources of folk tales 255
Indian • Celtic
Wide diffusion of the folk tales 256
Collections and collectors 257
French fairy tales • German folk tales • Norwegian popular tales • British folk tales
Other national groups of folk tales 263
Arabian Nights • Czechoslovakian stories • Finnish folk tales • Russian folk tales • Spanish stories
Folk tales in the United States 265
American Negro tales • North American Indian tales • Native variants of European tales • Tall tales and other native inventions
Predominant types of folk tales 269
Accumulative tales • Talking beasts • The drolls or humorous stories • Realistic stories • Religious tales • Romance • Magic
Fairies and other magic makers 272
The little people • Wise women, witches, and wizards • Giants and ogres • Fairy animals • Magic objects • Enchanted people
Distinctive elements of folk tales 275
The introduction • The development • The conclusion • Style • Character portrayal
Why use the folk tales with modern children? 281
Ethical truth • Satisfaction of needs • Variety
Misuses of the folk tales 283
Teaching morals • Forced retelling by young children • Introduced to children too early
Desirable uses of the folk tales 284
For entertainment • With national groups • For illustration • For dramatization • For storytelling by older children
Suggested reading, problems, and projects 287
References 288

11 FABLES, MYTHS, AND EPICS *298*

Moral tales: fables, parables, proverbs 298
Fable collections 300
Aesop • *The Panchatantra* • The *Jatakas* • La Fontaine
Using fables with children 303
With young children • With older children
Gods and men 305
Evolution of myths • Types of myth stories
Sources of mythologies 308
Greek myths • Roman myths • Norse myths
Why use the myths with children? 310
What versions of the myths to use 310
How to use myths with children 312
As the religion of a people • With the study of a people • As literature
Epic and hero tales 314
Characteristics of the epic • The *Odyssey* • *Sigurd the Volsung* • *Robin Hood* • *King Arthur and the Knights of the Round Table* • The *Ramayana* • Other epics
Suggested reading, problems, and projects 319
References 320

12 NEW MAGIC *326*

The beginnings of the modern fanciful tale 326
Hans Christian Andersen 327
Retelling of old tales • New stories in folk-tale style • Humorous tales • Inanimate objects personified • Talking beasts • Fantasy • Characteristics of style • Using Andersen's tales with children
Modern adaptations of old tales 332
Desirable adaptations • Undesirable adaptations
Modern tales in folk-tale style 333
Robert Southey • John Ruskin • Howard Pyle • Oscar Wilde • Helen Bannerman • Wanda Gág • Other examples
Stories of fantasy 337
Charles Kingsley • Lewis Carroll • George MacDonald • James Barrie • C.S. Lewis • Mary Norton • Lucy M. Boston • A. Philippa Pearce • Maurice Druon • Carolyn Sherwin Bailey • Julia Sauer • William Pène du Bois • Carol Fenner
Space fantasy 346
Robert Heinlein • Madeleine L'Engle
Modern stories of talking beasts 347
Beatrix Potter • Kenneth Grahame • Hugh Lofting • Walter de la Mare • Marie Hall Ets • Robert Lawson • E.B. White • Louise Fatio • Other examples of talking beasts
Inanimate objects personified 357
Richard Henry Horne • Carlo Lorenzini

• Margery Williams Bianco • A.A. Milne • Rachel Field • Rumer Godden
Modern examples of machinery personified 360
Virginia Burton • Hardie Gramatky • Norman Bate
"Funny books" 363
Lucretia Hale • Rudyard Kipling • P.L. Travers • Theodor Seuss Geisel • Richard and Florence Atwater • Astrid Lindgren • Maurice Sendak
Suggested reading, problems, and projects 367
References 368

13 STORYTELLING AND READING ALOUD 376

Is storytelling dead? 376
When to read stories and when to tell them 377
Why tell stories • Read the picture-stories; tell the folk tales • Read stories calling for exact words of author
Personal equipment for storytelling 380
Agreeable voice • Choice of words • Making vocabulary clear • Appearance • Living the story • Sharing the story • Selecting a story to tell • Adapting a story for telling
Learning and telling a story 389
The beginnings and endings • Dramatizing the tales
Four storytellers with contrasting styles 392
Marie Shedlock • Ruth Sawyer • Gudrun Thorne-Thomsen • Richard Chase
Reading aloud 394
Suggested reading, problems, and projects 395
References 396

part four

Fiction and Stranger Than Fiction

14 ANIMAL STORIES 398

Talking beasts—ourselves in fur 398
Toba Sojo • Munro Leaf • Else H. Minarik
Animals as animals but talking 400
Anna Sewell • Rudyard Kipling • Felix Salten • Alice Crew Gall and Fleming Crew
Animals as animals objectively reported 403
Dorothy Lathrop • E. Boyd Smith • Mary and Conrad Buff • Marjorie Flack • Lynd Ward • Clare Turlay Newberry • Tom Robinson • C.W. Anderson • Margaret and Helen Johnson • Glen Rounds • Marguerite Henry • Joseph Wharton Lippincott • Page Cooper • Philip Duffield Stong • Will James • Mary O'Hara • Theodore J. Waldeck • Marjorie Kinnan Rawlings • James Arthur Kjelgaard • Michel-Aimé Baudouy • John and Jean George • Emil E. Liers • Sheila Burnford • Lucy M. Boston
Criteria for judging animal stories 418
Suggested reading, problems, and projects 419
References 420

For March 10

15 HERE AND NOW 426

Realism for the youngest children 427
Here and now, cadence and awareness • Margaret Wise Brown • Ruth Krauss • Joan Walsh Anglund • Margery Clark • Elsa Beskow • Lois Lenski • Marjorie Flack • Alvin Tresselt • Leo Politi • Edward Ardizzone • Robert McCloskey • Will and Nicolas • Heidrun Petrides • Carolyn Haywood
Forerunners of realism for older children 434
Samuel L. Clemens (Mark Twain) • Louisa M. Alcott • Frances Hodgson Burnett
The modern scene in America and Great Britain 436
Arthur Ransome • Noel Streatfeild • Hilda Van Stockum • Eleanor Estes • Elizabeth Enright • Robert McCloskey • Beverly Cleary • E.C. Spykman • Archie Binns • James Street • Elizabeth Yates • Joseph Krumgold • Madeleine L'Engle • Jean George • Keith Robertson • Ester Wier
Stories about American Negroes 446
For children five to seven • For children eight to fourteen • Eleanor Frances Lattimore • Arna Bontemps • Marguerite de Angeli • Mabel Leigh Hunt • Jesse Jackson • John R. Tunis • Dorothy Sterling
American Indians 450
M. O'Moran • Eloise Jarvis McGraw • Laura Armer • Mary and Conrad Buff • Scott O'Dell • Ann Nolan Clark • Evelyn Sibley Lampman
Regional and religious minorities 454
Marguerite de Angeli • Virginia Sorenson • Sydney Taylor • Ellis Credle • Ruth and Latrobe Carroll • Jesse Stuart • Lois Lenski • Other minorities • Criteria for stories about minority groups
Mystery tales 459
Robert Louis Stevenson • Elizabeth Lansing • Belle Dorman Rugh • Keith Robertson • Isabelle Lawrence • Alice Lide, Margaret A. Johansen • Stephen Meader • Howard Pease
Stories of romance 463
Criteria for here and now stories 464
Suggested reading, problems, and projects 465
References 465

For March 17

16 OTHER TIMES AND PLACES 476

Correlating fiction and social studies 476
American historical fiction 477
Elizabeth George Speare • Rachel Field • Cornelia Meigs • Elizabeth Coatsworth • Walter D. Edmonds • Rebecca Caudill • Esther Forbes • William O. Steele • Evelyn Sibley Lampman • Harold Keith • Carol Ryrie Brink • Laura Ingalls Wilder • Alice Dalgliesh

Stories about the ancient world 488
Harry Behn • Elizabeth George Speare • Lucille Morrison • Eloise Jarvis McGraw • Olivia E. Coolidge • Isabelle Lawrence • Henry Winterfeld
European historical fiction 491
Rosemary Sutcliff • Erik Christian Haugaard • Howard Pyle • Elizabeth Janet Gray • Marguerite de Angeli • Marchette Chute
Some criteria for historical fiction 496
Early books about children of other lands 497
Mary Mapes Dodge • Johanna Spyri
Recent trends in books about other lands 499
Outstanding books about foreign lands 499
For the youngest • Ludwig Bemelmans • Eleanor Frances Lattimore • Taro Yashima • Esther Wood • Elizabeth Foreman Lewis • Margot Benary-Isbert • Armstrong Sperry • Kate Seredy • Monica Shannon • James Ramsey Ullman • Shirley Arora • Meindert DeJong • Natalie Savage Carlson
Suggested reading, problems, and projects 507
References 508

17 BIOGRAPHY 518

What is biography? 519
Biography as history 519
Authenticity • Objectivity • Sources
Biography as the individual 520
Typed characters unacceptable • The whole man • Vivid details
Biography as literature 522
Theme and unity • Style and pattern
Biographical types for children 525
Fictionalized biography • Biographical fiction
Biographies for young children 527
Ingri and Edgar Parin d'Aulaire • Alice Dalgliesh • Clyde Robert Bulla • Opal Wheeler and Sybil Deucher • Marguerite Henry • The Childhood of Famous Americans
The series multiply 531
Initial Biographies • Signature Books • Landmark Books • Clara Ingram Judson
Biographies for older children: exploration and settlement 533
Ronald Syme • Esther Averill
Colonial and Revolutionary periods 535
Elizabeth Janet Gray • Jeanette Eaton • Hazel Wilson • James Daugherty • Nardi Reeder Campion • Gene Lisitzky • Parallel biographies • Jean Lee Latham
Westward Ho! 539
Julia Davis • James Daugherty • Frances Joyce Farnsworth
Old Hickory and his colleagues 540
Marguerite Vance • James Daugherty • Shannon Garst • Constance Rourke • Marquis and Bessie James
Civil War period 542
Carl Sandburg • James Daugherty • Clara Ingram Judson • Bernadine Bailey • Henry Steele Commager • MacKinlay Kantor
Biographies which meet special interests 544
Heroines • Negroes • Artists, musicians, and writers • Scientists • Adventurers
Using biography with children 550
Correlation with school subjects • Discussion • Composition
Encouraging the reading of biography 552
Suggested reading, problems, and projects 553
References 554

part five

Reading Follows Many Paths

18 READING FOR INFORMATION 564

Criteria for informational books 564
Accuracy • Convenient presentation • Clarity • Adequate treatment • Style
Books for the social studies 566
For younger children • For older children
Books about man's past 569
Prehistoric and ancient times • The Middle Ages (476-1500 A.D.) • Discoveries in the New World (1492-1600) • Colonial America (1600-1775) • American growth and development (1775-1945) • The Civil War (1861-1865)
Books about man's present 575
North America • Latin America • Other cities and countries
Books about man's work 577
Science books for today's children 579
General science books 581
The world of living things 585
Life in various environments • Plant life • The animal kingdom • The human body
The earth and the universe 591
The earth's beginning years • Geology • The atmosphere and weather • Space
Matter and energy 595
Chemistry • Physics
Suggested reading, problems, and projects 597
References 598

19 READING AND CREATIVE EXPRESSION 606

Intelligence and creativity 607
Creative expression in the early years 607
Creative writing 610
Dramatization 613
With puppets • With social studies
Illustration 615
A rich experience with art and literature 617
The atmosphere for creativity 618
Suggested reading, problems, and projects 620
References 620

20 READING AND THE MASS MEDIA *622*

Television and radio 623
Evaluation of television and radio • Children's program choices • Educational television and radio • Television, radio, books, and children
Motion pictures 629
Commercial films • Educational films • Film selection and evaluation
Other audio-visual aids 633
Filmstrips • Recordings and tapes • Audio-visual aids and reading
Comics 635
Paperback books 637
Magazines and newspapers 639
Suggested reading, problems, and projects 641
References 642
Film companies 643
Filmstrip companies 643

21 READING IN THE FAMILY *644*

Home environment for reading 644
Reading aloud in the family 646
The reluctant reader 648
Religious books for children 650
Books of prayers • *The Bible* • Religious instruction
Using the public library 653
Buying books for children 654
Dictionaries and encyclopedias 656
The reading family 657
Suggested reading, problems, and projects 658
References 658

PUBLISHERS AND PUBLISHERS' ADDRESSES *664*

GUIDE TO PRONUNCIATION *666*

SUBJECT INDEX *669*

INDEX TO AUTHORS, ILLUSTRATORS, AND TITLES *673*

Children Discover Books

part one

1. *The Child and His Books*
2. *The Adult and the Child's Books*
3. *Children's Books: History and Trends*
4. *The Artist and the Child's Books*

chapter 1

The Child and His Books

Books are no substitute for living, but they can add immeasurably to its richness. When life is absorbing, books can enhance our sense of its significance. When life is difficult, they can give us momentary release from trouble or a new insight into our problems, or provide the rest and refreshment we need. Books have always been a source of information, comfort, and pleasure for people who know how to use them. This is as true for children as for adults.

In the last few years, writers, artists, and editors have joined forces to make children's books so varied in content and so beautiful to look at that adults as well as children enjoy them. The annual output is tremendous, reaching in recent years more than two thousand titles. These books, like those for adults, range from the unreliable and trashy to the scrupulously accurate and permanently significant. The treasures must be sought for, but they are there, a wealth of fine books old and new.

If we are to find these treasures, the best books for children, we need standards for judging them.[1] But two facts we need to keep constantly before us: a book is a good book for children only when they enjoy it; a book is a poor book for children, even when adults rate it a classic, if children are unable to read it or are bored by its content. In short, we must know hundreds of books in many fields and their virtues and limitations, but we must also know the children for whom they are intended—their interests and needs.

Certain basic needs are common to most peoples and most times. A child's needs are at first intensely and narrowly personal, but, as he matures, they broaden and become more widely socialized. Struggling to satisfy his needs, the child is forever seeking to maintain the precarious balance between personal happiness and social approval, and that is no easy task. Books can help him, directly or indirectly.

1. See Chapter 2, p. 17, for a discussion of standards for judging stories for children. Throughout this text, suggestions are given for introducing children to many of the classics of children's literature, books "too good to miss," but books they *may* miss without some wise, understanding guidance from adults.

Competence— the Need to Achieve

There is a new emphasis today upon competence as a motivating force in human behavior. Robert W. White in his study "Motivation Reconsidered: The Concept of Competence" states that

Something important is left out when we make drives the operating force in human behavior. I have chosen the word competence, *which . . . will refer to an organism's capacity to interact effectively with its environment.*[2]

The struggle to achieve competence begins with the infant's visual exploration, with his crawling, grasping, and other primitive activities and grows into the complex physical or intellectual performances of the expert housewife, athlete, mathematician, professional musician, or scientist. Competence, Mr. White states, is as satisfying as inhibitions and frustrations are disruptive. To be happy or well adjusted, the child or the adult must have a satisfying sense of competence in one area or another.

Mr. White's detailed psychological study lends support to Mary J. Collier and Eugene L. Gaier's study concerning "The Hero in the Preferred Childhood Stories of College Men."[3] The important factor which these book heroes had in common was that they performed their unique feats on their own. Whether it was Hänsel from the old fairy tale or the realistic Tom Sawyer, the hero's competence was achieved without help from adults, and his independent achievement was the quality that made him memorable and admired. This need to achieve may seem to contradict the need to belong, to be accepted by the group. On the contrary, it is the lack of competence that often causes rejection by the group and fosters withdrawal. Achieving competence may become the compensation for such rejection and a step toward acceptance. This is a frequent theme in stories for children—the lonely child or the shy teen-ager who develops competence in some field and so wins the admiration and acceptance of the group. Taro Yashima's *Crow Boy,*[4] Eleanor Estes' *The Hundred Dresses,* Armstrong Sperry's *Call It Courage,* and Betty Cavanna's *Going on Sixteen* are all built upon this theme.

The young child's first book heroes are doers, from Edward Ardizzone's Tim, who survives shipwreck and finds his lost parents, to David of the Old Testament, who slew the giant Goliath. In later childhood and adolescence young readers enjoy the competence of the heroes in adventure, mystery, and career stories and the achievements of famous men and women in biographies. *Carry on, Mr. Bowditch* by Jean Latham is a splendid, true record of competence independently achieved. Abraham Lincoln was poor, homely, uneducated, but he achieved competence at each stage of his life, first in his physical strength and later in law, politics, and letters. Certainly he was as much on his own as any human being could possibly be. This is the American ideal—the self-made man who "pulls himself up by his bootstraps," a homely phrase for competence independently achieved. Books about such heroes lead children gradually into an appreciation of emotional, intellectual, and moral competence. People who have conquered bad tempers or fears or lazy irresponsibility, heroes who have sacrificed personal comforts in devotion to research or exploration or some great cause—these stir in children and young people the desire not only to achieve tangible results but also to conquer self-indulgence and self-love.

There is a stern negative aspect to this hunger for achievement. The struggle for competence may involve failures and complete frustration. Physical handicaps or mental limitations must be faced and sometimes accepted. Johnny Tremain's maimed hand prevented him from becoming the master silversmith he had expected to be. Robin, a knight's son in *The Door in the Wall,* knew after he was lamed that he could never fulfill his father's expectations and become a knight. But both Johnny Tremain and Robin acquitted them-

2. *Psychological Review,* Vol. 66, No. 5, 1959, p. 297.
3. *American Imago,* Vol. 16, No. 2, 1959.
4. *Crow Boy,* as well as many of the other books mentioned in this chapter, is discussed elsewhere in the text. See the Index for relevant page references.

selves competently in other fields. George Washington Carver, despite poverty, frail health, and every social barrier raised against his progress, never gave up his almost superhuman struggles to achieve competence in his chosen field of science. Stories of such heroes who courageously accept defeats, handicaps, and even failures and achieve in spite of them help children in the task of growing up.

Material Security—the Need for Physical Well-Being

An important factor motivating the struggle for competence is, of course, man's hunger for material security, the desire for creature comforts. This begins for the child in his mother's or his father's arms, includes his routines of eating and sleeping, and comes gradually to embrace everything that gives him a sense of comfort and well-being. For both children and adults, material satisfactions may become the chief symbols of security. The old fairy tales were told by peoples who seldom had enough to eat or to keep them warm. So their tales are full of brightly burning fires, sumptuous feasts, rich clothes, glittering jewels, and splendid palaces. These are man's age-old symbols of security. Undoubtedly some of the appeal of the old *Elsie Dinsmore* stories and of Frances Hodgson Burnett's *Sara Crewe* and *The Secret Garden* lies in this same incredible affluence which the characters enjoy or achieve. Today, in this age of international upheavals and nuclear competition, material security is uncertain, but still people struggle for it.

So in books as in life, the lack of security and the hunger for it often supply the motive for the action and the theme of the story. The mythical hero Odysseus was struggling to reach home, his wife, his lands, his family—these spelled security after the perils of war. But the achievement of his goal was continually delayed and his personal safety repeatedly endangered. Hence the ageless appeal of *The Odyssey.* The three young men, adrift on the Pacific aboard the flimsy raft Kon-Tiki, were trying to prove their theory of the origin and migrations of the Polynesian people, and their goal was a safe landing on the South Sea Islands. Each day new dangers threatened their survival, and the enthralled reader cannot lay aside the book until he has learned its outcome. In *Kon-Tiki* there is a twofold struggle—partly for material security but particularly for intellectual security, the need to know.

Ease and abundance seldom lead to brilliant accomplishments unless there is a strong enough hunger for competence (achievement) or intellectual security (the need to know) or emotional security (the need to love and to be loved) to overcome the pleasant inertia of comfort and set off the struggle. Meanwhile, the search for snug security with its successes and frustrations will spellbind young readers of the old fairy tales or true adventure stories or the biographies of heroes, all the way from "Cinderella" to *Tom Sawyer* and the modern space men.

Intellectual Security—the Need to Know

Parents often complain about the bothersome curiosity of children, their eternal questions, and the scrapes they get into trying to find answers. But this need to investigate, to find out, to know for sure is a healthy sign of normal or better than normal intelligence. In fact, the keener the child is mentally, the wider and more persistent his curiosities will be. The need to know surely and accurately is a basic hunger and one which books help to satisfy. It is frequently the only justification adults see for buying books for children, and they are surprised and delighted at the range of fine informational books available for children today. Books about Alaska, desert Indians, birds, plants, stones, stars, rockets and jets, wild animals, care of pets, do-it-yourself books, and, of course, dictionaries and encyclopedias properly gauged to a child's needs are all available today. For the most part, modern informational books for children are prepared by experts and checked by other experts for complete accuracy and readability. Children's encyclopedias continue to improve and should be given serious consideration by book-buying parents of intellectually alert youngsters. Adults need only know a child's particular interests to find books that will answer his questions reliably, stimulate new curiosities, and set him to exploring further to satisfy his need to know and give him, momentarily at least, a certain intellectual security.

Caddie the tomboy is evident in this picture where the curved and diagonal lines heighten the effect of the action.
Illustration by Kate Seredy. Reprinted with permission of the publisher from Caddie Woodlawn *by Carol Ryrie Brink. Copyright 1935 by The Macmillan Company. (Book 5¼ x 8¼)*

Emotional Security—the Need to Love and to Be Loved

Every human being wants to love and to be loved. This need is so pressing that when it is frustrated in one direction it will provide its own substitutes, centering upon almost anything from lap dogs to antiques. Children, too, set up their own substitutes. A child who feels out of favor or rejected may lavish an abnormal amount of affection upon a stray cat, perhaps identifying himself with the unwanted animal.

It is in his family that the child learns his first lessons in the laws of affectionate relationships. Not only does his sense of security develop from these family patterns, but also his whole approach to other people and later his search for and treatment of a mate. The status of the mother and the father in the family circle provides a child with his first concepts of the woman's role and the man's role in life and often determines his consequent willingness or unwillingness to accept his own sex. Books such as *Caddie Woodlawn* can help in this necessary process of growing up, for tomboy Caddie, despite her love of boys' games and adventures, gradually learns to appreciate her woman's role. Family loyalties provide a basis for loyal friendships as the child's social life widens. When family relationships are normal and happy, a child starts life with healthy attitudes. If he feels loved and knows his love is accepted, he in turn is predisposed toward friendly relationships with people outside the family. When the reverse is true, his approach to other people is often suspicious or belligerent.

In either case—a happy or an unhappy home background—books can help. Stories about family life may interpret to the fortunate child the significance of his own experiences which he might otherwise take for granted. When a child finds traces of his father in Andy's father in *Onion John* or recognizes his mother in Mrs. March of *Little Women,* or shares the brother and sister fun of *Meet the Austins,* or shares the adventures of the cousins in *Gone-Away Lake,* his own family will mean more to him. On the other hand, children who have missed these happy experiences may find in family stories vicarious substitutes which give them some satisfaction and supply them with new insight into what families can be.

The engraving used in this illustration makes a precise, richly textured drawing. The thin, slight child is in striking contrast to the powerful gorilla with his haunting face full of intelligence and pain. Illustration by Peter Boston. From A Stranger at Green Knowe. *Copyright © 1961 by Lucy Maria Boston. By permission of Harcourt, Brace & World, Inc. and Faber and Faber Ltd. (Book 5¼ x 8)*

Another aspect of this need to love and to serve the beloved is the recognition of this same need in other creatures. Stories about wild animals defending their mates or their young or the herd are tremendously appealing. So, too, are stories of pets, steadfast not only in their affection for their own kind but for their human masters as well. Such stories as *Lassie Come Home* have played upon this appeal. The tragedy in most animal tales is always heightened by the inarticulateness of the creatures, which calls forth in children a tenderly protective response. *A Stranger at Green Knowe* by Lucy Boston is a moving example of a boy's understanding of and sympathy for an unhappy, caged young gorilla. Fine animal stories of all kinds will undoubtedly contribute to breaking down the young child's unwitting cruelties toward animals and to building up his sensitivity to their needs.

Finally, the need to love and to be loved, which includes family affection, warm friendships, and devotion to pets, leads the child to look toward romance. In children's literature, romance begins early but remains impersonal. The fairy tales, with their long-delayed prince or their princess on a glass hill, are little more than abstract symbols of what is to come. They do, however, help little girls to think of themselves in the girl's role and boys to identify themselves with the masculine role—an important task of later childhood.

By the time children are twelve years old the girls are biologically around two years older than the boys of the same chronological age. This means that when boys are absorbed in stories of adventure or sports, girls are looking for stories of romance. A few years ago the milder of the adult novels served for the good readers, but poor readers had to fall back on comic books, soap operas, or the lush lovemaking of moving pictures for information about this new and mysterious world of romance.

Now there is a great flood of novels for teen-agers. While many of them are incredibly stereotyped and predictable, there are growing numbers of competent authors who write well and respect their young readers. At least one of these novels—Maureen Daly's *Seventeenth Summer*—made history and is approved equally by youngsters and adults. As Professor Burton said, it "perhaps captures better than any other novel the spirit of adolescence."[5] It is a thoroughly wholesome introduction to vital problems of adolescence. Books by Betty Cavanna, Maud Lovelace, Margot Benary-Isbert, Mary Stolz, Margaret Bell, and others supply good examples of a fresh approach to romance in stories for teen-age and preadolescent girls. They supply wholesome pictures of family life, with boys and girls looking away from their families to a serious interest in someone of the opposite sex. The establishment of a desirable romantic attachment is one of the most important tasks of growing up. A well-written story that shows all the complications of romance, its pitfalls and disappointments as well as its happiness, can provide young people with needed guidance in an approach to one of life's most vital problems.

Out of family affection and trust grows a kind of *spiritual strength* that enables human beings to surmount dangers, failures, and even stark tragedies. Spiritual security is often but not always the result of a strong religious faith. Such books as *Little Women* and the Wilder stories, without referring to specific religious practices or creeds, leave children with the conviction that decent, kindly people can maintain an inner serenity even as they struggle with and master the evils that threaten them.

More often, in books as in life, this inner strength grows out of a belief in God and a universe in which moral law ultimately prevails. Particular religious groups and practices appear in children's books and reflect something of the diversities of belief in our modern world. *Thee, Hannah!* gives a charming picture of Quaker customs. *Daughter of the Mountains* by Louise Rankin is a story about a little Tibetan Buddhist girl's faith that she can accomplish her impossible mission because she is guided and cared for by Buddha. A camp meeting reforms Pa Slater in Lois Lenski's *Strawberry Girl. Young Fu of the Upper Yangtze* by Elizabeth Lewis gives a rich cross section of Confucian guides to conduct. Leo Politi's *Juanita* describes and illustrates the charming Blessing of the Animals, which is one of the yearly church festivals in some Catholic countries and on Olvera Street, Los Angeles. *All-of-a-Kind Family* by Sydney Taylor is a captivating picture of Jewish family life and religious observances. *Waterless Mountain* by Laura Armer and *Summer at Yellow Singer's* by Flora Bailey present the religion of the Navaho Indians with fidelity and beauty. Joseph Krumgold's *. . . and now Miguel* has a discussion of prayer between two teen-age boys that is unique in children's literature.

Reading such books, children can get an honest picture of religious diversity as it exists today—knowledge which should help them develop respect for different groups. However firm a family may be in its adherence to a particular religious sect or in its objections to all organized religion, it will find in these books a fair picture of the world as it is today. And when children read the biographies of heroes of such divergent religious beliefs as St. Francis of Assisi, John Wesley, Father Damien, Florence Nightingale, and George Washington Carver, they will understand that prayer and a sense of God give spiritual security and are impelling and creative forces in the lives of many men and women.

5. Dwight L. Burton, "The Novel for the Adolescent," *English Journal*, September 1951, p. 363.

Acceptance— the Need to Belong

Growing out of the need for security is the need of every human being to belong, to be an accepted member of a group. "*My* daddy," or "*My* big brother," the young child says with pride. At first these experiences are merely egocentric extensions of the child's self-love, but at least he is beginning to line himself up with his family, and this acknowledgment of others marks his growing sense of belonging to a group. Presently this same child will identify himself with his gang, his school, and later with his city and country, and perhaps with a world group.

So the child's literature should reflect this

The child's shyness, the parents' concern, the grocer's kindness are sensitively depicted in this pencil drawing.
Illustration by Paul Lantz. From Little Navajo Bluebird *by Ann Nolan Clark. Copyright 1943 by Ann Nolan Clark and Paul Lantz. Reproduced with permission of The Viking Press, Inc. (Book 6 x 8¾)*

expanding sense of the group. It should begin with stories about the family, the school, and the neighborhood in warm little books such as Carolyn Haywood writes for the primer age and Beverly Cleary carries on for the middle grades in her amusing *Henry Huggins* books. These represent happy, normal group experiences. But there are also stories about children who must struggle anxiously to be liked by the people whose acceptance they long for. The orphaned *Heidi,* Mary in *The Secret Garden,* Cissie in *Peachtree Island,* and *Santiago,* the Guatemalan Indian boy, are good examples. The story of the child who wins a respected place in groups that once rejected him is a satisfying theme from "Cinderella" to *Huckleberry Finn.*

With our growing consciousness of the true functioning of a democracy, stories about minority groups or individual members of such groups gaining respect, not just toleration, should be increasing but are not. Good ones are hard to find. John Tunis, in his popular sports stories for the preadolescent and teenager, makes his young readers face fully the extra difficulties that beset youngsters of minority groups in winning a place on the team or in the community. This is the general theme also of Eleanor Estes' *The Hundred Dresses.* Sometimes the problem is one not of winning acceptance but of accepting. For example, in Ann Nolan Clark's *Little Navajo Bluebird,* an Indian child passionately rejects the white man and all his ways and wants to belong only to her own tribal group. This unwillingness to go even halfway with a strange people is happily resolved. Books like these parallel the need of each individual not only to belong to his own group, but to identify himself warmly and sympathetically with ever widening circles of people. When a little girl from suburbia weeps over some of Joanda's difficulties in *Cotton in My Sack* or wishes she could know Hungarian Kate in *The Good Master,* her sense of belonging is widening. She is no longer narrowly provincial but is becoming a friendly well-wisher of different peoples.

Play— the Need for Change

Play is sometimes classified as a part of the desire for change, which is one of the basic needs of the human organism.[6] If we work hard, we need rest or play. If we are serious and intent, we need relaxation and gaiety. So, in our reading, after grave and factual books or books about everyday affairs we like something light or imaginative. If we are beset with personal anxieties, we look for a book of adventure

6. William E. Blatz and Helen Bott, *Parents and the Preschool Child,* p. 114.

or mystery or romance, lose ourselves completely, and come back to our own problems refreshed. "Ah, but that is reading for escape," someone protests. Of course it is a form of escape. Anything we do that lifts us out of ourselves or frees us from the doldrums is an escape, whether it is listening to music, taking a brisk walk, going to the movies, or reading a book. But what is wrong with that? Escape is reprehensible if it is a cowardly running away from responsibilities or an unwillingness to face reality, but escape becomes a sensible measure of safety when it means pausing to catch our breath on a hard climb or beating a hasty retreat before an onrushing truck. So when pressures bear down upon us too heavily, reading may create for us a little oasis of warmth or quiet or fun where we can relax, learn how to laugh again, and step forth with renewed buoyancy and courage.

Children also need such liberation. They suffer more than adults realize from the pressure of routines, adult coercion and tensions, and the necessity of conforming to a code of manners and morals whose reasonableness they do not always understand. Some children suffer from school failures, family troubles, or feelings of social or physical inferiority. They, too, may seek an escape in books and the escape will be wholesome or the reverse depending upon what they read. For instance, a little girl began to read one collection of fairy tales after another. She was running away from unhappy competition with a brighter, prettier, older sister. She escaped to a world of fantasy where the youngest daughter, the cinder girl, always comes into her own and triumphs. Mooning over her fairy tales, the child left her room in disorder, dodged study periods, and allowed herself to become more and more untidy. She was using books, good enough in themselves, as a screen between herself and the problems she would not face. She needed help rather than censure. When that help was forthcoming and when through a series of small successes and increasing acceptance by her school group she began to find her place in the world, she turned from her fairy tales, and *Heidi* replaced "Cinderella." Stories about girls who achieved in spite of difficulties helped her in her own struggle to achieve and to belong.

Sensational comic books, trashy reading material of any kind may provide children with temporary forgetfulness but will give them no help with their problems. For children identify themselves with their book heroes, and when those characters are sensible, courageous human beings, young readers discover new courage in themselves, new capacities for competent or noble action. In *The Door in the Wall* the hero accepts and rises above his handicap. In *Meet the Austins* the children face the tragedy of death and learn that life must go on. Such reading provides escape that is also fulfillment because it gives new insight and fortitude for life's difficulties.

Books of many kinds may be used to meet the child's need for healthy change. The old fairy tales are full of do-and-dare heroines and heroes who accomplish impossible tasks through their good deeds, courage, and persistence. These old tales have about them also a dreamlike quality that is a welcome change from the everyday world of here and now. Modern fantasies provide laughter and imaginative adventures that are sometimes rib-tickling nonsense and sometimes humor with overtones of beauty. These range from the fun of Dr. Seuss' rambunctious *Horton Hatches the Egg* to the beauty and tragedy of Mary Norton's *The Borrowers* and the compassionate self-sacrifice of *Charlotte's Web*. Absorbing adventure books such as Robert Du Soe's *Three Without Fear* or Thor Heyerdahl's dramatic tale *Kon-Tiki* are important to children and young people who may be finding life hopelessly dull or unchallenging. Fine poetry that arrests the attention and stirs the emotions, light verse and nonsense jingles now and then—these may supply a child with the inspiration or laughter for which he hungers. Our modern world, with its increased social tensions and fears, needs more than ever the safety valve of laughter. Laughter dissolves tensions. If we can laugh together, we can live together. The person with a sense of humor (not levity) is generally a balanced, sagacious person. The literature of humor and nonsense has a therapeutic value we cannot afford to overlook. It is the responsibility of adults to help children discover books that provide the wholesome delight to which they can escape when they need change.

Aesthetic Satisfaction—the Need for Beauty and Order

There is still another human need that seems curiously at odds with man's more utilitarian search for competence and security. It is the need to adorn, to make beautiful, and to enjoy beauty. The need to adorn begins primitively with the enjoyment of ornaments for self-glorification. With many people this remains a major source of satisfaction. For others the aesthetic sense expands rapidly beyond the purely personal to include expressions of the wonder and joy of life in the arts.

Whether in music, dancing, drama, story, painting, or sculpture, the artist seizes upon some aspect of life and re-creates it for us so that it is cleared of its confusions. We see it whole and understandable; people, events, and places, however sordid, assume a new dignity beyond the mere chronicling of facts. Lois Lenski, in her early regional books, gives children glimpses of underprivileged families whose lives are sordid but are dignified by family love and self-respect. These, too, are aesthetically satisfying because they seem true and right. Life is like a child's kaleidoscope: it changes too fast for us to capture the design. We are confused by the shifting colors and vanishing lines. We see this or that aspect of a man's character, but never the whole man. The artist can give us a long, clear view so that we see details in relation to the complete design. It is as if the kaleidoscope were held immovable. The colors and lines fall into logical relationship and the design stands out in bold relief, not necessarily beautiful but complete and therefore satisfying.

Men are continually seeking aesthetic satisfaction in one form or another and at varying levels of taste. One man may find it in the songs of Tin Pan Alley. Another finds it in a symphony which exalts the sorrows of life to heroic proportions. Aesthetic satisfaction comes to the small child as well as to the adult, and the development of his taste depends not only upon his initial capacities but also upon the material he encounters and upon how it is presented. When a child has chuckled over Miss Muffet and the spider, he is getting ready to enjoy Stevenson's *A Child's Garden of Verses,* and to progress to Walter de la Mare's poetry. After he has been charmed with *The Tale of Peter Rabbit,* he is on his way to appreciate the humor and beauty of *The Wind in the Willows* and the tragedy of *The Borrowers.*

In short, good reading can help every young human being to satisfy his basic needs vicariously if not in reality. Books mentioned here, and many others, may be used to give children the maximum enjoyment and often further their insight into their own problems and the problems of other people.

Child Guidance Through Books

To nurture these young spirits there must be books of many kinds. And they should be strong books, written with liveliness and honesty both in content and style, rather than little juvenile tracts designed to teach this lesson or that. There have been so many of these moralistic books in the last few years that they threaten the general quality of children's books. It is the old didacticism, which breaks out like a rash in every generation.[7] For instance, there is the story of little Dickie or Bobbie or Jimmy who goes to kindergarten, stamps around, yells, and knocks down other people's blocks or seizes their toys. He is isolated like the bubonic plague until one day he learns to share and is, forthwith, a beloved and accepted member of the group. A juvenile "how to make friends and influence people"!

7. See Chapter 3, p. 41.

Or there is the story of an obnoxious boy who says he wishes he didn't have a kid sister. But when she saves him in a social emergency his attitude changes for the better. The worst of such tracts is that children accept them and immediately assume an insufferably self-righteous attitude toward the sinner. "Isn't he awful?" they say virtuously. Such books may underscore a lesson, but they also encourage prigs. There are similar juvenile tracts, bogged down with preaching, in the field of race relationships. Such books, humorless and tame, offer nothing to lighten their dull didacticism.

Recently there has been a flood of small, pretty books for children four to seven years old about friendship, love, and similar abstractions. These precious trifles are purchased by nostalgic adults who hope to make the skipping, hopping child aware of the experiences he is bouncing through so heedlessly. But psychology makes it clear that for the young child such abstractions as unselfishness and kindness must be experienced objectively in this situation and that, not generalized in the large. These juvenile tracts seem thin indeed when compared with such robust tales as *Millions of Cats*, "Three Little Pigs," *Dick Whittington, Henry Huggins, Island of the Blue Dolphins,* and *Carry On, Mr. Bowditch,* to name just a few. Such books are timeless because they are built around universal themes or needs—the desire for competence or love or accurate knowledge.

There can be considerable danger in giving a child a story which deals with his particular behavior problem. In the process of growing older, a child may be confronted with pressures and problems too difficult for him to sustain or solve. As a result, he may lapse into temper tantrums or timid withdrawal or aggressiveness. To give such a child, already harassed, a story about a hero who conquers a similar fault may simply make the child more self-conscious or so resentful of the virtuous example in the book that he turns with increased fervor to the uninhibited excitement of television or the comics. A child going through one of these temporary periods of rebellion or withdrawal needs to discover books so absorbing, so alight with adventure or satisfying accomplishment that he is heartened in his own struggle to achieve and encouraged to believe that life is worth while in spite of its limitations. This is one form of indirect guidance. Another method of guidance is through informal discussions of the problems these books involve, rather than of the child's own personal difficulties.

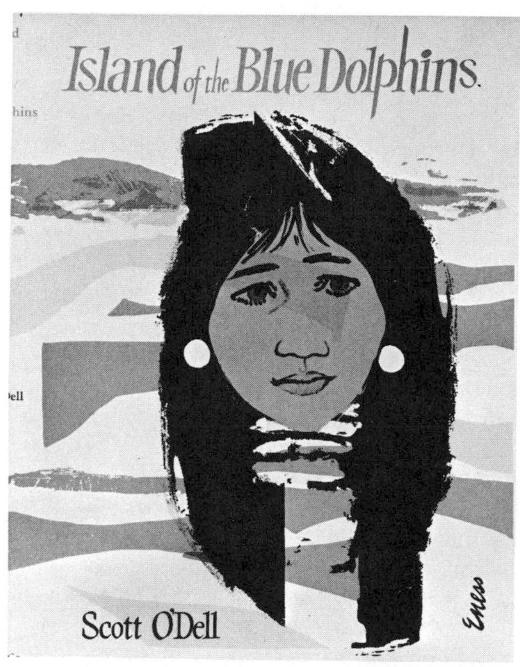

The hazy, abstract background helps focus attention on the grave, beautiful face of the Indian girl. Her suffering and hard won serenity are sensitively portrayed. Illustration by Eness. From Island of the Blue Dolphins *by Scott O'Dell. Copyright © 1960 by Scott O'Dell. Reproduced with permission of Houghton Mifflin Co. (Original in color, book 5⅞ x 8⅜)*

For instance, a group of children were discussing Elizabeth Enright's story of *Kintu,*[8] the son of an African chief, who was secretly afraid of the jungle. When the witch doctor gave him a charm to bury in the jungle in order to cure his fear, Kintu buried the charm but lost his way and had to spend the night in the trees. He saved himself from death by

8. This book, which unfortunately is out of print at this time, may perhaps be available in large libraries and is reprinted in *Time for True Tales,* revised edition, compiled by May Hill Arbuthnot, Scott, Foresman, 1961.

killing a leopard with his spear and afterwards discovered that he was no longer afraid of the jungle. The teacher asked the children what they thought cured Kintu of his fear—was it the charm? The children said "No," emphatically, and one child added, "That charm was just an old plum stone and I think the witch doctor gave it to Kintu so he'd have to go into the jungle and maybe stay there."

"Well, then, what cured him?" the teacher persisted.

The children discussed the question and concluded that after Kintu killed the leopard and found that he could take care of himself in the jungle, he wasn't afraid any more. The teacher agreed and asked, "Have any of you been afraid of something when you were younger that you aren't afraid of any more?"

There were plenty of responses—the dark, dogs, deep water—and a common fear was of a new school with strange children and teachers. Then the teacher led the children to tell how they got over their fears. The mother of the child who was afraid of the dark had played a game with her night after night until she could locate everything in her room in the dark and could even go around the house and find things quickly without any light. The children who were afraid of a new school felt that they might not be "up with the other kids" in arithmetic or reading, or that the teachers might not be friendly. They weren't afraid when they found the children and teachers friendly and they themselves better in some subjects even if they weren't so good in others. After considerable discussion with some teacher guidance, they arrived at these conclusions: first, that at some time or other everyone is afraid of something, and second, that to get over a foolish fear, you must do something about it. When you find you can take care of yourself, then you aren't afraid. Undoubtedly, there were still children in that group with fears, but here was a casual, impersonal kind of guidance by way of a book character that the children had thoroughly enjoyed.

At an older level, Sperry's *Call It Courage* would elicit similar discussions. Incidentally, in *Kintu,* although both text and pictures make it clear that the hero is a Negro boy, this aspect of the story was never mentioned. To white as well as Negro children he is another child like themselves, with a grave and understandable problem. He could not grow up to be respected unless he could conquer his secret fear.

A teacher who was reading aloud Beverly Cleary's *Henry Huggins* to her class stopped before she read them the solution of the ethical problem Henry faces when the original owner of his dog Ribsy turns up. "What would you do if you were in Henry's place?" she asked the children, and they played out the solution then and there, with different children taking Henry's part. Their varying interpretations told the teacher much about the children's standards and attitudes, and the activity provided a good deal of fun in the process.

A classroom group discussed Kate's outrageous behavior in the first chapter of *The Good Master*. Of course they thoroughly enjoyed her antics, but they came to the conclusion that she behaved that way because she was "mad" at her father for sending her away, and so she took it out on her uncle's family. It was further agreed that most of us are likely to behave foolishly when we think we have been unjustly treated. They supplied some rather hair-raising examples of their own. Kate, they thought, was just lucky to have someone like her uncle to be patient with her.

A problem not unlike Kate's is to be found in that splendid family story for eleven- and twelve-year-olds, *Meet the Austins,* by Madeleine L'Engle. What triggered the wretched quarrel between the older brother and sister that almost ended in tragedy for them both? The girl was the aggressor and completely unreasonable. But why, what set her off? Can the children see how the death of their beloved uncle and the arrival in their family of a spoiled brat of a girl had all the children emotionally upset and on edge? Such accumulative disturbances sometimes result indirectly in the worst explosions, as they did in this case. But the warmth and stability of family life are restored eventually in this heart-warming story.

Righteous anger over an injustice is one of the hardest emotions to quell, for both children and adults. It is important that children learn early that almost everyone suffers at one time or another from this difficulty. How to meet it? Julia Sauer's *The Light at Tern Rock* turns on such a problem and so affords an impersonal situation for discussion. It tells the story of Ronnie and his Aunt Marthy, who find themselves marooned on the lonely Tern Rock Lighthouse. They are substitute keepers of the light and they cannot leave because the regular keeper, Byron Flagg, has deliberately broken his promise to return and take them to the mainland December fifteenth. Ronnie is furious. "Aunt Marthy, isn't a broken promise the wickedest thing on earth?" he asks. Aunt Marthy thinks maybe cruelty is worse, cruelty to defenseless creatures. Unconvinced, Ronnie sulks, splutters about his wrongs, and nurses his anger toward Byron Flagg. Finally, Aunt Marthy announces, ". . . Christmas . . . is something in your heart. It's a feeling that doesn't go with anger and hatred. And my heart's got to be clean and ready for Christmas."

She sends Ronnie to his room, not to punish him, but to give him an opportunity to cool off and be alone. By Christmas Eve he comes out of his sulks and climbs with Aunt Marthy up the long stairs to light the great light. As its powerful beam shines out over the lonely sea and snowflakes drift softly down, Ronnie suddenly melts; the anger and hardness leave him. He turns to Aunt Marthy in surprise at his discovery. "We've lighted a candle tonight, too," he cries, "a big one. We've lighted the biggest candle we'll ever have a chance to light for Him—to help Him on His way."

It is a wholesome conclusion, but some questions still remain which children might well discuss. Should that "mean old man," as Ronnie called him, have lied as he did? Should Ronnie forgive him? Suppose you were Ronnie and had missed all the fun he had missed, how would you greet Byron Flagg when he arrived on the Rock three days after Christmas? This would be a choice scene to dramatize, and probably every child who played the part would have a different version of Ronnie's behavior.

Certainly such discussions or dramatizations can be too moralistic unless the presiding grownup gives the children plenty of latitude in drawing their own conclusions. Invaluable indirect guidance grew from reading aloud *Cheaper by the Dozen,* by Frank B. Gilbreth and Ernestine Gilbreth Carey. A young teacher had a sixth-grade group of boys and girls from about as undesirable homes as you could find. Divorce, desertion, drunkenness, and quarreling were the rule rather than the exception. The children were spellbound by the hilarious goings-on of that remarkable family. Their comments were revealing. Over and over they asked, "Is it really true? Did any family ever have fun like that?" One big overage boy commented, "A fellow wouldn't mind studying if he had a dad that helped him like that." And a girl said in surprise, "Why, those people really wanted their kids, didn't they?" Such comments gave the leader a chance not to moralize but to reassure those children. Yes, there really was such a family and these things did happen. Families have fun together when they share work, and plan and play together. He was trying to build into their concepts of family life the idea of family love and loyalty, the family group that stays together through thick and thin. By way of this book those children glimpsed, perhaps for the first time, the possible satisfactions and joys of family life.

Through such informal discussions of a variety of books, an adult can discover more about a child's attitudes than in almost any other way. Guidance may come casually as a part of a lively difference of opinion over such humorous situations as in the first chapter of *The Good Master* or some of Caddie Woodlawn's antics. Young tomboys who secretly sympathize with Caddie's aversions to the girl's role in life may, through Caddie's experiences, be helped to a happier acceptance of their sex.

Sometimes the best guidance is no guidance at all, a hands-off policy until the storm passes or the tensions are eased. Tales of laughter—for example, the books by Dr. Seuss or Keith Robertson's hilarious *Henry Reed, Inc.*—are invaluable. Invaluable too are grave books like *A Stranger at Green Knowe* or Scott O'Dell's *Island of the Blue Dolphins,* so absorbing that a young reader is carried out of himself and comes back recreated. Know your child and know books because for every child there is the right book at the right time.

SUGGESTED READING, PROBLEMS, AND PROJECTS

1. Read at least one of the following books and be prepared to give a brief report on it. *The Door in the Wall, Johnny Tremain, Tom Sawyer, Caddie Woodlawn, Henry Huggins, The Borrowers, Meet the Austins*. Read also the following picture-stories: *Juanita, Horton Hatches the Egg,* and *Millions of Cats*. (See the Preface for suggestions for keeping a record of your reading.)

2. Give examples of ways in which a child's need for security—material, intellectual, and emotional—should expand as he matures. Trace similar desirable changes in his other needs. What types of books might help at each stage?

3. How do you account for the various levels of taste adults have in music, art, and literature? How can teachers and parents help children develop good taste in their reading?

4. What kind of reading for escape do you enjoy? When is such reading desirable and when is it undesirable for an adult? For a child?

5. How does the need for competence explain young people's admiration for book heroes notable for their independent achievements? What happens when a desire for competence is completely thwarted?

6. From children's books you remember, give concrete examples of the influence reading may have in fostering useful social attitudes.

7. Suggest several books which could be used for guidance in a discussion with children. How would you direct the discussion?

8. Choose any well-remembered children's book and see if you can determine which basic needs it seems to satisfy.

REFERENCES

AMERICAN COUNCIL ON EDUCATION, COMMISSION ON TEACHER EDUCATION. *Helping Teachers Understand Children*. American Council on Education, 1945. This book represents the cumulative and anecdotal studies of children, both as individuals and in groups, made by their teachers.

ARTLEY, A. STERL. *Your Child Learns to Read,* ill. by Helen Carter and Eve Hoffman. Scott, 1953. A reading specialist discusses the learning-to-read processes from a developmental angle. Chapter 6 shows how the child's widening interests in many kinds of books are encouraged in schools and homes.

CLEARY, FLORENCE. *Blueprints for Better Reading: School Programs for Promoting Skill and Interest in Reading*. Wilson, 1957. Offers both inspiration and ideas to teachers and librarians.

CROSBY, MURIEL, ed. *Reading Ladders for Human Relations*. American Council on Education, 1963. This enlarged and revised edition contains an introduction and bibliographies on the role of reading in developing children's self-knowledge and social awareness.

DUFF, ANNIS. *"Bequest of Wings."* Viking, 1944. A pleasant account of one family's use of books, pictures, and music.

FRANK, JOSETTE. *Your Child's Reading Today*. Doubleday, 1960. Sensible advice from a pioneer in the child study movement concerning a child's reading, given from the standpoint of his social-emotional development. Don't deprecate his tastes, she advises, but capitalize on reading enjoyment.

GESELL, ARNOLD, and FRANCES ILG. *Child Development; An Introduction to the Study of Human Growth*. Harper, 1949. This research study considers child growth in its broadest sense—intellectual, emotional, and social—from infancy through adolescence. Lucid style and revealing case histories make this a readable and essential book for parents and teachers.

HYMES, JAMES LEE. *Understanding Your Child*. Prentice-Hall, 1952. This is a practical and entertaining discussion of child behavior and parent-child conflicts. It is built around these four major considerations: children grow, there is a plan to their growth, they want things out of life, and there is a reason for their behavior.

ILG, FRANCES L., and LOUISE BATES AMES. *Child Behavior*. Harper, 1955. Frances Ilg, M.D., and Louise Ames, Ph.D., give direct advice, based on their research at the Gesell Institute, to parents concerning problems of child behavior. The book is an extension of their popular and widely syndicated newspaper column.

JENKINS, GLADYS, HELEN SHACTER, and WILLIAM BAUER. *These Are Your Children*. Scott, 1953. A series of case studies with charts of normal child development and the special needs of children at various ages, enlivened by photographs of children in problem situations or normal activities.

MONROE, MARION, and BERNICE ROGERS. *Foundations for Reading: Informal Pre-Reading Procedures*. Scott, 1964. An idea book and guide for the kindergarten or first-grade teacher. Presents detailed descriptions of informal pre-reading procedures.

MOORE, ANNE CARROLL. *My Roads to Childhood*. Doubleday, 1939. A distinguished librarian and critic of children's books comments on outstanding books up to the year 1938.

MOTT, CAROLYN, and LEO B. BAISDEN. *The Children's Book on How to Use Books and Libraries,* ill. Scribner, 1961. Meets a wide variety of elementary grade needs ranging from writing a book review to using reference books and the library catalog.

WHITE, DOROTHY. *Books Before Five,* ill. by Joan Smith. Oxford, 1954. Written by a former librarian, this is a play-by-play account of the books her little girl loved, accepted, or rejected in the years between two and five.

WITTY, PAUL. *Reading in Modern Education.* Heath, 1949. A reading research expert sums up his point of view about the teaching of reading, and in Chapter V discusses children's books in a balanced reading program.

chapter 2

The Adult and the Child's Books

Books may be written for children, but it is the adults who buy the books. Parents, grandparents, uncles, and aunts select a choice volume for a favorite child. Teachers and librarians exhibit books, recommend them, and otherwise guide children's reading. But how can any adult know what book a child is going to enjoy?

Actually, adults can't know with any degree of certainty. Moreover, they must face the fact that youngsters are past masters at rejecting what is not for them. As Paul Hazard says in his delightful *Books, Children and Men:*

> *Children defend themselves, I tell you. They manifest at first a degree of inertia that resists the liveliest attacks; finally they take the offensive and expel their false friends from a domain in which they wish to remain the rulers. Nothing is done to create a common opinion among them and yet that opinion exists. They would be wholly incapable of defining the faults that displease them; but they cannot be made to believe that a book which displeases them* should *please them. Whatever their differences may be as to age, sex, or social position, they detest with common accord disguised sermons, hypocritical lessons, irreproachable little boys and girls who behave with more docility than their dolls. It is as though . . . they brought into the world with them a spontaneous hatred of the insincere and the false. The adults insist, the children pretend to yield, and do not yield. We overpower them; they rise up again. Thus does the struggle continue, in which the weaker will triumph.* (p. 49)

A book may be judged a juvenile classic by experts in children's literature, but if it is beyond the child's understanding or too subtle or sophisticated for his level of appreciation, he can turn it down with a stony indifference which leaves adults baffled and grieved. They needn't mourn. Two years later the child may accept that same book with enthusiasm. It is the same with music. A popular song will catch a child's ear, while a symphony may only confuse him. But as he matures and his musical experiences increase, he hears parts of the symphony, its different movements, over and over until he understands and enjoys them. Finally, when he hears the whole symphony, he can follow it with pleasure, and its great melodies sing in his memory. So some poems must be heard repeatedly, and some stories must be talked over in parts or listened to while someone who knows and loves them reads aloud.

Through this gradual induction into better and better literature, children catch the theme and savor the beauty or the subtle humor or the meaning that eluded them at first. Sometimes an adult has the privilege of seeing this discovery take place. The children's faces come suddenly alive; their eyes shine. They may be anticipating an amusing conclusion or a heroic triumph. There is a sudden chuckle, or breath is exhaled like a sigh. The book has moved them, perhaps even to laughter or tears, but in any case there is a deep inner satisfaction, and they will turn to books again with happy anticipation.

It is evident from the discussion of the child's needs in Chapter 1 that the first consideration in selecting books for a special child or a group of children must be the children themselves. The needs of each child are determined by his background and attitudes, his abilities and interests, and, of course, his reading skill. Adults should not feel restricted by a child's immediate interests, however, because these are often too narrow. Teachers, librarians, and parents should keep children exploring both the best of the old books and the most promising of the new. Since new titles alone number over two thousand a year, the adult needs a few general guideposts and some specific criteria to help him select wisely.

Certainly, children need books to widen their horizons, deepen their understandings, and give them broader social insights. They also need books that minister to their merriment or deepen their appreciation of beauty. They need heroism, fantasy, and down-to-earth realism. And they need books that, in the course of a good story, help to develop clear standards of right and wrong. Finally, children's books should have those qualities of good writing that distinguish literature for any age or group of people.

Criteria for Stories

Of course, a child's reading will not and should not be limited to stories, but stories are his first and most lasting literary love. He hears them with delight at three and will probably enjoy them throughout adolescence and maturity. What are the distinguishing characteristics of a well-written story? In general, stories should have an *adequate theme,* strong enough to generate and support a *lively plot;* they should also have *memorable characters* and *distinctive style.*

THEME

The theme is the idea of the story—what it is all about. Occasionally the theme is implied in the title, as in *Mike Mulligan and His Steam Shovel,* a story about the prodigious feat Mike performs with his steam shovel. *The Good Master* is the story of the gentling of a badly behaved little hoyden by the patience of the kindly master of the house. More often, the theme must be sought in the development of the story. *The Ark* tells of a family's search for security after the storms of war. The book entitled . . . *and now Miguel* is about one boy's struggle to attain competence in his chosen work and so be accepted as a responsible, mature person. Whatever the theme, it must be substantial, for a weak one results in a flabby story without unity or climax, a story which leaves the reader feeling "so what?" A strong theme, on the other hand, will support a vigorous plot with action, suspense, and a clear-cut conclusion.

PLOT

A good plot—the action of the story—grows out of a strong theme. Adults may like a

Drawn with posterlike simplicity, the "lovely light luscious delectable cake" of the Duchess has indeed risen! Notice the few interesting details of costumes and the cook rushing in with a spot of tea.
From Virginia Kahl's The Duchess Bakes a Cake. *Copyright 1955 by Virginia Kahl. Reproduced with permission of Charles Scribner's Sons. (Original in color, book 7½ x 10)*

stream-of-consciousness novel or a quiet character study, but children don't. They want heroes who have obstacles to overcome, conflicts to settle, difficult goals to win. It is the vigorous action in pursuit of these goals that keeps young readers racing along from page to page to find out how the hero achieves his ends. But achieve he must, in some way or other. All-round defeat is intolerable to youth, and rightly so, since youth is essentially the time for building both the courage to try difficult tasks and the faith to believe that high endeavor will succeed when properly reinforced with industry, planning, and persistence. In adult fiction it is possible to have a strong theme with little action or plot development, but in children's stories the two generally go hand in hand.

CHARACTERS

The characters in a story are no less important than the theme and the plot. It is true that children go through a stage during which mere tales of action, peopled with stereotypes, satisfy them. Adult readers of pulp fiction apparently never go beyond this stage. But, happily, most children do and consequently want characters that are not stereotypes of bravery or beauty but real flesh-and-blood individuals, unique and memorable. Although the story may be realistic or fantastic, the characters must be convincing. Mary Poppins is as fanciful as Cinderella, but Cinderella is a stereotype, whereas Mary Poppins is a severe and crusty individual that no child ever forgets. Wilbur, the "radiant pig" in *Charlotte's Web,* and Toad of Toad Hall in *The Wind in the Willows* are just as real to children as is Caddie Woodlawn, the redheaded tomboy. Long after details of plot have been forgotten, children and adults will recall with a chuckle or a warm glow of affection such characters as Jo in *Little Women,* Long John Silver, Heidi, Henry Huggins, Janey the middle Moffat, Arrietty in *The Borrowers,* and dozens of other salty book characters. And it is through such well-drawn individuals that children gain new insight into their own personal problems and their ever widening relationships with other people.

STYLE

Finally, there is style, difficult to define, a quality of which children are unconscious and yet one to which they respond as surely as they respond to a smile. In all too many stories for children, style is conspicuous by its absence, which accounts for the depressing mediocrity of so many books for children. By style we mean, in part, that the words, fraught with meaning, should also fall felicitously on the ear and read aloud comfortably and pleasantly. Read these excerpts aloud:

"Little pig, little pig, let me come in."
"No, not by the hair on my chinny-chin-chin."
"Then I'll huff and I'll puff and I'll blow your house in."

"Hundreds of cats, thousands of cats, millions and billions and trillions of cats."[1]

There are, of course, many styles. As Thrall, Hibbard, and Holman say in their *A Handbook to Literature,* "The best *style,* for any given purpose, is that which most nearly approximates a perfect adaptation of one's language to one's ideas."[2] When Virginia Kahl's Duchess baked a cake, it was to be "a lovely light luscious delectable cake," which it certainly was. The wise, cynical cat in *The Two Reds,* by Will and Nicolas, observes that "Idle paws will not fill an empty belly," and, after studying Polly the parrot, "All feathers and beak, nothing to eat." In contrast, note the quiet simplicity of the style in this excerpt from Laura Ingalls Wilder's *Little House in the Big Woods:*

She looked at Ma, gently rocking and knitting. She thought to herself, "This is now." She was glad that the cozy house, and Pa and Ma and the firelight and the music, were now. They could not be forgotten, she thought, because now is now. It can never be a long time ago.

Over and over again, Elizabeth Enright surprises her readers with her pat and amusing use of words that fit the situation or the character. In *Gone-Away Lake* five-year-old Foster is rescued from a dangerous bog of quicksand and explains that he is all right, "but I'm kind of weak from scaredness." And when Portia appears at the farm with braces on her teeth, her boy cousin comments, "When you smile it looks just like the front of a Buick!" Good prose style for any age level surprises and delights. And in children's books, too, good prose style is a genuine, even though unrecognized, source of pleasure for young readers or listeners.

So, then, in searching for children's fiction that is most worth while, look first for a substantial *theme* around which a lively *plot* can develop. Ask yourself what the book is about. Does it leave children with an added insight into their own problems or the problems of other people? Is the plot or action of the story absorbing, and does it add to the children's zest for living, their feeling that life is good? Consider the *characters* in the story—are they well drawn, unique, and unforgettable? Finally, is the *style* appealing and forthright with humor or beauty or those elements of the dramatic which are appropriate to the story? However, don't be too rigid in applying these standards. Even though a book does not measure up to every one, it should be considered if it has particular values for a particular child. These guides are generalizations. Wide reading at all levels and careful observation of children's reactions to stories and their individual and special interests will also help adults make wise choices in guiding young readers.

1. Wanda Gág, *Millions of Cats* (Coward-McCann, 1928).
2. William Flint Thrall and Addison Hibbard, *A Handbook to Literature,* revised and enlarged by C. Hugh Holmes (The Odyssey Press, 1960).

Criteria for Other Types of Books

The special criteria for the various types of children's literature—poetry, fairy tales, fables, myths, epics, fanciful tales, realistic stories, historical fiction, animal stories, and informational books—are discussed in succeeding chapters, and there are also evaluations of individual books, authors, and illustrators. Many different kinds of books should be judged by the criteria for stories—theme, plot, characters, and style. Biography, for instance, may be so evaluated, but it should also be judged by other equally important criteria (see Chapter 17). The essential criterion for judging informational books (see Chapter 18) is accuracy, but style, too, is important. Information can, and should, be presented in an interesting, lively fashion.

The Range of Stories for Children

Because childhood should be a time of exploring many kinds of books, adults who work with children should know the different types, both to prevent children from falling into reading ruts and to encourage them to try books of many varieties.

PICTURE-STORIES

For the prereaders and beginning readers, the picture-stories are enchanting. Their illustrations will be considered in Chapter 4. Significantly, the older stories which have lasted over the years are, for the most part, built around one or two general themes: love or reassurance, and achievement. *Peter Rabbit,* which is over sixty years old, has both. Peter has a daring adventure but returns safely to his home where his mother tucks him into bed with a justifiably punishing dose of camomile tea. Love and reassurance make Else Minarik's *Little Bear* books, and many other stories for the youngest, completely satisfying. And then, because the young child is always in an inferior position in his relations with older children and adults, he yearns for independent achievement or competence. Hence the long life of *Mike Mulligan and His Steam Shovel,* the popularity of *Madeline* and her achievements, and the success of *Little Tim,* who triumphs gloriously over his many mishaps, such as shipwrecks and mislaying his parents —all books with themes of satisfying achievement.

Any one of Maurice Sendak's Little Bear *pictures is marvelously interpretative. Here is sheer satisfaction, simply expressed in pen and ink with well drawn textures of nose, claws, and fur.*
Illustration by Maurice Sendak. Copyright © 1960 by Maurice Sendak. From Little Bear's Friend *by Else Holmelund Minarik. Reproduced with permission of Harper & Row, Publishers. (Original in color, book 5¾ x 8½, picture 3½ x 2½)*

FOLK TALES

Challenge and achievement are the heart of the folk tale themes. The heroes or heroines must perform stern tasks if they are to survive, but the fact that they deal competently with glass hills, giants, witches, wicked machinations, and come through modestly triumphant is both reassuring and encouraging. Stories such as "Cinderella," "Three Little Pigs," "Three Billy-Goats Gruff," and "Snow White" dramatize the stormy conflict of good and evil. And they reiterate the old verities that kindness and goodness will triumph over evil if they are backed by wisdom, wit, and courage. These are basic truths we should like built into the depths of the child's consciousness; they are the folk tales' great contribution to the child's social consciousness.

STORIES OF FAMILY LIFE

The themes of love, reassurance, and achievement continue in stories of family life. For the middle years, eight to ten or more, the pleasant and amusing adventures of *Little*

Eddie or *Henry Huggins* take place against a permissive family background of suburbia. So does that great family story for the twelves, *Meet the Austins.* The children in these stories have their problems and difficulties, some of them funny, some of them grave, but with the reassurance of family understanding and love. This is also true of such a fine regional book as *. . . and now Miguel,* the story of sheepherders of the Southwest, and it is true of books about underprivileged migrant workers such as *Blue Willow* and *Strawberry Girl.* These books broaden children's social understandings and deepen their sympathies. It is significant that the realistic stories for today's children have gone beyond such books as the once popular *The Bobbsey Twins* and *Nancy Drew* stories and present real people confronted with real problems—from earning money for a bike to rebuilding a fairly normal life in a postwar, bombed-out European city (*The Ark*).

This realistic fiction also acquaints the child with a wider world than the city suburbs or regional groups of our own country. Books begin to take him back in time and to introduce him to family life in other countries. Even in the picture-story stage, French *Madeline* or *Jeanne-Marie* are as familiar to American children as are the boys and girls of the United States in their preprimers. Presently the tens will be enjoying that strange French home-in-the-making *Family Under the Bridge,* and the twelves will find out what happens in the aftermath of a war when children who have been separated from their parents set out to find them—a three-year search which is recorded by Ian Serrallier in *The Silver Sword.* Gone are the fiesta stereotypes of foreign lands and gone are the stories about a country told by an author who has never seen it or who equates contemporary life with that of a hundred years ago. *Hans Brinker* has been replaced by Meindert De Jong's *Wheel on the School.* Today's India is re-created by Shirley Arora in *What Then, Raman?* Margot Benary-Isbert gives us a vivid picture of Germany as she knew it, a true picture of what happens to farms, cities, families in a war-bombed city. Here is modern reality, grim or terrible or confusing but gallant, too, because in such books as these children find human beings courageously building a better life out of the rubble.

A striking composition! See how much the artist's carefully selected details tell us about the girl—her poverty, loneliness, and love, all tenderly depicted.
Illustration by Paul Lantz. From Blue Willow *by Doris Gates. Copyright 1940 by Doris Gates. Reproduced with permission of The Viking Press, Inc. (Book 5½ x 8)*

HISTORICAL FICTION

Children may know Paul Revere in story or verse, but do they also know children of Revere's time—eight-year-old Sarah in *The Courage of Sarah Noble* and the twelve- or fourteen-year-old Johnny in *Johnny Tremain?* Historical fiction today is both historically authentic and well written. Indeed, in such books we find some of the best contemporary writing for children and youth. Both the 1961

The discomforts and dangers of pioneer travel are shown in this unusual composition, in which the delicate details of leaves and twigs are contrasted with the strong shapes of the figures, rocks, and tree trunks. Illustration by Leonard Weisgard. From The Courage of Sarah Noble *by Alice Dalgliesh. Copyright 1954 by Alice Dalgliesh and Leonard Weisgard. Reproduced with permission of Charles Scribner's Sons. (Original in color, book 5½ x 8)*

and the 1962 Newbery Medals were awarded to books of historical fiction—*Island of the Blue Dolphins* and *The Bronze Bow,* two books good readers of twelve and over should not miss. In each of the books mentioned in this brief sampling, the theme—from "Keep up your courage, Sarah Noble" to it is only love, not hatred, that can bend a bow of bronze—speaks strongly to children of today.

BIOGRAPHY

Historical fiction and biography may and should be used to reinforce each other. *Johnny Tremain* makes a biography of Paul Revere infinitely more real, and the homespun, frontier boys in William Steele's stories give vivid life to the scene and times of Daniel Boone. Both historical fiction and biography impress children with a sense of the reality of other days. "This really happened," they say, or "Those people really lived like that, didn't they?" Begin early to introduce children to these "real stories" we call biographies. Even the eights and nines can start with the d'Aulaires' picture-biographies and can then move on to many excellent biographies suitable for children of each age level. Books about Doctor Paracelsus, Galileo, Penn, Columbus, Patrick Henry, Washington, Lincoln, Lee, and many others are authentic and as fascinating as fiction, and they provide an antidote to the trivia and violence that beset our age.

ANIMAL STORIES

A teacher or parent confronted with a reluctant reader will find that the two most enticing baits to reading are animal stories and what the children describe as "funny books." Stories about animal heroes, either pets or wild creatures, are exceedingly popular. Does the child identify himself with the animal, helpless in the hands of men? Or, as some people think, does this very helplessness of the beast make the child feel superior in resourcefulness and competence? Whatever the answer, the fact remains that whether it is a horse story by Marguerite Henry, a dog story by Jim Kjelgaard, or the story of the young gorilla in *A Stranger at Green Knowe,* children read animal tales avidly even though they are generally filled with sadness or downright tragedy. The animal hero ordinarily has some unusual competence or achieves some special success which makes his vulnerability at the hands of master or hunter all the more heart-rending. Such stories call forth the young reader's desire to nurture and protect, and this is one of the values of the well-written animal tale for children. Compassion is close to love, and love is the most civilizing force in life. So let children weep over *King of the Wind* or *Brighty of the Grand Canyon*; they need the therapy of tears if they are to learn compassion.

FANTASY

Children need also the therapy of laughter, and often that is to be found in modern fantasy. Hence the value of the Seuss books from *Horton Hatches the Egg* to *The Cat in the Hat,* wild, daft nonsense matched at an older level by Astrid Lindgren's outrageously funny super-child *Pippi Longstocking.* There is also the subtler humor of *Winnie-the-Pooh* or *Charlotte's Web,* and the wry, close-to-tears humor and pathos of *The Borrowers.* For fantasy moves from nonsense to serious symbolism, as the *Narnia* stories or *The Wind in the Willows* proves. Children need fantasy as a corrective for the too tight literalness that is a frequent product of our mechanistic, science-conscious age.

Incidentally, there is delightful humorous realism too, as in Keith Robertson's *Henry Reed, Inc.* But whether laughter is found in a here-and-now story or in the wildest fantasy, it is so important in our grim days that we should search for it and use it.

Illustrations

Beautiful illustrations and format (the shape, size, type, paper, binding, and general arrangement) are among the most striking characteristics of modern books for children. Bright colors or soft pastels, quaint old-fashioned pictures or arresting modern designs—all clamor for attention. Even black and white drawings or pen and ink sketches have a drollery or a charm that delights children and carries the older generation back to its own childhood. Publishers know well the effect of gay-looking books. Grocery stores and newsstands are selling literally thousands of books for children on the strength of their eye-catching colors. Some of these are worth buying, but many of them are trivial in content and pictorially worthless. Temporary pacifiers in book form!

The crudities of the comics and of the advertisements and pictures in some of the slick magazines also confront children. How can we immunize them against the banal and vulgar and lead them into an increasing enjoyment of a variety of authentic styles and media? Only by exposing them to fine examples of graphic arts old and new. For, as Bertha Mahony says in *Illustrators of Children's Books,* "... art in children's books is a part of all art, not an isolated special field. In every period the greatest artists have shared in it." But in the evaluation of illustrations as in the evaluation of stories, the child himself must be the starting point if we are to meet his needs and improve his taste.

Here is photographic realism, thoroughly amusing in every detail, even to the book from which Henry is copying his designs. Illustration by Robert McCloskey. From Henry Reed, Inc. *by Keith Robertson. Copyright © 1958 by Keith Robertson. Reproduced with permission of The Viking Press, Inc. (Book 5¼ x 8¼)*

Children begin as stern literalists, demanding a truthful interpretation of the text. If the hero is described as red-headed, no child is going to accept a brown topknot without protest. When the child is told by Ludwig Bemelmans that there are twelve little girls who go walking from Madeline's school, he counts to see that the artist has put them all in.

Happily, with fantasy even young children forget their literalness. They accept all the cozy details of Caldecott's *Frog He Would A-Wooing Go* or Beatrix Potter's neat little fireside interior for *The Tale of Peter Rabbit* as readily as they follow the everyday drama of weather in Roger Duvoisin's pictures for Alvin Tresselt's *Follow the Wind* or *Sun Up*. If the illustrations interpret the story, the child will take to his heart such varied techniques as the splashy colors of Nicolas Mordvinoff's *Finders Keepers,* Robert Lawson's finely detailed pen and ink sketches of landscapes and small animals, and Arthur Rackham's inimitable gnomes, witches, wee folk, and strangely human trees.

Being literal, the young child also wants a picture synchronized precisely with the text. When *Make Way for Ducklings* has the mother duck leading her offspring across a busy Boston thoroughfare, the child is glad that Robert McCloskey placed his unforgettable picture with the description and not a page or two later. Even older children are irked by illustrations that appear before or after the episode they are supposed to represent.

Children are as fond of action in pictures as in stories. They love Ernest Shepard's gay action drawings of the skipping Christopher Robin, the flight of Virginia Kahl's impulsive Wolfgang, and the droll, carefree abandon of Maurice Sendak's capering children.

We know they also like bright colors, but not to the exclusion of muted hues or blacks and whites. A nursery school staff tested children on their color choices in clothes and in picture books and were surprised to find no conclusive preference for primary colors. To be sure, the brilliant reds and clear blues that the Petershams so frequently employ in their pictures are always eye-catching, but apparently children also respond happily to the gentle colors in Tasha Tudor's and Marguerite de Angeli's pictures for *Mother Goose*. On the whole, there is some evidence that children do prefer colors to black and white. Yet nothing could add to the young child's delight in Lynd Ward's powerful blacks and whites for *The Biggest Bear* or the older children's pleasure in the fine, clear minutiae of William Pène du Bois' drawings for his *Twenty-One Balloons* or *The Giant*.

Small children are generally not assumed to see details in a picture, but they do. For the older generation, half the charm of the pictures in the Palmer Cox Brownie books lay in their details. The illustrations seemed to have hundreds of Brownies, each doing something different, but every child always looked for his favorites, the Dude or the Policeman or the Cowboy. So children today look for the bespectacled twins or the Negro child in Elizabeth Orton Jones' group of children at play in *Small Rain*. But the same youngster who will gloat over small details in a picture may also enjoy the bold, uncluttered strength of a single figure by Rockwell Kent, or the sharp, clear outline of Artzybasheff's *Fairy Shoemaker*.

Young children, then, have some strong preferences regarding pictures, but they will accept a crude or saccharine drawing if it tells a story. However, if they are continuously exposed to authentic art of many varieties, they become more discerning and their taste improves. The captions for the illustrations reproduced throughout this book comment on the styles, techniques, and materials of the artists. They will help to guide adults in choosing children's books with worth-while illustrations. See also Chapter 4, which discusses some of the outstanding illustrators of children's books and their work.

Format

Although the content and the illustrations of a child's book are of first importance, format should also be considered. The books of children under six lead a rough life at best and survive only if sturdily made. Even the books of older children suffer more wear and tear than adult books. Children reread their favorites as adults rarely do. A beloved book goes to bed with a small child, to camp with an older child, and is generally lugged around and enjoyed at odd moments in odd places.

If a picture-story is to last through many readings, it should be clothbound with sturdy covers and firm stitching. Stout books with easy-to-turn pages of substantial, hard-to-tear paper are a comfort to young children, who like to pore over their picture books by themselves.

Size is another consideration. For the child under six, most books should be small and light enough for him to handle by himself. But, oddly enough, he does occasionally enjoy a book that he has to stand over at a table, leaning on his elbows. Or you will see him lying down comfortably on his stomach, propped up on his elbows, and browsing happily in a huge *Mother Goose*. Older boys and girls are much the same. Most of their books should be easy to hold and to read. But older children also like big science books or oversized art books whose large pictures add to their enjoyment and understanding of the text. Such books they should be taught to use on tables, both for their own comfort and for the preservation of the books.

The size of the type, the leading (the space between lines), and the number of words to a page are also important. Even in the picture-story for the nonreader, the small type used in adult books is undesirable. The words should be well spaced and in large enough type to attract the child's eye. Somewhere around five he begins to associate those printed symbols with word meanings, and one fine day he will recognize some particular word and be thrilled with his achievement. Reading has begun! On the other hand, boys and girls in the middle or upper grades of school will shy away from a book with large type. "Baby stuff!" they say at first glance. But children of all ages have one suspicion in common. They are afraid of a book page with too solid a printed pattern. Too many words to a page make the older child turn hastily to books with more conversation or shorter paragraphs. One three-year-old, bored with too many words, explanatory and descriptive, commanded the adult sternly, "Don't read the writing, read the pictures!"

Book Care

It is never too early to teach children the proper care of their books. Clean hands are the first requisite for handling books, and those hands, however small, should be taught to treat books carefully. A bookcase of his own is highly desirable, but, lacking that, a child should have a special shelf in the adults' bookcases or a section of a table or cupboard for his volumes. There they should be placed when he is through reading them, and there he should find them, uncluttered with adult magazines or papers, when he wants them. Willful destruction or excessively careless treatment of books should be corrected, but with exceeding caution. Accidents do happen, to books as well as to clothes. Let adults remember that tragic episode in *Cotton in My Sack* when Joanda drops a treasured book in the mud and doesn't dare go back to school. After all, one book mislaid or accidentally damaged should not frighten a child away from books. Its loss might make him value books more deeply.

The School Library

Choosing children's books for a school library presents some special problems. In general, schools need substantial collections of reference books, well selected and up to date. Children should be taught to use these informational books from the primary grades on. Schools should find a typical cross section of the varied types of children's books available—factual books of all kinds, poetry, biography, historical fiction, fairy tales, and all the other types of fiction. The school librarian or the library committee should consider the particular town or neighborhood in which the school is situated. If the children come largely from one particular European background, they will enjoy books about their national group. These books will be enriched by family anecdotes and will lend glamor and prestige to family customs and roots. But those same children will enjoy other stories as well. Children in a farming community will welcome stories about 4-H activities and farm animals, but they need books with an urban background, too. Whatever special subjects it may include, any good book collection will begin with a basic list of juvenile classics and other books that have stood the test of time and critical evaluation. How do you find these books? (See Chapter 21, Reading in the Family, for a discussion of the public library and its use.)

First Aids to Book Selection

Indexes and book lists will be found in the bibliography following this chapter, but several are of such immediate importance that it seems essential to mention them here. For instance, it is hard to think of any kind of book, old or new, for children of any age or special interest, that cannot be located with the help of the *Children's Catalog*. That big volume, with its yearly supplement, lists children's books alphabetically by title, author, and subject matter or kind. Books are well annotated, distinguished books are starred, and there are book lists by grades. Teachers will not always see eye to eye on the grouping, but it does indicate possibilities.

Next in importance and first in charm is *The Horn Book Magazine*. Published six times a year, it reviews current books for children and young people and includes copious illustrations from the books themselves. Delightful articles about or by famous illustrators and authors are its greatest contribution. The book reviews of new juveniles keep well abreast of publications but have tended to be so consistently laudatory that important books could scarcely be distinguished from the run of the mill variety. A wholesomely astringent criticism of several poor books by distinguished authors has corrected this state of affairs and reassured *Horn Book* readers. The summer number is of special value since it prints in full the acceptance speeches of the Newbery and Caldecott Medal winners. Pictures of the Medal winners are included, as well as articles about them written by people who know them intimately. Upper-grade children are as excited as their teachers about this August number. Certainly *The Horn Book Magazine* should be on the subscription list of every school.

An antidote to some of the laudatory reviews of *The Horn Book* are those in the *Bulletin of the Center for Children's Books,* published by the University of Chicago Press. The *Bulletin* reviews mediocre and poor books as well as fine ones and evaluates them realistically on the basis of the child's needs and interests as well as by literary standards. It is invaluable for book selection, and its frankness is reassuring. Without such corrective reviews, distinguished books are in danger of being overwhelmed by mediocre ones.

A valuable reference which stems from *The Horn Book* is its *Newbery Medal Books.* This handsome volume contains the acceptance speech of every winner from 1922 to 1955, an excerpt from the book, and a brief biography of the author. Some of these papers are as delightful to read as the books themselves, for adults and children alike.

The New York *Times,* New York *Herald Tribune,* Chicago *Tribune, Christian Science Monitor,* and other large city newspapers offer regular book sections which review new children's books. So do such popular magazines as the *Saturday Review, The Atlantic Monthly,* and *The New Yorker,* and such professional journals as *Elementary English* and *Childhood Education.*

For a different purpose is *Children's Books Too Good to Miss,* a booklet prepared by three specialists in children's literature and published by the press of Western Reserve University. Here, under four age groups, are listed books of such distinction and worth that children should at least be exposed to them, even if they reject some of them. It is a minimum list of juvenile classics and other fine books and is especially helpful to adults who are selecting books for a child to own or launching a school library.

As we evaluate these books, old or new, we shall keep the child's needs and interests in mind and try to determine to what extent books written for him have met or ignored these needs. The basic requirements—good design, competent writing, and attractive illustrations—are to be found in many books, books that help the child to grow and give him clearer insights. If adults bear in mind the criteria discussed in this chapter and throughout the rest of the book, they should be better able to appraise the suitability of a book for a special child or a class of children, and so bring children and books happily together.

SUGGESTED READING, PROBLEMS, AND PROJECTS

Suggested reading: The Ark, . . . and now Miguel, The Wheel on the School, King of the Wind, The Duchess Bakes a Cake, Mike Mulligan and His Steam Shovel.

1. How would you introduce a children's classic—*Wind in the Willows,* for instance—to a child who has not been attracted to the book? To a group of children? Why is a careful introduction to such books worth while?

2. Using the criteria given in this chapter, evaluate five children's books. In your notes on the books that you read throughout the course, you will find it helpful to include such brief evaluations.

3. Select several books with very different styles of illustrations and, if possible, show them to ten or more children of widely varying backgrounds. What are their reactions?

4. Contrast the earlier illustrations with the more modern ones reproduced in this chapter and in Chapter 4. What are some specific differences between them? In what ways might each picture appeal to children?

5. What tactics would you use to encourage children to take proper care of their books?

6. From the books which you have already read or with which you are already familiar, make a list of not more than twenty which you consider essential for a school or a child's library. Keep in mind the basic criteria given in this chapter. Save the list so that you can compare it with the list you will make at the end of the course.

7. Study the book lists and references discussed in this chapter. Which ones do you think will prove most useful to you?

REFERENCES

Note: For additional references related to this chapter, see also Bibliographies for Chapters 1, 3, and 4.

AMERICAN LIBRARY ASSOCIATION. *A Basic Book Collection for Elementary Grades.* American Library Assoc., 1960. Suggested as a minimum collection, this is a helpful annotated guide to books in subject fields as well as to fiction and picture books.
A Basic Book Collection for Junior High Schools. American Library Assoc., 1960. Similar in pattern to the book for elementary grades.
Best Books for Children. Bowker, 1959–. An annotated list published annually. Arranged by grade and subject.
Subject Index to Poetry for Children and Young People. American Library Assoc., 1957. Indicates grade level.

ARBUTHNOT, MAY HILL, MARGARET MARY CLARK, and HARRIET GENEVA LONG. *Children's Books Too Good to Miss,* ill., 4th ed. Western Reserve Univ. Press, 1963.

BREWTON, JOHN E. and SARA W. *Index to Children's Poetry.* Wilson, 1942. First supplement, 1954. Helpful in finding poem sources. Indexed by author, title, subject, and first line. Thorough analysis of book contents, number of poems in a book, and grade placement.

Bulletin of the Center for Children's Books. The Univ. of Chicago, Graduate Library School, Univ. of Chicago Press, Chicago 37, Ill. Published monthly except August.

Children's Catalog. Wilson, 1909 to date.

CHILD STUDY ASSOCIATION OF AMERICA. *The Children's Bookshelf.* Bantam Books, 1962. Annotated lists of 2000 juvenile titles and 300 adult books on many phases of family life and child care, together with brief authoritative articles by distinguished writers in these fields.

COLBY, JEAN POINDEXTER. *The Children's Book Field.* Pellegrini, 1952. An editor of juvenile books has written a lively and helpful book about writing, illustrating, producing, and editing children's books. Chapters on how not to write and how to begin writing are valuable, as are those about the whole field of illustration and design.

CROUCH, MARCUS. *Treasure Seekers and Borrowers: Children's Books in Britain, 1900-1960.* The Library Assoc., Chaucer House, Malet Place, London, 1962. Excellent brief appraisals of authors and books, chiefly British, published during the first sixty years of the twentieth century.

EAKIN, MARY K., comp *Good Books for Children 1948-1961.* Univ. of Chicago Press, 1962. This useful bibliography of 1300 titles, both fiction and nonfiction, is geared to primary through junior-high grades. Annotations are full and informative, carefully graded, subject indexed.

———, comp. *Subject Index to Books for Intermediate Grades,* 3rd ed. American Library Assoc., 1963. An index of 1800 titles with emphasis on trade books.

EAKIN, MARY K., and ELEANOR MERRITT, comps. *Subject Index to Books for Primary Grades,* 2nd ed. American Library Assoc., 1961. Approximately 1000 textbooks and trade books for primary grades are indexed under detailed subject headings useful for the classroom teacher and librarian.

EASTMAN, MARY HUSE. *Index to Fairy Tales, Myths and Legends.* Faxon, 1926. First supplement, 1937. Second supplement, 1952. Useful for locating various sources in which individual tales may be found. There are geographical and racial groupings and lists for storytellers.

EATON, ANNE THAXTER. *Treasure for the Taking.* Viking, 1957. First published in 1946, this revised, annotated bibliography is arranged according to many types of children's books.

FENNER, PHYLLIS. *The Proof of the Pudding.* Day, 1957. An entertaining discussion of many books children enjoy.

———, ed. *Something Shared: Children and Books.* Day, 1959. A spirited compilation from many authors interested in children and books offers genuine entertainment as well as inspiration.

FERRIS, HELEN, ed. *Writing Books for Boys and Girls.* Doubleday, 1952. Over two hundred authors of children's books tell how they happened to write their stories.

GUILFOILE, ELIZABETH. *Books for Beginning Readers,* ill. by Norma Phillips. National Council of Teachers of English, 1962. A useful and timely bibliography of over 300 easy-reading books for beginners. The majority have been published within recent years to meet the need for entertainment and information.

HAZARD, PAUL. *Books, Children and Men,* tr. by Marguerite Mitchell, 4th ed. Horn Book, 1960. A member of the French Academy and professor of comparative literature both in France and in the United States has written engagingly of the great children's books of many countries.

The Horn Book Magazine. Horn Book, Inc., 585 Boylston St., Boston 16. Published six times a year.

HUCK, CHARLOTTE, and DORIS YOUNG. *Children's Literature in the Elementary School.* Holt, 1961. A critique of books for children based on the psychology of child growth and development at different age levels. The evaluation of books is sound but not exhaustive.

HUUS, HELEN. *Children's Books to Enrich the Social Studies for the Elementary Grades.* National Council for the Social Studies, 1961. Excellent annotated bibliographies, topically arranged, cover world history and geography from ancient times to the present.

KUNITZ, STANLEY J., and HOWARD HAYCRAFT, eds. *The Junior Book of Authors,* 2nd ed. Wilson, 1951. Biographical sketches of outstanding authors and illustrators of books for children.

FULLER, MURIEL, ed. *More Junior Authors.* Wilson, 1963. Companion volume to *The Junior Book of Authors,* 1951, rev. ed. Contains biographical material on current juvenile authors and illustrators not included in that work.

LARRICK, NANCY. *A Parent's Guide to Children's Reading.* Hardcover ed., Doubleday, 1958. Paperback ed., Pocket Books, Inc., 1958. A popularly written advisory guide for adults on children's reading. Includes age-grouped annotated bibliographies.

———. *A Teacher's Guide to Children's books,* ill. Merrill, 1960. How to stimulate and develop reading interests in the elementary grades, accompanied by extensive bibliographies for the child and the teacher.

LINES, KATHLEEN, ed. *Walck Monographs.* Walck, 1961, 1962. Personal anecdotes and a delightfully informal style make these brief biographies and critical evaluations of internationally known British authors invaluable to the teacher or student of children's literature. The series includes:

J. M. Barrie, by Roger Lancelyn Green
Lewis Carroll, by Roger Lancelyn Green
Walter de la Mare, by Leonard Clark
Eleanor Farjeon, by Eileen H. Colwell
Rudyard Kipling, by Rosemary Sutcliff
Andrew Lang, by Roger Lancelyn Green

Beatrix Potter, by Marcus Crouch
Rosemary Sutcliff, by Margaret Meek

MAHONY, BERTHA E., and ELINOR WHITNEY FIELD, eds. *Newbery Medal Books, 1922-1955.* Horn Book, 1955. Elementary schools and libraries have for many years needed information about the Newbery winners. Here in one handsome volume are brief biographies of the authors along with their acceptance speeches. It would be hard to find more delightful reading.

NATIONAL COUNCIL OF TEACHERS OF ENGLISH. *Adventuring with Books* (frequently revised). National Council of Teachers of English. May be used with and by elementary grade children since it is carefully annotated for child appeal.

ROOS, JEAN CAROLYN. *Patterns in Reading,* 2nd ed. American Library Association, 1961. A useful selection of books for older children, youth, and young adults. The books are grouped around more than a hundred major reading interests and are well annotated and indexed. A valuable reference.

SMITH, LILLIAN. *The Unreluctant Years.* American Library Association, 1953. A Canadian librarian writes discerningly of children's literature from the standpoint of literary quality only. This is a sound but limited approach.

Subject and Title Index to Short Stories for Children. Subcommittee of the American Library Association Editorial Committee, 1955. Designed to assist librarians and teachers in locating stories on specific subjects. Approximate grades given.

WALSH, FRANCES, ed. *That Eager Zest; First Discoveries in the Magic World of Books.* Lippincott, 1961. Almost 50 delightful verses and sketches about their own childhood reading experiences by such well-known writers as Carl Sandburg, James Thurber, Sherwood Anderson, and Lewis Mumford.

chapter 3

Children's Books: History and Trends

The flood of recent publications in children's books is so overpowering that it is important to remind ourselves that there are old books in children's literature as fresh and serviceable today as they were fifty years ago. There are also old books for children which have been discarded, and properly so. Age is no guarantee of a book's excellence, nor recency of its significance. Some of the discards we shall glance at briefly, only to know their kind and to be wary of their reappearance in modern dress—because that is what happens. We have not arrived at our wealth of fine modern books for children without considerable trial and error, and the errors are difficult to eradicate. We need perspective in judging children's books. We need to look at the past with modern eyes and view the present with the accumulated wisdom of the past. Where and how did children's literature begin? What has it grown out of and where is it going?

Books Begin

Before a child can read, his acquaintance with literature begins, as it began for the race, through listening to the songs and stories of his people. Mothers of yesterday chanted or sang to their babies. In simpler days, old women told homely tales of the beasts and kept alive legends of strange events. Grandmothers have always been the custodians of traditional tales, both of families and of the larger group, the tribe or the village. The men told stories to the adults of daring exploits and great adventures, and we may be sure the children listened. The professional storytellers, the bards or minstrels, took these tales, embroidered and polished them, and made them into the ballads or the hero tales or the epics of the people. So unwritten folk literature grew and was passed on by word of mouth for centuries before the collectors gathered it together for printing. Much of it was bloody and terrible; some of it was romantic, some coarse and humorous, told by adults to adults. Undoubtedly the children listened and loved many of these tales never intended for their ears and begged for them again and again. We say this with confidence because that is the way they have acquired much of their literature in every generation, even our own.[1] They appropriate from adult material those things they understand and enjoy.

FOR GROWNUPS: FABLES, ROMANCES, ADVENTURES

William Caxton (1422-1491) was England's first printer. He issued a series of books which are still appearing on our publishers' book lists for children. These included, among other titles, Sir Thomas Malory's *Morte d'Arthur, The Recuyell of the Historyes of Troye, The Boke of Histories of Jason, The Historye of Reynart the Foxe,* and *Aesop's Fables.* Tales of King Arthur still give the older child a fine introduction to romance, the *Odyssey* remains a popular adventure story, and the fables are enjoyed by young children even if they do skip the morals. Although Caxton intended his books for adults, children appropriated many of them, and these same collections continue to delight each generation.

FOR CHILDREN: HORNBOOKS AND BATTLEDORES

While textbooks will not be discussed in detail, no account of children's books seems complete without a word about the hornbooks. These were not books at all but little wooden paddles on which were pasted lesson sheets. These sheets were covered with transparent horn and bound along the edges by strips of brass. Most of the hornbooks were two and three-fourths by five inches. The lesson sheets of vellum or parchment began with a cross followed by the alphabet (sometimes in both large and small letters) and by syllables: *ab, eb, ib,* and other vowel and consonant combinations. There would probably be "In the

1. Today, children watch adult television programs, attend adult moving pictures, take over adult popular songs, and read the same comics that the adults read.

This illustration is almost a design because of the careful arrangement and repetition of the leaf, grape, and tree forms. Illustration for the William Caxton edition of Aesop's Fables.

Name of the Father, the Son, and the Holy Ghost" and the Lord's Prayer. The hornbooks differed in content, but in general they were designed to teach the child his letters and their combinations and to continue his religious instruction. There is still in existence a little hornbook supposedly used by Queen Elizabeth I. We know that these first hornbooks made their way to the New World for the instruction of the Puritan children. Later, around 1746, the hornbooks became mere cardboard battledores with gilt-embossed Dutch paper on one side and the lesson on the other. Neither the hornbook nor the battledore ever carried anything that was even remotely entertaining; so the children still sampled what they could from adult books.

PEDLAR'S TREASURY: A TU'PENNY TREAT

Then came the chapmen, the pedlars of the seventeenth and eighteenth centuries, with news sheets, ballads, broadsides, and chapbooks tucked in among their trinkets. Chapbooks were cheap little books that could be bought for as little as a penny. They had from sixteen to thirty-two or sixty-four pages and were often not stitched but merely folded. F. J. H. Darton, in *Children's Books in*

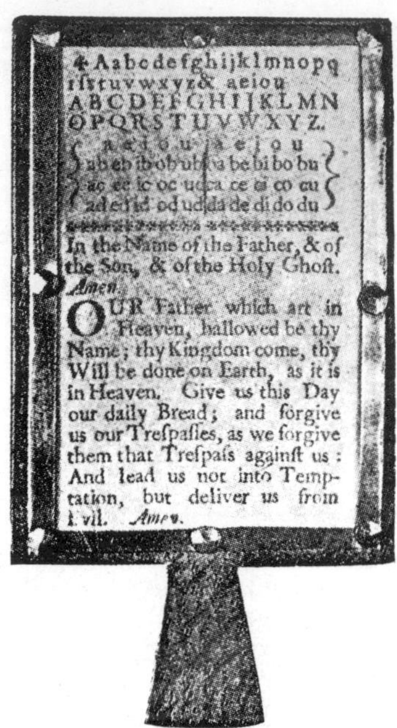

A photograph of a hornbook showing how learning to read was combined with religion. From a photograph in A Little History of the Horn-Book *by Beulah Folmsbee, The Horn Book, Inc., 1942.*

England, tells us that surviving copies have been found all carefully sewed with bits of silk or ribbon, perhaps by some child owner. The editors or compilers of these little books took the legends of antiquity, the old tales of the Middle Ages, elements of the fairy tales—any stories they could lay their hands on—and retold them in drastically condensed versions. All literary charm was lost; the grammar was often faulty, but what remained was a heightened sense of action with an adventure on almost every page. The educated upper classes of England may have frowned upon the chapbooks, but the common people of England loved them and bought them continuously. Of course the children discovered them and became ardent patrons of the pedlar's treasures, too.

The stories were the kind that children have always liked—adventure stories with heroes who do things. The account of their doughty deeds fills a book: *Chapbooks of the Eighteenth Century,* by John Ashton. "The History of Valentine and Orson" (see p. 34), is the story of twin brothers who were separated in infancy, Orson to be raised by a bear and Valentine to be reared by a king of France. Later Valentine captured the wild Orson and they performed great deeds together, each winning the hand of a lovely princess. Incidentally, the bear child, Orson, is a forerunner of Mowgli in Kipling's *Jungle Books.*

One favorite, "Tom Hickathrift," is a kind of early English Paul Bunyan. "At ten years old he was six feet high and three in thickness, his hand was like a shoulder of mutton, and every other part proportionable." He pulled up trees, slew giants, and felled four highwaymen at a blow.

In contrast to the colossal Tom Hickathrift, there is Tom Thumb, whose story is told in a chapbook rhymed version of "Tom Thumb His Life and Death." The woodcuts from 1630 show this Lilliputian hero early in his career falling into a bowl of pudding but later riding valiantly into battle atop an enormous war horse. (See p. 35.)

Another hero is the lusty "Sir Bevis of Southampton," who was cheated of his birthright and sold to the heathen Saracens. When he slew some sixty of the heathen for deriding the Christian religion, the king's daughter Josian won him her father's forgiveness and gave him a wonderful steed, Arundel, and a mighty sword, Morglay. With their aid he fought many brave battles, including one in which he captured the giant Ascapart. Eventually he married the beautiful "Heatheness," Josian.

The attitude of serious-minded adults of the day toward these crude, often vulgar little books was generally scornful. The clergy "viewed with alarm," but at least one man of letters spoke a good word for them. Richard Steele, in *The Tatler* (No. 95), tells how his young godson was "much turned in his studies" to these histories and adds:

> *He would tell you the mismanagements of John Hickerthrift, find fault with the passionate temper of Bevis of Southampton and loved St. George for being the champion of England: and by this means had his thoughts insensibly moulded into the notions of discretion, virtue, and honour.*

This may be a charitable interpretation of the effects of chapbook reading, but Florence Barry, in *A Century of Children's Books,* adds a cheerful note also. She says:

> *John Bunyan was the first to reconcile the claims of religion and romance, and he could never have written* The Pilgrim's Progress *if he had not been a good customer of the pedlar in his youth. (pp. 6-7)*

Badly written, crudely illustrated, unhonored though they were, the chapbooks preserved and popularized some of the precious elements of literature that children love. But their coarseness probably paved the way for the reaction against "tales, stories, jests," the reaction which produced children's books full of somber warnings and doleful examples.

The Puritans and Perdition

IN ENGLAND

Even while the chapmen were peddling their lurid, light-hearted "Histories," a religious movement was under way that was to affect life on both sides of the Atlantic. Beginning about the middle of Queen Elizabeth's reign, the English had become "the people of a book, and that book was the Bible." In London people went daily, in great crowds, to St. Paul's to hear the Bible read aloud, and small Bibles found their way into homes everywhere.

A group of deeply religious people whom we know as the Puritans studied their Bibles with a fervor that was increased by their honest horror at the licentiousness and depravity of the Restoration period and by their veneration for the victims of religious persecution. Foxe's *Book of Martyrs* (1563), with its details of death at the stake, was studied by the Puritans and given to their children.

As if this legacy of terror were not enough for small Puritans to endure, a clergyman, James Janeway, wrote in 1671 or 1672 a famous book that was long popular with the heaven-bent adults who ruled over Puritan nurseries. Its full title was:

> A Token For Children: *being an Exact Account of the Conversion, Holy and Exemplary Lives, and Joyful Deaths of several young Children. To which is now added, Prayers and Graces, fitted for the use of little Children.*

There were thirteen good little children in this gloomy book, and, considering their lives, it is small wonder that they died young. They spent their time trying to reform, convert, and generally improve everyone they encountered. They brooded on sin and eternal torment and the state of their souls. Morbid and unnatural as this book was with its continual dwelling on death, it grew from the earnest desire of the Puritans to make children happy—not in our modern sense of the word but in theirs. To be happy meant to be secure in the avoidance of Hell and in the assurance of Heaven. Unfortunately their method of instilling religious ideas was chiefly through the use of fear—the fear of Hell.

PILGRIM'S PROGRESS

Out of the Puritan world there emerged one great book for children—Bunyan's *Pilgrim's Progress.* This book was intended for adults and probably reached the children piecemeal as they listened to the adults read it aloud, or discuss it, or tell the more dramatic portions. Reviewing the story, we can easily understand why the children enjoyed the book. It is told in the best tradition of the old fairy tales which John Bunyan had enjoyed in chapbook form when he was a boy.

John Bunyan (1628-1688), a humble tinker, confessed that one of the sins of his youth was his delight in the "History of the Life and Death of that Noble Knight Sir Bevis of Southampton." As he grew more and more religious, he put away all such frivolous reading and turned to the Bible and to such fear-inspiring books as John Foxe's *Book of Martyrs.* These harrowing tales of "holy deaths" obsessed Bunyan to the point where he saw visions and dreamed horrible dreams of his own sins and the torments he was to suffer because of them. He began to preach such fiery and fearsome sermons that he was locked up for nonconformity to the established Church of England. In jail for years with his Bible and his *Martyrs,* he began to write the story of a Christian soul on its troublesome pilgrimage through this world to everlasting life. Sir Bevis was not forgotten but was reborn as Christian; the giant Ascapart became the Giant Despair; and so, in good fairy-tale style, Christian fought monsters and enemies with properly symbolic names. But no chapbook tale was ever so somber and so dramatic as this progress of a Christian pilgrim. It begins as a dream:

As I went through the wild waste of this world, I came to a place where there was a den, and I lay down in it to sleep. While I slept, I had a dream, and lo! I saw a man whose clothes were in rags, and he stood with his face from his own house, with a book in his hand, and a great load on his back.

Part one takes Christian through adventures, dangers, and despair until he loses the burden of his sins and joyously enters the Holy City. Part two deals similarly with Christiana and their sons. It is less exciting but seems to reflect Bunyan's love for his wife and children.

In its original form, with long interludes of theological moralizing, children would have difficulty reading this book, but when the dramatic story is cleared of these obstructions, it is a moving tale.

For children Bunyan composed some dull doggerels called *Divine Emblems, or Temporal Things Spiritualized.* The children would have none of them, and the only virtue we can find in them today is the absence of terror. These "good Godly books" of the Puritans must have developed in the children for whom they were intended either a lively resistance to books in general or a still livelier search for a comforting chapbook or some other treasure from the adult world.

IN THE NEW WORLD

The *Mayflower* reached our shores in 1620, but the great exodus of Puritans from England to the New World did not take place until

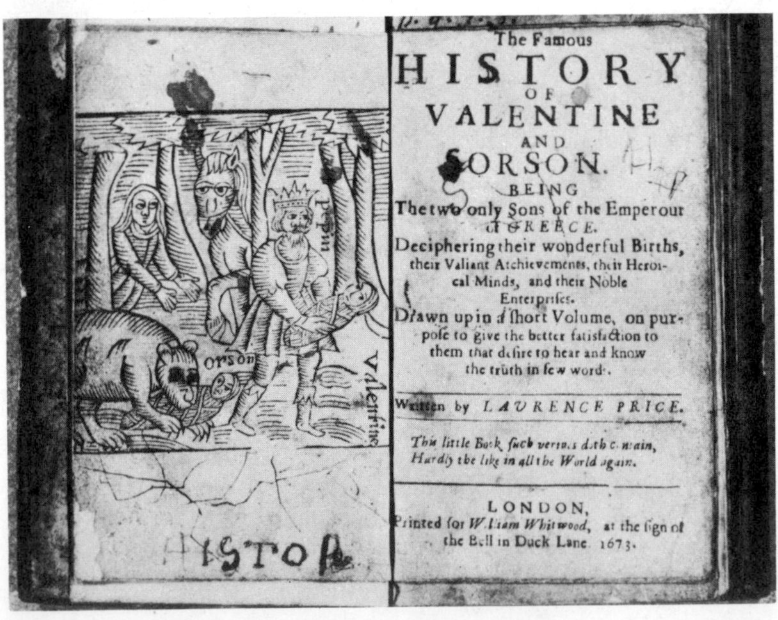

The Famous
HISTORY
OF
VALENTINE
AND
ORSON.
BEING
The two only Sons of the Emperour of GREECE.
Deciphering their wonderful Births, their Valiant Atchievements, their Heroical Minds, and their Noble Enterprises.
Drawn up in a short Volume, on purpose to give the better satisfaction to them that desire to hear and know the truth in few words.
Written by LAURENCE PRICE.
This little Book such various doth contain, Hardly the like in all the World again.
LONDON,
Printed for William Whitwood, at the sign of the Bell in Duck Lane. 1673.

Each stroke of the knife is visible in this simple woodcut; the effect on each object is to show its form rather than its texture. From Laurence Price's History of Valentine and Orson. *Reproduced from an edition in the D'Alte Welch Collection, Cleveland. (Book 3 x 5¼)*

around 1630. We can well imagine that those early years of colonization were too difficult for any excursions into book-producing for either children or adults, but the Puritans' passion for education could not long be submerged. Whatever else may be said of them, the history of their activities in New England is alive with a deep and growing concern for schools and the tools of education, books. As early as 1632, there are references to hornbooks, brought from England with the crosses blotted out—crosses being for the time a religious symbol to which the Puritans objected.

The first book for children to be published in the New World appeared in 1646. It was written by John Cotton and its full title was:

Milk for Babes, Drawn out of the Breasts of Both Testaments, Chiefly for the Spirituall Nourishment of Boston Babes in either England, but may be of like Use for any Children.

Beneath this title it adds *A Catechism in Verse,* and begins:

Who is the Maker of all things?
The Almighty God who reigns on high.
He form'd the earth, He spread the sky.

It continues with all the intricate details of Puritan theology.

Editions of the *New England Primer* published as early as 1691 have been found, although it is known to have been in print before that. Its famous rhyming alphabet begins:

In Adam's fall
We sinned all.

Thy life to mend
God's Book attend.

In addition, the book contains prayers, poems, the shorter catechism, the Ten Commandments, Bible verses, and pictures. One of these is a quaint woodcut of a Dame's school; another is the picture of a mournful figure contemplating a tombstone; and the prize is a graphic illustration of the burning of Mr. John Rogers, with his wife and ten children looking on, while a jaunty man-at-arms holds them

Tom Thumb.

How *Tom Thumb* fell into the Pudding-Bowl, and of his eſcape out of the Tinkers Budget.

He ſat upon the pudding-bowl, the Candle for to hold,

A 4 Of

In this interesting picture two separate events are depicted simultaneously—Tom falling into the pudding and the bird subsequently rescuing him.
From the chapbook Tom Thumb His Life and Death. *Reproduced from an edition (circa 1665) in the John G. White Collection, Cleveland Public Library.*

at bay. With tombs and torture, it is difficult to justify the subtitle, "An Easy and Pleasant Guide to the Art of Reading." (See p. 36.)

As late as 1832, Boston had its own descendant of Janeway's *Token.* It was written by Perkins and Marvin and the title page reads as follows:

Mary Lothrop
Who Died In
Boston
1831

The authors add in their preface that their Memoir was prepared "for the purpose of adding another to the bright pictures set before children to allure them into the paths of piety." This was a fairly large book for those days, about three by seven inches, and fully three fourths of it is devoted to the pious Mary's interminable death. The charming little frontispiece shows Mary and her little brother kneeling beside a chair, praying. The boy has struck his sister, and Mary is praying him into a state of repentance. Shortly after that, Mary becomes ill and begins her preparations for death. Gloom descends for the remaining pages. It is to be hoped that Boston children who were given this "bright picture" had recourse to the lusty nonsense of *Mother Goose*. For, despite the Puritans, a pirated edition of this cheerful volume was printed in the New World in 1785.

24 NEW ENGLAND PRIMER.

Thou shalt not see thy brother's ass or his ox fall down by the way, and hide thyself from them: thou shalt surely help him to lift them up again.

THE BURNING OF MR. JOHN ROGERS.

MR. JOHN ROGERS, minister of the gospel in London, was the first martyr in Queen Mary's reign; and was burnt at Smithfield, February the fourteenth, 1554. His wife, with nine small children, and one at her breast, followed him to the stake, with which sorrowful sight he was not in the least daunted, but with wonderful patience died courageously for the gospel of JESUS CHRIST.

This Easy and Pleasant Guide to the Art of Reading *was hardly conducive to a good night's sleep.*
From The New England Primer; or An Easy and Pleasant Guide to the Art of Reading. *Massachusetts Sabbath School Society.*

"Cheerfulness Creeps In"

FAIRY TALES IN FRANCE

Paul Hazard in his delightful *Books, Children and Men* calls attention to the early portraits of children clad in long velvet skirts, heavily plumed hats, corsets, swords, and ornaments, and he remarks, "If, for centuries, grownups did not even think of giving children appropriate clothes, how would it ever have occurred to them to provide children with suitable books?"

Yet around 1697 this miracle occurred in France with the publication of *Histoires ou contes du temps passé avec des moralités* (Histories and Tales of Long Ago with Morals), or, more familiarly, *Contes de ma Mère l'Oye* (Tales of Mother Goose). The stories were "La belle au bois dormant" (The Sleeping Beauty); "La petite chaperon rouge" (Little Red Riding Hood); "La Barbe Bleue" (Blue Beard); "Le maître chat, ou le chat botté" (The Master Cat, or Puss in Boots); "Les fées" (Diamonds and Toads); "Cendrillon, ou la petite pantoufle de verre" (Cinderella, or the Little Glass Slipper); "Riquet à la houpe" (Riquet with the Tuft); and "Le petit poucet" (Little Thumb).

Did Charles Perrault, member of the French Academy and author of many serious but forgotten works, collect these traditional tales, or was it Pierre Perrault d'Armancour, his eldest son? No author is listed in what is probably the first edition. Opinion favored the father for years, but he never admitted authorship. On the other hand, a publication privilege was granted to the eighteen-year-old "P. Darmancour." Percy Muir gives other evidence that the son was the compiler and adds, "Today informed opinion in France also favours the son and we may very well leave it at that" (*English Children's Books, 1600-1900,* p. 49). Perrault's Fairy Tales, we call them, and their immortality is due as much to the spontaneity and charm of the style as to the traditional content.

Perrault had imitators but no rivals. Mme. d'Aulnoy turned the old folk-tale themes into ornate novels for the court. "The Yellow Dwarf" and "Graciosa and Percinet" are sometimes adapted for modern collections but are rarely seen in their original form. Mme. de Beaumont, busy with the education of children, also took time to write some fairy tales for them. Of these, her "Beauty and the Beast" has survived deservedly. Still others took a hand at the fairy tales, but none with the freshness of Perrault.

JOHN NEWBERY IN ENGLAND

Meanwhile, in England, it was a happy day for children, steering a perilous course between the pedlar and the Puritan, when in 1729 R. Samber translated Perrault's *Tales of Mother Goose.* No chapbook was ever so thrilling as these eight tales, no "good Godly book" was ever so beloved. At the time, they must have attracted the attention of an English publisher by the name of John Newbery, because not only did his firm later use the title *Mother Goose,* but he may also have discovered through the popularity of the tales the importance of the child as a potential consumer of books.

John Newbery was what we would call today "a character." He dabbled in many things. He wrote; he published; he befriended indigent authors; he did a flourishing business manufacturing and dispensing medicines and a "Medicinal Dictionary." The caustic Samuel Johnson called him "Jack the Whirler," only to be pressed into service by busy Mr. Newbery as an occasional writer and literary adviser to a rapidly expanding publishing house. Then in 1744, along with Dr. James' Fever Powders, Newbery offered for sale his latest publication:

A LITTLE PRETTY
POCKET-BOOK
Intended for the
Instruction and Amusement
of
Little Master Tommy,
and
Pretty Miss Polly.
With Two Letters from
Jack the Giant-Killer;
As also
A Ball and a Pincushion;
The Use of which will infallibly make Tommy
a good Boy and Polly a good Girl.
To which is added,
A Little Song-Book,
Being
A New Attempt to teach Children
the Use of the English Alphabet,
by Way of Diversion.[2]

For the "*amusement*" of Tommy and Polly, "by way of *diversion*"—here is a new approach to books for children and a momentous one. It marks the beginning of English books for their delight! Of course, Jack the Giant-Killer wrote two exceedingly moral letters to the readers of the *Pretty Pocket-Book.* He had evidently reformed and settled down since the chapbook days, for his lectures are as mild as milk, with no threats anywhere. The letters are followed by a series of games with rhymed directions and morals: marbles, shuttle-cock, blindman's buff, thread the needle, leap frog, and many other old favorites. There are fables, proverbs, and rules of behavior, with a rhyming alphabet and a few poems thrown in for good measure. The morals to the fables are made more romantic and palatable by the signature of Jack the Giant-Killer. The success of the *Pocket-Book* evidently encouraged the publisher because other books for children followed rapidly.

2. No copies of the first English edition (1744) have survived. But in 1944, the two-hundredth anniversary of its first appearance, F. G. Melcher issued a reproduciton of the first American edition, which was a reprint by Isaiah Thomas published in 1787 in Worcester, Mass. You can now examine the *Pocket-Book* gaily bedecked with a flowery gilt paper cover after Newbery's custom.

In 1765 *The Renowned History of Little Goody Two Shoes, Otherwise Called Mrs. Margery Two Shoes,* appeared. This is a small juvenile novel, the first of its kind to be written expressly for children. Oliver Goldsmith is supposed to have written *Goody Two Shoes,* which tells the story of a virtuous and clever child, Margery *Meanwell.* At the opening of the book, Margery's father suffers "the wicked persecutions of Sir Timothy *Gripe* and Farmer *Graspall,*" who manage to ruin him and turn the whole family out of house and lands. The parents quickly die (evidently no Dr. James' Fever Powders available), leaving Margery and her brother Tommy destitute. Tommy goes to sea and Margery is rescued by charitable Clergyman Smith and his wife. When they buy her two shoes, the child is so overcome with pleasure that she keeps crying out, "Two shoes, Madam, see my two shoes"—hence her name.

This happiness is short-lived, for Gripe forces Smith to turn her out of the house. Back to the hedgerows once more, Margery teaches herself to read with remarkable ease by studying the schoolbooks of more fortunate children. Soon she knows more than any of them and decides to advance their learning. She makes up an alphabet of wooden blocks or "rattle traps" with both small and large letters, puts them into a basket, and goes from house to house helping children to read. The methods of the Trotting Tutoress apparently work like a charm, for all her young pupils respond immediately with never a "retarded reader" in the whole countryside.

Such pedagogical talent is bound to carry Mrs. Margery far, and soon she is made the head of a flourishing school. She meets the admirable Sir Charles Jones, whose love is won by "her virtue, good sense and prudent behaviour." As she is standing at the altar with this titled gentleman, who should come dashing in but Tommy, richly dressed—just in time to give his sister a handsome marriage settlement. After that, the Lady Margery lives happily and dies respected and beloved by all. "Her life was the greatest blessing and her death the greatest calamity that ever was felt in the neighborhood."[3]

Goody Two Shoes is full of sociological lessons; its characters are types rather than individuals. Nevertheless, it was entertaining and it was a child's book. Many adults, notably Charles Lamb, recalled the pleasure it gave them when they read it as children.

Between 1760 and 1766, John Newbery, according to many scholars, also published the first edition of *Mother Goose,*[4] but no trace of such a book remains and no contemporary reference to or advertisement of the book has ever been uncovered.[5] On the basis of their research, Jacques Barchilon and Henry Pettit[6] now assert that there was no such publication during those years. They assume that John Newbery may have planned such a book, but not until 1781 was there an advertisement announcing the first publication by his stepson, T. Carnan, of *Mother Goose's Melody.* John Newbery's firm remained in the family for many years and continued to publish books for children.

It is fitting that John Newbery, this first English publisher of books for children, is honored annually when the Newbery Medal is presented for the year's most distinguished literature for children. Frederic G. Melcher, a publisher, in 1922 created and named this award as a tribute to the genius and foresight of the Englishman who first believed in children as discriminating patrons of books.[7]

ADVENTURE AT LAST

One book emerged from the Puritan world to mark not only the increase of cheerfulness but the beginning of contemporary adventure tales. It was *Robinson Crusoe,* one of the most popular books in all English literature. It was written by Daniel Defoe, a gloomy reformer and pamphleteer who was in trouble most of his life.

Defoe (1659-1731), with a wisdom far in

3. *The Renowned History of Little Goody Two Shoes, Otherwise Called Mrs. Margery Two Shoes.* Attributed to Oliver Goldsmith. Edited by Charles Welsh.

4. Even the scholarly Opies give 1765-1766 in their *Oxford Dictionary of Nursery Rhymes* (Oxford, 1951), p. 33.

5. See Chapter 5 for a detailed account of *Mother Goose.* Other children's classics mentioned in this chapter are discussed more fully in later chapters. See the Index for relevant page references.

6. *The Authentic Mother Goose, Fairy Tales and Nursery Rhymes* (Alan Swallow, Denver, 1960), p. 11.

7. For the list of books which have been awarded the Newbery Medal see page 50.

advance of his times, wrote on banks, insurance companies, schools for women, asylums for the insane, and all sorts of social problems. He turned out bitter political and religious satires which landed him in the pillory. He rose to wealth and fame and sank to penury and prison more than once. Writing was his passion, and few men have written more continuously. His most famous book, *The Life and Strange Surprising Adventures of Robinson Crusoe,* appeared in 1719, when Defoe was sixty and nearing the end of his turbulent career. We are told four editions of it were printed in four months, and for once the old fighter enjoyed fame with no unhappy repercussions of any kind.

Why has this book commended itself to children of each succeeding generation? It was addressed to adults and originally contained masses of moral ruminations that the children must have skipped with their usual agility in the avoidance of boredom. Today children's editions generally omit these tiresome reflections and get on with the story.

There was, of course, an Alexander Selkirk, marooned for over four years on the island of Juan Fernandez, who not only told his story to Defoe but also gave him his papers. However, it is due to Defoe's skill that Selkirk, as Robinson Crusoe, emerges a favorite world hero. The theme itself is irresistible: man pitted against nature, one man with a whole world to create and control. He must obtain food, provide himself with clothes and shelter, fight off wild animals, reckon time, keep himself civilized and sane. We are given many details of how he makes his shelter and cultivates a garden, how he domesticates his little herd of goats and acquires a parrot, and finally how he discovers the savage who becomes "my man Friday," a symbol today of faithfulness and loyalty.

Here is a book that satisfies the child's hunger to achieve competence. Identifying himself with Robinson Crusoe, he wins an ordered, controlled place in the world by his own efforts and foresight. With the coming of Friday, he has the love of a friend whom he in turn nurtures and protects. No wonder children read and reread and dramatize this book. All the details are there; every question is answered. It is reasonable and clear—a design for living, complete and satisfying.

A SATIRICAL TRAVEL FANTASY

Another remarkable book emerged from this period, a political satire not intended for children but appropriated by them and known

Mother GOOSE's Melody. 37

JACK and *Gill*
Went up the Hill,
To fetch a Pail of Water;
Jack fell down
And broke his Crown,
And *Gill* came tumbling after.

Maxim.

The more you think of dying, the better you will live.

ARISTOTLE'S

38 Mother GOOSE's Melody.

ARISTOTLE'S STORY.

THERE were two Birds sat on a Stone,
Fa, la, la, la, lal, de; [one,
One flew away, and then there was
Fa, la, la, la, lal, de;
The other flew after,
And then there was none,
Fa, la, la, la, lal, de;
And so the poor Stone
Was left all alone,
Fa, la, la, la, lal, de.

This may serve as a Chapter of Consequence in the next new Book of Logick.

From The Original Mother Goose's Melody. *Reproduced in facsimile by W. H. Whitmore (Joel Munsell's Sons, 1899) from the edition reprinted by Isaiah Thomas of Worcester, Mass., about 1785. (Book 2½ x 3¾)* *(See also p. 80)*

today as *Gulliver's Travels.* The author, Jonathan Swift (1667-1745), was born in Dublin and died there, Dean of the Cathedral. But between his birth and death, he spent considerable time in London and took an active part in the political life of the times. Recognized today as one of the greatest satirists in English literature, in his own day he was known as a pamphleteer and misanthrope. Despite this forbidding reputation, he had deep and lasting friendships with such famous men as Sir William Temple, Bolingbroke, and Oxford. With his two close friends, the distinguished physician John Arbuthnot and the poet Alexander Pope, he founded the Scriblerus Club. From this group came the *Memoirs* of a fictional character known as Martinus Scriblerus. Dr. Arbuthnot wrote about Martinus' childhood and Swift was supposed to carry the hero through some fantastic journeys, but he never did so. However, this book may have furnished Swift with the idea for Lemuel Gulliver.

Swift wrote his book in Ireland to lampoon the follies of the English court, its parties, its politics, and its statesmen. Worried about the reception of the book, he published it anonymously in 1726 as *Travels into Several Remote Nations of the World,* in four parts, by Lemuel Gulliver. To Swift's surprise and relief, London society, the very society he was making fun of, was highly diverted. In writing these preposterous tall tales, Swift seems to have been caught up with the richness of his own invention, and the humor often overshadows the satire.

Children have always loved things in miniature, and they soon discovered the land of the Lilliputians. No one ever forgets Gulliver's waking to find six-inch people walking over him and Lilliputian ropes binding him. All the fascinating details are worked out to scale with logic and precision. Children are untroubled by any double meanings and like the fantasy for itself. The second journey, to the land of giants, Brobdingnag, is the next most popular, but man in an inferior position, treated like a toy, is not so appealing as the omnipotent Gulliver in Lilliput. The remaining books most children never read. Laputa is the land of the superminds, and a thoroughly repulsive lot they are. The country of the Houyhnhnms is strangest of all. It is ruled by beautiful and benignant horses, whereas men, the Yahoos, are horrid creatures, the beasts of the noble horses. As far as children are concerned, the first adventure makes the book, and it is Lilliput forever!

If Gulliver's travels had not fascinated artists, the book might not have survived in children's reading as long as it has. An early edition illustrated by Charles E. Brock (1894) and later editions illustrated by Arthur Rackham and by Fritz Eichenberg would lure anyone into reading the story.

POETS AND CHILDREN

About the time *Robinson Crusoe* and *Gulliver's Travels* were published, a gentle nonconformist preacher wrote a book of poetry for children. Isaac Watts moralized in verse about busy bees and quarrelsome dogs, but he also wrote tender and beautiful hymns, many of which are found today in most hymnals. His *Divine and Moral Songs for Children* (1715) dwelt not on the fearful judgments of God, but on God "our refuge," and many a child must have been comforted by his tender "Cradle Hymn."

Toward the end of the century a major poet, William Blake, published a book of poems for and about children. *Songs of Innocence* (1789) is now considered an epoch-making book, although it caused no stir at the time of its publication. A companion volume, *Songs of Experience* (1794), followed. These books may well mark the beginning of the Romantic Movement in English poetry. Although most of Blake's unique lyrics are for adults, the melody of his verses appeals to children also.

Ann and Jane Taylor's *Original Poems for Infant Minds: By Several Young Persons* (1804) teaches lessons in the manner of Watts' *Moral Songs,* but with a difference. The vigorous, fun-loving Taylors usually tell good stories in their verse and reveal something of the simple, pleasant life of rural England. The book enjoyed immediate popularity and was translated into various languages, but it is best known today for the familiar "Twinkle, twinkle, little star."

The Butterfly's Ball, published in book form in 1807, was written by William Roscoe (1753-1831), a lawyer and member of Parliament, for the amusement of his little son. There is no story, but there are such fascinating details as a mushroom table with a water dock leaf tablecloth, and there are William Mulready's charming pictures of the insect guests at the ball (see p. 56). However, the verse is tame, and the long popularity of the poem must have been due in part to lack of better verse for children.

Didacticism Again

ROUSSEAU, THE APOSTLE OF FREEDOM

In 1762 Rousseau proclaimed his theory of a new day for children through his book *Émile.* He believed in the joyous unfolding of a child's powers through a free, happy life. The fact that Rousseau's own life was sin-cursed and unhappy did not prevent his followers from accepting seriously this new glorification of freedom. The child Émile was the companion of his tutor; he was free of all books except *Robinson Crusoe;* and he lived vigorously out of doors, learning from experiences and activities. Schools today reflect Rousseau's emphasis on experiences and activities, but they have wisely retained both books and discipline.

To make a giant look gigantic, the artist puts an army between his feet, draws the city knee-high, and shows mountains barely up to his waist. It's a giant's-eye view of Lilliputia. Illustration by Louis Rhead. From Gulliver's Travels *by Jonathan Swift. Copyright 1913 by Harper & Brothers, copyright 1941 by Bertrand Rhead. Reproduced by permission of Harper & Row, Publishers. (Book 5¾ x 8½)*

DIDACTICISM IN FRANCE AND ENGLAND

In its day, *Émile* effected a revolutionary change in people's attitudes toward both children and education. To some people, Rousseau seemed like a breeze blowing away the clouds of Puritan morbidity. It was some time before his followers could see through the naïveté of his assumption that, given complete freedom, a child will develop both nobility and happiness. At any rate, one would naturally expect the ardent Rousseau converts, if they wrote books for children, to write only the gayest ones. Instead, in France, in England, and even in the United States, they began to write painfully didactic stories, sometimes to teach religion, sometimes to inform and educate. The only thing these writers seemed to have carried over from Rousseau was the idea of following and developing the child's natural interests. In practice, they went at the business hammer and tongs. If a poor child picked strawberries, the experience was turned into an arithmetic lesson. If he rolled a snowball, he learned about levers and proceeded from those to wedges. If he took a walk, he had to observe every bird, beast, stone, and occupation of man. Day and night these ardent authors stalked their children, allowing them never a moment for play or fancy but instructing and improving on every page. No longer did they threaten the child with the fear of Hell, but the pressure of Information hung almost as heavily over his hapless head.

Here was a revival of didacticism with a vengeance—not the terrifying theological didacticism of the Puritans but the intellectual and moralistic variety. Students who wish to read more about this period should study the works of the French Mme. de Genlis (1746-1830) and Armand Berquin (1749-1791) and those of such English writers as Laetitia Barbauld (1743-1825), Sarah Trimmer (1741-1810), and Hannah More (1745-1833). For most readers, a few examples of this writing will probably suffice.

One of the classic examples of the new didacticism is *The History of Sandford and Merton* in four volumes by Thomas Day (1748-1789). Tommy Merton was the spoiled, helpless, ignorant son of a rich gentleman, whereas Harry Sandford was the sturdy, industrious, competent child of an honest farmer. Harry was reared out of doors and trained to work and study; there was nothing he did not know and nothing he could not do. Father Merton, handicapped by wealth though he was, saw at once the advantage of having his young darling unspoiled and trained in the ways of the honest Harry. So poor Tommy, little knowing what was in store for him, was put in the charge of the same clerical tutor who had wrought such wonders with Harry. Mr. Barlow trained both boys, but Harry was always used as the perfect example to show up the ignorance, incompetence, and general orneriness of poor Tommy. All day that worthy pair, the omniscient Barlow and the admirable Harry, instructed, disciplined, and uplifted poor Tommy. Why Tommy did not have enough initiative to use one of his educational levers or wedges to haul off and clout his tormentors is beyond imagination; but no, through volume after volume, he was plagued and polished into Rousseau-like simplicity and competence. At the end of four volumes, there he was at last—Tommy Merton remodeled, divested of all his fine apparel, his curls gone, and his life to be given over to study and philosophy forever more. Could any reform go further?

Another and perhaps the most gifted exponent of didacticism in children's books was Maria Edgeworth (1767-1849), who told her moral tales with such dramatic realism that they are still remembered. She had an excellent laboratory for developing her stories as she was the second of twenty-two children. She not only helped her father with the education of the younger ones but wrote her stories in their midst, tried them out with the children, and modified them according to their suggestions. Thomas Day himself had a hand in Maria's early education, but her own father seems to have been a greater influence in her writings than anyone else.

Maria Edgeworth wrote many stories, some deadly dull and unnatural. But at her best, she was a born storyteller. She developed real plots—the first in children's stories since the fairy tales—with well-sustained suspense and surprise endings that took some of the sting out of the inevitable morals. The story that is most frequently quoted and that remained in the anthologies the longest is probably "The Purple Jar," which is sufficiently typical to relate here.

Rosamond, an amiable but thoughtless little girl, was out shopping with her mother. At the sight of all the delightful things displayed in the windows, Rosamond wanted something from each one, but a large purple vase in an apothecary's shop completely charmed her. She felt she could not do without it, although a large hole in her only pair of shoes made it evident that she needed shoes more than purple vases. Her mother, knowing well the fallacy of the jar, gave the guileless child her choice—shoes or jar. Rosamond chose the jar and received it in ecstasy. Once the treasure was in the house, Rosamond was sure she had made the right choice, but her mother bided her time. Wishing to put flowers in the vase, Rosamond emptied the purple liquid and lo, she had only a common white glass jar! In tears she begged her mother to take it back and purchase her shoes instead, but Mother insisted that Rosamond must bide by her choice, and so she did, limping miserably for a whole month. At the end of this sad tale Rosamond remarked:

How I wish I had chosen the shoes! They would have been of so much more use to me than the jar: however, I am sure, no, not quite sure, but I hope I shall be wiser the next time.

This proves that Rosamond, at least, was a real human being, even if her stern mother was not.

The mother annoys us today because she is insincere and unnatural. Rosamond, on the other hand, except for her language, is all child. The picture of the little girl, standing in the shoe shop in profound meditation over the choice of jar or shoes, is very childlike and genuine. Maria Edgeworth tells an interesting story. But her tales carry such a heavy and obvious burden of moral lessons that her characterizations and excellent plots are sacrificed to didacticism.

DIDACTICISM IN THE UNITED STATES

It was inevitable that the United States should develop its own brand of didacticism. Samuel G. Goodrich (1793-1860), who wrote under the name of Peter Parley and produced five or six volumes a year, wrote laudatory biographies of famous men and poured out a continuous stream of information in the fields of science, history, and geography. Jacob Abbott (1803-1879) launched a travel series in which a youth by the name of Rollo was dragged from one city and country to another, bearing up nobly under a steady barrage of travel talks and moralizing. Both men wrote well but pedantically. We shall detect some of their literary descendants in the books of today —information attractively sugared but oppressively informative nevertheless.

Our chief moralist was Martha Farquharson, pseudonym for Martha Finley (1828-1909), whose *Elsie Dinsmore* series began in 1868 and ran to twenty-six volumes. This pious heroine had a way of bursting into tears or fainting with such effect that adult sinners were converted and even Elsie's worldly father was brought to a state of repentance. Little girls cried their way through all twenty-six volumes. Most parents developed considerable resistance to Elsie but were baffled by her powers to charm their offspring. Elsie was a spellbinder, for her author had a sense of the dramatic. To this day sensible women remember weeping over Elsie's Sabbath sit-down strike at the piano, when she refused to play secular music for her erring father. She was made to sit on the piano stool until one of her best faints put an end to her martyrdom and Father repented. Elsie was a prig with glamour, and there is no telling how many more of her kind might have developed if certain pioneers had not appeared to clear away the artificiality and to bring laughter, fantasy, and realism to children's books.

Modern Books Begin

Even while Peter Parley was dispensing information, and Maria Edgeworth was teaching little Rosamond valuable lessons, and Martha Finley's heroine, Elsie Dinsmore, was piously swooning, epoch-making books in both England and the United States were appearing that were to modify the whole approach to children's literature. These children's classics, as popular today as when they were first published, not only brought laughter, fantasy, and realism into stories for young people, but they began the trend toward better illustrations in children's books. Each of these books will be discussed in greater detail in later chapters; they are reviewed here because they are milestones in the development of children's literature.

FAIRY TALES: THE GRIMMS AND ANDERSEN

Grimm's Popular Stories was translated into English by Edgar Taylor in 1823. Grimm's Fairy Tales, as they were called by the children, became as much a part of the literature of English-speaking children as their own *Mother Goose*. These stories, gathered by the Grimm brothers from the lips of the old storytellers, represented the accumulated wisdom of the race—tales that were grave, occasionally droll, but often somber and harrowing.

The *Fairy Tales* of Hans Christian Andersen appeared in England in 1846, translated by Mary Howitt. Many of these stories were Andersen's own adaptations of folk tales which he, too, had heard from the storytellers. But to these he added his own fanciful inventions and immeasurably enriched the child's world of the imagination. Andersen's stories have unusual literary and spiritual values, but they are, for the most part, in a minor key, melancholy and even tragic.

LAUGHTER AT LAST

One of the first notes of gaiety was a long story-poem by Clement Moore called "A Visit from St. Nicholas" (1822), but known to children as "The Night Before Christmas." This fast-moving, humorous ballad, full of fun, fancy, and excitement, with never a threat or a dire warning to spoil the children's delight, is as beloved now as it was in Moore's day.

Cruikshank had a feeling for action, humor, and lively details, a caricaturist's eye for the grotesque, and an artist's sense of composition. Illustration by George Cruikshank for Grimm's Popular Stories. *(Book 4½ x 6¾)*

Under Queen Victoria, England's industrial age flourished and grew prosperous and pompous. Adult society was never stuffier, children's books never more improving. Then suddenly two eminent men, by way of relaxation or reaction perhaps, broke into gibbering nonsense that sent the children off into gales of laughter. One of these gentlemen, Edward Lear, was an artist who earned his living by making scientific paintings of birds and reptiles. When he grew too bored with the drawing room, he took refuge with the children. For them he would write absurd limericks which he would illustrate on the spot. His *Book of Nonsense* (1846) not only was an unprecedented collection of amusing verses and pictures but perhaps paved the way for another excursion into absurdity.

In 1865 a book appeared that is generally considered the first English masterpiece written for children. It was *Alice's Adventures in Wonderland*. The author was an Oxford don, a lecturer in logic and mathematics, who used the pen name Lewis Carroll. *Alice* still remains a unique combination of fantasy and nonsense that is as logical as an equation. It was first told, and later written, solely for the entertainment of children, and neither it nor its sequel, *Through the Looking Glass,* has the faintest trace of a moral or a scrap of useful information or one improving lesson—only cheerful lunacy, daft and delightful. *Alice* launched the literature of nonsense and fantasy which is so gravely and reasonably related that it seems as real as rain, as natural as going to sleep.

ILLUSTRATIONS KEEP PACE

Both these laughter-provoking books have delightful illustrations—Lear's own outrageous caricatures for his *Book of Nonsense* and Sir John Tenniel's inimitable drawings for Carroll's *Alice*. Deservedly famous, too, are Walter Crane, Randolph Caldecott, and Kate Greenaway,[8] whose charming water colors brightened the pages of children's books with decorative designs, appealing landscapes, and figures which hold their own with the best in the modern books.

When Frederic G. Melcher in 1938 sponsored a second award—this time for the most distinguished picture book for children published each year in the United States—he named it the Caldecott Medal after Randolph Caldecott. The award is a fitting memorial to the man who drew a picture of himself surrounded by children, and who left those children a legacy of gay storytelling pictures.[9]

MYTHS: HAWTHORNE AND KINGSLEY

In the United States Greek myths were introduced to children by a gifted novelist, Nathaniel Hawthorne. Around 1852 *A Wonder-Book for Girls and Boys* was published, followed in 1853 by *Tanglewood Tales for Girls and Boys*. These books contain stories of the Greek gods and heroes, supposedly told to a group of lively New England children by a young college student, Eustace Bright. Eustace talked down to the children; his gods lost much of their grandeur, and his heroes were often child-sized. But the stories had a delightful style, and the chatty interludes of banter between Eustace and the children provided pleasant pictures of the New England outdoor world.

In England, Charles Kingsley, country parson, Victorian scholar and poet, also retold the myths for children. His adaptations not only are closer to the original myths than Hawthorne's but convey the inner significance and grandeur of the myths as no other translation for young people has ever done. Here are dreams of greatness, presented with the sensitive perception of a poet. Oddly enough, in Kingsley's own day these stories were less popular than his original fantasy, *The Water-Babies* (1863), which is marred for us today by its moralizing.

8. See Chapter 4 for a fuller account of illustrators of children's books.
9. For a list of the books which have been awarded the Caldecott Medal see page 51.

REALISM WITH CHARACTERS IN PLACE OF TYPES

In the United States our epoch-making book was a modest story of family life, *Little Women*. The author, Louisa M. Alcott, submitted the manuscript hesitatingly, and her publisher had to tell her as gently as possible how unacceptable it was. Fortunately, he felt some qualms about his judgment and allowed the children of his family to read the manuscript. They convinced him that he was wrong. Those astute little girls loved the book, and little girls have never ceased reading it since its publication in 1868. The story is as genuine a bit of realism as we have ever had. Family life is there—from the kitchen to the sanctuary of the attic, from reading to giving amateur dramatics in which the homemade scenery collapses. But right as all the details are, the reason that adults remember the book is the masterly characterizations of the four girls. No longer are people typed to represent Ignorance or Virtue, but here are flesh-and-blood girls, as different from each other as they could well be, full of human folly and human courage, never self-righteous, sometimes irritable but never failing in warm affection for each other. This ability to make her characters vividly alive was Louisa M. Alcott's gift to modern realism for children.

REALISM CROSSES THE TRACKS

So far, on both sides of the Atlantic, realistic stories for children were about eminently respectable characters. When Samuel Clemens, or Mark Twain as he signed himself, wrote *Tom Sawyer* in 1876, he carried realism across the tracks. In this book Huck and his disreputable father were probably the child's first literary encounters with real people who were not considered respectable but who were likable anyway. Moreover, they were not typed to show the folly of being disreputable, but Huckleberry Finn won all hearts and so nearly stole the book from Tom that he had to appear in a book of his own. Mark Twain in these two unsurpassed juveniles not only gave us realism with humor but also showed warm tolerance—for the first time in children's

The art of Norman Rockwell may be photographic in its realism, but its fidelity to American people and its rich humor make it generally beloved. His Tom Sawyer, *with its perfection of composition and droll details, masterfully portrays Mark Twain's young character.*
Illustration by Norman Rockwell. From Tom Sawyer *by Mark Twain. Copyright 1936 by Heritage Press. Reproduced with permission of George Macy Companies, Inc. (Original in color, book 6¼ x 9¼, picture 5 x 6⅜)*

books—in his presentation of socially undesirable people. We still find too few examples of such realism in children's books.

CHILDREN'S LITERATURE COMES OF AGE

The Victorian period saw the stream of cheerfulness in children's literature rise steadily. Many of the books written then are still popular and will be considered in detail later. This list is a reminder of these and others that are milestones in the development of children's literature.

1484 *Aesop's Fables,* translated and printed by William Caxton.
1646 *Spiritual Milk for Boston Babes,* John Cotton.
1657 or 1658 *Orbis Pictus,* Comenius (original in Latin).
1691 *The New England Primer.*
1697 *Contes de ma Mère l'Oye,* Perrault.
1715 *Divine and Moral Songs for Children,* Isaac Watts.
1719 *Robinson Crusoe,* Daniel Defoe.
1726 *Gulliver's Travels,* Jonathan Swift.
1729 *Tales of Mother Goose,* Perrault (first English translation).
1744 *A Little Pretty Pocket-Book.*
1765 *The Renowned History of Little Goody Two Shoes.*
1781 *Mother Goose's Melody.*
1785 *Mother Goose's Melodies* (Isaiah Thomas edition).
1789 *Songs of Innocence,* William Blake.
1804 *Original Poems for Infant Minds,* Ann and Jane Taylor.
1807 *The Butterfly's Ball,* William Roscoe.
1822 *A Visit from St. Nicholas,* Clement C. Moore.
1823 *Grimm's Popular Stories* (translated into English by Edgar Taylor).
1843 *A Christmas Carol,* Charles Dickens.
1846 *Book of Nonsense,* Edward Lear.
1846 *Fairy Tales,* Hans Christian Andersen (first English translation).
1852 *A Wonder-Book for Girls and Boys,* Nathaniel Hawthorne.
1865 *Alice's Adventures in Wonderland,* Lewis Carroll (Charles Lutwidge Dodgson).
1865 *Hans Brinker, or the Silver Skates,* Mary Mapes Dodge.
1867-1876 *Sing a Song of Sixpence, and other toy books,* illustrated by Walter Crane.
1868-1869 *Little Women,* Louisa M. Alcott.
1872 *Sing-Song,* Christina Rossetti.
1876 *The Adventures of Tom Sawyer,* Mark Twain (Samuel Clemens).
1877 *Black Beauty,* Anna Sewell.
1878 *Under the Window,* Kate Greenaway.
1878 *The House That Jack Built* and *The Diverting History of John Gilpin,* illustrated by Randolph Caldecott.
1880 *The Peterkin Papers,* Lucretia Hale.

1883 *Treasure Island,* Robert Louis Stevenson.
1883 *Nights with Uncle Remus,* Joel Chandler Harris.
1883 *The Merry Adventures of Robin Hood,* Howard Pyle.
1884 *Heidi,* Johanna Spyri (date of English translation).
1884 *The Adventures of Huckleberry Finn,* Mark Twain (Samuel Clemens).
1885 *A Child's Garden of Verses,* Robert Louis Stevenson.
1886 *Little Lord Fauntleroy,* Frances Hodgson Burnett.
1889 *The Blue Fairy Book,* Andrew Lang.
1894 *The Jungle Book,* Rudyard Kipling.
1899 *The Story of the Treasure Seekers,* E. Nesbit.
1900 *Little Black Sambo,* Helen Bannerman.
1901 *The Tale of Peter Rabbit,* Beatrix Potter.
1903 *Johnny Crow's Garden,* L. Leslie Brooke.
1908 *Wind in the Willows,* Kenneth Grahame.

These are individual books that were turning points in children's literature. They not only carry us into the twentieth century with distinction, but their influence is discernible in the writing of today. Laura Richards continued the deft nonsense verses of Lear and Carroll in her *Tirra Lirra* (1932). A. A. Milne's skillful light verse, *When We Were Very Young* (1924), did as much to popularize poetry for young children in schools and homes as Robert Louis Stevenson had done earlier. And the small, sweet lyrics of Christina Rossetti were followed by the exquisite poetry of Walter de la Mare (1922).

In the field of fairy tales and fantasy, *East o' the Sun* continued the interest in folklore that began with the Grimms. But with the Uncle Remus collections there came a new consciousness of the United States as a depository of regional and racial folklore. *Paul Bunyan* (1941) and other tall-tale heroes and *The Jack Tales* (1943), southern variants of European folk tales, stemmed from this interest. If the Italian fairy tale *Pinocchio* (1927) was the gay descendant of Andersen's somber toy stories, so too was the younger and equally light-hearted *Winnie-the-Pooh* (1926). Gulliver's Lilliput was never so fascinating as the miniature world of *The Borrowers* (1952). *Charlotte's Web* (1952) continued the great tradition of animal fantasy begun in *The Wind in the Willows.* And the daft world of *Alice's Adventures in Wonderland* grew perceptibly zanier in the fantastic dreams of Dr. Seuss.

True Americana began with *Tom Sawyer,* and continued to flourish in a different form in the *Little House in the Big Woods* (1932) series. It is there, too, in the great animal story *Smoky* (1926), written in the vernacular of a cowboy. And it is certainly alive in such regional stories as *Strawberry Girl* (1945), *A Place for Peter* (1952), and *...and now Miguel* (1953).

The picture stories so charmingly begun by Beatrix Potter continue in the varied books of Wanda Gág, Louise Fatio, Will and Nicolas, and many others. And if stories of other lands began auspiciously with *Hans Brinker* and *Heidi,* they have grown and strengthened in *The Good Master* (1935), *The Ark* (1953), *The Happy Orpheline* (1957), and *The Silver Sword* (1959). So the types of books that were turning points in children's literature at an earlier period are perpetuated today, although the kinship between the old and the new may sometimes seem remote.

Trends in Children's Books Today

What, we may ask, are the trends in writing for children today? A glance at the past makes it clear that nothing today is completely new, but certainly some types of books are better written today than ever before and are enjoying such tremendous popularity that they seem to mark a trend.

For instance, Hendrik Willem van Loon's *Story of Mankind* (1921) launched a fresh interest in biographies and informational books, both of which have developed into major trends. Authentic, well-written biographies are popular with adults today and equally popular with children and youth. Elizabeth Janet Gray's *Penn,* Jean Latham's *Carry On, Mr. Bowditch,* Sidney Rosen's *Doctor Paracelsus,* Elizabeth Yates' *Amos Fortune, Free Man,* Nardi Campion's *Patrick Henry*—these and many others mark biography as one of the most distinguished types of juvenile literature. Because of their great popularity, there is some danger at present that we will have a flood of stereotypes rather than authentic biography. Each year, however, a surprising number of well-documented, well-written biographies continue to appear.

Numerically, informational books threaten to outdistance all other types put together. From people and places to weather and worms, from stones to stars, from dinosaurs to missiles, from insects to astronauts, science and social studies books for children pour off the presses. The dust jackets assure us the information has been checked and double-checked by experts of eminence. The books are attractive and their content is designed for particular reading levels and understanding. Their numbers and variety are so staggering that they are more than a trend; they are practically an inundation. It may be that the emphasis on social studies and science books will be the most notable trend in children's literature of the second half of the twentieth century.

Another interesting phenomenon of recent years has been the rise of the picture book. Not since that famous triumvirate, Caldecott, Crane, and Greenaway, have so many artists lavished so much effort and talent on books for young children. Lynd Ward, himself an artist, wrote ". . . the book work of the thirties that is most significant in itself, and in terms of what it contributes to the world at large, was done in picture book form."[10] Mr. Ward's own *Biggest Bear* is an excellent example. Sharing such a book with children, adults find themselves as charmed with the pictures as are the children. Someone has said that a wonderful way to teach art appreciation would be through children's picture books which run the whole gamut of styles and techniques. Harold Jones' pictures for *Lavender's Blue (Mother Goose)* are in strong, dark colors and in an older style of realism with impressive composition. Marie Hall Ets' *Play with Me,* one of the most sensitive and perfect picture-stories ever made for the three- to seven-year-olds, is in delicate springtime colors that illumine each episode. Nicolas Mordvinoff, in a protest against prettified art for children, uses bold, bright colors and humorous composition. Tasha Tudor, Marguerite de Angeli, and Adrienne Adams are not afraid of delicate beauty of details and figures. And for complete contrast look at the modern, stylized art in the striking picture books illustrated by Nicolas Sidjakov. In short, today's picture book is exciting art with endless possibilities.

In contrast to the emphasis on informational books is the sudden and delightful interest in poetry both in and out of our schools. New books of poems appear often and, what is more, they sell. Many of the poets today may be "new singers of small songs," but there are authentic poets of childhood, too. Before his death, Robert Frost gave children and youth *You Come Too,* a fine selection from his poems. Harry Behn has composed some choice lyrics, and David McCord and John Ciardi enliven the scene with extraordinarily clever nonsense verse. Moreover, in the schools children are speaking poetry informally or in verse choirs with unfeigned enjoyment. Adults are reading poetry aloud and listening to poetry records and readings. Such delightful books as Aileen Fisher's *Going Barefoot* or Paul Galdone's beautifully illustrated edition of *Paul Revere's Ride* might have gone unsold twenty years ago. Today their popularity is assured.

Some people would say that both the easy-to-read books and the foreign-language books for children also constitute trends. But these, with a few exceptions, are closer to the primer category than to literature. Nor have they yet stood the test of time and usage. In the main, whether we talk about trends or modern emphases, one thing is certain: biography, pic-

10. "The Book Artist: Yesterday and Tomorrow," in *Illustrators of Children's Books, 1744-1945,* comp. by Bertha E. Mahony, Louise P. Latimer, and Beulah Folmsbee, 1947, p. 254.

ture books, poetry, and informational books for children are better today and more widely used than ever before.

SUGGESTED READING, PROBLEMS, AND PROJECTS

1. What did children read before they had books written expressly for them?

2. What modern publications are similar in some ways to chapbooks? How do the two types differ?

3. Read parts of the Robert Lawson edition of *Pilgrim's Progress* to a group of children, show them the pictures, and see if they are interested in reading on. What is their reaction? How do you explain it?

4. Do you think stories like "The Purple Jar" achieved the results desired? Why or why not?

5. Compare *Robinson Crusoe* and *Gulliver's Travels.* Did you enjoy them as a child? Why or why not?

6. Read Hawthorne's and Kingsley's adaptations of the myths. How do their treatments differ?

7. Name some other notable books you would add to the list on p. 46 if it were continued up to the present time.

8. How can this background of the history of children's books help you to evaluate new books for children? Do you see any other marked trends today?

REFERENCES

ADAMS, BESS PORTER. *About Books and Children.* Holt, 1953. A brief survey of early books for children and their modern descendants, with good chapters on juvenile magazines and on illustration. Almost half of the text is devoted to bibliographies without annotations.

ASHTON, JOHN. *Chap-Books of the Eighteenth Century.* London: Chatto, 1882. The author reproduces the stories and some of the pages and illustrations from the old chapbooks.

BARCHILON, JACQUES, and HENRY PETTIT. *The Authentic Mother Goose Fairy Tales and Nursery Rhymes* (see Bibliography, Chapter 5).

BARRY, FLORENCE V. *A Century of Children's Books.* Doran, 1923. A readable account of early English books for children, with unusually good evaluations.

DARTON, F. J. H. *Children's Books in England: Five Centuries of Social Life,* 2nd ed. Cambridge Univ. Press, 1958. A scholarly study of children's books, from the fables to Robert Louis Stevenson. Chapter VII is about John Newbery and the first English books for children.

FIELD, WALTER TAYLOR. *A Guide to Literature for Children.* Ginn, 1928. An early book on children's literature with many useful chapters.

FISHER, MARGERY. *Intent Upon Reading.* Watts, 1962. A refreshing and critical approach to children's books, both recent and standard selections. Though many of the titles are English publications, a great number are familiar to American readers.

FOLMSBEE, BEULAH. *A Little History of the Horn-Book.* Horn Book, 1942. A tiny book, beautifully printed, with a history of hornbooks in all their variations both in England and New England.

FORD, PAUL LEICESTER, ed. *The New England Primer.* Dodd, 1897. The subtitle explains the content: "A history of its origin with reprint of the unique copy of the earliest known first edition."

FRYATT, NORMA R., ed. *A Horn Book Sampler.* Horn Book, 1959. Selected articles on authors, artists, and books that appeared in *The Horn Book Magazine* between 1924 and 1948 provide illuminating background to some of the most significant years in children's book publication.

GREEN, ROGER LANCELYN. *Tellers of Tales,* enl. ed. E. Ward, 1953. This is a delightfully written discussion of English authors of children's books from 1839 to the present. Only twenty pages are devoted to modern writers.

HAZARD, PAUL. *Books, Children and Men* (see Bibliography, Chapter 2).

JORDAN, ALICE M. *From Rollo to Tom Sawyer.* Horn Book, 1948. Here in beautiful format with decorations by Nora Unwin are twelve little essays on some of the most important nineteenth-century writers for children.

KIEFER, MONICA. *American Children Through Their Books, 1700-1835.* Univ. of Pa. Press, 1948. The American child at the beginning of the eighteenth century was too insignificant for physicians to waste time on, the author tells us. She traces his developing place in the world through an examination of children's books.

LANG, ANDREW, ed. *Perrault's Popular Tales.* London: Clarendon, 1888. A careful study of Perrault and the tales he edited.

MAHONY, BERTHA E., LOUISE P. LATIMER, and BEULAH FOLMSBEE. *Illustrators of Children's Books, 1744-1945* (see Bibliography, Chapter 4).

MEIGS, CORNELIA, ANNE EATON, ELIZABETH NESBITT, and RUTH HILL VIGUERS. *A Critical History of Children's Literature*. Macmillan, 1953. Three librarians and an author of children's books have surveyed the field from ancient to recent times. The evaluations of books, authors, illustrators, and trends make this a valuable reference.

MUIR, PERCY. *English Children's Books, 1600 to 1900*. Praeger, 1954. Mr. Muir acknowledges his indebtedness to the books of Darton and the Opies, but his work adds to both. There are excellent indexes and lavish illustrations from the books discussed.

OPIE, IONA and PETER. *The Lore and Language of Schoolchildren* (see Bibliography, Chapter 5).

_____, eds. *The Oxford Dictionary of Nursery Rhymes* (see Bibliography, Chapter 5).

RICHARDS, GEORGE M. *The Fairy Dictionary* (see Bibliography, Chapter 10).

ROSENBACH, ABRAHAM S. W. *Early American Children's Books with Bibliographical Descriptions of the Books in His Private Collection*, foreword by A. Edward Newton. Southworth Press, Portland, Maine, 1933. Facsimile pages and illustrations (many in color) of American children's books published between 1632 and 1836. Probably the greatest and most comprehensive book on juvenile Americana.

SMITH, DORA V. *Fifty Years of Children's Books*, with an introduction by Muriel Crosby, ill. National Council of Teachers of English, 1963. From Dr. Smith's years of experience with children and books, she has selected and discussed significant titles which appeared between 1910 and 1959. Numerous illustrations are reproduced from the original books.

SMITH, IRENE. *A History of the Newbery and Caldecott Medals*. Viking, 1957. Excellent historical background material on the two annual medal awards for distinguished children's books in the United States.

ST. JOHN, JUDITH. *The Osborne Collection of Early Children's Books 1566-1910; A Catalogue*, intro. by Edgar Osborne. Toronto Public Library, 1958. Descriptive notes on this world-famous collection, illustrated with many facsimiles. Fascinating background material for scholars and students of children's literature.

TARG, WILLIAM, ed. *Bibliophile in the Nursery*. World, 1957. Articles by scholars, collectors, and authors have been combined into a delightful whole, highlighting developments in children's literature and the joys of collecting. Lavishly illustrated.

WELSH, CHARLES. *A Bookseller of the Last Century, Being some Account of the Life of John Newbery, and of the Books he published with a Notice of the later Newberys*. London: Griffith, Farran, 1885. A readable history of Newbery, his famous bookshop, and his varied activities.

_____, ed. *The Renowned History of Little Goody Two Shoes, Otherwise Called Mrs. Margery Two Shoes*, attributed to Oliver Goldsmith. Heath, 1930.

CHILDREN'S BOOKS

BUNYAN, JOHN. *Pilgrim's Progress*, ed. by Mary Godolphin, ill. by Robert Lawson. Lippincott, 1939. A skillfully shortened and well-illustrated edition. 8-12

CALDECOTT, RANDOLPH. *Randolph Caldecott's Collection of Pictures and Songs*. Warne, n.d.

_____. *Randolph Caldecott's Second Collection of Pictures and Songs*. Warne, n.d.

The material of these two volumes is also published by Warne in a four-volume set, *Randolph Caldecott's Picture Books*, and in the following sixteen separate paperbound volumes: *John Gilpin; House that Jack Built; Babes in the Wood; Elegy on a Mad Dog; Three Jovial Huntsmen; Sing a Song for Sixpence; Queen of Hearts; The Farmer's Boy; The Milkmaid; Hey Diddle Diddle, and Baby Bunting; A Frog He Would a-Wooing Go; The Fox Jumps Over the Parson's Gate; Come, Lasses and Lads; Ride a Cock Horse; Mrs. Mary Blaize; The Great Panjandrum Himself*. 4-14

DEFOE, DANIEL. *Robinson Crusoe*, ill. by J. Ayton Symington, 1920. Dutton, 1954 (Children's Illustrated Classics). A good standard edition. 10-14

PERRAULT, CHARLES. *All the French Fairy Tales*, retold by Louis Untermeyer, ill. by Gustave Doré. Didier, 1946. A fine source for storytelling. 8-12

_____. *Tales of Mother Goose*, as first collected in 1696, tr. by Charles Welsh, ill. by D. J. Munro after drawings by Gustave Doré. Heath, 1901. All of the eight stories are included, but the Doré illustrations suffer greatly from the copying. 8-10

SWIFT, JONATHAN. *Gulliver's Travels into Several Remote Nations of the World*, ill. by Arthur Rackham. Dutton, 1952 (Children's Illustrated Classics). An excellent edition with Rackham's pictures. 10-14

NEWBERY MEDAL BOOKS

1922 Van Loon, Hendrik. *The Story of Mankind*. Liveright.

1923 Lofting, Hugh. *The Voyages of Dr. Dolittle*. Stokes.

1924 Hawes, Charles Boardman. *The Dark Frigate*. Little.

1925 Finger, Charles J. *Tales from Silver Lands.* Doubleday.
1926 Chrisman, Arthur. *Shen of the Sea.* Dutton.
1927 James, Will. *Smoky.* Scribner.
1928 Mukerji, Dhan Gopal. *Gay-Neck.* Dutton.
1929 Kelly, Eric P. *The Trumpeter of Krakow.* Macmillan.
1930 Field, Rachel. *Hitty, Her First Hundred Years.* Macmillan.
1931 Coatsworth, Elizabeth. *The Cat Who Went to Heaven.* Macmillan.
1932 Armer, Laura Adams. *Waterless Mountain.* Longmans.
1933 Lewis, Elizabeth Foreman. *Young Fu of the Upper Yangtze.* Winston.
1934 Meigs, Cornelia. *Invincible Louisa.* Little.
1935 Shannon, Monica. *Dobry.* Viking.
1936 Brink, Carol Ryrie. *Caddie Woodlawn.* Macmillan.
1937 Sawyer, Ruth. *Roller Skates.* Viking.
1938 Seredy, Kate. *The White Stag.* Viking.
1939 Enright, Elizabeth. *Thimble Summer.* Rinehart.
1940 Daugherty, James. *Daniel Boone.* Viking.
1941 Sperry, Armstrong. *Call It Courage.* Macmillan.
1942 Edmonds, Walter. *The Matchlock Gun.* Dodd.
1943 Gray, Elizabeth Janet. *Adam of the Road.* Viking.
1944 Forbes, Esther. *Johnny Tremain.* Houghton.
1945 Lawson, Robert. *Rabbit Hill.* Viking.
1946 Lenski, Lois. *Strawberry Girl.* Lippincott.
1947 Bailey, Carolyn Sherwin. *Miss Hickory.* Viking.
1948 DuBois, William Pène. *The Twenty-One Balloons.* Viking.
1949 Henry, Marguerite. *King of the Wind.* Rand McNally.
1950 De Angeli, Marguerite. *The Door in the Wall.* Doubleday.
1951 Yates, Elizabeth. *Amos Fortune, Free Man.* Aladdin.
1952 Estes, Eleanor. *Ginger Pye.* Harcourt.
1953 Clark, Ann Nolan. *Secret of the Andes.* Viking.
1954 Krumgold, Joseph. *. . . and now Miguel.* Crowell.
1955 DeJong, Meindert. *The Wheel on the School.* Harper.
1956 Latham, Jean Lee. *Carry On, Mr. Bowditch.* Houghton.
1957 Sorensen, Virginia. *Miracles on Maple Hill.* Harcourt.
1958 Keith, Harold. *Rifles for Watie.* Crowell.
1959 Speare, Elizabeth George. *The Witch of Blackbird Pond.* Houghton.
1960 Krumgold, Joseph. *Onion John.* Crowell.
1961 O'Dell, Scott. *Island of the Blue Dolphins.* Houghton.
1962 Speare, Elizabeth George. *The Bronze Bow.* Houghton.
1963 L'Engle, Madeline. *Wrinkle in Time.* Farrar, Strauss.

CALDECOTT MEDAL BOOKS

1938 Lathrop, Dorothy. *Animals of the Bible.* Stokes.
1939 Handforth, Thomas. *Mei Li.* Doubleday.
1940 D'Aulaire, Ingri and Edgar. *Abraham Lincoln.* Doubleday.
1941 Lawson, Robert. *They Were Strong and Good.* Viking.
1942 McCloskey, Robert. *Make Way for Ducklings.* Viking.
1943 Burton, Virginia Lee. *The Little House.* Houghton.
1944 Slobodkin, Louis, ill. Thurber, James. *Many Moons.* Harcourt.
1945 Jones, Elizabeth Orton, ill. Field, Rachel. *Prayer for a Child.* Macmillan.
1946 Petersham, Maud and Miska. *The Rooster Crows.* Macmillan.
1947 Weisgard, Leonard, ill. MacDonald, Golden. *The Little Island.* Doubleday.
1948 Duvoisin, Roger, ill. Tresselt, Alvin. *White Snow, Bright Snow.* Lothrop.
1949 Hader, Berta and Elmer. *The Big Snow.* Macmillan.
1950 Politi, Leo. *Song of the Swallows.* Scribner.
1951 Milhous, Katherine. *The Egg Tree.* Scribner.
1952 Mordvinoff, Nicolas, ill. [Nicolas, pseud.]. Lipkind, William [Will, pseud.]. *Finders Keepers.* Harcourt.
1953 Ward, Lynd. *The Biggest Bear.* Houghton.
1954 Bemelmans, Ludwig. *Madeline's Rescue.* Viking.
1955 Brown, Marcia, ill. Perrault, Charles. *Cinderella.* Scribner.
1956 Rojankovsky, Feodor, ill. Langstaff, John. *Frog Went a-Courtin'.* Harcourt.
1957 Simont, Marc, ill. Udry, Janice May. *A Tree Is Nice.* Harper.
1958 McCloskey, Robert. *Time of Wonder.* Viking.
1959 Cooney, Barbara. *Chanticleer and the Fox.* Crowell.
1960 Ets, Marie Hall. *Nine Days to Christmas.* Viking.
1961 Sidjakov, Nicolas, ill. Robbins, Ruth. *Baboushka and the Three Kings.* Parnassus.
1962 Brown, Marcia. *Once a Mouse.* Scribner.
1963 Keats, Ezra Jack. *The Snowy Day.* Viking.

chapter 4

The Artist and the Child's Books

For children, books begin with pictures.[1] A small child is given a picture book of baby animals with no text at all except the indentifying labels, but with such books he learns to turn pages and to look at the pictures with increasing perception of pictorial details. In short, he is learning to "read" pictures and with their help will soon be able to follow a narrative read to him.

Beautiful pictures can sell a trivial book, and sometimes a first-rate story is overlooked because it lacks attractive illustrations. With today's offset printing and remarkable color reproduction, the eye-appeal of books is more important than ever before, and consequently the artist plays a very significant role in the production of books for children. The books he embellishes fall into at least three distinct categories: first, the pure *picture book* with little or no text (Bruno Munari's *ABC*, for example); second, the *picture-story* in which the pictures are so integral a part of the content that the story can actually be "read" by the child from the pictures (for example, Robert McCloskey's *Make Way for Ducklings*); and third, the *illustrated book* with fewer pictures but those interpretative of both characters and situations (*The Borrowers* with Beth and Joe Krush's illustrations is a good example).

Esther Averill, in her discriminating evaluation of the art of picture books as it is found in the Caldecott Medal winners, underscores the distinction further:

In an illustrated book the pictures are, as the term "illustrated" implies, a mere extension—an illumination—of the text. In a picture book, as the term implies, the pictures play a livelier role, and are an integral part of the action of the book.[2]

The "livelier role" generally means more pictures and a more complete interdependence

1. This is a reference chapter which discusses the history and development of illustrations in children's books and the styles of the artists responsible for them. It may be read as a whole or in parts. The alphabetical list of artists on page 71 will help you locate the discussion of the work of individual artists. Some cross references are provided, but see the Index to find additional examples and further discussion of the work of the artists discussed here.
2. "What Is a Picture Book?" in *Caldecott Medal Books: 1938-1957,* edited by Bertha Mahony Miller and Elinor Whitney Field, Horn Book Papers, 1957.

between pictures and text than is true in an illustrated book. Obviously then, the picture book and the picture-stories are limited in their appeal to the prereader groups from two to perhaps seven. But pictures, whether they are interpretative illustrations of a text or an integral part of a story, still belong to the total stream of art, just as stories written especially for children belong to the total stream of literature and should ultimately be evaluated in that context. For this reason artists who have contributed to children's books are discussed in the following pages of this chapter according to their overall artistic production. They are considered in chronological order, according to their birth dates.

The Beginning of Texts with Pictures?

When the ancient artists made their surprisingly modern paintings of animals on the cave walls at Lascaux, it seems more than likely that some of the children of the tribe got underfoot and clamored, "Tell me about that one." Then maybe one artist, blessed with a gift for words (a prehistoric Robert Lawson), might do so. But more likely, he would go on with his painting and say, "You get your grandfather to tell you about the hunt." So heroic deeds were preserved by oral tradition, just as the great paintings were preserved by the favorable climate of the caves. Perhaps this speculative example is close to the truth, because children are children, always pestering grownups for stories about pictures. Long before Comenius thought of bringing text and pictures together, these two forms of expression may have achieved an ancient and honorable union in the story of the great hunt or the successful battle illumined by the artist's brush.

JAPANESE SCROLL, TWELFTH CENTURY

In Japan in the twelfth century the artist Kakuyu (1053-1140), popularly known as Toba Sojo, produced a "Scroll of Animals" that for humor and storytelling power must have delighted both young and old. It is not in the heroic vein but is hilariously lighthearted, a sort of glorified comic strip drawn without any text by a superb artist. Velma Varner, an editor of children's books, reproduced the scroll in book form with brief commentaries that provide minimum clues to the action. She called the book *The Animal Frolic* (1954). The pictures show the creatures convening for a picnic and enjoying

In this ancient brush painting, the human postures and expressions of the animals engaging in an archery contest are humorous and appealing. Illustration by Toba Sojo for The Animal Frolic *by Velma Varner, G. P. Putnam's Sons. Copyright 1954 by the Temple of Kozanji, Kyoto, Japan.*

Flowers. XV. Flores.

Amongst the Flowers the most noted,	Inter flores notissimi,
In the beginning of the Spring are the *Violet*, 1. the *Crow-toes*, 2. the *Daffodil*, 3.	Primo vere, *Viola*, 1. *Hyacinthus*, 2. *Narcissus*, 3.
Then the *Lillies*, 4. white and yellow and blew, 5.	Tum *Lilia*, 4. alba & lutea, & cœrulea, 5.
and the *Rose*, 6.	tandem *Rosa*, 6.
and the *Clove gilliflowers*, 7. &c.	& *Caryophillum*, 7. &c.
Of these *Garlands*, 8. and *Nosegays*, 9. are tyed round with twigs.	Ex his *Serta*, 8. & *Serviæ*, 9. vientur.
There are added also *sweet herbs*, 10. as ***Marjoram***, ***Flower gentle***, ***Rue***, ***Lavender***, ***Rosemary***.	Adduntur etiam *Herbæ odoratæ*, 10. ut ***Amaracus***, ***Amaranthus***, ***Ruta***, ***Lavendula***, ***Rosmarinus***, (Libanotis).

In this charming illustration for what is probably the first picture book, the symmetry of the flower arrangement is contrasted with the view of the world beyond. From Comenius' Orbis Pictus.

swimming, feasting, athletic feats, a sword dance, and the choosing of a king-for-a-day. The characterization of each animal is droll and fascinating. Here, in spite of the original scroll form, is a true picture book with pictures that tell the story, show action, and reveal character without the necessity of words. How children who saw it some eight hundred years ago must have loved it, just as children love it today when they have the opportunity to see it and to "read" the pictures for themselves.

Woodcuts and Engravings Before 1800

In 1484 William Caxton issued the first English edition of *Aesop's Fables,* illustrated with woodcuts by some unknown artist or artists (p. 31). This was an adult book, but if the children saw the pictures and heard the stories, they were undoubtedly charmed and appropriated the book just as they have appropriated certain adult books in every generation. Since Caxton's publication of the fables these little moralities have been continuously reprinted, usually illustrated by outstanding artists, doubtless attracted by the dramatic situations the stories embody.

Between the Caxton edition of the fables and the epoch-making *Orbis Pictus,* there were hornbooks (p. 32) and battledores for children but with few or no pictures. There were also the popular chapbooks, enlivened with crude woodcuts, which were beloved by the story-hungry children of the sixteenth and seventeenth centuries (pp. 34-35).

COMENIUS AND HIS ORBIS PICTUS

The *Orbis Pictus* of Comenius is assumed to be the first picture book prepared for children. Today, we would say that it more nearly resembles a primer. It was written in Latin, in 1657 or 1658, by a Moravian bishop and translated into most European languages, including English in 1658. The pictures and text are stilted but not without charm. The word *Flores* appears above a small woodcut showing flowers in a vase and also in a field; the picture is followed by a pleasant commentary on spring flowers. Whatever the subject, there was a conscious effort to associate words and pictures and to use the latter to lead directly into the text. Compared with the gay, action-packed Japanese "Scroll of Animals," the *Orbis Pictus* seems tame and wooden, but for English-speaking children it marked the beginning of picture books planned especially for them.

Even the Newbery publications, important as they are in the history of children's books, did little to advance the art of illustration. It is generally agreed that only for *Little Goody Two Shoes* (1765) did the artist (possibly Thomas Bewick) execute his woodcuts with unusual grace and synchronize them with the text so that they are illustrations in the true sense of the word—interpreting or illuminating the story.

For the most part these earliest producers of crude woodcuts were minor artists, usually unknown. It was not until the advent of Thomas Bewick (pronounced Bū′ik) that children's books were adorned by a major artist.

THOMAS BEWICK 1753-1828

Although his brother John was also an engraver, Thomas Bewick is generally credited with being the greater artist. Thomas' first book designed for children was *A Pretty Book of Pictures For Little Masters and Misses or Tommy Trip's History of Beasts and Birds* (1779). This book, exceedingly rare today, is an example of the artist's skill in the use of the woodcut. He developed better tools for this work, made effective use of the white line, and carried the woodcut to a new level of beauty. Most of Thomas Bewick's finest drawings seem to have been for books originally planned for adults as, for instance, his various editions of Aesop's fables, particularly those of 1784 and 1818. The former was reprinted in 1878 by his publisher, T. Saint, from the original plates. It is called *Bewick's Select Fables of Aesop and Others.* These pictures show the artist's knowledge and love of the whole outdoor world—plants, trees, birds, and beasts. Certainly Thomas Bewick, and to a somewhat lesser extent his brother John, raised the woodcut to a new level of artistic achievement.

An interesting by-product of the Bewicks' contribution is that artists of established reputations began to sign their pictures for children's books.

WILLIAM BLAKE 1757-1827

The book that adds special luster to the artistic achievements of the eighteenth century is William Blake's *Songs of Innocence* (1789). The artist wrote the verses, illustrated them, engraved, hand-colored, and bound the book, with some help from his wife. It caused no great stir in its day, but it was nevertheless an epoch-making book. It is true that most of Blake's poetry and all of his finest engravings and water colors were for adults, but the artist thought of his *Songs of Innocence* as a book for children. He adorned it lovingly with garlands and scrolls. He gave it color and beautifully drawn figures of people, especially the active figures of children. The pictures are not realistic but delicate fantasies, almost dreamlike in character. They in no wise measure up to the greatness of his illustrations for adult books, *The Book of Job* (1825), for instance. But here are color and a tender perception of the artless grace of children. (See 1 in color section.)

FABLE XLVII.

The Fox and the Stork.

Note the grace of the figures and foliage in this beautifully designed illustration, enriched by the delicately arranged floral border. From Aesop's Fables, *Thomas Bewick edition. Faithfully reprinted from rare Newcastle edition. Published by T. Saint in 1784 with the original engravings by Thomas Bewick. From the John G. White collection, Cleveland Public Library. (Book 4½ x 7, picture 2½ x 2⅜)*

The Nineteenth Century

William Blake brought delicate colors into his book for children, not by color printing but by hand. Color printing, however, was widely used from about 1803 to 1835,[3] though at the beginning of the nineteenth century the most notable illustrators were still working in black and white.

Examine 2 and 4 in color section. These two early colored illustrations by unknown artists are interesting proof that publishers were beginning to recognize the lure of color in books for young children. *A Continuation of the Comic Adventures of Old Mother Hubbard and Her Dog* was issued in London in 1805 by John Harris, successor to Elizabeth Newbery. Harris was deservedly famous for his children's books. As Philip James says of him, "... the high quality of the illustrations in all of his books during the first quarter of the nineteenth century place him above his rivals."[4] The rare little book *The History of the House That Jack Built* has "15 elegant engravings on Copper Plate," brightly colored and amusing. In 1825, Fielding Lucas, a distinguished American publisher famous for his beautifully designed and decorated maps, was also publishing well-chosen children's books. They followed the English publications of Newbery or Harris, but we are told[5] he had his own plates made, some of them drawn by John Latrobe perhaps, but unsigned. Lucas' list of children's books advertised in a newspaper in 1824 includes twenty-four familiar English titles such as *Cock Robin, The Comic Adventures of Dame Trot and Her Cat, The Cries of London,* and *The History of the House That Jack Built.* Only seventeen examples of his children's books are extant, although he is known to have published seventy between 1820 and 1845.

Mulready's characterization of the bumblebee as a fat, sweet little boy is very appealing. Strong sense of form and rich texture always enhance his illustrations.
Illustration by William Mulready. From The Butterfly's Ball *by William Roscoe. Published by J. Harris, 1807.*

WILLIAM MULREADY 1786-1863

So the century began propitiously with some color printing for children's books, but it is the work of William Mulready that first brought distinction to those early years of the century.

This illustrator is remembered for his gay, fanciful drawings for *The Butterfly's Ball* (1807) by William Roscoe. This rhymed description of a fairy picnic enjoyed enormous popularity for over fifty years, aided no doubt by Mulready's amusing pictures in black and white. Some of his bees, snails, butterflies, and other guests of the party have human bodies with true-to-the-species creatures atop their heads or else they are well-drawn insects or animals piloted by elfish figures perched on their backs. The mole, for instance, has a fat blind gnome for a rider. Unfortunately, the children's books this gifted artist adorned do not stand the tests of time as his drawings do.

3. Percy Muir, *English Children's Books,* pp. 175-176.
4. *Children's Books of Yesterday,* edited by C. Geoffrey Holme, p. 44.
5. *Proceedings of the American Antiquarian Society.* At the Annual Meeting held in Worcester, October 19, 1955. "Fielding Lucas, Jr. Early 19th Century Publisher of Fine Books and Maps," by James W. Foster, pp. 202-207.

This is a fate that threatens the lasting fame of illustrators in each generation.

GEORGE CRUIKSHANK 1792-1878

A great artist of this period is George Cruikshank, satirist and cartoonist for England's famous *Punch.* In contrast to Mulready, Cruikshank had the good fortune to enter the field of children's book illustration by way of a classic that is ageless in its appeal—an English translation of the Grimms' *Collection of German Popular Stories* (1824 and 1826). In black and white, his humorous, lively, cleverly drawn pictures are the embodiment of the tales (see p. 44).

SIR JOHN TENNIEL 1820-1914

Inseparable from Lewis Carroll's *Alice's Adventures in Wonderland* (1865) and *Through the Looking Glass* (1871) are the illustrations by Sir John Tenniel, cartoonist for *Punch.* Other artists hopefully make pictures for this classic fantasy, but their illustrations usually seem inadequate when compared with the long beloved figures by Tenniel. Unforgettable are serious, pinafored, long-haired Alice, the smartly dressed, bustling White Rabbit, the Mad Hatter and his famous tea-party companions, Father William, the Cheshire Cat, and all the other mad, topsy-turvy characters of the Wonderland and the Looking Glass worlds. Strong in line and composition, drawn with beautiful clarity and poker-faced drollery, these illustrations enhance the fantasy and give it convincing reality.

ARTHUR HUGHES 1832-1915

The illustrations of Arthur Hughes are as strongly associated with George MacDonald's *At the Back of the North Wind* (1871) and *The Princess and the Goblin* (1872) as are Tenniel's illustrations with *Alice's Adventures in Wonderland.* Hughes worked in black and white and was an interpreter of fantasy, but his pictures are as different from Cruikshank's or Tenniel's as the MacDonald books

Here is pictured one of the most famous tea parties of all time. Tenniel's picture is as much a classic as the affair itself: the Dormouse sleeps; the Hatter spouts nonsense; the Rabbit listens wild-eyed; and prim little Alice is lost in gloom.
Illustration by Sir John Tenniel. From Alice in Wonderland, *by Lewis Carroll.*
(Original with color, book 5¾ x 8¾)

are different from the Grimms' fairy tales or Carroll's *Alice.* For MacDonald's two fairy tales the never-never land of the pictures is all mystery, gentleness, and lovely innocence. These qualities carry over to his more realistic pictures for Christina Rossetti's *Sing-Song* (1872), little masterpieces of tenderness and beauty (see p. 173).

WALTER CRANE 1845-1915

In *English Children's Books,* Percy Muir points out in the chapter "The Importance of Pictures" that it was ". . . in the sixties that publishers began first to attempt to sell books to children mainly for the interest of the illustrations." What a line of successors that movement launched! Mr. Muir then goes on to show how much modern color printing owes to Edmund Evans, a publisher and an artist in his own right. A pioneer in color printing, Evans had long inveighed against the cheap, gaudy illustrations used in books for children. He firmly believed that even an inexpensive paperback book planned for the nursery child could be beautiful in design and color. In

THE BROWNIES
TOBOGGANING
ONE evening, when the snow lay white
On level plain and mountain height,
The Brownies mustered, one and all,
In answer to a special call.

One of the first humorous American children's books, especially appealing because of the thin legs and fat bodies of the elves. From The Brownies: Their Book *by Palmer Cox. Century Publishing, 1887. (Book 6½ x 8¾)*

Walter Crane, Evans found an artist to carry out his theories.

Trained as a wood engraver, Walter Crane was greatly influenced by the work of the Pre-Raphaelites and also by his study of Japanese prints. Both of these influences are evident in his pictures—in the idealized figures of women and children and in the sparse, decorative landscapes. Between 1867 and 1876 Crane produced over thirty so-called "toy books,"[6] published chiefly by Routledge and generally undated. Crane took these books so seriously that he worked over every page, including the typography, so that it came out a well-composed whole. His *Baby's Opera* and *Baby's Bouquet* were a series of English nursery songs with words, music, and pictures. Later he decorated, also in color, Hawthorne's *Wonder Book* (1892). (See 5 in color section.)

KATE GREENAWAY 1846-1901

Edmund Evans was greatly taken with the delicate colors and decorative borders of Kate Greenaway's pictures for her own rhymes. He printed her book *Under the Window* (1878) by a costly process that reproduced the pictures with remarkable fidelity. To her surprise, the artist found herself famous almost overnight, and she outsold all the other artists of her day, the initial sales of *Under the Window* running to some 70,000 copies. It still sells, and Evans' firm is still printing her books from the original woodcuts.

Her style was unique—graceful figures in quaint old-fashioned clothes, at play, at tea, or otherwise decorously engaged. The pages are gay with garlands of fruits or flowers, mostly in delicate pastel colors. Her pictures often have a gentle humor, and their grace and charm still delight the eye. (See 3 in color section.)

RANDOLPH CALDECOTT 1846-1886

The work of Randolph Caldecott, for whom the Caldecott Medal is named, is much closer to modern tastes than Kate Greenaway's. He was the third of Edmund Evans' famous triumvirate and, like the others, owes much to that printer's bold experiments with color printing. Caldecott succeeded and far surpassed Walter Crane in the production of illustrated toy books.

Caldecott grew up in the Shropshire country, familiar with country fairs, the hunt, dogs, horses, and the lovely English landscape, all of which are evident in his pictures. As a young man he worked in a bank, but finally gave up the business world, settled in London, and devoted himself to his drawing and art classes. When in 1876 Washington Irving's *Old Christmas* appeared with Caldecott's illustrations, his reputation was established. But it was not until around 1878 that he began to work on the nursery toy books with which we associate his name and fame. Probably his most famous illustrations are those for William Cowper's *The Diverting History of John Gilpin* (1878), a rhymed picture-story, funny both to children and adults and a masterpiece

6. The term "toy book" is used today to mean books with pop-ups or cut-outs that make them more toys than books. The Crane "toy books" were simply books intended for the nursery of prereading child.

of droll action. No one ever drew such humorous horses or such recklessly inept riders. His illustrated *Mother Goose* rhymes in paper-covered book form are among his loveliest and most original creations. Caldecott did a number of these toy books, selling at one shilling, and they have never been surpassed by our best and most expensive modern picture books. (See p. 110 and 7 in color section.)

PALMER COX 1840-1924

Meanwhile, in the New World, interesting developments were taking place in the field of children's book illustration. From Canada came Palmer Cox's *The Brownies: Their Book* (1887). A rhymed narrative carried hundreds of brownies through a series of adventures that had children poring over the pen and ink drawings to find their favorite characters, the Frenchman or Dutchman or Chinaman or Policeman and, of course, the Dude. Although neither great literature nor art, these books have a charm that their descendants, the comics, have never achieved.

ARTHUR FROST 1851-1928

For that classic collection of Negro folk tales from our own South *Nights with Uncle Remus,* Arthur Frost made pen and ink pictures as comic and irresistible as that gay rogue, Br'er Rabbit himself. Whether he is "sashaying" down the road in his patched and droopy old pants or talking turkey to the Tar Baby, he is a picture of rural shrewdness. Frost's whole gallery of animal folk, "ourselves in fur," provides as marvelous characterizations as any Caldecott ever made.

HOWARD PYLE 1853-1911

Howard Pyle was another American artist who worked in black and white. His heroic and romantic pictures for such books as *Robin Hood* (1883), *Otto of the Silver Hand* (1888), and *Men of Iron* (1890) are meticulous in their fidelity to the historical costumes, weapons, and accoutrements of the period. Yet his elaborations of robes, courtly trappings, and tournament details are always subordinated to the interpretation of character or mood. The poignancy of young Otto's tragedy moves anyone who looks at those pictures, and, in contrast, the high good humor of Robin Hood is equally evident. Here was an artist with a gift for pictorial storytelling.

It always amuses children to see animals behaving like people. Frost focuses attention on the figures by simply darkening them and keeping the background suggestive and pale.
Illustration by Arthur Frost. From Nights with Uncle Remus *by Joel Chandler Harris. Published 1892 by Houghton Mifflin. (Book 4½ x 7)*

REGINALD BIRCH 1856-1943

Reginald Birch, an illustrator who lived and drew well into the twentieth century, is noted for his manipulation of beautiful details to make a striking composition. It is unfortunate that children should associate his work with the velvet knee breeches, curls, and lace collars of *Little Lord Fauntleroy.* These were true to the story, and the pictures of that impeccable little darling and his gouty grandsire, against backgrounds of grace or magnificence, show Birch's gift for characterization (p. 61).

LESLIE BROOKE 1862-1940

Although some of the work of the English Leslie Brooke was published as late as 1935, he is so much in the Caldecott tradition that he seems to belong to the earlier century of the famous triumvirate. In delicate pastel colors he provides glimpses of the English countryside, pictures as charming as any Caldecott produced. His *Mother Goose* characters in *Ring o' Roses* (n.d.) are delightful, and his pigs are triumphs of droll characterization. The three *Johnny Crow* books (1903, 1907, and 1935) are his own invention. Johnny Crow is the perfect host for two parties of birds and beasts so adroitly characterized both in verse and pictures that his books are classic examples of what picture books can be in the hands of a creative artist-writer. (See 6 in color section.)

The Twentieth Century

E. BOYD SMITH 1860-1943

An American artist and an innovator, E. Boyd Smith produced at the turn of the century but is now almost forgotten. In 1906 he wrote and illustrated *The Story of Pocahontas and Captain John Smith,* which could be considered the forerunner of the d'Aulaires' picture-biographies. It is a moving narrative with pictures that are beautiful in composition and wonderfully interpretative. In 1910 Smith wrote and illustrated *Chicken World,* a picture book as beautiful as anything we have today. Borders portraying the changes in season frame the large pictures which show the cock strutting grandly, his feathers all ashine, the hens sitting or proudly exhibiting their fluffy chicks. None of E. Boyd Smith's other work had the distinction of his biography of *Pocahontas* and his *Chicken World.* Both deserve to be in print today.

JESSIE WILLCOX SMITH 1863-1935

Jessie Willcox Smith was a student of Howard Pyle and, like his, her figures and backgrounds are strongly drawn, but here the resemblance ends. She used soft colors, dark rather than clear and light. The heart-shaped faces are idealized and all alike, and her pictures are completely feminine. And yet her illustrations for Stevenson's *Child's Garden of Verses* (1905) still seem as right for those poems as Shepard's for Milne's (p. 62).

BEATRIX POTTER 1866-1943

Beatrix Potter's *The Tale of Peter Rabbit* (1901), a milestone in children's literature, marks the beginning of the modern picture-story —the picture-story in which the pictures are so integral a part of the story that the nonreading child can soon "read" the story from the pictures. In Beatrix Potter's books, her clear water colors show the small animals dressed up like human country folks pursuing their activities through fascinating English lanes and meadows or within cozy interiors. The pictures are as beautifully composed as the texts, and in her little books there is a perfect union of the two arts. (See 9 in color section.)

ARTHUR RACKHAM 1867-1939

Arthur Rackham, whose distinctive work is easily recognized, illustrated well over fifty books but seemed most at home in the field of folklore. His pictures for *The Fairy Tales of Grimm* (1900) made an immediate impression, and Rackham enthusiasts and collectors began with that publication. There are no fluttering fairies to be found on his pages; instead, there are earthy old gnomes, ogres, and witches, eerie, mysterious, and sometimes menacing. In black and white or full color his pictures are alive with details that the casual observer may miss—small furry faces or elfin figures peering out from leaves or half hidden in grasses. His little girl heroines—like Snow White and Tattercoats—are fragile and lovely in a threatening world. Others, like Catskin and the heroines of the ballads, are lush, splendid creatures. We are told that Rackham drew his pictures before painting them, a technique that seems to strengthen them, because whether the colors are dark and somber or clear and light they have body and vitality. For *The Wind in the Willows* (1940), his characterizations of Mole, Ratty, Toad, and all the others are inimitable, and the details of picnics and cozy interiors enhance the warmth of that story. Here is an artist with unique gifts which he devoted almost entirely to the illustration of books for children. (See 8 in color section.)

ERNEST H. SHEPARD 1879-

The deft pen of Ernest Shepard was drawing for *Punch* as early as 1907, but not until the publication of A. A. Milne's *When We Were Very Young* (1924) with the Shepard illustrations were his pen and ink sketches widely and affectionately known. Milne's *Winnie-the-Pooh* followed in 1926, *Now We Are Six* in 1927, and *The House at Pooh Corner* in 1928, all illustrated by Shepard. Now Ernest Shepard's pen and ink sketches of Christopher Robin, Pooh, and their companions seem inseparable from the poems and stories. Whether it is Christopher Robin going hoppity or meditating "half way down the stair" or Pooh coming down on his head or trying to look like a cloud, these small pictures show mood, character, and situation. Shepard's interpretative ability is shown again in his illustrations for Kenneth Grahame's *Reluctant Dragon* (1938) and *The Wind in the Willows* (1931). Even Rackham's illustrations for this latter book cannot surpass some of Shepard's sketches. Mole "Jumping off all four legs at once, in the joy of living," Toad picnicking grandly or waddling off disguised as a washerwoman, or the mouse children singing carols, or the snug security of Badger's firelit kitchen after the cold of the Wild Wood—these pictures and many others are sheer perfection. In 1957 Shepard made eight color plates for *The World of Pooh* and followed, when he was eighty years old, with eight more for the Golden Anniversary Edition of *Wind in the Willows* (1959). His color plates are beautiful but add nothing to the virtuosity of his pen and ink sketches (p. 63).

NEWELL WYETH 1882-1945

Another pupil of Howard Pyle's, Newell Wyeth, brought to his illustrations a deep sense of drama and the heroic. Whether he illustrated *Robin Hood* (1917), *Robinson Crusoe* (1920), *The Odyssey* (1929), or *Treasure Island* (1911), his pictures are powerful in composition, almost three-dimensional in effect, and rich in color. None are more appealing than his pictures for *The Yearling* (1939), but in every one of these dissimilar books his fertile imagination interprets and illumines the story. (See 10 in color section.)

KURT WIESE 1887-

Sent to China on business, taken prisoner by the Japanese, back to Germany by way of Australia and Africa—somewhere along the line, German-born Kurt Wiese determined to be an artist. This background of travel and of

Here is the romantic realism of an earlier school of art. Notice the luxurious room, and see how the artist has made the small boy's figure sturdy despite the laces he wears. Illustration by Reginald Birch. From Little Lord Fauntleroy *by Frances Hodgson Burnett. Charles Scribner's Sons, 1955. Reprinted with permission. (Book 5½ x 7¾)*

knowledge of many peoples has given color and authenticity to his illustrations for such books as Elizabeth Lewis' *Young Fu of the Upper Yangtze* (1932), Kipling's *Jungle Books* (1932), and that classic little story by Marjorie Flack, *The Story About Ping* (1933).

Perhaps the most outstanding characteristic of Kurt Wiese's work is his amazing versatility. He has illustrated over a hundred books, and whether it is Ping, a Chinese duck waddling up the gangplank of his particular junk, or Felix Salten's wild and beautiful *Bambi* (1929), or two Middle Western small-town boys plus a moose in Phil Stong's *Honk: the Moose* (1935), or his own amusing stories *Rabbits' Revenge* (1940) and the Chinese *Fish in the Air* (1948), and whether he is working in black and white or full color, character and situations are illustrated with humor, fidelity to the story, and fine draughtsmanship. (See 16 in color section.)

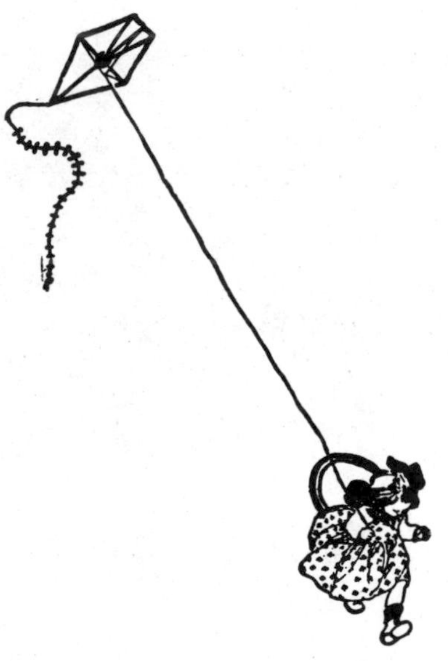

Foreshortening the body and using a diagonal composition make this picture of a child running with her kite effective and exciting. Illustration by Jessie Willcox Smith. From A Child's Garden of Verses *by Robert Louis Stevenson. Copyright, 1905, by Charles Scribner's Sons. Reproduced with permission of Charles Scribner's Sons. (Book 4 x 6, picture 3 x 4¾)*

To this group of artists, born in the nineteenth century but producing in the early or middle years of the twentieth century more names could be added. Thomas Handforth (1897-1948) won the Caldecott Medal for his major contribution to children's books, *Mei Li* (1938). His black and white illustrations are vigorous and full of action, and they make the little Chinese heroine seem real and understandable. Another Caldecott winner is the picture book *The Big Snow* (1948) by Berta and Elmer Hader (p. 64). It is typical of their work—a slight story, soft colors, and a warm feeling for birds, animals, and kindly people. Marie Hall Ets (1895-) did her amusing *Mister Penny* (1935) in black and white, but her sensitive and perceptive water colors for *Play with Me* (1955), about a little girl learning to be quiet with shy woodland creatures, are quite the loveliest she has ever produced. *Nine Days to Christmas* (1959) won the Caldecott Medal but is, in spite of full, bright colors, less interesting than her earlier books.

From the thirties on, there have been such numbers of picture books for the youngest children and such lavishly illustrated books for the older ones that the forties, fifties, and sixties may come to be known in the history of children's literature as the age of the illustrator. No book of this size can hope to name and appraise half the talented people who are doing fine and original illustrations for children's books. Of the sampling of these artists that follows, many were born in the nineteenth century, but most of them began their work in the thirties and have continued producing in the years following. The exception is Wanda Gág, whose epoch-making book *Millions of Cats* appeared before the thirties.

WANDA GAG 1893-1946

In 1928, Wanda Gág's picture-story *Millions of Cats* ushered in what came to be known as "The Golden Thirties" of picture books. It still outshines in strong story interest most of its successors. It is indeed about as close to perfection as a picture-story can be. It is told with all the rhythm and cadence of the old European storytellers and is illustrated with striking black and white lithographs that repeat the flowing rhythm of the text. Wanda Gág was steeped in European folk tales, which she heard told as a child, and so it is not surprising that her own completely fresh and original four stories have a folk flavor. They are, in addition to *Millions of Cats, Funny Thing* (1929), *Snippy and Snappy* (1931), and *Nothing at All* (1941). Her illustrations for *ABC Bunny* (1933) and the four small books of *Grimm's Fairy Tales* have the same flowing lines, dramatic black and white areas, and homely warmth that are characteristic of everything she did (1, p. 92).

CONRAD BUFF 1886-

Conrad Buff, a Swiss-born Californian, is primarily a landscape painter whose pictures hang in many of the great art museums in this country and abroad and in private collections. For his wife's stories he has made striking illustrations in black and white, sepia, or full color. His pictures for Mary Buff's *Big Tree* (1946), *Dash and Dart* (1942), and its sequel *Forest Folk* (1962) show not only his keen observation and love of nature but his primary concern with problems of light. The poetry of Conrad Buff's illustrations matches the cadenced prose of Mary Buff's stories. Theirs is a rare husband and wife collaboration. (See 15 in color section.)

The child and animals are very appealing. One would like to join these friends as they stand quietly watching the river in the sunshine.
Illustration by E. H. Shepard. From The House at Pooh Corner *by A. A. Milne. Copyright 1956, by A. A. Milne. Reproduced by permission of the publishers, E. P. Dutton & Co., Inc. (Book 5¼ x 7½, picture 4 x 5)*

MARGUERITE DE ANGELI 1889-

Whether Mrs. de Angeli gives us a rebellious young Quaker girl of long ago, kicking her bonnet down the stairs in *Thee Hannah!* (1940), or a too lively young pioneer schoolboy in *Skippack School* (1939) or whether she gives us some two hundred and sixty illustrations for her *Mother Goose* (1954), the people are always lovely to look at, the colors warm and soft, and the details of outdoor scenes or interiors authentic and beautifully composed. Although Mrs. de Angeli's illustrations may be somewhat reminiscent of the pretty quaintness of Jessie Willcox Smith's, they have much more vitality and action. Minority groups and historical subjects have held special interest for this artist. The Pennsylvania Dutch in *Henner's Lydia* (1936), the Amish in *Yonie Wondernose* (1944), the Polish children in *Up the Hill* (1942), and the hero of her splendid historical story *Door in the Wall* (1949, Newbery Medal) are most appealing. No matter whose story she is telling, Marguerite de Angeli's illustrations have grace, lovely colors, and eye-filling beauty. (See 13 in color section.)

JAMES DAUGHERTY 1889-

Thomas Handforth's *Mei Li* was awarded the Caldecott Medal in 1938, but another picture-story was also worthy of the award that year—*Andy and the Lion* by James Daugherty. Later, this author-artist received the Newbery

This is an accurate, close-up look at a blue jay in a tree, yelling his advice to his friends in good blue-jay style.
Illustration by Berta and Elmer Hader. From The Big Snow, *Copyright 1948 by Berta and Elmer Hader. Reproduced with permission of The Macmillan Company. (Original in color, book 8½ x 10, picture 5½ x 10)*

Medal for his *Daniel Boone* (1939). Both books are as distinguished for their illustrations as for the text. Warm earthiness and a tender appreciation of people mark his pictures. *Andy and the Lion* is entertaining, but the pictures are unforgettable. The rear view of young Andy reaching for a book on high library shelves, or Andy suddenly confronted with a lion in full roar, or Andy toppling over backwards as he extracts the thorn—these have a gusto that only Daugherty can impart to awkward, beautiful, absurd human beings. On the heroic side, his illustrations for *Daniel Boone* (1939) have vigor, and those for *Poor Richard* (1941) reveal his wonderful gift for characterization. James Daugherty uses no color, but his portraits are as colorful as the heroes they record.

MAUD 1890- AND MISKA PETERSHAM 1888-

Maud and Miska Petersham won the Caldecott Medal for their American Mother Goose, *The Rooster Crows* (1945). They celebrated the advent of a grandchild with the charming *The Box with Red Wheels* (1949), a book with bold, bright colors, strong composition, and a slight story with a surprise ending which appeals to children four to seven. However, it is their beautiful picture-story of the Nativity, *The Christ Child* (1931), that has especially endeared them to children, parents, and teachers. A year in Palestine gave them the inspiration and background for this classic, for which they wisely used the texts from St. Matthew and St. Luke. Their exquisite pictures, historically authentic in scene, costumes, and other details, have successfully caught and interpreted for young children the tender majesty of that matchless narrative. (See 11 in color section.)

FEODOR ROJANKOVSKY 1891-

Russian-born Feodor Rojankovsky has unforgettable illustrations with rich, earthy colors and homely, lovable, old peasant faces for Hans Christian Andersen's *The Old Man Is Always Right* (1940). There is this same earthy quality about all of Rojankovsky's people—the sturdy, unprettified children and the stocky, dumpy grownups with their warm, woolly scarfs or mittens. As for his animals there were never furrier kittens or fluffier feathered fowls. Texture, rich colors, and good draughtsmanship are hallmarks of this artist. He is at his best in his illustrations for that somber story of two lone, struggling children, Mikhail Prishvin's *Treasure Trove of the Sun* (1952). Yet it was Rojankovsky's gay, amusing illustrations for *Frog Went a-Courtin'* (1955), by John Langstaff, that won him a long deserved Caldecott Medal. He is one of the notable colorists among modern artists. (See 12 in color section.)

DOROTHY LATHROP 1891-

Primarily a worker in black and white, Dorothy Lathrop has illustrated many of Walter de la Mare's books, W. L. Hudson's *Little Boy Lost* (1920), and Sara Teasdale's *Stars To-night* (1930). These she has done with such beauty and interpretative power that story and pictures or poem and picture are a perfect whole. However, it is in the interpretation of animals that she has perhaps made her greatest contribution, and these pictures are all in pen and ink, sketched with remarkable fineness and integrity. *Animals of the Bible* (1937) was awarded the first Caldecott Medal but still remains the least popular of all her books. *Who Goes There?* (1935) is a picture book of small forest creatures who come to a winter feast spread for them in the woods. *Hide and Go Seek* (1938) is a record of those shyest of creatures, the flying squirrels. Both of these picture books are done with such exquisite details, such superb composition, that no colored illustration could do more. (See p. 176.)

ROBERT LAWSON 1891-1957

If pen and ink sketches can be described as witty, Robert Lawson's pictures certainly deserve the description. Who can ever forget his first glimpse of that mild young bull in *The Story of Ferdinand* (1936), peacefully inhaling the fragrance of flowers instead of snorting round the bull ring, or Mr. Popper blandly coping with his penguins in *Mr. Popper's Penguins* (1938), or the scene of the electric shock in *Ben and Me* (1939). In contrasting mood are Mr. Lawson's gravely beautiful drawings for *Pilgrim's Progress* (1939) and for *Adam of the Road* (1942), with boy and dog moving adventurously through thirteenth-century England. Robert Lawson was a master draughtsman, and every detail of scenes, costumes, and characterizations is meticulously executed. But not until he wrote as well as illustrated *Ben and Me* did his admirers realize the full scope of his talents and versatility. Text and pictures are equally amusing and full of the wry wisdom that appears again in his own *Mr. Revere and I* (1953), *Rabbit Hill* (1944, Newbery Medal), and its sequel, *The Tough Winter* (1954). (See p. 201.)

HELEN SEWELL 1896-1957

No illustrator ever varied her style more radically than Helen Sewell. She belongs both to the old and to the new in art. Her pictures for *The First Bible* (1934) are grave, realistic, and monumental. The pictures for her *Book of Myths* (1941) show an entirely new technique. Sharp lines give an effect of action, so that the pictures seem to be the recorded movements of a dance. Then for the illustrations of *Grimm's Tales* (1954), she used broad brush strokes and an almost abstract representation. This she used again in her pictures for *The Three Kings of Saba* (1955) by Alf Evers. At the beginning of the story the figures of the three kings are stonelike and unbending. After the kings see the Child, the lines are curved and yielding. (See p. 66.)

In addition to these modern illustrations of Helen Sewell, we have today the bold, vigorous pictures of Nicolas Mordvinoff and the strong, stylized ones of Nicolas Sidjakov. And here and there an occasional picture book displays a freer, more modern technique. However, the illustrators for picture books tend generally toward realistic representation.

LUDWIG BEMELMANS 1898-1962

The delightful author-artist Ludwig Bemelmans produced books for adults and for chil-

Tears, knotted tail, and bony knee make this one of the most appealing lions in children's literature. The rich black and whites give the bodies a three-dimensional look.
From James Daugherty's Andy and the Lion. *Copyright 1938 by James Daugherty. Reprinted by permission of The Viking Press, Inc. (Original with color, book 7½ x 10½)*

dren. His *Hansi* (1934) is a big book about a small boy who sent an unwilling dachshund off on a ski trip in the Alps. But it was *Madeline* (1939) that made Bemelmans famous. And with every succeeding Madeline book, Paris became more familiar to American children. Madeline falling into the Seine, Madeline grandly enjoying appendicitis, Madeline and the eleven other little girls searching for their dog, and Madeline in London—these big, handsome pictures, sketchily drawn but full of details and lovely color, have made Madeline and her creator forever beloved by children. (See 19 in color section.)

EDWARD ARDIZZONE 1900-

Only a man could spin the yarns about Tim, and only a first-rate artist like Edward Ardizzone could bless Tim with such splendid seascapes and glimpses of port towns. Whether the books come in the handsome, outsize edition of the first *Little Tim and the Brave Sea Captain* (1936) or in the small-size edition of *Tim All Alone* (1957), the pictures are water colors, beautifully reproduced, full of the relentless power of the sea and the jaunty courage of seafaring folk. Mr. Ardizzone's superb illustrations for *Don Quixote* (1959) have humor and pathos and, like those for *Little Tim,* show man forever confronted with something vast and beyond him, but struggling manfully nevertheless. (See 28 in color section.)

In Helen Sewell's stark uncluttered design there is also a powerful interpretative quality. The nonchalant strolling hen and the wistful Hänsel in his tiny cage tell a dramatic story.
Illustration by Helen Sewell from Grimm's Tales. *Reproduced with permission of Henry Z. Walck, Inc., Publishers. (Original in color, book 6 x 8½)*

ROGER DUVOISIN 1904-

Known as an artist's artist, Roger Duvoisin uses a variety of techniques but has an unfailing sense of strong composition and design. For Alvin Tresselt's books on weather and seasons, such as *White Snow, Bright Snow* (1947, Caldecott Medal), his colors are flat washes and the pictures simplified to a poster-like effect. For Louise Fatio's delightful series of stories about *The Happy Lion* (1954), Mr. Duvoisin's pictures are in soft colors with fascinating details. *Amahl and the Night Visitors* (1952) is illustrated in dark, rich colors with a somber, dramatic quality that is at one with the story. Here is a major artist giving his best to children's books. His own *Petunia* books have rare humor. (See 18 in color section.)

THEODOR SEUSS GEISEL (DR. SEUSS) 1904-

What shall we say of "Dr. Seuss" as an artist? He confesses that he cannot draw anatomy as it actually is, but in his pictures the fractured legs and gangling arms have made his nizzards and wizards, his Bartholomew, Horton, Thidwick the Moose, the Cat in the Hat, and all the rest of his mad characters so beloved by children that Dr. Seuss is synonymous with laughter. This is cartoon art, but when it accompanies rhymed stories of great originality, whose words run and leap with the rhythmic lines of the pictures, the combination is irresistible. There is also a strange, wild grace about some of the pictures, with their great heights and depths, bright clear blues and reds, decorative touches to costumes or scenes. These make the grotesque arresting and even beautiful.

1.

1. Warm colors, graceful use of curved lines, and unrealistic designs heighten the fantasy of these dreamlike pictures and poems. From the facsimile of Mr. Lessing J. Rosenwald's copy of William Blake's Songs of Innocence and of Experience, *published by the Trianon Press, London, for the William Blake Trust, 1955. (Book 5¼ by 8¼)*

2. The man's elegant and dramatic posture more than compensates for his tatters. No wonder the "Maiden all forlorn" was impressed. Notice the pleasing composition and clear, bright colors. From The History of the House That Jack Built. *Reproduced from the D'Alte Welch Collection, Cleveland. (Book 6 by 4)*

2.

4.

3.

Yes, that's the girl that struts about,
She's very proud,—so very proud!
Her *bow-wow's* quite as proud as she:
They both are very wrong to be
So proud—so very proud.

See, Jane and Willy laugh at her,
They say she's very proud!
Says Jane, "My stars!—they're very silly;"
"Indeed they are," cries little Willy,
"To walk so stiff and proud."

3. This is an amusing example of pictorial satire. A telling use of line contrasts the gentle, pretty girl and the haughty, ugly one to augment the satire of verses. From Kate Greenaway's Under the Window. *Reproduced with permission of Frederick Warne & Co., Inc. (Book 6½ by 9)*

4. This illustration is particularly amusing because it presents a fantastic idea in a meticulously realistic style. From A Continuation of the Comic Adventures of Old Mother Hubbard and Her Dog. *Reproduced from the D'Alte Welch Collection, Cleveland. (Book 4 by 4½)*

5. Delicate colors, good use of tone scale, interesting costume details, and a strikingly bold, simple composition of the whole, make this a typical example of Walter Crane's style. From Walter Crane's Baby's Bouquet. *Reproduced with permission of Frederick Warne & Co., Inc. (Book 7 by 7)*

6. Here is a hilarious dance. Notice that even the fiddler's foot is beating time and that the chicks are stepping as high as the lively old rooster and the woman. No wonder the cows look astonished. Illustration by Leonard Leslie Brooke. From Ring o'Roses. *Reproduced with permission of Frederick Warne & Co., Inc. (Book 7¾ by 10)*

7. This is one of Caldecott's illustrations that aroused Kate Greenaway's envy for its humorous inventiveness. The well-drawn legs of each figure not only characterize the creature but lend humor and dance movements to the whole composition. From Randolph Caldecott's Hey Diddle and Baby Bunting. *Reproduced from the D'Alte Welch Collection, Cleveland. (Book 7¼ by 8)*

6.

5.

7.

8. Rackham often distorted proportions for the sake of a dramatic storytelling effect. In this illustration, the purity of the maiden's face is in sharp contrast with the complex lines of the background and the grotesquerie of the faces in the well.
Illustration by Arthur Rackham. From English Fairy Tales. *Copyright 1918 by Macmillan & Co., London. Reproduced with permission of Macmillan & Co., London. (Book 6½ by 8¼)*

9

10.

9. Here is Peter Rabbit enjoying the forbidden pleasures of Mr. McGregor's garden. Beatrix Potter's delicate water colors, strengthened by her strong use of line, are as effective as her vigorous prose style. From Beatrix Potter's The Tale of Peter Rabbit. *Reproduced with permission of Frederick Warne & Co., Inc. (Book 4 by 5¼)*

10. The action in this scene, showing the parting of mother and son, is made more dramatic by the sharp division and contrast of light and dark areas. Illustration by Newell Wyeth. From Treasure Island *by Robert Louis Stevenson. Copyright 1911 by Charles Scribner's Sons, Copyright 1939 by N. C. Wyeth. Reproduced with permission of Charles Scribner's Sons. (Book 7 by 9¼)*

12.

11.

13.

11. In addition to good drawing, composition, and color this illustration gives a strong sense of moving toward a goal. This is accomplished through the use of lines in the background, the pointing hand, the bent knee, and the direction of the camels' heads. From The Christ Child. *Pictures copyright 1931 by Maud and Miska Petersham. Reproduced with permission of Doubleday and Company. (Book 8 by 10¾)*

12. The texture of feathers and fur and the popping fear-filled eyes of the fleeing bugs and beasts make the details of this picture worth studying again and again. What a helter-skelter flight it is! Even jaunty Frog is on the run, but he does have Miss Mousie by the hand. Illustration by Feodor Rojankovsky. From Frog Went A-Courtin'. *Copyright 1955 by John M. Langstaff and Feodor Rojankovsky. Reproduced by permission of Harcourt, Brace and World, Inc. (Book 7¾ by 10½)*

13. Light filtering through willow leaves, reflected in the water, and illuminating Yonie's happy face makes this picture beautiful. From Yonie Wondernose *by Marguerite de Angeli. Copyright 1944 by Marguerite de Angeli. Reproduced with permission of Doubleday and Company. (Book 8⅜ by 9¾)*

14. Here is a good example of white areas used to create depth. This is a very elegant picture, both rich and simple. Only four things are depicted, but each is in a blooming state: the trees are numerous and heavily leaved; Reynard has a sleek body, heavily furred; the grass is tall and lush; and Chanticleer, though in a dire predicament, is richly plumed. Illustration by Barbara Cooney in Chanticleer and the Fox, *adapted by Barbara Cooney from* Chaucer's Canterbury Tales. *Copyright 1958 by Barbara Cooney Porter. Thomas Y. Crowell Company, New York, publishers. (Book 7¼ by 9¼)*

15. In this unusual composition, the striking use of light and dark areas intensifies the drama of the old man telling a mysterious secret to the frightened boy. The bent, brooding postures of the man, boy, and bird against the stark background suggest fear and sadness. Illustration by Conrad Buff. From Hah-Nee *by Conrad and Mary Buff. Copyright 1956 by Conrad and Mary Buff. Reproduced with permission of Houghton Mifflin Company. (Book 7⅜ by 10½)*

14.

15.

16. 17.

16. *This illustration captures the excitement and beauty of the Chinese Lantern Festival. Notice how the blues and violets make the yellow lanterns glow. From* Fish in the Air *by Kurt Wiese. Copyright © 1948 by Kurt Wiese. Reprinted by permission of The Viking Press, Inc. (Book 10 by 8)*

17. *The artist makes excellent use of his colors in a three-color illustration. In addition to the abundance of action in the picture, the comic use of one kind of eye for everyone—girl, boys, and cats—adds wildness to the scene. Illustration by Nicolas Mordvinoff. From* Russet and the Two Reds *by Will and Nicolas. Copyright 1962 by William Lipkind and Nicolas Mordvinoff. Reproduced by permission of Harcourt, Brace & World, Inc. (Book 8¼ by 10¾)*

18. *In contrast to his light bright pictures for* The Happy Lion, *Duvoisin uses dark, jewel-like colors in this illustration for* Amahl and the Night Visitors. *The stately figures of the Three Kings emerge from the darkness illuminated by the glowing star that leads them. Illustration by Roger Duvoisin. From* Amahl and the Night Visitors *by Gian-Carlo Menotti, adapted by Frances Frost. Copyright 1952 by G. Sherimer. Reproduced with permission of Whittlesey House, McGraw-Hill. (Book 6 by 9)*

19. *Notice how the artist has deliberately distorted the perspective to make a more descriptive illustration that is all movement and humorous excitement. Even the statue looks as if it might take off at any moment. From* Madeline's Rescue *by Ludwig Bemelmans. Copyright 1953 by Ludwig Bemelmans. Reprinted by permission of The Viking Press, Inc. (Book 8⅜ by 12)*

18.

19.

20.

20. The effective use of color, shapes, and misty tones creates the atmosphere which distinguishes this picture. The onlooker can almost hear the lapping of water against the boat and the quiet splash of the paddles. The eye is gratified by the serenity of the total composition.
From Time of Wonder *by Robert McCloskey. Copyright © 1957 by Robert McCloskey. Reprinted by permission of The Viking Press, Inc. (Book 9¼ by 12)*

21. In Mike Mulligan and His Steam Shovel *Virginia Burton has used lettering of the text as well as pictorial line to give movement to the page. She has also managed to personify the steam shovel without gross exaggeration of its shape.*
From Mike Mulligan and His Steam Shovel, *by Virginia Lee Burton. Houghton Mifflin. Copyright 1939 by Virginia Lee Demetrios. (Book 8 by 9¼)*

22. In this picture the color is secondary to the effective use of sculptured shapes to provide impact. Even in black and white the illustration is striking and the strong opposite colors heighten the effect of the composition.
From Umbrella *by Taro Yashima. Copyright © 1958 by Taro Yashima. Reprinted by permission of The Viking Press, Inc. (Book 9 by 8)*

He had taken
such good care of her
that she could still dig
as much in a day
as a hundred men
could dig in a week;
at least he thought she could
but he wasn't quite sure.
Everywhere they went
the new gas shovels
and the new electric shovels
and the new Diesel motor shovels
had all the jobs. No one wanted
Mike Mulligan and Mary Anne any more.
Then one day Mike read in a newspaper that the town
of Popperville was going to build a new town hall.
'We are going to dig the cellar of that town hall,'
said Mike to Mary Anne, and off they started.

21.

22.

23.

24.

23. The fun of looking at this picture lies in the continual discovery of beautifully depicted detail—a butterfly, a lace collar, a pretty hand, a bird, an oak leaf. Illustration by Leonard Weisgard. From Alice in Wonderland *by Lewis Carroll. Reproduced with permission of Harper & Row. (Book 7¼ by 10¾)*

24. The wide-eyed child is obviously spellbound by the fantastic, unbelievable toys. These, together with the rich, muted colors, create a beautiful picture. From Leo Politi's Moy Moy. *Copyright 1960 by Leo Politi. Reproduced with permission of Charles Scribner's Sons. (Book 7½ by 10)*

25. Striking use of the woodcut medium and unusual composition are exemplified here. Putting the wise man and the tiger back to back is an effective way of revealing how they feel about each other. The body of the tiger blends with the grasses of the jungle, but the angry head has been isolated and given prominence. Notice also the wary eye of the wise man. From Once a Mouse *by Marcia Brown. Copyright 1961 by Marcia Brown. Reproduced with permission of Charles Scribner's Sons. (Book 8¾ by 9½)*

26. The artist has expressed the very essence of Cat—beautiful, inscrutable, and self-contained. The colors in this picture glow and vibrate; notice how that open door invites the eye to wander—even as Pussy Cat does. Illustration by Harold Jones. From Lavender's Blue, *Mother Goose rhymes compiled by Kathleen Lines. Copyright 1954. Reproduced with permission of Franklin Watts, Inc. (Book 7 by 9¾)*

27. Much of the appeal in Garth Williams' pictures lies in his ability to depict reality tenderly through delicate rather than sharp detail. Notice in this picture how subtly the poverty of the environment is suggested and how the loving concern of the Orpheline is shown. Illustration by Garth Williams. From jacket for A Brother for the Orphelines *by Natalie Savage Carlson. Copyright © 1959 by Garth Williams. Reproduced with permission of Harper & Row. (Book 7½ by 10)*

The tiger felt offended and humiliated. He forgot all the good he had received from the old man.
"No one shall tell me that I was once a mouse. I will kill him!"

25.

26.

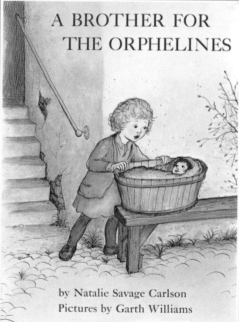

A BROTHER FOR THE ORPHELINES

by Natalie Savage Carlson
Pictures by Garth Williams

27.

28.

29.

28. This is a typical Ardizzone seascape—fresh color and all the lively staccato movement of a harbor scene.
From Little Tim and the Brave Sea Captain *by Edward Ardizzone. Reprinted by the permission of Henry Z. Walck, Inc. (Book 7¼ by 10)*

29. What an enchanting image Adrienne Adams has created of Thumbelina in a miniature world, surrounded by beautifully colored flowers.
Illustration by Adrienne Adams. From Thumbelina *by Hans Christian Andersen. Copyright 1961 by Adrienne Adams. Reproduced with permission of Charles Scribner's Sons. (Book 7⅜ by 9⅜)*

down into the water, in the middle of which floated a large tulip petal where Thumbelina could sit and row herself from one side of the plate to the other, using a couple of white horsehairs as oars. It was a most charming sight. She could sing, too, in the sweetest little voice you ever heard.

30.

31.

30. Besides good composition, color, and drawing, the artists have in this picture used two interesting devices for dramatic purpose: warped perspective and use of transparency to show things not visible in reality add greatly to the storytelling power of the illustration.
From Leif the Lucky *by Ingri and Edgar Parin d'Aulaire. Copyright 1951 by Doubleday, Doran & Company, Inc. Reproduced with permission of Doubleday and Co. (Book 7 by 10½)*

31. In this good example of monoprint, a technique seldom used in children's books, the texture created is reminiscent of old maps, appropriate for the story. Although the robot figures are austerely stylized, the conflict between the two men is dramatically evident, and so too is the helpless anxiety of the small drummer boy.
Illustration by Nicolas Sidjakov. From The Emperor and the Drummer Boy *by Ruth Robbins. Copyright 1962 by Nicolas Sidjakov and Ruth Robbins. Reproduced with permission of Parnassus Press. (Book 8 by 9¾)*

And he thought and thought
and thought about them.

32.

32. Here is a good example of collage used in illustration. This is a highly sophisticated drawing—the shapes are abstract and the colors are subtle. A nice touch of humor is provided by the eyes of the boy and the duckling looking at each other.
From The Snowy Day *by Ezra Jack Keats. Copyright © 1962 by Ezra Jack Keats. Reprinted by permission of The Viking Press, Inc. (Book 9 by 8)*

33. Through his unique use of water colors and particular choice of colors, Maurice Sendak in this book has created a world of shimmering light that heightens the fantasy of the story. In this picture there is something irresistibly droll about the figure of that earnest little girl escorted by that absurd, protective rabbit.
Illustration by Maurice Sendak. From Mr. Rabbit and the Lovely Present *by Charlotte Zolotow. Copyright 1962 by Maurice Sendak. Reproduced with permission of Harper & Row, Publishers. (Book 8 by 6¾)*

33.

INGRI 1905- AND PARIN D'AULAIRE 1898-

Ingri and Parin d'Aulaire are the artists who brought the picture-biography into its own. It is interesting that Norwegian-born Ingri and Swiss-born and French-educated Parin should have turned to the heroes of their adopted land for their subjects. Parin d'Aulaire in his Caldecott Medal acceptance speech for their *Abraham Lincoln* (1939) explained this. "We counted as our biggest asset just the fact that our conceptions of our American themes had never been shaped into school clichés." After the d'Aulaires make their first sketches, they work directly on the lithograph stone, which gives their pictures unusual strength and depth. These qualities were not so effective in their *George Washington* (1936), in which the pictures have always seemed wooden. But by the time they wrote the text and made the pictures for *Abraham Lincoln,* they were using this difficult medium superbly. The colors in this book are deep and rich, and the pictures are full of authentic factual details. The lines and composition have a sort of primitive simplicity that suggests folk art. *Benjamin Franklin* (1950) is particularly rich in storytelling details, *Leif the Lucky* (1951) and *Columbus* (1955) are the most colorful, *Pocahontas* (1946) and *Buffalo Bill* (1952), the most picturesque. Their large, handsome *The Book of Greek Myths* (1962) is another example of their versatility. (See 30 in color section.)

LYND WARD 1905-

The Biggest Bear (1952) won the Caldecott Medal for Lynd Ward, who was already a well-known illustrator, and that book seems to have overshadowed the lovely pictures he made for Hildegarde Swift's *The Little Red Lighthouse and the Great Gray Bridge* (1942). In spite of its long, awkward title, this is a significant picture-story that is made doubly moving by Mr. Ward's illustrations. In both books—*The Biggest Bear,* in black and white, and *The Little Red Lighthouse,* in dark blues and grays with touches of red—it is the artist's sure sense of dramatic contrast that tells the stories and grips and holds the children's attention.

LEO POLITI 1905-

Leo Politi is an artist whose pictures are deceptively simple, almost primitive. Both his figures and his landscapes are stylized, but the total composition makes a beautiful design. His children are colorful and appealing whether it is *Little Leo* (1951), capering gaily with his friends through Italian streets, or the lovely procession of children and pets in *Juanita* (1948), or the delightful little Chinese *Moy Moy* (1960). This generation needs the gentleness and decorative grace of Leo Politi's pictures. (See 24 in color section.)

Ninety-nine zillion,
Nine trillion and two
Creatures are sleeping!
So . . .
How about you?

The highly imaginative creatures and the bouncy rhythm of the composition make this a very lively illustration, full of new things to see.
From Sleep Book *by Dr. Seuss. Random House, 1962. Copyright © 1962 by Dr. Seuss. Reprinted by permission. (Original in color, book 8 x 11)*

VIRGINIA BURTON 1909-

Mike Mulligan and His Steam Shovel (1939) and *The Little House* (1942, Caldecott Medal) are landmarks in the field of picture-stories. Both have absorbing plots, perfect synchronization of text and illustrations, and both also have a social significance over and above their story appeal. Virginia Burton uses clear, bright colors and frequently a swirling line-pattern that suggests the ballet, from which she turned to illustrating. Every one of her books has been a delight to children, but artistically *Song of Robin Hood* (1947) is her *tour de force.* For these old ballads she produced hundreds of pictures of great intricacy and detail, and the whole composition makes striking patterns in black and white. This book is a collector's item. (See p. 99 and picture 21 in color section.)

NICOLAS MORDVINOFF 1911-

The team of "Will and Nicolas" made an immediate impression with their first book, *The Two Reds* (1950). It has a sequel now, *Russet and the Two Reds* (1962), and in between they have produced a number of picture-stories, including *Finders Keepers* (1951), which won the Caldecott Medal. William Lipkind's stories are fresh, humorous, and masculine. Nicolas Mordvinoff's pictures embody the same qualities. They are a protest against the prettified art that has accompanied too many books for children, especially the mass-produced variety. His animals and children are homely creatures except for *Chaga* (1955), which has a poetic quality not found in his other illustrations. Strong lines, bold composition, color dramatically employed, and plenty of action—these are characteristic of his work. (See 17 in color section.)

GARTH WILLIAMS 1912-

Garth Williams has won a formidable number of awards and prizes, including the Prix de Rome for sculpture, a field of art in which he still works. His first venture into children's book illustration was for E. B. White's *Stuart Little* (1945). He followed this with Mr. White's famous *Charlotte's Web* (1952)—a book that might well have received both the Newbery and the Caldecott Medals. For a new edition of Laura Ingalls Wilder's *Little House* books (1953), Garth Williams spent ten years making the pictures, getting acquainted with the author, going over all the country and learning to see the people, the scenes, and the action through her eyes. As a result the pictures and stories are one. Equally successful are his illustrations for Natalie Carlson's books about the French Orphelines and Jennie Lindquist's *Golden Name Day* (1955) and *Little Silver House* (1959). The artist works both in black and white and full color, and his pictures are always characterized by authenticity of details. The colors are fresh and soft, the composition vigorous. But whether the story he illustrates is realistic or pure fantasy, historical fiction or modern city life, his superb gift for characterization stands out. No pig could look more foolishly smug than Wilbur, no orphan could flee more desperately from the encircling bicyclists than Josine, no pioneers could look more cozy than the Little House dwellers, wherever they might be. Garth Williams' people live, his animals have personality, and the stories he illustrates come more vividly to life because they have been blessed with the interpretative skill of this splendid artist. (See 27 in color section.)

ROBERT McCLOSKEY 1914-

The first artist to be twice winner of the Caldecott Medal is Robert McCloskey, whose big, handsome picture-stories are as popular with adults as with children. *Lentil* (1940) is a juvenile *Main Street,* complete with Soldiers' Monument, a welcoming band, and a harmonica-playing hero. *Make Way for Ducklings* (1941, Caldecott Medal) vies with *Blueberries for Sal* (1948) in popularity. Only in *Time of Wonder* (1957, second Caldecott Medal) has this artist used color, but in his powerful black and whites you do not miss the color, so alive they are with realistic details and storytelling power. (See 20 in color section.)

LEONARD WEISGARD 1916-

Leonard Weisgard is a major illustrator whose wonderful pictures have sold many a second-rate text. He is a great colorist and his paintings are full of exquisite details of small flowers or frolicking animals or decorative birds. His illustrations for Margaret Wise Brown's *Little Island* (1946) won him the Caldecott Medal. The seascapes are in deep blues and greens, with the island sometimes lost in mist. The landscapes are in lush yellow greens and flashing blues. His illustrations for two books vie with each other for top place in his achievements. The first book is the large *The Golden Egg Book* (1947) by Margaret Wise Brown. To pore over those pictures is to discover springtime with the mystery of young life and beauty stirring everywhere. The other book is *Alice's Adventures in Wonderland* (1949), an edition which deserved far greater praise and recognition than it received. No one since Tenniel has interpreted the dreaming Alice and the lovely fantasy of her dream more perfectly than Leonard Weisgard. The nonsense of the dream is there, too, and all the lovely colors of that memorable summer day make this an unforgettable work. (See 23 in color section.)

BARBARA COONEY 1917-

Children were delighted by Barbara Cooney's black and white pictures for those two fine animal stories—Rutherford Montgomery's *Kildee House* (1949) and Barbara Reynolds' *Pepper* (1952). But in color she did not come into her own until she made the pictures for Lee Kingman's *Peter's Long Walk* (1953). They are in muted colors and interpret tenderly the child's long journey, the lovely New England countryside and village, the sad homecoming which turns out cheerfully. After this beautiful picture-story it was no surprise to have her win the Caldecott Medal for her illustrations for *Chanticleer and the Fox* (1958), adapted from Chaucer's *Canterbury Tales*. Every detail is historically accurate, but what the children love are those pages in bright clear reds, greens, and blues, alive with action, and old Chanticleer and Reynard equally gorgeous. This is one of the gayest, most exuberant picture-stories children have had. Her *Little Juggler* (1961) is done with the same painstaking accuracy and gorgeous colors, but the story is a gentler one with none of the humor and gaiety of *Chanticleer*. (See 14 in color section.)

MARCIA BROWN 1918-

No generalizations about the work of Marcia Brown are possible, for she varies her style to suit the content of the story she is illustrating. Her illustrations for *Stone Soup* (1947) are colorful, gay, and earthy, like the rogues who taught the villagers a more generous way of life. *Puss in Boots* (1952) is a gorgeous, flamboyant feline, well adapted to the court life into which he catapults his master. Both *The Steadfast Tin Soldier* (1953) and *Cinderella* (1954, Caldecott Medal) are in misty pinks and blues grayed down to the gentle mood of the tales. The sturdy woodcuts in brown and black for *Dick Whittington and His Cat* (1950) are as substantial as the hero. And the book that won her second Caldecott Medal, *Once a Mouse* (1961), is completely different from all the others. This fable of pride laid low is in jungle colors, the pictures are stylized, but with subtle details of expression or posture that tell the story and repay study. Marcia Brown has written and illustrated some charming stories of her own, but her major contribution to date is her brilliant interpretations of single folk tales. (See 25 in color section.)

MAURICE SENDAK 1928-

In spite of the fact that some of Maurice Sendak's first illustrations were for humorous books like Ruth Krauss' *A Hole Is to Dig* (1952), Marcel Aymé's fantasy *The Wonderful Farm* (1951), and Beatrice de Regniers' *What Can You Do with a Shoe?* (1955), they show also the tender appeal of children even when they are most absurd—round-faced children, grinning fiendishly or preternaturally solemn, dressed up in adult clothes or kicking up their heels and cavorting like

In bed you can have
your own little house
for a little while—
under the blankets.

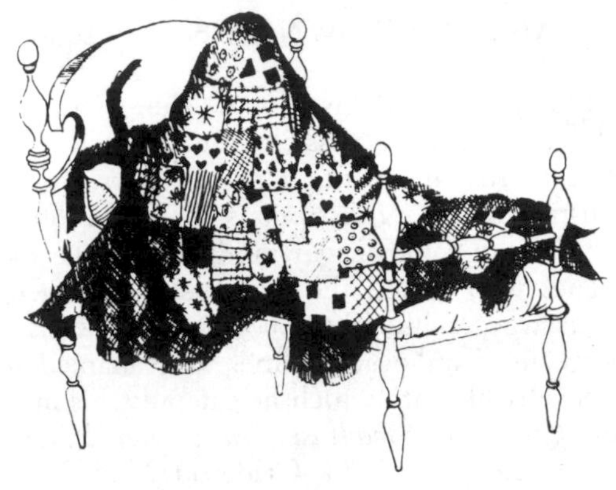

Just you and the pussy cat.

The simple graceful shape of the bed contrasts with the richly varied patterns of the quilt. Copyright 1954 by Irene Haas. From A Little House of Your Own *by Beatrice Schenk de Regniers. By permission of Harcourt, Brace & World, Inc. (Book 4½ x 9)*

young colts. Working mostly in black and white, this artist with his flair for comic exaggeration is tremendously popular. But in his illustrations for Meindert DeJong's books, *Wheel on the School* (1954), for example, and for his own book *Kenny's Window* (1956), he shows a sensitive perception of the lonely, imaginative, struggling side of childhood, too. One book in full color is a superb example of his versatility. His pictures for Janice Udry's *Moon Jumpers* (1959) are in the green-blues of a moonlit summer's night. The moon-mad children are running and leaping in ecstasy or dropping with exhaustion or going quietly home. These pictures are all beauty and the very poetry of childhood. The same could be said of his glorious color pictures for Charlotte Zolotow's *Mr. Rabbit and the Lovely Present* (1962). Mr. Sendak's four original stories for his tiny *Nutshell Library* (1962) are exceedingly funny both in texts and illustrations. Still, it will be unfortunate if he becomes typed with the comic, for he has a wide range of power and perceptiveness. (See 33 in color section.)

IRENE HAAS 1929-

Irene Haas also works in black and white and in a humorous vein. Her pictures for Paul Kapp's *A Cat Came Fiddling* (1956), for instance, show not merely children but some indescribably funny and well-characterized animals and adults. For Beatrice de Regniers' subtle little book about a child's need for privacy, *A Little House of Your Own* (1954), she has suggested the mood of quiet withdrawal in every picture. There are also sly touches of humor—for instance, in the picture of the child and cat covered up in bed, with only the cat's tail sticking out.

ADRIENNE ADAMS

Houses from the Sea (1959) by Alice Goudey includes some of the loveliest illustrations Adrienne Adams has made. Since then, her pictures for Grimm's *Shoemaker and the Elves* (1960) and Andersen's *Thumbelina* (1961) have been exceedingly popular. Her colors are warm and delicate, her pictures full of fascinating details. A most happy collaboration is evident in her delightful pictures for Aileen Fisher's *Going Barefoot* (1960) and *Where Does Everyone Go?* (1961), seasonal poems to which the pictures add lively charm. (See 29 in color section.)

NICOLAS SIDJAKOV 1924-

Three books illustrated by Nicolas Sidjakov are notable because the pictures are stylized and in the modern idiom. The illustrations for *The Friendly Beasts* (1957), *The Emperor and the Drummer Boy* (1962), and *Baboushka and the Three Kings* (1960, Caldecott Medal) are strikingly different from those in the general run of picture-stories. In all three books the figures are block-like and stylized. There is little realism in these pictures, but still they reveal character and mood. Baboushka is a flinty-looking old woman, the soldiers in the Emperor's story show a robot-like obedience in their mass marching, and the Friendly Beasts are gentle and sympathetic. Here is an artist who will make children see the world with new eyes and in new patterns. (See 31 in color section.)

Of course this list of artists should include Nora Unwin (1907-) and her powerful woodcuts, Tasha Tudor (1915-), who works with feminine grace in delicate pastel colors, Beth and Joe Krush (1918-), who have made *The Borrowers* so convincing, Helen Stone (1903-), Paul Galdone, Erik Blegvad, Ezra Jack Keats (see 32 in color section), and a dozen others. Their work will be mentioned later in connection with the books they have illustrated. From abroad, Jean de Brunhoff (1889-1937) delighted children with the adventures of that suave French elephant *Babar* (1933) in a series of large, handsome books. Bettina (Ehrlich, 1903-) introduces children to Italy in her big picture-stories of *Cocola* (1948) and *Pantaloni* (1957). Italian Bruno Munari (1907-) provides them with so magical a use of color against white spaces that he could train the color-blind to see and rejoice. Beginning with *Jeanne-Marie Counts Her Sheep* (1951), Françoise (Seignobosc, 1900-) has given us a number of books in bright decorative colors that are as fresh and pretty as a garden of pink petunias. In contrast, the illustrations of Felix Hoffmann (1911-) for *Sleeping Beauty* (1960) and *Rapunzel* (1961) are in the grand style, romantic and grave. So too are the pictures of English Harold Jones (1904-) for *Lavender's Blue* (1954). (See 26 in color section.) From Japanese-born Taro Yashima (1908-) have come the sensitive picture-stories of Japanese children in Japan, *Plenty to Watch* (1954), of a Japanese child in this country, *Umbrella* (1958), and others. (See 22 in color section.)

This is indeed the day of the artist in children's books, and their pictures should afford some protection from the flood of meretricious art that is so readily available. Better one good book with distinguished illustrations than a dozen stereotypes with flashy, poorly executed pictures. For children must be trained to see truly and subtly. They must be taught to look and look again at the illustrations in their books. Pictures can help them see the comic absurdities of life or its heroic struggles and tragedies. Pictures can give children a sudden breath-taking feeling for the beauty or the wonder of life. Such pictures deepen their perceptiveness and help them to grow.

ARTISTS DISCUSSED IN THIS CHAPTER

1. Adams, Adrienne, p. 70
2. Ardizzone, Edward, p. 66
3. Bemelmans, Ludwig, p. 65
4. Bewick, Thomas, p. 55
5. Birch, Reginald, p. 59
6. Blake, William, p. 55
7. Brooke, Leslie, p. 60
8. Brown, Marcia, p. 69
9. Buff, Conrad, p. 63
10. Burton, Virginia, p. 68
11. Caldecott, Randolph, p. 58
12. Comenius, p. 54
13. Cooney, Barbara, p. 69
14. Cox, Palmer, p. 59
15. Crane, Walter, p. 57
16. Cruikshank, George, p. 57
17. Daugherty, James, p. 63
18. D'Aulaire, Ingri and Edgar Parin, p. 67
19. De Angeli, Marguerite, p. 63
20. Duvoisin, Roger, p. 66
21. Frost, Arthur, p. 59
22. Gág, Wanda, p. 62
23. Geisel, Theodor Seuss, p. 66
24. Greenaway, Kate, p. 58
25. Haas, Irene, p. 70
26. Hughes, Arthur, p. 57
27. Lathrop, Dorothy, p. 64
28. Lawson, Robert, p. 65
29. McCloskey, Robert, p. 68
30. Mordvinoff, Nicolas, p. 68
31. Mulready, William, p. 56
32. Petersham, Maud and Miska, p. 64
33. Politi, Leo, p. 67
34. Potter, Beatrix, p. 60
35. Pyle, Howard, p. 59
36. Rackham, Arthur, p. 60
37. Rojankovsky, Feodor, p. 64

38. Sendak, Maurice, p. 69
39. Seuss, Dr., p. 66
40. Sewell, Helen, p. 65
41. Shepard, Ernest H., p. 61
42. Sidjakov, Nicolas, p. 70
43. Smith, E. Boyd, p. 60
44. Smith, Jessie Willcox, p. 60
45. Sojo, Toba, p. 53
46. Tenniel, Sir John, p. 57
47. Ward, Lynd, p. 67
48. Weisgard, Leonard, p. 69
49. Wiese, Kurt, p. 61
50. Williams, Garth, p. 68
51. Wyeth, Newell, p. 61

SUGGESTED READING, PROBLEMS, AND PROJECTS

This is distinctly a reference chapter to be consulted at need. But for students especially interested in art, it suggests fascinating areas for comparison or intensive study of an artist's total work. Furthermore, students will probably wish to discuss and perhaps argue about the appraisals, and they may wish to look for relationships not pointed out in the text.

1. Distinguish the three categories: picture book, picture-story, and illustrated book, with examples of each. Under which category would you place *The Animal Frolic, Orbis Pictus,* Caxton's edition of *Aesop's Fables?*

2. Why does Thomas Bewick seem to stand out among the early artists?

3. Discuss Blake's contribution to children's books as an artist. See also Chapter 7.

4. Compare three artists of the nineteenth century who worked entirely in black and white.

5. How did the use of color illustrations begin in children's books? What was the contribution of artist-printer Edmund Evans to the development of color illustrations? If possible, compare the price of his books with that of picture books in color today.

6. Discuss and compare the illustrations of Evans' famous triumvirate—Crane, Greenaway, Caldecott—and those of the closely related Leslie Brooke. Which is your favorite and why?

7. Choose one illustrator of children's books who interests you especially, look up a cross section of all his work, and report on him in detail.

8. Compare Rackham's *Wind in the Willows* with Ernest Shepard's. Which artist has the wider range?

9. Compare the pen and ink sketches of animals by any two of these artists: Toba Sojo, Arthur Frost, Robert Lawson, Dorothy Lathrop.

10. Compare the work of any two of these artists: Bemelmans, Duvoisin, Politi, Weisgard, Williams, Cooney.

11. Comment on the range of style in Marcia Brown's picture books.

12. Why should Maurice Sendak have been called the Picasso of children's books? Characterize his style and his strength both in black and white and in color.

13. What other contemporary artists would you like to include in this brief sampling? Justify your choice.

REFERENCES

ABBOTT, CHARLES D. *Howard Pyle: A Chronicle,* with an introduction by N. C. Wyeth, and many illustrations from Howard Pyle's works. Harper, 1925. An illuminating appraisal of Howard Pyle as both artist and author.

AMERICAN INSTITUTE OF GRAPHIC ARTS. *Children's Book Show 1961-1962.* AIGA. From 540 titles submitted by publishers these 95 were selected for artistic merit. For each chosen book there are a reproduction, descriptive information, and a critical evaluation of the illustrations.

The Art of Beatrix Potter, with an appreciation by Anne Carroll Moore. Warne, 1956. In a truly beautiful book, landscapes, still life, experimental drawings, and the tiny pictures for her children's classics are reproduced, giving new insight into the versatility of Beatrix Potter.

The Bewick Collector. A descriptive catalogue of the works of Thomas and John Bewick. . . . The whole described from the originals by Thomas Hugo, M.A., F.R.S.I., etc. Lovell Reeve, London, Vol. I, 1866. Supplement 1868.

BLACKBURN, HENRY. *Randolph Caldecott: A Personal Memoir of His Early Art Career,* ill. with reproductions and photographs. Sampson Low, London, 1886.

COLBY, JEAN POINDEXTER. *The Children's Book Field* (see Bibliography, Chapter 2).

CROUCH, MARCUS. *Beatrix Potter.* Walck Monographs (see Bibliography, Chapter 2).

DAUGHERTY, JAMES. *William Blake* (see Bibliography, Chapters 6-8, Biographies of Poets).

DAVIS, MARY GOULD. *Randolph Caldecott 1846-1886: an appreciation.* Lippincott, 1946. An evaluation of the great English artist's contribution to children's literature.

HUDSON, DEREK. *Arthur Rackham: His Life and Work.* Scribner, 1960. A handsome oversize book copiously illustrated with plates and sketches of Rackham's work for both children and adults.

LANE, MARGARET. *The Tale of Beatrix Potter: A Biography* (see Bibliography, Chapter 17, Biography-Artists).

MAHONY, BERTHA E., LOUISE P. LATIMER, and BEULAH FOLMSBEE. *Illustrators of Children's Books, 1744-1945.* Horn Book, 1947. A superb history of illustration in children's books considered as a part of the whole stream of art. Many pictures are reproduced from early books as well as from more recent ones. A major reference.

MILLER, BERTHA MAHONY, and ELINOR WHITNEY FIELD. *Caldecott Medal Books: 1938-1957.* Horn Book, 1957. Stories of artists who have won awards for the most distinguished picture book of each year, together with their acceptance speeches. An invaluable source for schools and libraries.

MONTGOMERY, ELIZABETH RIDER. *The Story Behind Modern Books* (see Bibliography, Chapter 17, Biography-Collections).

MOORE, ANNE CARROLL. *A Century of Kate Greenaway.* Warne, 1946. An appreciation of the artist and her distinctive contribution.

MUIR, PERCY. *English Children's Books, 1600-1900* (see Bibliography, Chapter 3, References).

NEWCOMB, COVELLE. *The Secret Door: The Story of Kate Greenaway* (see Bibliography, Chapter 17, Biography-Artists).

PITZ, HENRY C. *The Practice of American Book Illustration.* Watson-Guptill, 1947.

———, ed. *A Treasury of American Book Illustration.* Watson-Guptill, 1947. A distinguished artist discusses illustration as one of the seven lively arts. With many pictures from modern sources he proves his point. The second volume contains a good chapter on "Pictures for Childhood."

SCOTT, ALMA. *Wanda Gág: The Story of an Artist,* ill. with photographs and sketches. Univ. of Minn. Press, 1949. Written for youngsters in their early teens, this biography is a delightful introduction to the artist for the student of children's literature.

VIGUERS, RUTH HILL, MARCIA DALPHIN, and BERTHA MAHONY MILLER. *Illustrators of Children's Books, 1946-1956.* Horn Book, 1958. An outstanding supplement to *Illustrators of Children's Books, 1744-1945.* Includes current art trends, artists' biographies, and a wealth of illustrations from modern children's books.

Sing It Again

part two

5. Mother Goose and the Ballads

6. Poetry of the Child's World: Nonsense and Everyday

7. Growing Up with Poetry

8. Using Poetry with Children

9. Verse Choirs

chapter 5

Mother Goose and the Ballads

Small children acquire a love for poetry as naturally as did people of early times, through hearing poems spoken and through learning to say them, almost unconsciously, along with the speaker. Long, long ago, mothers, grannies, and nurses diverted crying babes by playing with their toes—"This little pig went to market," or making a game—"Pat-a-cake, pat-a-cake," or chanting a nonsense rhyme with a catchy tune—"Hickory, dickory, dock." In the same long ago, grownups were entertained by gifted minstrels chanting stories of heroic battles or sad romances or human absurdities. These old nursery ditties and ancient ballads were easily remembered and passed on by word of mouth for generations before they achieved the permanency of print and became known as *Mother Goose* and traditional (or popular) ballads. These folk rhymes are still important not only because children and youth continue to enjoy them, but because many are skillfully composed, exuberant or dramatic, and lead naturally into modern nonsense verse and narrative poems.*

Mother Goose

One of the opening pages of an old edition of *Mother Goose* contains a picture of an ancient crone admonishing two small children. The picture is followed by the text of her lecture. Mark its words well, for this is Ma'am Goose herself, addressing her "dear little blossoms." As you read, you discover that the good dame is distinctly irritated. She is relieving her mind in no uncertain terms concerning those misguided reformers who are forever pestering mothers to discard her soothing ditties in favor of more educational and uplifting verses. After defending her jingles

*Many of the poems discussed but not reprinted in this book can be found in the anthology Time for Poetry (gen. ed., comp. by May Hill Arbuthnot). The bibliography (p. 112) will also help you locate any poems not reprinted here. See also the bibliographies at the close of chapters 8 and 9.

lustily, the good dame rends her long-faced critics with a particularly withering blast:

Fudge! I tell you that all their batterings can't deface my beauties, nor their wise pratings equal my wiser prattlings; and all imitators of my refreshing songs might as well write a new Billy Shakespeare as another Mother Goose—we two great poets were born together, and we shall go out of the world together.
No, no, my Melodies will never die,
While nurses sing, or babies cry.[1]

The idea of Mother Goose calmly associating herself with Shakespeare and asserting an immortality equal to his is not so far-fetched as it may seem. Moreover, this spirited defense of a book that long ago proved itself a nursery classic is as timely today as it was in 1833. For earnest pedagogues are always arising to protest that *Mother Goose* is out of date, that her vocabulary is all wrong, that her subjects are not sufficiently "here and now." Despite these protests, the children go right on crying for her ditties, and mothers and nurses know well her power to soothe "won't-be-comforted little bairns."

2

HEAR WHAT MA'AM GOOSE SAYS!

My dear little Blossoms, there are now in this world, and always will be, a great many grannies besides myself, both in petticoats and pantaloons, some a deal younger to be sure; but all monstrous wise, and of my own family name. These old women, who never had chick nor child of their own, but who always know how to bring up other people's children, will tell you with very long faces, that my enchanting, quieting, soothing volume, my all-sufficient anodyne for cross, peevish, won't-be-comforted little bairns, ought to be laid aside for more learned books, such as *they* could select and publish. Fudge! I tell you that all their batterings can't deface my beauties, nor their wise pratings equal my wiser prattlings; and all imitators of my refreshing songs might as well write a new Billy Shakespeare as another Mother Goose — we two great poets were born together, and we shall go out of the world together.
No, no, my Melodies will never die,
While nurses sing, or babies cry.

From The Only True Mother Goose Melodies, *an exact and full-size reproduction of the original edition published and copyrighted in Boston in the year 1833 by Munroe and Francis (Lothrop, Lee and Shepard, 1905)*

Who Was Mother Goose?

Where did these verses come from? Who was Mother Goose? These are questions that occur to us as we turn over the pages of some beguiling modern editions. The answers are sometimes confusing; it is sometimes difficult to distinguish legends from facts, but it is illuminating to discover how these nursery songs are linked with our historical and literary past.

DAME GOOSE OF BOSTON

Boston children think they know quite well who Mother Goose was. In the Old Granary Burying Ground in the heart of downtown Boston, the caretaker will show you a flock of little tombstones bearing the name of Goose. He points to one particular stone and assures you that this is the resting place of none other than the famous Dame Goose herself. Many a Boston child, gazing with awe at this small tombstone, has visualized the beak-nosed old woman, with a suggestion of wings in her sharp shoulder blades, ready to go up in glory, chanting:

Old Mother Goose, when
She wanted to wander,
Would ride through the air
On a very fine gander.

It is a surprise to Boston children when they grow up to be told that their Boston Dame

1. *The Only True Mother Goose Melodies* (Reprinted by Lothrop, Lee and Shepard Co., Boston, 1905, from the Munroe and Francis edition, Boston, 1833).

Goose was not the author of these verses and that her son-in-law did not publish them in 1719. Both beliefs are wholly legendary. Indeed, the verses came chiefly from England and the name came from France.

MA MÈRE L'OYE

The name *Mother Goose,* as Chapter 3 explains, was first associated not with verses but with the eight folk tales recorded by Perrault. Andrew Lang, in *Perrault's Popular Tales,* tells us that the frontispiece of *Histoires ou contes du temps passé, avec des moralités* (Histories and Tales of Long Ago, with Morals) showed an old woman spinning and telling stories, and that a placard on the same page bore the words: "Contes de ma Mère l'Oye" (Tales of Mother Goose). But the name *Mother Goose* has now become so completely associated with the popular verses that most English translations of the Perrault tales omit it from the title of the collection.

The French also connect *Mother Goose* with Goose-footed Bertha, wife of Robert II of France. French legends represent the queen spinning and telling stories to children, as illustrators have sometimes pictured *Mother Goose.*

DAME GOOSE IN ENGLAND

Lina Eckenstein, in *Comparative Studies in Nursery Rhymes* (1906), says that the name *Mother Goose* was first used in England in connection with Robert Powell's puppet shows, exhibited in London between 1709 and 1711. Powell's plays included, among others, *Robin Hood and Little John, The Children in the Wood, Whittington and His Cat,* and one called *Mother Goose.* Perhaps it was Powell who popularized the name in England, for Joseph Addison in one of the *Spectator Papers* says that Powell set up his puppet show in London opposite St. Paul's and when the sexton rang his bell, many church-goers were deflected from piety to puppets. The sexton wrote to Addison to complain, "As things are now, Mr. Powell has a full Congregation, while we have a very thin House." What play did Mr. Powell present under the title of *Mother Goose*? It may have been one of Perrault's stories heard from a sailor. At any rate, Perrault's *Contes de ma Mère l'Oye* was translated into English in 1729, and the popularity of the eight tales undoubtedly helped establish still more firmly that delightful nonsense name, *Mother Goose.*

Early Editions of Mother Goose

NEWBERY EDITION, 1781

The next mention of the name in England is in connection with John Newbery, who is discussed in Chapter 3. At one time, Newbery was thought to have published an edition of *Mother Goose's Melody or Sonnets for the Cradle* between 1760 and 1765, but more recent research[2] suggests that he may have planned but did not publish such a book. In 1781 Newbery's stepson, T. Carnan, who continued the Newbery publishing business, advertised in the *London Chronicle* for January 2, "The first publication of *Mother Goose's Melody.*" No copy of that edition is extant, but the advertisement is considerable assurance of its one-time existence. The earliest extant edition of this famous little book is from

LONDON
Printed for Francis Powers, (Grandson to the late Mr. J. Newbery,) and Co.
No. 65. St. Paul's Church Yard, 1791.
Price Three Pence

For a complete reproduction of this rare edition we are indebted to Barchilon and Pettit in their book *The Authentic Mother Goose*

2. Jacques Barchilon and Henry Pettit, eds. *The Authentic Mother Goose Fairy Tales and Nursery Rhymes.*

Fairy Tales and Nursery Rhymes. Here the student will find the famous Preface by "a very great Writer of very little Books" (probably Oliver Goldsmith), fifty-two rhymes with their quaint and generally irrelevant "Maxims," and—a surprising inclusion—sixteen songs of Shakespeare, with a tiny woodcut for each verse or song. This pleasant juxtaposition of *Mother Goose* and Shakespeare reminds us of Dame Goose's boast, "We two great poets were born together, and we shall go out of the world together."

Whether the first Newbery edition was planned by John himself or by his stepson or grandson, we may be sure that, coming from the house of Newbery, it was "strongly bound and gilt," unlike the chapbooks which were merely "folded, not stitched" in pamphlet style. Leigh Hunt refers to these Newbery books as "certain little penny books, radiant with gold, and rich with bad pictures." So even on her first appearance in print, *Mother Goose* seems to have been brightly adorned.

ISAIAH THOMAS EDITION, 1785

The first American edition of *Mother Goose* was probably a pirated reprint of an early Newbery edition. It was published by Isaiah Thomas of Worcester, Massachusetts, who was in the habit of reproducing Newbery's books. W. H. Whitmore vouched for the fact that two copies of this Isaiah Thomas edition existed in his day, and in 1889 he reproduced the book in full, calling it *The Original Mother Goose's Melody.*[3] The little book is two and one-half by three and three-fourths inches. Preface, fifty-two jingles with maxims, sixteen songs of Shakespeare and small woodcuts are precisely the same as in the English edition. The maxims are surprising and often amusing, especially the one that follows "Margery Daw," which will surely he applauded by all bewildered readers of footnotes: "It is a mean and scandalous Practice in Authors to put Notes to Things that deserve no Notice."

3. W. H. Whitmore, ed. *The Original Mother Goose's Melody* (Albany: Joel Munsell's Sons, 1889). It is reproduced in facsimile from the Isaiah Thomas edition (Worcester, Massachusetts, 1785). Mr. Whitmore's introduction gives many interesting facts about the early collections of *Mother Goose.*

MUNROE AND FRANCIS EDITIONS, 1824, 1833

Two more notable American editions succeeded the Isaiah Thomas publication of 1785. Between 1824 and 1827, the Boston firm of Munroe and Francis published the *Mother Goose's Quarto, or Melodies Complete,* which contained many rhymes drawn from the Thomas reprint of Newbery's *Melody* but also many apparently old ones printed for the first time. In 1833 this firm made a reprint of the *Quarto* with the title *The Only True Mother Goose Melodies.* Fortunately, the second of these rare early editions has been made available in a modern facsimile edition with an introduction by Edward Everett Hale. It contains 169 rhymes illustrated with woodcuts. Both the *Quarto* and the 1833 edition are important sources for many of the later collections.

These editions include several fairly long poems such as "You owe me five shillings, say the bells of St. Helen's" and "London Bridge," each with eleven verses. They have such songs as "Johnny shall have a new bonnet" and "Lavender blue, Rosemary green." And as many of our modern editions do, they include some poems that are not traditional, such as Walter Scott's "Pibroch of Donnel Dhu" and Shakespeare's "Jog on, jog on, the foot-path way," which are obviously out of place in a collection of folk rhymes.

Origin of the Verses

The *Mother Goose* verses underwent many changes during the years when they were passed on by word of mouth, and later when they traveled from one printed edition to another. As with the ballads, variants of the same verses were recited or sung in different places, and which ones were the originals no one can say. Certainly they have led to considerable speculation and to some careful research. Undoubtedly many of the rhymes are mere nonsense jingles, but many others reveal interesting bits of history, old customs, manners, and beliefs. Some research studies help open our eyes to the hints these ditties give of other days and ways.

MOTHER GOOSE AND HISTORY

Attempts to find historical characters to fit the people of *Mother Goose* have shown more imagination than documented research. From 1834 with John Bellenden Ker's study to 1930 with Katherine Elwes Thomas' book, *The Real Personages of Mother Goose,* these romantic speculations caught the popular fancy and were repeated *ad infinitum.* Students were pleased to read that it was Queen Elizabeth I who rode the "cock horse to Banbury Cross" and danced to the tune of "Hey diddle diddle"; that dour old John Knox was the spider to poor Mary Queen of Scots' Miss Muffet; and that Anne Boleyn was the pretty maid hanging up her clothes and losing her head to the grim blackbird headsman. However, Iona and Peter Opie, in their book based upon scholarly research, *The Oxford Dictionary of*

Mother GOOSE's Melody. 25

PLATO's SONG.

DING dong Bell,
The Cat is in the Well.
Who put her in?
Little *Johnny Green.*
What a naughty Boy was that,
To drown Poor Puſſy Cat,
Who never did any Harm,
And kill'd the Mice in his Father's Barn.

Maxim. *He that injures one threatens an Hundred.*

LITTLE

26 Mother GOOSE's Melody.

LITTLE *Tom Tucker*
Sings for his Supper;
What ſhall he eat?
White Bread and Butter:
How will he cut it,
Without e're a Knife?
How will he be married,
Without e'er a Wife?

To be married without a wife is a terrible Thing, and to be married with a bad Wife is ſomething worſe; however, a good Wife that ſings well is the beſt muſical Inſtrument in the World. *Puffendorff.*

SE

Mother GOOSE's Melody. 27

SE ſaw, *Margery Daw,*
Jacky ſhall have a new Maſter;
Jacky muſt have but a Penny a Day,
Becauſe he can work no faſter.

It is a mean and ſcandalous Practice in Authors to put Notes to Things that deſerve no Notice. *Grotius.*

GREAT

28 Mother GOOSE's Melody.

GREAT A, little a,
Bouncing B;
The Cat's in the Cupboard,
And ſhe can't ſee.

Yes ſhe can ſee that you are naughty, and don't mind your Book.

SE

From The Original Mother Goose's Melody. *Reproduced in facsimile by W. H. Whitmore (Joel Munsell's Sons, 1889) from the edition reprinted by Isaiah Thomas of Worcester, Mass., 1785. (Book 2½ x 3¾)*

Nursery Rhymes, found little evidence for these deductions. Their comment is:

Much ingenuity has been exercised to show that certain nursery rhymes have had greater significance than is now apparent. They have been vested with mystic symbolism, linked with social and political events, and numerous attempts have been made to identify the nursery characters with real persons. It should be stated straightway that the bulk of these speculations are worthless. Fortunately the theories are so numerous they tend to cancel each other out. The story of "Sing a song of sixpence," for instance, has been described as alluding to the choirs of Tudor monasteries, the printing of the English Bible, the malpractices of the Romish clergy, and the infinite workings of the solar system. The baby rocked on a tree top has been recognized as the Egyptian child Horus, the Old Pretender, and a New England Red Indian. Even when, by chance, the same conclusions are reached by two writers the reasons given are, as likely as not, antithetical. This game of "interpreting" the nursery rhymes has not been confined to the twentieth century, though it is curious that it has never been so overplayed as in the age which claims to believe in realism. (p. 27.)

There is some evidence that several of the rhymes did originally refer to real people, and that some were once political lampoons. For instance, Miss Thomas gives a detailed and apparently documented account of "Little Jack Horner." The present Horner family, she says, showed her the deed to their estate, signed by Henry VIII and wrongly described as the "plum" their ancestor pulled out of the King's "pie"—a collection of deeds. According to the Opies, it is possible that this jingle did refer to a Horner ancestor, but on the whole a healthy skepticism is the safest approach to any attempts to identify nursery rhyme characters with real people.

COMPARATIVE STUDIES IN NURSERY RHYMES

Lina Eckenstein in *Comparative Studies in Nursery Rhymes* (1906), discusses a few historical origins but is mainly concerned with the ancient folk origins of the verses and their counterparts in other countries. For example, she traces "Sally Waters" from its present simple game-form back to its origin as part of a marriage rite in pre-Christian days. The name, she thinks, came from the Roman occupation of the city of Bath, where the temple was dedicated to Sulis-Minerva, Sul being the presiding deity at Bath. Sul of the Waters and Sally Waters do sound as if they might be related.

She devotes a whole chapter to cumulative tales—two of which have become a part of *Mother Goose,* "The house that Jack built" and "The old woman and her pig." She relates them to the Hebrew chant that begins:

A kid, a kid, my father bought
For two pieces of money,
A kid, a kid.
Then came the cat and ate the kid
That my father bought
For two pieces of money,
A kid, a kid.

The chant continues with the familiar sequence of dog, staff, fire, water, ox, butcher, then the angel of death, and the Holy One. This sequence, symbolizing the Hebrew people and their enemies at the time of the Crusades, is still recited as a part of the Passover liturgy and is probably older than "The old woman and her pig." Miss Eckenstein thinks that the latter is not merely what one scholar has called "a broken-down adaptation of the Hebrew poem" but that all these cumulative stories were originally incantations or rituals seriously performed.

Qualities That Charm the Children

VARIETY

Children enjoy the variety of subject matter and mood that continually surprises them in these verses. It ranges from the sheer nonsense of:

Hey! diddle, diddle,
The cat and the fiddle,
The cow jumped over the moon.

to the sad and tender ballad of "The babes in the wood":

My dear, do you know
How a long time ago
Two poor little children,
Whose names I don't know . . .

It is a rewarding task to make a list of the different kinds of verses in *Mother Goose.* Here are some obvious categories with only one or two examples of each, to which you can add dozens of others:

People (a rich gallery of characters)
Children—Little Miss Muffet
Grownups—Old King Cole
Imaginary—Old Mother Goose when she wanted to wander
Grotesque—There was a crooked man
Children's pranks—Georgie, Porgie, pudding and pie
Animals—I had a little pony
Birds and fowl—Jenny Wren; Higgledy, piggledy, my black hen
Finger play—Pat-a-cake
Games—Ring a ring o'roses
Riddles—Little Nancy Etticoat
Counting rhymes—One, two, buckle my shoe
Counting out—Intery, mintery, cutery-corn
Alphabets—A, is an apple pie
Proverbs—Early to bed, and early to rise
Superstitions—see a pin and pick it up
Time verses—Thirty days hath September
Days of the week—Solomon Grundy, born on Monday
Verse stories—The Queen of Hearts, she made some tarts
Dialogue—Who killed Cock Robin?
Songs—A frog he would a-wooing go
Street cries—Hot-cross Buns!
Weather—Rain, rain, go away
Tongue twisters—Peter Piper picked a peck of pickled peppers
Accumulative stories—This is the house that Jack built
Nonsense—Three wise men of Gotham

There is one little nature personification in *Mother Goose*:

Daffadowndilly
Has come up to town,
In a yellow petticoat
And a green gown.

And there is the charming

The North Wind doth blow,
And we shall have snow,
And what will poor Robin do then?

But on the whole, descriptive nature poems, in the modern sense, are conspicuously lacking. So are fairy poems; the only mention of fairies is usually:

Oh who is so merry
So merry heigh-ho,
As a light-hearted fairy?
Heigh-ho, heigh-ho.

Even this one fairy rhyme is lacking in many editions, but all the collections abound with characters absurd, grotesque, and fantastic. In what other collections of verse can you find such variety and surprise?

MUSICAL QUALITY

Lured on by the variety of these rollicking jingles, the child is also captivated by their musical quality. "Sing it again," he insists, when you finish reading one of his favorites. He nods his head or rocks his body or waggles a finger, marking time to the rhythm. He himself often suits the words to his own action.

A three-year-old was bouncing up and down on a spring-horse, chanting her version of "Ride a cock horse." If you read her chant aloud, you discover that while she mixed up the words, she never lost her rhythm, which is perfection for galloping:

Wide *a cock horse,* wh'ever *she goes,* wh'ever *she goes,* wh'ever *she goes.* She *make* moos*ic* wh'ever *she goes,* wh'ever *she goes,* wh'ever *she goes.* Wide *a cock horse, old* lady *wh'ever she goes,* wh'ever *she goes,* wh'ever *she goes.* Wide *a cock horse to* Bam*bury Cross.* See *'n old lady* on *a white horse.* Wings *on her fingers.* Bells *on her toes.* Ever *she make* moosic. Ever *she make* moosic. Ever *she make* moosic. Wh'ever *she goes!*

Children soon discover that the verses of *Mother Goose* skip, gallop, run, walk, swing, trot, and hop just as music does. "Hippity hop to the barber shop" is a high skip that swings along with gay vigor. Children often say it when they skip, and teachers sometimes have a group say it while others skip. It is fun to follow this idea and let the children march to "The Grand Old Duke of York," walk laggingly to the slow "A diller, a dollar," run hard to "Tom, Tom, the piper's son," run on tiptoe to "Wee Willie Winkie," tramp to "Hark, hark, the dogs do bark," rock or swing to "I saw a ship a-sailing," and so explore the musical aspect of these rollicking old verses. Because they are predominantly musical, they won't be injured by this kind of experiment.

Saying these verses, the child gets a happy introduction to rhyme—perfect and imperfect —to alliteration, onomatopoeia, and other sound patterns. Happily he gets these without the burden of their labels and so enjoys them light-heartedly. He likes the exact, neat rhyming of:

Georgie Porgie, pudding and pie,
Kissed the girls and made them cry.
When the boys came out to play
Georgie Porgie ran away.

But he is not disturbed by the far from perfect rhyme of:

Goosey, goosey, gander
Whither shall I wander?
Up stairs, down stairs,
And in my lady's chamber.

Alliteration tickles his sound sense to a degree that astonishes us. A three-year-old hearing "Sing a song of sixpence" for the first time laughed so hard over the alliteration that she would not allow the reading to proceed any further. All day long she went around hissing to herself "S-s-sing a s-s-song of s-s-sixpence" and then chuckling. Another child was fascinated by the staccato in "Higgledy, piggledy, my black hen" and by the explosive *tle* in "She lays eggs for gen*tle*men." Indeed, the brisk tune of this ditty turns upon its lively use of consonants, the *n* sounds making it ring delightfully. One of the many values of these melodious jingles is that they accustom the ear and the tongue to the musical aspects of our English language.

There are also in *Mother Goose* small lyrics of genuine poetic charm with a more subtle music than the examples already given: "I saw a ship a-sailing," "Bobby Shaftoe," "Hush-a-bye, baby," "Johnny shall have a new bonnet," "Lavender's blue," "The north wind doth blow," and the charming:

I had a little nut tree, nothing would it bear
But a silver apple and a golden pear;
The King of Spain's daughter came to see me,
And all for the sake of my little nut tree.
I skipped over water, I danced over sea,
And all the birds in the air couldn't catch me.

All in all, the verses offer many opportunities for the development of a fine sense of the musical quality of language.

ACTION

Still another characteristic of these verses that endears them to young children is their action. Jack and Jill fall down, Miss Muffet runs away, Mother Goose rides on her gander, the cow jumps over the moon, Polly puts the kettle on, the cat comes fiddling out of the barn, the Man in the Moon comes down too soon. Here are no meditations, no brooding introspections, no subtle descriptions to baffle the jumping, hopping, up-and-doing young child. In these verses things happen as rapidly and riotously as he would like to see them happening every day.

STORY INTEREST

Some verses contain simple stories. "The Queen of Hearts," for example, is a slight but

1.

2.

PETER, PETER, PUMPKIN-EATER

3.

1. Arthur Rackham's grotesquerie is an important part of his humor. Study this picture and you'll begin to see Rackham trees everywhere. Notice, too, the simplicity of his drawing of the pure child and the detail of the drawing of the man.
Illustration by Arthur Rackham. From Mother Goose. *Copyright, 1913, by Arthur Rackham, 1941, by Adyth Rackham. Reproduced by permission of D. Appleton-Century Company, Inc. (Original in color, book 7 x 9)*

2. A hungry wayfarer, a complacent cook, and a gluttonous feaster lend humorous contrast to this study in pigs.
Illustration by Leonard Leslie Brooke. From Ring o' Roses. *Reproduced with permission of Frederick Warne & Co., Inc. (Original in color, book 7¾ x 10)*

3. Circular forms repeated throughout this picture give it a gentle rhythm, and the predicament of Mrs. Peter Pumpkin Eater amuses the children.
Illustration by Blanche Fisher Wright. From The Real Mother Goose. *Copyright 1916, renewal 1944, by the publishers, Rand McNally & Co. (Original in color, book 9 x 11½)*

4. This homely, everyday Miss Muffet is centered completely and intensely upon the emotional problem of what to do about spiders. Rojankovsky's pictures usually illustrate, sometimes with exaggeration, often with humor.

Illustration by Feodor Rojankovsky. From The Tall Book of Mother Goose. *Copyright, 1942, by Artists and Writers Guild, Inc. Reprinted by permission. (Original in color, book 4¾ x 11¾)*

5. Here is a serene Miss Muffet, quaintly costumed. It is difficult to find the lurking spider, and we suspect he will leave Miss Muffet barely ruffled. This is the same pretty world we find in Kate Greenaway's illustrations.
Illustration by Tasha Tudor. From Mother Goose. *Copyright 1944 by Henry Z. Walck, Inc., Publishers. Reprinted by permission. (Original in color, book 6½ x 7½)*

5.

4.

Jay bird, Jay bird, settin' on a rail,
Pickin' his teeth with the end of his tail,
Mulberry leaves and calico sleeves
All school teachers are hard to please.

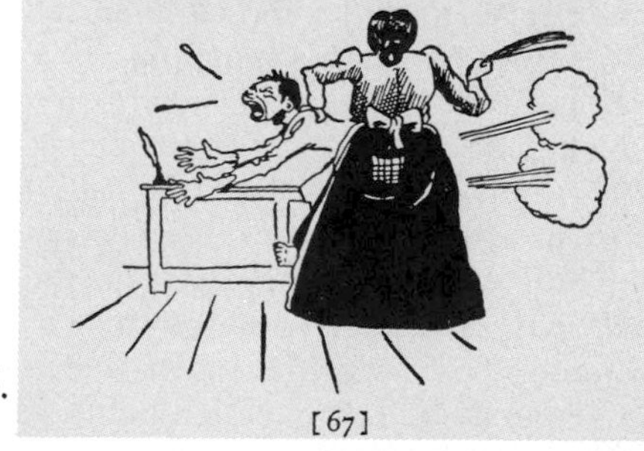

6.

[67]

6. Ed Hargis' homespun, humorous sketches have exactly caught the mood of the jingles in The American Mother Goose. *Here are frontier people—adults and children—who are neither graceful nor pretty but are full of fun and energy.*
Illustration by Ed Hargis. From The American Mother Goose *by Ray Wood. Reproduced with permission of J. B. Lippincott Company. (Book 6 x 8¼)*

complete account of the innocent and industrious queen, her tarts stolen, the villain caught, punishment administered, and the villain left in a properly penitent frame of mind. A child lends his pony and protests:

She whipped him, she lashed him,
She rode him through the mire,
I would not lend my pony now,
For all the lady's hire.

Old Mother Hubbard and her bare cupboard involve considerable suspense before the tale is told out. Froggy has all sorts of difficulties with his wooing. The bewildered old woman who wakes to find her skirts cut short and so is not sure of her identity makes a story that is funny to the last line. "The babes in the wood" is a tragic tale but endurable because it is brief and is gently and sweetly told. The brevity of these verse-stories makes them acceptable to children as young as two years old and they prepare children to enjoy longer and more involved prose and verse stories.

HUMOR

The sheer fun of *Mother Goose* keeps her verses alive in the hearts of every generation of children. Of course adults and children seldom see eye to eye on what is humorous. Our jaded ears, for instance, may have forgotten that the hissing *s*'s of "s-s-sing a s-s-song of s-s-sixpence" sound funny, but the child laughs at them as he laughs at other comical sounds our dull ears miss. The child, on the other hand, may stare gravely at the story of the dish running away with the spoon, which usually strikes adults as funny. Then he turns around and giggles at the crooked man, who seems a little sad to us. So it goes, but the fact remains that on almost every page of *Mother Goose* there is a smile or a chuckle for the child. What does he laugh at? It is hard to say; we can only watch and listen. Sometimes he laughs at the sound; often he laughs at the grotesque or the incongruous. Surprise tickles him, absurd antics amuse him, and broad horseplay delights him. There are plenty of examples of all these in *Mother Goose*. A man jumps into the bramble bush to scratch his eyes "*in* again"; a pig flies up in the air; Simple Simon goes fishing in his mother's pail; Humpty Dumpty has a fall (falls always bring a laugh); Peter, Peter pumpkin-eater keeps his wife in a pumpkin shell; Tom who "was beat" runs "roaring down the street." Such humor is far from subtle, but its absurdities must be a relief to the child beset on all sides by earnest adults.

ILLUSTRATIONS

Finally, and almost above all, the child loves the pictures that bedeck his favorite book. Whether the edition is so small he can tuck it into the pocket of his overalls, or so enormous that he has to spread it out on the floor, the numerous pictures enchant him. Here he shares his delight in *Mother Goose* with some of the finest illustrators of each generation, for artists also love the fun and action of these old rhymes and have lavished on them some of their best work. It has been said that the perfect edition of *Mother Goose* has not yet been made. Probably it never will be, because no two of us will ever see these famous characters in quite the same way. Just as there is endless variety in the stories, the mood, and the characters of these jingles, so there is a like variety in the size, the shape, the color, and the style of pictures that illustrate them. One adult prefers one edition, while a second adult greatly prefers another, but the children apparently like them all. What they ask for is *Mother Goose*—with colored pictures, simple or elaborate, commonplace or subtle.

Popular Modern Editions

It is impractical to list all the fine editions of *Mother Goose*, but the following choices are popular with parents, teachers, and children for a variety of reasons.

REALISTIC ILLUSTRATIONS

A good introduction to *Mother Goose* and her world is the tried and true *The Real Mother Goose,* illustrated by Blanche Fisher Wright. There are colored pictures on every page, often one picture fills a whole page, or sometimes there are two or three small ones. In either case, the illustrations are simple and clear and have only a few details. The characters are dressed in period costumes and can be seen distinctly by a large group of children. The colors are clear washes, sometimes soft and pale but more often bright and lively. It is a big book with a wide selection of traditional verses which the illustrations really illustrate. This is more important for young children than some artists have realized, because little children use pictures as clues to the meaning of the text. (See 3, p. 84.)

Marguerite de Angeli's *Book of Nursery and Mother Goose Rhymes* contains 376 jingles, 260 enchanting pictures, and innumerable decorations. It is a big book, and for the artist, it must have been a labor of love. Children and animals dance and prance across the pages. Little flowery bouquets and birds adorn the corners, and plump, pretty babies tumble here and there. The artist tells us that the faces of the family of "God bless the master of this house" were drawn from the laughing faces of her own family, and many of the other pictures seem to be sketches of real people. The book is too big for small children to handle alone, but it is fine for children and adults to look at together. The verses are not arranged in any particular order, so a nursery jingle is often followed by a ballad of sufficient substance to suit the oldest children. However, the rich offering of verses and illustrations makes this an edition to cherish and to pass on to the next generation.

From the rich store of their scholarly study Iona and Peter Opie have compiled *The Oxford Nursery Rhyme Book,* with eight hundred of the ditties that have delighted children for generations. The vast collection is skillfully organized. It begins with the simplest ditties and progresses to more mature riddles, songs, and ballads. Almost every verse has a picture—small and black only, but amazingly effective. Many of the illustrations are taken from the old chapbooks and toy books. The work of Thomas and John Bewick is well represented, and the distinguished drawings of contemporary artist Joan Hassall are in keeping with their style. Students of early children's books will find this an invaluable edition, and parents will also enjoy the book and its preface.

HUMOROUS ILLUSTRATIONS

One edition of *Mother Goose* that no child should miss is *Ring o' Roses,* illustrated by Leslie Brooke, who provides an imaginative and broadly humorous pictorial interpretation of the traditional verses. The lovely English countryside is painted in pastel colors, with yellows and tender greens giving a springtime brightness to the pages. The characters are in English period costumes and are utterly satisfying interpretations. Simple Simon *is* Simple Simon, daft and delightful. Goosey, Goosey, Gander and the outrageous old man "who would not say his prayers" will be forever your vision of that remarkable pair. But above all you will remember Leslie Brooke's pigs and after chuckling over them you will never again see pigs as plain pigs. Instead you'll see pigs with a smirk or a leer, pigs looking coy or shocked, pigs on the rampage, or pigs of complacence. This is, after all, the test of great illustrations: they do more than illustrate—they interpret the text so vividly that they become the visual embodiment of the words. There are only some twenty rhymes in *Ring o' Roses,* but every child should have the book to pore over and absorb until the pictures are his forever. (See 2, p. 84.)

The Tall Book of Mother Goose, illustrated by Feodor Rojankovsky, is an elongated book, approximately five by twelve inches, which can be easily held and handled by adults or children. The deep pages lend themselves either to delightful double-page spreads like the panoramic landscape of "One misty, moisty morning," or to a sequence of small pictures like those for "The three little kittens." Mr. Rojankovsky is a master of color and realistic texture. His furry kittens, feathery chicks, or woolly mufflers have a depth that almost creates a tactual sensation. His children are

I've got a rocket
In my pocket;
I cannot stop to play.
Away it goes!
I've burnt my toes.
It's Independence Day.
Suba

The airy pen sketches by Susanne Suba match the gay absurdities of the jingles in this book.
Illustration by Susanne Suba. From A Rocket in My Pocket *compiled by Carl Withers. Copyright 1948 by Carl Withers. Reproduced by permission of Holt, Rinehart, and Winston, Inc. (Book 5½ x 8)*

husky, everyday youngsters, never beautiful and often very funny. His pop-eyed Miss Muffet, viewing the spider with alarm, always brings laughter. On the other hand, Humpty Dumpty with the face of Hitler is a mistake since Hitlers are only passing phenomena and Humpty is immortal. Fortunately, the resemblance means nothing to young children. The illustration of "Ding, dong, bell" misses the point entirely. The freckled, rosy, good boy and the wan child with a cigarette not only do not illustrate the rhyme but introduce an adult line of thought completely irrelevant to the verse. Despite these two objectionable pictures, this book, with its 150 rhymes and twice as many pictures, remains justifiably popular. (See 4, p. 84.) And be sure to see Mr. Rojankovsky's pictures for *Frog Went a-Courtin'*, a Caldecott winner (see 12, color section, Chapter 4).

DECORATIVE, IMAGINATIVE ILLUSTRATIONS

Mother Goose; or, The Old Nursery Rhymes, illustrated by Kate Greenaway, is a tiny book to fit small hands and pockets and to fill small hearts with delight. It contains forty-four of the brief rhymes, each with its own picture in the quaint Kate Greenaway style. The print is exceedingly fine, but for nonreaders this does not matter. The illustrations are gently gay, the colors are soft, and the people exquisitely decorative.

Mother Goose; The Old Nursery Rhymes, illustrated by Arthur Rackham, one of England's great artists, is a splendid edition, now out of print, but well worth hunting up in any library that has it. It is a thick book, with both "The house that Jack built" and "The old woman and her pig." The illustrations are of three types: pen-and-ink sketches, silhouettes, and full-page color. The silhouettes are amazingly effective, for example, the dripping bedraggled cat of "Ding, dong, bell." The color plates are Rackham at his best and in many moods. These are pictures by an artist with imagination and a knowledge of folklore. (See 1, p. 84.)

Lavender's Blue, compiled by Kathleen Lines, is distinguished by Harold Jones' illustrations. Both in color and in black and white, they suggest old engravings. The pages are neatly bordered; the figures are stiffish, not stylized yet not realistic either. There are wonderful details, as in the double-page spread of "Goosey, goosey gander." Although the colors are muted and there is little humor, the composition of the pictures holds your attention. "I love little pussy" is an example. Puss sits tall, solemn, and mysterious, against an interior from which a door opens onto alluring streets. She is framed like a period portrait of a great lady (see 26, color section, Chapter 4). Show this book to the threes and fours to educate their young eyes. Use it with the fives, sixes, and sevens to discuss, mull over, and thoroughly enjoy pictures that are superlative in composition and color.

Tasha Tudor's illustrations have always been notable for her delicate imagination and for her use of quaint costumes. Her *Mother Goose* is six and one-half by seven and one-half inches, an agreeable size for small hands to hold. Of the seventy-seven verses, a number are unfamiliar. The costumes of the characters include Elizabethan, colonial, American pioneer, Kate Greenaway, and Godey styles, in pastel colors or soft grays. The action is interpreted both realistically and imaginatively. For instance, the illustration for "the cow jumped over the moon" pictures the cow running downhill with the distant moon showing through the cow's four legs. The cozy domesticity of many of the pictures is very appealing, as in the illustration for "One, two, buckle my shoe," which shows a mother tenderly dressing her little girl. (See 5, p. 85.)

Variants of Mother Goose

In addition to the many editions of *Mother Goose,* there are several collections of nursery rhymes which are fairly close in style and content to the old English jingles.

The American Mother Goose was compiled by Ray Wood and illustrated by Ed Hargis. Older children studying frontier life are interested in and amused by this collection. The verses are both rougher and funnier than the English nursery rhymes and are as indigenous to America as a "possum up a gum stump." Here are such familiar doggerels as "I asked my mother for fifteen cents," "How much wood would a woodchuck chuck," "Mother, may I go out to swim," the long "Obadiah jumped in the fire," "I went to the river," and a final section of riddles, games, and finger play. The pen-and-ink sketches (6, p. 85) are full of hilarious touches that delight adults as much as they do the children. This book is not for the youngest, but it is fun for older children.

Maud and Miska Petersham's *The Rooster Crows; A Book of American Rhymes and Jingles* was awarded the Caldecott medal in 1946. In spite of the inclusion of such American folk rhymes as "A bear went over the mountain" and "Mother, may I go out to swim," the subtitle is difficult to justify because the collection also contains such old-world rhymes as "Sally Waters" and "Oats, peas, beans and barley grows." Children enjoy the pictures of colts, kittens, and bunnies which adorn the pages, of children of long ago rocking wooden cradles or going a-hunting, and of modern children jumping off haymows and enjoying themselves generally.

A Rocket in My Pocket, compiled by Carl Withers, carries the subtitle *The Rhymes and Chants of Young Americans.* Some four hundred ditties, tongue twisters, derisive chants, and bits of pure nonsense, together with Susanne Suba's line drawings, make this an unusually beguiling book.

Lillian Morrison has made a delightful contribution to Americana with her small collections of riddles, auguries, school and playground chants, and amusing autograph album inscriptions. The two books in the last category—*Yours Till Niagara Falls* and *Remember Me When This You See*—are never on library shelves at commencement time.

Tongue Tanglers, compiled by Charles Francis Potter, is popular with both children and speech teachers. There are only forty-four tongue tanglers, but they are gems, and the illustrations in full color (p. 91) add to the hilarity. Dr. Potter's selection, chosen from thousands of tongue twisters, includes:

I Saw Esau kissing Kate.
Fact is we all three saw.
I saw Esau, he saw me,
And she saw I saw Esau.

and ends with that perfect conclusion:

Tongue twisters twist tongues twisted
Trying to untangle twisted tangles
My tangs tungled now.[4]

4. From *Tongue Tanglers* by Charles Francis Potter. Copyright 1962 by Charles Francis Potter. Published by The World Publishing Co.

ABC BOOKS

The pictorial ABC books of each generation are all variants of *Mother Goose*'s "A Apple Pie." Edward Lear wrote one of the funniest, all in nonsense phonetics, and it now appears in a delightful illustrated edition. Walter Crane made a charming *Baby's Own Alphabet,* and Kate Greenaway turned *A Apple Pie* into a thing of beauty.

Modern artists have also been intrigued by the austerity of a single letter and the possibilities of making it dramatic. Wanda Gág's *ABC Bunny* has a rhyming text with continuity unusual in such miscellanies. The dark woodcuts are relieved by large scarlet capital letters which suggest the small child's ABC blocks. The pictures (1, p. 92) and story make it a favorite.

Garth Williams' *Big Golden Animal ABC,* which is also available in a small edition, makes use of amusing contrast: for each letter Williams has provided a large realistic animal in full color and, on the same page, his unrealistic comic foil. The letter *A,* for instance, has a menacing Alligator with jaws agape and, near the bottom of the page, a wee rabbit on a bicycle, scuttling madly away.

Fritz Eichenberg's *Ape in a Cape,* "an alphabet of odd animals," is both funny and phonetic. The "Goat in a boat" looks properly wild-eyed (2, p. 92) like the "Fox in a box." The nursery crowd likes this book, and it inspires the older children to make rhymes of their own—"A llama in Alabama," for example.

Roger Duvoisin's *A for the Ark,* for children seven to nine, shows Noah calling the animals alphabetically. The ducks dawdle because they like the rain. Some bears come with the B's, others with U for ursus. On they come, comical or impressive, but all decorative in the artist's most colorful style. (See 4, p. 92.)

Also for older children is Phyllis McGinley's *All Around the Town,* an alphabet of city sights and sounds in lively verse, with Helen Stone's pictures as attractive as the text. The witty lyrics combine letter sounds with the maximum rhythm and meaning. For example, one verse begins "V is for the Vendor/A very vocal man." This book about city life delights all ages. (See 3, p. 92.)

In contrast to *All Around the Town,* Bruno Munari's *ABC* depends for its charm on his masterful use of color and design to build interesting associations around each letter—"A Fly/a Flower/a Feather/and a Fish" with "more Flies" at the top of the page to go buzzing on through the book (p. 93). So arresting are his colors and use of space that the visual impact of each page is a contribution to seeing.

Brian Wildsmith's ABC is a heady experience with color, an ABC book with the simplest of texts and the most glorious rainbow of subtle tints and hues. "cat CAT" says a fuchsia page with letters in three colors, and opposite, against a muted blue, is a green-eyed, black cat. One of the great pleasures of this book is to flip the pages slowly and enjoy the changing colors.

There are many other ABC books and undoubtedly more to come, but these major examples illustrate some of the various types.

Uses of Mother Goose

IN THE HOME

As soon as the baby attends to words, the mother can begin to say "Hush-a-bye baby" or "Bye baby bunting" at sleep time, or "Pat-a-cake" and "This little pig" at play time. As soon as he begins to like pictures, mother will have a *Mother Goose* to hold on her lap along with the baby. It is good to say the verses over and over as many times as he wishes, but never to force him to listen or to urge the book on him. He will come to it when he is ready. When the child begins to know the verses, the mother can say them with him at any time, with or without the book. The bathtub, the bed, the kitchen, the park, or the stroll: all are proper settings for a happy exchange of rhymes. One day it might be well to surprise the child with a new edition, quite different from the one he has had. Or perhaps he could be taken to a library to see several editions and choose one to take home.

Through the years from two to five, he should be encouraged to say these verses until they are his forever. Children entering kindergarten would have better speech habits, and first-grade children would have a greater power with and feeling for words, if more were done with *Mother Goose* in the homes. Knowing the verses expands the imagination, increases the vocabulary, and develops an ear for the music of words. Enjoying *Mother Goose* predisposes children to other books. Poring over the illustrations is an introduction to art appreciation. And meeting *Mother Goose* in the security of mother's or father's lap is a happy experience no child ever forgets.

IN THE SCHOOL

Occasionally, teachers get a little weary of *Mother Goose*. "The same old thing!" they say, and hurry the children to Dorothy Aldis or A. A. Milne, forgetting that to each crop of children *Mother Goose* is brand-new and endlessly diverting. So if you do find yourself a little tired of "Miss Muffet," try a new edition. Different illustrations will provide a fresh experience, and you will soon discover that you enjoy *Mother Goose* again.

In large cities there are many children with foreign accents. Everywhere, there are children whose speech is slovenly. These verses are the best possible speech exercise. Children can look at the pictures and say the rhymes effortlessly and the improvement in speech agility will be surprising.

These are utilitarian reasons for using the verses. The chief reason is enjoyment. Whole class periods may be devoted to going through a new edition, saying the verses, savoring the pictures, discussing and comparing different collections the children know. A book that is completely worn out, past all further patching and gluing, may be cut up and such pictures as you can retrieve mounted on boards. These may go up on the walls or be used as you

I saw Esau kissing Kate.
Fact is, we all three saw.
I saw Esau, he saw me,
And she saw I saw Esau.
37

This drawing is enlivened by white and black touches that contrast the various tones and textures. Illustration by William Wiesner. Reproduced from Tongue Tanglers, *copyright © 1962 by Charles Francis Potter. Illustration copyright © 1962 by William Wiesner. Reprinted by permission of The World Publishing Company. (Original in color, book 6¼ x 7¼)*

for Lizard – look how lazy

1.

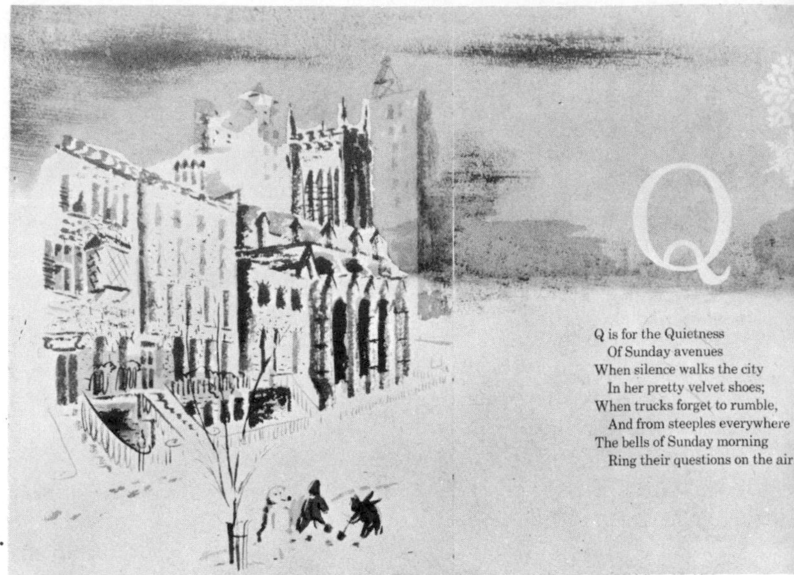

Q
Q is for the Quietness
Of Sunday avenues
When silence walks the city
In her pretty velvet shoes;
When trucks forget to rumble,
And from steeples everywhere
The bells of Sunday morning
Ring their questions on the air.

3.

2.

1. Contrasted masses of light and dark, rhythmic lines, and a strong center of interest make the pictures for The ABC Bunny *among the finest Wanda Gág has ever done.*
From Wanda Gág's The ABC Bunny. *Copyright 1933 by Wanda Gág. Used by permission of Coward-McCann, Inc. (Book 9½ x 11¾)*

2. Notice the effective curving lines of waves, boat, goat, windblown scarf, and beard, making an unusually striking composition.
From Ape in a Cape. *Copyright 1952 by Fritz Eichenberg. Reproduced by permission of Harcourt, Brace & World, Inc. (Original in color, book 8¼ x 10⅞)*

3. Beautiful in text and illustration, All Around the Town *is an alphabet book about city sights and sounds. In this two-page spread, Helen Stone uses snow to help capture the mood of Phyllis McGinley's lovely verse. See how the picture encloses the poem.*
Illustration by Helen Stone. From All Around the Town *by Phyllis McGinley. Illustration copyright 1948 by Helen Stone. Reprinted by permission of the publishers, J. B. Lippincott Company. (Original in color, book 7⅜ x 9½)*

4. This beautifully illustrated book is composed of two-page spreads containing pairs of animals on their way to the Ark. Some spreads are black line with yellow wash, and others are full muted color scenes of great beauty and dignity.
From Roger Duvoisin's A for the Ark. *Copyrighted 1952 and published by Lothrop, Lee & Shepard Co., Inc.*
(Original in color, book 8¼ x 10½)

"ABCDEFG—Now for the H,"
called Noah.
"H for the Horse,
the most beautiful of animals;
H for the Hyena, the ugliest;
H for the Hen, the busiest;
H for the Hare, the fleetest."
"ABCDEFGH—Ready for the I,"
called Noah.
"I for the Ibex who browse on mountain slopes;
I for the Izard who prances on mountain tops."

4.

5. This large, boldly illustrated picture book in clear, beautiful colors is especially suited for the younger child. Each page has several objects beginning with the letter shown, and all of the objects are easily identified. The flies beginning on this page go buzzing through many of the following pictures.
From Bruno Munari's ABC. *Copyright 1960 by Bruno Munari. Reproduced by permission of the publishers, The World Publishing Company.*
(Original in color, book 8½ x 11½)

5.

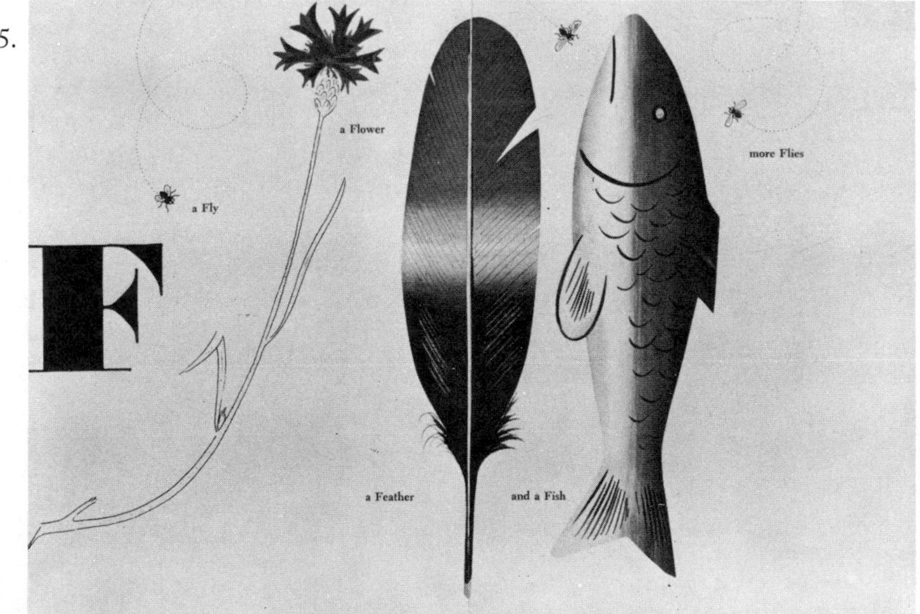

would use a book with the children. Sometimes older children "read" these to a younger group. Inexpensive editions should be on the children's own bookshelves for them to pick up in spare time.

Use *Mother Goose* to finish out a class period or to fill in a time of waiting, just saying the verses spontaneously without a book. Let the children dramatize some of the verses, with no set stage procedures. Of course, occasionally they are fun to use for an assembly, with the little children in the simplest costumes or just as usual. One kindergarten[5] had a big wooden book built by the manual training department. The cover opened and through the pages came the children as their favorite story-book characters. *Mother Goose* always supplied a group of these.

There are an infinite number of ways of using these old verses. Our goal is to see that no child goes out of our homes, our kindergartens, or our first grades without knowing by heart dozens of these artless, picturesque, lyrical rhymes that constitute the child's most entertaining introduction to English poetry.

Ballads and Story-poems

The ancient ballads have never been as beloved by children as *Mother Goose,* partly because their dialect and archaic language make them difficult to read. Yet children are universally fond of poems that tell a story, and a more hair-raising collection of stories would be hard to find. An eleven-year-old boy, after listening to his teacher read the old ballad of "Sir Patrick Spens," remarked, "That is the best poem I ever heard."

"Why?" asked his teacher, in some surprise.

"Oh, 'cause the author gets right into the story. He doesn't waste any time describing things. It's more exciting that way."

This young critic summed up neatly the appeal that ballads and story-poems have for children of all ages. They tell a story in concentrated form, with the maximum of excitement and the minimum of words. Many adults can recall similar childhood enthusiasm for poetry or songs that told a story.

The child makes no distinction between the types. He doesn't care whether a poem or a song is an old folk song or a folk ballad such as "The babes in the Wood" or "Bonny Barbara Allan," or a modern song like "Robin Adair," or a modern story-poem like "The Pied Piper of Hamelin." What he enjoys is the swift movement of verse or melody enhancing the dramatic appeal of a good story. The search for these story-poems carries us back into folk rhymes and forward to present-day narrative poems, ranging from hilarious nonsense to romance and noble tragedy.

Origins of the Popular Ballads

Like the *Mother Goose* verses and all other folk literature, the popular ballads were passed on by word of mouth long before they were printed. In England, Scotland, Germany, and Denmark, in particular, a great many ballads were passed on from person to person, village to village, and country to country. Sailors, too, would hear ballads and take them home, much as travelers carry popular songs from country to country today. So popular were these story-poems and so rapidly were they exchanged that it is difficult today to determine whether a ballad is Danish, Scottish, English, or German in origin.

THE MINSTRELS

When scholars began to wonder where the ancient ballads came from and who composed them, they thought first of the professional

5. Hazeldell School, Cleveland, Ohio; principal at that time, Miss Edith Peters; kindergarten teacher, Miss Helen McCormick.

entertainers who flourished at the same time in which the ballads were growing in number and popularity. The Danes had their scalds, who were the "smoothers" or "polishers" of the language. The scalds gave instruction and also furnished entertainment by singing or reciting stories and poems. England had the Teutonic scop, the "maker" or "poet," who was the forerunner of the gleeman or minstrel. As early as the fourth century, he traveled through the country singing and telling his stories in the mead halls. The minstrel, who succeeded the scop, rose to prominence in the tenth, eleventh, and twelfth centuries. Minstrels were attached to the households of kings and even to the religious houses. These men played the harp and sang songs of their own composition but were probably also the repositors and transmitters of songs heard from other minstrels, or from the ordinary people of their own and other lands.

Many scholars think that the ballads came to be what they are because they were composed and collected by minstrels, who were a more educated group than the mass of people and quite capable of polishing or even creating these poems. Bishop Percy (p. 98) and Sir Walter Scott (p. 98) believed the ballads were composed by individual minstrels, men whose names have been forgotten. The poems themselves offer significant testimony. The characters, for instance, are not so often rustics or villagers as kings, queens, knights, nobles, highborn ladies, pages, and harpers in the courts the minstrel himself was used to. The subjects with many adaptations from French romance and the Arthurian tales are also typical of the minstrel. The language includes court words, sophisticated phrases, and typical minstrel conventions: *burd* or *bryde* (maiden), *cramoisie* (crimson), *Christendie* (Christendom), *nourice* (nurse), *sheen* (beautiful), *brown brand* (sword), *merry men* (a standing phrase for companions in arms), *high-coled shoon* (high-cut shoes), and *bonie braes* (beautiful banks).

Probably the most convincing argument for the minstrel origin of the ballads is their literary artistry. For instance, many of them tell a story by questions and answers, a technique that came late, not early, in literary development. It is difficult to imagine such a use of the technique as in "Edward" being employed by any but a professional poet.

Edward[6]

'Why dois your brand sae drap wi bluid,
Edward, Edward,
Why dois your brand sae drap wi bluid,
And why sae sad gang yee O?'
'O I hae killed my hauke sae guid,
Mither, mither,
O I hae killed my hauke sae guid,
And I had nae mair bot hee O.'

'Your haukis bluid was nevir sae reid,
Edward, Edward,
Your haukis bluid was nevir sae reid,
My deir son I tell thee O.'
'O I hae killed my reid-roan steid,
Mither, mither,
O I hae killed my reid-roan steid,
That erst was sae fair and frie O.'

'Your steid was auld, and ye hae gat mair,
Edward, Edward,
Your steid was auld, and ye hae gat mair,
Sum other dule ye drie O.'
'O I hae killed my fadir deir,
Mither, mither,
O I hae killed my fadir deir,
Alas, and wae is mee O!'

'And whatten penance wul ye drie for that,
Edward, Edward?
And whatten penance will ye drie for that?
My deir son, now tell me O.'
'Ile set my feit in yonder boat,
Mither, mither,
Ile set my feit in yonder boat,
And Ile fare ovir the sea O.'

'And what wul ye doe wi your towirs and your ha,
Edward, Edward?
And what wul ye doe wi your towirs and your ha,
That were sae fair to see O?'
'Ile let thame stand tul they doun fa,
Mither, mither,
Ile let thame stand tul they doun fa,
For here nevir mair maun I bee O.'

6. The popular ballads quoted in this chapter are from *The English and Scottish Popular Ballads,* Student's Cambridge Edition, edited by George Lyman Kittredge.

'And what wul ye leive to your bairns and
your wife,
Edward, Edward?
And what wul ye leive to your bairns and
your wife,
Whan ye gang ovir the sea O?'
'The warldis room, late them beg thrae life,
Mither, mither,
The warldis room, late them beg thrae life,
For thame nevir mair wul I see O.'

'And what wul ye leive to your ain mither
deir,
Edward, Edward?
And what wul ye leive to your ain mither,
deir?
My deir son, now tell me O.'
'The curse of hell frae me sall ye beir,
Mither, mither,
The curse of hell frae me sall ye beir,
Sic counseils ye gave to me O.'

"Sir Patrick Spens," (or "Spence") with its economy of words, its dramatic episodes, and its controlled emotion is a little masterpiece of composition. It seems improbable that uneducated people were capable of either the subtle restraint that related only the bare outlines of that tragic tale, or the sense of drama that could devise the surprise ending. Many other ballads could be cited which, like "Edward" and "Sir Patrick Spens," represent an advanced level of literary composition. That such ballads as these were originated by the minstrels seems, therefore, a logical and justifiable conclusion.

THE CLERGY

Louise Pound in her *Poetic Origins and the Ballad* advances the theory that the ballads may well have begun with the clergy. She points out that the earliest ballads in the great collection by Francis Child have to do with Biblical history and legend. "Judas"—conceded to be the oldest surviving English ballad—is found in a thirteenth-century manuscript in the library of Trinity College, Cambridge. "Inter-Diabolus et Virgo," "The Carnal and the Crane," and "The Cherry Tree Carol" all occur early in Child's collection (p. 98). The religious character of these ballads is illustrated by:

The Cherry Tree Carol

Joseph was an old man,
and an old man was he,
When he wedded Mary,
in the land of Galilee.

Joseph and Mary walked
through an orchard good,
Where was cherries and berries,
so red as any blood.

Joseph and Mary walked
through an orchard green,
Where was berries and cherries,
as thick as might be seen.

O then bespoke Mary,
so meek and so mild;
'Pluck me one cherry, Joseph,
for I am with child.'

O then bespoke Joseph
with words most unkind:
'Let him pluck thee a cherry
that brought thee with child.'

O then bespoke the babe,
within his mother's womb:
'Bow down then the tallest tree,
for my mother to have some.'

Then bowed down the highest tree
unto his mother's hand;
Then she cried, 'See, Joseph,
I have cherries at command.'

O then bespoke Joseph:
'I have done Mary wrong;
But cheer up, my dearest,
and be not cast down.'

Then Mary plucked a cherry,
as red as the blood,
Then Mary went home
with her heavy load.

Then Mary took her babe,
and sat him on her knee,
Saying, My dear son, tell me
what this world will be.

'O I shall be as dead, mother,
as the stones in the wall;
O the stones in the street, mother,
shall mourn for me all.

'Upon Easter-day, mother,
my uprising shall be;
O the sun and the moon, mother,
shall both rise with me.'

These religious ballads may well have evolved from the clergy's desire to popularize scriptural stories. They may have come from the houses of the great religious orders as part of the medieval movement that also produced the carols, the lyrics, and the miracle plays. Many of the religious ballads show such artistic craftsmanship that they suggest individual authorship.

COMMUNAL COMPOSITION

A third source of the ballad is believed by reputable authorities to be a singing throng of simple people celebrating some common event such as a fine crop, a good haul of fish, a wedding, or perhaps lamenting some tragedy such as a murder, a drowning, or the sad ending of a romance.

Francis B. Gummere devoted his book, *The Popular Ballad,* to developing this theory. He pictures a group of people coming together to sing and dance and tell stories. Sometimes a talented leader, moved by an extraordinary event known to them all, begins to compose a story about it. The group answers with a chorus or refrain that gives the leader, or perhaps the next man in the circle, time to think up another verse. The refrain might be accompanied by gestures, fists or mugs banged on the table, or by skipping or dancing. These song-stories or dance-stories would then become the familiar property of the group. They might be carried from one village to another and handed on through generations. This process may have produced some of the ballads. It is difficult to imagine, however, a ballad of complex form or highly polished style developing from such spontaneous communal composition.

Here then are the three possible sources of the traditional ballad—minstrel, clergy, and communal composition. It seems possible and probable that each of these may have given rise to some of the popular ballads.

Printed Sources of the Popular Ballads

Whatever the origins of the ballads, it is known that they grew and flourished from the thirteenth to the middle of the sixteenth centuries. Eventually they must have reached the ears and captured the imaginations of the educated people, because references to the ballads become more and more frequent as modern times approach. Sir Philip Sidney in his *Defence of Poesie,* published in 1595, wrote of the ballad of Chevy Chase: "Certainly, I must confess my own barbarousnesse, I never heard the olde song of *Percy* and *Duglas,* that I found not my heart mooved more then with a Trumpet. . . ."

Joseph Addison devoted two papers in *The Spectator* (Nos. 70 and 71) to an excellent analysis of the moving qualities of this same ballad, commenting that: "The old song of Chevy-Chase is the favourite ballad of the common people of England, and Ben Jonson used to say he had rather have been the author of it than all of his works."

EARLY COLLECTORS

David Garrick, the famous English actor, collected ballads and no doubt recited or sang them with telling effect. Oliver Goldsmith, noted for his good voice, enjoyed singing them. Samuel Pepys, the jovial diarist, made one of the finest collections in existence, and in the 1720's Allan Ramsay, a Scottish poet, published three volumes of ballads. However, it was not until 1765, when Bishop Percy published his famous *Reliques* that the Scottish and English ballads became widely known and appreciated.

BISHOP PERCY, 1729-1811

Reliques of Ancient English Poetry

Reliques of Ancient English Poetry, the three-volume edition of the ancient ballads discovered by Bishop Percy contains the Bishop's own account of how he made his famous find. While visiting his friend Humphrey Pitt, in Shiffnal, Shropshire, Bishop Percy found an old manuscript lying on the floor under a bureau. Some of it had been used by the maids to start fires, and half of its fifty-four pages were torn away. This scrubby little book contained 195 handwritten ballads. The script of the copier placed the manuscript sometime before 1650, although the ballads were undoubtedly much older. The Bishop prepared the ballads for publication under the title *Reliques of Ancient English Poetry,* and the collection soon became extremely popular in England. Unfortunately, the good Bishop did not respect this ancient manuscript. He scribbled on the margins, struck out those ballads he thought indelicate, and, in his editorial capacity, wrote and rewrote ballads that he considered too crude for the "polished taste" of the day. It was not until 1867, over a hundred years after its discovery that scholars reprinted the original 195 ballads, and students could compare them with the Bishop's elaborations.[7]

Certainly no ballad is more exciting than the story of the discovery of this seventeenth-century manuscript with its ballads copied laboriously by some unknown lover of these story-poems. If Percy had postponed his visit to his friend for a few more weeks, perhaps the maids would have fed the whole manuscript to the flames. In that case, our present collection of traditional ballads and the romance of ballad collecting would have been much the poorer.

The Bishop's collection aroused enormous interest in ballads. Sir Walter Scott, for instance, by reading them in childhood was inspired to a lifelong search for them. Ballad "raids" he called his journeys into remote parts of Scotland to gather first hand from a shepherd or an old woman some little known ballad or variant of a familiar one. The publication of the ballads, though, distressed at least one of Scott's contributors, for the old woman who gave him so many of his ballads burst into tears when she first saw them in print. As she said, "They were made for singing and not for reading; but ye ha'e broken the charm now, and they'll never be sung mair."

FRANCIS JAMES CHILD, 1825-1896

The English and Scottish Popular Ballads

Since Scott's day other collectors have compared, criticized, and evaluated ballad sources, but the most notable compilation is the famous *The English and Scottish Popular Ballads,* in five volumes, edited by Francis J. Child of Harvard. Child not only carried on exhaustive investigations into manuscript sources and current versions but also studied the ballads of other countries. There are 305 ballads in his collection, with copious notes and with all known and accredited variants of each ballad. "Mary Hamilton" alone has twenty-eight variants. Child's five volumes represent the most thoroughly investigated collection of ballads that exists and are the final authority on the original sources of old ballads.

It is usually agreed that these volumes are principally for scholars, and yet if a sixth-grade teacher feels moved to read "Sir Patrick Spens" to her children, she can build up a richer background by consulting the introduction in Francis Child's great edition. She may not have the time or inclination to read all the eighteen variants, but her children will be interested at least to know that "Sir Patrick Spens" was remembered in so many places and by so many people, and that there exist today some eighteen ways of telling his story.

If these five volumes are not available, then teachers should become acquainted with the one-volume edition prepared by Child's student and successor, George Lyman Kittredge—*English and Scottish Popular Ballads, Student's Cambridge Edition.* It contains the 305 ballads with two or three variants of each, and brief notes that are invaluable.

7. *Bishop Percy's Folio Manuscript, Ballads and Romances.*

Characteristics of the Popular Ballad

MUSICAL QUALITY

The old ballad was a song-story and its singing quality is still evident in the lilting verses and refrains and in the lively tunes that accompany the words. "Bonny Barbara Allan," for example, tells a tragic tale swiftly and movingly, but the opening verse suggests at once that here is a song:

In Scarlet Town, where I was bound
There was a fair maid dwelling,
Whom I had chosen to be my own,
And her name it was Barbara Allan.

There are almost as many tunes to "Barbara" as there are variants to the words, and if you know any of the tunes it is difficult to read the words without singing them. This is also true of "The Gypsy Laddie," or its more familiar folk-song variant, "The Raggle, Taggle Gypsies." Its tune is a compelling one, but the ballad is also dramatic for reading. Even the most tragic ballads, like "Edward" or "Lord Randal," have wistful, tender airs that somehow soften the tragedy. The music of "Lizie Lindsay" has an attractive swing, and there are dozens of other ballads that seem to prove the old woman's contention that they were made for singing.

In many ballads this songlike quality is enhanced by refrains. The refrain of "The Cruel Brother" sounds like tripping dance steps:

There was three ladies playd at the ba,
With a hey ho and a lillie gay
There came a knight and played oer them a'
As the primrose spread so sweetly.

One version of the "The Gypsy Laddie" begins:

There was a gip come oer the land,
He sung so sweet and gaily;
He sung with glee, neath the wildwood tree,
He charmed the great lord's lady.
Ring a ding a ding go ding go da,
Ring a ding a ding go da dy
Ring a ding a ding go ding go da,
She's gone with the gipsey Davy.

"Robin Hood and Little John" starts out with a vigorous refrain:

When Robin Hood was about twenty years old,
With a hey down down and a down
He happened to meet Little John,
A jolly brisk blade, right fit for the trade,
For he was a lusty young man.

The second, fourth, and fifth lines suggest men banging on the table with their fists or with mugs of "nut brown ale," in jovial accompaniment to a familiar song.

Some of the ballad refrains are so lively that it is easy to imagine a still more vigorous bodily response. For instance, the refrain of "The Wife Wrapt in Wether's Skin" seems made for jig steps. Try reading the following

It took Virginia Burton over three years to make the intricate, sometimes verse-by-verse illustrations for this glorious edition of Robin Hood. The swirling lines, as you turn the pages, give almost the illusion of movement.
Illustration by Virginia Burton. From Song of Robin Hood *edited by Anne Malcolmson. Reproduced with permission of Houghton Mifflin Company. (Book 9 x 11)*

stanza aloud and perhaps even jigging or tap-dancing the refrain.

There livd a laird down into Fife,
Riftly, raftly, now, now, now
An he has married a bonny young wife.
Hey Jock Simpleton, Jenny('s) white petticoat,
Robin a Rashes, now, now, now.

Such a dancing, prancing refrain as this brings to mind at once Gummere's (p. 97) picture of a group of people stirring up a ballad by a kind of spontaneous combustion of high spirits, shouting and jigging while the next man thinks up another episode of the story. It reminds us also that the word *ballad* comes from *ballare,* meaning "to dance." Some of these refrains certainly seem made for dancing. It is a good idea to help children respond to the musical character of the ballads by having them sing some and suit gentle rhythmic movements to the words of others or even try lively dance steps to the lustier refrains.

DRAMATIC QUALITY

Perhaps the most striking characteristic of the ballads is their dramatic and rapidly unfolding plots. In "Edward," for example, you sense immediately that something is wrong; then you learn that Edward has killed his own father, but not till the last stanza do you know that the mother herself planned the crime and persuaded her son to commit it. "Lord Randal," opening peacefully with a mother questioning her son about his hunting, hints only in the melancholy last line of each verse—"For I'm wearied wi hunting, and fain wad lie down"—that all is not well. As the questioning goes on, you learn that Lord Randal's hawks and his hounds died of the food he gave them from his own plate. Then you find out that his "true love" is the poisoner and that Lord Randal will also die. The last-minute revelation of the villain is nowhere more strikingly employed than in "The Daemon Lover." In this ballad, it is only after the faithless wife has gone with her former lover on his ship that she "espies" his cloven hoof and knows she has eloped with the devil himself.

There are of course some comic plots too, but they are distinctly in the minority. "The Crafty Farmer" outwitting the thief is one of the children's favorites, and they like even better the broad slapstick farce of the stubborn old couple in "Get Up and Bar the Door." The folk-tale plot of trial by riddle with a bright person substituting for a stupid one is amusingly used in "King John and the Abbot of Canterbury" ("King John and the Bishop"). The charming "Wee Wee Man" is built on the folk-tale plot of the fairy who disappears if you take your eyes off him. "Lizie Lindsay" is mildly humorous, with the young Lord disguised as a shepherd's son and with poor Lizie tramping the soles off her shoes, but the conclusion of this ballad, where MacDonald reveals all his grandeur, turns it into a cheerful and dramatic romance.

On the whole, ballad plots are more likely to be tragic than humorous. They celebrate bloody and terrible battles, ghosts that return to haunt their true or their false loves, fairy husbands of human maids, infanticide, murder, faithless love punished, faithful love not always rewarded—sad, sad, romance and tragedies in every possible combination. Sadder still, there is not always the clear retribution characteristic of the fairy tales. Ballad villains are all too likely to make a go of their fell deeds, and their victims frequently die off with hardly time to curse them properly. Since children always disapprove of this lack of poetic justice, the ballads have to be combed carefully if you are to find a fair proportion with satisfactory, or just, endings. When you wish to use a sad one like "Bonny Barbara Allan" or "Lord Randal," then you should probably sing it. The gentle music leaves the children feeling so tender toward the victim that they almost forget the villain.

ABRUPT BEGINNINGS AND ENDINGS

The ballads often begin right in the middle of a complicated story. "The Daemon Lover" ("James Harris") opens with a brisk dialogue and not a "he said" to guide you:

'O where have you been, my long, long love,
This long seven years and mair?'

'O I'm come to seek my former vows
Ye granted me before.'

'O hold your tongue of your former vows,
For they will breed sad strife;
O hold your tongue of your former vows,
For I am become a wife.'

And there you are with a melodrama well under way. Three ragged gypsies sing at the door of a fine lady, and she comes promptly down the stairs—so the first verse of "The Raggle, Taggle Gypsies" ("The Gypsy Laddie") tells you, and you never do find out why. These are typical ballad beginnings; you have to keep reading to find out what on earth everyone is up to and why.

The conclusions are sometimes equally abrupt. In "Get Up and Bar the Door," after the old man breaks his vow and speaks first, the ballad concludes with the old woman skipping around in high glee. But what of those two roguish gentlemen? Nothing more is said about them, and you are left wondering mildly what happened next. Sometimes the ballad ends on a teasing note. What does that mean, you ask yourself, and go on wondering. In the last verse of "The Wife of Usher's Well," when the ghosts of the widow's three sons hear the cock crow and know they must be gone, one of them says:

Fare ye weel, my mother dear!
Fareweel to barn and byre!
And fare ye weel, the bonny lass
That kindles my mother's fire!

There is a suggestion of a sad romance in the last two lines—a poor ghost leaving behind not only his mother, his barn, and his byre, but his heart's delight as well! When these cryptic endings set the listener's imagination to work, they are almost as satisfactory as neat, thoroughgoing conclusions. They give the hearer a sense of making the story himself.

DESCRIPTION

Intent on telling a dramatic story, ballad makers were not concerned with either the details of the landscape or the emotions of the characters. Nature is used as a highly conventionalized setting for a tale. "It fell upon a Martinmass" or "at Lammas time" or "in the merry month of May" are favorite phrases. So, depending on the season, the nights may be "lang and mirk" or green leaves "a-springing" or lovers may walk along a green road "the greenest ever was seen." Maidens are "the fairest ever seen," and men are "lords of high degree" or "proper men." These are ballad conventions that made composition easy and memorizing even easier. When "Sir Patrick Spens" receives the "braid letter," "a loud lauch lauched he" and then "a tier blinded his ee." Such conventions take care of the emotions. The characters may "rive" their hair, and of course they die for love right on schedule, so that they can be buried side by side and roses can grow from their graves—

Until they could grow no higher,
And twisted and twined in a true lover's knot
Which made all the parish admire.

Today such standardized phrases are called clichés, but they served a useful purpose in the ballad by easing the strain of composition and centering attention on the action.

INCREMENTAL REPETITION

Incremental repetition is an aid to storytelling. This is a ballad convention in which each verse repeats the form of the preceding verse but with a new turn that advances the story. Its skillful use (see "Edward," p. 95) seems to suggest minstrel origin of the ballads. But because it simplifies storytelling, it is also used as an argument for communal origin. Here, for instance, is a portion of "The Cruel Brother." This ballad gives a breathing space for the composer with its formal refrains and leads up to the climax with its incremental repetition. The story concerns the fate of the fair lady whose lover forgets to ask her brother John for his consent to their marriage. This oversight is punished when John stabs the bride. To her lover the bride says:

'O, lead me gently up the hill,'
With a hey ho and a lillie gay
'And I'll there sit down, and make my will.'
As the primrose spreads so sweetly.

'O what will you leave to your father dear?'
With a hey ho and a lillie gay
'The silver-shode steed that brought me here.'
As the primrose spreads so sweetly.

'What will you leave to your mother dear?'
With a hey ho and a lillie gay
'My velvet pall and my silken gear.'
As the primrose spreads so sweetly.

'What will you leave to your sister Anne?'
With a hey ho and a lillie gay
'My silken scarf and my gowden fan.'
As the primrose spreads so sweetly.

'What will you leave to your sister Grace?'
With a hey ho and a lillie gay
'My bloody cloaths to wash and dress.'
As the primrose spreads so sweetly.

'What will you leave to your brother John?'
With a hey ho and a lillie gay
'The gallows-tree to hang him on.'
As the primrose spreads so sweetly.

Reading these ballads that use incremental repetition, you will find it easy to imagine a leader starting the pattern by asking the question, a crowd of people singing the refrain, and the same leader, or perhaps the next man in the circle, answering the question.

ANONYMITY

Whether a ballad was composed by a singing throng or a forgotten minstrel or a "curtal friar," its author remains strictly anonymous. Reference to the storyteller is comparatively rare, perhaps only in an opening line. The charming "Wee Wee Man" begins, "As I was walking all alone" and records the adventures of the speaker when he meets a fairy man. Nevertheless, the story concerns the fairy world and not the author of the tale. Who he was, how he felt, you never learn. He merely records the facts of the adventure as objectively as possible and remains himself completely anonymous. For the most part, the storytelling is impersonal and gives you not the slightest inkling of the author's point of view or station in life. It is "good reporting" in the modern sense.

SUBJECT MATTER

The ballads, as we have observed, run the whole gamut of subjects and emotions. Here are some categories with a few examples:

Farce—The Crafty Farmer; Get Up and Bar the Door
Comedy—King John and the Abbot of Canterbury (King John and the Bishop); A Gest of Robyn Hode (with the exception of the account of Robin Hood's death)
Crime—Edward; The Bonny Earl of Murray; Lord Randal; The Twa Sisters
Noble tragedy—Sir Patrick Spens; The Hunting of the Cheviot; The Battle of Harlaw; The Battle of Otterburn (the ballads of the great battles are generally too involved for the elementary school)
Romance—Lizie Lindsay; Bonny Barbara Allan; The Raggle, Taggle Gypsies (The Gypsy Laddie)
Fairylore—The Wee Wee Man; Tam Lin; Hind Etin
Ghost story—The Wife of Usher's Well
Melodrama—The Daemon Lover (James Harris); Lord Randal; Bonny Barbara Allan

Using the Traditional Ballad with Children

LANGUAGE DIFFICULTY

The old ballads are not for the primary grades but belong to the children of the middle and upper grades or of junior high school. One glance at these ballads shows the reading difficulties they present for even eleven- and twelve-year-old children. Not only do they employ difficult and obsolete words, but some of the ballads are in dialect, some are in a phonetic idiom that can only be guessed at, and others use familiar words which are so oddly spelled or abbreviated ("ba" for ball) that the average reader doesn't recognize the words when he sees them. Most of these difficulties, however, disappear when the child hears the ballads read aloud.

Children generally like dialect. If, then, you are going to read "Sir Patrick Spens" to the children, you can tell them that it is in Scottish dialect and old, old dialect at that. You might tell them something about the story first, or you might even read the ballad in modern English, either before or after reading the original version. This is the way the first two stanzas read in modern style:

The king sits in Dumferling town,
Drinking the blood red wine:
'O where will I get a good sailor,
To sail this ship of mine?'

Then up and spoke an elderly knight,
Sat at the king's right knee:
'Sir Patrick Spence is the best sailor
That sails upon the sea.'

In the fourth verse where "a loud laugh laughed he" and then "a tear blinded his eye," a good rhyme is upset but can be restored when you swing back to the "ee" of dialect. This may be a very unorthodox way of dealing with folk ballads, but the barrier of language should not keep these exciting story-poems from children. They like to hear the dialect if they know what it means. Translating it into modern English will make the meaning clear.

A BALLAD PROGRAM

A group of student teachers who had become ballad enthusiasts decided to give a ballad recital for fifth and sixth grades. They chose a school where the children not only were poor readers but ranked the second lowest in the city on their intelligence scores. One of the student teachers prepared an informal introduction, telling the children something of the history and origin of the old ballads. She also told them that many of the words might sound queer because some of them were an older form of English like "thou" and "thee" and some were dialect, and then she gave examples. She also said to them, "I rather think you will understand all the stories, but if you don't, we'll come around to your rooms later, and you can ask us about them."

The student teachers sang "Bonny Barbara Allan" to the children, gave a crude dramatization of "Get Up and Bar the Door" and "King John and the Bishop," and read "The Daemon Lover," "The Crafty Farmer," and "Lizie Lindsay" in parts—one girl reading the narration and other girls reading the speeches of the different characters. After presenting "Lizie Lindsay" as a drama, they sang part of it, for "Lizie" has a catchy tune. "The Wee Wee Man," "The Wife of Usher's Well," and "Sir Patrick Spens" were read as solos, and the program was concluded by the whole group of student teachers singing "Raggle, Taggle Gypsies."

CHILDREN'S RESPONSES TO THE BALLADS

The children were attentive throughout the program. They laughed at the funny ballads, gave "Sir Patrick Spens" and "The Wife of Usher's Well" breathless attention, applauded spontaneously and heartily at the end, and went out humming "The Raggle, Taggle Gypsies." The ballads they asked for in their rooms most often were, of course, the two broadly comic ones, "The Crafty Farmer" and "Get Up and Bar the Door," but they also wanted to learn to sing "Bonny Barbara Allan," and they asked to have "Sir Patrick Spens" read again. These responses, rather than their conventional expressions of enjoyment, were taken as evidence that they had liked the ballads. When the student teachers visited the children in their rooms, the discussion of the ballads was unforced and brisk. Checking up casually, they were astonished to find that no major point in any story had been missed. The plots of the ballads stood out clearly in the minds of the whole group of children. To be sure, the students had introduced each ballad carefully and had explained the meanings of obscure words in advance; but, as they said later, "We do the same thing in a history lesson and still the children don't get it all." Children's memory and understanding in the case of these traditional ballads are helped by the emotional impact of the startling and powerful plots.

A sixth-grade teacher had a group of overage children who were addicted to comic books and the more lurid movies. She started reading some of the old ballads aloud to them. The ones they liked best she read over and over, letting them say the verses along with her. To the children's surprise, they learned a number of the ballads in this way without consciously trying to memorize. When they commented on this, she told them she supposed people had always found ballads easy to learn, and had enjoyed repeating them. That is why they still exist today, after hundreds of years of being learned and passed on from one person to another.

There was a sudden burst of ballad subjects in the art activities, and the art teacher was taxed, not only for more help on figure drawing but for all sorts of information about costumes, furniture, armor, the great hall, and the like. Their ballad illustrations had a dramatic quality that testified to the moving character of the themes. Occasionally an anachronism would startle the teacher and would gradually dawn upon the children. One large and striking crayon sketch of "Sir Patrick Spens" showed some cautious "knichts" leaping overboard securely girdled with life preservers. This error was gravely explained to the young artist by the children themselves. Since the teacher kept the discussion unforced, a few of the ballads drew no comments from the children. If the children never asked for those ballads the teacher let them drop. On the other hand, with every saying of the favorite ballads, questions would come with a rush. "Did that old knight have it in for Sir Patrick Spens when he got the king to send him off to sea in the middle of the winter?" "Did Sir Patrick have to go to sea when he knew there was going to be a storm?" "Why couldn't he just throw the king's letter away and not go?" Such questions provoked considerable discussion and led to some wholesome conclusions about duty and courage. Another group argued at length about the conduct of the wife in "The Raggle, Taggle Gypsies." Why did a fine lady leave her home and her husband, they wondered. Was she just a faithless woman like the wife in "The Daemon Lover"? One of the girls thought not. "Perhaps," she said slowly, "perhaps she was a gypsy girl herself." Others caught the implication immediately and carried it further. "Maybe she thought it would be a fine thing to have a grand house and a rich husband, but when her own people came for her, she just couldn't stand being cooped up any longer; so she went with them." A logical and charitable conclusion!

CORRELATION WITH SCHOOL SUBJECTS

The Scottish and English ballads may be utilized in several ways. Sometimes, if the children are reading a prose version of Robin Hood, the teacher can read aloud to them the ballad sources of the tales. Or, in a dramatization of Robin Hood, Allen a Dale can sing some of the other old ballads, and the merry men can sing or say still others. The ballads make a fine center for English-class activities. A ballad assembly can be given by the children along lines similar to the student-teachers' assembly. In a dramatization of medieval life, a wandering minstrel can entertain the company in the great hall by saying or singing the ballads. Some of these he can say alone, but the company can join in with other ballads that have refrains. Many ballads lend themselves to choral speaking and to dramatization, and a few of the farcical ones are excellent for shadow or puppet plays. The heroic ballads, though, are usually better read or spoken by a single individual.

While the bulk of the ballads undoubtedly belongs to the high schools, a few have been effectively introduced into the elementary schools at the upper-grade levels. There is little doubt that the success of old ballads with children depends largely upon the teacher who presents them. She not only must know them well and like them but must be able to read them aloud with the simplicity and vigor they deserve. Ballads should be heard and not read silently. Any teacher who can read them aloud well will have children who not only like the ballads but develop a fresh faith in the fun and excitement that can be derived from various types of poetry.

Folk Ballads in the United States

AMERICAN DESCENDANTS OF THE POPULAR BALLAD

Early settlers brought the old Scottish and English ballads to this country, and children in states as remote from each other as Pennsylvania and Texas, or Wisconsin and the Carolinas, heard their parents and their grandparents singing the same ballads that *their* grandparents had sung in the mother country. "Bonny Barbara Allan," for example, was carried by the colonists and pioneer families from one end of the United States to the other.

The Child collection stimulated such an interest in these old story-songs that collectors began to search for and record their American variants. They found, as you might expect, a large number of ballads being sung or recited throughout the country, but especially in the Southern mountains. There the mountaineers, cut off from the main stream of immigration and changing customs, had preserved the songs their ancestors brought with them. Sometimes "Barbara Allan" was "Barbery Allen" or "Barbara Ellen," but in every version she was the same heartless girl whose cruelty caused her lover's death. "Lord Randal" might be hailed democratically as "Johnny Randall," or even "Jimmy Randolph," but he was still begging his mother to make his bed soon for he was "sick at the heart and fain wad lie down." Sometimes the verses had been so altered and patched together that they were incoherent. Most of the ballads had, however, come through with less change than you might naturally expect from several hundred years of oral transmission.

Cecil J. Sharp (1859-1924), an English musician, made early and outstanding collections of these survivals of the Scottish-English ballads in the Southern mountains of the United States. His books are valuable contributions to ballad literature in this country, and other collectors have followed his lead. Older children will enjoy the ballads in Sharp's first two volumes, while children as young as three and four are charmed with the *Nursery Songs.*[8]

These collections bear witness to the fact that the traditional ballads are still flourishing in places far removed from their source. Evidently the old woman who gave Sir Walter Scott so many of his ballads was overly pessimistic when she burst into tears at the sight of them in print. She would be surprised to hear voices of invisible singers, coming from boxes (phonographs, radios, and television), singing her ballads even as they were sung long ago. The traditional ballads of England and Scotland did not die between the covers of books but were kept gaily alive by the descendants of the early settlers who brought them to this country. Printing seems merely to have stimulated a greater pride and a more sustained interest in them.

NATIVE BALLADS

Once the collectors set to work gathering the American variants of the old-world ballads, they began to encounter new ballads and folk songs that are as native to the United States as buckwheat cakes and hominy grits. Lumberjacks, slaves, miners, cowboys, chain gangs, railroad men, cotton pickers, and sailors had all been singing at their work, it seemed, and they had been singing less of the sufferings of Barbara Allan than of their own

8. C. J. Sharp, compiler, *English Folk Songs from the Southern Appalachians; American-English Folk Songs; Nursery Songs from the Appalachian Mountains.*

toil and hardships. Here was a rich treasure of ballad-making still in the process of creation. These songs are not as finished or as noble as their Scottish-English predecessors. On the whole, they are rougher and sometimes more sordid in language and theme. They do, however, achieve a wistful melancholy or a happy-go-lucky philosophy or a sheer braggadocio that seems to distinguish certain groups of our hardy settlers or certain workers such as the Western cowboys.

The native ballads of the United States tell, on the whole, fewer coherent and dramatic stories than do the Scottish-English ballads; but they sing with or without the music. They usually have a chorus, but so completely gone are the "Hey nonny nonnies," that it is almost a shock to encounter a "Derry down, down, down, derry down," in "Red Iron Ore.[9]" The refrains are more likely to repeat a phrase or to be a three- or four-line chorus. The Negro spirituals reach heights of religious fervor never attained in any old-world ballad, but for their full beauty they need their music. The cowboy ballads have sometimes a philosophic or a wistful air that is more in the mood of a song than of a story. The language is easier for us, even the dialect or vernacular, but some of it is too rough for children. Among these ballads, as in the English and Scottish popular ballads, there is material composed by adults for adults with themes as well as language unsuited to children. No sensible youngster will be hurt by browsing through the collections, but ballads for use in the classroom should be selected by the teacher.

Once children realize that ballads are still remembered and treasured, they may turn collectors and discover some ballads in their own families or communities. Once they realize that ballads are still being made not merely by professional poets imitating old forms but by isolated peoples celebrating tragic, comic, or dramatic events, the children, too, may wish to try group composition of a ballad. It is fun and less difficult than it sounds. Certainly newspapers supply stories of heroes that are the very stuff of which these story-poems have always been made. Radio and television make constant use of such episodes for sketches and dramas. Why not try casting them into ballad form?

Using the Native Ballads with Children

In the Library of Congress, Washington, D.C., in the Archives of American Folk Song, are some 6000 records including of course many ballads. Some of these records contain apparently recent and as yet unpublished material. This is the greatest collection of native ballads in existence and one that should be known and used. Albums are available for loan or for sale and might provide a happy way of introducing children to ballad literature. Folk-song albums from the record companies are as varied in quality as they are numerous. In work with children you should avoid the obviously commercial.

The collections made by John and Alan Lomax and by Carl Sandburg are admirably classified for school use,[10] for example: "Pioneer Memories," "Great Lakes and Erie Canal," "Mexican Border Songs," "Railroad and Work Gangs," "Cowboy Songs," "Sailors and Sea Fights," "Lumberjacks, Loggers, and Shanty-Boys." Obviously such ballads will correlate with United States history and with the study of types of work that children find most picturesque and fascinating.

One group[11] studying the Great Lakes and using *Paddle-to-the-Sea* as the literary focus of a geography unit became so interested in lake lore and accumulated such a rich mass of factual material that an assembly was, of course, inevitable. "Red Iron Ore," with its vigorous lilt and dramatic story of shipping on the Great Lakes, was exactly what the children needed to make a lively interlude in their informative program.

Another group[12] studying Westward expansion enjoyed the tall tales for their English

9. This ballad is given in *The American Songbag* by Carl Sandburg.

10. Carl Sandburg, ed., *The American Songbag;* John A. Lomax and Alan Lomax, eds., *American Ballads and Folk Songs* and *Cowboy Songs and other Frontier Ballads.*

11. Benjamin Franklin School, Cleveland, Ohio. Principal at that time, Miss Aleda Ranft; teacher Miss Hulda Richardson.

12. Caledonia School, East Cleveland. Principal at that time, Miss Bertha Clendenin; teacher, Miss Ethel Hunter.

work and some of the cowboy ballads for their music period. Since they were reading the hilarious tall tale *Pecos Bill,* for their ballads they chose the contrasting melancholy of "Oh, Bury Me Not on the Lone Prairie," "As I Walked Out in the Streets of Laredo," and the two favorites, "A Home on the Range" and "Whoopee Ti Yi Yo, Git Along, Little Dogies." Other groups used records of the cowboy ballads, and memorized them in the course of playing them over and over. The Lomax section on "Breakdowns and Play Parties" might well be used with the study of the Daniel Boone, Davy Crockett, or Lincoln periods. All three men, the children like to remember, could dance at play-parties the whole night through.

So far, only those native ballads that are sung, or sung and danced, have been discussed. Our native ballads are more likely than the old English ballads to suffer if they are used apart from their characteristic melodies. The Negro spirituals or such a gentle, tender lyric as "Down in the Valley" have little significance without music. For these, the Lomax and Sandburg collections with their musical arrangements are invaluable.

There are a few story-ballads, however, that are delightful read aloud and may be used without music. Louise Pound's book, *American Ballads and Songs* (1922) is a good source for these. She gives, for instance, the droll ballad of "My Father's Gray Mare," in which young Roger, courting the farmer's daughter Kate, became more interested in the mare than the girl. "The Rich Young Farmer" is a much more satisfactory romance. (There is, by the way, something impersonal about these ballad love affairs that satisfies without embarrassing the adolescent who is interested in but self-conscious about romance.) In the Lomax *Cowboy Songs* there is an amusing burlesque on bad men called "The Desperado," which boys can read well. Or one boy can read the Desperado's lines while a verse choir does the chorus. Here is a sample of it:

The Desperado[13]

I'm a howler from the prairies of the West.
If you want to die with terror, look at me.
I'm chain-lightning—if I ain't may I be blessed.
I'm the snorter of the boundless prairie.
  He's a killer and a hater!
  He's the great annihilator!
  He's the terror of the boundless prairie.

These native ballads are rougher and cruder than most of the literature you will give children but, for that very reason, provide a wholesome change from the delicacy of most poetry. There is no doubt that children like ballads, and boys especially take them to their hearts.

Modern Narrative Poems

The story-poems and the old ballad form have proved as attractive to poets as they have to readers. The list of poets who have enjoyed writing narrative poems is a long one and includes such distinguished names as Scott, Allingham, Southey, Browning, Tennyson, Longfellow, Whittier, Swinburne, Rossetti, Kipling, and Masefield. The majority of these poems, however, belong to high school or even to college level. They are too long or the plots are too mature or the language too difficult for elementary school children to struggle with, even when the poems are read aloud. Still there are some narrative poems that not only are suitable for children but provide them with the fun, the thrills, and the satisfaction which only a dramatic verse-story can give.

POEMS FOR CHILDREN FIVE TO NINE

For the youngest children, from five to eight or nine, there are two masterpieces—"A Visit from St. Nicholas" by Clement Clarke Moore and "The Pied Piper of Hamelin" by Robert Browning.

13. From *Cowboy Songs* by John A. Lomax and Alan Lomax. Copyright 1910, 1916, 1918 by the Macmillan Co.; 1938 by Ludlow Music, Inc. Used by permission.

In 1822, Christmas Eve found a certain Mr. Clement Moore obliged to make a last-minute visit to the market. Darkness had come, sleigh bells jingled, snow crunched underfoot and, where the street lights fell upon it, sparkled and twinkled. Mr. Moore did his errand at the market, hurried home with his package, delivered it to his wife, and then hastened to his study where he shut the door and remained alone for several hours. When he rejoined his family, he brought with him "A Visit from St. Nicholas."

" 'Twas the night before Christmas," the children call it, and never recognize it by any other title. The three-, four-, and five-year-olds listen when you read it, chuckle, join in, and demand, "Read it again." The Santa Claus Mr. Moore gave to the world is a combination of an elfish Kris Kringle, the Dutch Saint Nicholas, and Mr. Moore's own exuberant imagination. His "Saint Nick" bounds and twinkles, winks, shakes with laughter, lays his finger "aside of his nose," whistles to his chargers, and appears and disappears with the speed of a hurricane. His reindeer team is no impersonal collection of reindeer but a mad, tearing crew, each with a name and a personality—Dasher, Dancer, Prancer, Vixen, Comet, Cupid, Donner, Blitzen. These names should trip off your tongue as readily as one, two, three. This Saint Nicholas with his reindeer has become the American Santa Claus. Clement Moore gave him a personality, a great dramatic role, a dreamlike existence all his own. The poem was not published until a year after it was written, but from 1823, no American Christmas which includes young children has been complete without it.

It is interesting to recall that Robert Browning wrote his "The Pied Piper of Hamelin" for the amusement of a sick child, with the special intention of supplying him with subject matter he could illustrate. Perhaps this accounts, in part, for the visual quality of the poem, which endears it to illustrators young and old. The story of "The Pied Piper" is too familiar to need reviewing, but particular qualities of the poem are worth noting. In the first place, the story moves rapidly. Words hurry and all but trip the reader's tongue; episodes follow each other swiftly; and lines have the racing tempo first of the scurrying rats and later of the skipping children. They slow down only for the pompous Mayor and his devious cogitations, and for the little lame boy's wistful account of being left behind. Some readers like to conclude with this episode, omitting the last two parts entirely. The dramatic conflict between greed and honor is sufficiently objective for children to understand, and they approve of the Piper's retributive revenge. Children usually dislike descriptions, but Part II, describing the destructiveness of rats, they roll over their tongues. Above all they like the mystery of the Piper himself. "Who was he? Was there ever such a person? Where did he take the children?" they wonder.

One little third-grade group[14] became so fond of the poem they decided to use it for a choral reading. After a few trials they invited one fifth-grade boy to be the Mayor and another to be the Piper, but the third graders read the long narrative. The choral reading was an ambitious undertaking, but those who heard it have never forgotten the young voices describing the tripping, skipping crowds of little children following the "wonderful music with shouting and laughter." The reading ended with one of the younger children speaking the lines of the little lame boy, left behind against his will and concluding sorrowfully:

"To go now limping as before,
And never hear of that country more!"

For broad comedy Eugene Field's "The Duel" (the tale of "The gingham dog and the calico cat") and Laura Richards' "The Monkeys and the Crocodile" are perennial favorites. William Allingham's "The Fairy Shoemaker" and Laura Richards' "Little John Bottlejohn" are unusual fairy and mermaid poems, the latter simple enough for the five-year-olds. The sevens like James Whitcomb Riley's "Little Orphant Annie," which is a rare mixture of scariness and nonsense, and they also like his "The Raggedy Man."

The eights will enjoy "The Pirate Don Durk of Dowdee" by Mildred Plew Meigs. The funny words and phrases tickle them: "squizzamaroo," "a floppety plume on his hat," "a parrot called Pepperkin Pye," "his

14. Benjamin Franklin School, Cleveland; teacher at that time, Miss Sackett.

Notice the contrast in these two interpretations of "The Pirate Don Durk of Dowdee." One child has caught the farcical tone of the poem; the other has pictured the gay, gallant pirate as he sees himself. Hazeldell and East Madison Schools. By children in the Cleveland Public Schools.

boots made a slickery slosh," "crook'd like a squash," and the dramatic "Oh jing! went the gold of Dowdee." In the same category of sheer nonsense is William Brighty Rands' poem about "Godfrey Gordon Gustavus Gore," the wretched boy who "never would shut a door."

Vachel Lindsay's "The Potatoes' Dance" and Walter de la Mare's "The Lost Shoe" are unique tales children also enjoy. Search your anthologies and books by single poets for more story-poems, because even the fives and sevens enjoy the swiftness and suspense which the rhythmic flow of verse gives to a story.

STORY-POEMS FOR OLDER CHILDREN

Older children will like many of the poems allotted to the younger ones. If, for instance, the twelves or fourteens have missed "The Pied Piper," give it to them, by all means. Another story-poem with a wide appeal is Ruth Crawford Seeger's *Let's Build a Railroad.* Six railroad work songs are connected by a cadenced narrative, with lively pictures by Tom Funk. The format suggests that the book is for children five to seven, but the text will have more meaning for ten- or twelve-year-olds. It would make a stirring class performance for an assembly, with solo voices and groups speaking or singing the narrative and the songs.

Children in the middle grades like Longfellow's moving "The Wreck of the Hesperus." Also tragic, and of high poetic beauty, is Edna St. Vincent Millay's "The Ballad of the Harp-Weaver." This the twelves and fourteens should not miss. It is a fantasy, eerie and wistful, built around a mother's love and sacrifice for her child. A poem as full of pity and tenderness as this lovely ballad will help to balance the stark and often brutal tragedies to which children are exposed through our newspapers and magazines. Children need the therapy of laughter; they need also the therapy of compassionate tears.

Scott's "Young Lochinvar," a gay, swashbuckling romance with a galloping tempo, is particularly enjoyed by older children, "The Highwayman" by Alfred Noyes is their favorite romance. Robert Southey's "The Inchcape Rock" tells a good pirate story, but unlike "Dowdee," it is a grim one. "Johnny Appleseed" by Stephen Vincent Benét and Rosemary Carr Benét is a simple and charming narrative. "John Gilpin" is only one of many humorous ballads they enjoy. And let's not forget that gem of Americana, Ernest L. Thayer's "Casey at the Bat."

For the eleven- to fourteen-year-olds there are many story-poems about great events in American history. Certainly they should know "The Landing of the Pilgrim Fathers" by Felicia Dorothea Hemans, with its unforgettable picture of that desolate arrival and its significance in our history. Children should also thrill to the galloping hoofbeats of Longfellow's "Paul Revere's Ride" before they meet the more complex and workaday Revere of the biographies. The gallantry of old "Barbara Frietchie" defying Stonewall Jackson is good, too, provided the children have a biography of Jackson and learn to appreciate him for the rare human being he was. Texas children should not be the only ones to tingle with pride over "The Defense of the Alamo" as Joaquin Miller relates it. Arthur Guiterman has written a number of fine historical ballads, but especially recommended are his "Daniel Boone" and "The Oregon Trail." These are significant, both as poems and as history. In the Benéts' *A Book of Americans,* which, by the way, should be in every elementary school, there are many poems you will wish to use with history, but the pair, "Nancy Hanks" and "Abraham Lincoln," are the great favorites. The plaintive, wistful ghost of Nancy asking if anyone knows her son, "did he have fun, did he get on," is poignantly moving, while the concluding lines of the Lincoln poem remain in your mind to be thought about over and over:

Lincoln was the green pine.
Lincoln kept on growing.[15]

These poems are typical of the fine narrative verse about people and events in United States history. Such poems can be introduced casually as the history chronology unfolds, or the children may become interested in the theme of heroism and start searching for hero poems of their own. Such a search will include other countries, of course. They will discover Browning's "Incident of the French Camp," brief, sharp tragedy, full of youthful gallantry, or they may find Henry Newbolt's "Drake's Drum" with its eerie, haunting verse:

"Take my drum to England, hand et by the shore,
Strike et when your powder's runnin' low;

15. "Abraham Lincoln." From *A Book of Americans* by Rosemary Carr and Stephen Vincent Benét. Copyright 1933 by the authors. Used by permission.

In this illustration for "John Gilpin's Ride," we see Caldecott's flair for humorous action and storytelling details at its best. Grace and helter-skelter action have made his pictures forever entrancing to children and adults. From R. Caldecott's Picture Book Number One. *Reproduced with permission of Frederick Warne & Co., Inc. (Original in color, book 7¼ x 8¾)*

If the Dons sight Devon, I'll quit the port o' Heaven,
An' drum them up the Channel as we drummed them long ago."

They should also discover Robert Nathan's "Dunkirk," a story-poem about two children who steered their little boat, along with sailors of other small craft, to bring the trapped soldiers home from that tragic beach. The return voyage with fourteen men finds the boy recalling the great English heroes of the sea, and the poem ends with the two lines:

There at his side sat Francis Drake,
And held him true and steered him home.[16]

Why do people fear that we will overromanticize history? The vision, the fortitude, and the selflessness of human beings can never be sufficiently celebrated. These put heart in youngsters, build their ideals, and help mold the temper of their minds and spirits. There cannot be too many such poems.

What a rich legacy children have inherited from the anonymous folk literature of the past! Young children listen to the lively verses of *Mother Goose,* say them, gallop to them, and pore over the pictures endlessly. So children begin poetry happily with *Mother Goose,* whose varied verses lead them naturally into modern lyric poetry and also into that other, more mature form of folk verse, the traditional ballad. These exciting story-poems belong chiefly to the older children, not only because of the difficult language but also because of the mature content. The ballads, too, lead into modern poetry. It may seem a far cry from "The Cruel Brother" to Robert Browning's "My Last Duchess," but, after all, both poems leave much unsaid, to be read between the lines, and Browning's sad lady won't seem unfamiliar to youngsters who have encountered "The Cruel Brother." These folk verses, both *Mother Goose* and the ballads, train the ear, challenge the imagination, and familiarize children with the fun, the excitement, and the sound and melody of English verse.

16. From *Dunkirk* by Robert Nathan, published by Alfred A. Knopf, Inc. Copyright 1941 by Robert Nathan.

This bold illustration of Admiral David Farragut conveys the spirit of a strong man. Illustration by Charles Child. From A Book of Americans *by Rosemary and Stephen Vincent Benét. Copyright 1933 by Rosemary and Stephen Vincent Benét. Copyright renewed © 1961 by Rosemary Carr Benét. Reproduced by permission of Holt, Rinehart and Winston, Inc.*

SUGGESTED READING, PROBLEMS, AND PROJECTS

1. Compare six editions of *Mother Goose* for (a) number of verses (note the proportion of well-known to little-known verses); (b) proportion of pictures to verses; (c) format (print, paper, binding, page size, durability, beauty); (d) illustrations (*types*—black-and-white, silhouettes, colored; *predominant colors*—primary or pastel, bright or dark; *costumes*—modern or period; *characters*—realistic, imaginative, humorous, prettified; *backgrounds*—period or modern, detailed or vague; *style of each artist*).

2. Give examples of some reflections in the

Mother Goose verses of earlier social customs and conditions. Would any of these interfere with children's comprehension of the verses? If so, how would you clear up such points?

3. Give two or more additional examples of each type of verse listed on p. 82.

4. Find examples of rhythms in *Mother Goose* which seem suitable for action such as skipping, galloping, running, walking, hopping, and trotting.

5. List *Mother Goose* verses which would be valuable for speech work on specific vowel, consonant, and combination sounds. Suggest verses suitable for dramatization.

6. Which is your favorite edition of *Mother Goose*? Why?

7. Which of the variants of *Mother Goose* do you find most usable? Why?

Note to students: The best preparation for the study of the ballads in this chapter is to listen to the records of Burl Ives, Jean Ritchie, Cynthia Gooding, Richard Chase, Alfred Deller, or any other of the ballad singers. *The English and Scottish Popular Ballads* (two records, Folklore Press) is an important source. Notice the source of the ballads, the subject matter, and the mood.

8. Quoting from ballads not cited in the text, give examples of ballad characteristics (musical quality, dramatic quality, abrupt beginnings and endings, description, incremental repetition, anonymity, subject matter).

9. Choose one of the old Scottish-English ballads and practice reading it aloud. Present it as you would to a group of children—first introduce the ballad and clear up any difficulties, and then read it aloud.

10. Compare our American variants of old-world ballads or our native inventions with the Scottish-English traditional ballads.

11. Choose a story-poem for the grade-level you plan to teach and work out an introduction which would grow naturally out of some classroom discussion or activity.

MOTHER GOOSE REFERENCES

ADAMS, BESS PORTER. *About Books and Children* (See Bibliography, Chapter 3).

The Annotated Mother Goose with introduction and notes by William Baring-Gould and Ceil Baring-Gould; the complete text and illustrations in a fully annotated edition, ill. by Caldecott, Crane, Greenaway, Rackham, Parrish, and historical woodcuts. With chapter decorations by E. M. Simon. Clarkson Potter, Inc., New York, 1962. Mother Goose and other rhymes, ditties, and jingles of the nursery run side by side with columns of absorbing historical notes. This impressively large, beautiful book contains over 200 illustrations and a first line index.

BARCHILON, JACQUES, and HENRY PETTIT. *The Authentic Mother Goose Fairy Tales and Nursery Rhymes.* Alan Swallow, 1960. Following a scholarly introduction to the history of Mother Goose and the Perrault fairy tales, there are facsimiles of the complete *Mother Goose's Melody,* and of the 1729 English translation of Perrault's *Tales.*

BARNES, WALTER. *The Children's Poets.* World Book, 1924. This valuable little book contains a fine chapter (II) on Mother Goose.

ECKENSTEIN, LINA. *Comparative Studies in Nursery Rhymes.* London: Duckworth, 1906. A study of the ancient folk origins of the Mother Goose verses and their European counterparts.

FIELD, WALTER TAYLOR. *A Guide to Literature for Children* (see Bibliography, Chapter 3), Chapter X is on Mother Goose.

MAHONY, BERTHA E., LOUISE P. LATIMER, and BEULAH FOLMSBEE. *Illustrators of Children's Books, 1744-1945* (see Bibliography, Chapter 4).

MEIGS, CORNELIA, ANNE EATON, ELIZABETH NESBITT, and RUTH HILL VIGUERS. *A Critical History of Children's Literature* (see Bibliography, Chapter 3). Chapter 6, Part I, deals with the early history of Mother Goose.

MUIR, PERCY. *English Children's Books, 1600-1900* (see Bibliography, Chapter 3).

OPIE, IONA and PETER. *The Lore and Language of Schoolchildren.* Oxford, 1959. "The curious lore passing between children about 6-14, which today holds in its spell some 7 million inhabitants of . . ." Great Britain, includes rhymes, riddles, childhood customs, and beliefs. Some can be traced back for generations and others are current. "The present study is based on the contributions of some 5000 children attending seventy schools."

______, eds. *The Oxford Dictionary of Nursery Rhymes.* Oxford, 1951. This is the most exhaustive and scholarly study yet made of the origins of the nursery rhymes, their earliest recordings, and variations through the years. Copious illustrations from old plates add to its real interest.

ST. JOHN, JUDITH. *The Osborne Collection of Early Children's Books 1566-1910* (see Bibliography, Chapter 3).

THOMAS, KATHERINE ELWES. *The Real Personages of Mother Goose.* Lothrop, 1930.

CHILDREN'S EDITIONS

BENÉT, WILLIAM ROSE, comp. *Mother Goose: A Comprehensive Collection of the Rhymes,* ill. by Roger Duvoisin. Heritage, 1936. This is a sprawling, riotously illustrated edition of four hundred rhymes. Children love the vivid colors and horseplay of the cartoon-like illustrations, although some adults detest them.

CALDECOTT, RANDOLPH. *Hey Diddle Diddle Picture Book,* ill. by the author. Warne, n.d. Some of Caldecott's finest pictures accompany favorite rhymes of the nursery.

The House That Jack Built, ill. by Antonio Frasconi. Harcourt, 1958. In a handsomely illustrated picture book, a favorite nursery rhyme is told in both French and English.

The House That Jack Built, ill. by Paul Galdone. Whittlesey, 1961. Colorful illustrations and picture book format give new life to an old favorite.

In a Pumpkin Shell, ill. by Joan Walsh Anglund. Harcourt, 1960. Familiar nursery rhymes are imaginatively arranged to achieve an alphabet book. Colorful illustrations.

LINES, KATHLEEN, ed. *Lavender's Blue,* ill. by Harold Jones. Watts, 1954.

Marguerite de Angeli's Book of Nursery and Mother Goose Rhymes, ill. by Marguerite de Angeli. Doubleday, 1954.

Mother Goose, ill. by Kate Greenaway. Warne, n.d.

Mother Goose, ill. by Arthur Rackham. Century, 1913.

Mother Goose, ill. by Tasha Tudor. Walck, 1944.

Mother Goose in Hieroglyphics. Houghton, 1962. An exact reproduction of an old edition of *Mother Goose* using words and rebus pictures, with an explanatory key for pictures that puzzle the reader! Originally published in Boston over a century ago.

OPIE, IONA, ed. *Ditties for the Nursery,* ill. by Monica Walker. Walck, 1954.

OPIE, IONA and PETER, comp. *The Oxford Nursery Rhyme Book,* ill. from old chapbooks, with additional pictures by Joan Hassall. Walck, 1955.

The Real Mother Goose, ill. by Blanche Fisher Wright. Rand McNally, 1916.

Ring o' Roses: A Nursery Rhyme Picture Book, ill. by L. Leslie Brooke. Warne, n.d.

The Tall Book of Mother Goose, ill. by Feodor Rojankovsky. Harper, 1942.

The Tenggren Mother Goose, ill. by Gustaf Tenggren. Little, 1940. Gay, Disney-like pictures which do not always illustrate the rhymes near which they appear.

A FEW VARIANTS OF MOTHER GOOSE

KAPP, PAUL, ed. and music arr. by. *A Cat Came Fiddling and Other Rhymes of Childhood,* ill. by Irene Haas. Harcourt, 1956. Here is enchantment for children and adults, at home or in school. The pictures are droll and perfect, and Burl Ives says of the music, "it sounds as though it had never been written but only sung." All ages

LANGSTAFF, JOHN. *Frog Went a-Courtin',* ill. by Feodor Rojankovsky. Harcourt, 1955 4-6

———. *Ol' Dan Tucker,* ill. by Joe Krush. Harcourt, 1963. Lively picture-book retelling of Ol' Dan Tucker's endless mishaps. Music included. 7-

———, ed. *Over in the Meadow,* ill. by Feodor Rojankovsky. Harcourt, 1957. The old counting rhyme of little creatures who lived "in the sand in the sun" is presented in a beautiful picture book. Music included. 3-8

LOW, JOSEPH and RUTH. *Mother Goose Riddle Rhymes,* ill. by Joseph Low. Harcourt, 1953. Mr. Low has made a modern rebus from nursery rhymes that is beautiful in design and clever in conception—a brain teaser for young and old. 6-9

MORRISON, LILLIAN, comp. *Black Within and Red Without,* ill. by Jo Spier. Crowell, 1953. A scholarly collection of rhymed riddles, wise, witty, and often as charming as poetry. Here are traditional puzzlers from ancient Egypt, Greece, the British Isles, the Orient, and our own Ozarks.

———, comp. *A Dillar a Dollar,* ill. by Marjorie Bauernschmidt. Crowell, 1955. Here is an exceedingly funny collection of anonymous "Rhymes and Sayings for the Ten O'clock Scholar." Over three hundred school riddles, sayings, derisive taunts, jokes, and proverbs will be sure to enliven classroom routines. 6-9

———, comp. *Touch Blue,* ill. by Doris Lee. Crowell, 1958. "Signs and spells, Love Charms and Chants, Auguries and Old Beliefs in Rhyme." All ages

PETERSHAM, MAUD and MISKA. *The Rooster Crows: A Book of American Rhymes and Jingles.* Macmillan, 1945. 5-7

POTTER, CHARLES FRANCIS, comp. *Tongue Tanglers,* ill. by William Wiesner. World, 1962. 5-

WITHERS, CARL, comp. *A Rocket in My Pocket,* ill. by Susanne Suba. Holt, 1948. 6-8

WOOD, RAY. *The American Mother Goose,* ill. by Ed Hargis, Lippincott, 1940. 8-12

ABC BOOKS

BROWN, MARCIA, ill. *Peter Piper's Alphabet.* Scribner, 1959. Billy Button, Inigo Impey, Peter Piper, and other old English tongue-twisting nonsense rhymes are brightly pictured. 4-10

CRANE, WALTER. *Baby's Own Alphabet,* ill. by author. Dodd, n.d. 5-7

DUVOISIN, ROGER. *A for the Ark,* ill. by author. Lothrop, 1952. 5-8

EICHENBERG, FRITZ. *Ape in a Cape,* ill. by author. Harcourt, 1952. 5-8

FRANCOISE [pseud. for Françoise Seignobosc]. *The Gay ABC,* ill. by author. Scribner, 1938. 5-7

GAG, WANDA. *The ABC Bunny,* ill. by author. Coward, McCann, 1933. 5-7

GORDON, ISABEL. *The ABC Hunt,* ill. by author. Viking, 1961. From the *A* in alphabet soup to the Z in the sign at the zoo, children will enjoy the game-like search for letters in this entertaining photographic alphabet book. 5-7

GREENAWAY, KATE. *A Apple Pie,* ill. by author. Warne, n.d. 5-7

LEAR, EDWARD. *A Nonsense Alphabet,* ill. by Richard Scarry. Doubleday, 1962. 5-7

MCGINLEY, PHYLLIS. *All Around the Town,* ill. by Helen Stone. Lippincott, 1948. 6-10

MUNARI, BRUNO. *Bruno Munari's ABC,* ill. by author. World, 1960. 4-6

NEWBERRY, CLARE. *The Kittens' ABC,* ill. by author. Harper, 1946. 5-7

ROJANKOVSKY, FEODOR. *Animals in the Zoo,* ill. by author. Knopf, 1962. A handsome zoo alphabet book in color with an animal for every letter. 4-6

SENDAK, MAURICE. *Alligators All Around* (see Bibliography, Chapter 12).

TUDOR, TASHA. *A is for Annabelle,* ill. by author. Walck, 1954. 5-7

WILLIAMS, GARTH. *Big Golden Animal ABC,* ill. by author. Golden, 1954, 1957. 4-7

WILDSMITH, BRIAN. *Brian Wildsmith's ABC,* ill. by author. Watts, 1963. 4-6

BALLAD REFERENCES

ALLINGHAM, WILLIAM. *The Ballad Book.* Cambridge: Sever and Francis, 1865. Contains seventy-six ballads with brief notes and an excellent introduction.

CHILD, FRANCIS JAMES, ed. *English and Scottish Popular Ballads,* 5 vols. Houghton, 1882-1898. This is our most authoritative source for all English and Scottish traditional ballads. Many variants are given for each ballad, together with copious notes.

GUMMERE, FRANCIS B. *The Popular Ballads.* Houghton, 1907. A detailed account of the origins, definitions, classifications, and sources of the ballads. An exposition of his theory of the communal composition of ballads.

HALES, JOHN W., and FREDERICK J. FURNIVALL, assisted by Francis J. Child. *Bishop Percy's Folio Manuscript.* London: Trübner, 1867. Here are the ballads that Bishop Percy found, together with the reproduction of an actual page of the manuscript with Percy's notes scribbled in the margin.

KITTREDGE, GEORGE LYMAN, ed. *English and Scottish Popular Ballads: Student's Cambridge Edition,* ed. by Helen Child Sargeant. Houghton, 1904. This is the invaluable one-volume edition of the Child collection. It contains the 305 ballads, a few variants of each, brief notes, and the excellent glossary giving the definitions and pronunciations of the difficult ballad words.

KRAPPE, ALEXANDER HAGGERTY. *The Science of Folk-Lore.* Dial, 1930. Chapter IX, "The Popular Ballad," discusses the ballad as part of the great stream of folklore, related to the epic, the carol, and the folk tale, migrating even as they have. Discredits Gummere's theory.

LOMAX, JOHN A. *Adventures of a Ballad Hunter.* Macmillan, 1947. An amusing account of the people and places from which Lomax gathered ballads.

_____, ed. *Songs of the Cattle Trail and Cow Camp.* Duell, 1950.

LOMAX, JOHN A., and ALAN LOMAX, comps. *American Ballads and Folk Songs.* Macmillan, 1946.

_____, eds. *Cowboy Songs and Other Frontier Ballads,* rev. and enl. Macmillan, 1948. The Lomax collections of our native ballads are of major importance as sources, not only because they were the first ones made, but also because they were gathered first-hand and the tunes were recorded on wax cylinders, on the spot, unedited.

POUND, LOUISE, ed. *American Ballads and Songs.* Scribner, 1922. A good collection of United States remnants of old ballads along with our native compositions. No music. Excellent introduction.

_____. *Poetic Origins and the Ballad.* Macmillan, 1921, Russell and Russell, 1961. The author furnishes lively evidence against the communal origin of the ballad, besides adding ballad history.

RITCHIE, JEAN. *Singing Family of the Cumberlands,* ill. by Maurice Sendak. Walck, 1955.

SANDBURG, CARL, ed. *The American Songbag.* Harcourt, 1927. While this collection borrows from others, Mr. Sandburg's illuminating notes make it a particularly useful and enjoyable volume.

SHARP, CECIL J., comp. *English Folk-Songs from the Southern Appalachians,* ed. by Maud Karpeles, rev. and enl., 2 vols. Oxford, 1953. A major contribution by an English collector and musician.

_____. *Nursery Songs from the Appalachian Mountains,* 2 vols. London: Novello, 1921-1923. A collection that should be better known in our schools. Many selections for the youngest children.

Some British Ballads, ill. by Arthur Rackham. Dodd, 1920. This is a superb edition for home and school.

OTHER BALLAD SOURCES

Most of the poetry anthologies listed on pp. 214-215 contain sections devoted to old ballads or to modern story-poems. Of these anthologies, *My Poetry Book,* by Huffard, Carlisle, and Ferris, contains an unusually large and well-selected group of story-poems for the elementary school.

BAKER, LAURA NELSON. *The Friendly Beasts,* ill. by Nicolas Sidjakov. Parnassus, 1957. Reverent and beautiful illustrations enhance this version of an old English carol of the first Christmas eve, when animals talked in the stable at Bethlehem. 4-

BONI, MARGARET BRADFORD, ed. *Fireside Book of Folk Songs,* arr. for piano by Norman Lloyd, ill. by Alice and Martin Provensen. Simon & Schuster, 1947. A beautiful collection of many types of folk songs to be enjoyed by the whole family. 8-

BROWNING, ROBERT. *The Pied Piper of Hamelin,* ill. by Kate Greenaway. Warne, n.d. Kate Greenaway made some of her loveliest pictures for this poem.

———. *The Pied Piper of Hamelin,* ill. by Harold Jones. Watts, 1962. An attractive, color-illustrated, new edition. 6-12

CHASE, RICHARD, comp. *Hullabaloo, and Other Singing Folk Games,* arr. for piano by Hilton Rufty, ill. by Joshua Tolford. Houghton, 1949. Eighteen singing games and dances with pictures and diagrams. All ages

COLE, WILLIAM, ed. *Story Poems New and Old,* ill. by Walter Buehr. World, 1957. Over 90 story-poems include traditional ballads, old favorites, and choice modern verses. 9-

FARJEON, ELEANOR. *Mrs. Malone,* ill. by Edward Ardizzone. Walck, 1962. Old Mrs. Malone had little of this world's goods, but she shared it with the hungry animals who had less. They saw to it that her reward was a heavenly one! 5-

FELTON, HAROLD W., ed. *Cowboy Jamboree: Western Songs and Lore,* music arr. by Edward S. Breck, ill. by Aldren A. Watson, foreword by Carl Carmer. Knopf, 1951. This small collection of only twenty songs is especially valuable because of the little introductions to each song. 6-

FERRIS, HELEN, comp. *Love's Enchantment,* ill. by Vera Bock. Doubleday, 1944. Romantic ballads, a collection especially popular with girls. 12-

LONGFELLOW, HENRY WADSWORTH. *Paul Revere's Ride,* ill. by Paul Galdone. Crowell, 1963. Illustrations in rich color capture the somber beauty of the night and the colonial countryside. 8-

MALCOLMSON, ANNE, ed. *Song of Robin Hood,* music arr. by Grace Castagnetta, ill. by Virginia Burton. Houghton, 1947. A collector's item, this beautiful book is invaluable as a source both for ballad text and music. 12-

MANNING-SANDERS, RUTH, ed. *A Bundle of Ballads,* ill. by William Stobbs. Lippincott, 1961. More than sixty traditional ballads, varied in mood and theme, introduce children to an absorbing poetic form. Given England's Kate Greenaway Award in 1959. 12-

MOORE, CLEMENT CLARK. *The Night Before Christmas,* ill. by Arthur Rackham. Lippincott, 1954. A new edition with Rackham's lovely pictures. 4-7

———. *The Night Before Christmas,* ill. by Leonard Weisgard. Grosset, 1949. Bold, bright colors and design characterize this big modern edition. 4-7

PARKER, ELINOR, comp. *100 Story Poems,* ill. by Henry C. Pitz. Crowell, 1951. All the favorite old story-poems are here. 8-14

———. comp. *100 More Story Poems,* ill. by Peter Spier. Crowell, 1960.

RITCHIE, JEAN. *The Swapping Song Book,* ill. with photographs by George Pickow. Walck, 1952. All ages

SEEGER, RUTH CRAWFORD. *American Folk Songs for Children: In Home, School and Nursery School,* ill. by Barbara Cooney. Doubleday, 1948. Contains an introduction for parents, songs and fun for everyone. Some of the ballads are of European origin, others seem to be native. 4-

———. *American Folk Songs for Christmas,* ill. by Barbara Cooney. Doubleday, 1953.

———. *Animal Folk Songs For Children: Traditional American Songs,* ill. by Barbara Cooney. Doubleday, 1950. An interesting introduction discussing our native animal folklore. Songs and illustrations are excellent. 4-

———, ed. *Let's Build a Railroad,* ill. by Tom Funk. Dutton, 1954. 4-9

SPIER, PETER, ill. *The Fox Went Out on a Chilly Night.* Doubleday, 1961. The old folk song enjoys a handsome picture-book setting of New England at harvest time. Illustrations in color and music appended. 5-

WIBBERLEY, LEONARD. *The Ballad of the Pilgrim Cat,* ill. by Erik Blegvad. Washburn, 1962. A lively tale of a stowaway Mayflower cat. 11-

chapter 6

Poetry of the Child's World: Nonsense and Everyday

In this chapter we consider poetry of the child's world, from nonsense and humorous verse by writers such as Edward Lear and A. A. Milne to more serious poems about the child's everyday experiences, observations, and feelings by writers such as Robert Louis Stevenson and Elizabeth Madox Roberts.*

The gay tradition of nonsense verse for children was given a rousing start by *Mother Goose*'s rhymes. Children enjoy these amusing jingles, and most adults find a lifelong source of fun in humorous limericks and verse. Nonsense verses may not represent the highest level of poetry, but they serve some useful ends in the child's personal and literary development.

Values of Nonsense Verse

RELEASE FROM TENSIONS

It is good for us to laugh. Someone has said that a teacher should count the day lost when her children have not, at one time or another, thrown back their heads and laughed spontaneously and heartily. This unknown philosopher should have added that teachers and parents need this release also; for a hearty laugh provides just that—a release from all the miserable little tensions that have gradually crept up on us and tied us in hard knots. We say that we are "weak with laughter," which means that our knots are untied, we are relaxed once more. If nonsense verse can provide such a release, blessed be nonsense!

Not all people and not all ages are amused by the same jokes. Two-year-olds may chuckle

* Many of the poems discussed but not reprinted in this book may be found in the anthology *Time for Poetry*, General Edition, compiled by May Hill Arbuthnot. The Bibliography (p. 214) will also help you locate any poems not reprinted here. See the Index for poems printed in other chapters of this book.

over the hissing *s*'s of "sing a song of sixpence." The hilarity of older children is roused by other forms of humor. Just listen to seven-year-olds enjoying Laura Richards' "Eletelephony." And try reading this traditional poem to the twelve-year-olds:

Whistle, Whistle[1]

"Whistle, whistle, old wife, and you'll get a hen."
"I wouldn't whistle," said the wife, "if you could give me ten!"

"Whistle, whistle, old wife, and you'll get a cock."
"I wouldn't whistle," said the wife, "if you gave me a flock!"

"Whistle, whistle, old wife, and you'll get a coo."
"I wouldn't whistle," said the wife, "if you could give me two!"

"Whistle, whistle, old wife, and you'll get a gown."
"I wouldn't whistle," said the wife, "for the best one in the town!"

"Whistle, whistle, old wife, and you'll get a man."
"Wheeple, whauple," said the wife, "I'll whistle if I can!"

RELIEF FROM REASON

The grotesque and the incongruous, which make up the content of nonsense verse, provide needed escape from the weight of the realistic and the reasonable. "The Jumblies" go to sea in a sieve and have a successful voyage instead of being properly drowned for their folly. The cow jumps over the moon and apparently her milk doesn't even curdle. The world of nonsense is a gay, exuberant world of irresponsible behavior and impossible results. It affords an innocent escape from gravity.

GOOD EAR-TRAINING

Humorous verse, if it is skillfully composed, introduces the child to rhyme, rhythm, and meter and to various types of verse patterns. The neatly turned limerick and the patter of humorous couplets or quatrains in exact meter train the ear to enjoy the sound of words and rhythms, a training that should carry over to catching similar sound patterns in poetry of a higher order.

BAIT TO BETTER POETRY

Sometimes children's first experience with poetry is made painful for them by too much analysis or by poems expressing adult moods or emotions.

One small boy admitted that he liked all kinds of books except books of poetry. The other boys in his group agreed with him. The consensus was that poetry is always "kind-a queer." They had other words for it, too, words that ran the gamut of their slang expressions for peculiar. With these boys the wise adult tried some humorous poems and promptly won their surprised attention and approval. After they had laughed, they admitted that funny poems weren't so bad. By the time their funny poems had progressed from the broadly nonsensical to a somewhat more subtle type of humor, their suspicions were broken down, and after some stirring narrative poems, they were ready to go further. In short, humorous verse is good introductory material to rouse interest in poetry and to allay the suspicion that poetry is always highbrow and peculiar.

Four Poets of Nonsense Verse

EDWARD LEAR, 1812-1888

The Book of Nonsense
Nonsense Songs and Stories

After *Mother Goose,* Edward Lear is chronologically the first poet to conjure up laughter. From the time *The Book of Nonsense* ap-

1. From *Choral Verse Speaking* by Elizabeth M. Keppie. Used by permission of the Expression Company.

peared in 1846, children and adults have been chuckling over Lear's limericks and verse-stories. Glancing at a chronology of poets who have contributed to the verse children enjoy, you will discover the hymns and moralistic maxims of Isaac Watts, the lyrics of William Blake, and the gentle moralizing of Ann and Jane Taylor—all before Lear's jingles, but there was no nonsense verse.

In England, about 1820, several small books of limericks appeared, the first of which, *Anecdotes and Adventures of Fifteen Gentlemen,* Lear probably read, because in his introduction to *More Nonsense* he writes:

> *Long years ago, in days when much of my time was passed in a country house where children and mirth abounded, the lines beginning "There was an old man of Tobago" were suggested to me by a valued friend as a form of verse lending itself to limitless variety for rhymes and pictures; and thenceforth the greater part of the original drawings and verses for the first* Book of Nonsense *were struck off with a pen, no assistance ever having been given me in any way but that of uproarious delight and welcome at the appearance of every new absurdity.*

> *There was an Old Man of Tobago,*
> *Lived long on rice gruel and sago;*
> *But at last, to his bliss,*
> *The physician said this—*
> *To a roast leg of mutton you may go.*

These were the lines that set Lear to writing some of the most famous nonsense in the English language and illustrating it with sketches so amusing that a Lear limerick without the Lear drawing is only half as funny as the two together. (See 4, p. 135.) Lear's own life and personality also gave impetus to his writing and drawing sheer nonsense. Older children, to whom most of Lear's verse belongs, will enjoy knowing something about him.

Edward Lear was one of twenty-one children, most of whom died in childhood or early youth. He was a pale, sickly child beset by an illness that he referred to all his life as the "Terrible Demon," a mild form of epilepsy. While he never allowed his illness to prevent him from doing anything he wished to do, we can readily imagine that it served as a stimulus to all sorts of activities that would help him forget it.

As a little boy, Lear knew the security of wealth. Then at thirteen he suffered the shock of seeing house, footmen, twelve carriages, and all the other luxuries disappear as if by magic. His father was imprisoned for debt and his mother plunged into poverty and anxiety. Eventually all the debts were paid, but by that time the family had scattered: the boys had left England, several of the girls had died, and the others had married except Lear's beloved Ann. This sister, twenty-one years older than Edward, raised the delicate little boy from the time he was a baby. He was more like her son than little brother, and when misfortune came to the family, Ann took Edward as her special responsibility and shared with him the small legacy that provided her with a modest living. By fifteen Lear was beginning to earn money with sketching. When he was in London he made scientific drawings for doctors, and when he was in the country he perfected his technique of drawing birds, butterflies, and flowers in the most minute detail. It was this latter skill that brought him an appointment to make drawings of the parrots at the zoo in Regent's Park. From the time of the publication of the book on parrots, with Lear's large colored drawings, his reputation as an artist was established, and he later prepared the drawings for another large volume, *Tortoises, Terrapins and Turtles.* It was while Lear was at work on the parrots that the Earl of Derby discovered him and invited the young artist to come down to his country estate and make drawings of his collection of birds and animals.

During his stay with this family (he was eventually employed by four Earls of Derby) he began the nonsense verses, and Lear the artist became also Lear the humorist.

Lear himself gives us a clue to this change. He sometimes grew a little tired of the formal gatherings to which he was subjected in the Earl's household and, as he wrote to a friend:

> *The uniform apathetic tone assumed by lofty society irks me* dreadfully; *nothing I long for half so much as to giggle heartily and to hop on one leg down the great gallery—but I dare not.*

So instead of giggling and hopping on one leg, Lear evidently took refuge with the innumerable grandchildren of the Earl. They adored him, and the Earl presently discovered that all the children on the place followed this serious-looking but irrepressibly gay young artist as if he were the Pied Piper. It was to these children that Lear must have shown his limericks as he produced them—limericks and sketches that were published in 1846 as the first *Book of Nonsense.* For Lear himself, writing them must have been great fun. They were a rest from those painstakingly detailed scientific drawings; they were a safe release for the high spirits and childlike mischief of the man who wanted to hop on one leg through the halls of the great; and, above all, they must have been a blessed escape from the illness which pursued but never conquered him.

The first book contained only limericks, and these became so famous it is sometimes erroneously assumed that Lear invented the form. Although he did not invent the limerick, he certainly became a master of its neat form and surprising content.

Narrative Poems

The second book, *Nonsense Songs and Stories,* published in 1871, includes a variety of humorous verses, among them the pseudoserious narrative poems that seem all the funnier because they are gravely told. Every generation of five- and six-year-olds delights in "The Owl and the Pussy-Cat," that begins:

The Owl and the Pussy-Cat went to sea
In a beautiful pea-green boat;
They took some honey, and plenty of money,
Wrapped up in a five-pound note.
The Owl looked up to the stars above,
And sang to a small guitar,
"O lovely Pussy! O Pussy, my love,
What a beautiful Pussy you are,
You are,
You are!
What a beautiful Pussy you are!"

Two sparkling editions of this single poem appeared in 1961 and 1962—*Le Hibou et la Poussiquette,* translated into French by Francis Steegmuller and illustrated by Barbara Cooney; and *The Owl and the Pussy-Cat,* illustrated by William Pène du Bois. The French poussiquette is a languishing siren. Mr. du Bois' feline is a bit flinty. Both are hilarious.

Another favorite with older children is "The Jumblies." The reason we like this wild crew is that we are sure we, too, have known Jumblies who set off to sea in a sieve and then triumphantly came home to look down their noses at all their cautious friends who never trusted sieves. Like most of Lear's narrative jingles, it seems overlong, and so the third and fourth verses may be omitted if you read it to children. The poem "The Duck and the Kangaroo," together with Lear's drawings, is popular with children from six years old to sixteen. It is characteristic Lear nonsense, merrily imagined and deftly written, and should be read with mock gravity.

The Duck and the Kangaroo

Said the Duck to the Kangaroo,
"Good gracious! how you hop!
Over the fields, and the water too,
As if you never would stop!
My life is a bore in this nasty pond,
And I long to go out in the world beyond!
I wish I could hop like you!"
Said the Duck to the Kangaroo.

"Please give me a ride on your back!"
Said the Duck to the Kangaroo.
"I would sit quite still, and say nothing but 'Quack,'
The whole of the long day through!
And we'd go to the Dee, and the Jelly Bo Lee,
Over the land, and over the sea;—
Please take me a ride! O do!"
Said the Duck to the Kangaroo.

Said the Kangaroo to the Duck,
"This requires some little reflection;
Perhaps on the whole it might bring me luck;
And there seems but one objection,
Which is, if you'll let me speak so bold,
Your feet are unpleasantly wet and cold,
And would probably give me the roo—
Matiz!" said the Kangaroo.

Said the Duck, "As I sate on the rocks,
I have thought over that completely,
And I bought four pairs of worsted socks,

1.

3.

2.

These three pictures are quite different and each is wonderful in its own way. Leslie Brooke's characterization is of two gay creatures stepping out for a big time; notice the disapproving onlookers. Barbara Cooney's pictures for the French translation are completely romantic; Owl is large and masculine, Pussy-Cat is small and languorous. Notice the elegant details of the spoon handle, the wine bottle and stem glasses, Pussy's head wreathed in flowers. William Pène du Bois' interpretation of the poem is different but equally charming. Here we have two daft characters who don't quite trust one another in a wild dance by the light of the moon.

1. Illustration by Leslie Brooke. From Nonsense Songs *by Edward Lear. Published and copyrighted by Frederick Warne & Co., Inc. Reproduced with the permission of the publishers. (Book 6¾ x 8¼)*

2. Illustration by Barbara Cooney. From Le Hibou et la Poussiquette *by Edward Lear, trans. by Francis Steegmuller. Illustration copyright © 1961 by Barbara Cooney. Reprinted by permission of Little, Brown and Company. (Book 6⅛ x 8⅜)*

3. Illustration by William Pène du Bois. From The Owl and the Pussy-Cat *by Edward Lear. Illustration copyright © 1962 by William Pène du Bois. Reproduced with permission of Doubleday and Company. (Book 5 x 7¼)*

Which fit my web-feet neatly;
And to keep out the cold I've bought a cloak,
And every day a cigar I'll smoke,
All to follow my own dear true
Love of a Kangaroo!"

Said the Kangaroo, "I'm ready!
All in the moonlight pale;
But to balance me well, dear Duck, sit steady!
And quite at the end of my tail."
So away they went with a hop and a bound,
And they hopped the whole world three times round;
And who so happy,—O who,
As the Duck and the Kangaroo?

Made-up Words

Lear's made-up words are one of the most obvious sources of amusement in these jingles. You find the Pobble who has no toes, the Quangle Wangle with the beaver hat, and the amorous Yonghy-Bonghy Bò. There's a Crumpetty Tree and a Dong with a Luminous Nose, and in the Torrible Zone you can get bottles of ring-bo-ree. The words in Lear's five different sets of alphabet rhymes are mostly of this tongue-twister variety. Of these five alphabet rhymes, none is better than the one that begins

A *was once an apple-pie,*
Pidy,
Widy,
Tidy,
Pidy,
Nice insidy,
Apple-pie!

B *was once a little bear,*
Beary,
Wary,
Hairy,
Beary,
Taky cary,
Little bear!

C *was once a little cake,*
Caky,
Baky,
Maky,
Caky,
Taky caky,
Little cake!

Singing Quality

Lear is an excellent craftsman. His meters are exact, his rhymes neat and musical, and his verse has a pleasant sound even at its wildest. Much of it is decidedly melodious. Undoubtedly part of the appeal of "The Owl and the Pussy-Cat" for young children is its melody. They chant it happily and linger over the refrains.

Lear's Caricatures

Children like the ridiculous and eccentric characters in these verses and are especially entertained by the mad troop that populates the limericks.

There was an Old Man with a beard,
Who said, "It is just as I feared!—
Two Owls and a Hen,
Four Larks and a Wren,
Have all built their nests in my beard!"

There was an Old Man in a tree,
Who was horribly bored by a Bee;
When they said, "Does it buzz?"
He replied, "Yes, it does!
It's a regular brute of a bee!"

There was a Young Lady of Norway,
Who casually sat in a doorway;
When the door squeezed her flat,
She exclaimed, "What of that?"
This courageous Young Lady of Norway.

Over and over Edward Lear caricatured himself with words and with sketches which must have convulsed his friends, both juvenile and adult. In a note protesting his inability to keep an engagement because, "Disgustical to say," he had a cold in his head, he added these words with an accompanying picture:

I have sent for 2 large tablecloths to blow my nose on, having already used up all my handkerchiefs. And altogether I am so unfit for company that I propose getting into a bag and being hung up to a bough of a tree till this tyranny is overpast.[2]

Another portrait of himself dancing, together with the poem beginning "How pleasant to

2. *The Complete Nonsense Book,* pp. 13-14.

know Mr. Lear!" might be a good way of introducing Lear to children.

LEWIS CARROLL, 1832-1898

Alice's Adventures in Wonderland
Through the Looking-Glass

In 1865 appeared the delightful and astonishing book *Alice's Adventures in Wonderland* by one Lewis Carroll, who was none other than Charles Lutwidge Dodgson, an Oxford don and a mathematician. The book was several degrees wilder than Lear's books at their wildest. There was the Duchess with her amazing advice:

"Speak roughly to your little boy,
And beat him when he sneezes:
He only does it to annoy,
Because he knows it teases."

CHORUS

"Wow! wow! wow!"

There was the gibberish poem, "Jabberwocky," which Alice found in the looking-glass book. Even Alice found it "*rather* hard to understand."

'Twas brillig, and the slithy toves
Did gyre and gimble in the wabe:
All mimsy were the borogoves,
And the mome raths outgrabe.

"Beware the Jabberwock, my son!
The jaws that bite, the claws that catch!
Beware the Jubjub bird, and shun
The frumious Bandersnatch!"

There were "You are old, Father William," "How doth the little crocodile," and many other nonsense verses interspersed throughout the prose of *Alice's Adventures in Wonderland* and later *Through the Looking-Glass.* To quote them is a temptation, but the fact is that these rhymes are much funnier in their context than they are apart from it. For this reason, Lewis Carroll will be considered later in this book, not merely as a writer of humorous verse, but as the author of one of the greatest fantasies ever written. The full flavor of his humor is in most cases best appreciated by boys and girls in their early teens rather than by younger children. For example, read "Father William" (see illustration 1, p. 156):

"You are old, Father William," the young man said,
"And your hair has become very white;
And yet you incessantly stand on your head—
Do you think, at your age, it is right?"

"In my youth," Father William replied to his son,
"I feared it might injure the brain;
But, now that I'm perfectly sure I have none,
Why, I do it again and again."

"You are old," said the youth, "as I mentioned before,
And have grown most uncommonly fat;
Yet you turned a back-somersault in at the door—
Pray, what is the reason of that?"

"In my youth," said the sage, as he shook his grey locks,
"I kept all my limbs very supple
By the use of this ointment—one shilling the box—
Allow me to sell you a couple?"

"You are old," said the youth, "and your jaws are too weak
For anything tougher than suet;
Yet you finished the goose, with the bones and the beak—
Pray, how did you manage to do it?"

"In my youth," said his father, "I took to the law,
And argued each case with my wife;
And the muscular strength, which it gave to my jaw,
Has lasted the rest of my life."

"You are old," said the youth, "one would hardly suppose
That your eye was as steady as ever;
Yet you balanced an eel on the end of your nose—
What made you so awfully clever?"

"I have answered three questions, and that is
enough,"
Said his father. "Don't give yourself airs!
Do you think I can listen all day to such stuff?
Be off, or I'll kick you down-stairs!"

Certainly Carroll gave the "gay nineties" a good start on their gaiety. And the gaiety was further increased by the operas of Gilbert and Sullivan, operas whose lyrics were chanted by adults in England and America, and were also taken over by the children. The satiric conversation in *H.M.S. Pinafore* between the boastful Captain, the "Ruler of the Queen's Navee," and the skeptical chorus has become a byword for all boasters.

Captain *For I'm never, never sick at sea!*
Chorus *What, never?*
Captain *No, never.*
Chorus *What, never?*
Captain *Well,—hardly ever!*

LAURA E. RICHARDS, 1850-1943

Tirra Lirra; Rhymes Old and New

Laura E. Richards, who is known as the American Poet Laureate of Nonsense for Children, came from an American home of unusual distinction and in turn added her unique contribution to its distinction. Her father was Samuel Gridley Howe, who devoted himself to such diverse social causes as the Greek War for Independence, the education of the blind, and the founding of the first school for feebleminded children. Her mother, the beautiful and gifted Julia Ward Howe, author of "The Battle Hymn of the Republic," was not only a poet but an excellent musician who "knew all the songs in the world," or so her children thought. Mrs. Howe sang to them in three languages, and she made a special song for each child.

Laura grew up with her brother and three sisters in a house called Green Peace. The children shared the family heritage of music, poetry, and wide interests, together with the companionship of happy, intelligent adults. It is not surprising that the children in turn scribbled stories and poetry and were bubbling over with ideas and fun. It was not, however, until after she was married and living once more in Green Peace with her own children that Laura thought much about writing. Then, remembering her own delight in her mother's songs, she, too, began to sing to her children. First she sang the old ballads she knew so well. Then she found herself making up her own ditties, just as her mother had done, probably because she could adapt them to the special demands of the child in her lap or at her knee. In her book, *Stepping Westward,* she tells about these songs. In the four years that saw the birth of her first three children (there were seven in all), she writes that she enjoyed

. . . contemporary with these births, the acquisition of my hurdy-gurdy . . . I had always rhymed easily; now . . . came a prodigious welling up of rhymes, mostly bringing their tunes (or what passed for tunes; the baby, bless it, knew no better!) with them. I wrote, and sang, and wrote, and could not stop. The first baby was plump and placid, with a broad, smooth back which made an excellent writing desk. She lay on her front, across my lap; I wrote on her back, the writing pad quite as steady as the writing of jingles required.

No wonder these "jingles" of Laura Richards have a spontaneity and a freshness that are only equaled by their lyric quality. Nor are we surprised to find that at eighty-one her "hurdy-gurdy" was still turning furiously, reeling out as delightful ditties for the third generation of babies as for the first.

It was Mrs. Richards' husband who suggested that she send some of her verses to the new magazine for children, *St. Nicholas,* and this she did. From then on, stories and poems came from her flying pen at an amazing rate. There was the long series known as the *Hildegarde* books, which were tremendously popular with an earlier generation but are somewhat dated now. *Captain January* told the story of a baby rescued from the sea and raised by a good old lighthouse keeper. Mrs. Richards' biographies are still read. They include such appealing heroines as *Elizabeth Fry, Florence Nightingale,* and *Joan of Arc.* Between stories and biographies, the verses continued to "bubble up" with undiminished charm. But it wasn't until 1932 that a book of her verses, called *Tirra Lirra; Rhymes Old and New,* was published—a book which she dedicated to her youngest grandchild and her eldest great-grandchild.

Funny Words

Mrs. Richards' verses abound in humorous, made-up words. Lear gave us "meloobious" and "torrible," and Carroll presented us with "galumphing," "beamish," "frabjious," and "whiffling," but Mrs. Richards matches them with "Muffin Bird," "Rummyjums," "bogothy-bogs," "Lolloping Lizard," "a Glimmering Glog," and those remarkable museum specimens, "Wiggledywasticums" and "Ptoodle-cumtumsdyl." Moreover, no one can play with words with more joyous confusion than she. Children from five to any age chuckle over

Eletelephony[3]

Once there was an elephant,
Who tried to use the telephant—
No! no! I mean an elephone
Who tried to use the telephone—
(Dear me! I am not certain quite
That even now I've got it right.)

Howe'er it was, he got his trunk
Entangled in the telephunk;
The more he tried to get it free,
The louder buzzed the telephee—
(I fear I'd better drop the song
Of elephop and telephong!)

Like "Eletelephony," "Some Fishy Nonsense," "Doggerel," "The Poor Unfortunate Hottentot," "Sir Ringleby Rose," and many others of Mrs. Richards' jingles depend for their fun upon this juggling with words.

Verse Stories

Mrs. Richards carries her fun beyond mere play with words. She has, in addition to the verse-maker's skill, the dramatic art of a first-rate storyteller. The gentle tale of "Little John Bottlejohn," lured away by a cajoling mermaid; the gory record of "The Seven Little Tigers and the Aged Cook" (see illustration 2, p. 134); the exciting "The Monkeys and the Crocodile"—these and a dozen others depend for their interest upon the skillful storytelling of the author as well as upon her irrepressible sense of the absurd. For example, here is the melodious

Little John Bottlejohn

Little John Bottlejohn lived on the hill,
And a blithe little man was he.
And he won the heart of a pretty mermaid
Who lived in the deep blue sea.
And every evening she used to sit
And sing on the rocks by the sea,
"Oh! little John Bottlejohn, pretty John Bottlejohn,
Won't you come out to me?"

Little John Bottlejohn heard her song,
And he opened his little door.
And he hopped and he skipped, and he skipped and he hopped,
Until he came down to the shore.
And there on the rocks sat the little mermaid,
And still she was singing so free,
"Oh! little John Bottlejohn, pretty John Bottlejohn,
Won't you come out to me?"

Little John Bottlejohn made a bow,
And the mermaid, she made one too;
And she said, "Oh! I never saw any one half
So perfectly sweet as you!
In my lovely home 'neath the ocean foam,
How happy we both might be!
Oh! little John Bottlejohn, pretty John Bottlejohn,
Won't you come down with me?"

Little John Bottlejohn said, "Oh yes!
I'll willingly go with you.
And I never shall quail at the sight of your tail,
For perhaps I may grow one too."
So he took her hand, and he left the land,
And plunged in the foaming main.
And little John Bottlejohn, pretty John Bottlejohn,
Never was seen again.

3. "Eletelephony" and the following poems: "Little John Bottlejohn," "Mrs. Snipkin and Mrs. Wobblechin," "The Umbrella Brigade." From *Tirra Lirra* by Laura E. Richards.

Mrs. Richards relates incongruous and surprising events with a convincing air of reality that heightens their humor. Little John Bottlejohn, for instance, seems to be a real person. He lives on a hill, he is a blithe little man, he hops and skips down his hill, he is a mannerly person with his courteous bow, but alas! he *will* talk to mermaids! The aged cook, who cooks for the seven little tigers, seems to be a harmless, mild old thing, and we are therefore doubly amazed when he hauls out his knife and cuts off the head of the tiger who intended to do the same for him. "My Uncle Jehoshaphat," who had a swimming race with his piggywig and divided the prize, might indeed be "*my*" uncle, so plausible he seems.

Absurd Characters and Situations

Mrs. Richards' absurd characters and situations are also a source of amusement for the children. They invariably chuckle when they hear the account of the quarrel between

Mrs. Snipkin and Mrs. Wobblechin

Skinny Mrs. Snipkin,
With her little pipkin,
Sat by the fireside a-warming of her toes.
Fat Mrs. Wobblechin,
With her little doublechin,
Sat by the window a-cooling of her nose.

Says this one to that one,
"Oh! you silly fat one,
Will you shut the window down? You're freezing me to death!"
Says that one to t'other one,
"Good gracious, how you bother one!
There isn't air enough for me to draw my precious breath!"

Skinny Mrs. Snipkin,
Took her little pipkin,
Threw it straight across the room as hard as she could throw;
Hit Mrs. Wobblechin
On her little doublechin,
And out of the window a-tumble she did go.

And little children, even four- and five-year-olds, feel superior when they giggle understandingly over the blunders of the two dogs "Jippy and Jimmy." The older children who know Kipling's "yellow dog Dingo" will also appreciate the ridiculous plight of "Bingo the Dingo," who fell in love with the "fatally fair flamingo." The funny situations in *Tirra Lirra* are laugh provoking, even without the funny words.

Lyrical Quality

Mrs. Richards has caught in her verses some of the singing quality of words that children enjoy. For example, "A Song for Hal," "A Legend of Lake Okeefinokee," "Little John Bottlejohn," "The Song of the Corn-Popper," "Talents Differ," "Will-o'-the-Wisp," and "Prince Tatters" are lyrics that almost sing themselves. To test this quality, read aloud the chorus of "The Umbrella Brigade":

But let it rain,
Tree-toads and frogs,
Muskets and pitchforks,
Kittens and dogs!
Dash away! plash away!
Who is afraid?
Here we go,
The Umbrella Brigade!

This lyric quality not only gives distinction to Mrs. Richards' most extravagant nonsense but makes children more sensitive to the musical qualities of words.

LESLIE BROOKE, 1862-1940

Johnny Crow's Garden
Johnny Crow's Party

Young children, four to six, are fortunate if they are introduced to their first nonsense after *Mother Goose* through the Johnny Crow books. Leslie Brooke always loved the stories about Johnny Crow, which his father, a novelist, used to tell him, and so when he grew up and had two sons of his own, he also made up stories about Johnny Crow. At his wife's suggestion he translated this genial bird into pictures and verse, and in 1903 published *Johnny Crow's Garden,* which he dedicated to his sons. A few years later came *Johnny Crow's Party,* but some thirty years passed before *Johnny Crow's New Garden* appeared, dedicated to young Peter Brooke, a grandson. These three books would amuse small children of any generation. The mannerly Johnny Crow himself, the "preposserous rhinoserous," the cow and the sow who sing "Squeal and Low"—these and other friendly beasts come and go with grave absurdity through the pages of the three picture books.

Children are great sticklers for details, and they find no slips in these books. Each animal runs true to form and costume through innumerable adventures. The lion in *Johnny Crow's New Garden* is even wearing the same necktie he wore to the first garden party thirty years before.

It seems a pity for today's children to miss the Johnny Crow books, but, sad to relate, they have almost vanished from juvenile bookshelves in the United States. Perhaps the language and the humor are too subtle or too British. More likely the books have disappeared because mothers and fathers don't know them or, if they do, don't take time to talk over and savor the jokes with the small children for whom they were intended. Good manners, though, are exemplified by Johnny Crow, the perfect host, and by the appreciative guests. In these famous picture books Leslie Brooke has created a choice array of illustrations and nonsense rhymes for children.

From Nonsense to Humor

Although no hard and fast line divides humor from sheer nonsense, there is, nevertheless, a difference. Nonsense is more daft, more impossible, with Pobbles, Jumblies, potatoes that dance, chickens that go out to tea, gargoyles and griffins—a wild crew close kin to the "cow that jumped over the moon." Humorous verse, on the other hand, deals with the amusing things that befall real people, or might conceivably befall them. Edward Lear and Laura E. Richards sometimes wrote humorous verse, but for the most part their verse is hilarious nonsense. In contrast, A. A. Milne wrote occasional nonsense, but on the whole his poems involve people and situations that are amusingly possible, however improbable they may be.

A. A. MILNE, 1882-1956

When We Were Very Young
Now We Are Six

A pleasant way to meet A. A. Milne is to read his *Autobiography*. This book contains more than the life of an author. It is a series of significant reminiscences of a man who not only enjoyed his own childhood but had a rare understanding of children. The opening paragraph is characteristic:

> *'Once upon a time there was a man who had three sons'—this was how we began, this was how the fairy stories began. And as our governess read them aloud to their inevitable end, Barry looked at Ken, and the two of them looked at Alan, and I looked as little complacent as I could, knowing that the third son was the good one, yet in a way sorry that his character was so blameless, his destiny so assured. Perhaps, after all, the others would get more fun out of life. In another moment Barry would be turned into a toadstool, and Ken into a two-headed bear; interesting, interesting; but the third son would only kill the same old dragon and come into the same old Kingdom, just as he had done a hundred times before. Oh, to be Barry or Ken for once, to miss this easy good-fortune by the simple and attractive method of being rude to a godmother, how exciting that would be!*[4]

Mr. Milne goes on to tell us that his mother, usually so competent and practical in most matters, *would* dress the three brothers like Little Lord Fauntleroys and keep their

4. Copyright 1939 by A. A. Milne. Reprinted by permission of the publishers, E. P. Dutton & Co., Inc., New York.

blond curls long. He testifies that old ladies instinctively adored them, and boys yearned to kick them. His father, to compensate for this, determined that they should be manly souls at all costs, and the boys were hard pressed to maintain their "manliness" with the handicap of floating curls.

Milne's father, the head of the first school the boys attended, was evidently a born teacher. A walk with him meant learning about caterpillars or the law of gravity, or doing fascinating problems. Here, evidently, was no dull pedant, because grown-up Alan testifies that he learned what his father taught and failed to learn what others taught. He recalls his brothers' and his great delight in the books their father read aloud to them. They loved *Uncle Remus* when their father read it and could not abide the sound of it when the nurse took it over. They found *Pilgrim's Progress* a thriller even though they suspected it was meant to be uplifting. Anything they did with their father they enjoyed.

After Cambridge, where Milne disappointed his father by coming out only third in mathematics instead of first, the two of them faced the fact that writing was the one thing Alan wished to do. With £320 he went to London and began writing a thousand words a day, sending his finished pieces to various magazines. By the end of the second year he was supporting himself, and the third year he was appointed assistant editor of *Punch* with an assured income and the chance to increase it. He was just twenty-four years old.

Financially secure, he married and had just started writing plays when the first World War came. He wrote of the needless brutality of war with understandable bitterness, but he managed to keep on writing and actually produced three plays during his years in service.

After the war, a son was born to the Milnes—Christopher Robin. As soon as he could talk he gave himself the name of "Billy Moon," and "Moon" he was called by everyone. For this reason, Milne explains, the name "Christopher Robin" always seemed to belong entirely to the public's little boy, not to his own.

At the time Milne was writing plays and other adult literature, he gave his wife a verse about Christopher Robin—"Vespers"—which she sent off to a magazine and which was accepted for publication. Then Rose Fyleman, who was publishing a magazine for children, asked Milne to contribute some children's verses. At first he firmly refused but finally changed his mind and sent them after all. When both the editor and the illustrator advised him to write a whole book of verses, he felt it was a foolish thing to do, but again he complied. He had, he said, as preparation for the task, three years of living with his son and "unforgettable memories of my own childhood." The result was *When We Were Very Young,* a major sensation in children's books both in England and America. It shares with the second book, *Now We Are Six,* an undiminishing popularity year after year. Milne's plays are amusing, but it is probable that Milne's reputation as a writer will rest more securely upon his two books of verse for children and his two books of stories about Pooh than upon any of his adult stories and dramas.

Knowledge of Children

Milne had a remarkable ability of presenting small children as they are. He gives us their bemused absorption in their private inner world of make-believe, their blithe egotism, their liking for small animals, their toys and games, and the peculiar angle from which they view the odd behavior of those adults who move vaguely on the fringe of their private world.

Christopher Robin speaks for the make-believe of children around four to six years old. His imaginative world is not peopled with the fairies of the eight-year-old but is just the everyday sort of play of the nursery age. One chair is South America and another is a lion's cage. When walking with his nurse becomes just too stale, flat, and unprofitable to be endured, Christopher scares himself into a pleasant spinal chill by imagining that bears are skulking around the corner and are watching his approach with a sinister smacking of the lips. This is characteristic play for a solitary child. So, too, are his imaginary companions. There is Binker, visible only to Christopher Robin, and there is the omnipresent Pooh, who appears both in the poems and in the prose adventures.

Much has been written about the egocentricity of the young child's thought and language, but it has never been recorded more accurately than by A. A. Milne. Christopher Robin goes to the market looking for a rabbit and is naïvely astonished that the market men should be selling mackerel and fresh lavender when *he*, Christopher Robin, wants rabbits. He catalogues his articles of clothing, fascinating because they are his. You can hear the smug emphasis on the personal pronoun. Changing the guard at Buckingham may be very impressive, but the child's only concern is, "Do you think the King knows all about Me?" This is a typical four-year-old, thinking and speaking of everything in terms of himself—an amusing and endearing little egotist!

Knowing children's interests, Milne reflects them in his writing. There we find the child's love of small animals: dormice, rabbits, puppies, snails, and goats, whose antics and vicissitudes enliven the verses. Toys are there, too —balls, tops, hoops, and the beloved teddy bear. The verses are full of the small child's activities, also. He walks, rolls, and plays. He gets sand between his toes. He stalks down the sidewalk missing all the lines. He sits on the stairs and meditates, or he goes hoppitty, hoppitty, hop. He enjoys complete happiness when he gets his mackintosh and waterproof boots on. He sometimes refuses rice pudding (or rather Mary Jane does), and he often resents foolish adult questions. On the whole, he is a busy, active child, immersed in his own affairs and oblivious of any world beyond his own horizon.

The readers soon realize that Christopher Robin is an only child. "Mummy" and "Daddy" are there, and Nana, the nurse, chaperones his every walk, but where are the other children? There are Mary Jane and John of the waterproof boots and Emmeline, whose hands are "purfickly clean," but these, too, are lone children with only supervising adults in the offing. None of these children plays with other children. There are no brothers or sisters or even neighbors' children, but neither Christopher Robin nor the young readers of these verses seem to miss them. Perhaps because the young child is so astonishingly egocentric and lives so completely within a world of his own, these verses that speak understandingly of one child speak adequately for all children alone or in groups.

Technique

Again we find, as in the poetry of all these humorists, a juggling with funny words: "sneezles and freezles," foxes who didn't wear "sockses," "biffalo-buffalo-bisons," "badgers and bidgers and bodgers," and a mouse with a "woffelly nose." The children seize upon them as their very own, for these words are exactly what they might have said. If you study Milne's funny words, you discover that they fall within the range of the child's own vocabulary. Here we find no "fatally fair flamingo" of the older child's level, but the measles and "sneezles" that "teasles" the funnybone of the little child because they are all close to words he recognizes.

No one can tell a better tall tale for children than Alan Alexander Milne. For examples, read "The King's Breakfast," "Disobedience," "Teddy Bear," "The Dormouse and the Doctor," and perhaps "Bad Sir Brian Botany." Some boys were convinced that they detested all "pomes," but, after listening to "Disobedience" read aloud several times, they were heard chanting it vociferously. After that, they wanted Milne and more Milne and progressed steadily in their respect and liking for "pomes."

Usually "The King's Breakfast" is the favorite with most Milne addicts. This starts reasonably with the king asking for a little butter on the "Royal slice of bread," and it moves along smoothly until the sleepy Alderney upsets all royal regularity by suggesting "a little marmalade instead." From then on the dialogue becomes entirely daft, reaching a joyous climax when the king bounces out of bed and slides down the banisters. This is, of course, the essence of the fun—the incongruity of a king who is so deeply concerned with marmalade that he whimpers, sulks, bounces, and slides down banisters. The verse pattern of each episode reinforces the mood.

Read Milne's two little books, *When We Were Very Young* and *Now We Are Six*, and you will discover an author who knew how to write verse that dances, skips, meditates, and changes to reflect changing moods.

We can analyze his tripping trochees, his iambics and dactyls, but those academic labels do not seem to convey any idea of the fluid and flashing use Mr. Milne made of words, rhyme, and rhythm to convey character, mood, and action. For example, read "Buckingham Palace" aloud and hear the marching of soldiers in the background throughout those brief descriptions and the whispered conversations of Alice and Christopher. The feet thud, thud, thud through every line. So, too, when Christopher Robin hops through the jingle called "Hoppity," the lines go in exactly the pattern of a child's hop, ending with a big one and a rest, just as hopping always does. But best of all is that juvenile meditation "Halfway Down." Ernest Shepard's sketch, too, has caught the mood of suspended action that is always overtaking small children on stairs. Why they like to clutter up stairs with their belongings and their persons only Mr. Milne knew, and he has told us with arresting monosyllables that block the way as effectually as Christopher Robin's small person blocks the stairs. In this first stanza from "Halfway Down"[5] notice "It" and "Stop," which sit as firmly in the middle of the verse as Christopher on the stair.

Halfway down the stairs
Is a stair
Where I sit.
There isn't any
Other stair
Quite like
It.
I'm not at the bottom,
I'm not at the top;
So this is the stair
Where
I always
Stop.

Over and over again, Mr. Milne makes a monosyllable or a single word equal by sheer intensity three or four words in a preceding line. It is a device that compels correct reading of the lines, regardless of scansion.

With all of these virtues, it is not surprising that some moderns have come to feel that Milne is the child's greatest poet, certainly his favorite poet. This enthusiasm would be harmless enough if it did not apparently curtail exploration of the work of other poets. Delightful as Milne's verses are, they do not cover the full range either of the child's interests or of his capacity for enjoying poetry. Many poets achieve greater lyric beauty, more delicate imagery, and deeper feeling for the child's inner world than A. A. Milne, but certainly we shall never encounter a writer who understood more completely the curious composite of gravity and gaiety, of supreme egotism and occasional whimsy that is the young child.

Illustrations by Ernest H. Shepard

We cannot leave Milne's books without considering the illustrations. Never was an author more happily paired with an artist than A. A. Milne with Ernest Shepard. The tiny pen-and-ink sketches capture the mood of every poem. You have only to glance at one of these tiny figures to know exactly what is happening inwardly as well as outwardly. In "Halfway Down," the small figure is planted in a dreamy, meditative but solid pose that makes you feel just how hard it's going to be to dislodge him. "Puppy and I" skip joyously; and Christopher Robin, looking pained and surprised at the absence of rabbits, catechizes the men in "Market Square." Pooh is there, too, the same solid, jaunty teddy bear we shall meet later on in the Pooh stories. The interpretative quality of these pictures makes them illustrations in the best sense of the word. (See 3, p. 134.)

ROSE FYLEMAN, 1877-1957

Picture Rhymes from Foreign Lands

Although most of Rose Fyleman's poems are dedicated to fairies, she also wrote amusing poems like "Mrs. Brown," "Mice," "The Dentist," or "Mary Middling."

In addition to these nonsense verses found in many anthologies, Rose Fyleman is respon-

5. From *When We Were Very Young,* published and copyrighted by E. P. Dutton & Co., Inc., New York. Copyright 1924.

sible for an international *Mother Goose* called *Picture Rhymes from Foreign Lands,* with translations of nursery rhymes from many countries. It is unfortunate that this treasury of nonsense is out of print, because young children who are exposed to it learn and like the galloping "Husky Hi" as much as they like "Ride a cock horse."

Husky Hi[6]

Husky hi, husky hi,
Here comes Keery galloping by.
She carries her husband tied in a sack,
She carries him home on her horse's back.
Husky hi, husky hi,
Here comes Keery galloping by!

The Dutch "Jonathan Gee" and the French "My Donkey" and "The Goblin" (p. 228) are among the dozen or more favorites. "My Donkey," with its delicate refrain, and the clumping, thumping "Goblin" make a pleasant contrast. Both poems are fine material for verse choirs. Rose Fyleman's musical gifts were never employed to better advantage than in these rollicking nursery rhymes which she translated so effectively.

VACHEL LINDSAY, 1879-1931

Vachel Lindsay enchants small children with his nonsensical "The Potatoes' Dance," which tells of the sad romance between the Irish lady and the hapless sweet potato. If children hear it twice, they begin to chant it with you, memorizing it in a jiffy. Lindsay himself calls it a "poem game." Here are the first twenty-eight lines:

The Potatoes' Dance[7]

"Down cellar," said the cricket,
"Down cellar," said the cricket,
"Down cellar," said the cricket,
"I saw a ball last night,
In honor of a lady,
In honor of a lady,
In honor of a lady,
Whose wings were pearly white.
The breath of bitter weather,
The breath of bitter weather,
The breath of bitter weather,
Had smashed the cellar pane.
We entertained a drift of leaves,
We entertained a drift of leaves,
We entertained a drift of leaves,
And then of snow and rain.
But we were dressed for winter,
But we were dressed for winter,
But we were dressed for winter,
And loved to hear it blow
In honor of the lady,
In honor of the lady,
In honor of the lady,
Who makes potatoes grow,
Our guest the Irish lady,
The tiny Irish lady,
The airy Irish lady,
Who makes potatoes grow.

Most of Vachel Lindsay's contribution belongs to youth and adults rather than to children. "Daniel," "The Santa Fe Trail," "General William Booth Enters into Heaven," and "The Congo" should not be missed by older boys and girls. These poems use repetition to develop a great swinging rhythm that is almost hypnotic in its effect. The two poems enjoyed by young children, "The Potatoes' Dance" and "The Mysterious Cat," develop this same hypnotic rhythm. One little group of six-year-olds who loved "The Potatoes' Dance" used to step it, from one foot to the other, as they said it. This brought a group swing that added greatly to the effect of the lines. Step, step, step, step, they went until they reached the line,

There was just one sweet potato.

Then their stepping ceased and that sudden cessation of all movement marked with dramatic intensity the coming of the mock tragedy. This was an entirely spontaneous, almost reflex response of young children to Vachel Lindsay's swinging rhythm that seems to demand a bodily response.

6. Copyright 1935 by Rose Fyleman. Reprinted by permission of the publishers, J. B. Lippincott Company.
7. From *Johnny Appleseed* by Vachel Lindsay. Reprinted by permission of the publishers, The Macmillan Company.

STEPHEN VINCENT BENÉT, 1898-1943
ROSEMARY CARR BENÉT, 1898-

A Book of Americans

Rosemary and Stephen Vincent Benét have contributed richly to the laughter and to the understanding of older children and adults with their *A Book of Americans.* It is a collection of Americana in verse: famous legends about famous people from Christopher Columbus, Pocahontas, and Johnny Appleseed to Theodore Roosevelt and Woodrow Wilson. The verse forms are uninspired, but the nonsense is hilarious and often penetrating.

"Pilgrims and Puritans" is a humorous presentation of the two sides of these colonists:

Pilgrims and Puritans[8]

The Pilgrims and the Puritans
Were English to the bone
But didn't like the English Church
And wished to have their own
And so, at last, they sailed away
To settle Massachusetts Bay.

And there they found New England rocks
And Indians with bows on
But didn't mind them half as much
(Though they were nearly frozen)
As being harried, mocked and spurned in
Old England for the faith they burned in.

The stony fields, the cruel sea
They met with resolution
And so developed, finally,
An iron constitution
And, as a punishment for sinners,
Invented boiled New England dinners.

They worked and traded, fished and farmed
And made New England mighty
On codfish, conscience, self-respect
And smuggled aqua-vitae.
They hated fun. They hated fools.
They liked plain manners and good schools.

They fought and suffered, starved and died
For their own way of thinking
But people who had different views
They popped, as quick as winking,
Within the roomy local jail
Or whipped through town at the cart's rail.

They didn't care for Quakers but
They loathed gay cavaliers
And what they thought of clowns and plays
Would simply burn your ears
While merry tunes and Christmas revels
They deemed contraptions of the Devil's.

But Sunday was a gala day
When, in their best attire,
They'd listen, with rejoicing hearts,
To sermons on Hell Fire,
Demons I've Met, Grim Satan's Prey,
And other topics just as gay.

And so they lived and so they died,
A stern but hardy people,
And so their memory goes on
In school house, green and steeple,
In elms and turkeys and Thanksgiving
And much that still is very living.

For, every time we think, "Aha!
I'm better than Bill Jinks,
So he must do just as I say
No matter what he thinks
Or else I'm going to whack him hard!"
The Puritan's in our backyard.

But, when we face a bitter task
With resolute defiance,
And cope with it, and never ask
To fight with less than giants
And win or lose, but seldom yell
—Why, that's the Puritan, as well.

Children like "Captain Kidd," "Peregrine White and Virginia Dare," and the larruping "Theodore Roosevelt." These are genuinely funny. The poem about the Wright brothers is particularly appreciated today by nine- and ten-year-olds for its humorous account of a momentous event in human history.

This book is Americana with a spice of homely wisdom and a pleasant veneration for the men and the legends that make our his-

8. From *A Book of Americans.* Copyright 1933 by Rosemary and Stephen Vincent Benét. Copyright renewed © 1961 by Rosemary Carr Benét. Used by permission

tory colorful. In the midst of the fun, "Nancy Hanks" is poignant and unforgettable. Lincoln, Hamilton, and Jefferson are also dealt with in serious vein. On the whole, however, the fifty-five verses in this book are amusing satires or plain rollicking nonsense. No American child should miss them.

JAMES WHITCOMB RILEY, 1849-1916

The popularity of James Whitcomb Riley's humorous verse seems to be waning, although a few of his children's poems persist in most of our anthologies. His verses have a homespun philosophy and a mild humor, but they rarely bubble or sparkle. They are newspaper verse with a rural flavor that appeals strongly to many people. At least two of his poems seem to be permanently popular with children—"The Raggedy Man" and "Little Orphant Annie."

EUGENE FIELD, 1850-1895

Another newspaper poet popular with the last generation is Eugene Field. While "The Rock-a-By-Lady," "Little Boy Blue," and "Wynken, Blynken, and Nod" are undoubtedly his best loved poems, "The Duel" occupies a special niche in the affectionate regard of the fives and sixes. This mock tragedy about the gingham dog and the calico cat who "ate each other up" has a pleasant swing to it and a delightful refrain.

OTHER WRITERS OF LIGHT VERSE

There are, of course, many other writers of light verse for children and many humorous poems to be found here and there in the books of serious writers. Shakespeare resorts to pure nonsense now and then, usually by way of a song. Christina Rossetti includes in her charming lyrics one or two which might have come from *Mother Goose.* Walter de la Mare in his subtle and highly imaginative poetry pauses to describe poor Henry taking a dose of physic, or to give us a startling account of the woebegone fish in "Alas, Alack!"

Alas, Alack![9]

Ann, Ann!
Come! quick as you can!
There's a fish that talks
In the frying pan.
Out of the fat,
As clear as glass,
He put up his mouth
And moaned "Alas!"
Oh, most mournful,
"Alas, alack!"
Then turned to his sizzling,
And sank him back.

This is typical of the occasional bright bits of hilarity you may find tucked in between the pages of serious poetry.

Light Verse Since the Fifties

DAVID McCORD, 1897-

Far and Few: Rhymes of the Never Was and Always Is
Take Sky: More Rhymes of the Never Was and Always Is

David McCord first began writing verse at fifteen, encouraged, he believes, by two solitary years on an Oregon ranch. After his school years at Harvard, his verses appeared frequently in newspaper columns and magazines. One of his books won the William Rose Benét Award of the Poetry Society of America. *Far and Few* is his fifteenth book of verse, a choice collection of poems for children. They

9. From *Collected Poems, 1901-1918,* by Walter de la Mare. Copyright 1920 by Henry Holt and Company, Inc. Copyright 1948 by Walter de la Mare. Reprinted by permission of the Literary Trustees of Walter de la Mare and the Society of Authors.

range from pure nonsense to quiet little meditations that reflect, perhaps, those solitary years out of doors. Here are two examples of this range of mood.

Notice[10]

I have a dog,
I had a cat.
I've got a frog
Inside my hat.

This Is My Rock

This is my rock,
And here I run
To steal the secret of the sun;

This is my rock,
And here come I
Before the night has swept the sky;

This is my rock,
This is the place
I meet the evening face to face.

Far and Few opens with a poem about "Joe," the greedy squirrel who keeps the birds waiting. It closes with "Fred," an intrepid flying squirrel, the original glider. Children and adults who provide feeding tables will recognize both these characters. Here is

Joe

We feed the birds in winter,
And outside in the snow
We have a tray of many seeds
For many birds of many breeds
And one gray squirrel named Joe.
But Joe comes early,
Joe comes late,
And all the birds
Must stand and wait.
And waiting there for Joe to go
Is pretty cold work in the snow.

Other small beasties are gaily presented—bats, grasshoppers, a snail, starfish, and an especially convincing crowd of crows "spilling from a tree." For sheer nonsense "Five Chants," "In the Middle," "Who Wants a Birthday?" and "Isabel Jones & Curabel Lee" are fun. Children under six like to roll the onomatopoetic refrains of "Song of the Train" and "The Pickety Fence" on their tongues. But it takes a perceptive older child to appreciate "The White Ships," "The Shell," "The Starfish," "Tiggady Rue," and "The Star in the Pail."

Mr. McCord's second book of verse for children is on the whole more completely humorous than *Far and Few,* although it begins seriously with

Take Sky[11]

Now think of words. Take sky
And ask yourself just why—
Like sun, moon, star, and cloud—
It sounds so well out loud,
And pleases so the sight
When printed black on white.

For fifty-six lines the poet plays with the sounds and meanings—denotations and connotations—of words. His "Write Me a Verse" should appeal to high-school youngsters wrestling with verse forms. In this poem, couplets, quatrains, limericks, and triolets are amusingly defined and illustrated. However, there is also much entertainment in this book for the youngest children. In "Sing Song," "Three Signs of Spring," "Sally Lun Lundy," and many other verses, Mr. McCord has a wonderful time playing with the sounds of words. He also makes many clever uses of dialogue. The series on "Food and Drink" opens with

Cup

"Cup, what's up?
Why, it's cocoa scum!
And who likes that?"
"Some."

The funniest of this series is the tongue twister, "Jug and Mug."

10. "Notice," "This Is My Rock" and "Joe." From *Far and Few* by David McCord. Copyright 1952 by David McCord. Reprinted by permission of Little, Brown & Co.
11. "Take Sky" and "Cup." From *Take Sky* by David McCord. Copyright 1961, 1962 by David McCord. Reprinted by permission of Little, Brown & Co.

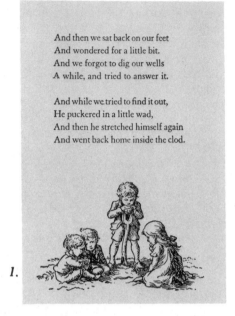

1.

And then we sat back on our feet
And wondered for a little bit.
And we forgot to dig our wells
A while, and tried to answer it.

And while we tried to find it out,
He puckered in a little wad,
And then he stretched himself again
And went back home inside the clod.

3.

2.

1. Judged by the large, colored illustrations of some children's books, this picture may seem a negligible example. Yet every significant detail of the poem is pictured in this small sketch. Check with the story told in "The Worm," and see how admirable the interpretation is. (See pp. 148-149.)
Illustration by F.D. Bedford. From Under the Tree *by Elizabeth Madox Roberts. Copyright 1930, 1958 by The Viking Press, Inc. and reprinted by their permission. (Book 6 x 9¼)*

2. The tigers may look ferocious and the cook look like a simpleton, but the artist, Marguerite Davis, cleverly provides a clue to the surprise ending of this poem. (See p. 125.)
Illustration by Marguerite Davis. From Tirra Lirra *by Laura Richards. Copyright, 1955, by Little, Brown and Company. Reprinted by permission of the publishers. (Book 4½ x 7¼)*

3. Ernest Shepard's Christopher Robin is usually pictured in lively action, but here he is shown lost in thought, even Pooh forgotten. The artist always catches the exact mood of

A. A. Milne's poems. (See p. 129.)
Illustration by E. H. Shepard. From the book When We Were Very Young *by A. A. Milne. Copyright, 1924, by E. P. Dutton & Co., Inc. Renewal, 1952, by A. A. Milne. Reproduced by permission of the publishers. (Book 4½ x 7)*

4. There is a nonchalance about Lear's cartoons that matches the rhymes. A Lear limerick without the Lear drawing is only half as funny as the two together. (See p. 121.)
From Edward Lear's The Complete Nonsense Book. *(Book 6 x 9)*

5. Here is bold, grandiloquent nonsense—a dragon toasting bread! With flowing outline, all angles and quirks, and with a saucy tail and ferocious flames, Juliet Kepes illustrates the extravagant metaphor of "The Toaster." (See p. 136.)
Illustration by Juliet Kepes. From Laughing Time *by William Jay Smith. Copyright, 1953, 1955 by William Jay Smith. Reprinted by permission of Little, Brown and Company. (Book 6¼ x 8¼)*

6. No one who looks at this illustration can miss the feeling of skittish exuberance in the upsurging lines. (See p. 160.)
From Jingle Jangle *by Zhenya Gay. Copyright 1953 by Zhenya Gay. By permission of The Viking Press, Inc. (Book 6 x 9¼, picture 5 x 7)*

4.

There was an Old Man on
whose nose
Most birds of the
air could repose;
But they all flew away at the closing of day,
Which relieved that Old Man and his nose.

5.

6.

I'd like to be a gnu,
Would you?
52

WILLIAM JAY SMITH, 1918-

Laughing Time
Boy Blue's Book of Beasts

"I like this book," said the King of Hearts.
"It makes me laugh the way it starts!"

"I like it also," said his Mother.
So they sat down and read it to each other.[12]

This is an ideal approach to verse, and, in the case of the verses in *Laughing Time,* repeat performances are inevitable. They are genuinely funny jingles, not too subtle for very young children and not too simple for the sevens and for the adults who must, perforce, read them aloud. "Laughing Time" is such infectious nonsense that you begin to smile as you look at the pictures and read the verses.

Laughing Time

It was laughing time, and the tall Giraffe
Lifted his head and began to laugh:

Ha! Ha! Ha! Ha!

And the Chimpanzee on the ginkgo tree
Swung merrily down with a Tee Hee Hee:

Hee! Hee! Hee! Hee!

"It's certainly not against the law!"
Croaked Justice Crow with a loud guffaw:

Haw! Haw! Haw! Haw!

The dancing Bear who could never say "No"
Waltzed up and down on the tip of his toe:

Ho! Ho! Ho! Ho!

The Donkey daintily took his paw,
And around they went: Hee-Haw! Hee-Haw!

Hee-Haw! Hee-Haw!

The Moon had to smile as it started to climb;
All over the world it was laughing time!

Ho! Ho! Ho! Ho! Hee-Haw! Hee-Haw!
Hee! Hee! Hee! Hee! Ha! Ha! Ha! Ha!

After the children have heard this once, the obvious next step is for the adult to read the narrative, with the child or children coming in on the laughing choruses.

Children enjoy the idea behind "The Toaster" (see illustration 5, p. 135):

A silver-scaled Dragon with jaws flaming red
Sits at my elbow and toasts my bread.
I hand him fat slices, and then, one by one,
He hands them back when he sees they are done.

"Moon" belongs to cat lovers of any age, from children to T. S. Eliot. This "proud, mysterious" feline is in the best tradition. But it may be that only adults will suffer from the full import of "People."

People

Hour after hour,
In many places,
People sit,
Making faces.

Boy Blue's Book of Beasts is equally good nonsense about animals wild and tame—considerably wilder in verse form! There is "a tough Kangaroo named Hopalong Brown/ Boxed all the badmen out of town" and "Trim my whiskers! Bless my soul!/Here comes a big brown one-eyed Mole." "A long-haired Yak" in a barber's chair presents a problem and so does a little Raccoon who wants to be something else. All the verses are cleverly written. Mr. Smith's *Typewriter Town* is less successful, but it is good to discover a writer of poetry for adults who starts his own children with the musical inventions of nonsense verse.

JOHN CIARDI, 1916-

The Reason for the Pelican
The Man Who Sang the Sillies
Scrappy the Pup
I Met a Man
You Read to Me, I'll Read to You

Another poet who starts his children with nonsense verse is John Ciardi. Like Edward

12. "The King of Hearts," "Laughing Time," "The Toaster," and "People." From *Laughing Time* by William Jay Smith. Copyright 1953, 1955 by William Jay Smith. Reprinted by permission of Little, Brown & Co.

Lear, Ciardi writes humorous verses that are often too long to sustain their humor. Somehow nonsense and light verses are funniest when they are on the brief side. However, the topics he develops are usually fresh and original, as, for example, "How to Tell the Top of a Hill," "The River Is a Piece of the Sky," "The Reason for the Pelican." And when he chooses a familiar subject like "Halloween," he treats it freshly, so that it is unlike any other Halloween poem ever written—dramatic and weird, and a brain-tickler for the oldest and best readers. Like Dr. Seuss and William Jay Smith, Mr. Ciardi delights in strange beasts such as "The Bugle-Billed Bazoo" or "The Saginsack" or the "Brobinyak."

Scrappy the Pup, in rollicking couplets, tells the story of a sleepy pup who was supposed to be a watch dog. One night a fox got into the hen house, which was responsible for the first of a series of noises that kept the farmer on the move all night while Scrappy drifted around in an "ocean of sleep."[13] The surprise ending will tickle children and adults who have owned such a pet.

The omission of words in "Summer Song" makes a good language game.

Summer Song[14]

By the sand between my toes,
By the waves behind my ears,
By the sunburn on my nose,
By the little salty tears
That make rainbows in the sun
When I squeeze my eyes and run,
By the way the seagulls screech,
Guess where I am? At the. . . . . !
By the way the children shout
Guess what happened? School is. . . !
By the way I sing this song
Guess if summer lasts too long?
You must answer Right or. . . . . !

One of Mr. Ciardi's interesting experiments in verse for children is *I Met a Man,* written with a controlled vocabulary of some four hundred words. It was planned as a first book for his daughter to read on her own, and it moves from easy to more difficult in both words and content. "Poetry," the author says, "is especially well designed to lead the child to such recognition" (of new words) "for rhyme and pattern are always important clues." For example,

I met a man that looked about
As sleepy as he could without
Falling over and starting to snore.
If he ever wakes up, I'll tell you some more.[15]

Decidedly more subtle is

The Cat Heard the Cat-Bird[15]

One day, a fine day, a high-flying-sky day,
A cat-bird, a fat bird, a fine fat cat-bird
Was sitting and singing on a stump by the highway.
Just sitting. And singing. Just that. But a cat heard.

A thin cat, a grin-cat, a long thin grin-cat
Came creeping the sly way by the highway to the stump.
"O cat-bird, the cat heard! O cat-bird scat!
The grin-cat is creeping! He's going to jump!"

—One day, a fine day, a high-flying-sky day
A fat cat, yes, that cat we met as a thin cat
Was napping, cat-napping, on a stump by the highway,
And even in his sleep you could see he was a grin-cat.

Why was he grinning?—He must have had a dream.
What made him fat?—A pan full of cream.
What about the cat-bird?—What bird, dear?
I don't see any cat-bird here.

Mr. Ciardi continued his experiment with a limited vocabulary in *You Read to Me, I'll Read to You,* in which he alternates a poem the child is supposed to read with one for the adult to read, unrestricted by word lists. These, too, are clever verses. But at the rate Mr. Ciardi is publishing, his humor may be running thin. Children see, touch, smell, taste, hear, and feel the beauty and the wonder of life. Mr. Ciardi could give children more of this sort of poetry, also, and we hope he will.

13. From *Scrappy the Pup* by John Ciardi. Copyright 1961 by John Ciardi. Published by J. B. Lippincott Company.
14. From *The Man Who Sang the Sillies* by John Ciardi. Copyright 1961 by John Ciardi. Published by J. B. Lippincott Company.
15. "I Met a Man" and "The Cat Heard the Cat-Bird." From *I Met a Man* by John Ciardi. Reprinted by permission of Houghton Mifflin Co.

OGDEN NASH, PHYLLIS McGINLEY, WILLIAM COLE

Ogden Nash is, of course, one of the most successful modern practitioners of the art of nonsense verse and a master of the outrageous surprise rhyme. Most of his verses are sophisticated adult humor, but it is a poor anthology that cannot find among Mr. Nash's riches a rib-tickling selection or two for children.

The Love Letters of Phyllis McGinley is a treasury of light verse for adults and clever teen-age youngsters but not for children. Only the delightful verses of Phyllis McGinley's ABC book, *All Around the Town,* belong to them. This alphabet and her stories for children prove she can write for them if she will.

William Cole's *Humorous Poetry for Children* is a large, unusual anthology. In spite of the title, more of the selections are for teenagers and adults than for children. But there are enough funny ones for the tens to twelves to make the book decidedly worth adding to the library of laughter both in elementary schools and in homes.

Since anthologists have not found all the humorous verse that has been written, it is a rewarding activity for teachers to make a collection of favorites, or to encourage children to make such a collection. Clever, well-written verses which provoke a chuckle are worth having not only because they bring laughter into this grave old world, but because their rollicking jingles cultivate the ear and lead naturally and painlessly to the enjoyment of lyric poetry.

Poetry of the Child's Everyday World

The world of fantastic nonsense and the child's everyday world of people, pets, and the outdoors may seem far apart. Yet many poets move easily from one to the other and, like the child, are at home in both worlds.

Actually, in the years before Edward Lear introduced children to his madcap world of nonsense, they had been given to understand that life was not only real but decidedly earnest. Poems were written and read to children for the purpose of improving their manners and uplifting their morals. Yet didactic as some of these early efforts seem today, they marked a dawning recognition of the child's everyday world of people and play, both real and imaginative. Slowly the idea took form and grew, the idea of a child, not as a small adult, but as an intensely active person, functioning in a world of his own. Poetry for children arrived at this point of view slowly. It began as their stories began, with the idea of teaching them moral lessons.

Early Poets of Manners and Morals

ISAAC WATTS, 1674-1748

Divine and Moral Songs for Children

Isaac Watts, a nonconformist preacher, was famous in his own time for his textbooks on *Logick* and *Principles of Geography and Astronomy*. Today he is best known for his hymns and for certain little moralistic verses for children. Old school readers and anthologies always included such selections as this:

Against Idleness and Mischief[16]

How doth the little busy bee
Improve each shining hour
And gather honey all the day
From every op'ning flow'r.

How skilfully she builds her cell;
How neat she spreads her wax,
And labors hard to store it well
With the sweet food she makes.

In works of labor or of skill,
I would be busy too;

For Satan finds some mischief still
For idle hands to do.

In books, or work, or healthful play,
Let my first days be past;
That I may give for ev'ry day
Some good account at last.

In his "Introduction to Parents and all who are concerned in the Education of Children," Watts wrote:

What is learnt in verse, is longer retained in memory, and sooner recollected.

This will be a constant furniture for the minds of children that they may have something to think of when alone; and may repeat to themselves.

He concluded, then, that since a child learns and recalls rhymes so easily, he might as well learn moral lessons in that form. So he composed his *Divine and Moral Songs for Children.* It was first published in 1715, and so many succeeding editions have been published that there is a whole book devoted to its history and the listing of the numerous editions.[16] Read over the Watts hymns to be found in any modern hymnal and see how meaningful most of them still are: "Joy to the world," "Come, Holy Spirit," and "O God, our help in ages past." Little children also like the first verse of his "Cradle Hymn":

Hush! my dear, lie still and slumber,
Holy Angels guard thy bed!
Heavenly blessings without number,
Gently falling on thy head.

Such hymns make a center of peace and encouragement for children.

ANN TAYLOR, 1782-1866
JANE TAYLOR, 1783-1824

Original Poems for Infant Minds
Rhymes for the Nursery
Hymns for Infant Minds

Ann and Jane Taylor are credited with being the first English authors to write wholly for children. They were literary descendants of Isaac Watts at his most moralistic, although they never achieved the serene beauty of his best religious poetry. They did, however, venture further into the child's world, and they wrote some nature lyrics without moral lessons.

Ann and Jane were the daughters of intellectual parents and enjoyed a happy family life in the lovely English countryside. The sisters wrote so much alike that only the initial which sometimes follows a verse identifies the author.

The titles of the verses indicate their improving content: "The Vulgar Little Lady," "Dirty Jim," "Meddlesome Matty," "Contented John." But the sisters had a gift for storytelling, and many of their narrative poems profit by cleverly sustained suspense. "Ball" is a good example:

Ball

"My good little fellow, don't throw your ball there,
You'll break neighbor's windows, I know;
On the end of the house there is room, and to spare,
Go round, you can have a delightful game there,
Without fearing for where you may throw."

Harry thought he might safely continue his play
With a little more care than before;
So, heedless of all that his father could say,
As soon as he saw he was out of the way
Resolved to have fifty throws more.

Already as far as to forty he rose,
And no mischief had happened at all;
One more, and one more, he successfully throws,
But when, as he thought, just arrived at the close,
In popped his unfortunate ball.

"I'm sure that I thought, and I did not intend,"
Poor Harry was going to say;
But soon came the glazier the window to mend,
And both the bright shillings he wanted to spend
He had for his folly to pay.

16. Wilbur Macy Stone, *The Divine and Moral Songs of Isaac Watts: An Essay thereon and a tentative List of Editions.* Privately printed for *The Triptych,* 1918.

When little folks think they know better than
great,
And what is forbidden them, do,
We must always expect to see, sooner or late,
That such wise little fools have a similar fate,
And that one in the fifty goes through.
A. T.

Children will listen to these little sermons because of their story interest, but the poems are commonplace. The nature lyrics are sometimes genuinely pleasing when they are not too lengthy or marred by extraneous "lessons." "The Snowdrop" is one of the prettiest; and "Twinkle, twinkle, little star" is the enduring favorite.

KATE GREENAWAY, 1846-1901

Under the Window
Marigold Garden

Like Jane and Ann Taylor, Kate Greenaway wrote undistinguished verse for children, but she did write with artless gaiety, and her illustrations have all the lyric grace the verses lack. Her balanced pages—decorated with flowers, fruits, merry children, and pleasant landscapes—possess a freshness and charm, and a kind of rhythmic grace that seem to lift the accompanying quatrains into the realm of genuine poetry. Without the pictures, the rhymes probably would not have survived, but the two in combination constitute a unique contribution to children's books.

This modest and charming woman was born in London and worked there most of her life. The daughter of an artist, she began her own study of art as a matter of course. When she was still only twenty-two years old, her exhibitions of water colors were exciting favorable comment, but it was her Christmas cards which started her vogue. From the Christmas cards she turned to the illustration of children's books and soon enjoyed a tremendous popularity.

The tiny *Mother Goose* with the Greenaway pictures and decorations still remains an exquisite edition of the old favorite. The artist's popularity reached new heights with the publication of her own book of verses and drawings, *Under the Window* (1879), which is said to have sold 150,000 copies. This, together with her *Birthday Book, Marigold Garden,* and her *Almanacs,* brought her a large income and made her famous in every great city of Europe and of the United States.

Although Kate Greenaway's verses are often wooden and occasionally unchildlike, most of them have a gentle gaiety and exhibit a real understanding of children which at the time was rare; for example, this one from *Under the Window*[17]:

In go-cart so tiny
My sister I drew;
And I've promised to draw her
The wide world through.

We have not yet started—
I own it with sorrow—
Because our trip's always
Put off till to-morrow.

It is typical Kate Greenaway—simple in language and idea, but with a spark of humor that brings a smile. When she moralizes, as she does frequently, it is not with the heavy hand of the Taylors but with sly humor. Here is a good example, also from *Under the Window:*

Yes, that's the girl that struts about,
She's very proud,—so very proud!
Her bow-wow's *quite as proud as she:*
They both are very wrong to be
So proud—so very proud.

See, Jane and Willy laugh at her,
They say she's very proud!
Says Jane, "My stars!—they're very silly";
"Indeed they are," cries little Willy,
"To walk so stiff and proud."

The verses, together with the gentle caricature that illustrates them, are an excellent satire on pride as children see it. (See 3 in color section.)

The following poem might have come out of *Mother Goose.* Children like it for the contagious excitement of its lines.

17. "In go-cart so tiny," "Yes, that's the girl that struts about," "Higgledy, piggledy! see how they run!" and "School is over." From *Under the Window* by Kate Greenaway, published by Frederick Warne & Co. United States rights by permission of Frederick Warne & Co., Inc. Canadian rights by permission of Frederick Warne & Co., Ltd.

Higgledy, piggledy! see how they run!
Hopperty, popperty! what is the fun?
Has the sun or the moon tumbled into the sea?
What is the matter, now? Pray tell it me!

Higgledy, piggledy! how can I tell?
Hopperty, popperty! hark to the bell!
The rats and the mice even scamper away;
Who can say what may not happen to-day?

"Susan Blue" is a little conversation piece—two small girls talking over a garden gate and wondering where to play. "Tommy was a silly boy" relates the amusing mishap of a small boy who thought he could fly. "Blue Shoes," "Shall I Sing!" "Under the Window," and "My House Is Red" are all pleasant, if uninspired, little verses. But one characteristic makes them important: they reflect a new consciousness of the real child and his everyday play. In the Greenaway books, we see and read about children racing and skipping, dancing to the piper's tune, flying kites, rolling hoops, chasing each other, going primly to tea, or quietly enjoying their own little red house—in short, real children.

School is over,
Oh, what fun!
Lessons finished,
Play begun.

Who'll run fastest,
You or I?
Who'll laugh loudest?
Let us try.

Poets of the Child's World

The poems of Kate Greenaway marked the transition from verse written for children's instruction to verse written for their entertainment, verse which records the child's play world from his point of view. "What is Tommy running for?" she asks, and sagely concludes that Tommy is running so that Jimmy can run after him. Reason enough for any child! Other poets caught this new point of view and began to write a new kind of verse for and about children. Their poems reflect both the child's everyday world of active play and his inner world of imaginative play.

ROBERT LOUIS STEVENSON, 1850-1894

A Child's Garden of Verses

The title "poet laureate of childhood" has often been bestowed upon Robert Louis Stevenson and until A. A. Milne appeared, there was no real contender for it. Stevenson first captivated adult readers with his essays and fiction, then caught and held the affectionate regard of children with *A Child's Garden of Verses*. There was nothing comparable to these verses when they were written, no literary precedents, even though Stevenson himself said that the idea for his book came to him while he was glancing over one of Kate Greenaway's little books. *A Child's Garden of Verses* goes far beyond Greenaway at her best, both in its reflection of the child's point of view and in its poetry.

The facts of Stevenson's life are too well known to need much reviewing. There has been, however, far too much emphasis on the pathology of his life, and on his recurrent illnesses, and not enough emphasis on the indomitable spirit that kept him working and playing with tremendous energy and enjoyment to the very end of his short life.

He was always a frail child, to be sure, and the sullen, severe climate of Edinburgh could not have helped his health. One glimpse of that high, dark house in which he lived, with its walls touching the walls of the houses on either side, suggests still another reason why a delicate child needing the sun could grow no stronger there. Fortunately, Louis sometimes got away from it for visits to his grandfather Balfour's house at Colinton on the Water Leith. There he played outdoors with his cousins, and made friends with all the small creatures and with the garden blossoms he names so lovingly in his poem "The Flowers." There he discovered the "thrushes on the lawn," the lilacs, and the lawn itself which he later said was "a perfect goblet of sunshine." There, too, at the foot of the garden, flowed the dark brown river over its golden sand "with trees on either hand," just as he recalls it in "Where Go the Boats?"

Fortunately, too, the young Louis went on journeys with his father to visit the great lighthouses of the Scottish coast, many of them built by the grandfather, Robert Stevenson, for whom he was named. These lighthouses and the daring feats of engineering which they represented captured the imagination of the child and helped his spirit grow robust.

Perhaps these journeys with his father helped to establish the boy's lifelong passion for travel and outdoor life, and his capacity for enjoying the companionship of all kinds of people.

Of his adult life more tales can be told than he himself ever wrote. He studied law but soon turned to writing, and no author ever took his profession more earnestly nor worked at it more zealously. We know of his continual travels all over the world for health and for pleasure, and we know how his notebooks went with him everywhere and how there was never a journey that did not yield fat notes to be used later in essays, poems, plays, novels, short stories, and letters.

In France he fell in love with an American, a Mrs. Osbourne, and followed her to California, where they were married in 1880. Their life together was remarkably happy, and Stevenson found himself in a kind of family partnership for writing. He dictated to his stepdaughter Isobel; he read everything he wrote to his wife, who was one of his best critics; and on Lloyd Osbourne, his stepson, he tried out his boys' stories, chapter by chapter. *Treasure Island* grew and flourished by way of Lloyd's enjoyment, Lloyd's criticism, Lloyd's robust approval. "No women in the story, Lloyd's orders," wrote Stevenson. Again—"the trouble is to work it off without oaths. Buccaneers without oaths—bricks without straw. But youth and the fond parent have to be consulted. . . . It's awful fun boys' stories; you just indulge the pleasures of your heart; that's all; no trouble, no strain."

Stevenson's last four years were spent in Samoa, and no part of his brief life is more picturesque. He built himself a great house in the midst of a tropical estate, which he cultivated with astonishing success. He gathered round him a kind of feudal clan of natives who adored him and whom he protected like a kindly patriarch. He aided their deposed king, wrote a book in behalf of his native friends, hoping to help their cause in England, and was himself a sort of island king and judge.

When Stevenson died suddenly, his native friends came from all over the island to look upon the face of the dear friend they called "Tusitala," teller of tales. They brought their finest mats to honor the dead, they filled his room with their brightest flowers, and they carved a road up the great mountain to a peak where Stevenson had said he wished to lie. Sixty Samoans carried their friend up that precipitous road and left him forever in the land he loved. "Talofa, Tusitala," one of them said, "Sleep, Tusitala."

A Child's Garden of Verses appeared in 1885 as *Penny Whistles,* with sixty-three poems and this fond dedication to Stevenson's childhood nurse: "To Alison Cunningham (From Her Boy)." Not all these poems are for children; a few of them are merely about children or are adult reminiscences of childhood. Such poems creep into almost every collection of juvenile poetry but are nevertheless to be avoided; for example, Stevenson's "Keepsake Mill," "Whole Duty of Children," and the rarely included "To Any Reader" and "To Willie and Henrietta."

Fidelity to Child Nature

With these exceptions, no careful reading of the poems can fail to leave you impressed with the author's genuine understanding of children. The opening poem, "Bed in Summer," is every child's complaint:

And does it not seem hard to you,
When all the sky is clear and blue,
And I should like so much to play,
To have to go to bed by day?

His children get up shivering with cold on winter mornings; they yearn to travel; they discover the sea miraculously filling up their holes on the beach; they struggle with table manners; they have a deep respect for "System," an orderly world; they enjoy good days and bad ones, mostly good; they can't understand why the gardener doesn't want "to play at Indian wars" with them; they watch for the lamplighter; they wonder why they can't see the wind; and they enjoy a world of play and a world of the imagination as well. Children's interest in tiny things is found not only in "The Little Land" but over and over again in other verses. Here are real children, many-sided and with many interests.

Dramatic Play

Especially true to child life are the poems involving dramatic play. Imagination transfers a clothes basket into a boat. Climbing up in the cherry tree, the child glimpses not merely the next-door garden but foreign lands and even fairyland. In "A Good Play," the children explain:

We built a ship upon the stairs
All made of the back-bedroom chairs,

The sick child's fleets go "all up and down among the sheets" in "The Land of Counterpane"; and in "The Land of Story Books," he has a forest adventure, "Away Behind the Sofa Back." The poems bristle with the properties and imaginative transformations of that arch magician, the child of about four to seven years old.

Group Play

People have complained that this child of the *Verses* is a solitary child, and they have read into the poems some of the pathos of the sick Louis. But if you study these verses, you will find several children playing pirates in the "Pirate Story"; building ships together in "A Good Play"; being "mountaineers" in "The Hayloft"; crawling "through the breach in the wall of the garden" to "Keepsake Mill"; tramping round the village in the "Marching Song" with Johnnie, Willie, Peter, and "great commander Jane"; and in "Northwest Passage," facing together the "long black passage up to bed." These give us a fair proportion of other children and of social play. They emphasize also the normal play activities of healthy children. Nothing of the invalid here!

Night Poems

Perhaps the largest group of poems under a single general classification is made up of those concerned with night. What an imaginative group it is, and sometimes scary, too: "Young Night Thought," "My Bed Is a Boat," "The Land of Story-Books," "Night and Day," "The Moon," "Windy Nights," "Shadow March," "The Land of Nod," "Escape at Bedtime," "Good-Night," and "In Port." Of these, "Escape at Bedtime" is one of the most interesting (see illustration 2, p. 156).

Musical Qualities

There are two poems in this night group which are also notable for their rhythm. "Shadow March" is in perfect marching time but it is an eerie, frightening march of bogies and shadows, not to be used before the children are seven or eight years old and stout enough to stand it. Less scary and still finer is that pounding gallop called

Windy Nights

Whenever the moon and stars are set,
Whenever the wind is high,
All night long in the dark and wet,
A man goes riding by.
Late in the night when the fires are out,
Why does he gallop and gallop about?

Whenever the trees are crying aloud,
And ships are tossed at sea,
By, on the highway, low and loud,
By at the gallop goes he,
By at the gallop he goes, and then
By he comes back at the gallop again.

Another fine example of the use of rhythm to suggest the subject is "From a Railway Carriage." Notice that the verse has the tempo and the driving speed of the train.

Faster than fairies, faster than witches,
Bridges and houses, hedges and ditches;
And charging along like troops in a battle,
All through the meadows the horses and cattle:
All of the sights of the hill and the plain
Fly as thick as driving rain;
And ever again in the wink of an eye,
Painted stations whistle by.

These examples of rhythm illustrate another of the outstanding qualities in Stevenson's *Child's Garden of Verses:* the poems are markedly lyrical. Of course, numbers of them have been set to music, but they sing anyway, without benefit of notes. Take the concluding line of "A Good Boy": "And hear the thrushes singing in the lilacs round the lawn." It does sing, doesn't it? Or read the familiar

Singing

Of speckled eggs the birdie sings
And nests among the trees;
The sailor sings of ropes and things
In ships upon the seas.

The children sing in far Japan,
The children sing in Spain;
The organ with the organ man
Is singing in the rain.

Or listen to the refrain in "The Wind":

O wind, a-blowing all day long,
O wind, that sings so loud a song!

Go through page after page of these poems and you'll find them singing in your memory with their own melody. One of the most lyrical of them all is

Where Go the Boats?

Dark brown is the river,
Golden is the sand.
It flows along forever,
With trees on either hand.

Green leaves a-floating,
Castles of the foam,
Boats of mine a-boating—
Where will all come home?

On goes the river
And out past the mill,
Away down the valley,
Away down the hill.

Away down the river,
A hundred miles or more,
Other little children
Shall bring my boats ashore.

Notice the slow, smooth-flowing melody of the first two verses, like the flow of the river. In the third verse, the repetition of "Away" gives an impetus to the lines as if the current were really flowing faster and carrying the boats farther until, abruptly, as if in a little eddy, the boats come to anchor in the last two lines. Except that the poem has no gaiety, the smooth glide of the lines suggests the flowing melody of "The Moldau," by Smetana.

Stevenson was evidently fond of the poem pattern which seems to begin close at hand and go farther and farther away. He uses it again effectively in "Foreign Lands," and, for the youngest, in the brief

Rain

The rain is raining all around,
It falls on field and tree,
It rains on the umbrellas here,
And on the ships at sea.

Although teachers and mothers who were raised on *A Child's Garden of Verses* may feel that the verses are overfamiliar, they must not forget that these poems are new to each generation of children. "The Cow," "My Shadow," "The Swing," "Winter-time," and "Time to Rise," in addition to the verses already quoted, are perennial favorites, and children should not miss them. New poets of childhood may make their contributions, but Robert Louis Stevenson has left to young children a legacy of small lyrics, just their size.

CARL SANDBURG, 1878-

Early Moon
Wind Song

Carl Sandburg was almost forty years old before he began to be recognized as a writer. Now he is the author of what is certainly one of the greatest biographies of Abraham Lincoln, *The Prairie Years* and *The War Years,* and he occupies a secure position in American letters.

When Sandburg was thirteen, his schooling was apparently over and he went to work. His occupations were numerous and carried him all through the Midwest and eventually to Puerto Rico. As porter, dishwasher, trucker, driver, scene-shifter, harvest hand, and soldier in the Spanish-American War, he learned to know workingmen and people of all kinds. He saw poverty and brutality, along with the nobility and vision that make life in the United States the curious composite that it is. After the Spanish-American war was over, he worked his way through college and went into newspaper work. He was with the Chicago *Daily News* for many years, and some of his poems first appeared in that paper. The publication of his *Chicago Poems* in 1915 created a sensation and brought down upon his head both hostility and enthusiasm. Critics seemed to feel either that poetry was going rapidly downhill or that here was another Walt Whitman, a prophet of a new day. So with readers today, either they like Sandburg's gusty, lusty verse or they find it contrived, self-conscious, and continually disappointing. His two books for children will be so evaluated, either plus or minus. However, the books are worth trying with eleven-and twelve-year-olds. Boys are especially apt to like them. Here are a few examples:

Bubbles[18]

Two bubbles found they had rainbows on
their curves.
They flickered out saying:
"It was worth being a bubble just to have held
that rainbow thirty seconds."

Between Two Hills[19]

Between two hills
The old town stands.
The houses loom
And the roofs and trees
And the dusk and the dark,
The damp and the dew
Are there.

The prayers are said
And the people rest
For sleep is there
And the touch of dreams
Is over all.

Older children can also appreciate the ironical "Southern Pacific." Its biting brevity is exceedingly effective. Easier for them to understand are "Paper 1" (writers and wrappers), "Children of the Desert," "Summer Grass" (waiting for rain), "Again?" (about the Woolworth building), "Buffalo Dusk" (good for Western units), "People Who Must" (about a steeplejack), "Manual System" (about a switchboard operator), and the fine "To Beachey, 1912" (which might be about any aviator of any year).

Sandburg has given some good advice to the children themselves in "Primer Lesson." If you read this to children, let them talk it over. It is good advice for anyone.

Primer Lesson[20]

Look out how you use proud words.
When you let proud words go, it is not easy to
call them back.
They wear long boots, hard boots; they walk
off proud; they can't hear you calling—
Look out how you use proud words.

ELEANOR FARJEON, 1881-

Eleanor Farjeon's Poems for Children
The Children's Bells
Kings and Queens

The poetry of Eleanor Farjeon cuts across any classification which could be devised. She writes skillful nonsense verse, her lyrics are tender and beautiful and her verses reflect a sure knowledge of the child's world and wonderment.

18. "Bubbles" by Carl Sandburg. Reprinted from his volume, *Wind Song* by permission of Harcourt, Brace & World, Inc. Copyright © 1960 by Carl Sandburg.
19. From *Chicago Poems* by Carl Sandburg. Copyright 1916 by Holt, Rinehart and Winston, Inc. Copyright renewed 1944 by Carl Sandburg. Reprinted by permission of Holt, Rinehart and Winston, Inc.
20. From *Slabs of the Sunburnt West* by Carl Sandburg. Copyright 1922 by Harcourt, Brace and World, Inc.

Surely no child ever grew up in a more amusing household than little "Nellie" Farjeon enjoyed. For a picture of childhood in a family which was as brilliant as it was unusual, you should read her delightful *Portrait of a Family*.

Although the four Farjeon children grew up on friendly terms with many of London's distinguished people, none seemed as wonderful to them as their gentle mother and their gay, irrepressible father. The mother was the daughter of America's beloved actor, Joseph Jefferson of Rip Van Winkle fame. From the Jeffersons, Eleanor thinks, the four children inherited their love of music, which was strong in all of them and developed into a profession with Harry, the oldest. Certainly pretty "Maggie" Jefferson gave them a good start, singing for them all the American songs with which she had grown up and which they soon learned to know and love as well as she did.

Nellie adored her father, a popular novelist of his day and the friend of all the notables in the world of the theater, music, literature, and art. When Nellie was about ten years old, her father began the pleasant custom of presenting each child with a book after Sunday dinner. Nellie's first one was *In Memoriam*, and she remembers her father telling her about Tennyson and reading her parts of the poem. He read aloud much poetry, and of all the poets Shakespeare was their favorite.

When Eleanor Farjeon began to write, she always took her manuscripts to her father's study, pushed them under the door, and then ran away. "I had a stomach-ache till he came and told me if he liked it," she writes. "He never kept me waiting. Even if he was writing his own stories, he stopped at once to look at my last poem, and came straight to the Nursery to talk it over with me. He taught me how to correct proofs and to be particular in the clearness of my 'copy' for the printers, long before I had any printers to consider." Once, when she was ill, Nellie wrote a twenty-thousand-word story, sent it down to her father, and then waited in bed fearful and anxious to learn his opinion. When he came, he exclaimed, "I have hopes of you, Nell! I have hopes of you!" and she knew complete satisfaction. The story might not win a prize but she was on her way. Her father thought she might be a writer!

After the death of their father, the children spent one year in the United States with their grandfather, Joseph Jefferson. Then Harry received an appointment to the faculty of the Royal Academy of Music in London, and Eleanor returned with him. Her first book was published shortly after she returned to London. It was the amusing *Nursery Rhymes of London Town*, for which she wrote her own music. This was followed by the lively historical nonsense, *Kings and Queens*, by her brother and herself, and from then on she has written prolifically, both prose and poetry.

Kings and Queens, written with her brother Herbert, was republished in 1953 and will delight children wrestling with the solemnity of English history. For instance, "Henry VIII"[21] opens with:

Bluff King Hal was full of beans;
He married half a dozen queens;
For three called Kate they cried the banns,
And one called Jane, and a couple of Annes.

And it continues with blithe irreverence to account for the six ladies and their much-marrying spouse.

At her best, Eleanor Farjeon's poems for children, whether nonsense or serious lyrics, are skillfully written. Her rhythms are often as lively as a dance; her meters and rhyme schemes are varied and interesting; and her subject matter has exceptional range.

Unfortunately, the quality of her poems is uneven. She is not, for instance, so adroit at describing the modern child's everyday activities as A. A. Milne, although such poems as "Bedtime," "Breakfast," and "What I've Been Doing" are well liked by the children.

Imagination and the Everyday World

But the moment she turns imaginative, something wonderful happens. Take, for example, that curious and lovely night poem, whose very title arrests attention:

21. From *Kings and Queens* by Herbert and Eleanor Farjeon. Copyright 1933 by E. P. Dutton & Co., Inc.; © 1961 by Eleanor Farjeon. Reprinted by permission of the authors.

The Night Will Never Stay[22]

The night will never stay,
The night will still go by,
Though with a million stars
You pin it to the sky.
Though you bind it with the blowing wind
And buckle it with the moon,
The night will slip away
Like sorrow or a tune.

Mr. Milne has given us "Hoppity" and Mrs. Aldis, "Hiding," but it takes Eleanor Farjeon to turn an ordinary night into something as perishable and precious as life itself. This poem might well give a child his first sense of time, rushing irresistibly along in a pattern of starry nights that will not stand still. Not that the child can so translate the poem, but he will say it and say it again, because both the ideas and the words are as haunting as a melody. In *The Children's Bells,* her "What Is Time?" supplements this poem in a gayer mood. Children like the sound of her companion poems, "Boys' Names" and "Girls' Names" (p. 232), and the surprise endings amuse them.

Of her fairy poems, "City Under Water" is perhaps the loveliest and the most usable for children. There are not many of these, but they are invariably good fairy lore and are well written.

Nature Poems

Nature poems occur throughout the books. Of these, children like especially "The Kingfisher," "A Dragon-Fly," "Heigh-Ho, April," "Farewell to Summer," and the favorite, "Mrs. Peck-Pigeon." Read it aloud and notice how the words and lines of this poem suggest, ever so subtly, the funny little bobbing, teetering gait of the pigeon pecking for crumbs:

Mrs. Peck-Pigeon[23]

Mrs. Peck-Pigeon
Is picking for bread,
Bob-bob-bob
Goes her little round head.
Tame as a pussy-cat
In the street,
Step-step-step
Go her little red feet.
With her little red feet
And her little round head,
Mrs. Peck-Pigeon
Goes picking for bread.

Christmas Poems

One of Eleanor Farjeon's most valuable contributions is her Christmas poetry, which is unique in its variety and spirit. Sometimes the poems have the hushed reverential mood of a Christmas hymn; sometimes they are gay and rollicking. Often she uses contrast to point ever so gently the lesson of Christmas, as in "For Christmas Day." "The Shepherd and the King" is filled with tender joy, and young children will like the spirited "In the Week When Christmas Comes." There are no poems more true to the Christmas spirit, thoughtful, tender, imaginative. Her "Prayer for Little Things" is often used at Christmas but is actually timeless in its appeal. Even though Eleanor Farjeon had written nothing else, her Christmas poems would still give her a high place among the poets who have written poetry that children love.

JAMES S. TIPPETT, 1885-1958

I Live in a City
I Go A-Traveling
I Spend the Summer

James S. Tippett's numerous small books, just pocket size, make an immediate appeal to the young child. For him the author is interpreting the skyscraper environment of a large city—elevators, endless stairways, switchboard girls, the subway—all the complexities of New York City experienced through the eyes of an inquiring child. Some of this subject matter in *I Live in a City* might be incomprehensible to a suburban child of another large city, but some of the verses make a general appeal, for instance:

22. From *Gypsy and Ginger* by Eleanor Farjeon. Used by permission of Eleanor Farjeon.
23. Reprinted by permission of the publishers, J. B. Lippincott Company, from *Over the Garden Wall* by Eleanor Farjeon. Copyright 1933 by Eleanor Farjeon.

The Park[24]

I'm glad that I
Live near a park
For in the winter
After dark
The park lights shine
As bright and still
As dandelions
On a hill.

I Go A-Traveling opens with a chant which the child himself might have spoken. If a child had chanted such words, we would accept them as interesting speech play, but we would not call the result poetry, nor read it back to the child as such. Mr. Tippett's virtue is that he is never arch. His directness and sincerity are admirable. His books are records of a modern child's curiosities, his response to his environment, both in the city and in the country. As language records, these books have their place. Most of the favorites are in the anthologies.

ELIZABETH MADOX ROBERTS, 1886-1941

Under the Tree

Elizabeth Madox Roberts was born and grew up in Perryville, Kentucky, where her forebears had settled in Daniel Boone's time. From her novels we know that she must have been steeped from childhood in the balladry, the folklore, and the history of her state. From her poems we guess she must have had an unusually happy childhood with the other children in her family—enjoying the normal village experiences of picnics, church, lessons, and the glorious treat of the circus.

From 1917 to 1921, she attended the University of Chicago and graduated not only with Phi Beta Kappa but with the McLaughlin prize for essay and the Fisk prize for poetry. The poetry was later published in the book called *Under the Tree,* about which Louis Untermeyer has remarked, "few American lyricists have made so successful a debut." After her graduation from the university, she lived in New York for a while and began writing her novels. Later she retired to her own Kentucky and continued her work there. She won several poetry prizes while writing her novels, but she is best known as the author of *The Time of Man, Jingling in the Wind, The Great Meadow,* and other stories of Kentucky. A year before her death, a second volume of poems, *Song in the Meadow,* appeared.

One reviewer, J. Donald Adams, has said of Elizabeth Madox Roberts: "Everything she writes bears the unmistakable mark of her highly individual gifts; nothing she has ever done could possibly be mistaken for the work of another writer."

Child's Point of View

This is particularly true of her one book of poems for children, which is unlike any other juvenile poetry. It has a deceptive air of simplicity that gives the unwary reader no immediate clues to the artistry which makes these poems emotionally satisfying and full of everyday enchantment. "The Worm"[25] will serve as an example:

Dickie found a broken spade
And said he'd dig himself a well;
And then Charles took a piece of tin,
And I was digging with a shell.

Then Will said he would dig one too.
We shaped them out and made them wide,
And I dug up a piece of clod
That had a little worm inside.

We watched him pucker up himself
And stretch himself to walk away.
He tried to go inside the dirt,
But Dickie made him wait and stay.

His shining skin was soft and wet.
I poked him once to see him squirm.
And then Will said, " I wonder if
He knows that he's a worm."

24. Acknowledgment is hereby made to Harper & Row, Inc. for the use of "The Park" from *I Live in the City* by James S. Tippett. Copyright, 1927, by Harper & Brothers.
25. "The Worm," "The Butterbean Tent," "Crescent Moon," "Firefly," "The People," "Horse," "Mr. Wells," and "Strange Tree." From *Under the Tree* by Elizabeth Madox Roberts. Copyright 1922 by B. W. Huebsch, Inc., 1930 by The Viking Press, Inc., New York.

And then we sat back on our feet
And wondered for a little bit.
And we forgot to dig our wells
A while, and tried to answer it.

And while we tried to find it out,
He puckered in a little wad,
And then he stretched himself again
And went back home inside the clod.

Here is a narrative as direct as prose, with no "proud words," no fancies, no ethereal theme—just worm and children. The children are digging; but, notice that they are digging with a broken spade, a piece of tin, and a shell—tools so characteristic of children that this first verse startles the adult and is accepted as a matter of course by the child. Then the worm distracts them from their original plan of digging a well, and they experiment with it for a while until a strange idea makes them forget their experiments. They sit back and wonder if "he knows that he's a worm"—an idea that only a child could think of. The ability to think, see, and feel as a child is the first characteristic of Elizabeth Madox Roberts that strikes you as unerringly right and true. She makes even the language seem much as the child might talk, although only an artist could choose words as descriptive as those about the worm: "pucker up himself," "stretch himself to walk away," "his shining skin was soft and wet," and finally "he puckered in a little wad." These are masterly descriptive phrases, and yet they sound as if the child might have spoken them. So in "The Cornfield," "Mumps," "Father's Story," "The Picnic," "The Butterbean Tent," and a dozen others, you encounter a real child telling seriously of what he sees, feels, and does. (See illustration 1, p. 134.)

Child Wonder and Delight

The Roberts child ruminates about things, wonders, and has several scares, but she is never fairy-conscious or full of those delicate whimsies so frequently found in British juveniles. This child has a wholesome earthiness and a healthy identification with and delight in nature. She enjoys milking time; she makes herself a little house under

The Butterbean Tent

All through the garden I went and went,
And I walked in under the butterbean tent.

The poles leaned up like a good tepee
And made a nice little house for me.

I had a hard brown clod for a seat,
And all outside was cool green street.

A little green worm and a butterfly
And a cricket-like thing that could hop went by.

Hidden away there were flocks and flocks
Of bugs that could go like little clocks.

Such a good day it was when I spent
A long, long while in the butterbean tent.

She has all the fun of wading in "The Branch." She listens to the "Water Noises" that seem to say, "And do you think? And do you think?" She grows suddenly joyous over the "Crescent Moon," and the verse skips as ecstatically as the children:

Crescent Moon

And Dick said, "Look what I have found!"
And when we saw we danced around,
And made our feet just tip the ground.

We skipped our toes and sang, "Oh-lo.
Oh-who, oh-who, oh what do you know!
Oh-who, oh-hi, oh-loo, kee-lo!"

We clapped our hands and sang, "Oh-ee!"
It made us jump and laugh to see
The little new moon above the tree.

She shares her shelter from a "Little Rain" with a shivery chicken and a ladybug. She is haunted by stars, amazed at the miracle of a

Firefly
(A Song)

A little light is going by,
Is going up to see the sky,
A little light with wings.

I never could have thought of it,
To have a little bug all lit
And made to go on wings.

And she is struck by the odd three-layer cake arrangement of the universe:

The People

The ants are walking under the ground,
And the pigeons are flying over the steeple,
And in between are the people.

A very tidy arrangement when you come to think of it!

Then there is talk, back and forth, between the child and her world. She listens to the hens going to roost and speaking their "little asking words." Twice a bush speaks to her, quite naturally, just a passing word. Around sleep time there is a gay little brown jug that talks, and in broad daylight an old horse, in the poem called "Horse," gives her a piece of his mind and sends her on her way:

He didn't talk out with his mouth;
He didn't talk with words or noise.
The talk was there along his nose;
It seemed and then it was.

He said the day was hot and slow,
And he said he didn't like the flies;
They made him have to shake his skin,
And they got drowned in his eyes....

And then he shut his eyes again.
As still as they had been before.
He said for me to run along
And not to bother him any more.

So children interpret dog or cat talk in their earnest and commendable efforts to reach the animal's point of view. This poem is horse-talk indeed, and you can fairly hear the snort with which horse asserts. " 'I'm horse,' he said, 'that's what!' "

People

The poems are full of pleasant people and reflect the child's interest not only in other children, but in the grownups at home and abroad. Father fills the little girl's mug at milking time and sings or tells stories to all the children. Mother sends them on picnics and corrects their manners. There are brothers: Clarence, Charles, and the twins, Will and Dick. In "Christmas Morning" the child recalls the details of the Nativity in terms of her own mother and baby John—as naïve and lovely an interpretation as you can find! Sundry other relatives are remembered in the poems. The townspeople vary from pretty "Miss Kate-Marie," the Sunday school teacher, and another "Beautiful Lady," to Mr. Pennybaker, who makes faces when he sings bass, and the notable Mr. Wells:

Mr. Wells

On Sunday morning, then he comes
To church, and everybody smells
The blacking and the toilet soap
And camphor balls from Mr. Wells.

He wears his whiskers in a bunch,
And wears his glasses on his head.
I mustn't call him Old Man Wells—
No matter—that's what Father said.

And when the little blacking smells
And camphor balls and soap begin,
I do not have to look to know
That Mr. Wells is coming in.

The intense curious interest that children feel toward the strange antics of grownups is reflected in poem after poem and is summarized in the amusing "People Going By."

Fidelity to Child Nature

Reading and rereading these poems, you realize their integrity. No word, no line is dressed up or prettified to sound "cute." Cuteness afflicts much modern verse for children and is indeed the curse of juvenile poetry. Here in these poems by Elizabeth Madox Roberts is complete fidelity to child nature. The poems are grave, simple, and full of the unconscious beauty of a child's narrative when he is moved to tell you earnestly of something he enjoys. You can live with these poems, use them year after year, and never exhaust their richness. No adult can read them without knowing much more about children when he finishes, and no child can hear them without feeling a kinship with that child who likes to play with wiggletails, smell the aromatic herbs of fennel, and eat cherry pie, but who occasionally suffers from fears no less intense from being imaginary.

Strange Tree

Away beyond the Jarboe house
I saw a different kind of tree.
Its trunk was old and large and bent,
And I could feel it look at me.

The road was going on and on
Beyond to reach some other place.
I saw a tree that looked at me,
And yet it did not have a face.

It looked at me with all its limbs;
It looked at me with all its bark.
The yellow wrinkles on its sides
Were bent and dark.

And then I ran to get away,
But when I stopped to turn and see,
The tree was bending to the side
And leaning out to look at me.

MARY AUSTIN, 1868-1934

The Children Sing in the Far West

Mary Austin's *The Children Sing in the Far West* is our only collection of children's poems about our great Southwest. Yet the Indian lore, flora, fauna, desert, and mountains are as important to the children of that region as the landscape and creatures of New England are to the children there. "Grizzly Bear" is a joke children of any age enjoy. "Texas Trains and Trails," "A Song of Western Men," and "A Feller I Know" are satisfying Westerns. "Seven Rhyming Riddles" are delightful, but Mary Austin's finest poems are her interpretations of Indian feeling and philosophy. Perhaps the children will prefer her at her second best, in the rollicking "Texas Trains and Trails" style, but teachers should slip in some of her best and most characteristic poems now and then—"Charms," "Prayers," and "A Song of Greatness," for example—and at least a few of the children will respond.

A Song of Greatness[26]

When I hear the old men
Telling of heroes,
Telling of great deeds
Of ancient days,
When I hear that telling
Then I think within me
I too am one of these.

When I hear the people
Praising great ones,
Then I know that I too
Shall be esteemed,
I too when my time comes
Shall do mightily.

Mary Austin's own mysticism and her sympathetic understanding of the Indian's religion make "Morning Prayer" and "Evening Prayer" particularly fine.

The old Indian wisdom of killing only for food, never for the mere sport of killing, is expressed in

For Going A-Hunting[26]

O my brothers of the wilderness,
My little brothers,
For my necessities
I am about to kill you!
May the Master of Life who made you
In the form of the quarry
That the children may be fed,
Speedily provide you
Another house;
So there may be peace
Between me and thy spirit.

These poems give young readers a new understanding of and respect for our American Indians. At her best, Mary Austin transcends local color and writes with universal significance.

WINIFRED WELLES, 1893-1939

Skipping Along Alone

The poems of Winifred Welles and Mary Austin have been out of print for so long

26. "A Song of Greatness" and "For Going A-Hunting." From *Children Sing in the Far West* by Mary Austin. Used by permission of the publishers, Houghton Mifflin Co.

that there seems little hope of their return. They survive chiefly in the larger libraries and partially at least in anthologies.

Winifred Welles' *Skipping Along Alone* contains poems that are highly imaginative with a lovely lyric quality that suggests Walter de la Mare. Her quiet, mysterious "Green Moth" has a melody quite different from that of the crotchety "Stocking Fairy" or the mysterious "Behind the Waterfall" or the popular "Dogs and Weather." Each has its unique musical pattern perfectly suited to the mood or the content of the poem. Read them aloud, to appreciate fully their lyricism.

RACHEL FIELD, 1894-1942

Taxis and Toadstools
Poems

Rachel Field must have been a delightful human being, judging from the amusing account of her early years she wrote for *The Junior Book of Authors,* and from the varied tributes paid her in the Memorial edition of the *Horn Book* (July-August 1942). These give you the impression of a warm, vivid personality, full of exuberance, loving people and the outdoor world. She worked at top speed, as if from some inner compulsion, and gave to her books the vigor and integrity that were hers. With curly red hair and bright eyes, she was "just like Christmas," said Laura Benét, a fellow poet.

Rachel Field was born in the lovely old town of Stockbridge, Massachusetts. There she started school and, she confides, did so poorly that she dreaded the days when report cards were due. But teachers and townspeople remember her as a gifted child, absorbed by dramatics and playing well such contrasted characters as Shylock in *The Merchant of Venice* and the title role of *Rebecca of Sunnybrook Farm.* She began to write poetry at an early age, but mathematics was forever a mystery and a terror. In high school in Springfield, Massachusetts, she won an essay prize and determined to go to college if she could avoid mathematics. Radcliffe accepted her as a special student, and throughout four happy years she took all the English she could get, both literature and composition. Eventually she became a member of the famous English 47, George P. Baker's "Dramatic Workshop," which produced many notable playwrights.

After Radcliffe, Rachel Field settled in New York to begin the serious business of writing. Her *Six Plays* were published in 1924, and that same year the Yale University Press published her poems for children, *The Pointed People.* These attracted favorable attention even though they appeared at the same time that A. A. Milne's *When We Were Very Young* was creating a sensation. Rachel Field illustrated her book with her own cut-out silhouettes, and in 1926 did the decorations for her second book of poems, *Taxis and Toadstools.* This clever title signified her own way of life: eight months in New York City, with taxis, street-vendors, and skyscrapers; four months on an island off the coast of Maine with fogs, wood-strawberries, and toadstools.

From 1924 to 1942, in a period of only eighteen years, she published some thirty-six books, many of which she herself illustrated. She ended with two popular novels for adults. It is pleasant to think that boys and girls recognized her ability when they bestowed upon *Calico Bush,* the historical novel she wrote for them, their wholehearted approbation. *Hitty,* which is the story of a hundred-year-old doll, won the Newbery Medal, but Rachel Field's finest prose contribution to children's literature is the unusual and powerful *Calico Bush* (see Chapter 16).

The last six years of her sunny life must have been among the happiest. After her marriage she went to California with her husband and there she wrote the adult novel *All This, and Heaven Too,* which was made into a successful moving picture. In California, when their daughter Hannah was only two-and-a-half years old, Rachel Field died. In the closing paragraph of her last novel, *And Now Tomorrow,* she writes, "Once I might have faltered before such a transplanting. But that was yesterday. Now I am ready for tomorrow."

A Child's Sense of Wonder

Of Rachel Field's books of poems for children, *Taxis and Toadstools* is the one that children like best. Here are poems as direct and forthright as their author.

An inland child once said with awe that she was going to spend the summer on an *island.* "A real island with the sea all around; just think, with sea on every side of us!" she breathed, recalling:

If once you have slept on an island
You'll never be quite the same.

How could Rachel Field know so unerringly the child's sense of the miracle of islands? Over and over, she catches the curious wonderment of children. She shows a child turning back to look at the china dog with the "sad unblinking eye" and wishing for magic words to bring him to life; or a child wondering what the ring of the doorbell may bring forth; or feeling "strange and shivery" when a parrot looks at him with his "bead-bright eyes"; or wondering if skyscrapers ever want to lie down and never get up! These are authentic child-thoughts, and the children respond to their integrity with spontaneous pleasure.

A Child's Kinship with Nature

Out-of-doors, the children of her poems voice that curious kinship with birds, beasts, and growing things that is part of the magic of childhood. Some people, like Rachel Field herself, keep this all their lives. In "Barefoot Days" the child is "glad in every toe," and the first verse is alive with the feeling of cool grass and curly fern under small, naked feet. Her children lie down in meadow grass and expect to hear the bluebells ring. They go to the woods for wild strawberries and forget that there is anything else in the world to do but "fill my hands and eat." They think that perhaps if they sit still long enough—the whole summer through—they may take root in the ground with the bay and the juniper trees. They understand the wild creatures, and when they see "The Dancing Bear," they know at once something is wrong, for his eyes look bewildered "like a child's lost in the woods at night."

The City Child

Rachel Field's unique contribution to children's verse is perhaps the three groups of city poems in *Taxis and Toadstools,* called "People," "Taxis and Thoroughfares," and "Stores and Storekeepers." Of course the city child likes automobiles, just as a country child likes horses and cattle. A ten-year-old boy of the city streets used to recite Rachel Field's "Taxis" with a shine in his eyes and a gusto that seemed to say, "Now listen to this. Here's something!"

Taxis[27]

Ho, for taxis green or blue,
Hi, for taxis red,
They roll along the Avenue
Like spools of colored thread!

Jack-o'-Lantern yellow,
Orange as the moon,
Greener than the greenest grass
Ever grew in June.
Gayly striped or checked in squares,
Wheels that twinkle bright,
Don't you think that taxis make
A very pleasant sight?
Taxis shiny in the rain,
Scudding through the snow,
Taxis flashing back the sun
Waiting in a row.

Ho, for taxis red and green,
Hi, for taxis blue,
I wouldn't be a private car
In sober black, would you?

In the recently published collection of her verses called *Poems,* "Song for a Blue Roadster" is equally popular. So the city child likes "Good Green Bus," "At the Theater," "The Florist Shop," "The Animal Store," and the favorite "Skyscrapers."

One of the pleasantest poems in this group is "City Rain." The first verse is so clear a picture that children always want to illustrate it. The cozy feeling in the second verse is heightened by the rainy sound of that next-to-the-last line, with its humming *n*'s or *ing*'s:

27. "Taxis" and "City Rain." From *Taxis and Toadstools* by Rachel Field. Copyright 1926 by Doubleday & Company, Inc.

City Rain

Rain in the city!
I love to see it fall
Slantwise where the buildings crowd
Red brick and all.
Streets of shiny wetness
Where the taxis go,
With people and umbrellas all
Bobbing to and fro.

Rain in the city!
I love to hear it drip
When I am cosy in my room
Snug as any ship,
With toys spread on the table,
With a picture book or two,
And the rain like a rumbling tune that sings
Through everything I do.

The Child Looks at People

The child who speaks in the first person throughout these poems likes people and watches them with friendly keenness even as Rachel Field must have done. Interest in people is characteristic of children, and it is recorded in these poems with sensitive perception. When the child sees "Sandwich Men," there is a recognition of something wrong. The men are "dreary round the eye" with something about them that makes her "want to cry." And this is not an unchildlike observation. Children study lame people or anyone who deviates from the normal with a passionate intentness that seems bent upon finding out why, at all costs.

Rachel Field's poetry never attains the power and sureness of her best prose, but the complete absence of artificiality or juvenile cuteness in these poems commends them to both children and adults.

DOROTHY ALDIS, 1897-

All Together;
A Child's Treasury of Verse
Quick as a Wink
Hello Day

Dorothy Aldis' verses are popular with children six to eight years old, although her verse patterns, compared with Milne's, are neither varied nor interesting, and she rarely achieves anything unusual either in form or content. Yet she makes a sure appeal to young children. Her strength lies in her knowledge of the small child's everyday interests, his play, and his observations. Mrs. Aldis' verse-children keep pets, have brothers and sisters, wonder about their hands and feet, celebrate Fourth of July, and enjoy a happy relationship with their parents. "Hiding," which is the most popular verse she ever wrote, can be found in most anthologies. A prime favorite with six- and seven-year-olds, it is beloved in part because it reflects a parent-child relationship that every child longs for. Here are a mother and father playing with their child, entering into his make-believe with proper gravity and no condescension.

HARRY BEHN, 1898-

The Little Hill
Windy Morning
The Wizard in the Well

Harry Behn's three small books of verse, attractively decorated by the author, speak to young children, five to nine, with lyric charm and unusual variety. There are a few nonsense jingles like "Mr. Pyme," "Dr. Windikin," "Shopping Spree," and the lively

Tea Party [28]

Mister Beedle Baddlebug,
Don't bandle up in your boodlebag
Or mumble in your jimblejug,
Now eat your nummy tiffletag
Or I will never invite you
To tea again with me. Shoo!

There are also comparatively few fairy poems. Particularly pleasing are the imaginative "The Merry-Go-On," "The Fairy and the Bird," the philosophical "The Wizard in the Well," and the gentle, wistful "Undine's Garden." In quite a different mood of conscious make-believe is the amusing:

28. "Tea Party" and "The Gnome." From *Windy Morning,* copyright 1953 by Harry Behn. Reprinted by permission of Harcourt, Brace and World, Inc.

The Gnome

I saw a gnome
As plain as plain
Sitting on top
Of a weathervane.

He was dressed like a crow
In silky black feathers,
And there he sat watching
All kinds of weathers.

He talked like a crow too,
Caw caw caw,
When he told me exactly
What he saw,

Snow to the north of him
Sun to the south,
And he spoke with a beaky
Kind of a mouth.

But he wasn't a crow,
That was plain as plain
'Cause crows never sit
On a weathervane.

What I saw was simply
A usual gnome
Looking things over
On his way home.

There are many verses about the child's play world, both real and imaginative. "The New Little Boy" is refreshingly antisocial. "Picnic by the Sea" is a child's view of the queer grownups who sit sunning themselves when there are so many wonders to be explored. "Hallowe'en" is a particularly shivery celebration of that favorite festival and is delightful for verse choirs to speak. "Pirates," "The Kite," "Growing Up," "Visitors," "Teddy Bear," "Old Grey Goose," and "Surprise" are all good examples of this group of verses.

Mr. Behn's unique contribution is found in those poems where he is helping the child to look at his everyday experiences with the eyes of the spirit. Notice the philosophy in

Others[29]

Even though it's raining
I don't wish it wouldn't.
That would be like saying
I think it shouldn't.

I'd rather be out playing
Than sitting hours and hours
Watching rain falling
In drips and drops and showers,
But what about the robins?
What about the flowers?

Read aloud "Early Awake," "Trees," "Spring," "Spring Rain," "The Little Hill," "Lesson," and you will feel the reassurance, the acceptance, and the happy peace that emanate from these and many other poems. "This Happy Day" begins with a child's cheerful greeting to the sun on a bright new day and concludes with a note of thanksgiving. Without any religious pronouncements, these are religious poems in which the poet helps children to appreciate their everyday experiences, the sheer magic of being alive. One of the finest of these is "Gardens." The young child may not understand its full meaning without a little explanation, but it is a reverent expression of the mystery of creation.

Gardens[30]

Clouds are flowers
Around the sun.

The summer breeze
Hums with bees.

One drop of dew
Holds only me,

29. From *The Wizard in the Well,* copyright 1956 by Harry Behn. Reprinted by permission of Harcourt, Brace and World, Inc.
30. From *The Little Hill,* copyright 1949 by Harry Behn. Reprinted by permission of Harcourt, Brace and World. Inc.

In this picture, shapes are stylized and repeated to create a design with rhythm and charm. From Windy Morning. *Copyright 1953 by Harry Behn. By permission of Harcourt, Brace & World, Inc. (Book 5 x 7¼, picture 1¾ x 1)*

1.

3.

2.

1. Fine lines, strong lights and darks give interesting textures to this picture of "Father William" turning "a back-somersault in at the door." (See pp. 122-123.)
Illustration by John Tenniel. From Alice in Wonderland and Through the Looking Glass *(one-volume edition) by Lewis Carroll. Copyright 1941 by Heritage Press.*
Reproduced by permission of Heritage Press. (Book 6 x 9)

2. In this imaginative illustration of "Escape at Bedtime," the night sky is beautifully decorated with constellations.
Illustration by Martin Provenson. Reproduced by permission from A Child's Garden of Verses *by Robert Louis Stevenson. © Copyright 1951 by Golden Press, Inc.*
(Original in color, book 8½ x 11, two-page picture 14¾ x 5)

4.

6.

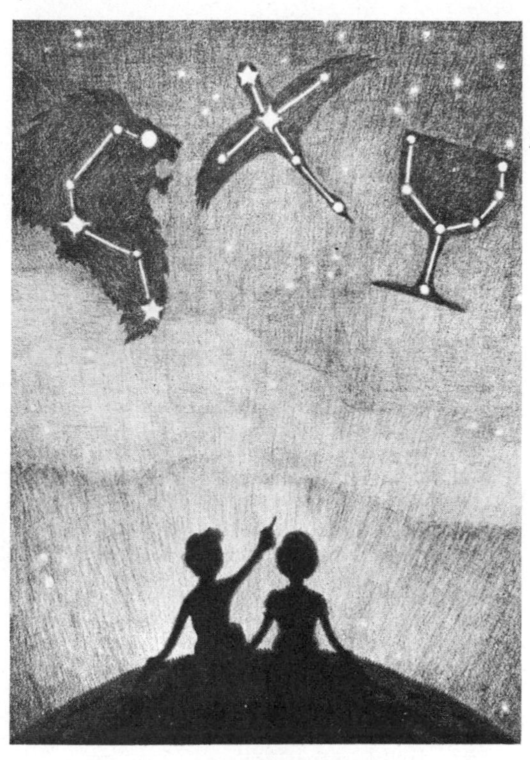

5.

3. *In this illustration for "Vern," the boy's face tells the story of his sadness. Only his dog understands at this moment. (See p. 159.) Illustration by Ronnie Solbert. From* Bronzeville Boys and Girls *by Gwendolyn Brooks. Copyright © 1956 by Gwendolyn Brooks Blakely. Reproduced with permission of Harper & Row. (Book 6⅜ x 8⅛)*

4. *Simple line, contrasting areas of black and white, and effective details make this picture of a yawning cherub with a bare middle very fetching. (See p. 161.) Illustration by Jacqueline Chwast. Reproduced from* Wide Awake and Other Poems, *© 1959, by Myra Cohn Livingston, by permission of Harcourt, Brace & World, Inc. (Book 4⅝ x 6¾)*

5. *In this lovely crayon drawing, the children are silhouetted against a luminous sky, are awed as they gaze at the constellations. (See p. 133.) Illustration by Henry B. Kane. From* Take Sky *by David McCord. Copyright © 1961, 1962, by David McCord. Reprinted by permission of Little, Brown and Company. (Book 5¼ x 8¼)*

6. *Wonderful line portrait of "Silas Pie," that almost extinct person, the fruit peddler, and his good old horse. (See p. 162.) Illustration by Rita Fava. From* Speaking of Cows *by Kaye Starbird. Copyright © 1960 by Kaye Starbird. Reproduced by permission of the publishers, J. B. Lippincott. (Book 5¼ x 8)*

But there is one
That holds the sun

And clouds and flowers
And everyone.

This quiet note of reassurance is characteristic of Mr. Behn's poetry for children.

FRANCES FROST, 1905-1959

The Little Whistler
The Little Naturalist

Frances Frost's two small books of verses are not so well known as they deserve to be. The title poem of *The Little Whistler* is an account of a child's vain attempts to produce a whistle. The poems of the four seasons in this book reveal the author's delight in seasonal changes and her enjoyment of the outdoor world. But her best observations of nature are to be found in the posthumous book, *The Little Naturalist*. Both books are written from a child's point of view. Typical is her

Green Hill Neighbors[31]

When I look at our green hill,
I think of all the wild
Small hearts that live inside it:
The woodchuck's chubby child,

Rabbits with busy whiskered faces
Peering out of rocks,
The big-eared meadow mouse, the dainty
Gold-eyed baby fox.

When I look at our green hill
Beneath the sunny sky,
I'm pleased to have such friends inside—
And glad I live nearby!

"Green Afternoon" is an account of two nervous mothers, a cow and a doe, anxiously watching their youngsters frolicking together. "Fox Cub Goes Home" is the dramatic account of a fox baby following a child. Otters at play seem almost neighbors in

Otter Creek

Watch the little otters
Playing in the sun!
On the snowy riverbank
They have great fun

Sliding down an otter-
Fashioned chute-the-chutes,
Silver on their whiskers
And their small gay suits.

Up they hitch and waddle,
Down they swoop and squeak!
We've named the river after them,
We call it Otter Creek.

"The Foxes" playing ball is a beguiling picture. Every poem reflects Frances Frost's love for and close observation of the small creatures of field, forest, and meadow. These poems will enrich science courses and should make a young naturalist of any child who reads them.

New Singers of Small Songs

A Negro poet, Gwendolyn Brooks, has twice been recipient of a Guggenheim Fellowship. She has also received the Pulitzer Prize for her book of adult poems, *Annie Allen*, and an award from the Academy of Arts and Letters. Her book of poems for and about children, *Bronzeville Boys and Girls*, will have a universal appeal because the poems speak for any child of any race. They show a rare sensitivity to the child's inner life—his wonderments, hurts, and gay sense of make-believe and play. Here are two in contrasting mood.

Cynthia in the Snow[32]

It SUSHES.
It hushes
The loudness in the road.
It flitter-twitters,
And laughs away from me.
It laughs a lovely whiteness,

31. "Green Hill Neighbours" and "Otter Creek." With permission of McGraw-Hill Book Co., Inc. Whittlesey House from *The Little Naturalist* by Frances Frost and Kurt Werth. Copyright © 1959 by the Estate of Frances Frost, and Kurt Werth.
32. "Cynthia in the Snow" and "Vern." From *Bronzeville Boys and Girls* by Gwendolyn Brooks. Copyright 1956 by Gwendolyn Brooks Blakely. Reprinted by permission of Harper & Row, Inc.

And whitely whirs away,
To be
Some otherwhere,
Still white as milk or shirts.
So beautiful it hurts.

Vern

When walking in a tiny rain
Across the vacant lot,
A pup's a good companion—
If a pup you've got.

And when you've had a scold,
And no one loves you very,
And you cannot be merry,
A pup will let you look at him,
And even let you hold
His little wiggly warmness—

And let you snuggle down beside.
Nor mock the tears you have to hide.

Beatrice Schenk de Regniers' books, whether in prose or verse, are unique and imaginative. A good example is *Something Special* with its ten beguiling verses and the gay, interpretive drawings by Irene Haas. "If You Find a Little Feather" is sensitive fancy that trips off the tongue delightfully.

If You Find a Little Feather[33]

If you find a little feather,
a little white feather,
a soft and tickly feather,
it's for you.

A feather is a letter
from a bird,
and it says,
"Think of me.
Do not forget me.
Remember me always.
Remember me forever.
Or remember me
at least
until
the little feather
is
lost."
So . . .

. . . if you find a little feather,
a little white feather,
a soft and tickly feather,
it's for you.
Pick it up
and . . .
put it in your pocket!

"If We Walked on Our Hands" is childlike nonsense. Every one of the ten poems is a pleasant surprise, including "Keep a Poem in Your Pocket" (p. 192), with a philosophy suitable for the four-year-old but equally sound for the octogenarian.

Aileen Fisher has been a prolific writer of verses for children. Her topics cover the seasons, children's pets, nature as the child encounters it. Typical of her earlier work is

My Cat[34]

My cat rubs my leg
and starts to purr
with a soft little rumble,
a soft little whir
as if she had motors
inside of her.

I say, "Nice Kitty,"
and stroke her fur,
and though she can't talk
and I can't purr,
she understands me,
and I do her.

With *Going Barefoot* Miss Fisher has attained a new freedom of verse patterns, a lighter, gayer touch, and a melodic line that makes this book a delight to read aloud either at one sitting or in parts day by day. It begins with the boy's question—

How soon
how soon
is a morning in June,
a sunny morning or afternoon
in the wonderful month
of the Barefoot Moon?[35]

33. Copyright 1958 by Beatrice Schenk de Regniers. Reprinted from *Something Special* by Beatrice Schenk de Regniers and Irene Haas by permission of Harcourt, Brace & World, Inc.
34. Reprinted from *Runny Days, Sunny Days* by Aileen Fisher, by permission of Abelard-Schuman Ltd. All rights reserved. Copyright 1933, 1938, 1946 by Aileen Fisher.
35. "How soon" and "June." From *Going Barefoot* by Aileen Fisher. Copyright 1960 by Aileen Fisher. Thomas Y. Crowell Company, New York, publisher.

Then the young philosopher observes that rabbits go barefoot all year round, so do raccoons, bees, cats, deer, and other creatures, while he must suffer the handicap of socks, shoes, and even galoshes. At last comes the day when he and his mother consult the calendar and the narrative reaches a triumphant conclusion—

June!

The day is warm
and a breeze is blowing,
the sky is blue
and its eye is glowing,
and everything's new
and green and growing . . .

My shoes are off
and my socks are showing . . .

My socks are off . . .

Do you know how I'm going?
BAREFOOT!

This is free and melodic and as full of movement as the restless child waiting for the big day of emancipation from shoes. The poetry about the rabbits, the kangaroos, and other creatures may be read and enjoyed separately or enjoyed as part of the whole. Adrienne Adams' illustrations in full color, with authentic paw prints adorning the end pages, add enchantment to this delightful book. The autumnal *Where Does Everyone Go?* is not quite so exhilarating but exceedingly pleasant to hear and look at. New books in this style continue to appear.

Zhenya Gay, like Kate Greenaway, is primarily an artist. Her verses are pedestrian, but her accompanying pictures (see 6, p. 135) are so full of zestful action and reveal so true an observation of the capering grace of young children and animals that to use her books is a joyous experience. *Jingle Jangle* is the best of them so far. Through its pages she helps the child to touch, taste, smell, see, hear, and enjoy the outdoor world: "Night things are soft and loud," "The world is full of wonderful smells," "Going barefoot is lots of fun." She also does some really giddy nonsense verses, and throughout her books the pictures bring oh's and ah's of delight from children and adults. She writes for the three- to six-year-olds, but the sevens and eights enjoy a few of her verses also.

Mary Ann Hoberman's *Hello and Good-By* has forty-one brief verses. The title poem voices an intriguing idea and "Brother" will undoubtedly find many sympathizers. It is an amusing patter verse to say.

Karla Kuskin's *In the Middle of the Trees* is a large, handsome book with twenty-one verses, the best of which is the double-page spread for

Spring[36]

I'm shouting
I'm singing
I'm swinging through the trees
I'm winging skyhigh
With the buzzing black bees.
I'm the sun
I'm the moon
I'm the dew on the rose.
I'm a rabbit
Whose habit
Is twitching his nose.
I'm lively
I'm lovely
I'm kicking my heels.
I'm crying "Come dance"
To the fresh water eels.
I'm racing through meadows
Without any coat
I'm a gamboling lamb
I'm a light leaping goat.
I'm a bud
I'm a bloom
I'm a dove on the wing.
I'm running on rooftops
And welcoming spring!

Another pleasant one, challenging for the children to illustrate, is "The Gold-Tinted Dragon." New books by this author appear frequently.

Myra Cohn Livingston's several books of verse for the youngest children—*Whispers, I'm Hiding, Wide Awake,* and *See What I Found*—deal with the sensory experiences,

36. "Spring" from *In the Middle of the Trees* by Karla Kuskin. Copyright 1958 by Karla Kuskin. Reprinted by permission of Harper & Row, Publishers.

activities, and imaginings of young children. The rhymed comments are as discerning as the pen and ink sketches by Jacqueline Chwast (see 4, p. 157) and Erik Blegvad.

Whispers[37]

Whispers
tickle through your ear
telling things you like to hear.
Whispers
are as soft as skin
letting little words curl in.
Whispers
come so they can blow
secrets others never know.

Wide Awake[38]

I have to jump up
out of bed
and stretch my hands
and rub my head,
and curl my toes
and yawn
and shake
myself
all wideawake!

Mary O'Neill's *Hailstones and Halibut Bones* is a happy experiment with words and colors. The intriguing title comes from the opening lines of

What Is White?[39]

White is a dove
And lily of the valley
And a puddle of milk
Spilled in an alley—
A ship's sail
A kite's tail
A wedding veil
Hailstones and
Halibut bones
And some people's telephones.

This is typical of the humorous and often subtle associations of colors with objects or moods or feelings. The children have taken to these verses with enthusiasm, sometimes trying to guess what next, sometimes making their own associations, and sometimes carrying the notion home to see the grownups playing the game also.[40] Perhaps the subtlest is "What Is Black?" which concludes:

Think of what starlight
And lamplight would lack
Diamonds and fireflies
If they couldn't lean against
Black . . .

Of the verses, one of the children's favorites is the gay and childlike "What Is Yellow?" The poems are a delight to read aloud; they set the children's imaginations to working, and they also lend themselves to choral speaking. Leonard Weisgard's decorative illustrations in the appropriate color for each poem make this an all-round distinguished book.

In *Speaking of Cows,* Kaye Starbird, one of the most promising new poets for children, has written twenty-nine amusing poems from the child's-eye view of everyday experiences. The casual, ruminative pace of these verses is well illustrated by the title poem.

Speaking of Cows[41]

Speaking of cows
(Which no one was doing)
Why are they always
Staring and chewing?
Staring at people,
Chewing at clover,
Doing the same things
Over and over.

Once in awhile,
You see a cow mooing,
Swishing her tail
At a fly that needs shooing.

37. From *Whispers and Other Poems,* copyright 1958, by Myra Cohn Livingston. Reprinted by permission of Harcourt, Brace & World, Inc.
38. From *Wide Awake and Other Poems,* copyright 1959 by Myra Cohn Livingston. Reprinted by permission of Harcourt, Brace & World, Inc.
39. Excerpts from "What Is White?" and "What Is Black?" From *Hailstones and Halibut Bones* by Mary O'Neill. Copyright © 1961 by Mary Gibbons O'Neill. Reprinted by permission of Doubleday & Company, Inc.
40. Miss Leslie Newton, Head of the Children's Division, Lakewood Public Library, Lakewood, Ohio, records these experiences with the poems.
41. "Speaking of Cows" and "Silas Pie." From *Speaking of Cows* by Kaye Starbird. Copyright 1960 by Kaye Starbird. Published by J. B. Lippincott Company.

Most of the time, though,
What's a cow doing?
Munching and looking,
Staring and chewing.
Eyes never blinking,
Jaws always moving.
What are cows thinking?
What are cows proving*?*

Cows musn't care for
New ways of doing.
That's what they stare for;
That's why they're chewing.

These poems present a child voicing his honest opinions or questions about the bugs, beasts, people, and ideas he encounters. There is the unloved lizard "O'Toole," "Living his life in a quiet way," but still unloved. There is "My Cousin Kitty," who no matter what wonders you show her continues to cry "I want a balloon." The poems about the kitten in the mailbox, the toad that needed a baby sitter, Patsy Doolin, the naughty, imaginary sprite who takes over the body of a child who is misbehaving—these and many others are inventive and skilfully composed.

Silas Pie

Buicks all blue and shiny,
Plymouths all red and tan
Go zooping by
Old Silas Pie
The Fruit-and-Garden Man.
But Si just guides his wagon
Along the humming highways,
Steering his course
And telling his horse,
"These modern ways ain't my *ways"*

Instead of gas," says Silas,
"I've got my good horse, Bella.
And if it rains
I take the pains
To raise my red umbrella.
There's no place in the country
That Bella, here, can't walk to.
And what's so fine
In speed and shine
Without a horse to talk to?"

Chevrolets green and glossy,
Pontiacs pale or black,
Go tootling by
Old Silas Pie
Who never tootles back.
Summer and spring and autumn
Silas just steers his course,
Traveling slow,
Watching things grow
And talking to Bella,
His horse.

Children and adults were introduced to the world of laughter by the hilarious verses of Edward Lear, and the tradition of nonsense and humorous verse has been kept healthy and flourishing by many talented writers. Laura E. Richards gave children some of the best and wildest nonsense verse. And A. A. Milne, with his knowledge of children, gave them some of their most amusing poetry. With poets such as David McCord, William Jay Smith, and John Ciardi writing today, we need not worry about nonsense and humor dying out in children's poetry.

Poetry of the child's everyday world began primly enough with the intent to teach manners and morals in a form that would be remembered. To this end, Isaac Watts wrote his little verse-sermons. The Taylor sisters also rhymed their advice, but their verses reflected more awareness of the real child. This awareness of the living child became still more evident in Kate Greenaway's mildly humorous verses. She showed children chatting, skipping, rolling hoops, and enjoying life.

But Robert Louis Stevenson with his *A Child's Garden of Verses* broke completely with moralistic verse. Stevenson's verses are imaginative and musical, with an easy flowing grace and a sure knowledge of the child's world. Stevenson showed the way, and later Eleanor Farjeon, Mary Austin, Elizabeth Madox Roberts, and many others brought their lyric gifts to interpret the everyday world the child sees and wonders about. Today many new singers of small songs are adding here and there a gay bit of nonsense, a sparkling lyric, a sage observation, or a joyful mood in the best tradition. So for the child, nonsense and reality and everyday play and imaginings go skipping along together in gaily adorned books of verse.

SUGGESTED READING, PROBLEMS, AND PROJECTS.

Note to students: To appreciate the humor or beauty of any poem, read it aloud. You will not only increase your appreciation of the poem but also gain perceptibly in interpretative ability.

Remember that the poems given in this text are only samples and no substitute for reading a poet's whole offering. Use this text merely for clues to the types, style, and range of poetry you will find.

For class discussion and later for use with children you will need far more poems from each writer than this book gives. If you plan to teach the primary grades, start now with this chapter to make your own collection.

1. Cite instances from your own experiences of the way laughter can relax tensions or relieve boredom. Think of some school situations in which a funny poem might come in handy.

2. What incidents from the lives of Lear, Carroll, Richards, Farjeon, and Milne might you tell children to enhance their enjoyment of the poems?

3. Compare the verses of Lear with those of Carroll. Do their verses seem dated in any way?

4. Give examples (not quoted in this text) from Laura Richards' *Tirra Lirra* of poems about animals, fairies, and nature. What are the qualities of the verses, and to what ages does the book appeal?

5. What do you know about Chistopher Robin from the verses in *When We Were Very Young* and *Now We Are Six*? Cite poems that give you information about his home and its location, his play and playmates, his pets and toys, and his attitudes.

6. Cite the different types of humor found in *A Book of Americans*. Notice also the penetrating and even serious characterizations scattered throughout the humorous verse.

7. Find five poems by David McCord or John Ciardi or William Jay Smith which you would like to use with children. Introduce each to the class in a sentence or two.

8. Turn the class into a Light Verse Clinic and have each member present her candidates for diagnosis from magazines, newspapers, or other sources. Does the poem have genuine humor, lively and musical rhythm, and fresh, childlike subject matter, or is it arch or falsely "cute," with pedestrian meter and forced rhymes?

9. Examine Greenaway's *Under the Window* and *Marigold Garden* and pick out your favorite verses. How would you use Kate Greenaway's books with young children? With middle-grade children?

10. Is Stevenson's child as solitary as Christopher Robin? Support your answer with evidence from the poems. After you know *A Child's Garden of Verses* thoroughly, select a group of poems to introduce and read to a group of children.

11. Select a poem by Sandburg not given in this text and prepare an introduction for it which will insure the children's understanding of its significance. Present the poem to the class.

12. Choose some of your favorite Farjeon poems not given in this text to read to the class. Evaluate them.

13. How does the little girl in Elizabeth Madox Roberts' poems compare with Stevenson's child or Milne's Christopher Robin in age, activities, way of living, interests, play, attitudes?

14. Give some specific examples of how Rachel Field's poems reflect the child's sense of wonder and delight.

15. Find five or six poems by Harry Behn which would help the young child interpret his everyday experiences.

16. Which of Frances Frost's poems do you think children would enjoy and how would you introduce and use them?

17. Look over the selections from "New Singers of Small Songs" or, better still, their books, if available. Which appeal to you especially and why? Which show promise of continued writing of special value to children?

18. From the work of all the poets considered in this chapter, find examples of lyrical quality, unusual imagery, fresh ways of expressing and enjoying everyday experience, modern insight into the psychology of childhood, useful subject matter, gaiety and humor, response to the child's needs for security. Divide these items among a group and pool the results.

REFERENCES

A combined bibliography for this chapter and chapters 7 and 8 appears on pages 214-219.

chapter 7

Growing Up with Poetry

Ask any teacher or parent who reads aloud to children what kind of poems they like and the answer will be, "Funny ones." The made-up words in so many of the nonsense poems and the amusing characters and situations in the humorous narratives always delight children. A mouse running up a clock or somebody going to sea in a sieve and coming safely home are surprises that tickle the funny bone. The rhythm and melody of verse are also primary sources of satisfaction to children just as are the rhythm and melody of music. But it is a long way from the tumpity-tump skips and gallops of early childhood to Bach and Beethoven and it is just as far from *Mother Goose* and Edward Lear to Walter de la Mare and Robert Frost. How can we help children grow up in poetry as successfully as music teachers help them grow up in music? Like the music teachers, we should start where the children are.

For instance, children begin as young as two years old to play with words and respond to their sounds. "Pickle-lillie, pickle-lillie," chants one child, savoring the ear-tickling *l*'s with evident enjoyment. "Upsey-daisy," sings another with broad smiles. Such responses to the humor of sounds are fairly common. But when a four-year-old repeated over and over in a soft, sad little voice, "Far, far away, far, far away!" everyone was surprised because none of the nursery-school stories or poems had included such a phrase or such a mood. Although he was ordinarily a rambunctious little boy, he spoke the words wistfully. He never added to the phrase, but throughout the day he would murmur, always in the same sad tone, "Far, far away!"[1] So other children are caught by the charm of other words and phrases, and without knowing why, they respond to the mood invoked by the words. In some such accidental way, children's taste for lyric poetry may begin. It is the responsibility of parents and teachers to provide poetry experiences for children that will help them grow up happily with poetry.

1. Marie L. Allen, *A Pocketful of Rhymes.*

Response to Mood and Melody

Reading aloud to a group of nursery-school children, Miss Jean Wheeler[2] tried Coleridge's "Kubla Khan":

In Xanadu did Kubla Khan
A stately pleasure-dome decree:
Where Alph, the sacred river, ran
Through caverns measureless to man
Down to a sunless sea.

When she concluded, a two-year-old remarked sagely, "Know what? That's nice." Of course he did not know what the verse meant, and of course its "niceness" for him consisted in the flow of words so beautiful and hypnotic to hear that even understanding adults can scarcely attend to their meaning. "But this is all wrong," say the earnest ones. "It is dangerous to encourage children to respond to words they do not understand. Words should convey meaning." Of course they should, but not all meaning is factual. Sometimes words induce a mood or feeling which cannot be wholly accounted for by their literal meanings but results from their sound, combined with their associative meaning. Certainly the two-year-old sensed the quiet beauty of "Kubla Khan" as truly as the most analytical critic.

A group of seven-year-olds who had enjoyed Milne's poetry and other humorous verse heard for the first time some poems by Walter de la Mare, among them "The Horseman." It was read to them twice with no comment.

I heard a horseman
Ride over the hill;
The moon shone clear,
The night was still;
His helm was silver,
And pale was he;
And the horse he rode
Was of ivory.[3]

After the second reading a boy spoke slowly, "That makes me think of knights . . . it has a sort of nice sound." When these children had an opportunity to receive a copy of the poems they had enjoyed the most and wished to hear again, "The Horseman" was one of their most frequent choices. Why? Its meaning is open to debate, but its mood of quiet and mystery somehow reaches young children, partly because of the associative qualities of such words as *horseman, still, helm,* and *ivory* but mostly because of the poem's gently melodic sound.

These examples are not intended to suggest that lyric poetry is characteristically obscure or that its sound is more important than its meaning. But they do imply that authentic poetry not only conveys meaning but generally evokes an emotional response. Children who have the good fortune to hear a poem that gives them a shiver up their backbones or a swift upsurging flood of elation or a sense of quiet and peace are discovering some of the joys of poetry.

Meaning is also important. After the early years of exploring poetry, children can and should profit from a close study of some poems for their ideas, secondary meanings, and possible implications. The study of poetic form can probably wait for high school and college. Just when this more intellectual approach to poetry should begin depends upon the child or group of children, their poetry experiences, and general background. But certainly, even within the elementary school years, they should grow in poetry appreciation both aesthetically and intellectually.

Meanwhile, the adult's responsibility is to find for the child at each age level those rich treasures of authentic poetry that suit his emotional range, cultivate his ear for the more subtle music of verse, and give him fresh ideas that are the essence of an experience.

Fortunately, the stream of English lyric poetry flows brighter than that of almost any other country. From this great body of verse, the child will appropriate certain poems that suit him, and when he has spoken them repeatedly until he knows them, they become

2. "Poetry for Children," *Childhood Education,* January 1930.

3. From *Peacock Pie* by Walter de la Mare, published by Holt, Rinehart and Winston, Inc. Reprinted by permission of the Literary Trustees of Walter de la Mare and the Society of Authors.

truly his. He will ask about them, too, and through discussions meaning will be enriched. If most children still prefer the lightest of light verse, just remember that most adults do, too. But a child's acceptance of one lovely lyric poem means he is on his way to greater appreciation of authentic poetry. The poems in this chapter will not be as easy as those in the preceding chapters, but reading them aloud to children, discussing them informally, rereading them, and encouraging the children to speak them with you will help children grow up in poetry.

Singers of Songs

William Shakespeare, William Blake, and Christina Rossetti are all associated in our minds with song. Different as they were, they had one gift in common, the gift of gay, childlike song. Their works are as sharply contrasted as their lives, yet children enjoy the songs of all three poets. Their lyrics must be heard over and over, casually and without pressure or catechizing but often enough so that they begin to sing in the children's memories.

WILLIAM SHAKESPEARE, 1564-1616

The great English dramatist is one of those poets who, although writing for adults, have songs that children enjoy. Children hearing the songs of Shakespeare without being forced to analyze or memorize them soon know the poems by heart, and the words sing in their heads like a popular tune. "Under the greenwood tree," from *As You Like It,* seems to belong with Robin Hood:

Under the greenwood tree
Who loves to lie with me,
And tune his merry note
Unto the sweet bird's throat,
Come hither, come hither, come hither:
Here shall he see
No enemy
But winter and rough weather.

Who doth ambition shun,
And loves to live i' the sun,
Seeking the food he eats
And pleased with what he gets,
Come hither, come hither, come hither:
Here shall he see
No enemy
But winter and rough weather.

"Jog on, jog on," from *The Winter's Tale,* is a good march for any excursion of children, and Ariel's song, "Where the bee sucks," from *The Tempest,* is a pleasant fairy poem. "Who is Sylvia?" from *The Two Gentlemen of Verona;* "When icicles hang by the wall," *Love's Labour's Lost;* and "Hark, hark! the lark," *Cymbeline*—these poems have a singing quality and a simplicity of content that bring them within the enjoyment range of our older children, especially if they hear the poems before they read them.

WILLIAM BLAKE, 1757-1827

Songs of Innocence

Blake's *Songs of Innocence* is a landmark in English literature as well as in children's literature. The average child may not particularly enjoy some of the more difficult poems, but he will enjoy many of them if he hears them read aloud by someone who likes their melodies. For Blake's poems are songs, full of cadences and lovely sounds.

It has always seemed easier to understand Blake's poems, their beauty and their limitations, if we know something not only of the man himself but of his art, for Blake was primarily an artist. Some of the stories about Blake's life, particularly his childhood, might well be told to the older children as an introduction both to his poems and to his illustrations. For younger children, we omit biographical data and expose them only to those poems they are capable of enjoying.

William Blake was the second of five children. His father had a small hosier's shop in

London, and in the rooms over the shop Blake lived until he was a young man. He was ordinarily an amiable, gentle child, but when roused sometimes showed a violent temper. From the time he was four years old he saw visions, and he continued to see them throughout his seventy years. At four, he saw the face of God looking at him through the window. A few years later, he saw a tree full of angels. He told his mother he had met and talked with Ezekiel, and she punished him for telling a lie. As a man, he insisted that he talked with his dead brother, with the poet Milton, the Apostle Paul, and other great ones, who, though dead, gave him continual guidance. All his life he told people about his visions as a matter of course, and so he was called "mad Blake" by the skeptical.

As a little boy, William was educated at home, but he showed such an unusual talent for drawing that his father, limited as his funds probably were, sent the boy to the drawing school of Henry Par. The ten-year-old boy worked devotedly at his drawing and further enriched his art experience by haunting the shops and exhibitions of the great art dealers of London. These men, recognizing the extraordinary interest and discrimination of the child, used to encourage him to talk about the prints he pored over so eagerly. He was soon known in these famous salesrooms as "the little connoisseur"—for he was already starting his own collection of prints by Michelangelo, Raphael, and Dürer.

Blake was apprenticed at fourteen to a famous engraver, James Basire, who appreciated and understood his strange pupil. Blake's descriptions of his conversations with the prophets made him the butt of ridicule among the other students, and his temper led to frequent fights. Basire, wishing to rescue this odd and talented boy, sent him off to the cathedrals to make drawings in solitude. After seven years of apprenticeship, Blake studied for a short time at the newly formed Royal Academy, and this completed his art education.

At twenty-five, Blake married Catherine Boucher, the daughter of a market-gardener. This young woman was uneducated but was lovely both in physical appearance and in character. She had a gentle, affectionate disposition that promised well for Blake's happiness but gave no hint of the fortitude and the unswerving loyalty of the woman who was to endure every hardship in her long life with her gifted husband. Blake taught his wife to read and write, shared with her his visions, and loved her throughout his life.

In the early days of their marriage the young couple seems to have enjoyed a prosperous and happy time. Blake was showing pictures yearly at the exhibitions of the Royal Academy. The rising young artists of the day were his friends, and he was a welcome visitor at the home of the Reverend Mr. and Mrs. Matthews, patrons of the arts. Besides painting his pictures, Blake was writing poems at this time and composing the music to accompany them. None of this music has survived, but Blake is said to have entertained the notables at the Matthews' home by reciting and singing his own compositions.

Then suddenly Blake turned against the people who were making much of him and withdrew completely from society. The companionship of "the mighty dead" was more important to him than the society of his lighthearted contemporaries. He felt that his friends interfered with his visions; so he turned away from people despite their kindness.

In 1789, *Songs of Innocence* was published. This book was a labor of love on the part of both William and Catherine Blake and was literally a handmade book. Blake wrote the poems and made the decorative designs that accompanied each one, engraving them upon copper plates. He published his own book, with his wife helping him print, add the hand-coloring, and even bind it. Notable as this book seems to us now, imaginative and lovely as were its poems and decorations, it was not appreciated at the time.

For us, *Songs of Innocence* marks a turning point in English poetry. The classical school had run thin; Wordsworth was already writing, but the Romantic Movement had not yet become consciously articulate. Then, suddenly, *Songs of Innocence* appeared—fresh, simple, unique. *Songs of Experience* was not published until five years later, but between the two collections of *Songs* came many of those poems Blake called his works of prophecy. Their mysticism and their incoherence

"Oberon and Titania" by William Blake

led people to judge Blake insane. This judgment was reversed even during Blake's lifetime, and today—however people regard his visions and his more confused writings—the best of Blake's poems are ranked among England's finest lyric poetry and a large proportion of his illustrations among the world's greatest engravings.

The remainder of Blake's life is of little interest to children. He had some periods of intense productivity as well as six long years of abject poverty and silence when he did no work at all but communicated only with his visions and his voices. During this period many people in England thought he was dead; only his wife sustained and comforted him. The years of obscurity were brought to an end when some artists (especially one by the name of John Linnell) discovered the genius of Blake's illustrations and decided to find the man who had created them, if he was still alive. In 1818 they found him, a quiet, serene old man of sixty, full of his dreams. Then Linnell seems to have been responsible for getting Blake commissions again and for launching him on another period of creative work that lasted until his death ten years later. In the years that followed his meeting with Linnell, Blake was cheered by the friendship and understanding of several artists. When he was sixty-five, the Royal Academy made him a small grant of money, and, best of all, he had the satisfaction of finding his creative powers unimpaired. During those last ten years, Blake turned out some of his finest illustrations. Toward the end of his life, he was too feeble to get out of bed, but eye, hand, and brain worked together more skillfully than ever.

Blake seems to have known when his life was nearing its close. On his last day he sang songs of praise to his Creator and assured his wife that he would always be near her. All his life he had been too close to another world to have any fear of death. He is said to have remarked, "I cannot think of death as more than going out of one room into another."

Blake's Illustrations[4]

If Blake's pictures for the Book of Job are available to you, examine them by all means; or study the illustrations reproduced by Darrell Figgis in *The Paintings of William Blake,* and those found in that useful little book by Philippe Soupault, *William Blake.* For purposes of comparison, consider "Oberon and Titania" and "The Procession from Calvary." These are typical engravings but do not, of course, represent his great range of subject matter.

Look first at "Oberon and Titania." The fairy figures have the dancing lightness of those in Botticelli's "Spring" but seem more unearthly because of the way both faces and bodies melt into the landscape. Only the impish Puck is sharply drawn. His smiling face attracts the eye immediately and not only is a center of interest but suggests the mood of the whole picture—light-hearted merrymaking. The four fairies dancing in a ring at his right are dimly drawn—one is only half visible—but their movement and speed are unmistakable. The whirling effect of their dance is heightened by contrast with the static figures of Oberon and Titania at the extreme left. So Blake, using no photographic details, suggests the rushing movement of an elfin dance and a mood of heedless gaiety. This he does through his use of whirling lines: follow them with your finger until you feel them rising and falling.

Look now at "The Procession from Calvary," which makes use of lines and masses to produce an opposite effect—not light gaiety but majestic power. The men in the proces-

4. See Chapter 4, p. 55, for another comment on Blake's illustrations.

sion are carrying the body of the dead Christ and they are followed by three sorrowing women. They are moving against a gloomy background: faintly suggested tree trunks and tree tops, buildings, and distant hills, one of which is surmounted by three black crosses. Dark masses and severe vertical lines are repeated over and over with increasing emphasis and growing clarity, from the dim background to the foreground of marching figures. The robes on the figures sweep downward with columnlike strength and solidity except at the head and feet, where they break into curving lines that produce an astonishing illusion of movement. This procession moves strongly and majestically forward. The body of Christ is borne unrealistically by the men, each using one supporting hand and shoulder that scarcely touch the bier. Indeed, that prostrate figure of the dead Christ seems to move forward of itself. The broad horizontal lines of the bier support it; horizontal clouds point to it and follow it, so that as the rigid body of the Christ is propelled forward, the eye travels with the procession out of the picture and onward. Here, again, Blake has given us not a realistic representation but a powerful interpretation of an idea and a feeling.

Blake's Poetry

Blake uses in his poetry the same interpretative rather than realistic method. In verse his mediums are no longer lines and masses but the sounds and the associative meanings of words and the rhythmic flow of lines. These he uses to create a mood or to convey an idea or feeling—not through a logical reporting of facts, but through words and rhythms that speak to the emotions and the imagination. For example, read aloud the first verse of

Spring

Sound the flute!
Now 't is mute;
Birds delight,
Day and night,
Nightingale
In the dale,
Lark in sky,—
Merrily,
Merrily, merrily to welcome in the year.

"Procession from Calvary" by William Blake

This opening verse suffices to set the mood of joy for the whole poem. The short, tripping lines and the brief words are like quick dance steps. The clear vowel sounds and the refrain, with its thrice-repeated "merrily," make a melody of every verse. Titania's fairies might dance to this song—the lines move with the same lightness and speed. But should children get every picture in every line, each in turn? Should they be told that larks and nightingales are not American but British birds? Heaven forbid! Four-year-old children like the sound of this poem with its rushing movement. Older children will like it, too, if it is read to them for just what it is: a song that suggests the exuberance of spring.

For contrast in mood, turn to those two companion poems, "The Little Boy Lost" and "The Little Boy Found." Read the former aloud. Doesn't it remind you, in both mood and tempo, of Schubert's famous song "The Erl King"?

The Little Boy Lost

"Father, father, where are you going?
Oh, do not walk so fast!
Speak, father, speak to your little boy,
Or else I shall be lost."

The night was dark, no father was there,
The child was wet with dew;
The mire was deep, and the child did weep,
And away the vapour flew.

Do you feel the terror of a lost child crying out to his father? The poem does not say where the father is or how the child lost him; its rapidly moving eight lines convey only the feelings of anguish and mystery. Notice how the metrical lines suggest the running of the child, just as Blake's graphic lines suggest movement in his pictures. Now turn to the tender reassurance of

The Little Boy Found

The little boy lost in the lonely fen,
Led by the wandering light,
Began to cry, but God, ever nigh,
Appeared like his father, in white.

He kissed the child, and by the hand led,
And to his mother brought,
Who in sorrow pale, through the lonely dale,
The little boy weeping sought.

This poem begins on a minor note, but the hurry and the terror are gone. The words and lines move quietly and gently, telling how God, appearing to the child in the guise of his father, leads him safely into the arms of his mother. Was the father dead? Blake never says, because in these two poems he is concerned not with reporting facts but with conveying powerfully and briefly (with no distracting details) the terror of being lost, the sense of guidance and comfort outside ourselves, and the blessed relief of coming home to love and security. Not circumstance but emotion is important in these poems—one a poem of terror, one a poem of reassurance.

Again, rhythm in the "Laughing Song" produces emotion.[5] Here Blake induces merriment through lines that rise steadily to a crescendo just as a laugh rises and increases. They never come to a rest until they burst into the hearty "Ha ha he" of the last line. The mounting gaiety is infectious, and children invariably smile with that laughing conclusion. What all the descriptive lines mean they can sense only hazily when they first hear them. The details grow in richness with repeated hearings, but to the contagious fun the children respond immediately. Here Blake captures laughter in the words and metrical lines of poetry, just as he captured gaiety in the masses and graphic lines of his fairy pictures.

This is a typical page from Blake's own edition of the Songs of Innocence. *The colors are the palest pastels, added by hand. From William Blake's* Songs of Innocence *(facsimile from British Museum copy, published by Minton, Balch, 1926)*

Using Blake's Poems with Children

These examples perhaps are sufficient to emphasize that Blake is not striving for realistic effects in his poems any more than he was in his illustrations. So when you read the *Songs* with children, do not bear down heavily on the factual details. Read the poems aloud for their melody and for the feeling-response

5. Many of the poems discussed but not reprinted in this book can be found in the anthology *Time for Poetry* (gen. ed., comp. by May Hill Arbuthnot). The bibliography (p. 214) will also help you locate poems not reprinted here. See the Index for poems printed in other chapters of this book.

Till the little ones, weary,
No more can be merry;
The sun does descend,
And our sports have an end.
Round the laps of their mothers
Many sisters and brothers,
Like birds in their nest,
Are ready for rest;
And sport no more seen
On the darkening Green.

In this picture the eye is led from the mother and children, to the older couple under the tree, to the children going home, and finally to the focus of the scene, the setting sun. Illustration by Harold Jones for William Blake's "Echoing Green" from Songs of Innocence. *Copyright 1961 by A. S. Barnes & Company, Inc. By permission of A. S. Barnes & Company, Inc., and Faber & Faber, Ltd., of London. (Book 6 x 8¼)*

they invariably arouse. If the children hear them read well enough, they experience a momentary feeling of gaiety or wonder, terror or peace. Then Blake speaks to them as he wished to speak—in terms of universal feeling. Of course, if the children ask questions or comment on a poem, encourage them to discuss it.

The effortless melody of many of these songs makes them sing in your head with a few readings. That is true of "Piping down the valleys wild," in which Blake describes the feeling that brought him to write these poems. Blake called this poem "Introduction," and so it may serve to introduce children to his *Songs*.

"The Shepherd" and "The Lamb" (p. 229) are in a quiet mood—the latter, with "The Little Boy Lost" and "The Little Boy Found," belongs to the religious literature of early childhood. Pictures of children at play are found in "Nurse's Song" and "The Echoing Green." Isn't that title—"Echoing Green"—a melody in itself? Young children like "Infant Joy," an imaginary dialogue between a two-day-old baby and a grownup who is wondering what to name it. This poem is typical of Blake's unrealistic style, as you can readily discover if you try to imagine how Dorothy Aldis or A. A. Milne would present the same situation. It is not with the question of naming a baby John or Peter that Blake is concerned but with the feeling of joy that a baby arouses. This little dialogue is not easy to read but is worth your best efforts to bring it to a child's understanding. (See p. 197.)

"The Little Black Boy" is a most sensitive presentation of the racial problem. It belongs to the upper grades or high schools, as do "The Chimney Sweeper," "Holy Thursday," and the religious poem "The Divine Image." These four poems illustrate the remarkably modern character of Blake's social and religious ideas.

There are perhaps only nine or ten of Blake's *Songs* that belong in the literature of the elementary school, and not more than four or five of these can be used in the primary grades. But if, through hearing them read aloud, the children like one or two of these songs well enough to ask for them at poetry time, or if they discover that they can say some of them aloud with you, or if they find that one of the songs is running through their heads, then you have accomplished all you could hope for. Their liking for authentic poetry is beginning and may become a permanent source of refreshment.

CHRISTINA ROSSETTI, 1830-1894

Sing Song

Christina Rossetti gave to children a small treasury of verses called *Sing Song*. Only a few incidents in her life will appeal to children, but to students of English literature and art she is interesting not only because she was the sister of the poet and painter Dante Gabriel Rossetti, and the model for several Pre-Raphaelite paintings, but also because she was an artist in her own right. Christina Rossetti contributed a fresh, if melancholy, note to English lyric poetry.

The Rossetti family was unusual in several ways. Apparently every member was beautiful to look at, highly intelligent, and uniquely gifted. The father, a distinguished Italian scholar, came to London as a political exile and found there not only the opportunity of continuing his writing on Dante, but also a charming wife, Frances Polidori. Even when Mrs. Rossetti was an old woman, visitors commented on her beauty and her intelligence. Her husband and her four children adored her, and the children—Maria Francesca, William Michael, Dante Gabriel, and Christina Georgina—quoted her word as final authority, painted her portrait, and wrote poems to and about her. Christina wrote a series of valentine poems all dedicated to her mother. It is amusing to discover that the recipient of this adoration found her artistic family a bit trying now and then. Mrs. Rossetti wrote:

I had always a passion for intellect, and my wish was that my husband should be distinguished for intellect, and my children too. I have had my wish; and now I wish that there were a little less intellect in the family, so as to allow for a little more common sense.[6]

The Rossettis lived in a shabby house on a down-at-the-heel London street. There was no glimpse of beauty in any direction, but the father often took the children to walk in the parks and to see some of the notable sights of historical old London. What a charming picture they must have presented—the grave, handsome man with the four dark-eyed, sparkling children! The Rossetti house was the rendezvous for Italian political refugees and Italian writers, musicians, and artists; so whatever the outer world of the little Rossettis lacked in beauty was compensated for by the highly exciting intellectual life of their family and friends.

The little country home of Christina's grandparents, the Polidoris, in Buckinghamshire, provided her with her only rural experiences. There on her occasional visits the city child made the acquaintance of frogs, toads, moles, caterpillars, birds, and flowers. These she recalled over and over in her poems. She learned to love the small "beasties," and in a day when girls were absurdly squeamish, she could pick up toads and caterpillars with calm tenderness.

Christina was always delicate, but the gay, "skittish" child grew gradually into a melancholy, deeply religious young woman, something of a recluse, unnaturally indifferent to clothes, wrapped up in her adored family, her books, and her writings. There were good reasons for this change, chief of them the unhappy conclusion of two love affairs. During her years of emotional vicissitudes, Christina must have found release and satisfaction in the recognition and praise given to her poetry. *Goblin Market and Other Poems* appeared in 1862 and immediately attracted wide attention, particularly the title poem, which was praised by the leading critics of the day.

But Christina Rossetti became more and more of an invalid until her death in her sixty-fourth year. Oddly enough, it was during these years of sadness and pain that she wrote her gayest poems and dedicated to a baby, "without permission," that nursery classic *Sing Song*, which appeared in 1872. The light-hearted verses of this little book she herself translated into Italian under the title *Ninna Nanna*—a charming gift for the children of her father's country!

Lyric Quality

Sing Song verses provide the young child with an ideal introduction to lyric poetry because they lead him imperceptibly from the patter of nonsense verse to the subtle and lovely cadences of authentic poetry. "If a pig wore a wig" might have come out of *Mother Goose* and so might the popular

Mix a pancake,
Stir a pancake,
Pop it in the pan;
Fry the pancake,

6. Dante Gabriel Rossetti, *His Family Letters,* p. 22.

Toss the pancake,—
Catch it if you can.[7]

But Christina Rossetti's little songs have a music which is obviously more subtle than that of *Mother Goose,* and they express more complex ideas. For instance, the personification of the daffodil as a lady in yellow and green is found in both *Mother Goose* and *Sing Song,* but notice the difference. *Mother Goose* gives us the briefest personification with no embellishments:

Daffadowndilly
Has come up to town,
In a yellow petticoat
And a green gown.

But Christina Rossetti gives us hills and vales, a chilly springtime, and the suggestion of the daffodil's fragility in those clear, clipped words "straight and frail" and the delicate sounds of "chilly," "hilly," "dilly"—all slight as the flower.

Growing in the vale
By the uplands hilly,
Growing straight and frail,
Lady Daffadowndilly.

In a golden crown,
And a scant green gown
While the spring blows chilly,
Lady Daffadown,
Sweet Daffadowndilly.

Christina Rossetti makes subtle and repeated use of vowel and consonant sounds to suggest the feeling or idea described by the words. Take her wind poems, for instance. There is quite a group of them and each one describes a different kind of wind, which you can almost hear in the sounds of the words. There is a stormy, ominous wind from the sea:

The wind has such a rainy sound
Moaning through the town,
The sea has such a windy sound,—
Will the ships go down?

The apples in the orchard
Tumble from their tree.—
Oh will the ships go down, go down,
In the windy sea?

Notice the use of the *n* and *d* sounds, which heighten the minor note of the poem. Then there is the poem about a tender little breeze:

O wind, where have you been,
That you blow so sweet?
Among the violets
Which blossom at your feet.

The honeysuckle waits
For summer and for heat;
But violets in the chilly spring
Make the turf so sweet.

And, finally, there is that gentle wind you can hear whispering in the soft, slight words of "Who has seen the wind?"

Tone Color

Every reader of *Sing Song* will have favorite examples of the skillful use of tone color. This

In this pen-and-ink drawing the sweep of the cape and the curve of the tree partially frame the tender faces of mother and child. Illustration by Arthur Hughes for Sing Song *by Christina Rossetti (1872 edition).*
(Book 4⅛ x 6¼, picture 3½ x 2⅞)

7. "Mix a pancake," "Daffodil," "The wind has such a rainy sound," "O wind," "What is pink?" "Angels at the foot," "Lullaby," "Seldom 'can't,' " and "An emerald is as green as grass." From *Sing Song* by Christina Rossetti, published by The Macmillan Company and used with their permission.

is worth noting because the way in which word sounds fit the mood or sensory impression of the poems largely determines how they should be read. For instance, with just the slightest exaggeration in emphasis you will discover that the words actually hop in that amusing couplet describing a rabbit:

And timid, funny, brisk little bunny
Winks his nose and sits all sunny.

Or read aloud the couplets of that remarkable color poem "What is pink? A rose is pink," noticing particularly these last four verses:

What is yellow? pears are yellow,
Rich and ripe and mellow.

Roll these words over your tongue and you can fairly taste pears

What is green? the grass is green,
With small flowers between.

Sounds delicate and small like spears of grass

What is violet? clouds are violet
In the summer twilight.

Slow, clinging words, quiet as the twilight

What is orange? why, an orange,
Just an orange!

Explosive, staccato words like a sudden laugh

Subject Matter

Young children respond with delight to the music of Christina Rossetti's slight, exquisite little lyrics, and, fortunately, most of the subject matter is understandable and appealing to them. There are, to be sure, a number of elegies about dead babies which should be omitted, but her live babies are delightful from the first poem:

Angels at the foot,
And angels at the head,
And like a curly little lamb
My pretty babe in bed.

to "I know a baby, such a baby" and the lullaby that begins

Lullaby, oh lullaby!
Flowers are closed and lambs are sleeping;

She also brings in other members of the family circle: there is Father "hot and tired, knocking at the door," Mother shaking the cherry tree, "Minnie and Mattie and fat little May," and an eight o'clock visit from the postman. Then there are all the small creatures the child delights in: a cock crowing "Kookoorookoo," "a frisky lamb and a frisky child," "hopping frogs," "plodding toads," pussy, doggy, white hen and her chicks, the "brown and furry caterpillar," and robins and wrens. There is a whole garden full of flowers, the sun, moon, and stars, and the rainbow seen in the poem "Boats sail on the rivers." Moralizing is rare but amusingly handled. If the verse is gaily read, children will invariably smile at

Seldom "can't,"
Seldom "don't";
Never "shan't,"
Never "won't."

For the most part, Christina Rossetti keeps to the small creatures and objects of the young child's world and to the family and playmates he knows the best.

Bits of Wisdom

For older children, there are some choice bits of wit and wisdom that the young child cannot grasp. In these poems the same idea or play on words is repeated several times. For example, "A pin has a head, but has no hair" is a pattern that occurs again in "The peacock has a score of eyes." The weighing of values in "A diamond or a coal?" is repeated in this still finer comparison:

An emerald is as green as grass;
A ruby red as blood;
A sapphire shines as blue as heaven;
A flint lies in the mud.

A diamond is a brilliant stone,
To catch the world's desire;
An opal holds a fiery spark;
But a flint holds fire.

It takes an older child to interpret such fables as these, but what vivid, colorful bits of wisdom they are!

Christina Rossetti's masterpiece is undoubtedly her fairy poem *Goblin Market.* While the occasional child of twelve or fourteen might enjoy hearing this poem, the folklore is too unfamiliar and the narrative too complex for the average.

Poets of Nature

Sara Teasdale, Elizabeth Coatsworth, and Hilda Conkling are dissimilar in most respects, and the unknown authors of the Eskimo poems are totally unlike these three poets. Still all of them have one characteristic in common: they observe nature and record its beauty and its effect with an imaginative turn which kindles a responsive spark in the reader. The form of their poetry varies from the pure lyric to free verse. Certainly Elizabeth Coatsworth, Hilda Conkling, and the Eskimo poets are less melodious than Sara Teasdale, yet they arouse—through the precision of their observation and their sensitive interpretation of experience—a response which, even though more intellectual than that produced by most of our singing poets, is no less moving.

SARA TEASDALE, 1884-1933

Stars To-night

In the death of Sara Teasdale, America lost a fine lyric poet. If children can suddenly catch the charm of even one or two of her poems, they will have a surer sense of poetry and the stirring of the spirit that it can bring.

Sara Teasdale was born in St. Louis of wealthy parents. She was a delicate child who went to school irregularly, and she never had to face the bread-and-butter struggle which has a stabilizing effect on most people. She read and traveled widely, and after her marriage lived in New York. The summer before she died she was in London in search of material for a biography of Christina Rossetti.

Her poems have something of the cryptic brevity of Emily Dickinson's but are richer in sensory beauty and emotion. She wrote much about love, the stars, the night, and the sea. In her last book with its enigmatic title, *Strange Victory,* the concluding poem ends with these lines:

I shall find the crystal of peace,—above me
Stars I shall find.

Those stars shine all through her poetry, and to the selection from her poems made for boys and girls she gave the title *Stars To-night.* When Macmillan added to this unusual collection the illustrations of Dorothy Lathrop, the result was a book of rare beauty. These pen-and-ink drawings have a frosty, sparkling quality that is as delicate and sensitive as the poems themselves.

The first poem in the book is one of the favorites and is characteristic of Sara Teasdale's highly individual style and mood:

Night[8]

Stars over snow,
And in the west a planet
Swinging below a star—
Look for a lovely thing and you will find it,
It is not far—
It never will be far.

For the second poem, "Stars," Miss Lathrop has captured the enchantment of the experience with a picture of a child alone, looking up at the night sky and awed by the great procession of stars marching up the dome of heaven, "stately and still." You can almost imagine the child whispering to herself the concluding lines of "Stars":

Up the dome of heaven
Like a great hill,
I watch them marching
Stately and still,

8. "Night," "Stars," "The Falling Star," and "The Coin." From *Stars To-night* by Sara Teasdale. By permission of The Macmillan Company, publishers.

And I know that I
Am honored to be
Witness
Of so much majesty.

In the winter when the zenith is ablaze with stars, older children should have these poems. But even a five-year-old child can enjoy

The Falling Star

I saw a star slide down the sky,
Blinding the north as it went by,
Too burning and too quick to hold,
Too lovely to be bought or sold,
Good only to make wishes on
And then forever to be gone.

While the poems of Sara Teasdale are largely descriptive and are often too subtle for the child under fourteen, no child should miss this book. Don't force the poems. Read the easier ones first—those already mentioned, along with "Winter Noon," "February Twilight," and "Redbirds." You will probably not use all these at once but will read just one poem several times and then leave the book around where the children can look at it. Poring over the pictures helps establish the mood of the poems, and presently some child will bring you the book and say, "Read this one." So the range of appreciation will grow. If the children appropriate only one of these poems but really enjoy it and make it their own, then you have given them a treasure.

Night, space, and frosty stars are delicately suggested in this pen-and-ink drawing. Illustration by Dorothy P. Lathrop for Stars To-night *by Sara Teasdale. Copyright, 1930, by Sara Teasdale Filsinger. Reprinted by permission of the publishers, The Macmillan Company. (Book 5½ x 8½)*

Oh, better than the minting
Of a gold-crowned king
Is the safe-kept memory
Of a lovely thing.

ELIZABETH COATSWORTH, 1893-

Elizabeth Coatsworth (Mrs. Henry Beston) was born in Buffalo, New York. She enjoyed the double blessing of an excellent education and wide travel. She went to a private school as a child and comments that its "English system" resulted in severe, scholarly discipline. After graduation from Vassar, she took her M.A. at Columbia University. Meanwhile she had traveled in this country, in Mexico, Europe, and Egypt, and, after her graduate degree, spent a year in the Orient. Today, Mr. and Mrs. Beston divide their time between an old house in Massachusetts and a hundred-acre farm on a lake in Maine. Both husband and wife write books for children.

Elizabeth Coatsworth's *The Cat Who Went to Heaven* won the Newbery Medal for 1930 but is not as popular with children as her historical tales such as *Away Goes Sally, Five Bushel Farm,* and *The Fair American.* Within the pages of these books are some of her best poems.

Characteristics of Style

A certain style in her poetry is well illustrated by the frequently quoted "Swift things are beautiful," from *Away Goes Sally*[9]:

9. "Swift things are beautiful," "Hard from the southeast blows the wind," "Away Goes Sally," and "When all the other leaves are gone." From *Away Goes Sally* by Elizabeth Coatsworth. Copyright 1934 by The Macmillan Company and used with their permission.

Swift things are beautiful:
Swallows and deer,
And lightning that falls
Bright-veined and clear,
River and meteors,
Wind in the wheat,
The strong-withered horse,
The runner's sure feet.

And slow things are beautiful:
The closing of day,
The pause of the wave
That curves downward to spray,
The ember that crumbles,
The opening flower,
And the ox that moves on
In the quiet of power.

Here are the comparisons that the author uses, not incidentally but as the theme of the entire poem. You can find other examples of contrasts in all three books. From *Five Bushel Farm* there is another one on swiftness, but treated differently—"Swift comes the summer." In *The Fair American* there is a comparison of sorrow, danger, and courage, long ago and today, in the poem beginning "So long ago," and in a still more striking poem there is a comparison of a clipper ship with flame, bird, deer, and horse. Building a poem around a series of comparisons seems then to be a favorite pattern for Elizabeth Coatsworth. It is an exceedingly provocative one for children to study and to try for themselves.

Another aspect of her style is the smooth, flowing lines that fall so gently on the ear. Poem after poem has this quietness. From *Away Goes Sally* read "Hard from the southeast blows the wind," with its description of a gathering storm without and the cozy comfort of an open fire within. Note these lines, for example:

And the cat comes to bask herself
In the soft heat,
And Madame Peace draws up her chair
To warm her feet.

With those concluding lines, you can fairly feel yourself relaxing and stretching a bit. "No leaf is left," "How gray the rain," and "In the forest it is cool" are only a few examples of that quietness with which the poems abound. Although the lines can frolic now and then, slow-moving calmness predominates. For this reason, reading many of the poems at a time is monotonous.

Both in her prose and in her poetry, Elizabeth Coatsworth makes an effective use of words, often rich with associative meaning, such as "Madame Peace" drawing up her chair to the fire to "warm her feet"—not extraordinary words but laden with associations of peace, warmth, and comfort. Sometimes the words are pleasant sounding, as "the quiet of power" or

All, all waits. Up hill, down valley—
The time is ripe, and away goes Sally!

On the whole these poems are not markedly musical, but they are rich in sensory words; for instance: fallen apples that "smell cidery on the air," sleigh bells that ring "icily sweet," children with their "mouths stained with berry juice," "bright-veined lightning," and little buds "no larger than a mouse's ear." You can find examples of her use of words which make you see, smell, taste, touch, and hear.

Nature

The single lines and phrases already quoted reveal her sensitive response to nature. Her nature poems seem to fall into two classes. Some are straight nature descriptions, and others are brief, lovely descriptions which lead toward, or climax in, a human mood or situation. One of the finest examples of the second type, "How gray the rain," from *Five Bushel Farm,* ends with

Serene and bright
The rainbow stands
That was not anywhere before,
And so may joy
Fill empty hands
When someone enters through a door.[10]

These poems linking together nature and human concerns are notable but they may prove

10. From *Five Bushel Farm* by Elizabeth Coatsworth. Copyright 1939 by The Macmillan Company and used with their permission.

a bit subtle for children and may require discussion before the literal-minded children catch their implications. But the nature descriptions are understandable to all children. For those who know salt marshes, the first poem in *Away Goes Sally,* "This is the hay that no man planted," is particularly good. In that same book there is the memorable characterization of oak leaves that most children will recognize:

When all the other leaves are gone
The brown oak leaves still linger on,
Their branches obstinately lifted
To frozen wind and snow deep-drifted.

But when the winter is well passed
The brown oak leaves drop down at last,
To let the little buds appear
No larger than a mouse's ear.

In this group of nature poems there is an interesting pair that might start the children writing their own poetry. In *Away Goes Sally,* the autumn poem beginning "When the pumpkin yellows" (page 38) is repeated in *Five Bushel Farm* (page 19) except that the last two verses of the poems are different. Here is an experiment children might try. Ask them, "How else could the poem be concluded? What would you put in your verses?" The books also contain two fire poems that are worth comparing (*The Fair American,* page 18, and *Five Bushel Farm,* page 30).

Wisdom

The following verse from *The Fair American* is typical of a small group of the poems that present an occasional bit of homely wisdom:

He who has never known hunger
Has never known how good
The taste of bread may be,
The kindliness of food.[11]

Such verses lack the epigrammatic and sparkling quality of similar poems by Christina Rossetti but have instead a straightforward simplicity. In this same book there is the philosophic

To have nothing at all
Is to have much still.

and the interesting application to human life of the plant:

The plant cut down to the root
Does not hate.
It uses all its strength
To grow once more.

Turn, boy, to the unknown field
Beyond the gate.
Never look back again
To the bolted door.

There are examples of everyday wisdom in her other books, but these suffice to illustrate this type of poem and the style in which it is written.

Animals

Small animals appear throughout the poems, but cats are favorites. There are a number of poems about them, usually in a humorous mood. The gayest of these from *Away Goes Sally* begins, " 'Who are you?' asked the cat of the bear," and contains a dialogue that is thoroughly amusing. Certainly one of the loveliest poems about animals, also from *Away Goes Sally,* is "The Rabbit's Song Outside the Tavern." All the gay wildness of small beasts on a moonlit night is in these lines.

The poetry of Elizabeth Coatsworth is more ideational than most juvenile verse. It belongs chiefly to older children and will stretch their minds and imaginations.

HILDA CONKLING, 1910-

Poems by a Little Girl
Shoes of the Wind

That a little girl living much in the company of her poet-mother should begin "talking" her own poems is not surprising, but the

11. "He who has never known hunger" and "The plant cut down to the root." From *The Fair American* by Elizabeth Coatsworth. Copyright 1940 by The Macmillan Company and used with their permission.

quality of Hilda Conkling's poems *is*. They are beautiful both in ideas and in expression.

Hilda's mother, Mrs. Grace Hazard Conkling, was a professor of English at Smith College, a gifted musician, and a writer of poems in free verse. Her two little girls, Elsa and Hilda, grew up in the lovely New England country of Northampton, Massachusetts, with daily enjoyment of garden and countryside, books and music. Not only must the companionship of the three have been unusually close, but the whole environment was favorable to creative expression. At first, both little girls "dictated" their poems to their mother. For Hilda poetry remained the favored mode of expression, but the other child, Elsa, turned gradually to music.

When Hilda was ten years old, *Poems by a Little Girl* was published with a laudatory introduction by the poet Amy Lowell. Since it created something of a sensation, Mrs. Conkling gave occasional lectures on how the poems happened. She said the poems often came when they were walking or just conversing. Hilda never hesitated for a word, and the mother made notes as best she could. Later she read her copy to Hilda, who would correct any word that had been inadvertently changed. The poems stand exactly as the child spoke them. When Hilda was twelve, her second book, *Shoes of the Wind,* was published; then, after that, so far as we can discover, no more poetry from Hilda! Speculations as to why she ceased writing are beside the point. Our concern is with these poems that have for children important qualities.

Free Verse

First of all, their lack of rhyme is sometimes an asset. The time always comes when children are obsessed with rhyming everything and calling it poetry; then it is a good thing to read them some of young Hilda's verses and say, "Here is poetry written by a little girl. It has no rhyme. Why do you suppose it is called poetry?" That question is a poser. It sometimes disconcerts college students, but eventually children and students both arrive at certain unmistakably poetic qualities in these unrhymed stanzas. "She *sees* things good," one child said after hearing

Moon Song[12]

There is a star that runs very fast,
That goes pulling the moon
Through the tops of the poplars.

Another child, hearing "Chickadee" and "Red Rooster," thought the poet remembered how things *sounded.* Eventually, they discover that it is the fresh or different way in which she tells something with just a few words that makes these little verses different from prose. For instance:

Tree-toad is a leaf-gray shadow
That sings.
Tree-toad is never seen
Unless a star squeezes through the leaves,
Or a moth looks sharply at a gray branch.

Hilda Conkling's largely unrhymed but sensitively perceptive verses are, then, a salutary antidote for the rhyming passion when it produces only doggerel and seems to handicap the development of original observation and expression. Her limitation for children is that she is predominantly descriptive. She is chiefly concerned with finding the precise words that tell how something looked or felt or appealed to her imagination. That the short feathers along the rooster's back

Are the dark color of wet rocks
Or the rippled green of ships
When I look at their sides through water.

is a remarkably fine and discriminating observation, but too much of this kind of detailed description swamps children. They cannot see rooster for words, or, rather, after a number of these short, highly descriptive verses, children cannot follow the idea. Their attention is gone.

Using the Poems with Children

The most effective way to use the poems is singly, slipped in with other poetry of a less

12. "Moon Song," "Tree-Toad," and "Red Rooster." From *Poems by a Little Girl* by Hilda Conkling. Reprinted by permission of the publishers, J. B. Lippincott Company. Copyright 1920 by J. B. Lippincott Company.

analytical sort. Or use a particular poem when the occasion demands it. The first dandelions of spring could hardly be welcomed by a more charming verse than Hilda Conkling's "Dandelion." Or when gardens get under way the children will appreciate "Little Snail." And for introducing fairies to children, there is no verse better than her "Fairies."

Everyone will have favorites among her poems. Young children like her "Velvets," "Mouse," and both the "Butterfly" verses, particularly the one with the mildly contrary ending: "I have to go the opposite way." They like the poems already quoted and the unusual "Easter." On this subject there is almost nothing in literature for young children except general spring poems, but Hilda Conkling has recorded the sensory impressions a child receives from Easter Day: bells ringing, people, lilies, a sense of joy!

For older children, "Red Rooster," "The Old Bridge," "Tree-Toad," "Gift," and "I Am" are a few of the favorites. The last-named poem might well start the children writing their own "I Am." One important reason why it is good to use these imaginative verses with children is that they encourage more boldness in trying to think and write freshly.

A BOOK OF ESKIMO POEMS

Beyond the High Hills

The Danish explorer Knud Rasmussen brought back from his fifth expedition to the Arctic a large collection of Eskimo poetry. A selection from these has been made into a rarely beautiful book for children, illustrated with breath-taking color photographs by a missionary priest, Father Guy Mary-Rousselière. The result is sheer beauty pictorially and verbally, with a dramatic re-creation of Eskimo thoughts, feelings, and way of life.

Like Hilda Conkling's verses these are in free form but they have greater strength and maturity. The bitter contrast between the two seasons is evident in this—

There is joy in
Feeling the warmth
Come to the great world
And seeing the sun
Follow its old footprints
In the summer night.

There is fear in
Feeling the cold
Come to the great world
And seeing the moon
—Now new moon, now full moon—
Follow its old footprints
In the winter night.[13]

Some of the poems sing the joys of the hunt and of food after famine, some are warmly personal—a first kill, the mood of approaching womanhood. This is a rune of hospitality.

The lands around my dwelling
Are more beautiful
From the day
When it is given me to see
Faces I have never seen before.
All is more beautiful,
All is more beautiful,
And life is Thankfulness.
These guests of mine
Make my house grand.

To quote briefly from this book gives no conception of its sweep. Here are the joys, terror, and casual everyday heroism of a people who have maintained life under almost unendurable hardships. To read these poems with the loneliness and beauty of the photographs is a moving experience. They will give children more of Eskimo life and thought than many factual books.

Poets of Fairyland

Our next group of poets, William Allingham, Rose Fyleman, and Walter de la Mare, includes one modern voice of major

13. "There is joy" and "The lands around my dwelling." From *Beyond the High Hills* by Knud Rasmussen. Copyright 1961 by the publishers, World Publishing Company.

importance. It is the voice of Walter de la Mare, who is often compared to William Blake in the lyric beauty of his poetry and the otherworldliness of much of his subject matter. He occupies a position of unique importance in the modern world of adult poetry, and his contribution to children's literature is a treasure all should know and cherish. Beside De la Mare, William Allingham and Rose Fyleman are only pleasant minor voices. It is significant that all three of these poets of fairyland are Irish or British. Somehow the fairies seem never to have emigrated to the New World and it is chiefly in England and Ireland that we hear of them today.

WILLIAM ALLINGHAM, 1824-1889

Robin Redbreast

The name of William Allingham immediately brings to mind one poem, "The Fairies." The perfection of its fairy lore is accounted for by the fact that the author was an Irishman and so, by birth, a natural authority on "the wee folk." Why the Irish should know more about fairies than any other people we cannot say, but so it is.

Allingham was born in Ballyshannon, Donegal, Ireland—surely by the sound of it the very seat and center of fairyland or at least of folklore and balladry. Because of financial difficulties, Allingham was forced to combine his literary interests with various "white-collar" jobs. It was not until he was forty-six that he resigned his civil-service post to become an editor of the well-known *Fraser's Magazine*. During his life he published not only his own poems but collections of songs, ballads, and stories, and a book on the ballads, *The Ballad Book*. Today, Macmillan's "Little Library" has reprinted his poems for children under the title *Robin Redbreast*.

This book contains "The Fairies," which is a fine lyric poem children enjoy. They like it first because it sings, and second because it contains the vital statistics they should know about the good people—what they wear, where they live, what they eat, what tricks they play. Read it aloud to catch the dancing, tripping rhythm of the trooping fairies, and the sudden change to the grave, sober narrative of little Bridget:

The Fairies[14]

Up the airy mountain,
Down the rushy glen,
We daren't go a-hunting
For fear of little men;
Wee folk, good folk,
Trooping all together;
Green jacket, red cap,
And white owl's feather!

Down along the rocky shore
Some make their home,
They live on crispy pancakes
Of yellow tide-foam;
Some in the reeds
Of the black mountain lake,
With frogs for their watch-dogs,
All night awake.

High on the hill-top
The old King sits;
He is now so old and gray
He's nigh lost his wits.
With a bridge of white mist
Columbkill he crosses,
On his stately journeys
From Slieveleague to Rosses;
Or going up with music
On cold starry nights
To sup with the Queen
Of the gay Northern Lights.

They stole little Bridget
For seven years long;
When she came down again
Her friends were all gone.
They took her lightly back,
Between the night and morrow,
They thought that she was fast asleep,
But she was dead with sorrow.
They have kept her ever since
Deep within the lake,
On a bed of flag-leaves,
Watching till she wake.

By the craggy hill-side,
Through the mosses bare,

14. From *Robin Redbreast* by William Allingham. By permission of The Macmillan Company, publishers.

They have planted thorn-trees
For pleasure here and there.
If any man so daring
As dig them up in spite,
He shall find their sharpest thorns
In his bed at night.

Up the airy mountain,
Down the rushy glen,
We daren't go a-hunting
For fear of little men;
Wee folk, good folk,
Trooping all together;
Green jacket, red cap,
And white owl's feather.

It has always seemed a pity to give five-year-olds only the first verse of this poem, when by waiting until they are six or seven they will like it all. At that age, they also enjoy Allingham's "The Fairy Shoemaker," especially with the Artzybasheff illustrations.

ROSE FYLEMAN, 1877-1957

Fairies and Chimneys

When Rose Fyleman visited the United States and read her poems to the children in schools and libraries, she captivated her young hearers both because of her readings and because of her attractive personality. The children murmured their favorite poems with her and fixed fascinated and incredulous eyes upon this handsome person who had written them. How could anyone know so much about fairies? Had she really seen the fairy queen herself riding a bus in Oxford Street? Listening to Rose Fyleman, they believed. Here, at last, was a high authority on fairies; she *had* heard them, she *had* seen them, and she made them so real in her verses that American children were entranced.

Rose Fyleman had a trick of combining fairies with the children's everyday, modern world in a way that is both amusing and convincing. Take as simple an idea as "Differences," where Miss Fyleman contrasts the things Daddy does with the amazing things fairies do quite easily. Daddy rides in a "snorty" motor, but the fairies ride on the backs of bumble bees. Daddy sails in a "jolly wooden boat," but the fairies sail on a mere "scrap of foam." Daddy climbs hard, rocky mountains, but the fairies "go a-climbing on the mountains in the clouds." Doesn't this juxtaposition of Daddy and the fairies make them natural and seeable? Or take the favorite "Yesterday in Oxford Street," where the bus, the shops, and the busy people build up a substantial world of reality. Then, suddenly, into this everyday world comes the fairy queen and alights on the rail of the bus, and is accepted as a part of the substantial realities. She is the credible surprise that turns an otherwise humdrum day into something worth gloating over.

Besides the fairy poems, Miss Fyleman wrote some amusing light verse about the modern child and the things he is interested in. Small children like her cheerful, four-line "Singing-Time," which tells about waking up in the morning. "Mrs. Brown," with her imaginary children, and "Mice," with its brevity and highly personal note, are both favorites. Since there are not many of these everyday verses, it is chiefly as ambassador extraordinary to fairyland that Rose Fyleman will be remembered.

WALTER DE LA MARE, 1873-1956

Rhymes and Verses:
Collected Poems for Children
Peacock Pie

Adults and children of the English-speaking world lost a great lyric poet when Walter de la Mare died in Twickenham, England, on June 22, 1956. He was born in the little village of Charlton in Kent. When he was only seventeen, he finished his schooling and went into the London office of the Anglo-American (Standard) Oil Company. For eighteen years he worked in the statistical department of that company, during which time he wrote stories and poems and published them under the pseudonym of Walter Ramal. The treasured *Songs of Childhood* was published in 1902 when he was still engaged in this statistical work.

When he was thirty-five, he received a

small civil pension and had sufficient income from book reviewing to enable him to retire from business. Later an interesting legacy enabled him to drop all work except his own creative writing. When the English poet Rupert Brooke went into the war (1914), he made a will leaving his money and the proceeds of his books to be divided among three of his poet friends, Wilfrid Gibson, Lascelles Abercrombie, and Walter de la Mare. The terms of this generous bequest are particularly touching in view of the great promise of the donor. Speaking of his three friends, Rupert Brooke told his mother, "If I can set them free to any extent to write the poetry and plays and books they want to, my death will bring more gain than loss."[15] Rupert Brooke's death was a grievous loss to English letters, but Walter de la Mare's poetry and prose do honor to the foresight of the friend who recognized his worth.

Walter de la Mare has left behind him a rich legacy of both poetry and prose, for children and adults. If *Memoirs of a Midget* is brilliant fiction for mature readers, *The Three Royal Monkeys* is equally distinguished fantasy for children. If his adult poetry is frequently compared to William Blake's, many of his poems for children merit the same comparison and have, besides, a range and variety not found in Blake. That his work for children has the same beauty found in his books for adults is not surprising when he himself said in his Introduction to *Bells and Grass,* "I know well that only the rarest kind of best in anything can be good enough for the young." If anyone has given children "the rarest kind of best" in poetry, it is Walter de la Mare.

All of his poems for young people are now collected in *Rhymes and Verses.*[16] *Peacock Pie* has been reissued and is a choice book for the special child to own. Many of his poems are beyond the comprehension of children. Nevertheless, this work yields a precious residue of pure poetry that no child should miss. Choose your favorite poems; try them with the children; then try certain others that are beautiful but that are not so sure to be enjoyed at first hearing. Who knows what words will catch the imagination of children and set their spirits winging? When you are using the poetry of a great lyric poet, be adventurous and try a wide selection for the sake of that occasional child who may suddenly be carried out of himself by the magic of poetry.

The Unanswered Question

One characteristic of Walter de la Mare's poems is the use of the unanswered question which leaves the reader wondering. Reading the gravely beautiful "The Horseman," you discover that the content is slight, the melody is utterly satisfying, but the picture it produces is an enigma. "Is it a knight?" "Maybe it's the moon." "Or maybe it's white clouds," the children say. When you read them the last lines of "Someone"—

So I know not who came knocking,
At all, at all, at all.[17]

the children ask, "But who *was* knocking?" and immediately start answering their own question. Many of Walter de la Mare's poems have this enigmatic quality. Whether he is writing for children or adults, his poems frequently leave you possessed and wondering. You keep on saying them, trying to find the answer from the poet himself, or, failing in this, supplying first one answer of your own and then another. Children speculate over "The Mocking Fairy," "Jim Jay," and "The Little Green Orchard," to mention only a few. Adults are similarly haunted by "The Song of the Secret," "The Song of Finis," and "Farewell."

Of course, too much ambiguity in children's literature may be a dangerous quality, children being rather literal creatures and liking things straight and plain. A little, however, stimulates their imagination and provokes not only a healthy speculation but the ability to transcend the factual and go over into the world of dreams. Some people make this transition with music. Why not with poetry as well?

15. Edward Marsh, *Rupert Brooke, a Memoir,* p. 141.
16. There is also *Come Hither,* De la Mare's own selection of poems for children.
17. "Someone," "Chicken," "The Bandog," "Tired Tim," "The Barber's" and "Tillie." From *Peacock Pie* by Walter de la Mare, published by Holt, Rinehart and Winston, Inc. Reprinted by permission of the Literary Trustees of Walter de la Mare and the Society of Authors.

The Child's World

Walter de la Mare could be straight and plain when he wished to, and his children are real flesh-and-blood children. The account of "Poor Henry" swallowing physic is as homely a bit of family life as you can find anywhere. Little Ann waking up and tumbling out of her bed in the morning is any child waking happily. Small children enjoy the matter-of-fact subject matter and the straightforward treatment of such poems as "Chicken," "The Cupboard," "Bread and Cherries," "Tired Tim," "The Bandog," "The Barber's," and the Elizabeth Ann parts of "A Child's Day." Even these poems for the youngest children, however, are illumined with little touches that invariably lift them above the commonplace. Listen to the amusing *l* sounds in the opening line of "Chicken":

Clapping her platter stood plump Bess,

Notice the admirable description of the dog's teeth in

The Bandog

Has anybody seen my Mopser?—
A comely dog is he,
With hair of the colour of a Charles the Fifth,
And teeth like ships at sea,
His tail it curls straight upwards,
His ears stand two abreast,
And he answers to the simple name of Mopser,
When civilly addressed.

Contrast the dragging words of "Tired Tim" with the gay, skipping words of "The Barber's":

Tired Tim

Poor tired Tim! It's sad for him.
He lags the long bright morning through,
Ever so tired of nothing to do;
He moons and mopes the livelong day,
Nothing to think about, nothing to say;
Up to bed with his candle to creep,
Too tired to yawn, too tired to sleep:
Poor tired Tim! It's sad for him.

The Barber's

Gold locks, and black locks,
Red locks and brown,
Topknot to love-curl,
The hair wisps down;
Straight above the clear eyes,
Rounded round the ears,
Snip-snap and snick-a-snick,
Clash the Barber's shears;
Us, in the looking-glass,
Footsteps in the street,
Over, under, to and fro,
The lean blades meet;
Bay Rum or Bear's Grease,
A silver groat to pay—
Then out a-shin-shan-shining
In the bright, blue day.

Walter de la Mare wrote many of these poems for his own children. He knew what caught their fancy and what jokes they liked. So he sometimes gave them rare nonsense in the preposterous vein they appreciated, for example, "Alas, Alack!"

The poet also knew children's curious penchant for names. In nursery schools they can be heard sometimes chanting each other's names, not for the sake of calling or addressing each other but just for fun: "Sandy Anderson, Lois, Lois, Lois Calhoun." Walter de la Mare must have observed this delight in saying names, for he wrote several poems using them. The introduction to "The Child's Day" and "O Dear Me!" are examples of this use of names as is the favorite

Bunches of Grapes[18]

"Bunches of grapes," says Timothy;
"Pomegranates pink," says Elaine;
"A junket of cream and a cranberry tart
For me," says Jane.

"Love-in-a-mist," says Timothy;
"Primroses pale," says Elaine;
"A nosegay of pinks and mignonette
For me," says Jane.

18. "Bunches of Grapes" and "Sleepyhead." From *Collected Poems* by Walter de la Mare. Copyright 1920 by Holt, Rinehart and Winston, Inc. Reprinted by permission of the Literary Trustees of Walter de la Mare and the Society of Authors.

"Chariots of gold," says Timothy;
"Silvery wings," says Elaine;
"A bumpity ride in a wagon of hay
For me," says Jane.

This last poem illustrates another virtue in Walter de la Mare's children. They are indeed real, from pert little Mima and her taunting sister, to the hammering and sawing small boy who speaks from "The Little Green Orchard," and to the three children in "Bunches of Grapes." Can't you see them? Timothy is a gentle, dreamy boy; Elaine, fair, golden-haired, and dainty; and bouncing Jane, rosy and plumpish. These are children the poet knew, and we know them, too, from the verses.

The World of Nature

There are many so-called "nature" poems in *Rhymes and Verses*. There are "The Hare," "Quack!" "Come–Gone," "The Warbler," "A Goldfinch," "Mrs. Earth," "The Pool in the Rock," "The Snowflake," "Silver," "Full Moon," "Wanderers" (the planets), "Snow," the simple and beautiful "The Rainbow," and many others. Throughout the poems you find intimate glimpses of flowers, birds, beasts, the sea, and the countryside—all caught and colored with the poet's own peculiar insight. No poetry is more intensely visual than Walter de la Mare's. A "sun-washed drift of sea-birds," the "knobble-kneed" old donkey—"Nicholas Nye," "horned snails," "four-clawed moles," "moths like ghosties," a "martin's sun-baked nest," "rain-sweet lilac on the spray," the "yeasty surf," "sunshine sweet and pale," and, for another sensory experience, those "chuffling" pigs making their "grizzling, gruzzling and greedy" sounds. Sometimes you feel as if Walter de la Mare shared his famous midget's ability to stand grass-high and look intimately at bluebells and beetles, cobwebs and dewdrops, so vividly did he record them.

The World of Fairy

Forrest Reid characterizes Walter de la Mare's poetry by saying that it is chiefly "poetry of imagination and *vision* with its hints of loveliness belonging to a world perhaps remembered, perhaps only dreamed, but which at least is not *this* world."[19] Certainly when you read *Rhymes and Verses*, you are impressed with the large number of fairy poems and with their great range of mood and style. They begin at nonsense level with such delightful absurdities as "Tillie," the old woman who swallowed some magic fern seeds when she yawned and has ever since been floating around on the wind.

Tillie

Old Tillie Turveycombe
Sat to sew,
Just where a patch of fern did grow;
There, as she yawned,
And yawn wide did she,
Floated some seed
Down her gull-e-t;
And look you once,
And look you twice,
Poor old Tillie
Was gone in a trice.
But oh, when the wind
Do a-moaning come,
'Tis poor old Tillie
Sick for home;
And oh, when a voice
In the mist do sigh,
Old Tillie Turveycombe's
Floating by.

Or for older children, there is that hilarious "The Dwarf," which is almost a study in laughter. "The Hare" is a favorite, also "Bluebells," "The Ride-by-Nights," and the charming "Berries," "Sam," and "The Three Beggars." One of the children's favorite fairy poems is "Sleepyhead," with its interesting contrast between the child's matter-of-fact narrative and the wild, sweet singing of the "gnomies." By the way, this is one of those poems of which there are at least three variants in the different editions. The version given below was the first one, in the 1902 printing. It was called "The Gnomies" in that edition but is "Sleepyhead" in most of the books.

19. *Walter de la Mare: A Critical Study.* Faber and Faber Ltd., 1929.

Sleepyhead

As I lay awake in the white moonlight,
I heard a faint singing in the wood—
'Out of bed,
Sleepyhead,
Put your white foot now,
Here are we,
'Neath the tree
Singing round the root now!'

I looked out of the window in the white moonlight,
The leaves were like snow in the wood—
'Come away
Child and play,
Light wi' the gnomies;
In a mound,
Green and round,
That's where their home is!
Honey sweet,
Curds to eat,
Cream and fruměnty,
Shells and beads,
Poppy seeds,
You shall have plenty.'

But soon as I stooped in the dim moonlight
To put on my stocking and my shoe,
The sweet, sweet singing died sadly away,
And the grey of the morning peep'd through:
Then instead of the gnomies there came a red robin
To sing of the buttercups and dew.

Boris Artzybasheff's illustrations are often too stylized for children to enjoy. This picture, however, is an understandable interpretation. Illustration by Boris Artzybasheff for Walter de la Mare's "Sleepyhead" from The Fairy Shoemaker and Other Fairy Poems. *Copyright, 1928, by The Macmillan Company. Reprinted by permission of the artist. (Book 7¼ x 8½)*

If you read all of the poems mentioned in this group and add "Melmillo," "Bewitched," "The Pedlar," "As Lucy Went A-Walking," and half a dozen others, you soon discover that here are no fairies with gauzy wings and jeweled wands, but rather the witches, the dwarfs, the occasionally droll, homely wee women or wee men of ancient folklore. If you have not seen witches that "straddled their brooms 'neath a louring sky," or met at twilight a strange pedlar with "glittering eyes" and a "sugared song," you feel once you have read these poems as if you *might* at any moment. Too many of them make too highly spiced a literary diet for children, but the simpler ones mentioned in the first group are among the best poems of fairy lore that we have for children. Hearing them, children will discover that Walter de la Mare's poems can put a spell upon them, compounded of wonder, melody, and sheer beauty.

"Earth's the Best Place for Love"

ROBERT FROST, 1874-1963

You Come Too

Robert Frost is the American poet our children should grow up to, and that means grow up with. More than any other poet he spoke for America in the rhythms and idiom of American speech. To have heard him read his own poems was to hear America talking—not urban or academic America, but the America of farmers, villagers, people close to the earth, speaking simply of everyday events or sometimes of world events and concerns in everyday words. The language and phrasing of his poetry have a deceptive simplicity. Each poem yields a story or a picture or an episode, readily grasped in one reading. But when the poem is read again and again, deeper meanings and richer implications begin to emerge. Children should encounter some of Robert Frost's poems so that they can live with the poetry over the years. The poems will grow in significance as the children grow in years and experience.

Everyone thinks of Robert Frost as a New Englander, but he was born in San Francisco and did not arrive in New England until he was eleven years old. However, his forebears had been there for generations and his spirit was so completely akin to the region that he spoke with the laconic wit, plain words, and arresting understatements of a native.

At Lawrence High School, he was at the head of his class until in his senior year a young lady overtook him. Robert Frost and Elinor Miriam White were co-valedictorians, and when Robert was twenty-one they were married. That marriage, marked in the beginning by poverty and struggle, gave them four handsome children and forty years of mutual happiness.

Frost seems to have taken college lightly, with less than one term at Dartmouth and two years at Harvard. In later years Dartmouth, Harvard, Amherst, Yale, Michigan, Indiana, and other universities honored him with positions on their faculties and with honorary degrees. Some forty academic hoods might have been gathering dust in his closets except that he had them made into a splendid patchwork quilt, commenting, "It's knowing what to do with things that counts"[20]—a line that sounds as if it came from one of his

The rich detail about the "Road not taken" makes it mysterious and alluring. This wood engraving particularly suits the poem. Illustration by Thomas W. Nason from You Come Too *by Robert Frost. Copyright, © 1959, by Holt, Rinehart and Winston, Inc. Reproduced by permission of Holt, Rinehart and Winston, Inc. (Book 5⅜ x 8¼)*

poems! Besides holding professorships in many universities and colleges, Robert Frost traveled the lecture circuit throughout the United States to literally hundreds of institutions, clubs, and groups of every sort. He read his own poems inimitably, he talked wisely and simply about poetry, and he charmed everyone.

Robert Frost was four times the recipient of the Pulitzer Prize for poetry. In 1950 the United States Senate adopted a "resolution of felicitation" on his seventy-fifth birthday, and in 1961, President-elect John F. Kennedy invited Frost to read one of his poems at the inaugural ceremony, the first time a poet had been so honored.

In 1962, the poet's eighty-eighth year, a new book of his poems was published, *In the Clearing,* an arresting title for a last book. Robert Frost died early in 1963. John F. Kennedy said of the poet, "... he will live as a poet of the life of man, of the darkness and despair, as well as the hope. . . ."[21] And the poet John Ciardi wrote of Frost, "If he is half radiance he is also half brimstone, and praise be. His best poems will endure precisely because they are terrible—and holy."[22] But the poet himself had the last word. In a poem

20. Lawrence Thompson, "A Native to the Grain of the American Idiom," *Saturday Review,* March 21, 1959, p. 55.
21. Quoted from President Kennedy's "Comments" on "Accent," February 24, 1961, in *Saturday Review,* February 23, 1963, p. 18.
22. "Robert Frost: American Bard," *Saturday Review,* March 24, 1962, p. 15.

called "Into My Own," he wrote of death as walking deeper and deeper into "those dark trees" that "stretched away unto the edge of doom" and he prophesied that for those who missed and followed him—

They would not find me changed from him they knew—
Only more sure of all that I thought was true.[23]

"Favorite Poems for Young Readers"

Which of Robert Frost's poems are simple enough for young children? The poet answered this question with the title of his own selections—*You Come Too, Favorite Poems for Young Readers.* The title is a wonderful phrase for all of us. "You come too"—let's explore together, let's share our tasks, our fun, our interests. Isn't that a good definition of friendship? In this book young children will enjoy the riddle about the grasshopper, "One Guess," and the amusing "Fireflies in the Garden." Children can understand "Blue-Butterfly Day" with that wonderful line, "But these are flowers that fly and all but sing"; and of course they chuckle over "Last Word of a Bluebird." They'll like to know that the little girl, Lesley, is Mrs. Ballantine, daughter of the poet, with two daughters of her own. If the nines are given help with the unusual word "rue" they like "Dust of Snow," just as an episode. But they, too, can think of days that have gone wrong and suddenly are right when something pleasant unexpectedly happens. Here is a poem that will be just as perfect at eighty-nine as at nine, which is one test of a good poem.

For the nines and tens and older, almost any poem in this selection will carry meaning, more meaning perhaps for the rural than for the urban child. The latter probably has never "out-walked the furthest city light," nor watched "A Hillside Thaw," nor tried "Mending Wall," nor discovered how thrush music from a woods can seem "Almost like a call to come in/To the dark and lament." But fortunately, we can all learn by vicarious experiences, and in every poem, the pictures or episodes or ideas are sharply and clearly told with words that have a tonal beauty as captivating as music. So whether children are rural or urban these poems are for them all.

Robert Frost once said, "Every poem is a new metaphor inside or it is nothing"[24]—which implies that the surface meaning of a poem is only the beginning. Frost's poems grow in richness with thoughtful rereading. We may not wish to discuss the possible double meaning in every poem with children but it would be a pity to leave intelligent children with nothing more than the obvious scenes the verses report. "A Drumlin Woodchuck" is, for instance, the amusing soliloquy of a canny old denizen of a hilltop (drumlin) telling how he has managed to evade the hunters. Here is the last verse—

It will be because, though small
As measured against the All,
I have been so instinctively thorough
About my crevice and burrow.[25]

Here is obviously more than meets the eye. The poet himself referred to it as "my most Vermonty poem." And it is obviously rich, good-humored satire. It might be the poet speaking for himself or any other human being who is trying to maintain a little privacy, to protect his own right to be himself, to live his own life, to keep his own secrets, to protect his spirit from unwanted intrusions. Older boys and girls fighting for a place of their own can appreciate this. In a different vein, "The Death of a Hired Man" is a dramatic, poignant story none too tragic to confront the insensitivity that sometimes marks youth. Discuss with them how the husband must have felt at the close of that dialogue, after his harsh, unpitying words. Even if all had been well with Silas, wouldn't you rather be victimized once more than to have those bitter words to be sorry for? "The Road Not

23. From *Complete Poems of Robert Frost.* Copyright 1916, 1921, 1923, 1928, 1930, 1934, 1939 by Holt, Rinehart and Winston, Inc. Copyright 1936, 1942 by Robert Frost. Copyright renewed 1944, 1951, © 1956, 1962 by Robert Frost. Copyright renewed © 1964 by Lesley Frost Ballantine. Reprinted by permission of Holt, Rinehart and Winston, Inc.
24. Charles R. Anderson, "Robert Frost," *Saturday Review,* February 23, 1963, p. 20.
25. From *You Come Too* by Robert Frost. For copyright information, see footnote 23.

Taken" has a different meaning for every human being. Even twelve-year-olds can sense the choices that lie ahead. "The Tuft of Flowers" is the delightful discovery of a kindred spirit, a heart-warming experience at any age, and fairly easy for children to parallel. "Two Tramps in Mud Time" is more difficult—must we *not* work at work we love, if someone else needs such work? That is a difficult social problem. What should the poet have done?

Poems such as these from this one small collection of Frost's poetry will help the children move gradually from the purely objective to deeper meanings. Slipped in among the lighter fare, these poems should be read and reread, discussed, paralleled with personal experiences or the experiences of people we know or of people from history, and then they should be reread still again for pure enjoyment and enriched meaning.

In this process children and adults will note many memorable lines, for Robert Frost is almost as "full of quotations" as Shakespeare:

Proclaimed the time was neither wrong nor
right

And miles to go before I sleep.

Earth's the right place for love:
I don't know where it's likely to go better.

"Men work together," I told him from the
heart,
"Whether they work together or apart."

Home is the place where, when you have to
go there,
They have to take you in.
....
Something you somehow haven't to deserve.

All these are from one small selection of Robert Frost's poems, and there are many more priceless bits of wisdom, pithily phrased for the delight of children, young people, and adults. To know the poetry of Robert Frost is to grow with and through poetry.

Here, then, are some of the poets who have written seriously for children in words that sing. Not all of them have been gifted with lyric genius, but each one of them has made a contribution which serves to underscore the fact that *children like poetry.* If the lesser of our poets are at first more popular with children than our major poets, it is because they are direct and clear; they choose subjects children can understand easily, and they treat the subject briefly and cheerfully. These are standards we must respect in our choice of verse for children. We must remember, too, that they turn away from obscurity in a poem; that they will endure length only in narrative verse that is swift-moving and exciting; and that, in general, they shun long descriptions and the somber mood. So lyric poets who catch their favor generally do so with poetry that is brief and gay, or markedly melodious.

Allowing for these preferences, we can select for children a lyric offering that has variety and charm. Shakespeare with his blithe songs, William Blake with his strange and subtle melodies, Christina Rossetti with her small lyrics—these older writers speak as freshly to children today as they ever did. Sara Teasdale, Elizabeth Coatsworth, and Hilda Conkling share with the child their delight in the face of nature, her moods and surprises. William Allingham, Rose Fyleman, and Walter de la Mare carry children over into that half-world of fairy so vividly, so convincingly that even the modern child sees, hears, and is charmed. Of all the poets of childhood Walter de la Mare and Robert Frost have given them poetry to grow on—to begin with in the early years, to study, to say over, and to be haunted by. To these poets we would add selections from Emily Dickinson, Edna St. Vincent Millay, Langston Hughes, John Ciardi, and a dozen others. To our children, English poetry offers a unique lyric treasure. It is our adult responsibility to know this heritage of great poems and to use it to the fullest possible extent.

SUGGESTED READING, PROBLEMS, AND PROJECTS

Note to students: Listen to the poems in this chapter as you would listen to songs or to a Chopin prelude. Remember that a prelude or a song or a poem may convey a feeling of sadness, mystery, gaiety, peace, or sheer joy. If you lose the meaning of the words in the melody at first, that is all right. Try to feel the melody and mood of the words just as you respond to these in music.

1. Read Blake's poems until you feel the movement of the lines and catch the moods. After you have read them aloud and heard them, do they mean any more to you? Do you find that certain lines stay with you, or are these poems just not for you at this time? Be honest but explicit. People may have excellent literary taste and still not like the same things. What poems of Blake's minister to the child's need for security?

2. Find examples of lyrical qualities and tone color in some of Rossetti's verses which are not quoted in the text. If you are with a group of children, read her poem "What is pink?" and then ask them to try to find examples for "What is soft?" or "What is cold?" or other qualities.

3. How can you make the philosophy of Sara Teasdale's "Night" concrete and understandable to children so that they can give their own examples of "lovely things" that are "not far"? What other poems do you find in *Stars To-night* which may need to be made concrete for children? Plan how you would present a group of these poems.

4. Try some of Elizabeth Coatsworth's contrast or comparison poems with older children, and let them find other pairs, such as softness and hardness, wetness and dryness, sweetness and bitterness. It will be easier to try these in prose, although you may end up with charming free verse.

5. How and when would you use the free verse of Hilda Conkling or the Eskimo poems?

6. From reading the Eskimo poems what do you know about the Eskimos' lives that would make you like these people? Give definite examples.

7. Why do you think fairy poems are less popular in the United States than in Great Britain? How would you introduce the fairy poems of Allingham and Fyleman to a typical group of children?

8. Summarize De la Mare's lasting virtues as a poet for children. Point out some of the problems his poetry presents to the teacher of an average group of unpoetic children. Why is it worth while to introduce the poems of De la Mare to children who are not immediately interested? What poems would you choose for introducing his work, and how would you launch your readings?

9. Select four poems by Robert Frost suitable for the six to nines and four for the older children. Plan the way you would use the poems so that the children will grow in their understanding and enjoyment of them.

10. How do you justify the statement that children of the United States should grow up to and with Robert Frost's poems? Treat yourself to the paperback copy of his poems, or the *Complete Poems,* or at least the selection for youth, *You Come Too.* Read a group of his poems about trees—"Birches," "Tree at My Window," "Come In," "Into My Own," "The Sound of Trees," and others. How does Frost feel about trees? Read also a group of his dialogue poems such as "Home Burial," "The Death of the Hired Man," "The Housekeeper," "The Star Splitter," "The Fear," "The Mountain," and others. From these narratives, what do you know about New England people and what do the poems tell you about Frost himself?

11. From the poets' collections discussed in this chapter, try to find outstanding examples of melody and mood (poetry that expresses gaiety, joy, excitement, peace, wonder, or mystery) or some negative emotion.

REFERENCES

A combined bibliography for this chaper and Chapters 6 and 8 will be found on pp. 214-219.

chapter 8

Using Poetry with Children

Keep a poem in your pocket
and a picture in your head
and you'll never feel lonely
at night when you're in bed.

The little poem will sing to you
the little picture will bring to you
a dozen dreams to dance to you
at night when you're in bed.

So—
Keep a picture in your pocket
and a poem in your head
and you'll never feel lonely
at night when you're in bed.[1]

Here in the lightest of light verses, Beatrice Schenk de Regniers gives us one reason for using poetry with children and youth. Like music, it carries its own therapy. To cold or timid hearts it can bring warmth, reassurance, even laughter. It can stir and arouse or quiet and comfort. Above all it gives significance to everyday experience. To miss poetry would be as much of a deprivation as to miss music. For these reasons it is essential that we know poetry and that we know how to introduce it to children and youth. The experience of poetry should come with so much pure pleasure that the taste for it will grow and become a permanent part of a child's emotional and intellectual resources.

Definitions of poetry are, of course, valueless to children, but they are valuable to adults since they throw light on the manner in which to present poetry. For instance, Eleanor Farjeon asks

What is Poetry? Who knows?
Not the rose, but the scent of the rose;
Not the sky, but the light in the sky;
Not the fly, but the gleam of the fly;
Not the sea, but the sound of the sea;
Not myself, but what makes me
See, hear, and feel something that prose
Cannot: and what it is, who knows?[2]

1. From *Something Special* by Beatrice Schenk de Regniers and Irene Haas. Copyright © 1958 by Beatrice Schenk de Regniers. Reprinted by permission of Harcourt, Brace & World, Inc.
2. "Poetry." Reprinted by permission of the publishers, J. B. Lippincott Company, from *Sing for your Supper* by Eleanor Farjeon. Copyright 1938 by Eleanor Farjeon.

This is a poet's way of saying that a poem is a distillation of an experience: not the rose but the essence of the rose, not the sea but its light and sound.

Robert Frost develops the same idea when he says that "A poem is momentary stay against confusion. Each poem clarifies something. . . . A poem is an arrest of disorder."[3] Frost implies that our experiences come pell-mell, but a poem sorts them out, gives them order and meaning—not merely the essence of an experience but its significance.

Here are a few more definitions of poetry:

Absolute poetry is the concrete and artistic expression of the human mind in emotional and rhythmical language.—Encyclopaedia Britannica

The essence of poetry is invention; such invention as, by producing something unexpected, surprises and delights.—Samuel Johnson

If I read a book and it makes my whole body so cold no fire can ever warm me, I know that is poetry. If I feel physically as if the top of my head were taken off, I know that is poetry. These are the only ways I know it. Is there any other way?—Emily Dickinson

I always know it is a good poem when the small hairs rise on the back of my neck.—William Rose Benét

A living poem begins with a lump in the throat; a homesickness or a lovesickness. It is a reaching out toward expression to find fulfillment. A complete poem is one where an emotion has found its thought and the thought has found words.—Robert Frost

If you examine these definitions and others, you will discover certain ideas recurring: poetry surprises and delights; it sings like music; it makes you feel intensely; poetry gives you an arresting thought in rhythmic words, plus a shiver up your backbone. When poetry means these things to you, you have genuinely enjoyed it; it is poetry to you. When it leaves you just where you were, neither aroused nor amused, neither enchanted nor solaced, then poetry has not happened to you; it has passed you by. So it is with children.

3. John Ciardi, "Robert Frost: Master Conversationalist at Work," *Saturday Review,* March 21, 1959.

Elements of Good Poetry

But how about adults who enjoy doggerel, and children who accept anything that rhymes? Does their enjoyment make the jingles they read poetry? Perhaps for them it does temporarily, but doggerel need not remain their top level of appreciation. Good taste in any field—music, interior decoration, clothes, poetry—is a matter of experience. As a person becomes familiar with the best in one field, he gains discrimination there, while in another field in which his experience is limited he may show very poor taste. So we should be patient with children's enjoyment of poor poetry. Their taste will improve if they have repeated experiences with good poetry. This means that adults must know what *is* good and must also be able to recognize the characteristics of hackneyed doggerel not worth the children's time or attention.

SINGING QUALITY: MELODY AND MOVEMENT

One of the most important characteristics of good poetry is its singing quality, its melody and movement. In the nonsense jingles and humorous verse, for example, words and lines trip along with the lightness of children jumping rope. Clumsy doggerel—in contrast to the verses of Lear, Richards, and Milne—is heavy footed, and its words and lines have no sparkle. If a poem is in a mysterious or meditative or wistful mood, the lines move slowly and the words fall subtly on the ear. These are clues to reading poetry aloud—emphasize the musical pattern. The poems of Blake, Rossetti, and De la Mare contain many examples of the perfect accompaniment of melody and movement to mood. On the whole the poetry children like is more lively and dancing than poetry for adults—no blank verse for children and very little free verse. The fact that children enjoy marked rhythms and crisp rhymes accounts for their ready acceptance of second-rate verse if it has these characteristics. But if their ears become attuned to the subtleties and varieties of rhythmic patterns found in poems like those by Stevenson, De la Mare, and Behn, they may detect the labored rhythms and forced rhymes which characterize masses of mediocre verse.

Blacks and whites are carefully balanced in this picture of a small boy wondering about life. Notice the rhythmical design of the tree in contrast to the treatment of sky and rock. Illustration by Henry B. Kane for Far and Few *by David McCord. Copyright 1925, 1929, 1931, 1941, 1949, 1952, by David McCord. Published by Little, Brown & Co. (Book 5 x 8)*

WORDS OF POETRY

Poetry uses strong, vigorous words or warm, rich words or delicate, precise words that define with accurate perfection. Of course, prose may employ the same words, but poetry ordinarily uses them with greater condensation and in more melodious combinations so that their effect is more striking. Remember the amusing "sneezles and freezles" of Christopher Robin or Blake's "the echoing green," which suggests the calls and shouts of children at their play. Read through these poems and notice both the exact, descriptive words and the sensory, connotative words and phrases which distinguish good poetry from the ordinary: "the still dark night," "skipping along alone," "rain in the city" falling "slantwise where the buildings crowd," "soaked, sweet-smelling lane," "Apple trees are snowing." Words that stir the imagination, that speak to the senses, that provoke laughter, that move us deeply and strongly—such words are part of the secret of good poetry.

CONTENT OF POETRY

While poetry is primarily emotional in its appeal, it is built around subjects or ideas, and appeals to the intellect as well as the emotions. Even a slight verse like "Little Miss Muffet" has a well-defined idea—security, fright, escape. The child's emotional response to this unit depends upon his grasp of the content. Of course poetry may have almost as varied subject matter as prose, but like any of the other arts, it must invest that content with arresting significance. A slippery baby in a bathtub is Carl Sandburg's "fish child." Rachel Field sees city "Taxis"—"Scudding through the snow," "flashing back the sun," and rolling along "like spools of colored thread." A vivid picture to city children! When mother cooks fish, the child chuckles over the memory of De la Mare's "a fish that *talks* in the frying pan." John Ciardi's "thin grin-cat" stalking a bird is ominous in its suggestion of hunger and anticipated satisfaction. So poetry takes the strange or everyday facts of life and gives them fresh meaning. We see new colors in the world because poetry has revealed them.

When we choose a poem for children, we may well test it with these questions: First, *does it sing*—with good rhythm, true, unforced rhymes, and a happy compatibility of sound and subject—whether it is nonsense verse or narrative or lyric poetry? Second, *is the diction distinguished*—with words that are rich in sensory and connotative meanings, words that are unhackneyed, precise, and memorable? Third, *does the subject matter of the poem invest the strange or the everyday experiences of life with new importance and richer meaning?* When a poem does these three things, it is indeed good poetry—it may add to the child's day one brief moment of laughter or give him a new dream to dream over in solitude or bring him a sharpened awareness of life.

Why Poetry Is Difficult for Children

Many people, however, do not enjoy poetry. When college students are asked why so few of them read poetry voluntarily, their responses each year are invariably the same: They had too much analyzing of poems, or they were given many selections that were boring. "Lots of poems are too long," they complain, or "Poetry is hard to understand and it's hard to read." Sometimes, when poetry is read aloud to children, it is badly read—in a dull singsong or with unnatural affectations or with a "holy tone." Any one of these afflictions is enough to induce a permanent distaste for poetry.

SUBJECT MATTER

Many children have learned to distrust the subject matter of poetry largely because of our blundering choice of selections for them. We have given them pedantic verse designed to teach manners or morals or safety or health. In some adaptations of nursery rhymes, Jack and Jill fall down because they didn't look both ways before they started up the hill. Then we have given children poems that voice the philosophy of old age rather than that of exuberant childhood:

Tell me not, in mournful numbers,
Life is but an empty dream!

So speaks middle age, or perhaps dreams wistfully of Innisfree:

I shall have some peace there, for peace comes dropping slow.

But the last thing a child wants is peace. What he yearns for is action, and if we are going to foster children's natural liking for poetry we had better avoid these elderly daydreams and find selections that speak to youth.

We have also given children poetry whose meaning is obscure. If these obscurities cannot be cleared up in a brief discussion, then we should drop such poems for the time being. A selection may be great literature, but if it leaves the children baffled and suspicious, it is not good literature for them at that point.

In choosing poetry for children, select poems whose subject matter is sufficiently common to their experiences and emotions so that they can understand what the poem is about and share the feeling underlying the words. We need not be too literal about this. The child need not have shared every experience he encounters in poetry, but there should be some common ground between the child and the poem.

The city child, for example, may not know meadows and cowslips, but he knows all about trying to decide where to go and what to do; so he understands this little conversation piece by Kate Greenaway:

Susan Blue[4]

Oh! Susan Blue,
How do you do?

4. From *Marigold Garden* by Kate Greenaway. United States rights by permission of Frederick Warne & Co., Inc. Canadian rights by permission of Frederick Warne & Co., Ltd.

Please may I go for a walk with you?
Where shall we go?
Oh! I know—
Down in the meadow where the cowslips
grow!

The city child might make his own ending and say, "Over in the park where the tulips grow," or "over on the hill to slide in the snow." So, too, the child may never have had a ride on a merry-go-round, but the sense of action that Dorothy Baruch's irresistible "Merry-Go-Round"[5] gives him will make it joyously comprehensible.

FIGURES OF SPEECH

Figures of speech have proved particularly baffling to young children. Blanche Weekes, in a study called *Influence of Meaning on Children's Choices of Poetry,* found that the literal-minded child does not understand most figures of speech and tends to misinterpret them rather consistently. Sixth-grade children, for instance, interpreted "the lion of thunder roared" to mean that the lion roared at the thunder. So if the young child hears a poem about the stars looking like daisies that "dot the meadows of the night," he may visualize a topsy-turvy world with daisies sticking head-first down from heaven instead of popping up from the ground as self-respecting daisies should. In short, involved figures of speech are more likely to muddle than to inspire the young. One reason Stevenson and A. A. Milne are successful with young children is that they rarely use figurative language, but maintain an understandable directness most of the time.

Not that we are herewith going to abandon every poem for children that uses figurative language—not at all. But it is safe to say that the younger the child the fewer and simpler the figures of speech should be, particularly since many of them are decidedly platitudinous. Magazines abound with endless ditties about mewing pussy willows, sprightly Jacky Frost, and willful autumn leaves—outworn expressions which probably never appealed to children and which can well be discarded.

LONG DESCRIPTIONS

Long descriptions are another stumbling block to an easy enjoyment of poetry. Children have always skipped descriptions in prose, and they have always spoken out fully and frankly about how much they dislike them. Yet adults have never hesitated to give them poetry that is little else. They may enjoy a few descriptive poems if they are brief, but too many and too long descriptions send them away from poetry bored and discouraged.

FORM

The form of poetry presents even more reading problems than the content. The mere look of a page of poetry is strange with its short lines and stanza patterns, so different in appearance from a page of prose. Attacking it gingerly, the child encounters both rhythm and rhyme, which do odd things to his reading. For instance, they heighten the child's tendency to pause at the end of each line, a pause usually marked by dropping the voice. This, in turn, results in singsong that frequently destroys the meaning.

Inverted sentences also cause singsong reading and a consequent loss of meaning. Read these lines of Stevenson's:

When to go out, my nurse doth wrap
Me in my comforter and cap . . .

Drop your voice conclusively after "wrap," and you have a strange second line. Or if the poet delays the completion of his sentence for several lines, the young reader is immediately befuddled. Take, for example, the familiar opening lines of William Cullen Bryant's "To a Waterfowl":

Whither, 'midst falling dew,
While glow the heavens with the last steps
of day,

5. Many of the poems discussed but not reprinted in this book can be found in the anthology *Time for Poetry* (gen. ed., comp. by May Hill Arbuthnot). The bibliography (p. 214) will also help you locate poems not reprinted here. To locate poems reprinted in other chapters of this book, turn to the Index.

Far, through their rosy depths, dost thou pursue
Thy solitary way?

The exclamatory question that begins with "Whither," is not completed until "dost thou pursue thy solitary way?"—a conclusion that is distributed over two lines. Such examples emphasize the pitfalls that await the unskilled reader of verse. The child, lost in such entanglements, knows he isn't making sense and becomes suspicious of this thing called poetry.

DIALOGUE

Dialogue is another source of trouble in verse, because the poets have a way of blithely omitting the helpful "said he" or "said she." Look at the little conversation piece by Kate Greenaway (page 195). Does Susan Blue's unknown friend speak all the lines, or does Susan herself break in with the question and then the joyous solution of the last two lines? This latter interpretation turns the poem into a charming little dialogue which seems sufficiently appealing to justify such a reading. In Blake's imaginary dialogue between an adult and a tiny baby, the words are simple, but who says what? Read the poem aloud with the proper interpretation of the dialogue, and it is immediately understandable.

Infant Joy

Baby *"I have no name;*
I am but two days old."
Narrator *What shall I call thee?*
Baby *"I happy am,*
Joy is my name."
Narrator *Sweet joy befall thee!*

Narrator *Pretty joy!*
Sweet joy, but two days old.
Sweet joy I call thee;
Thou dost smile,
I sing the while;
Sweet joy befall thee!

The moral of all this is that children still in the process of learning to read should get most of their poetry through their ears before they are asked to cope with it on the printed page.

To Make Poetry-Lovers of Children

KNOW WHAT CHILDREN LIKE ABOUT POETRY

This brings us to the heart of the difficulty and to the delight of using poetry with children. We must know what they like about poetry and how to expose them to it so the liking grows. Fortunately, its first and strongest appeal is its *singing quality,* the *melody* and *movement* of the word patterns and the lines. Walter de la Mare calls these qualities "tune and runningness," and they make poetry an aural art like music, to be heard and spoken just as music is to be heard and played. Our business as adults is to savor this singing quality of verse and to learn how to maintain it in our reading.

Next, children like the *story element* in poetry, from "Little Miss Muffet" to "The Highwayman." This is so strong an interest that we should search for fine narrative poetry for every age level. Children will accept the feeblest doggerel if it tells a story. Often the surprising and provocative little story suggestions in the lyric poetry of Walter de la Mare account for the children's enjoying subtler and lovelier verse than they would otherwise appreciate. Perhaps some of the gifted modern poets will respond to this need and write some stirring narrative poems of the quality of "The Pied Piper."

Nonsense and *humor* in poetry have great appeal to children. They delight in the daft lunacy of cows jumping over the moon and they move happily from the gaiety and nonsense of *Mother Goose* and Edward Lear to the modern hilarity of Ogden Nash and John Ciardi. But on the way, nonsense merges naturally into light verse. Children chuckle over the gay drama of "The King's Breakfast" and a few years later are grinning over the more intellectual humor of "Macavity the Mystery Cat." For humor can be subtle, and well-written humorous verse is an exercise not only in ear-training but also in quick associations, double meanings, satire, or witty implications.

The *sensory content* of poetry constitutes one of its strongest appeals, or, in some cases, accounts for its failure with certain children. If the sensory content is familiar or understandable, then they respond with zest to the words of seeing, smelling, feeling, hearing, and tasting with which poetry abounds. Unfortunately, over half the children in the United States are from urban areas while a large proportion of our poetry is distinctly rural in its sensuous imagery. The city child and the country child have certain experiences in common—wind, rain, snow, sun, moon, stars, heat, cold, fog—but how differently these experiences impinge on the consciousness of each of them. Take snow, for instance, which in the crowded areas of the city is soon a blackish, soggy slush. How, then, can the city child, who knows neither down, nor lambs, nor even clean, soft snow, respond to the feeling of stepping upon "white down," of walking upon "silver fleece," as described in Elinor Wylie's "Velvet Shoes"? By the time these are laboriously explained to him, there is not much left of the dreamlike quality of that walk

At a tranquil pace,
Under veils of white lace.[6]

Often it seems as if more time should be spent providing city children with some of the lovely sensory experiences that crowded city streets deny them. Somewhere they should see frisky lambs and colts at play, smell the good smells of earth after a spring rain, bury their noses in lilies of the valley, or hear a wood thrush calling at twilight. They should have the fun of plopping through mud, wading creeks, getting lost in a cornfield, or whooping down a hillside on a windy autumn day. But lacking these experiences, which are the very stuff of dreams, of poetry, and of a lifetime of sensory joys, children in the big cities find their own beauty—skyscrapers against scudding clouds, rainy streets at night reflecting the lights of the cars, the whine of wind around tall buildings, airplanes heard when still unseen, and over the roar of city noises the eerie sound of fog horns or boat whistles. These are good experiences, too, and well worth savoring and expressing in words or colors. These, too, are the stuff of dreams.

ENSURE DESIRABLE RESPONSES

Children's encounters with poetry should include three types of response—*enjoyment, exploration,* and *deepening understandings.* These do not occur as separate steps but simultaneously. Certainly, the child must start with enjoyment or his interest in poetry dies. But if from the beginning, he finds delight in the poems he hears, he is ready and eager to explore further—more books and more poems of different sorts. Even the youngest children can learn to read between the lines. For example, they can be helped to decide what is back of the conversation between "Pussy cat, pussy cat" and his owner: Is Cat telling a tall tale as an excuse, or did he really see the queen? Does Cat's owner believe the runaway? To read between the lines is to identify oneself with the poet, to ask the poet's questions. This is reading for deeper understanding, taking a thoughtful look at what lies beneath the surface. Enjoyment, exploration, and deeper understanding must all be part of children's experience with poetry if we are to build poetry-minded children.

READ POETRY TO CHILDREN

Because poetry is an aural art like music, children should listen to it before they encounter it on the printed page. Poetry began as a spoken art; people listened to it, enjoyed it, and remembered it because rhyme and meter make it much easier to recall than prose. So it should begin for children. Adults should read or speak it aloud and encourage

6. From *Collected Poems of Elinor Wylie.* Reprinted by permission of Alfred A. Knopf, Inc. Copyright 1921, 1932 by Alfred A. Knopf.

the children to join in until, without even realizing it, they have memorized effortlessly dozens of poems which they can speak naturally and gaily. Saying or reading poetry to children should continue all through their first twelve years. By that time they will have mastered the mechanics of reading for themselves; they will also be steeped in poetry; and they will have the habit of saying it so well established that they will go right on reading it and enjoying it on their own.

Poetry should never be used as a reading exercise. When children have to struggle with a poem as a reading lesson, they are baffled and discouraged. John Erskine, writing for older students, says in *The Kinds of Poetry*: "The office of the teacher of poetry is easily defined; it is to afford a mediation between great poets and their audience." With children, effective oral reading is the surest mediation.

The poets themselves agree. At the turn of the century, the Irish poet William Butler Yeats wrote:

> *I have just heard a poem spoken with so delicate a sense of rhythm, with so perfect a respect for its meaning, that if I were a wise man and could persuade a few people to learn the art I would never again open a book of verse.*[7]

Yeats implies that to read a poem silently is to miss the potent appeal of its music and perhaps even its meaning. He himself read poetry with spellbinding charm, and John Masefield in his autobiography, *So Long to Learn*, testifies to Yeats' powerful influence on the young poets of the day. He convinced them of the importance of the aural effect of poetry on the reader or listener. Later, Robert Frost, in a series of cryptic comments on poetry, said:

> *The eye reader is a barbarian. So also is the writer for the eye reader, who needn't care how badly he writes since he doesn't care how badly he is read.*

Mother Goose is a natural starting point with children from two to six or seven years old. Her pages are alive with "tune and runningness" and the children respond with vigor.

This young artist has chosen "Tired Tim" for illustration. The picture shows Tim, appropriately lethargic, creeping bedward. Illustration by a child in Moses Cleveland School.

They soon discover that "Ride a cock horse" is a gallop and "To market, to market" is an everyday walk, quite unlike the military tread of "The grand Old Duke of York." Children may try marching, skipping, galloping, hopping, running, rocking their babies, with most of the group speaking the poem while two or three respond to its rhythm. They don't know that it is meter and rhyme, line and word patterns that produce these contagious rhythms, but they feel the "goingness" of the verses. They discover that the words hop like the rabbit in Christina Rossetti's

> *And timid, funny, brisk little bunny,*
> *Winks his nose and sits all sunny.*

The introduction to poetry for older children should begin as painlessly as it begins for the nonreaders. That is, they should hear many poems read aloud vigorously for sheer pleasure, with no analysis during this exploratory stage. As this casual exposure to a variety of verses continues, lovely bits of authentic poetry should be slipped in and introduced with a comment like this: "A new poem is like new music. Sometimes you have to hear it several times before you know whether or not

7. William Butler Yeats, *Ideas of Good and Evil* (Macmillan, 1907), p. 16.

you like it." Children of eight or older should not be asked to respond to poems with bodily rhythms, but they may well identify the gallop of Stevenson's "Windy Nights" or the clacking rhythm of the trains in Mary Austin's "Texas Trains and Trails." So, too, they will show you by their response that they feel the tranquility of Elizabeth Madox Roberts' "Evening Hymn," even though they cannot analyze the mood in words.

Just as young children begin to chant *Mother Goose* ditties with you, so the older boys and girls should begin to speak their favorites as you read. A new poem should always be read several times when you first present it, and then reread on successive days. By the second day, if the children obviously enjoy the poem, it is time to say, "I saw some of your lips moving, so I think you almost know the poem. I'll read it slowly and you say the words with me." Try this for a few days, and they will memorize a poem with the maximum enjoyment and the minimum effort. Don't let them memorize only the humorous verse, as they may begin to do, but encourage this painless mastery of a variety of verses with emphasis on quality.

It may be asked, "How long must children have their poetry read to them? Aren't they ever going to explore books of poetry on their own?" Of course they are! That is what this program is for. If, during the years when they are still trying to master their reading skills, children hear poetry well read by someone who thoroughly enjoys it, they too enjoy it unabashedly and begin to accept it as naturally as they accept stories. If they hear enough authentic poetry over these formative years, they will never suffer from what the poet W. H. Auden calls a "tin ear"[8] for merely tin pan alley verses. Instead they will develop, or at least some of them will, a sensitivity to the beauty and power of the spoken word, and by the time they are eleven and twelve years old and competent readers they will explore poetry for themselves. This is the goal of the aural and oral approach to poetry for sheer enjoyment. When it succeeds, children will enter high school with trained ears, good diction, and the ability to interpret and enjoy the major poets to whom they will be exposed.

EXPLORE POETRY BOOKS WITH CHILDREN

In the process of enjoying poetry, children will encounter many books and different types of verse. Their explorations will include books by a single author and anthologies of poetry by many poets.

Anthologies are invaluable, and there is no reading experience more satisfying, either in a classroom or at home, than to settle down with your children to explore a new anthology. Needless to say, you will have explored it first to know its range and contents and to have chosen in advance a group of poems that you feel sure the children will understand and enjoy. Modern anthologies usually provide a high quality of poetry selections and convenient subject matter arrangements, and they rescue from oblivion such out-of-print treasures as "The Pirate Don Durk of Dowdee," "Overheard on a Saltmarsh," and the best of Winifred Welles and Mary Austin. Camps, classrooms, and homes should own not less than two anthologies. Here are a few criteria for selecting an anthology from among the many excellent ones available:

1. Examine the author index to discover the range and quality of writers represented. Does it lean heavily on poets of the past, Eugene Field, Riley, Stevenson, Longfellow, or are the best of these balanced by many good modern poets?

2. How many poems does the book contain? Oddly enough one anthology will contain over seven hundred poems while another at approximately the same price will include two to three hundred. If the quality of the two books is equally good, the first is obviously a better choice.

3. Look for indexes and classifications. The indexes should include authors, titles, and, preferably, first lines. Teachers will find classifications by subjects equally important—such groupings as people, animals, nonsense, magic, our country, seasons, and the like. Organization by subjects is far more important than organization by grades. Indeed, grade levels for poems are impossible and undesirable, no

8. W. H. Auden, "An Appreciation of the Lyric Verse of Walter de la Mare." *New York Times Book Review*, Feb. 26, 1956, p. 3.

matter how teachers yearn for them, because children's tastes and capacities vary as much as the poems themselves and depend on their varied experiences.

4. Format is important. A heavy volume may be useful in the school library as a reference book, but it will not be good for a child to use or an adult to handle with the child. Good paper, clear type, well-spaced pages, all add to the attractiveness of a book.

Some anthologies not only meet these basic criteria, but provide extra dividends in the form of attractive illustrations, brief introductions to or explanations of poems, and suggestions for reading aloud and choral speaking.

Teach children how to explore and use an anthology. The first snowstorm should send them to look for snow or winter poems. A forthcoming festival means a search for the best Halloween or Christmas poems. Undoubtedly the greatest value of a fine anthology is the feeling it gives the child for the range and variety of poetry. He will look, browse further, and make discoveries.

In the same way, children should become acquainted with the books of single poets, not merely Stevenson's *A Child's Garden of Verses,* but David McCord's *Far and Few,* Harry Behn's *Little Hill,* and others. This exploration of the works of individual poets guarantees that the child will encounter a range of poetry from the imaginative and subtle lyrics of Walter de la Mare to the robust nonsense of John Ciardi. Such exploration will also help children to grow emotionally and intellectually with poetry.

DEEPEN CHILDREN'S UNDERSTANDING OF POEMS

A third phase of poetry experience involves a more intellectual response than either enjoyment or exploration. It is what John Ciardi has called "reading in depth" or reading for a more complete understanding of the poet's meaning. With the youngest children this begins with talking about word meanings and background experiences and with older children it progresses to a fuller consciousness of implications, double meanings, and possible

Robert Lawson, with a fine pen for details, pays a tribute to the lure of music. Illustration by Robert Lawson for Gaily We Parade, *edited by John Brewton. Copyright, 1940, by The Macmillan Company. Reproduced with permission of The Macmillan Company. (Book 6 x 9, picture 4 x 4¼)*

symbols, and even to some analysis of form; in short, it involves reading a poem at different levels of meaning.

To help younger children understand the meaning of a poem, we often need to *evoke or supplement their background of experience.* For instance, suppose a child has never been on an escalator or even seen one, real or pictured. Explain to him, "It looks like a stairway, but when you step on the first step, *you* stand still and the whole stairway moves upward, carrying you along until you hop off at the next floor." Then, Phyllis McGinley's "E is the escalator" becomes amusingly real. Or suppose a city child has never seen a snail. Show him a picture of a snail or bring one to school. Then Hilda Conkling's "Little Snail" with "his house on his back" will be visually clear. Walter de la Mare never says in his poem "The Huntsmen" that it is about three boys riding their hobbyhorses upstairs, and so unless children understand this, the "clitter clatter" of those wooden sticks on the stair and the whole meaning of the poem will be obscure. Older children who have never seen a great bird swoop downward, stop himself in full flight, and then slowly ascend may not understand the averted crash in Robert Frost's

Questioning Faces[9]

The winter owl banked just in time to pass
And save herself from breaking window glass.
And her wings straining suddenly aspread
Caught color from the last of evening red
In a display of underdown and quill
To glassed-in children at the window sill.

But almost every child knows about braking a car suddenly and swerving sharply to avoid a crash or may have watched airplanes bank for a landing. If he understands that word *bank* in the sense of descending and then making a corrective ascent, he can visualize what those watching children saw through the window pane when the great owl saved herself from a crash. Most children can illustrate this with a swift movement of arm and hand. These are just a few examples of evoking or amplifying background experiences to clarify meaning.

Sometimes the musical pattern of a poem affects its meaning in ways even very young children can sense. For instance, the fives know that the words in Stevenson's "The Swing" really swing and that the words of Milne's "Hoppity" do hop with Christopher Robin to the very last line which hops to a standstill. Their young ears can also be trained to hear the quietness of Winifred Welles' "Green Moth," the hushed quality of the words in De la Mare's "Some One" or "The Horseman," and the very place in Edna St. Vincent Millay's "The Ballad of the Harp-Weaver," where the spinning music begins—as truly a spinning song as Schubert's. Hearing poetry read with an emphasis on its musical patterns, young children can be trained to the point where they are aware, consciously or unconsciously, of what the patterns are making them feel or understand. For instance, an upper grade boy who especially liked "The Snare" by James Stephens said to his teacher, "Everytime you read that poem or I say it to myself it makes me feel as if I were running and had to hurry faster." His teacher replied, "Well, that is what the poem is about; that is the idea the poet wanted you to understand." If the boy had asked "But what makes me feel that way?" the teacher could have shown him how the repetition of the last line of each verse as the first line of the next verse compels an emphasis that hurries one on. If you read the poem without that first line repetition, you will discover that the push has gone out of the poem completely. Should the teacher have raised the question herself? This depends on the boy. In some instances, it would be enough that he had felt the poem's meaning and the teacher had praised his thoughtful response. But a boy that intelligent and inquiring could probably be carried one step further to understand the effect of pattern on feeling response.

Or take Elizabeth Coatsworth's beautiful study in contrasts—"Swift things are beautiful," p. 177. Help the children to hear how the words and lines of the first stanza hurry along, with no long, sonorous vowels or words to delay the crisp, brisk movement. But in the second verse, the long vowels in such mouth-filling phrases as "The pause of the wave/ That curves downward to spray" and the heavy last lines, "And the ox that moves on/ In the quiet of power," compel a slow deliberate reading. You simply cannot dash off those last lines briskly.

Having helped the children discover Elizabeth Coatsworth's effective use of words to enhance contrast, let them explore some of her other poems for contrasts. They will find "The sea gull curves his wings," in which the first couplet is smooth as silk and as gentle as the sailing flight of the gull; the second, a sharp, harsh staccato like the cry of warning, which it is. The second verse repeats this contrast. See also "Cold winter now is in the wood" and again note the contrasts.[10] Eleanor Farjeon uses similar contrasts in "For Christmas Day," and many other examples can be found.

These brief, simple examples of the way poets use the words and patterns of their verse to suggest action, mood, or meaning are ob-

9. From *In the Clearing* by Robert Frost. Copyright 1942, 1951, © 1962 by Robert Frost. Reprinted by permission of Holt, Rinehart and Winston, Inc.
10. See pages 176-178 for a discussion of Elizabeth Coatsworth's poetry.

vious enough for children and are the beginnings of a deeper look at the poetry they enjoy. This deeper look will carry them into the below-the-surface meaning or implications or symbols the poet uses.

In the discussion of the traditional ballads in Chapter 5, there was continual emphasis upon reading between the lines. Why did the Lady leave her fine house and go off with the Raggle Taggle Gypsies? Why did the King choose Sir Patrick Spens to sail overseas in the stormiest time of the year? Why in the last lines of "The Wife of Usher's Well" that sad reference to the maid? For children from sixth grade on, these old ballads with their cryptic condensations are good exercises in reading for meanings that are implied but never fully stated, and therefore not to be settled neatly and without questions and differing speculations.

From a gifted teacher of English in the Montreal schools comes this interesting experience with Robert Frost's

Stopping by Woods on a Snowy Evening[11]

Whose woods these are I think I know.
His house is in the village though;
He will not see me stopping here
To watch his woods fill up with snow.

My little horse must think it queer
To stop without a farmhouse near
Between the woods and frozen lake
The darkest evening of the year.

He gives his harness bells a shake
To ask if there is some mistake.
The only other sound's the sweep
Of easy wind and downy flake.

The woods are lovely, dark and deep.
But I have promises to keep,
And miles to go before I sleep,
And miles to go before I sleep.

The teacher read it to the children of his seventh grade, and they discussed it first as a scene so vividly sketched that you could draw or paint it. The teacher said, "Do you think it is only a description of a scene, an incident?" And he read the poem again. They thought it was more than a scene. It referred to the feeling of lateness with still many things to do. Perhaps they were thinking of homework, but at least they caught the idea that "miles to go" might well mean many things to do, night coming, and the day's work still unfinished. The teacher agreed. Then he said, "Listen again and see if it says anything more to you," and he read it once more. A child spoke slowly, "Could the poet be thinking of death, do you suppose?" The discussion was lively. Some thought "before I sleep" might well mean death. Others disagreed and still preferred the idea of unfinished work. John Ciardi, in his provocative analysis of this poem, "one of the master lyrics of the English language," in *The Saturday Review,* referred to the dark and the snowfall as fairly obvious symbols of the death-wish.[12] This may be true, but to many older people, "and miles to go before I sleep" refers to all the wonderful things still to do, to see, to learn, to express—all the richness of life—and so little time left. By the way, it is more than likely that those children, in their own silent reading of the poem, would never have looked below the surface of this scenic description. But hearing the poem repeatedly—"lovely, dark and deep... And miles to go before I sleep," the children discovered meanings that they would never have found in a cursory silent reading. They were able to find at least three levels of meaning: (1) a simple episode, a scene vividly described, (2) the day nearly over and much work still to do, (3) the nearness of the long sleep of death, with still so many things to see and do and time running out.

With high-school students it might be interesting to go through Frost's poems and see how he has repeatedly used trees as symbols. (This might be an individual assignment or a class project.) One verse in "Come In" suggests "Stopping by Woods," for again the poet is at the edge of a woods, listening—

Far in the pillared dark
Thrush music went—

11. From *Complete Poems of Robert Frost.* Copyright 1923 by Holt, Rinehart and Winston, Inc. Copyright renewed 1951 by Robert Frost. Reprinted by permission of Holt, Rinehart and Winston, Inc.
12. John Ciardi, "Robert Frost: The Way to the Poem," *Saturday Review,* April 12, 1958.

Almost like a call to come in
To the dark and lament.[13]

The same idea recurs in the first verse of

Into My Own[14]

One of my wishes is that those dark trees,
So old and firm they scarcely show the breeze,
Were not, as 'twere, the merest mask of gloom,
But stretched away unto the edge of doom.

And the poet goes on to imagine that "into their vastness I should steal away"—another image of death.

There is a remarkable sense of companionship with "Tree at My Window" ending—

That day she put our heads together,
Fate had her imagination about her,
Your head so much concerned with outer,
Mine with inner, weather.[15]

And finally, there is "Birches" with the unforgettable conclusion—

. . . Earth's the right place for love:
I don't know where it's likely to go better.[16]

Undoubtedly, some teacher has already helped her students discover the remarkable likeness of themes in Gerald Johnson's superb *America Is Born* and Robert Frost's poem "The Gift Outright." In his book Mr. Johnson says:

At the start nobody intended to become an American, but everybody did if he stayed in this country. They were changed simply by living [here]. . . . George Washington still thought of himself as a trueborn Englishman, although it was impossible for him to be anything of the sort.

What made us Americans was not long and careful thinking about it, but simply seeing what had to be done and doing it. What had to be done here was not exactly what had to be done in England; and in doing it we became something different from Englishmen. (p. 140)

Read the children this and then read "The Gift Outright" several times until they see the connection.

The Gift Outright[17]

The land was ours before we were the land's.
She was our land more than a hundred years
Before we were her people. She was ours
In Massachusetts, in Virginia,
But we were England's, still colonials,
Possessing what we still were unpossessed by,
Possessed by what we now no more possessed.
Something we were withholding made us weak
Until we found out that it was ourselves
We were withholding from our land of living,
And forthwith found salvation in surrender.
Such as we were we gave ourselves outright
(The deed of gift was many deeds of war)
To the land vaguely realizing westward,
But still unstoried, artless, unenhanced,
Such as she was, such as she would become.

The relation between this poem and the Johnson passage lies, of course, in the lines, "She was our land more than a hundred years/ Before we were her people." Why? Because we were "Possessed by what we now no more possessed"—in other words, England. Which is just another way of saying what Gerald Johnson said. The children can readily fill in the wars involved in "(The deed of gift was many deeds of war)," but it is more important to challenge the children with those enigmatic last lines—"Such as she was, such as she would become." What would they like our country to become, our United States? This is important because the answer may well lie with them, the children of today, the adults of tomorrow. What would they have our country

13. From *You Come Too* by Robert Frost and *Complete Poems of Robert Frost.* Copyright 1916, 1921, 1923, 1928, 1930, 1934, 1939 by Holt, Rinehart and Winston, Inc. Copyright 1936, 1942 by Robert Frost. Copyright renewed 1944, 1951, © 1956, 1962 by Robert Frost. Copyright renewed © 1964 by Lesley Frost Ballantine. Reprinted by permission of Holt, Rinehart and Winston, Inc.
14. *Ibid.*
15. *Ibid.*
16. *Ibid.*
17. From *In the Clearing* by Robert Frost. Copyright 1942, 1951, © 1962 by Robert Frost. Reprinted by permission of Holt, Rinehart and Winston, Inc.

become that she is not today? The children's answers won't be profound, neither would the answers of average adults, but at least the poem will have made them look beneath the surface of evolving life in their own country and sense the fact that they, too, are going to play a part in its future. This poem is a perfect example of Frost's own pronouncement that "Each poem clarifies something."

Incidentally, "The Gift Outright" could lead easily and naturally into "A Cabin in the Clearing" (p. 231), which is the title poem of Frost's last book, *In the Clearing*. In that poem, the dialogue between Mist and Smoke concerns the settlers, asleep in their wilderness cabin. Mist thinks they don't know where they are, and Smoke says that "If the day ever comes when they know who/They are, they may know better where they are." Still Smoke "will not have their happiness despaired of." This curious dialogue will be more meaningful to children who have read "The Gift Outright." "A Cabin in the Clearing" can also be read and reread for underlying implications: (1) the predicament of our early settlers—lonely, hungry for neighbors with whom they could talk over their difficulties and bewilderments; (2) ourselves, confused also by personal anxieties, reaching out for understanding, for friends; (3) our own United States, "too sudden to be credible," facing such threats and fears as mankind has never faced before, trying "to push the woods back . . . /And part them in the middle with a path," trying to push back "woods," or misunderstandings, to find friends who will reach out a hand to reassure or help, only to find them "equally bewildered." Not to lead children to these underlying meanings through rereading and discussion and an occasional question is to hold them back so that they miss the growth in understanding and interpretative skill they are ready for.

The poems of Frost have a deceiving simplicity, which is good for children. They catch meaning with the first reading or listening. But as children grow chronologically, they also grow intellectually. In their reading of poetry this growth includes a more perceptive grasp of undertones of meaning. No poet offers them richer food for growth than Robert Frost.

How to Read Poetry Aloud

Throughout this chapter there has been an emphasis on reading poetry aloud to children as long as their own reading fluency is limited. This puts a heavy responsibility on adults, and the question is often asked, "How can a person with little knowledge of poetry and less knowledge of oral interpretation learn to read poetry acceptably?" The answer is, only by reading a poem aloud repeatedly until its tune and its meaning grow. Fortunately, the nonsense ditties of *Mother Goose,* Lear, and Laura Richards, with their crisp or explosive consonants and brisk rhythms, practically force the reader into vigorous, precise speech and give him a sense of tempo and variety. Milne, too, writes his lines so that they compel a correct interpretation. The subtle lyrics of Blake, Rossetti, and De la Mare, and the thought-provoking poetry of Robert Frost, however, require something more than vigor and swing. The works of these poets demand delicate, precise interpretation, and such interpretation must be grown into. So read a poem aloud to yourself first to get the general mood or feeling. Obviously, Blake's "Laughing Song" carries a gentle gaiety with it; listen to your own reading and see if you hear the suggestion (and only a suggestion) of laughter growing and finally coming to a climax in the last line. "Some One" by Walter de la Mare is mysterious and hushed—you can almost hear the speaker listening and whispering his speculations about the unseen knocker-at-his-door.

You make many such discoveries when you read poetry aloud, because skilled poets write for the ear, and they employ melody and movement consciously for specific ends: (1) Sometimes melody and movement are used to suggest the action described in the poem. (2)

Sometimes they help to establish the mood of the poem, or (3) they may even furnish clues to its meaning. When you read a poem aloud, therefore, you catch elements you miss when you read it silently, and the second time you try it orally you will interpret it better because you understand it better.

Melody and movement are used to suggest action. Read aloud Dorothy Baruch's "Merry-Go-Round" and you discover that the carousel winds up, gains momentum, and obviously runs down to a full stop as her line patterns suggest. Or read aloud the running of the rats in Browning's "Pied Piper of Hamelin":

And the muttering grew to a grumbling;
And the grumbling grew to a mighty
rumbling;
And out of the house the rats came tumbling.
Great rats, small rats, lean rats, brawny rats,
Brown rats, black rats, gray rats, tawny rats,
Grave old plodders, gay young friskers,
Fathers, mothers, uncles, cousins,
Cocking tails and pricking whiskers,
Families by tens and dozens,
Brothers, sisters, husbands, wives—
Followed the Piper for their lives.

As you read, you find yourself biting off the words in fine staccato style and gaining momentum as the thunderous race goes on. This is quite different from the broken, tripping, skipping, helter-skelter of the children's procession later in the poem. In still sharper contrast is this Greek lament, written over two thousand years ago, for a little dog. It moves slowly, gravely.

A Maltese Dog[18]

He came from Malta; and Eumêlus says
He had no better dog in all his days.
We called him Bull; he went into the dark.
Along those roads we cannot hear him bark.

This suggests the broken, halting movement of Ravel's music "Pavane for a Dead Princess," and the melody is in the same minor key. These auditory qualities force you to a reading very different from the ones you would use for the spinning music of Edna St. Vincent Millay's "The Ballad of the Harp-Weaver" or the nonsense of Milne's "The King's Breakfast."

Melody and movement help to establish mood. A galloping rhythm suggests excitement, and in Stevenson's "Windy Nights" it heightens the mystery of the unseen rider. In Browning's "How They Brought the Good News from Ghent to Aix" it makes the ride almost unbearably exciting and full of suspense. And in Alfred Noyes' "The Highwayman" it adds enormously to the romantic thrill and tragedy of that perennial favorite. But there are subtler rhythms and tunes that are just as potent. Read Langston Hughes' "April Rain Song" slowly, thoughtfully, and feel the tranquillity it induces:

Let the rain kiss you.
Let the rain beat upon your head with silver
liquid drops.
Let the rain sing you a lullaby.

The rain makes still pools on the sidewalk.
The rain makes running pools in the gutter.
The rain plays a little sleep-song on our roof
at night—

And I love the rain.[19]

So, in contrast, Ivy Eastwick's "Where's Mary?" (p. 232) is a comic study of irritability, a nagging woman getting more and more shrewish with every line. You find yourself growing sharper with every word. Heaven help poor Mary!

For an example of two entirely different poems about the same general subject, look at "Something Told the Wild Geese" by Rachel Field, and "The Last Word of a Bluebird" by Robert Frost. Both poems are about the migration of birds in the autumn, but their tunes and rhythms are as unlike as possible, and each one induces a completely different mood. "Something Told the Wild Geese" has caught the wild poignancy of the autumn flight of geese southward. The last

18. Tymnes (2nd century B.C.). From *From the Greek,* translated by Edmund Blunden. Used by permission of The Clarendon Press.
19. Reprinted from *The Dream Keeper* by Langston Hughes, by permission of Alfred A. Knopf, Inc. Copyright 1932 by Alfred A. Knopf, Inc.

two lines almost give you the shiver up the backbone that you feel when you hear wild geese honking overhead. Now look at "The Last Word of a Bluebird." It sounds as colloquial as two old men meeting on a street corner to discuss the late lamented cold snap. Only it happens to be a crow talking. It is laconic, earnest, and comic. Two different tunes compel two different moods and do something to your reading if you explore them orally a time or two.

Melody and movement furnish clues to meaning. Although these clues are not always apparent, we often use them unconsciously. For example, the minor note in that last verse of Robert Frost's "Stopping by Woods on a Snowy Evening" is the clue to its meaning. Look also at the small, quiet words of Elizabeth Madox Roberts' "Firefly" (p. 149). Words and lines suggest the idea of a small, evanescent creature, the "little bug all lit."

Notice, for contrast, the hammer stroke of the words in T. S. Eliot's

The world turns and the world changes,
But one thing does not change.
In all of my years, one thing does not change.
However you disguise it, this thing does not change:
The perpetual struggle of Good and Evil.[20]

This is the sound of the preacher, pounding home a moral truth. Even if you understood no English, you would know that you were being preached at, and that is the idea back of the words. So the beat of words and lines helps to convey the meaning and clarifies obscurities.

Reading poems aloud will, then, help to train your ear, improve your diction, and develop your taste for poetry. But, for your own sake, do not confine yourself to poetry for children; explore adult poetry as well. Treat yourself to a book by a modern poet—Archibald MacLeish or T. S. Eliot or Robert Frost —or to books by some of the younger poets. Treat yourself to at least one fine anthology of poetry. Walter de la Mare's *Come Hither,* Helen Plotz's *Imagination's Other Place,* and

20. From *Collected Poems 1909-1935* by T. S. Eliot, copyright 1936 by Harcourt, Brace & World, Inc. and reprinted with their permission. Canadian rights by permission of Faber and Faber Ltd.

There could have been no happier choice of illustrator for this remarkable anthology than Clare Leighton, a master of design. Here, the upturned faces, slanting lines, and glaring white spaces against the black carry not only the eye but the imagination upward with the telescope. Her striking pictures for this book use both mass and line to induce a feeling or to suggest an idea.
Illustration by Clare Leighton in Imagination's Other Place, *compiled by Helen Plotz. Copyright 1955 by Thomas Y. Crowell Company, New York, publishers. (Book 6 x 8¾)*

Elinor Parker's *The Singing and the Gold* are three treasures to be used by the whole family through the years. Between the covers of one anthology you will find excitement when you feel dull, peace when you are harassed, refreshment when you are weary.

Poetry has the same power of healing that music has. Prove it for yourself. Some night when you find yourself exhausted or disturbed or "all tied in knots," take out your anthology and read aloud, slowly and quietly, these first lines of John Keats' "Endymion":

A thing of beauty is a joy forever:
Its loveliness increases; it will never
Pass into nothingness; but still will keep
A bower quiet for us, and a sleep
Full of sweet dreams, and health, and quiet breathing.
Therefore, on every morrow, are we wreathing
A flowery band to bind us to the earth,
Spite of despondence, of the inhuman dearth
Of noble natures, of the gloomy days,
Of all the unhealthy and o'er-darkened ways
Made for our searching: yes, in spite of all,
Some shape of beauty moves away the pall
From our dark spirits. Such the sun, the moon,
Trees old and young, sprouting a shady boon
For simple sheep; and such are daffodils
With the green world they live in; and clear rills
That for themselves a cooling covert make
'Gainst the hot season; the mid-forest brake,
Rich with a sprinkling of fair musk-rose blooms:
And such too is the grandeur of the dooms
We have imagined for the mighty dead;
All lovely tales that we have heard or read:
An endless fountain of immortal drink,
Pouring unto us from the heaven's brink.

Visualize these lines as you read; then, start memorizing the selection as a whole, that is, going through all the lines each time. You won't learn it perfectly the first night, perhaps, but by the time you have mulled over it four or five times, savoring the words, catching new meanings that escaped you at first, you will discover that your tenseness is gone, that you are relaxed, renewed, healed. For those who have cultivated a listening ear, poetry has the same therapeutic quality as music. When you have made this discovery, you will be ready to use poetry with children as it should be used.

CREATING THE MOOD

With children the success of a poem depends in part upon the way you read or say it, and in part upon the mood and the setting in which the poem is introduced. One father used to settle down in the evening with his small boy in his lap. Sometimes there was an open fire, and always the child was undressed, ready for bed, comfortably snug in bathrobe and slippers. Then, in a leisurely, rumbling voice, the father would read or say the poems they both enjoyed. Occasionally the boy's thin treble would chime in, making a piccolo-bassoon duet. Invariably, along with requests for Stevenson and Milne, the child would demand, "Now say that about 'cloud-capp'd towers.' " Father would roll out those sonorous lines in his rich, deep voice, and the boy would listen intently but without comment. Occasionally he would murmur, "Say it again."

The cloud-capp'd towers, the gorgeous palaces,
The solemn temples, the great globe itself,
Yea, all which it inherit, shall dissolve
And, like this insubstantial pageant faded,
Leave not a rack behind. We are such stuff
As dreams are made on; and our little life
Is rounded with a sleep.—The Tempest.

Do you suppose that small boy would have listened to or been absorbed by those lines of Shakespeare had his father tried saying them to him on an automobile trip or at the breakfast table? Probably not. Mothers have always known the value of words spoken quietly at the going-to-sleep period, and the stories they have told and the prayers they have taught then are remembered always. So that small boy will probably carry with him as long as he lives "cloud-capp'd towers" happily associated with the warmth and security of his father's arms.

Schools usually have no such period of peace and affection, but perhaps they should create one. Of necessity a schoolroom must be functional; it must be a workshop, a study, a playroom, and a laboratory, all combined. But it is still possible to create a small area that suggests relaxation and enjoyment. In one classroom there was a little spot of ordered beauty—a table placed against a wall on which hung a bright-colored textile. On the table there was sometimes a bowl of flowers, or a vase with bare twigs, or some shining brasses borrowed from home, or a copy of a fine bit of sculpture. The children took turns arranging this table, which was a continual source of interest and pride. In another room, a teacher had one narrow window to the north. This she had turned into a glowing feast for the eyes, with glass shelves on which she and the children arranged colored glass vases. Some of them were from the ten-cent store, some the children brought from home as temporary loans, but the result was eyefilling sparkle and color. In still another classroom, there was space for a rug and some easy chairs over in a corner with the piano nearby. Such areas in the midst of our busy classrooms invite the imagination and are ideal settings for both music and literature.

For poetry, teachers and children should make themselves as comfortable as possible. Let there be no sitting up straight with hands folded. If there are any rockers or easy chairs, sit in them. If not, be as relaxed as classroom chairs permit. If the children sit on their feet, loll around, or curl up in strange postures, let them. You can assuage your conscience by giving them some setting-up (or even sitting-up) exercises at another period. Get the children close to you for poetry; relax, and let it be known that this is the time for enjoyment.

INTRODUCING POETRY

In poetry, as in music, some of us will like certain selections better than others. You will want to make this clear to the children, so that they will not feel forced to approve of every poem they hear. Nor do you want them glibly disapproving. Perhaps if you are introducing a new collection of poems to the children, or if you have a new group of children, you might say to them, "Do you know that the first time you hear a poem you can't always tell whether or not you like it? Sometimes you have to hear it several times before you know. That is why I always read new poems twice or even three times. Then we can see which poems we remember, or think about, or would like to hear again." This suggests a positive reaction, rather than the negative one which comes all too easily to children and to adults as well.

ANTICIPATING DIFFICULTIES

Even with two hearings some poems still remain obscure to children unless you clear up in advance the baffling words that block their comprehension. Poets have a high regard for words and employ no vocabulary studies to inhibit the use of them. They fling words around with blithe disregard for the audience to whom they are addressed. "Aye, marry, two," says *Mother Goose,* and talks nonchalantly in terms of "farthings," "sixpence," "tuffet," "grenadier," "dun," "mare," and dozens of other words that never yet crashed the gate of any respectable vocabulary list for the young. Here are a few more unorthodox words chosen at random from some of the poems already quoted: "helm," "vapour," "dale," "fen," "strong-withered," "disdain," "furled," "comely," "civilly," "louring." What are we to do with such words and the consequent obscurity which they may occasion for young readers?

First, there are the unimportant words which are not essential to the meaning. In all the times that children have heard "Is John Smith within?" not one ever seems to have inquired about "Aye, marry, two." Here, obviously, is just an explosive affirmative to the question, "Can he cast a shoe?" Well, of course he can, my goodness, yes,—*two* of them, all condensed into "Aye, marry, two." There is no use being heavily pedantic about trivia. Any sensible child gets the meaning of that expletive without your going into the ancient and honorable lineage of "marry." On the other hand, no child is anything but bewildered by Elizabeth Coatsworth's "strong-withered horse." If he is to see anything but a "wrinkled" horse, you will have to explain "withered" and "withers" before you read the poem. Any key word which is obscure should be explained casually in advance.

Sometimes it is better to read a poem first, letting children catch its sound and movement, and then go back to clear up obscurities. Take Winifred Welles' "Dogs and Weather." Decidedly this is a poem to read first and then go back and mull over, dog by dog, in some such manner as this:

"The greyhound for grey fog, a wolfhound with 'a tail like a silver feather' for snowy, wintry nights, a golden cocker spaniel to match the red-gold of autumn—these you can understand. She is matching her dogs to the time of year or the weather. But why did she want a terrier for rain? She speaks of him trotting through the rain with 'fine disdain'—that means he scorned rain; he never noticed it; rain did not bother him the way it bothers a cat. Do you know why? It is because a terrier has wiry hair, like a thistle, and that hair sheds water better than any raincoat you ever saw. That is why the terrier was able 'To trot with fine disdain/Beside me down the soaked, sweet-smelling lane.' "[21]

In short, children need not know the meaning of every word—some they can deduce from the context; some are too unimportant to bother about. Key words, however, should be cleared up before reading the poem, while other meanings may be developed casually after reading. Indeed, savoring the full flavor of the unusual words in poetry is part of the pleasure it gives and can result in an astonishing enrichment of vocabulary and a livelier feeling for words.

WAITING FOR CHILDREN'S REACTIONS

When you finish reading a poem, *wait for the children's questions or comments.* Don't ask, "Children, did you like that poem?" because the poor lambs, earnestly trying to please teacher, will all chorus docilely, "Yes!" Or if you don't have the group really with you, this question will invariably bring forth a strong-lunged "No!" that will set you back for a week. Instead of embarrassing children with such interrogations, wait for them to speak or to ask a question or to make an honest if hesitant comment that is really their own. If nothing comes, read on and don't worry. Do *you* burst into sprightly comments the first time you hear a new symphony? Probably not. You are still mulling it over—a little baffled, or too much under its spell to be capable of marshaling your reactions and translating them into words. In short, you are feeling something, but what it is you are not too sure. It is the same way with children listening to a poem for the first time. The words are not always heard or apprehended even with two readings. For this reason, if the children make no comments and never ask to hear a poem again, slip it in a day or two later and perhaps once again. Then, if there is still no response, no request for it, just tuck it away and say to yourself, "This may be good poetry, but if my children don't like it, it is not for them, at least not now."

21. From *Skipping Along Alone* by Winifred Welles. By permission of The Macmillan Company, publishers.

Children show you whether or not they like a poem in a variety of ways which you soon begin to watch for. Smiles, chuckles, and laughter are recognizable tributes to the kind of humor they enjoy. A certain intentness often testifies to a feeling they cannot put into words. Also their reactions are frequently delayed, like the boy's comment on "The Snare," which came weeks after he first heard the poem but showed he had been thinking about it. Sometimes a quick change of mood is an equally unmistakable sign of appreciation. Children who have been growing restless or apathetic or discouraged may suddenly come to life with a rousing poem in which they can participate. Or children who have been overstimulated and are keyed too high, relax and quiet down under the magic of poetry. Laughter, quiet, "say it again" questions about the poem, a sparkle in the eyes, speaking it with you—these are all signs that the contagion of poetry has caught.

Poetry in the Schoolroom

WITH SCHOOL SUBJECTS

While an unexpected event may be made more significant by saying the right poem at the right time, it is also obvious that there are many predictable uses of poetry for which suitable verses can be collected. We know, for instance, most of the child's nature interests: the change of seasons; the weather; birds, flowers, and insects; the sun, moon, and stars. For all of these interests we may well collect matching poems and have them ready. So much poetry is devoted to nature subjects that we can find excellent material to correlate with the children's science experiences throughout the year. In social studies it is not so easy. Of course there are many poems about the farm; and a few about boats, trains, airplanes, and buses; but for the fire department, colonial life, and many other "units" there are no poems worthy of the name. When good poetry is lacking, do not yield to the temptation to introduce any old doggerel because it is conveniently titled "The Fireman" or "When George Washington Was a Boy." If there is fine poetry available, use it. If not, don't waste time with the second-rate. Instead, introduce the children to all the splendid informational books now available for almost any subject you can think of. Then for their literature period, use poetry that is a complete contrast. For instance, when you are having a particularly factual unit of work—transportation or post office or tropical countries, for example—that might be the very time to treat the children to a satisfying feast of nonsense verse, or to investigate fairy lore and the delicately imaginative poetry that "correlates" with no facts but is precious in its own right. In short, correlate school subjects with poetry when you can legitimately do so with authentic poetry, and when you can't, use poetry for contrast and enjoy the change.

WITH FESTIVALS

Celebrate festivals with poetry as well as with music and art. Beginning with the first festival of the school year, Halloween, teachers give the children a background of fairy lore and set them to looking for fairy poems and the favorite jack-o'-lantern verses. They may start with Sandburg's "Theme in Yellow," but they progress to the idea of fairies abroad on Halloween and use Walter de la Mare's "Little Green Orchard," "Tillie," "Some One," and (for the older children) "The Rides-by-Nights," and John Ciardi's or Marie Lawson's poems called "Halloween."

For Thanksgiving, develop the real meaning of the word—literally, "giving thanks"—and introduce the children to that great body of Thanksgiving hymns, the Psalms. The smallest children can learn such verses as:

Praise ye the Lord: for it is good to sing praises unto our God; for it is pleasant; and praise is comely (147:1).

Blow up the trumpet in the new moon, in the time appointed, on our solemn feast day (81:3).

Bless the Lord, O my soul: and all that is within me, bless His holy name.
Bless the Lord, O my soul, and forget not all His benefits (103:1-2).

With the older children, use Psalms 23, 95, 100, 147, 150, or the first five verses of 103. Children and teacher also talk over what they have to be thankful for today, and this discussion almost always culminates in the children's own song of Thanksgiving,[22] composed individually or more often as a group. Over the years, these psalms of the children's own making have been varied and moving and have well deserved a hearing along with David's words of praise. Perhaps you are wondering why hale and hearty children should be interested in the Psalms or why schools should use Biblical literature. One boy answered that question, speaking unconsciously for many children who find life none too secure or comfortable. His verse choir had been practicing two of the Psalms for a Thanksgiving assembly. Walking from the classroom to the auditorium, this boy confided quietly to his teacher:

"You know, I like to say those Psalms just before I go to sleep."

"I do, too," she replied. "Why do you like them?"

The boy thought a moment and then said slowly, "Well, they make me feel sort of safe."

And that is what the Psalms have been doing for people all these years, making them feel "sort of safe."

Christmas is actually richer in poetry than

22. Thanks to the example of Miss Nell Curtis' methods of developing such a psalm. Hughes Mearns, "Childhood's Own Literature," *Progressive Education*, Jan., Feb., Mar., 1928.

Every teacher should know and use several good anthologies of poetry. A number of excellent ones have appeared in recent years, some of them general collections and many of them with a unifying idea such as William Cole's superb collection of animal poems, The Birds and the Beasts Were There, *or his* Poems for Seasons and Celebrations. *Johannes Troyer's illustrations for the latter book are simple, sensitive pen-and-ink. Illustration by Johannes Troyer for* Poems for Seasons and Celebrations *by William Cole. Copyright © 1961 by William Cole. Reprinted by permission of The World Publishing Company. (Book 6⅛ x 9¼)*

in stories. Indeed, the offering is so wide and splendid that there is no excuse for wasting time on the multitude of trivialities that afflict us with rhymes about Santa bringing *toys* for girls and *boys*. From Clement Moore's " 'Twas the night before Christmas" (which is a perennial command performance for the youngest children) to the second chapter of St. Luke (which is for children of all ages), the poetry of Christmas is both gay and rich in meaning. Some of the old carols are good to say aloud: "I saw three ships come sailing," or "As Joseph was a-walking," or

Beggar's Rhyme

Christmas is coming, the geese are getting fat,
Please to put a penny in the old man's hat;
If you haven't got a penny, a ha' penny will do.
If you haven't got a ha' penny, God bless you!

For the older children, Robert Herrick's "Ceremonies for Christmas" makes lusty reading. The youngest should have—along with Martin Luther's "Cradle Hymn"—Eugene Field's

Song[23]

Why do bells for Christmas ring?
Why do little children sing?

Once a lovely shining star,
Seen by shepherds from afar,
Gently moved until its light
Made a manger's cradle bright.

There a darling baby lay,
Pillowed soft upon the hay;
And its mother sang and smiled,
"This is Christ, the holy Child!"

Therefore bells for Christmas ring,
Therefore little children sing.

All these and many others are to be found in the best anthologies of children's poetry. And it will be especially worth while to look at *Come Christmas,* the collection of poems of Eleanor Farjeon.

YOUR OWN COLLECTION

To be ready with the right poem at the right moment means two first-rate anthologies on the teacher's desk or the home bookshelves, but in addition to these, it is a great satisfaction to have a choice poetry selection of your own making. Cards four by six inches are con-

23. Reprinted from *Sharps and Flats* by Eugene Field; copyright 1900, 1901, 1928 by Julia Sutherland Field. Used by permission of the publisher, Charles Scribner's Sons.

venient for this purpose. They are enough to take a poem of several stanzas on one card if you use both sides, and they can be conveniently filed in a shoe box, which the ingenious teacher decorates attractively and keeps on her desk. Poems should be copied accurately and clearly so that you won't stumble over words when you read from your cards. You may file them alphabetically, according to authors, or under subject-matter heads. Many people use both classifications—they file the full text of the poems according to author, and then make a cross-reference index under subjects, copying on these subject cards only the titles and authors. Blake's poem "The Lamb," for instance, would be copied and filed under Blake, but its title might appear on two different cards in the subject-matter index, perhaps once under animals and once under religious poems. Your subject index will include all those areas of interest that you have discovered both in the children and in your curriculum. Each person's index will be different, although animals, the four seasons, play, just-for-fun, going places, and several other topics will occur rather universally.

The reward for having your own collection is that on the day when there is a gale of wind that goes swooshing round the building with such a noise that you are bound to be aware of it, you can go over to your decorative shoe box and produce not one, but six, wind poems. "What have the poets said about wind?" you may ask. "What kind of wind do you think this author was feeling? Are any of these like our gale today? Perhaps, then, not everything has been said about the wind that might be. Perhaps one of you can think of something else about the wind."

The children themselves are fascinated with these handmade anthologies. In group after group where they have been used, a child or two has started his own collection, and, whenever the teacher has permitted it, the children have used her file themselves, lovingly and with pride in the teacher's unique possession. Few of us can reach a library and get out six books by six authors on the particular morning when the daffodils have bloomed and we must celebrate with poems on the bulletin board and with poems to be said together. Then you will be thankful for your cards. You will be equally grateful each year when "Indian" appears on your program, or "Westward Expansion," or "The Farm," and you know that tucked away in your anthology you have the very best poems you need, the ones last year's children liked best, and a few new ones to try out.

Finally, since poetry is difficult to read and since its strongest appeal is to the emotions, whether children are going to grow up liking poetry or not depends largely upon how wisely adults have chosen poems, how well they have read poetry aloud, and how all-around-happy an experience they have made of hearing, understanding, and saying poetry. Children must both hear and say poetry before they have really tasted the richness of great verse. For these reasons, verse choirs, which can provide valuable and exciting poetry experiences, are discussed in the next chapter.

SUGGESTED READING, PROBLEMS, AND PROJECTS

1. Which definition of poetry means the most to you? Why? Apply Frost's "momentary stay against confusion" to life today.

2. Can you recall any poem that gave you "a new enthusiasm," perhaps opened your eyes to fresh meanings, restored your emotional equilibrium, or gave you a sudden sense of well-being? Can you explain why the poem had this effect?

3. Choose and read three poems which you think illustrate the three important elements of good poetry: (a) singing quality—melody and movement, (b) distinguished or appropriate diction—words that are unhackneyed, precise, and memorable, (c) subject matter which invests life with new significance.

4. Have you had difficulties with poetry for any of the reasons suggested in the text, or for any other reasons? What might have been done, do you think, to have aroused and kept your interest in verse? Make a list of practical suggestions for stimulating genuine enjoyment of poetry.

5. Using the suggestions in this chapter, prepare a fifteen-minute poetry program for the age group you plan to work with. Practice reading the poems aloud to make the best use of their melody and movement, and plan the introductions to clear up as many difficulties in advance as possible. Allow some

flexibility in your program, so that if it seems necessary to do more, or less, rereading or explaining than you had planned, you will be prepared.

6. Plan a ten-minute period introducing Robert Frost's poems to primary children or a twenty-minute period introducing his poems to upper-grade children. Don't forget to allow time for rereading the poems as you present them.

7. Examine two anthologies and judge them on the basis of the criteria on page 200.

8. Select one poet of childhood whose book you would like to introduce to a class. How would you go about it? Which poems would you use? Read them aloud.

9. Do you sense any danger in helping children read, discuss, and reread poetry for different levels of meaning? Does it sound too analytical or too difficult for children? How can you avoid going too far with close analysis?

10. Find three poems not cited in the text to illustrate melody and movement which suggest (a) the action the poem describes, (b) the mood of the poem, and (c) the meaning or idea of the poem.

CHILDREN'S BOOKS: ANTHOLOGIES

There are so many good anthologies of poetry for children that it is not possible to list them all here. The following are especially useful for reasons the notes make clear.

ADSHEAD, GLADYS L., and ANNIS DUFF, eds. *An Inheritance of Poetry,* ill. by Nora S. Unwin. Houghton, 1948. A large collection of unusual poems, chiefly for adolescents, but with some exquisite bits for children. 10-16

ARBUTHNOT, MAY HILL, ed. *Time for Poetry,* General Edition, revised, ill. by Arthur Paul. Scott, 1961. Trade ed., A. Whitman. There are more than seven hundred poems in this newest edition of a favorite collection, ranging from *Mother Goose* to T. S. Eliot. The introductions for reading poetry to children and using poetry in verse choirs and the notes throughout the text are invaluable for adults. Also included in *The Arbuthnot Anthology.* 4-14

Association for Childhood Education, Literature Committee. *Sung Under the Silver Umbrella,* ill. by Dorothy Lathrop. Macmillan, 1935. A small collection of choice poetry, including selections from the Bible, modern poems, nonsense verse, and Japanese *hokku.* 4-9

BREWTON, SARA and JOHN, comp. *Birthday Candles Burning Bright; A Treasury of Birthday Poetry,* ill. by Vera Bock. Macmillan, 1960. A delightful anthology of poems arranged by age groups, illustrating the general fun of birthdays and including a choice selection of Christmas poems. 5-

———, comp. *Sing a Song of Seasons,* ill. by Vera Bock. Macmillan, 1955. 6-12
The Brewtons are excellent anthologists. Their books generally contain around three hundred well-chosen poems. *Gaily We Parade, Under the Tent of the Sky, Sing a Song of Seasons,* and *Birthday Candles Burning Bright* are especially useful in school libraries.

COLE, WILLIAM, ed. *The Birds and the Beasts Were There,* ill. by Helen Siegl. World, 1963. A choice and lovely collection of verses about animals, birds, and insects, both real and fantastic. Only a few poems are duplicated in this collection and John Brewton's *Under the Tent of the Sky,* so that they make excellent companion volumes of animal poetry. 6-

———, ed. *Humorous Poetry for Children,* ill. by Ervine Metzl. World, 1955. Laughter unlimited! This collection ranges from wild nonsense to the cleverest of light verse, sometimes more adult than "for children." 8-

———, ed. *Poems for Seasons and Celebrations,* ill. by Johannes Troyer. World, 1961. From the year's beginning to its end, poems follow the cycle of seasons and holidays in a refreshing collection of modern and traditional verses. Well indexed and attractively illustrated. 8-15

———, ed. *Poems of Magic and Spells,* ill. by Peggy Bacon. World, 1960. Goblins and ghosts, witches and other magical creatures are highlighted in a novel and attractive anthology. 9-13

DE LA MARE, WALTER, ed. *Come Hither,* 3rd edition, ill. by Warren Chappell. Knopf, 1957. A completely reset and newly illustrated edition of a great poet's selection of poetry. De la Mare's own notes add richness to this choice collection. 14-

———, ed. *Tom Tiddler's Ground,* ill. by Margery Gill. Knopf, 1962. First American edition of a choice compilation of verses for younger children. As in *Come Hither,* De la Mare's perceptive notes distinguish his anthologies. 9-

EATON, ANNE THAXTER, comp. *Welcome Christmas!* ill. by Valenti Angelo. Viking, 1955. A garland of some fifty Christmas poems, chosen with exquisite taste and given format and decorations of fitting beauty. All ages

FERRIS, HELEN, comp. *Favorite Poems Old and New,* ill. by Leonard Weisgard. Doubleday, 1957. Here is a splendidly varied collection of over 700 poems to appeal to the tastes and interests of children and grownups, too. 5-

GARNETT, EVE, comp. *A Book of the Seasons,* ill. by the compiler. Bentley, 1953. Brief excerpts, sometimes only two lines long, chiefly from adult English poems, will give children a taste of authentic poetry. The exquisite pencil sketches show younger children than those to whom the verses may appeal. 6-12

GREGORY, HORACE, and MARYA ZATURENSKA, eds. *The Crystal Cabinet,* ill. by Diana Bloomfield. Holt, 1962. A refreshingly original anthology of lyric poetry, wide in range, from Chinese translations to poems by Edith Sitwell, chosen for special appeal to children and young people. 12-

HUFFARD, GRACE T., and others, eds. *My Poetry Book,* rev. ed., ill. by Willy Pogány. Holt, 1956. A well-organized collection of some five hundred poems, with plenty of moderns. 6-14

MC DONALD, GERALD D., comp. *A Way of Knowing; A Collection of Poems for Boys,* ill. by Clare and John Ross. Crowell, 1959. A varied and popular collection, representative of modern and traditional poets. Appeals to girls as well as to boys. 10-

PARKER, ELINOR, comp. *The Singing and the Gold,* ill. by Clare Leighton. Crowell, 1962. A distinguished anthology of translations from over 30 countries and historic periods. The book's rich variety leaves the reader with new insight into the universality of human emotions and aspirations. 12-

PLOTZ, HELEN, comp. *Imagination's Other Place; Poems of Science and Mathematics,* ill. by Clare Leighton. Crowell, 1955. The most unusual anthology in this bibliography is a book for the whole family. With excerpts from the Bible and from old and modern poems written about science and mathematics, this collection ranges from atoms to relativity, Euclid to Einstein, and from modern surgery to God. 12-

READ, HERBERT. *This Way, Delight,* ill. by Juliet Kepes. Pantheon, 1956. A poet's choice of over 100 poems within the understanding of younger readers. Selected to delight children, they are followed by a distinguished essay on *What Is Poetry?* 8-

SECHRIST, ELIZABETH, comp. *One Thousand Poems for Children,* based on the selections of Roger Ingpen, ill. by Henry C. Pitz. Macrae-Smith, 1946. A tremendous collection, excellent for a library reference in school or home. All ages

SMITH, JANET ADAM, comp. *The Faber Book of Children's Verse.* London: Faber, 1953. Eight- to fourteen-year-old English children may rise to this collection, but in this country it will fit chiefly the high-school levels. An unusual selection of fine poetry makes it well worth knowing. 12-

SNELL, ADA L., comp. *Where Birds Sing,* ill. by Freda Reiter. Bookman, 1959. A welcome collection of bird poems, each illustrated with an identifying bird picture in black-and-white. 10-

THOMPSON, BLANCHE, ed. *More Silver Pennies,* ill. by Pelagíe Doane. Macmillan, 1938. 10-16

———, ed. *Silver Pennies,* ill. by Winifred Bromhall. Macmillan, 1925. Small collections of choice modern poetry for children and youth, with brief introductions to each poem. 8-12

UNTERMEYER, LOUIS, ed. *Rainbow in the Sky,* ill. by Reginald Birch. Harcourt, 1935. Mr. Untermeyer was one of the first and most indefatigable anthologists for children. This is only one of his many books. They lean heavily on old and familiar poems. 7-12

VAN DOREN, MARK, ed. *Anthology of World Poetry,* rev. and enl. ed. Harcourt, 1936. A collection of choice poems on an international scale, including ancient literatures and modern poetry as well. 12-

CHILDREN'S BOOKS: BY INDIVIDUAL POETS

ALDIS, DOROTHY. *All Together: a Child's Treasury of Verse,* ill. by Helen D. Jameson. Putnam, 1952. 5-9

———. *Hello Day,* ill. by Susan Elson. Putnam, 1959. A recent collection of verses by the author of such earlier favorites as *Everything and Anything* and *Here, There and Everywhere.* 4-7

———. *Quick as a Wink,* ill. by Peggy Westphal. Putnam, 1960. 4-7

ALLINGHAM, WILLIAM. *The Fairy Shoemaker and Other Fairy Poems,* ill. by Boris Artzybasheff. Macmillan, 1928. Poems by Allingham, Walter de la Mare, and Matthew Arnold. 9-12

———. *Robin Redbreast and Other Verses,* ill. by Kate Greenaway, Helen Allingham, Caroline Paterson, and Harry Furness. Macmillan, Little Library, 1930. 7-12

AUSTIN, MARY. *The Children Sing in the Far West,* ill. by Gerald Cassidy. Houghton, 1928. 8-12

BEHN, HARRY. *The Little Hill,* ill. by author. Harcourt, 1949.

———. *Windy Morning,* ill. by author. Harcourt, 1953.

———. *The Wizard in the Well,* ill. by author. Harcourt, 1956. 5-9

BENÉT, ROSEMARY and STEPHEN VINCENT. *A Book of Americans,* rev. ed., ill. by Charles Child. Holt, 1952. 8-14

BLAKE, WILLIAM. *Songs of Innocence,* ill. by Harold Jones. Barnes, 1961. A welcome new edition which contains nineteen of Blake's more childlike poems. 6-

BROOKE, L. LESLIE. *Johnny Crow's Garden*. Warne, 1903.

———. *Johnny Crow's New Garden*. Warne, 1935.

———. *Johnny Crow's Party*. Warne, 1907. 3-7

———. *Leslie Brooke's Children's Books,* 4 vols. Warne, n.d. 5-12

———. *Ring o' Roses* (see Bibliography, Chapter 5).

BROOKS, GWENDOLYN. *Bronzeville Boys and Girls,* ill. by Ronni Solbert. Harper, 1956. 7-11

CARROLL, LEWIS. *Alice's Adventures in Wonderland* (see Bibliography, Chapter 12).

———. *The Annotated Snark,* with an introduction and notes by Martin Gardner. Simon & Schuster, 1962. The full text of Lewis Carroll's great nonsense epic *The Hunting of the Snark* and the original illustrations by Henry Holiday.

CIARDI, JOHN. *The Reason for the Pelican,* ill. by Madeleine Gekiere. Lippincott, 1959. 5-9 Nonsense verses and imaginative poems in this collection launched John Ciardi's books for children. Others are:

———. *I Met a Man,* ill. by Robert Osborn, Houghton, 1961. 4-8

———. *John J. Plenty and Fiddler Dan* (see Bibliography, Chapter 10—Modern Fables).

———. *The Man Who Sang the Sillies,* ill. by Edward Gorey. Lippincott, 1961. 4-8

———. *Scrappy the Pup,* ill. by Jane Miller. Lippincott, 1960. 4-8

———. *You Read to Me, I'll Read to You,* ill. by Edward Gorey. Lippincott, 1962. 5-8

COATSWORTH, ELIZABETH. *Away Goes Sally* (see Bibliography, Chapter 16).

———. *The Fair American* (see Bibliography, Chapter 16).

———. *Five Bushel Farm* (see Bibliography, Chapter 16).

———. *Mouse Chorus,* ill. by Genevieve Vaughan-Jackson. Pantheon, 1955. Mostly mouse and not up to the author's best but worth looking over for a few choice verses. 4-6

———. *Poems,* ill. by Vee Guthrie. Macmillan, 1957. Poems of nature, animals, and the outdoors, including poems found in the pages of the author's stories. 8-

CONKLING, HILDA. *Poems by a Little Girl*. Lippincott, 1920.

———. *Shoes of the Wind*. Lippincott, 1922. 6-10

DE LA MARE, WALTER. *Peacock Pie,* ill. by Barbara Cooney. Knopf, 1961. Barbara Cooney's distinguished illustrations add beauty and appeal to this new edition of a classic De la Mare collection. 6-

———. *Rhymes and Verses: Collected Poems for Children,* ill. by Elinore Blaisdell. Holt, 1947. 5-

DE REGNIERS, BEATRICE SCHENK. *Something Special,* ill. by Irene Haas. Harcourt, 1958. 3-6

EASTWICK, IVEY. *Fairies and Suchlike,* ill. by Decie Merwin. Dutton, 1946. This book should not have gone out of print. The author has a true lyric gift, her fairy lore is authentic, and her nature poems have unusual charm. 5-12

EDEY, MARION. *Open the Door,* ill. by Dorothy Grider. Scribner, 1949. The outdoor world pleasantly recorded for young children in a small book of lilting verse. 5-10

FARJEON, ELEANOR. *The Children's Bells,* ill. by Peggy Fortnum. Walck, 1960. Verses about a magical world of saints and heroes, children and nature, fantasy and fun. 9-14

———. *Eleanor Farjeon's Poems for Children*. Lippincott, 1951. 5-12

———. *Mighty Men,* ill. by Hugh Chesterman. Appleton, 1926. 10-12

———. *Prayer for Little Things,* ill. by Elizabeth Orton Jones. Houghton, 1945. 5-12

FARJEON, ELEANOR and HERBERT. *Kings and Queens,* rev. ed., ill. by Rosalind Thornycroft. Lippincott, 1955. 10-12

FIELD, EUGENE. *Poems of Childhood,* ill. by Maxfield Parrish. Scribner, 1904. 8-12

FIELD, RACHEL. *Poems,* ill. by author. Macmillan, 1957. Favorite selections from this versatile author's earlier books with a few new poems. 6-12

———. *Taxis and Toadstools,* ill. by author. Doubleday, 1926. 7-12

FISHER, AILEEN. *Going Barefoot,* ill. by Adrienne Adams. Crowell, 1960. 4-8

———. *Up the Windy Hill*. Abelard, 1953. 5-8

———. *Where Does Everyone Go?* ill. by Adrienne Adams. Crowell, 1961. 4-8

FROST, FRANCES. *The Little Naturalist,* ill. by Kurt Werth. Whittlesey, 1959. 8-12

———. *The Little Whistler,* ill. by Roger Duvoisin. Whittlesey, 1949. 8-12

FROST, ROBERT. *You Come Too,* ill. by Thomas W. Nason. Holt, 1959. 11-

GAY, ZHENYA. *Jingle Jangle,* ill. by author. Viking, 1953. 3-5

GREENAWAY, KATE. *Marigold Garden,* ill. by author. Warne, 1910.

———. *Under the Window,* ill. by author. Warne, 1910. 4-7

HOBERMAN, MARY ANN. *Hello and Good-By,* ill. by Norman Hoberman. Little, 1959. 4-9

KUSKIN, KARLA. *The Bear Who Saw the Spring,* ill. by author. Harper, 1961. A most amiable bear inducts a small dog into the beauties of each of the four seasons. Rhyming text makes this a delightful read-aloud picture book. 5-6

———. *In the Middle of the Trees,* ill by author. Harper, 1958. 5-8

———. *James and the Rain,* ill. by author. Harper, 1957. A novel illustrated counting rhyme about a little boy and the animals he meets on a rainy day excursion. 4-7

LEAR, EDWARD. *The Complete Nonsense Book,* ed. by Lady Strachey. Dodd, 1942. This volume includes both books referred to in the text: *The Book of Nonsense* and *Nonsense Songs and Stories.* These are available in the original attractive separate volumes from Warne. 8-14

———. *Le Hibou et la Poussiquette,* trans. by Francis Steegmuller, ill. by Barbara Cooney. Little, 1961.

———. *Nonsense Book,* sel. and ill. by Tony Palazzo. Doubleday, 1956. For this companion volume to his handsome edition of Aesop's fables, Mr. Palazzo has selected one of the nonsense alphabets, eight long narrative jingles, and some of the best of the limericks. The colored pictures are gay and lively. 3-

———. *The Owl and the Pussy Cat,* ill. by William Pène du Bois. Doubleday, 1962.

LINDSAY, VACHEL. *Johnny Appleseed, and Other Poems,* ill. by George Richards. Macmillan, 1928. 10-

LIVINGSTON, MYRA COHN. *Whispers and Other Poems,* ill. by Jacqueline Chwast. Harcourt, 1958. This book has been followed by a number of others for young children. 5-7

MC CORD, DAVID. *Far and Few: Rhymes of the Never Was and Always Is,* ill. by Henry B. Kane. Little, 1952. 5-10

———. *Take Sky: More Rhymes of the Never Was and Always Is,* ill. by Henry B. Kane. Little, 1962. 8-

MC GINLEY, PHYLLIS. *All Around the Town* (see Bibliography, Chapter 5).

———. *The Year Without a Santa Claus,* ill. by Kurt Werth. Lippincott, 1957. In verse as sparkling as the season, Phyllis McGinley tells of the Christmas when poor, tired Santa Claus nearly took a vacation. Richly colored pictures frame each page. 6-12

MERRIAM, EVE. *There Is No Rhyme for Silver,* ill. by Joseph Schindelman. Atheneum, 1962. Jaunty little verses full of rhythm, nonsense, and child appeal, for the youngest. 5-7

MILLER, MARY BRITTON. *Give a Guess,* ill. by Juliet Kepes. Pantheon, 1957. Rhymes and pictures of twenty-five animals and birds which offer amusing stimulus to nature observation. 3-6

MILNE, A. A. *Now We Are Six,* ill. by Ernest Shepard. Dutton, 1927.

———. *When We Were Very Young,* ill. by Ernest Shepard. Dutton, 1924. These verses were reprinted in 1961, in larger type and more attractive format.

———. *The World of Christopher Robin,* ill. by Ernest Shepard. Dutton, 1958. The complete verses from *Now We Are Six* and *When We Were Very Young* appear in attractive single-volume format with eight new color illustrations. 5-10

NOYES, ALFRED. *Daddy Fell into the Pond, and Other Poems for Children,* ill. by Fritz Kredel. Sheed, 1952. After the hilarity of the first poem, this small collection reflects the world of nature and child activities. Its British flavor makes it difficult for average children. 6-

O'NEILL, MARY. *Hailstones and Halibut Bones,* ill. by Leonard Weisgard. Doubleday, 1961. 6-

RASMUSSEN, KNUD, comp. *Beyond the High Hills: A Book of Eskimo Poems,* ill. by Guy Mary-Rousselière. World, 1961. Color photographs of exceptional beauty illustrate this very special collection of short Eskimo poems gathered by the Danish explorer Knud Rasmussen. 7-

REEVES, JAMES. *Prefabulous Animiles,* ill. by Edward Ardizzone. Dutton, 1960. Extraordinary, fantastic animals of a poet's creation make this a fun-filled collection of nonsense verse. In more varied vein is the poet's *Blackbird in the Lilac* (1959), an excellent selection of some fifty poems. 4-8

RICHARDS, LAURA E. *Tirra Lirra; Rhymes Old and New,* ill. by Marguerite Davis, foreword by May Hill Arbuthnot. Little, 1955. 5-12

RIEU, E. V. *The Flattered Flying Fish,* ill. by E. H. Shepard. Dutton, 1962. Lovely light verses that savor of Milne and Lewis Carroll and yet have a special quality of their own. There is a tenderness when touching on a child's woes and a happy imaginativeness in the nonsense rhymes that will charm children and grownups, too. 7-12

ROBERTS, ELIZABETH MADOX. *Under the Tree,* ill. by F. D. Bedford. Viking, 1922. 6-10

ROSSETTI, CHRISTINA. *Sing Song,* ill. by Marguerite Davis. Macmillan, Little Library, 1924. 4-10

SANDBURG, CARL. *Early Moon,* ill. by James Daugherty. Harcourt, 1930. 10-14

———. *Wind Song,* ill. by William A. Smith. Harcourt, 1960. Poems chosen for child appeal cover a wide range of subjects from prayers and people to nature and nonsense. 11-14

SHAKESPEARE, WILLIAM. *Seeds of Time,* comp. by Bernice Grohskopf, ill. by Kelly Oechsli. Atheneum, 1963. Presented in most attractive format are nearly fifty brief selections from Shakespeare, chosen for young readers. 11-

———. *Under the Greenwood Tree, Songs from the Plays,* comp. by Julia Louise Reynolds, ill. by Leonard Weisgard. Oxford, 1940. 6-

SMITH, WILLIAM JAY. *Boy Blue's Book of Beasts,* ill. by Juliet Kepes. Little, 1957. 5-

———. *Laughing Time,* ill. by Juliet Kepes. Little, 1955. 4-

STARBIRD, KAYE. *Don't Ever Cross a Crocodile,* ill.

by Kit Dalton. Lippincott, 1963. Refreshingly original in their approach and distinctively rhythmic are these poems of personable people and animals. 5-10

———. *Speaking of Cows,* ill. by Rita Dava. Lippincott, 1960. 5-10

STEARNS, MONROE. *Ring-A-Ling,* ill. by Adolf Zábransky. Lippincott, 1959. The verses, adapted from folk songs, are uneven in quality, but the illustrations are unforgettably beautiful. 4-8

STEVENSON, ROBERT LOUIS. *A Child's Garden of Verses.* There are many editions of this classic. These are representative.
Ill. by Jessie Willcox Smith. Scribner, 1905. A large book with appealing pictures in soft colors.
Ill. by Tasha Tudor. Walck, 1947. A full edition with pictures in soft pastels using the young Robert Louis himself as the child. 4-10

TEASDALE, SARA. *Stars To-night,* ill. by Dorothy Lathrop. Macmillan, 1930. 8-12

WATTS, ISAAC. *Divine and Moral Songs for Children.* Page, 1901.

BIOGRAPHIES OF POETS

AUSLANDER, JOSEPH, and FRANK ERNEST HILL. *The Winged Horse; The Story of Poets and Their Poetry.* Doubleday, 1927. Written for older children and young people, this is a thoroughly interesting book for teachers and parents as well.

BALFOUR, GRAHAM. *The Life of Robert Louis Stevenson.* Scribner, 1915.

BARNES, WALTER. *The Children's Poets.* World Book Co., 1924. Chapter I, "Children's Poetry and Children's Poets," should not be missed.

———. "Contemporary Poetry for Children." *The Elementary English Review,* January 1936, 13:3. See the continuation of these articles throughout the year.

BENET, LAURA. "Rachel Field: A Memory." *Horn Book,* July-August 1942, 18:227.

CLARK, LEONARD. *Walter de la Mare.* Walck Monographs (see Bibliography, Chapter 2).

COLWELL, EILEEN H. *Eleanor Farjeon.* Walck Monographs (see Bibliography, Chapter 2).

DAUGHERTY, JAMES. *William Blake,* ill. Viking, 1960. One of today's outstanding illustrators writes an appreciative biography of the great eighteenth-century artist-poet. Although directed to teen-age readers, it is also a welcome source for teachers and students of children's literature.

DAVIDSON, ANGUS. *Edward Lear, Landscape Painter and Nonsense Poet.* Dutton, 1939.

FARJEON, ELEANOR. *Portrait of a Family.* Stokes, 1936.

FIELD, ISOBEL. *This Life I've Loved.* Longmans, 1937. About Robert Louis Stevenson, by his stepdaughter.

GITTINGS, ROBERT, and JO MANTON. *The Story of John Keats* (see Bibliography, Chapter 17).

GURKO, MIRIAM. *Restless Spirit; The Life of Edna St. Vincent Millay* (see Bibliography, Chapter 17).

LENNON, FLORENCE BECKER. *Victoria Through the Looking-Glass.* Simon & Schuster, 1945. Reissued as *The Life of Lewis Carroll,* Collier Books, 1962, paperback. A fine biography of Lewis Carroll.

MILNE, A. A. *Autobiography.* Dutton, 1939.

MUNSON, GORHAM. *Robert Frost,* ill. by Dan Siculan. Encyclopaedia Britannica Press, 1962. Enriched with examples of Frost's own poetry, this entertaining biography concludes with the award to Frost of the Congressional Medal, March 1962. 13-

NEWCOMB, COVELLE. *The Secret Door: The Story of Kate Greenaway.* Dodd, 1946. A fictionalized biography of Kate Greenaway, a good source of stories to tell to children. The illustrations by Addison Burbank are free copies of Greenaway's own pictures.

REID, FORREST. *Walter de la Mare: A Critical Study.* Holt, 1929.

RICHARDS, LAURA E. *Stepping Westward.* Appleton, 1931.

SERGEANT, ELIZABETH SHEPLEY. *Robert Frost, The Trial by Existence.* Holt, 1960. A definitive biography of the poet, full of fascinating details about the circumstances that occasioned many of the poems.

SOUPAULT, PHILIPPE. *William Blake,* tr. by J. Lewis May. Dodd, 1928.

SPIELMANN, M. H., and G. S. LAYARD. *Kate Greenaway.* Black, 1905. A definitive study.

STEVENSON, ROBERT LOUIS. *The Letters of Robert Louis Stevenson,* 4 vols., sel. and ed. by Sidney Coloin. Scribner, 1921-1923.

SYMONS, ARTHUR. *William Blake.* Dutton, 1907.

OTHER ADULT REFERENCES

ABERCROMBIE, LASCELLES. *Poetry: Its Music and Meaning.* Oxford, 1932. A detailed analysis of the elements involved in the music of poetry and the relation of music to meaning. Difficult but rewarding reading.

ARNSTEIN, FLORA. *Adventure into Poetry.* Stanford Univ. Press, 1951. A teacher's careful record of her step-by-step procedures in conducting an experiment in creative writing with a group of elementary school children. Her sound literary taste, knowledge of children, and endless patience and tact make this an invaluable study.

BARROWS, HERBERT, HUBERT HEFFNER, JOHN CIARDI, and WALLACE DOUGLAS. *How Does a Poem Mean?* Houghton, 1959. A college text for the study of poetry in general with an analysis of specific poems. The examples from traditional ballads, nonsense verse, and fine English poetry make the book a good anthology also.

DEUTSCH, BABETTE. *Poetry in Our Time.* Holt, 1952. This book brings the author's earlier study of *The Modern Poetry* more nearly up to date. It concludes with a chapter called "Science and Poetry" and an analysis of the work of W. H. Auden. This is a detailed and scholarly analysis of new trends in poetry and the output of individual poets, from Thomas Hardy to Cummings, Stevens, Williams, and their contemporaries.

DREW, ELIZABETH, and GEORGE CONNOR. *Discovering Modern Poetry.* Holt, 1961. "There is no single 'meaning' to much poetry. Different interpretations are always possible. . . . Analysis is not destructive, it is creative." These are clues to the authors' approach to the interpretation of modern poetry. Modern authors are examined with an appreciation that should help the most skeptical to a better understanding of modern poetry.

EASTMAN, MAX. *The Enjoyment of Poetry.* Scribner, 1921. This book is an excellent introduction to the pleasures of poetry. "Poetic People" (Chapter I), in which he gives his reasons for listing the child as one of the "poetic people," and his "Practical Values of Poetry" (Chapter XV) should be noted.

ERSKINE, JOHN. *The Kinds of Poetry.* Bobbs, 1920. There is a particularly good chapter on the teaching of poetry, much of which applies to any age, although the author has young people in mind.

FRANKENBERG, LLOYD. *Pleasure Dome: On Reading Modern Poetry.* Houghton, 1949. In his Foreword the author says, "I hope to provide a bridge to modern poetry for readers like myself, brought up on prose." It is a rainbow bridge with a detailed analysis of the poetry of James Stephens, T. S. Eliot, Marianne Moore, E. E. Cummings, and Wallace Stevens, and briefer discussion of seven other modern poets.

FROST, ROBERT. *In the Clearing.* Holt, 1942, 1962. This new edition of a choice collection includes "The Gift Outright," which the poet read at the Kennedy Inaugural in 1961.

GUMMERE, FRANCIS B. *The Beginnings of Poetry.* Macmillan, 1901. A basic study of origins of poetry. Read Chapter II, "Rhythm As the Essential Fact of Poetry."

HILLYER, ROBERT. *In Pursuit of Poetry.* McGraw, 1960. A distinguished poet and winner of the Pulitzer Prize, Robert Hillyer has written an entrancing introduction to the appreciation of poetry, old and modern, with unforgettable examples from some of the finest English poetry.

ISAACS, J. *The Background of Modern Poetry.* Dutton, 1952. Scholarly first aid to adults who find modern poetry hard to take.

MC GINLEY, PHYLLIS. *The Love Letters of Phyllis McGinley.* Viking, 1954.

NASH, OGDEN. *The Selected Verse of Ogden Nash.* Modern Library, 1946.

———. *Versus.* Little, 1949.

PARKHURST, HELEN HUSS. *Beauty: An Interpretation of Art and the Imaginative Life.* Harcourt, 1930. This is one of the most readable books we have on aesthetics. The illustrations add much to the text. Chapter III, "Sensuous Qualities of the World," Chapter VII, "Prose and Poetry," and Chapter IX, "Beauty and the Aesthetic Essence," are of particular importance to the discussion of poetry.

STONE, WILBUR MACEY. *The Divine and Moral Songs of Isaac Watts: An Essay Thereon and a Tentative List of Editions.* Privately printed for *The Triptych,* 1918.

chapter 9

Verse Choirs

Verse choir or choral speaking is an art that is comparatively new in our schools but old in the history of the race. "A speaking choir," according to Marion Robinson and Rozetta Thurston, "is a balanced group of voices speaking poetry and other rhythmic literature together with a unity and beauty born of thinking and feeling as one."[1]

However, a verse choir is more than a group of people speaking poetry in unison. Like a singing choir, a verse choir is made up of several groups of blended voices that may speak together or separately. These small choirs within the large group will not be so exact a blend in range and quality as the soprano, contralto, tenor, and bass sections of a singing choir, but they will be grouped as low and high voices, or in three groups—low, medium, and high voices. These three groups of well-blended voices are as essential to a genuine verse choir as the four sections of singers are to a singing choir.

In the singing choir so much emphasis may be placed on beauty of tone that some words are blurred or even lost in the effort to preserve a pure musical quality. In contrast, the speaking choir must project every word clearly and expressively. If words are blurred, the choir is a failure, no matter how charming the voices may be. Moreover, children who do not have adequate voices or musical skill for a singing choir may belong to a speaking choir with success and satisfaction. They may not be musicians, but when they speak poetry together they become music makers in a unique and exciting way.

Certainly nothing has ever demonstrated the singing quality of the spoken word more strikingly than the modern verse choir. Audiences are hushed as they hear a poem intensified by the united voices of a verse choir. Just as the combined instruments of an orchestra can develop certain melodies with a richness beyond the power of any single instrument, so a blend of many voices can clarify the melody of certain poems and magnify their rhythm. Children practicing in a verse choir are suddenly electrified by their own effects, while other children listening to them want to participate.

Anyone who regards verse choirs as just a

1. *Poetry Arranged for the Speaking Choir*, p. 13.

stunt should work with them. Children forget themselves completely; they discipline themselves, trying for an exact tone or inflection. They will listen to each other critically or with warmest enthusiasm; apparently practice periods are almost as enjoyable as a performance before an audience. From little second-grade beginners to college students, the work in verse choirs is marked by the most intense enjoyment and is an exhilarating experience.

Ancient and Modern Choric Speech

Poetry has been spoken, or perhaps chanted, by groups of people in many different parts of the world. The ancient Greek drama consisted first of odes chanted by a chorus with rhythmic bodily movements. Later a leader was added, who spoke certain lines alone; then there were two leaders, each speaking alone. Even with these solo voices added, the chorus continued to play an important part in the drama, sometimes speaking in unison, sometimes dividing and speaking in antiphonal style—one choir and then the other. But in Greek drama, the words of the chorus were as important as those spoken by the leaders. Choric lines advanced the plot and so had to be delivered with the utmost clarity and dramatic intensity if the audience was to follow the developing action.

There are passages in the Old Testament that read as if they were intended for solo and choral voices. For example,[2] in Psalm 24 it is easy to imagine a procession outside the gates demanding entrance and chanting joyously:

Lift up your heads, O ye gates; and be ye lifted up, ye everlasting doors; and the King of glory shall come in.

When the keeper of the gate challenges,

Who is this King of glory?

the chorus replies,

The Lord strong and mighty, the Lord mighty in battle.

Long, long ago, before speaking choirs had been heard of in our schools, a little New England teacher used to let her children say the Psalm in precisely that way. The children could never decide which was the more glorious part, the dramatic challenge or the robust and reassuring reply. Perhaps the Hebrew people never spoke the words in this manner, but it sounds as if they might have, and those children were sure of it.

Some of the ballads probably were recited by a leader carrying the narrative while a chorus thumped on the table with their flagons and chanted a lusty response. American Indians, with their rain chants or chants to promote the growth of the crops, may also have followed the pattern of solo speech and choric refrains. But, unlike the Greek chorus, the choruses of the ballads and the Indian chants did not carry the burden of meaningful lines that develop the story. The modern speaking choir seems, then, to owe more of its form to the Greek drama with its leaders and choruses than to any other source.

Speaking poetry in unison is nothing new, but verse choirs, as we know them today, are a comparatively recent development. They came to us chiefly from England, where they were suggested by John Masefield and initiated by Miss Marjorie Gullan. Her inspiration seems to have stemmed from the Greek drama, because in one of her earlier accounts of her experiment she writes:

The author first had the opportunity of making an experiment in choral speaking on the occasion of the Glasgow Musical Festival of 1922, when she trained a group of speakers in Greek drama choruses for a poetry speaking contest. It was subsequently found by experiment that the old Scottish ballads, with their haunting refrains or their vivid dialogue, gave just the inspiration needed for Scottish choric speakers.[3]

2. Robinson and Thurston, *Poetry Arranged for the Speaking Choir*, p. 95.
3. Marjorie Gullan, *Choral Speaking*, p. xi.

Her first experiments with choral speech were so successful that they were applauded and encouraged by such English writers as John Masefield, Poet Laureate of England, and Gordon Bottomley, playwright and critic. John Masefield established the Oxford Recitations, where speech choirs could come together to speak poetry, hear each other, and receive the expert criticism and advice of Miss Gullan. Later the London Recitations were established for the same purpose. Miss Gullan trained teachers for this work, and choral speaking swept England and Scotland, resulting in a fresh interest in poetry and in a wholesome improvement in speech.

In this country Miss Gullan herself gave tremendous impetus to the movement by her lectures, classes, books, and, above all, by the sincerity and power of her own unsurpassed interpretations of poetry. To hear Miss Gullan was to hear English poetry in its full vigor and beauty. To watch her direct a choir of children was to see them suddenly animated with new life. They spoke better than they ever spoke before; they reflected Miss Gullan's vitality and sincerity, and they responded to her leadership with complete enjoyment and self-forgetfulness. Yet in spite of her personal inspiration, in spite of the detailed reports of her methods in her many books, American choral speaking differs from the English choirs. The methods are less uniform and results often less finished. However, here and there throughout the country, sound and beautiful work is under way. For instance, in Milwaukee, under the able direction of Professor Agnes Curren Hamm of Mount Mary College and Marquette University, annual assemblies of choral-speaking groups meet together to hear each other and to receive constructive criticism and help. Such poetry-speaking assemblies have given impetus to the work in England and will do the same in this country if other cities encourage them.

Verse choirs have generated enough enthusiasm in the United States and Canada to deserve praise and much more encouragement than they have received. Teachers report that speaking poetry together makes it live for the children, does wonders for the improvement of their speech and voices, and gives them the keenest pleasure. For these reasons it seems worth while to scrutinize briefly the methods that are bringing good results and to formulate some standards of performance by which teachers can continually test and improve their own choirs.

Laying a Foundation for Choir Work

First of all, working with children in the elementary schools is different from working with adults, or even with high-school boys and girls. The objectives of choral speaking in the elementary schools are the children's enjoyment of poetry and their development, rather than a polished, finished performance. The approach with children must be more informal than with older people, and practice should not come so frequently or be so intensive as it often is with young people and adults.

KINDERGARTEN-PRIMARY

The kindergarten and first grade—perhaps the second, too—are merely periods of preparation for choir work, building toward it but involving none of the intensive drill that a real choir necessitates. In these early years, saturate the children with poetry; let them say *Mother Goose* and other simple poetry with you, keeping their voices soft and light just as you do in their singing. When you read a poem with a refrain, let the children come in on the chorus and then *mark the time as you do when they sing* to prevent them from dragging. Let the children discover that a poem can be as good a march or walk or skip or run as music. While the group says "Hippity hop to the barber's shop," let one or two children skip it—a high, free skip with arms swinging. They may gallop to "Ride a cock horse" or march to Milne's "Buckingham Palace" or walk laggingly to "A dillar, a dollar" or rock to "Hush-a-bye-baby." In this way they discover varieties of rhythm in poetry and respond appropriately. Even in the kindergarten, you might take such a little conversation piece as "Susan Blue" (p. 195), and let half of the children say the first three lines and the other half the concluding three lines. But at this early period you won't drill them for perfect timing or perfect speech.

Hearing a great variety of poems from nonsense verse to lyrics, developing a sense of rhythm, entering into the saying of these verses individually and in a group, never letting poetry drag or turn into singsong but keeping it light, crisp, and clear in sound and meaning, the children will have as much of a foundation for choral speaking as you should expect at the five- and six-year-old levels. If the results of your efforts are the children's whole-hearted enjoyment of poetry and the feeling that it is fun to speak together, then you are happily on your way.

MIDDLE AND UPPER GRADES

If you are starting this work with older children, begin in much the same casual way. First, there must always be a preliminary saturation with all types of poetry until the children acquire an ear for rhythm and a quick sense of mood. The informal speaking of some of their favorites follows naturally. This is one of the tests of their genuine liking for a poem —they begin to say it with you. With these older children, always mark the time (with hand or finger, as you do for singing) when they speak together and hold them to standards of suitable tempo and of light, pleasant voices. Never, even on the lustiest chorus, should the children's voices become harsh or loud. Sweet, light voices are, for children, one mark of good choral speaking. Their vocal cords are immature, and volume can strain and injure these cords with a resultant injury to voice quality. Long ago, public school music teachers began to insist upon light singing for young voices. But too often the child was encouraged to *talk* louder, as if a loud speaking voice were a virtue instead of an unmitigated evil. In verse choirs, children naturally tend to become shrill or loud and harsh; so it is important to remember the warning—*keep these young voices light.*

These older children may explore the rhythms of poetry, and they are mature enough to find their own examples of poems that swing, run, walk, hop, gallop, or skip. They may discover, too, the silent beat in poetry that is like the silent beat in a bar of music. Read aloud to them Stevenson's "Windy Nights," asking them to tap on their desks with one finger tip or to mark time in any way that is natural and noiseless. They will soon discover the silent beat between certain lines and realize that it must be observed in poetry just as the rest is in music.

Whenever the moon and the stars are set,
*Whenever the wind is high,**
All night long in the dark and wet,
*A man goes riding by.**

This discovery of the silent beat is important for the correct reading of poetry, and many children are soon able to recognize it independently.

Beginnings of Choir Work with Children

At this point, when the children are used to poetry, when they have discovered how much like music it is in its variety of rhythms, moods, and melodies, and when they like it well enough to explore further, you may tell them something about speaking choirs. Perhaps you will tell them that just as there are choirs for singing together, so there are choirs for speaking together, called verse choirs or choral speaking.

UNISON

To begin choir work, try contrasted examples of short verses that cannot be spoiled by speaking them in unison. While unison speech in its finished form is extremely difficult and requires the greatest precision and sensitivity, nevertheless, start with it in its simplest form for several reasons: first, because ever since the children could say the words of *Mother Goose* with you they have been speaking in unison; second, because such choral speech loosens their tongues and increases their speech agility without any conscious drill; finally, because there is a contagion and fun about speaking poetry together that delights the children and gets the choir off to an excellent start.

If you have seven-, eight-, or nine-year-old children, you might begin with this rousing march from *Mother Goose:*

The grand Old Duke of York
He had ten thousand men,
He marched them up a very high hill
And he marched them down again.
And when he was up he was up
And when he was down he was down
And when he was only half way up
He was neither up nor down.

Say it to the children first with the spirited marching rhythm the verse demands, and then let them say it with you, keeping the voices light. After they have it on the tips of their tongues, let half of the children say it and, as the last word is spoken, see if the other half can pick up the first line in perfect rhythm and say the verse through. Later, when the children are used to speaking together, it is fun to begin this march softly as if far away, to grow louder as if the marchers were coming nearer, and then, on a second saying, to carry it far away again and fainter and fainter. A child suggested this variation and the group thoroughly enjoyed it.

A gallop guaranteed to rouse the most apathetic is Rose Fyleman's "Husky Hi" (p. 130). Say this to the children and let them say it with you. Make the "husky hi" a vigorous staccato from way down in the diaphragm. You probably won't mention diaphragm to the children, but you will suggest that they get the feel of this gallop into their voices and into the words. Then let half the children take imaginary reins in their hands and "cluck" to their horses while the other children say the words. Or two or three children might be Keery and gallop to the verse. Don't use more than three, because the noise of their feet will drown out the speakers or force them to get louder and louder. If the gallopers don't get back to their chairs on the last word, just keep on

Galloping by, galloping by,
Here comes Keery galloping by.

For a contrast to these lively rhythms, try this one from *Mother Goose:*

Blow wind, blow, and go mill, go,
That the miller may grind his corn;
That the baker may take it,
And into bread bake it,
And bring us a loaf in the morn.

Say this to the children first, giving full value to the long vowel sounds and the sustained tone in the opening lines. Note the interesting contrast between the long, slow beat of the first two lines and the light staccato of the next two. The children can soon say this smoothly, bringing out the contrast that falls so pleasantly on the ear.

If you are beginning this work with children ten, eleven, and twelve years old, you might want to start with Shakespeare's walking song:

Jog on, jog on, the footpath way,
And merrily hent the stile-a:
A merry heart goes all the day,
Your sad tires in a mile-a.

Of course, say it to the children first. Doesn't it sound like a detachment of Boy Scouts on a hike? *Stile* may have to be explained—steps over a fence—but even though *hent* is not used today, every child can tell from the context that it means climb over, or get over the stile. Use this song much as you did "The Grand Old Duke of York."

With adults, you can use "Jog on" to illustrate an important distinction between a metrical singsonging of verse and the natural rhythmic emphasis that is desirable. If you mark the metrical beat, you will discover that in the last line it falls on *in*—"Your sád tires ín a míle-a." If you read it that way or let the children do it, you get a droning singsong that is tiresome and meaningless. You should speak it as you would naturally, accenting *sad* and prolonging the emphasis on *tires*—"Your *sad tires*—in a mile-a." Over and over again, you will discover that when the children singsong, it is because they strike the metrical beat so hard that they destroy the meaning. Here meaning depends on the contrast between the *merry* heart that goes all day and the *sad* that *tires* in a mile-a.

For a gallop, use "Husky hi" or the unfamiliar "Master I Have." This you can label "traditional," and so avoid the older children's reproach that *Mother Goose* is "baby stuff":

Master I have, and I am his man,
Gallop a dreary dun;
Master I have, and I am his man,
And I'll get a wife as fast as I can;
With a heighly gaily gamberally,
Higgledy, piggledy, niggledy, niggledy,
Gallop a dreary dun.

Say it to the children first, explaining that here is a young man who is delighted to have a job, "a master." He may have to ride a dreary old dun-colored horse, doing errands, but he doesn't care. A master means wages; wages mean a chance to get married. So he pounds along, celebrating his good luck with a song—and a rollicking, hard-riding song it is! Let half the children say it and, as the last word dies away, let the other half pick it up and say it again. Notice if you prolong the *n* sounds in the final words of the lines, you make them sing. This verse is especially good for learning breath control, which you may or may not call to the children's attention. They generally discover they have difficulty when they try to say those last three lines all on one breath. When the children can say "Master I Have" well, you might try Robert Louis Stevenson's "Windy Nights" (p. 143), another good gallop but much harder to say.

For a contrast, try the amusing surprise of Mary Austin's "Grizzly Bear," which tickles children of any age.

These are a few examples of the way you may begin your speaking choirs with either younger or older children. Say a poem first so that they are clear about the words, the mood, the tempo, and the meaning. Then let them say it with you, keeping their voices soft and light. When they know the words, they should speak the poem without your voice to help them, although you will still mark the time.

Probably no one should go much further than this with a speaking choir unless she has studied and acquired some knowledge of the detailed techniques of developing the work. Listening to well-trained verse choirs or to records of choir work is a great help to the amateur. The following pages will suggest the varieties of choir work and the techniques involved in developing them. These procedures are as nearly foolproof as years of working with children as well as adults can make them.

GROUPING CHILDREN IN CHOIRS

After you have worked with your children for two or three weeks, you will be conscious of certain voices that stand out, very high voices and very low voices. Children's voices do not have the extremes of range found in adults' voices but still they have more range than you would expect. As you work with large numbers of children under twelve years of age, you find that they divide into three groups—high, medium, and low voices. *Boys will be found in the high choir as well as in the low, and girls in the low choir as well as in the high.* Grouping the children is fairly easy. Listen for your one or two extreme voices at each end of the scale and start with them. You have to be very careful that the children get no sense of being out of line because they have the highest or the lowest voices in the room. To prevent this, you might say, "To have a good verse choir, children, we need high voices, low voices, and medium voices, each in a group or choir. As I have listened to you, I have heard some lovely high voices, some rich low voices, and some fine medium voices, but I can't tell to whom they belong. Now it is time to try out and see which choir you should be in. After we have our three choirs we shall be able to get much better effects when we speak together."

Take any simple poem that the children know, such as "Jack and Jill" or "The friendly cow all red and white" or "How would you like to go up in a swing?" and begin with the two voices you think are the highest. Let them say a verse together; then add a third and fourth voice and try to get a blend in which no single voice stands out. Keep trying until you have eight or ten children in one group. Follow the same procedure for the lowest voices and for the medium voices. Of course, you may find later that some children have to be shifted to another choir. In these trial periods, children often pitch their voices unnaturally, without meaning to, and have to be moved after a practice period or two.

Some people prefer to get the average range of the voice by the piano. To do this, you have a child read or say a poem near the piano, where you pick out his tonal range very softly on the keyboard. Children are surprised to discover that their speaking voices, like their singing voices, have a characteristic range, although a more limited one.

Whichever method of matching voices you use, children invariably become interested in the process, and some of them develop surprisingly keen ears. Have them listen and judge with you. Older children are a great aid in this process and enjoy helping.

Eight to twelve makes a good group in each choir, although you can use more or fewer if you need to. Sometimes you will get a blend of voices that is so smooth you can scarcely believe it, and sometimes, alas, one voice will be sufficiently atypical to stand out noticeably wherever you put it. When this happens, don't fuss with the child who has the unfortunate voice, but let him practice (softly) and have the fun of choir work with the others. If you give a program, let him do the announcing or distribute programs or do something sufficiently necessary to justify his being temporarily out of the choir. After all, human values are always more important than assembly programs.

You might occasionally, with a large class, find your choirs falling into four groups, but three is the usual pattern. With three choirs you have a flexible working basis for all the varieties of choral speaking. In a program these three choirs move around or are broken into other units according to the demands of the poems. For instance, you may turn your three choirs—which, for convenience, are referred to as high, low, and medium—into two choirs for antiphonal work. For this, you generally divide your medium voices and let the higher half go with the high voices and the lower half with the low voices. Again, you may wish to keep part of your low voices for a narration and part for a refrain, repeating this pattern in the high voices. Then you would really have five choirs temporarily. Below is a diagram of the three groupings just described.

USUAL FORM

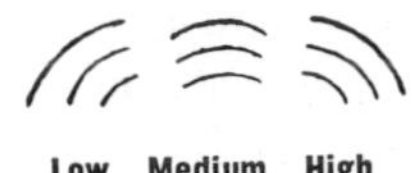

ANTIPHONAL

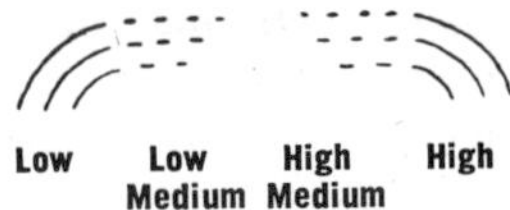

GROUPS AND CHORUSES

Experience will probably lead you to form other groups now and then. A solo voice may speak from a group or stand a little apart. There should not be too much moving around, especially in a program with children, but different combinations add to the effectiveness of your choir performance and are interesting both to the children and to audiences. Such changes in your groups you will find necessary if your program includes any variety of poems.

Having three choirs immediately brings color and contrast into choral speaking. Try to divide your voices by the second or, at the latest, the third week of working together. You may do it sooner if you know the children well. Make each choir feel its value to the whole group. High voices take the lines which suggest delicacy and lightness. They also ask a question, unless the questioner in the selection is a man. The low voices answer the question, unless the answerer is a woman. Low voices read lines which suggest mystery, terror, gloom, or solemnity. They are also used to give richness and warmth, or a reassuring quality to a passage. The medium voices are of great importance to the blending of all voices. They often have a bright, clear quality not so evident in the other two choirs. The medium voices usually carry the narrative, introduce the characters or explanations, and restore the everyday mood. After your three choirs have worked together for a while, you will hear the children in one choir admiring the tone and effect of the other choirs. They are soon able to recognize the particular contribution of each group.

Problems in Casting a Poem

Casting a poem is best learned in a class where you can try a poem several different ways before deciding on the most effective method. Casting a poem means deciding how it shall be read—unison, solo and chorus, line-a-child, group work, or antiphonal—and determining how the lines shall be distributed, which choirs shall take which lines. During your early work with a choir you will have to allocate the parts. But the trial-and-error method is good to use with children after they have had considerable experience. Cast a poem one way; then call for suggestions for other possible ways of speaking it, and try some of the children's suggestions. In the beginning they will propose all sorts of impos-

FIRST CASTING	*The Wind*	SECOND CASTING
Low	*I saw you toss the kites on high*	Medium
	And blow the birds about the sky;	
	And all around I heard you pass,	
	Like ladies' skirts across the grass—	
Medium	*O wind, a-blowing all day long!*	Low
	O wind, that sings so loud a song!	
High	*I saw the different things you did,*	High
	But always you yourself you hid.	
	I felt you push, I heard you call,	
	I could not see yourself at all—	
Medium	*O wind, a-blowing all day long,*	Low
	O wind, that sings so loud a song!	
Low	*O you that are so strong and cold,*	Medium
	O blower are you young or old?	
	Are you a beast of field and tree,	
	Or just a stronger child than me?	
Medium	*O wind, a-blowing all day long,*	Low
	O wind, that sings so loud a song!	

The Goblin[4]

High *A goblin lives in our house, in our house,*
in our house,
A goblin lives in our house all the year round.

Low *He bumps*
And he jumps
And he thumps
And he stumps.

Medium *He knocks*
And he rocks
And he rattles at the locks.

High *A goblin lives in our house, in our house,*
in our house,

All *A goblin lives in our house all the year round.*

FIRST CASTING		SECOND CASTING
1st choir	*A farmer went trotting upon his gray mare;*	1st choir
2nd choir	*Bumpety, bumpety, bump!*	2nd choir
1st choir	*With his daughter behind him so rosy and fair;*	1st choir
2nd choir	*Lumpety, lumpety, lump!*	3rd choir
	A raven cried "Croak!" and they all tumbled down,	
	Bumpety, bumpety, bump!	
	The mare broke her knees, and the farmer his crown,	
	Lumpety, lumpety, lump!	
	The mischievous raven flew laughing away,	
	Bumpety, bumpety, bump!	
	And vowed he would serve them the same the next day,	
	Lumpety, lumpety, lump!	

sible divisions, but they will gradually develop a sense of proportion, a good ear for effects, and a feeling for difficulties and limitations.

Page 227 gives two ways of casting Robert Louis Stevenson's "The Wind," using your three choirs in group work. Another plan for casting "The Wind" is to assign each verse to a solo voice and have the chorus spoken by a blend of voices. But group work on the verses gives more practice to more children and produces a pleasant effect besides. In this poem the *n* sound in the chorus should be prolonged just enough to give a sense of humming wind. Don't exaggerate this. It should only be suggested. Any overemphasis tends toward a stagy effect, which is the bane of verse choirs.

"The Goblin," from Rose Fyleman's *Picture Rhymes from Foreign Lands,* offers some interesting casting possibilities but falls most often into group-work form, using three choirs (above). There can be a very pretty graduation in tone on those three middle stanzas—"He bumps," "He knocks," "A goblin"—if each chorus comes in just a half tone higher than the preceding one. All three choirs speak the last line lightly but conclusively.

4. From *Picture Rhymes from Foreign Lands* by Rose Fyleman. Reprinted by permission of the publishers, J. B. Lippincott Company.

In casting a poem, be careful not to break the lines too frequently, especially with young children. Also, it is not usually advisable to have too sharp a contrast from the very high to the very low. And remember that each of the choirs has its own range from low to high, so that considerable variety can and should be obtained within any one group.[5]

REFRAINS OR CHORUSES

You will find that poems with refrains are easy for beginners. From *Mother Goose* we have "A farmer went trotting" (see suggested castings, p. 228). In this poem, one group of children may read the narrative, another the "bumpety" chorus, and a third the "lumpety" chorus; or you can keep it within the two groups, one reading the narrative while the other does both choruses. The responsibility of the chorus is always to come in with the same mood as the preceding line. In this first verse all is serene, but in the second verse a mischievous raven cries "croak"—they all tumble down, and various catastrophes result. The chorus therefore becomes proportionately tragic. This is one of the uses of the chorus—to emphasize or anticipate or heighten a mood.

Other easy examples for beginners are to be found in Rose Fyleman's *Picture Rhymes from Foreign Lands.* One of the prettiest is "My Donkey." The moment you read this poem aloud to the children in a mock-serious manner, they catch the idea that the donkey is faking his ailments in order to get attention. The first and third verses can be taken by the low choir, the second verse by the medium choir, and the refrain by the high choir. Be sure to keep the refrain as light and soft as the little syllables themselves: "Lav-lav-lavender." This poem is a good medium for establishing a sweet voice quality and for learning to suggest, by way of the voice, a characterization—in this case, the comical invalidism of the pampered donkey.

A rather complicated but exceedingly effective poem for choirs and choruses is A. A. Milne's "Shoes and Stockings" from *When We Were Very Young.* A decided contrast to this poem is William Blake's "The Lamb," which is best to use with the older children.

5. See "Using Poetry in Verse Choirs," The *Arbuthnot Anthology,* p. LXX, for other examples of casting poems.

The Lamb

High	*Little lamb, who made thee?*	**High**
	Dost thou know who made thee?	
Medium	*Gave thee life, and bid thee feed*	**Medium**
	By the stream and o'er the mead;	
Low	*Gave thee clothing of delight,*	
	Softest clothing, woolly, bright;	
Medium	*Gave thee such a tender voice,*	
	Making all the vales rejoice?	
High	*Little lamb, who made thee?*	**High**
	Dost thou know who made thee?	
Low	*Little lamb, I'll tell thee;*	**Low**
	Little lamb, I'll tell thee;	
Medium	*He is callèd by thy name,*	**Medium**
	For He calls Himself a Lamb.	
High	*He is meek, and he is mild;*	
	He became a little child.	
Medium	*I a child and thou a lamb,*	
	We are called by His name.	
Low	*Little lamb, God bless thee!*	**Low**
	Little lamb, God bless thee!	

Remembering that high voices usually ask a question and low voices answer, you will assign the opening and closing couplets of the first verse to the high voices. Lines three through eight can be given to the medium voices, or they can be assigned by couplets as indicated—medium, low, medium. Which casting you use will depend upon the quality of your medium voices. If that choir is particularly good, with clear voices and good diction, it can carry the whole six lines. Try it both ways in practicing until you know which is better. In the second verse, follow the same pattern, only begin and close with the low voices speaking warmly and reassuringly in answer to the question in the first verse.

After these examples, it should be evident that there are many possible forms for the choral interpretation of a poem. When the group is fairly experienced, it is fun to try out a variety of forms and let the group choose the most effective one. A particularly beautiful solo voice or a choir with an unusually rich quality will often determine the main pattern of the interpretation.

DIALOGUE OR ANTIPHONAL

A happy change from plain unison or unison and refrains is a verse with simple two-part dialogue. "Susan Blue," already mentioned for use in the kindergarten, is an example. In *Mother Goose* there are many simple dialogue poems; for instance, "Little Tommy Tucker's Dog," or the more interesting:

1st choir *"Is John Smith within?"*
2nd choir *"Yes, that he is."*
1st choir *"Can he set a shoe?"*
2nd choir *"Aye, marry, two."*
All *"Here a nail and there a nail,*
Tick, tack, too!"

This poem may be spoken as indicated. Of course the second chorus could speak the last three lines, but bringing in all the voices on the last two lines makes a more rounded conclusion. Elizabeth Coatsworth's dialogue between a cat and a bear, "Who are you?" Harold Monro's "Overheard on a Saltmarsh," Eleanor Farjeon's "Choosing," and Marie Lawson's "Halloween" are favorites with older children. Lucy Sprague Mitchell's "It Is Raining" is also good dialogue with choirs responding to the questions. Try it this way. Assign the first and third "It is raining" lines to the medium choir, the second "It is raining" line to the high choir. Assign the first and third questions to the high choir, the second question to the medium. Assign the first answer to the low voices, the second answer to the high voices, the third answer to the low voices, and the last two lines to all.

A dialogue set in a story is handled differently. A choir carries the narrative and a solo voice the speeches. If "he said" is in a line containing the speech, let the solo voice of the speaker rather than the narrative choir say it. Otherwise you get an absurdly choppy reading. A simple example is Rowena Bennett's "Conversation Between Mr. and Mrs. Santa Claus" where Mrs. Santa also carries the explanatory line following her first words:

Conversation Between
Mr. and Mrs. Santa Claus
(Overheard at the North Pole
Early Christmas Morning)[6]

"Are the reindeer in the rain, dear?" **High**
Asked Mrs. Santa Claus.
"No. I put them in the barn, dear, **Low**
To dry their little paws."

"Is the sleigh, sir, put away, sir, **High**
In the barn beside the deer?"
"Yes. I'm going to get it ready **Low**
To use again next year."

"And the pack, dear, is it back, dear?" **High**
"Yes. It's empty of its toys, **Low**
And tomorrow I'll start filling it,
For next year's girls and boys."

This poem may be spoken with high and low choirs or with two children. It is fun to do either way. "The Raggle, Taggle Gypsies" is another example of dramatic dialogue. The narrative is carried by a choir; a small choir

6. From *Jack and Jill.* Copyright 1947 by the Curtis Publishing Company, Philadelphia. By permission of the author.

speaks for the frightened servants, and solo voices take the parts of the lady and her outraged husband. These dialogue poems are popular with children because they are dramatic and effective.

By junior and senior high school age, boys and girls should have grown up in poetry to the place where they can handle as subtle and magnificent a bit of dialogue as Robert Frost's "A Cabin in the Clearing." When the poem is presented to an audience, it needs an introduction, which one of the students can deliver, and perhaps some other student can prepare.

A Cabin in the Clearing[7]

(for Alfred Edwards)

MIST
I don't believe the sleepers in this house
Know where they are.

SMOKE
They've been here long enough
To push the woods back from around the house
And part them in the middle with a path.

MIST
And still I doubt if they know where they are.
And I begin to fear they never will.
All they maintain the path for is the comfort
Of visiting with the equally bewildered.
Nearer in plight their neighbors are than distance.

SMOKE
I am the guardian wraith of starlit smoke
That leans out this and that way from their chimney.
I will not have their happiness despaired of.

MIST
No one—not I—would give them up for lost
Simply because they don't know where they are.
I am the damper counterpart of smoke
That gives off from a garden ground at night
But lifts no higher than a garden grows.
I cotton to their landscape. That's who I am.
I am no further from their fate than you are.

SMOKE
They must by now have learned the native tongue.
Why don't they ask the Red Man where they are?

MIST
They often do, and none the wiser for it.
So do they also ask philosophers
Who come to look in on them from the pulpit.
They will ask anyone there is to ask—
In the fond faith accumulated fact
Will of itself take fire and light the world up.
Learning has been a part of their religion.

SMOKE
If the day ever comes when they know who
They are, they may know better where they are.
But who they are is too much to believe—
Either for them or the onlooking world.
They are too sudden to be credible.

MIST
Listen, they murmur talking in the dark
On what should be their daylong theme continued.
Putting the lamp out has not put their thought out.
Let us pretend the dewdrops from the eaves
Are you and I eavesdropping on their unrest—
A mist and smoke eavesdropping on a haze—
And see if we can tell the bass from the soprano.

Than smoke and mist who better could appraise
The kindred spirit of an inner haze.

As the students work with the poem, let the higher choir speak for Mist and the lower for Smoke. The final couplet should come slowly and gravely from all the voices. Notice, there is no question mark after those lines. Smoke, mist, and inner haze!

When the children have become used to each other and have lost their self-consciousness, these dialogue poems may occasionally be tried with two solo voices; but, on the whole, the development of all the children is greater when the choirs take the two parts.

Poems which fall into two parts, but are not dialogues, are read antiphonally. Often they are poems of contrast like Elizabeth Coatsworth's "Cold winter now is in the wood," in which the lonely cold of the outdoors (lower voices) is contrasted with the snug comfort of life indoors (higher voices).

7. From *In the Clearing* by Robert Frost. Copyright 1942, 1951, 1962 by Robert Frost. Reprinted by permission of Holt, Rinehart and Winston, Inc.

The same antiphonal contrast is to be found in her "The sea gull curves his wings," in which the higher choir will speak the smooth first couplets of each verse and the lower will come in with a quick, harsh staccato cry of warning in the second couplets.

LINE-A-CHILD OR LINE-A-CHOIR

Another variety of choral speech Miss Gullan appropriately called "line-a-child." It differs from antiphonal works only in that it engages not two but three or more individual children or choirs. With this little verse of Kate Greenaway's you might use three children, a different child speaking each of the first three lines and all three saying the fourth line together. Or it can be spoken in the same way using three choirs:

1st *Little wind, blow on the hill-top;*
2nd *Little wind, blow down the plain;*
3rd *Little wind, blow up the sunshine;*
All *Little wind, blow off the rain.*[8]

A favorite with English choirs which is equally popular in the United States is Queenie Scott-Hopper's "Amy Elizabeth Ermyntrude Annie." "Where's Mary?" from *Fairies and Suchlike* by Ivy O. Eastwick is a pleasant poem, too, for this work. Like "Amy Elizabeth," it is prettier line-a-child rather than line-a-choir. A single voice may speak two lines at a time, or with an expert group only one line. Remember, this is a nagging woman, growing crosser and crosser, so bite off the lines peevishly.

Where's Mary?[9]

1st *Is Mary in the dairy?*
Is Mary on the stair?
2nd *What? Mary's in the garden?*
What is she doing there?
3rd *Has she made the butter yet?*
Has she made the beds?
4th *Has she topped the gooseberries*
And taken off their heads?
5th *Has she the potatoes peeled?*
Has she done the grate?
6th *Are the new green peas all shelled?*
It is getting late!
7th *What? She hasn't done a thing?*
Here's a nice to-do!
8th *Mary has a dozen jobs*
And hasn't finished two.
9th *Well! here IS a nice to-do!*
Well! upon my word!
All *She's sitting on the garden bench*
Listening to a bird!

Line-a-child or line-a-choir is always popular with children because of its variety and because of the challenge of picking up lines quickly in exact tempo. Eleanor Farjeon's "Boys' Names" and "Girls' Names" are good for this type of work. How effectively your children speak these poems will depend largely upon how well you read them in the first place.

Girls' Names[10]

All *What lovely names for girls there are!*
Medium *There's Stella like the Evening Star,*
High *And Sylvia like a rustling tree,*
Low *And Lola like a melody,*
Medium *And Flora like a flowery morn,*
High *And Sheila like a field of corn,*
Low *And Melusina like the moan*
Of water.
All *And there's Joan, like Joan.*

All three choirs say the first line together. It is spoken with slow tempo and sustained tone which are maintained throughout the poem until the concluding line, which makes a gay, humorous climax. *Stella* should be given to a medium voice. There is serenity in that line. *Sylvia* goes to a high voice, a little breathy. *Lola* is low and rich; *Flora*, gentle, soft, and medium in tone. *Sheila* is high and light—sun on the corn—with those sharp long-*e* sounds. Finally, the low or low-

8. From *Under the Window* by Kate Greenaway. United States rights by permission of Frederick Warne & Co., Inc. Canadian rights by permission of Frederick Warne & Co., Ltd.
9. Taken from *Fairies and Suchlike*, by Ivy O. Eastwick, published and copyright 1946 by E. P. Dutton & Co., Inc., New York.
10. From *Over the Garden Wall* by Eleanor Farjeon. Reprinted by permission of the publishers, J. B. Lippincott Company. Copyright 1933 by Eleanor Farjeon.

GREEN HILL NEIGHBORS
When I look at our green hill,
I think of all the wild
Small hearts that live inside it:
The woodchuck's chubby child,
Rabbits with busy whiskered faces
Peering out of rocks,
The big-eared meadow mouse, the dainty
Gold-eyed baby fox.
When I look at our green hill
Beneath the sunny sky,
I'm pleased to have such friends inside—
And glad I live nearby!
6
7

Children listening to the poem have fun picking out the animals as they are mentioned. Notice the fine, proud posture of the fox, alert and ready to go. Illustration by Kurt Werth for "Green Hill Neighbors." With permission of McGraw-Hill Book Co., Inc. Whittlesey House from The Little Naturalist *by Frances Frost and Kurt Werth. Copyright © 1959 by the Estate of Frances Frost, and Kurt Werth. (Original in color, book 6 x 9).*

est voice take *Melusina* (Mel-ū-seen′-a) on a minor note. This intensifies the sudden, humorous contrast of "Joan, like Joan"—spoken gaily by everyone. *Joan* is one syllable, pronounced *Jōn*. The companion poem, "Boys' Names," follows the same pattern. These are beautiful demonstrations of the different tone colors of your three choirs.

Frances Frost's "Green Hill Neighbors" is a pleasant example of line-a-child with narrative choirs for the beginning and the end.

Green Hill Neighbors[11]

Medium *When I look at our green hill,*
I think of all the wild
Small hearts that live inside it:
1st *The woodchuck's chubby child,*

2nd *Rabbits with busy whiskered faces*
Peering out of rocks,
3rd *The big eared meadow mouse,*
4th *the dainty*
Gold-eyed baby fox.

High *When I look at our green hill*
Beneath the sunny sky,
Low *I'm pleased to have such friends inside—*
And glad I live nearby!

11. With permission of McGraw-Hill Book Co., Inc. Whittlesey House from *The Little Naturalist* by Frances Frost and Kurt Werth. Copyright © 1959 by the Estate of Frances Frost, and Kurt Werth.

An exciting example of line-a-choir for older choristers is Sir Walter Scott's "Hie Away" (see the two castings below).

You may let all the voices say the opening and closing couplets, or you may divide your voices—letting the high choir and the high half of the medium group do the first line, while the low half of the medium choir and the low voices take the concluding couplet. Lines three through ten you may assign in couplets or by single lines according to the agility and precision of your choirs. The couplet assignment is a little easier, but the single line break gives more color and variety.

SOLO VOICES WITH CHOIRS

In some poems, it is highly effective to have certain lines spoken by a solo voice. In Vachel Lindsay's *The Potatoes' Dance,* for instance, different choruses carry the absurd narrative until they come to the third verse:

There was just one sweet potato.
He was golden brown and slim.[12]

Having a low-pitched solo voice speak those lines with portentous solemnity heightens and prepares for the mock-tragedy that follows. Another appropriate use of a single voice is in asking the two questions that open Eugene Field's "Song":

Why do bells for Christmas ring?
Why do little children sing?[13]

Then the various choirs follow, answering the questions. In some of the Psalms, several solo voices may be used effectively. "Taking Off" offers an opportunity for dramatic use of a solo voice with choirs. The excitement mounts throughout the eight lines, with the first couplet spoken by the low choir, the second by the medium, the third by the high, a single clear voice crying out the seventh line, "It's just a speck against the sky," and the whole group sighing the last line, "—And now it's gone!"[14] Because the contrast of the single voice against the choral groups is so striking, it should be sparingly employed, and only when there seems to be a real reason for it.

GROUP WORK

Most poems are cast into some form of group work, which may involve three, four, or five choirs, combinations of line-a-child, or dialogue. Group work is not a separate technique or form of choral speaking but merely the use of any or all types of this work for the most effective casting of a poem.

Group work may begin with extremely simple poems and progress to subtle and intricate material requiring real skill in interpretation.

12. From *The Potatoes' Dance* by Vachel Lindsay. By permission of The Macmillan Company, publishers.
13. Reprinted from *Sharps and Flats* by Eugene Field; copyright 1900, 1901, 1928 by Julia Sutherland Field; used by permission of the publishers, Charles Scribner's Sons.
14. Reprinted from *Very Young Verses,* published by Houghton Mifflin Company. "Taking Off" is also reprinted in May Hill Arbuthnot's *Time for Poetry.*

Hie Away

High Med.	*Hie away, hie away!*	**All**
Med. Low	*Over bank and over brae,*	
High	*Where the copsewood is the greenest,*	**High**
Medium	*Where the fountains glisten sheenest,*	
Low	*Where the lady fern grows strongest,*	**Medium**
Medium	*Where the morning dew lies longest,*	
High	*Where the blackcock sweetest sips it,*	**High**
Medium	*Where the fairy latest trips it:*	
Low	*Hie to haunts right seldom seen,*	**Low**
Low	*Lovely, lonesome, cool, and green;*	
High Med.	*Over bank and over brae,*	**All**
Med. Low	*Hie away, hie away!*	

An easy example to begin with is Rose Fyleman's "Mice." The opening and concluding couplets of this poem may be spoken either by a solo voice or by all three choirs. A single voice can set the quiet, meditative mood of the poem a little easier than a lot of voices. Lines three through fourteen can be taken in twos by low, high, medium, high, medium, and low choirs respectively. This sixteen-line poem is fun to use because of its interesting contrast.

An interesting example of incremental effect is "Until We Built a Cabin" by Aileen Fisher. This begins with a simple statement, increases in enthusiasm, and ends exultantly. Try this two different ways to see which you prefer—begin the first verse with high choir, second verse medium, and last verse low, or reverse the progression. Notice that the fourth line of the second verse should be spoken by the choir that speaks the last verse. The effect you are working for is a climactic feeling of wonder and delight in that last verse. Some prefer to have those concluding lines, "I never knew how many/many/stars there really are!"[15] spoken by all three choirs.

Another easy but somewhat more subtle example of group work is described for "The Goblin" on page 228. In that poem there is a steadily ascending tone in the middle portion of the poem, a pattern also used in Mrs. Baruch's "Merry-Go-Round," where after the ascent it slows down to the end.

For children ten and over, Herbert Asquith's "Skating" can be used for more difficult group work. You may cast it in several ways, but the following plan is one possiblity:

Skating[16]

All *When I try to skate,*
My feet are so wary
They grit and they grate:
High *And then I watch Mary*
Easily gliding,
Like an ice-fairy;
Medium *Skimming and curving,*
Out and in,
With a turn of her head,
And a lift of her chin,
And a gleam of her eye,
And a twirl and a spin;
Low *Sailing under*
The breathless hush
Of the willows, and back
To the frozen rush;
Medium *Out to the island*
And round the edge,
Skirting the rim
Of the crackling sedge,
Low *Swerving close*
To the poplar root,
And round the lake
On a single foot,
High *With a three, and an eight,*
And a loop and a ring;
Where Mary glides,
The lake will sing!
Low *Out in the mist*
I hear her now
Under the frost
Of the willow-bough
Easily sailing,
Light and fleet,
All *With the song of the lake*
Beneath her feet.

This whole poem must be said with a light swinging rhythm; the tempo must never drag or grow heavy or dull. And notice, in lines seven through eleven, *the rhetorical commas which should be completely ignored in reading*. The attention to the comma is a continual stumbling block to good reading, and accounts for much singsonging and monotony. Children have often been told to pause or drop their voices slightly at a comma. Occasionally this rule may hold, but in oral reading the rhetorical comma may mean nothing at all. It doesn't in this poem. These lines remain up and unfinished, until the charming "twirl and a spin"—where there is a semicolon, a drop in the voice, and a breathing space. Then the skater is off again. This time, the comma after "willows" (line fifteen) is oratorical as well as rhetorical; so you *do* pause; but, again, in lines twenty-four and twenty-five ignore the comma. See that the ringing *ing* sounds in lines twenty-six and twenty-eight really sing. Finally, on the concluding

15. From *That's Why* by Aileen L. Fisher, published by Thomas Nelson & Sons. Reprinted by permission of the author.

16. From *Pillicock Pie* by Herbert Asquith. By permission of The Macmillan Company, publishers.

Psalm 103

Medium 1 *Bless the Lord, O my soul: and all that is within me, bless his holy name.*

High 2 *Bless the Lord, O my soul, and forget not all his benefits:*

Low 3 *Who forgiveth all thine iniquities; who healeth all thy diseases;*

Medium 4 *Who redeemeth thy life from destruction; who crowneth thee with loving-kindness and tender mercies;*

High 5 *Who satisfieth thy mouth with good things; so that thy youth is renewed like the eagle's.*

Low and Medium 6 *Bless the Lord, O my soul, and forget not all his benefits:*

All 7 *Bless the Lord, O my soul: and all that is within me, bless his holy name.*

The Good Samaritan

Medium 30 *A certain man went down from Jerusalem to Jericho, and fell among thieves,*

High *which stripped him of his raiment, and wounded him, and departed, leaving him half dead.*

Low 31 *And by chance there came down a certain priest that way: and when he saw him,* he passed by on the other side.

Medium 32 *And likewise a Levite, when he was at the place, came and looked on him, and passed by on the other side.*

High 33 *But a certain Samaritan, as he journeyed, came where he was; and when he saw him,* he had compassion on him,

Medium 34 *And went to him, and bound up his wounds, pouring in oil and wine,*

Low *and set him on his own beast, and brought him to an inn, and* took care of him.

Medium 35 *And on the morrow when he departed, he took out two pence, and gave them to the host, and said unto him,*

Solo *Take care of him; and whatsoever thou spendest more, when I come again, I will repay thee.*

All 36 *Which now of these three, thinkest thou, was* neighbor *unto him that fell among the thieves?*

couplet, with all the choirs coming in lightly and triumphantly, let the voices make a bow with the three concluding words:

Be—neath—her—feet.

Does that sound absurd? It really isn't. "Beneath-her" is gently sustained on a descending scale, or tone, until the voice drops conclusively on that last word. In this way the voice makes a bow—a good way to end many poems.

A wonderful description of a powerful American river, undoubtedly our Mississippi, is T. S. Eliot's, "I do not know much about gods"—also for older children. Let the first couplet be spoken by the low choir, the second couplet by the medium choir, the next lines through "dwellers in cities—" by the high choir, then medium through "choose to forget" and close with all the voices speaking slowly,

Choirs	Four Little Foxes[17]	Choirs and solo
High	*Speak gently, Spring, and make no sudden sound;*	High choir
Medium	*For in my windy valley, yesterday I found*	Solo voice
Medium	*New-born foxes squirming on the ground—*	Solo voice
High	*Speak gently.*	High choir
Low	*Walk softly, March, forbear the bitter blow;*	Low choir
Low	*Her feet within a trap, her blood upon the snow,*	Low solo
Low	*The four little foxes saw their mother go—*	Low solo
Medium	*Walk softly.*	Medium choir
High	*Go lightly, Spring, oh, give them no alarm;*	High choir
Medium	*When I covered them with boughs to shelter them from harm,*	Solo voice
Medium	*The thin blue foxes suckled at my arm—*	Solo voice
High	*Go lightly.*	High choir
Medium	*Step softly, March, with your rampant hurricane;*	Medium choir
Low	*Nuzzling one another, and whimpering with pain,*	Low solo
Low	*The new little foxes are shivering in the rain—*	Low solo
Medium	*Step softly.*	Medium choir

rhythmically, and softly the concluding lines. Throughout these lines there is the flow and push of water, increasing in the last lines.

Since most poems useful for choral speaking are cast for group work, it seems worth while giving a few more contrasted examples. Psalm 103 (the first five verses with the first and second repeated at the close) makes a simple, understandable song of thanksgiving for young children (see page 236). Don't drop the voice after every phrase, in the usual manner of congregational readings. The voices stay up after each phrase, beginning with verse two, until the conclusive period of verse five. There should be a swelling lift to the voices in that last verse.

The parables lend themselves admirably to choral speaking, and they embody great ideals for children to carry with them all their days. The parable of the Two Houses (Matthew 7:24-27) is easily cast for verse choirs. The Good Samaritan (Luke 10:30-36) is not quite so easy but presents an ideal children need to know. (See page 236.) The Bible verse form is altered in this copy in order to make it easy to cast for verse choirs. Roman type has been used for some phrases which must stand out—not in loudness but with the gravity of their implications. In verses thirty and thirty-four keep the voices up after the phrases set off by commas until the period terminates the series. The speech of the Samaritan should go to the voice that speaks it best, regardless of its lowness or highness. That speech is the heart of the parable. The final question, asked gravely by all the choirs, is a tremendously dramatic conclusion.

Lew Sarett's touching poem "Four Little Foxes" is an interesting example of a poem which verse choirs may interpret differently. A group of Canadian children loved this poem, cast it for verse choir, and spoke it beautifully. A group of American children decided it was better spoken quietly by a single voice. Above are two different ways in

17. From *Slow Smoke* by Lew Sarett. Copyright 1925 by Holt, Rinehart and Winston, Inc.; copyright 1953 by Lew Sarett. Reprinted by permission of Mrs. Lew Sarett.

which it may be spoken. When a choir speaks the lines, it must say the lines quietly and with great restraint; otherwise the poem is almost unbearably sad. The final words of each verse should come gently, with the last words almost a whisper but clear, and with, perhaps, a rising inflection on "softly" as if the story were not finished. For children, speaking such a poem is an unforgettable experience.

The fox poem by Marion Edey and Dorothy Grider is amusing, and is good for eliciting from the children round, full tones and clear diction. For further examples of poems cast into group-work form, see the General Edition of *Time for Poetry* or *The Arbuthnot Anthology,* which provides footnotes and an introduction "Using Poetry in Verse Choirs."

The Little Fox[18]

High *Who came in the quiet night,*
Trotting so lightly?
Low *It was the russet fox who came*
And with his shadow played a game;
Medium *Where the snow lay whitely*
And the moon shone brightly
There he wrote his name.

High *Who spoke in the winter night,*
A cold sound and lonely?
Medium *The clock-faced owl, so round and hunchy,*
The yellow-eyed owl, in a voice so crunchy:
Low *"Who-oo-oo-oo, are you?*
I like to be only
Squat and bunchy–
All *Do you-oo-oo-oo, too?"*

UNISON SPEECH

Only an alert and disciplined choral group is capable of good unison speech. Unison speech, as contrasted with the speaking together of one choir, is the sustained speaking together of all three choirs. It requires a smooth blend of voices, an ability to speak together with perfect timing, and a control of tone and volume. The poems you choose for this form of choral speaking may be as varied as those for any other forms. Children five to seven or eight years old may speak in unison Kate Greenaway's "Little Wind" or Christina Rossetti's "And timid, funny, brisk little bunny" or Leroy F. Jackson's "O, it's hippity hop to bed" or the more restrained and exacting "Who has seen the wind?" by Rossetti. With even as simple material as this, there must be practice in beginning and keeping together, so that every word comes out clearly and the voices are light and pleasant to hear.

Older children may begin with Victor Hugo's "Good Night," which takes a warm, round tone throughout.

Good Night

Good night! good night!
Far flies the light;
But still God's love
Shall flame above,
Making all bright.
Good night! Good night!

The first "good nights" are not conclusive, but the last one is, and bows the poem out reassuringly. The tempo is even and the mood serene. It is a comforting good-night thought to leave with a child and is well worth his memorizing. College students enjoy this poem just as much as the children do. Because unison timing must be exact, diction and voice quality beyond reproach, short poems are best to begin with—"Heap on more wood," "But give me holly, bold and jolly," "If humility and purity be not in the heart," or even the charming "Hold Fast Your Dreams." When your choir is really experienced and well trained, let them speak in unison Robert Frost's exquisite "Dust of Snow." The children should have heard it several times, and should understand those concluding lines, "And saved some part/Of a day I rued." Perhaps they should also translate this into their own experiences—going home after a bad day at school to find a welcome and unexpected guest for dinner, or after a bad game, praise from the coach for their good sportsmanship, perhaps. They might also like to know that another poet, miles and countries and time

18. From *Open the Door* by Marion Edey and Dorothy Grider, copyright 1949 by Marion Edey and Dorothy Grider. Reprinted by permission of Charles Scribner's Sons.

away from Robert Frost, expressed this same idea. Then read John Keats' lines from "Endymion"

. . . yes, in spite of all,
Some shape of beauty moves away the pall
From our dark spirits.

When they know "Dust of Snow," let them try speaking it together smoothly, with clear thoughtful precision. Notice, these lines have no commas. Only the break in verses gives a breathing space for that wonderful concluding idea to develop.

Unison, refrains, dialogue, line-a-choir, choirs with solo voices, and group work are all different ways of using your choirs in certain poems. Of course you do not develop them in any precise order; that is, you do not develop all poems with refrains one week and all dialogue or line-a-choir the next. Rather, after the work is well under way, you choose, for each practice, poems that involve different styles of interpretation. Variety in the work makes practice more colorful and more fun.

Ordinarily you do not drill on special sounds, sustained breathing, or pure tone as such, particularly during the early stages of your work. But you will deliberately choose certain poems that give the children the practice you know they need. Nor do you stress speech exercises. In fact it is to be devoutly hoped you will never have to use them because you don't want to make your children self-conscious and you hope above all that they will enjoy their choral speaking and like poetry better because of it.

The Choir Leader: Teacher or Student

In the beginning, the teacher must lead the choir. She gives the signals for beginning and ending, she marks the time, and she may signal for crescendo or diminuendo exactly as she would for a singing choir. Some choral speaking authorities give specific gestures for each signal. This seems a bit pedantic, since no two orchestra leaders use exactly the same movements, nor do any two leaders of choirs. In general, the fewer signals a choir needs, the better trained it is. At first you may wave your hands and arms with large gestures and considerable vehemence[19] until you get your choir loosened up and fired with some enthusiasm. As a choir learns a poem and practices it for greater precision, the leader's movements should become quieter and less observable from the audience. A finished performance usually involves only the signal to begin, the signal for the entrance of each choir in turn, and occasionally a gesture to increase or diminish the tone. These signals can be given so inconspicuously that the audience is hardly conscious of them. Older children should have the pleasure and practice of directing also. In every group you will usually find one or two excellent directors. A child can often handle the choir so successfully that you can trust him to take over the leadership for a public performance. This is most desirable. But during practice periods when you are working for good diction, precision, and clear interpretation, you should, of course, do all the directing.

A Public Performance

Some directors allow the children to be seated during practice periods, but most teachers find they get better results if the children stand in good position, even for practice. Choirs may sit while you run through a poem together, clear up meaning, and try out the reading of the parts. Posture is important. Children should stand erect with heads up and eyes alert for signals. Encourage the children to let their hands hang loosely and naturally by their sides. If children practice on their feet, they will become so accustomed to the standing position that it will cease to cause

19. The degree of vehemence depends upon the temperament of the leader. Some work quietly from the beginning.

them any self-consciousness, and they can actually relax—in the sense of being at ease but never to the point of slumping.

It is certainly not necessary or even desirable to have special costumes for a public performance. Little girls in blue skirts and white blouses and little boys in blue trousers and white shirts, all with red ties, or blue ties, are attractive, but the costume is not an important element in a good performance. One choral-speaking group came from a desperately poor neighborhood in the depths of the 1930's depression. These children were clean but downright ragged. They loved their choral speaking, and the poetry they had learned together carried them out of themselves. Their voices were pure beauty, and their eyes shone; they spoke their poems with understanding and such a sense of enjoyment that they swept the audience along with them. Had they been clad in choir robes of celestial blue, they could not have been more effective or more beautiful. Children who are simple, natural, and intent on doing their best are wonderful to behold, regardless of what they wear. If, however, you wish to use costumes for some state occasion, be sure to have several practice periods in those costumes. Strange clothes can do strange things to easily diverted children; so take no chances. Ordinarily there is no reason for costuming a choir and certainly there is no excuse for ethereal lighting effects or background music. All these accessories smack too much of a stunt, and verse choirs ought to grow out of the children's everyday work. If choral speaking does not have forthright sincerity, nothing is worse.

Suitable Poems for Verse Choirs

In the books about verse choirs, lists of poems are usually included under each type of work, and sometimes minute directions for choir performance of these selections are given. Try them, by all means, but do not be limited by these lists. Our splendid American anthologies of poetry for children are rich sources of material that you should explore and try for yourself. But it is only fair to warn you that some of your choices may not work. Teachers ask, "But how can I tell in advance whether or not a poem is good for verse-speaking?" The answer is complicated.

Were you to have a list of all the poems which have been spoken effectively by verse choirs, you still could not be sure that your group would achieve success with these same poems. What goes well with one choir may not go well with another, even with the same director. Performance abilities differ and tastes differ. However, there are certain characteristics of poems which suggest at once that they are going to be effective or ineffective for choral speaking.

There seems to be a relationship between poetry that is good for choral speaking and music that is suitable for a dance. A dance usually requires music that is markedly rhythmic, and choral speaking needs strongly rhythmic poetry. But there must also be contrast in the music for a dance, or there is no dance; so also contrast is a basic necessity in a poem for choral speaking. When you read a poem through and find a lively rhythm, so far so good. But does the tempo change, or is there variety in mood, or in the persons speaking, or in the ideas presented? It is this lively change, this dramatic variety or contrast, upon which effective choral speaking depends.

Monro's "Overheard on a Saltmarsh," for example, has broad contrasts in the voices and characteristics of the nymph and the goblin, and subtle and delightful changes of mood within the dialogue of each of the two speakers. Best of all, there are striking contrasts between the pleading and cajoling of the goblin and the sharper and sharper negatives of the nymph. Obviously, this poem lends itself to choir production. "Sleepyhead," too, provides contrast between the child's matter-of-fact narrative and the lilting, eerie song of the fairies. These are unusually dramatic examples of contrast, but within every poem effective for this type of work there must be some variety.

Not all poems that have contrast lend themselves to choral speaking. Take William Blake's "Introduction," in which you find gaiety and sadness, a dialogue between a phantom child and a human being, and a charming descriptive narrative. Here are all the elements for effective choral speaking. Yet this poem is generally ruined by a choir because it is too subtle, too delicate, and too highly imaginative for group interpretation. The sheer weight of numbers rests too heavily on the light-as-air mood of the verses. The vision, which should be delicately suggested and clearly sustained throughout the poem, is blurred by the inability of a group to hold that vision. On the whole, verse choirs, particularly of children, need poems where broader, less subtle effects can be employed. Choirs add little to some of our finest lyric poetry, and they may even make it seem prosaic and commonplace. Not that it would hurt your choir to try "Introduction" or Robert Frost's "Stopping by Woods on a Snowy Evening" or any other lyric dear to the hearts of you or your students. But the moment you discover that a single voice gives more color, depth, or delicacy to a poem than a choir does, be courageous and abandon that poem as choir material. Use only those poems that are truly suitable.

Possible Dangers of Choral Speaking

SINGSONG DELIVERY

Choir speaking undoubtedly has its limitations and possible dangers. One danger is the children's tendency to singsong their lines. You work, in the beginning, for a strong rhythmic swing, and invariably the children begin to hit the metrical beat too hard and to drone their verses. The best way to correct this is to turn attention to the story or idea of the poem. Take the second verse of Stevenson's "The Wind." Children almost invariably singsong this verse, and so destroy the meaning. Say to your children something like this: "In that second verse, the boy was talking to the wind. 'It was strange,' he said to the wind, 'that I was able to see all the things you *did,*

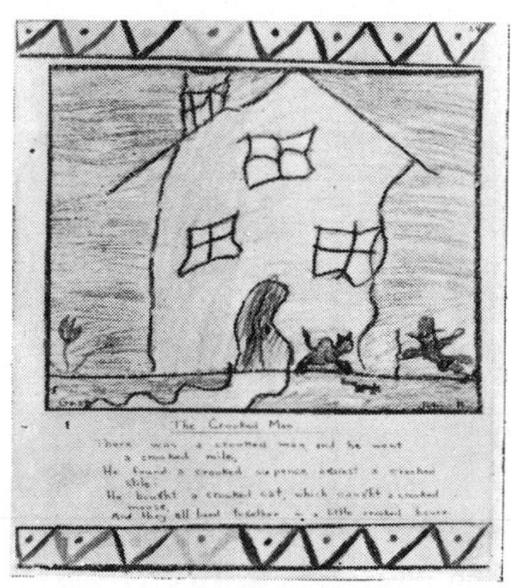

These pictures may be crude, but they show that the young artists have understood and enjoyed the poems the drawings illustrate. "The Crooked Man" is indeed crooked, the fairy queen drawn for "Yesterday in Oxford Street" is obviously a queen, and certainly the goblin for "Overheard on a Saltmarsh" is a devilish-looking fellow.
Mayfair School, East Cleveland, first and second grades; teacher, Miss Ada L. Hauck.

but always *you yourself,* you—*hid!*' Now can you children speak the boy's words so that people understand just how queer it is that we can *hear* wind and *feel* wind but never *see* the wind?" So you focus attention on meaning, rather than on a certain emphasis. Another conspicuous example is Walter de la Mare's "The Cupboard," which children ruin by hitting the metric beat—"I knów a líttle cúpboard"—with hammer strokes and then concluding with a pause for every comma in "For me, me, me." Actually, this is as gaily syncopated as the jubilant, prancing child who speaks the lines, so say to your children, "This is a little boy speaking, and he is telling us a wonderful secret." Then, you speak the lines in the fluid, natural rhythms of conversation, speaking the triumphant "For me me me!" with never a comma. Always stop your choirs the moment they begin to singsong and try to make them conscious of meaning and aware of what happens when they cease to think the words they are saying. Work continually to help them realize that speaking a poem to an audience means only one chance to make the people understand what it is about. This means that every member of the choir must *think* the words as he says them. If this suggestion is followed, then the audience is bound to catch the meaning.

CHOICE OF MEDIOCRE VERSE

Another unfortunate tendency of verse choirs is to use second-rate verse because it is "cute" or timely or strongly rhythmic. A poem may have the contrast and the rhythm suitable for choral work, but if it has no merit as poetry, it is a pity to waste time and effort on it. It is true that the finest lyric poetry is too difficult for the average choir, but this does not necessitate lapsing into a choice of mediocre material. Clever nonsense verse is a legitimate starting point. With a little practice, choirs can soon progress to good narrative poetry, heroic ballads, charming light verse, Bible selections, and a few simple lyrics. Avoid the banal, the newspaper type of verse; in short, avoid poor poetry no matter how rhythmic or timely it may be.

OVERDRAMATICS

Perhaps the unhappiest by-product of verse choirs is the lapse into the overdramatics of old-fashioned elocution. Natural, forthright youngsters are sometimes trained to arch their eyebrows on a given line, roll their eyes heavenward, gesticulate, and oversay and overact every line. Such exhibitions are enough to make any person who respects the integrity of children and the integrity of the spoken word condemn all such work. Of course, small children—four, five, and even six years old—use gestures spontaneously. They can hardly say "Rock-a-bye baby" without rocking their imaginary babies, or "Choo, choo, choo" without shuffling their feet and going into action. But children cease to do this somewhere around seven years of age. To put big eight- and nine-year-olds through pantomimic action in the speaking of every poem is to violate not only our code of sincere, thoughtful delivery of lines but good taste as well. An occasional gesture that comes spontaneously to add humor to a nonsense verse may tickle the children as well as the audience. But generally speaking, gestures detract from the meaning of poetry, attract attention to the speakers, and contribute to an artificial stunt-performance that is poor taste and bad for the children.

LOUD VOICES, INCREASED SPEED

Another danger when children speak together is the mounting volume of voices. With a chorus like "Way-hey, blow the man down," children get enthusiastic and bellow the words if you let them. Or, just in the course of practicing together, you will find there is always a tendency to grow louder and faster. If you let this go on, you will soon have a choir with a shrill or harsh tone that is unpleasant and will damage children's voices. Or the tempo will be so fast that words and meaning will be blurred. It is the feeling back of the words, the intensity and precision of the speech, not the volume of voices, that set the mood. In choruses like "Way-hey, blow the man down," work for round, vigorous tone but not loudness. In verses like "Who has seen the wind?"

work for quiet precision and for directing voices out over the audience to the farthest persons—a technique which will make every word carry even though the whole poem is in a hushed minor key. Never let the choirs gain momentum until they suggest a runaway. Mark the time firmly, and keep the voices warm, rich, pleasant, and light, but never loud.

Standards for Judging Choir Work

SPEECH AND VOICE IMPROVEMENT

Teachers will be helped in judging the results of their verse choirs if they will ask themselves certain questions. First ask yourself if there has been an improvement in the speech and voice quality of the children. You will probably not practice formal speech exercises before or during your speaking-choir activities, nor will you do the "lipping" or the breathing exercises recommended by many of the early books on this work. Pure vowels, vigorous consonants, and sustained breath are all essential to good speaking choirs, but they may be gained in the course of poem practice rather than in formal exercises. Choral speaking is very like singing. A song depends for its effectiveness upon clear diction, proper breathing, and good tone quality, but with children these are not practiced as exercises alone. Rather they are achieved through the song. Children can laugh at themselves when they run out of breath on such a chorus as the "Heighly gaily" of "Master I Have." They understand, then, the necessity for a good deep breath before starting the chorus, and they develop pride in having enough breath left over to "gallop a dreary dun, gallop a dreary dun" for a couple of extra rounds. When they listen to each other—and this is a privilege the children should have every so often—they can detect immediately the one voice using a long *a* sound in "Gallop *a* dreary dun," when the short sound of the *a* is obviously indicated.[20] Or they can hear one voice saying the usual "Christ*mus,*" and then understand the reason for pure vowels which everyone in the choir should speak alike.

The problem of local diction was sensibly dealt with by Miss Gullan, who, though Scottish by birth, worked in London and in all sections of the United States. She advised us to accept the best and the most cultured diction of our own locality as our standard, and not to try to force the speech of one geographic section upon another. This means that we should not expect a Southern child to speak like a New Englander, or vice versa, but in each case should accept the best standards of the community, try to overcome marked local impurities of speech, and work for vigorous, natural diction. Sweet, rich voices are an objective everywhere, and the choir work will help realize this objective, especially if the children have opportunities to listen to each other and to notice voice quality. Good choral speaking will correct many individual speech faults and will improve children's diction in general. It will not, however, take care of children who have special disabilities of voice or word-production. Those children need clinical help, or work with a speech teacher.

INCREASED ENJOYMENT OF POETRY

Next, and this might well come first, you should ask, Do the children have a greater enjoyment of poetry because of speaking it together, and are they genuinely eager for more and better poetry? There is something curiously exciting about a good speaking choir. Apparently, the members stimulate each other; the rhythm, the rich body of tone, the dramatic contrasts in choirs and individual voices all help make the experience enlivening and delightful. In schools where choir membership is voluntary, children will skip their lunches

20. In reading aloud, such words as *a, and,* and *the* are usually elided unless the meaning calls for an emphasis, as in "There are many cats, but this is *the* cat."

if they aren't watched or will miss special treats for the sake of choir practice. Young choir members read through books of poetry eagerly for new poems that might lend themselves to verse speaking. Children memorize dozens of poems easily with no urging. When such things happen, it is fairly evident that the children are enjoying poetry and that it is becoming a living part of them. Whether or not their taste improves depends largely on the teacher's own good taste and her tact in guiding the children. When they bring in poor, cheap little doggerels because they think they are "cute," be patient; even try the verses rather than hurt the children, but lead them to feel that they can do "harder" things, poems that are more beautiful and difficult. Gradually, the children will bring better poetry to try in practices, and then you can take heart; their taste is developing.

GROWING ABILITY TO INTERPRET POETRY

Are they also developing growing powers of interpretation, so that they speak their poems with understanding and vitality? At first, the teacher sets the pattern of the interpretation when she reads a poem to the children. With older children, she may read it two or three times, discuss it with them, and then let individual children read it to the group. A fresh voice or a different point of view will often bring out new beauties in a poem. Both younger and older children may suggest different ways of casting a poem that are real contributions to interpretation. Every child in the group should be able to read alone unselfconsciously and with pleasure. This power comes gradually, but it will come.

BETTER PERSONAL ADJUSTMENTS

Has the anonymity of choir work helped individual children? This is one of the invaluable by-products of a speaking choir. The shy child forgets himself. Lost in the group, he lifts a timid voice; under the surge and swing of great poetry, he speaks with authority and presently discovers that this new confidence stays with him: he can really do things on his own. On the other hand, the exhibitionist has to learn to submerge himself in the group. This is not so irksome as might be expected, because he presently finds himself carried along by the energizing excitement of the choir. The show-off, along with the other children, develops a pride in group performance —a shared sense of achievement.

ABILITY TO LEAD

Are some of the children able to take over the leadership of the choir? It is amazing how quickly certain children develop an ear for tone and tempo that makes it possible for them to give sound suggestions which add color and meaning to the interpretation. Others develop, in addition to a keen sense of tempo, an equal sensitivity to the contributions of the three choirs. They can lead certain poems as well as the teacher, and the scope of their directing grows with practice. Opportunities for leadership should be provided. Many groups work toward student leadership for public performances. Certainly it is a desirable goal.

SINCERITY

Are the children completely simple, natural, and sincere in their work? Costumes are not needed, nor footlights, nor background music. Can your choir speak for the assembly or on a school picnic with exactly the same self-forgetfulness and the same intent absorption that possess them in their practice periods? Intelligent, sincere poetry-speaking under any circumstances is an important goal.

If your speaking choir seems to be achieving these results, then you are doing sound and careful work. A love of fine poetry, the pleasure of sharing it, vigorous speech, light, agreeable voices, and complete simplicity and honesty of interpretation are the essentials of a good speaking choir.

Among adults, there is no unanimity of feeling about the values of choral speaking. Some adults are enthusiastic. One teacher remarked that after she launched her verse choir the children "simply ate up poetry" which they had scrupulously avoided before. "They memorized yards of poems," she added, "and they want to try everything in their verse choir." A principal likes the work for the same reasons, and adds that in their foreign neighborhood it has done more to get rid of accents and establish correct English diction than did all their formal speech drills put together.

Many people dislike the work violently. Perhaps they have heard poor examples—loud, strained voices or exaggerated emphasis. Others feel that altogether too much of the poetry spoken by the choirs is trivial and not worth the effort. Their criticisms may be valid. Choral speaking can be disastrously bad; it may employ poor verse, and, at best, it is no guarantee that good taste or good voice and speech habits will prevail. However, one thing is certain: there are few children who have been in verse choirs under able leadership who do not love the work and turn to poetry habitually and happily ever after. The same is true of college students, who beg for a chance to be in a choir. If choral speaking, when it is well done, can generate enthusiasm both for poetry and for a cooperative enterprise, it is certainly worth studying. Look over the catalogue of your nearest university. If it offers classes in choral speaking, treat yourself to such a class, for a genuine treat it will be. Then return to your children and launch the work with them. Our responsibilities are to know what is good choral speaking, how to achieve it, and what poetry will lend itself to this work and be worth while as literature.

SUGGESTED PROBLEMS AND PROJECTS

This chapter can aid you in elementary work with choral speaking. But if you plan any extensive choir activities, you will need more direction. Find out if the speech department of your college has any special classes or extracurricular work in choral speaking. If so, enroll in a group if possible or at least try to obtain permission to listen to some of its rehearsals. Attend any choral-speaking programs you can (it's possible that some of the teachers in the elementary schools are experimenting with choir work). Listen to any records of verse choirs now available.

Organize a group of your friends, or turn the class into a temporary choral-speaking laboratory. Follow the directions through, step by step. Keep checking your work with the "dangers" ascribed to choral speaking on pages 241-243. Try out all the suggestions for each type of work. You should find the Supplementary List of Poems in the bibliography helpful for more practice. Take turns directing. Also, sit out occasionally and listen carefully to the others. Take plenty of time for criticism of the work. Read and reread the standards for judging results, pages 243-245.

When you feel that you can direct a group, that you have the different types of work in mind, and that you know some good poems for the group to work with, go ahead. You will gain power, and both you and the children will have a good time.

REFERENCES

ABNEY, LOUISE. *Choral Speaking Arrangements for the Junior High School,* rev. ed. Expression, 1959.

———. *Choral Speaking Arrangements for the Upper Grades,* rev. ed. Expression, 1952.

ABNEY, LOUISE, and GRACE ROWE. *Choral Speaking Arrangements for the Lower Grades,* rev. ed. Expression, 1953. Useful books for the grades indicated.

BROWN, HELEN A., and HARRY J. HELTMAN, eds. *Choral Readings for Fun and Recreation.* Westminster Press, 1956.

DE WITT, MARGUERITE E., and others. *Practical Methods in Choral Speaking.* Expression, 1936. A compilation of papers by American teachers covering methods from the primary grades through the university, with many practical suggestions.

GARRISON, GERALDINE. "Bibliography of Choral Speaking in the Elementary School." *The Speech Teacher,* March 1954.

GULLAN, MARJORIE. *Choral Speaking.* Expression, 1931.

———. *The Speech Choir.* Harper, 1937. This is one of the most useful of Miss Gullan's books because it is both an anthology and a methods text. It contains American poetry as well as English ballads, with a detailed description of the presentation and development of each poem. Most of the poems are for upper-grade children and the high schools.

———. *Spoken Poetry in the Schools.* Expression, n.d. There is considerable repetition of methods and objectives in these early books of Miss Gullan's, yet each one repays reading because of the emphasis upon certain phases of the work, and for the sake of the different poems she uses for illustrations.

GULLAN, MARJORIE, and PERCIVAL GURREY. *Poetry Speaking for Children.* Expression, n.d., in 3 parts.

HAMM, AGNES C. *Choral Speaking Technique,* 3rd ed. Tower Press, 1951. A sound handbook of choral speaking methods by an excellent teacher who also conducts an annual verse choir festival in Milwaukee.

ROBINSON, MARION P., and ROZETTA L. THURSTON. *Poetry Arranged for the Speaking Choir.* Expression, 1936. While this anthology is for adult choirs and advises some of the embellishments Miss Gullan disapproves of, it contains such a choice selection of poetry that it should not be missed. There is a fine section answering questions concerning choir work, and a useful discussion of the speaking choir for religious services.

SUPPLEMENTARY LIST OF POEMS

Because most anthologies for choral speakers are for upper grades and high school, this brief list is added for elementary school children. The original source of a poem is generally given if it is in print. Page references are given for poems in this book. Many of these, as well as numerous others, appear in *Time for Poetry* (1961, gen. ed., comp. by May Hill Arbuthnot), which is cited for convenience. Many of the poems, of course, may be found in other anthologies.

Refrains and Choruses

ALLEN, MARIE LOUISE. "The Mitten Song." *Time for Poetry.*

ALLINGHAM, WILLIAM. "A Swing Song." *My Poetry Book.*

AUSTIN, MARY. "Texas Trains and Trails." *Time for Poetry.*

BLAKE, WILLIAM. "The Lamb." P. 229; *Songs of Innocence.*

CAMPBELL, JOSEPH. "I Will Go with My Father A-Ploughing." *Time for Poetry.*

CARROLL, LEWIS. "The Lobster Quadrille." *Alice's Adventures in Wonderland, Time for Poetry.*

CLARK, BADGER. "Cottonwood Leaves." *Time for Poetry.*

EASTWICK, IVY. "Waking Time." *Time for Poetry.*

EDEY, MARION, and DOROTHY GRIDER. "Open the Door." *Time for Poetry.*

FYLEMAN, ROSE. "My Donkey." *Picture Rhymes from Foreign Lands, Time for Poetry.*

———. "Well, I Never!" *Picture Rhymes from Foreign Lands.*

LEAR, EDWARD. "The Jumblies." *Complete Nonsense Book, Time for Poetry.*

———. "The Owl and the Pussy-Cat." *Complete Nonsense Book, Time for Poetry.*

MAC DONALD, WILSON. "A Song to the Valiant." *Poems Worth Knowing,* C. E. Lewis, ed.

MC CORD, DAVID. "Tiggady Rue." *Far and Few.*

MEIGS, MILDRED PLEW. "The Pirate Don Durk of Dowdee." *Time for Poetry.*

MILNE, A. A. "Shoes and Stockings." *When We Were Very Young.*

MOTHER GOOSE. "A farmer went trotting." P. 228.

———. "Up at Piccadilly, Oh!"

———. "Young Roger and Dolly."

NEWLIN, EDITH H. "Tiger-Cat Tim." *Time for Poetry.*

REESE, LIZETTE WOODWORTH. "The Good Joan." *Time for Poetry.*

RICHARDS, LAURA E. "The Baby Goes to Boston." *Tirra Lirra, Time for Poetry.*

———. "Kindness to Animals." *Tirra Lirra, Time for Poetry.*

———. "The Umbrella Brigade." *Tirra Lirra, Time for Poetry.*

RITTER, MARGARET. "Faith, I Wish I Were a Leprechaun." *Time for Poetry.*

ROUNDS, EMMA. "The Ballad of the Merry Ferry." *My Poetry Book.*

SANDBURG, CARL. "The Makers of Speed," Sec. 16 from *Good Morning, America. Panoramas,* Scott, Foresman Basic Readers 8^1.

STEVENSON, ROBERT LOUIS. "The Wind." P. 227; *A Child's Garden of Verses.*

TENNYSON, ALFRED, LORD. "Ring Out, Wild Bells." *Time for Poetry.*

TIPPETT, JAMES S. "Up in the Air." *I Go A-Traveling, Time for Poetry.*

WISE, WILLIAM. "What to Do." *Time for Poetry.*

Refrains and Choruses: Christmas

CHESTERTON, GILBERT. "A Christmas Carol." *Time for Poetry.*

FARJEON, ELEANOR. "In the Week When Christmas Comes." *Eleanor Farjeon's Poems for Children, Time for Poetry.*

———. "Now Every Child." *Eleanor Farjeon's Poems for Children.*

———. "The Shepherd and the King." *Eleanor Farjeon's Poems for Children, Time for Poetry.*

UNKNOWN. "The Christmas Pudding." *Time for Poetry.*

———. "Here We Come A-Caroling." *Time for Poetry.*

———. "Long, Long Ago." *Time for Poetry.*

———. (Old Broadside). "Sunny Bank, or, I Saw Three Ships." *Welcome Christmas!*

Dialogue and Antiphonal

COATSWORTH, ELIZABETH. "Cold winter now is in the wood." *Time for Poetry.*

———. "The sea gull curves his wings." *Time for Poetry.*

———. "The Rabbits' Song Outside the Tavern." *Time for Poetry.*

———. "Swift things are beautiful." P. 177.

———. " 'Who are *you?*' asked the cat of the bear." *Time for Poetry.*

EDEY, MARION. "The Little Fox." P. 238.

———. "Open the Door." *Time for Poetry.*

FARJEON, ELEANOR. "Choosing." *Eleanor Farjeon's Poems for Children, Time for Poetry.*

———. "Moon-Come-Out." *Eleanor Farjeon's Poems for Children, Time for Poetry.*

FROST, ROBERT. "A Cabin in the Clearing." P. 231.

FYLEMAN, ROSE. "Momotara." *Picture Rhymes from Foreign Lands, Time for Poetry.*

GREENAWAY, KATE. "Oh, Susan Blue." P. 195; *Marigold Garden.*

LAWSON, MARIE. "Halloween." *Time for Poetry.*

MC CORD, DAVID. "Cup." P. 133; *Take Sky.* P. 133.

MILLAY, EDNA ST. VINCENT. "Wonder Where This Horseshoe Went." *Poems Selected for Young People, Time for Poetry.*

MILLER, JOAQUIN. "Columbus." *Time for Poetry.*

MILNE, A. A. "Puppy and I." *When We Were Very Young, Time for Poetry.*

MITCHELL, LUCY SPRAGUE. "It Is Raining." *Time for Poetry.*

MONRO, HAROLD. "Overheard on a Saltmarsh." *Time for Poetry.*

MOTHER GOOSE. "Bell horses." *Time for Poetry.*

———. "Blow wind, blow." *Time for Poetry.*

———. "Bow, wow, wow!" *Time for Poetry.*

———. "Is John Smith within?" P. 230.

———. "Jennie come tie my bonny cravat."

———. "The North Wind doth blow."

———. "Old woman, old woman, shall we go a-shearing?" *Time for Poetry.*

———. "Pussy-cat, pussy-cat." *Time for Poetry.*

———. "What are little boys made of?"

———. "Whistle, whistle, old wife." P. 117.

RICHARDS, LAURA E. "Mrs. Snipkin and Mrs. Wobblechin." P. 125; *Tirra Lirra.*

———. "Talents Differ." *Tirra Lirra, Time for Poetry.*

ROSSETTI, CHRISTINA. "What does the bee do?" *Time for Poetry.*

———. "What is pink?" *Sing Song, Time for Poetry.*

———. "Who has seen the wind?" *Sing Song, Time for Poetry.*

UNKNOWN. "The Big Clock." *Time for Poetry.*

YOUNG, ELLA. "Holiday." *Time for Poetry.*

Dialogue and Antiphonal: Christmas

ALDIS, DOROTHY. "The Grasshoppers." *All Together.*

BENNETT, ROWENA. "Conversation Between Mr. and Mrs. Santa Claus." P. 230.

CHESTERTON, FRANCES. "How far is it to Bethlehem?" *Welcome Christmas!*

FARJEON, ELEANOR. "The Children's Carol." *Eleanor Farjeon's Poems for Children.*

———. "Earth and Sky." *Eleanor Farjeon's Poems for Children.*

MORRIS, WILLIAM. "Carol." *Welcome Christmas!*

SAYERS, DOROTHY. "Carol." *Welcome Christmas!*

SIMPSON, EDITH. "The Ox and the Ass." *Welcome Christmas!*

Line-A-Child or Line-A-Choir

ABBEY, HENRY. "What do we plant?" *Time for Poetry.*

BEHN, HARRY. "Spring." *Time for Poetry.*

BEYER, EVELYN. "Jump or Jiggle." *Time for Poetry.*

BIBLE. "For, lo, the winter is past." The Song of Songs, 2:11, 12, *Time for Poetry.*

———. "Whatsoever things are true." Philippians 4:8, *Time for Poetry.*

BLAKE, WILLIAM. "Laughing Song." *Songs of Innocence, Time for Poetry.*

BUSH, JOCELYN. "The Little Red Sled." *Time for Poetry.*

DAVIES, WILLIAM H. "Leisure." *Time for Poetry.*

DE LA MARE, WALTER. "Bunches of Grapes." P. 184; *Rhymes and Verses for Children.*

———. "O Dear Me!" *Rhymes and Verses for Children, Time for Poetry.*

EASTWICK, IVY. "Where's Mary?" P. 232.

FARJEON, ELEANOR. "Boys' Names." *Eleanor Farjeon's Poems for Children, Time for Poetry.*

———. "Girls' Names." P. 232; *Eleanor Farjeon's Poems for Children.*

FYLEMAN, ROSE. "Have You Watched the Fairies?" *Fairies and Chimneys, Time for Poetry.*

GREENAWAY, KATE. "Higgledy, piggledy! see how they run." P. 141; *Under the Window.*

———. "Little Wind." P. 232; *Under the Window.*

HOPPER, QUEENIE SCOTT. "Amy Elizabeth Ermyntrude Annie." *Time for Poetry.*

HOWARD, WINIFRED. "White Horses." *Sung Under the Silver Umbrella.*

HUGHES, LANGSTON. "April Rain Song." P. 206; *The Dream Keeper.*

MOORE, VIRGINIA. "Epic." *This Singing World,* Louis Untermeyer, ed.

MOTHER GOOSE. "Bow-wow, says the dog."

_____. "For want of a nail."

_____. "I won't be my father's Jack."

_____. "One, two, buckle my shoe." *Time for Poetry.*

NEWBOLT, SIR HENRY. "Finis." *Time for Poetry.*

O'NEILL, MARY. "White." *Hailstones and Halibut Bones.*

_____. "Black." *Hailstones and Halibut Bones.*

_____. "Yellow." *Hailstones and Halibut Bones.*

ROBERTS, ELIZABETH MADOX. "The People." P. 150; *Under the Tree.*

ROSSETTI, CHRISTINA. "Eight o'clock." *Time for Poetry.*

_____. "Ferry me across the water." *Sing Song, Sung Under the Silver Umbrella.*

_____. "Oh, Fair to See." *Time for Poetry.*

SANDBURG, CARL. "Buffalo Dusk." *Time for Poetry.*

SCOTT, SIR WALTER. "Hie Away." P. 234.

TEASDALE, SARA. "The Falling Star." *Time for Poetry.*

TIPPETT, JAMES. "Trains." *Time for Poetry.*

UNKNOWN. "The Green Grass Growing All Around." *My Poetry Book.*

_____. "Taking Off." *Time for Poetry.*

WHITMAN, WALT. "I Hear America Singing." *Leaves of Grass, Time for Poetry.*

WORDSWORTH, WILLIAM. "My Heart Leaps Up." *Time for Poetry.*

_____. "Written in March." *Time for Poetry.*

WYNNE, ANNETTE. "Ring Around the World." *Time for Poetry.*

Line-A-Child or Line-A-Choir: Christmas

FIELD, EUGENE. "Song" ("Why do bells for Christmas ring?"). P. 212.

MOTHER GOOSE. "Christmas" ("Christmas is coming, the geese are getting fat"). *Time for Poetry.*

MUHLENBERG, WILLIAM. "Carol, Brothers, Carol." *Time for Poetry.*

UNKNOWN. "Gladde Things." *Time for Poetry.*

_____. "An Old Christmas Greeting." *Time for Poetry.*

Group Work, Sometimes with Solo Parts

ASQUITH, HERBERT. "Skating." P. 235.

BARUCH, DOROTHY. "Merry-Go-Round." *Time for Poetry.*

_____. "Stop–Go." *Time for Poetry.*

BEHN, HARRY. "Halloween." *Little Hill, Time for Poetry.*

BENÉT, ROSEMARY and STEPHEN. "Abraham Lincoln." *Book of Americans, Time for Poetry.*

BENNETT, HENRY HOLCOMB. "The Flag Goes By." *Time for Poetry.*

BIBLE. Psalms 23, 24, 100, 103, 147, 150. *Time for Poetry.*

BROWN, BEATRICE CURTIS. "Jonathan Bing." *Time for Poetry.*

CHIPP, ELINOR. "Wild Geese." *Time for Poetry.*

CIARDI, JOHN. "Halloween." *Time for Poetry.*

_____. "The River Is a Piece of the Sky." *Time for Poetry.*

_____. "The Cat Heard the Cat-Bird." P. 137.

DE LA MARE, WALTER. "The Ship of Rio." *Rhymes and Verses for Children, Time for Poetry.*

_____. "Sleepyhead." P. 186; *Rhymes and Verses for Children.*

_____. "The Three Beggars." *Rhymes and Verses for Children.*

EDEY, MARION, and DOROTHY GRIDER. "The Little Fox." P. 238.

FARJEON, ELEANOR. "News! News!" *Eleanor Farjeon's Poems for Children.*

FIELD, EUGENE. "The Duel." *Time for Poetry.*

_____. "The Rock-a-by Lady." *Time for Poetry.*

_____. "Song." *Time for Poetry.*

FISHER, AILEEN. "Until We Built a Cabin." *Time for Poetry.*

FOLLEN, ELIZA LEE. "The Little Kittens." *Time for Poetry.*

FROST, FRANCES. "Valentine for Earth." *Time for Poetry.*

FYLEMAN, ROSE. "The Goblin." P. 228.

_____. "Have You Watched the Fairies?" *Time for Poetry.*

GREEN, MARY MCB. "Aeroplane." *Time for Poetry.*

GUITERMAN, ARTHUR. "The Pioneer." *Time for Poetry.*

HEMANS, FELICIA D. "The Landing of the Pilgrim Fathers." *One Thousand Poems for Children, Time for Poetry.*

KIPLING, RUDYARD. "Seal Lullaby." *Collected Poems, An Inheritance of Poetry, Time for Poetry.*

MEIGS, MILDRED PLEW. "The Pirate Don Durk of Dowdee." *Time for Poetry.*

MILNE, A. A. "The Christening." *When We Were Very Young.*

_____. "The King's Breakfast." *When We Were Very Young.*

_____. "Market Square." *When We Were Very Young.*

RANDS, WILLIAM BRIGHTY. "Godfrey Gordon Gustavus Gore." *Time for Poetry.*

RICHARDS, LAURA. "Little John Bottlejohn." P. 124; *Tirra Lirra.*

———. "The Monkeys and the Crocodile." *Tirra Lirra, Time for Poetry.*

SANDBURG, CARL. "To Beachey." *Time for Poetry.*

STEVENSON, ROBERT LOUIS. "Where Go the Boats?" *A Child's Garden of Verses.*

———. "The Wind." P. 227; *A Child's Garden of Verses.*

———. "Windy Nights." P. 143; *A Child's Garden of Verses.*

UNKNOWN. "The Crafty Farmer." *Time for Poetry.*

———. "Get Up and Bar the Door." *Time for Poetry.*

———. "The Squirrel." *Time for Poetry.*

———. "Taking Off." *Time for Poetry.*

WELLES, WINIFRED. "Dogs and Weather." *Time for Poetry.*

WOLFE, FRIDA. "Choosing Shoes." *Time for Poetry.*

Group Work: Christmas

HERRICK, ROBERT. "Ceremonies for Christmas." *Time for Poetry.*

REESE, LIZETTE W. "A Christmas Folk-Song." *Time for Poetry.*

Unison

AUSLANDER, JOSEPH. "A Blackbird Suddenly." *Time for Poetry.*

AUSTIN, MARY. "Grizzly Bear." *Time for Poetry.*

BEHN, HARRY. "This Happy Day." *Little Hill, Time for Poetry.*

BIBLE. "For, lo, the winter is past." *Time for Poetry.*

COATSWORTH, ELIZABETH. "He who has never known hunger." P. 178; *The Fair American.*

CONKLING, HILDA. "Loveliness." *Time for Poetry.*

———. "Water." *Time for Poetry.*

———. "Weather." *Time for Poetry.*

DE LA MARE, WALTER. "The Horseman." P. 165; *Rhymes and Verses for Children.*

———. "Some One." *Rhymes and Verses for Children, Time for Poetry.*

DRISCOLL, LOUISE. "Hold Fast Your Dreams." *Time for Poetry.*

FARJEON, ELEANOR. "Down! Down!" *Eleanor Farjeon's Poems for Children, Time for Poetry.*

———. "Mrs. Peck-Pigeon." P. 147; *Eleanor Farjeon's Poems for Children.*

———. "The Tide in the River." *Time for Poetry.*

FROST, ROBERT. "Dust of Snow." *Time for Poetry.*

FYLEMAN, ROSE. "Singing Time." *Time for Poetry.*

GREENAWAY, KATE. "Little wind, blow on the hill-top." *Under the Window, Time for Poetry.*

GUTHRIE, JAMES. "Last Song." *Time for Poetry.*

HUGHES, LANGSTON. "Heaven." *Dream Keeper, Time for Poetry.*

HUGO, VICTOR. "Be Like the Bird." *Time for Poetry.*

———. "Good Night." P. 238.

ISE, LADY. "The Rains of Spring." *Time for Poetry.*

JACKSON, LEROY F. "Hippity Hop to Bed." *Time for Poetry.*

JOYCE, JAMES. "The Noise of Waters." *Time for Poetry.*

KIKURIO. "Daffodils" (Japanese *hokku*). *Time for Poetry.*

KIPLING, RUDYARD. "Seal Lullaby." *Time for Poetry.*

MASEFIELD, JOHN. "Sea River." *Story of a Round House, Time for Poetry.*

MILNE, A. A. "Happiness." *When We Were Very Young, Time for Poetry.*

———. "Hoppity." *When We Were Very Young, Time for Poetry.*

MOTHER GOOSE. "Daffadowndilly." P. 173.

———. "Higgledy, piggledy." *Time for Poetry.*

———. "I had a little nut tree." P. 83.

———. "Master I have." P. 225.

———. "One misty moisty morning." *Time for Poetry.*

———. "Rain, rain, go away." *Time for Poetry.*

———. "Wee Willie Winkie." *Time for Poetry.*

NEWBOLT, SIR HENRY. "Finis." *Time for Poetry.*

ROBERTS, ELIZABETH MADOX. "Firefly." P. 149; *Under the Tree.*

ROSSETTI, CHRISTINA. "And timid, funny, brisk little bunny." P. 174.

———. "Who Has Seen the Wind?" *Time for Poetry.*

SANDBURG, CARL. "Buffalo Dusk." *Time for Poetry.*

SCOTT, SIR WALTER. "Heap on more wood." *Time for Poetry.*

SHERMAN, FRANK DEMPSTER. "The Snow-bird." *Time for Poetry.*

SILBERGER, JULIUS. "A Reply to Nancy Hanks." *Time for Poetry.*

STEVENSON, ROBERT LOUIS. "Happy Thought." *A Child's Garden of Verses, Time for Poetry.*

Unison: Christmas

UNKNOWN. "Bethlehem." *Welcome Christmas!*

Once Upon a Time

part three

10. Old Magic

11. Fables, Myths, and Epics

12. New Magic

13. Storytelling and Reading Aloud

chapter 10

Old Magic

Folk tales, like the nursery rhymes and ballads, are a part of that great stream of anonymous creation known as "folklore"—the accumulated wisdom and art of simple everyday folk. In the broadest sense of the word, folklore includes superstitions, medicinal practices, games, songs, festivals, dance rituals, old tales, verses, fables, myths, legends, and epics. Folklore is sometimes called the "mirror of a people." It reveals their characteristic efforts to explain and deal with the strange phenomena of nature; to understand and interpret the ways of human beings with each other; and to give expression to deep, universal emotions—joy, grief, fear, jealousy, wonder, triumph.

Of the many varieties of folklore, the folk tale is the most familiar and perhaps the most appealing. Interest in folk tales developed in the eighteenth century, along with the interest in old ballads, but in the nineteenth century a romantic interest in the old tales grew so strong that many thousands were collected from all over the globe. Striking similarities were then noticed among the folk tales found in different parts of the world, and many theories were advanced to explain these similarities.

Theories of Folk-Tale Origin

REMNANTS OF MYTH AND RITUAL

One of the earliest explanations for the similarities among folk tales of different peoples was the *"Aryan myth"* theory. It involved several ideas which have now been thoroughly discredited. For instance, this theory held that the language group sometimes called the "Aryans" was a pure racial strain descended from a common stock. We know today that there is no such thing as a pure racial strain.

The theory held too that the people in this language group (which included not only Teutonic-Germanic but also Greek, Latin, Slavonic, Celtic, and Sanskrit) constituted a superior race. This also is discredited by later scholars. But most important for this discussion, the theory asserted that all folk tales came from the nature myths of this single ancestral group. This is sometimes referred to as the theory of "monogenesis" or "single origin." Although the "Aryan myth" theory has been thoroughly refuted, it is interesting today because it has been the springboard for some other theories of folk-tale origin.

Some students, convinced that the folk tales preserved the *remnants of nature myths,* continually interpret any traditional story as a nature allegory—whether it is about sleep or forgetfulness, about a hero battling with a dragon, or about a lassie being carried off by a polar bear. "Little Red Riding Hood," for instance, has been interpreted as an allegory of sunset and sunrise. The wolf is supposed to symbolize night, and in many versions he succeeds in devouring the little girl, who in her red cape represents the setting sun. This symbolic interpretation is extended in the Grimm version of the story, in which the hunters cut open the wolf and release "Little Red-Cap," the sun, from her imprisonment in the wolf, or night. Perrault's version of "The Sleeping Beauty," with its oddly extraneous part about the ogress, was considered another embodiment of this night and day myth. The ogress (night) first wishes to devour Beauty's two children, Dawn and Day, and then Beauty herself (the sun). The Norse "East o' the Sun" with its polar bear and its disappearing Prince was, like the Balder myth, supposed to explain the disappearance of the sun. But as Andrew Lang caustically remarked about these theories, "One set of scholars will discover the sun and dawn, where another set will see the thundercloud and lightning. The moon is thrown in at pleasure."

Other folklorists, while not interpreting all the old stories as nature allegories, believed that many of these tales preserved *remnants of other kinds of religious myth and ritual.* For instance, Sir George Webbe Dasent thought that the Norse folk tales contained many of the elements of the Norse myths. He explained that after Christianity came to the Scandinavian countries, the old Norse gods lost their prestige and were gradually changed into the fabulous creatures of the folk tales. Odin became the Wild Huntsman riding through the sky with his grisly crew. And perhaps the nursery tale of "The Three Billy-Goats Gruff" preserves the memory of Thor's battle with the Frost Giants, for the billy goat was the ancient symbol of Thor, and the huge, stupid trolls could easily be the inglorious descendants of the Frost Giants.

Some scholars believe that the accumulative tales like "The House That Jack Built" and "The Old Woman and Her Pig" have ritualistic origins (p. 81). Other stories too, they think, preserve fragments of spells or incantations. In the Grimms' dramatic "The Goose-Girl," the heroine puts a spell on Conrad's hat:

Blow, blow, thou gentle wind, I say,
Blow Conrad's little hat away . . . .

Ancient superstitions and customs surrounding christenings and marriage ceremonies may also be found in the folk tales. So may propitiations of spirits, witches, the devil, or certain powerful animals (like the bear in the Norse tales).

POLYGENESIS

Another group of scholars stoutly opposed the "Aryan myth" theory ("monogenesis"), which implied that all the folk tales came from a single prehistoric group. Their theory was one of "polygenesis," or "many origins." They asserted that human beings everywhere in the world are moved by much the same emotions—love and pity, fear and anguish, jealousy and hatred; that every people can observe the results of greed, selfish ambition, or quiet courage and kindliness; that they have seen the ways of cruel stepmothers (were there no loving ones in the old days, one wonders); and that they saw the neglected child come into his own. So Andrew Lang and other believers in polygenesis insisted that similar plots could develop in different parts of the world from similar situations common to all men. Lang used the widely disseminated story of Jason to prove his point. This theory would seem to account for the 345 variants of "Cinderella" found in Egypt, India, all parts of Europe, and even among the North American Indians.

However, modern social anthropologists point out that people are *not* the same the world over. In some cultures, for instance, stepmothers may not be feared at all. The Andaman Islanders are apparently indifferent to whether the children they bring up are their own or other people's—no stepmother problem there! Another objection made to polygenesis is that the same story in all its peculiar details and chains of events could scarcely have grown up quite independently among entirely different groups isolated from each other. But whether or not there is any validity to the theory of polygenesis, one thing is certain: almost all peoples have produced stories and there are striking similarities among the tales of different peoples.

ORIGINS IN DREAMS AND UNCONSCIOUS EMOTIONS

Psychoanalytic writers have studied those objects and ideas which appear frequently in fairy tales from all over the world and have asserted that they are *symbols of emotional fantasy* which all people experience. Among such supposedly universal feelings are unconscious sexual love for the parent, hatred of paternal or maternal authority, love or jealousy among brothers and sisters. The ideas and objects representing these feelings are supposed to be the same in folk tales the world over and to explain the similarities among these stories. But social anthropologists object to this theory, too. They maintain that unconscious emotions vary among different peoples and so do the symbols which represent them. The unconscious emotions described, they say, may be the characteristic product of modern urban life and not universal among all peoples and times.

Some authorities think that the stories originated in the *wonderful dreams or nightmares* of the storytellers. Stories about a poor girl sent out to find strawberries in the middle of winter (some versions clothe her in a paper dress) might well grow from the bad dreams we have when the night turns cold and we find ourselves with too few blankets. Haven't you dreamed that you were out-of-doors, inadequately clothed, and waked up to find yourself shivering? Did the story of "Snow White" emerge from such a dream? Or consider the story of the poor lassie in "East o' the Sun," who kissed the prince and then found herself out on a lonely road—the prince gone, the castle vanished, the little bell that fulfilled her every wish lost forever, and she in rags once more. Is she the embodiment of our anxieties and our reluctance to return from our dreams to a workaday world? So the fatal questions, impossible tasks, and endless discomforts in the folk tales may suggest some of the anxieties that haunt us in our sleep now and then. Perhaps the primitive quality of some of our dreams may also explain the shocking elements in some of the tales. These always seem less horrible in the stories than they actually should seem because they are seldom attended by any realistic details but are indeed vague, dreamlike, and evanescent.

Another phase of the psychological interpretation of folk-tale origin is the idea that the people who created them found in fancy the *satisfaction of unconscious frustrations or drives.* These imaginative tales provide *wish fulfillment.* That is, the oppressed peasants who produced some of the tales were "motivated by naïve dreams of the success of the despised," and so they told stories about cinder lads and lassies going from wretched hovels to fabulous castles, or about a goose girl marrying the prince. Certain it is that fairy tales do satisfy deep human needs, particularly the needs for security and competence (pp. 3-4). In the folk tales, banquets, servants, glittering jewels, and rich clothes are concrete symbols of success. Granting that these tales are primarily for entertainment, there seems to be little doubt that they contain a deeper meaning and an inner significance which the child or adult feels without being conscious of the cause. Barchilon and Pettit in discussing Perrault's fairy tales say, "Just as the dream expresses innermost wishes in disguised form, the fairy tale masks our real wishes with the appearance of a free fantasy." And again they emphasize the symbolic character of the tales saying, "... the veiled symbolism of the fairy tale and its violence fulfill a need in the child's life. The fairy tale is his apprenticeship to life."[1]

Psychoanalysts also hold that "the child, through the comparison between the fantastic and the real, gradually learns to test reality. When the child realizes that the fairy tale is fictitious he learns to enjoy it as fiction. This is one giant step not only in the process of rational maturation but in aesthetic development as well."[2]

CEMENT OF SOCIETY

In recent times the science of folklore has merged more and more into the science of social anthropology. To understand the why and wherefore of folk tales, anthropologists have lived intimately with many peoples, visiting their homes, markets, religious ceremonies, and festal celebrations. Of course they cannot visit the early European people who produced the folk tales we are most interested in, but their studies of modern folk societies can cast light on the origin of European folk tales. Their conclusion may be summed up in one sentence: folk tales have been the *cement of society*. They not only expressed but codified and reinforced the way people thought, felt, believed, and behaved.

Folk tales taught children and reminded their elders of what was proper and moral. They put the stamp of approval upon certain values held by the group, and thus cemented it together with a common code of behavior. They taught kindness, modesty, truthfulness, courage in adversity—and they made virtue seem worth while because it was invariably rewarded and evil just as invariably punished. This idea of the folk tales as the carriers of the moral code helps explain the ethical significance and emotional satisfaction they still hold for us today (p. 282).

Some of the explanations for the origins of folk tales are dubious, but many of them are reinforced by enough reasonable evidence to make them seem both plausible and probable. Folklorists now agree that the folk tale is created by most peoples at an early level of civilization. Historically, it may contain elements from past religions, rituals, superstitions, or past events. Psychologically, it serves to satisfy in symbolic form some of man's basic emotional needs. Ethically, it serves as "the cement of society"—reinforcing our faith in morality and the ultimate triumph of good over evil.

1. Jacques Barchilon and Henry Pettit, *The Authentic Mother Goose Fairy Tales and Nursery Rhymes* (Denver: Swallow, 1960), p. 27.
2. *Ibid.*, p. 26.

Sources of Folk Tales

Where did the European folk tales come from? Their ingredients seem to have been "compounded with themes from the Cloister and the Castle, mixed with elements from the Bible and from the heathenness of the Orient, as well as the deep pre-Christian past." In the thirteenth century there was a major development of this literature of the people, and it was then that many of the European folk tales as we know them today took form. But these tales had many and diverse origins. In this rich potpourri most scholars distinguish two main ingredients: the Indian and the Celtic.

INDIAN

From India came a multitude of talking-beast tales and other stories which retained their entertainment value despite the moral and religious lessons sometimes added to them. During the twelfth century, manuscripts of these stories were transmitted to the West through Arabic and Persian translations. These were carried by merchants and Crusaders and circulated throughout Europe. So we can understand why some scholars have thought that ancient India was the source of all the folk tales. Many of the elements in tales we hear today or read in various racial collections did come from India. But there is no telling the original home of the tales which may have been first written down in India but not necessarily created there. Some have been traced back to ancient Egypt.

CELTIC

From Ireland the European folk tales acquired many of the elements that make children call them "fairy tales"—fairies and witches, spells and enchantments, romance between the two worlds of fairies and humans. The Irish stories are very old—some say they go back to 400 B.C., but Patrick Kennedy, the Irish Grimm, is content with the general statement that they existed long before the Christian era and were preserved by oral tradition. Their number is staggering. Joseph Jacobs estimated it as around two thousand stories, of which only two hundred fifty were in print in his day. Undoubtedly Ireland's isolation helped preserve her tales. Dependence for many centuries upon traveling storytellers kept the tales alive and vital in Ireland long after print had superseded the spoken word in most countries. By the eleventh and twelfth centuries many of them had been recorded in the great vellum manuscript volumes written in Gaelic or Old Irish. As they circulated through Europe, they mingled with the Indian stories, court romances, religious myths, epics, and the local droll tales to form the almost endless permutations and combinations that the Grimms and their modern successors have tirelessly collected. These collections in turn have been scattered to every corner of the globe.

Wide Diffusion of the Folk Tales

Students have found recognizable variants of such tales as "Nicht Nocht Naething" ("Nix Nought Nothing"), "Jason and the Golden Fleece," and "Cinderella" in the manuscripts of ancient India, Egypt, and Greece and on the lips of storytellers in Zulu huts, Indian hogans, and Samoan villages—from the Russian steppes to African jungles and the mountains of South America. The three tasks, the flight, the pursuit, the lost slipper or sandal, and the undoing of a spell are found in innumerable racial groups. How were they carried?

First, of course, they were carried orally by the migrations of whole peoples. Later they traveled from one country to another with sailors and soldiers, women stolen from their tribes, slaves and captives of war, traders, minstrels and bards, monks and scholars, and young gentlemen on the grand tour. Some storytellers no doubt polished and improved the tales, while others debased them. If the folk tales traveled by land, they were passed on by many peoples and greatly changed in the process; but if they traveled by sea, they stayed closer to the originals. Sometimes one story theme would combine with others, producing either a variant of the original tale or a relatively new one. So ancient storytellers preserved old stories, produced variants of others, and occasionally dreamed up new ones to pass on. This process continues today as missionaries and sailors, teachers and salesmen tell their own versions of the classic tales to children and adults in distant places.

As we have noted, the literary (or written) sources of the popular tales did not begin to circulate in Europe until around the twelfth century. Then came the Indian and Irish manuscript collections, vivid and lively importations which were no doubt partly responsible for the flowering of folk art in the thirteenth century. Ballads and stories began to bubble up everywhere, often with the same plots or themes.

During the sixteenth century, popular literature in England made a dignified beginning in print with Caxton's fine English translations of Aesop's fables, the King Arthur stories, the Homeric epics. In England, too, the chapbooks picked up fragments of tales from everywhere and kept them alive in garbled but recognizable versions, dearly beloved by the people. In the late seventeenth century, Perrault, with the blessing of the French court, ushered the fairy tales into print. These mark the beginnings of our written sources of folk literature in Europe. Their more ancient written sources are still the debating ground for scholars. Our major concern is with the tales themselves in the collections we use today.

For however fascinating the theories of how and where folk tales originated and spread, the tales themselves have the real magic. Children call them "fairy tales," and adults rather stuffily classify them as folk tales. But fairy tales they are—tales of enchantment and wonder, flowing from all the peoples of the globe.

Collections and Collectors

Four national groups of folk tales include the children's favorites: these are the French, German, Norwegian, and English. These tales have so colored our thinking and entered into our language that we call them classics. Adults should know these collections well enough to select from them the great tales no child should miss. But they should also be familiar with the collections of similar tales now available from almost every country in the world. Not that all of these can or should be used with children, but any one of them may prove an open sesame to a neighborhood. Adults using the major national groups of tales will be interested in the collectors and their methods of gathering and handling their materials.

FRENCH FAIRY TALES

Perrault

The history of Perrault's unique *Contes de ma Mère l'Oye,* published in 1697 and translated into English in 1729, has already been discussed (p. 36). This is the appreciative tribute paid to Perrault by his countryman,

Here is the cat of cats as no one else has ever quite portrayed him—gallant, intrepid, and a fine, romantic fellow to boot. Notice the lighting effects in this picture, which serve to pinpoint interest on the great cat. Illustration by Gustave Doré. From Charles Perrault's French Fairy Tales *retold by Louis Untermeyer. Reproduced by permission of Didier, Publishers. (1946) (Book 7½ x 9½)*

Paul Hazard, a distinguished member of the French Academy:

> *Perrault is as fresh as the dawn. We never reach the end of his accomplishments. He is full of mischief, humor and charming dexterity. He never seems to be achieving a* tour de force, *lifting a weight, looking for applause, but he seems to be having more fun than anyone, relating these prodigious stories entirely for his own pleasure.* (Books, Children and Men, p. 9.)

Mr. Hazard comments on the tenderness and the terror in "Hop o' My Thumb," the suspense and despair in "Blue Beard," and the sly drollery of "Puss in Boots." He reminds us that Puss "profits by every circumstance—a bath, a stroll, or a call," and, finally, wheedling the ogre into taking the form of a mouse, gobbles him up. "We shall laugh over that the rest of our lives," he concludes.

Perrault's eight stories are in perfect style, which means, of course, that they possess rather more polish and sophistication than is usual in the folk tales. It does not matter to children whether it was Perrault father or son who collected and rewrote the tales; it is their sprightly style the children have always loved. In place of dull narrative, they are lively with conversations. Cinderella's haughty sisters talk about their own finery; Cinderella has earnest discourse with "her godmother, who was a fairy," about her needs for the ball. There is hardly a child who cannot reproduce these dialogues in the very spirit of the original.

Every necessary detail is logically provided for, or its omission underscored as a pivotal point in the plot. In "The Sleeping Beauty," for instance, the fairy touches everyone with her sleep-inducing wand "and little Mopsey, too, the Princess's little spaniel, which was lying on the bed" so that the Princess will not wake "all alone in the old palace." Or, again, we see how Little Thumb finds the way home from the forest for himself and his brothers and sisters by the white pebbles he has collected and dropped. But the next time, the door is locked and he can get no pebbles; he has only one piece of bread to crumble and let fall—disaster is near. Everywhere is the perfect logic of the French—no loose ends, no incredible happenings. Magic is there, but used so sparingly and with such reasonable preparation that conviction is never disturbed.

Like most adults, young Perrault could not resist "improving" these traditional tales. Sometimes he dabbled with the plot, as in the moralistic conclusion of "Little Thumb." Sometimes he added contemporary touches—"hairdressers" and "patches." Often he slipped in sly bits of satire, as the offer of the king to make the Marquis of Carabas his son-in-law on the spot once he has seen the vast estate of the Marquis. The erotica of these tales is discussed by Barchilon and Pettit, who think Perrault drove it skillfully underground for children but made it slyly evident to adult readers. On the whole, these tales are related with so masterly a sense of the dramatic that they continue to be the children's favorites.

Barbara Leonie Picard

Oddly enough, after Perrault's book there was no major collection of French folk tales until Barbara Leonie Picard's *French Legends, Tales and Fairy Stories* was published in 1955. This contains four hero tales, six courtly tales of the Middle Ages, and thirteen legends, or folk tales, with no repetition of Perrault's famous eight.

Although there is more magic in these tales than in Perrault's, they will appeal to older children. The epic tales are full of battles and various complexities, the courtly tales are highly romantic, and the folk tales, although they contain some variants of familiar themes, are more mature in style than the stories they resemble. Good readers will enjoy this collection, and the storyteller will find fresh and exciting material in such stories as "The Grey Palfrey," "The Mouse-Princess," "The Stones of Plouhinec," and "Ripopet-Barabas."

GERMAN FOLK TALES

Jacob Ludwig Carl Grimm, 1785-1863
Wilhelm Carl Grimm, 1786-1859

The Grimm brothers may be said to have started the modern science of folklore. They had a scholarly respect for sources which kept them from tampering with the language or the plots as they wrote down the stories from the dictation of the people.

While Perrault altered his tales to suit the tastes of the times, the conscientious Grimms began with a passionate concern for sources. They were university professors—philologists—and their interest in sagas, ballads, popular tales, and all forms of traditional literature was at first secondary to their interest in the roots and development of the German language. This interest in grammar remained paramount with Jacob, but Wilhelm gradually became more interested in the tales than in any other phase of their work. When they began their collection, it was not with children in mind. They undertook their research as a part of a vast and scholarly study of language origins which was to climax in the German grammar (*Deutsche Grammatik*) and the dictionary (*Deutsches Wörterbuch*). They were not only meticulous about recording the tales exactly as the people told them, writing down every variant separately, but they were so afraid that some publisher might refine the stories that they carefully avoided their publisher friend Brentano, whose predilection for "touching up" they well knew. The Grimms were determined that the language of the people should get into print exactly as it was, and it did. Their kind of scrupulous accuracy in recording folk literature is the standard by which other collections are now judged. The Grimms established folklore as a field for scholars.

The brothers themselves were as unusual as their work. As children, they must have known pinching times, with their widowed mother trying to support her brood of six. The two little boys, only one year apart in age, were inseparable. They shared the same bed and table, attended the same school, and grew up with the same interests, each intending to be a lawyer like their father. If it had not been for the generosity of an aunt, they might never have reached the university, and the world would have lost two scholars. In the University of Marburg, Jacob fell under the influence of Savigny, a celebrated scholar who was responsible for Jacob's early absorption in the literature of the Middle Ages. Wilhelm, of course, followed his brother's lead. After Wilhelm's marriage, the two were still inseparable. "Uncle Jacob" lived in his brother's house, shared the same study, the same books, and the same contented family life.

Yet the brothers were not alike except in their amiable dispositions. Jacob was perhaps the greater scholar of the two, working with tremendous energy and initiative, completely immersed in his studies. Wilhelm was the artist. He loved music and was much sought after socially, for he was a gifted storyteller and a gay, animated companion. The four years after Wilhelm's death was their longest separation. "Die Brüder Grimm," they signed themselves, and so we think of them—the Grimm brothers, scrupulous scholars, cheerful human beings, happily devoted to their work and to each other.

When the *Kinder- und Hausmärchen*[3] appeared in 1812 (the second volume in 1815), it caused no particular stir in literary circles. Some critics considered the stories boorish; Brentano thought them slovenly; and yet somehow, in spite of the reviews, the stories were received with an unprecedented enthusiasm. Edition followed edition; translations began, first into Danish, Swedish, and French, then into Dutch, English, Italian, Spanish, Czech, and Polish—in all, some seventeen different languages.

The plots of these tales appeal to all ages from the seven-year-olds to adults, while the style has the peculiarly spellbinding quality of the great storytellers. The Grimms were fortunate in their sources. Besides the "story-wife," Frau Viehmann, there were Wilhelm Grimm's wife, Dortchen Wild, and her five sisters, who had been raised with these old tales and could tell them with effortless fluency. Other relatives, in-laws, and neighbors contributed to the collection also, but were not equally gifted storytellers. If you check in the Pantheon edition of *Grimm's Fairy Tales* the index of the tales with Mr. Campbell's list of the people who told them, you will discover that most of your favorites—"Hänsel and Gretel," "Mother Holle," "The Goose-Girl," "Rumpelstiltskin," to mention only a few—were related either by Frau Viehmann or the members of the Wild family.

To reread these stories is to find strange refreshment. Here are somber tales of children who are turned out to fend for themselves but who find love and security after all their hardships. Here are morons, cheerful and irresponsible, and royal youths and maidens, dispossessed, reduced to misery and humiliation, but keeping their innate kindness and tenderness, and so finding love. Here youth responds to the call of great tasks and accomplishes the impossible. Here a girl looks upon Holiness unmoved and is stricken dumb for her hardness, and Godfather Death stalks his prey and

3. *Nursery and Household Tales* is the usual translation, but for the German *Märchen* we have no precise translation. *Märchen* is legend, fiction, a cock-and-bull story, romance—in short, a fairy tale.

is never outwitted. These stories have colored the attitudes of readers toward life, toward human relationships, and toward moral standards. They are both fantasy and reality, and they are supremely entertaining.

NORWEGIAN POPULAR TALES

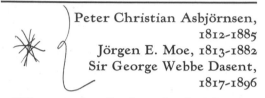

Peter Christian Asbjörnsen, 1812-1885
Jörgen E. Moe, 1813-1882
Sir George Webbe Dasent, 1817-1896

When people talk about the Scandinavian folk tales, they usually mean a particular book, *East o' the Sun and West o' the Moon,* the collection most people have known and loved, in one edition or another, all their lives. These stories probably rank with *Grimm's Fairy Tales* in their continuous popularity, and for similar reasons. They have the ring of complete sincerity and the oral charm of the storyteller's art at its best, for they were gathered from old wives who were still telling them to their children or grandchildren. They were recorded by two scrupulous scholars, Peter Christian Asbjörnsen and Jörgen E. Moe, and turned into matchless English by a British scholar, Sir George Webbe Dasent, who was influenced by no other than Jacob Grimm himself. The names of these three men—Asbjörnsen, Moe, and Dasent—are so inextricably bound up with the tales that the book is sometimes listed under Asbjörnsen and Moe, the collectors, and sometimes under Dasent, the translator.

Peter C. Asbjörnsen and Jörgen Moe were devoted friends from early boyhood, and death separated them by only three years. Although Asbjörnsen was a zoölogist and Moe a poet and a theologian, both became interested in gathering the popular tales of their native Norway from the lips of old storytellers who were still relating them as they had received them from the lips of preceding generations. When Asbjörnsen started out on a scientific expedition, he followed his folklore hobby in his spare time. Indeed the two activities could be admirably combined. Searching for specimens and studying the terrain of the countryside carried him into the isolated districts where storytelling was still the chief source of indoor entertainment. Moe spent his holidays similarly employed, traveling to remote parts of the country and gathering the legends and stories of the district from the storytellers. Dasent said of them, "For these Norse Tales one may say that nothing can equal the tenderness and skill with which MM. Asbjörnsen and Moe have collected them."

While in Stockholm in a diplomatic post, Sir George Webbe Dasent had the great good fortune to meet Jacob Grimm, who urged him to begin a thorough study of the language of the North, especially Icelandic. This Dasent did, and his first publication was an English translation of the *Prose, or Younger Edda,* followed by his *Grammar of the Icelandic or Old Norse Tongue,* and eventually an *Icelandic-English Dictionary.* In the midst of a remarkably strenuous life of study, translations, journalism, and travel, he became interested in the Norse folk tales and made his masterly translations of the Asbjörnsen-Moe collections, *Popular Tales from the Norse* (1859) and *Tales from the Fjeld* (1874), the two sources for all subsequent English editions.

Mrs. Gudrun Thorne-Thomsen (p. 392), who taught and was herself one of the great exponents of the storytelling art, used to say that she enjoyed the Dasent translations of these tales as much as she did the originals. Other Norwegians have made similar comments and have remarked about the translator's ability to catch the folk flavor of the language, even to the idioms. Like the Grimm stories, the tales were told by adults to adults, and some changes have to be made in the text when they are told to children. Dasent, in his translations, made no such adaptations but gave the stories exactly as they were in the Asbjörnsen-Moe collections. The Dasent books are, therefore, English sources for adult students of folklore, but you will find that most of the children's editions have altered them as little as possible.

While the general mood of the Norwegian tales is serious, which is true of most folk tales, there is much more humor, or buoyancy, in the Norse collection than in the German. The people make the best of things with an amusing nonchalance. In "The Princess on the Glass Hill," Boots, or Espen Cinderlad, with the barn almost falling about his ears, reassures himself that if things get no worse he can stand it. Gudbrand's old wife, instead of clouting her husband as the German "Mrs. Vinegar" does, makes cheerful alibis for his bad management. Nothing daunts these people, and nothing quells their firm conviction that they will make out somehow.

There are no fairies in the gauzy-winged tradition, but there is a great deal of magic. Trolls, hill folk, giants, hags, and witch-wives are plentiful. There are magic objects—fiddles, axes, tablecloths, rams, and sticks. Winds talk and take a hand in the affairs of men now and then. A polar bear (another symbol of the North) and a great dun bull are both men under enchantments, and there are the colossal horse Dapplegrim, the kindly wolf Graylegs, and talking beasts of every variety.

Rhymes are infrequent, but one of the prettiest of them is the spell "Katie Woodencloak" casts on the Prince:

Bright before and dark behind,
Clouds come rolling on the wind;
That this Prince may never see
Where my good steed goes with me.

For storytelling, "The Pancake" is probably the finest of all accumulative stories because of its humor and rollicking movement. "The Cock and Hen That Went to Dovrefell" has a witty surprise ending that is far more satisfying than its English equivalent, "Henny Penny." These tales, like the Grimms', run the whole gamut from sheer nonsense to the romantic and heroic. They are classics and matchless entertainment which all children should have a chance to hear.

BRITISH FOLK TALES

Joseph Jacobs, 1854-1916

When Joseph Jacobs began compiling the English folk tales, his objective was different from that of the Grimms or of the men who had preceded him in the English field. He intended his collection not for the archives of the folklore society but for the immediate enjoyment of English children. So Jacobs omitted incidents that were unduly coarse or brutal, adapted the language somewhat, especially dialect, and even deleted or changed an occasional episode. Jacobs also "prosed" some of the ballads and left one, "Childe Rowland," in the sing-and-say, or prose-and-verse, style of the original cante-fable. He admitted cheerfully that his editing was all very horrifying to his folklorist friends but observed that every one of them, even the Grimms, had made similar modifications. Jacobs was scrupulous in recording these alterations. At the back of his books, in a section for adult readers called "Notes and References," he gives the sources

The strength and simplicity of the d'Aulaires' style are particularly effective in this interpretation of the massive troll and the powerful third Billy-Goat.
From East of the Sun and West of the Moon *by Ingri and Edgar Parin d'Aulaire. Copyright 1938 by Ingri and Edgar Parin d'Aulaire. By permission of The Viking Press, Inc. (Book 7¾ x 11)*

for each tale and its parallels, and then notes precisely what changes he has made. Studying these notes, you soon discover that his adaptations are not too heinous, and reading the stories, you realize that he has indeed attained his goal, which was "to write as a good old nurse will speak when she tells Fairy Tales."

Jacobs obtained a few of his tales from oral storytellers—some from Australia and one from a gypsy are mentioned. But most of his tales he obtained from printed sources. He acknowledged the use of stories collected by his predecessors, notably Patrick Kennedy for the Celtic group, Robert Chambers for Scotland, and James Orchard Halliwell for England. Jacobs also credited "How Jack Sought His Fortune" to the *American Folk-Lore Journal* and added "I have eliminated a malodorous and un-English skunk." It was not until 1943 that a whole collection of the American Jack tales[4] was published, "malodorous and un-English" skunks and all! All in all, Joseph Jacobs was a sound enough folklorist. As a matter of fact, he was editor of the British journal *Folk-Lore*. But his greatest contribution is probably in selection and adaptation. Had it not been for his collections, many of these tales might still be gathering dust in antiquarian volumes.

These English tales of Jacobs' are remarkable for three things: the giant killers, the humor, and the large number suitable for the youngest children. From these collections of Jacobs come the favorites, "The Story of the Three Bears," "The Story of the Three Little Pigs," "Henny Penny," "Johnny-Cake," "The Old Woman and Her Pig," and many others. "Tom Tit Tot," one of the stories which Jacobs rescued from the dusty oblivion of the journal *Folk-Lore,* is undoubtedly the most hilarious of all the variants of "Rumpelstiltskin." This story is indeed an admirable example of the way cheerfulness creeps into these British stories. The German tale is grave throughout, even somber. The English tale opens with a bit of low comedy between a mother and her greedy, witless daughter. There is a light touch throughout, and yet the story is every bit as exciting and satisfying as "Rumpelstiltskin." The superiority of this version lies in the full and consistent characterization of the silly girl, the impishness of "that," and the amusing hints as to the personality of the king.

The tales of giant killers are another striking feature of the English collections, beginning with the old national hero story "St. George and the Dragon," and continuing through "Tom Hickathrift," "Jack the Giant Killer," and their only feminine rival, the resourceful "Molly Whuppie." These stout heroes who make away with monsters were multiplied and perpetuated by the chapbooks, and their adventures have remained popular with British children ever since.

Oxford Myths and Legends

Jacobs remained the chief source of English folk tales until, beginning in 1954, volumes of English, Scottish, and Welsh folk tales were issued in the Oxford Myths and Legends series. Beautifully told, handsome in format and illustrations, these three books have greatly expanded the range of British folk tales.

James Reeves' *English Fables and Fairy Stories* includes many of the old favorites as well as such delightful additions as "The Pedlar's Dream," "The Two Princesses," and "The Fish and the Ring." The style is distinguished, the stories are varied in mood, and they read or tell beautifully.

Welsh Legends and Folk Tales by Gwyn Jones includes some of the hero tales of King Arthur and his knights. There are such romances as "Pwyll and Pryderi," "How Trystan Won Esylit," and three about the fairy "Woman of Llyn-Y-Fan." The folk tales are full of magic, incantations, fairy folk, and difficult names.

The *Scottish Folk Tales and Legends* by Barbara Ker Wilson are largely unfamiliar. There are simple nursery tales for small children, broadly comic stories for older children, a few horrific scare tales, and stories of romantic beauty. Through them all runs the Gaelic fairy lore—spells, enchantments, magic, and many sorts of fairy creatures, sometimes kind, often menacing.

Two delightful books by Sorche Nic Leodhas, *Heather and Broom* and *Thistle and*

4. *The Jack Tales.* Told by R. M. Ward and others. Edited by Richard Chase.

Thyme, will further enrich the Scottish lore with both humor and romance. These stories have been written in such perfect storytelling form that they may be read or told without modification, and their charm is irresistible.

Black, gray, and white are used to create a variety of patterns. Notice that the three main objects are bold—the one important tree and the two figures are black. Illustration by Evaline Ness. From Thistle and Thyme *by Sorche Nic Leodhas. Copyright © 1962 by Leclaire G. Alger. Reproduced by permission of Holt, Rinehart and Winston, Inc. (Book 6 x 9)*

Other National Groups of Folk Tales

In addition to the groups of folk tales already discussed—Indian, Celtic, French, German, Norwegian, and English—there are stories from innumerable other national groups. Should you wish to use a collection not mentioned here, look it up in the *Children's Catalog,* that unfailing reference for librarians and all harried makers of bibliographies, or in the *Index to Fairy Tales, Myths and Legends* by Mary Huse Eastman. A discussion of a few of these national collections can perhaps give some idea of the richness and variety of folk tales available today fror all countries.

ARABIAN NIGHTS

Do you remember from your childhood a thick book of exceedingly long stories which were notable for their flying carpets, glittering jewels, a genie of the lamp, oil crocks concealing robbers, the mystic password of "Open sesame"? The book was, of course, *The Arabian Nights.*

The origin of these "thousand and one" tales is confused and lost in antiquity, partly because they belonged to the people and were not considered polite literature. In the Moslem world they circulated only in the coffee houses and the market place. The stories are very old, some of them seeming to stem from ancient India, others from North Africa, with an early collection from Persia. A Frenchman, Antoine Galland, made his translation of them in 1704 from a manuscript sent to him from Syria but written in Egypt. So here again are old stories which have been inveterate travelers, with sources so ancient and varied that it is impossible to determine their true origin. We do know that Galland's translation of the tales into French, under the title *Les mille et une nuit,* was so popular that it was immediately translated into other languages, including English. Indeed, some of Galland's translated stories were even translated back into Oriental languages. The stories were fortunate in falling into the hands of a translator who was also a skillful storyteller. These tales of

Vera Bock has relied upon the Persian style of drawing—stylized bodies and many opulent details and patterns.
Illustration by Vera Bock. From Arabian Nights, *edited by Andrew Lang. Copyright, 1898, 1946 by Longmans, Green and Co. Reproduced by permission of David McKay Company. (Book 5⅜ x 8)*

the Orient were given a Gallic touch, so they lack nothing of drama or color.

Today, children have turned away from most of these exceedingly long stories. However, certain of these stories have entered permanently into our speech and our thinking. A child who does not know a few of them is distinctly the poorer.

CZECHOSLOVAKIAN STORIES

The Czech stories are unusually amusing and have been translated into clear, vigorous English. They include many variants of the Grimm stories but often are more interesting than the German. "Clever Manka," for instance, is a far better story than Grimms' "The Peasant's Daughter." Parker Fillmore's lively English translations of these stories have been out of print, but *The Shepherd's Nosegay* has been reissued and contains the favorite tales—"Budulinek," "Smolicheck," "Katcha and the Devil," and of course, "Clever Manka."

FINNISH FOLK TALES

Joseph Jacobs used to say that the Finns at Helsingfors had in manuscript form the largest group of folk tales in existence, a group that he believed exceeded twelve thousand. But John Wargelin, President of Suomi College, stated that over thirty thousand tales had been collected although only a small portion of them had been published. In spite of this wealth of stories, the Finnish tales have not been well known or much used in this country, possibly because they are both long and descriptive, and the Finnish names are undoubtedly difficult. But this strong group of tales will repay study and will be enjoyed by older children.

RUSSIAN FOLK TALES

A. M. Afanasiev collected the Russian folk tales as the Grimm brothers collected the German, and there is now an English translation of the complete Afanasiev collection in the Pantheon edition. These stories are for adult students of folklore, not for children. They are bloody and horrible but full of excitement and color. Certain of these tales are rather generally familiar to American children —"The Snow Maiden" (sometimes called "Snegourka"), "The Firebird," and "Sadko." Every one of these lends itself to dramatization as well as to storytelling. These and other popular Russian stories are found in a good storytelling form in Arthur Ransome's *Old Peter's Russian Tales.*

SPANISH STORIES

One American storyteller, Ruth Sawyer, thinks the Irish stories are matched only by the Spanish, and her own collection seems to bear out her opinion. New and delightful stories for telling can be found in every one of the collections of Spanish tales listed in the bibliography for this chapter. The stories for the youngest children are full of fun, those for the older ones full of grace. *Padre Porko,* for instance, is one of the most enchanting series of talking beast tales to be found anywhere. The Padre, the gentlemanly pig, is both astute and benignant, and his canny solutions of neighborhood difficulties are made with great elegance.

So delightful folk tales come to us in translation from Italy, Poland, Mexico, Yugoslavia, Burma, Turkey, Korea, China, Japan, Persia, Africa, many South American countries, and from the Pacific and Caribbean islands. Indeed it is almost a case of name the country and your librarian can match it with native folk tales. Some of these have been better translated and adapted than others, but there is scarcely a collection that will not yield two or three memorable stories for reading or telling.

Folk Tales in the United States

The United States is the fortunate recipient of folklore and folk tales from all over the world. Americans should be proud of this rich heritage, which they can discover merely by taking the pains to visit one of the intercultural libraries of the large cities, or, better still, by meeting and making friends with different racial groups throughout the country. American Indians have woven beautiful baskets and rugs decorated with characteristic tribal symbols, and they still tell their own old tales, some of which are strangely reminiscent of European ones. There are embroideries from Bulgaria and Hungary, with intricate designs that for generations have been passed on from mother to daughter along with legends still more ancient. The Southern mountaineers are still weaving the Tudor rose into their textiles and still singing ballads that were already time-honored in the days of Queen Elizabeth I. Boys and girls of Swedish, Russian, Polish, and Scottish ancestry still dance the old dances, sing the old songs, and hear the old stories that have been handed down from their grandparents' grandparents. An Irish neighborhood abounds with stories straight from the Gaelic, tales that were old when Christianity was young. The Sicilian puppet shows sometimes play the popular stories of the people. A Negro grandmother may be heard telling a story which goes back to the mythology of West Africa. And a Bohemian child may hear her father's version of a story which the Grimm brothers found in Germany over a hundred years ago.

The fox is furious with the mischievous squirrel; Porko smiles indulgently. Notice the wonderful texture and form in the tree, fox, grass, and Padre Porko.
Illustration by Fritz Eichenberg. From Padre Porko *by Robert Davis. Copyright 1939 by Robert Davis. Reproduced by permission of Holiday House. (Book 5 x 7)*

Folklore in the United States falls into four large categories: (1) tales from the American Negro, especially the collections known as the Uncle Remus stories; (2) tales from the North American Indians; (3) variants of the European stories; and (4) native tall tales of the Paul Bunyan variety. In the general discussion of folk tales (p. 269) few references are made to these American types, for definite reasons. In the first place, the European collections came into print long before ours began, and so they rather set the standard or pattern of such tales. Moreover, our collected tales differ in so many respects from those of the European groups that they often prove the exception to the very principles discussed as typical. They are, besides, far from being a homogeneous group—no generalizations will cover all four varieties. An Uncle Remus tale differs from a tall tale, and a tall tale from an Indian story, quite as much as all of them differ from their European relatives. In short, each of the four types of American folk tales needs to be considered separately.

AMERICAN NEGRO TALES

Joel Chandler Harris, 1848-1908

Joel Chandler Harris became interested in collecting the tales he heard the plantation Negroes telling. Born in Georgia and raised on such stories as a child, he knew the Negro's dialect, humor, and picturesque turns of speech. Moreover, he had a deep love for the stories and for the fine people who told them. In the character of Uncle Remus, a plantation Negro, Harris embodied the gentleness, the philosophy, the shrewd appraisal of character, and the rich imagination of all Negro storytellers to whom he had listened. Into the mouth of Uncle Remus, he put the stories he gathered first-hand. It was a labor of love performed with sensitive perception and fidelity.

The stories are mostly talking-beast tales, and the hero is Brer Rabbit, the weakest and most harmless of animals, but far from helpless. Through his quick wit, his pranks, and his mischief, he triumphs over the bear, the wolf, the fox, and the lesser animals. Like the French "Reynard the Fox," he is a trickster, but unlike Reynard, he is never mean or cruel, only a practical joker now and then, a clever fellow who can outwit the big brutes and turn a misfortune into a triumph. No matter what happens to him or what he does, he remains completely lovable.

These stories are, of course, reminiscent of the talking-beast tales of other countries. Some of them may have had their roots in India, but it is generally agreed that most of them originated in Africa or were created in this country. Variants of "The Tar Baby" are found in many lands, but there is a special flavor to the Uncle Remus stories. They show a homely philosophy of life, flashes of poetic imagination, a shrewd appraisal of human nature, a childlike love of mischief, a pattern and style unsurpassed by any other beast tales.

These stories do have their limitations, and the dialect is chief of them. Children in the South may be fortunate enough to hear these tales read by adults who can do justice to the flavorsome dialect. A. A. Milne's British father read these tales aloud to his children, dialect and all, and they loved them. However, it is the dialect that makes the stories almost unintelligible to most children and adults. When the stories are turned into standard English, they retain their witty folk flavor, just as tales translated from the Norwegian or East Indian or American Indian do. Perhaps translation is the answer here, too.

Other objections to these stories are raised by modern American Negroes. In an article entitled "Uncle Remus for Today's Children" (*Elementary English,* March 1953), Margaret Taylor Burroughs points out that the tales are full of offensive terms for Negroes. She objects to the intrusion of old "Uncle's" personality and point of view. These sometimes add to the wit and wisdom of the stories, but she cites some deplorable examples also.

These objections point up the fact that the great body of seven hundred *Uncle Remus Tales* will survive chiefly as source material for gifted storytellers. Where else in any collection of folk tales can you find such droll revelations of human nature—antic, sagacious, witty? And where else can you find a colorful dialect so lovingly and perfectly recorded by a scholar with an ear for the euphony of speech?

NORTH AMERICAN INDIAN TALES

Occasionally it strikes someone as strange that American children know European folk tales better than they know the tales of the native American Indians. It is actually not strange at all—most of our children are more closely related to Europeans in race, customs, and ways of thinking than they are to our native Indians. Another reason for the less frequent use of Indian stories is that they are, by and large, neither sufficiently dramatic nor well enough organized to command interest. Indeed, Alexander Krappe remarks that "the variants of old-world tales collected among the North American Indians give one an impression that their narrators were incapable even of preserving a good tale, to say nothing of inventing a new one." While this may sound like an extreme statement, as a matter of fact it is largely true. Unless the Indian tales are considerably edited and adapted as in the case of the Olcott and Kennedy collections, there are few which are sufficiently memorable to make a deep impression or to be genuinely popular with young people.

Indian stories include many mythlike *why stories*—why the robin has a red breast, why the bear has a short tail, why the woodpecker had a red head. These little explanatory stories are usually simple, brief, and somewhat moralistic. A few of them are interesting to young children; many of them are monotonous. There is a whole cycle of them concerned with the creation of the earth, sun, moon, the stars, and man, but they lack the grandeur of other creation myths.

The long, unedited tales of the Indians, recorded verbatim, are long indeed. The tales were sometimes told night after night around campfires, so that the episodes follow one another endlessly. They often lack the conclusive endings dear to young listeners. These unadapted tales are also filled with cruelties and tortures more realistically related, and therefore more horrifying, than the conventional "off with his head" of the European tales. Fortunately, we have some good collections of Indian stories made with children in mind (see the bibliography). These preserve the spirit of the tales and the atmosphere and customs of the Indians but are sufficiently edited to be entertaining. These stories may be used in connection with an Indian unit about some particular tribe, along with realistic stories about that same tribe today.

NATIVE VARIANTS OF EUROPEAN TALES

Kindergarten teachers who have delighted their children by telling them "Epaminondas" have long known that it is a Negro variant of the English "Lazy Jack" or the German "Clever Hans." They know, too, that it is a much wittier and more satisfying tale than either of the European tales. The Southern "The Gingerbread Boy," printed in *St. Nicholas* in 1875, "Johnny-Cake," in Jacobs' *English Fairy Tales,* and Ruth Sawyer's "Journey Cake, Ho!" are American variants of the Scotch "The Wee Bannock" or the Norse "The Pancake." As was noted before, Jacobs included in his English collection the story of "How Jack Sought His Fortune" from the *American Folk-Lore Journal.* There are undoubtedly dozens of other European folk tales extant in this country in characteristically modified form, but so far the most amusing and significant collection of them is *The Jack Tales* by Richard Chase, collected from American mountain people. Mr. Chase's account of these gay-hearted people makes you wish there were more of the stories. Old Counce "was a sight to dance. . . . Seventy years old, he could clog and buck-dance as good as a boy sixteen." And he could also spellbind the mountaineer children with tales—tales that should never be *read*—"You've got to tell 'em to make 'em go right."

The stories are recorded in the vernacular of the mountain people who have modified them to local speech and customs. The god Wotan or Woden appears, ancient, mysterious, but as helpful to Jack as he was to Sigurd or Siegfried. Jack is a country boy, unassuming but resourceful, and never nonplussed by the most fantastic adventures. The language is ungrammatical and sometimes rough, but it is humorously effective when handled by as gifted a storyteller as Richard Chase. The mood is decidedly comic, the setting rural.

AND HE WAS A GREAT LOGGER, THAT'S SURE—AND I GUESS THERE AIN'T NOBODY PRETENDS THERE EVER WAS ANYBODY LIKE HIM . . .

Notice the clean, powerful lines of Rockwell Kent's pictures, the subordination of details, the resultant clarity and strength of the whole composition. Observe how the hand grasps the ax handle, how those firmly planted feet support the heroic figure, and how the jutting-jawed face turns the whole picture into broad comedy.
Illustration by Rockwell Kent. From Paul Bunyan *by Esther Shephard. Harcourt, Brace & World, Inc., 1941. Reproduced by permission of the artist.*
(Book 5¾ x 8¼)

City children may not know "The Old Sow and the Three Little Shoats," but they'll recognize it as the "Three Little Pigs." The book's appendix by Herbert Halpert predicted that many of the tales would be found elsewhere in this country, and they have been.

TALL TALES AND OTHER NATIVE INVENTIONS

It is no accident that in this vast country, where people think and say "The sky's the limit," the two national symbols are a super-tall, benignant old giant known as "Uncle Sam" and the biggest bird in the country, the eagle. This is a pioneer land which—by our proud notions at least—has the biggest rivers, the tallest mountains, the vastest plains, and the humblest individuals skyrocketing to highest fame and fortune. So its people are bound to think expansively. They naturally express themselves with exaggeration and develop a sense of humor that is untrammeled and exuberant. And naturally the American stories follow the pattern of the biggest, the most heroic, even the most preposterous, from Davy Crockett, Paul Bunyan, Pecos Bill, and Captain Stormalong to Superman.

Our native tall tales—with their outrageous exaggeration, their poker-faced humor, and their swaggering heroes who do the impossible with nonchalance—are the natural expressions of our native optimism and our unshakable belief that our countrymen can do anything and then some. These tales also embody delusions of power: dreams of riding a cyclone or mowing down forests, or, in short, blithely surmounting any and every obstacle. These stories appeal to Americans because they are success epics with a sense of humor. They are such flagrant lies that the lyingest yarn of all is the best one, provided it is told with a straight face and every similitude of truth. Babe, Paul Bunyan's blue ox, measures "forty-two axhandles between the eyes—and a tobacco box—you could easily fit in a Star tobacco box after the last axhandle." Pecos Bill, after riding the cyclone successfully, must figure a convenient way of getting down. In short, one characteristic of American humor is that there must be a great show of reasonableness and accuracy in the midst of the most hilarious lunacy.

There are no complete or satisfying answers to the questions about where all these tales came from or who started them. The New England coast produced Captain Stormalong. Paul Bunyan and his blue ox came from the lumber camps, perhaps of Canada or Wisconsin or Michigan. The Western plains started Pecos Bill and his horse the Widow Maker on their careers. Mike Fink was a keelboatman on the Mississippi, while Davy Crockett, Tony Beaver, and John Henry all belong to the South. One artist has covered a map of the

United States with these heroes,[5] and it is the most astonishing array of rip-roaring, snarling, snorting he-men that any country ever produced. These tall-tale heroes are not only broadly and wildly funny, but they are also these United States in person, "large as life and twice as natural." Certainly American children should not miss reading about the soaring achievements of America's early supermen.

Predominant Types of Folk Tales

While children care nothing about the names for the different types of stories found in any fairy-tale collection, no adult can read these tales, particularly the French, German, Norwegian, and English, without being conscious of the varied groups into which they fall: accumulative tales, talking-beast stories, the droll stories, realistic stories, religious tales, tales of romance, and, of course, tales of magic. Many classifications have been made, but this one seems to bring in most of the types and to emphasize their characteristics.

ACCUMULATIVE TALES

Very young children enjoy the simplest of all stories, the accumulative tale or repetitional tale. Its charm lies in its minimum plot and maximum rhythm. Its episodes follow each other neatly and logically in a pattern of cadenced repetition. Sometimes, as in "The Old Woman and Her Pig," the action moves upward in a spiral and then retraces the spiral downward to the conclusion. Sometimes, as in the American-English "Johnny-Cake," the Norse "Pancake," and the American "Gingerbread Boy," the action takes the form of a race, and the story comes to an end with the capture of the runaway. Fortunately, the runaway in such stories has forfeited our sympathy by his stupidity ("Henny Penny"), or by his impudence ("The Pancake"), so that his capture becomes merely the downfall of the foolish or the proud.

"The Pancake" is one of the most delightful of these tales. The pancake—having jumped out of the frying pan and escaped from the mother, the father, and the seven hungry children—meets a series of creatures and becomes more insolent with each encounter. The following excerpt is typical of the racing-chasing style of these little tales:

> *"Good day, pancake," said the gander.*
> *"The same to you, Gander Pander," said the pancake.*
> *"Pancake, dear, don't roll so fast; bide a bit and let me eat you up."*
> *"When I have given the slip to Goody Poody, and the goodman, and seven squalling children, and Manny Panny, and Henny Penny, and Cocky Locky, and Ducky Lucky, and Goosey Poosey, I may well slip through your feet, Gander Pander," said the pancake, which rolled off as fast as ever.*
> *So when it had rolled a long, long time, it met a pig.*
> *"Good day, pancake," said the pig.*
> *"The same to you, Piggy Wiggy," said the pancake, which, without a word more, began to roll and roll like mad.* (Tales from the Fjeld.)

Here, in the last four lines, the storyteller by her ominous tone of voice warns the children that for the pancake the jig is up. Piggy Wiggy is Fate itself.

Accumulative stories move imperceptibly from mere chants, such as "The House That Jack Built," to stories with more and more plot. "The Three Little Pigs" and "The Bremen Town-Musicians" are repetitional and sequential, but they have the well-rounded plots of a more advanced type of story.

Incidentally, the popularity of these accumulative tales with young children has led to a tiresome number of modern imitators. These have often missed the fun, the element of surprise, and the swift movement of the old

5. Sgt. Glen Rounds' end pages for Walter Blair's *Tall Tale America,* an amusing group of fabulous stories.

stories. Modern examples of the happy use of this pattern are Marjorie Flack's *Ask Mr. Bear,* Wanda Gág's *Millions of Cats,* and Maurice Sendak's extremely funny *One Was Johnny.*

TALKING BEASTS

Perhaps young children love best of all among the old tales the ones in which animals talk. Sometimes the animals talk with human beings as in "Puss in Boots" and "The Three Little Pigs," but more often with other animals as in "The Cat and the Mouse in Partnership." Oddly enough, these creatures talk every bit as wisely as humans, or as foolishly. Possibly their charm lies in the opportunity they give the reader to identify himself with the cleverest of the three pigs or the most powerful and efficient member of "The Three Billy-Goats Gruff." Perhaps the credulity of "Henny Penny" or of the two foolish pigs ministers to the listener's sense of superiority. Certainly children are amused by these old tales for the same reasons that modern adults and children laugh at "Mickey Mouse" and "Donald Duck." The animals in both the old and the modern creations are exaggerated characterizations of human beings, and in that exaggeration lie their humor and fascination.

These beast tales generally teach a lesson—the folly of credulity and the rewards of courage, ingenuity, and independence—though their didacticism does not stand out so much as in the fables. The stories are so lively and diverting that they are primarily good entertainment. Perhaps the most successful of the modern descendants of the ancient beast tales are Beatrix Potter's *The Tale of Peter Rabbit, The Tale of Benjamin Bunny,* and all her other "Tales." These have joined the ranks of the immortals, along with "The Three Little Pigs."

THE DROLLS OR HUMOROUS STORIES

A small body of the folk tales are obviously meant as fun and nonsense. These are the stories about sillies or numskulls, who are, no doubt, the ancestors of the "dimwits" in our moron tales of a few years back. Grimm's "Clever Elsie" is a classic example.

As you remember, Elsie had a wooer who demanded a really clever bride. Her family sent her down to the cellar to draw some beer, and there, just over her head, she saw a pick-axe that had been left thrust into the masonry. Immediately she began to weep, thinking to herself,

> *"If I get Hans, and we have a child, and he grows big, and we send him into the cellar here to draw beer, then the pick-axe will fall on his head and kill him."*

She cried so hard and so long that first one member of the household and then another came down cellar, listened to her tale, and began to weep, too. Finally, Hans came and, hearing how things were, decided that Elsie was indeed a thoughtful, clever girl and married her. After the marriage Hans, who had evidently taken his bride's measure at last, gave Elsie a task to do in the field and left her there alone. But Elsie, unable to decide whether to work first or sleep first, finally fell asleep in the field and slept until night. Returning home in a great fright, she asked,

> *"Hans, is Elsie within?" "Yes," answered Hans, "she is within." Hereupon she was terrified, and said: "Ah, heavens! Then it is not I."*

And so she ran out of the village and was never seen again.

The English "Lazy Jack," another type of numskull story, is the ancestor of the American "Epaminondas." These are stories of boys sent to bring something home and told exactly how to carry it. When they are given a different object from the one they were sent for, the results are disastrous. So Epaminondas carries the butter on his head where it melts, cools the puppy dog in the water until it dies, drags the loaf of bread by a string in the dusty road, and steps in the middle of every mince pie! That ending invariably brings squeals of shocked enjoyment from young listeners.

Like the accumulative stories, the drolls or humorous stories vary in the amount of plot they develop. Some have well-rounded plots;

for instance, in "The Husband Who Was to Mind the House" (he does so with disastrous results) and in "Mr. Vinegar" (who trades off his cow as the start of a series of barters which bring him less and less until he has nothing left but a good cudgeling from his wife). The favorite Norse story "Taper Tom" has not only all the droll antics to make the princess laugh but real adventure as well. Finally, the Norse "Squire's Bride" is not only a droll story but also a capital bit of adult satire on elderly wooers of young girls.

These drolls are sometimes the only realistic stories in a folk-tale collection. Realistic stories, of course, are those in which all of the episodes, however improbable, are possible. They *could* have happened. The astonishing sillies, the dolts, and the ninnies are painful possibilities. So the reader thinks uneasily, "There, but for the grace of a few extra coils of gray matter, go I." Perhaps this is why the droll tale is not so popular as some others. The portraits are all unpleasant: there are no heroes with whom the reader can comfortably identify himself, and the noodles seem only too familiar. Is the storyteller poking fun at us? We are amused for a while, but our egos are deflated and we turn with relief to other types of stories.

REALISTIC STORIES

For the most part, the peoples who created these old tales seem to have had no great taste for using as story material their own "here and now," the stuff of everyday living. Even when they omit all elements of magic, they still tell a fabulous tale: the monster in "Blue Beard," for example, seems to have had some historic basis, but to young readers he is a kind of cross between an ogre and a giant. His English variant, "Mr. Fox," is even less realistic, though strictly speaking there is nothing in either story that could not have happened. Perhaps the prettiest of all realistic stories in our folk-tale collections is the Norse "Gudbrand on the Hill-side." This is "Mr. Vinegar," with a loving wife instead of a shrew. Gudbrand's old wife knows her man can do no wrong; so, secure in this knowledge, Gudbrand makes a wager with a neighbor that his wife will not blame him no matter what he does. Just as Gudbrand expects, his wife's tender responses to his series of disastrous trades reaches a climax with her heartfelt exclamation:

> *"Heaven be thanked that I have got you safe back again; you do everything so well that I want neither cock nor goose; neither pigs nor kine."*
>
> *Then Gudbrand opened the door and said,*
>
> *"Well, what do you say now? Have I won the hundred dollars?" and his neighbour was forced to allow that he had.*

Is this realism? Strictly speaking, the story is possible, but it hardly belongs to the modern school of acid realism. On the whole, folk tales pay scant attention to the laws of probability, and stories with even a remote claim to realism are few and far between.

RELIGIOUS TALES

Folk tales using elements of religious beliefs are rarely found in children's collections but are fairly frequent in the complete editions of almost any racial group. Coming down from the morality plays of the Middle Ages, the devil and St. Peter appear usually in comic roles. The Czech tales have an especially large number of devil stories, in which the devil is always worsted. The story of the devil who begged to be taken back to hell in order to escape from a shrew of a wife is a popular plot throughout Europe.

The Virgin is usually introduced respectfully and even tenderly. Grimm has several stories in which Our Lady appears, intervening in human lives, kindly and with pity.

St. Joseph is also introduced as a figure of compassion and as the administrator of poetic justice. The religious folk tales are generally either broadly comic or didactic and are, on the whole, not well adapted to children.

ROMANCE

Romance in the folk tales is usually as remote and impersonal as the waves of the sea.

Like them, romance is a cause—things happen because of it. But the characters are stereotypes. Aucassin and Nicolette are less interesting than their adventures. Enchantments and impossible tasks separate folk-tale lovers, and magic brings them together, whether they be Beauty and the Beast, the Goose Girl and the King, or the lassie who traveled east o' the sun and west o' the moon to find her love.

MAGIC

Tales of magic are at the heart of folk tales. These are the stories which justify the children's name for the whole group—"fairy tales." Fairy godmothers, giants, water nixies, a noble prince turned into a polar bear, the North Wind giving a poor boy magic gifts to make good the loss of his precious meal, three impossible tasks to be performed, a lad searching for the Water of Life—these are some of the motifs and some of the fairy people that give the folk tales a quality so unearthly and so beautiful that they come close to poetry. A large proportion of the folk tales is based upon magic of many kinds—so it is worth while to study these motifs and the fairy folk who flit so mysteriously through the tales.

Fairies and Other Magic Makers

The modern word *fairy* comes from the French word *fée,* a name for a variety of supernatural creatures who inhabited a world known in Old French as *faierie*. Into the word have been read wider meanings, borrowed from the medieval Latin word *fatare,* "to enchant," and the older Latin *fatum,* "fate" or "destiny." These ideas all enter into our concepts of fairies as supernatural creatures—sometimes little and lovely, sometimes old witch wives, or sometimes wise women like the Fates who have the power to enchant or to cast spells on human beings. To these concepts, the Celtic fairy lore has added rich details. Indeed, though the word *fairy* may come from the French, our fairy lore is predominantly Celtic.

THE LITTLE PEOPLE

The belief in fairies is astonishingly widespread and persistent among Celtic peoples (particularly in Ireland and Scotland). Even when serious belief is gone, certain superstitions remain. From these countries comes the idea of trooping fairies, ruled over by a fairy queen, dwelling underground in halls of great richness and beauty. These fairy raths (or forts) are the old subterranean earthworks remaining today in Ireland and Scotland, with the gold and glitter of jewels added by the Celtic imagination. From these hiding places, according to tradition, the fairies emerge at night to carry off men, maidens, or children who have caught their fancy. They may put spells on the cattle or on the work of humans they dislike, or they may come to the assistance of those who win their gratitude. To eat fairy food or to fall asleep in a fairy ring (a ring of especially green grass) or under a thorn tree on May Eve or Halloween is to put yourself in the power of the fairies for a year and a day. May Eve (the evening before the first of May) and All Hallows Eve (the night before All Saints' Day) are the two nights when the fairies ride abroad and human beings had best beware. Leave food on the doorstep for them, by all means; keep away from their rings and their raths; and you may avoid their anger and escape their wiles.

The name by which you refer to these "blithe spirits" is also a matter of importance in Celtic lore. If you want to play safe, you will never use the word f-a-i-r-y, which reminds them of the unhappy fact that they have no souls. On the Day of Judgment when humans have a chance (however slight) of going up in glory, the wee folk know full well, poor soulless creatures that they are, that they will simply blow away like a puff of down in a strong wind. So address them tactfully as "the good people," "the little people," or "the wee folk," if you would be well treated in return.

Other countries have these little creatures, too. In Cornwall, they are called pixies or piskeys, and they, like their Irish relatives, ride tiny steeds over the moors. In the Arabian tales you meet the jinns, who also live in deserted ruins, often underground, and are respectfully addressed as "the blessed ones." The German dwarfs are usually subterranean in their work and sometimes in their dwelling, too. Although they seem not to insist upon any special form of address, to treat them disrespectfully is to incur sure punishment.

The Norse hill folk live underground also, as do some of the small fairy folk of England and Scotland. There are other resemblances among these three groups. The Norse countries have a house spirit, the Tomten, much like the English Lar or Lob-Lie-by-the-Fire and the Scotch Aiken-drum. Astrid Lindgren has described their kindly guardianship in a book titled *The Tomten,* so beautifully and convincingly illustrated that even our most skeptical young skeptics will secretly hope to have a Tomten on hand. All these household spirits take up their abode in a house where they are well treated and make themselves useful in many ways. They may be propitiated by bowls of milk or offerings of parsley, chives, and garlic. But woe to the misguided soul who gives them clothes! Such a gift usually offends them and always drives them away, never to return. Oddly enough, the elves in Grimm's "Shoemaker and the Elves" were not insulted by the tiny garments, but they did depart, forever, even though they had manifested a most unorthodox delight in the offering.

One reason for the sense of motion in this drawing is the use of S and C forms. Accent is provided by the black window, the spinning wheel, and Tom Tit Tot's body. Textural contrast is provided by the window patterns and the pleats of the gown. Illustration by Joan Kiddell-Monroe. From English Fables and Fairy Stories, *retold by James Reeves. Henry Z. Walck, Inc., Publishers, 1954. Reprinted by permission. (Original with color, book 5 x 8¼)*

WISE WOMEN, WITCHES, AND WIZARDS

A few of the fairy folk are consistently evil, but most of them fluctuate in their attitude toward human beings and may be either helpful or ruthless. The wise women, who come to christenings or serve as fairy godmothers to bedeviled cinder lassies, are, on the whole, a grave and serious group. They are not unlike our idea of the Fates, or Norns, who mark off the life span and foretell coming events. One of these wise women aided Cinderella, while a peevish one sent Beauty off to sleep for a hundred years.

Witches and wizards are usually wicked. They lure children into their huts to eat them, or they cast spells on noble youths and turn them into beasts. Russia has a unique witch, Baba Yaga, who lives in a house that walks around on chicken legs. When she wishes to fly, she soars off in a pestle and sweeps her way along with a besom (two objects which have to be explained to children in advance, by the way). She has some other unique powers that make her quite as fascinating as she is gruesome.

The magicians and sorcerers cast spells but may sometimes be prevailed upon to do a kind deed and help out a worthy youth bent on the impossible. The Celtic "Merlin" is the most romantic of all the sorcerers, but he is seldom mentioned in the folk tales. The English "Childe Rowland," however, enlists Merlin's aid in rescuing Burd Ellen from Elfland.

Occasional imps, like the German "Rumpelstiltskin" and the English "Tom Tit Tot," are hard to classify. They seem to be a kind of hybrid elf and fiend, perhaps just one of the earth dwellers turned sour, hoping to get hold of a gay, laughing child to cheer his old age.

GIANTS AND OGRES

Ogres and ogresses are always bloodthirsty and cruel. Giants, however, are of two kinds: the children call them "bad" and "good." The "bad giants" are a powerful clan using brute force to mow down all opponents. They swallow their antagonists whole, as tremendous power seems always to do in any age. They are ruthless and unscrupulous and must be dealt with on their own terms—deceit and trickery. But fortunately they are often thickheaded and rely too much on force, so that clever boys like Jack or the one girl gianttamer "Molly Whuppie" can outwit them and leave them completely befuddled. The other tribe of giants is the helpful one. They aid the lad who shares his last crust of bread with them, and of course their aid is magnificent. They can drink up the sea and hold it comfortably until it is convenient to release it again. They can see a fly blinking in the sun five miles away or hear a blade of grass growing. They feel cold in the midst of fire and suffer from heat in solid ice. They can step lightly from mountain to mountain, break trees like twigs, and shatter rocks with a glance. They are the ancestors of Paul Bunyan and other supermen. The lad who lines up these giants on his side is guaranteed to win the princess and half the kingdom into the bargain. But no sluggard, no pompous pretender, no mean soul ever secures this aid. It is freely given only to honest lads about whom shines the grace of goodness.

FAIRY ANIMALS

In the world of fairy, domestic animals are as kindly disposed toward human beings as they are in the world of reality. For example, there is that handsome cat of cats, "Puss in Boots"—surely a child given a magic choice of one handy assistant from all the gallery of fairy helpers would choose the witty and redoubtable Puss. The Norse "Dapplegrim" is a horse of parts and does fully as well for his master as the Russian Horse of Power in "The Firebird."

Occasionally wild animals take a hand in the magic events of the folk tales. In the Norse story, a gray wolf carries the king's son to the castle of "The Giant Who Had No Heart in His Body," and, in the Czech story, old Lishka the fox gives "Budulinek" a ride on her tail, to his sorrow. Wild animals may be for or against human beings. Sometimes they serve merely as transportation, but often they are the real brains of an enterprise.

MAGIC OBJECTS

"Little Freddy with His Fiddle" makes magic music which no one has the power to resist. People cannot stop dancing even though they land in the midst of a thorn bush, even though their bones ache until they fall down exhausted. Freddy knew how to make magic with that frivolous fiddle of his, and it carried him a long way. In "Herding the King's Hares," Espen Cinderlad receives a remarkable whistle for his kindness to an old hag. With it he can bring order to every runaway bunny in the king's herd, and finally to the royal family as well:

Then the king and queen thought it best to give him the princess and half the kingdom; it just couldn't be helped.

"That certainly was some whistle," said Espen Cinderlad.

"Molly Whuppie," pursued by the double-faced giant, runs lightly across the Bridge of One Hair, on which the giant dares take not so much as a single step. That is the kind of power every one of us needs to develop—the power to find a bridge, however slight, on which we can run lightly away from the ogres pursuing us. The folk tales are full of these "Fools of the World," who learn how to use magic tools as the pompous and pretentious never learn to do. Espen Cinderlad, with three impossible tasks to perform, hunts around until he finds the self-propelled axe, the spade, and the trickling water that could be stopped or let loose by him alone. Each of these magic objects told him it had been waiting a long, long time, just for him. Magic is always waiting for those who know how to use it.

ENCHANTED PEOPLE

Being put under a spell is just one of the many complications that beset the heroes and heroines of the fairy tales. Childe Rowland's sister unknowingly courted disaster by running around the church "widershins"—counterclockwise—and so put herself under the power of the fairies. "Rapunzel," of the long, long hair, was locked up in a tower by a cruel enchantress who was so clever that only a super-prince could worst her. And there are many variants of the folk tale about the royal brothers who are changed into birds, and who can be released from their enchantment only after their little sister has gone speechless for seven long years and spun each of them a shirt of thistledown. The Russians tell the marvelous story of "Sadko," who lived at the bottom of the ocean in the palace of the Czar of the Sea—this story has all the curious elusiveness of a dream. Grimm's touching "The Frog-King" is one of the many tales in which either the husband or the wife is a fairy creature or is in the power of some witch or sorcerer. Of these, Grimm's "The Water-Nixie" is perhaps the most exciting and the Norse "East o' the Sun and West o' the Moon" the most beautiful. In all such stories only love, loyalty, and self-sacrifice can break the enchantment and restore the beloved.

On the whole, the good and evil supernatural forces in the folk tales act according to certain laws. If magic makes wishes come true and points the way to happiness, it does so only with struggles and hardships on the part of the hero or heroine. The true princess suffers pitifully before magic opens the king's eyes and he sees her for what she is—the rightful bride for his son and a gentle, loving girl. These stories are not didactic, but one after another shows that courage and simple goodness work their own magic in this world, that evil must be conquered even if it carries us to the gates of death, and that grace and strength are bestowed upon those who strive mightily and keep an honest, kindly heart.

Distinctive Elements of Folk Tales

For generation after generation, folk tales have continued to be popular with children. Modern youngsters, surrounded by the mechanical gadgets and scientific wonders of our age, are still spellbound by their magic. What needs can they satisfy and what elements in these old stories give children pleasure?

The form, style, and character portrayal in folk tales are distinctly different from those of the modern short story. A brief examination of these distinctive elements may help explain the charm of the old tales for children and may help measure the probable appeal of modern stories being written for children today. First of all, the form or pattern of the folk tales is curiously satisfying both to children and adults. Folk-tale form is as clear cut and definite as that of the old drama which it closely resembles.

THE INTRODUCTION

The introduction to a folk tale does exactly what its name implies. It *introduces* the reader to the leading characters, the time and place of the story, the theme, and the problem to be solved, or the conflict which is the very breath of the story.

Usually the folk tales have *robust themes* which are capable of supporting good plots. The theme is the idea of the story, the center of interest—what the story is about. Often it is expressed in the title or in a slight amplification of the title. For instance, "The Lad Who Went to the North Wind" to get his rights for the stolen meal is a strong theme, around which a good action story is bound to develop. "Taper Tom" and how he made the princess laugh, "The Sleeping Beauty in the Woods," and "Hänsel and Gretel" and the wicked witch—here are three very different themes, each capable of exciting development.

The themes often involve the element of *contrast*. Sometimes there is the uneven conflict, which always makes a story more exciting: "Hänsel and Gretel" and the wicked witch—two little children pitted against an evil power; "The Three Little Pigs" and the wicked wolf. You realize at once that if pigs are going to survive in a wolf-infested world, they will have to keep their wits about them. Sometimes the contrast lies within a like group; for example, in "The Three Little Pigs," there are not only pigs and wolf but also a wise pig and foolish pigs. So in "Boots and His Brothers" (or, as it is sometimes entitled, "Per, Paal, and Espen Cinderlad") the humble Cinderlad shows the wisdom his older brothers lack. "One-Eye, Two-Eyes, and Three-Eyes" has a strange theme with a most unusual contrast in the three sisters. Obviously, contrast heightens the conflict and rouses the reader's sympathy for the weaker or less fortunate or more kindly member of the group.

Folk-tale themes are never abstract but *objective* and *understandable*. They have to do with winning security, earning a living or a place in the world, accomplishing impossible tasks, escaping from powerful enemies, outwitting wicked schemes and schemers, and succeeding with nonchalance. These themes are as vital today as ever and account for the vigor of these old tales. Weak themes enfeeble some of our modern juveniles. Going to the store to get Mother's groceries can usually suggest only a negligible plot. But *"The 500 Hats of Bartholomew Cubbins,"* murmurs Dr. Seuss, and forthwith launches a tale that would spellbind any generation. Or Edward Ardizzone's *Little Tim and the Brave Sea Captain* fairly breathes adventure.

Time is effectively accounted for by a conventional phrase like "Once upon a time," "Long ago and far away," "In olden times when wishing still helped one," "A thousand years ago tomorrow," or "Once on a time, and a very good time too." Such folk-tale conventions do more than convey an idea of long ago; they carry the reader at once to a dream world where anything is possible.

The *scene* is even more briefly sketched. It is a road, a bridge, a palace, a forest, or a poor man's hut, and that's all—no interior decorations, no landscapes, just a place where something is going to happen and soon. No wonder these introductions catch the child's attention. They launch the conflict with no distracting details.

Sometimes the folk tales, like the ballads, get off to such a brisk start that the introduction is almost imperceptible. This one for "The Three Billy-Goats Gruff" is a masterpiece of brevity:

> *Once on a time there were three Billy-goats, who were to go up to the hill-side to make themselves fat, and the name of all three was "Gruff."*
>
> *On the way up was a bridge over a burn they had to cross; and under the bridge lived a great ugly Troll, with eyes as big as saucers, and a nose as long as a poker.*

There you are! The scene is a bridge with a pleasant stretch of grassy hillside just beyond. The characters are three earnest billy goats of the Gruff family who are desirous of getting fat on the hillside. Obstacle, Conflict, Problem lives under the bridge in the person of an ugly Troll. In the fewest possible words, you have all the makings of a good plot. Obviously, only the simplest tale can get under way as rapidly as this. "The Sleeping Beauty," still a fairly uncomplicated story, must introduce the king, queen, courtiers, the grand christening for the baby princess in the palace, the good fairies for whom plates of gold have been prepared, and the evil fairy who is uninvited and minus a gold plate and therefore thoroughly angry. What will happen? This is the mark of a good introduction: it whets the appetite for more; you "go on" eagerly. For children, brevity of introduction is an important part of the charm of these folk tales. The excitement gets under way with minimum description. In comparison, the introductions of many modern stories are tiresomely wordy.

THE DEVELOPMENT

The development, sometimes called the body of the story, carries forward the note of trouble sounded in the introduction. The quest begins, the tasks are initiated and performed, the flight gets under way, and the obstacles of every kind appear, with the hero or heroine reduced to despair or helplessness or plunged into more and more perilous action. This is the heart of the story—action that mounts steadily until it reaches a climax, when the problem or conflict will be resolved one way or the other.

The development of the story is really the *plot*—what happens to the theme. The vigorous plots of the folk tales, full of suspense and action, appeal strongly to young readers. The heroes *do* things—they ride up glass hills, slay giants who have no hearts in their bodies, outwit wolves, get their rights from the North Wind, or pitch an old witch into an oven she intended for them. Here are no brooding introspectionists but doers of the most vigorous sort. And the plots that unfold their doings have logic, unity, and economy.

First, their *logic*. If these action plots are to carry conviction, the development must be both logical and plausible. When in "The Three Little Pigs" one pig is so foolish as to build a house of straw and another to build a house of sticks, you know they are doomed. But when a pig has sufficient acumen to build his house stoutly of bricks, you know perfectly well he will also be smart enough to outwit his adversaries, for such a pig will survive in any society. Another example of a logical, plausible plot development is "Clever Manka," the witty Czech story that is a favorite with older children. Manka by her cleverness wins a fine husband, a judge and burgomaster; but

Wealth and security for the homeless musicians at last! Only the nocturnal cat lies awake in her handsome new bed. Hans Fischer, with freely sketched pen lines filled in with bright colors, tells the story in details that reduce words to second place. Illustration by Hans Fischer. Reproduced from Grimm's Traveling Musicians, *by permission of Harcourt, Brace & World, Inc. (Original in color, book 8¼ x 12)*

he warns her that she will be banished from his house if she ever uses her cleverness to interfere with his business. Knowing Manka and realizing that no one can help using what wit the Lord gave him, you feel the conflict approaching. Of course Manka learns of a case where her husband has rendered a flagrantly unfair judgment, and in the interest of justice she interferes. She is found out and banished, but in the face of this ultimate catastrophe, she uses her wit and saves both herself and her husband from permanent unhappiness. Here is a realistic folk tale of clever mind against duller mind, with the clever one saving them both. The ending is surprising but completely logical.

A good folk-tale plot must also preserve *unity of interest,* which means the centering of attention on the theme. Every episode in "The Lad Who Went to the North Wind" concerns the boy's struggles to get his rights for the meal that the North Wind blew away. "The Three Little Pigs" never deflects the reader from his intense preoccupation with the third pig's attempts to win security in a wolf-haunted world. In "Cinderella," the activities of the two spiteful sisters only heighten our concern for Cinderella and our desire to have her win the place she deserves in the world. And in "The Bremen Town-Musicians," interest in the forlorn musicians is not drawn away by the new interest in the robbers. The robbers may be ever so picturesque; they may even be kind to their families—we don't know or care. Our only concern with them is that the musicians shall drive them out of the neighborhood for good and all. So the best of the fairy tales maintain a strict unity.

To achieve this unity, a story must preserve a decent *economy of incidents.* Too many episodes, too long-drawn-out suspense, or too much magic destroys the unity of the tale. The development often contains three tasks or three riddles or three trials. Perhaps there is no particular significance in the "three" except that the old storyteller, always properly audience-conscious as a good storyteller should be, could see for himself that suspense can be endured just so long before people get impatient. After the hero rides three times up a glass hill, the listeners demand results. Molly can use her bridge of one hair three times and after that she had better finish things off and get home. For it is on *suspense* that the successful development of folk-tale action depends. Suspense is built up and maintained until it reaches a peak in the climax, after which it declines and the action ends with a flourish.

The Arabian tales, the American Indian stories, and many of the Russian tales develop too many incidents. One involved episode follows another until you almost forget what the hero was up to in the first place. Magic is piled upon magic until your credulity gives out under the strain.

THE CONCLUSION

The third part of the story, the conclusion, usually comes swiftly and is as brief as the introduction. In "The Three Billy-Goats Gruff," the ringing challenge of the biggest billy goat announces the climax. The fight ensues, the biggest billy goat is the winner, and the Gruff family is now free to eat grass and get fat for the rest of its days. In "The Sleeping Beauty," the kiss breaks the spell for the princess and the whole court, the royal wedding quickly takes place, and that ought to be all except for the conventional blessing "and they lived happily ever after." But the old folk tale thought otherwise, for a second story begins, a kind of sequel in which poor Beauty finds herself with an ogress for a mother-in-law and another conflict to be resolved. Whether or not the nature-symbolism theory or the bad-dream theory accounts for this second part is of small importance. It is poor story form and children don't like it, as the storytellers have discovered. Most versions now conclude with the wedding of Beauty and the prince.

The conclusion, then, should follow swiftly on the heels of the climax and should end everything that was started in the introduction. Not only must the heroes and heroines achieve a happy solution for their troubles and a triumphant end to their struggles, but the villains must also be accounted for and satisfyingly punished. Such conclusions satisfy the child's eye-for-an-eye code of ethics and apparently leave his imagination untroubled—probably because they usually have no harrowing details and are so preposterous that they move cheerfully out of reality.

The fairy tale has some conventional endings that are as picturesque as the openings. "The Three Billy-Goats Gruff" concludes

Snip, snap, snout
This tale's told out.

Other endings are: "If they haven't left off their merry-making yet, why, they're still at it"; "A mouse did run, the story's done"; "And no one need ask if they were happy"; "Whosoever does not believe this must pay a taler" (or as we should say, a dollar); "And the mouth of the person who last told this is still warm"; "And now the joy began in earnest. I wish you had been there too." For little children, the chance to vary the name in the last line of the following conclusion makes it one of their favorites.

My tale is done,
Away it has run
To little Augusta's house.

STYLE

One of the charms of the folk tale is its characteristic style—the language and manner of telling the story. For these tales were never read silently; they were told until their form and language patterns were fixed. Consider: "Go I know not whither, bring back I know not what," or

"Little pig, little pig, let me come in."
"No, no, by the hair of my chinny chin chin."
"Then I'll huff and I'll puff and I'll blow your house in."

Or in the Scotch tale "Whippety Stourie," read the conversation with the wee fairy ladies that turned the stern husband from trying to make a spinner of his wife:

"Would you mind telling me," he asked them, "why it is that your mouths are all as lopsided as a fir-tree leaning against the wind?"

Then the six wee ladies burst into loud, lopsided laughter, and Whippety Stourie herself replied:

"Och, it's with our constant spin-spin-spinning. For we're all of us great ones for the spinning, and there's no surer way to a lopsided mouth."

Or read that matchless ending, "As for the Prince and Princess, they . . . flitted away as far as they could from the castle that lay East o' the Sun and West o' the Moon." These are brief examples of fairy-tale style—frequently cadenced, sometimes humorous, sometimes romantic—with the words suited to the mood and tempo of the tale.

The beginnings and endings of the stories, of course, are particularly good examples of the storyteller's skill in establishing the predominant mood of the story, or breaking off and sending the listeners back to their workaday world. But dialogue in these old stories is also a part of their style—it runs along so naturally that real people seem to be talking. Read aloud the conversation between the old man and his wife in "Gudbrand on the Hill-side." Never once does the swift interchange of news and comments falter for a descriptive phrase such as "said he *uneasily*," or "said she *reassuringly*." Here is just a rapid, natural give-and-take between two people:

"Nay, but I haven't got the goat either," said Gudbrand, "for a little farther on I swopped it away, and got a fine sheep instead."

"You don't say so!" cried his wife; "why you do everything to please me, just as if I had been with you. What do we want with a goat! . . . Run out child, and put up the sheep."

"But I haven't got the sheep any more than the rest," said Gudbrand; "for when I had gone a bit farther I swopped it away for a goose."

"Thank you! thank you! with all my heart," cried his wife. . . .

So they proceed from disaster to disaster without a single literary interpolation. Notice, too, that the words suffice to establish unmistakably the attitude of each speaker. Words so perfectly chosen make long descriptions unnecessary.

Another characteristic of fairy-tale style is the use of rhymes. Indeed, the stories are sometimes part prose and part verse in the old sing-and-say pattern of "Aucassin et Nicolette." Cante-fables, such stories are called—that is, singing stories or verse stories. The frequency of rhymes in some of the old folk tales has caused some speculation about whether the fairy tales came from the ballads or the ballads from the tales, since both often have the same subjects ("Earl Mar's Daugh-

Fine pen-and-ink with one color wash. No living thing in the picture looks at another. A tangle of hair frames the lovely, unshadowed, drooping, sad face of the Goose-Girl. Illustration by Johannes Troyer. From Grimm's Household Stories, *translated by Lucy Crane. Copyright, 1954, by The Macmillan Company. Reprinted by permission of the publishers. (Book 5½ x 8¼)*

ter," "Binnorie," "Childe Rowland," and "The Laidly Worm," to mention a few). This is a matter for the specialists to settle, but certainly the little rhymes add greatly to the interest of the tales.

"The Well of the World's End" ("The Frog-King") alternates prose and verse, with the frog singing over and over the same words except for the request in the first two lines in which he raises his demands each time:

"Give me some supper, my hinny, my heart,
Give me some supper, my darling;
Remember the words you and I spake,
In the meadow, by the Well of the World's End."

Some of the prettiest verses in the fairy tales are in Grimm's "The Goose-Girl" and in the English "The Black Bull of Norroway." The former breaks into rhyme when the faithful horse, Falada, speaks to his mistress. And after he has been killed and his head nailed to the dark gateway, the Goose-Girl, who is really the princess, weeps beneath the gateway saying:

"Alas, Falada, hanging there!"

Then the head answered:

"Alas, young Queen, how ill you fare!
If this your mother knew,
Her heart would break in two."

This piteous dialogue is followed by the song of the Goose-Girl, putting a spell on young Conrad, because he takes too much delight in her golden hair:

"Blow, blow, thou gentle wind, I say,
Blow Conrad's little hat away,
And make him chase it here and there,
Until I have braided all my hair,
And bound it up again."

Grimm's "Cinderella," "Hänsel and Gretel," "The Fisherman and His Wife," the tragic "The Juniper Tree," "Little Snow-White," and many others have memorable rhymes which some adults can still recite. The English tales are especially full of them. But many other folk tales are marked by the subtle art of the storyteller who has perfected a fine oral pattern in which rhymes frequently appear.

CHARACTER PORTRAYAL

The interest of the modern short story frequently depends far more upon characters than upon plot or action. This is not true of the fairy tales. Plot is of first importance, and the characters are more or less typed. The good people in these stories are altogether good, and the wicked are so completely wicked that we waste no sympathy on them when, in the end, they are liquidated. So, too, the animals in the folk tales stand for simple traits like loyalty, cleverness, slyness, cruelty.

But look for brief flashes of characterization here and there. Cinderella is a teen-age girl with her mind on balls and fine clothes. Red Riding Hood is good-hearted but irresponsible. The Lad who went to the North Wind to get his rights for the wasted meal is one of those dogged, stick-to-itive boys who, with right on his side, is going to get his way in the world or know the reason why. And as for the lad's mother, you can just see her, the old skeptic, shaking her head and saying, "All very true, I daresay, but seeing is believing, and I shan't believe it till I see it." There, in a flash, is a character sketch of the doubter, the cynic.

Sometimes the characters are passive—like the Sleeping Beauty, or the remote princess on the glass hill—but they are still sufficiently individual so that each one arouses different reactions. Beauty's doom, hanging over her youth and loveliness like a black cloud, inspires only pity. But the silly, feckless girl in "Tom Tit Tot," with her big appetite and meager wit, is so absurd that you don't particularly mind the hard bargain "that" drives with her.

So while fairy-tale people are strongly typed as "good" or "bad" with no subtle distinctions between, they are also individualized. Sympathy or antagonism is aroused in different degrees by the brief characterizations. A whole portrait gallery of lads and lassies, goose-girls and princes, kings and queens remains in your memory, distinct and convincingly true to human nature.

Why Use the Folk Tales With Modern Children?

A famous English poet, W. H. Auden, reviewed the Pantheon edition of *Grimm's Fairy Tales* for the New York *Times* (November 12, 1944). He made this rather startling statement:

For, among the few indispensable, common-property books upon which Western Culture can be founded—that is, excluding the national genius of specific peoples as exemplified by Shakespeare and Dante—it is hardly too

Felix Hoffmann's illustrations for The Sleeping Beauty *are reminiscent of Howard Pyle's style in their heroic characters and their suggestion of magnificence. Illustration by Felix Hoffmann. From Grimm's* The Sleeping Beauty, *copyright 1959, by H. R. Sauerlander & Co., Aarau. Reprinted by permission of Harcourt, Brace & World, Inc. and Oxford University Press. (Original in color, book 5⅝ x 11⅝, picture size 8 x 6½)*

much to say that these tales rank next to the Bible in importance.

Later in the review he added:

It will be a mistake, therefore, if this volume is merely bought as a Christmas present for a child; it should be, first and foremost, an educational "must" for adults, married or single, for the reader who has once come to know and love these tales will never be able again to endure the insipid rubbish of contemporary entertainment.

Yet some people raise a great hue and cry about the ethics of the fairy tales. They wonder whether children should read about Bluebeard's gory collection of ex-wives, or about a girl who tricks a giant into killing his own offspring in place of the trembling human children who had taken refuge in his castle. People so protective of children might also inquire whether they should read about Jacob tricking his brother Esau out of his birthright, or about the terrors of Daniel in the den of lions.

ETHICAL TRUTH

Of course, the fairy-tale ethics are not always acceptable to the modern moral code. These stories were told by adults to adults in an age when using wits against brute force was often the only means of survival, and therefore admirable. But even today, in wars upon crime—whether crimes against individuals or nations—trickery, ruthlessness, and killing are accepted as necessary. Not a pretty code, but a realistic one. In the fairy tales, then, witches and ogres are destroyed or defeated according to the common-sense code of survival.

But fairy tales are predominantly constructive, not destructive, in their moral lessons. "The humble and good shall be exalted," say the stories of "Little Snow-White," "Cinderella," "The Bremen Town-Musicians," and dozens of others. "Love suffereth long and is kind" is the lesson of "East o' the Sun" and "One-Eye, Two-Eyes, and Three-Eyes." In "The Frog-King," the royal father of the princess enforces a noble code upon his thoughtless daughter. "That which you have promised must you perform," he says sternly, and again, "He who helped you when you were in trouble ought not afterwards to be despised by you." Indeed, so roundly and soundly do these old tales stand for morality that they leave an indelible impression of virtue invariably rewarded and evil unfailingly punished. Here, in fairy tales, is the world as it ought to be—sometimes ruthless of necessity but sound at the core. Can this world and this code hurt a child?

SATISFACTION OF NEEDS

Most adults rereading these stories begin to understand Mr. Auden's feeling that they are timeless in their appeal. Plumbing, kitchen gadgets, and modes of transportation may change, but human desires and human emotions continue strong and unchanging. These old fairy tales contain in their "picture language" the symbols of some of the deepest human feelings and satisfy in fantasy human desires for security, competence, and love.

Everyone longs for security, the simple physical security of a snug house, warmth, and good food. In the fairy tales, the little hut in the forest is cozy and warm, safe from ravening wolves, and full of the peace of the fireside, with a loaf of bread baking on the hearth and a flavorsome kettle of soup on the hob. And of course there are castles, too; they may be a bit cold and drafty, but Jack or Tattercoats or Espen Cinderlad always seems to settle down very comfortably in the new grandeur. Children identify themselves with either the elegance of the castle or the snug security of the house in the woods. Both are satisfying: the castle speaks of achievement, the little hut of peace and safety.

Human beings are always in search of love. There will never be a time when people do not need loving reinforcement against the hostile world and the frightening thought of death. The old tales are full of loving compensations for fears and hardships. Hänsel reassures his little sister and protects her as long as he is able, and Gretel comes to his rescue when he is helpless and in peril. Commoners and royalty alike pursue their lost loves and endure every kind of suffering to free them from unhappy enchantments. A competent peasant boy rescues a lonely princess from her glass hill, and a prince gives all his love to Cinderella. There is cruelty in these old tales and danger, too, but the real world, like the fairy world, can be cruel and perilous. In reassuring contrast are the symbols of love, lending strength to the weak, offering sanctuary to those in peril, and in the end rewarding their faithfulness or their struggles.

People long not only for love and security but for competence. They are eager to overcome difficulties, to right wrongs, and to stand fast in the face of danger—abilities essential for heroes of any generation. The fairy tales supply unforgettable stories of wicked powers defeated and of gallant souls who in their extremity are granted supernatural strength. Whether or not children are conscious of it, these stories may become sources of moral strength—a strength which is part faith, part courage, and wholly unshakable.

VARIETY

There is a fairy story for every mood. There are drolls and romances, tales of horror and of beauty. Fairy tales cover every range of feeling.

Undoubtedly their first appeal to children is *exciting action*. Things happen in these stories with just the hair-raising rapidity that children yearn for in real life and rarely find. For this reason, a child who reads too many fairy tales may find everyday life painfully dull and static—no beanstalks to climb, no giants to kill, no witches to outwit. The action in the fairy tales does fill a definite need, however. Before the child is ready to understand and follow character development, these active heroes are lads after his own heart.

There is sometimes a strange quiet about these stories. The forest is so still you can hear one bird singing; a little lamb speaks softly to a fish in a brook; the enchanted castle is silent; and the prince falls asleep by the fountain from which gently flows the water of life. Reading some of these strange tales, you feel yourself relaxing. Here there is time for everything, even a little nap by magic waters. Compared with any moving-picture version of fairy tales, the old words make immeasurably better pictures, create stronger moods, and refresh and relax to a degree which only music or poetry can approach. The three are closely related: children who have learned to love the fairy tales will be equipped to enjoy music and poetry, too. Moreover, they will have discovered the wonders of tranquillity and quiet in the midst of a noisy, restless world. As adults they will have inner resources because their spirits have been fed richly and well.

Misuses of the Folk Tales

TEACHING MORALS

Every so often, adults are seized by an attack of earnestness and feel that the fairy tales should either be abolished entirely or related only for some useful end. Because some of the tales have a strong moral flavor, they were occasionally selected and told for moral lessons. For instance, some storytellers related "Little Red Riding Hood" chiefly in order to stress the moral of disobedience properly punished. But one of England's great illustrators carried this unpleasant practice still further. George Cruikshank (p. 57), who produced the pictures for the first English edition of the Grimms' tales and also for many of Dickens' novels, issued his own collection of fairy tales —*The Cruikshank Fairy-Book*. He took four old tales—"Puss in Boots," "The Story of Jack and the Bean-Stalk," "Hop-o'-My-Thumb and the Seven-League Boots," and "Cinderella and the Glass Slipper"—and rewrote them completely, making them carry some of the useful moral lessons he felt they lacked. "Cinderella" was interrupted for three pages of "Temperance Truths, with a fervent hope that some good may result therefrom." Librarians keep this book only as a curiosity.

Fortunately, methods like Cruikshank's

have been defeated by their obvious absurdity and by children's healthy resistance to them. The great moral truths inherent in many of the tales will take effect without hammering them home. Occasionally children make their own applications of the morals. A group of children had been listening to "The Princess on the Glass Hill," and after a violent electrical storm, one six-year-old remarked complacently, "We were just like Boots, weren't we? We stood it." The teacher laughed and said, "Sure enough you did stand it." The morals speak for themselves and need no underscoring.

FORCED RETELLING BY YOUNG CHILDREN

A second misuse of folk tales is to expect young children to retell them for language development and practice. One or two children are always eager to retell their favorite stories and often do it acceptably, but in the primary grades such a task is a catastrophe for many children. Not only are the plots too complex and the dialogue too fast moving and subtle, but the polished perfection of the style of these old tales is beyond the little child's powers of narration. It is as if he were asked in his music periods to sing a Brahms waltz or a Chopin prelude, which he may thoroughly enjoy hearing but is incapable of reproducing. The worst of having young children laboriously retell folk tales is that their unfortunate listeners are bored beyond endurance. The tale is ruined for both narrator and audience. Your older child may tell a story well, but on the whole, it is better for primary children to have their oral language practice with easier materials.

INTRODUCED TO CHILDREN TOO EARLY

Children reach the peak of interest in fairy tales when they are around seven, eight, and nine years old, not four or five as people once thought. There are some stories, of course, that the youngest children ask for again and again: a few beast tales like "The Three Little Pigs" and "The Little Red Hen," and also the accumulative stories. The prereading child should not miss these nursery classics. But for the most part, he is passionately concerned with his own realistic world of trains and autos, stores and houses, real dogs and real goats. Fairies and giants are not for him as yet, although he accepts the troll under the bridge matter-of-factly enough. For him, apparently the troll is just something to wheedle or to fight with.

"Cinderella," "Hänsel and Gretel," "East o' the Sun," and "Mollie Whuppie" are far better for children of eight or nine than for those of five or six. And some folk tales are best for ten- and eleven-year-olds and even older—tales like "Clever Manka," "The Most Obedient Wife," and the American tall tales. Since there are some fairy stories right for every age, it is unnecessary to force the stories on children who are too young for them.

Desirable Uses of the Folk Tales

FOR ENTERTAINMENT

First and foremost, these old tales should be told or read just for fun. The relaxation and entertainment in the promise of "Once upon a time" are a justification for the stories at any age or any hour. They are so close to poetry that all that has been said about the use of verse applies again to the fairy tales. When things have been tense or difficult, try a story and relax. Have the kindergarten children just had their first fire drill? Tell them "The Pancake" and make them laugh. Or when a factual study has pressed the older children hard, read them "Urashima Taro and the Princess of the Sea" and they will be refreshed. Keep a book of these tales in the room to pick up at any time just for pleasure. These stories do not have to "correlate" with any study unit; they do not have to teach something. Whether romance or sheer nonsense, nursery tale or allegory, their power of entertainment is their first reason for existence and our first reason for using them.

WITH NATIONAL GROUPS

As suggested before, the folk tales may become a teacher's open sesame to friendship in a neighborhood made up of a somewhat homogeneous national group. One teacher will never forget telling Irish fairy tales at a mothers' and daughters' party where most of the mothers had been born in Ireland. When she began, the girls looked a bit self-conscious, but the mothers' eyes were bright and responsive.

"I heard that story another way," said one mother when the teacher had finished.

"How did yours go?" she asked. The mother outlined the differences clearly, but added, "Mrs. O'Connor's the one for stories. She knows dozens of them."

Between them, they persuaded the reluctant Mrs. O'Connor to tell a story. Proud of her art, she told "Hudden and Dudden and Donald O'Neary" to perfection. They all laughed, and the girls lost their self-consciousness. Over the refreshments, everyone compared notes on the Irish stories she knew and agreed to exchange some of her favorites the next time they met. One of the girls said, "I've a young aunt just over from Ireland and you should hear *her* tell stories. May I bring her next time?" Of course the teacher agreed, and so began a series of storytelling exchanges ranging from the hilarious "King O'Toole and His Goose" to bits of the Cuchulain epic. Even by the second meeting, they were no longer teacher, pupils, and mothers; they were just friends.

Another teacher, finding that the children in her class were principally of Czech descent, began to tell them the English versions of some of the old Czech tales. She consulted the children about the pronunciation of proper names, and they patiently set her straight and enjoyed the reversal of roles, teacher turned pupil. Presently they were saying, "My mother knows 'Budulinek,' " or "My grandfather knows stories like those and lots more, too." The stories led to reports on Czech customs, festivals, and special treasures the families had brought with them from the Old World. Finally an all-school exhibition and party was inevitable. Beautiful costumes, embroideries, glassware, and pottery were displayed; parents sang songs in Czech and danced the folk dances, while the children told and dramatized the stories. The refreshments included Czech breads and pastries. Not only did everyone have fun, but there was a new and warmer relationship between school and family, based on respect and friendly interest.

So folk tales may lead straight into the homes of the children and develop a common bond between two generations and between two or more national groups. In a school where different nationalities mingle, a rich and beautiful program can be developed around "Folk Tales of Many Countries," with typical stories told, dramatized, played by puppets and marionettes, and illustrated by the children with paints and clay modeling. The likenesses as well as fascinating differences among all peoples will be dramatically evident.

FOR ILLUSTRATION

As subjects for modeling or painting, the fairy tales are unsurpassed. One man's guess is as good as another's in illustrating them, because no one can tell anyone else the precise measurements and equipment of a fairy godmother. A third grade illustrated "Budulinek"[6] with diverse artistic effects. One child portrayed Granny wearing a frivolous hat and carrying a large pocketbook in modern style. Other young artists drew the interior of the room with the closed door and a bowl on the table. But everyone wanted to paint Budulinek going for a ride on Lishka's tail. Each picture shows Lishka as genuinely foxlike with a fine brush of a tail on which the naughty Budulinek perches jauntily. The pair are pictured hurrying through some dramatic landscapes, the best these third-graders had ever done. "Hänsel and Gretel," "Mother Holle," "Cinderella," and dozens of others are beautiful subjects for illustration and send the

6. Roxboro School, Cleveland Heights; teacher at that time, Miss Evelyn Brockway.

The Three Bears
The Three Bears went for a walk—
Baby Bear, Mother Bear, and Father Bear

children's imaginations soaring. Needless to say, no book pictures should be visible when the children are making their own illustrations.

FOR DRAMATIZATION

Most of the folk tales have a dramatic quality, and any discussion of children and these old tales eventually leads to the possibilities of dramatization. Chapter 19, "Reading and Creative Expression," offers suggestions for classroom dramatization.

FOR STORYTELLING BY OLDER CHILDREN[7]

Upper-grade children had unusual fun with fairy tales in one school which was an experiment station for English activities of all kinds. The fifth-grade children had listened to stories

7. See Chapter 13 for a discussion of storytelling.

Children's imaginations have full play in illustrating fairy tales. The drawing for "The Three Bears" shows as jaunty a bear family as ever went strolling woodsward. The picture for "Mother Holle" suggests the timid, lonely girl and the mystery of trees which talk. Exciting moments in the story of "Budulinek" are pictured in the last three illustrations. Drawings are from (1) Mayfair School, East Cleveland; (2) Charles Dickens School, Cleveland; (3, 4, and 5) Roxboro School, Cleveland Heights.

told over the radio by Miss Margaret Clark,[8] one of the best storytellers in the city, and had read other tales as well. They decided to tell some of their favorites to younger children. They formed themselves into the Children's Storytelling Club, learned their stories well, and told them to the primary grades with such zest that the primaries were charmed. The fifth-grade storytellers carried on this activity for a whole semester and not only enjoyed themselves thoroughly but grew in poise, language power, and ability to interest and hold an audience.

Try rereading these folk tales. They will move you sometimes to laughter and sometimes to tender pity. They will give you a better understanding of other people and yourself also. When you have finished, you will find that you have grown accustomed to looking at life with the eyes of a poet, searching for the spirit behind the rags or behind the fine clothes, for the selfishness or the nobility that makes the man. You will find that your ears have grown accustomed to the language of poets speaking in prose. You can never forget the measured cadence of these tales, the words dancing or stepping gravely to the mood. All the rest of your life you will unconsciously measure other prose and other stories by the fairy tales.

The multiplicity of folk-tale collections does not mean that we should use more of them. Most teachers are probably using them less than they once did because other types of fiction for children have improved in quality. But we should know that there are now available many national collections of these old tales, and we should select from them a moderate number of suitable variety and use them in balanced proportion to realistic stories and informational reading. They are fantasy, and too much fantasy can make Jack a confused boy, a runaway from reality. Still, in moments of discouragement, let's be grateful for the reassuring message these old tales carry. They say to the child, "Don't be too depressed about brute force and wickedness, because you will live to see them overthrown. Kindness and courage work their own magic in this world. Just remember the glass slipper in your pocket. It is your talisman of the triumph of virtue."

8. Librarian in charge of the Lewis Carroll Room, Cleveland Public Library.

SUGGESTED READING, PROBLEMS, AND PROJECTS

Suggested Reading: In order to follow the discussions in this chapter and in Chapter 13, read a fair sampling of the following stories:

Perrault: "Cinderella," "Sleeping Beauty," "Little Red Riding Hood," "Little Thumb," "Puss in Boots."

Grimm: "Cinderella," "Little Briar-Rose," "Little Red-Cap," "Hänsel and Gretel," "Bremen Town-Musicians," "Mother Holle," "The Frog-King," "The Goose-Girl," "Rumpelstiltskin," "Clever Elsie," "Little Snow-White," "The Water of Life," "The Twelve Brothers," "The Fisherman and His Wife," "The Shoemaker and the Elves."

Asbjörnsen: "Three Billy-Goats Gruff," "The Pancake," "Taper Tom," "The Lad Who Went to the North Wind," "Boots and His Brothers" ("Espen Cinderlad"), "Gudbrand on the Hill-side," "East o' the Sun," "Twelve Wild Ducks," "Little Freddy and His Fiddle."

Jacobs: "Three Little Pigs," "Old Woman and Her Pig," "Henny Penny," "Lazy Jack," "Tattercoats," "Jack and the Beanstalk," "Molly Whuppie," "Little Red Riding Hood," "Tom Tit Tot," "The Black Bull of Norroway."

Ransome: "Sadko," "The Firebird."

Fillmore: "Budulinek," "Smolicheck," "Clever Manka."

Harris: Any of the Uncle Remus stories, probably "Tar Baby."

Arabian Nights: "Aladdin" or "Flying Carpet."

American Tall Tales: Paul Bunyan, Pecos Bill ("Pecos Bill and His Bouncing Bride").

1. Which theories of folk-tale origins sound most plausible to you? Take some familiar folk tale (not used as an example in the discussion of origins) and tell to which theory or theories it seems to be related.

2. What ancient beliefs or customs are suggested by the story "The Goose-Girl"? What dreamlike qualities do you find in "Tattercoats," "Sadko," and "The Frog-King"?

3. Read the stories in any two collections of folk tales and compare their (a) plots; (b) style; (c) types of characters; (d) use of rhyme; (e) propor-

tion and kind of humor and tragedy; (f) proportion of accumulative tales, talking beasts, drolls, religious tales, romance, tales of magic; (g) variations within the same story.

4. Read one other national collection of folk tales (not U.S.). Evaluate the collection for use with children.

5. Compare one American variant of a European tale with its possible source. Read enough of Paul Bunyan or Pecos Bill or *The Jack Tales* to get the swing of the tales. What qualities account for their popularity with American children?

6. Report on any one of the following topics as it is exemplified in several folk-tale collections: unforgettable characters, notable animals, cinder lads and lassies, the misunderstood, human nature, the will to achieve, poetic justice, "Lover, come back to me," democratic romances, humor, pathos and farce, types of fairy creatures.

7. If you had never read about Paul Bunyan, what would you know about this hero from Rockwell Kent's picture (p. 268)? What are some of the outstanding elements of strength in this illustration?

8. Review the needs discussed in Chapter 1. Choose five or six folk tales (not discussed in the text) that seem to answer these needs.

9. Be able to analyze the form of each of these tales as follows: introduction (theme, conflict); development (plot, logic, unity, economy); conclusion (brevity, completeness, justice); style (beginning and ending, dialogue, use of rhymes or repetitional phrases); characterization (much or little?).

10. Have you encountered any of the misuses of the folk tales discussed in this chapter? What were the results?

11. Describe any particularly enjoyable uses of folk tales which you have observed. Suggest additional ways of using the folk tales.

12. Of the artists who have illustrated single folk tales, which one's work do you like best and why?

REFERENCES

AFANASIEV, ALEXANDER N. *Russian Fairy Tales,* tr. by Norbert Guterman, ill. by A. Alexeieff. Pantheon, 1945. See the valuable "Folkloristic Commentary" by Roman Jakobson.

ANDREWS, ELIZABETH. *Ulster Folklore.* Dutton, 1919. Here are all the historical ramifications of the theory that fairy dwellers in raths and mounds are survivors of an inferior race.

ARBUTHNOT, MAY HILL. *Time for Fairy Tales, Old and New,* ill. by John Averill and others. Scott, 1961. A large collection of favorite folk tales, fables, myths, epics, and modern fanciful tales with introductions concerning their origins, history, and uses. Also included in *The Arbuthnot Anthology.*

ASBJÖRNSEN, PETER C., and JÖRGEN MOE. *Norwegian Folk Tales,* tr. by Pat Shaw Iversen and Carl Norman, ill. by Erik Werenskiold and Theodor Kittelson. Viking, 1961. Thirty-six folk tales in an excellent recent translation which reintroduces the original Asbjörnsen illustrators.

______. *Popular Tales from the Norse,* tr. by Sir George Webbe Dasent. Putnam, n.d. A long and rich introduction by the translator is particularly good on changes from myth to fairy tale.

______. *Tales from the Fjeld,* tr. by Sir George Webbe Dasent, ill. by Moyr Smith. Putnam, 1908. A source book found only in large libraries.

BARCHILON, JACQUES, and HENRY PETTIT. *The Authentic Mother Goose Fairy Tales and Nursery Rhymes* (see Bibliography, Chapter 5).

BENEDICT, RUTH. "Folklore." *Encyclopedia of the Social Sciences,* 6:288-293. A leading student of world cultures discusses and criticizes theories of folklore. An excellent exposition of the modern anthropological and psychological theories.

BETT, HENRY. *Nursery Rhymes and Tales.* Holt, 1924. A comparative study of nursery rhymes and folk tales of many countries, tracing their origins to ancient customs, myths, and rituals.

BOTKIN, BENJAMIN A., ed. *A Treasury of American Folklore.* Crown, 1944. A valuable source for students interested in our native variants of European ballads and tales and our own American tall-tale inventions.

BUNCE, JOHN THACKERY. *Fairy Tales, Their Origin and Meaning.* London: Macmillan, 1878. Based on the discredited theory of Aryan origin but interesting because it traces the parallels of such universal themes as Eros and Cupid.

COLUM, PADRAIC, ed. *A Treasury of Irish Folklore.* Crown, 1954. This book gives insight into Irish history and heroism as well as folklore.

COX, MARIAN ROALFE. *Cinderella, Three Hundred and Forty-Five Variants.* Published for the Folk Lore Society by Nutt, 1893. Marian Cox has pursued the story of "Cinderella" through some forty-three countries and their peoples.

DAVIDSON, LEVETTE J. *A Guide to American Folklore.* Univ. of Denver Press, 1951. A useful introduction to American folklore, with excellent definitions and interpretations of its many aspects, together with bibliographies of outstanding books and periodical materials.

DE AUGULO, JAIME. *Indian Tales,* ill. by author, foreword by Carl Carmer. Hill and Wang, 1953. The author lived forty years among the Pit River Indians and thinks as they think and writes in English as they speak in their language. The time of these stories is the historic dawn, "when men and animals were not so distinguishable as they are today." Chiefly an adult source book.

EASTMAN, MARY HUSE. *Index to Fairy Tales, Myths and Legends* (see Bibliography, Chapter 2).

Funk and Wagnalls Standard Dictionary of Folklore, Mythology and Legend, 2 vols., ed. by Maria Leach and Jerome Fried. Funk and Wagnalls, 1949. Working with a staff of internationally known folklorists and anthropologists the editors have compiled an invaluable source on national folklores, characters, and symbols in folklore and mythology.

GRIMM, JACOB and WILHELM. *Grimm's Fairy Tales,* tr. by Margaret Hunt, rev. by James Stern, ill. by Josef Scharl. Pantheon, 1944. The "Introduction" by Padraic Colum and "Folkloristic Commentary" by Joseph Campbell are important contributions.

———. *Popular Stories,* tr. by Edgar Taylor, ill. by George Cruikshank, a reprint of the first English edition. London: Clowes, 1913. This edition is interesting to adults as a reproduction of the first English translation of the Grimm tales with matchless Cruikshank illustrations.

HARTLAND, EDWIN SIDNEY. *The Science of Fairy Tales.* Stokes, n.d. This, a tribute to the storytellers whose art has preserved the fairy tales, pursues the origins discussion further.

HAZARD, PAUL. *Books, Children and Men* (see Bibliography, Chapter 2).

JACOBS, JOSEPH. See listings in other sections of Bibliography, this chapter. His collections of English, Celtic, and Indian folk tales contain significant introductions, and the notes in each appendix are treasures of folklore information.

KEIGHTLEY, THOMAS. *The Fairy Mythology.* London: Bell, 1892. A fascinating account of the fairies and fairy lore of many countries and times, illustrated with tales recorded from the people.

KRAPPE, ALEXANDER HAGGERTY. *The Science of Folk-Lore* (see Bibliography, Chapter 5). This book covers various types of folk literature, evaluates theories of origin and content, and analyzes motives.

LANG, ANDREW. *Custom and Myth.* Longmans, first printed in 1884. An early study of "the oldest stories" by a brilliant folklorist.

———. *Myth, Ritual and Religion,* 2 vols., Longmans, first printed in 1887. The author traces the wilder and more abhorrent elements in myths and folk tales to their origin in or survival from savagery or barbarism. Chapter XIX, "Heroic and Romantic Myths," discusses the nursery tales.

PERRAULT, CHARLES. *Perrault's Complete Fairy Tales,* tr. by A. E. Johnson and others, ill. by W. Heath Robinson. Dodd, 1961. The unabridged fairy tales of Perrault, together with tales by Mme. de Beaumont and Mme. d'Aulnoy.

RANK, OTTO. *The Myth of the Birth of the Hero: A Psychological Interpretation of Mythology,* trans. by F. Robbins and Smith Ely Jellife. Brunner, 1952. A classic exposition of the connection between the form of myths and the unconscious emotions of the child. Studies the myths of the birth of the hero from Moses to Lohengrin, interpreting each myth in terms of the Oedipus complex.

RICHARDS, GEORGE M. *The Fairy Dictionary,* ill. by author. Macmillan, 1932. Illuminating definitions and sketches of the different types of folk that inhabit fairy land.

(Note: T. Crofton Croker printed his *Fairy Legends and Traditions of the South of Ireland* in 1825, but finer collections were made by Patrick Kennedy, a Dublin bookseller whose *Legendary Fictions of the Irish Celts* was published in 1866 and followed by two more collections in 1867 and 1869. Kennedy's notes prefacing the tales are invaluable for students of Irish folklore, but unfortunately his books have been allowed to go out of print. Lady Wilde's *Ancient Legends of Ireland* (1887) is a good source for adult students of folklore.)

COLLECTIONS OF TALES

African and Ethiopian

AARDEMA, VERNA. *Tales from the Story Hat,* ill. by Elton Fax. Coward, 1960. Folk tales from South Africa told with spontaneity and humor. 8-12

ARNOTT, KATHLEEN. *African Myths and Legends,* ill. by Joan Kiddell-Monroe. Walck, 1963. Tales from south of the Sahara, thirty-four in all, tell of "animals, humans, and superhumans." 11-

BURTON, W. F. P. *The Magic Drum; Tales from Central Africa,* ill. by Ralph Thompson. Criterion, 1962. Short tales with a fablelike quality that are favorites in the Congo. Illustrated with humor and imagination. 9-12

COURLANDER, HAROLD. *The King's Drum and Other Stories,* ill. by Enrico Arno. Harcourt, 1962. Almost thirty stories from Africa identified by tribal sources. Excellent notes are appended on the origins or interpretations of these folk tales. 9-13

COURLANDER, HAROLD, and GEORGE HERZOG. *The Cow-Tail Switch, and Other West African Stories,* ill. by Madye Lee Chastain. Holt, 1947. Seventeen tales, told in lively style and revealing much about the customs of the people. 10-12

COURLANDER, HAROLD, and WOLF LESLAU. *The Fire on the Mountain and Other Ethiopian Stories,* ill. by Robert W. Kane. Holt, 1950. Outstanding in style, illustrations, and content. 10-14

COURLANDER, HAROLD, and ALBERT PREMPEH. *The Hat-Shaking Dance, and Other Tales from the Gold Coast,* ill. by Enrico Arno. Harcourt, 1957. Humorous, droll, or wise are these twenty-one tales of Anansi. 9-12

GILSTRAP, ROBERT, and IRENE ESTABROOK. *The Sultan's Fool and Other North African Tales,* ill. by Robert Greco. Holt, 1958. Eleven wise and witty tales, excellent for reading aloud and storytelling. 9-12

MOZLEY, CHARLES. *First Book of Tales of Ancient Egypt,* ill. by author. Watts, 1960. Folklore of Egypt, richly illustrated in color, offers a cultural supplement to the study of this ancient land. 9-12

Arabian

Arabian Nights, retold by Amabel Williams-Ellis, ill. by Pauline Diana Baynes. Criterion, 1957. Lively retellings of the children's favorites together with several lesser known tales. 10-13

The Arabian Nights, ill. by Earle Goodenow. Grosset, 1946. An attractive and inexpensive edition. 10-14

BROWN, MARCIA. *The Flying Carpet,* ill. by author. Scribner, 1956. This story, so much a part of our language and so difficult to find, is beautifully retold and illustrated. 6-10

COLUM, PADRAIC, ed. *The Arabian Nights: Tales of Wonder and Magnificence,* ill. by Lynd Ward. Macmillan, 1953. Republished after thirty years, in a new and attractive edition, this outstanding collection will appeal to younger readers. 10-14

LANG, ANDREW, ed. *Arabian Nights,* ill. by Vera Bock. McKay, 1946. Fine black-and-white drawings and large print make this a favorite edition for children's reading. 10-14

Tales from the Arabian Nights, ed. by E. O. Lorimer, ill. by Brian Wildsmith. Walck, 1962. Outstanding retellings based on the Lang translation, illustrated in lush color by a noted British artist. 11-15

WIGGIN, KATE DOUGLAS, and NORA SMITH, eds. *Arabian Nights, Their Best Known Tales,* ill. by Maxfield Parrish. Scribner, 1909. Here are the favorite stories—"Aladdin," "Ali Baba," "The Voyage of Sinbad the Sailor"—gorgeously illustrated in color and well told." 10-14

Canadian

BARBEAU, MARIUS. *The Golden Phoenix; and Other French-Canadian Fairy Tales,* retold by Michael Hornyansky, ill. by Arthur Price. Walck, 1958. Notes as to their origin give these eight tales a special interest for the student. Told with humor and zest. 10-13

CARLSON, NATALIE SAVAGE. *The Talking Cat and Other Stories of French Canada,* ill. by Roger Duvoisin. Harper, 1952. Tales told with vitality and humor and excellent for reading aloud. 8-11

Chinese

BIRCH, CYRIL. *Chinese Myths and Fantasies,* ill. by Joan Kiddell-Monroe. Walck, 1961. Ghosts and magicians and plain folk, too, are characters in this absorbing collection of tales. 11-

BISHOP, CLAIRE. *The Five Chinese Brothers,* ill. by Kurt Wiese. Coward, 1938. This Chinese version of five brothers, each with a magical gift, has been a favorite ever since it appeared. 5-10

CARPENTER, FRANCES. *Tales of a Chinese Grandmother,* ill. by Malthé Hasselriis. Doubleday, 1937. The "Grandmother" series for different racial groups is a reliable source, with many good stories. 9-12

LIM, SIAN-TEK. *Folk Tales from China,* ill. by William Arthur Smith. Day, 1944. An excellent selection of folk and legendary tales.

______. *More Folk Tales from China,* ill. by William Arthur Smith. Day, 1948. 12-16

MERRILL, JEAN. *The Superlative Horse,* ill. by Ronni Solbert. W. R. Scott, 1961. An unassuming stable lad becomes head groom in the royal stables when he selects the perfect horse. Based on a Taoist legend and illustrated in ancient Chinese style. 9-11

RITCHIE, ALICE. *The Treasure of Li-Po,* ill. by T. Ritchie. Harcourt, 1949. These six original fairy tales are told with all the sincerity and dignity of the folk tales which they resemble. 10-14

Czechoslovakian

FILLMORE, PARKER. *Shepherd's Nosegay,* ed. by Katherine Love, ill. by Enrico Arno. Harcourt, 1958. Eighteen tales of Finland and Czechoslovakia compiled from Fillmore's out-of-print collections. Excellent for telling and reading aloud. 9-12

Danish

HATCH, MARY COTTAM. *13 Danish Tales, Retold,* ill. by Edgun (pseud.). Harcourt, 1947. These stories are excellent for reading or storytelling, and are carefully adapted from the Bay translation. 9-13

______. *More Danish Tales, Retold,* ill. by Edgun (pseud.). Harcourt, 1949. 9-13

JONES, GWYN. *Scandinavian Legends and Folk Tales* (see Bibliography, Norwegian tales).

English, Scottish, and Welsh

BROWN, MARCIA. *Dick Whittington and His Cat,* ill. by author. Scribner, 1950. A lively, readable adaptation of this classic hero tale with strong linoleum cuts in two colors. 4-8

GALDONE, PAUL, ill. *The Old Woman and Her Pig.* McGraw, 1960. The old nursery favorite is reintroduced as a lively picture book. Another nursery classic made into a picture book by the artist is *Old Mother Hubbard and Her Dog* (1960). 4-7

HAVILAND, VIRGINIA, ed. *Favorite Fairy Tales Told in Scotland,* ill. by Adrienne Adams. Little, 1963. Six of the more familiar tales retold for the reading of younger children. 8-10

JACOBS, JOSEPH, ed. *English Fairy Tales,* ill. by John D. Batten. Putnam, n.d.

______. *More English Fairy Tales,* ill. by John D. Batten. Putnam, n.d.

These not only are reliable sources for the favorite English tales but are also appealing to children in format and illustrations. 9-12

______. *Favorite Fairy Tales Told in England,* retold by Virginia Haviland, ill. by Bettina (pseud.). Little, 1959. Six tales in attractive large-print format imaginatively illustrated. 8-9

JONES, GWYN. *Welsh Legends and Folk Tales,* ill. by Joan Kiddell-Monroe. Walck, 1955. Retellings of ancient sagas as well as folk and fairy tales are included. Illustrations in color are particularly outstanding. 11-14

LEODHAS, SORCHE NIC (pseud.). *Heather and Broom,* ill. by Consuelo Joerns. Holt, 1960. Highland tales of wee folk and of the clans, rich in imaginative quality, are retold from the Gaelic. 10-12

______ (pseud.), ed. *Thistle and Thyme,* ill. by Evaline Ness. Holt, 1962. Ten Scottish tales of romance and magic which are a delight to read, but more difficult for storytelling than the compiler's earlier *Heather and Broom.* 10-12

REEVES, JAMES. *English Fables and Fairy Stories,* ill. by Joan Kiddell-Monroe. Walck, 1954. An attractive collection of nineteen tales illustrated in two colors. 10-14

SHEPPARD-JONES, ELISABETH. *Scottish Legendary Tales,* ill. by Paul Hogarth. Nelson, 1962. Forty traditional tales of folk and fairy people, vividly told for both storyteller and reader. A companion volume is *Welsh Legendary Tales* (1960). 10-13

STEEL, FLORA ANNIE. *English Fairy Tales,* ill. by Arthur Rackham, with an afterword by Clifton Fadiman. Macmillan, 1962. This book has the imaginative pictures of Rackham and the excellent adaptations of Mrs. Steel. All the favorites are here. 8-12

TREGARTHEN, ENYS (pseud. for Nellie Sloggett). *Piskey Folk, A Book of Cornish Legends.* Day, 1940. A rare collection for the storyteller, full of the pranks of the piskeys. 8-12

______. *The White Ring,* ed. by Elizabeth Yates, ill. by Nora S. Unwin. Harcourt, 1949. An exquisite Celtic fairy tale about Cornish fairies. To be read aloud. 7-12

WILSON, BARBARA KER. *Scottish Folk Tales and Legends,* ill. by Joan Kiddell-Monroe. Walck, 1954. In addition to the folk tales, a section of stories on the legendary exploits of the Fians is included. Attractive format and illustrations. 11-14

Eskimo

GILLHAM, CHARLES EDWARD. *Beyond the Clapping Mountains: Eskimo Stories from Alaska,* ill. by Chanimum. Macmillan, 1943. Illustrated by an Eskimo girl, these are unusual and highly imaginative tales. 10-12

Filipino

SECHRIST, ELIZABETH H. *Once in the First Times; Folk Tales from the Philippines,* ill. by John Sheppard. Macrae-Smith Co., 1949. This small book includes fifty Filipino folk tales—"why" stories, tales of the creation, legends, hero tales, and romances. 8-12

Finnish

BOWMAN, JAMES CLOYD, and MARGERY BIANCO. *Tales from a Finnish Tupa,* from a tr. by Aili Kolehmainen, ill. by Laura Bannon. Whitman, 1936. Here are the everyday folk tales of the Finnish people, not the epic stories. Beautifully told, with effective illustrations. 10-14

French

COONEY, BARBARA. *The Little Juggler,* ill. by author. Hastings, 1961. In this appealing picture-story version of the old legend, an orphan boy is the little juggler who offers his only skill at the monastery altar. 8-11

DOUGLAS, BARBARA, comp. *Favourite French Fairy Tales; Retold from the French of Perrault, Madame d'Aulnoy, and Madame Leprince de Beaumont,* ill. by R. Cramer. Dodd, 1952. "Beauty and the Beast" and "Prince Darling" by Mme. de Beaumont, and "The White Cat" and "Goldenlocks" by Mme. d'Aulnoy are included with the Perrault tales. 9-12

PERRAULT, CHARLES. *All the French Fairy Tales,* retold by Louis Untermeyer, ill. by Gustave Doré. Didier Pubs., 1946. The reproduction of the superb Doré illustrations makes this edition a notable one. 9-12

______. *Cinderella; or The Little Glass Slipper,* ill. by Marcia Brown. Scribner, 1954. Attractive pastel illustrations. Caldecott Medal. 5-9

______. *Favorite Fairy Tales Told in France,* retold by Virginia Haviland, ill. by Roger Duvoisin. Little, 1959. Five well-loved tales include "Puss in Boots," "Beauty and the Beast," and "Sleeping Beauty." Large print and attractive illustrations. 8-10

______. *Puss in Boots,* ill. by Marcia Brown. Scribner, 1952. Wonderful pictures enliven this story of the faithful cat who helps to make a lord of his poor young master. 6-9

______. *Puss in Boots,* ill. by Hans Fischer. Harcourt, 1959. A noted Swiss artist interjects a subtle humor of his own into the pictures and his retelling of Perrault's tale. 5-8

PICARD, BARBARA LEONIE. *French Legends, Tales and Fairy Stories,* ill. by Joan Kiddell-Monroe. Walck, 1955. A rich and varied source of folklore ranging from epic literature to medieval tales; from legends to fairy tales. 10-14

POURRAT, HENRI, ed. *A Treasury of French Tales,* tr. by Mary Mian, ill. by Pauline Baynes. Houghton, 1954. A collection of over forty tales told with vitality and humor. 10-14

German

ANGLUND, JOAN WALSH. *Nibble Nibble Mousekin,* ill. by author. Harcourt, 1962. Mrs. Anglund's drawings of guileless children add an appealing note to this colorful picture-book tale of "Hänsel and Gretel." 5-8

GRIMM, JACOB and WILHELM. *Gone Is Gone,* retold and ill. by Wanda Gág. Coward, 1935. Lively retelling of the old tale about the man and wife who exchanged household duties for a day. 6-8

______. *Snow White and the Seven Dwarfs,* freely tr. and ill. by Wanda Gág. Coward, 1938.

______. *Tales from Grimm,* freely tr. and ill. by Wanda Gág. Coward, 1936.

______. *Three Gay Tales from Grimm,* tr. and ill. by Wanda Gág. Coward, 1943. Wanda Gág's narration is lively, natural, and simple. So are the illustrations. Both text and pictures preserve the folk flavor of the tales, and children feel at once that these books belong to them. 8-12

______. *Favorite Fairy Tales Told in Germany,* retold by Virginia Haviland, ill. by Susanne Suba. Little, 1959. "Hänsel and Gretel," "Rapunzel," and "Frog Prince" are among the seven selections in this attractive, large-print edition. 5-8

______. *Grimm's Fairy Tales.* Pantheon (see References).

______. *Grimm's Fairy Tales,* tr. by Mrs. E. V. Lucas and others, ill. by Fritz Kredel. Grosset, 1945. An edition that is thoroughly satisfactory to children. The excellent translation is supplemented by bright, appealing pictures. 9-12

______. *Grimm's Tales,* ill. by Helen Sewell and Madeleine Gekiere. Walck, 1954. Fine format and distinctive modern illustrations characterize this collection of sixteen tales. 10-12

______. *Household Stories from the Collection of the Brothers Grimm,* tr. by Lucy Crane, ill. by Johannes Troyer. Macmillan, 1954. Thirty-two favorite tales are included in this attractive, large-print edition. 10-12

______. *The Shoemaker and the Elves,* ill. by Adrienne Adams. Scribner, 1960. Colorful illustrations add new beauty to one of the Grimms' best-loved tales for little children. 3-6

______. *The Sleeping Beauty,* ill. by Felix Hoffmann. Harcourt, 1960. The richly toned pictures make a rare contribution to this American edition, originally published in Switzerland. Other Grimm tales illustrated by this artist include *The Wolf and the Seven Little Kids* (1959) and *The Seven Ravens* (1963). 5-9

______. *The Traveling Musicians,* ill. by Hans Fischer. Harcourt, 1955. Distinctive illustrations in color make this an outstanding folk-tale picture book. 5-8

HAUFF, WILHELM. *Dwarf Long-Nose,* tr. by Doris Orgel, ill. by Maurice Sendak. Random, 1960. Poor Jacob displeases a witch and spends years as an ugly dwarf before regaining his true form and a handsome bride as well. An excellent translation, appealingly illustrated. 9-11

PICARD, BARBARA LEONIE. *German Hero-Sagas and Folk-Tales,* ill. by Joan Kiddell-Monroe. Walck, 1958. *Siegfried* and other sagas, as well as such folk tales as *Ratcatcher of Hamelin,* give children a broader background of German lore than the more familiar Grimm tales. 11-14

India and Pakistan

BABBITT, ELLEN C. *The Jataka Tales,* ill. by Ellsworth Young. Appleton, 1912.

______. *More Jataka Tales,* ill. by Ellsworth Young. Appleton, 1912.

These are valuable sources of East Indian fables. Recently reissued in school editions. 6-10

BROWN, MARCIA. *Once a Mouse,* ill. by author. Scribner, 1961. The timid mouse was changed by a kindly hermit into a cat, a dog, and then a tiger who became so cruel he had to be punished. Caldecott Medal. 5-8

GRAY, JOHN E. B. *India's Tales and Legends,* ill. by Joan Kiddell-Monroe. Walck, 1961. Truly distinguished retellings of India's rich lore, which will appeal to older children. 11-

JACOBS, JOSEPH, ed. *Indian Fairy Tales,* ill. by J. D. Batten. Putnam, 1892. Like Jacobs' other collections, these stories are selected from manuscript sources. They also throw light on fable and folktale origins. 9-12

QUIGLEY, LILLIAN. *The Blind Men and the Elephant; An Old Tale from the Land of India,* ill. by Janice Holland. Scribner, 1959. The popular and often quoted tale of the blind men who, in describing an elephant, "saw" only what they could feel. 5-9

SIDDIQUI, ASHRAF, and MARILYN LERCH. *Toontoony Pie, and Other Tales from Pakistan,* ill. by Jan Fairservis. World, 1961. Stories gathered at first hand from the ancient regions that are now Pakistan. There are lively tales of the royal and the poor and fable-like tales of animal wisdom. 9-12

TURNBULL, E. LUCIA. *Fairy Tales of India,* ill. by Hazel Cook. Criterion, 1960. Sixteen magical tales from India, attractive for reading aloud as well as for the children's own reading. 9-12

Irish

BENNETT, RICHARD. *Little Dermot and the Thirsty Stones, and Other Irish Folk Tales,* ill. by Richard Bennett. Coward, 1953. Eight lively tales with appeal for younger readers. The title story is especially good for storytelling. 9-12

COLUM, PADRAIC. *The King of Ireland's Son,* ill. by Willy Pogány. Macmillan, 1921, 1962. Seven Irish folk tales about a brave young royal lad. 10-12

HAVILAND, VIRGINIA, ed. *Favorite Fairy Tales Told in Ireland,* ill. by Arthur Markovia. Little, 1961. "Old Hag's Long Leather Bag" and "Billy Beg and the Bull" are among the popular tales included in this attractive, large-print collection. 8-11

JACOBS, JOSEPH, ed. *Celtic Fairy Tales,* ill. by John D. Batten. Putnam, 1892.

———. *More Celtic Fairy Tales,* ill. by John D. Batten. Putnam, n.d. Jacobs includes Welsh, Scotch, Cornish, and Irish in his two Celtic collections. His copious notes are of great value. 9-12

MACMANUS, SEUMAS. *Hibernian Nights,* ill. by Paul Kennedy. Macmillan, 1963. The "last of the great Irish storytellers" compiled this rich collection of twenty-two of his favorite tales chosen from his earlier books. Padraic Colum's introduction is a gracious tribute to MacManus and his storyteller's art. 11-

MASON, ARTHUR. *The Wee Men of Ballywooden,* ill. by Robert Lawson. Viking, 1952. Humorous and enchanting fairy tales the author remembers hearing as a child. 10-14

O'FAOLAIN, EILEEN. *Irish Sagas and Folk-Tales,* ill. by Joan Kiddell-Monroe. Walck, 1954. This distinguished collection contains epic tales and folk tales to delight both reader and storyteller. 10-14

Italian

CHAFETZ, HENRY. *The Legend of Befana,* ill. by Ronni Solbert. Houghton, 1958. The old Italian Christmas legend beautifully retold and illustrated. 5-9

JAGENDORF, M. A. *The Priceless Cats and Other Italian Folk Stories,* ill. by Gioia Fiamenghi. Vanguard, 1956. An attractive and gay collection for the children's own reading. 10-13

VITTORINI, DOMENICO. *Old Italian Tales,* ill. by Kathryn L. Fligg. McKay, 1958. Twenty short tales alive with humor and wisdom offer fine reading-aloud fun. 7-12

Japanese

BARUCH, DOROTHY. *Kappa's Tug-of-War with Big Brown Horse,* ill. by Sanryo Sakai. Tuttle, 1962. Retelling of an old legend of a little water-imp who steals what he wants, and is at last outwitted by Farmer Shiba. 6-8

EDMONDS, I. G. *Ooka the Wise: Tales of Old Japan,* ill. by Sanae Yamazaki. Bobbs, 1961. Ooka, the shrewd old Japanese judge, solves with wisdom and humor the problems that beset his fellow townsmen. An intriguing series of tales for reading and telling. 9-12

MCALPINE, HELEN and WILLIAM, comp. *Japanese Tales and Legends,* retold by the McAlpines, ill. by Joan Kiddell-Monroe. Walck, 1959. A choice selection from the folklore, legends, and epic tales of Japan. 10-14

STAMM, CLAUS, ed. *Three Strong Women: A Tall Tale from Japan,* ill. by Kazue Mizumura. Viking, 1962. A sturdy girl, her mother, and her grandmother train a cocky young wrestler to new heights of strength for a court performance. A humorous read-aloud, color illustrated. 8-11

———. *The Very Special Badgers; A Tale of Magic from Japan,* ill. by Kazue Mizumura. Viking, 1960. An amusing and humorous tale of how two badger clans settle a dispute. 8-10

UCHIDA, YOSHIKO. *The Dancing Kettle and Other*

Japanese Folk Tales, retold, ill. by Richard C. Jones. Harcourt, 1949. Fourteen Japanese folk tales, some of them familiar, many of them new, make this a welcome addition to folklore collections.

______. *The Magic Listening Cap, More Folk Tales from Japan,* ill. by author. Harcourt, 1955. The author-artist has illustrated this second collection with the distinctive simplicity characteristic of Japanese art. 9-12

YAMAGUCHI, TOHR. *The Golden Crane,* ill. by Marianne Yamaguchi. Holt, 1963. When a sacred golden crane is injured, a small boy rescues it and risks his life to save it from the avaricious who want it as a trophy. Based on a Japanese folk tale, both story and illustrations are artistically lovely. 8-10

Korean

JEWETT, ELEANORE MYERS. *Which Was Witch? Tales of Ghosts and Magic from Korea,* ill. by Taro Yashima [pseud. for Jun Iwamatsu]. Viking, 1953. Fourteen stories with sparkle and suspense, excellent for storytelling. 9-13

Mexican and South American

FINGER, CHARLES J. *Tales from Silver Lands.* Doubleday, 1924. The author gathered these outstanding folk tales from the Indians during his South American travels. Newbery Medal. 10-14

HENIUS, FRANK, ed. *Stories from the Americas,* ill. by Leo Politi. Scribner, 1944. Twenty folk tales and legends which are favorites of the peoples in Mexico, Central and South America. 9-11

JAGENDORF, M. A., and R. S. BOGGS. *The King of the Mountains; A Treasury of Latin American Folk Stories,* ill. by Carybé. Vanguard, 1960. More than fifty tales, listed by country of origin. 10-14

JORDAN, PHILIP D. *The Burro Benedicto and Other Folk Tales and Legends of Mexico,* ill. by author. Coward, 1960. This handsomely color-illustrated book contains eighteen legends and tales, many of which illustrate Christian and Aztec beliefs. 9-11

LOVELACE, MAUD and DELOS W. *The Golden Wedge,* ill. by Charlotte Anna Chase. Crowell, 1942. Myths and legends of the South American Indians which had their origin before the white man came. 10-14

Norwegian

ASBJÖRNSEN, PETER C., and JÖRGEN MOE. *East o' the Sun and West o' the Moon,* ill. by Hedvig Collin. Macmillan, 1953. A new and attractive edition of a title which appeared twenty-five years ago. Based on the Dasent translation. 10-14

______. *East o' the Sun and West o' the Moon,* ill. by Kay Nielsen. Doubleday, 1922. Fifteen favorite stories with highly imaginative illustrations. 10-14

______. *Norwegian Folk Tales* (see References, this chapter). 10-13

______. *The Three Billy Goats Gruff,* ill. by Marcia Brown. Harcourt, 1957. A favorite folk tale appears in brightly colored picture-book format. 4-7

HAVILAND, VIRGINIA, ed. *Favorite Fairy Tales Told in Norway,* retold by Virginia Haviland, ill. by Leonard Weisgard. Little, 1961. Seven familiar tales, handsomely illustrated in three colors. Includes "Why the Sea Is Salt," "Taper Tom," and "Princess on the Glass Hill." 8-11

JONES, GWYN. *Scandinavian Legends and Folk Tales,* ill. by Joan Kiddell-Monroe. Walck, 1956. Another Oxford contribution to folk-tale collections, this contains several of the familiar stories. Others are hero tales and unusual examples of folklore told with humor and impressive art. 8-12

THORNE-THOMSEN, GUDRUN. *East o' the Sun and West o' the Moon,* rev. ed., ill. by Frederick Richardson. Row, 1946. The stories are adapted from the original by a famous storyteller. 7-12

UNDSET, SIGRID, ed. *True and Untrue and Other Norse Tales,* ill. by Frederick T. Chapman. Knopf, 1945. A good collection for storytelling and for children's own reading. The author's foreword on the subject of folklore will appeal to the student. 10-13

Polish

BORSKI, LUCIA M., and KATE B. MILLER. *The Jolly Tailor, and Other Fairy Tales,* ill. by Kazimir Klephacki. McKay, 1957. Reissued after many years, this collection translated from the Polish offers fine material for reading and storytelling. 9-12

HAVILAND, VIRGINIA, ed. *Favorite Fairy Tales Told in Poland,* ill. by Felix Hoffmann. Little, 1963. Six tales appealingly retold and illustrated. Large-print format appeals to younger readers. 8-10

Russian

ARTZYBASHEFF, BORIS. *Seven Simeons; a Russian Tale,* retold and ill. by the author. Viking, 1961. 7-10

DOWNING, CHARLES. *Russian Tales and Legends,* ill. by Joan Kiddell-Monroe. Walck, 1957. Epic, folk, and fairy tales gathered from many areas of Russia. 11-

GRISHINA-GIVAGO, NADEJDA, *Peter Pea.* Lippincott, 1926. This is the Russian Hop o' My Thumb—no bigger than a pea. He is adopted by a princess and has many amusing adventures in the palace. When the princess plants him on his request, he grows into a handsome young man and they live happily ever after. A charming picture-story. 6-7

HAVILAND, VIRGINIA, ed. *Favorite Fairy Tales Told in Russia,* ill. by Herbert Danska. Little, 1961. Among the five tales included in this color-illustrated, large-print book are "The Straw Ox," "Flying Ship," and "To Your Good Health." 8-11

PROKOFIEFF, SERGE. *Peter and the Wolf,* ill. by Warren Chappell. Knopf, 1940. Delightful picture-book story about young Peter, who outwitted the wolf to rescue the duck. Excerpts from the musical score accompany the text. 7-10

RANSOME, ARTHUR. *Old Peter's Russian Tales,* ill. by Dmītriĭ Mītrokhīn. Nelson, 1917. This is the teacher's most practical source for the Russian tales. They are in admirable style for telling or reading aloud or dramatizing. 8-12

ROBBINS, RUTH. *Baboushka and the Three Kings,* ill. by Nicolas Sidjakov. Parnassus, 1960. The familiar Russian folk tale of the selfish old woman and the Wise Men is enhanced by striking modern illustrations. Caldecott Medal. 5-10

WHEELER, POST. *Russian Wonder Tales,* ill. by Bilibin. Beechhurst Press, Inc., 1946. Serving in diplomatic posts in various parts of the world, Post Wheeler gathered the folklore of the people. 11-14

Spanish

BOGGS, RALPH STEELE, and MARY GOULD DAVIS. *The Three Golden Oranges and Other Spanish Folk Tales,* ill. by Emma Brock. McKay, 1936. Stories for older children, romantic and exciting. One remarkable ghost story. 10-12

DAVIS, ROBERT. *Padre Porko,* ill. by Fritz Eichenberg. Holiday, 1948. Padre Porko, the gentlemanly pig, has all the benignance of the Buddha animals, and a certain mannerly elegance besides. Amusing tales, enhanced by good pen-and-ink sketches. 8-12

EELLS, ELSIE SPICER. *Tales of Enchantment from Spain,* ill. by Maud and Miska Petersham. Dodd, 1950. These are romantic tales, rich in magic. 10-14

HAVILAND, VIRGINIA, ed. *Favorite Fairy Tales Told in Spain,* ill. by Barbara Cooney. Little, 1963. Six delightful Spanish tales retold. 8-10

Swiss

DUVOISIN, ROGER. *The Three Sneezes and Other Swiss Tales,* ill. by author. Knopf, 1941. Humorous tales, many of which are based on the theme of the stupid fellow who succeeds. 9-12

MÜLLER-GUGGENBÜHL, FRITZ. *Swiss-Alpine Folk-Tales,* tr. by Katharine Potts, ill. by Joan Kiddell-Monroe. Walck, 1958. These tales are a distinguished collection of national folklore in the Oxford series of Myths and Legends. 10-14

United States: North American Indian

BELL, CORYDON. *John Rattling-Gourd of Big Cave: A Collection of Cherokee Indian Legends,* ill. by Corydon Bell. Macmillan, 1955. An outstanding collection of twenty-four legends, many of them about natural phenomena. Fine black-and-white illustrations. 10-14

BELTING, NATALIA M. *The Long Tailed Bear and Other Indian Legends,* ill. by Louis F. Cary. Bobbs, 1961. Animal legends of twenty-two tribes make this a valuable source. The large-print format will appeal to children, and storytellers will welcome the tribal identification preceding each story. 8-10

BROUN, EMILY (pseud. for E. G. Sterne). *A Ball for Little Bear,* ill. by Dick Mackay. Aladdin, 1955. How the world was rescued from darkness after Big Bear took the sun from the sky for Little Bear to play with.

______. *How Rabbit Stole Fire,* ill. by Jack Ferguson. Aladdin, 1954. A humorous Cherokee legend of how Rabbit stole sacred fire and gave it to the people. 7-10

FISHER, ANNE B. *Stories California Indians Told,* ill. by Ruth Robbins. Parnassus, 1957. A dozen Indian myths told with zest and ranging from creation myths to such humorous tales as "Why Women Talk More Than Men." 9-12

GRINNELL, GEORGE BIRD. *Blackfoot Lodge Tales.* Univ. of Nebr. Press, 1962. Authentic, unadapted tales, taken down from the tribal storytellers. Originally published in 1892. 10-14

HARRIS, CHRISTIE. *Once Upon a Totem,* ill. by John Frazer Mills. Atheneum, 1963. Five superb tales of the Indians of the North Pacific. 9-12

MACFARLAN, ALLAN A. *Indian Adventure Trails; Tales of Trails and Tipis, Ponies and Paddles, Warpaths and Warriors,* ill. by Paulette Jumeau and Bob Hofsinde (Gray Wolf). Dodd, 1953. These stories offer more plot and action than many of the Indian folk tales. 11-14

MACMILLAN, CYRUS. *Glooskap's Country, and Other Indian Tales,* ill. by John A. Hall. Walck, 1956. First published in 1918 as *Canadian Wonder Tales,* this is one of the finest collections of Indian stories available. They range from simple "how" stories to complex and mystical tales of magic, superbly told and illustrated. 8-12

MARTIN, FRAN. *Nine Tales of Coyote,* ill. by Dorothy McEntee. Harper, 1950. Authentic tales of Coyote, the Indian animal god. The stories are lively and have a quality of suspense. Illustrations are in color.

———. *Nine Tales of Raven,* ill. by Dorothy McEntee. Harper, 1951. These tales of the Northwest Coast Indians appear in attractive format. 8-11

PENNEY, GRACE. *Tales of the Cheyennes,* ill. by Walter Richard West. Houghton, 1953. Long-ago legends explaining nature and customs, and a group of humorous tales chiefly about the Indian Wihio, who liked to play tricks. 10-14

United States: North American Negro

DUNCAN, EULA G. *Big Road Walker,* ill. by Fritz Eichenberg. Lippincott, 1940. A collection of Negro tall tales as told to the author by Alice Cannon. Big Road Walker is a giant who goes "steppin' a mile a step" but can't keep out of trouble without the help of his little wife Hokey. Traditional folklore, written in dialect. 8-10

HARRIS, JOEL CHANDLER. *Complete Tales of Uncle Remus,* ed. by Richard Chase. Houghton, 1955.

———. *Uncle Remus: His Songs and Sayings,* rev. ed., ill. by A. B. Frost. Appleton, 1947.

———. *Uncle Remus: His Songs and His Sayings,* with a foreword by Marc Connelly and woodcuts by Seong Moy. Heritage, 1959. 10-

United States: tall tales and other native inventions

BLAIR, WALTER. *Tall Tale America: A Legendary History of Our Humorous Heroes,* ill. by Glen Rounds. Coward, 1944. These tales, collected, retold, and sometimes originated by the author of *Native American Humor,* range from Leif the Lucky, who discovered America and then misplaced it, to a mythical Professor Blur lost in the Pentagon Building. 10-14

BONTEMPS, ARNA, and JACK CONROY. *The Fast Sooner Hound,* ill. by Virginia Lee Burton. Houghton, 1942. How this tall-tale hound could outrun any train, even the Cannon Ball, is gravely related and hilariously pictured. 8-12

———. *Sam Patch, the High, Wide and Handsome Jumper,* ill. by Paul Brown. Houghton, 1951. Another tall tale enhanced with wonderful action pictures. 10-12

BOWMAN, JAMES CLOYD. *Mike Fink,* ill. by Leonard Everett Fisher. Little, 1957. Mike Fink was one of the greatest legendary riverboatmen, and his adventures are related in tall-tale tradition. 11-

———. *Pecos Bill,* ill. by Laura Bannon. Whitman, 1937. Pecos Bill is the gayest of our heroes and the closest to the child's sense of humor. The illustrations add to the book's appeal. 9-12

CREDLE, ELLIS. *Tall Tales from the High Hills,* ill. by author. Nelson, 1957. Lively folk tales from the North Carolina Blue Ridge country, fine for reading and telling. 9-12

FELTON, HAROLD W. *Bowleg Bill, Seagoing Cowpuncher,* ill. by William Moyers. Prentice-Hall, 1957. Tall-tale nonsense about a cowboy who solves his problems in his own cowboy way. 10-

———. *John Henry and His Hammer,* ill. by Aldren A. Watson. Knopf, 1950. The author has compiled a dramatic and effective account of the Negro superman's life, a part of our railroad epic. 10-13

FIELD, RACHEL. *American Folk and Fairy Tales,* ill. by Margaret Freeman. Scribner, 1929. An early collection of such diverse items as Indian legends, Negro stories, tall tales, Southern mountaineer stories, and two classics, "Rip Van Winkle" and "The Great Stone Face." 10-14

JAGENDORF, MORITZ. *New England Bean Pot: American Folk Stories to Read and to Tell,* ill. by Donald McKay. Vanguard, 1948. Folk tales of six New England states told with zest and humor. Two other titles in this regional series are: *Sand in the Bag and Other Folk Stories of Ohio, Indiana and Illinois,* ill. by John Moment. Vanguard, 1952; and *Upstate, Downstate; Folk Stories of the Middle Atlantic States,* ill. by Howard Simon. Vanguard, 1949. 10-14

MALCOLMSON, ANNE. *Yankee Doodle's Cousins,* ill. by Robert McCloskey. Houghton, 1941. This is one of the finest collections of real and mythical heroes of the United States. 10-14

MARGOLIS, ELLEN, ed. *Idy, the Fox-Chasing Cow and Other Stories,* ill. by Kurt Werth. World, 1962. Seven humorous folk tales from the Ohio region that will be welcomed by storytellers. 9-12

PECK, LEIGH. *Pecos Bill and Lightning,* ill. by Kurt Wiese. Houghton, 1940. A brief edition with copious illustrations to aid the slow reader. 8-12

ROUNDS, GLEN. *Ol' Paul, the Mighty Logger,* ill. by author. Holiday, 1949. These Paul Bunyan stories are retold with an earthy, exuberant zest. 10-

SHAPIRO, IRWIN. *Heroes in American Folklore,* ill. by Donald McKay and James Daugherty. Messner, 1962. Five tall-tale heroes include Casey Jones, Joe Magarac, John Henry, Steamboat Bill, and Old Stormalong.

———. *Yankee Thunder, the Legendary Life of Davy Crockett,* ill. by James Daugherty. Messner, 1944. The author is torn between writing about the real Davy and the mythical Davy, but chooses the latter—"Yaller blossom of the forest, half horse, half snapping turtle, the ring-tailed roarer.

. . ." The pictures are as vigorous as the hero. 10-14

SHEPHARD, ESTHER. *Paul Bunyan,* ill. by Rockwell Kent. Harcourt, 1941. The most complete edition of these tales, this book also has Rockwell Kent's superb pictures. 10-14

United States: variants of European tales

CHASE, RICHARD, ed. *Grandfather Tales,* ill. by Berkeley Williams, Jr. Houghton, 1948. 9-12

———. *Jack and the Three Sillies,* ill. by Joshua Tolford. Houghton, 1950. 8-10

———. *The Jack Tales,* ill. by Berkeley Williams, Jr. Houghton, 1943. 9-12

———. *Wicked John and the Devil,* ill. by Joshua Tolford. Houghton, 1951. 9-12

The American versions of the old-world tales are as vigorous as the mountain folk of the Cumberlands and the Smokies from whom they came.

COTHRAN, JEAN, ed. *With a Wig, With a Wag, and Other American Folk Tales,* ill. by Clifford N. Geary. McKay, 1954. Many of these tales suggest variants in European and other folklores. A final chapter describes their parallels. 9-12

SAWYER, RUTH. *Journey Cake, Ho!* ill. by Robert McCloskey. Viking, 1953. Mountain folk-tale version of *The Pancake.* Lively illustrations make this an attractive picture book. 6-10

Other countries

BAKER, AUGUSTA, comp. *The Golden Lynx and Other Tales,* ill. by Johannes Troyer. Lippincott, 1960. Sixteen folk tales from around the world that are excellent for storytelling. 10-13

CARPENTER, FRANCES. *The Elephant's Bathtub; Wonder Tales from the Far East,* ill. by Hans Guggenheim. Doubleday, 1962. Burma, Cambodia, Malaya, Vietnam, and other lands of the Far East are represented in the twenty-four tales of humor and enchantment. 11-14

COURLANDER, HAROLD. *The Tiger's Whisker and Other Tales and Legends from Asia and the Pacific,* ill. by Enrico Arno. Harcourt, 1959. More humorous and philosophic tales gathered by a folklorist who has made a significant contribution to the lore of faraway lands. 9-13

CURCIJA-PRODANOVIC, NADA. *Yugoslav Folk-Tales,* ill. by Joan Kiddell-Monroe. Walck, 1957. 10-14

DE LA MARE, WALTER. *Tales Told Again,* ill. by Alan Howard. Knopf, 1959. This collection of nineteen familiar tales retold by De la Mare was first published over twenty years ago as *Told Again.* 9-13

DEUTSCH, BABETTE, and AVRAHM YARMOLINSKY. *Tales of Faraway Folk,* ill. by Irena Lorentowicz. Harper, 1952. A unique collection of tales from Baltic, Russian, and Asiatic lands. 9-12

———. *More Tales of Faraway Folk,* ill. by Janina Domanska. Harper, 1963. Fifteen more tales, many from Iron-Curtain lands. 7-11

KELSEY, ALICE GEER. *Once the Hodja,* ill. by Frank Dobias. McKay, 1943. Twenty-four tales from Turkey filled with humor and simple wisdom.

———. *Once the Mullah,* ill. by Kurt Werth. McKay, 1954. Stories told by the Mullah give insight into Persian life and folklore. 9-12

MCNEILL, JAMES, comp. *The Sunken City,* ill. by Theo Dimson. Walck, 1959. Tales from around the world provide an excellent and varied collection for storytelling and reading aloud. 9-12

ROSS, EULALIE STEINMETZ, ed. *The Buried Treasure and Other Picture Tales,* ill. by Josef Cellini. Lippincott, 1958. A compilation of some of the choicest tales that appeared in the small separate volumes of the Picture Tales series, each of which had selected stories from a single country. 8-10

SHERLOCK, PHILIP M. *Anansi, the Spider Man; Jamaican Folk Tales,* ill. by Marcia Brown. Crowell, 1954. These stories are told by Jamaicans with simplicity and charm. 9-12

Anthologies

ARBUTHNOT, MAY HILL. *Time for Fairy Tales, Old and New* (see References, this chapter).

Association for Childhood Education Literature Committee. *Told Under the Green Umbrella,* ill. by Grace Gilkison. Macmillan, 1930. Favorite nursery tales such as "The Three Billy-Goats" and "The Sleeping Beauty." 3-8

BROOKE, L. LESLIE, ed. *The Golden Goose Book,* ill. by editor. Warne, 1906. "The Golden Goose," "Tom Thumb," "Three Little Pigs," and "Three Bears" are delightfully illustrated. 5-10

HUBER, MIRIAM BLANTON. *Story and Verse for Children,* ill. by Lynd Ward. Macmillan, 1955. A general anthology of children's literature with a good chapter on the values of folk tales.

HUTCHINSON, VERONICA, ed. *Chimney Corner Stories,* ill. by Lois Lenski. Putnam, 1925. 3-8

———. *Fireside Stories,* ill. by Lois Lenski. Putnam, 1927. 8-12

Authentic, well-written, and well-illustrated adaptations, suitable for storytelling or reading aloud.

JOHNSON, EDNA, EVELYN SICKELS, and FRANCES CLARKE SAYERS. *Anthology of Children's Literature.* Houghton, 1959. The chapter on "Folk-Tales, Literary Fairy Tales, Myths and Legends" contains a good selection.

ROJANKOVSKY, FEODOR. *The Tall Book of Nursery Tales.* Harper, 1944. This collection of old tales is notable for Mr. Rojankovsky's illustrations. 5-8

chapter II

Fables, Myths, and Epics

Fables, myths, and epics, like the ballads and fairy tales, are also a part of the great stream of folklore. While they are not generally so popular with children as the fairy tales, they have made an equally important contribution to our literary heritage. The fables have colored our attitudes toward moral and ethical problems. The myths and the epics have become a part of our everyday symbols and speech. All these three types of literature, while fundamentally different from each other, have one characteristic in common: they have a strong moral flavor.

Moral Tales: Fables, Parables, Proverbs

Fables are brief narratives which take abstract ideas of good or bad, wise or foolish behavior and attempt to make them concrete and striking enough to be understood and remembered. Whether the characters are men or beasts, they remain coldly impersonal and engage in a single significant act which teaches a moral lesson. These are the essential elements of the true fable. Here is an example of the simplest type:

The Crow and the Pitcher[1]

A thirsty Crow found a Pitcher with some water in it, but so little was there that, try as she might, she could not reach it with her beak, and it seemed as though she would die of thirst within sight of the remedy. At last she hit upon a clever plan. She began dropping pebbles into the Pitcher, and with each pebble the water rose a little higher until at last it reached the brim, and the knowing bird was enabled to quench her thirst.

"Necessity is the mother of invention."

The chief actor in most fables is an animal or inanimate object which behaves like a

1. From *Aesop's Fables,* translated by V. S. Vernon Jones, p. 17. Copyright 1912 by Doubleday & Company, Inc.

human being and has one dominant trait. G. K. Chesterton insists that there can be no good fables with human beings in them, and it is true that most fables are not concerned with people. Yet there are a substantial number of fables which tell about human beings and still retain their fable quality. Remember "The Boy Who Cried Wolf," and

The Milkmaid and Her Pail[2]

A farmer's daughter had been out to milk the cows, and was returning to the dairy carrying her pail of milk upon her head. As she walked along, she fell a-musing after this fashion: "The milk in this pail will provide me with cream, which I will make into butter and take to market to sell. With the money I will buy a number of eggs, and these, when hatched, will produce chickens, and by and by I shall have quite a large poultry-yard. Then I shall sell some of my fowls, and with the money which they will bring in I will buy myself a new gown, which I shall wear when I go to the fair; and all the young fellows will admire it, and come and make love to me, but I shall toss my head and have nothing to say to them." Forgetting all about the pail, and suiting the action to the word, she tossed her head. Down went the pail, all the milk was spilled and all her fine castles in the air vanished in a moment!

"Do not count your chickens before they are hatched."

Here again is a single episode pointing to a moral, as briefly and impersonally related as "The Crow and the Pitcher." It is a true fable.

Fables have a teasing likeness to proverbs and parables. All three embody universal truths in brief, striking form; and all three are highly intellectual exercises, as exact as an equation. Of the three, the *proverb* is the most highly condensed commentary on human folly or wisdom. It tells no story but presents a bit of wisdom succinctly:

A soft answer turneth away wrath: but grievous words stir up anger.[3]

The wicked flee when no man pursueth: but the righteous are bold as a lion.[4]

He that diggeth a pit shall fall into it.[5]

He that is slow to anger is better than the mighty; and he that ruleth his spirit than he that taketh a city.[6]

Boast not thyself of tomorrow; for thou knowest not what a day may bring forth.[7]

Better is a dry morsel and quietness therewith, than an house full of feasting with strife.[8]

He that diligently seeketh good procureth favour: but he that seeketh mischief, it shall come unto him.[9]

Certainly the sixth proverb is a perfect moral for "The Town Mouse and the Country Mouse," and either the third or seventh would fit Marcia Brown's *Once a Mouse.*

It is interesting to find many examples in *Japanese Proverbs* by Rokuo Okada that are amazingly like our proverbs in their implications:

He who wants to shoot the general must first shoot his horse.

A sparrow (suzume) will never forget to dance till it is a hundred years old.

A cornered mouse bites the cat.[10]

Perhaps the fable grew out of the proverb, to dramatize its pithy wisdom in story form.

The *parable* is like the fable in that it tells a brief story from which a moral or spiritual truth may be inferred. But its characters, unlike the personified animals or objects of most fables, are generally human beings, like the Wise and Foolish Virgins, or the Prodigal Son, or the Good Samaritan. If the story is told in terms of animals or objects, they are never personified but remain strictly themselves. That is, the seed that falls upon rocky ground has nothing to say for itself, and the

2. *Ibid.,* p. 25.
3. Proverbs 15:1.
4. Proverbs 28:1.
5. Ecclesiastes 10:8.
6. Proverbs 16:32.
7. Proverbs 27:1.
8. Proverbs 17:1.
9. Proverbs 11:27.
10. From *Japanese Proverbs* by Rokuo Okada. Copyright by the Japan Travel Bureau. In *Japan Times Weekly,* December 1, 1962.

house that was built upon sand goes down in the flood strictly a house. The parables use people or things as object lessons, and the matchless parables of Jesus point out and amplify the moral.

There are obvious differences among the stories discussed in the following pages under *Fable Collections.* Some are typical fables, some are parables, others resemble folk tales, and many contain maxims or proverbs. All of them, however, embody moral or spiritual wisdom.

Fable Collections

If you say "fables" to an English-speaking child, he thinks at once of *Aesop's Fables,* the source of the two stories quoted on pages 298-299. To a French child, La Fontaine and "fables" are inseparably associated, and so in the Orient it is *The Panchatantra, The Fables of Bidpai,* or the *Jatakas.* These major collections of fables, while resembling each other, show also striking differences.

This leopard's pride is written all over his face. Note how Artzybasheff, a master of intricate design, repeats curved lines. From Aesop's Fables *by Boris Artzybasheff. Copyright 1933 by Boris Artzybasheff. Reproduced by permission of The Viking Press, Inc. (Book 6 x 9¼)*

AESOP

Planudes, a fourteenth-century monk, prefixed a story of Aesop's life to a book of fables, supposedly those of Aesop. Some modern scholars not only doubt the authenticity of this account, but doubt whether Aesop really existed. G. K. Chesterton suggests that he may be as completely a fictitious character as that other slave, Uncle Remus, who also told beast tales. But his name and fame persist through one edition of the fables after another. Aesop is said to have lived in Greece between 620 and 560 B.C. and is thought to have been a Samian slave. Because free speech under the Tyrants was risky business, Aesop is supposed to have used the fables for political purposes, protecting himself and veiling his opinions behind the innuendoes of these little stories. Legend has it that he was deformed and that he was hurled off a cliff, whether for his deformity or for his politics it is not known. All we know is that the picturesque legends about Aesop have survived with his name.

Translated into Latin in the first and third centuries, the Aesop fables became the textbooks of the medieval schools. In Latin they found their way into England, France, and Germany, were translated into several languages, and were among the first books to be printed by Caxton when he started his famous press in England. Evidently there was infiltration from other sources. Joseph Jacobs said he could mention at least seven hundred fables ascribed to Aesop, although the first known collection of them, made by Demetrius of Phalerum about 320 B.C., contained only about two hundred. Since India, like Greece, had long used the beast tale for teaching purposes, undoubtedly some of the Indian fables gravitated, in the course of time, to the Aesop collection. From whatever source they came, once included in Aesop they assumed the Aesop form, which is now regarded as the pure fable type. It is a brief story with inanimate objects or animals most frequently serving as the leading characters, and with the single action of the narrative pointing to an obvious moral lesson. James Reeves in his *Fables from Aesop* points out that the virtues which Aesop praises are not the heroic ones but rather "the peasant virtues of discretion, prudence, moderation and forethought.... That is why Aesop... has always had the affection and regard of ordinary people."

AND THEY LAUGHED LOUD AND LONG

In spite of the beautiful sweep of wings, there is something irresistibly comic in these soaring creatures.
Illustration by E. Boyd Smith. From The Tortoise and the Geese and Other Fables of Bidpai, *retold by Maude Barrows Dutton. Houghton Mifflin Company, 1936. Reproduced by permission of the publishers. (Book 4¾ x 7½)*

THE PANCHATANTRA

The Panchatantra, meaning "five books," was composed in Kashmir about 200 B.C.,[11] and is the oldest known collection of Indian fables. *The Hitopadesa,* or Book of Good Counsel, is considered only another version of *The Panchatantra,*[12] and still another is called *The Fables of Bidpai.* These collections were translated into Persian, Arabic, Latin, and many other languages. In the Latin version the tales became popular throughout medieval Europe.

After the extreme condensation of Aesop, the stories of *The Panchatantra* seem long and involved. They comprise a textbook on "the wise conduct of life" and are intricate stories-within-stories, interrupted with philosophical verses so numerous that the thread of the story is almost forgotten. Some of these poems are sixteen or twenty verses long, but the quatrain is the more usual type.

A friend in need is a friend indeed,
Although of different caste;
The whole world is your eager friend
So long as riches last.

When arrows pierce or axes wound
A tree, it grows together sound;
From cruel, ugly speech you feel
A wound that time will never heal.

Make friends, make friends, however strong
Or weak they be;
Recall the captive elephants
That mice set free.[13]

These verses are summaries of the stories which seem more like folk tales than fables. On the whole, *The Panchatantra* is for adults rather than children, but some thirty-four of the best of these stories are well illustrated by E. Boyd Smith in *The Tortoise and the Geese and Other Fables of Bidpai.* This is a book children enjoy.

THE JATAKAS

Another ancient collection of Indian fables is the group called the *Jatakas.* The time of their origin is not definitely known. They were in existence in the fifth century A.D., but carvings illustrating Jataka stories have been found which were made as early as the second or third centuries B.C. In modern India, crowds of attentive people still listen to these old tales.

11. *The Panchatantra,* translated by Arthur W. Ryder (University of Chicago Press, 1925), p. 3.
12. *The Fables of India* by Joseph Gaer, p. 53.
13. *The Panchatantra,* op. cit., pp. 5, 322, 273.

King Tawny of Hard-to-Pass Forest is simply and realistically portrayed.
Illustration by Randy Monk. From The Fables of India *by Joseph Gaer. Copyright 1955, by Joseph Gaer. Reproduced with the permission of Little, Brown and Company. (Book 5¾ x 8½)*

Jatakas is a Buddhist name for stories concerning the rebirths of Gautama Buddha, who according to tradition was reincarnated many times in the forms of different animals until he became at last Buddha, the Enlightened One. These beast stories, then, are really about a man living briefly as an animal, consorting with other animals, and deriving from these experiences certain ethical lessons.

Joseph Gaer tells us that there are two or three thousand of these stories. Generally, the introduction and body of the tale are in prose, but the conclusions are often verses. Comparatively few of them are suitable for children and then only with considerable adaptation. Ellen C. Babbitt's two books of the Jatakas were made with children in mind and so omit all reference to the Buddha. Joseph Gaer's versions, in *The Fables of India*, keep closer to the original form of the Jatakas, as you can see by comparing his tale of "The Talkative Tortoise," with this version by Ellen C. Babbitt:

The Turtle Who Couldn't Stop Talking[14]

A Turtle lived in a pond at the foot of a hill. Two young wild Geese, looking for food, saw the Turtle, and talked with him. The next day the Geese came again to visit the Turtle and they became very well acquainted. Soon they were great friends.

"Friend Turtle," the Geese said one day, "we have a beautiful home far away. We are going to fly back to it to-morrow. It will be a long but pleasant journey. Will you go with us?"

"How could I? I have no wings," said the Turtle.

"Oh, we will take you, if only you can keep your mouth shut, and say not a word to anybody," they said.

"I can do that," said the Turtle. "Do take me with you. I will do exactly as you wish."

So the next day the Geese brought a stick and they held the ends of it. "Now take the middle of this in your mouth, and don't say a word until we reach home," they said.

The Geese then sprang into the air, with the Turtle between them, holding fast to the stick.

The village children saw the two Geese flying along with the Turtle and cried out: "Oh, see the Turtle up in the air! Look at the Geese carrying a Turtle by a stick. Did you ever see anything more ridiculous in your life!"

The Turtle looked down and began to say, "Well, and if my friends carry me, what business is that of yours?" when he let go, and fell dead at the feet of the children.

As the two Geese flew on, they heard the people say, when they came to see the poor Turtle, "That fellow could not keep his mouth shut. He had to talk, and so lost his life."

14. From *Jataka Tales* by Ellen C. Babbitt. Copyright 1912, by The Century Company; 1940, by Ellen C. Babbitt. Reprinted by permission of D. Appleton-Century Company, Inc.

This is, of course, a true fable. Other Jatakas remind us of familiar parables from the Bible. Still others are like short folk tales with self-evident morals. Because the tales in Joseph Gaer's *The Fables of India* keep closer to the original form of the Jatakas, they are more suitable for children of ten or older, while Ellen C. Babbitt's *Jatakas* appeal to the younger children. All three books are delightfully illustrated in the spirit of the text.

LA FONTAINE, 1621-1695

In the twelfth century, Marie de France introduced and popularized the fable in France. Others followed her lead, but Jean de La Fontaine, a contemporary of Charles Perrault, made the fable so completely and gracefully his own that the French coined a word for him, *le fablier,* "the fable-teller."

He was born in the lovely district of Chateau-Thierry in Champagne, but after his separation from his wife, who continued to live there with their son, La Fontaine settled in Paris under the protection of first one wealthy patron and then another.

La Fontaine was a skilled poet and wrote his fables in graceful verses which are delightful to read and easy to memorize. Unfortunately, they lose some of their appeal when translated into English. It is a lucky child who can have them in French with the illustrations of Boutet de Monvel. There are charming bits of description in these fables which reveal the birds and little beasts and the forests and meadows of the beautiful Champagne countryside where La Fontaine grew up. The courtier and the man of the world show themselves in the shrewd appraisals of character and the worldly philosophy that permeate the *Fables:*

Now, as everyone knows, white paws do not grow on wolves.

My dear Mr. Crow, learn from this how every flatterer lives at the expense of anybody who will listen to him. This lesson is well worth the loss of a cheese to you.

But among all the fools the human kind excels. We have the eyes of a lynx for the faults of others and the eyes of moles for our own. We forgive ourselves much more easily than we do our neighbor.[15]

Doesn't this remind you of the New Testament admonition, "And why beholdest thou the mote that is in thy brother's eye, but considerest not the beam that is in thine own eye?"[16]

La Fontaine used for his sources the Latin versions of Aesop and *The Fables of Bidpai,* and the versions of his predecessor, Marie de France. In spite of the verse form and the characteristic bits of philosophy, these *Fables* of La Fontaine's are closer to the Aesop pattern than to the tales from India. They maintain the brevity, the predominant use of animal characters, and, above all, the single striking episode which points the moral. Reading them in French, you readily understand why the school children of France have for generations memorized them with delight and remembered them always.

Using Fables with Children

The highly intellectual quality of fables, proverbs, and parables is quite apparent when they are compared with the folk tales. Just because the fables happen to use characters that sound like those of the folk tales, and because large, colored illustrations usually play up this resemblance, and because they are brief, they have often been given to small children for entertainment. Then we are surprised when the children don't warm up to them. But let's keep our definitions clearly in mind. All three of them—proverbs, parables, and fables—are attempts to make abstract ideas sufficiently striking or objective to be understood and

15. From *The Fables of La Fontaine,* translated by Margaret W. Brown (Harper, 1940), pp. 6, 8, and 19.
16. St. Matthew 7:3.

remembered. Every one of them *is* an abstraction—a maxim, an adage, a brief sermon on morality—and, because of this, the least appealing of all story types with children.

If you try to compose an original fable yourself, you will discover at once what a mathematical procedure it is. Suppose you take "Pride goeth before a fall" and choose a rabbit for your leading character. Your rabbit cannot be little Peter Rabbit, own brother to Flopsy, Mopsy, and Cotton-tail; but he will be an impersonal creature known as Proud Rabbit. Then your equation is merely: *Proud Rabbit* + *X* = *Pride goeth before a fall.* All you have to do is to devise a single episode for X in which the Proud Rabbit takes a well-deserved tumble. No one will care about his misfortune either, because you give Proud Rabbit no family to grieve for him, no personality. He isn't a family man, kind to his wife and children, with just one slight weakness, his pride. No, this fable rabbit is all PRIDE and nothing else. Your heart never beats with sympathy for fable creatures. They remain impersonal, unemotional exemplifications of virtue or folly.

WITH YOUNG CHILDREN

These are some of the reasons why, in spite of the bright-colored pictures which adorn many an edition of Aesop or La Fontaine, the fables should be used chiefly with the older children. To be sure, a few may be told to young children in anticipation of the whole books later on, but they should be the ones which have the most story appeal or an obvious bit of humor: for instance, "The Lion and the Mouse," "The Town Mouse and the Country Mouse," "The Hare and the Tortoise," and "The Fox and the Crow." Two or three such fables a year, slipped in among warmly appealing folk tales and modern realistic stories, are about as many abstractions as the primary school child enjoys.

WITH OLDER CHILDREN

On the other hand, children ten, eleven, and twelve years old can read for themselves and enjoy a good collection of the Aesop fables. They like to tell a fable to the class, omitting the moral to see how closely the group can come to supplying it. This, by the way, is no mean intellectual feat but is one item often used in intelligence tests. Try the project suggested on this page: take a maxim or proverb (see those given on page 299) and try to evolve a fable. This is too hard for children to do individually but can be great fun for a whole class. Because the pithy maxims of Aesop and La Fontaine have passed into our language and our thinking, every child should have some experience with them—"What's bred in the bone will never come out of the flesh."

With a study of India, introduce the stories of *The Panchatantra* and *Jatakas* as told by Ellen C. Babbitt and Joseph Gaer. Their three books have stories that are worth using at any time, with or without a unit on Indian life. "Greedy and Speedy," "The Lion and the Wily Rabbit," "The Hermit and the Mouse," "The Merchant of Seri," "Grannie's Blackie," and "The Banyan Deer" are all entertaining tales.

There are now available many beautifully illustrated editions of the fables, notably James Reeves' *Fables from Aesop,* and editions of single fables by well-known artists. Marcia Brown won her second Caldecott Medal with *Once a Mouse* and Barbara Cooney won the same award with *Chanticleer and the Fox.* Katherine Evans has retold and illustrated a series of fables including *A Camel in the Tent* ("Give the foolish a little and they want too much") and *The Man and the Boy and the Donkey* ("In trying to please everyone you please no one"). All of the books in the series are well told and pleasantly illustrated.

James Daugherty made some of his finest and funniest pictures for *Andy and the Lion,* a modern version of the old fable of "Androcles and the Lion." Now the indefatigable John Ciardi has come up with a delightful new version of "The Grasshopper and the Ant," told in verse. It is called *John J. Plenty and Fiddler Dan.* John J. is, of course, the earnest go-getter ant, and Fiddler Dan, the happy, improvident grasshopper. But from there on the story takes a new turn. Poor John J. nearly starves himself to death trying to save for the future while Dan enjoys a romance and weathers the bad winter with love and a song. Here is one of three sprightly morals to the tale:

Say what you like as you trudge along,
The world won't turn without a song.

After the older children have had some experience with the fables and one or both of these fable adaptations, they may discover the fable-like qualities of such stories as Wanda Gág's *Nothing at All,* Munro Leaf's *The Story of Ferdinand,* and Anita Brenner's *A Hero by Mistake.* For the moral of this last story they may think of that popular song from *The King and I* "Whenever I feel afraid, I whistle a happy tune." A few experiments with double meanings will go a long way with children. Even so, these old moralities, these priceless bits of wisdom we call fables, are an essential part of their literary heritage, too good to miss.

Gods and Men

The fables are simple, highly condensed lessons in morality. The myth is far more complicated. It attempts to explain—in complex symbolism—the vital outlines of existence:

(1) cosmic phenomena (e.g., how the earth and sky came to be separated); (2) peculiarities of natural history (e.g., why rain follows the cries or activities of certain birds); (3) the origins of human civilization (e.g., through the beneficent action of a culture-hero like Prometheus); or (4) the origin of social or religious custom or the nature and history of objects of worship.[17]

It also attempts to make more acceptable the painful realities of existence—danger, disease, misfortune, and death—by explaining them as part of a sacred order in the universe.

The "explanations" may seem irrational and inconsistent to the science-minded modern. This is because they are not scientific hypotheses but were created by and appeal to the imagination. The truth of the myth was unquestioned by primitive peoples because it was so closely associated with their sacred beliefs. For them, both nature and society were areas of reverent acceptance[18]—not of objective study, as they are in this age of science and social science.

EVOLUTION OF MYTHS

A number of writers have called attention to the various levels of myth development, their evolution from primitive to highly complex symbolic stories. These developmental stages are important to us because they throw light upon the various types of stories included in myths and help to explain their suitability, or lack of it, as story material for children.

The early part of this evolution is, of course, shrouded in the darkness of prehistoric times. Much research has been devoted to it, but the outlines are still only dimly understood. For one thing, the evolution of myth and religion differs from people to people. Suffice it to say that the Greeks, like many other peoples, passed through a primary stage in which they worshiped an impersonal force believed to pervade all aspects of the universe: sun, moon, crops, rivers. The early Greeks performed rites to propitiate these bodiless forces so that they would grant to the world fertility and life. Later these nature forces were personified in the myths.

Myths, then, did give body—both animal and human—to the mystic forces that early people felt in the universe. As these ideas developed, the tendency was to give complex human form to these impersonal forces. These bright sky-dwellers were created in man's own image but surpassed him in beauty, wisdom, and power. All the warmth and glory of the sun were embodied in the Greek ideas of

17. William Reginald Halliday, "Folklore," *Encyclopaedia Britannica.*

18. At the adult level, an excellent example of this would be the religious beliefs and practices found in Mary Renault's *The Bull from the Sea.*

Apollo, all the terror of storms in their ideas of Zeus and his fearful thunderbolts. Not only are the myths the "earliest recorded utterances of men concerning the visible phenomena of the world into which they were born," but myths also express men's wonder, fear, and sense of the beauty and majesty of nature.

Imagining these supernatural beings in their own likeness, the people interpreted a flood to mean that the river god was angry with man and intended to punish him. Drouths, earthquakes, good crops, and bad crops were all dependent on how man stood in the graces of these nature gods. These primitive beginnings of myth were polytheistic; that is, they developed many gods. G. K. Chesterton, speaking of the Greek deities, commented that "the Greeks could not see trees for dryads."

Presently these beings developed relationships among each other, assumed certain powers, and suffered limitations of power. Thus in the Greek mythology the first gods were all brothers and sisters—Hestia, Demeter, Hera, Poseidon, Hades, and Zeus. Because Zeus saved them from destruction, he was chosen the supreme ruler, the sky god, while Poseidon ruled the waters and Hades, who dwelt below the earth, ruled the dominion of the dead. From their matings, their children, and the powers and limitations of each of these three powerful brothers arose endless squabbles that bear a melancholy resemblance to the earthly rows of man himself.

Each god or goddess came to assume certain powers. For instance, Hera, the wife of Zeus, was the jealous guardian of the marriage state. She kept an eagle eye on her faithless spouse, wrought bitter vengeance on his unfortunate loves, and generally waged a strenuous, if unavailing, war on anything that threatened the dignity of the lawful wife.

But every god, except Zeus, knew distinct limitations to his powers and was vulnerable to misfortunes in certain respects, even as man. Balder, the Norse sun god, whose mother Frigga made everything except the mistletoe promise not to harm him, was slain by the insignificant shrub which Frigga had thought too harmless to bother about. Balder the Beautiful died; he went out to sea in his fiery ship, burning like the autumn foliage; the earth wept for him, and cold and darkness followed —a picture of the coming of autumn and winter in the north country. So these man-made deities developed relationships and powers but were subject to certain limitations from other powers.

The extension of a god's powers soon turned him into a symbolic figure, standing for certain abstract virtues. So Zeus, from being at first merely a sky god, became the symbol of power and law. Apollo began as the sun god, a beautiful young man with a fiery chariot to drive across the sky daily. Then he became also the god of health and healing, the patron god of physicians. Finally this idea of healing was expanded to include the related but less physical concept of purification, and Apollo then stood for the abstract idea of purity. In some such way as this, many of the gods evolved from mere nature personifications to become symbols of abstract moral attributes.

Of course, this evolution into symbolism was not true of all gods. Pan remained ever

> *. . . the dear son of Hermes, with his goat's feet and two horns—a lover of merry noise. Through wooded glades he wanders with dancing nymphs who foot it on some sheer cliff's edge, calling upon Pan, the shepherd-god . . .*[19]

Pan never became an abstraction but remained always the joyous earthy denizen of woods and meadows, the lover of high song.

In some mythologies less sophisticated than the Greeks' the deities have never signified anything more than spirits of earth, sky, sun, moon, or even animals. The Indian "Old Man Coyote" is such a deity. On the other hand, the Navaho "Turquoise Woman" is not merely a sky goddess but seems to be also a symbol of beauty in the highest sense, meaning harmony and goodness.

Finally, when the gods had come to stand for moral attributes and powers, the next and last stage of myth-making was the development of a priesthood, temples, and a ritual of worship. Then the myth was an organized religion. Apollo had a great temple at Delphi

19. Hesiod, *The Homeric Hymns and Homerica,* translated by Hugh C. Evelyn-White, p. 443.

with priests, an oracle, vestal virgins, and elaborate ceremonies and rituals. There were temples to Zeus, to Demeter, and to the splendid Pallas Athena, until by the time the Apostle Paul arrived in Athens, temples had been built to so many gods that there was even an altar to "The Unknown God" lest one be overlooked. Few gods had as elaborate ramifications to their worship as Apollo. The Apollo cult represents the last and most complex stage of myth-making, to which only the mythologies of highly civilized people attain.

TYPES OF MYTH STORIES

Among the simplest of myth stories are the little *why* stories, or *pourquoi* tales. Why the woodpecker has a red head and how the arbutus came to be are from the North American Indians. Why the sunflower turns to the sun (the story of Clytie) and how a flower was born of the blood of Apollo's accidental victim (the story of Hyacinthus) are from the Greek. Yet these Indian and Greek tales are similarly naïve and childlike. Children enjoy a few such stories in connection with the study of a people and accept them with a comfortable sense of superiority—they know better!

In both Greek and Norse myths these *why* stories become more complex than in the American Indian woodpecker and arbutus examples. Take, for instance, the Greek explanation of summer and winter; the story goes that Demeter (the earth mother) has been deprived of her beautiful child Persephone (the grain), who has been carried off by Hades to his realm below the ground. Demeter seeks her child, weeping, but Persephone must remain in Hades' dark world for six months of each year, leaving earth to darkness and cold. Such a story is neither simple nor explanatory for a child. For him, it is a good fairy tale, but if he is to catch any glimpse of its seasonal significance, it has to be explained in careful detail. Similar to this tale is the story told of Balder the Beautiful, the Norse sun god, at whose death the whole earth weeps and falls into darkness. So our North American Indians of the Southwest have their desert seasonal story of little Burnt-Face, the scorched earth, who sees the invisible chief, the spring rains, and is made beautiful by him and becomes his bride. To children, these three are just good fairy tales, as interesting and objective as "Cinderella." However, if in the study of Greeks, or Romans, or Norsemen, or Desert Indians, you explain to the children the possible meaning of these stories for the people who created them, they are surprised and charmed with the secondary meaning.

A second type of myth story is the *allegory*. Niobe, for example, boasts of her divine descent, is insolently proud of her powers and, above all, of her seven sons and seven daughters. She sets herself up as the equal of the goddess Leto, and, for this impious pride, Apollo and Artemis, Leto's twins, avenge their mother by striking down all fourteen of Niobe's children. Her pride brought low, frozen with grief, Niobe turns into a stone fountain, weeping forever for her children.

Human pride seems to be particularly offensive to the gods. Arachne was turned into a spider because she boasted of her weaving. Bellerophon, after he captured the winged horse, Pegasus, became so sure of himself that he attempted to ride into Zeus' dwelling and was promptly struck blind for his presumption. Some of these myths are almost like fables, and, like the fables, they could be summarized with a maxim or proverb. Others, like "Arachne," are little *why* stories with a moral. Still others are involved adult allegories. "Cupid and Psyche," standing for Love and the Soul, is such a tale. Fortunately, we have it in folk-tale form as our favorite "East o' the Sun and West o' the Moon." Pandora is another adult allegory—sin brought into the world by the "beautiful bane," woman.

The allegories are, on the whole, too adult in content and significance to be appropriate story material for children. But the simpler tales among them are accepted by the children exactly as they accept any folk tale. One of their favorites is "King Midas," who wished that everything he touched would turn into gold and soon found himself starving in the midst of plenty. And there is the charming tale of "Baucis and Philemon," the old couple who entertained the gods with their humble best and were granted their two wishes—to serve the gods and to be taken out of this world together. At the hour of death they were changed into an oak and a linden tree, growing side by side. Well-told versions of such stories are as suitable for children as any other fairy tales and may be used with or without the background of the people and their mythology.

The *ways of the gods with men* make another group of stories which includes the two just mentioned, "King Midas" and "Baucis and Philemon." One of the most delightful of these is "Bellerophon and Pegasus." Bellerophon, a handsome youth, is sent by his host, Iobates, to kill the chimera, which is devastating Lycia. Although Iobates is sure the mission will mean the boy's death, the gods take pity upon Bellerophon and send him the winged Pegasus. That Pegasus, the winged horse of the gods, means "poetry" does not enter the children's heads, but that Bellerophon could not kill the terrible chimera until he had first captured and tamed Pegasus makes a good adventure story of unusual beauty. "Daedalus" is an interesting myth today, because it is an early story about men flying. "Jason and the Golden Fleece" is another good tale into which the gods enter indirectly. These are really hero tales with a background of myth and they comprise a particularly good group of stories for children. Some of them, like those in the *Odyssey,* later developed into national epics.

The gods' amatory adventures among men are legion and are the ones we do not adapt for children. Zeus, Apollo, Aphrodite, and, in fact, most of the deities succumbed repeatedly to the charms of mortals. Their godly mates also wreaked ungodly vengeance on the poor humans; so these tales are both scandalous and cruel. Stories about the ways of nymphs and dryads with men are much like fairy lore. Sometimes they deserted their mortal mates; sometimes the men fled from them. On the whole, the earthly loves of the gods are inappropriate tales for children.

Finally, the *ways of the gods with other gods* furnish us with another body of myth-stories, often complex in their significance and adult in content. Here we encounter nature myths which even the folklorists interpret differently and which leave the layman baffled and a bit weary with all the things which aren't what they seem. Frazer's *Golden Bough* is a repository for these stories. Turning to the Greek stories again, we find involved and often repellent tales of creation whose interpretation is decidedly speculative. Consider Cronus, who swallowed all his children at birth, until the last son, Zeus, was saved by a deception. Later Zeus gave his cannibalistic father a potion which caused him to regurgitate the five sons and daughters he had kept handily tucked away in his divine interior. These young gods made war upon their unnatural father and, once victorious, divided the world among themselves and dwelt in godlike glory on a glittering Olympus. Brothers marrying sisters, matings with monsters, the birth of monsters, continual infidelity among the deities, jealousy and vengeance—these are the ways of the gods with other gods.

These are the least suitable for children of all the myths. Back of such accounts of the gods and their escapades are endless double meanings which may start simply with Gaea, a personification of the Earth, who is touched by Eros (Love) and bears Uranus (Heaven). Other stories, like "Cupid and Psyche," take on more abstract significance. Moving and profound is the story of Prometheus, the Titan, who dared the wrath of the gods to bring man fire and suffered endless tortures as a result. Prometheus is so noble a symbol of sacrifice that poets and painters have repeatedly used his story as a theme. But these myths, with their symbolism and inner meanings are both complex and abstract, and many people feel they have no place in children's literature.

Sources of Mythologies

GREEK MYTHS

The Greek myths came to us by way of the poet Hesiod, who is supposed to have lived during the eighth century B.C. He was a farmer and a bachelor with an abiding love of nature and an equally firm dislike of women. While he was guarding his father's flocks, so the story goes, the Muses themselves commissioned him to be their poet. So a poet he became, winning a contest and gratefully dedicating a tripod to the Muses, who had shown him the way.

His first famous poem, *Works and Days,* is largely didactic but is also a kind of farmer's calendar, telling when to sow or plant or harvest and what seasons are most propitious for different kinds of work. There are ethical lessons on industry and honest toil, some biting criticisms of women, and the earliest known fable in Greek, "The Hawk and the Nightingale."

Theogony, another poem attributed to Hesiod, contains the Greek myths of the creation and the history of Zeus and Cronus, including Zeus' great battle with the Titans. Hesiod's picture of the defeated Titans, confined and guarded by giants and by Day and Night, is a convincing one.

Hesiod is credited with bringing together in organized form the major portion of Greek mythology. The English translation, although in prose, is good reading.

ROMAN MYTHS

The Roman versions of the Greek myths are available to us in the more familiar *Metamorphoses* of the Latin poet Ovid. Born in 43 B.C., Ovid belonged to a wealthy and privileged family. He was educated under famous Roman teachers, became a poet against his father's wishes, and, in contrast to Hesiod, was married three times. Only his last marriage was happy, but he seems never to have taken love or the ladies seriously. He belonged to the pleasure-bent, dissolute set which the Emperor Augustus was trying to discourage. When the poet's *Ars amatoria* appeared, its scandalous nature, coupled with some offense whose nature is not known, furnished sufficient cause for Ovid's banishment. He was forced to live in a barbarous little town, where his writing must have been his only consolation. Since his sentence was never rescinded despite frequent petitions, Ovid died in exile.

The *Metamorphoses* consists of fifteen books recounting tales of miraculous transformations, hence the title. It begins with the metamorphosis of Chaos to order, follows the Greek development of gods and men, recounts innumerable *why* stories of flowers, rivers, rocks, and the like. It concludes, appropriately enough, with Julius Caesar turned into a star, and Ovid himself on his way to some form of immortality. These stories, even in our English prose translations, are amazingly dramatic. It is interesting to check modern versions with these stirring tales of Ovid, which are the source of most adaptations.

NORSE MYTHS

Whether the Norse myths began in Norway, Greenland, Ireland, Iceland, or England, it was in Iceland that they were preserved orally and first written down. Iceland, remote from the rest of the world and settled largely by Norwegians, held to the old language, once the speech of all Northern peoples, and so kept the stories alive in their original form. The two collections are the *Elder* or *Poetic Edda,* and the *Younger* or *Prose Edda.*

The *Poetic* and the *Prose Eddas* follow the sing-and-say style, with the difference that the *Poetic Edda* is mostly verse with brief prose passages, and the *Prose Edda* is mostly prose with interspersed poetic passages. Both are difficult books, but there are several adaptations to use with children.

The word *Edda* was originally the name or title for a great-grandmother. In time it came to stand for the Norwegian court-meter or the art of poetry. In both senses it seems to imply something traditional. The *Elder* or *Poetic Edda* (thirty-four poems) contains the Prophecy, which tells how the world was created, how the gods came to be, and how they fell. There is a book of proverbs, and finally there is the story of Sigurd the Volsung, the Norse epic. These heroic lays were supposedly collected from oral tradition by Saemund the Learned and committed to writing about the eleventh or twelfth century. By then they must have been exposed to Christian ideas and to other cultures, but they remain, nevertheless, primitive and vigorous.

The *Younger* or *Prose Edda* was not collected until the thirteenth century. The first book, "The Beguiling of Gylfi," contains the bulk of the Norse myths. It was the work of Snorri Sturluson, an Icelander who combined a greedy and traitorous character with a real reverence for the traditional literature he recorded so faithfully.

Why Use the Myths with Children?

It is the rare child who is not enchanted with the stories of mythology. The sky-dwellers of the Greeks and Romans not only left a mark on our language, but they continue to spellbind each succeeding generation of children. Bellerophon taming the winged horse, Icarus plummeting through the sky into the sea, Hermes stepping cloudward on his winged sandals—these somehow catch the imagination with their dramatic beauty. It is not an accident that most of the examples of myth in the preceding pages have been from the Greek. If the children can sample only one mythology, it should be the Greek or its Roman adaptation. Our language and our thinking are full of words and ideas derived from these sources.[20] For example, *titanic* comes from the powerful Titans; *erotic* from Eros, the god of love; *panic* from the god Pan; and *cereal* from Ceres, the grain goddess. Men "steer between Scylla and Charybdis" or "cut the Gordian knot." Travelers who cross the equator for the first time must endure a lively hazing at the court of King Neptune, while any delayed wanderer may be dubbed a Ulysses. Minerva with her owl gazes down on us from our libraries. Hermes, or Mercury, with winged sandals, adorns our railroad terminals. Venus, rising from her sea shell, advertises bath salts or cosmetics. Our sandals and sun suits emulate Diana. We swear "By Jove!" The Muses preside over our concert halls, and young ladies used to study the terpsichorean art. There is a dramatic quality about the myths which has so captured the imaginations of poets that poetry, and English poetry in particular, is filled with classical allusions. To not know Greek-Roman mythology is to grope more or less blindly through the arts, particularly literature.

But the Norse myths too should be part of the experience of English-speaking children. The people who composed them were a vital source of our customs, laws, and speech. Yet the myths which are their finest expression and the clearest mirror of their life are not nearly so familiar to most of us as the myths of the ancient civilizations of Greece and Rome. The Norse gods do not have the beauty and grace of the classic deities, but they are cast in heroic mold, and there is a grandeur about the tales that is hard to match. Such stories as "How Odin Lost His Eye," "How Thor Found His Hammer," "The Apples of Iduna," "Thor's Visit to the Giants," and "The Death of Balder" are fascinating with or without a study of the people.

Both Greek and Norse mythologies, moreover, furnish the background for the great national epics of those countries. Children must know Greek mythology in order to understand the *Iliad* or the *Odyssey,* and they must know Norse mythology in order to understand the ideals and motives of the heroic characters in the Norse epic *Sigurd the Volsung,* or in Wagner's opera cycle *The Ring of the Nibelungs,* the Teutonic form of the Sigurd epic.

These are a few of the reasons why myths should be used with older children, but the chief reasons are, after all, the beauty and the imaginative quality of the tales themselves.

What Versions of the Myths to Use

The chief difficulty in using mythology with children is to find satisfactory versions of the stories. Hawthorne, consummate artist

20. There is a book devoted to such sources: Isaac Asimov, *Words from the Myths* (Houghton, 1961).

that he was, did not scruple to turn the gods into petulant children. He told an entrancing story, but he lost almost completely the dignity of the gods, and sometimes he even lost the significance of the story. One writer protests:

When one reads Hawthorne's version of Pandora and Prometheus and realizes the mere babble, the flippant detail, under which he has covered up the grim Titanic story of the yearnings and strivings of the human soul for salvation here and hereafter, the very deepest problems of temptation and sin, of rebellion and expiation, he must see clearly what is most likely to happen when a complex and mature myth is converted into a child's tale.[21]

Persephone (or Proserpina), in Hawthorne's version, is turned into a child carried off by Pluto to live underground for six months in the year and be his "little girl." While Hawthorne's versions have delighted generations of children, such writing down to children too young to hear the real stories plays havoc with any literature. The myths suffer especially from such treatment. Of course, even the best modern versions are not wholly free from interpretations that are unnecessarily childish. But on the whole no one has taken such devastating liberties with mythology as Hawthorne except Walt Disney, who turns it into something cute or coy.

Good versions of the myths for children have been made and new ones are still appearing. A few general standards should help us in selecting the best of these:

First, although some adaptation is necessary, myths should not be written down to children. When this is done, the author is usually trying to retell myths to children who are too young for them. Six- and seven-year-old children can take only the bare bones of these stories, but children from nine or ten years old to fourteen can enjoy rich versions of some of the originals. In the home, individual children may read myths earlier, but in the mixed groups of the average classroom, the appeal of myths is distinctly to older children.

Second, select those stories which have themes children can understand. Never risk a story about which you cannot answer all the questions curious young minds can ask. For the most part, the children's editions of myths have taken care of that problem and have toned down or omitted the peccadillos of the gods.

Finally, adaptations should be simple enough to be thoroughly comprehensible to children without sacrificing either the spirit or the richness of the originals. Too often, in order to simplify these stories, the adapter reduces the colorful details of the original to drab outlines devoid of charm. Simplification of some of the words is permissible enough and even essential. For example, Henry T. Riley's literal translation of Ovid's account of Phaëthon's rash entrance into the presence of his father, the Sun, describes the youth standing at a distance because "he could not bear the refulgence nearer." Sally Benson's adaptation has "for the light was more than he could bear"—a legitimate substitution. Words may be simplified, paraphrased, or explained in advance. But reject an adaptation that omits the rich, descriptive details of Ovid's tale. It would be a pity to miss the pictures of the palace, the chariot, and the horses of the Sun, the account of Apollo's love and anxiety for the reckless youth, the portrayal of the boy's terror of the lonely heavens, and the descriptions of the rushing speed, the earth aflame, finally the Jovian bolt, and then:

. . . Phaethon, the flames consuming his yellow hair, is hurled headlong, and is borne in a long tract through the air; as sometimes a star from the serene sky may appear to fall, although it really has not fallen. . . . The Hesperian Naiads commit his body, smoking from the three-forked flames, to the tomb and inscribe these verses on the stone:—"Here is Phaethon buried, the driver of his father's chariot, which if he did not manage, still he miscarried in a great attempt."[22]

Another version translates the last lines:

21. From *Literature in the Elementary School* by Porter Lander MacClintock (University of Chicago Press, 1907), p. 122.

22. *The Metamorphoses of Ovid,* literal translation into English prose by Henry T. Riley, p. 59.

He could not rule his father's car of fire,
Yet was it much so nobly to aspire.[23]

According to these standards, what versions of the myths are best to use with children? There has been a flood of new adaptations and some new editions of old versions. Of the latter, one of the best is *The Heroes* by Charles Kingsley, Victorian scholar and poet. His stories of Perseus, Theseus, and Jason have a nobility that should prove a wholesome antidote to the banality of much of our mass entertainment. Padraic Colum's *The Golden Fleece* is superb storytelling for good readers, and Sally Benson's *Stories of the Gods and Heroes,* in spite of some disturbing modern touches, is still one of the best and most popular versions. A recent edition, the d'Aulaires' big, handsome *Book of Greek Myths,* represents years of preparation. The stories are brief but have continuity; the copious and colorful illustrations are uneven in quality but imaginative. This will be a splendid book for classroom use. It is also interesting to see how the myths appeal to poets, beginning with Kingsley and Colum. In 1960, the British poet Robert Graves brought out his version, called *Greek Gods and Heroes,* a lively text that makes clear what is often confusing. And Ian Serraillier, another poet, has told the story of Perseus, *The Gorgon's Head,* and Theseus, *The Way of Danger,* with dramatic beauty. Both can be read by the children or may serve as sources for storytelling. The illustrations suggest the figures on Greek vases. Examine these editions and choose the one or two that best suit your needs as sources for storytelling or references for the children to read themselves.

When you want to use the Norse myths and hero tales, turn again to Padraic Colum, to his *Children of Odin,* a stirring and understandable version of those complex tales. An early adaptation that still serves well is Abbie F. Brown's *In the Days of Giants,* while Dorothy Hosford's *Sons of the Volsungs* and *Thunder of the Gods* cover the myths and the hero cycles in superb style, either for storytelling or reading by the children themselves. These are, however, the most difficult of all stories to tell.

23. *A Book of Myths* by Helen Sewell, p. 39.

How to Use Myths with Children

AS THE RELIGION OF A PEOPLE

Some people believe that myth should be studied as the religion of a people. As a matter of fact, many church schools are using mythology in this way, including the myths in a comparative study of religions for adolescent boys and girls. *The Tree of Life* is a collection of myths from many peoples compiled for such study. The selections show the emergence, here and there throughout the centuries, of great religious ideals which are universal and command our respect today. Ideas of sin, repentance, expiation, and purification, and ideals of faithful love and self-sacrifice are all to be found in the old symbolic myths. This sort of study probably belongs to late adolescence but is certainly a matter for church schools and families to decide individually.

WITH THE STUDY OF A PEOPLE

The elementary schools often use the myths in connection with the study of a people. That is, the children who are studying the Vikings explore the Norse myths in order to understand the motives for and the standards of behavior, the moral code of the Vikings. Or, if they are following the vicissitudes of the Greek hero Odysseus, they study the Greek mythology in order to understand the Olympian battle of the gods—some ranged on the hero's side and some opposed to him. A study of certain forest Indians reveals a far less advanced mythology than that of the Navahos, but no tribe can be understood without the background of its particular ideology of the supernatural. It is, then, not only desirable but essential that any unit about a people shall include a study of its religious ideals.

AS LITERATURE

Reading the myths in connection with the study of a people would seem to take care of these stories. Unfortunately, in many school systems the studies of early peoples are being replaced by units that are either "here and now," or tied into United States history or civics. Since the high schools generally take for granted that something has been done with myths in the elementary schools, secondary schools may also omit them from the curriculum. The result is that many college freshmen today have no knowledge of mythology. They don't know Jupiter, let alone Zeus. They see trees but no dryads, and they assume that the Delphian oracle was probably some kind of old-time fortuneteller. The glory that was Greece has no reality for them. This is not to suggest to the teachers of social studies that a unit of Greek life might have more lasting significance for elementary-school children than the study of the local garbage-disposal plant—both are important. Rather our problem is to see what can be done with mythology if Greek units are no more.

Certainly, if the high-school curriculum does not include myth, then the elementary schools should—if not as the study of a people, then only as literature. In the literature periods we need not give children all the involved and confusing ramifications of the gods' genealogies, but we could introduce the major gods to them through stories which illustrate the characteristics and powers of the gods. Older children will be interested in the following Greek gods (Roman names in parentheses):

Zeus (Jove or Jupiter), the chief of the Olympian gods
Hera (Juno), wife of Zeus, goddess of women and marriage
Athena (Minerva), goddess of wisdom
Aphrodite (Venus), goddess of love and beauty
Eros (Cupid), god of love
Artemis (Diana), the virgin huntress, who is associated with the moon
Poseidon (Neptune), the god of the sea
Hades or *Pluto* (Dis), god of the underworld
Dionysus (Bacchus), god of wine and the harvest
Hermes (Mercury), messenger of the gods
Ares (Mars), god of war
Hephaestus (Vulcan), god of fire and metal-working
Demeter (Ceres), goddess of agriculture
Persephone (Proserpina), goddess of the underworld, spring

Decide to use consistently either the Greek or Roman names. The Greeks created the gods and the stories about them; the Romans merely adapted them, but the Roman names are more familiar and more generally used. Even the Greek hero Odysseus is better known to most people as Ulysses. To give children both sets of names is generally confusing; so keep to one or the other, perhaps according to the central book you may be using with the children.

The myths are indeed entirely appropriate for the literature period. Many stories about the gods are much like the finest of the fairy tales and are perhaps, in some cases, the sources of certain fairy tales. In "Baucis and Philemon," the gods, Zeus and Hermes, are glorified versions of the folk-tale godmothers or mysterious strangers who grant wishes as the rewards of hospitality or goodness. Older children who know "The Sleeping Beauty" find that the Greek "Demeter and Persephone" is a mature edition of their old friend. Incidentally, this myth lends itself to superb dramatization by a mettlesome fifth or sixth grade. "Cupid and Psyche" may well be the source of "East o' the Sun," while "Jason and the Golden Fleece" is another search for "The Water of Life" or the destruction of "The Giant Who Had No Heart in His Body." Older children find the myths even more beautiful and memorable than their favorite fairy tales. Certainly they have a more intellectual appeal.

To conclude with a question—are we in danger of forgetting that childhood and youth should be fed on greatness if young people are to dream and achieve greatness? In the story which opens Charles Kingsley's *The Heroes,* the goddess Pallas Athene confronts Perseus with a choice of two ways of life. He can choose, she says, to be one of those souls of clay that

". . . fatten at ease, like sheep in the pasture, and eat what they do not sow, like oxen in the

stall . . . and when they are ripe death gathers them, and they go down unloved into hell, and their name vanishes out of the land.

But to souls of fire I give more fire, and to those who are manful I give a might more than man's. . . . For I drive them forth by strange paths, Perseus, that they may fight the Titans and the monsters, the enemies of Gods and men. . . ."

For every generation there are Titans and monsters to be conquered. For children of ten and older, mythology opens new imaginative vistas. These mortals who aspire to immortal deeds, these bright gods, and these "cloud-capped towers, the gorgeous palaces" of Olympus are indeed "such stuff as dreams are made on," and every child should have them.

Epic and Hero Tales

In the source collections of myths, both Greek and Norse, there are (in addition to the stories of the gods) tales of human heroes, buffeted violently by gods and men but daring greatly, suffering uncomplainingly, and enduring staunchly to the end. Some of these heroes (for instance, Odysseus) accumulated so many stories about their names that the collection of these tales makes an epic. The word *epic* comes from the Greek *epos* meaning "a saying or a song," but it has now come to signify, according to Helen Guerber in *The Book of the Epic,* "some form of heroic narrative wherein tragedy, comedy, lyric, dirge, and idyl are skillfully blended to form an immortal work."

CHARACTERISTICS OF THE EPIC

Epics are sometimes written in verse, as the *Iliad* or the *Sigurd Saga,* and sometimes in prose, as Malory's *Morte d'Arthur*. The adventures of the legendary hero Robin Hood were preserved by the ballads. Miss Guerber's definition allows for a wide flexibility in the form and content of the epic; she includes such dissimilar materials as the great philosophical poem from the Hebrew, the Book of Job, the slight and romantic *Aucassin and Nicolette* from the medieval French, and the comparatively modern *Paradise Lost* by the English poet, John Milton.

Most of us, however, think of epics as a cycle of tales gathered around one hero, such as the *Odyssey* or the *Iliad.* These two heroic narratives have come to typify this particular field of literature. In them legendary heroes pursue legendary adventures, aided or hindered by partisan gods who apparently leave Olympus for the express purpose of meddling in human affairs. In short, myth may still be with us in the epic, but the dramatic center of interest has now shifted from the gods to a human hero. We have moved from Olympus to earth; we have transferred our sympathies from gods to men, from divine adventures to human endeavors.

The epic is strongly national in its presentation of human character. Odysseus may never have lived, but he is the embodiment of the Greek ideals of manly courage, sagacity, beauty, and endurance. Sigurd is the personification of Norse heroism; King Arthur is the code of chivalry in the flesh; and Robin Hood is the mouthpiece for England's passionate love of freedom and justice, as he is the ideal of hardy, jovial English manhood. Study the epic hero of a nation and you discover the moral code of that nation and era—all its heroic ideals embodied in one man.

Teachers sometimes say that the epics take up too much time, that there isn't space in the curriculum for such intensive living with one piece of literature. Yet it is that very time element which is important to the richness of feeling that the epic builds. Many individual stories like "Ulysses and Circe" are good stories, but it is Ulysses' struggles day after day, his resourcefulness, his vision, and his tireless endeavor that make the pathos of his homecoming and the triumph of his final bout with the wastrels a memorable experience for children. It is this living with greatness day after day that gives the epics their value for children.

THE ODYSSEY

The *Iliad* and the *Odyssey* are attributed to Homer, a legendary Greek poet. Songs about the siege of Troy are known to have been sung shortly after the events took place, although the first written forms of the epics did not appear until some six hundred years later. What Homer composed and what he compiled cannot be established, but the great epics known by his name were studied and recited by educated Greeks and there were apparently texts or arrangements of them from around 560 to 527 B.C. Authentic texts are established by 150 B.C. The date of Homer's birth has been variously estimated as from 1159 B.C. to 685 B.C., but by the time stories of Homer's life began to appear, nothing was authentically known about him. Legend has it that he was blind and poor and wandered from city to city singing his great songs. Seven cities vie with each other for the honor of being the place of his birth, but legend agrees only that his birthplace was somewhere in Ionia. George Gilbert Aimé Murray sums up this disputable evidence in the following fashion:

> *The man "Homer" cannot have lived in six different centuries nor been born in seven different cities; but Homeric poetry may well have done so. The man cannot have spoken this strange composite epic language, but the poetry could and did.*[24]

The *Iliad* is certainly complex and long, but the adventures in the *Odyssey*, or *Ulysses*, are exciting and understandable to children. If units of Greek life have vanished from your school, there is still no reason why the children should not have the *Odyssey*. Prompt the librarian to give it to them in her story hour—a serial, one story a week, till the suitors are all wiped out and Odysseus is happily reëstablished in his home with his faithful Penelope and his son Telemachus. If the librarian can't do it, why not try it yourself? No story is more rewarding to tell than this one. Superior readers can read it for themselves in the sixth or seventh grade, but it makes a strong appeal to younger children, as young as ten, and therefore seems to call for telling.[25]

24. George Gilbert Aimé Murray, "Homer," *Encyclopaedia Britannica.*

25. See suggestions on p. 387 in Chapter 13, "Storytelling and Reading Aloud."

Alice and Martin Provenson by every line of eyes, limbs, jutting profiles, and deadly spear, show violent action by desperate men. Here is the climax of the Cyclops story graphically told.
Reproduced by permission from The Iliad and the Odyssey *adapted by Jane Werner Watson. Illustration by Alice and Martin Provenson. Copyright © 1956 by Golden Press, Inc. Reproduced by permission of the publisher. (Original in color, book 9⅞ x 12¾, picture 9⅞ x 4)*

THE MERRY FRIAR CARRIETH ROBIN ACROSS THE WATER

Howard Pyle's almost photographic realism for his Robin Hood, *first published in 1883, is tremendously appealing in its lively details. The two clever, laughing faces, the costumes, and the castle in the background all catch the eye and the imagination.*
From The Merry Adventures of Robin Hood *by Howard Pyle. Copyright, 1946, by Charles Scribner's Sons. Reproduced by permission of the publishers. (Book 7 x 9)*

In this epic the Greek ideals of cool intelligence, patience, and resourcefulness are found in both Penelope and Odysseus. They exhibit these qualities and hold tenaciously to their goals even when men and gods are arrayed against them. Over "the misty sea," "the wine-dark sea," Odysseus sailed for twenty years and none could stay him. This is a story of fortitude which every generation of children should know.[26]

SIGURD THE VOLSUNG

The Norse epic *Sigurd the Volsung* is not so well known in this country as it deserves to be. There is a rugged nobility about the saga stories which boys especially appreciate. Because these tales reflect a simpler social order, many people consider them better suited to children than the Greek epics. This is a debatable point, since anyone who has ever tried to tell the saga of Sigurd knows all too well its difficulties. Obscurities in the text, difficult names much alike, and unpalatable social relationships upon which the main action of the story depends make this an epic which calls for expert handling.[27]

Certainly the saga has some elements of violence in common with those crime stories which the modern child may be reading in the newspapers or seeing in moving pictures. But their differences are important. In the latter, the tales of blood and murder are sordid, horrifying, and uninspired. In the Sigmund-Sigurd stories, there is the nobility of great heroism, of keeping your word even though it costs you your life, of self-sacrifice for a great cause, of death rather than dishonor, of ideals of race and family, of intrepid courage and perseverance. These justify the violence and leave the impression of nobility uppermost. If children must have blood and thunder and continually seek it in their television programs, movies, and comics, why should we expurgate all of their literature? Should we not, instead, give them violence in noble form, the great national epics which have left their mark on our moral code?

ROBIN HOOD

Of all the hero cycles, *Robin Hood* is unquestionably the children's favorite. It may not be the loftiest epic, and Robin Hood may not be the noblest hero, but his mad escapades, his lusty fights, his unfailing good humor when beaten, his sense of fair play, and, above all, his roguish tricks and gaiety practically define "hero" for children. Chil-

26. George H. Palmer's prose translation of the *Odyssey* is a splendid source of these tales.
27. See suggestions on p. 388 in Chapter 13, "Storytelling and Reading Aloud."

dren should read *Robin Hood,* see it in a moving-picture or television version, and read it again. Indeed, no other hero lends himself so readily to dramatization on screen or in classroom as does this gallant leader of the outlaws. School dramatizations of *Robin Hood* may be out-of-door affairs when the landscape includes enough trees. Otherwise the children can paint their own sets for an assembly program, or the story can be happily lived in any classroom, with a few props and plenty of spirit.

One grownup still remembers her childhood visits to her grandmother, when a flock of cousins and a nearby woods became the Outlaw Band and Sherwood Forest. The props were not exactly right; the bows and arrows were passable, but a coonskin cap and a powder bag were pressed into service and worn with authority. Their greens were motley until the children persuaded their mothers to equip them with green caps adorned with feathers from the chicken yard. These were sufficient. All summer they skulked and leapt through the trees, shot arrows into space, ran madly from the sheriff, and perspired mightily in the service of whoever had the good luck to be the Robin Hood of the day. This honor was passed around. To be sure, the youngest children never got an inning, but the older ones took turns, consoled in losing the lead by the richness of such roles as Little John, Friar Tuck, and all the others. That is the beauty of Robin Hood for dramatization; all the parts are fat parts, and everyone can star who has an imagination. This brief outline recalls only the main points of the story:

Robin Hood, wrongly accused of shooting the King's deer, is deprived of his estates and driven into hiding. He takes refuge in Sherwood Forest, where he organizes an outlaw band of heroes as lusty as himself. A giant of a fellow, Little John, worsts Robin Hood in a battle of staves and joins the band forthwith. A curtal friar, fat, jolly, and a good fighter, Friar Tuck by name, is another useful member of the band. So, too, are Will Scarlet, Allan a Dale, Midge the Miller's son, and all the others! This gay band continually harries its enemy the Sheriff of Nottingham, robs the rich to feed the poor, and generally conducts itself gallantly and triumphantly. Finally, there comes to Sherwood Forest a stout fellow who joins in the sports, quaffs ale with the fat friar, listens to the tales of wrongs righted and of the sheriff's downfall, and reveals himself as King Richard of the Lion Heart. To him the band swears loyalty. Lands and title are restored to Robin Hood and all ends merrily.

Or so you usually end a dramatization. But if the children read for themselves the Howard Pyle version, they will discover and weep over the tragic end of Robin Hood at the hands of the false Prioress. This is omitted in most school editions, but it is all right if the children discover it. They must learn that treachery and death exist, and that nothing lasts in this world except that little legacy of character a man leaves behind. With Robin Hood, this was so great a legacy that his name has never died, and today Robin Hood still means to us gallantry, gentleness, justice, and a warm gaiety which cannot be downed.

Children enjoy hearing some of the ballads of Robin Hood read aloud, but the prose version by Howard Pyle, with his spirited illustrations, is the text they should know. It is hard reading for most children, and if they can't read it for themselves, they should hear it. For the lucky superior readers, it remains for generation after generation of children one of the most exciting narratives in all literature.

KING ARTHUR AND THE KNIGHTS OF THE ROUND TABLE

Opinions differ as to the appropriateness of the King Arthur stories for young children. Certainly they are more mature in content and significance than either the *Odyssey* or *Robin Hood.* The individual adventures of some of the knights are as understandable as those of the Sherwood Forest band, but the ideals of chivalry are far subtler than the moral code of Robin Hood and his men. Too often brave deeds are performed for the love of a fair lady, and the Guinevere-Launcelot theme must be glossed over. For these reasons, many feel the cycle is better for the adolescent period when

Since the Ramayana *is often danced in ballet form, the artist has very properly illustrated the episodes in the style of the conventional postures of Oriental ballet. Illustration by Randy Monk. From* The Adventures of Rama *by Joseph Gaer. Copyright 1954, by Joseph Gaer. Reproduced by permission of Little, Brown and Company. (Book 5⅜ x 8)*

romance is uppermost and a code of chivalry needs to be established.

On the other hand, there are unusually good juvenile editions of the Arthur tales for children, which, simplified though they are, satisfy the child's love of knights and knightly adventures and make an excellent introduction to the cycle which they will encounter later in Tennyson's *Idylls of the King*. Teachers who love the Arthur stories will have children who enjoy them. Certainly a saturation with any of these hero cycles is an enriching experience. Among the stories popular with the children are: "How Arthur Became King," "The Winning of the Sword Excalibur," "The Winning of a Queen," "The Story of Merlin," "Sir Launcelot," "Sir Gawaine," "Sir Galahad's Search for the Holy Grail," and "The Passing of Arthur."

It is the gentleness and beauty of these stories and the idealistic character of King Arthur and his knights which sometimes furnish children with their first idea of strength in gentleness, of the power that comes through disciplined restraint. Not that they can put these qualities into words, but they are there, embodied in the strong, gentle men who are the heroes of these tales.

THE RAMAYANA

There was no version of the *Ramayana* suitable for children until Joseph Gaer's *The Adventures of Rama* was published. This myth-epic of India tells how the god Vishnu came down to earth as Prince Rama, a mortal, to save mankind from the evil powers of Ravan. Once on earth, Rama behaves much like other epic heroes. He fights innumerable battles, marries the beautiful Sita, suffers banishment, gives way to suspicion and jealousy, and is put to shame by the gentle Sita's trial by fire. After that, all goes well, and throughout the ten thousand years of Rama's reign

Unknown were want, disease and crime,
So calm, so happy was the time.

The individual stories resemble Greek myths rather more than the usual epic does. Older girls will enjoy the strongly romantic flavor of the tales, while boys will appreciate the thread of brotherly loyalty that runs through them. The illustrations suggest the dance, in which form the adventures of Rama are often shown in India.

OTHER EPICS

The Irish *Cuchulain the Hound of Ulster*, the French *Story of Roland*, and even the English *Beowulf*, while of tremendous importance to folklorists and to students of literature, are not necessarily important for children. Not all the epics can be crowded into the child's experience, and they shouldn't be. We must choose those which are the most appropriate for the years before adolescence. *Beowulf,* for instance, is in the heroic mold, but the fact that there is a dragon to be killed does not guarantee the suitability or the value of the story for children. It is, as a matter of fact, one of the bloodiest of all the sagas, with far less characterization of the persons involved and less nobility of action than are found in other epics. "St. George and the Dragon" is a more childlike tale of dragon-slaying, and the *Odyssey* and *Sigurd the Volsung* are richer in deeds and moral implications than the Beowulf stories.

Perhaps, in the schools, two epics in the years from ten to fourteen are about as many as the children can comfortably enjoy, living with them for weeks and savoring them thoroughly. Of the rich offering available, the *Odyssey* is of first importance and *Robin Hood* is the most popular and the easiest. These may be supplemented with such single hero tales as the stories of Moses, Jacob and Esau, and Joseph and his brethren, since those also have entered into our speech, our thinking, and our moral code. Choose, then, from the epics the one or two which you yourself enjoy and which you believe will give the children the greatest enjoyment and enrichment. Then live with these, joyously and intensively, for six or eight weeks.

Fable, myth, and epic are different from each other in many ways, yet all three are a part of the great stream of folk literature and are also embodiments of moral truths in story form.

The *fable* teaches briefly and frankly and provides the child with his first excursion into the realm of abstract ideas, intellectual speculations about conduct.

The *myth* teaches through symbols which grow more and more complex. The symbolism soon ceases to have the simple, obvious moral of a fable and becomes as complicated as life, and it is then proportionately difficult for a child to understand. Fortunately, the myth stories possess a beauty that is satisfying in itself.

The *epic* embodies national ideals in the person of a human hero, a doer of mighty deeds. A long cycle of stories about such a hero allows time for real characterizations, for a continual reiteration of the moral code. The hero lives up to this code and he succeeds, or he fails with glory. It is good for children to consort with greatness over a long period of time. Ideas and ideals have a chance to take hold.

So we leave traditional literature at a high level. Children have been treated to a progressively richer and richer legacy from *Mother Goose* to *Odysseus,* from "The Three Little Pigs" to "Phaëthon." Yet these gifts follow naturally—each good in its place, each offering new enjoyment. By the time the child reaches fable, myth, and epic, he must be capable of deeper feeling and understanding; for fable is a theorem, myth an allegory, and epic the glorification of man the doer, the hero.

SUGGESTED READING, PROBLEMS, AND PROJECTS

Suggested Reading: In addition to the fables included in the chapter read the following: "The Town Mouse and the Country Mouse," "The Lion and the Mouse," "The Hare and the Tortoise," "The Fox and the Grapes," "The Boy Who Cried Wolf," "The Wind and the Sun," "The Ox Who Won the Forfeit," "Granny's Blackie," "The Banyan Deer," and "The Hare That Ran Away."

Read the following myths in one of the editions discussed in the chapter or listed in the Bibliography: "Clytie," "Pandora," "Phaëthon," "Demeter and Persephone," "Daedalus," "Bellerophon and Pegasus," and "The Death of Balder."

If you have read *Robin Hood* and the *Odyssey,* review both. If not, read one.

1. What do folk tales, fables, myths, and epics have in common? In what ways are the last three types unlike the folk tales? Why are folk tales usually the most popular with children?

2. Why is it important that children know at least the more common fables, myths, and epics? What modern references to or uses of the fables, myths, and epics have you encountered recently? (See advertisements.)

3. Compare any two collections of fables (Aesop, La Fontaine, *The Panchatantra,* the *Jatakas*). What might children enjoy hearing about the backgrounds of these collections?

4. Give concrete examples which illustrate the differences between the proverb, the parable, and the fable. What have they in common? Divide the class into groups of five or six, choose a familiar proverb, and try to turn it into a fable. Compare results. Or write a proverb which summarizes the moral lesson taught in one of the modern stories listed on page 321.

5. Which types of myth stories are suitable for children and which ones are unsuitable? Would you read or tell myths? Why?

6. Evaluate any of the editions of myths discussed in the text.

7. What might children enjoy hearing about Homer or Greek life in general as preparation for the study of the *Odyssey*?

8. Divide the class into groups and have each group read and report on various editions of one epic other than the *Odyssey*. Consider illustrations, print, reading ease. What parts of each epic would lend themselves to dramatization?

9. On the whole, which epic seems to have greatest child appeal? Why?

GENERAL REFERENCES

ASIMOV, ISAAC. *Words from the Myths.* Houghton, 1961. From the Greek myths come many word roots used in science and daily language. Mr. Asimov tells the legends briefly and explains origins of current usage.

AUSLANDER, JOSEPH, and FRANK HILL. *The Winged Horse,* ill. by Paul Honoré. Doubleday, 1927. The story of poets and their poetry for children. Fine references on ballads and epics.

Funk and Wagnalls Standard Dictionary of Folklore, Mythology and Legend (see Bibliography, Chapter 10).

GUERBER, HELENE A. *The Book of the Epic.* Lippincott, 1913. A summary of all the national epics, copiously illustrated with paintings from the old masters and with interesting excerpts from poetry.

SMITH, RUTH, ed. *The Tree of Life,* ill. by Boris Artzybasheff. Viking, 1942. A distinguished text for a comparative study of religious ideas. It is a compilation of the "testaments of beauty and faith from many lands." Excerpts from the expressions of religious ideals of the Navaho Indians, the Norse, Hindu, Buddhist, Confucianist, and other religions (including the Hebrew and Christian) make up the content of the book, which is for adolescents or for adults to use with older children.

AESOP'S FABLES

Aesop for Children, illustrated by Milo Winter. Rand McNally, 1919. The fables have been expanded in this edition, making them more like stories. Children enjoy them, and the illustrations are beautiful. 10-14

Aesop's Fables, tr. by V. S. Vernon Jones, ill. by Arthur Rackham. Doubleday, 1912. One of the most satisfactory editions both for children and adults. Chesterton's introduction should not be missed. The illustrations appeal to older children. 10-14

Aesop's Fables, ill. by Fritz Kredel. Grosset, 1947. An attractive, readable edition which contains over 150 fables. Illustrated in color and black and white. 10-14

EVANS, KATHERINE. *A Bundle of Sticks,* ill. by the author. Whitman, 1962. An amusing modern picture book adaptation of the Aesop fable for younger readers. Other adaptations by this author include *The Boy Who Cried Wolf* (1960) and *A Camel in the Tent* (1961). 5-8

Fables from Aesop, retold by James Reeves, ill. by Maurice Wilson. Walck, 1962. In his selection of fifty fables, the narrator has introduced brief dialogue and descriptive phrases to enliven them, while keeping to the spirit of the original. Illustrations, many in color, are exceptional in quality. 9-13

The Fables of Aesop, as first printed by William Caxton, 1484, ed., intro. by Joseph Jacobs, 2 vols. London: Nutt, 1889. Found only in unusual collections. Contains Jacobs' history of the fables in full.

The Hare and the Tortoise, ill. by Paul Galdone. McGraw, 1962. Action-filled color illustrations for this Aesop fable heighten suspense for the youngest. 4-7

JACOBS, JOSEPH, ed. *The Fables of Aesop,* ill. by Kurt Wiese. Macmillan, 1950. This classic edition of the fables includes Jacobs' short history and is delightfully illustrated. 10-12

The Miller, His Son, and Their Donkey, ill. by Roger Duvoisin. McGraw, 1962. Fun in story and picture as the poor miller tries hard to please everyone and ends pleasing no one. 5-7

TOWNSEND, GEORGE TYLER, and THOMAS JAMES, tr. *Aesop's Fables,* ill. by Glen Rounds. Lippincott, 1949. The translation used in this edition is simpler than Jacobs' and the humorous illustrations appeal strongly to children 10-12

FRENCH FABLES

LA FONTAINE. *The Fables of La Fontaine,* tr. by Marianne Moore. Viking, 1954. These fables retain their original verse form in this translation. A scholarly edition which includes La Fontaine's twelve books of fables and his own original preface. Chiefly an adult source.

NORTON, ANDRÉ. *Rogue Reynard,* ill. by Laura Bannon. Houghton, 1947. Stories from the French beast epic of Reynard the Fox. 9-12

INDIAN FABLES

BABBITT, ELLEN C. *Jataka Tales* (see Bibliography, Chapter 10).

———. *More Jataka Tales* (see Bibliography, Chapter 10).

BROWN, MARCIA. *Once a Mouse* (see Bibliography, Chapter 10).

GAER, JOSEPH. *The Fables of India,* ill. by Randy Monk. Little, 1955. Beast tales from three outstanding collections of Indian fables: the Panchatantra, the Hitopadesa, and the Jatakas. The stories are entertainingly presented, and there is excellent background material on the known history of fable literature for the student. 12-16

The Panchatantra, tr. by Arthur W. Ryder, Univ. of Chicago Press, 1925. Adult students of the fables will be interested in discovering here the sources of many Aesop and La Fontaine fables. The proverbs in verse form might provide themes for new fables.

MODERN FABLES

ANDERSEN, HANS CHRISTIAN. *The Ugly Duckling, The Emperor's New Clothes,* and others (see Bibliography, Chapter 12).

BRENNER, ANITA. *A Hero by Mistake,* ill. by Jean Charlot. W. R. Scott, 1953. Afraid of his own shadow, this little man accidentally captures some bandits, is hailed as a hero, and learns to behave like one. 6-8

CIARDI, JOHN. *John J. Plenty and Fiddler Dan,* ill. by Madeleine Gekiere. Lippincott, 1963. 4-9

CHAUCER, GEOFFREY. *Chanticleer and the Fox,* adapted and ill. by Barbara Cooney. Crowell, 1958. Pictures of colorful beauty and design add delight to the old fable of the crafty fox and the vain cock. Caldecott Medal, 1959. 6-9

DAUGHERTY, JAMES. *Andy and the Lion* (see Bibliography, Chapter 12).

FRISKEY, MARGARET. *Seven Diving Ducks* (see Bibliography, Chapter 12).

GÁG, WANDA. *Nothing at All* (see Bibliography, Chapter 12).

LEAF, MUNRO. *The Story of Ferdinand* (see Bibliography, Chapter 14).

MCGINLEY, PHYLLIS. *The Plain Princess* (see Bibliography, Chapter 12).

GREEK AND ROMAN MYTHS AND EPICS: REFERENCES

BENEDICT, RUTH. "Folklore" (see Bibliography, Chapter 10). A complete and authoritative discussion of various theories of the myth.

BULFINCH, THOMAS. *Age of Fable; or, Stories of Gods and Heroes,* intro. by Dudley Fitts, ill. by Joe Mugnaini. Heritage, 1958. This handsome edition of Bulfinch is almost completely devoted to the Greek and Roman myths, though it does include brief materials from the Norse, Celtic, and Hindu lore.

FISKE, JOHN. *Myths and Myth Makers.* Houghton, 1900. A comparative study of the myths of many peoples, classical and primitive.

GREEN, ROGER LANCELYN. *Andrew Lang,* Walck Monographs (see Bibliography, Chapter 2).

GUERBER, HELENE A. *Myths of Greece and Rome.* American Bk., 1893. A standard reference, retelling and interpreting the myths.

HESIOD. *The Homeric Hymns and Homerica,* tr. by Hugh G. Evelyn-White. Putnam, 1914. An invaluable source to be found in large libraries.

HOMER. *The Odyssey,* tr. by George H. Palmer, ill. by N. C. Wyeth. Houghton, 1929. This cadenced prose will sing in your memory like poetry. For children who are superior readers, this edition illustrated by Wyeth is a superb source for these tales.

OVID. *The Metamorphoses,* tr. by Henry T. Riley. McKay, 1899. A literal prose translation of the Latin versions of the Greek myths and hero tales, with copious notes explaining their fable or allegorical significance.

REINACH, SALOMON. *Orpheus: A History of Religions,* rev. ed. Liveright, 1933. A fascinating study, though dated in some respects. Pages 84-93 contain the core of his theory explaining the evolution of Greek religion and myth.

SCHWAB, GUSTAV. *Gods and Heroes,* tr. by Olga Marx and Ernst Morwitz, ill. with designs from Greek vases. Pantheon, 1946. This large and beautiful book still omits a few favorite myths. The English translation from a German adaptation is not always satisfactory, but the book is an excellent source nevertheless.

TATLOCK, JESSIE M. *Greek and Roman Mythology.* Appleton, 1917. Although intended for high school study, this is a useful book for teachers. Miss Tatlock retells the myths, gives excerpts from the "Homeric Hymn" and modern poetry, and presents some fine photographs of Greek sculpture.

WOODBERRY, GEORGE E. *The Torch.* Macmillan, 1905. Two chapters on "The Titan Myth" are devoted to an analysis of the significance of the Prometheus idea, its likeness to Christian ideas, and its use in English poetry. Found in large libraries.

GREEK AND ROMAN MYTHS AND EPICS: CHILDREN'S BOOKS

BENSON, SALLY. *Stories of the Gods and Heroes,* ill. by Steele Savage. Dial, 1940. 10-14

CHURCH, ALFRED JOHN. *The Odyssey of Homer,* ill. by John Flaxman. Macmillan, 1951. First published in 1906, this attractive recent edition is an excellent source for children to read or adults to tell. Stories are arranged in chronological order. 10-14

COLUM, PADRAIC. *The Children's Homer,* ill. by Willy Pogány. Macmillan, 1925, 1962. A distinguished version in cadenced prose, simple but in the spirit of the original. Vigorous illustrations and handsome enlarged format.

______. *The Golden Fleece,* ill. by Willy Pogány. Macmillan, 1921, 1962. A companion edition to *The Children's Homer,* and equally fine. 10-14

COOLIDGE, OLIVIA E. *Greek Myths,* ill. by Edouard Sandoz. Houghton, 1949. Mrs. Coolidge has retold twenty-seven of the most widely known Greek myths. Here the gods are not idealized, but the stories have authenticity. For young people rather than children. 10-16

D'AULAIRE, INGRI and EDGAR PARIN. *Book of Greek Myths,* ill. by authors. Doubleday, 1962. 8-12

DE SÉLINCOURT, AUBREY. *Odysseus the Wanderer,* ill. by Norman Meredith. Criterion Bks., 1956. A lusty, modern retelling of the *Odyssey* that should lure many young readers into an acquaintance with this epic before high-school days. 11-

GALT, TOM. *The Rise of the Thunderer,* ill. by John Mackey. Crowell, 1954. An absorbing retelling of the ancient Greek story of creation. The language is modern and the narrative moves at a swift pace as it tells of gods who fought for power, sons against fathers. 10-14

GRAVES, ROBERT. *Greek Gods and Heroes,* ill. by Dimitris Davis. Doubleday, 1960. 12-15

______. *The Siege and Fall of Troy,* ill. by C. Walter Hodges. Doubleday, 1963. An easy-to-follow narrative history of the Trojan War. 12-16

GREEN, ROGER LANCELYN. *Heroes of Greece and Troy; retold from the Ancient Authors,* ill. by Heather Copley and Christopher Chamberlain. Walck, 1961. The tales of the Heroic Age have been woven into a unified whole, from the coming of the Immortals to Odysseus, the last of the heroes. Beautifully written, and with an introduction that will give insight into the great variety of classic sources used in this fine version. 12-

HAWTHORNE, NATHANIEL. *The Golden Touch,* ill. by Paul Galdone. McGraw, 1959. The old tale of King Midas is imaginatively illustrated with gold-toned pictures. 6-9

______. *A Wonder Book, and Tanglewood Tales,* ill. by Maxfield Parrish. Dodd, 1934. Although not good interpretations of the old myths, these stories are nevertheless worth examining for their storytelling qualities. Editions illustrated by Walter Crane and Arthur Rackham are available in many libraries. 10-14

KINGSLEY, CHARLES. *The Heroes,* ill. by Vera Bock. Macmillan, 1954. Beautifully retold tales which make a fine cycle for the storyteller. 10-14

LANG, ANDREW. *The Adventures of Odysseus,* ill. by Joan Kiddell-Monroe. Dutton, 1962. Andrew Lang's distinguished retellings of Homer's *Iliad* and the *Odyssey* are reissued in handsome new format. Originally published in his *Tales of Greece and Troy* (1907). 12-

MACPHERSON, JAY. *Four Ages of Man,* ill. St. Martin's Press, 1962. Beautifully narrated stories from the Greek myths organized around four periods: "creation and the coming of the gods; pastoral life and the ordering of the seasons; the adventures and the labors of the heroes; war, tragic tales, and decline into history." Illustrations have been drawn from ancient vases. 13-

PICARD, BARBARA LEONIE. *The Iliad of Homer,* ill. by Joan Kiddell-Monroe. Walck, 1960. A truly distinguished retelling of the *Iliad,* with characters sympathetically portrayed. *The Odyssey of Homer* (1952) is an equally fine companion volume. 12-15

SELLEW, CATHARINE. *Adventures with the Gods,* ill. by George and Doris Hauman. Little, 1945. An introduction to the more familiar myths, simply written for younger children. 9-12

SERRAILLIER, IAN. *The Gorgon's Head; the Story of Perseus,* ill. by William Stobbs. Walck, 1962. 12-14

______. *The Way of Danger; The Story of Theseus,* ill. by William Stobbs. Walck, 1963. 12-14

SEWELL, HELEN. *A Book of Myths,* sel. from Bulfinch's *Age of Fable,* ill. by Helen Sewell. Macmillan, 1942. Some people dislike, others are enthusiastic about the stylized illustrations in black and white, or sharp blue, black, and white. They are undeniably authentic in spirit and detail. For a Greek ballet or dramatization, these are worth study. A recommended edition. 10-14

TAYLOR, N. B. *The Aeneid of Virgil,* ill. by Joan Kiddell-Monroe. Walck, 1961. The epic of Aeneas and his journeys after the burning of Troy, retold in an excellent prose version. 13-15

NORSE MYTHS AND EPICS: REFERENCES

EDDA SAEMUNDAR. *The Poetic Edda,* tr. by Lee M. Hollander. Univ. of Texas Press, 1928. Another good translation with notes on verse form.

______. *The Poetic Edda,* tr. by Henry Adams Bellows, American-Scandinavian Foundation, 1923. Not only a fine translation but good background and evaluation of material.

MUNCH, PETER A. *Norse Mythology, Legends of Gods and Heroes,* rev. by Magnus Olsen, tr. by Sigurd B. Hustvedt. American-Scandinavian Foundation, 1926. Authoritative and complete interpretation of sources.

Volsunga Saga: The Story of the Volsungs and Niblungs, with Certain Songs from the Elder Edda, tr. by Eirikr Magnusson and William Morris. London: Walter Scott, n.d. This prose translation of the difficult verse form of the *Elder Edda* is easy to read and is the basis for Morris' beautiful verse version of the saga. (In 1962 Collier Bks. published a paperback version using the Morris translation.)

NORSE MYTHS AND EPICS: CHILDREN'S BOOKS

BROWN, ABBIE FARWELL. *In the Days of Giants,* ill. by E. B. Smith. Houghton, 1902. This is a sterling adaptation of the Norse myths. 10-14

COLUM, PADRAIC. *Children of Odin,* ill. by Willy Pogány. Macmillan, 1920, 1962. Norse myths and hero tales retold in a continuous narrative ending with the death of Sigurd. Our best source for children. In fine modern format. 10-14

COOLIDGE, OLIVIA. *Legends of the North,* ill. by Edouard Sandoz. Houghton, 1951. A wide variety of stories includes tales of the northern gods and heroes, the Volsungs, and other sagas. 12-14

HOSFORD, DOROTHY G. *Sons of the Volsungs,* ill. by Frank Dobias. Holt, 1949. A splendid version of the Sigurd tales adapted from William Morris' *The Story of Sigurd the Volsung and the Fall of the Niblungs.* 11-14

______. *Thunder of the Gods,* ill. by George and Claire Louden. Holt, 1952. Distinguished retellings of the Norse myths: stories of Odin, Thor, Balder, Loki, and other familiar tales. Excellent for storytelling or reading aloud. 11-14

SELLEW, CATHARINE. *Adventures with the Heroes,* ill. by Steele Savage. Little, 1954. Retold in simple language are the stories of the Volsungs and Nibelungs. 9-12

ENGLISH EPICS

HOSFORD, DOROTHY G. *By His Own Might; the Battles of Beowulf,* ill. by Laszlo Matulay. Holt, 1947. A distinguished retelling of *Beowulf* for boys and girls. 11-16

LANIER, SIDNEY. *The Boy's King Arthur,* ill. by N. C. Wyeth, ed. from Sir Thomas Malory's *History of King Arthur and His Knights of the Round Table.* Scribner, 1942. An authoritative and popular version of this hero cycle; the best one to use for reading or telling. 10-14

MCSPADDEN, J. WALKER. *Robin Hood and His Merry Outlaws,* ill. by Louis Slobodkin. World, 1946. While the McSpadden versions of the Robin Hood tales are not so satisfying as Howard Pyle's, they are good, and much easier to read. Mr. Slobodkin's illustrations are humorous and appealing. 9-12

MALORY, SIR THOMAS. *Le Morte d'Arthur,* ill. by W. Russell Flint. London: Warner, publisher to the Medici Society [1921], 2 vols. Children who are superior readers are fascinated with this source of the Arthur stories. 12-16

PYLE, HOWARD. *The Merry Adventures of Robin Hood of Great Renown in Nottinghamshire,* ill. by author. Scribner, 1946. This is the great prose edition of the Robin Hood tales, the best source for reading and telling. 12-14

______. *Some Merry Adventures of Robin Hood,* rev. ed., ill. by author. Scribner, 1954. This book contains a dozen stories adapted from the longer book, and would serve as an introduction for younger readers. 10-13

______. *The Story of King Arthur and His Knights,* ill. by author. Scribner, 1933. Any Pyle edition is written with grace and distinction. This is no exception. 12-14

SERRAILLIER, IAN. *Beowulf, the Warrior,* ill. by Severin. Walck, 1961. The Anglo-Saxon epic is retold in stirring verse by the distinguished British poet. The episodes of Grendel, Grendel's mother, and the Fire Dragon are included in this handsomely illustrated book. 12-

Song of Robin Hood, ed. by Anne Malcolmson, music arr. by Grace Castagnetta, ill. by Virginia Lee Burton. Houghton, 1947. Eighteen ballads in rhythmic text illustrated with distinguished black-and-white drawings. Traditional music for many of the ballads is included. The book is the result of careful research in art and music as well as in selection of the ballads. 10-14

SUTCLIFF, ROSEMARY. *Beowulf,* ill. by Charles Keeping. Dutton, 1962. This magnificent prose version retains the true spirit of the ancient epic, and yet is told with restraint, concluding with the death of Beowulf. 11-

OTHER NATIONAL EPICS

DAVIS, RUSSELL, and BRENT K. ASHABRANNER. *Ten Thousand Desert Swords; The Epic Story of a Great Bedouin Tribe,* ill. by Leonard Everett Fisher. Little, 1960. The Bani Hilal were a great and ancient warrior tribe, and their legends are superbly retold for the discriminating reader. 12-

DEUTSCH, BABETTE. *Heroes of the Kalevala,* ill. by Fritz Eichenberg. Messner, 1940. This version has not only literary distinction but continuity. Text and illustrations bring out the lusty humor of the tales. 10-14

GAER, JOSEPH. *The Adventures of Rama,* ill. by Randy Monk. Little, 1954. One of the best-loved epics of India is the story of Prince Rama and of his wife Sita, stolen from him by a demon king. The careful selection of incidents makes this an absorbing and unified tale. 12-14

HAZELTINE, ALICE, ed. *Hero Tales from Many Lands,* ill. by Gordon Laite. Abingdon, 1961. A sampling of the epic literature of many countries introduced through thirty tales of Greek, Anglo-Saxon, Celtic, Persian, Spanish, and many other heroes. Handsomely illustrated. 11-15

HULL, ELEANOR. *The Boys' Cuchulain,* ill. by Stephen Reid. Crowell, 1910. (published in England as *Cuchulain, the Hound of Ulster.*) Cuchulain and King Nessa are supposed to have lived about the first century, but the earliest documents about them are from the eleventh and twelfth centuries. Cuchulain stands for the highest ideal of Irish hero. This is a fine cycle of tales for older boys and girls. 11-14

NORTON, ANDRÉ [pseud. for Alice Mary Norton]. *Huon of the Horn,* ill. by Joe Krush. Harcourt, 1951. An episode of the Charlemagne saga retold with distinction. This adaptation is based on a sixteenth-century translation and tells of a cruelly betrayed knight who tries to regain his emperor's favor. 12-14

The Song of Roland, tr. by Merriam Sherwood, ill. by Edith Emerson. McKay, 1938. This is one of the finest translations of the story of Roland for younger readers, and is illustrated with distinctive line drawings. 12-16

chapter 12

New Magic

The distinction between the old folk tale and the modern fairy tale is of no importance to the child. Magic is magic to him whether he finds it in Grimm, Andersen, or Dr. Seuss. Children do not think of their stories in the conventional categories of literature or of libraries but describe their favorites broadly as animal stories or funny stories or true stories or fairy tales, by which they mean any tale of magic, old or modern. The elements in the folk tales which make them particularly appealing to children are the same ones which make the fanciful tales attractive. In fact, interesting story patterns, style, and characterizations are elements essential to any good story for children. Many of the old folk tales were unsuitable for children because of their bawdiness, their violence, or their adult themes and situations. Some modern fanciful stories err because they are overwhimsical or unduly sophisticated or, worse still, because they talk down to children. As we select from the new fanciful stories being published each year, let's keep in mind (along with good story patterns, style, and characterizations) sincerity and directness as essential characteristics.

The development of modern fanciful tales has been so astonishing and varied that it merits detailed examination. Because there are so many of these tales, this chapter can consider only a few—stories which have remained favorites over the years, recent ones which have attained great popularity, and certain ones which illustrate trends.

The Beginnings of the Modern Fanciful Tale

Hans Christian Andersen is generally credited with launching the literary fairy tale. Actually, it began in the French court of the seventeenth century, with elaborations of traditional tales. Fairy tales moved boldly from the hut in the woods to the fashionable drawing rooms of the court and became the vogue of the sophisticates in the century of Louis XIV. Perrault's eight little *contes* were the rage, but adorned though they were with the gentle art of a skilled writer, they remained genuine folk tales, perhaps a shade too simple for the intelligentsia. So the cultivated ladies of the court began their embroideries.

Mme. d'Aulnoy with her "White Cat," "Graciosa and Percinet," "The Yellow Dwarf," and others turned the fairy tale into an involved story full of double meanings and romance. Published around 1700, these stories in adapted or shortened form are still found in modern collections.

Mme. Leprince de Beaumont wrote chiefly in a didactic vein for children, but happily she had her lighter moments, and her "Beauty and the Beast" (1757) was one of these. With this charming adaptation of a famous folk-tale theme, she forgot her need to improve children's manners and morals; sheer enchantment was the result. Her story is of course strongly reminiscent of the Norse "East o' the Sun and West o' the Moon" and Grimm's "Bearskin." But Beauty seems more human and convincing than the lassies in the older stories, and neither of the four-footed heroes in the folk tales has the heart-wringing pathos of Beauty's sighing Beast. Although this is not an original tale, Mme. de Beaumont has retold it so tenderly and with such inventive touches that it has long been the favorite version of that theme. Andersen, too, began with skillful adaptations of traditional tales, but his creative genius lifted the modern fairy tale to greatness and he is deservedly called its originator.

Hans Christian Andersen, 1805-1875

Andersen's life was as incredible as his fairy tales. He was born at Odense, Denmark. His father, a poor shoemaker, disappointed because he could never be a scholar, cherished a shelf of the classics which he shared with his son. The mother was an uneducated peasant with a protective tenderness for the strange boy whom she could only partially understand. After the father died, the mother married again but was obliged to support her son as a washerwoman. Up to her knees in the cold water of the river, suffering from the rheumatic pains which afflicted all the washerwomen of Odense, this poor soul helped her son as long as she lived. There was a feeble-minded grandfather, of whom Hans was horribly ashamed, and a cheerful little grandmother, who tended the gardens of the insane asylum and told Hans fantastic tales of his family. The boy heard also the stories and superstitions of the peasants, and the weird imaginings of the patients in the insane asylum.

Poor and ignorant, romantically vain and proud, young Hans avoided school and lived in a dream world of his own creation. He made a puppet theater, dressed his puppets with remarkable skill, and dramatized the stories and the plays he was reading so avidly. He was spellbound by Shakespeare's plays and soon imagined himself becoming a great dramatist. With equal ease, he imagined himself as a ballet dancer, a great actor, a singer, a poet, in spite of the fact that he was as strikingly ugly and awkward as he was uneducated. He was overtall for his age, with big hands and feet, a big nose, a shock of yellow hair over his eyes, and a gangling body which was always outgrowing the poor clothes he somehow managed to keep clean and neat. But none of these limitations disturbed him, so strong were his dreams.

At fourteen he set off for Copenhagen alone to seek the fortune which he never doubted would await him. The disillusioning years which followed would have crushed a less intrepid soul. He literally broke in upon opera singers, ballet masters, and men of literature, and sang, danced, or recited poetry for them whether they wished it or not. He was considered mildly mad, was snubbed on all sides, and was reduced to near starvation; but here and there someone always believed in the strange boy. Musicians helped him first, until his high, sweet soprano voice changed and he was of no use to the choir. Then Jonas Collin, director of the Royal Theater, obtained a small pension for the boy and made him go back to school. Before starting to school again, he published his first book, *The Ghost at Palnatoke's Grave*. At the grammar school at Slagelse and at another school in Elsinore, he remained for some five or six years. These were the bitterest years of his entire life, and the schoolmaster who humiliated and tortured him used to appear in the nightmares which haunted Andersen's old age.

Returning to Copenhagen, educated in some degree, he resumed his writing of plays and poetry with only moderate success. In 1833 Andersen traveled on a modest stipend, granted to him by the king, and visited all those countries whose glories he was to give back to the world in his *Fairy Tales*. The first volume of these was published in 1835. They created no special stir, but, as more of them appeared in the ensuing years, their fame grew and spread to other countries until Hans Andersen found himself famous as the author of the *Fairy Tales,* which became as much the vogue as the *Contes des fées* in eighteenth-century France and completely eclipsed all of the author's more pretentious works. Andersen was never wholly resigned to the allocation of his fame to his stories for children. He continued to struggle with other types of writing which never succeeded as his fairy tales did. These were translated into almost every European language and brought Andersen the friendship of notable artists all over the world. The most poignant of all his triumphs must have been his return to his native Odense. There he was carried on the shoulders of his countrymen, who filled the streets to do him honor.

Except for the bad dreams, Andersen's old age was as peaceful and happy as his youth had been tragic. The world, which had laughed at the vain, childlike boy, now cherished and revered the famous old man, the favorite son of Odense and Copenhagen.

The stories themselves, probably the greatest fairy tales ever written, have a freshness and range that are just as astonishing to readers today as they were to those of Andersen's generation. He may have started retelling the old folk tales and combining folk-tale motifs into new tales, but he was soon creating original patterns of his own. His stories fall into rather obvious classifications, which are worth noting because we shall find that modern tales of magic can be grouped under these same headings.

RETELLING OF OLD TALES

First, there are Andersen's versions of familiar folk tales such as "What the Good-Man Does Is Sure to Be Right!" which is our Norse friend "Gudbrand on the Hill-side"; "Hans Clodhopper," which is "Lazy Jack"; "Great Claus and Little Claus," which is "Hudden and Dudden"; "The Wild Swans," which is Grimm's "The Six Swans" and Asbjörnsen's "Twelve Wild Ducks." When Andersen retold these old tales, he never destroyed the essential elements of the original plots but merely added little embellishments, little characterizations so charming and so right that they are never forgotten. For instance, in "What the Good-Man Does Is Sure to Be Right!" you get a foretaste of the happy end when the old wife prepares her husband for his trip to the market:

So she tied on his neckerchief—for that was a matter she understood better than he—she tied it with a double knot, and made him look quite spruce; she dusted his hat with the palm of her hand; and she kissed him and sent him off, riding the horse that was to be either sold or bartered. Of course, he would know what to do.

NEW STORIES IN FOLK-TALE STYLE

Andersen was so steeped in folk-tale motifs and style that his own stories seem to have come out of some old folk collection. "The Elfin-Mount" sounds curiously like an Asbjörnsen tale. "Thumbelina" might be a feminine version of the Russian "Peter Pea," the English "Hop-o'-My-Thumb," or Grimm's "Thumbling," but is, of course, an original tale. "The Little Mermaid" is remotely reminiscent both of the water nixies who desire human husbands and of the wives and sweethearts who go through untold sufferings to rescue their beloveds. Yet these and other Andersen tales are not retellings but completely new stories in the old manner, using familiar motifs in new combinations.

HUMOROUS TALES

When Andersen retells a folk tale or improvises in folk-tale style, he often falls into the hearty, slapstick humor of the old stories. Good examples are his genuinely droll "Great Claus and Little Claus" and some of the fantastic episodes in "The Elfin-Mount." But the moment he begins to write original stories, his humor becomes more subtle, less childlike, often satirical. "The Real Princess," "The Swineherd," and "The Emperor's New Clothes" are all satires on adult foibles, and the humor is ironical. After presenting a picture of a princess atop twenty mattresses under which is one little pea that causes her acute suffering, Andersen concludes, with tongue in cheek, "Was not this a lady of real delicacy?" This is as sly a jibe at snobbery and the myth of blue-bloodedness as can be found anywhere.

He uses "The Swineherd" to make fun of false standards and people who prefer the artificial and the trivial to the durable satisfactions of life. In "The Emperor's New Clothes," Andersen relieves his mind of all its pent-up bitterness against the pompous pretentiousness of the rogues and fools who sometimes inhabit high places. This is not childlike humor, but the irony of an adult lampooning some of the cruel foibles from which he has suffered. Fortunately, most of the satire goes over the children's heads, and they take the stories literally. They are perfectly serious over the absurd princess on her twenty mattresses, and they accept the emperor as the broadest kind of farce. Nevertheless, Andersen's humor is adult rather than childlike and is predominantly satirical rather than truly and obviously funny.

INANIMATE OBJECTS PERSONIFIED

Stories about inanimate objects seem to have been Andersen's invention and special delight. "The Darning Needle," "The Drop of Water," "The Flax," "The Fir Tree," "The Constant Tin Soldier," and "The Top and the Ball" are only a few of the stories in which Andersen endows objects with life and turns their exploits into stories. They are good sto-

Erik Blegvad revisited his native Denmark before he began to illustrate the Andersen fairy tales. His pictures are full of delicate details, and the luminous light gives them clarity and color. Illustration by Erik Blegvad. Reproduced from Hans Christian Andersen's The Swineherd, *© 1958, by Erik Blegvad, by permission of Harcourt, Brace & World, Inc. (Original in color, book 6½ x 7½, picture 4½ x 3)*

ries, too, though many of them are sad and adult in theme and therefore not popular with children. Modern authors have picked up Andersen's innovation and put it to happier and more childlike uses.

TALKING BEASTS

The story with animals that talk is an old form which Andersen uses less frequently than others but carries to a more complex and symbolic level than is found in the folk tales. The traditional story "The Three Little Pigs," for instance, tells a simple tale of brains against brawn and is understandable and childlike. When Andersen told the story of "The Ugly Duckling," he wrote his own biography in symbols which are strangely moving. Writing of the ugly duckling, he says, "The poor little thing scarcely knew what to do; he was quite distressed, because he was so ugly, and because he was the jest of the poultry-yard." The duckling went out into the world to seek his fortune, but there also he was snubbed, laughed at, persecuted, and left bitterly alone. He saw the swans flying "so very high . . . he could not forget them, those noble birds!" When he could no longer see them, "he plunged to the bottom of the water, and when he rose again was almost beside himself . . . the poor, ugly animal!"

Finally, after an almost unendurable winter, the spring came again and with it the swans. He approached them expecting they would kill him, but they welcomed him as one of themselves, and when he looked in the water, he saw his own reflection—not that of an ugly duckling, but of a swan! "It matters not to have been born in a duck-yard, if one has been hatched from a swan's egg." "The Ugly Duckling" is no folk tale but a touching allegory. Do we not see ourselves as ugly ducklings, waiting for that marvelous moment of recognition when the swans shall welcome us into their noble company? This theme goes deeper than the Cinderella motive, for it shows us a human soul struggling pitiably and fiercely against its own limitations. Fortunately, it is also a convincing story of a misplaced swan baby, which pleases children eight to twelve years old, even while it gives them a sense of larger meaning, felt, if not clearly apprehended. "The Nightingale" is Andersen's old sermon against the false standards of society, but it is less satirical and more tender than "The Swineherd."

FANTASY

Finally, Andersen took the make-believe and the magic of the folk tales and developed tales of pure fantasy which have never been surpassed—"The Marsh King's Daughter," "The Little Mermaid," "The Girl Who Trod on the Loaf," "The Little Match Girl," and, finest of them all, "The Snow Queen." What tales these are! Every one of them is allegorical; but, in most cases, they are excellent stories despite their secondary meanings. "The Marsh King's Daughter" is a weird tale of a changeling—a savage, cruel girl by day, a kindly, hideous frog by night. Here is man's dual nature in perpetual conflict until love and pity conquer the evil. The story is not for children, but is a first-rate tale and perhaps an ancestor of *Dr. Jekyll and Mr. Hyde.*

"The Little Mermaid" concerns the old folklore conflict of a fairy creature who loves a human being. The selfless love of the mermaid endures every suffering for the sake of her beloved. Finally, losing her life, she wins the hope of immortality. Love is never wasted and carries its own benediction, Andersen seems to be saying. Again, this is a story for older children and adults and so, too, is that tale of sin "The Girl Who Trod on the Loaf," despising God's gifts and suffering a terrible punishment. It recalls Grimm's "Our Lady's Child," though it is a completely new story. On the other hand, children understand and love "The Little Match Girl" and "The Snow Queen." The former may be too sad for many children, and certainly they have wept over it ever since it was written, but there is no story in all literature that speaks more movingly of God's mercy and pity for suffering.

"The Snow Queen" is almost a novelette and, aside from its rather subtle symbolism, is an exciting adventure tale in a dream world of strange beauty. Like all of the other fantasies, this begins realistically. Two real children, sitting on their roof-top under a real rose vine, share a real picture book and a loving companionship. Then a glass splinter gets into Kay's eye and the magic begins. The splinter stabs his heart, too, which becomes as cold as ice. He sees faults in everything that he used to find good, even his little friend Gerda. Finally he is whisked away to the Snow Queen's palace, where the empty iciness suits him perfectly and he can play "the ice-puzzle of reason" to his heart's content. Meanwhile Gerda, hurt by Kay's unkindness but still loving him, sets out to find him. Her adventures are like a series of dreams, each strange and incredible but linked together by Gerda's determination to rescue her little friend. She finds him at last, stonily, icily cold, but her hot tears of grief melt the mischievous splinter, and Kay is restored to joy and love.

CHARACTERISTICS OF STYLE

"The Snow Queen" is often ranked as Andersen's masterpiece, and indeed it exhibits Andersen's characteristic style at its best. Here are conversations so lively and natural that whether a Robber-maiden, a Buttercup, or a Reindeer speaks, you feel you have known her well. Like Gerda, you are even a bit apologetic because you cannot speak Ravenish to the Raven. No one has ever handled dialogue more easily and happily than Andersen. The characterizations often suggested by a conversation are swift and masterly. For instance, Kay's sudden change of heart after the splinter strikes him is apparent in his spiteful, angry words to poor Gerda:

"Why do you cry?" asked he; "you look so ugly when you cry. . . . Fie!" exclaimed he again, "this rose has an insect in it, and just look at this! after all they are ugly roses! and it is an ugly box they grow in!" Then he kicked the box and tore off the roses.[1]

The wild Robber-maiden is curiously convincing with her biting and kicking, her sudden, grave reaching out toward kindness, but with her dagger handy, just in case. The weird people in this tale all come to life, sketched briefly, sometimes with a line of description but more often only through their own words. Andersen used description most often for the landscape, and certainly nothing he has written excels the paragraph picturing the Snow Queen's palace:

The walls of the palace were formed of the driven snow, its doors and windows of the cutting winds; there were above a hundred halls, the largest of them many miles in extent, all illuminated by the Northern Lights; all alike vast, empty, icily cold, and dazzlingly white. No sounds of mirth ever resounded through these dreary spaces; no cheerful scene refreshed the sight—not even so much as a bear's ball, such as one might imagine sometimes takes place; the tempest forming a band of musicians, and the polar bears standing on their hind-paws and exhibiting themselves in the oddest positions. Nor was there ever a card-assembly, wherein the cards might be held in the mouth, and dealt out by the paws; nor even a small select coffee-party for the white young lady foxes. Vast, empty, and cold were the Snow Queen's chambers, and the Northern Lights flashed now high, now low, in regular gradations.[2]

USING ANDERSEN'S TALES WITH CHILDREN

Whether or not children enjoy these stories depends upon the children and their age and upon how the stories are presented. Obviously, they are not for young children. A few eight-year-olds may enjoy them, but the ten- and eleven-year-olds are more likely to appreciate them. Probably such a story as "The Snow Queen" should be read aloud to children over a number of days. Then it will not seem overlong, and the children can enjoy its strange beauty. "The Ugly Duckling," "The Tinder Box," "What the Good-Man Does Is Sure to Be Right!" and others of the simpler type they can read for themselves.

Because of the double meanings, the adult

1. Rex Whistler edition of *Andersen's Fairy Tales*, p. 122. Published by Oxford University Press.
2. *Ibid.*, p. 147.

themes, and the sadness of many of these stories, the whole collection is usually not popular with children. It has indeed almost dropped out of our schools. Children are direct, forthright creatures, and ambiguity makes them uneasy. As one child said sadly about an allegory, "It's a story where everything is what it ain't," and they soon get tired of speculating about which is which. Too many double meanings, too much sadness are not good for children, and for that reason Andersen's stories should not be presented in a mass, but one or two stories should be given in the fourth grade, two or three more in the fifth, and two or three in the sixth. Then, if some child wishes to explore the whole collection on his own, well and good. There are always a few children who love these tales above all others.

Andersen's *Fairy Tales* are not only good literature but they have about them a wholesome goodness which children need to believe in. The tales are moralistic but unobtrusively so, and the morals they exhibit are the humble ones of kindness, sincerity, and faith in God. The deeply religious note in many of these tales never seems forced or dragged in but is there as naturally as sunshine on the sand, warming everything. Andersen was not afraid to show children cruelty, sorrow, even death, but they are presented so gently that the children understand and are not hurt. He shows them rogues and fools along with hosts of kind, loving people, and he seems to be saying, "Well, this is the world. Which group will you join?" Then he makes them laugh at the rogues, but when he shows them the goodness of people he brings tears to their eyes or smiles of tenderness. Their young hearts are touched, and "The Little Match Girl" or "The Ugly Duckling" or Gerda they never forget. Paul Hazard says:

It is this inner life that gives the Tales *their deep quality. From it also comes that exaltation which spreads through the soul of the readers. From it comes, finally, a marked quality of serenity. . . .*

The children are not mistaken. In these beautiful tales they find not only pleasure, but the law of their being and the feeling of the great role they have to fill. They themselves have been subjected to sorrow. They sense evil confusedly around them, in them; but this vivid suffering is only transitory and not enough to trouble their serenity. Their mission is to bring to the world a renewal of faith and hope. (Books, Children and Men, *pp. 104-105*)[3]

Beautifully illustrated editions of single stories, such as Marcia Brown's *Steadfast Tin Soldier,* Johannes Larsen's *Ugly Duckling,* Erik Blegvad's *The Swineherd,* and Adrienne Adams' *Thumbelina* (see 29 in the color section for Chapter 4), are good introductions to Andersen's tales for children who might find the whole collection too formidable.

Modern Adaptations of Old Tales

Andersen set such an admirable standard for the retelling of old tales that it is worth keeping in mind when we are called upon to judge the modern versions which are continually appearing. Andersen's adaptations are right because they make the stories suitable and understandable for children while maintaining the integrity of the source. Of course, there must be some changes in these old tales, created by adults for adults, if they are to be read or told to children. Dialect or coarse language must be altered, cruelties toned down, biological facts of mating and infidelity omitted or obscured. Andersen in "Great Claus and Little Claus" endows the husband of the faithless wife with a special antipathy for "sextons"; so the infidelity motive is amusingly glossed over. Yet this change does not interfere in any way with the essential body or style of the story. This is the standard Joseph Jacobs adhered to and de-

3. Used by permission of The Horn Book Magazine.

fended. He altered a folk tale in such ways as to make it suitable and understandable to children without changing the core of the story. In using the sources of traditional material, Jacobs and Andersen set a commendable standard. On the other hand, if the tale requires many changes, it is probably unsuitable for children either in content or style.

DESIRABLE ADAPTATIONS

Next to Hans Andersen's sensitive and intelligent adaptations, Howard Pyle's *Wonder Clock* is one of the happiest collections of old tales retold that we have. The stories are chiefly from Grimm but include some legends, too, such as stories of St. Nicholas and St. Christopher. Pyle took more liberties with his material than Andersen did, but the essence of the story is there. His conversations are so lively and humorous that this book is a favorite with storytellers.

Chapter 10 commented upon the successful adaptations of Russian folk tales by Arthur Ransome, Czech tales by Parker Fillmore, and the Grimm tales by Wanda Gág. These are all admirably done in the Andersen-Jacobs style. So, too, are the more recent adaptations Marcia Brown has made of *Dick Whittington, Puss in Boots, Cinderella,* and the droll *Stone Soup*. These retellings seem easy to achieve until you explore other modern adaptations and discover how much easier it seems to be to destroy the simplicity and directness of the originals and to end up with something unpleasantly sophisticated.

UNDESIRABLE ADAPTATIONS

As we have seen, Nathaniel Hawthorne provided a pattern for this drastic type of adaptation. In his *Tanglewood Tales* he rewrote the Greek myths completely, turning the gods into willful little boys and girls, and modernizing and domesticating them in strange ways. Because Hawthorne was an artist, his tales are beautifully and excitingly written, but his willingness to violate sources produced stories that are dramatic but somehow not myth.

So Walt Disney had this classic precedent for the liberties he has taken with both folk tales and myth. He began beautifully with his film version of "The Three Little Pigs," which was perfection. In that picture he was true both to the spirit and the letter of the tale. No film has ever been more beloved by adults and children alike, and it ought to be revived yearly for each new crop of moviegoers.

In Disney's film and text versions of "Snow White," on the other hand, the elaborations and distortions of the old tale were so evident that many discerning children and adults were disappointed. "Bambi," "Peter Pan," "Uncle Remus," and "Pinocchio" suffered still more from excessive embellishments in the film and attenuation in the text. This oversimplification of a story together with an elaboration of pictorial details may possibly make good theater, but it certainly results in deplorable books. The Disney versions of these stories now on the market are incredibly meager and flat. All the imaginative quality of the old tales seems to have disappeared from the texts and to have been transferred to the charming illustrations. Children who know the full-bodied originals resent these texts in spite of the pictures.

When Disney's original inventions, Mickey Mouse, Donald Duck, Dumbo, the Singing Whale, and The Lady and the Tramp, are so delightful, why does he play such havoc with traditional or well-known stories?

Modern Tales in Folk-Tale Style

Hans Andersen was steeped in folk-tale tradition. He could create new stories in a similar vein, and his inventions seem to have inspired a few writers in almost every generation.

Fritz Kredel has caught the feeling of Ruskin's story in his colorful pictures. The spirit of the mug is a round, golden little man, and the lad is a handsome, fairy-tale hero. Clear type and fine paper make this an outstanding edition. Illustration by Fritz Kredel. From The King of the Golden River *by John Ruskin. Copyright 1946 by The World Publishing Company. Reprinted by permission of the publisher. (Original in color, book 5¼ x 8½)*

ROBERT SOUTHEY

The Three Bears

To discover that "The Three Bears" was written by the poet Robert Southey is something of a shock. It has all the earmarks of a folk tale. Certainly Southey's version with a nosey old woman instead of a little girl is characteristic of folk tales. But when someone somewhere substituted a snooping little girl—"Silver-hair" in England, "Goldilocks" in the United States—she captured the nursery crowd forever. Now no one ever tells the Southey version. The present-day version of "The Three Bears," however, rivals "The Three Little Pigs" in popularity and is generally classified as a folk tale.

JOHN RUSKIN

The King of the Golden River

John Ruskin tried writing "The King of the Golden River" in the old fairy-tale style. It is for children ten to fourteen, but many of them avoid it because of its length and reading difficulty. This powerful tale with something of the somber, frightening air of the medieval legends tells the story of little Gluck, a cinder lad tormented by his cruel older brothers, Hans and Schwartz. A mysterious visitor, the South-West Wind, is treated kindly by Gluck and meanly by the brothers, and the stranger vows revenge. How Gluck discovers in the melting golden mug the King of the Golden River and with the King's help wins back his inheritance makes an exciting tale. The evil brothers are disposed of in good folklore style and Gluck is safe forever. This story is well written and genuinely dramatic. Children should have it read aloud to them or if they wish to read it themselves, they may need a simpler version than the original.

HOWARD PYLE

Pepper and Salt

No one, not even Andersen, has been more successful in creating new fairy tales in the old folk-tale patterns than Howard Pyle has been in his delightful *Pepper and Salt.* This is a favorite book with teachers and parents who like to tell stories or read them aloud. There are eight stories interspersed with clever verses and equally clever drawings by the author. Humor is the prevailing tone of the whole book. Older children like to read it for themselves as well as to hear the stories read or told.

The first tale is typical of the way Pyle used old folk motifs with new and humorous invention. In "The Skillful Huntsman," Jacob, a poor and supposedly stupid lad, wishes to marry Gretchen, the Mayor's daughter. The Mayor, to get rid of him, sets Jacob a series of tasks, the first of which is to shoot the whiskers off a running hare. Jacob meets a stranger clad in red with cloven hoofs. The stranger offers to make Jacob the greatest of all hunters and to obey his commands for ten years if at the end of that time Jacob will go with him. The lad agrees on one condition: at the end of the ten years, if the stranger cannot answer Jacob's question, Jacob is free. The bargain is made; Jacob accomplishes every task and marries Gretchen. At the end of the fateful ten years, the stranger comes for Jacob. They agree to enjoy one last hunt, and the stranger is to tell Jacob what to shoot. Gretchen appears in the far distance, all covered with feathers, and he of the cloven hoof commands Jacob to shoot. "But what is it?" asks Jacob innocently. The baffled gentleman in red is obliged to admit he does not know, and so Jacob is free. The whole tale is lightly and wittily told, with old motifs in new and amusing dress.

OSCAR WILDE

The Happy Prince and Other Fairy Tales

"Beauty and the Beast," "The Three Bears," "The King of the Golden River," and Pyle's stories are all written with the directness of traditional tales and legends. But Oscar Wilde's fairy tales are art forms, polished and adult. Two of Wilde's allegories, "The Happy Prince" and "The Selfish Giant," have been rather generally used for storytelling in the elementary school. The former is so sentimental and morbid it clearly does not belong to children, but "The Selfish Giant" has all the earmarks of a child's fairy tale. The story is about a beautiful garden enjoyed by the children until its owner, a very selfish giant, comes home and puts up a sign, "Trespassers Will Be Prosecuted." Then winter comes to the garden and remains there as long as the children are locked out. One day the giant discovers that the garden is blooming with flowers and children. He rushes out and encounters a little boy who touches the giant's hard heart. He lifts the child into a tree and bids him come daily to the garden with his little friends. After the giant has grown old, he sees his little friend again. Hastening to the child, he discovers the prints of nails on the hands and on the little feet.

"Who hath dared to wound thee?" cried the Giant; "tell me, that I may take my big sword and slay him."

"Nay!" answered the child; "but these are the wounds of Love."

"Who art thou?" said the Giant, and a strange awe fell on him, and he knelt before the little child.

And the child smiled on the Giant, and said to him, "You let me play once in your garden; to-day you shall come with me to my garden, which is Paradise."

And when the children ran in that afternoon, they found the Giant lying dead under the tree, all covered with white blossoms.

If children understand that the Child is supposed to be Jesus, they are still baffled by this conclusion and uncomfortable because of the mixture of religious ideas with a fairy tale. But most children miss the point entirely and find the nail prints merely confusing and irrelevant. The significance of "the wounds of Love"—that only those we love and care for can wound us deeply—is also difficult for children.

Almost seventy years later, in 1955, Clyde Bulla told a similar story in *The Poppy Seeds.* A suspicious old man who in an arid land kept his clear spring to himself learned that to share is to be rich. The poppy seeds that the boy Pablo had dropped in fright grew and blossomed by the spring. The moral is evident, but not underscored, and children can understand every aspect of the conflict.

This renewed simplicity is characteristic of children's literature in the twentieth century. One possible explanation is that beginning in the early nineteen hundreds there was a growing awareness of the child. G. Stanley Hall had launched a new science, Child Study, and the consciousness of the child as a child rather than as a small adult was penetrating the literate world. Whatever the cause, the turn of the century brought some delightful new fanciful tales for children.

HELEN BANNERMAN

Little Black Sambo

One of the first of these twentieth-century books was a small one, only about four by five and one-half inches in size, called *Little Black Sambo.* The author, Helen Bannerman, was a Scotchwoman stationed in India. Because the climate of that country is especially trying for children, she had, like so many of her countrywomen, taken her two little daughters back to their native land to be educated. On the long return journey to India, torn by this separation from her two children, Helen Bannerman wrote and illustrated *Little Black Sambo,* partly to amuse her daughters and partly to comfort herself. It was published about 1900, caused no particular stir, and, at the time Stokes published it in the United States, was not even copyrighted. But American children took it to their hearts with a fervor and unanimity that have necessitated reprint after reprint ever since its first appearance in the United States.

This story, which might almost have come out of some folklore collection, has about it an effortless perfection which baffles analysis. Its extreme simplicity is deceiving. Just try to duplicate it! It begins by introducing Sambo and his family, one sentence and one picture to a page: "And his Mother was called Black Mumbo. And his Father was called Black Jumbo." Then the clothes appear, piece by piece: first, blue trousers; next, red coat; then, grand green umbrella; finally, the climax—"Purple Shoes with Crimson Soles and Crimson Linings." (Now those were shoes!) Sambo's walk in the jungle wearing all his "Fine Clothes" brings out the tigers, and they take Sambo's apparel away from him and wear it in amusing and ingenious ways. How Sambo gets his clothes back and eats 169 pancakes into the bargain is certainly the best substitute for getting "the princess and half the kingdom" ever invented for children.

In this age of color and race consciousness, some people wish that Mrs. Bannerman had not woven the word *black* into her repetitive cadence of colors. Indeed its use, together with the stylized pictures, has brought about the exclusion of the book from most reading lists. If *black* applied to people is a cause of grief to some of our children, then the book should be omitted from school lists. But Sambo is happy and completely triumphant, the envy of all young hero worshipers—he outwits the tigers over and over. He has the right kind of parents, just the kind every child would like to have. And in the history of children's literature *Little Black Sambo* remains an important innovation. It has theme, plot, and felicitous style. The text of the story and the pictures are perfectly synchronized. It remains a model for the picture-story type of literary composition.

They came to a pond.
"Mew, mew! We are thirsty!" cried the
Hundreds of cats,
Thousands of cats,
Millions and billions and trillions of cats.

The rhythm of Wanda Gág's text, "Hundreds of cats, thousands of cats, millions and billions and trillions of cats," is reflected in the rhythmic lines of her drawings with their curving, flowing, up-and-down pattern. Illustration from Wanda Gág's Millions of Cats. *Copyright 1928 by Coward-McCann, Inc. Reproduced with permission of the publisher. (Book 8½ x 6¼)*

WANDA GAG

Millions of Cats

It was almost three decades after the publication of *Sambo* that the inimitable *Millions of Cats* (1928) appeared, another modern invention in folk-tale style. Wanda Gág had been brought up on the traditional tales; so she had the feeling for plot and also for the fine flowing rhythms of storytelling. This same rhythm is as characteristic of her illustrations as it is of her text and makes a strong appeal to young children. They welcomed Wanda Gág's first story with the same joyous approval that they bestowed upon *Peter Rabbit* and *Little Black Sambo,* and already it has entered the ranks of nursery immortals.

Wanda Gág always tells a good story. *Millions of Cats* concerns a little old man and a little old woman who wanted a little cat. The old man went out to choose one, but because he could not decide which was the prettiest he came home with "hundreds of cats, thousands of cats, millions and billions and trillions of cats."[4] Notice the walking rhythm of that refrain which goes all through the story. How the jealous creatures destroyed each other and left only one scrawny little cat, too homely to be in the fight, and how the little old man and woman petted and fed the skinny little thing until it became a creature of beauty make the tale. Ah, but the text and the pictures! There are strength and tenderness in these illustrations, simplicity and directness in the words. Together they make a picture-story so gently humorous in content, so pleasant to the eyes and the ears, so happily concluded, that adults who read it aloud and show the pictures enjoy it quite as much as the children.

Snippy and Snappy, The Funny Thing, and *Nothing at All* are all good stories in Miss Gág's own particular rhythms, and the pictures have the same deceptive simplicity found in the text. Children enjoy every one of them and should probably have them all, but *Millions of Cats* is a must.

OTHER EXAMPLES

On the whole, not many stories are being written in folk-tale style today, but some exceedingly good ones appear from time to time. Marjorie Flack's *Ask Mr. Bear* and Margaret Friskey's *Seven Diving Ducks* have long been popular. Will and Nicolas' *Finders Keepers,* the amusing story of two dogs that found the same bone and asked for advice to decide which should keep it, belongs to this same group of picture-stories for the youngest children.

4. Wanda Gág, *Millions of Cats,* Coward-McCann, 1928.

In Richard Bennett's Irish fairy tale *Shawneen and the Gander,* Shawneen catches a leprechaun and gets a goose's egg. It hatches into a very demon of a gander, which is eventually the cause of Shawneen's getting the bugle he wants. These adventures tickle children eight to ten, the same group that delights in Dr. Seuss' *The 500 Hats of Bartholomew Cubbins.* In *Alphonse, That Bearded One,* Natalie Carlson tells children ten to twelve the entertaining story of a woodsman who trains a bear to drill like a soldier and to take his place in the army. The situations are hilarious, with Alphonse the bear always triumphant.

These are just a few typical examples of the original modern tales in traditional style which are successful with children. There are plenty of contrived examples available also, but these come and go in short order. Unless an author has grown up with the oral tradition of folk tales, his own stories are not likely to come out in that style. If he tries consciously to reproduce it, the results are likely to be obviously labored.

Stories of Fantasy

One of Andersen's most successful story types is the fantasy, and the most spectacular juvenile book of the nineteenth century, *Alice's Adventures in Wonderland,* is also a fantasy. Fantasy here means a tale of magic, often beginning realistically but merging quickly into adventures strange, astonishing, and dreamlike. Andersen's stories of this type are invariably melancholy or tragic—for example, "The Marsh King's Daughter," "The Snow Queen," and "The Little Mermaid." In England, the best examples of this type of tale are exactly the reverse. Just as the humorous "Tom Tit Tot" contrasts with the somber "Rumpelstiltskin," so Alice, the English equivalent of Gerda, starts on her dreamlike adventures, not in pursuit of an icy-hearted boy but of an utterly frivolous rabbit wearing a fancy waistcoat and carrying a gold watch. Before following Alice down her famous rabbit hole, let's look briefly at one of her predecessors.

CHARLES KINGSLEY

The Water-Babies

Charles Kingsley, a clergyman and a scientist, wrote a book for his own little boy which enjoyed great popularity for many years. It told the story of Tom, a poor little chimney sweep who was carried off by the fairies to the world under the waters, where he became a Water-Baby. For the most part this story makes little appeal to modern children. It is interesting historically not only because it embodies magic, but because the water creatures are true to their species. Here, perhaps, is the ancestor of the modern animal tale which permits the creatures to speak but keeps them otherwise true to their kind. Unfortunately, *The Water-Babies* also teaches moral lessons, and the unwieldy combination of magic, morals, and lessons in science is enough to account for its waning popularity.

LEWIS CARROLL

Alice's Adventures in Wonderland
Through the Looking Glass

The "Alice" books cannot be accounted for on the basis of anything that had preceded them, nor does any knowledge of the author's adult life help to explain them. The comfortable, solid life of Charles Lutwidge Dodgson, author of *Alice's Adventures in Wonderland*, was as different from the tragic irregularities of Hans Andersen's as it could well be. Yet in the end both men achieved somewhat similar fame. Both loved children and were loved by them; both were bachelors; and both were disconcerted when their fame was attached not to their serious work but to their books for children. Here the likeness ends.

Dodgson's father was an Archdeacon in the Church of England. The boy enjoyed the finest possible education, first at Rugby and then at Oxford, where he took orders for the ministry. At Oxford he remained for forty-seven of his sixty-five years. There he was remembered as a dry, perfunctory lecturer in mathematics and as an early experimenter with photography. His well-composed, well-lighted photographs of famous contemporaries are now invaluable. They include not only pictures of Tennyson, Ruskin, Faraday, the Rossettis, and other celebrities but also many of little Alice Liddell, for whom he spun his story.

As a child, young Charles complicated the family garden with an elaborate miniature railroad, which he built and ran. He also launched a newspaper, wrote poems for it, and drew the illustrations. He made a puppet theater, and he kept all sorts of curious animals for pets. Indeed, it is hard to believe that this active, enterprising boy could grow up to be a sober, sedate cleric with ambitions toward mathematical research. But his childhood may account in part for *Alice*.

Fortunately, Dr. Liddell of Christ Church, where Dodgson lectured, had three little girls called by their mathematical friend, Prima, Secunda, and Tertia. Secunda was Alice, evidently Dodgson's favorite:

Child of the pure unclouded brow
And dreaming eyes of wonder!

So he described her, in the introductory poem to *Through the Looking Glass*. The charming photographs he has left of her bear out his description. To these little girls, Dodgson used to tell stories, teasing them by breaking off in the middle with "And that's all till next time." Whereupon "the cruel Three" would cry, "But it *is* the next time!"

Then came that famous summer afternoon (the fourth of July, by the way) when Dodgson rowed his little friends up the Cherwell River to Goodstow, where they had tea on the riverbank. There the young man told them the fairy tale of "Alice's Adventures Under Ground." Secunda hoped there'd be nonsense in it, and no hopes ever materialized more gloriously. The next Christmas, Dodgson wrote his story as a gift for "a dear child in memory of a Summer day." The story was exquisitely written in clear script, as legible as print, and charmingly illustrated by the author. Years later that little green volume of ninety-two pages was sold to a private collector in the United States for £15,400 or about $77,000, "the highest price which any book has ever brought in an English auction room."

Three years after the famous picnic, the story appeared in book form, somewhat enlarged, with the new title *Alice's Adventures in Wonderland* and with Sir John Tenniel's matchless illustrations. That was 1865, and six years later the companion volume appeared, both books under the pseudonym Lewis Carroll. Then a strange thing happened. Charles Lutwidge Dodgson, still an obscure mathematician, found Lewis Carroll a famous person—sought after, praised, discussed, even advertised. Gentle, sensitive soul that he was, Dodgson was horrified. He announced firmly that "Mr. Dodgson neither claimed nor acknowledged any connection with the books not published under his name." Autograph hunters hunted in vain. He wrote several more books under his pseudonym, but when Queen Victoria asked for the rest of his works, he sent her all his learned treatises on mathematics and nothing else. If the name "Lewis Carroll" was supposed to provide Charles Dodgson with a shield against publicity, it was a dismal failure. Instead, it practically obliterated the mathematician. Like Andersen's, Dodgson's declining years were serene and uneventful. Nothing else he ever wrote enjoyed the success of his two companion volumes about Alice.

The Story about Alice

Does anyone who has read the *Adventures in Wonderland* ever forget those opening paragraphs, with the child's comment on books?

Alice was beginning to get very tired of sitting by her sister on the bank, and of having nothing to do: once or twice she had peeped into the book her sister was reading, but it had no pictures or conversations in it, "and what is the use of a book," thought Alice, "without pictures or conversations?"

Then plop! Right into the third short paragraph comes the White Rabbit, with waistcoat and watch. Down he goes into the rabbit hole, murmuring "Oh dear! Oh dear! I shall be too late!" And down the rabbit hole after him goes Alice, "never once considering how in the world she was to get out again." From then on madness takes over.

Alice finds a little glass table on which is a tiny golden key that unlocks the door to more bewilderment. She drinks from a little bottle and shrinks to ten inches, swallows a piece of cake and finds she is "opening out like the largest telescope that ever was!" This goes on, but never is Alice the proper size for the place she is in. She nearly drowns in a lake of her own tears; she is forever catching glimpses of the hurrying White Rabbit, but hurrying where? She encounters strange creatures. There is the smiling Cheshire Cat who can vanish leaving only his grin behind. There is the Queen of Hearts who disposes of all who disagree with her with a simple "Off with her head!" and the Red Queen who has to run for dear life in order "to keep in the same place." All these characters talk nonsense in the gravest way. The best example is "A Mad Tea-Party," where the conversation reminds you uncomfortably of some of the disjointed small talk which you have not only heard but perhaps, horrid thought, even contributed to. The characters appear and disappear, behave with a kind of daft logic, and burst into verses which sing in your head in place of the serious poetry you might prefer to recall. Here are some verses from a typical poem:

The Walrus and the Carpenter

The sun was shining on the sea,
Shining with all his might:
He did his very best to make
The billows smooth and bright—
And this was odd, because it was
The middle of the night.

The moon was shining sulkily,
Because she thought the sun
Had got no business to be there
After the day was done—
"It's very rude of him," she said,
"To come and spoil the fun!"

The sea was wet as wet could be,
The sands were dry as dry,
You could not see a cloud, because
No cloud was in the sky;
No birds were flying overhead–
There were no birds to fly.

The Walrus and the Carpenter
Were walking close at hand;
They wept like anything to see
Such quantities of sand:
"If this were only cleared away,"
They said, "it would be grand!"

"If seven maids with seven mops
Swept it for half a year,
Do you suppose," the Walrus said,
"That they could get it clear?"
"I doubt it," said the Carpenter,
And shed a bitter tear.

There are eighteen verses of this mock tragedy relating how the Walrus and the Carpenter lured some young oysters to a "dismal" end. Equally delightful nonsense are "The Lobster-Quadrille," "Jabberwocky" (p. 122), and "Father William" (p. 122).

When Do Children Enjoy Alice?

These ditties, which occur every few chapters, are memorized with ease and are popular with children. They represent a kind of humor which some people enjoy and others find hard to understand. Paul Hazard in *Books, Children and Men* says of the English people and *Alice:*

The English are a calm and cold people. But let them relax, for a single day, that compulsion for self-control which governs them and they will show a capacity for boisterous unrestraint that is surprising.... It is the same with laughter. When they enjoy looking at the universe on its fantastic side, distorting it with deforming mirrors, there is no stopping them.... A foreigner can try to understand Alice in Wonderland; *but to appreciate fully this marvelous story one must be English. (p. 140)*

This last statement should be qualified by adding "or American." For many Americans revel in the book. The puzzling question is when do children enjoy *Alice?* Needless to say, it should never be required reading. In the first place, some children heartily dislike fantasy and to make them read *Alice* would be turning reading into a penalty instead of a delight. In the second place, Alice was intended to be a light-hearted excursion into nonsense. If for certain children it rouses no laughter, it is worse than useless for them. When college students are asked what books they remember enjoying as children there is more disagreement over *Alice* than over any other book. Some disliked it heartily or were bored by it; some say *Alice* was one of their favorite books, not as children but at the high-school age. This is perhaps where it really belongs. Most of those who liked *Alice* as children, ten or under, had heard it read aloud by adults who enjoyed it. Those who had to read the book for themselves rarely found it funny until they were older. Here are some clues. Try reading *Alice* aloud to the children if you yourself like it. If the story captures their interest, keep on; if it rouses no enthusiasm, put it away until later. But somewhere, sometime, children should be exposed to this fantasy and allowed to accept it joyously or reject it without apologies. And as adults they may reread it as political satire and find to their astonishment famous contemporary figures neatly caricatured.

Illustrations by Sir John Tenniel

Sir John Tenniel in his illustrations for *Alice* has fixed forever the face, figure, and dress of this beloved little girl. Long, straight hair, a grave, prim face, a neat, perky dress covered with a pinafore, and the straight, slim legs clad in horizontally striped stockings make an appealing little figure which no one ever forgets. This is Alice, the Alice who remains impeccably Alice even when her neck has grown as long as a giraffe's. The Tenniel rabbit is an equally unforgettable figure with his sporty tweed coat, his massive gold watch and chain, his swagger walking stick, just the kind of fellow who *would* keep the Duchess waiting. For Tenniel does not merely illustrate. He interprets, giving the mood and the manner of the creature as well as his outer appearance. (See illustrations pp. 57 and 156.)

You also have to admire the remarkable technique of these pictures. Tenniel draws Alice stepping through the looking glass, with curious and plausible ease, half of her on one side, half on the other. The Cheshire Cat disappearing, leaving only his grin behind, and the playing-card and chess people are only a few of his pen-and-ink wonders. These sketches are so alive, so profoundly interpretative that no one has ever wished for colored illustrations of Alice, at least not until Leonard Weisgard created them color-drenched and beautiful (see 23 in the color section of Chapter 4). But certainly no artist has illustrated Alice with greater magic than Tenniel. If possible, let children's first experience with Alice include the drawings of her first illustrator, Sir John Tenniel, most excellent interpreter of Wonderland.

GEORGE MacDONALD

At the Back of the North Wind

George MacDonald was a personal friend of Charles Dodgson, and *Alice* was read to the MacDonald children when it was still in manuscript form. However, when MacDonald began to write fairy tales himself, he turned back to the more serious vein of Hans Christian Andersen. Indeed his first book, *At the Back of the North Wind,* is reminiscent of "The Snow Queen." This story of Diamond's adventures is a long one, carrying the little boy through thirty-eight adventures (chapters), some with the North Wind herself, some with his flesh-and-blood friends or foes. The North Wind first comes to Diamond in his hayloft bed. She carries him out into the night, teaches him to follow her through the air and to go from his dream life with her to play a brave part in his difficult everyday life. This continual change from fantasy to reality and back again to fantasy confuses many children. Some like the North Wind parts but others prefer the earthly adventures of the boy.

Diamond is an appealing little figure when he is not being too angelic. His flesh-and-blood adventures are often as incredible as those with the North Wind: he reforms a drunkard, rescues a street sweeper from slavery to an infamous old woman, drives his father's cab through the London streets, and generally guides and improves all the adults with whom he comes in contact. Despite the moralistic side of the book, many of the chapters tell an imaginative and thrilling story. The chapter that tells how the real Diamond was seriously ill and the other Diamond miraculously passed through the North Wind herself and came to the country which lies at her back is a beautifully related bit of mysticism implying, perhaps, death. It is one of the most moving episodes in the book. Probably few children ever catch this inner meaning, but whether they do or don't, the chapter is reassuring.

The other MacDonald books, like this one, seem overlong. *The Princess and the Goblin* and *The Princess and Curdie* present interminable adventures above and below ground with cobs and humans and with considerable general moralizing into the bargain. The books are well written and have a strong imaginative appeal, but because of their length and complexity they are enjoyed today only by the exceptional child.

JAMES BARRIE

Peter Pan

Of all Sir James Barrie's delightful plays and books, none has been so beloved as *Peter Pan* (1904). Exquisitely performed by Maude Adams at the beginning of the century and by Mary Martin on stage and television in the middle of the century, it has been as popular with adults as with children. The book *Peter and Wendy* was made from the play but was never so successful, probably because the writing was too subtle for the average child. The play makes dramatically clear the story of Peter Pan, the boy who will not grow up; Tinker Bell, the fairy who loses her shadow; and the three children—Wendy, John, and Michael—who go off with Peter

Pan to Never Never Land. Their adventures with pirates, redskins, and a ticking crocodile are exciting, but in the end they return to their parents to begin the serious business of growing up. Peter Pan is left alone with Tink, whose life is in danger. Only one thing will save her, and so Peter calls through the dusk to all children, "Do you believe in fairies?" Always, at this point in the play, a great cry goes up from the audience, "*I* do!" "*I* do!"—the children's testimony of faith!

C. S. LEWIS

The Lion, the Witch, and the Wardrobe

British authors have always had a way with fantasy, and in the midst of serious work distinguished literary figures like C. S. Lewis have stopped to write books for children. Well known as a theologian, poet, and author, he has created for children a strange new world—Narnia—which they first enter through an old wardrobe. *The Lion, the Witch, and the Wardrobe* (1950) is the first of a series of books about the adventures of four children. Narnia is no Utopia. In fact, once the children have become kings and queens of Narnia, they find themselves engaged in the endless conflict between good and evil symbolized by the benignant Lion Aslan and the malicious Witch. After reigning for many years, the children return to their own world, only to find that they have not even been missed.

Prince Caspian carries the children back to Narnia for further adventures. *The Magician's Nephew* goes back to the creation of Narnia by the Lion. When the Lion sings into existence the world, the stars, the land, and then the creatures, the sheer goodness of creation is too much for the Witch. She flees, but the reader knows she will return. *The Last Battle* concludes the series. As the title implies, the loyal followers of the king of Narnia are making their last stand against the forces of evil which seek to destroy the noble Lion Aslan and the world he has created. Another theologian, Chad Walsh, considers this the best of the series, a book full of Christian symbolism, and a "deeply moving and hauntingly lovely story apart from its doctrinal content." Children never suspect the doctrine, but a world of good and evil seems strangely plausible.

This very fine line pen-and-ink drawing is filled with wonderful details, each one important to the story.
Illustration by Pauline Baynes. From The Lion, the Witch and the Wardrobe *by C. S. Lewis. Copyright, 1950, by The Macmillan Company. Reproduced with permission. (Book 5¼ x 8)*

MARY NORTON

The Borrowers

In 1943 a book called *The Magic Bed-knob* appeared. It caused no great stir but was well liked by children who encountered it. Then in 1953 came *The Borrowers* by the same author, Mary Norton. Most reviewers agreed that here was a treasure of lasting value. As British as tea for breakfast, but with action, suspense, and characters of universal appeal, it was immediately popular.

Borrowers are not fairies but small creatures who live in old houses and take their names from the places they inhabit—the Overmantels, for instance, the Harpsichords, and the Clocks, who live under a huge old grandfather's clock in the hall. Homily, Pod, and their daughter Arrietty Clock are the only surviving family of Borrowers in the old house. When a Borrower is *seen,* there is nothing for him to do but emigrate. Only Pod, climbing curtains with the aid of his trusty hatpin, borrowing a useful spoon now and then or a bit of tea or a portrait stamp of the Queen, only Pod has escaped detection. Arrietty is the problem now. Arrietty wants to see the world and she goes exploring, happily and trustingly even after the boy sees her. They become fast friends, but even the boy cannot prevent the tragic ending. It was so catastrophic that children could not accept it as final. There had to be a sequel, and so we follow the fortunes of these fascinating characters in *The Borrowers Afield, The Borrowers Afloat,* and *The Borrowers Aloft,* with which the series ends.

No briefing of these stories can give any conception of their quality. Every character is unforgettably portrayed. There is poor Homily with her hair forever awry, loving but a chronic worrier, "taking on" first and then going capably to work. Pod is the sober realist, a philosopher and a brave one. Arrietty is youth and adventure, springtime and hope, too much in love with life to be afraid even of those mammoth "human beans." To read these books aloud is to taste the full richness of their humor and good writing. Children read and reread them and presently, in classrooms, homes, and camps, they create their own versions of a Borrower's house. None is ever as clever as Pod's under-clock domain, but each one, done with loving inventiveness, is a tribute to Pod, Homily, Arrietty, and Mary Norton.

Other books of fantasy distinguished by their excellent writing and convincing realism have come to us from England. English fantasy often has more whimsy, more adult overtones, and more humor than American fantasy. And for sheer storytelling enchantment and delight, the best of these English books are hard to match.

See how subtly unreality is suggested by the background lines that show right through Pod's plump body. The details in this picture may be more appreciated by adults than by children, but the dramatic import of Pod's acceptance by that ancient crone is evident. Illustration by Beth and Joe Krush. Reproduced from The Borrowers, *copyright, 1952, 1953, by Mary Norton, by permission of Harcourt, Brace & World, Inc.* **Inc.**
(Book 4¾ x 7¾)

LUCY M. BOSTON

The Children of Green Knowe
Treasure of Green Knowe
The River at Green Knowe

Another distinguished English fantasy, beautifully written and completely absorbing, is *The Children of Green Knowe* (1955), by Lucy M. Boston. It is a juvenile *Berkeley Square,* going back in time from the present and a boy named Tolly to the seventeenth century and three children of his family who lived and died in the great plague.

A lonely child, Tolly is sent to live with his great-grandmother, Mrs. Oldknow, at the family's ancient manor house The Green Knowe. He is soon aware of the presence of other children who come and go. He hears them but cannot see them although he knows his grandmother sees them. She shows him the portrait of the three and tells him the story of each child and their great horse Feste, and presently Tolly sees them also, but he can never touch them. Play with these children from the past involves Tolly in a terrifying situation. He is saved by St. Christopher, and the story ends serenely. It is safe to say that no reader young or old will ever forget Mrs. Oldknow or Tolly or the mysterious and beautiful old manor house.

There are more books in this setting—*Treasure of Green Knowe,* in which Tolly and his great-grandmother again appear, and *The River at Green Knowe,* in which a new set of characters appears—and in both of these stories real life and fantasy are successfully mingled. *A Stranger at Green Knowe,* one of the most moving boy and animal tales ever written, is discussed in Chapter 14, page 418.

A. PHILIPPA PEARCE

Tom's Midnight Garden

Known to American children as the author of a fascinating English mystery story *The Minnow Leads to Treasure,* Philippa Pearce won the Carnegie Medal for *Tom's Midnight Garden* (1959), an equally engrossing fantasy, with time as a theme. Young Tom, much bored by life in his aunt and uncle's apartment, hears an ancient clock strike thirteen. Immediately he slips into an enchanting garden where he plays with Hatty, a child from the past. Their play is imaginative but made credible because of the logic of "Time no longer," the motto on the clock. These strange midnight adventures of Tom's are later half explained by what adults might call thought-transference. However, they seem quite clear and uncomplicated to young readers once they accept Tom's timeless midnight garden.

MAURICE DRUON

Tistou of the Green Thumbs

From France comes a subtle allegory called *Tistou of the Green Thumbs* (1958). As a little boy, Tistou is different from other children but it is the gardener who discovers that the child has green thumbs which cause flowers to bloom immediately. The old man says, "Hidden talent often leads to trouble. . . . Well, keep it to yourself." And the two of them do, only Tistou can not help using his talent. When he sees the misery of prisoners, he makes the prison courtyards blaze with roses, and likewise the slums, the zoo, and, finally, even the guns in his father's munition factory. Only on the last page does the reader discover Tistou's identity, and the little parable ends gently. Children will miss the social satire of the story, but the joyous changes Tistou brings about are memorable pictures.

CAROLYN SHERWIN BAILEY

Miss Hickory

Miss Hickory, a mere twig with a hickory nut head and personality plus, begins as a doll left behind by the children. Waspish, but sound as a nut, she faces adversity bravely and with Crow's help makes a home for herself in a robin's nest. Her adventures come to a strange end when a squirrel bites off her head and is then frightened out of his wits when the twig that was Miss Hickory walks serenely away. That this twig becomes the graft on an old tree and gives it new life is a conclusion that leaves most children baffled. Perhaps a few of them get the suggestion of the continuity of life, but whether they do or don't, the characters are amusing, and the story of tart, competent Miss Hickory is beautifully told.

JULIA SAUER

Fog Magic

Before Tolly played with his ancestors at Green Knowe, a Nova Scotian child, Greta Addington, abroad in a fog, walked straight into Blue Cove, a village of long ago. There she finds a friend her own age to play with and is accepted by the family as one "from over the mountain." Greta can find the village only on days of heavy fog, so she hopes her twelfth birthday will be foggy. But it isn't, until nightfall. Then she hurries to Blue Cove, where her friends give her a kitten for a birthday gift with a wish for "Safe passage for all the years ahead." Somehow Greta knows this is goodbye to fog magic and she is not surprised to discover that her father on his twelfth birthday had received a small knife for a gift and had never seen the village again.

Notice how Tolly, Tom, and Greta, in these stories that go back and forth in time, are temporarily lonely children in search of companionship. Psychologists say such stories vicariously fill a need, but *Fog Magic* (1943) does one thing better than the others. It terminates the play with finality. Maturity lies ahead and reality must be accepted. *Fog Magic,* which is mainly a girl's story, has rare beauty and significance.

WILLIAM PENE DU BOIS

Twenty-One Balloons

The fantasies of William Pène du Bois are as orderly and logical as mathematics, and his illustrations have the same graceful balance. He himself credits his passion for order to his regimented school life at Lycée Hoche, for which he is as grateful as he is for glorious weekly excursions to the French circus. These and other lifelong interests are reflected in his books—his love of France, the circus, all forms of mechanized transportation, islands, Utopias, and explosions! Look at some of his most notable books: *Bear Party* is a reasonable fable of some quarrelsome bears who grow genuinely fond of each other when they have a fancy dress party. A bear Utopia results. *The Giant* is a logical story of an eight-year-old giant, already seven stories tall but wistfully amiable. He can disrupt a whole city and send the people into a panic by picking up streetcars or automobiles or people for a better look. It is all drawn to scale as precisely as an architect's plan.

And best of all there is his Newbery Medal book, *Twenty-One Balloons* (1947). When its hero, Professor William Waterman Sherman, tires of teaching little boys arithmetic, he sets off in a balloon to see the world and be alone. He tells his story of landing on the island of Krakatoa (a real island, by the way) and finding its inhabitants inventors of the most amazing super-gadgets. These are described in detail and drawn meticulously, and the reader wonders why we don't have them. Since the island is volcanic, the people have planned a machine for escape should the volcano erupt, and of course it does. And off they go in their airy-go-round. Related with the utmost simplicity, the story piles up suspense until the explosion is a relief.

CAROL FENNER

Tigers in the Cellar

For the youngest children *Tigers in the Cellar* (1963), written and illustrated by Carol Fenner, relates a delicious fantasy of a child's own making. A little girl is sure there are tigers in the cellar. They do not bother her by day, but she hears them every night. When she tells her mother about the tigers, her mother just says "Nonsense!" and then, "Now go pick up your clothes." But that very night the little girl hears the tigers again, padding around, snuffing and growling. Down to the cellar goes the little girl and there are the tigers, two of them. One of them is a weepy fellow and the other one sings delightfully. They are soon good friends and best of all they take her tiger-back riding. The next day, when the little girl tells her mother, she says, "Nonsense!" and then, "Now go pick up your clothes." So the little girl's problem is how to pick up those disgusting clothes and still hang on to her dream of tigers. The illustrations add to the charming text. Children four to eight years old will like this book for different reasons at different age levels.

The most convincing modern fantasies have come chiefly from England, but American writers are working in this field with increasing success. May Massee spoke soundly when she said: "The right story of fantasy has its feet on the ground."[5] That is, the more real and everyday the setting and the people, the more reasonable and convincing the story.

Space Fantasy

There is one field that American writers with characteristic inventiveness seem to have cornered, and that is space fantasy. At their best, these tales are so convincing that the reader is all prepared to "tesseract" or take off for the Mushroom Planet or Ganymede on a moment's notice. To be sure, some of the earlier tales are already dated. Children have had visual close-ups of long, laborious flight preparations, count downs, take-offs, and flight hazards until they challenge anything that does not measure up to the facts they know. But space stories that are more fantasy than science can still hold their own.

ROBERT HEINLEIN

Rocket Ship Galileo

The fun and danger of *Rocket Ship Galileo* (1947) and Robert Heinlein's many other books about interspace travel is that they seem completely reasonable and factual. No "airy-go-rounds" in these tales. Instead the reader has to pinch himself to remember that we are not pioneering on Mars, sending colonies to Ganymede, or commuting to Hespera. Most space fiction falls into predictable patterns but not Robert Heinlein's. His characters are well-drawn human beings, with human faults, unique problems, and moments sometimes of despair and sometimes of triumph. The stories are so well told they swing the reader along in a state of almost unbearable suspense. No one writing in this field surpasses Robert Heinlein. Nevertheless, even with the best space stories, a few too many and the reader gets tired of being duped. The fad passes and the fact remains that no classic has yet emerged from this field of imaginative writing unless time and young readers bestow that honor on the 1963 Newbery Medal winner, *A Wrinkle in Time.*

MADELEINE L'ENGLE

A Wrinkle in Time

Mrs. L'Engle's first notable book, *Meet the Austins,* is a fine realistic family story. The opening of *A Wrinkle in Time* suggests that it will be a similar kind of story. A storm is raging outside, but within the cozy kitchen Meg Murry and her brother, precocious five-year-old Charles Wallace Murry, are having hot cocoa with their mother. Into this family group comes a strange old woman, Mrs. Whatsit. She explains that she was "caught in a down draft and blown off course." But having finished her cocoa, she departs with one final word to the mother, ". . . there *is* such a thing as a tesseract." That is what the children's scientist father had been working on for the government when he disappeared. The next day, Meg, Charles Wallace, and Calvin O'Keefe, a friend, meet Mrs. Whatsit and two other strange old women, who warn the children that their father is in grave danger and that only they can save him and only if they are willing to tesseract. This involves

5. Bertha Mahony Miller and Elinor Whitney Field, eds., *Newbery Medal Books: 1922-1955,* p. 297.

the "fact" that the shortest distance between two points is not a straight line, but a fold or wrinkle. The children agree to try it. It proves to be a solitary, painful experience of blackness and terrifying force, which lands them on a dark planet that casts its ominous shadow on earth. It is a land of robots controlled by an evil force called simply IT. The three old women warn the children that they are in great danger. They warn Charles Wallace especially against arrogance and all three against despair. Then the children are on their own. IT takes over the mind and body of Charles. Meg and Calvin find and free her father and then they are brought into the presence of IT—a raw, horrible, pulsating brain that beats through all the inhabitants of this shadow land. There follows in the complex course of the rest of the book a battle between good and evil, love and hate, that in spite of being complicated with science, philosophy, religion, satire, and allegory, carries the story on at a horrifying pace. In the end Meg's love triumphs and Charles is saved. All of them tesseract back to earth where their lives pick up as they were except for their new found knowledge of good and evil.

This space allegory is neither as clear nor as beautiful as the Narnia series, but it is written in terms of the modern world in which children know about brainwashing and the insidious, creeping corruption of evil. The last third of the book is confused, but the fact that children and young people read it avidly suggests that they get more of its underlying significance than might be expected. It is a tribute to their growing maturity and to Madeleine L'Engle's writing, which is spellbinding.

For much younger children, anywhere from eight to ten or eleven, there are no science-fiction masterpieces but numerous thoroughly amusing and plausible space fantasies. Ruthven Todd's *Space Cat,* Louis Slobodkin's *Space Ship Under the Apple Tree,* Ellen McGregor's *Miss Pickerell Goes to Mars,* and Eleanor Cameron's *Wonderful Flight to the Mushroom Planet,* together with their sequels, make absorbing reading and good introductions to this popular pseudo-scientific field of space adventures.

Modern Stories of Talking Beasts

The talking beasts in the old tales were, on the whole, a cheerful lot. Silly creatures were liquidated, but the wise pig survived, and smart billy-goats gained the grassy hillside in spite of the troll. There were no brooding and no melancholy until Andersen's *Fairy Tales.* The Ugly Duckling not only was mistreated by others but suffered spiritually. In the two English talking-beast masterpieces, *The Tale of Peter Rabbit* and *The Wind in the Willows,* there are also animals with limitations, who make mistakes and commit follies but who shake them off with blithe determination. It is these lively tales free from introspection and melancholy rather than "The Ugly Duckling" which have set the pattern for recent beast tales.

BEATRIX POTTER

The Tale of Peter Rabbit

Beatrix Potter, English novelist of the nursery and cheerful interpreter of small animals to small children, has left her own account of how she happened to write her classic, *The Tale of Peter Rabbit.* In a letter to *The Horn Book,* May 1929, she said:

> *. . . About 1893 I was interested in a little invalid child. . . . I used to write letters with pen and ink scribbles, and one of the letters was Peter Rabbit.*
>
> *Noel has got them yet; he grew up and became a hard-working clergyman in a London poor parish. After a time there began to be a vogue for small books, and I thought "Peter" might do as well as some that were being published. But I did not find any publisher who*

agreed with me. The manuscript—nearly word for word the same, but with only outline illustrations—was returned with or without thanks by at least six firms. Then I drew my savings out of the post office savings bank, and got an edition of 450 copies printed. I think the engraving and printing cost me about £11. It caused a good deal of amusement amongst my relations and friends. I made about £12 or £14 by selling copies to obliging aunts. I showed this privately printed black and white book to Messers. F. Warne & Co., and the following year, 1901, they brought out the first coloured edition.

Commenting on her method of writing, Miss Potter adds:

My usual way of writing is to scribble, and cut out, and write it again and again. The shorter and plainer the better. And read the Bible (unrevised *version and Old Testament) if I feel my style wants chastening.*

These apparently simple little stories[6] of Beatrix Potter's the children learn by heart in no time, and how they relish the names of her characters: Flopsy, Mopsy, and Cottontail, Jemima Puddle-Duck, Pigling Bland, Mrs. Tiggy-Winkle, Benjamin Bunny, Peter Rabbit. The stories are invariably built on the never-fail formula of a beginning, a middle, and an end, with plenty of suspense to bring sighs of relief when the conclusion is finally reached. Children chuckle over the funny characters, the absurd predicaments, and the narrow escapes. They pore over the clear water-color illustrations, which are full of action. Even at four they absorb delightedly the lovely details of landscape, old houses, fine old furniture and china, and at forty, learn why they liked them. (See 9 in color section.)

If you were to play one of those wretched games in which you can choose only two books for a five-year-old marooned on a desert island, you would feel obliged to choose *Mother Goose* and *The Tale of Peter Rabbit.* These are the child's favorites. Peter's adventures he can soon "read" for himself, he knows them so well; but the charms of that humorous and exciting plot never grow stale; disobedient Peter in Mr. MacGregor's cabbage patch, very complacent at first, then pursued and thoroughly frightened but still keeping his wits about him; next, Peter hiding in the watering can, and, finally, Peter at home, properly repentant, chastened by his mother, but snug in bed at last and secure. Here is a cheerful Prodigal Son, child-size.

When Beatrix Potter died in December 1943, such papers as the London *Times* and the New York *Herald Tribune* praised the reality of the little world she had brought so vividly to life and praised her excellent prose. Certainly the children for whom her little books provide an introduction to the world of animals are never going to see a rabbit skipping hurriedly out of their gardens without amusement and sympathy, for children who have known Beatrix Potter's books know this world of timid, scampering creatures as a world touchingly like their own.

KENNETH GRAHAME

The Wind in the Willows

Another pleasant thing about Peter Rabbit is that he paves the way for *The Wind in the Willows* (1908). Children who loved Peter are more likely to adopt Mole and Rat and Toad a few years later.

Kenneth Grahame was a lovable, literary, out-of-doorish sort of Englishman with a gift for storytelling. For his small son, nicknamed "Mouse," he used to spin continuous tales at bedtime. Once Mouse refused to go to the seaside because his trip would interrupt the adventures of Toad, to which he was listening. In order to persuade the child to go, his father promised to send him a chapter in the mail daily, and this he did. Sensing their value, the nursery governess who read the chapters to Mouse mailed them back to Mrs. Grahame for safekeeping. From these letters and bedtime stories grew *The Wind in the Willows.*

Each chapter tells a complete adventure of the four friends, Mole, kindly old Water Rat, shy Badger, and rich, conceited, troublesome

6. Among the companion volumes to *Peter Rabbit* are *The Tale of Benjamin Bunny, The Tailor of Gloucester, The Tale of Squirrel Nutkin, The Tale of Jemima Puddle-Duck, The Tale of Mrs. Tiggy-Winkle,* and *The Tale of Tom Kitten.*

Toad. The friends "mess around in boats," have picnics, dine elegantly at Toad Hall, get lost in the Wild Wood, rescue Toad from his life of folly, and even encounter once "The Piper at the Gates of Dawn." But how explain the appeal of this book? Of course, not all children like it, but those who do are likely to value it above most other books. One boy, faced each summer with the problem of choosing one book to take with him to camp, took *The Wind in the Willows* four consecutive seasons. Why?

Sensory Appeal

In the first place, the sensory experiences make the reader one with Mole or Ratty. You can just feel the sunshine hot on your fur; you, too, waggle your toes from sheer happiness or stretch out on some cool dock leaves or explore the silent silver kingdom of the moonlit river. Earth and water, a green world of woods and meadows speak to you from every page. There are also the most succulent foods in this book. The friends are forever dining, or supping, or breakfasting, or taking tea. They feast on rich flavorsome stews, rashers of bacon, plates of fried ham, potted lobster, or tea with hot toast that is dripping with butter. You find your mouth watering and your appetite rising. Sights, sounds, tastes, feels, smells—a rich sensory world!

Humor

The humor of *The Wind in the Willows,* particularly the humor of the conversations, is a little subtle for some children but delights those who do catch it. Fortunately, Toad's antics, his bemused pursuit of his latest fad, his ridiculous conceit, the scrapes he gets into, and the efforts of his friends to reform him furnish enough broad comedy to satisfy everyone.

Conversations

Children invariably flip over the pages of a strange book to see if it has enough conversation to suit them. So they enjoy Mole, Rat, Badger, and Toad, for the friends talk continually. The dialogue is so easy and natural you might know that it grew not from written but from oral composition. It is that of the born storyteller, used to children's predilection for talk, improvising dialogue in his own fluent, individual vein. What talk it is—funniest when it is most grave, revealing more of the speaker than any explanatory paragraph.

For example, Toad, having dragged his friends Rat and Mole on an uncomfortable journey across the country in a cart, remarks fatuously:

". . . This is the real life for a gentleman! Talk about your old river!"

"I don't talk about my river," replied the patient Rat. "You know *I don't, Toad. But I* think *about it," he added pathetically, in a lower tone: "I think about it—all the time!"*

*The Mole reached out from under his blanket, felt for the Rat's paw in the darkness, and gave it a squeeze. "I'll do whatever you like, Ratty," he whispered. "Shall we run away to-morrow morning, quite early—*very *early—and go back to our dear old hole on the river?"*

"No, no, we'll see it out," whispered back the Rat. "Thanks awfully, but I ought to stick by Toad till this trip is ended. It wouldn't be

Whether Shepard is drawing Christopher Robin or Toad, he can suggest with a few strokes of the pen a particular mood, action, or personality. Here Toad's huge mouth, wide stance, pompous pose, and absurd costume tell the tale—Toad the playboy!
Illustration by E. H. Shepard. From The Wind in the Willows *by Kenneth Grahame. Published by Charles Scribner's Sons, 1954. Reproduced with permission of the publisher. (Book 5¼ x 7¾, picture 1¼ x 1⅝)*

safe for him to be left to himself. It won't take very long. His fads never do. Good night!"[7]

No preaching about the duties of a friend, just patient, enduring friendship, loyal in service and understanding!

Descriptions

These conversations are as much a part of the style as the descriptions which make the book one of the masterpieces of English for readers of any age. The famous chapter in which Rat and Toad meet "The Piper at the Gates of Dawn" is shot through with descriptions that for simplicity and beauty cannot be surpassed. After the black darkness of the river at night the friends see the moon rise:

The line of the horizon was clear and hard against the sky, and in one particular quarter it showed black against a silvery climbing phosphorescence that grew and grew. At last, over the rim of the waiting earth the moon lifted with slow majesty till it swung clear of the horizon and rode off, free of moorings; and once more they began to see surfaces—meadows widespread, and quiet gardens, and the river itself from bank to bank, all softly disclosed, all washed clean of mystery and terror, all radiant again as by day, but with a difference that was tremendous. Their old haunts greeted them again in other raiment, as if they had slipped away and put on this pure new apparel and come quietly back, smiling as they shyly waited to see if they would be recognized again under it.

The dawn comes with equal beauty and strangeness. City children may never have seen such beauty, but to hear this prose is to hear beauty. As the river was "gemmed" with flowers, so this book is "gemmed" with effortless, flawless description.

Inner Significance

None of these things—sensory appeal, humor, dialogue, or descriptions—accounts for the hold this book takes upon the heart and the imagination. As in Andersen's *Fairy Tales,* it is the inner significance of the story that counts. First of all, there is the warm friendliness of the animals. Each one makes mistakes, has his limitations, but no one ever rejects a friend. The three put up with Toad's escapades as long as they can; then they join together and reform him in spite of himself. Together they endure perils and pitfalls and come safely through only because they help each other. This continual kindliness, the overlooking of other people's mistakes, and the sympathetic understanding which pervade every page warm the reader's heart. No allegory here, just decent people who happen to wear tails and fur treating each other with decent kindliness. The book also gives the reader a heartening sense of sanctuary. Mole gets lost in the Wild Wood, frighteningly lost and hurt, but Ratty comes to his rescue. Then just as the two of them despair of reaching home before the cold overcomes them, they find Badger's house. Good old Badger takes them in, warms them beside his roaring fire, clothes them, and feeds them sumptuously; their sense of peace and security is restored. So it is with the rescue of the lost Otter baby in "The Piper at the Gates of Dawn."

This is a warm book, a book to read when the heart is chilled or the spirit shaken. It is one of the most reassuring and comforting books in all literature.

Why did Kenneth Grahame write only this one story for children?[8] Talking to an American admirer, he said:

I am not a professional writer. I never have been, and I never will be, by reason of the accident that I don't need any money. I do not care for notoriety: in fact, it is distasteful to me. . . .

What, then, is the use of writing for a person like myself? . . . A large amount of what Thoreau called life went into the making of many of these playful pages. To toil at making sentences means to sit indoors for many hours, cramped above a desk. Yet, out of doors, the wind may be singing through the willows, and

7. This passage and the following one are from *The Wind in the Willows* by Kenneth Grahame; copyright 1908, 1935 by the publishers, Charles Scribner's Sons.
8. He also wrote *Dream Days* and *The Golden Age,* which were about children.

my favourite sow may be preparing to deliver a large litter in the fullness of the moon.[9]

So he left children only one book, a little masterpiece, and an American admirer and critic said of him when he died:

And yet it is a truth that, on that day, the translators of the King James version of the Bible, seated at an eternal council-table, admitted to their fellowship the last great master of English prose. . . .[10]

Not all children like this book, but most of them do if it is read aloud to them as it was told to Mouse, a chapter at a time. For this is decidedly a book to be shared. Its richness grows when it is mulled over, discussed, and savored to the full. If a child likes it, then it is one book he ought to own—in his favorite edition, illustrated by Arthur Rackham, or Ernest Shepard, or Paul Bransom, or whichever artist he prefers. Certainly if *The Wind in the Willows* is enjoyed in childhood, it will be reread when the child is grown up, and it will be passed on to his children as a precious inheritance.

HUGH LOFTING

The Story of Dr. Dolittle

Hugh Lofting's *The Story of Dr. Dolittle* (1920) is a favorite, too, but it is as unlike Kenneth Grahame's masterpiece as it could well be. If Mole and Ratty are a little on the highbrow side, certainly Polynesia, Gub-Gub, and their friends are distinctly lowbrow. If the former are witty and urbane, the latter are downright ridiculous. Dr. Dolittle is the center of an animal saga which is hilarious and unique, and it is a rare child who does not enjoy the Doctor.

World War I produced him, Hugh Lofting tells us. He says there was little news at the front suitable to write his children, and so he had to make up something or not write at all. He was continually concerned with the animals forced into the war and suffering fear, wounds, and death without ever being able to speak for themselves. Obviously, to take care of horses properly, a doctor ought to understand horse language, Mr. Lofting thought, and such a character, Dr. Dolittle, began to grow in his letters to his children. After the war, the book was made from the letters and illustrated by the author. Other Dolittle adventures followed, and the whole series has continued to make a wide appeal to children ten or twelve years old.

Dr. John Dolittle of Puddleby-on-the-Marsh gave up doctoring "the best people" and became a doctor of animals. Polynesia, the parrot, suggested that if Dolittle would really settle down to learn animal languages, which she could teach him, he might become an animal doctor of some account. The good Doctor went to work immediately and soon discovered how right Polynesia had been. His first patient was a horse who told him in good strong horse terms that a stupid man had been treating him for spavins when all he needed was glasses. Dr. Dolittle fitted him with a splendid pair of glasses and from then on the Doctor's fame as a physician who could converse with his animal patients spread like wildfire and carried him into adventures which fill some eight books. These adventures of the Doctor are wildly impossible and very funny.

The charm of these books lies partly in the humorous reversal of roles—the animals, guiding, assisting, and generally taking care of the helpless human beings—and partly in the characterizations of both animals and people. Hugh Lofting also has a sly way of relating utterly preposterous events with a complete gravity that makes the rare "pushmi-pullyu" as plausible as a panda. This pseudo-serious style strikes children as exceedingly funny. Adults today are disturbed by the racial epithets and incidents that occur in some of the books, particularly the first one. These could be so easily deleted that it seems a pity not to edit the books and remove the offending sections. Although these stories lack literary distinction, they have a grave logic and a straight-faced humor that appeal to large numbers of children.

9. Quoted by Elspeth Grahame, in *First Whisper of "The Wind in the Willows,"* pp. 31-32, from an article by Clayton Hamilton in *The Bookman*, January 1933.
10. *Ibid.*, p. 33.

Notice the wild racing action emphasized by the decorative moving branches at the top of the picture, and notice, too, the dramatic contrast of the savage leaping zebra and the frightened monkey. The drawing is stylized but strangely convincing.
Illustration by Dorothy Lathrop. From The Three Mulla-Mulgars *by Walter de la Mare. Copyright, 1919, by Alfred A. Knopf, Inc. Reproduced by permission of the publisher. (Original in color, book 5½ x 8¼)*

WALTER DE LA MARE

The Three Royal Monkeys

It is difficult to classify *The Three Royal Monkeys* (originally entitled *The Three Mulla-Mulgars*) of Walter de la Mare. It could be called animal fantasy, but since it seems a not-too-distant relative of "The Ugly Duckling," it is grouped here with the other talking beasts. It has the same curious blend of realism and fantasy that characterizes the poet's novel *Memoirs of a Midget*. Grave and completely convincing fantasy is characteristic of Walter de la Mare's verse and prose, and is bewildering to some readers.

The Three Royal Monkeys is a long story dealing with the adventures of three little monkeys, or Mulgars, of the Blood Royal, who go in search of their father, a prince from the Valley of Tishnar. Tishnar stands for hope and beauty and peace beyond our world. Little Nod, the youngest of the royal monkeys, is a Nizza-neela; that is, he has magic about him, and he carries the Wonderstone, which marks him as a true prince. The brothers suffer endless hardships, but always their bravery and Nod's magic bring them through. They know that they have reached their father's land of Tishnar when they suddenly meet "a Mulgar of a presence and a strangeness, who was without doubt of the Kingdom of Assasimmon."

The book is full of wise sayings. The unhappy panther, dressed in man's clothes, is asked if she is comfortable and replies:

> *"O my friend, my scarce-wise Mulgar-royal, when did you ever hear that grand clothes were comfortable?"*

Later, Nod remarks philosophically,

> *"Who is there wise that was not once foolish?"*

But it is the descriptions that give it a strange eerie beauty unlike any other:

> *Over the swamp stood a shaving of moon, clear as a bow of silver. And all about, on every twig, on every thorn, and leaf, and pebble; all along the nine-foot grasses, on every cushion and touch of bark, even on the walls of their hut, lay this spangling fiery meal of Tishnar—frost.*

Comparatively few youngsters—probably none under twelve—will read this long story for themselves. But those who have the capacity to enjoy such a book will discover that when a poet tells a fairy tale, the result is often a strange and heady enchantment.

MARIE HALL ETS

Mister Penny

The hero of *Mister Penny* (1935) has to work hard in the factory of Friend-in-Need Safety-Pins in order to support his family of lazy, good-for-nothing animals. He loves them all—Limpy the horse, Mooloo the cow with beautiful eyes, Splop the goat, Pugwug the pig, Mimkin the lamb, Chukluk and Doody the hen and rooster. Yet the varmints do nothing to assist Mr. Penny. Instead, they get into the most expensive kind of mischief. Finally, when they destroy the rich neighbor's garden, old Thunderstorm delivers his frightful ultimatum. He'll take the worthless animals unless his garden is completely restored. The animals decide that even work is preferable to falling into the hands of old Thunderstorm. So they firmly resolve to work! A completely black page bears the caption "Here they are working in the neighbor's garden"—at night. Before the time limit elapses they have not only completely restored old Thunderstorm's garden, but they have become so enthusiastic over their labors and their successes that they go right on and make a splendid garden for Mr. Penny, too.

The story ends on a note of triumph. Mister Penny is out of the Friend-in-Need factory forever. He is installed in a fine new house, too, which everyone comes to look at because, besides climbing roses and a superb garden, the pink house boasts a separate door for each one of the animals and one for Mr. Penny—seven doors in all. The villagers think it a little queer, but they have to admit "They're the happiest family in Wuddle." This little fable about the satisfaction that comes from working and helping is a kindly tale and is delightfully humorous.

In similar vein is Marie Hall Ets' story of the animals who saved the hero of *Mr. T. W. Anthony Woo* from the interference of a meddlesome sister. *In the Forest* and *Another Day* are slight but charming stories for the nursery child, for whom Mrs. Ets is writing and illustrating some beautiful books. Her talking beasts have been admirable, and in *Play with Me* they have ceased to talk but are equally effective.

ROBERT LAWSON

Ben and Me
Rabbit Hill

Robert Lawson, with his easy storytelling style and beautiful illustrations, added much to the glory of the talking-beast tale. The children consider *Ben and Me* (1939) one of the genuinely "funny books." These biographical memoirs of Benjamin Franklin are supposedly written by Amos, a cheeky mouse who modestly admits that he supplied Ben with most of his ideas. Take that little matter of the stove, for instance. They were almost frozen and Ben had a bad case of sniffles when Amos thought out the idea of a stove. Ben was a little slow at catching on but finally worked out a very satisfactory contraption. Amos admits that he thoroughly disapproved of Ben's experiments with electricity, but he stuck by his friend in spite of many a shock and some novel results caused by Amos' interference. The mouse, tucked snugly away in the famous fur cap, appeared at the French court with Ben. What Amos did there is too fearful to relate.

A series of these fantastic biographies followed, of which the best one by far is *Mr. Revere and I* (1953). Notice the improved English. Unlike *Ben and Me,* Paul Revere's story is told by a cultured English horse who loathed the "American peasants" when he first landed in Boston. But after he falls into Revere's hands, he becomes an ardent patriot. He even carries Revere on his fateful ride in spite of the silversmith's atrocious horsemanship. It is quite possible that children will get as much from this picture of the American Revolution as from some of their histories.

Good as these humorous biographies are, Mr. Lawson really came into his own as a creative writer with *Rabbit Hill* (1944), a Newbery Medal winner. This is the story of Father and Mother Rabbit, their high-leaping son, Little Georgie, and an aged Uncle Analdas, who are the leading characters, with Willie Fieldmouse and Porkey the Woodchuck playing important parts. The story begins with the pleasant rumor that new folks are moving into the big house. The question is, what kind of folks will they turn out to be—mean and pinching, or planting folks with a thought for the small creatures who have always lived on the hill? The new folks begin well with a sign "Please Drive Carefully on Account of Small Animals." They plant gardens without fences, sow fields without traps, provide generous "garbidge," and permit no poison. They rescue little Willie from drowning and Little Georgie from an automobile accident. Their crowning beneficence is a beautiful pool and feeding station for their furry and feathered friends, presided over by the good St. Francis—a little sanctuary which bears the kindly legend "There is enough for all."

The Tough Winter (1954) is the sequel to *Rabbit Hill.* It tells a moving story of what happens to small beasts when snow and ice last too long and there are no kind-hearted human beings to help. If ever there was a plea for aid to winterbound beasts, it is this story.

These books may not have the superlative literary qualities of *The Wind in the Willows,* but they are exceedingly well written and marvelously illustrated. All of the animals, from suspicious Uncle Analdas to worrying Mother Rabbit, are delightfully individual-

New Folks co-ming, Oh my! New Folks co-ming, Oh my! New Folks co-ming, Oh my! Oh my! Oh my!

This picture is a beguiling contrast to Mr. Lawson's drawings of Little Georgie's wild leaping. The gentle landscape, the floating clouds, the completely relaxed Georgie—all suggest peace and contentment.
From Rabbit Hill *by Robert Lawson.*
Copyright 1944 by Robert Lawson. Reprinted by permission of The Viking Press, Inc.
(Book 6 x 9¼, picture 5¼ x 4½)

ized. Their precarious lives, their small needs, and their many hardships are sympathetically related, and the happy conclusions are not too idealistic, as anyone can testify who has harbored wild creatures. These stories and their illustrations should do more than any lectures to develop in young children a feeling of tenderness and regard for small animals.

Robert Lawson's Illustrations[11]

To fully appreciate the range and power in Mr. Lawson's pictures of animals, you will need to examine all of his illustrated books. *Rabbit Hill,* which was also the name of his own country home, is a pleasant assembling of all the small creatures he watched and recorded with humorous understanding in his own books as well as those by other authors which he illustrated. Even in *Pilgrim's Progress* they bob up gaily. Mr. Lawson evidently enjoyed mice, because not only is little Willie engagingly recorded in *Rabbit Hill,* but the redoubtable Amos in *Ben and Me* is a very prince of mice and as chummily convincing as Ferdinand, the languishing bull. Mr. Lawson's illustrations show his creatures not as types but as individuals in varying moods. In *Rabbit Hill,* Porkey's out-thrust, drooping lower lip is stubbornness personified; Georgie, leaping with a powerful push from those hind legs of his, is very different from the relaxed Georgie, hands folded over his fat paunch, making up his happy chant about "New Folks coming, Oh my!" In any group of the animals you can pick out Father, the bluegrass gentleman of the old school, and Uncle Analdas, the agitator.

Because Mr. Lawson drew with exquisite detail and complete clarity, he is sometimes characterized as old-fashioned. But Helen Dean Fish tells of another appraisal of Robert Lawson by a small boy who was looking at an exhibit of contemporary illustrations. He said, "I like *his* best. He draws them up neat, and you can see what they mean."[12] So you can, and there is meaning in every line and a humor that will set you to chuckling.

11. See Chapter 4 for another brief discussion of Robert Lawson's illustrations.
12. "Robert Lawson," *The Horn Book,* January-February 1940, p. 20.

E. B. WHITE

Charlotte's Web

E. B. White, essayist and editorial writer for *The New Yorker,* noted for his lucid, effortless prose, wrote *Stuart Little,* the story of a baby who resembled a mouse, "in fact he was a mouse." Some children liked Stuart's adventures, but most adults were disturbed by the biology of this mouse-child of a human family. *Charlotte's Web* (1952), on the other hand, had the distinction of being enthusiastically reviewed in both the adult and children's sections of our most important literary magazines. It is a delight to read aloud, and adults as well as children enjoy it.

Fern, a farmer's child, persuades her father to give her a runt of a pig he is about to liquidate. "Wilbur," Fern names her pet, and she raises him in a doll buggy with a doll's nursing bottle for a feeder. But when Wilbur gains girth, Father firmly banishes him to the barnyard, and here the fantasy begins. Fern spends long periods of time with her pet daily and discovers that she understands what the animals are saying to each other. Wilbur has learned about the fall butchering and he doesn't want to die. Charlotte, the aloof, intelligent spider, feels sorry for the silly little pig and promises to save him. Her devices for doing this are unique and exceedingly funny. The progress of Wilbur, the "radiant pig," involves all the people on two farms and most of the barnyard creatures, including Templeton, the selfish rat. In the end, Wilbur is saved but Charlotte dies, true to her kind, leaving hundreds of eggs. Birth and death and life go on in their strange and moving cycles.

Children laugh hilariously over this story, but they weep at its conclusion—even the ten-year-olds. Said one seven-year-old whose grandmother had read him the book, "Mother, Charlotte died."

CHAUSSURES
CHARCUTERIE
CAFE
TABAC
MODES
AMEUBLEMENT
Now the lion
began to hear the joyous sounds of a military march.
He turned around the next corner,
and there was the town band, marching down the street
between two lines of people.
Ratatatum ratata ratatatum ratatata boom boom.
Before the lion could even nod and say, "Bonjour,"
the music became screams and yells.
What a hubbub!
Musicians and spectators tumbled into one another
in their flight toward doorways and sidewalk cafes.
Soon the street was empty and silent.

A baffled lion and a band in headlong flight—Duvoisin's pen has created a hilarious situation. Illustration by Roger Duvoisin. From The Happy Lion *by Louise Fatio. Copyright, 1954, by Louise Fatio Duvoisin and Roger Duvoisin. Reprinted by permission of Whittlesey House (McGraw-Hill). (Original in color, book 8 x 10)*

And his mother, not knowing about Charlotte, replied casually, "Oh, did she?"

Shocked, the boy cried, "Mother, don't you care?" and burst into tears.

A book that can so delight and so move children carries with it the therapy of laughter and a growing compassion as well.

LOUISE FATIO

The Happy Lion

In the series of *Happy Lion* books, who can say which is better—the stories by Louise Fatio or the illustrations by Roger Duvoisin? This husband and wife team has produced inimitable picture-stories, witty and beautiful. The first book, *The Happy Lion* (1954), introduces the Lion at home in a small French park, greeted daily and politely by his friends, in particular the zoo keeper's little boy. One day, when someone inadvertently leaves the gate unlocked, the Lion saunters out to find his friends, and people flee, women faint, and the band panics. Only the little boy greets the Lion as usual and leads him gently home to his place in the park. Through the succeeding three books the Lion travels, roars, and, after kidnaping a beautiful lioness, has himself a family (*The Three Happy Lions*). Not only are these stories well told with good plots, sly humor, and surprise endings, but the pictures are rich in details that children pore over. A *Happy Lion* devotee could find his way to every shop in that particular French village and would know at precisely which street corner the panic began.

OTHER EXAMPLES OF TALKING BEASTS

Three other series, like the *Happy Lion* books popular with the nursery-kindergarten children, are the *Curious George* books by Hans A. Rey, the *Anatole* books by Eve Titus, and the old favorites the *Babar* books by Jean de Brunhoff. *Curious George* (1941), illustrated by the author, is a monkey who gets in and out of scrapes with a successful agility children envy. *Anatole and the Cat* (1957), gloriously illustrated by Paul Galdone, is the story of a French cheese-tasting mouse, complete with beret and brief case. His enemy the cat is a source of considerable danger and must be put in his place by Anatole. *The Story of Babar* (1937), illustrated by the author, was the first of innumerable books about Babar, now being continued by Jean de Brunhoff's son Laurent. Babar is a sophisticated elephant who comes to Paris, obtains a wealthy patroness, is outfitted with an elegant wardrobe, and returns to Africa to set up such a dynasty as never was before or since. *Babar and Father Christmas* is one of the favorites.

There have been an enormous number of talking-beast stories for two- to six-year-old children in the last three decades. All sorts of creatures, from pandas to goldfish, are talking and adventuring. Many of these tales are thin in content and undistinguished in style, but some are delightful. Margaret Friskey's *Seven Diving Ducks*, a story of the one little duck who was afraid to take the plunge, is worn out with rereadings. One of the best of these stories is Margaret Wise Brown's *The Runaway Bunny*. In this brightly colored picture-story, a young bunny warns his mother that he is going to run away:

"If you run away," said his mother, "I will run after you. For you are my little bunny."

"If you run after me," said the little bunny, "I will become a fish in a trout stream and I will swim away from you."

"If you become a fish in a trout stream," said his mother, "I will become a fisherman and I will fish for you."

So they play the game of make-believe, and Clement Hurd's pictures show the bunny as a little fish with his mother as a fisherman, or the bunny as a bird with his mother as a big rabbit-shaped tree. The word-pattern goes on like a song until it ends reassuringly:

"Shucks," said the bunny, "I might just as well stay where I am and be your little bunny."

And so he did.

Marjorie Flack's *Ask Mr. Bear* is the nursery-school and kindergarten favorite. A small boy, not knowing what to give his mother for a birthday present, asks a series of animals for advice. Finally Mr. Bear whispers just the right thing in his ear. He hurries home and gives his mother—a great big Bear Hug. The surprise ending never fails to bring pleasure no matter how many times the children have heard it.

The Country Bunny and the Little Gold Shoes is a choice Easter rabbit story by Du Bose Heyward. More recently, Roger Duvoisin has written and illustrated a droll series about Petunia, a genius of a goose, whose predicaments delight her young followers.

Modern talking-beast tales should be chosen with discrimination. If Beatrix Potter went back to her Bible-reading when she felt her style needed chastening, we had better reread Beatrix Potter and *The Wind in the Willows* when we are in doubt about choosing from the multitude of these new beast tales.

Inanimate Objects Personified

Although the fanciful story about the secret life of toys and other inanimate objects was Andersen's invention, it took the writers of the twentieth century to use this form at the child's level, with an inventiveness and charm that already have made some of these stories children's classics. Andersen's tales of the little china shepherdess and the chimney sweep or the rusty tin soldier are faintly sad and decidedly adult. Later writers have avoided both these pitfalls. Their dolls, trains, and airplanes are cheerful and lively.

RICHARD HENRY HORNE

Memoirs of a London Doll

In the nineteenth century there was one popular example of this type of story, the English *Memoirs of a London Doll* (1846) by Richard Henry Horne (pseudonym Mrs. Fairstar). In this book, Maria Poppett, the doll, tells her own story.

Tom Plummy traded an elegant Twelfth-cake for Maria as a present for his little sister, Ellen Plummy. The doll tells all the things she and her mistress did and saw together in the London of a hundred years ago. The Christmas pantomime, the Lord Mayor's show, a typical Punch and Judy entertainment, the food, and the clothes of long ago are described. Although some little girls enjoy this early doll story, it is not an important book today, but it is interesting to adults as the ancestor of the American *Hitty*, the Newbery Medal winner written by Rachel Field (p. 359).

CARLO LORENZINI

The Adventures of Pinocchio

The strongest impetus to the modern personification type of story may well stem not from Hans Andersen's tales but from that popular Italian classic *Pinocchio*. Written in 1880 by a witty Tuscan, Carlo Lorenzini (pseudonym Collodi), it was apparently first translated into English and published in this country in 1892. From then on, it has held a high place in the affections of American children and has undoubtedly influenced American writers.

The story concerns a rogue of a puppet which old Geppetto painstakingly carves out of wood. Hardly has the poor wood carver finished his manikin when the saucy creature kicks him, leaps down from the bench, and makes off through the door in pursuit of life, liberty, and his own sweet way. Pinocchio is full of good resolutions: to buy new clothes for his dear papa Geppetto, to go to school, to learn his lessons, and to be a good boy generally. Instead, he wastes his money, lies about it, plays hooky from school, and chooses for his companions the villains and the boobies. Every time he lies to his friend the Blue Fairy, his nose grows longer, until soon he can't turn around in a room without colliding with the walls. Neither the Talking Cricket nor the Blue Fairy can check his follies. The climax is his journey to the Land of Toys, where there is never any school and where he finds presently that he has grown a fine pair of donkey ears and a body to match. Saved again and again by the good Blue Fairy, he learns that she is ill and starving. He is roused at last, earns money to feed and care for both Geppetto and the Fairy, and wakes in the morning to find himself no longer a puppet but a real boy, living with Geppetto in a well-kept home. Geppetto explains,

". . . when bad boys become good and kind, they have the power of making their homes gay and new with happiness."

And the irrepressible Pinocchio, looking at the remains of the puppet dangling on the wall, remarks to himself with great complacency:

"How ridiculous I was as a marionette! And how happy I am, now that I have become a real boy!"

Despite all the sinning and repenting, here he is—still cocky, still vain and boastful! This is the children's own epic, themselves in wood, full of good resolutions, given to folly, sliding through somehow, but with one difference—Pinocchio always comes out on top and never quite loses face.

No child's book of the nineteenth century in any country is more completely on the child's level. Pinocchio's wickedness is bloodcurdling from the child's angle—kicking his good papa, running away, lying like a trooper—but then the swift punishments which follow every misdeed are equally bloodcurdling and objective. Suppose our noses started growing every time we told a lie? The children giggle a little uneasily and can hardly wait to read what happens next. Even the jokes are understandable, which is not always true in the great English classics, and there are laughs on almost every page.

MARGERY WILLIAMS BIANCO

The Velveteen Rabbit

Margery Williams Bianco's books have the same sensitive, imaginative quality that Andersen's tales have, and they are often similarly moving.

The Velveteen Rabbit (1926) is built upon the theme that toys come to life if they are loved enough. The Velveteen Rabbit suffers more than the ordinary vicissitudes of toys and is finally, during the illness of his little owner, thrown out on the ash pile. But the child misses his companion. It does not matter to him that his toy is dilapidated and dirty; he loves his Velveteen Rabbit and wants him more than anything else. Then, out-of-doors once more, he sees a tame rabbit. The two gaze at each other. There is no doubt in the child's heart—here at last is his dear Velveteen Rabbit come to life.

A. A. MILNE

Winnie-the-Pooh
The House at Pooh Corner

A. A. Milne's *Winnie-the-Pooh* (1926) and *The House at Pooh Corner* (1928) are different from anything that has preceded them. They seem to have grown as a natural sequence to the poems about Christopher Robin and Pooh, and they also developed, as the author says, from his small son's demands to hear a story for Pooh:

"What sort of stories does he like?"
"About himself. Because he's that *sort of Bear."*
"Oh, I see."...
So I tried.

The accommodating Mr. Milne forthwith begins to spin a series of tales about Pooh, when he lived in the forest "under the name of Sanders." He calls on Rabbit and eats so much that he sticks in the door and can't get out. He flies up in a balloon to get some honey out of a tree, tries to imitate a cloud in order to distract the suspicious bees, and finally has to have the balloon shot in order to get down. There are adventures with Piglet, Eeyore the old donkey, Kanga, and Little Roo. *The House at Pooh Corner* introduces Tigger, a new and amusing character, but the tales go on in much the same vein.

Ernest Shepard's illustrations make it clear that most of the animals are really toys like Winnie-the-Pooh. Christopher appears in their midst rallying them for an "expotition" to the North Pole, or rescuing them from various mishaps, but he, too, lives in a tree in the forest in quite a cozy bearlike den. The pictures are full of the fascinating details Mr. Shepard knows how to put in. For instance, Mr. Owl's house has two signs at the door. One, under the knocker, says

PLES RING
IF AN RNSER
IS REQIRD

The other, under the bell rope, reads

PLEZ CNOKE
IF AN RNSR
IS NOT REQID

The stories are unusual in that Christopher goes in and out of them on a familiar forest-dwelling level with the animals, but in the end he brings everything back to reality when he sets off up the stairs of his own house, headed for a bath, dragging Pooh by one leg. The stories are finished, Christopher is himself, and Pooh is Pooh. This is not only a tale about toys come to life, but also a clever fantasy for the youngest—not too complicated, no fairies, just a little boy sharing make-believe adventures with his toys and the little creatures of the woods, but knowing all the time that they *are* make-believe. It's a game of "let's pretend" put into story form, and children anywhere from five to nine or even ten enjoy both of these books.

Gideon's head, being large, might have dominated the scene, but it is softly drawn and kept as a background to the strong blacks and whites of doll and snail. Illustration by Adrienne Adams. From Impunity Jane *by Rumer Godden. Copyright 1954 by Rumer Godden. By permission of the Viking Press, Inc. (Original with color, book 5 x 7¾, picture 4 x 4¼)*

RACHEL FIELD

Hitty, Her First Hundred Years

Rachel Field and the artist Dorothy Lathrop were fascinated by an old doll in a New York antique shop. She was carved from mountain ash and dated back to whaling days in Maine. Rachel Field bought the doll, started a book about her to be illustrated by Dorothy Lathrop, and prophesied, as a justification for her extravagance, that this story was going to win the Newbery Medal. Indeed, *Hitty* (1929) was so honored and was present in person when Rachel Field made her acceptance speech and received the medal.

The book, which is enjoyed by girls ten to twelve years old, records Hitty's numerous adventures which range all the way from being shipwrecked and serving as a heathen idol on a remote island to hearing Jenny Lind sing and to being on exhibition in New Orleans.

RUMER GODDEN

The Dolls' House
Impunity Jane
Miss Happiness and Miss Flower

The novelist Rumer Godden has written a series of doll stories that are unsurpassed in variety and charm, for her dolls have distinct personalities and in her books they talk and act in character. Only in one respect are they alike. In the hands of their owners they are often misunderstood and badly treated, and always helpless, except for the sheer force of their unique personalities. The first of the series, *The Dolls' House* (1947, 1962), is one of the most dramatic. An exquisite old Victorian doll house is inhabited by proper, genteel dolls. When a strange, haughty doll is added to the group, a doll-sized tragedy takes place, but this ending is as gentle as the spirit of the old house.

Perhaps the most popular of the books is *Impunity Jane* (1954), so called because the clerk tells the buyers that this finger-sized doll can be dropped "with impunity." But her owner does not think much of Jane; so she relegates her to a stuffy old doll house where she sits for years, bored and pining for adventure. When a small boy named Gideon carries her off in his pocket, life begins for Jane. What that boy thinks up for Jane to do is a caution. She sails his boats, flies his airplanes, rides on his bicycle, dwells in igloos and wigwams, and generally enjoys life. When Gideon's conscience forces him to own up to his kidnaping, the solution is a joyous one, and he and Jane return happily to a life of exploration and adventure.

In contrast to the intrepid Jane, *Miss Happiness and Miss Flower* (1961) are two exquisite Japanese dolls, too gentle it would seem to enjoy any adventures. Yet they are the promoters of a long series of activities, which help a homesick, timid little girl and quell a jealous one. They are the inspiration for a carefully constructed, authentic, and exquisite Japanese doll house. What is more, these dolls give rise to another series of adventures in a book called *Little Plum*. In this story the interest centers less on the dolls and more on their owner Belinda's naughty curiosity and behavior in relation to a new child next door. However, the culmination of the amusing action is a most felicitous Feast of the Dolls in Japanese style. Doll-loving little girls should indeed be grateful to Rumer Godden for these varied and absorbing doll books. These books would convince any reader that dolls are not as inanimate as they seem.

Modern Examples of Machinery Personified

Tales in which modern machinery is personified furnish the child with something he desires and seems likely to enjoy permanently. There were a few forerunners of these recent stories about machinery. Every kindergarten teacher told "The Little Engine That Could" to delighted groups of five-year-olds. This story with its refrain, "I think I can, I think I can, I think I can," is still popular and still fun to tell. Lucy Sprague Mitchell followed with another repetitional engine story, "How the Engine Learned the Knowing Song," which, if not as spontaneous as its predecessor, is still enjoyed by the youngest children. Then in 1939 *Mike Mulligan and His Steam Shovel* took the five-year-olds by storm and was almost equally popular with older children. Virginia Burton, the author-artist of *Mike Mulligan*, has repeated her success with other books.

VIRGINIA BURTON

Choo Choo
Mike Mulligan and His Steam Shovel
The Little House
Katy and the Big Snow

If artists have any facility with words, they should make good storytellers, because graphic representation requires the ability to see clearly and to bring to life for others what is taking place. Virginia Burton (Mrs. George Demetrios, in private life) uses her brush and words in the happiest possible combination. In her picture-stories, the pictures are an integral part of the text, interpreting and even adding to the text. Her subjects are machines, very likely a natural response to the interests of her sons when they were small.

A Steam Shovel, a Snow Shovel, and a Train

Mike Mulligan and His Steam Shovel tells the story of Mike, who owns a fine steam shovel with which he does important jobs of excavation until his machine, Mary Anne, is outmoded by new and more powerful models. Jobs no longer come his way, and Mike and his faithful shovel are in a bad state. Then Mike reads about a town which wishes to have its Town Hall excavation dug in a great hurry. Mike and Mary Anne hasten to the scene of action and offer to dig it in one day or no pay. The city fathers agree, seeing a chance to get their excavation done for nothing, since such a feat seems obviously impossible. The next morning Mary Anne and Mike go to work. Dirt flies in all directions, and the watching crowds grow to a mob and hang breathlessly over the heaving, bouncing Mary Anne, driven by Mike. At last, exactly on the hour, the excavation is finished, deep and well squared off at the corners. The crowd bursts into loud cheers. The only trouble is that Mike, in his excitement, has dug himself in, and there is no way of getting Mary Anne out. So Mary Anne just becomes the furnace of the new Town Hall and Mike her attendant. Both live a warm, prosperous, and respected life ever after. (See 21 in the color section for Chapter 4.)

Katy and the Big Snow, the story of a snow shovel, has a similar format and manner but is not so popular as *Mike. Choo Choo,* the story of a runaway engine, preceded *Mike* by two years and is a favorite also.

It is significant that Virginia Burton studied for the ballet. There is certainly something of the dance in her swirling spirals and her repeated use of circular design. This view of "the little house" shows a stage in its eventful life.
From The Little House *by Virginia Lee Burton. Houghton Mifflin Company, 1942. Caldecott Medal. Reproduced with the permission of the publisher. (Original in color, book 9½ x 9)*

Appeal of Machine Stories

These machine stories have certain marked characteristics which help to explain their popularity. The plot always involves a staggering task or action and has considerable suspense. The illustrations heighten the feeling of action by swirling, circular lines that rush across the page and stem from or center on the cause of it all. You can almost see movement in the pictures of Mary Anne tearing around that hole with dirt flying in all directions and of the crowd of tiny figures with their gaze focused on the snorting steam shovel. In the pictures of *Choo Choo,* trees, bridges, and telegraph poles yield to the onrushing momentum of the reckless runaway. The eye follows Choo Choo past or into or out of the next set of obstacles. The action in the text and pictures keeps young readers (or read-tos) fairly breathless.

Biography of a Little House

The Little House, the winner of the Caldecott Medal for 1943, is Virginia Burton's finest and most distinguished book so far. It tells the story of a house in the country which presently finds itself in the center of a village, and then in the midst of a great city where it is an insignificant obstruction between skyscrapers, with elevated trains overhead, subways beneath, and swarms of people everywhere. Rescued by the descendants of its builder, the little house is taken back to the country where it can once more watch the cycle of the four seasons revolving in comely and ordered beauty.

There is a significance to this book that

should make it permanently valuable both as literature and art. The evolution of cities in all their complexity and the resultant loss of some of the sweetness of earth and sky are implied in text and picture. The house has only a delicately suggested face, and the personification is subordinate to the pattern of these illustrations, something for children and adults to study with growing astonishment and delight. The pattern of every picture is the same—rhythmical curving lines which in the country are gracious and gentle but in the city become more and more violent and confused. The children's activities on the farm in each of the four seasons, the new event in each picture of urban growth, and the hundreds of dashing, darting people in the city are a part of the rich panorama and minute details which make this a book to be looked at again and again.

Children delight in Hardie Gramatky's personifications of tugboats, fire engines, and airplanes. Done in water colors, these pictures have a fresh, bright beauty.
From Little Toot *by Hardie Gramatky. Copyright, 1939, by Hardie Gramatky. Reproduced with permission of G. P. Putnam's Sons. (Original in color, book 7 x 7¾)*

HARDIE GRAMATKY

Little Toot
Hercules
Loopy

The same year that *Mike Mulligan* appeared, another artist launched the first of a popular series of fanciful personifications of machinery. Hardie Gramatky is a water colorist of distinction. His story of *Little Toot,* an irresponsible tugboat, appeared in 1939. Toot is hilariously personified, as are all his tugboat relatives. Toot is a lazy youngster, a disgrace to his hard-working family. How he finally reforms and makes a heroic rescue is amusingly told and pictured. Toot was followed by *Hercules,* the story of a horse-drawn fire engine forced to retire. Hercules comes into his own for one last grand run, and the pictures, in the loudest, fieriest colors, are as exciting as the text. *Loopy* is the story of an airplane used by student pilots for practice, but Loopy yearns to be a skywriter. Mr. Gramatky's personifications are extremely funny, and his tales have a breezy, masculine touch that all children—especially boys—enjoy.

NORMAN BATE

Who Built the Highway?
Who Built the Bridge?

Six- to eight-year-old boys like the more serious personifications of Norman Bate's books. He takes the tremendous machines and building projects of our modern age and personifies them ever so slightly. In *Who Built the Bridge?* (1954), Old Bridge creaks and groans. He knows just how mean Big Sleepy the river can be, and he knows there must be a new bridge to stand against the river. So the great bulldozers, the pile drivers, and the huge cranes go to work. In *Who Built the Highway?* (1953) the pictures show the huge machines that tear up the landscape and put it together again in a new form. Young readers identify themselves with the men who drive these machines. They, too, the children think, will drive piles, build highways, and dredge rivers when they grow up. Almost

realism, these fine books and stirring illustrations have a rhythmic style that gives a sense of movement. They are factual and poetic; their values are both informational and aesthetic.

Certainly Virginia Burton, Hardie Gramatky, Norman Bate, and other gifted writers and illustrators have taken full advantage of the fact that to the modern child a machine is something alive and individual. These books prove beyond doubt not only that machines are one of the child's liveliest and most continuous interests but that they can be a thrilling center of a good story.

"Funny Books"

Adults may speak of "drolls" or "tales of laughter" or "humorous stories," but the children say to librarians, "I want a *funny* book," and so do all of us now and then. Chapter 6 discusses the therapeutic value of nonsense and the need to break our tensions with laughter. One of the best ways to get a double dose of this curative property is to read aloud to a child one of his favorite "funny books." He laughs so hard you have to stop reading, and presently you find yourself beginning to give way to the rib-tickling humor that captivates the child. Just to discuss a funny book with a child or to hear him tell about it is to regain instantly your sense of the wholesome gaiety of life. One eight-year-old, reporting on Hugh Lofting's *Mrs. Tubbs* in a classroom, would tell an episode, then go off into contagious chuckles, and, finally, when she could scarcely speak for laughter, would show a picture and murmur, "Honestly, it's awful funny; you'll just have to read it yourself." Before she got through, she had the whole room full of children laughing, too, and of course every one of them read *Mrs. Tubbs.*[13]

These humorous books are not a class by themselves but cut across all other groups. Some are talking beasts, some are fantasies, some are told in folk-tale style, some are personifications, and some, like the folk-tale drolls, are improbable but almost realistic. Many adults would head the humorous list with *Alice's Adventures in Wonderland,* but, on the whole, its humor is a little subtle for children; they smile rather than laugh at *Alice.* On the other hand, all of Hugh Lofting's books could be grouped here as well as with the talking beasts. The following discussion of funny books, then, includes only a few types—stories written primarily for sheer fun, even nonsense, with no morals anywhere and no double meanings of a serious nature. Funny books they were intended to be and funny books they are.

LUCRETIA HALE

The Peterkin Papers

In the latter part of the nineteenth century, Lucretia Hale began to create for her friends' children a series of tales about a certain Peterkin family. These stories continue to seem as fantastically funny as the day they were published. Miss Eliza Orne White tells us that the episode which furnished Mrs. Hale with the idea for her stories was as absurd as any in the book. While visiting the White family, Mrs. Hale was about to start for a drive with her friends when the horse refused to go. They discovered, after all efforts to move him had failed, that he was still tied to the hitching post. Hence the story "Mrs. Peterkin Wishes to Go to Drive."

The Peterkin family consists of Mr. and Mrs. Peterkin, Solomon John, Agamemnon, Elizabeth Eliza, and the little boys in india-rubber boots. They learn wisdom by consulting "the lady from Philadelphia." For instance, Mrs. Peterkin puts salt instead of sugar in her morning coffee. They call the chemist who makes it worse. The herb woman puts in a little of everything, and the coffee is frightful. The lady from Philadelphia suggests that they throw it out and make a fresh cup of coffee. A happy solution! A new piano is moved into the house, but the movers

13. Mount Auburn School, Cleveland, Ohio.

leave it with the keyboard against a window. Elizabeth Eliza, seated on the porch, plays the piano through the window, a satisfactory arrangement as long as the weather is warm. When winter comes, it takes the lady from Philadelphia to suggest that they turn the piano around. The stories continue in this vein.

Here is "Clever Elsie" multiplied into a whole family. The humor is so obvious and robust that an upper-grade class can even make up its own *Peterkin Papers.*

RUDYARD KIPLING

Just So Stories

Living in India for many years and thus familiar with the Indian Jatakas and the usual pattern of a "why" story, Rudyard Kipling wrote his own collection of explanatory tales in amusing imitation of the old form. "How the Whale Got His Throat" and "How the Leopard Got His Spots" begin seriously and end with a logical kind of nonsense that reminds us of *Alice.*

"The Sing-song of Old Man Kangaroo" explains that the Kangaroo got his long tail because a certain Yellow-Dog Dingo chased him halfway across the world, ending in Australia, where they were both too exhausted to run another step. By that time, the Kangaroo's hind legs had lengthened, and he had grown a long and powerful tail which helped him to jump, but he complained to the god Nqong:

"He's chased me out of the homes of my childhood; he's chased me out of my regular meal-times; he's altered my shape so I'll never get it back; and he's played the Old Scratch with my legs."

Yellow-Dog Dingo complains, too, and, when left together, each says, "That's *your* fault."

"The Cat that Walked by Himself, walking by his wild lone through the Wet Wild Woods and waving his wild tail" is droll and subtly true, but the children's favorite is "The Elephant's Child." This story explains how the elephant's "blackish, bulgy nose, as big as a boot" grew to the long trunk we see today. It was all because of the " 'satiable curtiosity" of the Elephant's Child, who, after innumerable spankings, ran away to seek knowledge by the banks of "the great grey-green, greasy Limpopo River."

These are stories to be read aloud. They are cadenced, rhythmic, and full of handsome, high-sounding words, which are both mouth-filling and ear-delighting. It isn't necessary to stop and explain every word. The children will learn them, even as they learn "Hey diddle diddle," and the funny meanings will follow the funny sounds, gradually. The mock-serious tone of these pseudo-folk tales adds to their humor. Once children catch on to the grandiloquent style and absurd meanings, they love them. These stories are a good cure for too tight, humorless literalness. No child should miss hearing some of them, certainly "The Elephant's Child" for one.

P. L. TRAVERS

Mary Poppins
Mary Poppins Comes Back

P. L. Travers grew up in Australia, where high, wild winds blow everyone into a dither and make almost anything possible. So it is an east wind that blows Mary Poppins straight into the nursery of the Banks family, and a west wind that carries her off. The children first see her coming up the walk, bag in hand, and the next thing she strikes the house with a bang. Once their mother has engaged her as a nurse, Mary slides lightly *up* the banisters as neatly as the children slide down. When she opens her bag, they see it is quite empty, but out of it she takes everything from a folding cot to a bottle of medicine from which she doses the children with incredibly delicious liquid, tasting of strawberry ice or lime-juice cordial or whatever you prefer. "You won't leave us, will you?" Michael asks her anxiously, and she replies, "I'll stay till the wind changes," and she does.

Strange things happen during her stay. Having inhaled a little laughing gas, the children enjoy an elaborate tea party sitting comfortably on nothing at all around a table suspended in mid-air. They find a compass and journey north, south, east, and west without an effort. But a day comes when there is a wild west wind, and Mary is all gentleness. Her manner troubles the children and they beg her to be cross again. "Trouble trouble and it will trouble you!" she replies tartly and leaves them. Then they see her in the yard, the wind tugging at her skirts, her umbrella lifted. Suddenly she smiles at the wind, and it lifts her steadily and swiftly up and away from the children—Mary Poppins is gone. But, of course, she comes back in another book.

The Poppins books are extremely British, with cooks, gardeners, maids, nanas, nurseries, and teas. The humor is sometimes adult and sometimes whimsical, but children who like these books like them enormously and wear them to shreds with rereadings; others dislike them with scornful heartiness. These violent differences seem to occur more often about fanciful books than about any others. At any rate, the Poppins books have enjoyed a continuous popularity and are now being paid the compliment of rather frequent imitations. The character of Mary Poppins herself has a flavor all its own. Vain, stern, crotchety, continually overtaken by magic but never admitting it, adored by the children she disciplines and enchants, Mary is indeed what the Irish would call "a char-ácter."

Floating away over the roofs of the houses

Mary Poppins looks so down-to-earth with her bag and umbrella that, although she is ascending heavenward, we know that heaven is not her destination. "Just a bit of a blow!" we can hear her say.
Illustration by Mary Shepard. Reproduced from Mary Poppins, *copyright, 1934, © 1962, by P. L. Travers, by permission of Harcourt, Brace & World, Inc. (Book 4¾ x 7½)*

THEODOR SEUSS GEISEL

And to Think That I Saw It on Mulberry Street
The 500 Hats of Bartholomew Cubbins

Theodor Seuss Geisel chose his middle name for a pen name and then added the "Dr." as a purely honorary touch. But Dartmouth, his own college, decided to make it official. The college said he had long possessed a D.D.C.—doctor of delighted children—so it would merely add a doctor of humane letters!

Dr. Geisel and his wife live atop a precipitous hill from which they look down upon the city of La Jolla. They can see the ocean where the whales go by every spring, watch the fog roll in almost any day, and, when it's clear, have a view of the mountains of Mexico. Perhaps this unusual setting helps to explain the fantasies and, in the drawings, the continual use of hair-raising heights and precipices. Certainly the imagination of Dr. Seuss is never stopped by earthbound limitations.

His first book for children, *And to Think That I Saw It on Mulberry Street* (1937), is still a favorite. A small boy sees only a horse and a wagon on Mulberry Street but begins working up a bigger and bigger yarn to tell his father. Each succeeding page pictures the next addition to his tale until finally two pages across are necessary to get everything in. Then his father fixes him with a cold stare and his tale diminishes suddenly, leaving only the horse and wagon on Mulberry Street.

This rhymed narrative was only a sample of more and better nonsense to come. Of all the Seuss books *The 500 Hats of Bartholomew Cubbins* (1938) is certainly one of the best. Bartholomew Cubbins takes off his hat to the King only to find the royal coach stopping, and the King commanding him to take off his hat. Puzzled, he puts his hand to his head and finds a hat there. He jerks it off hastily only to find another in its place, and another, and another, and another. He is seized and threatened with death, but still the hats continue to crown his bewildered head. The horrid little Grand Duke Wilfred assures the King that it will be a pleasure to push Bartholomew off the highest parapet. Up the stairs they go, hats falling at every step. Finally the King sees upon the boy's head the most gloriously regal hat he has ever beheld. In exchange for this hat of elegance, he spares Bartholomew's life, and, as the befeathered hat goes on the King's head, Bartholomew finds his own head bare at last. The outline of this story gives no idea of the humor of both pictures and text—Bartholomew bewildered, helpless, wild-eyed; the King outraged and frustrated; the headsman unable to behead because his clients must take their hats off. All of these are hilariously pictured and solemnly described. This story has a lively sequel, *Bartholomew and the Oobleck.*

This photograph shows the Nutshell Library *with* One Was Johnny *nestled in a four-year-old's hands.*
Photograph courtesy of Harper & Row, publishers. Nutshell Library: One Was Johnny, Pierre, Alligators All Around, *and* Chicken Soup with Rice *by Maurice Sendak. (Each book is 2½ x 3¾)*

Most children and adults think *Horton Hatches the Egg* is the funniest. *Dr. Seuss's Sleep Book* is also good fun (see p. 67). But these stories are all funny and most of them are delightful. Unfortunately, when Dr. Geisel harnesses his original genius to the bandwagon of the easy-to-read, the resulting books lack the sparkle and gaiety of his other work.

RICHARD AND FLORENCE ATWATER

Mr. Popper's Penguins

Another funny book is *Mr. Popper's Penguins* (1938), written by Richard and Florence Atwater. This wild yarn is a nonsense tale narrated with gravity and giving every indication of being a simple, realistic story. Strictly speaking, nothing in the book is impossible, but because the narrative carries improbability to its uttermost limits it ends where Mr. Popper himself began—in the realm of the fanciful.

It tells the story of Mr. Popper, an untidy paperhanger with a passion for the Antarctic. An explorer rewards his admiration with a penguin. That one becomes twelve, and then the penguins revolutionize the lives of the entire Popper family. Eventually, the children return to school, Mrs. Popper gets to the meeting of the Ladies' Aid and Missionary Society, but Mr. Popper——? Well, when last seen, Mr. Popper and his penguins were headed due north.

ASTRID LINDGREN

Pippi Longstocking

A Swedish writer of excellent detective stories for children (the *Bill Bergson* series) is also responsible for creating a superchild, the heroine of *Pippi Longstocking* (1950). Pippi is an outrageous and delightful orphan who lives competently with her monkey and horse and takes control of any situation in which she finds herself. She cows some bullying boys, disrupts a school session, and manhandles two policemen when they try to take her to an orphanage. (Indeed, after carrying one in each hand, she sets them down so hard that it is some time before they can get up.) Then they report she is not a fit child for the orphanage!

Pippi's antics are exceedingly funny to children and to most adults. However, a few adults do have their doubts.

MAURICE SENDAK

Nutshell Library

How can the four irresistible books that make up Maurice Sendak's *Nutshell Library* (1962) be classified? Approximately two and one-half by three and three-fourths inches, they are tidily contained in a small box, and the box, the book jackets, and the books are illustrated with Mr. Sendak's impish, round-faced boys. Only flinty-hearted old Scrooge himself could resist this offering. The text of the four little books is as original as the pictures. *One Was Johnny* is a counting book, which winds up and unwinds in fine, accumulative style. *Pierre,* subtitled "a cautionary tale," describes the horrible fate of a boy who keeps saying "I don't care." But the ending is droll. *Alligators All Around* is one of the funniest alphabet books yet, and *Chicken Soup with Rice* is hilarious nonsense about the months of the year. These are "funny books," original and beguiling in miniature form.

Under each category of modern fanciful tales many more stories could be listed. Most of the examples discussed in this chapter are outstanding because they pointed the way or were exceptions or became classics or seem likely to attain that distinction. Even with innumerable omissions, the list is a long one, and the numbers of these books are increasing yearly.

These fanciful stories are not to be given as a special group to children, but they should be brought in for variety between poetry and geography or between realistic fiction and science. They are perhaps the dessert on the child's literary menu, although the best of them are sustaining food in themselves. Occasionally you find a child who likes to read fairy tales and nothing else. Perhaps, temporarily, they are what he needs, and he will swing back to realistic stories when he can hold his own and has a little happiness to spare. Generally, children enjoy these books as a change from the here and now, as a breathing space in the serious process of growing up. It is a rare child who does not like some of them, and most children enjoy many of them. Adults sometimes wonder why. The probable reason is that they provide children with another kind of flight, a flight into other worlds, incredible, exciting, satisfying. A little boy is driving an airplane when his mother calls him to come in for his bath. She can't see the pilot affronted by this indignity. Or someone says to a little girl, "No, you can't take that battered old doll downtown," and the child has to comfort the mutely hurt and unhappy doll. Children walk about their own yards as pirates, princesses, and fire engines, and we who have eyes do not see them thus transformed and free. Most children are "wind-runners" by nature and if they aren't, what a pity! These tales will help the swift wind-runners soar higher and will teach those who have never learned to run on the wind at least how to walk a little more boldly, with more faith in the unseen. Hans Christian Andersen, Kenneth Grahame, Beatrix Potter, Mary Norton, E. B. White, C. S. Lewis, Lucy Boston, and the others can reach a hand to the child and teach him to turn somersaults in the clouds or climb skyward on the rainbow.

SUGGESTED READING, PROBLEMS, AND PROJECTS

Suggested Reading: Read the following stories by Andersen: "The Ugly Duckling," "The Emperor's New Clothes," "The Real Princess," "The Little

Match Girl," "The Swineherd," "The Brave Tin Soldier," "The Wild Swans," "The Marsh King's Daughter," "The Little Mermaid," "The Girl Who Trod on a Loaf," and "The Snow Queen." Also read *Alice's Adventures in Wonderland, The Wind in the Willows, Winnie-the-Pooh,* "The Elephant's Child," and several of Theodor Seuss Geisel's books.

Kindergarten-primary: *Little Black Sambo, Peter Rabbit, Mister Penny, Ask Mr. Bear, The Little Red Lighthouse,* all of Wanda Gág's books, *Runaway Bunny,* one book by Norman Bate, and all of Virginia Burton's books.

Middle and upper grades: *Pinocchio, Dr. Dolittle* (one book), *Mary Poppins* (one book), *The Borrowers,* one of C. S. Lewis' Narnia books, one book by Robert Heinlein or Madeleine L'Engle's *A Wrinkle in Time, Charlotte's Web, Mr. Revere and I,* and *Rabbit Hill.*

1. What elements in Andersen's life account for or are reflected in the stories by him listed above? Which of them would you like to use with children nine to fourteen? Why do children like "The Emperor's New Clothes"? How would you use the stories for reading aloud, for children to read, for illustrating, for dramatizing, for puppetry?

2. What qualities in *Millions of Cats* remind you of folk tales?

3. As a child, how did you feel about *Alice's Adventures in Wonderland?* Can you account for your opinion? Try reading parts of it to children of different ages and note their reactions.

4. How do C. S. Lewis' Narnia books make use of religious symbolism? What effect do you think this would have on children's enjoyment of the books?

5. Read part of *The Borrowers* to a group of children. What seem to be the chief sources of interest in this book?

6. Quote from *The Wind in the Willows* to illustrate its rich sensory appeal, sly humor, exuberance, sense of leisure, sense of security after peril, and warm kindliness and loyalty. Why does the average child usually enjoy *Dr. Dolittle* more than *The Wind in the Willows?* How could adults help children to the enjoyment of the latter?

7. How does the appeal of *The Tough Winter* differ from that of *Rabbit Hill?*

8. How do you like *Charlotte's Web?* Why do children find it so moving?

9. Compare any of the following with *Pinocchio:* Andersen's stories about inanimate objects, the Pooh books, or Rumer Godden's doll stories. Consider humor, dramatic interest, action, style, age appeal, convincing quality.

10. Why are the Virginia Burton, Hardie Gramatky, and Norman Bate books so satisfying to modern children, especially boys?

11. Upon what characteristics does the humor of the following books depend: *The Peterkin Papers,* "The Elephant's Child," *Mary Poppins, The 500 Hats of Bartholomew Cubbins, Mr. Popper's Penguins,* and *Pippi Longstocking.*

12. The examples cited in this chapter are only samplings of good fantasy, both old and new. Name other books not discussed in this chapter which you feel have special values. Justify your choices.

REFERENCES

CARROLL, LEWIS [pseud.]. *The Annotated Alice; Alice's Adventures in Wonderland & Through the Looking Glass,* ill. by John Tenniel. With introduction and notes by Martin Gardner. Clarkson N. Potter, 1960. Significant quotations from Carroll biographies and other sources are placed parallel to the story text. An enriching background source for students.

CREWS, FREDERICK C. *The Pooh Perplex; A Freshman Casebook,* ill. by E. H. Shepard. Dutton, 1963. Brilliant parodies using Milne's stories and verses to illustrate how profound meanings can be read into even such childlike books.

CROUCH, MARCUS. *Beatrix Potter.* Walck Monographs (see Bibliography, Chapter 2).

GODDEN, RUMER. *Hans Christian Andersen: a Great Life in Brief.* Knopf, 1955. "Life itself is the most wonderful fairy tale." So wrote Andersen, and no one could have told his fairy tale more poignantly than Rumer Godden, the English novelist.

GREEN, PETER. *Kenneth Grahame,* ill. with photographs. World, 1959. This very welcome biography is authoritatively and perceptively written about the author of *Wind in the Willows.*

GREEN, ROGER LANCELYN. *J. M. Barrie.* Walck Monographs (see Bibliography, Chapter 2).

______. *Lewis Carroll.* Walck Monographs (see Bibliography, Chapter 2).

SUTCLIFF, ROSEMARY. *Rudyard Kipling.* Walck Monographs (see Bibliography, Chapter 2).

WILLIAMS, SIDNEY H., and FALCONER MADAN. *The Lewis Carroll Handbook,* rev. and enl. by Roger Lancelyn Green. Oxford, 1962. A valuable and comprehensive bibliography of Lewis Carroll's own writings and what others have written about his life and works. Descriptive notes are comprehensive and scholarly.

CHILDREN'S BOOKS

ALDEN, RAYMOND MACDONALD. *The Christmas Tree Forest,* ill. by Rafaello Busoni. Bobbs, 1958. A charming new picture-book edition of an old Christmas favorite, *The Great Walled Country.* 6-8

ANDERSEN, HANS CHRISTIAN. *The Complete Andersen,* tr. by Jean Hersholt, ill. by Fritz Kredel. Heritage, 1952. Jean Hersholt captures both the spirit and fine literary style of Andersen in this translation of 168 tales. 12-

———. *Fairy Tales,* ed. by Svend Larsen, tr. by R. P. Keigwin, ill. by Vilhelm Pedersen. Scribner, 1951. The Danish literary folk consider this translation, together with those of the late Paul Leyssac and Jean Hersholt, the closest to the original manuscript. The book contains nineteen favorite tales. The small print would discourage younger readers, but the Andersen enthusiast will delight in its content. 12-

———. *It's Perfectly True, and Other Stories,* tr. by Paul Leyssac, ill. by Richard Bennett. Harcourt, 1938. This translation of twenty-eight stories by a famous Danish storyteller has been a favorite collection for younger readers. 11-14

———. *Seven Tales,* tr. by Eva le Gallienne, ill. by Maurice Sendak. Harper, 1959. Favorite stories chosen for their appeal to younger readers. 7-12

———. Other editions:

Ill. by George and Doris Hauman. Macmillan, 1953.

Ill. by Arthur Szyk. Grosset, 1945.

Ill. by Tasha Tudor. Walck, 1945. 10-14

———. Single-story editions:

The Emperor's New Clothes, ill. by Virginia Burton. Houghton, 1949. 7-10

The Steadfast Tin Soldier, tr. by M. R. James, ill. by Marcia Brown. Scribner, 1953. 6-10

The Swineherd, tr. and ill. by Erik Blegvad. Harcourt, 1958. 5-9

Thumbelina, tr. by R. P. Keigwin, ill. by Adrienne Adams. Scribner, 1961. 6-9

The Ugly Duckling, tr. by R. P. Keigwin, ill. by Johannes Larsen. Macmillan, 1955. 6-9

The Wild Swans, ill. by Marcia Brown. Scribner, 1963. 6-10

ASSOCIATION FOR CHILDHOOD EDUCATION. *Told Under the Magic Umbrella.* Macmillan, 1939. This collection of fanciful tales includes such favorites as "Ask Mr. Bear" and "Peter the Goldfish." 8-12

ATWATER, RICHARD and FLORENCE. *Mr. Popper's Penguins,* ill. by Robert Lawson. Little, 1938. 8-12

AYME, MARCEL. *The Wonderful Farm,* tr. by Norman Denny, ill. by Maurice Sendak. Harper, 1951. The wonderful farm is quite an ordinary French farm except that the animals happen to talk. This is a book both children and adults will enjoy. 7-10

BAILEY, CAROLYN. *Miss Hickory,* ill. by Ruth Gannett. Viking, 1946. 10-13

BANNERMAN, HELEN. *The Story of Little Black Sambo,* ill. by author. Lippincott, 1923 (first pub. in 1900). 4-7

BARRIE, SIR JAMES. *Peter Pan,* ill. by Nora Unwin. Scribner, 1950. Peter Pan and all his delightful companions are visualized for the children by Nora Unwin's illustrations for this new edition. 9-12

BATE, NORMAN. *Who Built the Bridge? A Picture Story,* ill. by author. Scribner, 1954.

———. *Who Built the Dam?* ill. by author. Scribner, 1958. Dramatically told picture tale of the building of a hydroelectric dam.

———. *Who Built the Highway? A Picture Story,* ill. by author. Scribner, 1953.

———. *Who Fishes for Oil? A Picture Story,* ill. by author. Scribner, 1955. A restless little shrimp boat shifts its activities to a project for drilling oil under the sea. Action, imaginative illustrations, and cadenced texts that make good reading. 5-9

BEATTY, JEROME, JR. *Matthew Looney's Voyage to the Earth,* ill. by Gahan Wilson. W. R. Scott, 1961. Science fiction with a novel and humorous approach. A young moon boy journeys by rocket to earth to see if life exists. 10-12

BENNETT, RICHARD. *Shawneen and the Gander,* ill. by author. Doubleday, 1937, 1961. 6-8

BIANCO, MARGERY. *The Velveteen Rabbit,* ill. by William Nicholson. Doubleday, 1926. 6-9

BOND, MICHAEL. *A Bear Called Paddington,* ill. by Peggy Fortnum. Houghton, 1960. A small brown bear from Peru arrives complete with hat and suitcase, and upsets a conservative English household with his unusual activities. Further humorous incidents follow in *Paddington Helps Out* (1961) and *More about Paddington* (1962). 9-11

BOSTON, L. M. *The Children of Green Knowe,* ill. by Peter Boston. Harcourt, 1955.

———. *Treasure of Green Knowe,* ill. by Peter Boston. Harcourt, 1958.

———. *The River at Green Knowe,* ill. by Peter Boston. Harcourt, 1959. 11-15

BROOKS, WALTER. *Freddy and the Men from Mars.* Knopf, 1954.

———. *Freddy Goes to Florida.* Knopf, 1949. Between these two books lies a long series of Freddy stories that enjoy enormous popularity. Whether Freddy the pig is leading the animals of Mr. Bean's farm to Florida or playing detective, he can be counted on for fun and excitement. 9-12

BROWN, MARCIA. *Stone Soup,* ill. by author. Scribner, 1947. Three soldiers reform a selfish village by persuading the people to make a remarkably inexpensive soup—with a few additions! 7-10

BROWN, MARGARET WISE. *The Runaway Bunny,* ill. by Clement Hurd. Harper, 1942. 4-6

BRUNHOFF, JEAN DE. *The Story of Babar, the Little Elephant,* ill. by author. Random, 1937. A series of these books follows and has been continued since the author's death by his son Laurent. 5-8

BULLA, CLYDE. *The Poppy Seeds,* ill. by Jean Charlot. Crowell, 1955. 7-10

BURTON, VIRGINIA. *Choo Choo,* ill. by author. Houghton, 1937. 5-7

______. *Katy and the Big Snow,* ill. by author. Houghton, 1943. 4-9

______. *The Little House,* ill. by author. Houghton, 1942. Caldecott Medal. 5-8

______. *Mike Mulligan and His Steam Shovel,* ill. by author. Houghton, 1939. 6-8

BUTTERWORTH, OLIVER. *The Enormous Egg,* ill. by Louis Darling. Little, 1956. The village of Freedom, New Hampshire, is thrown into a twitter when young Nate Twitchell's hen hatches a dinosaur egg. The creature's incredible growth soon makes it a national concern. Humorous drawings capture the mood of this funny story. 9-13

CAMERON, ELEANOR. *Stowaway to the Mushroom Planet,* ill. by Robert Henneberger. Little, 1956. A journey into space is complicated by the intrusion of a stowaway.

______. *The Wonderful Flight to the Mushroom Planet,* ill. by Robert Henneberger. Little, 1954. Two small boys and their inventive neighbor build a space ship and take off to aid the people of a dying planet. 9-11

CARLSON, NATALIE. *Alphonse, That Bearded One,* ill. by Nicolas [pseud. for Nicolas Mordvinoff]. Harcourt, 1954. 8-11

CARROLL, LEWIS [pseud. for Charles Lutwidge Dodgson]. *Alice's Adventures in Wonderland* and *Through the Looking Glass,* ill. by John Tenniel. Heritage, 1944 (first pub. in 1865 and 1871). One of the best-loved and most quoted fantasies for children.
Ill. by John Tenniel. Grosset, 1946.
Ill. by John Tenniel. Macmillan, 1923.
Ill. by John Tenniel, 2 vols. Peter Pauper, 1940.
Ill. by John Tenniel. World, 1946.
Ill. by Leonard Weisgard. Harper, 1949. 10-

CLARKE, ARTHUR C. *Dolphin Island.* Holt, 1963. A fine science fiction tale of teen-age Johnny Clinton, who becomes interested in dolphins when they rescue him from drowning. 12-15

COATSWORTH, ELIZABETH. *The Cat Who Went to Heaven,* ill. by Lynd Ward. Macmillan, 1930 and 1959. A humble Japanese artist risks his future to include the portrait of his cat in a painting for the temple. A miraculous change in the picture rewards his unselfish act. Newbery Medal. 10-14

COLLODI, CARLO [pseud. for Carlo Lorenzini]. *The Adventures of Pinocchio,* tr. by Carol Della Chiesa, ill. by Attilio Mussino. Macmillan, 1951.
Ill. by Richard Floethe. World, 1946.
Ill. by Anne Heyneman. Lippincott, 1948.
Ill. by Fritz Kredel. Grosset, 1946. 9-12

CROWLEY, MAUDE. *Azor,* ill. by Helen Sewell. Walck, 1948.

______. *Azor and the Blue-Eyed Cow,* ill. by Helen Sewell. Walck, 1951.

______. *Azor and the Haddock,* ill. by Helen Sewell. Walck, 1949.
Azor is a small, everyday sort of boy who happens to understand animals when they talk to him. Their confidences sometimes get him into trouble, but his complete honesty and good will invariably save the day. 7-9

DAUGHERTY, JAMES. *Andy and the Lion,* ill. by author. Viking, 1938. Young Andy has read about lions but never expected to meet one. The encounter ends in high adventure for both of them, and for enthusiastic young readers. 6-8

DAVIS, ALICE. *Timothy Turtle,* ill. by G. B. Wiser. Harcourt, 1940. All Timothy Turtle's animal friends rally to his aid when he falls on his back and cannot turn over. 5-8

DE LA MARE, WALTER. *A Penny a Day,* ill. by Paul Kennedy. Knopf, 1960. Walter de la Mare brings poetic beauty to his prose style in six tales of fantasy which offer choice reading aloud. Followed by a companion volume, *The Magic Jacket* (1962). 10-13

______. *The Three Royal Monkeys,* ill. by Mildred Eldridge. Knopf, 1948. Originally published as *The Three Mulla-Mulgars.* 12-15

DOLBIER, MAURICE. *Torten's Christmas Secret,* ill. by Robert Henneberger. Little, 1951. The freshest, gayest Christmas story in years involves Santa's toy factory, hard-working gnomes, lists of good and bad children, and lovely glimpses of Santa's frosty, sparkling arctic world. 4-8

DRUON, MAURICE. *Tistou of the Green Thumbs,* ill. by Jacqueline Duhème. Scribner, 1958. 9-11

DU BOIS, WILLIAM PENE. *Bear Party,* ill. by author. Viking, 1951 and 1963. 5-8

______. *The Giant,* ill. by author. Viking, 1954. 9-12

______. *Great Geppy,* ill. by author. Viking, 1940.

______. *Peter Graves,* ill. by author. Viking, 1950. 10-14

______. *Three Policemen; or, Young Bottsford of Farbe Island,* ill. by author. Viking, 1938 and 1960. 10-12

______. *Twenty-one Balloons,* ill. by author. Viking, 1947. 10-12

DUVOISIN, ROGER. *Petunia,* ill. by author. Knopf, 1950. The first of a number of books about the adventures of that silly goose Petunia. 5-8

EAGER, EDWARD M. *Half Magic,* ill. by N. W. Bodecker. Harcourt, 1954. The finding of an old coin provides four children with some startling vacation adventures. 9-11

ELKIN, BENJAMIN. *Six Foolish Fishermen,* ill. by Katherine Evans. Childrens Press, 1957. At the end of their day on the river each of the six fishermen forgot to count himself and was sure one had drowned. A small boy points out their foolish mistake. A perfect read-aloud. 4-7

ENRIGHT, ELIZABETH. *Tatsinda,* ill. by Irene Haas. Harcourt, 1963. As an infant, Tatsinda was left by an eagle in the mountain land of the Tatrajanni. How she overcame the people's distrust and won the love of their prince is beautifully narrated in this modern fairy tale. 9-12

ESTES, ELEANOR. *The Witch Family,* ill. by Edward Ardizzone. Harcourt, 1960. Their pleasant game of drawing witches leads two small girls into incredible adventures when their witches come alive! 10-12

ETS, MARIE HALL. *Another Day,* ill. by author. Viking, 1953. 4-7

______. *In the Forest,* ill. by author. Viking, 1944. Walking through the forest, a small boy has a highly satisfying time meeting imaginary wild animals in friendly mood. 4-7

______. *Mister Penny,* ill. by author. Viking, 1935. 6-8

______. *Mister Penny's Race Horse,* ill. by author. Viking, 1956. All the animals get into mischief going to the Fair, and Limpy finds that he can be a race horse. 6-8

______. *Mr. T. W. Anthony Woo,* ill. by author. Viking, 1951. 6-8

______. *Play with Me,* ill. by author. Viking, 1955. An exquisite picture-story showing how a little girl makes many animal friends when she learns to be still in the woods. 3-6

FAIRSTAR, MRS. [pseud. for Richard Horne]. *Memoirs of a London Doll,* ill. by Emma L. Brock. Macmillan, 1922 (first pub. in 1846). 9-12

FARMER, PENELOPE. *The Summer Birds,* ill. by James J. Spanfeller. Harcourt, 1962. It was a glorious summer for the children of an English village when a strange bird-boy taught them to fly. In this haunting and lovely fantasy, the children are at last faced with a sad choice, whether to follow him forever, or to remain behind. 9-12

FATIO, LOUISE. *The Happy Lion,* ill. by Roger Duvoisin. Whittlesey House (McGraw), 1954. Other titles in this consistently popular series include: *The Happy Lion in Africa* (1955), *The Happy Lion Roars* (1957), *The Three Happy Lions* (1959), *The Happy Lion's Quest* (1961). 5-8

______. *Red Bantam,* ill. by Roger Duvoisin. McGraw, 1963. Bullied by the big red rooster, the little bantam is quite miserable until he proves his courage. 5-7

FENNER, CAROL. *Tigers in the Cellar,* ill. by author. Harcourt, 1963. 5-7

FIELD, RACHEL. *Hitty: Her First Hundred Years,* ill. by Dorothy P. Lathrop. Macmillan, 1929. Newbery Medal. 11-14

FISCHER, HANS E. *The Birthday,* ill. by author. Harcourt, 1954. The animals in *Pitschi* fete their old mistress, Lisette, with a wonderful surprise party on her seventy-sixth birthday. 5-8

______. *Pitschi, the Kitten Who Always Wanted to Be Something Else,* ill. by author. Harcourt, 1953. A dissatisfied little kitten tries to emulate every creature on the farm, with discouraging results. The color illustrations are beautiful and appealing. 5-8

FLACK, MARJORIE. *Ask Mr. Bear,* ill. by author. Macmillan, 1932. 3-7

______. *Walter the Lazy Mouse,* ill. by Cindy Szekeres. Doubleday, 1963. The reform of a naughty little mouse who was always tardy. A welcome reissue. 4-7

FRANCOISE [pseud. for Françoise Seignobosc]. *Jeanne-Marie at the Fair,* ill. by author. Scribner, 1959. Jeanne-Marie enjoyed every minute at the village fair, but her runaway pet lamb Patapon was most unhappy until he was rescued. Illustrated with appealing pastel drawings. One of several books about the quiet adventures of Jeanne-Marie. 4-6

FRIEDRICH, PRISCILLA and OTTO. *The Easter Bunny That Overslept,* ill. by Adrienne Adams. Lothrop, 1957. The sleepy Easter bunny arrived with eggs for every holiday but his own until Santa gave him an alarm clock. An endearing story. 5-8

FRISKEY, MARGARET. *Seven Diving Ducks,* ill. by Lucia Patton. McKay, 1940. 5-7

GAG, WANDA. *Millions of Cats,* ill. by author. Coward, 1928. 5-8

______. *Nothing at All,* ill. by author. Coward, 1941. Through the use of a magic phrase, a lonesome little invisible puppy becomes "see-able," and finds a happy home. 5-7

______. *Snippy and Snappy,* ill. by author. Coward, 1931. Two unwary little field mice are rescued by their wiser father from the baited mouse trap. 5-8

GANNETT, RUTH S. *The Dragons of Blueland,* ill. by Ruth Chrisman Gannett. Random, 1951.

———. *Elmer and the Dragon,* ill. by Ruth Chrisman Gannett. Random, 1950.
The adventures of Elmer and the candy-striped baby dragon he rescued from Wild Island are popular favorites with younger readers.

———. *My Father's Dragon,* ill. by Ruth Chrisman Gannett. Random, 1948. 7-10

GODDEN, RUMER. *The Dolls' House,* ill. by Tasha Tudor. Viking, 1962. 8-10

———. *The Fairy Doll,* ill. by Adrienne Adams. Viking, 1956. Elizabeth, the youngest of four, is not very clever, quite clumsy, and often naughty until the fairy doll takes her in hand. She is only the doll from the top of the Christmas tree, but it is surprising what she does for Elizabeth. 5-8

———. *Impunity Jane,* ill. by Adrienne Adams. Viking, 1954. 8-10

———. *Miss Happiness and Miss Flower,* ill. by Jean Primrose. Viking, 1961. 8-11

———. *The Mousewife,* ill. by William Pène du Bois. Viking, 1951. Expanded into a story from a note in Dorothy Wordsworth's Journal, this is an exquisitely written little fable of the friendship of a mouse and a dove. 7-10

GRAHAME, KENNETH. *The Wind in the Willows,* ill. by Ernest H. Shepard. Scribner, 1933 (first pub. in 1908).

———. *Wind in the Willows,* intro. by A. A. Milne, ill. by Arthur Rackham. Heritage, 1944. 10-

GRAMATKY, HARDIE. *Hercules,* ill. by author. Putnam, 1940.

———. *Homer and the Circus Train,* ill. by author. Putnam, 1957.

———. *Little Toot,* ill. by author. Putnam, 1939. 5-7

———. *Loopy,* ill. by author. Putnam, 1941. 5-8

HALE, LUCRETIA P. *Peterkin Papers,* ill. by Harold Brett. Houghton, 1924 (first pub. in 1880). 10-12

HEINLEIN, ROBERT A. *Have Space Suit—Will Travel.* Scribner, 1958. An incredible but convincing tale of two youngsters who journey through space and save humanity from immediate destruction. 12-16

———. *Rocket Ship Galileo,* ill. by Thomas Voter. Scribner, 1947. Working together with an inventor, a trio of teen-age boys complete a rocket ship and make a trip to the moon. Entertaining science fiction based on a background of scientific knowledge. 12-

———. *Space Cadet,* ill. by Clifford N. Geary. Scribner, 1948. It is the year 2075, and at the rocketship training school at Terra Base, Colorado, boys from different planets come to train as cadets for Solar Patrol's interplanetary communication system. 12-

HEYWARD, DU BOSE. *The Country Bunny and the Little Gold Shoes,* ill. by Marjorie Flack. Houghton, 1939. A fanciful Easter story of a mother rabbit who became one of the Five Easter Bunnies and was rewarded with golden shoes. 5-9

HOFF, SYD. *Oliver,* ill. by author. Harper, 1960. Poor Oliver was the surplus elephant in a circus shipment. How his unexpected talents won him a place on the program offers delightful reading. 6-7

HOLT, ISABELLA. *The Adventures of Rinaldo,* ill. by Erik Blegvad. Little, 1959. Rinaldo was a shabby knight who had to seek his fortune. How he wins a bride and a castle, and overcomes a fierce enemy makes humorous reading. 9-12

JANICE [pseud. for Janice Brustlein]. *Little Bear's Sunday Breakfast,* ill. by Mariana. Lothrop, 1958. Little Bear steps right out of the old folk tale and hurries to Goldilocks' house, he is so hungry. Color illustrated, this novel picture book will have popular appeal. 3-6

JOHNSON, CROCKETT [pseud. for David J. Leisk]. *Harold's Trip to the Sky,* ill. by author. Harper, 1957. Little children enjoy this Martian tale and other stories of Harold, who crayons himself and his equipment into one lively adventure after another. 5-7

JONES, ELIZABETH ORTON. *Twig,* ill. by author. Macmillan, 1942. When Twig found the red tomato can in the yard, she thought it would make a beautiful home for a fairy. And a fairy did come to delight a city child. 8-10

JOSLIN, SESYLE. *What Do You Do, Dear?* ill. by Maurice Sendak. W. R. Scott, 1961. Delightful nonsense situations inspire the correct thing to *do* in this gay sequel to her 1958 book. 5-7

———. *What Do You Say, Dear?* ill. by Maurice Sendak. W. R. Scott, 1958. Manners for the youngest in a delightful read-aloud in which simple phrases of courtesy become memorable through the nonsense situations which inspire them. Children will invent others. 4-7

KAHL, VIRGINIA. *Away Went Wolfgang!* ill. by author. Scribner, 1954. Wolfgang was the least useful dog in the tiny Austrian village, until the housewives discovered that when Wolfgang ran, he could churn a whole cartful of milk into butter! 5-8

———. *The Baron's Booty,* ill. by author. Scribner, 1963. Amusing rhyming tale of a wicked robber baron who steals for ransom the thirteen little daughters of the Duke and Duchess. His frantic efforts to return his troublesome booty provide good read-aloud entertainment. 6-9

———. *Droopsi,* ill. by author. Scribner, 1958. In far off Bavaria, a most untalented little boy named Droopsi and his cat Schnurrli unexpectedly win the music contest for their village. 6-9

———. *The Duchess Bakes a Cake,* ill. by author. Scribner, 1955. There was consternation in the kingdom when the duchess was carried skyward atop the light fluffy cake she had baked. The story is told in lively rhyme and bright pictures and is satisfyingly funny. 6-10

———. *Maxie,* ill. by author. Scribner, 1956. When the baron held a competition for the biggest, bravest, and swiftest dog in the village, Maxie the dachshund used his wits and won. 4-8

———. *The Perfect Pancake,* ill. by author. Scribner, 1960. A clever beggarman wins an unlimited supply of pancakes from the town's best cook by always belittling the last batch! Told in lively rhyme and bright pictures. 5-8

KENDALL, CAROL. *The Gammage Cup,* ill. by Erik Blegvad. Harcourt, 1959. Children who enjoy Tolkien's *The Hobbit* will appreciate this tale of mild revolt among the Minnipins, or little people, and its surprising outcome. A protest against conformity. 10-13

KIPLING, RUDYARD. *Just So Stories,* ill. by author. Doubleday, 1902.
Ill. by J. M. Gleeson. Doubleday, 1912.
Ill. by Nicolas [pseud. for Nicolas Mordvinoff]. Doubleday, 1952. 8-12

KUMIN, MAXINE W. *Sebastian and the Dragon,* ill. by William D. Hayes. Putnam, 1960. "Sebastian John Alexander Brown was the littlest boy in his home town," but he captured a dragon (small size) for the zoo. A clever rhyming easy reader, profusely illustrated. 5-8

LANGTON, JANE. *The Diamond in the Window,* ill. by Erik Blegvad. Harper, 1962. This is a beautifully written tale of fantasy and suspense for the exceptional reader. The background is Concord, Massachusetts, with numerous allusions to Emerson and Thoreau. 11-14

LAUGHLIN, FLORENCE. *The Little Leftover Witch,* ill. by Sheila Greenwald. Macmillan, 1960. The reform of Felina, a mean little witch, whose broken broomstick led her into the garden and into the hearts of the kindly Doon family. 7-10

LAWSON, ROBERT. *Ben and Me,* ill. by author. Little, 1939. 9-12

———. *Mr. Revere and I,* ill. by author. Little, 1953. 11-14

———. *Rabbit Hill,* ill. by author. Viking, 1944. 9-12

———. *The Tough Winter,* ill. by author. Viking, 1954. 9-12

L'ENGLE, MADELEINE. *Wrinkle in Time.* Farrar, 1962. 11-14

LEWIS, CLIVE STAPLES. *Horse and His Boy,* ill. by Pauline Baynes. Macmillan, 1954.

———. *The Last Battle,* ill. by Pauline Baynes. Macmillan, 1956.

———. *The Lion, the Witch, and the Wardrobe,* ill. by Pauline Baynes. Macmillan, 1950.

———. *The Magician's Nephew,* ill. by Pauline Baynes. Macmillan, 1955.

———. *Prince Caspian,* ill. by Pauline Baynes. Macmillan, 1951.

———. *The Silver Chair,* ill. by Pauline Baynes. Macmillan, 1953.

———. *The Voyage of the Dawn Treader,* ill. by Pauline Baynes. Macmillan, 1952. 8-12

LIFTON, BETTY JEAN. *Joji and the Dragon,* ill. by Eiichi Mitsui. Morrow, 1957. Poor Joji, the discarded Japanese scarecrow, was restored as guardian of the rice fields through a scheme of his loyal friends, the crows. 5-8

LINDGREN, ASTRID. *Pippi Longstocking,* tr. by Florence Lamborn, ill. by Louis S. Glanzman. Viking, 1950. 9-12

———. *The Tomten,* adapted from a poem by Viktor Rydberg, ill. by Harald Wiberg. Coward, 1961. Unforgettably lovely pictures of the wintry Swedish countryside illustrate the story of the kindly little troll who secretly goes about helping the people and animals. 5-7

LIONNI, LEO. *Inch by Inch,* ill. by author. Obolensky, 1960. A wise little inch worm escapes becoming a robin's dinner by proving his talents. A nature theme ingenuously framed in fantasy and illustrated with humor and imagination. 4-6

LOFTING, HUGH. *The Story of Dr. Dolittle,* ill. by author. Lippincott, 1920. 9-12

———. *The Story of Mrs. Tubbs,* ill. by author. Lippincott, 1923. 6-8

———. *The Voyages of Dr. Dolittle,* ill. by author. Lippincott, 1922. Newbery Medal. 9-12

MAC DONALD, GEORGE. *At the Back of the North Wind,* ill. by George and Doris Hauman. Macmillan, 1950.

———. *The Light Princess,* ill. by William Pène du Bois. Crowell, 1962.

———. *The Princess and the Goblin,* ill. by Nora S. Unwin. Macmillan, 1951. Attractive editions of old favorites. 10-12

MC GINLEY, PHYLLIS. *The Horse Who Had His Picture in the Paper,* ill. by Helen Stone. Lippincott, 1951. Joey, the discontented horse, yearns for publicity that will silence the policeman's boastful horse. 4-8

———. *The Plain Princess,* ill. by Helen Stone. Lippincott, 1945. A charming fable about a homely princess who was made beautiful. 6-8

MAC GREGOR, ELLEN. *Miss Pickerell Goes to Mars,* ill. by Paul Galdone. McGraw, 1951. Hilarious tale of a determined old lady's adventures when she unwillingly goes to Mars. 8-11

MAC KELLAR, WILLIAM. *Ghost in the Castle,* ill. by Richard Bennett. McKay, 1960. Young Angus Campbell stunned the village of Aberdour with an unknown story of its past. 10-13

MC LEOD, EMILIE WARREN. *Clancy's Witch,* ill. by Lisl Weil. Little, 1959. Small Clancy has the startling experience of having a witch for a next door neighbor! 5-8

MILNE, A. A. *The House at Pooh Corner,* ill. by Ernest Shepard. Dutton, 1928.

______. *Winnie-the-Pooh,* ill. by Ernest Shepard. Dutton, 1926.

These stories were reprinted in 1961, with larger type and more attractive format. 8-10

______. *The World of Pooh,* ill. by E. H. Shepard. Dutton, 1957. Distinctive color illustrations give a festive air to this new large-print volume, containing *Winnie-the-Pooh* and *House at Pooh Corner.* 5-10

NORTON, MARY. *Bed-Knob and Broomstick,* ill. by Erik Blegvad. Harcourt, 1957. Prim Miss Price was studying how to be a witch when the Wilson children discovered her. The bit of magic she gave them to ensure silence leads to some enchanting adventures. 9-13

______. *The Borrowers,* ill. by Beth and Joe Krush. Harcourt, 1953. This book was followed by *The Borrowers Afield* (1955), *The Borrowers Afloat* (1959), *The Borrowers Aloft* (1961). 9-12

PEARCE, A. PHILIPPA. *Tom's Midnight Garden,* ill. by Susan Einzig. Lippincott, 1959. 10-13

PICARD, BARBARA LEONIE. *The Lady of the Linden Tree,* ill. by Charles Stuart. Criterion, 1962. Told in traditional folk-tale style, these twelve original fairy tales have the flavor of European and Oriental folklore. 10-12

POTTER, BEATRIX. *The Tale of Peter Rabbit,* ill. by author. Warne, 1903. Between 1903 and 1930, 19 books were published in this series. 3-8

PYLE, HOWARD. *Pepper and Salt,* ill. by author. Harper, 1923 (first pub. in 1885).

______. *Wonder Clock,* ill. by author. Harper, 1943 (first pub. in 1887). 10-12

RESSNER, PHIL. *August Explains,* ill. by Crosby Bonsall. Harper, 1963. A very small bear loses all desire to be changed to a human when he hears about all the complexities of a boy's life. 5-7

REY, HANS A. *Curious George,* ill. by author. Houghton, 1941. The first of a well-liked series. 4-8

RICE, INEZ. *The March Wind,* ill. by Vladimir Bobri. Lothrop, 1957. Playing with the old hat he discovered in the gutter, the little boy becomes a cowboy, a soldier, and other heroic figures until the March wind whisks the hat away. 5-8

RUSKIN, JOHN. *The King of the Golden River,* ill. by Fritz Kredel. World, 1946. 10-14

SAINT-EXUPÉRY, ANTOINE DE. *The Little Prince,* tr. by Katherine Woods, ill. by author. Harcourt, 1943. When an aviator is forced down in the Sahara desert, he is startled at meeting the prince of a very small asteroid. In the days that follow, the aviator gains new insight from the little prince's spiritual and aesthetic values. 12-

SANDBURG, CARL. *Rootabaga Pigeons,* ill. by Maud and Miska Petersham. Harcourt, 1923.

______. *Rootabaga Stories,* ill. by Maud and Miska Petersham. Harcourt, 1922. 8-12

SAUER, JULIA. *Fog Magic.* Viking, 1943. 10-12

SAWYER, RUTH. *The Enchanted Schoolhouse,* ill. by Hugh Troy. Viking, 1956. When Brian Boru Gallagher came to America he brought a fairyman with him to show the glories of Ireland. They turned Lobster Cove topsy-turvy. 9-12

SCHLEIN, MIRIAM. *The Big Cheese,* ill. by Joseph Low. W. R. Scott, 1958. Proudly bearing his prize cheese to the king, the farmer shares it too generously and arrives with but a taste for His Majesty. A humorous read-aloud. 5-8

SELDEN, GEORGE. *The Cricket in Times Square,* ill. by Garth Williams. Farrar, 1960. Chester from Connecticut, a musical cricket of rare talent, is the hero of this heart-warming fantasy centered in a Times Square subway station. 9-12

SENDAK, MAURICE. *Nutshell Library,* ill. by author. Harper, 1962. 4-7

SEUSS, DR. [pseud. for Theodor Seuss Geisel]. *And to Think That I Saw It on Mulberry Street,* ill. by author. Vanguard, 1937. 5-8

______. *Bartholomew and the Oobleck,* ill. by author. Random, 1949. 7-10

______. *The Cat in the Hat,* ill. by author. Random, 1957. The Cat provides novel entertainment for two house-bound children.

______. *The Cat in the Hat Comes Back!* ill. by author. Random, 1958. More fun with the Cat and his twenty-six alphabetically named cat helpers. Easy-to-read stories. 5-8

______. *Dr. Seuss's Sleep Book,* ill. by author. Random, 1962. 7-10

______. *The 500 Hats of Bartholomew Cubbins,* ill. by author. Vanguard, 1938. 6-10

______. *Horton Hatches the Egg,* ill. by author. Random, 1940. 5-8

______. *Horton Hears a Who!* ill. by author. Random, 1954. 5-8

______. *McElligot's Pool,* ill. by author. Random, 1947. 7-10

______. *Scrambled Eggs Super!* ill. by author. Random, 1953. 5-8

SHARP, MARGERY. *The Rescuers,* ill. by Garth Williams. Little, 1959. Witty fantasy of three brave mice who rescue a Norwegian poet from imprisonment in a deep, dark dungeon. *Miss Bianca* (1962) relates another brave rescue. 10-13

SLEIGH, BARBARA. *Carbonel: The King of the Cats,* ill. by V. H. Drummond. Bobbs, 1957. Humorous magical tale of two children who rescue the king of cats from the spell of an old witch. 9-12

———. *The Kingdom of Carbonel,* ill. by D. M. Leonard. Bobbs, 1960. Carbonel battles for the rights of his royal kittens. 9-12

SLOBODKIN, LOUIS. *The Late Cuckoo,* ill. by author. Vanguard, 1962. Amusing nonsense tale of a harried Swiss clockmaker who solves the problem of the sleepy little cuckoo. 6-8

———. *Space Ship Under the Apple Tree,* ill. by author. Macmillan, 1952. Eddie's farm vacation at grandmother's proves anything but quiet when he is joined by Marty, the little man from Martinea, complete with his space ship. 8-10

STEELE, WILLIAM O. *Andy Jackson's Water Well,* ill. by Michael Ramus. Harcourt, 1959. Andy Jackson achieves the incredible by bringing back water to drought-ridden Nashville. A hilarious tall tale that is ideal for storytelling. 9-13

STOCKTON, FRANK R. *The Griffin and the Minor Canon,* ill. by Maurice Sendak. Holt, 1963. The lonesome last griffin, curious as to how he looks, flies far from his native haunts to see his statue image on an old church. His reception by the people, and especially by the Minor Canon, make this an intriguing tale. 6-10

STOLZ, MARY S. *Belling the Tiger,* ill. by Beni Montresor. Harper, 1961. Two timid little mice, ordered to bell the housecat, bell far bigger game while in flight from their enemy. 7-10

———. *Pigeon Flight,* ill. by Murray Tinkelman. Harper, 1962. Sulky Mr. Pigeon, indignant over a fancied slight, departs to the country from his established roost in Central Park. His brief bout with country living is engagingly funny. 7-10

SWAYNE, SAMUEL F. and ZOA. *Great-Grandfather in the Honey Tree,* ill. by authors. Viking, 1949. Pioneer days in Indiana are the background of this amusing tall tale. 5-12

THURBER, JAMES. *Many Moons,* ill. by Louis Slobodkin. Harcourt, 1943. Told in fairy-tale style, this is the appealing story of a little princess who yearned for the moon. Caldecott Medal. 7-10

TITUS, EVE. *Anatole and the Cat,* ill. by Paul Galdone. McGraw, 1957.

———. *Anatole over Paris,* ill. by Paul Galdone. Whittlesey, 1961. 5-7

TODD, RUTHVEN. *Space Cat,* ill. by Paul Galdone. Scribner, 1952. Flyball was a daring cat, and when he accompanied his favorite pilot on a trip to the moon, he not only saved his life but made an important scientific discovery. 8-10

TOLKEIN, JOHN R. R. *Farmer Giles of Ham,* ill. by Pauline Diana Baynes. Nelson, 1962. Humorous tale of a simple farmer who finds himself rescuing his village from dragons! 9-12

———. *The Hobbit,* ill. by author. Houghton, 1938. A rare fantasy of dwarfs, trolls, elves, and other such creatures who lived in the long ago. For the discriminating and imaginative reader. 5-8

TRAVERS, P. L. *Mary Poppins,* ill. by Mary Shepard. Harcourt, 1934.

———. *Mary Poppins Comes Back,* ill. by Mary Shepard. Harcourt, 1935.

———. *Mary Poppins in the Park,* ill. by Mary Shepard. Harcourt, 1952.

———. *Mary Poppins Opens the Door,* ill. by Mary Shepard and Agnes Sims. Harcourt, 1943. 8-12

TRESSELT, ALVIN. *The Frog in the Well,* ill. by Roger Duvoisin. Lothrop, 1958. Forced to leave his home in the well, the little frog discovers what a very small part of the world it was. 4-7

TREVOR, MERIOL. *Sun Slower, Sun Faster,* ill. by Edward Ardizzone. Sheed, 1957. A superbly written story of special interest to young Catholic readers. Two modern English children go back into their country's past and live in historically significant religious periods. 11-14

UNGERER, TOMI. *Emile,* ill. by author. Harper, 1960. Emile was an octopus with as many talents as appendages. 5-8

VALENS, EVANS G., JR. *Wingfin and Topple,* ill. by Clement Hurd. World, 1962. Young Topple is taught the art of being a proper flying fish by the knowledgeable Wingfin. 5-8

WHITE, E. B. *Charlotte's Web,* ill. by Garth Williams. Harper, 1952. 10-

WILL and NICOLAS [pseuds. for William Lipkind and Nicolas Mordvinoff]. *The Christmas Bunny.* Harcourt, 1953. On Christmas eve, young Davy brings gifts of food to the little woodland creatures. 4-7

———. *Finders Keepers.* Harcourt, 1951. Caldecott Medal. 4-7

———. *The Little Tiny Rooster.* Harcourt, 1960. Despised because he is undersized. Little Tiny Rooster becomes the barnyard hero when he outwits a cunning fox. 4-7

ZIMNIK, REINER, and HANNE AXMANN. *Little Owl,* ill. Atheneum, 1962. In a lushly colorful picture-story from Germany, Little Owl leaves his dark park niche to warn his human friends of fire. 5-7

ZOLOTOW, CHARLOTTE. *The Bunny Who Found Easter,* ill. by Betty Peterson. Parnassus, 1959. The bunny's quest for Easter did not end until he discovered that spring and Easter meant the beginning of all things beautiful. 5-7

———. *Mr. Rabbit and the Lovely Present,* ill. by Maurice Sendak. Harper, 1962. Aided by Mr. Rabbit, who makes the most impractical suggestions, a little girl finally decides on a gift for her mother's birthday. 4-6

chapter 13

Storytelling and Reading Aloud

Is Storytelling Dead?

In his introduction to the Pantheon edition of *Grimm's Fairy Tales,* Padraic Colum describes the quiet evenings in an Irish cabin of yesterday. Only a small fire on the hearth lighted the woman at her spinning and the face of the storyteller weaving his tale. For those who sat in the shadows, the dimness must have enhanced the mystery or the sorrow or the wonder of the tale. Then, presently, the time came when kerosene lamps moved into the cabin and with them books and newspapers. The household arts came to an end and so did the professional storytellers. With this picture Mr. Colum seems to imply that the art of storytelling is pretty well finished and so it seems to be at first glance.

Ask a young elementary teacher of some ten or eleven subjects if she tells stories to her class, and she may reply indignantly, "And when would I have time to prepare a story to tell?" Or ask a young mother pushing her two-year-old around in the supermarket cart, "Do you tell stories to your children?" When she recovers from the shock, she will probably say, "Of course not. I don't have time to learn stories, but I do read aloud to them. In fact I am going to pick up a book right now, over by the detergents. The children are tired of the ones we have." This last statement, which is a common one, is interesting because children will ask for a *good* story —if it is well told—over and over again.

Is anyone telling stories today? The answer is a strong affirmative.

Kindergarten teachers have always told stories and will, it is hoped, continue to do so. To be sure, they are probably reading six picture-stories to one they tell, but certain stories are always told—"The Gingerbread Boy," "The Three Little Pigs," and "Henny Penny," for example. Children's librarians continue their wonderful story hours in the libraries all over the country, little centers of culture and delight. A hard pressed teacher may find the children's librarian willing to come into her classroom to tell, over a number of weeks, a hero cycle such as *Robin Hood* or the *Odyssey,* or to tell the folk tales of the country the children are studying. Camp counselors know the spell of stories told around a camp fire, and not only tell stories themselves but encourage the young people to try storytelling also. Social workers use storytelling for neighborhood meetings with children and even with adults. Museum directors have discovered that storytelling is good bait to attract children's interest to science or history or art. And, finally, both radio and television make frequent and often exceedingly effective use of storytelling on their programs.

So it seems the art of storytelling is far from dead. It may have moved from the firelit cabin to the fluorescent-lighted classroom or the marble corridors of a museum or some other equally unlikely spot, but the old, old art of storytelling still has power to charm. To practice this art is sheer delight for the teller, and to observe the profound impression it makes on the listeners is a gratifying bonus. Still, some teachers will protest, "But why tell stories in this day of many books?"

Whether Louis Slobodkin is "making Moffats" or illustrating epics, you can always sense the sculptor's sure modeling of figures underneath the clothes. Robin Hood and Little John are indeed two solid fellows. Note the interesting use of angles to give vigor and movement to the whole.
Illustration by Louis Slobodkin. From Robin Hood and His Merry Outlaws *by J. Walker McSpadden. Copyright 1923, 1946 by The World Publishing Company. Reprinted by permission of the publishers. (Book 5¼ x 8¼)*

When to Read Stories and When to Tell Them

WHY TELL STORIES

It would be reassuring to say that reading stories aloud is just as satisfactory as telling them, but unfortunately it is not true. Of course stories are better read well than told poorly, but children miss a unique experience with literature if they never hear a gifted storyteller. The folk tales, particularly, should be told, for they were created orally and kept alive for generations by oral transmission.

Storytelling is more direct than reading. *There is no book between you and your audience,* and you can give the story plus your own enjoyment of it unhampered by following the precise words on the page. Your facial expression, your occasional gestures, and your inflections all respond to the audience just as they do when you regale your family or friends with an account of some exciting experience you have had. The younger the children, the more they need this intimate approach to literature, because words are still difficult symbols for them. When you are free of the book, you can observe their confusions and throw in the much needed parenthetical phrase which never occurred to the editor. "Then the princess—the king's little girl," you add hastily for the sixes. Even with ten-year-olds, when you mention "a well of scythes" and see their bewildered expressions, of course you interpolate "a well whose walls were lined with sharp knives or scythes," and go blithely on. Or, when you observe Peter's unflattering yawn, you take your narrative at a livelier tempo or style. *More spontaneity is possible in storytelling than in reading aloud,* and hence the storyteller imparts a more natural, informal quality to the stories. This intimacy is especially good for little children in school for the first time.

It is good even for older children to hear stories told now and then, and it is good for *you* to tell them. Nothing else will give you so sharp and sure a sense of style. This fact was emphasized by Wanda Gág, who said:

When I was a child my favorite funny Märchen was one about a peasant who wanted to do housework. I have never forgotten either the tale itself or the inimitable way in which it was told to me in German. . . . No doubt this tale exists in some German collections. There must be English versions of it too, for by questioning various children, I found them to be familiar with it, but only vaguely so. From this I concluded that it had never been presented to them as it had been to me—that is, in a full-flavored conversational style and with a sly peasant humor which has made the tale unforgettable to me.

This is a faithful description of good storytelling: conversational, humorous, or grave according to the tale, with something of the storyteller's unique personality. There is a chance for more subtle characterizations and for an unconscious building up of suspense. Both teller and listener develop a keener feeling for words. Telling "Clever Manka" to the oldest children in the elementary school plays upon their ability to anticipate the results of certain actions, builds up their wonder at what Manka will think up next, and, finally, leaves them amused and satisfied. Telling "Urashima Taro" is different. Here are strange people and places, a subtle and beautiful style, and an ending sad and enigmatic. Telling these stories to older children gives you more fun than you ever had from reading the tales. They are somehow your own creation when you tell them, as they can never be when you stand with book in hand.

It is true that most of the storytelling and reading aloud is done in kindergarten and primary grades, especially for the fives and sixes. For them, *storytelling or reading aloud are important baits to books.* If a child has heard "The Bremen Town-Musicians" or "Snow White" or "Sonny Boy Sims" and knows that they are to be found in books, then he is encouraged to read and is ready for the struggle. But in the first grade when his reading vocabulary is limited and his reading materials something less than enthralling, he may experience a sense of defeat. Then the well told story, dramatic, full of suspense, and rising to a breath-taking climax and conclusion, fills the gap between what he can read and what he would like to read. This lag between reading skill and appreciation may, by fourth grade, be as much as two years or more. Hence the importance of some oral presentation of literature throughout the elementary school years.

Storytelling is very important, too, because *through listening, children develop their powers of aural comprehension.* The ability to hear, comprehend, and react intelligently to the spoken word is of great importance. In one nursery school where many picture-stories were available, the children, it was discovered, required pictures in order to attend to or understand a story that was told or read. This is a serious limitation in learning a language. Picture clues are valuable first aids to reading in the beginning years. But children should also have continuous practice in hearing poetry and stories which are not illustrated. With such balanced experience, their vocabularies will grow and so will their ability to comprehend the meaning of the spoken word.

Moreover, *a word that has been heard and understood is more easily recognized when a child encounters it in print.* So actually a storytelling, reading-aloud program, used in moderation, is just one more device for promoting word recognition when reading begins.

These are utilitarian reasons for storytelling and reading aloud, but there are equally important aesthetic reasons. Unconsciously, *children's ears are becoming accustomed to the tune and cadence of good English,* such English as they may not hear on the streets or perhaps even in their homes. And *they hear and enjoy types of literature they might never read for themselves,* but find delightful when they listen to it interpreted by someone who understands and thoroughly enjoys it. Tastes are broadened, and enjoyment is raised to a higher level, if literature is taught by the sheer contagion of shared pleasure.

READ THE PICTURE-STORIES; TELL THE FOLK TALES

The younger the child, the more he needs the informal, intimate approach to literature that storytelling provides. But even the youngest child should hear stories read from books. All the so-called picture-stories should be read with the book. A picture-story, of course, is one told with pictures as an integral part of the text, like Marjorie Flack's *Ping,* or Beatrix Potter's *Tale of Peter Rabbit,* or Louise Fatio's *Happy Lion* series. Such stories actually lose a great deal if they are told without the accompanying illustrations. But except for these tales in which the pictures are as important as the text, stories for small children should be told, as intimately and comfortably as a mother tells her child stories at night when she puts him to bed. There is no excuse for reading "The Little Red Hen," "The Three Billy-Goats Gruff," or "The Three Little Pigs," since they are as easy to tell after two or three trials as *Mother Goose* verses are to say. As a matter of fact, they are so easy to learn that by about the third round the child is telling them with you. Learn four or five of them one year, and they will be with you for life. Learn a few more the next year, and soon you will have a storytelling repertoire that will surprise you and delight the children. Never will you have to lug books to a picnic, because the stories will be in your head. Never will an unexpected wait for the school nurse or the promised tester find you searching wildly for a book to read to the children. You are equal to any emergency, and when your store of tales gives out, usually some of the children can take over.

Teachers of older children say, "Oh, well, that's all right for those little, short, repetitional tales which please the kindergarten or primary children, but stories for older children are long; teachers don't have time to learn them; surely they should be read aloud." The folk tales *are* long, but they are surprisingly easy to learn. However, rather than omit such stories because you feel it is impossible to sit down and learn to tell a complex and lengthy story as it deserves to be told, tell only one or two and read the others. It is far, far better to read a story beautifully than to tell it poorly. But learn to tell perhaps only two stories a year and read the others. Then learn two more the next year. Your children will be changing while your repertoire is growing, and the old stories will be new to each oncoming group. Meanwhile, your powers of storytelling will be kept alive and will improve steadily.

READ STORIES CALLING FOR EXACT WORDS OF AUTHOR

Stories which you never tell but always read from the book are those which depend upon the exact words of the author for their charm and meaning. Rudyard Kipling's *Just So Stories* are good examples. No word of these should be altered; so telling them would mean memorization, which is never storytelling but something much more formal. Although separate episodes from *Alice in Wonderland* or *Wind in the Willows* can be selected for telling, they should not be. Such stories should be read, because the style of the author ought not to be tampered with—no words can be altered without a loss. Probably even Hans Christian Andersen's retelling of folk tales are better read, because his matchless style is lost unless the story is memorized. Marie Shedlock, the famous English storyteller, always told the Andersen tales to perfection, but she memorized them as an actress memorizes her lines and then recreated them in telling with apparent spontaneity and captivating charm. She was an artist to her finger tips, but hers was the art of the platform, with five hundred or more in the audience, not the intimate art of the fireside, the cribside, the library, or the schoolroom with a few children close to the teller and the tale keyed in the low tone of friend to friend. For most of us, the rule still holds that a story which must be memorized becomes a recitation and a recitation is not storytelling. It is better always to read the tale that requires the exact words of the author.

Personal Equipment for Storytelling

The successful storyteller must have two types of equipment for his art. First, he must possess those outward and visible evidences of fitness for the task—good voice, clear diction, adequate vocabulary, and pleasant appearance. Second, he must achieve a certain elusive inner and spiritual grace made up of complete sincerity, delight in his tale, self-forgetfulness, and a respect for his audience and for his storytelling art. The first equipment can be attained through patient practice. The second must grow from living and from loving both literature and people.

AGREEABLE VOICE

An agreeable voice and clear, pure diction are perhaps the first requisites for the storyteller to consider. Needless to say, there should not be a special voice reserved for storytelling. You have sometimes heard the saccharine voice that talks down to the "Dee-ah lit-tel chil-dren." You should take stock of your own vocal equipment. Ask others to evaluate your voice honestly. Record it if possible, so that you can listen to it yourself. If your voice is nasal, harsh, or monotonous, try to improve it for everyday use to the point where it is agreeable and lovely for special use. Women tend to pitch their voices higher and shriller than they should. Try your speaking voice at the piano and see where it falls in relation to middle C. Most women can profitably pitch their everyday speaking voices a key or so lower, and both they and the children will be more peaceful as a result. Go to the theater, turn on the radio or television, or play some recordings of gifted readers, and deliberately listen to and compare voices. Be critical of the oversweet voices of some radio or television personalities, both male and female. Try to discover what makes the voices of artists like Katharine Cornell, Helen Hayes, Sir Lawrence Olivier, Richard Burton, Maurice Evans, and Dylan Thomas so moving and satisfying. Lessons with an expert in voice placement and production will help you, but by cultivating a listening ear you can do much for yourself.

A good voice is invariably supported by deep and controlled breathing. Breath must come from the diaphragm, not from the upper chest. Read aloud sustained passages from the Psalms or from Shakespeare. Put on Maurice Evans' recording of the lines from *Richard II* or Sir John Gielgud's "Ages of Man," and read the lines with the record. You can then tell when you run out of breath and shouldn't. Breathe deeper, and not only will you be able to sustain those long sonorous passages, but your voice will grow in richness and resonance. Shallow breathing makes thin, tired voices, which are apt to become shrill and sharp. Deep, controlled breathing gives to the voice both support and increased range and color.

When you can read Shakespeare's Sonnet XXIX and phrase it correctly without running out of breath, then you have good breath control, which will make your voice grow in depth and power as you use it. Notice that this sonnet has only the final period and two semicolons to break the sequential phrases. Try lines 2, 3, and 4 on one breath, and, of course, lines 11 and 12.

When, in disgrace with fortune and men's eyes,
I all alone beweep my outcast state,
And trouble deaf heaven with my bootless cries,
And look upon myself and curse my fate,
Wishing me like to one more rich in hope,
Featured like him, like him with friends possess'd,
Desiring this man's art and that man's scope,
With what I most enjoy contented least;

Yet in these thoughts myself almost despising,
Haply I think on thee, and then my state,
Like to the lark at break of day arising
From sullen earth, sings hymns at heaven's gate;
For thy sweet love remember'd such wealth brings
That then I scorn to change my state with kings.

Now, after having huffed and puffed self-consciously as you worked for breath control, read the sonnet for enjoyment.

Clear articulation of words is as essential as an agreeable voice. Of course, nothing is worse than an artificial, overprecise enunciation, except perhaps an attempt to imitate the speech of another district that is quite foreign to us. If we are New England, Southern, Midwestern, or Western, let's not try for Oxford English or any other accent unnatural to us. Instead, let's eradicate the impurities of our own particular region (every region has them), and try to speak the purest, most vigorous pattern of English that obtains in our section of the country. Storytelling is ruined if it sounds artificial or pretentious, for it is the homiest of all the arts.

In telling stories, you should always maintain the quiet, intimate tone of friendly conversation, but you must also speak so that every one in your audience can hear you easily. This is easy enough in a small classroom or a corner of a library, but telling stories in a school auditorium or outdoors on a picnic or around a campfire is quite another matter. How can you be heard by those farthest from you without shouting at the people sitting nearby?

Deep, controlled breathing should build up resonance in your voice, and resonance plays a large part in the carrying quality of the spoken word. But it is not the whole secret. Light, sweet voices are often perfectly audible in the most remote corners of a theater or an auditorium. To be clearly heard at a considerable distance, you must consciously *direct or send your voice* to the most remote people in your audience. If it is possible to see their faces, watch to determine whether they are hearing comfortably. It they are leaning forward, tense or uneasy, they are not hearing. When this happens, women, in particular, tend to pitch their voices higher and shriller. Don't do it. Instead, take a deep breath, keep your voice pitched low and then consciously send your words to the farthest members of the audience. The old actors knew how to do this and so did the political orators of long ago who addressed vast audiences without benefit of microphones. These people were not always possessors of big, bellowing voices; some of the women had light, high voices, but they possessed remarkable breath control and this hard-to-describe ability to send the voice wherever it should go. "Carrying quality" they called it, and that is precisely what the voice did—it carried.

CHOICE OF WORDS

Storytelling is an art that requires disciplines of many kinds, and one of these is the choice of words. As a storyteller, you can not go far with a meager vocabulary; moreover, you must develop a sensitivity to words, so that you cannot possibly tell an Irish tale with the same vocabulary and cadence you use for a Norwegian story. Read the story aloud first until you get the feel and flavor of its peculiar vocabulary and word patterns. While exact memorizing is usually the wrong approach to the folk tale, the other extreme is much worse —a slipshod telling, a careless use of words. Such modern colloquialisms as "Boots got real mad," or "the princess looked perfectly lovely," or " 'O.K.,' said the lad," can ruin the mood and magic of a tale. Words must be chosen with a sensitive perception of the individual style of each tale. The dreamlike romance of "Sadko" calls for a very different choice of words from the rural dialogue of the old man and his good wife in "Gudbrand on the Hillside." Voice, diction, and vocabulary demand the training of your ear. Listen to yourself—to your voice, your speech, and, above all, to the appropriate words for your story.

MAKING VOCABULARY CLEAR

A second aspect of the word problem is the effect the peculiar language of the folk tales has upon children. For instance, consider words like "pate," "goody," "lassie," "mare," "foal," "tapers," "minstrels," "spindle." As this text has already suggested, one of the easiest ways to explain these baffling words to young listeners is just to paraphrase them casually as you tell the story: "Just then he met a lassie—a young girl—'Good day, lassie,' said he." And the word is established. A teacher once told the story of "Clever Manka" to a group of college students, and, when she had finished and they had all commented pleasantly on the story, she asked them what it meant when it said, "the mare foaled in the market place." Only one girl in the class knew, although an important point in the story turns on that phrase. Why should the students have understood it? They were city girls and it is a rural phrase. Children would be even more confused by such language. In telling it to children, paraphrase by all means: "The mare foaled in the market place—gave birth to a little colt or foal." Or if you wish, since it relates to an important episode in the tale, clear it up before telling the story. Since the tale is for older children, the latter procedure is probably better. Write the words on the board and discuss the power of newborn colts or foals to get on their feet and even walk a little way. Explain that the foal in this story probably tottered over to a nearby wagon and lay down. There is no reason why children should not hear a much wider range of words than they are going to use, but there is every reason why you should help them to understand the words as they hear them, either by paraphrasing or systematical explanation before or after the storytelling.

APPEARANCE

Your particular style of beauty or plainness is of no consequence to successful storytelling, but certain other elements of appearance are. Whether you sit or stand, you must be relaxed and easy. If you have to stand to tell your stories, then practice them standing until you are at ease and so can enjoy yourself. If you sit with your children grouped comfortably close to you, then practice telling your story sitting down until you are used to telling stories in that position. For most of us, it is safest to practice both ways, so that we can forget ourselves in either position and be ready for any storytelling situation in which we may find ourselves. Forgetting ourselves does not mean that we can afford either to sit or to stand sloppily. Practice in front of a mirror for a little while until you know what a comfortable good posture looks like; then hold it. Either sitting or standing, you should keep your hands free of handkerchiefs or pencils or other impedimenta, free for the occasional gesture most people make now and then. Your clothes should be the kind your audience forgets the moment the tale begins. If you wear chains or necklaces, don't fuss with them and don't wear clanking bracelets. In short, avoid any distracting element in your dress that centers attention on you and takes it away from the story.

LIVING THE STORY

The important elements of your appearance come from within. These are your genuine, unaffected smile of enjoyment, the twinkle in your eye, the sudden gravity, the warning frown—in short, those slight but unmistakable responses to the changing mood or matter of the tale. The elaborate pantomime and large dramatic gestures of the stage have no place in storytelling. You need only the subtle expressions of the face and eyes, responding even as the voice responds to the import of the story. Mousy girls are often illumined with the zest and fun of a great story, timid girls are often lifted and inspired by a hero tale until they actually seem to grow in stature and impressiveness. This comes from within. This comes from living and loving your story until you are a flexible instrument for its full and best expression. It is not something to be learned by standing in front of a mirror and twinkling your eyes at the right moment—heaven forbid! It means something far more difficult.

First, you must genuinely desire to tell your story. You must fall in love with the content or style or both. Never try to tell a story which barely interests you. Ruth Sawyer put this positively in *The Way of the Storyteller,* when she said that she was *always trying out with others something that had moved me deeply; always finding out that what had been for me a spiritual feast usually fed others.*

Of course, if you have not the emotional capacity to be deeply moved by these stories, then do not try to tell them, for there must be warmth and a loving appreciation in every word of a story if it is to touch an audience. To hear Mrs. Gudrun Thorne-Thomsen tell "Gudbrand on the Hill-side" was to know how she loved that tender old wife and how she relished the complete faith of that absurd and canny old man. She was sincerely entertained and touched by the pair, and her feeling captured her audience.

To love a story in this way means that the teller not only has learned the story intellectually and lived with it for some time but has learned it with her heart, brooding over it and fussing with the phraseology until words and voice convey precisely what she feels. She does not rattle through it merely to learn the words but recreates it imaginatively. She tells it slowly and thoughtfully to the darkness after she has gone to bed or thinks it through, scene by scene, on the bus until finally it is her story. Such solitary preparation for telling is a process of disciplining herself until she can give an honest interpretation of the way the story makes her feel.

SHARING THE STORY

Telling a story to an audience, however large or small, requires another quality which is difficult to name. Perhaps friendliness is as good a word for it as any other—a reaching out to people, a desire to share with them something that you enjoy.

Once when I was still very new at storytelling, I was asked to give a Christmas Eve program in a detention home for girls. When I saw the girls marching in, I was suddenly in a panic. Most of them were there for the worst possible reasons, and it was as sad a group as you could well imagine. Some of them were far too young to look as hard as they did; some were making a pitiful show of bravado and sophistication, but the majority of them looked out of dull eyes with a kind of hopeless apathy. How could these girls be reached by stories about fairies and wee red caps, or about a goldfish that talked back? Probably my beginning was as weak as possible, because I was beset by doubts. Then "Peter the Goldfish" began to absorb my entire attention, as he always does, and I forgot the peculiar quality of these girls; they were just girls to enjoy what I enjoyed. Suddenly one of them chuckled spontaneously, and we were friends sharing a common joke. After that there was no more panic for the teller. We shared the humor and charm of both Peter and "The Voyage of the Wee Red Cap" (blessings on Ruth Sawyer for that inimitable tale!). We sang some carols together, and I ended with the second chapter of St. Luke, read quietly, as I read it at home. The room was still, and the girls were at ease. Afterward they came up to shake hands, and one of them said simply, "You done real good. I hope you come again."

This is what storytelling will help you do —reach out to people impersonally but with the friendliness that comes from pleasures shared. It is one of the most heart-warming experiences in the world.

SELECTING A STORY TO TELL

Selecting a story to tell is almost as complex a matter as the selection of a hat for a woman. The story, like the hat, must be becoming. It must do something for the teller, and the teller must do something for the story. There are some stories that are perfect for one person and perfectly awful for another. For instance, the Jack Tales that Richard Chase tells with inimitable style—masculine humor, wry characterizations, mountaineer turns of speech—would be quite unsuited to a storyteller of Marie Shedlock's delicate style. And born storyteller though he is, Richard Chase might not do so well with the highly polished form of Hans Andersen's tales. So each person, by the process of trial and error perhaps, must discover the type of stories most compatible with his unique storytelling personality.

The easiest stories to begin with are the folk tales. They are easy because they were created orally by storytellers and have perfect form for narration. The form is invariable: a clear, brief introduction that launches the conflict or problem; the development or body of the story with a rising action, increasing suspense, and an exciting climax that marks the turning point in the story and the fortunes of the hero; and, finally, a satisfying conclusion that winds up everything—problems, conflicts, and villains all suitably disposed of. From the simplest accumulative "Pancake" type of story, through "Snow White" and "The Bremen Town-Musicians," to the more subtle "Clever Manka" for the oldest children, these folk tales tell with ease and will help you fall into the storytelling habit and develop your own unique style.

But which folk tales will you choose from the myriads? Try a variety and see. The German, Norwegian, English, and Czech are similar in form, the French and Spanish are more polished. Perhaps you are attracted by that offbeat Caribbean hero, *Anansi, the Spider Man*. You can hear some of these tales on records told by their collector, Philip Sherlock. If you are from the South, it should be your privilege to keep alive the Uncle Remus stories which can be cruelly damaged by Northern tongues. The Jack Tales and the tall tales seem to come more naturally and effectively from men. However, women who like them may tell them remarkably well. Some people have no taste for the tales of the wee folk found so frequently in the folk lore of Ireland and Scotland, though it is hard to imagine anyone failing with the stories in Sorche Nic Leodhas' *Heather and Broom* or *Thistle and Thyme*. The moral is, select what you have a genuine liking for and what seems compatible with your personality.

The next richest source of stories to tell are the myths, but here there is a problem of adapting your story, generally from several sources, until you have a version you thoroughly enjoy. Many of the myths are long and may take two or three story periods to tell, for example, the stories of Perseus and of Theseus. Fortunately these two tales have been well told by Ian Serraillier in *The Gorgon's Head* and *The Way of Danger*. Reading these books will show you why even the simplest myths demand more imagination in the telling

In this scene, Polydects, because he insists upon seeing the Gorgon's head, is turned to stone as are all in the chamber who see the Gorgon's head. In this simple line drawing, with black for accent, the figures and details are classically stylized. Illustration by William Stobbs. Reproduced from The Gorgon's Head. *© 1961 by Ian Serraillier. By permission of Henry Z. Walck, Inc. (Book 5 x 7¾)*

and a more choice vocabulary than the folk tales.

The hero cycles or epics, such as the *Odyssey, Sigurd, Beowulf,* and *Robin Hood,* are the hardest of all stories to tell. They demand long and careful preparation, a study of sources, a comparison of versions, and considerable practice before they are ready for telling. The *Odyssey* and *Robin Hood* are the easiest, *Sigurd* the most difficult. Which do you care about so strongly that you are willing to study and work long and hard on the adaptation and telling? The epics are well worth your time and the children's, because as you tell them over a number of weeks the children are steeped in heroic struggles and noble achievement as they never are in listening to a short story.

Whether you will tell or read Andersen depends on you. If you decide to tell the tales, you must be prepared to absorb a good deal of the language verbatim, because Andersen is a great stylist. Most stories written these days are for reading, not for telling, but here and there you will find little stories that are as perfect for telling as any folk tale. "Paddy's Three Pets" by Mary Phillips is a good example, also *Torten's Christmas Secret* by Maurice Dolbier, "Peter the Goldfish" by Julian Street, and *The Bears on Hemlock Mountain* by Alice Dalgliesh. These are all marvelous for telling and you will find others. If you begin with your favorite folk tales and tell enough of them to get the feel and fun of storytelling in your very bones, then you will be better able to spot a likely candidate for your repertoire, whether it is a tale as old as old or as new as today.

The stranger's countenance still wore a smile, which seemed to shed a yellow luster all about the room, and gleamed on little Marygold's image, and on the other objects that had been transmuted by the touch of Midas.
"Well, friend Midas," said the stranger, "pray how do you succeed with the Golden Touch?"

With dramatic use of black, red, and gold, Paul Galdone has illustrated King Midas. Notice that the child is simply drawn, but the King's woes are emphasized by the heavy drooping lines of face and head. Illustration by Paul Galdone. Reproduced from The Golden Touch *by Nathaniel Hawthorne. Copyright © 1959 by Paul Galdone. By permission of Whittlesey House (McGraw-Hill). (Original in two colors, book 5¾ x 8)*

ADAPTING A STORY FOR TELLING

Before learning a story, read it carefully to see if it needs some adaptation. The folk tales are in fairly good form for telling except for an occasional adult frankness. For instance, in "East o' the Sun and West o' the Moon" the stranger who comes every night gets into bed with the lassie. For this you substitute something of this sort: "Every night after the lassie had gone to bed, she could hear someone go into the room next to hers, and yet all day long she never saw a living soul except the great white bear."

The myths, on the other hand, need almost a complete remaking of the story. Bulfinch is the usual English source, but it is astonishing how bare and dull his versions can be. Adaptation is essential and it requires a complete visualization, using all your creative imagination to see and hear the situations and characters as they might have been. Sally Benson's versions help and so do Hawthorne's. Hawthorne's versions are masterful storytelling, when pruned of the asides and the touches that make the characters seem juvenile. His "King Midas" and "Philemon and Baucis" are among his best, but many of the others are too adorned. Between Hawthorne and Bulfinch there is a happy medium which Sally Benson almost achieves. There are, however, some stories for which you have a feeling that no version quite represents. Here, for instance, is an example of how the story of "Bellerophon and Pegasus" might be recreated:

Bellerophon and Pegasus

In the ancient country of Lycia, reigned over by King Iobates, a terrible monster called a Chimaera had suddenly appeared. It had three horrible heads, one of them a goat's, one a lion's, and the third a snake's head. All three belched out flame and smoke that burned and laid waste the country wherever the creature went. So it happened that at the beautiful spring of Pirene, where the people came to get their water, they were talking not about the cold sparkling waters of the spring, but about the fearful Chimaera. Would it burn their fields and vineyards next? Who could ever kill so terrible a creature? Already many heroes had tried unsuccessfully and perished in the attempt.

Suddenly a handsome stranger appeared in their midst, carrying in his hand a golden bridle.

"You are troubled because of the Chimaera," he said to the people. "Do not be afraid. It will not burn your crops and orchards much longer. I am Bellerophon, sent from King Iobates to slay the monster. But tell me first, is this the fountain of Pirene?"

They said it was, and they stared at the young man with pity, thinking how soon he would perish like all the others.

"Then if this is the spring of Pirene," Bellerophon continued, "perhaps tonight I shall see Pegasus, the winged horse of the gods, for I am told the creature drinks only the clear waters from this spring."

Some of the people laughed at the idea of a winged horse, others said they had heard of it, and a few said gravely, "Yes, Pegasus drinks here," and they noticed again the jeweled bridle the young man held in his hand. "Does he hope to capture the winged horse?" they whispered among themselves, as they filled their pitchers with water and, one by one, set off for home.

Bellerophon was alone by the bubbling spring, but he was not afraid, for no less a one than the goddess Minerva had given him the golden bridle and told him he would see Pegasus at the fountain of Pirene. Bellerophon lay quietly, half hidden in the long grasses, watching the big, white clouds sail lazily by. But was that a cloud, way off there? It moved more swiftly than any cloud. Then it caught the last golden rays of the sun, and there was no mistake about it, it was not a cloud. Those great white wings flashed back the sun as the snowy white horse galloped and cavorted airily down to earth. When the small, polished hooves landed lightly on the ground, the winged horse pranced gaily over to the spring, snuffled and blew the water playfully, and drank his fill, and then looked around.

Slowly Bellerophon rose from his hiding place and held out the golden bridle. Immediately Pegasus, the winged horse of the gods, came quietly to his hand and allowed Bellerophon to slip the bridle over his head. Of course, Bellerophon must have patted him and talked as horse lovers always talk, "Steady there, my beauty, easy does it," and "Good boy!" The winged horse stood perfectly still and allowed Bellerophon to mount him. Then off they went like the wind, where no rider had ever gone. This was cloud climbing, star chasing, wind racing such as no man had ever known before. It was glorious, and now Bellerophon knew how he would deal with the Chimaera. Such speed and lightness as this would be able to dodge the smoke and fire if he managed rightly. Bellerophon patted the winged steed and talked to Pegasus as they galloped and cavorted through the clouds. When at last they came to rest atop a mountain, the two slept side by side, the man sheltered and warm beneath one of Pegasus' great wings.

The next day from a safe height they had a good look at the three frightening heads of the Chimaera. Bellerophon had buckled on his sword. Now he held it in his hand as they came down to earth at terrible speed, moving in sideways on the monster. As they flew by, the sword flashed fast and sure and the goat's head fell to the ground. Back they came from the other side and the lion's head fell with a great roar and burst of fire and smoke. Then they waited a bit until the smoke cleared and they could see the snake's head writhing and rearing itself high and fierce, the green eyes scanning the skies for any sign of the return attack. Bellerophon patted Pegasus reassuringly and spoke words of encouragement before they started on their swift descent earthwards. With all the speed at Pegasus' command they flew by that horrible, hissing serpent and Bellerophon decapitated it with one sure stroke of his sword.

The Chimaera was dead. King Iobates' land was saved, and now the people could resume their usual tasks of cultivating their vineyards and their orchards and tilling the soil in peace and security.

What became of Bellerophon and his beautiful winged horse, Pegasus? There are different stories told about them. The King seems to have rewarded them and feared them. But horse and rider performed many heroic deeds together and were so evidently favorites of the gods that the treacherous King Iobates dared do nothing against them. It is said that Bellerophon married the King's daughter. It is also told that he offered Pegasus his freedom, but as long as they two lived, Pegasus would come flashing down through the clouds at his master's call. Perhaps that is the way their lives ended—Bellerophon mounted on the back of Pegasus, the winged horse of the gods, soaring off into the high clouds together.

This is the way one person sees and hears the story of Bellerophon and his winged horse. If you make your own adaptation or even if you tell this one, it will be different. But look once again at the Bulfinch outline of the story after you have read this version and you will see that adapting a story means living it imaginatively until it comes to life in dialogue, scene, and characterization.

Telling epics or hero cycles generally requires the same drastic adaptation. Some are easier than others. The *Odyssey* requires, for example, a complete reordering of the episodes. A serial telling of the stories may be divided into some such chapters as these:

By means of the famous Trojan horse, the Greeks conquer the Trojans, divide the spoils, and set off for their homes. Odysseus, ruler of Ithaca, sails hopefully. He loses some of his men to the strange Lotus-eaters but travels on.

Landing on the rude island of the Cyclops, Odysseus and his men fight for their lives with a one-eyed giant named Polyphemus. Odysseus saves the day by a clever trick.

To aid him on his journey, Odysseus is given a sack by Aeolus containing the winds. But through his men's curiosity and cupidity, they are stranded on the island of Circe. This enchantress turns some of them into swine, but Odysseus rescues all but one of them.

Odysseus offends the gods and is almost lost in trying to steer his course between the terrible whirlpool, Scylla, and the rock, Charybdis.

Clinging to the keel of his ship, Odysseus drifts at last to the island of the nymph, Calypso, who holds him as her unwilling guest for seven long years. Then at Zeus' command she bids him build a raft and be gone.

Drifting about on his raft, he comes to the land of the friendly Phaeacians, and is rescued by the beautiful Nausicaä, daughter of the King. Odysseus is brought to the king's palace and tells his tale. The Phaeacians, after games and feasts, equip him for his homeward journey and Odysseus says farewell to the lovely Nausicaä and sets sail.

Once on his native soil he hides in the hut of a swineherd until he can learn what has been happening. Only his old dog knows him. He meets his son Telemachus grown to manhood, learns of the wretched suitors' laying waste to his kingdom, and of the faithfulness of his wife Penelope. Disguised as a beggar, he enters his own hall. Telemachus brings forth the great bow of Odysseus, but none can bend it until the beggar tries and succeeds. Throwing off his disguise, Odysseus announces himself, and with his son beside him, takes aim at the suitors, who are killed or driven away. Odysseus proves his identity and is reunited with Penelope.

In the original story the actual chronological beginning does not appear until the ninth book, an arrangement which is at first confusing. Fortunately, most children's versions relate the story in the easier chronological form outlined above. Even this brief outline should make it evident that here is an adventure tale after the child's own heart. What no outline can reveal is the exciting quality of the hero and the beauty of the style.

The Norse epic *Sigurd the Volsung* is difficult to adapt for children and calls for expert handling. This you can understand from the following summary:

The first book, Sigmund, *opens with the wedding of Signy, the daughter of King Volsung, to the wily Goth king, Siggeir. Suddenly into the great hall strides a man "one-eyed and seeming ancient." Deep into the tree, Branstock, he thrusts a gleaming sword with word that it is his gift to the man who can pluck it from the tree. Then the god Odin vanishes, and the men try to take the sword from the tree. The Goth king is enraged when he fails with all the others only to see Sigmund, the twin brother of the bride, take it easily. After the wedding, Signy's villainous husband extracts a promise from King Volsung that he, with his sons and his men, will come to the Gothland for a visit. Signy suspects foul play, but Volsung, having promised, will not break his word. The Volsungs go and are treacherously slain, only Sigmund escaping. He hides in the forest, biding his time until he can avenge the death of his kinsfolk and rescue his twin sister, Signy, from her villainous mate.*

To her brother, Queen Signy sends each of her sons to be tested for courage. The boys fail dismally. Then she knows that only a child of pure Volsung blood will have the mettle to aid her brother in his revenge. So she disguises herself as a beautiful witch and takes refuge with Sigmund. When the son of this union is born, she names him Sinfiotli and later sends him to Sigmund to be tested. The boy meets every trial and Sigmund begins his training. When Sinfiotli reaches manhood, the plan is made. They lay siege to the Goth King's hall, slay the men, and fire the hall. Sigmund calls to his sister to join them, but Signy appears on the balcony, tells her brother that Sinfiotli is his son, and bids them both farewell. She then returns to the burning hall and perishes with her husband. The book of Sigmund *closes with his return to the land of the Volsungs, to reign once more in his father's hall. Sinfiotli is tragically poisoned, and as Sigmund bears his son's body to the sea, a boat draws near, bearing a one-eyed stranger, "grey-clad like the mountain-cloud."*

" 'My senders,' quoth the shipman, 'bade me waft a great kin o'er. So set thy burden a shipboard . . .' "[1]

Sigmund does as he is told, and ship and burden vanish. Later Sigmund marries a noble woman but perishes in battle before their son is born. So ends the book of Sigmund.

The book of Regin *is about Sigmund's second son, Sigurd, whose adventures are no less stormy than his father's. He wins a great horse, Greyfell; he is instructed by the wise Regin in the secret of warfare of the gods; he is told about their hoard of gold, guarded by the serpent Fafnir. For Sigurd, Regin forges a mighty sword, but the young hero breaks the blade easily. Regin finally forges a sword from the fragments of Sigmund's blade. Mounted on Greyfell, armed with his Odin-given blade, Sigurd slays the serpent Fafnir on the Glittering Heath and drinks his blood, which enables him to understand the speech of the birds. Led by them, he discovers the sleeping Brynhild, a Valkyr or battle maiden, who had defied Odin and been condemned to a long sleep by the god. She was surrounded by a barrier of flames through which only a great hero could come to waken her. Sigurd kisses the sleeping Valkyr; she wakes, loves her rescuer, and accepts the magic ring he gives her to seal their love.*

For children, the story is usually terminated here, although many dangers and adventures follow. The ride through the flames to wake the sleeping Valkyr makes the properly triumphant note on which to close this stirring saga. Only adults can endure the tragic aftermath.

Even so sketchy an outline as this makes the difficulty of the material fairly evident, but it is magnificent to tell. The *Odyssey*

1. William Morris, *The Story of Sigurd the Volsung,* pp. 54-55.

and *Robin Hood*[2] are the easiest and most rewarding epics to tell, but if you have a special fondness for *Sigurd, Cuchulain, Beowulf,* or *King Arthur,* work on your favorite by all means.

Learning and Telling a Story

Probably no two people learn and re-create stories in quite the same way, but visualizing characters and scenes has always helped me not only to learn a story but to tell it. In "The Pancake," I see a snug kitchen with a mother standing close to the stove, her seven hungry children crowding much too near her to watch that fat sizzling pancake. An old grandfather is sitting over in the corner smoking his pipe. Through the open door—it must be open because the pancake rolled through it— I see a road winding over the hills and across the country and clear out of sight. I see the characters, too, some in more detail than others, depending upon how dramatic their words or their roles are in the tale. Seeing them undoubtedly helps in characterizing them; so if you see the sneering faces of Cinderella's sisters, undoubtedly something of the sneer gets into your interpretation of their words and behavior. Not that you do actually sneer, of course—that is stage business, not storytelling—but still a sneerful suggestion undoubtedly creeps in. And if you are telling a hero tale, something noble and serious comes into your voice, face, and manner.

Obviously, if you are going to tell a story you must know it thoroughly. This involves overlearning to such a degree that you cannot possibly forget the tale, but you can stand aside and play with the interpretation of your story because you have no worries about the mechanics of recall. Some people feel that memorizing is the only solution. Others consider memorizing a dangerous approach to the folk tales for two reasons: First, these naïve tales do not have the formal perfection of the literary story; they were always kept fluid and personal by the old tellers. If they are memorized, they are likely to sound stilted and impersonal. Ruth Sawyer, in *The Way of the Storyteller,* pays a tribute to the storytelling of her Irish nurse, who was proud of her art and used it with great dignity. She would close a story with the saying, "Take it, and may the next one who tells it better it." This is exactly what happens. A young student will tell one of the tales which I have loved and told and, although she follows the same text, the story becomes as uniquely hers as if no one had ever told it before. This is the way it always has been and always will be.

A second reason why exact memorizing is dangerous is that the forgetting of a single phrase or a connecting sentence will throw the teller completely off, so that she has to stop or start over or pause awkwardly while she racks her brain for the lost words. This of course spoils a story. On the other hand, if it is thoroughly learned but not memorized it will remain in your memory for years. Sometimes when I am going to tell a story which perhaps I have not told for several years, I will read it over only once to recall it, or if the manuscript is not handy I will start in solitude, bringing it back to the threshold of consciousness and speech. It may come haltingly in spots, but with one or two retellings it is as smooth and sure as it ever was. How is it done?

Psychologists say that the greatest carry-over in learning and the least loss through forgetting are insured by practicing in the same way in which you are going to use your material. Since storytelling is oral, learn your story orally, in the sitting or standing position you expect to employ, and with an imaginary audience around you. Of course you read your tale once or twice silently until you are thoroughly familiar with its sequential action, its mood, its areas of suspense, and its climax. You may then read it aloud once or twice if you wish to hear it, listening especially for its peculiar cadences, its folk flavor. Then begin telling it aloud, with the book at hand

2. See Chapter 11, p. 317, for an outline of the story of Robin Hood.

to refer to when you forget. It will be heavy going at first, with more rough spots than smooth, but go through the tale as a whole once or twice. Then polish the beginning and the end until both are easy and sure. Dialogue is the most difficult and the most fun. The dialogue sections you must lift out and work at until you make the right connections and they come naturally and spontaneously. Every time you single out a special section for practice, go back and tell the whole story again until it comes to life as a whole.

Perhaps my experience will illustrate the difference between memorizing and the process just described. In telling "The Pancake," I have no idea when and to whom the pancake says, "How do you do," or "As well as I may," or "Good day to you," or "The same to you." The pancake and the characters he encounters exchange all these various forms of greetings and responses. These I know in general and apply as I wish. As a matter of fact, after years of telling, my own use of them seems to follow a definite pattern that is mine, never the modern "Hi-yah," or the stately "God rest you, stranger" of some other tale. My version is both the pattern of the "Pancake" and my own personal pattern. It is learned, but not memorized. Does this make the distinction any clearer?

The other spots in the story which you lift out for special practice are those which stir the emotions. Listen to yourself. If you are waxing overemotional, tone down; or if you muff the climax, go back and heighten the suspense that leads up to it, bringing out the climax on a fine crescendo. The great virtue of working orally is that you can hear your weak spots and strengthen them. You can hear where the story becomes a little dull or slow, where your dialogue halts or the vocabulary is obscure for the particular group you have in mind. In short, oral practice for oral presentation is the safest, the quickest, and the most effective method of learning, whether you memorize your material or not.

THE BEGINNINGS AND ENDINGS

The beginnings and endings of your stories should be polished until they are smooth and sure. The beginning requires special care because it establishes the mood of your tale. You announce your story informally in any of a dozen ways: "Today we are going to hear about our old friends, 'The Three Billy-Goats Gruff.'" "I've a new story for you today, and it's called 'The Fox and His Travels.'" "You have all heard stories about 'Jack the Giant Killer,' but do you know there was one *girl* who got the best of a powerful giant? Our story is about her, and her name is 'Molly Whuppie.'"

Then, having announced your story, pause a moment—not too long, not long enough to let the children start squirming again, just long enough for a deep, quiet breath—and then begin. The beginning of a nonsense tale is very different from the beginning of a romance, as you can hear when you read these lines aloud:

> *Once upon a time there was a man who had a goody who was so cross grained that there was no living with her.* ("*Goody Gainst the Stream*" *from* Tales from the Fjeld.)

> *Once, in the golden time, when an Irish king sat in every province and plenty covered the land, there lived in Connaught a grand old king with one daughter. She was as tall and slender as the reeds that grow by Lough Erne, and her face was the fairest in seven counties.* ("*The Princess and the Vagabone,*" *from* The Way of the Storyteller.)

> *There was once upon a time a Fisherman who lived with his wife in a pig-stye close by the sea, and every day he went out fishing; and he fished, and he fished.* ("*The Fisherman and his Wife*" *from* Grimm's Fairy Tales.)

> *As Chicken-Licken went one day to the wood, an acorn fell on her poor bald pate, and she thought the sky had fallen.* ("*Chicken-Licken,*" *from* Popular Rhymes and Nursery Tales.)

Here are the beginnings of a droll, a romance, a comic-tragedy, and a nursery tale. In your telling, you establish the right atmosphere for your whole story with these opening lines; you put your audience in the right mood and build up anticipation.

So with the endings you should leave your audience satisfied, with a sense of completion. Good stories have been spoiled by a weak, inconclusive telling of the end. It must come with conviction, whether it is nonsense, romance, poetic justice, or one of those surprise endings which are fun for everyone. The noisy grunt or inhalation with which you finish off "The Pancake" ought to make the children jump and then laugh. This is primitive slapstick humor but well worth practicing for its gratifying results. Very different are the surprise endings of "Clever Manka" and "Sadko," or the romantic conclusions of "The Princess and the Vagabone" and "East o' the Sun," or the poetic justice of "The Fisherman and His Wife." These satisfying conclusions are characteristic of the folk tales and should be enhanced by the way you tell them.

If you are telling a cycle of hero tales, the conclusion of one episode may serve as a lead into the next adventure, a promise of new dangers to be conquered. The first story of Theseus concludes:

"No traveller who took that road has ever reached Athens alive," said Aithra.

"Then I will be the first," said Theseus. "If I can bring my father proof of my manhood, he will honour me and love me all the more."

Aithra did not dissuade him. Her son was no longer a boy but a man, and he knew his mind.[3]

DRAMATIZING THE TALES

The preceding discussion suggests the question of how far you should go in dramatizing these tales as you tell them and points, perhaps, to a limit beyond which too much is decidedly too much. Storytelling is essentially the art of the fireside, the campfire, the cribside, and the classroom. It should be kept simple and informal, or else it goes over into the realm of the stage, where it does not belong. Yet the folk tales are dramatic and should be dramatically told in the restrained drama of everyday talk.

Young children are so motor-minded that they can't talk about a train without "choo-chooing" and making the appropriate scuffing, shuttling motions of feet and arms. So in telling stories to them, you unconsciously use more gestures and more pantomime than you would ordinarily. It may not be necessary, but it seems entirely natural to roll the pancake out of the door with a big circular motion of the hand when you say "and rolled out of the door like a wheel," or to suggest the length of the troll's nose with hand to nose and then hand extended full arm's length away as you say, "and a nose as long as a poker." Most nursery-school and kindergarten teachers and most mothers of young children do something of the sort. If such gestures are not overdone, they are natural and legitimate. But they probably should diminish to the vanishing point with older children. With them, any overdramatization turns storytelling into elocutionary absurdity. "The lassie made a low bow" is most decidedly not accompanied by such a bow. Nevertheless, the lassie's fear or humility is conveyed by the voice, which speaks the words gravely or humbly. Or suppose there was mockery in that bow; so, too, the voice can suggest the lassie's frame of mind in the speaking of those same words. Try it. In short, you never dramatize literally; you suggest ever so simply but unmistakably the dramatic element in the narrative. The moment you forget this restraint so essential to the integrity of a story, something artificial and stagy comes in, and the art of storytelling is destroyed.

So far most of the examples given to illustrate storytelling techniques have been taken from the folk tales, but precisely the same techniques apply to other types of stories. Realistic stories often have less exciting action but may be just as absorbing in a quieter way. If you tell rather than read Andersen's fairy tales, you will find yourself cutting some of the long descriptions (particularly in "The Snow Queen") but try to preserve the beauty of scene and language as best you can.

Whatever stories you choose to tell, may you have a golden tongue for the telling.

3. Ian Serraillier, *The Way of Danger,* Walck, 1963.

Four Storytellers With Contrasting Styles

Perhaps some of these points about storytelling can be illustrated by sketching briefly the techniques of four distinguished storytellers: the English Marie Shedlock, the American Ruth Sawyer, the Norwegian Gudrun Thorne-Thomsen, and the American Richard Chase. These four were as unlike as possible in personality, in manner of telling their stories, and even in the type of tales they told, but they did have certain characteristics in common. All had a deep love for the old stories and presented them with an evident sincerity and enjoyment. And all were sensitive to words and used them with precision and telling effect. Their art was as individual as their voices.

MARIE SHEDLOCK

Marie Shedlock was a tiny woman used to appearing before enormous audiences. As a result she used the large gestures of the stage and dramatized her material to a greater extent than would be necessary by the fireside or in a schoolroom. If the story called for a curtsey, she curtsied. She also memorized her stories, probably because she was preëminent as an interpreter of the stories of Hans Christian Andersen, whose words she felt should not be tampered with. She was of the stage or platform rather than the home or schoolroom, and hers was a literary rather than a folk art. Nevertheless, it was great storytelling, rich in characterizations, full of subtly suggested implications, and sparkling with infectious gaiety. Her eyes shone, her voice was clear and rich, and her flawless diction fell on the ears like music. Marie Shedlock will be remembered for her ebullient humor, her disciplined art of narration, her sense of the dramatic, and her unaffected delight in telling a good story. These qualities won her audiences old and young.[4]

RUTH SAWYER

Ruth Sawyer is known not only as a collector and editor of folk tales but as a storyteller. People comment on her warm friendliness, which reaches out to an audience immediately. There is no one else who can relate Irish stories as she does, and there is perhaps no other storyteller with so wide a range of tales from many lands, representing many types and moods. If she is sometimes a bit sentimental, she has also a sense of fun and wonderful flashes of wit. While her stories are folk tales, collected from the lips of native storytellers, Miss Sawyer tells them in literary form that is quite different from the stark simplicity of a Norwegian folk tale. Perhaps this is because she has listened to the Irish storytellers, who use language richly and melodiously, making a more frequent use of the cadenced line than any others. Her stories are music on the printed page and in her telling them. Only a fine storyteller with an unerring sense of words, mood, and the music of narration could have produced that Christmas masterpiece, "The Voyage of the Wee Red Cap." It is characteristic of her art both in editing and in telling stories.

GUDRUN THORNE-THOMSEN

Gudrun Thorne-Thomsen has given us the greatest expression of the folk art of storytelling that this generation has known. Neither here-and-now fashions in children's literature nor Hollywood's cult of distorting folk literature has ever touched the purity of her art. Recordings of her storytelling have been made for the Library of Congress, and commercial recordings are available too. Mrs. Thomsen has trained innumerable librarians and teachers in the meticulous disciplines of

4. *Horn Book,* May 1934, is devoted to the art of Marie Shedlock.

storytelling, and these recordings of hers should extend her influence to still other practitioners of the art.[5]

Two forces in her childhood help to explain her unique art. She was Norwegian born, the daughter of the distinguished actress who created the roles of Ibsen's heroines as each of his plays was written and produced. We can imagine the child of that mother, highly intelligent and sensitive to beauty, growing up in an atmosphere where devotion to the integrity of the spoken word was taken for granted. Storytelling was also a part of each day's experience, so that the child, Gudrun, stored away in her heart an abiding love for the sagas and the homely tales of her country. This love she expressed in a lifetime of storytelling.

Mrs. Thomsen was small and plain with the beautiful plainness of fine silver. Her brow was high and serene, her features delicate and mobile, and her eyes Northern blue, clear, and honest. She stood quietly with rarely a gesture; she spoke slowly and gravely and her voice captured you immediately. It was a light voice—with no heavy resonance, no ringing tones, but a rare sweetness. Here was a tempered instrument which had been used in the service of beauty and spoke to the spirit even more effectively than the carefully chosen words. She had a quiet sense of humor, which expressed itself subtly in just a hint of a smile or a droll turn of phrase. She developed the drama of her tales with astonishing effectiveness, considering her restraint. She used no exaggerated inflections and few gestures. It was the quality of the voice, the minor note of fear or loneliness, the crescendo of happiness or exultation, and the steady sustained tone of courage which told the story. Whether it was a lassie searching for her lost love or a Pancake growing cockier and cockier or a Sigurd winning his sword, the voice laid its spell on every audience.

Gudrun Thorne-Thomsen was the quietest of all the storytellers, and the least humorous. Sometimes in telling a saga she seemed almost austere, and her stories were apt to fall continuously into a minor key. Her art was the essence of dramatic simplicity.

5. Five records can be obtained through the American Library Association, 50 East Huron Street, Chicago 11.

RICHARD CHASE

Lest these examples imply that the great storytellers have all been women, let it be said at once that some of the best storytelling in the world comes from men—fathers, grandfathers, uncles, and great-uncles. Listen to Philip Sherlock's recording of his Anansi stories. Even without his facial expression and occasional gestures, here is a great storyteller. Another is Richard Chase, folklorist and collector and editor of the Jack, Will, and Tom stories of our Southern Appalachian mountains.

Richard Chase is a tall, lean, good-looking man who dances the old play party reels and square dances with easy grace and sings the ballads with compelling charm. But the moment he begins to tell one of the Jack Tales, you see at once "old Uncle Mon-roe, sitting on hard clods in the middle of a tobacco patch" or "leaning in the corner of a rail fence," spellbinding his audience. His gestures are few but angular and effective. He uses the easy drawl and the language of the mountaineers. His eyes twinkle with appreciation at the fixes Jack gets himself into but the audience shares his certainty that Jack will get himself out of trouble come what may. The language is not dialect but is full of the characteristic words and phrases of the region —"rarin'," "piggin," "querled," "shadder," and "get shet of" (for "get rid of"). These heighten the humor of the tales and make them more colorful. The storyteller's voice is rich and his facial expression reflects the drollery of the tales. Richard Chase has a deep love for these stories and for the fine sturdy folk who kept alive these mountain variants of the European folk tales. His deep appreciation for each tale gives warmth and integrity to the telling. He can capture audiences from children to word-weary professors of English. His is distinctly a masculine performance and there has yet to be found a woman who can do these stories with the same gusto.

These four great storytellers—Marie Shedlock, Ruth Sawyer, Gudrun Thorne-Thomsen, and Richard Chase—had different gifts and different styles but an equal devotion to their art. They are proof that different personalities will succeed with different methods

—in storytelling as well as in other activities. Marie Shedlock, in the tradition of the stage rather than the fireside, had a dramatic quality and an unaffected gaiety that no child could resist. Ruth Sawyer gives a literary, ornamented touch to folk tales that makes them sheer poetry and carries the children to new appreciation of the beauty of words. Mrs. Thomsen might seem overserious for children, but her simplicity and her quietness were right, both for the folk tales she told and for her listeners. Richard Chase's storytelling is homespun art with more humor than that of the women and great warmth. Your own storytelling will take on still a different pattern. Only two specific qualities you must share with these four—you must be sincere and you must enjoy telling stories.

Reading Aloud

It may seem easier to read a story aloud than to tell it, but telling and reading require similar disciplines. Everything that has been said about appearance, dramatic simplicity, voice, and diction for storytelling applies also to reading aloud. There must also be some preliminary preparation, because when you read to children you have a book between you and them, and you can easily lose their attention if yours is confined to the text. You must know your book so well that you can look over it directly into the eyes of the children. Acquaint yourself with the text in advance so that you can anticipate a change in mood, the introduction of a new character, the building up of suspense, a smashing climax, or a surprise ending. You simply cannot do justice to a story unless you know what's coming. A parent or a teacher who reads well can brighten an otherwise dull day for children. A poor reader is just another pain for them to endure and forgive if they can.

The wonderful picture-stories for the kindergarten and primary children are generally a delight to read aloud but require certain techniques for the maximum enjoyment. Seat the children comfortably around you so that everyone can see the pictures, and hold the book in front of you with the pages facing the children and with its back to you. You can do this with such glorious picture-stories as *Ping* or *Curious George* or *Petunia* or *The Happy Lion* or *Madeline* because, after a couple of readings, you will know the text so well that an upside-down clue suffices. If you don't know it that well, hold the book up and off to the side, so that you can take a long look at the text while the children study the pictures. This method will work unless you choose a picture-story where words and illustrations are not synchronized. This can cause a minor riot which is not your fault but which will continue until you say firmly, "Now children, wait a minute. These pictures don't always match what it says on the page; so I am going to read you the whole story first without pictures. Then when I finish, we will look at the pictures and you can tell me what is happening."

Some people prefer to read all books in this way. Certainly it is the best method for handling the pictures in a well illustrated story for older children—show the pictures after you have finished the chapter or the book. Remember, of course, that no suggestions for "best methods" are infallible. You will probably be unable to resist interrupting *Charlotte's Web* while you show the children Garth Williams' hilarious pictures of Wilbur the pig taking off in full flight from the top of the manure pile or trying to look "terrific." Children can laugh harder at the rest of the story because they can visualize ridiculous Wilbur in terms of Mr. Williams' inimitable drawings. With a book like the D'Aulaires' big, handsome *Book of Greek Myths,* which is for older boys and girls, it might be well to let the children pore over the pictures for several days before you read the first story. They will undoubtedly read parts of the text, here and there, and so with the help of the illustrations will build up their own introduction to myths to help them visualize Olympus and its bright skydwellers. Pictures in a book you are reading aloud may be a hazard or a tremendous asset, depending on how skillfully you are able to use them.

After studying the chapters on poetry, you know that all poetry for children is most thoroughly understood and enjoyed when it is read aloud by someone who can read it well.[6] In the classroom let the children hear it read casually every day until they are so accustomed to its musical patterns, its fun, beauty, surprise, and all-round variety that they join in when you repeat their favorites and learn in this way, almost unconsciously, a great many poems of different sorts. Repeating certain poems not only encourages this effortless memorizing on the part of the children, but gives a start, even in the primary grades, to reading in depth—that is considering a poem at more than one level of meaning. It is doubtful if children's understanding of poetry grows from silent reading as it does from hearing poems read aloud, properly interpreted, and from speaking the poems themselves. And actually for you, meaning develops at deeper levels as you read aloud striving for an honest interpretation. In no field of literature is reading aloud so essential as in poetry.

Reading aloud in the family[7] is one of the most precious memories a child can have. It means enjoyment shared—the younger children trying hard to understand what makes the older children and the grownups laugh or weep, the adults stopping for a moment to explain the joke or the tragedy or to help the young members of the family understand what is at stake. This is the family at one, united warmly and happily through shared enjoyment.

Garth Williams' pen-and-ink drawings make the activities of these creatures entirely believable. Note the realistic touches—the old shovel, the feeding trough, the peaceful cows.
Illustration by Garth Williams. From Charlotte's Web *by E. B. White. Copyright 1952 by E. B. White. Reprinted by permission of Harper & Row, Publishers. (Book 5⅜ x 8)*

One college boy remembered his father reading Shakespeare aloud to the whole family, young and old, so beautifully that as long as they lived those children felt at home with Shakespeare. They read Shakespeare again for themselves, but with the sound of their father's voice in their ears. Another student remembered asking her mother over and over again to read the "Death of Minnehaha" while she, the child, crawled under a well draped table to weep in private. There was something about her mother's low, gentle voice that made this part of the "Hiawatha" story piteously real and so lovely it must be heard again and again. A grandmother recalled gratefully, as long as she lived, the family evenings devoted to reading the novels of Charles Dickens aloud, so that everyone could share in this treat. And then, because books were scarce and hard to come by in their small town, the books were circulated to family after family to be shared in the same way. Good books, shared by families reading together, will do much to create in children not only a liking for literature but warm memories of companionable family life.

6. Chapter 8 in particular discusses the techniques of reading poetry aloud.
7. Also see Chapter 21, "Reading in the Family."

SUGGESTED READING, PROBLEMS, AND PROJECTS

1. What has happened to the intimate art of storytelling in the last hundred years?

2. At a time when movies and television have great impact and influence, why should the oral presentation of fine literature be important to (a) nonreaders, (b) beginning readers, (c) older children who can read for themselves?

3. On what basis will you decide whether to tell or to read a story?

4. Which of the items of "personal equipment for storytelling" seem most difficult to achieve? Discuss.

5. What kinds of adaptations are necessary for telling folk tales, myths, fables, or epics?

6. Choose an Andersen story you would genuinely like to share with a group of children. How will you present it?

7. When you learn a story for telling, does your method of learning differ from those described in this text? Actually no two people probably learn a story in quite the same way. Why are the beginnings and endings of the story so important?

8. Choose one story for telling. It may be a folk tale, a myth, an episode from an epic, or it may be a realistic story. Learn it for class presentation; try it out on children, if you can, before class presentation. Note: If the class is large, it may be necessary to break up into groups of five or six, so that everyone has a chance to tell a story to an audience, to be listened to by his peers, and to have his efforts constructively evaluated. Another possibility is to arrange for storytelling once a week at children's hospitals or detention homes. It is better to make these visits in groups of four or five at a time both to listen and to see what succeeds or fails and also to be able to provide the audience with at least two stories in an afternoon.

9. (a) Introduce and read part of a picture-story, showing how you will manage the pictures with, before, or after the story. (b) Do the same with a book for upper grade children. What would be your reason for reading aloud to them? For reading aloud choose from any type of book, realistic or fanciful, just so you like it well enough to wish to share it with children. Which do you find easier, reading aloud or telling a story? Why?

REFERENCES

NEW YORK LIBRARY ASSOCIATION. *Once upon a Time . . .* Association, 1955. Help for librarians with pre-school hours, picture-book hours, and story hours. Suggested programs and bibliographies are included.

SAWYER, RUTH. *The Way of the Storyteller.* Viking, 1942 and 1962. Informally written in Ruth Sawyer's fine style, this is a contribution both to the art of storytelling and to the history of the old tales. It also contains eleven unusual stories, including a favorite, "The Princess and the Vagabone."

SHEDLOCK, MARIE. *Art of the Story-Teller,* 3d ed., bibl. by Eulalie Steinmetz. Dover, 1951. Guidance in selection of material, techniques of storytelling, and useful bibliographies are included.

Stories to Tell to Children. Carnegie Library of Pittsburgh. Frequent Revisions. One of the outstanding bibliographies of folk and fairy literature available for the storyteller.

TOOZE, RUTH. *Storytelling.* Prentice, 1959. Extensive bibliographies add to the value of this helpful guide for storytellers.

Fiction and Stranger Than Fiction

part four

14. Animal Stories

15. Here and Now

16. Other Times and Places

17. Biography

chapter 14

Animal Stories

All children are interested in animals. As babies they follow them with their eyes, they reach out to them, and after they have said "ma ma" and "da da" they may burst forth with "doggy" or "kitty." Rhymes about "The Three Little Kittens" or the mouse that ran up the clock are early favorites. *Mother Goose* is supplemented by the more realistic animal picture books, first in linen or heavy paper and later in well-bound editions. With these picture books, children learn to name all the beasts under the sun from hippopotamuses to anteaters. The folk tales with animal heroes come next and seem never to wear out their welcome. "The Three Little Pigs," "The Little Red Hen," and all the other favorites are heard over and over with endless satisfaction.

From these, children progress to the more complex, realistic stories about animals, and for most people the interest lasts a lifetime. Consider the tremendous popularity—in book form, in films, and in television—of such animal stories as *Lassie Come Home* and *My Friend Flicka.* Ernest Thompson Seton probably launched this favorite type of story with his *Lives of the Hunted* and other animal sagas. Certainly in recent years the influx of animal stories has grown steadily both in numbers and in quality. Today there are many fine books in this field worthy of serious consideration.

Talking Beasts—Ourselves in Fur

Animal stories fall into three distinct groups—talking beasts, animals true to their species but with the power of speech, and animals objectively reported. The oldest type is the folk tale (talking beast) in which the animals are given the characteristics of human beings—they are ourselves in fur. These stories are completely unscientific. "Little Pig" belongs to no Poland China nor any other swine species. He is called Pig, but he is really our industrious and capable selves, triumphing over every difficulty. So in the modern talking-beast stories, *Curious George,* the irresponsible, mischievous monkey is a four-footed Andrewshek or a Little Pear or a Johnny Jenks next-door, always in hot water. The animals in *The Wind in the Willows* (p. 348) are more like our neighbors than they are like moles and toads and river rats. Toad is the perfect picture of some vacuous and reckless young playboy, and Ratty is the Good Samaritan, the guardian angel which such young scamps seem always to acquire.

There is a great variety in these animal take offs on human behavior. Some of them are close to fables. *Ping* shows children that home is best even with a spank—a moral for four-year-olds, without any moralizing. In *Rabbit Hill* (p. 353) pompous Father Rabbit, worrying Mother, and suspicious, complaining Uncle Analdas are thoroughly entertaining—and they are also satires on types of people we have known. The same characters in *The Tough Winter* reveal the helplessness of creatures in the grip of natural forces more effectively than a factual account could do.

In hilarious contrast to *The Tough Winter* is Anne H. White's *Junket,* a story about a canine who teaches a city family the proper ways of farm living from a dog's eye view. Junket is all dog, but he has the determination of a wise, patient great-uncle who gets things done, one way or another. This is a lastingly popular story.

From the talking tortoise and Balaam's ass to Mickey Mouse, these unscientific talking-beast tales have had a long life. Why have they lasted, and why does the stream of new ones continue? Apparently it is the fun of their exaggerated pictures of human foibles. Donald Duck, with his hoarse roarings, is so ridiculously like someone we know that he makes us chuckle. Or the timid seventh duck in *Seven Diving Ducks* makes the timid child feel brave by comparison, and he is consoled. Or the Babar stories offer children amusing pictures of the adult world and social relationships.

In the chapters on the old folk tales, the fables, and the modern fanciful tales, many of the talking-beast stories have already been reviewed. A few more examples of the type, then, will suffice—Else Minarik's *Little Bear* books and two unusual talking-beast stories: Toba Sojo's *The Animal Frolic* and Munro Leaf's *The Story of Ferdinand.*

Junket and Montgomery are determined to keep the two hens. All the illustrations in this book are spirited and lively. The body of Junket is always well drawn. Notice the determination it speaks here, and notice the smug look of the hens.
Illustration by Robert McCloskey. From Junket *by Anne H. White. Copyright 1955 by Anne H. White and Robert McCloskey. Reprinted by permission of The Viking Press, Inc. (Book 5¾ x 9)*

TOBA SOJO

The Animal Frolic

If you have a chance to share with children that collector's item *The Animal Frolic* (1954),[1] you will doubly enjoy some of the most subtle and beautiful satires on human behavior you have ever seen. The book is a reproduction of a twelfth-century scroll by a famous Japanese artist. Here is the officious rabbit as chairman of the hospitality committee and master of ceremonies. The text does

1. See p. 53 for an additional discussion of this book.

not say he is, but he must be, because throughout this animal picnic he welcomes, bosses, organizes, interferes, and decides. Contests are set up to choose the king of the picnic. (Evidently beauty contests had not yet troubled twelfth-century Japan.) Some of the contests are fair and square, but the frog wins on an undetected foul. He bites the rabbit's ear and hangs on. However, he does make a very decent king, after all. The text is slight, but children can provide their own interpretations of what is happening. And the droll antics of the animals in these matchless pictures will delight both children and adults.

MUNRO LEAF

The Story of Ferdinand

No adult ever forgets his first surprised examination of the small pink book bearing the picture of a mild-looking bull and the title *The Story of Ferdinand* (1936). Munro Leaf's brief, succinct text, together with some of Robert Lawson's finest drawings, achieves a droll perfection that is hard to account for.

Ferdinand, the peaceful bull, accidentally sits down on a bee, is stung into wild action, and is mistaken for the "fightingest" bull of the whole countryside. He is carted off to the city for a bullfight, but once in the arena he merely returns to his favorite occupation, smelling flowers, and so is ignominiously sent back to his meadow.

Why does this small tale induce such prolonged chuckles? First, it has a genuinely funny situation: peaceful Ferdinand cast in the role of a frightful monster! Ferdinand's plight suggests amusing human parallels. Probably every adult has at one time or another found himself in the thick of some battle for which he was never intended; some awful committee he should never have been put on; some exalted public task he is supposed to work at brilliantly when all he really wants is a little spare time to go his own way and sniff peacefully at such fine flowers of leisure as life affords. So adults, identifying themselves with the absurdly miscast Ferdinand, are much amused with his tribulations. But children like this story, too. The youngest take it literally. They say gravely, "Did the bee hurt Ferdinand?" Older children are entranced by the drawings and catch the fine humor of the text.

ELSE H. MINARIK

Little Bear

Else Minarik's series of books about Little Bear, his mother, father, friends, and activities have enjoyed a well-deserved popularity. Little Bear is any small child. He pretends he is going to take off for the moon, but after falling kerplop, he approaches his mother who enters into his make-believe by asking him who he is. When this pretending goes a little too far for his comfort,

Little Bear put his arms around Mother.
He said, "Mother Bear, stop fooling.
You are my Mother Bear
And I am your Little Bear,
And we are on earth, and you know it.
Now may I have my lunch."

These books are of the easy-to-read variety, but they are completely satisfying stories, with Maurice Sendak's irresistible pictures.

Animals as Animals but Talking

The second type of animal story is a paradox. In these tales the animals are scientifically true to their species, but they are given the human abilities of thoughts and speech. The boy Mowgli, in the *Jungle Books,* first learns the language of each kind of animal; then he converses with his four-footed friends much as he might talk with his parents. But Bear always advises from the standpoint of bear experience, and Panther from panther experience. *Bambi,* the deer, thinks and speaks only of deer matters, never of human. Except that we are told the thoughts of the animals, the story is scientifically true to deer life and to the lives of the other creatures.

This is a difficult type of story to tell convincingly, for it is easy to sentimentalize or humanize the animals falsely. But if these stories are honestly written, they are good for children to have. Told from the standpoint of the animal, they dramatize the creature and point up his hardships, his fears, and his tragedies. The children gain from such stories a closer kinship with animals, more tenderness for them, and a greater desire to help them.

Hans Christian Andersen's "Ugly Duckling" (p. 330) is generally classified as an allegory, but it is also an admirable example of this type of animal tale. The young swan, in a barnyard full of cackling hens, chickens, ducks, and turkeys, is confronted with the problems of being a swan. He is rejected because he is different; he suffers the perils of being outcast and alone; he yearns to belong to his own kind without knowing why; and when his maturity is accomplished, he is welcomed by the swans to whom he belongs. This is an allegory, but it is also the story of a swan, scientifically true to its species except that we are told what this swan thinks and says.

Of course, children have always thought of their pets' noises as talk. "Soot says he is hungry," they interpret helpfully when the dog barks. And this is good, because it means they are developing a sensitivity to the needs of animals and to their discomfort or suffering when they are neglected or mistreated. These talking-beast tales which are also authentic animal lore speak for the vulnerability of all animals—the fear of the hunted creature as well as the joy of the pet in the companionship of his beloved master.

ANNA SEWELL

Black Beauty

In contrast to "The Ugly Duckling," there is that old animal classic *Black Beauty,* by Anna Sewell, first published in 1877. It enjoyed tremendous popularity for many years. Some children wept over Beauty's sufferings and were never thereafter able to ride or drive a horse without being haunted by its probable agonies of mind or body. Only parents with a sense of humor could laugh and talk them out of Black Beauty vapors.

Black Beauty was written as a protest against the tight checkrein and other more serious cruelties to horses. It relates, in the first person, a good story of the ups and downs of a carriage horse. Black Beauty tells us about his childhood, his training, the mishaps that overtook him at the hands of a young and inexperienced groom in a fine stable, and the praise and affection he received in his happy years. Then things go wrong. Black Beauty is sold farther and farther down the horse social scale. People inexperienced with horses handle him; he is whipped, abused, underfed, and neglected. He is made to haul loads far too heavy for him, until finally he collapses in the street. Through a series of happy accidents he falls into the hands of Joe, the now prosperous man who as an unskilled groom almost killed him. He makes amends to the old horse, and Beauty lives in clover ever after.

This story sounds all right, yet *Black Beauty* is rarely listed in careful bibliographies in spite of new and beautiful editions of it. One reason is that Black Beauty, while presumably a real horse, thinks and talks out of horse character. He is humanly sensitive to the social and moral tone of the people with whom he lives. His social judgments are those of a genteel lady, not a horse. He is ultraconservative about such habits as smoking, of which he heartily disapproves. Bad language, dirty clothes, and the smell of liquor offend his refined sensibilities—not as a horse, which might associate these things with cruel treatment, but as a perfect Victorian lady. Black Beauty is so full of human proprieties that he ceases to be convincing as a horse. The story is also morbidly sad, but it is the sentimentality and the overhumanizing of the species that make *Black Beauty* unconvincing as a horse story.

RUDYARD KIPLING

Jungle Books

The greatness of Rudyard Kipling's *Jungle Books* lies in part in his scrupulous avoidance of this temptation to overly humanize the animals. Mowgli, the human baby, is raised by the wolves and vouched for by them at the council rock. Later he is repudiated by his foster brothers because he is not wolf. They remain true to their wolfishness, knowing that Mowgli can never be one with them. Thereafter Mowgli hunts alone. Another example from these stories of the way Kipling scrupulously reveals the nature of the animal and never permits sentimentality to mar the picture is "Kaa's Hunting." Usually the animals avoid the great snake, Kaa. They know his wiles and have a healthy respect for his powers, but when Mowgli is stolen by the irresponsible monkeys, his protectors, the Bear and the Panther, have to summon Kaa to help them. He graciously consents, only because of the prospect of a delectable feast on the silly monkeys. All goes well. Mowgli is released, but before he and his protectors can depart, Kaa has begun his dance before the monkeys. Spellbound, they watch him, and spellbound, the Bear and the Panther watch also. Mowgli has to bring them out of their trance and get them away, or they, too, like the helpless monkeys, would soon find themselves a part of Kaa's feast.

It would have been easy for a less skillful writer to have made Kaa altruistic, or at least temporarily loyal to his friends of the hunt, but Kipling knew his jungle animals too well and was too scrupulous a writer to make any such mistakes. It is for these reasons, as well as for the exciting episodes in the stories and for their powerful imaginative appeal, that no recent books ever displace the *Jungle Books*. Children get from these stories an insight into wild-animal nature, into the curious likeness of animals and humans, and into the still more curious lines of demarcation.

FELIX SALTEN

Bambi
Bambi's Children

Bambi and *Bambi's Children* by Felix Salten are also fine animal stories. Bambi is a deer, and we follow him from his first day of life in a little forest glade to the absentee parenthood of the mature male deer. The books are exquisitely written and the animals well characterized. They are all there, from little field mice and rabbits to foxes and great elk. There is also "He," the enemy of all the forest creatures. His scent carries terror; his pale, hairless face chills them with horror because just beneath it are "legs" which reach out with a stick, and the stick shoots fire and death far beyond its reach. *Bambi* tells a story of man's hunting from the standpoint of the hunted and is therefore desperately tragic in places. The account of the hunters encircling the animals and then frightening them from their hiding places with terrible noises and constant shooting is so horrible it should make readers hate this barbarous practice. Fortunately, the larger proportion of the two Bambi books has to do with the training of the young deer, with the relationship of the males and females in the organization of the herd, and with some of the idyllic qualities of forest life as well as with the hard struggle for existence in the winter months. Older children twelve to fourteen can read these books, but younger children enjoy hearing them, too.

ALICE CREW GALL FLEMING CREW

The Tail books

The *Tail* books by Alice Crew Gall and Fleming Crew are an important contribution to animal stories. The first of the series, *Wagtail* (1932), is the story of pond life, told from the standpoint of a polliwog. Wagtail's universe is the Blue Pool and the bordering banks, where he must learn to distinguish between friends and foes. Once Wagtail has achieved legs, the old Patriarch frog teaches him the basic law of his kind, which is to jump first at the sight of a strange creature and find out about him afterward. Wagtail remembers this advice when he is idly wondering about an approaching heron. He jumps just as the heron opens his mouth to catch the frog—"another second would have been too late." Decidedly, action is the thing. From the friendly woodchuck, he learns a strange fact: the Blue Pool is not there in the cold months. It is gone completely; only white snow is everywhere. This is baffling, particularly since the Patriarch has told Wagtail about their long winter sleep, buried in mud at the bottom of the pond. But Wagtail is no introspective brooder. He is too busy leaping for life, liberty, and the pursuit of food. The pond is teeming with satisfactions and dangers, but after all, the Patriarch has survived, and so, too, Wagtail feels, will he. The Patriarch hints very gently of a still longer sleep, a sleep from which some warm spring the old frog will not return, and Wagtail will take his place on the old log and be the new Patriarch. This, too, is baffling, but something to be accepted without anxiety. Meanwhile, the sun shines hot and comforting on Wagtail's back, and the pond is clear and blue. Frog life is good, despite these mysteries. Whether it is *Ringtail* the raccoon or *Flat Tail* the beaver, these talking-beast stories are true to the species, and each book gives the reader a clear understanding of a particular species and its ways of life.

Following *Bambi* and the *Tail* books there were no outstanding contributions to this type of animal story until E. B. White wrote his *Charlotte's Web,* which has been discussed in Chapter 12 under fantasy. To be sure, each animal in the book remains true to his species. Wilbur, the silly pig, fights death in every way he knows. Templeton, the rat, fattens happily on the rich garbage of the county fair. And Charlotte, the spider, dies according to the biological laws of her species. But the animals are also embodiments of human folly, greed, and selflessness, and this distinguished contribution to children's literature remains more fantasy than animal lore.

Animals as Animals Objectively Reported

The third type of animal story is the one told from observation, with fidelity to all the modern knowledge of a species. It may deal with animals by themselves in their own world, as reliable observers have seen them, holding their own against their particular enemies and solving their own problems. Or it may deal with human beings and animals together. In this case the animals are most frequently pets—dogs, kittens, or horses—recorded objectively as human beings see them. The animals are permitted no thoughts, except as people guess at them, and no language other than the barks or whines or purrs or cringing or hissing or exuberant cavortings appropriate to their kind.

Such stories are appearing in increasing numbers and are on the whole the most popular of all types of animal books with children over seven or eight. In these stories, the child finds himself a spectator in a humorous or tragic or dramatic series of events whose import he cannot always fathom. He finds himself looking in on an unfamiliar world, enough like his own so that it rouses his curiosity and sympathy but so strange that he cannot predict what will happen. He knows the mother creature will defend her young at the risk of her life, even as the human mother will, but the animal mother's means of defense will be strange to him and her defeat or triumph uncertain. He tries to guess at what his dog is pleading with him to do, but he may not guess right and so may blunder on a happy or a tragic solution of the dog's difficulty. It is the element of uncertainty in these objective modern animal tales that makes them more convincing and more exciting than other types. If such stories are genuinely true to animal nature and abilities, they constitute an excellent source of enlightenment and engrossing entertainment for the modern child, especially the city child.

DOROTHY LATHROP

Who Goes There?
Hide and Go Seek

There are some outstanding picture books designed for the youngest child which give equal delight to adults and to all ages in between. Dorothy Lathrop's *Who Goes There?* (1935) pictures in exquisite drawings the

No modern artist can draw the small, furry creatures of field and forest more exquisitely than Dorothy Lathrop. Beautiful in composition, in line and balance, in the fidelity of every detail, her pictures arouse in the observer a feeling for the spirit and beauty of these small animals.
From Who Goes There? *by Dorothy Lathrop. Copyright, 1935 by The Macmillan Company. Reprinted by permission of the publisher. (Book 9¼ x 8)*

small creatures who come to eat the food left for them in the snowy forest. Chipmunks, red squirrels, gray squirrels, rabbits, field mice, a crow, a porcupine, and even flying squirrels come to the feast. By way of an index, their tracks are recorded behind each animal. Here is a book to take out and look at again every winter. Children who study these pictures will know these animals intimately. In *Hide and Go Seek* (1938), Miss Lathrop has drawn the flying squirrels from birth to maturity, in every type of activity, until this tiny nocturnal animal is as familiar as a pet dog. One teacher, never having seen flying squirrels in the flesh, knew them instantly from these pictures when they began to come and go on her window sill after dusk, for all the world like small flashes of furry lightning. In time, the food and quiet allayed their fears, and she could observe how truly Miss Lathrop had recorded her own living models. Miss Lathrop's art has already been discussed (p. 64), but nowhere is it finer than in these two books.

E. BOYD SMITH

Chicken World

An old picture book that should never have gone out of print is E. Boyd Smith's *Chicken World* (1910). It should be chosen to introduce every city child to domestic fowls. In brilliant colors, the old rooster struts proudly with every fiery feather shining. The hens are soft, motherly creatures with their fluffy chickens to train and guard. Ducks and turkeys add variety, but interest centers on the chicken family, which is carried through perils and escapes. Along the border of each colorful page, flowers, fruits, or vegetables mark off the succeeding months. Here information and beauty go hand in hand.

MARY AND CONRAD BUFF

Dash and Dart
Forest Folk
Hurry, Skurry, and Flurry
Elf Owl

Mary and Conrad Buff have made a number of beautiful picture-stories for young readers and pre-readers. *Dash and Dart* (1942) tells about the first year in the lives of twin fawns. *Forest Folk* (1962) continues the story of Dash to the time when he fights his way to become king of the herd. *Hurry, Skurry, and Flurry* (1954) are three forest squirrels, frolicsome but aware of the lurking danger which always threatens them and finally catches up with one. The tiny *Elf Owl* (1958) looks out of his home in a spiny saguaro cactus and views the drama of desert creatures from a safe distance. The pictures in these books have a poetic beauty that matches the cadenced text. The stories read aloud beautifully and provide a background of understanding for the more complex animal stories to come. (For additional discussion, see p. 63.)

MARJORIE FLACK

The Angus books
The Story about Ping

Realistic animal stories for the youngest children are on the whole a cheerful group containing some excellent pictures and some of the children's favorite tales. Early favorites were the dog stories of Marjorie Flack.

The *Angus* books are worn to shreds by athletic young devotees of four or five. *Angus and the Ducks* (1930), the first of the series, is typical. Angus is a small, curious Scotch terrier. Even as he dozes on or under his favorite sofa he wishes to get out and discover things for himself. One day his chance comes. He runs out the open door, through the hedge, into the next garden. There he encounters some strange creatures who go "Quack, quack, quack." He barks at them and they run away. This is very satisfactory to Angus, and he feels well pleased with himself. He explores the ducks' territory, but suddenly they turn on him, both of them, and, with a terrible "sssing" and flapping of wings, they chase him through the garden and through the hedge back to his own house. There the terrified Scottie takes refuge under the sofa and forgets to be curious for all of three minutes. A simple enough narrative, you may think, but just try to do something like it. Here at the simplest level are all the elements of a good plot—a problem, action, and a surprising, humorous climax and conclusion.

The Story about Ping (1933), with pictures by Kurt Wiese, carries the children to China, and so it is generally allocated to the sixes and sevens, although the fours enjoy it thoroughly. Ping is a duck, a youthful member of a large duck family living on a boat in the Yangtze River. In the morning all the ducks walk down a gangplank and go swimming in the river. Toward evening they return to their boat, and the last duck to waddle up the gangplank always gets a little spank from a small switch. Ping, returning late one evening, decides that he won't submit to this spank, and so he hides in the rushes all night. The next day all sorts of things happen to him. Finally, he is captured by a strange family which intends to cook him, but a kind-hearted boy sets him free. Ping hastily returns to his own family. Home and security, even with a spank, look good to the adventurous young duck after the dangers he has endured.

The story is told with a directness that makes ducks on the Yangtze River as understandable and homey as ducks on the local duck pond, and the prodigal Ping receiving his spank gratefully is an amusing final touch. No need to moralize. "Home's best after all" is written all over Ping's contented acceptance of the family pattern. Kurt Wiese's pictures add to the fun of the story.

LYND WARD

The Biggest Bear

A delectable comedy is Lynd Ward's *The Biggest Bear* (1952), which won the Caldecott Medal almost by public acclamation. Young Johnny is so mortified because his family has no bearskin nailed up on their barn door that he sets off to capture a bear all by himself. He does it, too, and brings it home alive. That bear grows and grows and grows, and Johnny's problems grow right along with the bear. The solution, like most things in life,

Conrad Buff can be counted on for a beautiful portrayal of wildlife in its natural setting.
From Elf Owl *by Mary and Conrad Buff. Copyright © 1958 by Mary Marsh Buff and Conrad Buff. By permission of The Viking Press, Inc. (Book 6⅝ x 9⅞)*

Lynd Ward's magnificent picture of a docile but ungainly bear and a determined boy has a droll humor that tells the whole story.
From The Biggest Bear *by Lynd Ward.*

(Book 7¾ x 10½)

is a compromise, but not half bad for either Johnny or the bear. Adults are as captivated by this story and its heart-warming pictures as the children are. (For an additional comment on Mr. Ward's illustrations, see p. 67.)

CLARE TURLAY NEWBERRY

Mittens
Babette
Barkis
Percy, Polly, and Pete

Clare Turlay Newberry's little books have no importance as literature, but as exquisite picture books for the youngest they are unexcelled. Her cats have a fluffy, furry look that fairly tempts you to touch them, and so have the woolly snowsuits and the hair of the children. There is a softness, a rotundity, and a depth of textures in her pictures to which children and adults respond with equal delight. These pictures are made by a person who loves the feel of cats, puppies, and babies. She draws them lovingly and happily, and children respond with "Ohs" and "Ahs" of delight.

Mittens, Babette, Barkis, and *Marshmallow* are cat stories, but they also include one puppy, one rabbit, and the children. *Percy, Polly, and Pete* is the amusing story of an old mother cat who tries to hide her three kittens, in order to protect them from the strenuous affection of two-year-old Shasha. This is Mrs. Newberry's nearest approach to a plot, but the tender appeal of her pictures and the kindliness that pervades the stories make them worth while.

TOM ROBINSON

Buttons

A distinguished picture-story which has never enjoyed the popularity it deserves is *Buttons* (1938) by Tom Robinson, superbly illustrated by Peggy Bacon. There have been innumerable stories about fluffy kittens, Siamese exotics, and felines of various ages and colors, but *Buttons* is the first tale about an alley cat, the son of an alley cat, a hero to the last scratch. Born in an ash can, orphaned at six weeks, fighting his way to the kingship of the alley mousers—how he managed to leave all this behind and attain cleanly security makes a grand tale. These are not pretty cats, and starvation looks out of their gaunt faces, but they have desperate courage and the will to live. Perhaps for these reasons *Buttons* shouldn't be given to all four-year-olds, but from five on children can well afford to pore over these pictures and sympathize with the forlorn but unquenchable hero, Buttons.

C. W. ANDERSON

The Blaze stories
Salute

The first author to give young children adequate horse stories is C. W. Anderson. His books range in their appeal from the five-year-old level to high school. They are good, substantial stories with splendid drawings of horses by a man who knows every muscle, every stance, and every cavorting of these big, amiable creatures. The books begin for the five-year-olds with *Billy and Blaze* (1936), the simple story of a little boy who gets his first pony and names it Blaze for the star on its forehead. Children of five like the *Blaze* stories, but slow readers of eight and nine or even ten will read them with pleasure also, because of the horse pictures and the direct style of the narratives.

In addition to the *Blaze* books, Mr. Anderson has written stories of the race horses he knows so well. He has child characters in these books, too—horsy children who read everything there is to read about the great racers and study horse training humbly and devotedly. One value of these books is the picture they give of the patience needed to make a racer. *Salute* and *High Courage* are great favorites. Fine human relationships are to be found in all the Anderson stories.

He wasn't dressed like a king,
But he was King of the Alley.

Notice the background details of this picture —alley trash, desperate cat motherhood, feline starvation! These heighten the effect of the central figure, Buttons, cat desperado, powerfully drawn, complete in every detail of battle-scarred courage.
Illustration by Peggy Bacon. From Buttons *by Tom Robinson. Copyright 1938 by Tom Robinson and Peggy Bacon. Reprinted by permission of The Viking Press, Inc.*
(Book 8¾ x 12)

MARGARET AND HELEN JOHNSON

Barney of the North

Each of the many dog stories written and illustrated by Margaret Johnson and her mother, Helen Johnson, deals with a particular species, and the plot turns upon that species' peculiar abilities in a particular line. For instance, the collie's latent talent for herding sheep and the Newfoundland's swimming power are turning points in *Black Bruce* and *Barney of the North*. Too many of these books at once are tiresome because the plots are so similar. But young dog lovers may enjoy a few of them, and they are useful with slow readers.

GLEN ROUNDS

The Blind Colt

The Blind Colt (1941) by Glen Rounds is a mildly sad horse story for children eight to twelve. It is humorous and moving, and is, besides, a completely satisfying "Western."

Whitey watches a blind colt until he wants it more than any other colt on the range. His uncle tells him it must be shot, and the boy is inconsolable. Finally he wins a reprieve for the blind but spirited animal. When it survives all the dangers of a hard winter and marauding wolves, Whitey begins the colt's training. His success convinces Uncle Torval that this is really a smart colt and will make a good "Sunday horse" at least. So Whitey keeps his colt and the colt finds security.

Written in the cowboy vernacular, this book makes an instant appeal to boys. The pictures by the author convey some of the excitement of the colt's adventures. *Blind Colt* is followed by several good Westerns with young Whitey as the resourceful hero.

MARGUERITE HENRY

King of the Wind
Brighty of the Grand Canyon

Today's children and many adults believe that Marguerite Henry is probably the most successful writer of horse stories we have ever had. Her success rests on a sound basis. Every book represents careful research, the stories measure up to the highest standards of good storytelling, the animal heroes are true to their species, and the people in her books are as memorable as the animals.

Justin Morgan Had a Horse (1954) is an example of the careful research Mrs. Henry puts into a book. For this book she conducted an intensive search for information about the ancestor of the Morgan breed and the people responsible for establishing it. It is the story of a poor teacher and singing master who accepted two horses in payment for a debt. One of them was a big, handsome creature and the other was a runt of a colt. It was Justin Morgan's young pupil, Joel, who saw in the colt a rare combination of intelligence, strength, and willingness. In fact, Joel loved the colt, which he called Little Bub, and began to train him. When the horse showed that he had both strength and speed, men began to exploit him. Joel, because he was too poor to buy his beloved horse, had to stand by and see Little Bub overtaxed but a winner in a pulling bee. After that the horse was matched against thoroughbreds in a race, and later he was sold out of the state. The story of the reunion, years later, of Joel and Bub is as moving as the Clint and Smoky reunion. Bub lived to achieve new honors, sire innumerable colts, and establish the Morgan line.

The artist's love for and knowledge of fine horses shows in every line of his horse pictures. Here a handsome mare guards her foal. And even in the lines of that coltish body, we see, in the alert ears and proud lift of the head, the makings of a great horse. Illustration by Wesley Dennis. From King of the Wind *by Marguerite Henry. Copyright 1948 by Rand McNally & Company, publishers. Reproduced by permission of the publisher. (Book 6½ x 9¼, picture 2¾ x 2⅛)*

Misty of Chincoteague followed the history of the little wild horses on the island of Chincoteague, Virginia. Mrs. Henry wrote *Sea Star, Orphan of Chincoteague* a few years later, but in between was the Newbery winner, *King of the Wind* (1948). For this story, the author pursued the history of the great Godolphin Arabian, which changed the physical conformation of race horses and sired a line of thoroughbreds from which Man o' War was descended. It is one of the most exciting and moving horse stories ever written, and it is enormously popular with both children and teachers.

If *King of the Wind* had not won the Newbery Medal, *Brighty of the Grand Canyon* (1953) certainly would have. It is the story of the legendary burro, wild and solitary, whose hoofs galloping up and down the walls of the Grand Canyon are said to have made that terrifying path known as Bright Angel Trail. Brighty is the most winning of all Mrs. Henry's four-footed heroes. He is a comic, like all burros, but lonely too. His search for companionship, his loyalty to those who are kind to him, and his gay flights back to freedom make a thrilling story of animal and human adventure.

What gives these books by Marguerite Henry their unique quality? First of all, she can make the true pattern of animal life so vivid that readers identify themselves with it. Yet the animals are never humanized. With complete integrity to their species, these creatures exhibit traits that children most admire in human beings—fortitude, loyalty, and a blithe zest for life.

In every book there are memorable people. There is the mute in *King of the Wind,* who suffers doubly with his horse because he cannot tell people what they are too stupid to discover. And there is Joel, a bound boy unable to save Little Bub from sale but loyal in his search for the Morgan. Grandpa and Grandma and Maureen and Paul in *Misty* and *Star* are as endearing as the horses and as true. No reader will ever forget Uncle Jimmy Owen, who befriends and aids Brighty but lets him go his own free way. Finally, Mrs. Henry creates such absorbing stories that her remarkable writing skill has never received due credit. Reread the dialogue in these books. It moves and flows with the fluidity of real speech, with delightful overtones of homely philosophy. The descriptions are vivid and often beautiful, and they never bog down the story nor the reader's interest in the action and characters. In *King of the Wind,* read the dramatic account of the rape of Roxana, the famous mare, by the Godolphin Arabian. The facts are made clear, yet with so light and swift a touch that the chapter can be read aloud without embarrassment. Marguerite Henry's vigorous prose never lapses into sentimentality or overemotionalism, even in such moving scenes as Joel's dramatic reunion with the broken-down Bub. All these qualities mean good writing.

Children are delighted to learn that on Mrs. Henry's little farm there is a fine Morgan horse and a modern near-relation of Brighty. Moreover, the real Misty lived there in clover, adored by young Brighty, until Mrs. Henry decided to take Misty back to the island from which she came. There Misty now has foals of her own, stronger perhaps because of Misty's years of good care and feeding on the Henry farm.

On a mountainside near Warrenton, the horsiest of Virginia's horse-loving communities, lives Wesley Dennis, the illustrator of Marguerite Henry's most famous books. So remarkable are Mr. Dennis' identification with and interpretation of these stories in his pictures that both children and adults think of text and illustrations as an inseparable whole. Beautiful color and a feeling for the country as well as the characters make the illustrations a delight. And the humor and tenderness of his *Brighty* pictures are something special. Together, this gifted author and artist have also made the beautiful *Album of Horses* and *Wagging Tails; an Album of Dogs.* May their good books continue.

JOSEPH WHARTON LIPPINCOTT

Wilderness Champion

Joseph Lippincott, publisher by vocation and naturalist by avocation, writes engaging stories, chiefly about wild creatures. *Wilderness Champion* (1944) is the story of a red setter pup which is lost in the mountains and raised by a black wolf. Through field glasses his master sees the dog hunting with the wolves. Reddy is a powerful dog in prime condition, and his companion is a huge black wolf the men call King. His master recovers Reddy only because he comes upon the dog caught in an illegal trap. Nursing the dog back to health in the forest where he found him, the master is conscious of the black wolf hovering near. One morning he discovers that Reddy has been moved and his wounds thoroughly licked; so the master knows that King, the old wolf, has been there in the night helping his friend. Meanwhile, the dog is developing a fondness for the man and goes with him to his cabin, where the other dogs, which are actually his brothers, help establish Reddy's liking for the place and his sense of belonging there. Reddy becomes a man's dog, and his friend the wolf disappears for a while from that part of the mountains. Reddy is taught to hunt with men and is taken south and entered in field trials where he wins all contests—but he is dispirited. Finally his master takes him back to his own mountains and turns him loose. Reddy sets off at once at his old wolf pace, loping up the mountains toward wolf country. How he finds King and stays with him faithfully until his death is the most thrilling part of the tale. With King gone, Reddy is lost for a while; then he returns to his master, a man's dog again.

Wahoo Bobcat is the still more unusual story of the friendship that developed between a huge bobcat and a small, solitary boy. The story centers on the bobcat's struggle to survive in a changing environment where he is ceaselessly pursued by the hunters and their dogs. *Phantom Deer* deals with the battle one old man wages to save the gentle miniature deer of the Florida Keys from total extermination. It takes government action to save the deer and old Hickey too. For younger or less skilled readers Mr. Lippincott has written *Striped Coat, the Skunk.* It is the story of a war between skunk and farmer, with humor and final success for the skunk.

The human characters in these stories are of secondary importance. However, these tales of the wilderness life of hunted creatures are scientifically accurate, and in the process of reading them children develop deeper understanding and sympathy.

PAGE COOPER

Amigo, Circus Horse

Franz is the fifteen-year-old son of a famous rider of Lippizan horses, meticulously trained in the advanced techniques known as *haute école.* Franz too is learning this art. Why then should he have lost his heart to Amigo, a nervous and unreliable palomino horse? Two other circus youngsters are Franz' best friends. Mulk is the son of a Hindu lion tamer and expects to be an animal man also. Dolores is an Argentine orphan, cared for by the snake charmer and studying to be an equestrienne like her famous mother. In their brief leisure the three young people are boon companions, but first and foremost they are professionals, each one dedicated to perfecting his art. There is a friendly rivalry among them to see which one will make the big center ring first.

In the course of time and after some harrowing experiences, Franz obtains Amigo for his own and undertakes his training both in stability and in *haute école.* It is a study in patience and persistence. In the end, all three youngsters have made the big center ring, each in a star act. This book gives children the most intimate picture of circus life we have. They see the domestic life of the performers and their daily self-disciplined work. The animal handlers are there, brave, patient, and knowing. There are terrifying emergencies. The animals—the big cats, the horses, the elephants—are as individual as the human performers. The farewell performance of the trained elephant, old Sadie, a wonderful trouper, is a moving climax to a colorful story.

PHILIP DUFFIELD STONG

Honk: the Moose

There is so much inevitable sadness about animal stories that it is a satisfaction to remind readers young and old that *Honk: the Moose* is a tale of sheer hilarity. Written in 1935 and joyously illustrated in color by Kurt Wiese, it is the story of a huge moose which insists upon being housed and cared for during the Minnesota winter. There is no attempt to present scientific animal lore in this perennial favorite—just a problem moose on the loose!

WILL JAMES

Smoky

One of the greatest animal stories for children is the Newbery winner for 1927, *Smoky,* told and illustrated by the cowboy Will James. Fussy adults are sometimes shocked when they read the author's preface:

> *I've never yet went wrong in sizing up a man by the kind of a horse he rode. A good horse always packs a good man, and I've always dodged the hombre what had no thought nor liking for his horse or other animals, for I figger that kind of gazabo is best to be left unacquainted with. (p. v)*[2]

Then the story begins:

> *It seemed like Mother Nature was sure agreeable that day when the little black colt came to the range world, and tried to get a footing with his long wobblety legs on the brown prairie sod.*

2. Selections from *Smoky, the Cowhorse* by Will James, copyright 1926 by Charles Scribner's Sons. Used by permission of the publishers, Charles Scribner's Sons.

Smoky is written in the vernacular of the Western cowboy, his everyday speech, with something of the easy, loping style of his riding too. There are such verbs as *knowed, figgered, throwed, sashayed*—not academic English, but the cowboy's lingo! And there are horsy words like *stud, mare, stallion,* and *gelding.*

If a teacher is going to use *Smoky* with a class, particularly one made up of city children, she had better clear up the horsy words in advance. List on the board all the new words that are likely to cause difficulty and refer the children to the dictionary. Then tell them something about horses: how the stallion is responsible for the herd of mares and colts that follow him; how his leadership depends upon fighting off not only enemies but young stallions who would like to take over his leadership; and how the mares and the young colts he has fathered are loyal to him only as long as he can maintain his supremacy against all newcomers. Then remind the children that even if they sometimes forget the words they have looked up and are confused by other words, they should go on reading and the story will usually make the meaning clear.

In *Huckleberry Finn,* Mark Twain uses a vernacular which includes several dialects. *Smoky* is not nearly so hard to read as *Huck,* but it is difficult for the child who has become word conscious to the point where he is held up by each unfamiliar phrase. A good reader will swing along in spite of individual words, because *Smoky* reads as people talk, with an ease that carries some of the spellbinding qualities of a good storyteller. You don't interrupt *him* to get the meaning of every word, but you catch the main intent and action of his story.

This writing as people talk has been popularized by such authors of adult fiction as Ernest Hemingway and John Steinbeck. Will James did it effortlessly in *Smoky.* Don't let the bad grammar deceive you into thinking for one moment that this is a crudely written story. It is composed with consummate art. If children are troubled by the large number of strange words or such highly descriptive phrases as *crowhopped, hightailed,* and the like, a little help in the beginning will tide them over these minor difficulties, and they will get from this easy narrative a portrait of a horse they will never forget.

The story is simple, but the details are rich and absorbing. Smoky is a little range colt "fetched up" by his mammy and by his own high spirits and intelligence. When it comes his turn to be broken, he puts up a terrific fight, but he has the luck to fall into the skillful hands of the cowboy Clint, who loses his heart to this spunky, handsome pony. Smoky is broken and trained but will allow no one to handle him except Clint. The little horse gains a reputation for being the finest cow pony on the range and is Clint's special pride. Then Smoky is stolen by a vicious half-breed who treats the horse so cruelly that he turns into a killer. Under the name of The Cougar, he fights all rodeo riders until he is worn out.

Who but Kurt Wiese could draw a huge, ungainly moose with a soulful eye that pleads for all the comforts to which he is unaccustomed? Fierce jungle animal, powerful sea creature, or hopeful moose, Wiese draws them all with sure skill. Illustration by Kurt Wiese. From Honk: the Moose *by Phil Stong. Copyright, 1935, by Phil Stong. Reprinted by permission of the publisher, Dodd, Mead and Company. (Original in color, book 8 x 9¾)*

Then he is sold to a livery stable. There he is overworked and uncared for, and he is foundered by an ignorant rider. From this experience he recovers only partially and is sold to a vegetable vendor, whose cruelty equals the half-breed's. Clint, in town for a rodeo, discovers his horse at last, a broken-down nag. Clint beats up the vendor and takes his horse. Smoky does not even know him. Back at the range where he was born, old Smoky is fed, rubbed, doctored, and presently turned out in the spring sunshine with the colts. Still he does not know Clint, but the little colts—yes, he knows just what to do about them:

The cowboy could near see the horse smile at the little colts. . . .

"Daggone his old hide," says the cowboy, "it looks to me like he's good to live and enjoy life for many summers yet. . . ."

Weeks pass before Smoky returns to the barn and nickers for Clint:

Clint dropped his bucket in surprise at what he heard and then seen. For, standing out a ways, slick and shiny, was the old mouse-colored horse. The good care the cowboy had handed him, and afterwards the ramblings over the old home range, had done its work. The heart of Smoky had come to life again, and full size.

No briefing of this book and no excerpts give any idea of its power. The sad parts are so moving it is almost impossible to reread them in detail, but lovers of this book will read over and over the colt days and the happy youth of Smoky. Never once does the author sentimentalize or humanize his horses. If children are going to weep over animal stories, here is one that is worth their tears.

MARY O'HARA

My Friend Flicka
Thunderhead
Green Grass of Wyoming

My Friend Flicka, Thunderhead, and *Green Grass of Wyoming,* a trilogy by Mary O'Hara (Mary Sture-Vasa), were written for adults but have been appropriated by the children who can read them. They deal with the biology of horse breeding on the McLaughlins' ranch, where the problems are complicated by a bad wild-horse strain from a white stallion they call the Albino. Ken, the juvenile hero of *My Friend Flicka* (1941), falls in love with a colt from this strain. When he is finally allowed to choose a young horse for his very own he chooses—to his father's distress—this half-wild filly, which he later calls Flicka. His father warns him that he will never be able to break her, that the whole breed is "loco"—crazy. When the boy begins to work with the horse, she lives up to her reputation. Her fights for freedom are harrowing to read about. She nearly kills both Ken and herself. Finally, the boy is told Flicka is dying from her self-inflicted injuries. Unable to sleep, Ken gets up in the night and finds the horse half under water in a stream to which she has dragged herself. All night long he holds her in that icy water, keeping her head up. When the family finds the pair in the morning, Flicka is on the mend, but the boy is desperately ill from the exposure. Ken lives to see his horse gentled at last, as tractable and intelligent as any. Ken apparently is right about Flicka, but the father is not convinced. Through both of these books runs the conflict of the strong-willed father and son, much alike, loving each other dearly, but critical of each other, too, because they are so much alike. Family relationships are strained from time to time but on the whole are understanding and affectionate. The horses are the center of interest for the whole family.

Thunderhead (1943) is the name given to Flicka's first colt, which, to everyone's horror, turns out to be pure white. This means that Flicka has mated with the Albino, and the loco strain will be intensified in the colt. Indeed, Thunderhead has intelligence, tremendous speed, but complete instability. This story of Thunderhead runs off in three directions. First there are the falling fortunes of the father with his horses and the consequent rift between him and his devoted wife. Then there are Ken's ups and downs in trying to make a racer of Thunderhead. Finally, there are Thunderhead's own excursions back to the great canyon and the mesa, where he encounters his father, the Albino. In the end Thunderhead goes back to the wild strain from which he came. Ken and his father complete the separation. They blow up the rocks in the gorge, dividing, so they think, the wild horses from the ranch and bidding farewell to the untamable Thunderhead. *Green Grass of Wyoming* shows Ken growing up, and includes a teen-age romance.

THEODORE J. WALDECK

On Safari
The White Panther

Theodore J. Waldeck has written some unusually fine stories of jungle animals in their native haunts. His autobiographical *On Safari* (1940), besides being an amusing account of himself as a cub explorer, contains some unforgettable pictures of the jungle creatures. This book is popular with teen-age boys. Of the stories, *The White Panther* (1941) is a favorite. It follows this rare, beautiful, and hunted creature from cub days to maturity. Life is mostly eating, sleeping, stalking prey, killing, and eating again, broken only by fights with enemies and accompanied by a continual alert against man. Ku-Ma, with his coat like faintly dappled white velvet, is an appealing creature only because of his uncanny beauty. He is a sleek bundle of appetite and ferocity, though, unlike man, he kills only to eat or to preserve his life. His perils are many, especially from man, who hunts his rare pelt. How Ku-Ma escapes even the clever man-made trap is the triumphant conclusion of the book. The Waldeck stories leave the reader with no delusions about the possible sweetness and light of these wild creatures. Rather they build up in his mind a respect for their skill, resourcefulness, and courage.

MARJORIE KINNAN RAWLINGS

The Yearling

Although *The Yearling* (1938) by Marjorie Rawlings was written for adults, many children have appropriated it even as they have appropriated adult books in every generation. It is a beautifully written story of a lonely boy, living in the primitive wilds of inland Florida with his family and his pet deer, Flag. Jody is only a boy when the story begins, as full of play as his fawn. But life as hard as that of the Baxters makes for an early maturing of young things. Penny Baxter, the father, realizes that his son's period of play will be almost as brief as the deer's, and he watches Jody and Flag with sad tenderness. Together the boy and the deer frolic and grow, make mistakes and are punished, only to forget and play again. Finally Flag, the year-old deer, begins to eat the family's scanty crops as fast as they grow. There is not enough food for the maturing deer and the family. Penny knows the dreaded time has

In all the pictures Wyeth made for this book, the light has an almost incandescent quality. Notice how the lashing storm is emphasized by the dark frame of the barn and the boy's tense figure.
Illustration by N. C. Wyeth. From The Yearling *by Marjorie Kinnan Rawlings. Charles Scribner's Sons, 1939. Reprinted by permission of publisher. (Original in color, book 6¾ x 9)*

come to make Jody face facts; Flag must be shot. The boy is frantic and will not listen to his father. Penny is bedridden and so cannot do what needs to be done. The tragedy of those last hours of the boy with his deer are too much for Jody, and he runs away. When he returns, father and boy talk together for a long time. Penny says, "You've takened a punishment. You ain't a yearlin' no longer." That night, in the beginning of his sleep, Jody cries out, "Flag!"

It was not his own voice that called. It was a boy's voice. Somewhere beyond the sinkhole, past the magnolia, under the live oaks, a boy and a yearling ran side by side, and were gone forever.

This poignant story of growing up is more boy than deer, but it turns upon a child's devotion to a pet. Not all adults understand how deeply rooted such a love can be. The child feels that the animal not only loves him but depends upon him and trusts him. Yet he may be called upon to give up his pet, send it away, or have it "put to sleep." A child so forced to betray the creature which loves him may suffer just as passionately as Jody did over Flag. And that suffering, as adults also fail to realize, is compounded of bitter, if temporary, hatred for those who demand such a sacrifice, as well as of lacerating sorrow over the loss of the loving and beloved creature. Not all children have the wise tenderness of a father like Penny to come back to. There was a father who could help his son grow up. Penny could not spare his son pain, but he could help him understand the reason for the pain and give him the courage to stand it. Children who have suffered these heartbreaking separations from a loved and loving pet may read *The Yearling* or *Sea Pup* or *Good-bye, My Lady* over and over. A better catharsis for such pent-up emotions could hardly be found.

No comment on *The Yearling* is complete without a word about its illustrator, Newell Convers Wyeth. A happier choice of an artist to interpret this story could not have been made. Wyeth journeyed down to the hammock country of Florida to study both the land and the people. The results were pictures so true and yet so imaginative that they represent a high point in the remarkable achievement of this dean of illustrators of children's books: Jody running over the sandy road with the sunlight on his blond hair and Flag stepping daintily, the sunlight making an aureole around his pretty head and lean, graceful body; or Jody and Penny in a wild, ecstatic dance of triumph over the slaying of old Slewfoot, the bear; or Jody sitting on the floor in front of the fire with his arms around Flag, boy and deer older now—dangerously older—with something of the gaiety of fawn and little boy gone out of them. These are beautiful pictures, pictures which interpret this splendid story of a boy's maturing as perhaps no other artist could have done.

N. C. Wyeth has created a Jody as he created a Long John Silver in *Treasure Island*, a Robinson Crusoe, and many other juvenile heroes so that they remain forever the image of the character. (See 10 in color section, Chapter 4.)

JAMES ARTHUR KJELGAARD

Big Red
Snow Dog
Swamp Cat
Haunt Fox

Jim Kjelgaard, as he always signs himself, writes dog stories as excellent as Marguerite Henry's horse stories. His books are equally absorbing, with fine literary quality and the very breath of the wilderness blowing through the pages. His dogs are so lovable and courageous, so true to their breeds and devoted to the men who love them, that the people in these books are of less importance than the dogs.

Beginning with *Big Red* (1945), Mr. Kjelgaard has written three books about the champion Irish setters in Mr. Haggin's kennels. Ross Pickett and his son Danny care for, train, and completely devote themselves to the "Irishmen" above all other breeds of dogs. In the first story, Danny and Big Red both prove their mettle in a series of exciting adventures culminating in the tracking down of a great bear.

In *Irish Red, Son of Big Red,* Mr. Haggin imports some English setters and a new trainer. When the Picketts leave, Mike, the "mutton-headed" son of Big Red, trails them. Their winter in the woods is rugged for all of them, but when they return to the kennels, Mike is a disciplined and worthy son of Big Red and maintains the glory of the Irish dogs against the English. *Outlaw Red,* the third book, is almost all dog. Pampered Sean, another son of Big Red, is lost in the wilderness and is almost shot as a suspected sheep killer. Bewildered and lonely, the dog makes a painful adjustment to his new life. The story of how he manages to survive, secure a mate of his own breed, and raise his pups may stretch the long arm of coincidence a bit, but it is convincingly told. This is an enthralling series of books for dog lovers.

Snow Dog (1948) tells a haunting story of a wilderness pup, part Husky and part staghound, that lives wild until a trapper befriends it. This is a dramatic tale of hardships, courage, and devotion.

Jim Kjelgaard has written other dog stories and stories about other animals. His *Swamp Cat* is a remarkable story of an independent wilderness cat's devotion and aid to a hard-pressed woodsman. And in *Haunt Fox* the much hunted fox wins the admiration of the boy and dog who have pursued him. In all his books, Jim Kjelgaard interprets the world of nature truthfully and shows the nobility and courage of animals.

MICHEL-AIME BAUDOUY

Old One-Toe

Old One-Toe (1959) is a variant of the master fox versus the master hunter, but it is enlivened by four delightful children, two unique adults, an earnest hunting dog, and a clown of a city dog intoxicated with country life. The four children, who have come from Paris to live on their aunt's chicken farm, are horrified when a fox destroys her whole brood of young chickens. They vow they will get the fox, old One-Toe. Under the master hunter, the boy Piet begins to track the fox without a gun. Observing the creatures of the forest, including the fox, Piet comes to love their wildness and resourcefulness. By the time the big hunt is organized, Piet and the other children are secretly on the side of old

Here is a powerful picture of a predatory owl making off with Andy's muskrat. Contrasting areas of black and white, swirling lines, and bright lighting of the owl against the darkness reveal the conflict. Illustration by Edward Shenton from Swamp Cat *by Jim Kjelgaard. Copyright, 1957, by Jim Kjelgaard. Reprinted by permission of the publisher, Dodd, Mead & Company. (Book 5¼ x 7⅝)*

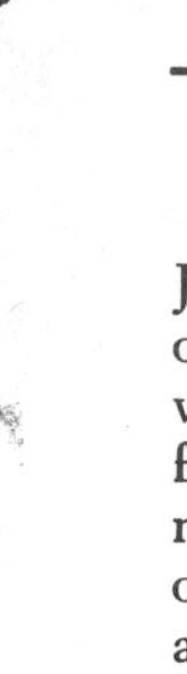

In all the books by this remarkable husband-and-wife team, Jean George's pictures invariably capture the wildness and wariness of forest creatures. With a few brush strokes she makes them so real you can sense the bone and sinew that lie under their fur. The beauty of the wilderness is suggested as well.
From the book Masked Prowler: The Story of a Raccoon *by John and Jean George. Illustrated by Jean George. Copyright, 1950, by John and Jean George. Reproduced by permission of E. P. Dutton & Co., Inc. (Book 5½ x 7¾)*

One-Toe. The hunt is a comedy of errors for the hunters, complicated by the children and their wildly excited, unsportsmanlike dog. It is near tragedy for One-Toe and his vixen, but the children save them. This well-written book is full of the outdoor magic of fields and forests, the gallantry of hunted creatures, and lively characterizations of both the children and the adults.

JOHN AND JEAN GEORGE

Vulpes, the Red Fox

John George, zoologist, and his artist wife, Jean, have turned their unusual combination of talents to the production of books about wild animals. In most of the books the story follows the animal's life cycle: his discoveries, mistakes, and escapes; his mating and raising of young; and his continual search for food and struggle against enemies—always with death just around the corner.

The hero of *Vulpes, the Red Fox* (1948), for instance, is known to every hunter for his superb pelt, his raids on barnyards, and his skillful escapes from both dogs and men with guns. Actually, Vulpes is so swift and so powerful that he sometimes courts the hunt to enjoy the befuddlement of the hounds, or at least so the hunters think. Meanwhile, readers follow his search for a mate. Rejecting a nervous weakling, he courts a strong, handsome vixen, a worthy mate. Cubs are born, and the relentless battle for food continues. Finally, one unwary moment, death comes to Vulpes at the hands of the hunters. Yet somehow this inevitable ending is not sad. Vulpes has lived a zestful life. He has loved the sun on his fur, the excitement of the chase, and the sweetness of mate and cubs. And death comes swiftly, a good end.

Masked Prowler follows a similar pattern except that at the finish old Procyon, the aged raccoon, after an epic battle with the dogs, retires in triumph to lick his wounds and become a forest myth. The animal hero in *Vison, the Mink* is too bloodthirsty to be appealing. *Bubo, the Great Horned Owl* is one of the most dramatic of these stories. Most of us know little about great horned owls, the "tigers" of the forest. Their size and the ferocity of their hunting would seem to make them invulnerable. Instead, they are hunted by every creature in the forest in one way or another. Twice Bubo's fledglings are destroyed. With a third brood, Black Talon, the female, is killed, but Bubo manages to raise his young to maturity. The book ends with Bubo facing the winter alone.

Although *Meph, the Pet Skunk* follows the amusing development of the skunk, it is chiefly the story of the reclamation of an eroded farm, and of an unhappy farmer and his disturbed teen-age boy. It is a fine story for young people. This book foreshadows Mrs. George's immensely popular *My Side of the Mountain* (see p. 445).

In all of these books, both the writing and the wonderful illustrations show acute observation and a scientific knowledge of these woodland creatures and their habitat.

EMIL E. LIERS

An Otter's Story

A more lovable creature than the playful, affectionate, fresh-water otter doesn't exist. That it should be so ruthlessly hunted by farmers is hard to understand. Mr. Liers tells a delightful story of one otter family and makes clear their harmlessness as well as their usefulness to the balance of nature both for farmers and fishermen. The story is based upon long observation, and every incident is vouched for. Tony Palazzo's handsome illustrations are as spirited as the text.

SHEILA BURNFORD

The Incredible Journey

The year 1961 saw the publication of two remarkable animal stories, *The Incredible Journey* and *A Stranger at Green Knowe.* The former is a detailed account of three heroic animals who travel through two hundred and fifty miles of Canadian wilderness to the place and people that mean home and love to them. A young red-gold Labrador retriever instigates the journey and leads the way. A Siamese cat and an old English bull terrier complete the triumvirate. The old bull dog gives out first, and the cat feeds him till he regains his strength. The cat is the most competent of the trio, and even after he is half drowned he manages to rejoin his companions and keep them going. The retriever gets a face full of porcupine quills which fester. Then cat and terrier bring him the kill, so he can lap the blood when he cannot chew anything. Mauled by bears, nearly starved, attacked by a bobcat, delayed by the blandishments of occasional human beings they encounter, the trio, led by the retriever who never loses his sense of direction or purpose, traverse a final fifty miles of such hazardous forest terrain the rangers say they cannot possibly survive. The reunion with the human beings they love is an unforgettable scene, written with restraint and integrity. The animals are never humanized or sentimentalized, and this beautifully written saga of three gallant animals is a superb story to read aloud either in the home or classroom.

In his illustrations for The Incredible Journey, *Carl Burger has captured perfectly the noble, invincible spirit of these three animals. His drawings have a marvelous three-dimensional quality. The artist, like the author, has a sure knowledge of animals—notice the resting dog's alert ears.*
Illustration by Carl Burger. From The Incredible Journey *by Sheila Burnford.*

(Book 5½ x 8¼)

LUCY M. BOSTON

A Stranger at Green Knowe

Green Knowe, an old English manor house, is associated with three remarkable fantasies, the most notable of which is *The Children of Green Knowe* (p. 344), so it comes as a surprise to find that *A Stranger at Green Knowe* (1961) is completely realistic. It is the story of Ping, a small Chinese refugee, and Hanno, a thirteen-year-old gorilla, two displaced creatures who have known years of dreary gray cement. They meet in a dismal zoo, the gorilla inside a cage, the boy outside. The boy gives the gorilla his peach, and they eye each other with what seems to the boy complete understanding. Later, by a series of coincidences, they meet in the small, dense forest of Green Knowe. Both have escaped their prisons, both are happy in the freedom of this green wildness, and they adopt each other. But they are too close to civilization to be safe, and the story moves inevitably toward a tragic conclusion. It is nobly met by both Ping and Hanno. The peace of Green Knowe is temporarily shattered, but there is new hope for Ping, thanks to the remarkable Mrs. Oldknow. The introductory picture of the gorilla tribe in its native jungle and the horrible hunt that leads to the capture of Hanno are scenes no reader will ever forget. Mrs. Boston is one of the most distinguished writers in the juvenile field, and while this book will not enjoy the popularity of *The Incredible Journey*, *A Stranger at Green Knowe* is a powerful and original book no child should miss. It too reads aloud magnificently. (See illustration, p. 6.)

Criteria for Judging Animal Stories

These three groups of animal stories (discussed under Ourselves in fur, Animals as animals but talking, and Animals as animals) could be subdivided, but there is no point in spinning the distinctions too fine. These categories are important only because they call attention to diverse purposes and points of view in these stories and because they suggest somewhat our approach to and judgment of such stories.

Unquestionably, the group of books in which the animals strut about with the same virtues and foibles as human beings is the gayest. In the stories about Babar and Ferdinand, in *Horton Hatches the Egg* and *Rabbit Hill,* these absurd animals are doubly funny because they parody the people we know. The stories in this group are mostly animal comics, with *Rabbit Hill* and *The Wind in the Willows* striking more serious and mature notes. These beast tales are chiefly for children three to seven years old, with a few for the tens and even twelves. Of the folk-tale type we ask only good entertainment and good style. Such stories to be sound must be true to human, not animal, nature, and they must be told with light-hearted wisdom.

The stories of animals scientifically represented, with the exception of their power to think and speak, are a more serious group. In the *Tail* series and similar stories for children from seven to ten, disasters and death are gently suggested but unmistakably present. *Charlotte's Web* remains light-hearted until death impinges at the end. In the stories for older children, nine to twelve, there are the real hardships and suffering, the cruelty and tragedy of books like *Bambi*. Such stories induct children into the hard lives of animals, constantly threatened by other animals, natural forces, and man.

This hybrid literary form is likely to become sentimental or to present an overly humanized animal. But the *Jungle Books* are scrupulously true to the nature and the ways of each species, in spite of endowing it with speech. In short, when animals are described as animals but talking, their behavior and their problems must be only those of their animal world.

The third type of story in which the animals are objectively portrayed must be completely scientific and convincing. This means that the criteria for these and the second type of animal story (Animals as animals but talking) are much alike. The difference lies in the fact that in this third type the author may never interpret the animals' motives or behavior through giving the animal speech or thought. He may guess at the motives of his animal hero, but those guesses must accord with the interpretation of animal behavior as reliable observers have recorded it.

The books in which animals are objectively recorded as animals are a growing and increasingly popular body of stories for children from seven or eight to maturity; these stories range from mere thrillers to substantial literature. They may be as gay and humorous as *Honk: the Moose,* but they are likely to be harrowing or tragic. The authors do not necessarily wish to play on the reader's emotions merely to rouse or hold interest, but the lives of most animals, whether wild or domestic, run into tragedy sooner or later. It has been said that wild creatures rarely die a natural death. The books show this to be true. Even pets are subject to the changing fortunes and whims of the human beings to whom they belong. They may be sold or given away or misunderstood to a tragic degree. Such dramatic situations make up the plots of many of these tales, and such stories are almost unavoidably melancholy.

If the animal hero is sufficiently appealing or the human and animal relationship sufficiently strong, such tragedies will attract readers even to a poor story. In these strongly emotional plots we need to be more than ordinarily alert to what is a true and consistent story, and to what is pure animal melodrama. A little melodrama or a few trashy books are not going to hurt children, but they should not miss the great animal tales in a welter of second-rate ones.

There is rarely any need to urge children to read stories about animals. From Marie Ets' entrancing *Play with Me* they discover how shy the wild creatures are and how quiet must be the approach of human beings. Pet stories bring out the child's desire to nurture and protect, and, as he matures, he learns about the piteous vulnerability of animals at the hands of cruel masters or hunters and trappers. Such stories encourage a compassionate sense of kinship with animals. Many of these books teach sex casually in the course of an absorbing story. This is true of *My Friend Flicka,* the books by John and Jean George, and many others. For city children who have little or no knowledge of breeding and the raising of young, these stories are especially valuable. From the stories that center on the proper training of dogs and horses, young readers gain a background for the training of their own pets.

Some of these books have special values. *The Yearling, Sea Pup* (see p. 443), and *Good-bye, My Lady* (see p. 443) are all centered on boy heroes but involve a relationship with a unique pet that is so full of mutual love and dependence that it could retard the boy's development. Why it doesn't makes these stories especially worth while.

Best of all, these four-footed heroes display the very qualities that children most admire in human beings–courage in the face of danger, fortitude in suffering, loyalty to cubs, mate, or master, and finally, a gay, frolicsome zest for life that is much like the child's own frisky, coltish enjoyment of each day. These are all good reasons why the child enjoys fine books about animals.

Since the mere nature of the wild animal's life means chiefly pursuit or being pursued, escape or death; and since the drama of a pet's life turns upon the upsetting of its happy security with a tragic or triumphant outcome, there is bound to be a certain similarity in these tales. Too many of them in a row are monotonous or overly harrowing. Such stories should be read along with other books. But any child is the richer for having had his sympathies expanded and his tenderness stirred by such great animal books as *Smoky, Big Red, Buttons, Sea Pup,* and *The Yearling.* Any child is the poorer for having missed the drama of the *Jungle Books, King of the Wind, The Incredible Journey,* and *A Stranger at Green Knowe.*

SUGGESTED READING, PROBLEMS, AND PROJECTS

Suggested Reading: *Story about Ping, Ferdinand, Who Goes There? Buttons, The Biggest Bear, Billy and Blaze, Elf Owl,* one of the Marguerite Henry books, one of the Jim Kjelgaard books, *Honk: the Moose, Wagtail* or *Bambi, The Jungle Books, Smoky, The Incredible Journey* or *A Stranger at Green Knowe.*

1. Give examples, from the books you have read, of each category discussed in this chapter. How well does each fulfill the standards for its type? Have you discovered a preference for any particular type among preschool or middle-grade or upper-grade children?

2. Which of the animal picture-stories did you like best? Why?

3. If you were using *Smoky* or *King of the Wind* or *My Friend Flicka* with children eleven or twelve years old, how would you handle the special vocabulary and the questions the new words provoke?

4. How do Wesley Dennis' illustrations for the Henry books or Wyeth's for *The Yearling* contribute to the story? Have you discovered any animal book that could be helped by better pictures?

5. If you read *The Jungle Books* as a child, how does the opinion you had then of the books compare with the one you have now? Why?

6. What special values did you find in either *The Incredible Journey* or *A Stranger at Green Knowe?*

7. Can you justify the popularity of either the Henry or the Kjelgaard animal books?

8. The examples cited in this chapter are only samplings of good animal stories of different types. Give examples not discussed in this chapter which you feel have special values. Justify your choices.

REFERENCES

Note: For other stories about animals, see also Bibliographies for Chapters 12 and 15.

PICTURE-STORIES

ANDERSON, CLARENCE. *Billy and Blaze,* ill. by author. Macmillan, 1936.

———. *Blaze and the Forest Fire,* ill. by author. Macmillan, 1938.

———. *Blaze and the Gypsies,* ill. by author. Macmillan, 1937.

———. *Blaze Finds the Trail,* ill. by author. Macmillan, 1950. 5-8

BUFF, MARY and CONRAD. *Dash and Dart,* ill. by Conrad Buff. Viking, 1942.

———. *Elf Owl,* ill. by Conrad Buff. Viking, 1958.

———. *Forest Folk,* ill. by Conrad Buff. Viking, 1962.

———. *Hurry, Skurry, and Flurry,* ill. by Conrad Buff. Viking, 1954. 5-8

DELAFIELD, CLELIA. *Mrs. Mallard's Ducklings,* ill. by Leonard Weisgard. Lothrop, 1946. A beautiful picture book with brief text of the seasonal cycle from egg to winter flight. 5-8

DENNIS, MORGAN. *Burlap,* ill. by author. Viking, 1945. A worthless farm dog suddenly proves himself by helping to capture an escaped circus bear. 6-8

FLACK, MARJORIE. *Angus and the Cat,* ill. by author. Doubleday, 1931.

———. *Angus and the Ducks,* ill. by author. Doubleday, 1930.

———. *Angus Lost,* ill. by author. Doubleday, 1932. 4-7

———. *Restless Robin,* ill. by author. Houghton, 1937. Mr. Robin starts north in February and finally arrives in New Hampshire with the spring. 6-8

———. *The Story about Ping,* ill. by Kurt Wiese. Viking, 1933. 5-8

———. *Tim Tadpole and the Great Bullfrog,* ill. by author. Doubleday, 1934. 5-8

———. *Topsy,* ill. by author. Doubleday, 1935. 4-6

———. *Wag-Tail Bess,* ill. by author. Doubleday, 1933. 4-6

FREEMAN, DON. *Fly High, Fly Low,* ill. by author. Viking, 1957. Scenic San Francisco offers a colorful background for this picture tale of a pigeon which temporarily loses its mate when their electric-sign home is moved. 6-8

FRITZ, JEAN. *Fish Head,* ill. by Marc Simont. Coward, 1954. Fish Head was a scarred old wharf cat full of fight and swagger. By accident, he went to sea and found that it was the life for him. 7-10

GEORGE, JEAN. *Snow Tracks,* ill. by author. Dutton, 1958. Distinctively illustrated nature picture-story of animal tracks and of a boy who followed them to acquire a whitefoot mouse for a pet. 6-8

HADER, BERTA and ELMER. *The Big Snow,* ill. by authors. Macmillan, 1948. Beautiful pictures of small animals preparing for a winter that was worse than they dreamed. With the aid of human friends they survive. Caldecott Medal. 6-9

———. *Squirrely of Willow Hill,* ill. by authors. Macmillan, 1950. A lost baby squirrel winters luxuriously in the McGinty home, and in the spring returns to his own world. 7-9

HOLLING, HOLLING C. *Pagoo,* ill. by author and

Lucille W. Holling. Houghton, 1957. A quietly paced, beautifully illustrated life story of a hermit crab. 9-12

JOHNSTON, JOHANNA. *Penguin's Way,* ill. by Leonard Weisgard. Doubleday, 1962. In the cold bleakness of the Antarctic, Emperor Penguins care for their young. A life-cycle picture book of unusual charm and distinction. 5-8

KRASILOVSKY, PHYLLIS. *The Cow Who Fell in the Canal,* ill. by Peter Spier. Doubleday, 1957. After a tumble into the canal, Hendrika, the cow, climbs on a raft and is soon drifting down to the city. Beautiful Dutch scenes in crisp clear colors. 6-8

LATHROP, DOROTHY. *Bouncing Betsy,* ill. by author. Macmillan, 1936. 6-10

______. *Hide and Go Seek,* ill. by author. Macmillan, 1938. 7-10

______. *Who Goes There?* ill. by author. Macmillan, 1935. 6-10

LEAF, MUNRO. *The Story of Ferdinand,* ill. by Robert Lawson. Viking, 1936. 5-

MCNEER, MAY. *My Friend Mac,* ill. by Lynd Ward. Houghton, 1960. An orphaned and fast-growing moose provides plenty of diversion for lonely little Baptiste of the Canadian woods. 7-9

MINARIK, ELSE. *Little Bear,* ill. by Maurice Sendak. Harper, 1957. Other books in the series include *Father Bear Comes Home* (1959), *Little Bear's Friend* (1960), and *Little Bear's Visit* (1961). 4-8

NEWBERRY, CLARE. *April's Kittens,* ill. by author. Harper, 1940. When April's cat Sheba has kittens, April's father agrees to move from a one-cat to a two-cat apartment.

______. *Babette,* ill. by author. Harper, 1937.

______. *Barkis,* ill. by author. Harper, 1938.

______. *Marshmallow,* ill. by author. Harper, 1942.

______. *Mittens,* ill. by author. Harper, 1936.

______. *Percy, Polly, and Pete,* ill. by author. Harper, 1952.

______. *Smudge,* ill. by author. Harper, 1948. A mischievous kitten grows into a cat. 5-8

PALAZZO, TONY. *Bianco and the New World,* ill. by author. Viking, 1957. A gentle little Sicilian donkey and an unruly circus horse become inseparable friends after an encounter in a blacksmith's shop. Large, impressive brown-toned drawings. 5-8

ROBINSON, TOM. *Buttons,* ill. by Peggy Bacon. Viking, 1938.

______. *Greylock and the Robins,* ill. by Robert Lawson. Viking, 1946. A gay story, with a happy ending, of a battle between an old cat and a mother robin. 6-9

SMITH, E. BOYD. *Chicken World,* ill. by author. Putnam, 1910. 4-10

SOJO, TOBA. *The Animal Frolic,* ill. with reproductions from the drawings of Kakuyu. Text by Velma Varner. Putnam, 1954. 6-8

TRESSELT, ALVIN. *The Rabbit Story,* ill. by Leonard Weisgard. Lothrop, 1957. The little wild rabbit lost her freedom to become a pet and then escaped to raise her own family. An appealing nature story beautifully illustrated in brown tones. 4-7

______. *Under the Trees and Through the Grass,* ill. by Roger Duvoisin. Lothrop, 1962. Scurrying one by one through colorful tree-filled pages, woodland creatures tell of their activities. Last of all comes a little boy who has been happily observing them all. A childlike nature tale in Tresselt's lilting prose. 5-7

WARD, LYND. *The Biggest Bear,* ill. by author. Houghton, 1952. Caldecott Medal. 5-8

BOOKS FOR READERS EIGHT-ELEVEN

ANDERSON, CLARENCE. *High Courage,* ill. by author. Macmillan, 1941. 10-13

______. *Salute,* ill. by author. Macmillan, 1940. 9-12

ARUNDEL, JOCELYN. *Simba of the White Mane,* ill. by Wesley Dennis. McGraw, 1958. In an exciting tale of Africa young Toki saves a lion from the ruthless safari leader. Handsomely illustrated, and with an underlying theme of animal conservation. 9-12

BELL, THELMA HARRINGTON. *Yaller-Eye,* ill. by Corydon Bell. Viking, 1951. Through Randy's negligence his cat loses a foot, and there is conflict between father and son as to whether the cat should be spared. A good story of mountaineer life and of a boy's love for his pet. 8-11

BULLA, CLYDE. *Star of Wild Horse Canyon,* ill. by Grace Paull. Crowell, 1953. The disappearance of the wild white horse which Danny has so carefully trained creates a mystery in this easy-to-read Western story. 7-9

CLARK, BILLY C. *The Mooneyed Hound,* ill. by Nedda Walker. Putnam, 1958. Jeb's handicapped dog proves his mettle as a hunter in the field trials.

______. *The Trail of the Hunter's Horn,* ill. by Veronica Reed. Putnam, 1957. Jeb's happiness in his new hunting dog was crushed when the puppy proved to be half blind. Two distinctive stories of Kentucky mountain life, rich in human values. 9-11

COGGINS, HERBERT. *Busby & Co.,* ill. by Roger Duvoisin. McGraw, 1952. Keeping a beaver as a pet is not easy, as Jerry Gardner soon realizes when the beaver's instinct to chew creates situations both funny and tense. 8-10

COOPER, PAGE. *Amigo, Circus Horse,* ill. by Henry Pitz. World, 1955. 12-16

DE JONG, MEINDERT. *Along Came a Dog,* ill. by Maurice Sendak. Harper, 1958. The sensitive reader will respond to this slowly paced, beautifully told story of a crippled red hen and the stray dog who protected her. 10-12

______. *The Last Little Cat,* ill. by Jim McMullan. Harper, 1961. The timid seventh kitten strays away from his friend, the old blind dog, and encounters many cat enemies before he reaches home and safety. 8-10

______. *The Little Cow and the Turtle,* ill. by Maurice Sendak. Harper, 1955. This story of a friendly little cow who follows her turtle companion onto the railroad tracks reaches a powerful climax as both barely escape an oncoming train. A beautifully written book with a fascinating rhythmic quality for reading aloud. 8-12

ENGELHARD, GEORGIA. *Peterli and the Mountain,* ill. by Madeleine Gekiere. Lippincott, 1954. No one really knows what made Peterli, the cat, climb the Matterhorn, but climb it he did, with the aid of a friendly guide. An amusing tale based on a true incident. 8-12

GALL, ALICE CREW, and FLEMING CREW. *Flat Tail,* ill. by W. Langdon Kihn. Walck, 1935.

______. *Ringtail,* ill. by James Reid. Walck, 1933.

______. *Splasher,* ill. by Else Bostelmann. Walck, 1945. A flood is a great adventure for a young muskrat and his friends.

______. *Wagtail,* ill. by Kurt Wiese. Oxford, 1932. 8-10

GATES, DORIS. *Little Vic,* ill. by Kate Seredy. Viking, 1951. When Pony River, a Negro boy, sees Little Vic, he believes the colt will be as great as his sire, Man O' War. The boy endures every hardship willingly in his devotion to the colt. 9-12

HENRY, MARGUERITE. *Black Gold,* ill. by Wesley Dennis. Rand McNally, 1957. Because his trainer opposed an operation, a gallant horse died at the height of his racing fame. Another true horse story by a popular author-artist team. 10-13

______. *Born to Trot,* ill. by Wesley Dennis. Rand McNally, 1950. The true story of Ben and Gib White, trainer and owner of a famous trotting mare, with a good deal of history of trotting races.

______. *Brighty of the Grand Canyon,* ill. by Wesley Dennis. Rand McNally, 1953.

______. *Justin Morgan Had a Horse,* ill. by Wesley Dennis. Rand McNally, 1954.

______. *King of the Wind,* ill. by Wesley Dennis. Rand McNally, 1948. Newbery Medal.

______. *Misty of Chincoteague,* ill. by Wesley Dennis. Rand McNally, 1947.

______. *Sea Star; Orphan of Chincoteague,* ill. by Wesley Dennis. Rand McNally, 1949. 9-14

JOHNSON, MARGARET and HELEN. *Barney of the North,* ill. by authors. Harcourt, 1939.

______. *Black Bruce,* ill. by authors. Harcourt, 1938. 7-10

LIPPINCOTT, JOSEPH WHARTON. *Gray Squirrel,* ill. by George F. Mason. Lippincott, 1954.

______. *Little Red, the Fox,* ill. by George F. Mason. Lippincott, 1953.

______. *Striped Coat, the Skunk,* ill. by George F. Mason. Lippincott, 1954.

Authentic life stories of native animals. 9-11

MOWAT, FARLEY. *Owls in the Family,* ill. by Robert Frankenberg. Little, 1962. A funny and heartwarming story of two owls of Northern Canada, told by their youthful rescuer. 9-12

REYNOLDS, BARBARA. *Pepper,* ill. by Barbara Cooney. Scribner, 1952. This amusing story of Alec's attempt to domesticate a baby raccoon and the complications that develop as Pepper matures is especially popular with boys. 8-12

RIETVELD, JANE. *Wild Dog,* ill. by author. Follett, 1953. Jerry's beloved Eskimo puppy, the gift of a Canadian Indian, develops hunting instincts that are a menace in a farm community, and Jerry faces the hard decision of returning him to his natural environment. 10-13

ROUNDS, GLEN. *The Blind Colt,* ill. by author. Holiday, 1941.

______. *Stolen Pony,* ill. by author. Holiday, 1948. Two stories with a background of the Dakota Badlands. With the care and training given by a ten-year-old boy, the blind colt earns his right to live. The sequel tells how the pony was stolen by horse thieves and then abandoned, to make his way home with the aid of a faithful dog. 9-12

______. *Whitey's First Roundup,* ill. by author. Holiday, 1960. Maybe it was an accident that small Whitey roped his first cow, but he had all the fun of feeling like a first-class cowhand. 8-10

SALTEN, FELIX. *Bambi,* ill. by Kurt Wiese. Grosset, 1931.

______. *Bambi's Children,* ill. by Robert Kuhn. Grosset, 1948. 10-14

STOLZ, MARY S. *A Dog on Barkham Street,* ill. by Leonard Shortall. Harper, 1960. In a fine family and animal tale, the visit of Uncle Josh and his handsome collie helps troubled Edward to cope with such problems as the neighborhood bully. 10-12

______. *Fredou,* ill. by Tomi Ungerer. Harper, 1962. Fredou, a Parisian cat of great wisdom, takes a homesick young American boy in hand and provides him with a memorable summer. The French background is a joy in this most delightful tale. 8-10

STONG, PHIL. *Honk: the Moose,* ill. by Kurt Wiese. Dodd, 1935. 9-10

TOMPKINS, JANE. *The Polar Bear Twins,* ill. by Kurt Wiese. Lippincott, 1937. 8-9

WEEKS, SARA. *Tales of a Common Pigeon,* ill. by Eric von Schmidt. Houghton, 1960. In a nature story of rare charm and humor, an "elderly" pigeon recounts the exciting adventures he shared with animal friends in a Boston park. 10-13

WHITE, ANNE H. *Junket,* ill. by Robert McCloskey. Viking, 1955. 9-11

BOOKS FOR READERS TWELVE AND OLDER

BALL, ZACHARY. *Bristle Face.* Holiday, 1962. Orphaned Jase tells his own tale of the unexpected talents of his homely dog, Bristle Face, and of the kindly storekeeper, Lute Swank, who found a home for them. Background is rural Mississippi in the early 1900's. 12-16

BAUDOUY, MICHEL-AIMÉ. *Old One-Toe,* tr. by Marie Ponsot, ill. by Johannes Troyer. Harcourt, 1959. 10-13

BOSTON, LUCY M. *A Stranger at Green Knowe,* ill. by Peter Boston. Harcourt, 1961. 11-14

BURNFORD, SHEILA. *The Incredible Journey,* ill. by Carl Burger. Little, 1961. 11-

CHIPPERFIELD, JOSEPH E. *Wolf of Badenoch,* ill. by C. Gifford Ambler. McKay, 1959. An outstanding tale of the Scottish Highlands and of the vindication of a great sheep dog who was suspected of being a killer. 12-16

CLARK, DENIS. *Black Lightning,* ill. by C. Gifford Ambler. Viking, 1954. Black Lightning, a rare black leopard of Ceylon, regains his jungle freedom after harsh captivity in a shabby little circus. An exciting and well-written wild animal story.

______. *Boomer,* ill. by C. Gifford Ambler. Viking, 1955. An absorbing tale of an Australian kangaroo, orphaned and adopted as a household pet, who later returns to the wild and becomes a leader of his kind. 12-16

GEORGE, JEAN. *The Summer of the Falcon,* ill. by author. Crowell, 1962. A unique story of growing up, in which a sixteen-year-old loses interest in the falcon training that has absorbed her earlier years. The descriptions of the sparrow hawk and its training are the highlights of the book. 12-15

GEORGE, JOHN and JEAN. *Bubo, the Great Horned Owl,* ill. by Jean George. Dutton, 1954.

______. *Masked Prowler; the Story of a Raccoon,* ill. by Jean George. Dutton, 1950.

______. *Meph, the Pet Skunk,* ill. by Jean George. Dutton, 1952.

______. *Vison, the Mink,* ill. by Jean George. Dutton, 1949.

______. *Vulpes, the Red Fox,* ill. by Jean George. Dutton, 1948. 11-14

GIPSON, FRED. *Old Yeller,* ill. by Carl Burger. Harper, 1956. Travis' mongrel dog is bitten by a rabid wolf while loyally defending his family. He becomes infected and has to be destroyed. This is a moving tale of a boy and his dog, set in pioneer Texas of the 1870's. In a sequel, *Savage Sam* (1962), Travis, now fifteen, is aided by Old Yeller's equally gallant son in rescuing two small children from Apache captivity. 11-14

JAMES, WILL. *Smoky, the Cowhorse,* ill. by author. Scribner, 1926. Newbery Medal. 11-16

JOHNSON, JAMES RALPH. *Utah Lion,* ill. by author. Follett, 1962. The wild rugged country near the Grand Canyon is the background for this powerful story of an orphaned mountain lion and his struggle for survival. 11-15

KIPLING, RUDYARD. *The Jungle Book,* ill. by Kurt Wiese. Doubleday, 1932. Ill. by Fritz Eichenberg. Grosset, 1950. 12-14

KJELGAARD, JIM. *Big Red,* ill. by Bob Kuhn. Holiday, 1956.

______. *Haunt Fox,* ill. by Glen Rounds. Holiday, 1954.

______. *Irish Red, Son of Big Red.* Holiday, 1951.

______. *Outlaw Red, Son of Big Red.* Holiday, 1953.

______. *Snow Dog,* ill. by Jacob Landau. Holiday, 1948. 11-14

______. *Swamp Cat,* ill. by Edward Shenton. Dodd, 1957. 12-16

KNIGHT, ERIC. *Lassie Come Home,* ill. by Marguerite Kirmse. Holt, 1940. Lassie, the collie dog, had to be sold because the Yorkshire collier's family was impoverished. The dog's loyalty impelled her to journey back four hundred miles, from Scotland, and her return brought good fortune to the family. 10-16

LEIGHTON, MARGARET. *Comanche of the Seventh,* ill. by Elliot Means. Farrar, 1957. In the life story of Comanche, the horse that survived Custer's Last Stand, the author achieves fine historical fiction and an absorbing animal tale. 11-15

LIERS, EMIL. *An Otter's Story,* ill. by Tony Palazzo. Viking, 1953. 10-13

LINDQUIST, WILLIS. *Burma Boy,* ill. by Nicolas Mordvinoff. Whittlesey, 1953. A thrilling tale of an elephant of the teakwood forests who goes wild, and of young Haji, the elephant boy, who wins his confidence and saves the villagers from disaster. 10-13

LIPPINCOTT, JOSEPH WHARTON. *The Phantom Deer,* ill. by Paul Bransom. Lippincott, 1954.

______. *The Wahoo Bobcat,* ill. by Paul Bransom. Lippincott, 1950.

______. *Wilderness Champion,* ill. by Paul Bransom. Lippincott, 1944. 12-15

LOKEN, ANNA BELLE. *The Colt from the Dark Forest,* ill. by Donald Bolognese. Lothrop, 1959. Sensitively written story of a young Norwegian farm boy who overcomes every obstacle to feed and train the newborn red colt he found in the forest. 10-13

MCMEEKIN, ISABEL. *Kentucky Derby Winner,* ill. by Corinne Dillon. McKay, 1949. A boy-centered horse story of unusual value. It concerns young Jacky Spratt and his devotion to Aristides, the horse which eventually won the first Kentucky Derby. Fine people, good horse lore, and considerable humor make this a memorable story for young readers. 9-13

MAXWELL, GAVIN. *The Otters' Tale,* ill. with photographs. Dutton, 1962. A juvenile edition of the author's memorable nature tale of his otter pets, *Ring of Bright Water.* 12-15

MONTGOMERY, RUTHERFORD. *Kildee House,* ill. by Barbara Cooney. Doubleday, 1949. Story of an elderly would-be hermit who, building a house in the redwood forest, soon finds it filled with small animals and visited by warring children. The tragicomic episodes make this a nature story of unusual sensitivity and beauty. 10-13

MUKERJI, DHAN GOPAL. *Gay-Neck,* ill. by Boris Artzybasheff. Dutton, 1927. Gay-Neck's training as a carrier pigeon in India made him valuable as a messenger in France during the war. Newbery Medal, 1928. 11-14

———. *Hari, the Jungle Lad,* ill. by Morgan Stinemetz. Dutton, 1924.

———. *Kari, the Elephant,* ill. by J. E. Allen. Dutton, 1922. These two stories of East India are rich in atmosphere. The first book is the story of a boy of the jungle and how his meeting with Kari brings good fortune to his family. The second book tells of elephant life and adventure. 11-14

O'BRIEN, JACK. *Silver Chief, Dog of the North,* ill. by Kurt Wiese. Holt, 1933. Silver Chief, half wolf and half husky, is trained by Jim Thorne of the Canadian Mounted Police, and heroically shares his master's adventures in the wild Northwest. 10-14

O'HARA, MARY [pseud. for Mary Sture-Vasa]. *My Friend Flicka.* Lippincott, 1941. 12-

———. *Thunderhead.* Lippincott, 1943. 14-

———. *Green Grass of Wyoming.* Lippincott, 1946. 12-

RAWLINGS, MARJORIE KINNAN. *The Yearling,* ill. by N. C. Wyeth. Scribner, 1939. 12-

VIKSTEN, ALBERT. *Gunilla,* tr. by Gustaf Lannestock. Nelson, 1957. In the loneliness of an Arctic trapper's life, Gunilla, the polar bear cub, becomes an endearing but often dangerous companion. 11-

VOORHOEVE, RUDOLF. *Harimau,* tr. from the Dutch by Jan Fabricius. Day, 1959. A powerful and suspense-filled story of a Sumatran tiger which culminates when he is relentlessly hunted after killing a villager. 12-

WALDECK, THEODORE J. *Lions on the Hunt,* ill. by Kurt Wiese. Viking, 1942. A young lion becomes the leader of his pack, hunted by the people of a Zulu village on the South African veldt.

———. *On Safari,* ill. by Kurt Wiese. Viking, 1940.

———. *The White Panther,* ill. by Kurt Wiese. Viking, 1941. 11-15

chapter 15

Here and Now

"Here and now" may suggest dull and prosaic stories, but actually realistic stories may be every bit as exciting or humorous or romantic or imaginative as fanciful tales. Realistic stories, however, are always plausible or possible. In a realistic story everything that happens *could* happen. Sometimes the adventures of the hero may seem rather improbable but still merit the classification of realistic because they are possible. Sometimes the hero's exploits may be possible but are so extravagant that they are classified as fanciful. On the whole, a realistic story may be defined as a tale that is convincingly true to life.

Modern realistic fiction for children was off to a spirited start with such books as *Hans Brinker, or the Silver Skates, Heidi, The Adventures of Tom Sawyer, The Adventures of Huckleberry Finn,* and *Little Women.* Indeed, later authors of realistic stories for children and youth have produced nothing that is better and a great deal that is distinctly poorer. Strangely enough, this group of notable books had been preceded by such heavy-handed moralizing of the didactic school as "Spiritual Milk for Boston Babes," "The Purple Jar," and *Elsie Dinsmore.* Even more strange, *Hans Brinker, Heidi,* and *Tom Sawyer* were followed by the sentimental sweetness of *Little Lord Fauntleroy* and *Sara Crewe.* While there are signs that moralistic and sentimental didacticism is not wholly dead, present-day realistic fiction is predominantly honest. Authors now assume, as did Samuel Clemens, that children are sensible, normal human beings, interested in how other children and adults get along in the world. On the whole, modern realistic fiction for children includes, along with a great number of mediocre stories, some of the finest children's books ever written.

Realistic stories for children are divided into many categories. There are innumerable stories about peoples of other lands and a growing body of historical novels for children (Chapter 16), animal stories (Chapter 14), and a steadily improving selection of fiction about contemporary life in our own country—the major concern of this chapter. These stories are particularly valuable to children because they throw over everyday life something of the excitement and charm of fiction.

Realism for the Youngest Children

HERE AND NOW, CADENCE AND AWARENESS

Our youngest children, anywhere from two years old to seven, seem to have special need for stories that are as factual and personal as their fingers and toes and the yards and neighborhoods they are beginning to explore. At the beginning of the nineteen twenties, Lucy Sprague Mitchell in her *Here and Now Story Book* called attention to the fact that there were few if any stories for children under five concerned with their modern world. The four- and five-year-olds were given "The Three Little Pigs," "The Gingerbread Boy," and "The Three Billy-Goats Gruff" over and over again. Of course they liked these stories and still do, regardless of motor buses and airplanes. But they should also have been supplied with stories about children like themselves and about the everyday things of their everyday world.

Mrs. Mitchell set out to supply these tales. She did her best with earnestness and sincerity, but she turned away from plot, centered on the child's own activities, and wrote from the child's own talk—using many sensory-motor words and repetitional phrases. She launched the purr, purr, pat, pat school of writing, which offers the young child pitter-patter in place of plot. Nevertheless, her idea of a modern realism for the youngest was sound, and she soon had a devoted group of followers. Mrs. Mitchell's work fulfilled a need which few adults had noticed before.

Dr. Dorothy Baruch, at the beginning of her distinguished career as a writer, carried her notebook and pencil to the nursery-school playground and recorded the children's chants and their picturesque comments on what was happening to them. These she put together with, we assume, some editorial touches, and in book form they were read back to the children in lieu of other literature. Most of these little books are now out of print. They were interesting to adults as examples of the child's way of thinking.

MARGARET WISE BROWN

The City Noisy Book

The most notable of the early followers of Lucy Sprague Mitchell's pattern was, of course, Margaret Wise Brown, who wrote also under the name of Golden MacDonald. It was said that at the peak of her remarkable productivity she turned out some fifty-four books in two years. One of them, *The Little Island,* was so beautifully illustrated by Leonard Weisgard that it won the Caldecott Medal in 1947, and many of the others probably sold because of the irresistible appeal of the artists' pictures. The style of her books was cadenced, the goal was to stimulate the sensory perceptions and awareness of young children.

The Noisy Book (1939) was a pioneer in this awareness school of writing. It was followed by several more *Noisy* books. Then there was a series contrasting bigness and littleness. The hero of *The Little Fisherman* caught little fish and the big fisherman caught big fish, and so it went with *The Little Cowboy* and *The Little Farmer.* Of all these innumerable picture books, some in bright colors, some in pastels, one bound in real fur, and all of them cadenced, two will probably outlive or at least outdistance in popularity all of the others. These are *Little Lost Lamb* and *The Runaway Bunny.* The former tells a real story about a shepherd boy and his dog who retrace their steps up a dangerous mountain after dark to find a lost lamb. This provides substance for Leonard Weisgard's beautiful pictures. *The Runaway Bunny* is a delightful talking-beast tale (p. 356), with the nearest approach to humor that Margaret Wise Brown ever made. Posthumous books have appeared in considerable numbers since her death. Her contribution lies chiefly in her sensitive perception of the child's sensory responses to the big booming confusion of the world. Her cadenced style comes close to poetry now and then, but her attempts at verse never quite reach poetry.

The books by Margaret Wise Brown launched a torrent of awareness compositions for the young. There were books about night sounds, day smells, wetness, coldness, colors, and "plink plink goes the water in the sink." By the nineteen fifties it began to look as if we were in for a kind of pernicious anemia of theme and plot, with language experiences in place of stories and pitter-patter in place of events. These books give the child back himself with little more—no rich entertainment, no additional insight, and no laughter. In the beginning a paucity of humor was characteristic of the here and nowists, and it was not until Beatrice Schenk de Regniers (see Bibliography for this chapter) and Ruth Krauss began their books that hilarity entered in.

RUTH KRAUSS

A Hole Is to Dig
A Very Special House

In 1947 Ruth Krauss' *Growing Story* caused no great stir. It is about a small boy who sees various things growing but does not realize that he too is lengthening until he tries on his last year's clothes. With *A Hole Is to Dig* (1952) Ruth Krauss proved herself a lineal descendant of Dorothy Baruch and became an author whom adults argue about pro and con. This book is a series of definitions by children: "a hole is to dig," "a face is so you can make faces," "mud is to jump in and slide in and yell doodleedoodleedoo."[1] Adults immediately said, "How cute! And just like children." Boys and girls in the upper grades enjoyed experimenting with their own definitions: "ice is to suck and to fall down on," "trees are what you tear your pants on." This is conscious language play for children old enough to know what they are doing and to enjoy giving vent to their pent-up silliness.

A Very Special House (1953) is an imaginative spree by a small child who for once in his life does everything he shouldn't, such as drawing on the walls, jumping up and down on a bed, and shouting "ooie ooie ooie." And nobody ever says "stop stop stop." It ends riotously with a jump and a cadenced "dee dee dee oh." Herein lies Ruth Krauss' particular skill. These examples are not sufficiently extensive to show it, but she uses cadence so cleverly that it is as orderly and lyrical as verse.

Maurice Sendak's hilarious action pictures would predispose anyone to the texts. Like Margaret Wise Brown, Ruth Krauss has been fortunate in all her illustrators.

JOAN WALSH ANGLUND

Love Is a Special Way of Feeling

Then came Joan Anglund, a delightful person who out-wrote, out-drew, and out-sold all the other abstractionists put together. *A Friend Is Someone Who Likes You, Love Is a Special Way of Feeling, Christmas Is a Time of Giving, Spring Is a New Beginning*—the titles suggest the concepts each book develops. Sometimes the examples are objective, but all too often they are nebulous. The children in the pictures are bulging browed and chinless. The total effect is "cute" or "sweet"—both adjectives are used. These books are tiny and pretty and have enjoyed a tremendous vogue. Nostalgic adults buy them for children hoping to make the youngsters conscious of the experiences they are bouncing through so heedlessly, or they buy them for other adults to recall the sweetly precious days of childhood.

The trend toward awareness or mood or abstract concepts can result in books that are painfully monotonous. Scarcely one of these books has a text that can stand on its own without its illustrations. But what about the children for whom the books are intended? When you finish one of these cadenced repetitional abstractions, the child often eyes you with a "So what?" expression, but rarely if ever gives the firm command, "Read it again."

Meanwhile, side by side with the authors of this juvenile stream-of-consciousness kind of writing, other authors were proving that even though stories for children did not follow the "stylized conventions of the fairy tale," they could still be about something of significance and interest to the child. Taking the modern world for a setting, skilled writers have told stories with plot and substance and meaning

1. Copyright 1953 by Ruth Krauss.

that give the child fresh insight into the cause and effect of behavior and, in the process, furnish him with the kind of entertainment that prompts him to command the willing adult, "Read it again."

MARGERY CLARK

The Poppy Seed Cakes

One book of realistic tales which appeared a few years after Mrs. Mitchell's stories was nothing short of epoch-making. *The Poppy Seed Cakes* (1924) broke every one of the canons of realism which had been developed by Mrs. Mitchell. The stories have a Russian atmosphere with beautifully unfamiliar and mouth-filling names like Andrewshek, Erminka, and Auntie Katushka. The children roll them under their tongues and wish they had been given such splendid names. Every story in the series has a lively plot—something happens. Mostly the stories turn upon Andrewshek's irresponsibility. He starts bouncing on the feather bed, and the goose walks in and gobbles up Auntie Katushka's poppy seed cakes. Andrewshek repents, but the next time he forgets to watch the picnic basket. Off it goes down the lake, propelled by a predatory swan. Every story involves plenty of action and laughter.

Here are no stories by a formula but a book full of tales as gay and funny as any fanciful tale could possibly be. Boys recognize themselves in Andrewshek and so delight in his mishaps. Girls see themselves in Erminka with her passion for red boots. The stories have a warm, human atmosphere, which is enhanced by Maud and Miska Petersham's gay illustrations.

BOUNCING UP IN THE AIR FOR THE NINTH TIME

The Petershams' illustrations for The Poppy Seed Cakes *are as lively and vigorous as the gay, humorous text.*
Illustration by Maud and Miska Petersham. From The Poppy Seed Cakes *by Margery Clark. Copyright, 1924, by Doubleday and Company, Inc. Reprinted by permission of publisher. (Original in color, book 5¼ x 7¼)*

ELSA BESKOW

Pelle's New Suit

Another example of realism for the youngest came from the Swedish. It was a translation of *Pelle's New Suit* (1929), told and illustrated by Elsa Beskow.

Text and beautiful pictures in color tell how the little boy Pelle needs a new suit. He raises his own lamb and then, for each person who helps him with his suit, he performs some useful service. He also watches the shearing of the sheep and sees the wool washed, carded, and spun into yarn. He helps with the dyeing and weaving and watches anxiously the important process of cutting the beautiful blue cloth into a suit to his measure. He follows the tailoring even as he assists the tailor. Finally, for his Sunday best he triumphantly wears his beautiful blue suit. This process of making cloth and clothes may be dated, but pictures and text make it understandable and give children a sense of the sequential activities involved in producing a suit of clothes. This is what Mrs. Mitchell was moving toward. A plot for small children need not have elaborate complications if it has enough significance.

LOIS LENSKI

The Little Auto and other stories

Books for the youngest children owe much to the work of Lois Lenski, who pioneered in realism at this level. Her series, beginning with *The Little Auto* in 1934 and continuing with such books as *The Little Sail Boat, The Little Train,* and *The Little Airplane,* tells with lively pictures and the briefest of texts how Mr. Small steers and manages these various forms of locomotion. Trains, airplanes, and all the rest have changed, and unfortunately, even for preschool children, these books are dated. But they pointed the way, and it is easy to understand their great popularity. Mr. Small convinces every child that he too will some day run a train or drive a fire engine. In such books as *Cowboy Small* and *Policeman Small* Mr. Small's varied duties are described. The writing is direct, with no wasted words.

MARJORIE FLACK

Wait for William

Even before the earnest Mr. Small had appeared in *The Little Auto,* Marjorie Flack had begun her famous series about the Scotch terrier, Angus (see Chapter 14). Unlike the Lenski series, every one of Marjorie Flack's little books has a clearly defined plot and delightful humor.

Wait for William (1935) is a delightful "here and now" story whose whole plot turns on a small boy's struggle to get his shoelaces tied. Any four-year-old can understand and sympathize with William's predicament, and so can adults.

On his way to watch a circus parade, being hurried of course by the older children, who never pay any attention when he pleads with them to wait, William just *has* to stop to tie his shoelaces. When he finishes, the children have vanished. Things look dark for William, until suddenly the parade he was waiting for overtakes him. Moreover, he is lifted high on the top of the elephant by a sympathetic circus man and allowed to ride with the parade. Imagine the amazement of the older children when William goes by and waves to them from his exalted post on the elephant's back. Never, never again will they run away from him. From then on they'll gladly "wait for William." A more joyous story of the humble being exalted and the meek inheriting the earth was never told.

Then he dyed his wool himself until it was all, all blue.

Even lacking the vivid colors of the original, this picture shows Elsa Beskow's illustrative strength. Interest is centered on the activity of the boy dipping the skeins in the dye pot and hanging them up to dry. The whole composition is a thing of beauty.
Illustration by Elsa Beskow from Pelle's New Suit. *Harper & Row, Publishers, 1929. Reprinted by permission of Stig Beskow, Stockholm. (Original in color, book 12 x 8¾)*

Marjorie Flack, it is said, not satisfied with privately working over her little story patterns, always submitted them to the critical responses of two different school groups, whose reactions helped her to determine the final form of these tales. This perhaps accounts for their unfailing popularity with children everywhere. Some of these books, certainly *Ping* (p. 405), have become permanent nursery favorites.

ALVIN TRESSELT

White Snow, Bright Snow

Midway between the awareness and the theme-plot schools of writing for young children lie the charming picture-stories of Alvin Tresselt and Leo Politi. Mr. Tresselt constructs his stories from the thinnest of threads —a change in the weather or season. But with Roger Duvoisin's pictures, these themes develop a real sense of drama. In rhythmic prose Mr. Tresselt tells about the coming of snow or rain, wind or a big storm, spring or autumn. These little everyday miracles of the weather he makes exciting, something to be watched and enjoyed, never feared. Text and pictures are full of reassurance and beauty. *White Snow, Bright Snow* won the 1948 Caldecott Medal for Mr. Duvoisin. Charlotte Zolotow does similar books, of which *The Storm Book* is the most dramatic and satisfying.

LEO POLITI

Juanita and other stories

Leo Politi's beautiful picture-stories are simple in theme and plot, frequently centered on the activities of small children living in a homogeneous racial group in the midst of one of our big cities. *Pedro, the Angel of Olvera Street* and *Juanita* (1948) are both about the Mexican-Americans of Los Angeles. The latter describes the pre-Easter ceremony, the Blessing of the Animals, which is celebrated each year on Olvera Street. *Moy Moy* is a little Chinese-American girl celebrating the Chinese New Year (see 24 in color section). In *Little Leo* this author-artist carries his Italian-American child back to the Old World from which his parents came. The story of little Leo teaching all the little Italians how to be cowboys is gay and amusing. A tender understanding of children is reflected in every book and every picture Leo Politi has made, and his smiling, skipping children are a delight.

EDWARD ARDIZZONE

Little Tim and the Brave Sea Captain

Even young children need a touch of wildness now and then, which is precisely what the English Mr. Ardizzone gives them in his spirited account of Tim's adventures at sea. It all starts with Tim, who plays in and out of boats on the beach. How he becomes a stowaway, learns to be an efficient if reluctant deck hand, and experiences shipwreck and a hair-raising rescue in company with the Captain makes a thrilling story for the five- to eight-year-olds. Mr. Ardizzone's water colors are as vigorous as his tale. No wonder his own small boy liked the book. Here is realism for the youngest at its most adventurous level. Tim is a do-it-yourself hero if ever there was one, and his competence and achievements through a series of stories rouse the admiration of his young devotees. Mr. Ardizzone's books introduce other heroes, but Tim is the favorite, and for boys especially the process of identification is valuable. (See additional discussion, p. 66.)

ROBERT McCLOSKEY

Make Way for Ducklings
Time of Wonder

Robert McCloskey was the first artist to win the Caldecott Medal twice, 1942 and 1958. If you look over his beautiful picture-stories—*Make Way for Ducklings* (1941), *Blueberries for Sal* (1948), *One Morning in Maine* (1952), and *Time of Wonder* (1957)—you discover that they are all built on a theme of reassurance. Children know the ducklings will safely come through their first perilous trip in city traffic because their mother has them in charge. Sal, picking blueberries, somehow loses her own mother and follows a much astonished mother bear, but Sal gets safely back to mother. In *One Morning in Maine,* Sal has shed her first tooth and life is plainly ruined. But her mother reassures her, she is merely getting bigger and better teeth like the rest of the family. And finally in that superb book in full color *Time of Wonder,* the safe, secure world of woods and beach is threatened by the oncoming darkness of a hurricane. How the family prepares for and survives this menace is so convincingly told and pictured that children feel they too can meet and endure danger. The black and white pictures in the first three books have humor and strength, and some of the paintings in *Time of Wonder* have a breathtaking beauty. These are all good stories that delight young children and their parents, too. (See comment, p. 68.)

WILL AND NICOLAS

The Two Reds
Russet and the Two Reds

William Lipkind's stories and Nicolas Mordvinoff's pictures guarantee something unique in picture-stories for the youngest. Their first collaboration was the amusing *The Two Reds* (1950), in which Red a city boy and Red an alley cat are pursued by a militant gang known as the Signal Senders. In the second book (1962), Russet, another redhead but a girl, has moved upstairs over the two Reds. They ignore her, but when the Signal Senders pursue again, Russet proves her worth. Once secure, the three go home, a united trio. These are slight stories but they have the realism of city streets. (See comment, p. 68.)

He planted himself in the center of the road, raised one
hand to stop the traffic, and then beckoned with the other,
the way policemen do, for Mrs. Mallard to cross over.

The realistic details in Robert McCloskey's illustrations always provoke an appreciative chuckle. Michael, the policeman, rises to the emergency, and the ducks are safely conducted across the street.
From Make Way For Ducklings *by Robert McCloskey. Copyright, 1941, by Robert McCloskey. By permission of The Viking Press, Inc. (Book 9 x 12)*

HEIDRUN PETRIDES

Hans and Peter

Here is a grave and beautiful book about two little boys who make a dream come true. Written by a fifteen-year-old girl, young enough to know about the fierce urgency of childhood dreams, *Hans and Peter* is one of the most significant picture-stories we have had in many years.

Hans lives in an attic where he can see nothing but roofs. Peter lives in a basement where he can see only people's feet. The boys agree that when they grow up they will build their dream house from which they can see fields and meadows. Their dream seems possible when they accidentally discover a deserted shed workmen had used. It is dirty and dilapidated, but the view is there. After a desperately difficult interview with Mr. Dingelmeyer, the important owner of the shed, the boys carry the project through with brains, brawn, determination, and remarkable ingenuity. Step by step the beautiful pictures in full color, the small pencil sketches, and the text record their efforts. When the dream house is finished, the boys invite Mr. Dingelmeyer, their families, and all who have helped them, to enjoy the view and to join in a celebration.

To dream and to create is the essence of living, and Hans and Peter discover this at an early age.

These beautifully colored pictures by a fifteen-year-old girl are free and fresh. In this particular scene the boys' parents have their first look at the house which has two red walls, a red ceiling, pale blue and white stripes on one wall, and elegant newspaper lace curtains.
From Hans and Peter *by Heidrun Petrides, © 1962, by Atlantis Verlag, Zurich © 1962 translation Oxford University Press, London. Reproduced by permission of Harcourt, Brace & World, Inc. and Oxford University Press, London. (Original in color, book 11 x 10½)*

CAROLYN HAYWOOD

"B" Is for Betsy
Little Eddie

With the *Betsy* and the *Little Eddie* books of Carolyn Haywood, children progress from the picture-story to the illustrated story, with the pictures of secondary importance to the tale. Another mark of increasing maturity is that against a familiar background of family life, the heroes or heroines are moving into a widening circle of neighborhood and school adventures, camps, even travel.

"B" Is for Betsy (1939) launched the series of books about the everyday activities of an everyday little girl in suburbia. Children took Betsy to their hearts immediately. As she grew with each succeeding book, her experiences widened, much as they do in any good set of readers. Other books, about other characters in Betsy's circle of friends, appeared each year. But whether the story was about Betsy or Star or Peter and Penny or the twins, the characters remained very close to stereotypes. It was the interpretation of their activities or the problems connected with school or camp or the school policeman or vacation or typical mistakes and accidents that held the attention of young readers. These gave the child greater self-knowledge, more understanding of other people and experiences, and a greater confidence in approaching the next level of life.

With *Little Eddie* (1947) Carolyn Haywood developed a real boy, and laughter began. Eddie is as earnest as Betsy, but much more alive. He is an avid collector of "valuables," which his long-suffering family calls "junk." But the family endures patiently even an old but full-sized fire engine. However, Gardenia the goat is too much for Father, and Eddie and his pet are banished to an uncle's ranch, far, far away. The picture of ranch life is a bit vague, but not Eddie. He saves Gardenia's life but remains definitely Eddie, traveling home with the largest miscellany of "valuables" ever collected. In the next book, *Eddie's Pay Dirt,* our hero is confronted with a grave ethical problem. His father helps him to see it, but leaves the decision to Eddie. *Eddie and His Big Deals* shows many signs of maturity.

These well-written stories have a warmth and a directness that win and hold young readers.

Forerunners of Realism for Older Children

Before examining present-day realistic stories for older children, it will be helpful to review some of the classics of this group—*Tom Sawyer* (1876), *Huckleberry Finn* (1885), and *Little Women* (1868). The innumerable stories of children of other lands began with *Hans Brinker* (1865) and *Heidi* (1884), which will be discussed in the next chapter.

SAMUEL L. CLEMENS (MARK TWAIN)

Tom Sawyer
Huckleberry Finn

Compared with the Mark Twain pair, recent fiction for children is far tamer, more cleaned-up and respectable, less adventurous. Tom introduced children to the seamy side of village life ninety years ago. At that time, moving pictures, radios, superhighways, super cars, and super gasoline had not tied the small towns so intimately to the large cities that there was little difference between the two. There in *Tom Sawyer* was the isolated country town Samuel Clemens himself had grown up in with respectable churchgoers on one side and the village ne'er-do-wells on the other. Tom was the link between the two groups. By way of his friendship with Huck, the son of the town drunkard, he knew all the shady characters as well as his Aunt Polly's churchgoing friends. He saw a grave robbery and a murder and had other adventures which to the modern child are as incredible as those in any television program he may watch and quite as hair-raising.

Since *Tom Sawyer* was written, children's literature has fallen largely into the hands of women—teachers, librarians, and juvenile editors. Would *Tom* have passed some of these modern censors of subject matter for children's books? Perhaps not, but at least the book is still recommended. It has, however, been pushed higher and higher in the schools until it has finally come to rest in junior or senior high-school book lists—partly because it is stiff reading for the masses of poor readers, who probably will not be able to read it at high-school level either. Its appeal is to children around ten, eleven, and twelve. At those ages, it gives them chills up and down their spinal columns. Few books do this for children today. For spinal chills, they go unerringly to the comics, radio thrillers, and movie horror tales. Men produce these, with no punches pulled. Let's be sure we do not so overrefine children's literature that youngsters have to hunt their robust thrills outside books.

Reread *Tom Sawyer* and see if it doesn't give you a thrill, too. But it is not lurid sensationalism. Along with the excitement and the humor, notice the steady emergence of the boy's code. He keeps his word to a friend; he may be scared to death, but he sees things through. In real peril, he protects a weaker person. He uses his head, keeps cool, and keeps trying. This is as good a code today as it ever was, and for youngsters who are never going to be able to read about Tom and Huck, moving-pictures or television should show authentic versions of these books yearly.

Adult critics are likely to consider *The Adventures of Huckleberry Finn* superior to *Tom,* but most children like *Tom* better. *Huckleberry* is written in the first person, for one thing, and the vernacular is harder to read. Also *Tom* is closer to the average child, more understandable than *Huck,* although to some of our city gangs, *Huck,* if they could read him, might make a stronger appeal. *Tom Sawyer* is one book every American should have at some stage of his life.

LOUISA M. ALCOTT

Little Women

Little Women deals with a family of four girls of teen age, but it is the preadolescent girls to whom this book makes the greatest appeal, because of their interest in what lies just ahead, their first sense of romance, their dream of being grown up. Many girls still enjoy *Little Women* as much as their grandmothers did. There are several books in the series, but none of them, not even *Little Men,* has quite the ageless quality of *Little Women,* and none is so dear to each generation. Here is the first great juvenile novel of family life—a warm, loving family group, struggling with poverty and with individual problems but sustained by an abiding affection for each other and an innocent kind of gaiety that could make its own fun. This is just the kind of home group every child would like to belong to—struggles and all. Not until the Laura Ingalls Wilder series or perhaps Hilda Van Stockum's *The Cottage at Bantry Bay* or Margot Benary-Isbert's *The Ark* or Madeleine L'Engle's *Meet the Austins* do we again encounter such a picture of a family. None of these recent examples is any better, and in no one of them is each member of the group so distinctly drawn as are the unforgettable Beth, Jo, Meg, and Amy. Here is characterization that makes each girl a real human being—exasperating, lovable, heroic, absurd, delightful. Modern writers may well go back to this old book to study its vivid portrayal of people.

In spite of the fact that the March family is eminently respectable and that the girls are idealistic and often noble, the story never lapses into sentimentality. It is quite as full of humor, of a different sort, as *Tom Sawyer.* The humor is decidedly feminine, but it bubbles up in almost every chapter. There is tragedy in the story, too, but not even the sadness of Beth's dying has a false note in it or is even remotely sentimental. In all juvenile literature there is no better example of facing the poignancy of a family loss.

Little Women also provides a wholesome introduction to romance, to the responsibilities and joys of a happy marriage, and to the inevitability of death even among loved ones, who, because they are loved, seem somehow invulnerable. There is a continuity in social relationships, with the home as the necessary core of all happy living. These concepts are as important to growing girls as the boys' code in *Tom Sawyer* is to boys. Both provide insight into group loyalties and group living, not didactically analyzed and underscored but emerging unobtrusively in absorbing stories.

FRANCES HODGSON BURNETT

The Secret Garden and other stories

For a long period after *Tom Sawyer* and *Little Women* appeared, there was as little substantial realism for older children as there was for the youngest. Of course the books by Frances Hodgson Burnett, which began in 1877 with *That Lass o' Lowrie's* and continued until the last book came out in 1922, span the gap between these older books and those realistic stories which are comparatively recent.

When *Little Lord Fauntleroy* was published in 1886, it is said to have "caused a delirium of joy." The moving pictures did beautifully by it in recent years and on the strength of that performance big, husky sixth-graders got it out of the library to read. Their disillusionment was violent. Cedric, they said, was "a pill," a "creep," and worse. Not so the girls. They thought he was "sweet." Probably, even in 1886, the "delirium" sounded a soprano note. *Editha's Burglar,* published the same year, was almost as wildly popular, and *Sara Crewe* (1888) equaled *Fauntleroy.* On stage and in films as *The Little Princess, Sara Crewe* many years later enjoyed a second period of popularity. Other books followed in rapid succession, and little girls of the decorous nineties acquired sets of Frances Hodgson Burnett which were the envy of their less fortunate friends.

These stories purported to be realistic, but what fairy tales they were! Both Fauntleroy and Sara Crewe began by being painfully "poor" but ended, through sheer personal charm and the long arm of coincidence, in almost regal opulence. The Fauntleroy lad passed out of the common sphere entirely by landing in the peerage. Editha encountered a burglar, a hard-looking crook, who after one visit with the girl was restored to the good life. Even her unhappy dolls in that delightful fantasy *Rakketty Packetty House* achieve opulence.

About a quarter of a century after *Fauntleroy,* Mrs. Burnett wrote *The Secret Garden* (1909), which has maintained a following of devoted readers to this very day. It, too, tells a fairy tale of unimaginable riches, of children misunderstood and suffering but conquering all. Mrs. Burnett enjoys describing great wealth and then showing how it often brings neither a normal nor a happy life—very consoling to those who do not possess such wealth. The heroine of *The Secret Garden,* Mary, is plain and bad tempered as well as orphaned and neglected. In the huge estate where she is sent to live, Mary discovers a secret garden, a master with a crooked back, and his ailing son, Colin. Martha, the hearty Yorkshire maid, provides a poor but healthy contrast, and Martha's little brother, Dickon, is the very spirit of the earth as is his wise, kind mother, who has love enough for her own brood of twelve and for the poor little rich children besides. Among them, they get the wretched Colin into the secret garden with Mary. Under Dickon's guidance, the children make the garden grow and bloom once more, without realizing that in the process they, too, will grow and bloom.

Dickon is as unreal as Fauntleroy, but Mary, sour and homely, and Colin, with his temper tantrums, are convincing. In spite of the heavy metaphysical suggestion at the close of the story about the "magic" of the earth and right thinking, this book is probably Mrs. Burnett's most lasting contribution. She could write a spellbinding story, a romantic kind of childhood fantasy, Cinderella almost possible, a dream come true! Reread one of these books today and discover what a spell good writing can weave.

The Modern Scene in America and Great Britain

Samuel L. Clemens and Louisa M. Alcott wrote good realistic stories for children during the nineteenth century, but few authors of children's books in the years that followed could get away from the curse of didacticism. Youngsters, not being articulate about their literary needs, could not say, "Isn't it high time someone wrote stories about just plain everyday children like us?" It was time, and finally someone did, and then others followed suit. Today, children have a wide selection of lively realistic stories which reflect excitingly their own modern world.

ARTHUR RANSOME

Swallows and Amazons and other tales

After the publication of *Old Peter's Russian Tales* (p. 264), Arthur Ransome started a series of stories about English children living in the Lake district of England. These were so popular for a while that children read every book in the series. Now, although their popularity has declined, they still have special values.

Swallows and Amazons (1931) is the first of the series. "The Swallows" are the four Walker children, who wish to camp out completely on their own. When Mother cables their seafaring father for permission, he cables back, "Better drowned than duffers if not duffers won't drown." Decidedly the children are not duffers. They set up shipshape living quarters on their island, establish a regular schedule, get their supplies by sailing to the mainland in their own boat, and have as little to do with the "natives" (adults) as possible. The Blackett girls are the "Amazons," and quite as seasoned sailors as the Walkers. The two tribes agree to make war on each other, with amusing results and considerable excitement. City children may wonder why they weren't all drowned, but lake-raised or seacoast children will understand. A whole series follows. Some of the adventures are genuinely hair-raising, but they are possible for well-trained, competent children, and they are just such adventures as every normal child dreams of. The outstanding characteristic of these Ransome children is their competence. They know how to cook, clean fish, sail a boat, do their own laundry, scour their pans with sand, take care of themselves in a storm, on land or lake. They meet every emergency with resourcefulness and intelligence. No one talks about courage. It is taken for granted like cleanliness and a decent sense of responsibility.

The outdoor atmosphere of these stories is invaluable for indoor children. Everything happens outdoors. It is indeed almost impossible to imagine the Walkers and Blacketts cribbed and confined in schoolrooms or houses. You wonder if they don't perhaps carry their mattresses to the roofs for the winter and become arctic explorers. You also hope their mothers ply them with sufficient greens and milk during the winter to compensate for their somewhat sketchy holiday diets and their amazing consumption of strong British tea.

Two arcs of foliage frame the happy Dickon and Mary as they regard the first crocuses. The rook and fox nestling against Dickon reveal much about the boy. Soft, warm colors and accurate details are typical of Tasha Tudor's distinctive style.
Illustration by Tasha Tudor. From The Secret Garden *by Frances Hodgson Burnett. Copyright 1911 F. H. Burnett. Copyright renewal 1938 by Verity Constance Burnett. Illustrations copyright © 1962 by J. B. Lippincott Company. Reprinted by permission of the publishers, J. B. Lippincott Company. (Original in color, book 6⅜ x 8⅜)*

NOEL STREATFEILD

The Shoes stories

Another Britisher and another popular series are Noel Streatfeild and her "Shoes" books. These extremely gay tales are all vocational in their themes, but they manage to avoid the heavy earnestness that generally pervades such books. The two best ones are *Ballet Shoes* and *Circus Shoes*.

In the first story, *Ballet Shoes* (1937), the three Fossil children determine to become famous, so famous that their names will be in every history book. One is going to be a dancer, one a moving-picture star, and one an aviator. This book follows particularly the training of the would-be ballerina in the Academy of Dancing and Stage Training. The work is hard; there are bitter disappointments and also moments of triumph as brief as they are rare, but always the child's own unwavering determination to succeed keeps her working. How such a story manages to be as gay as it is rests entirely with Noel Streatfeild's ability to make everyday events somehow amusing.

In *Circus Shoes* (1939) we meet poor Peter and Santa, who have been raised to be excessively genteel and never to appear outdoors without their gloves! Suddenly they find themselves running away to the only relative they have left in the world, an unknown Uncle Gus, of Cob's Circus. Uncle Gus is as horrified by his genteel relatives as the poor children are by the rough and ready life of the circus. Presently it begins to dawn upon Peter and Santa that they are surrounded by experts and perfectionists. These circus people are artists, as are even the seals and the poodles; and the children realize their own clumsy helplessness. The account of their getting acquainted with their circus friends, who help them make a beginning in this new life, and the story of their struggles and meager successes make glorious reading for the nine- to twelve-year-olds.

For the child with a special interest in ballet or any sort of theatrical life, these books are valuable. They take a serious attitude toward professions and amplify the difficulties without minimizing the satisfactions.

HILDA VAN STOCKUM

The Cottage at Bantry Bay and other stories

Having spent a childhood divided between Holland and Ireland, and later raising her own family in the United States, Hilda Van Stockum writes delightful stories of family life in all three countries. Children never think of the Irish twins, Francie and Liam, or the tomboy Pegeen as children of a foreign land. They are merely country children, like the mountaineer children of *Down Down the Mountain.*

The Cottage at Bantry Bay (1938) is the first of the series dealing with the O'Sullivan family. The mother and father are poor in this world's goods but rich in understanding and love. Michael and Brigid are resourceful older children, who, entrusted with considerable money, successfully negotiate a perilous journey over the mountains. The twins are alike only in being forever in hot water, and their dog is in more scrapes than the twins. Francie has a clubfoot and there is no money to have it cared for, but this misfortune bothers only his mother and father, not Francie. There are mishaps and sadness, gaiety and triumph in this charming story, but the center of it all is the love of the family for each member of the group. Every episode is satisfying, and the fine human relationships of these obscure people make the book memorable.

Francie on the Run (1939) is a surprising sequel. Money is obtained to have Francie's foot taken care of. A successful operation is performed, but before Francie can be officially discharged from the large city hospital, he walks out. Of course he heads in the wrong direction. Everyone tries to aid this beguiling imp; he has a wonderful time and goes farther and farther astray. He gets home eventually no worse for his travels and much richer in experiences.

In the story of *Pegeen* (1941), Francie is safely home, and a new child Pegeen, an orphan, shares the love of the O'Sullivan family. Always there hangs over their heads the dread day when Pegeen will have to leave them and go to her only relative in America. The happy solution of this problem makes a heart-warming conclusion to the trilogy.

ELEANOR ESTES

The Moffat stories

Within the United States one of the most captivating book families is unquestionably "the Moffats," created by Eleanor Estes. There are three of these books now—*The Moffats* (1941), *The Middle Moffat* (1942), and *Rufus M.* (1943). Some adults consider either *Rufus M.* or *The Middle Moffat* the best of the series, but the children like them all. Here are books in which, for once, children and adults see eye to eye on humor.

The adults in these stories are relegated to the dim background. They are usually in a dither or a fog and rarely understand what the children are up to. The children are equally baffled by the adults, who, well-meaning but oddly dense, wander in and out of their lives, adding to the confusion. Meanwhile, the children go their own way and live their own secret lives, planning intensely and always surprised at the way things turn out.

There is no general theme, no long suspense, and no exciting climax to these books. Each chapter is a complete episode in the life of one of the Moffats. There is dancing school in the genteel atmosphere of Moose Hall with a moose's head looking down severely upon the agonized contortions of the young. Or there is Janey's well-meaning attempt to give a recital, where the ladies she has lured in to listen to her find themselves suddenly enveloped in a cloud of moths from the old organ. All the children do their earnest best. Rufus M. is fired with ambition to possess a library card, but his vicissitudes in trying to get one rival those of Odysseus. Indeed, Odysseus was probably no more surprised to end up in Polyphemus' cave than was Rufus M. to land finally in the bowels of the library coal cellar.

The funniest episode, however, is Janey's performance in a dramatization of "The Three Bears." She carries on mostly without her middle-bear's head, which she mislaid, and she finishes with it on backward, after it has been hastily retrieved and chucked over her head.

Eleanor Estes was awarded the Newbery Medal for *Ginger Pye*. It is not up to the standard of the Moffat books, but she well deserved the Medal as an accumulative award for a unique contribution to children's books.

Louis Slobodkin with only a few lines puts vigor, movement, and personality into small figures. These apparently careless drawings are so rich in meaning that beside them, many an elaborate illustration seems empty. In the Moffat books you will find invariably funny children and adults in every kind of mood and action.
Illustration by Louis Slobodkin. Reproduced from The Middle Moffat, *copyright, 1942, by Eleanor Estes, by permission of Harcourt, Brace & World, Inc. (Book 5 x 7¾)*

Louis Slobodkin—Moffat-maker

The ultimate humor in these Moffat situations is touched off, like a firecracker with a match, by the artist—Louis Slobodkin. The Moffat tales and Mr. Slobodkin's illustrations represent the perfect union of story and pictures. Probably even Mrs. Estes cannot see one of her own Moffats other than as Mr. Slobodkin has drawn him. Rufus M. leaping for a deadly catch in a baseball game; Janey catapulting through big girls with her middy up and her bloomers down, to say nothing of her stockings; Janey, again, viewing the world amiably from an upside-down angle, looking between her own stout legs, head almost on the ground—these are children you see daily. These pictures are obviously drawn by an artist who likes people, who enjoys them as they are without wishing to tidy them up and make them quite otherwise. They are also drawn with a sense of a body under the clothes. Here are legs which support a well-rounded and substantial frame, postures so full of suggested movement that the child seems ready to break into a run. The Caldecott Medal was given to Mr. Slobodkin for his illustrations of James Thurber's *Many Moons* with its frail, wishy-washy princess. Obviously, he should have received it for his hundreds of stout, rambunctious Moffats.

ELIZABETH ENRIGHT

The Saturdays
Gone-Away Lake

Elizabeth Enright has a gift for realism, and her Melendy children in *The Saturdays, The Four Story Mistake,* and *Then There Were Five* are as popular with the ten-, eleven-, and twelve-year-olds as *The Moffats* are with children just a little younger. *The Saturdays* (1941) introduces the four Melendys, ranging in age from six to thirteen, and deals with their $1.60 Saturdays. These are achieved by pooling all their allowances and by permitting one child to use the whole amount for a Saturday on his own. The results are often startling and always amusing. Their adventures in New York City are characteristic of each child, and only poor Mona comes to grief with her experiment. The *Four Story Mistake* and *Then There Were Five* continue the family activities in the country and lead to the adoption of a country boy. All three books show these Melendy children not only playing as children do but also carrying regular responsibilities, learning new types of work, and, like the Streatfeild youngsters, thinking of future careers.

Even so, the Melendy family has been almost superseded by the popular cousins in *Gone-Away Lake* (1957) and its sequel. In the first book, Portia and her cousin Julian discover an abandoned colony of summer cottages near a swamp that was once a lovely, sparkling lake. Two of the cottages are inhabited, one by an old man, the other by his sister, both of whom spent summers there as children. They welcome the cousins, warn them about the treacherous bog, and tell them stories of the past. Most of the chapters provide mild adventures, with several thrillers. In the second book, *Return to Gone-Away* (1961), the family makes the joyous decision to restore one of the old houses and live there the year round. Mrs. Enright's style is so forthright and lively that this unusual setting becomes completely real and the reader shares the family's joy in that final decision.

The Newbery Medal was given to Mrs. Enright's *Thimble Summer* (1938). Here is the germ of a family story which developed more successfully in her Melendy family. The setting of *Thimble Summer* is a Midwestern farm in the midst of a burning drouth. Just as the drouth is broken by a drenching rain,

The expectancy on the faces of the crowd as they await the moment when the safe will be opened is as amusing as the interesting background details in this sketchy pen-and-ink drawing. Illustration by Beth and Joe Krush. Reproduced from Return to Gone-Away, *© 1961, by Elizabeth Enright, by permission of Harcourt, Brace & World, Inc. (Book 5¼ x 8)*

Garnet finds a silver thimble, which she is convinced will bring her a lucky summer. Certainly exciting events follow rapidly. Garnet, her friend Citronella, the boys, and the adults are an entertaining group, and Mrs. Enright's illustrations are pleasant additions.

ROBERT McCLOSKEY

Homer Price

Perhaps Robert McCloskey's most popular book is *Homer Price* (1943). This book, for older children, is a rare commentary on the modern child. In one picture, the "soda jerker" is wiping glasses; Homer is inhaling a coke through a straw; another boy is lost in the pages of the "Super-Duper" comic magazine, while a small child sits on his heels in front of a rack of comics. He is luxuriously licking an ice-cream cone as he broods lovingly over "Crime Does Not Pay," "Marvelous Men of Mars," "General Brave," and "Super-Duper," in endless poses of power and action. Here is a modern American scene, with not a detail missing, even to the cylinder of straws and the old twisted-metal drugstore chairs. But the picture is more than photographic; it is an interpretation of what a child is up to today—his odd credulity, his absorption in this new streamlined magic of the comics.

This is one of the first stories to spoof the comics and their devotees with hilarious results. Homer tried reading the comics but was soon fed up:

"Gosh, Freddy, these Super-Duper stories are all the same," said Homer.

"No, they're not!" said Freddy. "Sometimes the Super-Duper smashes airships and sometimes he smashes ocean liners. Then, other times he just breaks up mountains." . . .

"Shucks!" said Homer. "Let's go pitch horse shoes."

But the Super-Duper made a personal appearance in town, red tights, blue cape, and all. He was almost as terrific as his picture—all about the ELECTRIC RAY. Even Homer might have been impressed if the boys had not later encountered his Super-Duperness with his fancy automobile in the ditch. They hid and watched to see him heave it lightly back on the road again. But he did nothing of the sort. All he did was to get badly tangled up in a barbed-wire fence from which with many "ouches" the boys had to rescue him. Their old horse, Lucy, was also necessary to get his car back on the road again. The boys' disillusionment was complete.

Homer Price shows that Robert McCloskey is not only an artist with a rare gift for humor and interpretative details but a writer who knows today's children. Whether Homer is following a "Sensational Scent," part skunk and part robbers, or assisting with a doughnut machine that can't be stopped, or joining in a pageant celebrating the new prefabricated allotment to the town, the tales and the pictures are caustically amusing. Some of these yarns are a shade too extravagant and too incredible, but they have an astringent humor.

Children eight to twelve like *Homer Price,* and all ages enjoy *Lentil* (1940), which is a juvenile *Main Street.* It is chiefly big pictures of a small town, with a slight tale centered on Lentil's inability to sing and on his consequent devotion to playing the harmonica. Every picture is a gem. You find yourself absorbed in the details: Lentil practicing in the bathtub, the familiar architecture of the small town, the exalted Soldiers and Sailors Monument with the squirrels beneath looking scandalized at Lentil's tootling—these and innumerable other little touches keep you looking and looking again.

BEVERLY CLEARY

Henry Huggins

Probably no reviewer of children's books has forgotten the excitement and fun of reading the first of Beverly Cleary's *Henry Huggins* books in 1950. Pure Americana, from supermarkets to backyard barbecues, the stories are delightfully humorous and they also present a picture of life in these United States that might well represent us to other peoples.

The Huggins family is an average group. The parents are sympathetic to Henry's enterprises but not overly indulgent. All the children in the stories are pursuing their own goals with the frustrations usual to children. The first book begins with Henry's determination to keep and support a stray dog he has acquired and named Ribsy. After Ribsy has been accepted, the next problem concerns the speedy multiplication of a pair of guppies Henry buys at a sale. By midsummer the neighborhood is glutted with guppies and they are occupying his mother's entire supply of mason jars. This is a dilemma, in the canning season! Then when the original owner of Ribsy turns up and claims his dog, Henry is in a still more serious spot. He earnestly wants to do the right thing, but he also wants Ribsy. The solution is a masterly piece of diplomacy.

In *Henry and Beezus,* our hero is trying to earn a bicycle. When he trusts Beezus (Beatrice) to pick him out a second-hand bike at an auction, she gets a fair specimen, but unfortunately it is the wrong sex! Again Henry is cheered when he wins a door prize at the supermarket opening, until he discovers it is fifty dollars' worth of work at a beauty shop! But eventually Henry gets his bicycle, and his family rejoices with him. Each book is built around a real struggle on Henry's part and involves some hilarious situations before a hard-won success.

Beverly Cleary's girl stories are good, too. *Ellen Tebbits'* difficulties are thoroughly appreciated by girls. *Beezus and Ramona* seems a bit more contrived, and Ramona's tantrums seem less interesting than Henry's projects. But the problem of tag-along younger brothers and sisters is a real one to many children, who sympathize with Beezus.

These books may not be gems of literary style, but the characters are real boys and girls, convincingly alive. The picture of a family that must work and plan for its luxuries is a wholesome one. And the situations are thoroughly enjoyable. For example, one boy said to his teacher, who had been reading *Henry and Ribsy* aloud, "I hate to have you finish in case there won't be another Henry book."

E. C. SPYKMAN

A Lemon and a Star

Superior readers ten to fourteen years old will enjoy *A Lemon and a Star* (1955), a unique and genuinely funny book, though a long one for the average child. More completely individualized, flesh-and-blood children than the four motherless Cares youngsters are not to be found in literature.

Thirteen-year-old Theodore is the pompous elder of the tribe, against whom the three younger children are united in a book-long feud. It all starts with Jane's tenth birthday, when Ted gives her a magnificent-looking

Henry and Ribsy brood over the possible profits in guppy raising. The Darling pictures show enterprising young America in realistic and humorous predicaments. Illustration by Louis Darling. From Henry Huggins *by Beverly Cleary. Copyright, 1950, by William Morrow & Company, Inc. Reprinted by permission of the publisher. (Book 5½ x 7¾, picture 4 x 2½)*

package which turns out to be only a lemon! War is on. These children live in the country, and their adventures abroad and in the nearby village are often hair-raising. When the final revolt against Ted gets under way, complete with battle axes, that young man knows it is time to move. He heads for the marsh, and the result is more mud than gore. But Janey, returning from her near-triumph dirty and disheveled, barges right in on a brand-new stepmother. In the end it is "Madam," as Janey calls her, who finally unites the tribe in affectionate amity. *The Wild Angel* and *Terrible, Horrible Edie* continue the adventures of the Cares children.

ARCHIE BINNS

Sea Pup

For most children there comes a time when they are called upon to put away childish things. *The Yearling* (p. 413) and . . . *and now Miguel* (p. 444) both turn upon this necessity. Growing up means taking on responsibility, making decisions with a long-range view of life, and turning away from pleasant immediacy. Because this is hard to do, it is important that children gain some insight into this problem of coming into man's estate before they have to meet it. Fortunately, there are a number of fine books to help them.

In Archie Binns' *Sea Pup* (1954) Clint is a budding oceanographer. He lives on a remote shore of Puget Sound. When Clint finds a day-old seal pup, the family accepts the orphan with many dire warnings. But from the first, Buster is so friendly and so funny that he wins the affection of the whole family, in spite of such misdemeanors as milking the neighbor's cows. Clint is sure he can control his pet by one method or another. Meanwhile, boy and seal swim together, fish, sail, explore, and hunt specimens. The climax comes when a Seattle professor urges Clint to come to the city where he can get the proper pre-college course in science. But what about Buster? Clint's father talks it over with his son but leaves the decision to him, and Clint grows up by facing his problem.

This book has rare values as a family story, as a record of a beguiling pet, and as a presentation of the deep love that can develop between a lonely boy and an animal. It also gives an unusual picture of an intellectual boy living competently in an outdoor world that is beautiful, dangerous, and thrilling. Few children will ever forget Clint's night at sea in the midst of a school of killer whales.

JAMES STREET

Good-bye, My Lady

Good-bye, My Lady (1954) by James Street presents a boy entirely different from Clint in *Sea Pup*. Skeeter lives on the edge of a great swamp. He has never possessed anything of his own in his whole life. Yet he is rich and secure, secure because he shares Uncle Jesse's one-room cabin and his love, rich because now he has a dog, and what a dog! At first, she is only a weird sound of laughter in the moonlit swamp. Then she is a small tigress fighting for her life against a cruel pack of hog dogs. And finally, she is his dog, a small, trembling creature that laughs instead of barks, licks herself clean like a cat, and sheds tears when she is scolded. Even Uncle Jesse has never seen her like.

Skeeter trains his dog painstakingly, and people come from miles around to watch her phenomenal performance in the field. But her spreading fame brings tragedy to Skeeter. She turns out to be an African Basenji, lost from a famous kennel that has been advertising for her. No one will tell on Skeeter if he decides to keep the dog, but loving his "Lady" has made Skeeter grow up. Their parting is a heartbreaker, and after the truck has gone with Lady, Uncle Jesse's old friend Cash speaks up: "Figured a little coffee might go good before y'all went back." He pours three cups, stout and black, a man's drink. Skeeter downs it, bitter though it is. After all, he *is* grown up, a man among men. Then he and Uncle Jesse head for home.

The lonely beauty of river and swamp are in this book, and the kindliness of humble people to each other.

ELIZABETH YATES

A Place for Peter

A Place for Peter (1952) deals with another kind of growing-up problem, a conflict between a father and son. Peter who has appeared in an earlier book, is now a sturdy thirteen-year-old fighting for recognition as a mature human being. But his father keeps him at small-boy chores which he does sloppily or neglects. When the understanding mother is called away from home for a long period of time, Peter faces with dread the prospect of life with his father alone. Added responsibilities and sheer necessity challenge all of Peter's energies and good sense. He swings the sugar bush alone, makes a difficult trail, plants a garden, deals with rattlesnakes, and manages to enjoy himself in the process. He has the comfort of his devoted dog and a philosophic old hired man. By spring, Peter discovers to his surprise that he and his father are friends as they never were before, partners in the demanding tasks of running the farm. The succession of seasons and seasonal work, the beauty of woods, meadows, hills, and sky, and, above all, the closeness of these men to their farm animals make this a warm and beautiful story.

This realistic pen-and-ink drawing of Peter tapping maple trees has much interesting and informative detail. Illustration by Nora S. Unwin. From A Place For Peter *by Elizabeth Yates. Copyright, 1952, by Coward-McCann, Inc. Reprinted by permission of the publisher. (Book 5½ x 8⅜)*

JOSEPH KRUMGOLD

. . . and now Miguel
Onion John

Joseph Krumgold has given the preadolescent two fine stories of growing up, both winners of the Newbery Medal.

The members of Miguel's family have been sheepherders for generations, first in Spain, now in the Southwest country around Santa Fe, New Mexico. Twelve-year-old Miguel is struggling to prove to his father that he is as mature and competent a sheep man as his adored brother Gabriel, who is eighteen. This is a universal problem, differing only in its symbols for the city boy, the coastal boy, or Miguel, the sheepherder. His attempts to prove his maturity and responsibility supply the action of the story. After many disheartening blunders, success comes, but it is tempered with regret. This book, written in the first person, will have to be introduced to children, but it is well worth the time and effort. Here are strong family love and loyalty with a profound respect for the family tradition of work, and here is pride in the expert performance of that work. Here too is the hero worship of a younger for an older brother. There is a feeling for the cycle of the seasons, each one bringing its special work and special satisfactions. And finally there is a closeness to God that makes prayer a natural part of life.

This remarkable book began as a documentary film and is still available in that form.

Onion John (1959) was not so universally approved as *Miguel,* but it too is concerned with problems in family relationships that are part of growing up. Andy is temporarily fascinated by a picturesque old hobo who lives in a shanty at the edge of town. This absurd hero worship causes the first rift between Andy and his father. The story of the whole town trying to uplift and "do good" to the old tramp is an exceedingly funny and characteristic bit of Americana. But not until Onion John has fled from his do-gooders, does Andy realize that he would rather be exactly like his father than anyone else—the respected owner of the town hardware store.

Here is an important theme—hero worship centered in the home. It was "Pa" for Jody in *The Yearling* and for the girls in the *Little House* books. It was his brother Gabriel for Miguel and the father again for Peter and Andy. Such family love and respect can ease the pangs of growing up as nothing else can and in addition can give the child a picture of his own life stretching ahead of him, rich with promise.

MADELEINE L'ENGLE

Meet the Austins

Still another important family-centered book is *Meet the Austins* (1960), and isn't this the first book in children's literature since *Little Women* in which the death of a loved one is handled so well?

The story begins in a modern kitchen where mother is preparing a gala dinner for a visiting relative. The small children are underfoot with dog and toys, the twelve-year-old daughter is doing her homework, and the record player is midway through Brahms' Second Piano Concerto when the telephone rings. It announces the death in an airplane crash of a beloved uncle, a distinguished test pilot, and his copilot. The scene that follows is handled with graphic details. The next night, realizing that the two oldest children are not sleeping, the mother gets them up and dressed and they drive up the mountain to talk. The children demand bitterly why God had to take a good man like Uncle Hal, and the mother replies, "Sometimes it's very hard to see the hand of God instead of the blind finger of Chance. That's why I wanted to come out where we could see the stars." They talk it out quietly in between long healing silences, and then they go home. Life goes on, but changed, with the spoiled orphaned child of the copilot in their home. The children's ups and downs, a serious brother-sister conflict, some funny and some grave situations—all develop against a background of family love. This is a fine family story, as unusual and provocative throughout as is its first chapter.

In this interesting sketch the artist has omitted such details as the chin, arm, hand, and tree trunk lines with a resulting strong emphasis on the boy's concentration. The illustration is fresh and beautiful. From the book My Side of the Mountain, *written and illustrated by Jean George. Copyright, © 1959, by Jean George. Reproduced by permission of E. P. Dutton & Co., Inc. (Book 5 x 7⅝)*

JEAN GEORGE

My Side of the Mountain

Quite the opposite of a family-centered story, *My Side of the Mountain* (1959) is the record of a New York City boy who breaks away from his family to prove that he can maintain life completely on his own in a mountain wilderness for a year. This competent young nonconformist writes, "I am on my mountain in a tree home that people have passed without ever knowing I am here. The house is a hemlock tree six feet in diameter, and must be as old as the mountain itself." How fourteen-year-old Sam perfects his house and how he makes a lamp from deer fat in a turtle's shell, clothes from deer skins, flour from acorns, and a balanced diet from roots, wild onions, leaves, and livers of animals make absorbing reading. Only the concluding reunion with his family seems mildly contrived. Jean George, an artist and a naturalist, not only writes well but knows what she is writing about.

KEITH ROBERTSON

Henry Reed, Inc.

Children need books also which demonstrate that life is not always earnest, that it can in fact be highly entertaining. *Henry Reed, Inc.* (1958) is such a book. It is Henry's private journal. He observes that explorers and pirates keep journals—not diaries because "diaries are kept by girls and tell all about their dates and what they think of their different boy friends." On a visit to his uncle and aunt who live in the country near Princeton, Henry hears all about the research at that University; so he decides to go into research. He takes over an old barn and paints an enormous sign: HENRY REED, RESEARCH. To the sign a girl who forces her way into this intellectual domain adds: PURE AND APPLIED. She wants her name added too, but Henry is adamant—she must prove her worth first. Worthy or not, their research activities are as hilarious reading as any book in the juvenile field. No lessons in this book, just laughter—pure and applied.

ESTER WIER

The Loner

The year 1963 brought children a new book and a new author of unusual promise. This story of the reëducation of a "loner" is a notable one.

Boy—with no name, no family, and no home—has picked crops as long as he can remember. He learns early that the only way to get along in this world is to look out for yourself and no one else. So when different families he travels with take all his money and finally leave him behind, sick and hungry, he does not blame them—they are just taking care of themselves. Then yellow-haired Raidy comes along and shows him warmth and kindness, a new experience for Boy. But when Raidy's looking after him causes her death, Boy has more than he can stand. Starving, heartbroken, and at the end of his strength, he curls up in a little hole in the earth, somewhere in the lonely grazing lands of Montana. There Boss, a big, competent sheep woman, finds him, carries him to her wagon house, and feeds and cares for him until he is on his feet once more. She names him "David" and thinks he will be a shepherd like her dead son, but David's training is far too brief to permit him to move easily into this new role. He yearns to please Boss and stay with her, but over and over he fails her.

Another influence in his life is a cowboy friend, Tex, who has also been a loner. Tex tries to explain why caring only for oneself is poor business. "There's always people who need you just as much as you need them. . . . you're happier carin' about someone else." From his dismal failures to measure up and from Boss herself, he learns what it means to give oneself completely to a job, to do it perfectly and completely.

It is his growing love for the helpless sheep, the wonderful dogs, and above all Boss herself that pulls the boy through. "David the shepherd boy" is a name worth living up to and his work is work worth doing.

The characterizations of people, dogs, and sheep are so vivid that even an ornery old ewe called Cluny becomes memorable. The hardships of sheepherding demand deep devotion. The details of this life Mrs. Wier has made clear in a story with a noble theme.

Stories About American Negroes

Stories about Negro children have always presented unique difficulties. For one thing, many of them are written in broad dialect, as incomprehensible to Northern

Negro children as it is to Northern white children. Then there is the natural sensitiveness of the Negro—a race making rapid strides toward better education and standards of living for all of its people—to stories which hold up to the Negro child only the poverty stricken and the less educated members of its group. White children may smile at Lois Lenski's vagrant families, because they have dozens of books about more sensible and successful families. They can enjoy drawings of white children which are almost caricatures, like Louis Slobodkin's *Moffats* and Robert McCloskey's *Lentil,* because they have dozens of other books in which white children are shown to be idealistically beautiful and noble. In order to laugh at ourselves wholeheartedly, we must feel secure socially and confident personally. The Negroes are trying to develop such a sense of dignity and self-respect in their children and so feel, quite properly, that books for and about them should foster such self-respect.

In recent years the problems of writing an acceptable and appealing story about Negro children have increased enormously. The integration problems both in the North and in the South have broken into violence that have engendered bad feeling on both sides. Anything that is said today will be dated tomorrow as either too evasive or timid or too controversial an approach. So what is happening to the children's books in this field? Charming picture-stories that portray but never mention color are appearing for the youngest children and show a normal, everyday world. For older children the controversy is met head on, from the Negro point of view. But all too often the terror and the humiliation are resolved too quickly and too easily. Perhaps that is the only way in a book for children at this point.

Adults who guide children's reading should follow certain criteria in selecting books in this field. Certainly, any story about Negro children should take them seriously and present pictures either of average families or of families solving their problems intelligently and successfully. Stories and pictures may be humorous but never caricatures. The speech should be average or better than average modern speech, neither dialect nor illiterate. If the story is centered in the struggle for the dignity of every human being and the right to equal opportunities, it should if possible reflect also the joyous zest for life and the warm, generous personalities that so many Negroes have kept in spite of the formidable problems they are still facing. It does not seem too much to ask these things of children's books for and about a group that is advancing so courageously and that has contributed so richly to the music, literature, and science, the kindliness, and the gaiety of our national life.

FOR CHILDREN FIVE TO SEVEN

Two Is a Team (1945) by Lorraine and Jerrold Beim is equally popular with Negro and white children because the story it tells has universal appeal. It is a simple enough theme—two small boys discover that they can accomplish more together than singly. The fact that they are of two different races makes no difference. It is teamwork that counts. This sounds moralistic, as indeed it is, but the story is a very natural one.

My Dog Rinty (1946) by Ellen Tarry and Marie Hall Ets is a still better story of a small boy who faces the heartbreaking issue of disposing of a beloved but destructive dog. This is a problem any child understands and sympathizes with. The family is appealing, David is a winning personality, and the pictures are attractive presentations of likable boys. The problem is the dog, not color.

The Snowy Day, written and illustrated by Ezra Jack Keats, won the 1963 Caldecott Medal, and a beautiful book it is. A little boy wakens to find snow falling and faces the joyous prospect of a snowy world to explore. He plays outdoors, and later in the bath tub and in his warm bed he remembers all the fun of his snowy day. Best of all the snow is still falling. This is another mood book. That he is a beautiful little Negro boy is not mentioned, why should it be? What he sees, says, thinks, and plays are common experiences of all children on snowy days. (See illustration 32 in color section.)

Tobe (1939) by Stella Gentry Sharpe is not a story but a series of documentary photographs of a Southern Negro farm family. The simple, easily read text, together with the fine pictures, carry the reader to Tobe's home, his school, church, holidays, and work activities.

Books like these protect our youngest school children from stereotypes of Negroes. But they do more than this. They show Negro children facing problems common to all children and solving them sensibly and happily.

FOR CHILDREN EIGHT TO FOURTEEN

Books for children eight to fourteen also present Negro children facing problems common to all children. Some, however, show them facing the tragically difficult problems of racial prejudice. Should children's books about Negroes avoid all controversial issues? There are yes and no answers to this question, and the division of opinion is reflected in differing appraisals of some of the books discussed in the following pages. One thing is essential—you must know the content of the book before you use it with children.

ELEANOR FRANCES LATTIMORE

Junior, a Colored Boy of Charleston

A single book of unusual appeal is *Junior, a Colored Boy of Charleston* (1938) by Eleanor Lattimore. It is the story of a little boy's efforts to help his family during the pinching times when his father is out of work. Sometimes Junior does well; sometimes he fares badly. His greatest success is singing for the old shrimp man, who gets weary chanting his wares all day. This job leads to Junior's largest earnings and helps change his family's ill fortune. Children from seven to ten will be amused by some of Junior's efforts.

April is tenderly comforted by Mrs. Cole. The tree encloses them, framing their heads in a gentle curve. This is a fine drawing with a good variety of texture.
From Bright April. *Copyright ©, 1946, by Marguerite de Angeli. Reprinted by permission of the publishers, Doubleday & Company, Inc. (Book 8 x 8)*

ARNA BONTEMPS

Sad-Faced Boy

Arna Bontemps' *Sad-Faced Boy* (1937), with its amusing illustrations by Virginia Burton, is popular, particularly with children ten to fourteen years old. It tells the story of a trio of Alabama boys, Slumber, Willie, and Rags, who decide to go to Harlem. They beat their way North, explore the wonders and discover the limitations of the city. When life gets too baffling they can always make music and dance. They are a little annoyed by the bossy Daisy Bee, who shows them a trick or two with the drums and tap dancing, but they profit by her tips. Ultimately they decide there is more contentment for them in Alabama; so they return as they came. The boys are an appealing trio, and Mr. Bontemps catches the exact cadence of their speech. It is beautiful to hear and to read.

MARGUERITE DE ANGELI

Bright April

This attractive book has the virtue of showing a cultured Negro family. They live in a beautiful, well-kept house. They are prosperous, intelligent, and handsome. Little April, the youngest child, is a heart-stealer. But each episode in the book involves a racial issue. There are no moments of family fun minus a problem. The family meets each difficulty courageously and well, and for little April there is a happy solution to her humiliations. Some people object seriously to the conclusion of the story, others feel that the multiplicity of problems is excessive. One thing is certain: Mrs. de Angeli's pictorial presentation of her characters makes them both appealing and convincing.

MABEL LEIGH HUNT

Ladycake Farm

Ladycake Farm (1952) is a better story, with well-drawn characters and a theme that turns upon family achievement. But so serious are the issues involved that the book was praised and attacked by both Negro and white reviewers. It concerns a family of Negroes who have accumulated sufficient funds to buy a farm. The unique process of moving their house with everything in it makes an entertaining beginning. The farm more than fulfills their dreams until they find a sign by a lovely brook, "Niggers unwelcome. Keep out." The children never go near that beautiful stream again. Fortunately, the Freeds' hard work and courage win them a respected place in the community, and eventually the hateful sign comes down. The mother is an unforgettable character in this story, but some Negroes have objected to the father's advice to smile in the face of insults. Certainly this is no book to be used without careful reading and a full realization of the seriousness of the issues involved.

JESSE JACKSON

Call Me Charley

Jesse Jackson has given a full and moving account of the kind of discriminations a Negro boy encounters. In *Call Me Charley* (1945), the young Negro, the only one in the neighborhood, is not welcome in the school but is tolerated. He has some bitter disappointments but gradually wins the respect and friendship of some of the boys. It is a touching story made more poignant by Charley's quiet, patient acceptance of his lot. When his friends finally sense his heartbroken disappointment over his exclusion from the school play, they do something about it. Charley is in the play and happy for the present. The author has too realistic an approach to suggest a complete solution, but he tells a good story of a brave, likable boy in a difficult world.

Charley Starts from Scratch, a sequel, finds Charley graduated from high school and trying to find a job in a strange city. Many doors are closed to him, but coming in first in Olympic trials gives Charley fresh courage and convinces several employers of the boy's worth and perseverance. Like the first book, this story is sensitively told.

JOHN R. TUNIS

All-American

Boys will tell you that John Tunis knows his sports; parents will tell you he knows his adolescent boys; teachers will add, "and our American schools, too." He writes in the slangy vernacular of the modern boy, and he tells an exciting story. And in the process he does some unobtrusive propagandizing for the workings of democracy. In *All-American* (1942), Ronny, a private-school boy, transfers to a public high school and plays football with the usual mixed racial groups. He comes to value each boy for his worth and becomes aware of the special difficulties of the one Negro player. How Ronny helps solve the problem of discrimination is courageous and realistic. In the *Horn Book* for May 1946, Howard Pease says of this book, "Its story rings and echoes in our minds for weeks and months afterwards. I myself found *All-American* one of the most exciting junior novels I have ever read. To me it remains a milestone in juvenile book publication."

DOROTHY STERLING

Mary Jane

Dorothy Sterling's *Mary Jane* faces fully the violence that met the first Negro children to try out school integration in a segregated community. Mary Jane's grandfather is a scientist and former college professor, living in quiet retirement on his farm. When Mary Jane tells him that in the autumn she is going to enter the white high school in order to get certain subjects not taught in their segregated school, her grandfather tries gently to prepare her for trouble. When she returns home, her lawyer father tries to do so also, but Mary Jane is adamant. Nothing, not even her father and the police escort, has prepared her for the jeering, howling mob shouting, "Go back to Africa," or the white mothers' faces distorted with hate, yelling, "Pull her black curls out," or the boys inside the school chanting, "We don't want her. . . . She's too black for me." Mary Jane is frightened right down to the pit of her stomach, but along with one Negro boy, she keeps her chin up and stays in school.

The indignities they suffer in and out of school are many, but Mary Jane wins the friendship of one white girl. With Sally's encouragement and the understanding kindness and backing of two teachers, Mary Jane hangs on. By the year's end, things are better and the future a shade more hopeful. Is this too easy and too quick a conclusion? Who can say? Both Negro and white children must have courage and hope. Books can help to build both. But again you must know this book and how you wish to use it, before giving it to children.

Certain qualities are still lacking in children's books about Negroes. For example, there is little suggestion of the deep religious faith that permeates many Negro homes. Nor is there an adequate picture of their sense of fun and the gaiety of their family and community celebrations. These qualities have carried many Negroes far and help to account for their special success in the arts. Their talented boys and girls have struggled against unusual odds to achieve recognition in the entertainment field. *Steppin and Family* by Hope Newell is built around this theme. It is a pity this book has been allowed to go out of print, because it is the kind of realistic success story that is greatly needed.

Finally, the motivation that activates intelligent Negro families today to continue the struggle for equal rights must be respected. And equal rights must be balanced by equal responsibilities for the manners and morals of youth, both white and Negro. Equal rights and equal responsibilities are two themes that should go hand in hand in these stories.

American Indians

Indian stories for young people and children have undergone an interesting evolution. They began with such romantically idealized stories as James Fenimore Cooper's *Last of the Mohicans,* dear to the boys of an earlier generation. Then came early settler stories which emphasized the scalping, warpath Indian. He was the personification of all that was bloody and terrible, with an eye on scalps and a tomahawk ready for all white people, especially women and children. *The Matchlock Gun* (p. 480) is this type of story. In none of them was there any hint that the Indian might have some justification for harrying the white settlers. No mention is made of the period when treaty after treaty was broken with the Indians and they were driven ruthlessly off their land farther and farther west to poorer and poorer lands. Only recently in either adult or juvenile literature has there been any attempt to present the Indian living his own life with his own tribal customs, religion, and code of behavior. Now, having ignored the treaty-breaking past, writers are also turning their backs upon the bloody massacres of the Indians.

The new books for children are showing the modern Indian of the reservation or the farm, coping with many difficulties, holding his self-respect and his dignity. The books do not deal with Indians in general but with specific tribes. Characteristic dwelling places, foods, religious beliefs and practices, and ways of making a livelihood vary with each tribe; and they are presented authentically. Recently, some books have included the Indians' prejudices against the white men. The Indians described in these stories are very different from the James Fenimore Cooper Indians or the scalping, war-whooping Indians. There is a sincere attempt to interpret honestly and sympathetically the present-day problems of these native Americans.

M. O'MORAN

Trail of the Little Paiute

Books that give children authentic pictures of how Indians in the past lived, thought, and felt are important in building a background for understanding Indians today. One of these is *Trail of the Little Paiute* (1952), which shows the struggle for survival after white men invade the arid hunting grounds of the Paiute Indians. When famine comes, the law of the tribe is that the old ones must leave the camp and walk out into the wilderness alone, which of course means death. But the motherless boy, Inyo, when he finds his grandmother is the first to be sent away, rebels against the tribal law and follows his grandmother. The story of their hardships and adventures crossing mountains and desert is almost incredible. Inyo becomes an important go-between for his tribe and the white men. This story is remarkable for its vivid characterizations of individual Indians, especially the old grandmother and the Paiute chief. It is also an important record of the Paiute's courageous but hopeless last stand against the encroaching white men.

ELOISE JARVIS McGRAW

Moccasin Trail

Moccasin Trail, a well-written and absorbing story (1952), marks the end of the era of mountain men and the beginning of settlements and farms in the Far West. It is also the story of a white boy, rescued and raised by Crow Indians until he thinks and feels completely Indian. Or so he believes, until one day the braves return to camp with some scalps, and among them is one with blond hair—the color of his mother's. In a flash Jim knows he is not Indian and he must go back to his own family. But readjusting to settled life is harder than Jim anticipated. Jim helps his family, but he hates their continual industry and orderly ways. He knows too that his wild restlessness, his long braids with his coup feather, are deeply offensive to his young sister. Only to his little brother Daniel is Jim a hero, but the boy's worshipful admiration and imitation which are balm to Jim are sources of anxiety to Sally. Once, in Jim's absence, young Daniel runs away to the Indians. Then Jim knows that Daniel must be saved and he himself must turn his back forever on the Moccasin Trail. This story of a personal conflict is important because through Jim's troubled thinking the author shows both the attractions and virtues of Indian life and its limitations and inevitable doom.

LAURA ARMER

Waterless Mountain

Laura Armer's books about the Navaho Indians were written for children twelve to fifteen years old. The hero of her Newbery winner, *Waterless Mountain* (1931), is Younger Brother, whose secret name is Dawn Boy. Younger Brother knows that he is going to be a medicine man when he grows up, and the story tells much about his training in the mysticism of the Navaho religion. It is a beautifully written story but decidedly difficult for many children to understand and share. To be sure, teachers who love this book can have a whole roomful of young Navaho mystics completely in sympathy with Younger Brother, but most children must be helped to an enjoyment of this unusual story. The everyday life of the tribe emerges clearly, and there is one exciting adventure when the boys catch horse thieves and reclaim a beloved pony.

MARY AND CONRAD BUFF

Dancing Cloud

Mary and Conrad Buff lived among the Indians, and in *Dancing Cloud* (1937) they tell about the Navahos in story and in wonderful pictures. The story is not so memorable as the pictures. Each chapter is a separate episode dealing with the activities of these people and their children—weaving, herding and shearing sheep, making jewelry, preparing food.

Magic Maize (1953) by this talented husband-and-wife team is about Guatemalan Indians, but their problems are much like those faced by some of the remote tribes in this country. The characters in this story are more fully realized than those in *Dancing Cloud*. And again Mr. Buff has captured the calm strength of the Indians and the glowing colors of their country.

Hah-Nee (1956) goes back in time to explain why the great Pueblo cities of the Southwest were abandoned. Hah-Nee does not quite emerge as a flesh-and-blood boy but is chiefly a name to carry the story. The effect of long-continued drouth will be understood by modern desert dwellers. To other children the book will supply an exciting background for the enigma of those vast, empty Pueblo cities. (See illustration 15 in color section.)

SCOTT O'DELL

Island of the Blue Dolphins

There seem to be more good realistic stories about the American Indian set in the past than in the present. Of these stories of the past, the most powerful is *Island of the Blue Dolphins* (1961 Newbery Medal).

In the early 1800's off the coast of California, a twelve-year-old Indian girl boarded a ship that was to carry the tribe away from their island home where they were being harried and destroyed by Aleutian seal hunters. But when Karana saw that her little brother had accidentally been left behind, she jumped off the moving ship and swam back to him and their island home. A pack of wild dogs killed her brother and began to stalk the solitary girl. This is the beautifully told story of her survival on the island for eighteen years. She had to prepare her own weapons, build a shelter with a strong fence, maintain a continual search for food, replace her worn out clothes, all with an eye on the savage pack of dogs. The need to love and nurture was strong. So when she wounded the leader dog, she nursed him back to health and he became her inseparable companion and defender. Shining through her struggles and hardships are her quiet resignation, her endurance, her genuine love for her island home, and the great fortitude and serenity she developed. The story of Karana is historically true. Her incredible battles with a bull sea elephant, a devilfish, and the ferocious dogs, and above all her years of solitude command the reader's humble admiration for human courage. (See illustration, p. 11.)

ANN NOLAN CLARK

In My Mother's House
Secret of the Andes

In My Mother's House and *Secret of the Andes* represent something of Mrs. Clark's range of experience with primitive peoples. Furthermore, she is able to interpret their ways of life so that modern children respect them. She was at one time a teacher of Southwestern Indian children, has been a supervisor of Indian Schools, and has traveled under the Inter-American Educational Foundation in various countries of Latin America training native teachers. Her writing reflects her love for these peoples. *Secret of the Andes* (1952), a Newbery Medal winner, is the story of a dedicated Peruvian Indian boy, the last of a royal line. *Santiago* is about a Guatemalan youth, raised in a Spanish home but determined to find his place in the world as an Indian. Both of these perceptive stories are for children eleven to fourteen.

For younger children Mrs. Clark has written three books that give authentic pictures of the life and ideals of our desert Indians. *In My Mother's House* (1941) is written as if a Tewa child were speaking simply and beautifully of the small world he knows and holds dear. The cadenced prose of the text is matched by the rhythmic beauty of the illustrations. The last page summarizes the content of the book:

The pueblo,
The people,
And fire,
And fields,
And water,
And land,
And animals—
I string them together
Like beads.

They make a chain,
A strong chain,
To hold me close
To home,
Where I live
In my Mother's house.

Little Navajo Bluebird (1943) tells the dramatic story of a Navaho child who loves her home, her family, and the old ways of life. She sees her brother and sister changed by the white man's school, and she hates the idea that she will ever have to go there and lose the old ways so dear to her. Through the sympathy and wisdom of her brother's young wife, she comes to see that the Red Man's Trail and the White Man's Trail may meet. She knows that when her time comes to go to the white man's school she will go gladly. Children nine to eleven enjoy little Doli, and through her story acquire a better understanding of the Indian's problems of adjustment. (See illustration, p. 8.)

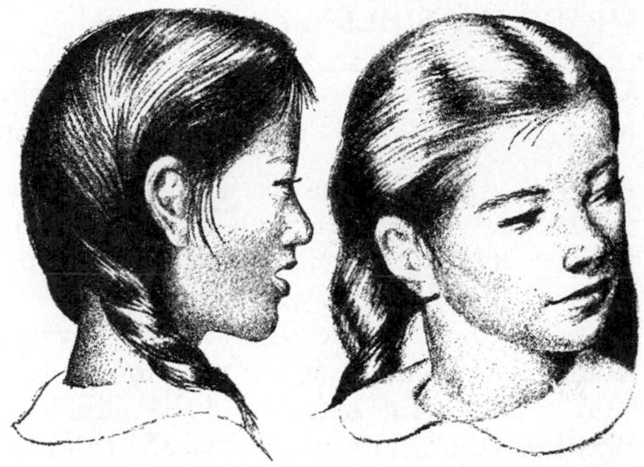

The light reflected on the skin and hair of the two girls gives them a three-dimensional look. The look of dislike on the face of the girl at the right is sadly revealing.
Illustration by Paul Lantz. From Navaho Sister, *copyright ©, 1956, by Evelyn Sibley Lampman. Reprinted by permission of publisher, Doubleday and Company, Inc. (Book 5¼ x 8)*

Blue Canyon Horse (1954) is about the Havasu Indians, who, with neither roads nor wagons, must depend on horses in their canyon home. The book begins with the flight of a young mare to the high mesa above the canyon, where the wild horses live. All winter the hero grieves for his lost horse but never loses hope that she will return. And sure enough, in the spring she comes back with her colt to the friendship of her master. No outline can give a fair picture of the beauty and simplicity of this story, with its account of the little mare running wild and free and the interludes of the boy's hurt and longing, his dream "misted, unreal, unfinished, but in it flickers a spark of hope." For the oldest or the youngest children, Mrs. Clark writes with a sense of the inner life and ideals of a people. Her cadenced prose is beautiful and unique.

EVELYN SIBLEY LAMPMAN

Treasure Mountain
Navaho Sister

Evelyn Lampman has been unusually successful in writing stories about the modern Indian child who is faced with conflicting ways of life. In *Treasure Mountain* (1949) an Indian brother and sister from a government school spend a summer with their great-aunt who is a full-blooded "blanket Indian." Accustomed to white men's ways, the children at first are shocked by their aunt's customs and beliefs, but as the summer passes their respect and love for her grow. The title comes from the children's hunt for treasure to raise the money for taxes, but the primary interest in this story lies in their deepened appreciation of values in the old ways of Indian life as well as in the new.

Navaho Sister (1956) is a girl story and a good one. Orphaned Sad Girl goes to a government school where she feels isolated and is thoroughly unhappy. The episodes in the book bring out the difficult adjustment an Indian child must make to a modern school. Sad Girl's need to be more outgoing and tolerant is a problem in social adjustment most children can understand.

Regional and Religious Minorities

No other country in the world shelters the variety of peoples to be found in the United States. We have such regional groups as the mountaineers, the Cajuns, and the migrant groups that follow the crops—picking cotton or beans or strawberries or oranges. Then there are the close-knit communities of immigrants and their descendants making a little Italy or Hungary or Sweden within a larger community. And this still does not exhaust the varieties of groups in the United States; there are other groups representing all the major and innumerable minor religious sects—Jewish, Catholic, Protestant, Amish, Quaker, Mormon, and many more.

Since all of these diverse peoples have contributed richly to our national life, it is important that children should meet them vicariously in books in order that they may meet them in person sympathetically and with respect. Whether the story is about the family of a migrant cotton picker, a Pennsylvania-Dutch farmer, a mountaineer, or a Jewish storekeeper, the book should be first of all a good story, not a sociological tract for children. And the young hero or heroine of the story should be so appealing and understandable that young readers will sympathetically identify themselves with him in his ups and downs. Of all these regional books *...and now Miguel* is still the finest, but there are others that have special values.

MARGUERITE DE ANGELI

Henner's Lydia

Mrs. de Angeli was one of the pioneers in relating stories about the minority groups around her home in Philadelphia. Her stories are slight, but the warm pictures she paints, both with colors and words, of Amish, Quaker, and Pennsylvania-Dutch children are important. *Henner's Lydia, Skippack School, Yonie Wondernose,* and *Thee, Hannah!* contribute to youngsters' feeling that these people are even as you and I, only perhaps a bit more interesting.

Yonie Wondernose (1944) with his wondering is the favorite, especially when, like the hero of the folk tale, his wondering pays off and he proves his courage as well. Particularly appealing, too, is the little Quaker girl in *Thee, Hannah!* (1940), who despises her Quaker garb until she finds herself chosen, because of it, to serve a great cause. This book goes back in time to the Civil War.

Up the Hill (1942) is about a modern Polish colony in one of our large cities. We know their food, their fetes, their dances, their old-world treasures, and new-world ambitions. In this, as in all of Mrs. de Angeli's books, the great value lies less in the story than in the author's warm and affectionate appreciation of the people she writes about.

Of first importance are her illustrations. These are beautiful in color with springtime freshness and innocence. To be sure, her children—whatever their sex, nationality, or disposition—have always the same little heart-shaped faces and wistful beauty, but they have also a skipping gaiety which is the very essence of all childhood. Grace, lightness, and pure, clear colors give her illustrations an eye-filling loveliness. (See illustration 13 in color section.)

VIRGINIA SORENSON

Plain Girl

Plain Girl (1955) is another delightful story about a Pennsylvania minority group. Ten-year-old Amish Esther is both worried and pleased when she knows she must attend a public school. But she makes friends and is surprised to find that her very best friend, she of the glorious pink dress, actually admires Esther's plain clothes. There is conflict for Esther, too. She is worried because her brother has run away from the plain ways. Was it because of what he learned in school? The pink dress presents a minor but very real problem also. How these conflicts are resolved makes a good story which earned the Child Study Award for a significant and well-told tale.

SYDNEY TAYLOR

All-of-a-Kind Family

One of the large religious groups in this country is, of course, Jewish. And books that are models of what authors should strive for in presenting such groups to children are Sydney Taylor's *All-of-a-Kind Family* (1951), *More All-of-a-Kind Family*, and *All-of-a-Kind Family Uptown*. The fact that the children are all girls accounts for the titles, although to Papa's great delight a boy arrives eventually.

The family lives on New York's lower East Side in a Jewish neighborhood, but the adventures of the girls are such as might happen to any city children anywhere. The first book opens with the despair of the five over the loss of a library book. How can they ever face the library lady? Will they be barred from getting more books? This incident as well as the others are the kind that might happen in any family. The difference lies in the fact that their warm home life is deeply rooted in Jewish religious customs. Hard-working Papa and pretty, capable Mama keep all the fasts and feasts of the Jewish year with deep reverence and thanksgiving. These and the family gaiety, together with Mama's mouth-watering foods, make every reader wish he might be a part of the family group. A pleasanter emissary for Jewish culture, religious piety, and family love than these entertaining and heart-warming books could hardly be found.

ELLIS CREDLE

Down Down the Mountain

Reading about Southern mountaineers in the books of Ellis Credle, the two Carrolls, and Jesse Stuart gives the city child some of the insight a camp experience does. If mountaineer children have greens for dinner, it is because they have helped plant them, tend them, pick, wash, and cook them. If they want new shoes or a present for granny, they must earn the money. If a little girl has a polka-dot dress, it is because her clever granny knows how to splatter dash it with a daub stick. If she has a doll, it is made of corn shucks, and a "sight pretty" too. If life grows dull, the mountain child can always dream over the "wish book," the mail-order catalog, or listen to ballads sung by granny or a neighbor. He may even dream of going "far beyant," which is much farther than the far side of the mountains. Some of the children's adventures are scary, but their resourcefulness sees them through.

A favorite is Ellis Credle's *Down Down the Mountain* (1934), a story about two Southern mountaineer children, Hetty and Hank, who yearn to possess a pair of squeaky shoes. They must earn them, but how? Their mountain is so steep that pumpkins might roll right off the side; so they plant turnips, which flourish. But on the way to town to exchange their crop for shoes, the children find hungry people who seem to have more need for their turnips

"A-hunting we will go" is the obvious intent of this young man and his pup. To her pictures of woodlands and steep mountainsides the artist gives a sense of mystery and peace. Illustration by Ruth Carroll. Reproduced from Beanie. *Copyright 1953 by Ruth and Latrobe Carroll. By permisison of Henry Z. Walck, Inc (Original with color, book 8 x 10)*

than they themselves have for shoes. By the time Hetty and Hank finally reach the town they have given away all their turnips except one, their biggest one to be sure but still only one. Obviously they can't have shoes. Then the fair with prizes for the finest specimens unexpectedly provides shoes for Hetty and Hank. Their turnip of turnips wins a prize! They get the most elegantly squeaky shoes in town and enjoy a triumphant return home, with shoes and presents.

These mountaineer children are resourceful, enterprising youngsters. They expect to earn what they get and do their own dickering into the bargain. They take disappointments cheerfully and receive good fortune with delighted amazement. There are action, energy, good humor, and a nice generosity about these children which make them likable but never priggish. The author's vigorous crayon sketches in blues and browns have action and humor.

RUTH AND LATROBE CARROLL

Beanie

The Carrolls have continued their annals of the Tatum family through a number of lively books glorified by magnificent sketches of the great Smoky Mountains. The hero is young Beanie. Complications in the first story stem from his frisky pup, Tough Enough, and the adventures include an encounter with a bear, a spring freshet, and sundry other unexpected excitements. There is an unobtrusive emphasis on character. Everyone must do his share of work. Mother is loving and competent, and she expects competence of her children. Father is independent and is a hard worker, but he has patience and understanding. Young Beanie must use his head to survive. It takes courage to face a bear, but it takes more courage to tell father his dire suspicions of his pet's misdemeanors. Back of everything are the love of the Tatums for each other and the fun and solidarity of the Tatum tribe. For children six to nine, these are fine family stories, with considerable variety in their plots.

JESSE STUART

The Beatinest Boy

Jesse Stuart, a mountain man, poet, and author of that charming autobiography, *The Thread That Runs So True,* is not yet at ease in the juvenile field, but his books are improving. *The Beatinest Boy* (1953) was somewhat disjointed, but it has a delightful episode about a Christmas gift. Granny and the boy are well worth knowing. *Penny's Worth of Character* shows that the wages of cheating are a bad conscience and the need to make amends—too obviously moralistic to be much of a story. The story element in *Red Mule*—mule versus tractor—is livelier and more successful. Mr. Stuart's plots are too contrived to be first-rate, but he has so deep a love for the people of the country that they are always convincing.

LOIS LENSKI

Strawberry Girl

In 1940 *Blue Willow,* a tender and beautifully written book by Doris Gates, was a runner-up for the Newbery Medal. It is a story of migratory farm workers and their camps. It centers on ten-year-old Janey's longing for a permanent home where her family will be a settled part of a settled community. Then in 1946 when the Newbery Medal was given to Lois Lenski's *Strawberry Girl,* it called attention to a unique series of books about regional groups of many kinds, all over this country.

Lois Lenski began her series with *Bayou Suzette,* a story about the French-speaking people in the bayou section of Louisiana. After *Strawberry Girl* of Florida came *Blue Ridge Billy,* about the North Carolina mountaineer group, and *Judy's Journey,* which followed the crop-pickers from California to Florida and back to New Jersey. There have been more of these books in succeeding years. *Strawberry Girl* is still one of the best, with *Boom Town Boy* and *Cotton in My Sack* equally strong stories about highly individual characters and places. Other authors have written regional stories, but no one has approached the task with greater sincerity and sense of dedication than Lois Lenski.

"Seeing Others As Ourselves" was the title of her acceptance paper for the Newbery Medal, and it is her approach to each of these books. She moves into a community literally and spiritually. Sketching outdoors is the magnet which draws and enchants the children as they watch a scene or people developing on her paper. The children in turn pave the way for her informal visits with the adults in markets, on stoops and porches, or in kitchens and yards. From Florida to Texas, people tell about her warmth and kindliness. "I shall recollect you . . . in all pleasantness. . . ." one old man told her. And many have thought it.

Strawberry Girl (1945) is typical of these books at their best. It is the story of Birdie Boyer's family, newly moved to Florida's backwoods for the purpose of raising small crops of "sweet 'taters," strawberries, oranges, and the like. Birdie has courage and spunk, and the Boyers are a close-knit, competent family. They take their ups and downs philosophically, and the Slaters next door are the worst pests they encounter. Pa Slater drinks and is deliberately and maliciously mean. Ma Slater is slatternly, and the children are unkempt and rough. But Shoestring Slater, under Birdie's relentless guidance, begins to see the light. In the end, a revival meeting reforms Pa, at least temporarily, and the Slaters, especially Shoestring, taste the sweetness of group acceptance and even approval. Meanwhile, the Boyers are on their way to a modest success.

This is grimmer realism than anything since *Tom Sawyer,* and it continues in the other books. In *Cotton in My Sack* the mother can't cook or keep her house and children clean. Everyone in the family, except the baby, toils endlessly picking cotton, only to indulge in a weekly orgy of aimless spending. So in *Boom Town Boy,* Orvie's family when it strikes oil goes on a spending spree that is silly and purposeless. Only Gramp saves them from demoralizing idleness. Yet these books have a wry humor about them, and children like the stories.

What is it that lifts these uneducated, close-to-vagrant families above the squalor in which they live? It is partly their courage but chiefly their fierce family pride and love that bind them together through thick and thin. Joanda would not touch the school lunches until Ma

Here is Joanda, with sunbonnet and sack, pictured in Lois Lenski's simple, direct style. From Cotton in My Sack. *Copyright, 1949, by Lois Lenski. Published by J. B. Lippincott Company. Reprinted by permission of author. (Book 6½ x 8¾)*

told her to, because they seemed to be a reflection on Ma's cooking, as indeed they could hardly help but be. Orvie is ashamed of his family but loyal to them and sure Gramp will pull them through. This abiding love for each other and sense of the solidarity of the family group gives warmth to what might otherwise be a too somber realism.

There are dangers in such a series of books. They might easily turn into obvious propaganda and stereotypes. The values of this series are to be found in its objective realism and compassion. Young members of underprivileged families meet their own kind in these regional stories of Lois Lenski's. And they take heart, because always the ups and downs of these hard-pressed people yield a ray of hope. Things are, or give promise of becoming, better. As for the well-cared-for children of suburbia, these books give them a picture of family love and loyalty that makes these families worthy of respect.

OTHER MINORITIES

Clara Ingram Judson has written a splendid series of books subtitled *They Came from Sweden, They Came from Scotland,* and so on. These follow the course of sturdy immigrants to these shores and show their difficulties and adjustments to life here.

In *Nino* Valenti Angelo, a master of decorative design, has given children a delightful picture of his own childhood in Italy; in later books he has followed the family adventures in this country. *Paradise Valley* tells about families who because of unemployment or seasonal work are forced to live in temporary homes, shantytowns, or camps. *The Bells of Bleecker Street* is the amusing story of boys in the "Little Italy" of a big city, with a background of Italian customs centering in the neighborhood church.

To our knowledge of a little known religious group, Virginia Sorenson has contributed a substantial novel called *The House Next Door.* Teen-agers will find this story of the Utah Mormons, in the critical period of transition from polygamy to its abolition, a powerful one. The characters are vividly alive, and their problems sympathetically dealt with.

Stories about our so-called "aliens," a sad word for the newcomers to our shores, are beginning to multiply. The Literature Committee of the Association for Childhood Education edited an excellent anthology of such stories, including tales about most of our racial and religious minorities. *Told under the Stars and Stripes* is a valuable introduction to the unhappy miscarriages of our democracy and to the children's solutions of some of these problems—democracy in action.

So the picture grows. Here are groups, set apart by race, geography, special work, or religion, differing widely in beliefs and customs but living side by side in comparative amity. Through this very diversity all are contributing to the richness of our national life.

CRITERIA FOR STORIES ABOUT MINORITY GROUPS

How shall we appraise these books about minority groups? The books cited in this chapter may well serve as criteria for evaluation.

They are all primarily good stories with strong child appeal, substantial themes, and good plots. They are also alive with unique and memorable characters. Lois Lenski's people might easily slip into stereotypes of the poor or depressed. Instead they are vividly and often cantankerously alive. In the story of Miguel even the minor characters are remembered—the wise and wonderful old Padre de Chavez and the irrepressible Faustina with her "Okeydokee" one week and "GalgoGalgalena" the next. Nor in any of these books is there any patronizing attitude toward the "poor aliens" or "poor fruit pickers" or the Mormon or Jewish child. Instead, all these people are presented with warmth and understanding, and their tragedies, struggles, anxieties, and brief moments of triumph or fun are characteristic of most families. If, within the framework of lively, well-written stories, young readers can discover that people in reality are more alike than different, more akin to each other than alien, then these are good books. They do not have to preach democracy. They are showing it in action—many different kinds of peoples living peaceably and happily side by side, all good citizens of this country.

Mystery Tales

A current classification of children's books which cuts across all groups of realistic fiction in all countries and times is the mystery story. The mystery tale is certainly a striking example of the way in which children's books parallel predominant trends in adult reading interests. With mothers, fathers, and even grandparents all devoted to the "Whodunit" school of writing, it is not surprising to find a seven-year-old marching into the children's room of a great library and demanding a good mystery story.[2] In libraries today, older children can find racks upon racks of juvenile mysteries which include, along with mediocre ones, some fine books by authors whose names are a guarantee of wholesome, well-written fiction.

The extreme popularity of the mystery tale at present is undoubtedly a fad as far as children are concerned, artificially stimulated by adult emphasis. Indeed, librarians say that the juvenile demand for a "mystery" is beginning to diminish even now. An element of mystery has always been a source of interest in a story and always will be. But when innumerable books are written merely for the sake of the mystery, the pattern and mood of such tales are liable to become tiresomely repetitious and the stories are likely to be mere trash. This is happening in adult mysteries today and in juveniles as well. At their worst, such books are marked by preposterous plots, details left unaccounted for, too many episodes, violence piled upon violence, typed characters, and, finally, poor style.

The virtues of good mystery tales for children are numerous, but first among these is the atmosphere of excitement and suspense which serves as the most tempting of all baits for nonreaders. Comic-strip-addicted and television-fed children demand a highly spiced book fare if they are going to read at all, and these mystery tales are usually adventure stories with plenty of breath-taking action to keep young thrill-seekers absorbed. Another useful feature of such stories is that they help establish a much needed reading skill—rapid silent reading. Children unconsciously speed up their usual reading rate under the stimulus of an agreeable suspense. They will cover pages of a mystery tale at breakneck speed in their desire to find the answers and solve the mystery. This rapid rate of silent reading, together with a little skipping or skimming on the way, is a useful habit for fiction readers to establish —the younger the better.

Finally, if children can be supplied with mystery stories which are also well written and not too difficult for them to read, unbookish children can be persuaded to read a better type of literature than they might otherwise attempt. A superb example of good adventure literature is Robert Louis Stevenson's *Treasure Island.* This is for the fourteen-year-old and is not easy to read. But younger children sometimes finish it, lured on by its superior thrills and its picturesque characters. The virtues of this story are worth noting as standards for what a good mystery story can be.

ROBERT LOUIS STEVENSON

Treasure Island

Treasure Island is the tale of some guileless gentlefolk who fall into the hands of a villainous pirate crew headed by an ingratiating leader, Long John Silver. They sail on the *Hispaniola* to look for buried treasure, the exact location of which is on a map the boy Jim Hawkins gets possession of and turns over to the doctor for safekeeping. Jim overhears the pirates plotting with Silver to get the map, kill off the men they are serving, and take the treasure and the ship. Jim warns his friends, and once on the island the fight is on—captain, doctor, squire, Jim, and a few decent members of the crew versus Long John Silver and the pirates. It is a battle of wit and strategy as well as of violence, for the one-legged Silver with his parrot Captain Flint riding on his shoulder is a formidable foe—cool, brainy, and ruthless. How the captain, the squire, the doctor, and Jim finally win the battle, capture the treasure, and set sail once more is surprising enough. But to

2. Reported by Miss Margaret Clark, head of the Lewis Carroll Room, Cleveland Public Library.

find the redoubtable Silver amiably lined up on the side of the victors is a curiously natural and satisfying conclusion.

The virtues of this absorbing story are greater than the mere solution of the treasure mystery or the suspense of the many parts of a wholly thrilling tale. Here is masterly characterization. The leading persons in the story are convincing composites of strength and weakness, bravery and wickedness. Jim Hawkins is a real boy, full of curiosities, good intentions, and a youthful but often mistaken confidence in his own abilities. The well-intentioned squire gets them all into their scrape in the first place by his chatty indiscretions. The doctor and the captain are the brains of the expedition, each forthright and competent in his own way. Long John Silver, hobbling about on his wooden leg and crutch as agilely as a monkey, is as fascinating a villain as ever dominated a tale. Silver is intelligent, clever, cruel, treacherous, and impatient with the stupid, greedy wretches he commands, and he always has his eye on the best course for John Silver.

There is an adroit contrast in moral codes in this assembly of decent folk and rogues. Silver and his band are ever ready to betray or kill each other. Silver is redeemed from being completely despicable by his courage and his ebullient spirits. The doctor and the captain exemplify the virtues of gentlemen. The doctor will give medical aid to the enemy but will give no quarter to the wretches personally. The captain organizes and disciplines his handful of men, not only for battle but for morale between times. It is the captain who rebukes Jim gravely for the desertion of his post to carry out one of his own reckless enterprises. And it is the squire who roundly denounces the turncoat Silver when the latter joins the very company he had been fighting:

> *"John Silver," he said, "you're a prodigious villain and impostor—a monstrous impostor, sir. I am told I am not to prosecute you. Well, then, I will not. But the dead men, sir, hang about your neck like millstones."*

From then on, no member of the group treats Silver as anything but the villain he is, and his escape is welcomed by them all as good riddance of a man who, having in him the element of greatness, was nevertheless a traitorous brigand.

This book, with its gallery of finely drawn characters and a narrative that surpasses any other pirate or buried treasure story ever composed, has the additional virtue of good writing. The characters talk and the reader is spellbound. A scene is described and the reader is there:

> *. . . for I had heard in the silent, frosty air, a sound that brought my heart into my mouth—the tap-tapping of the blind man's stick upon the frozen road. It drew nearer and nearer, while we sat holding our breath. Then it struck sharp on the inn door, and then we could hear the handle being turned. . . .*

Descriptions, action, characterization, dialogue —these carry the reader completely out of his own world with the sweep and vigor of a well-told tale.

If stories of this caliber could be found, no one would have any complaint against mystery tales. However, it is unfortunate if a child limits his reading to mystery stories—or to any other type of reading, for that matter. Youth should be the time for sampling many types. Happily, although there is only one *Treasure Island,* many good mystery and adventure stories have been written for younger and less skilled readers. Most of these are not mystery stories in the adult sense of the word. Rather, the author has introduced an incidental vein of mystery with exciting results. The children call them mystery stories, and teachers and librarians don't quarrel with them about classifications but are thankful for the combination of good writing, exciting plots, and wholesome stories.

While most of these books are for the teen age with a fair number for the ten- to twelve-year-olds, there are a few that will probably satisfy readers under ten.

ELIZABETH LANSING

Deer Moutain Hideaway

Fred and Hank, the young heroes of *Deer Mountain Hideaway* (1953) and *Deer River*

Raft, do not set out to be detectives. They just blunder into mysteries so sinister that their expert help is obviously needed. Their only handicap is Fred's snooping little sister Janey, who, in spite of the limitations of her age and sex, has a maddening way of landing in the thick of things. In the first book, the boys are building a hut on Deer Mountain when they stumble on some desperate deer poachers. The boys' sleuthing involves several grave mistakes and considerable danger. But the hair-raising climax is a triumph for the boys, tempered only by the fact that the ever-active Janey reaches the scene of action first.

Deer River Raft is an exciting tale of cattle rustlers, and again the solution of the mystery turns upon the irrepressible Janey, who astonishes even the boys. These are excellent outdoor stories as well as mysteries. The characters are very much alive, and although Fred and Hank have the major roles, Janey's casual successes will tickle the girls. These books are good reading for children eight to ten and a boon to slow readers of twelve.

Astrid Lindgren's *Bill Bergson* stories are similar to Mrs. Lansing's in plot construction but Swedish in background. For this reason they are not so easily read and understood, although they are exciting and amusing stories.

BELLE DORMAN RUGH

Crystal Mountain

Crystal Mountain (1955) is a beautiful story about life in another land, for only slightly older children. This book about four American boys and one English girl living in Lebanon was a Newbery runner-up. The boys speak Arabic, are friendly with the Lebanese, and live an active life exploring the mountain. Boadie, the English child, and her unique governess join but do not handicap the boys. Between them, they also manage to discipline a spoiled brat whose reëducation is most satisfying. How the children slowly uncover the mystery of an oddly built hut up in the rocks involves many people– English, American, and Lebanese. The story ends with the unfolding of a tender and tragic tale and the deepening friendship of all these different people. Unique characters, dialogue that is outstanding in its lively naturalness, and glimpses of the wild beauty of the country make this a distinguished book.

The Path Above the Pines brings back the lively children from *Crystal Mountain.* This time, still in Lebanon, they investigate thoroughly the mystery of some strange sounds rising from a rocky area near their home. The setting for these two stories is almost as fascinating as the active children who would undoubtedly stir up wonder and action in any place they found themselves.

KEITH ROBERTSON

Three Stuffed Owls

Keith Robertson's mysteries for older children and young people are not only well written, but humorous and exciting, too. *Three Stuffed Owls* (1954) begins with the two youthful detectives of the "Carson Street Detective Agency" yawning idly as they wait

Five-year-old Danny, with sailor cap and knapsack, accompanies his older brothers in their exciting adventures. With his humorous pen drawings, Shepard has developed an easily recognizable style.
Illustration by E. H. Shepard. From Crystal Mountain *by Belle Dorman Rugh.*
Copyright 1955 by Belle Dorman Rugh and Ernest H. Shepard. Reprinted by permission of Houghton Mifflin Company.
(Book 5½ x 8⅛, picture 1 x ⅞)

in their "office" over the garage for business to begin. Ginny, their first client, wants Swede and Neil to find her brother's bicycle. When the boys go to work on the case, they get into more than they bargained for. There is a mysterious taxidermist and his assistant, who is conspicuously missing a finger. There is a barn with a dungeon-like pit, a stuffed owl that hoots horrifically, and sundry other birds, stuffed and otherwise. As the action gains momentum the suspense increases, and the case will keep young readers guessing to the end.

An earlier book, *The Mystery of Burnt Hill,* is also a good yarn, involving carrier pigeons, invisible ink, and a sure-enough gunfight at the end.

Ice to India (1955) is the best of Mr. Robertson's mysteries, with the most colorful and villainous villain since Long John Silver. When Captain John Mason is struck down by some cargo on the eve of sailing, there is plenty of reason to believe it is not an accident. His father comes out of retirement to replace him and adds young Nathaniel Mason to the crew, though Nat is only a boy. Their cargo is a desperate speculation—ice to India—and the Masons soon find out that in addition to ice they are carrying as villainous a crew as ever sailed a ship. But old Captain Mason proves that once a commander, always a commander, and young Nat learns to sail and to use his head. How the two Masons get their cargo of ice to India and come safely home makes as thrilling a sea story as we have had in many years.

ISABELLE LAWRENCE

A Spy in Williamsburg

Spy stories make good mysteries, and *A Spy in Williamsburg* (1955), with its background and such historical figures as Thomas Jefferson and Patrick Henry, has special values. Its authenticity of detail is vouched for by Colonial Williamsburg, and the story is a rouser. Will Budge the smith is none too prosperous; his family gratefully welcomes Patrick Henry as a lodger. When he is followed by a youth who applies for work as an apprentice and lodging besides, things really look better. The boy Ben Budge is surprised to find that the ever-helpful apprentice slips out of the house nights, and when Ben begins to follow him, things happen thick and fast. The conclusion of the story is a rousing blend of fact, fiction, and excitement.

ALICE LIDE
MARGARET A. JOHANSEN

Mystery of the Mahteb
The Wooden Locket

Amlak, the hero of *Mystery of the Mahteb* (1942), is the son of a conquered king of thirteenth-century Ethiopia. Amlak hates the oppressors of his people but sees no hope of overthrowing them. Then his dying father sends Amlak on a search for "that which is lost," a mysterious symbol of power. Amlak's journey is thrilling. He encounters a people ruled by a woman who helps him when she is convinced that he is worthy to rule. Finally Amlak becomes the new king of an independent people. This is a colorful, dramatic tale about an interesting hero and period.

The Wooden Locket (1953) employs a much milder mystery to tell a modern story of Polish displaced persons trying to make a new life for themselves in this country. One of them carries the scars of her terrifying war experiences in the form of blind panic which now and then overtakes her. All of them suffer from their unfamiliarity with the language, but the children learn fast, and each member of the family has a contribution to make to his new home, as young Jan proves with the mysterious contents of his wooden locket. The community crisis precipitated by Tilka's panic will tell children something about mob psychology. The whole story has qualities that will deepen children's social understandings and sympathies.

STEPHEN MEADER

Who Rides in the Dark?

Stephen Meader is another author who not only writes well but can include a mystery that keeps the reader guessing from the first page to the last. *Red Horse Hill* has a problem of a lost will, but chiefly it is a good story of a boy and the horses he loves. *Who Rides in the Dark?* (1937) does not explain the mystery of the masked rider until the last chapter. It is a good tale about early days in New Hampshire. Daniel Drew, an orphaned stable boy at an old stagecoach inn, helps solve the mystery of the swift night rider on the fine horse. Poor Dan'l nearly loses his own life in the process but lives to enjoy happier days. *Shadow in the Pines* is a thriller which fathers have been known to borrow from their sons. Ted Winslow lives with his grandfather in the Pine Barrens of New Jersey. Like any healthy boy, he knows every inch of the country, and this knowledge, together with his insatiable curiosity, enables him to be of service to the FBI. Between them they round up a gang of saboteurs who were plotting to destroy Fort Dix. *Jonathan Goes West* is about a boy's adventures in the days of the first railroad. Mr. Meader writes so well it is a pleasure to read any of his books. His boys are real boys, well characterized and convincing. His stories are action tales, fast moving and exciting. They are clearly written and not difficult to read. Boys who would reject other more subtle tales might be lured into reading Mr. Meader's books. Yet in giving boys Stephen Meader's books, you give them good prose and wholesome stories. Particularly worth while is the relationship which usually exists in these stories between adults and boys.

HOWARD PEASE

Secret Cargo and other stories

Howard Pease is a writer of good mysteries. *Hurricane Weather, Jungle River,* and *Wind in the Rigging* are only a few of his titles. The outdoor settings, particularly in the sea stories, make an especial appeal. No matter how wild his plot may be, the reader is treated to glimpses of the New Guinea jungles or a storm at sea which are refreshingly real. *Secret Cargo* (1946) will perhaps serve as well as any of these stories to indicate their type. Larry Mathews, finding his family without funds, sets off for New Orleans to earn his own living somehow. His only companion is a mongrel dog named Sambo. Larry finally ships on a wretched old trading vessel bound for the South Seas. He manages to smuggle Sambo aboard, too. Larry is a timid boy to begin with, very shy and self-effacing. He is dubbed "Mouse" and is the butt of considerable razzing and rough treatment. Finally, when the bullying boatswain throws Sambo overboard, Mouse goes after his dog. Both are hauled back on board, and that is the beginning of Mouse's growth in courage and backbone. There has been a death on board which Larry suspects was not so accidental as it seemed. Eventually, he solves the mystery of what was in reality a murder. This is a good sea story. There is a desirable character development in Larry which adds to the satisfaction of the conclusion.

Many more examples could be given, but these should suffice to show how the mystery story cuts across most forms of fiction—here and now, other lands, historical, and outdoor adventures. Unlike adult "whodunits" the juveniles rarely involve murder. Rather, the element of mystery is introduced to heighten interest and suspense. For the most part these books are not marked by literary distinction, although many of them are very competently written, and *Crystal Mountain* has unusual beauty of style and content. The great value of such stories is that in the course of exciting action they also emphasize desirable attitudes and social relationships.

Stories of Romance

By twelve or fourteen, while boys are still avidly reading adventure stories and biography, girls are turning to stories of romance. In Chapter 1 (pp. 6-7), the preadolescent's hunger for this type of reading was discussed with a few suggestions of outstanding books and authors. More are listed in the bibliography for this chapter. Such books are generally to be found in the youth collections of our libraries.

There is considerable difference of opinion about the value of this body of teen-age books. Some teachers, librarians, and parents argue that by twelve or fourteen, children should have attained enough reading skill and social maturity to make the transition to selected choices from adult fiction and nonfiction. They say plenty of boys and girls of these ages can and do read *Gone with the Wind* or *To Kill a Mockingbird* or *Kon-Tiki* or *Ring of Bright Water*. And we know that young readers have taken to their hearts such powerful books as *Catcher in the Rye* and *Lord of the Flies,* beside which even the best of the teen-age fiction will seem wan, weak, and unrealistic.

However, there remain many older boys and girls who are unable to read such books or too immature to like them. Among this group, the girls generally betake themselves to the lush fiction of popular magazines. Some of these stories are all right, but many of them are considerably less than all right. Few give youngsters the wholesome insight into their own approaching maturity and first brush with love, that the books of Betty Cavanna, Margaret Bell, and Mary Stolz provide. (See Bibliography.) As a substitute for the fiction magazine habit or the blatant sex appeal of sensational moving pictures, let's find the best of the teen-age books to help these girls grow up with normal, healthy ideas of romance, marriage, and family life.

Criteria for Here and Now Stories

How can we evaluate this wealth of realistic fiction for children, when it ranges from picture-stories for the youngest to mystery stories and romance for young people? Turn again to the general criteria in Chapter 2 and ask of a book, whether for the youngest or the oldest, the same questions: Does it have a substantial theme, about something of real significance to a child? Is there a good plot with plenty of action, suspense, and a satisfying conclusion? Are the characters alive and memorable, or are they merely stereotypes of the poor or the alien or just names upon which to build the mystery or romance or regional story? Has the book a style that makes for comfortable reading, captivates the reader, and keeps him tearing along from page to page? And has it some literary distinction that develops the child's taste even as it enchants him?

In addition to fulfilling these familiar standards, good realistic stories should satisfy some of the child's basic needs. From *One Morning in Maine* to *Strawberry Girl* there is continual emphasis on winning or holding security.

The satisfaction of belonging is very important in *Plain Girl, Little Navajo Bluebird,* and the picture-story, *Wait for William.* Loving and being loved is a powerful motive in *Good-bye, My Lady, Moccasin Trail,* and *Cotton in My Sack*. Children's love of change and fun is a motivating force in *Henry Huggins,* the Ransome books, and *Little Eddie*. Of course the need to know is not so prominent in fiction as in informational books, but it is important in *The Little Auto, Tom Sawyer,* and *. . . and now Miguel,* as well as in the mystery tales.

And the need for competence is a strong motivating force in *Yonie Wondernose, Beanie, My Side of the Mountain, Island of the Blue Dolphins,* and many other realistic stories both of the past and today. If these books center on the child's basic needs; if they give him increased insight into his own personal problems and social relationships; if they make absorbing reading but still fulfill the standards of good literature; if they convince young readers that they can do something about their lives—have fun and adventures and get things done without any magic other than their own earnest efforts; then they are good and worth-while books for a child to read.

SUGGESTED READING, PROBLEMS, AND PROJECTS

Suggested Reading: Tom Sawyer or *Little Women, Secret Garden* or *Treasure Island, My Side of the Mountain* or *Island of the Blue Dolphins.* The complete offering of each author given in the following lists might be covered in brief class reports by individual students. In the same way one student might report on the books in a special group, such as Negro stories, Indian stories, mysteries.

Kindergarten-primary: Read several books by Kraus or De Regniers or Anglund, *The Poppy Seed Cakes,* one Tresselt book, one by Politi, one by Ardizzone, and two recent picture-stories not mentioned here.

Middle and upper grades: Read one book each by any five of the following authors—Tunis, Cleary, De Angeli, Enright, Estes, McCloskey, Van Stockum, Ransome, Streatfeild.

1. What are the main virtues of realistic stories for children? Did you find certain weaknesses?

2. How do you rate Carolyn Haywood's contribution to this field?

3. When you read or reread *Tom Sawyer* or *Little Women* how did it impress you? Compare *Tom Sawyer* with *Henry Huggins,* or *Little Women* with *Pegeen,* or *Little Women* with *Meet the Austins.*

4. How and where would you use such a story as *Mary Jane* or *Bright April* or *Call Me Charley?* What special problems do the books about Indians present?

5. Read *Sea Pup* or *Good-bye, My Lady* and discuss the value either might have for an older child.

6. Read one mystery story discussed in the text. Why did you like or dislike it? What standards for a substantial thriller emerged from your reading of *Treasure Island?*

7. Read one romance by one of the authors suggested in the text. What contribution do you think it makes to the development of the preadolescent girl?

REFERENCES

Realism for the Youngest

ALDRIDGE, JOSEPHINE H. *A Penny and a Periwinkle,* ill. by Ruth Robbins. Parnassus, 1961. Old Sy's day spent fishing near his Maine coast home proves more satisfying than any city adventure. 7-9

ARDIZZONE, EDWARD. *Little Tim and the Brave Sea Captain,* ill. by author. Walck, 1955 (first pub. in 1936). First of several books about Tim's adventures at sea. 4-6

———. *Nicholas and the Fast Moving Diesel,* ill. by author. Walck, 1959. Two small boys avert a train wreck when fireman and engineer become ill. High adventure for the youngest. 5-7

Association for Childhood Education Literature Committee. *Told Under the Blue Umbrella,* ill. by Marguerite Davis. Macmillan, 1933 and 1962. A collection of realistic stories. Mary G. Phillips' "Paddy's Three Pets" is a gem for storytelling. 4-10

AUSTIN, MARGOT. *Barney's Adventure,* ill. by author. Dutton, 1941. A good circus story for the kindergarten age. 4-8

BATE, NORMAN. *Vulcan,* ill. by author. Scribner, 1960. Vulcan was an outmoded train engine which emerged after a trip to the steel mills as a handsome warning buoy for ships at sea. A colorfully illustrated introduction to industry for the youngest. 5-8

BESKOW, ELSA. *Pelle's New Suit,* ill. by author. Harper, 1929. 4-8

BORTEN, HELEN. *Do You See What I See?* ill. by author. Abelard, 1959. A provocative picture book which may be used to stimulate children's observation of "lines and shapes and colors everywhere around." *Do You Hear What I Hear?* (1960) offers a parallel treatment of sound. 4-7

BROWN, MARCIA. *The Little Carousel,* ill. by author. Scribner, 1946. Into the crowded tenement neighborhood comes the little traveling merry-go-round. Its kindly owner lets Anthony earn the rides he cannot pay for. 5-8

BROWN, MARGARET WISE. *The City Noisy Book,* ill. by Leonard Weisgard. Harper, 1939.

———. *The Little Cowboy,* ill. by Esphyr Slobodkina. W. R. Scott, 1948.

———. *The Little Farmer,* ill. by Esphyr Slobodkina. W. R. Scott, 1948. 4-6

———. [Golden MacDonald, pseud.]. *The Little Island,* ill. by Leonard Weisgard. Doubleday, 1946.

———. [Golden MacDonald, pseud.]. *Little Lost Lamb,* ill. by Leonard Weisgard. Doubleday, 1945. 4-8

———. *The Runaway Bunny* (see Bibliography, Chapter 12).

BULLA, CLYDE R. *A Ranch for Danny,* ill. by Grace Paull. Crowell, 1951.

———. *Surprise for a Cowboy,* ill. by Grace Paull. Crowell, 1950.

A story and its sequel about a little city boy who wanted to be a cowboy, and how his desired ranch became a reality. 7-9

CLARK, MARGERY [pseud. for Mary E. Clark and Margery C. Quigley]. *The Poppy Seed Cakes,* ill. by Maud and Miska Petersham. Doubleday, 1924. 4-9

COLLIER, ETHEL. *The Birthday Tree,* ill. by Honore Guilbeau. W. R. Scott, 1961. The joy of replanting her very own tiny tree climaxes a little girl's birthday trip to the country. For younger readers. 6-8

COOK, BERNADINE. *Looking for Susie,* ill. by Judith Shahn. W. R. Scott, 1959. Gay repetitive tale of a family that set off one by one to bring young Susie home and stayed instead to play with the new litter of kittens. 4-6

DE REGNIERS, BEATRICE. *A Little House of Your Own,* ill. by Irene Haas. Harcourt, 1955. A childlike introduction to the importance of being alone at times. 5-7

______. *The Snow Party,* ill. by Reiner Zimnik. Pantheon, 1959. On a lonely Dakota farm, a blinding snowstorm brings a houseful of company to a little old woman who pined for a party. 5-9

ETS, MARIE HALL. *Gilberto and the Wind,* ill. by author. Viking, 1963. Bronze-skinned little Gilberto tells his own story of how the wind helps and hinders his play. Rhythmic, childlike text and distinctive illustrations. 4-7

FELT, SUE. *Rosa-Too-Little,* ill. by author. Doubleday, 1950. It is an important day for Rosa when she can at last write her name and have a library card. 5-7

FLACK, MARJORIE. *Wait for William,* ill. by author and R. A. Holberg. Houghton, 1935. 4-8

GOUDEY, ALICE. *The Day We Saw the Sun Come Up,* ill. by Adrienne Adams. Scribner, 1961. Two children view the beauty of the sunrise and the sunset and learn from their mother the causes of day and night. Beautiful color illustrations and distinguished text. 5-7

______. *Houses from the Sea,* ill. by Adrienne Adams. Scribner, 1959. Pastel-toned illustrations of exceptional charm and an imaginative text introduce the joys of shell collecting in this story of two children at the seashore. 5-8

GUILFOILE, ELIZABETH. *Nobody Listens to Andrew,* ill. by Mary Stevens. Follett, 1957. Humorous cumulative tale of Andrew's attempts to tell everyone there was a bear in his bed! An easy to-read book for the primary. 6-7

HAYWOOD, CAROLYN. *"B" Is for Betsy,* ill. by author. Harcourt, 1939. First in an extensive "Betsy" series of appealing home- and school-life stories. 6-10

______. *Little Eddie,* ill. by author. Morrow, 1947. Beginning title in another Haywood series. Popular with both boys and girls. 7-9

______. *Here's a Penny,* ill. by author. Harcourt, 1944.

______. *Penny and Peter,* ill. by author. Harcourt, 1946.

______. *Penny Goes to Camp,* ill. by author. Morrow, 1948. 6-9

HEILBRONER, JOAN. *The Happy Birthday Present,* ill. by Mary Chalmers. Harper, 1962. Peter and Davy, with little money and endless time, shop thoroughly for mother's birthday gift. One of the most delightful of the beginning readers. 6-7

HOBAN, RUSSELL C. *Herman the Loser,* ill. by Lillian Hoban. Harper, 1961. A most refreshing picture-story of a little boy with a talent for losing who one day becomes a victorious finder. 5-6

KOCH, DOROTHY. *I Play at the Beach,* ill. by Feodor Rojankovsky. Holiday, 1955. A little girl gives a vivid description of all the events of her day at the seashore. Illustrations have color and atmosphere. 5-8

KRAUSS, RUTH. *The Growing Story,* ill. by Phyllis Rowland. Harper, 1947. 4-6

______. *A Hole Is to Dig: a First Book of First Definitions,* ill. by Maurice Sendak. Harper, 1952. 4-

______. *A Very Special House,* ill. by Maurice Sendak. Harper, 1953. 4-7

LENSKI, LOIS. *Cowboy Small,* ill. by author. Walck, 1949. Here is the life of a cowboy, riding the range, rounding up cattle, and cooking outdoors.

______. *Let's Play House,* ill. by author. Walck, 1944. Molly and Polly imitate the household duties of grownups.

______. *The Little Farm,* ill. by author. Oxford, 1942.

______. *The Little Train,* ill. by author. Walck, 1940. One of several transportation stories in which popular Mr. Small plays the leading role. Others are *The Little Auto* (1934), *The Little Sailboat* (1937), *The Little Airplane* (1938), *The Little Fire Engine* (1946).

______. *Papa Small,* ill. by author. Oxford, 1951. The activities of the Small family throughout the week.

______. *Policeman Small,* ill. by author. Walck, 1962. The versatile Mr. Small is back in a new role. His day of varied duties will fascinate young readers, and will do valiant service in "community helper" units. 5-7

LIANG, YEN. *The Skyscraper,* ill. by author. Lippincott, 1958. The skyscraper replaced many old buildings that crowded the city, and left spacious grounds for everyone to enjoy. A striking picture book with a unique theme. 5-8

LINDMAN, MAJ. *Snipp, Snapp, Snurr and the Red Shoes,* ill. by author. Whitman, 1932. The humorous adventures of three small boys earning money to buy their mother a pair of red shoes. 4-8

MC CLOSKEY, ROBERT. *Blueberries for Sal,* ill. by author. Viking, 1948.

———. *Make Way for Ducklings,* ill. by author. Viking, 1941. 4-8

———. *One Morning in Maine,* ill. by author. Viking, 1952. 3-7

———. *Time of Wonder,* ill. by author. Viking, 1957. 6-9

PETRIDES, HEIDRUN. *Hans and Peter,* ill. by author. Harcourt, 1963. 7-9

POLITI, LEO. *Juanita,* ill. by author. Scribner, 1948. 6-9

———. *Little Leo,* ill. by author. Scribner, 1951. 6-9

———. *Moy Moy,* ill. by author. Scribner, 1960. 7-9

———. *Pedro, the Angel of Olvera Street,* ill. by author. Scribner, 1946. 6-9

———. *Song of the Swallows,* ill. by author. Scribner, 1949. Little Juan, anticipating the yearly return of the swallows to Capistrano on St. Joseph's Day, is allowed to help ring the mission bells and welcome them back. Caldecott Medal. 6-9

RAND, ANN and PAUL. *Sparkle and Spin,* ill. by Paul Rand. Harcourt, 1957. A rare picture book that conveys at the young child's level the importance of words. Highly stylized illustrations by a master of design. 4-7

SAUER, JULIA. *Mike's House,* ill. by Don Freeman. Viking, 1954. The library is "Mike's House" to young Robert because it houses his favorite book, *Mike Mulligan and His Steam Shovel.* 5-7

SLOBODKIN, FLORENCE and LOUIS. *Too Many Mittens.* Vanguard, 1958. Small mitten-losers will delight in this humorously repetitive picture tale of Ned and Donny, the twins, who were also mitten-losers. 5-7

STOLZ, MARY S. *Emmett's Pig,* ill. by Garth Williams. Harper, 1959. A delightful easy-to-read story about a little city boy's happy long-distance ownership of a farm piglet. 6-8

TRESSELT, ALVIN. *Autumn Harvest,* ill. by Roger Duvoisin. Lothrop, 1951.

———. *Bonnie Bess, the Weathervane Horse,* ill. by Marylin Hafner. Lothrop, 1949.

———. *Follow the Wind,* ill. by Roger Duvoisin. Lothrop, 1950.

———. *Hi, Mister Robin!* ill. by Roger Duvoisin. Lothrop, 1950.

———. *I Saw the Sea Come In,* ill. by Roger Duvoisin. Lothrop, 1954.

———. *Johnny Maple-Leaf,* ill. by Roger Duvoisin. Lothrop, 1948.

———. *Rain Drop Splash,* ill. by Leonard Weisgard. Lothrop, 1946.

———. *Sun Up,* ill. by Roger Duvoisin. Lothrop, 1949.

———. *White Snow, Bright Snow,* ill. by Roger Duvoisin. Lothrop, 1947. Caldecott Medal. 5-8

TUDOR, TASHA. *Pumpkin Moonshine,* ill. by author. Walck, 1938 and 1962. This Halloween story makes a good introduction to the other beautifully illustrated books of Tasha Tudor. Reissued in larger format. 4-7

UDRY, JANICE MAY. *The Moon Jumpers,* ill. by Maurice Sendak. Harper, 1959. Beautiful color illustrations enhance this mood picture book which describes children frolicking in the moonlight until bedtime interrupts their imaginative play. 5-8

WILL and NICOLAS. *Russet and the Two Reds,* ill. by authors. Harcourt, 1962.

———. *The Two Reds,* ill. by authors. Harcourt, 1950. 5-8

YASHIMA, TARO (pseud. for Jun Iwamatsu). *Umbrella,* ill. by author. Viking, 1958. To small Momo it seemed that rain would never come so that she might use her new blue umbrella and bright red boots. New York background. 4-6

ZION, GENE. *Dear Garbage Man,* ill. by Margaret Bloy Graham. Harper, 1957. Popular for community units as well as highly entertaining is this picture-story of Stan, the brand-new rubbish collector. 5-8

———. *The Plant Sitter,* ill. by Margaret Bloy Graham. Harper, 1959. Tommy crowded the house with the plants of vacationing neighbors, and his zeal in their care precipitates a family crisis! A novel and humorous picture book. 5-7

ZOLOTOW, CHARLOTTE. *The Storm Book,* ill. by Margaret B. Graham. Harper, 1952. Little boy and his mother share the beauty and excitement of a summer storm. Brief text and charming illustrations. 5-7

REALISM FOR OLDER CHILDREN

Forerunners

ALCOTT, LOUISA M. *Little Women,* ill. by Jessie Willcox Smith. Little, 1934 (first pub. in 1868).

———. *Little Women,* ill. by Barbara Cooney. Crowell, 1955. 12-16

BURNETT, FRANCES HODGSON. *The Secret Garden,* ill. by Tasha Tudor. Lippincott, 1962 (first pub. in 1909). 8-12

TWAIN, MARK [pseud. for Samuel Clemens]. *The Adventures of Tom Sawyer* and *The Adventures of Huckleberry Finn,* ill. by Norman Rockwell, 2 vols. in 1. Heritage, 1952 (first pub. in 1876 and 1885). 10-14

American, British, and Irish stories

BINNS, ARCHIE. *Sea Pup,* ill. by Robert Candy. Little, 1954. 10-14

BRAGDON, ELSPETH. *That Jud!* ill. by Georges Schreiber. Viking, 1957. Outstanding in its background and characterization is this story of an orphaned Maine boy who loses and regains his village's good will. 10-13

BUTLER, BEVERLY. *Light a Single Candle.* Dodd, 1962. The stirring story of Cathy Wheeler, blinded at fourteen, and her courageous struggle to regain her place in the school crowd. 12-15

CARSON, JOHN F. *The Coach Nobody Liked.* Farrar, 1960. A basketball coach who puts sportsmanship ahead of winning finds himself the central focus of a divided community. 12-15

CHURCH, RICHARD. *Five Boys in a Cave.* Day, 1951. Five boys carefully plan their expedition into an old tunnel. When an accident occurs, it is the quiet unassuming lad who takes over leadership of the group and brings them to safety. 11-14

CLEARY, BEVERLY. *Emily's Runaway Imagination,* ill. by Beth and Joe Krush. Morrow, 1961. In between her zealous efforts to start a town library, imaginative Emily frequently finds herself the victim or the heroine of some very funny situations. A lively story of Oregon in the 1920's. 9-11

______. *Henry Huggins,* ill. by Louis Darling. Morrow, 1950.

______. *Ellen Tebbits,* ill. by Louis Darling. Morrow, 1951.

______. *Henry and Beezus,* ill. by Louis Darling. Morrow, 1952.

______. *Henry and Ribsy,* ill. by Louis Darling. Morrow, 1954.

______. *Beezus and Ramona,* ill. by Louis Darling. Morrow, 1955. 8-12

______. *Henry and the Paper Route,* ill. by Louis Darling. Morrow, 1957. 9-12

______. *Henry and the Clubhouse,* ill. by Louis Darling. Morrow, 1962. 9-11

DILLON, EILIS. *The Fort of Gold,* ill. by Harper Johnson. Funk, 1962. Three Irish lads outwit the outlanders who are searching for Spanish gold long hidden in an ancient fort. A suspenseful tale rich in Irish atmosphere, humor, and good characterization. 11-14

ENRIGHT, ELIZABETH. *Gone-Away Lake,* ill. by Beth and Joe Krush. Harcourt, 1957. 9-12

______. *Return to Gone-Away,* ill. by Beth and Joe Krush. Harcourt, 1961. 10-13

______. *The Saturdays,* ill. by author. Holt, 1941.

______. *The Four-Story Mistake,* ill. by author. Holt, 1942.

______. *Then There Were Five,* ill. by author. Holt, 1944.

______. *Thimble Summer,* ill. by author. Holt, 1938. Newbery Medal. 8-12

ESTES, ELEANOR. *The Moffats,* ill. by Louis Slobodkin. Harcourt, 1941.

______. *The Middle Moffat,* ill. by Louis Slobodkin. Harcourt, 1942.

______. *Rufus M.,* ill. by Louis Slobodkin. Harcourt, 1943. 7-10

______. *Ginger Pye,* ill. by author. Harcourt, 1951. Newbery Medal. 8-12

GAGE, WILSON. *Dan and the Miranda,* ill. by Glen Rounds. World, 1962. Dan chose spiders for his school science project, and the family, especially his sister, regarded the choice with mixed feelings! A delightful family tale developed around a nature theme. 9-10

GARNETT, EVE. *The Family from One End Street,* ill. by author. Vanguard, 1960. A grand family story of the seven Ruggles children who found their meager existence quite full of adventure. This popular English story received the Carnegie Medal award in 1938. 10-13

GEORGE, JEAN. *My Side of the Mountain,* ill. by author. Dutton, 1959. 11-15

HALL, ROSALYS HASKELL. *Young Fancy,* ill. by Donald Bolognese. McKay, 1960. Rebecca's "growing up" in a New England rectory is complicated by four lively brothers. 11-14

KRUMGOLD, JOSEPH. *...and now Miguel,* ill. by Jean Charlot. Crowell, 1953. Newbery Award. 9-12

______. *Onion John,* ill. by Symeon Shimin. Crowell, 1959. Newbery Award. 12-14

LANGTON, JANE. *The Majesty of Grace,* ill. by author. Harper, 1961. Even her family's straitened finances did not discourage young Grace Jones, for she was convinced she was heir to the British throne! 10-12

LE GRAND [pseud. for Le Grand Henderson]. *Augustus Rides the Border,* ill. by author. Bobbs, 1947. Augustus and his ever wandering family travel down to the Mexican border in a broken-down old car, and with a minimum of cash. 9-11

L'ENGLE, MADELEINE. *Meet the Austins.* Vanguard, 1960. 10-12

LOVELACE, MAUD HART. *Betsy-Tacy,* ill. by Lois Lenski. Crowell, 1940. One of a popular series including *Betsy-Tacy and Tib* (1941), *Betsy and Tacy Go over the Big Hill* (1942), *Betsy and Tacy Go Downtown* (1943). Betsy, Tacy, and Tib are close friends in a Minnesota town at the turn of the century, and their warm friendship continues into their romantic years. The first four titles tell of their grade-school years. (See Romance for others in series.) 7-12

MC CLOSKEY, ROBERT. *Centerburg Tales,* ill. by author. Viking, 1951. Further adventures of Homer Price and reminiscences by his grandfather.

———. *Homer Price,* ill. by author. Viking, 1943.

———. *Lentil,* ill. by author. Viking, 1940. 8-12

MAC KELLAR, WILLIAM. *Wee Joseph,* ill. by Ezra Jack Keats. McGraw, 1957. Young Davie prayed hard, and a small miracle and a great scientific event combine to save Wee Joseph, his runt puppy, from being drowned. A heartwarming story of Scotland. 8-10

MC LEAN, ALLAN CAMPBELL. *Storm over Skye,* ill. by Shirley Hughes. Harcourt, 1957. A story rich in Scottish atmosphere tells of two brothers' efforts to solve the sheep stealing that has thrown their community into an uproar. A bit of romance, too. 13-16

MAYNE, WILLIAM. *A Swarm in May,* ill. by C. Walter Hodges. Bobbs, 1957. The author achieves a unique continuity with the past in this story of young John Owen, who is chosen as the traditional Beekeeper in an English Cathedral Choir School. 11-14

NASH, MARY. *While Mrs. Coverlet Was Away,* ill. by Garrett Price. Little, 1958. Light-hearted nonsense tale of the three Persever children, whose cat-food formula opens the road to modest riches. 9-11

NORDSTROM, URSULA. *The Secret Language,* ill. by Mary Chalmers. Harper, 1960. The events of eight-year-old Victoria's first year at boarding school are told with sympathy, humor, and keen insight. 8-10

RANSOME, ARTHUR. *Swallows and Amazons,* ill. by Helene Carter. Lippincott, 1931. The first title in a popular series. 12-14

ROBERTSON, KEITH. *Henry Reed, Inc.*, ill. by Robert McCloskey. Viking, 1958. 11-13

ROBINSON, TOM. *Trigger John's Son,* ill. by Robert McCloskey. Viking, 1949. Trigger is an orphan in the process of being adopted when he decides to inspect his future parents. He gets off the train prematurely and the action begins. Robert McCloskey's sensitive drawings add to the fun. 10-14

SPYKMAN, E. C. *A Lemon and a Star.* Harcourt, 1955. 11-14

———. *The Wild Angel.* Harcourt, 1957. Written with the same forthrightness and humor as *A Lemon and a Star,* this sequel recounts the further adventures of the Cares children temporarily away from home and eager to return. *Terrible, Horrible Edie* (1960) finds the Cares children at the seashore with storm and flood adding to the summer excitement. 11-14

STREATFEILD, NOEL. *Ballet Shoes,* ill. by Richard Floethe. Random, 1937.

———. *Circus Shoes,* ill. by Richard Floethe. Random, 1939. 10-14

STREET, JAMES. *Good-bye, My Lady.* Lippincott, 1954. 12-

TUNIS, JOHN. *All-American,* ill. by Hans Walleen. Harcourt, 1942. 10-16

———. *The Duke Decides,* ill. by James MacDonald. Harcourt, 1939.

———. *The Iron Duke,* ill. by Johan Bull. Harcourt, 1938.

Among the best college stories we have for the precollege boy. *The Iron Duke* is about an Iowa boy's adjustments to Harvard. *The Duke Decides* finds him a member of the Olympic track team. 12-16

———. *The Kid from Tomkinsville,* ill. by J. H. Barnum. Harcourt, 1940. Roy Tucker, a small-town boy, makes a big-league baseball team. Fine story of his training, mistakes, and triumphs. The Tunis books are popular sports stories with a strong emphasis on community ideals. 11-15

VAN STOCKUM, HILDA. *Canadian Summer,* ill. by author. Viking, 1948. Adventures of the Mitchell family in a summer cottage near Montreal.

———. *The Cottage at Bantry Bay,* ill. by author. Viking, 1938.

———. *Francie on the Run,* ill. by author. Viking, 1939.

———. *The Mitchells,* ill. by author. Viking, 1945.

———. *Pegeen,* ill. by author. Viking, 1941. 10-14

WIER, ESTER. *The Loner,* ill. by Christine Price. McKay, 1963. 12-15

WILSON, HAZEL. *Herbert,* ill. by John N. Barron. Knopf, 1950. Followed by *Herbert Again* (1951) and *More Fun with Herbert* (1954). Herbert is a younger Homer Price; and his adventures and vicissitudes are equally funny. 8-12

YATES, ELIZABETH. *Mountain Born,* ill. by Nora Unwin. Coward, 1943. Young Peter cares for Biddy, the little black lamb, proudly wears a coat woven from her wool, and endures the grief of losing her after she dies in a mountain storm. 8-11

———. *A Place for Peter,* ill, by Nora Unwin. Coward, 1952. 10-14

Stories about American Negroes

BAKER, AUGUSTA. *Books about Negro Life for Children.* New York Public Library, N.Y. A frequently revised and useful annotated bibliography prepared by the New York Public Library's Supervisor of Work with Children.

BEIM, LORRAINE and JERROLD. *Two Is a Team,* ill. by Ernest Crichlow. Harcourt, 1945. 6-9

BONTEMPS, ARNA. *Sad-Faced Boy,* ill. by Virginia Burton. Houghton, 1937. 8-10

BURGWYN, MEBANE HOLOMAN. *Lucky Mischief*, ill. by Gertrude Howe. Walck, 1949. This book combines the virtues of being a good mystery, a story about 4-H activities, and a picture of a substantial, rural Negro community. The feud between two boys is finally dissolved in their devotion to their pet steers. 10-14

DE ANGELI, MARGUERITE. *Bright April*, ill. by author. Doubleday, 1946. 8-10

EVANS, EVA KNOX. *Araminta*, ill. by Erick Berry [pseud. for Allena Best]. Putnam, 1935. First in a trio of stories of city and country life, including *Jerome Anthony* and *Araminta's Goat*. 7-10

FAULKNER, GEORGENE, and JOHN BECKER. *Melindy's Medal*, ill. by Elton C. Fax. Messner, 1945. A humorous and tender story of a little Negro girl, Melindy, who is boundlessly happy when the family moves to a new housing project. When a fire breaks out at her school, Melindy proves her bravery. 8-10

HAYES, FLORENCE. *Skid*, ill. by Elton C. Fax. Houghton, 1948. 10-13

HUNT, MABEL LEIGH. *Ladycake Farm*, ill. by Clotilde Embree Funk. Lippincott, 1952. 9-12

JACKSON, JESSE. *Call Me Charley*, ill. by Doris Spiegel. Harper, 1945. 10-13

______. *Charley Starts from Scratch*. Harper, 1958. 12-

KEATS, EZRA JACK. *The Snowy Day*, ill. by author. Viking, 1962. Caldecott Medal. 5-7

LATTIMORE, ELEANOR. *Junior, a Colored Boy of Charleston*, ill. by author. Harcourt, 1938. 8-10

MEANS, FLORENCE CRANNELL. *Great Day in the Morning*, Houghton, 1946. A lovable Negro girl experiences the sadness of racial prejudice but has the courage to go on. At Tuskegee she comes to know Dr. Carver and decides to become a nurse. 12-14

______. *Shuttered Windows*, ill. by Armstrong Sperry. Houghton, 1938. A Northern Negro girl adjusts to more primitive Southern life. 12-14

NEWELL, HOPE. *A Cap for Mary Ellis*. Harper, 1953. Two young nursing students enter as the first Negro trainees in a New York State hospital. There they make a happy adjustment to the new life, their fellow workers, and the patients. The story is told with warmth and humor. Followed by *Mary Ellis, Student Nurse* (1958). 12-16

SHARPE, STELLA G. *Tobe*, ill. with photographs by Charles Farrell. Univ. of N. C. Press, 1939. 6-8

STERLING, DOROTHY. *Mary Jane*, ill. by Ernest Crichlow. Doubleday, 1959. 11-14

TARRY, ELLEN, and MARIE HALL ETS. *My Dog Rinty*, ill. by Alexander and Alexandra Alland. Viking, 1946. 8-10

TUNIS, JOHN R. *All-American* (see American, British, and Irish stories).

Stories of American Indians

Note: A few historical stories are included for background.

ARMER, LAURA. *Waterless Mountain*, ill. by author and Sidney Armer. McKay, 1931. 12-14

BAKER, BETTY. *Little Runner of the Longhouse*, ill. by Arnold Lobel. Harper, 1962. Little Runner finally gains his reward of maple sugar in the Iroquois New Year rites. An amusing repetitive Indian tale for beginning readers. 6-7

BUFF, MARY. *Dancing Cloud*, rev. ed., ill. by Conrad Buff. Viking, 1957. 8-10

______. *Hah-Nee*, ill. by Conrad Buff. Houghton, 1956. 8-10

BUFF, MARY and CONRAD. *Magic Maize*, ill. by authors. Houghton, 1953. 9-12

BULLA, CLYDE. *Eagle Feather*, ill. by Tom Two Arrows. Crowell, 1953. Eagle Feather, a young Navaho, loved the outdoor life of a shepherd and had no wish to go to school until changed circumstances made school a longed-for goal. 7-10

______. *Indian Hill*, ill. by James Spanfeller. Crowell, 1963. Adjustment of a Navaho Indian family moved from a reservation to a city apartment. 8-10

CLARK, ANN NOLAN. *Blue Canyon Horse*, ill. by Allan Houser. Viking, 1954. 8-10

______. *In My Mother's House*, ill. by Velino Herrera. Viking, 1941. 8-12

______. *Little Navajo Bluebird*, ill. by Paul Lantz. Viking, 1943. 8-12

______. *Santiago*, ill. by Lynd Ward. Viking, 1955. 12-15

______. *Secret of the Andes*, ill. by Jean Charlot. Viking, 1952. 10-14

DAVIS, RUSSELL G., and BRENT K. ASHABRANNER. *The Choctaw Code*. McGraw, 1961. By tribal law Choctaw Jim had one year before he must die for violating his Indian code. This is the moving story of that year which he spent sharing his Indian wisdom and skills with a young pioneer boy. 12-15

LAMPMAN, EVELYN. *Navaho Sister*, ill. by Paul Lantz. Doubleday, 1956. 10-13

______. *Treasure Mountain*, ill. by Richard Bennett. Doubleday, 1949. 12-14

LAURITZEN, JONREED. *The Ordeal of the Young Hunter*, ill. by Hoke Denetsosie. Little, 1954. A distinguished story of a twelve-year-old Navaho boy who grows to appreciate what is good in the cultures of the white man and the Indian. Background of the story is Flagstaff, Arizona. 11-14

MC GRAW, ELOISE. *Moccasin Trail*, ill. by Paul Galdone. Coward, 1952. 11-14

MC NICKLE, D'ARCY. *Runner in the Sun*, ill. by Allan Houser. Holt, 1954. The background of this story is the Southwest before the coming of the white men. A young Indian lad realizes the needs of his people and makes a hazardous journey to the lands of the Aztecs to find a hardier maize. 12-14

MEANS, FLORENCE CRANNELL. *Whispering Girl,* ill. by Oscar Howard. Houghton, 1941. A Hopi family adopts three children. The sixteen-year-old girl helps solve the problems which make up the story. 12-15

O'DELL, SCOTT. *Island of the Blue Dolphins.* Houghton, 1960. Newbery Medal. 12-16

O'MORAN, M. [pseud. for Mabel O. Moran]. *Trail of the Little Paiute,* ill. by Claire Davison. Lippincott, 1952. 10-13

SANDOZ, MARI. *The Horsecatcher.* Westminster, 1957. Young Elk, the Cheyenne, dreamed of taming wild horses rather than of becoming a great warrior. In spite of going against tradition, he won the respect of his tribe. Written with beauty and distinction. 12-16

SHARP, EDITH LAMBERT. *Nkwala,* ill. by William Winter. Little, 1958. Stirringly written historical tale of a young Spokane Indian who at last wins his adult name. 11-13

Regional and Religious Minorities

ANGELO, VALENTI. *The Bells of Bleecker Street,* ill. by author. Viking, 1949.

______. *Big Little Island,* ill. by author. Viking, 1955. A war orphan learns to feel at home among the Italian-Americans of Manhattan. 10-13

______. *Nino* (see Bibliography, Chapter 16).

______. *Paradise Valley,* ill. by author. Viking, 1940. 8-12

Association for Childhood Education. *Told under the Stars and Stripes,* ill. by Nedda Walker. Macmillan, 1945. 8-12

BUFF, MARY and CONRAD. *Peter's Pinto,* ill. by Conrad Buff. Viking, 1949. A Utah ranch summer is highlighted for Peter when he acquires a wild pinto pony of his own. Mormon background. 9-11

CARROLL, RUTH and LATROBE. *Beanie,* ill. by authors. Walck, 1953. Followed by *Tough Enough* (1954), *Tough Enough's Trip* (1956), *Tough Enough's Pony* (1957), *Tough Enough and Sassy* (1958), and *Tough Enough's Indians* (1960). 8-11

CREDLE, ELLIS. *Down Down the Mountain,* ill. by author. Nelson, 1934. 7-8

DE ANGELI, MARGUERITE. *Henner's Lydia,* ill. by author. Doubleday, 1936.

______. *Skippack School,* ill. by author. Doubleday, 1939 and 1961. 8-12

______. *Thee, Hannah!* ill. by author. Doubleday, 1940.

______. *Up the Hill,* ill. by author. Doubleday, 1942. 8-12

______. *Yonie Wondernose,* ill. by author. Doubleday, 1944. 5-7

ESTES, ELEANOR. *The Hundred Dresses,* ill. by Louis Slobodkin. Harcourt, 1944. A touching story of a little girl with a "funny foreign" name and not many dresses. 7-10

GATES, DORIS. *Blue Willow,* ill. by Paul Lantz. Viking, 1940. 10-12

JUDSON, CLARA INGRAM. *Bruce Carries the Flag; They Came from Scotland,* Follett, 1957.

______. *The Green Ginger Jar; They Came from China,* ill. by Paul Brown. Houghton, 1949. A young Chinese-American brother and sister thought their grandmother and parents adhered too closely to old country ways, and so they set out to change them.

______. *The Lost Violin; They Came from Bohemia,* ill. by Margaret Bradfield. Follett, 1958. The story of a Bohemian family who brought their creative skills and love of music to America. Background is Chicago in the 1890's.

______. *Michael's Victory; They Came from Ireland.* Follett, 1957.

______. *Petar's Treasure; They Came from Dalmatia,* ill. by Ursula Koering. Follett, 1958. All the difficulties that face the non-English-speaking and impoverished immigrant were encountered by the newly arrived Petrovich family from Dalmatia, before they found security in the new land.

______. *Pierre's Lucky Pouch; They Came from France;* ill. by Lois Lenski. Follett, 1957.

______. *Sod-House Winter; They Came from Sweden,* ill. by E. C. Caswell. Follett, 1957. 9-12

JUSTUS, MAY. *Children of the Great Smoky Mountains,* ill. by Robert Henneberger. Dutton, 1952. 7-10

______. *Here Comes Mary Ellen,* ill. by Helen Finger. Lippincott, 1940. 8-12
These stories give an all-around picture of life in the Tennessee mountains.

Land of the Free Series. This series includes several fine stories which highlight contributions of different nationalities to American development:

HAVIGHURST, WALTER and MARION. *Song of the Pines; A Story of Norwegian Lumbering in Wisconsin,* ill. by Richard Floethe. Holt, 1949.

LUNDY, JO EVALIN. *Tidewater Valley; A Story of the Swiss in Oregon,* ill. by Margaret Ayer. Winston, 1949.

MEANS, FLORENCE and CARLETON. *Silver Fleece; A Story of the Spanish in New Mexico,* ill. by Edwin Schmidt. Winston, 1950.

OAKES, VIRGINIA (VANYA). *Footprints of the Dragon; A Story of the Chinese and the Pacific Railways,* ill. by Tyrus Wong. Winston, 1949.

ROBINSON, GERTRUDE. *Sign of the Golden Fish; A Story of the Cornish Fishermen in Maine,* ill. by Frederick T. Chapman. Winston, 1949.

ZIEGLER, ELSIE. *The Blowing-Wand; A Story of Bohemian Glassmaking in Ohio,* ill. by Jacob Landau. Holt, 1955. 11-15

LAWRENCE, MILDRED. *Peachtree Island,* ill. by Mary Stevens. Harcourt, 1948. After having been passed about among numerous relatives, nine-year-old Cissie finds a real home with Uncle Eben in the Great Lakes peach-growing area. Cissie loves the work, Uncle Eben, and the happy winter when the harvest is in. 8-10

______. *Sand in Her Shoes,* ill. by Madye Lee Chastain. Harcourt, 1949. The family move to the east coast of Florida brings a new kind of life to an eager young brother and sister for whom the sea and scenery are a totally different experience. 9-12

LENSKI, LOIS. *Bayou Suzette,* ill. by author. Lippincott, 1943.

______. *Blue Ridge Billy,* ill. by author. Lippincott, 1946.

______. *Boom Town Boy,* ill. by author. Lippincott, 1948.

______. *Cotton in My Sack,* ill. by author. Lippincott, 1949.

______. *Judy's Journey,* ill. by author. Lippincott, 1947.

______. *Strawberry Girl,* ill. by author. Lippincott, 1945. Newbery Medal. 9-12

LIDE, ALICE, and MARGARET JOHANSEN. *The Wooden Locket* (see Mystery tales).

LINDQUIST, JENNIE D. *The Golden Name Day,* ill. by Garth Williams. Harper, 1955. Nancy's visit to Grandma and Grandpa Benson and their Swedish neighbors reaches its joyous climax when a name day is found for her. A heart-warming story with fine characterization. Followed by *The Little Silver House* (1959). 9-12

MUSGRAVE, FLORENCE. *Robert E.,* ill. by Mary Stevens. Hastings House, 1957. Moving to a Midwestern city from a lonely existence in the Southern Mountains, Robert E. finds adjustment extremely difficult. 10-13

SEREDY, KATE. *A Tree for Peter,* ill. by author. Viking, 1941. A story of shantytown complicated by a rather confusing symbolism, but with some of Kate Seredy's finest pictures. 9-12

SORENSEN, VIRGINIA. *Plain Girl,* ill. by Charles Geer. Harcourt, 1955. 9-12

STONG, PHIL. *Honk: the Moose* (see Bibliography, Chapter 14).

STUART, JESSE. *The Beatinest Boy,* ill. by Robert Henneberger. McGraw, 1953. 8-12

______. *A Penny's Worth of Character,* ill. by Robert Henneberger. McGraw, 1954. 7-10

______. *Red Mule,* ill. by Robert Henneberger. McGraw, 1955. 8-12

TAYLOR, SYDNEY. *All-of-a-kind Family,* ill. by Helen John. Follett, 1951.

______. *More All-of-a-kind Family,* ill. by Mary Stevens. Follett, 1954.

______. *All-of-a-kind Family Uptown,* ill. by Mary Stevens, Follett, 1958. 9-12

TUNIS, JOHN R. *Keystone Kids.* Harcourt, 1943. A fine sports story for the teen age—the happy resolution of anti-Semitic feeling is achieved by the students. 12-16

Mystery Tales

ANCKARSVARD, KARIN. *The Robber Ghost,* tr. from the Swedish by Annabelle Macmillan, ill. by Paul Galdone. Harcourt, 1961. The disappearance of money from the post office housed in a wing of an old and supposedly haunted Swedish castle arouses the detective instincts of young schoolmates Michael and Cecilia. Good atmosphere and suspense for both boys and girls. 10-12

CAMERON, ELEANOR. *The Terrible Churnadryne,* ill. by Beth and Joe Krush. Little, 1959. Did a strange prehistoric creature really stalk San Lorenzo peak? Tom and Jennifer and the whole town of Redwood Cove are caught up in the strange controversy. A unique well-written tale of suspense. 9-12

DILLON, EILIS. *The Singing Cave,* ill. by Stan Campbell. Funk, 1960. Suspense and mystery abound in this outstandingly written tale of the discovery and disappearance of Viking remains from a cave on an Irish isle. 12-15

HALL, AYLMER. *The Search for Lancelot's Sword.* Criterion, 1962. An outstanding mystery tale with Welsh background. Somewhere at Llanvair Castle a legendary sword may have been concealed centuries ago, and three modern youngsters set out to find it. 11-14

HIGHTOWER, FLORENCE. *Dark Horse of Woodfield,* ill. by Joshua Tolford. Houghton, 1962. The Woodfield home was a shabby relic, but it housed Buggsie and Maggie Armistead, who trained a horse, solved a mystery, and even bred cocoons to restore the family fortunes. A highly humorous and substantial family story with a background of New England. 11-13

______. *The Ghost of Follonsbee's Folly,* ill. by Ati Forberg. Houghton, 1958. The newly bought dilapidated house in the country soon had the young Stockpoles trying to solve the mystery of its strange sounds and another puzzle as well. 11-14

______. *Mrs. Wappinger's Secret,* ill. by Beth and Joe Krush. Houghton, 1956. Eccentric Mrs. Wappinger of a Maine resort island is quite sure she has ancestral buried treasure somewhere on her property. Young Charlie Porter, summer visitor, is more than delighted to aid her in a secret treasure-hunting alliance. 11-14

JEWETT, ELEANORE. *Cobbler's Knob,* ill. by Christine Price. Viking, 1956. A girl solves the mystery of a haunted house with exciting results. 9-12

———. *Mystery at Boulder Point,* ill. by Jay H. Barnum. Viking, 1949. Good characterization and atmosphere mark this exciting tale of two girls who solve the mystery of an abandoned house. 11-13

KASTNER, ERICH. *Emil and the Detectives,* tr. by May Massee, ill. by Walter Trier. Doubleday, 1930. Robbed while traveling to Berlin to visit his grandmother, young Emil, with the lively assistance of a group of boys, tracks down the thief. 10-13

KYLE, ELISABETH [pseud. for A. M. Dunlop]. *Holly Hotel,* ill. by Nora Unwin. Houghton, 1947. A Scotch family opens its home to boarders and the children of the family soon become involved in the mystery of the lost manuscript. Unusually good background of the country, convincing characters. 10-13

LANSING, E. H. *Deer Mountain Hideaway,* ill. by Marc Simont. Crowell, 1953.

———. *Deer River Raft,* ill. by Marc Simont. Crowell, 1955. 9-12

LAWRENCE, ISABELLE. *A Spy in Williamsburg,* ill. by Manning Lee. Rand McNally, 1955. 9-12

LIDE, ALICE A., and MARGARET JOHANSEN. *The Mystery of the Mahteb,* ill. by Avery Johnson. Longmans, 1942. 12-14

———. *The Wooden Locket,* ill. by Corydon Bell. Viking, 1953. 11-14

LINDGREN, ASTRID. *Bill Bergson Lives Dangerously,* tr. by Herbert Antoine, ill. by Don Freeman. Viking, 1954.

———. *Bill Bergson, Master Detective,* tr. by Louis Glanzman. Viking, 1952.

These two mystery stories from the Swedish are told with considerable humor in spite of their dramatic plots. In *Bill Bergson, Master Detective* Bill and his friends Anders and Eva Lotta track down stolen jewels and restore them to the police. In the other book they identify a murderer. 10-13

MC LEAN, ALLAN CAMPBELL. *Master of Morgana.* Harcourt, 1959. Sixteen-year-old Niall solves the mystery of his older brother's injuries in this suspense-filled tale of fishermen and poachers on the Isle of Skye. 13-15

MEADER, STEPHEN. *The Fish Hawk's Nest,* ill. by Edward Shenton. Harcourt, 1952. Exciting tale of smuggling on the New Jersey coast in the 1820's. Good characterizations and background. 11-14

———. *Jonathan Goes West,* ill. by Edward Shenton. Harcourt, 1946. 11-14

———. *Red Horse Hill,* ill. by Lee Townsend. Harcourt, 1930.

———. *Shadow in the Pines,* ill. by Edward Shenton. Harcourt, 1942. 14-16

———. *Who Rides in the Dark?* ill. by James MacDonald. Harcourt, 1937. 14-16

ORTON, HELEN F. *Mystery at the Little Red School House,* ill. by R. Emmett Owen. Lippincott, 1941.

———. *Mystery of the Secret Drawer,* ill. by Sandra James. Lippincott, 1945.

———. *Mystery up the Chimney,* ill. by Robert Doremus. Lippincott, 1947.

———. *The Secret of the Rosewood Box,* ill. by Robert Ball. Lippincott, 1937.

———. *The Treasure in the Little Trunk,* ill. by Robert Ball. Lippincott, 1932.

A mild element of mystery in all these historical tales. 8-11

PEASE, HOWARD. *Jungle River,* ill. by Armstrong Sperry. Doubleday, 1948.

———. *Secret Cargo,* ill. by Paul Forster. Doubleday, 1946. 12-14

ROBERTSON, KEITH. *The Crow and the Castle,* ill. by Robert Greiner. Viking, 1957. A superior mystery tale involving two youthful amateur detectives. 11-14

———. *Ice to India,* ill. by Jack Weaver. Viking, 1955.

———. *The Mystery of Burnt Hill,* ill. by Rafaello Busoni. Viking, 1952. 12-14

———. *Three Stuffed Owls,* ill. by Jack Weaver. Viking, 1954. 10-14

RUGH, BELLE D. *Crystal Mountain,* ill. by Ernest H. Shepard. Houghton, 1955. 11-14

———. *The Path above the Pines,* ill. by Dorothy Bailey Morse. Houghton, 1962. 11-13

STEVENSON, ROBERT LOUIS. *Treasure Island,* ill. by C. B. Falls. World, 1946 (first pub. in 1883). 12-16

WHITNEY, PHYLLIS. *Mystery of the Green Cat.* Westminster, 1957. The discovery of a message long hidden in a ceramic cat brings peace to an old neighbor. 11-14

———. *Mystery of the Haunted Pool,* ill. by H. Tom Hall. Westminster, 1960. A well-paced mystery tale of a long-lost necklace, and of a brother and sister who help recover it while vacationing in a Hudson River town. 11-14

WINTERFELD, HENRY. *Detectives in Togas* (see Bibliography, Chapter 16).

Romance

ALLAN, MABEL ESTHER. *"On Stage, Flory!"* Watts, 1961. At the Edinburgh Festival, young Flory

Ronald finds both romance and the start of a stage career. Good atmosphere and a convincing plot. 12-

_____. *Strangers in Skye.* Criterion, 1958. Forced to postpone her entrance to Oxford, shy, serious seventeen-year-old Elizabeth Falcon joins her brother in running a youth hostel in the Hebrides. Here, the beauty of the country, kindliness of the people, and romantic affection of two brothers open a new world for Elizabeth. 12-16

BELL, MARGARET. *Love Is Forever,* Morrow, 1954.

_____. *Watch for a Tall White Sail.* Morrow, 1948. An Alaskan author has written two fine junior novels with the background of her country. In *Watch for a Tall White Sail,* sixteen-year-old Florence Monroe is meeting with true pioneer courage the harsh existence in wild Nicols Bay where her father and brothers have started a salmon industry. Here she meets her future husband when he rescues her from drowning in the bay. In *Love Is Forever,* Florence marries at eighteen and leaves for a distant wilderness home. The first year ends in happy unity after considerable conflict. 14-

CAVANNA, BETTY. *Fancy Free.* Morrow, 1961. Her father's archaeological expedition to Peru reveals to teen-age Fancy Jones a new world of sights and sounds, and of human values too. 12-15

_____. *A Girl Can Dream.* Westminster, 1948. Shy, oversensitive Lorette wins a block of flying lessons for writing an essay in the high-school contest. Her love for planes gives her a new zest for living, and a more outgoing personality in her relations with boys and other girls. 12-16

_____. *Going on Sixteen.* Westminster, 1946. Julie forgets some of the miseries of her social failures by plunging into her favorite occupations. In the process of dog training and drawing she finds herself. 12-16

CLEARY, BEVERLY. *Fifteen,* ill. by Beth and Joe Krush. Morrow, 1956. Jane at fifteen wants above all a handsome boy friend. Her progress, along with the essential family life of fifteen-year-olds, is told with a light and satisfying reality. 12-15

_____. *Jean and Johnny,* ill. by Beth and Joe Krush. Morrow, 1959. The author creates a sympathetic family life around fifteen-year-old bespectacled Jean and the cocky senior who temporarily captures her heart. 12-15

_____. *The Luckiest Girl.* Morrow, 1958. Shelley and her two teen-age romances highlight a story rich in good family relationships and sound in its handling of the crises which accompany "growing up." 12-15

COLEMAN, PAULINE. *The Different One.* Dodd, 1955. Freckles and a father who does not approve of dates or high heels are two major worries of fifteen-year-old Ella Dillon, self-absorbed in the problems of growing up. 12-15

CRAIG, MARGARET MAZE. *Now That I'm Sixteen.* Crowell, 1959. A teen-age story of real substance, in which Chip, a boy classmate, steers timid, insecure Beth on the road to genuine popularity and success. 12-15

DALY, MAUREEN. *Seventeenth Summer.* Dodd, 1942. Vacation days bring Angie Morrow a full calendar of activities, and all the joys and sorrows of first love. When time for college approaches, Angie realizes how much she has grown emotionally during that summer holiday. 14-

LOVELACE, MAUD HART. *Betsy and Joe,* ill. by Vera Neville. Crowell, 1948. Other titles include *Heaven to Betsy* (1945), *Betsy in Spite of Herself* (1946), *Betsy Was a Junior* (1947), *Betsy and the Great World* (1952), *Betsy's Wedding* (1955). The high-school years bring new friends, and activities, and problems too, to Betsy, Tacy, and Tib. Betsy discovers her affection for steadfast Joe growing, and the series concludes with their marriage. (See American, British, and Irish stories for earlier titles in series.) 12-15

SELLARS, NAOMI. *Cross My Heart.* Doubleday, 1953. Kathy Barnum feels she has "arrived" when she joins the high-school sorority. Soon she discovers that the group's ideas and activities do not coincide with the school's best interests. She resigns, and finds a happier and freer companionship with other girls and boys. 12-16

STOLZ, MARY. *The Organdy Cupcakes.* Harper, 1951. In this happy career and romance story, three student nurses in their final year of training anticipate a bright future.

_____. *The Sea Gulls Woke Me.* Harper, 1951. Overprotected Jean Campbell, a sorry wallflower at the school dance, welcomes a chance to spend the summer at her uncle's seashore resort as a waitress where her latent social qualities develop. Mrs. Stolz' stories face youthful problems at a somewhat more adult level, and are for the more mature young reader. 14-

chapter 16

Other Times and Places

Children's books have always reflected the predominant interests of the adults. Cataclysmic wars, intimate acquaintance with many countries, and interest in their relationships to each other have widened the horizons of adults and made them world-conscious, people-conscious, and history-conscious as never before. It is only natural that their reading should follow these absorbing new interests and that they should encourage children to undertake similar reading. Teachers include historical fiction and books about other lands on their preferred reading lists; librarians promote such books with children; and parents approve heartily of these books. Committees of educators even approach publishers with the new subject-matter needs of the schools and ask for books which reflect them. Whether the predominant concern is "Hands Across the Border" or "One World" or "Integration," there is a flourishing crop of new juveniles devoted to the current theme. Their brightly colored pictures are attractive, and the blurbs on the jackets assure the reader of the authenticity of the content.

Correlating Fiction and Social Studies

This present-day zeal may suggest that the didactic school of writing is overtaking us once again. Although the emphasis is not on theology or on impossibly moralistic behavior, the pressure for information or propaganda may be just as heavy-handed and overzealous. It is increasingly important for adults to be able to distinguish a good story from synthetic, made-to-specification fiction. To reinforce our judgment, we have enough fine realistic fiction for children, which was created not because a slogan or a curriculum outline seemed to require it but because an author had something to write about, a robust story to tell. The children themselves, given the opportunity, pick out these books unerringly, regardless of Newbery Medals or social-studies' endorsement.

Along with this adult obsession to provide realism in books for children has gone the emphasis on correlation of literature with social studies. Many social-studies units can be greatly enriched by good fiction related to the unit under consideration. But correlation of literature and social studies should not become constant. It is necessary to remember that a good story is a good story regardless of whether or not it correlates with social-studies outlines, and a poor story is a poor story even if it was written with a particular outline in mind. To fail to promote fine literature because it does not happen to fit curriculum units is as short-sighted as to promote commonplace, second-rate fiction because it was written particularly for such a unit. It is far better to turn to the substantial factual books in this field and allow the child to take his fiction along other lines. Certainly it would be just as absurd to expect all the child's reading to correlate with his social studies as it would be to expect adults to forego their favorite novels because such reading did not correlate with their workaday interests.

Perhaps by being aware of the richness of the whole offering in the realistic field and of its wide range and variety, we can develop a feeling for what is substantial and fine and a corresponding sensitivity to what is thin, labored, or trivial. It should not trouble us if right in the middle of his study of the Congo or of medieval times some child wishes to read *Tom Sawyer*. Why shouldn't he? Often a change is a good thing. It is quite conceivable that he is temporarily fed up on jungles or knights and wants to get back to his own boy's world. Let him read *Tom Sawyer*, by all means. He'll return to his geography or his castles and moats with a fresh perspective. So, whether children are at the moment following the rise of the guilds in medieval days or good neighboring with South American countries or being interracially conscious, they should have the best realistic fiction available, let the slogans and the units fall where they will!

Today, when historical fiction for adults contains much that is sensational and erotic, historical fiction in the juvenile field includes some of our finest books. And though adults flit from one historical novel to another, children read and reread their favorites. Such stories as *Calico Bush, Johnny Tremain, Caddie Woodlawn, The Courage of Sarah Noble, Tree of Freedom, Winter Danger*, and the fine Laura Ingalls Wilder series are good literature and are also continuously popular with young readers. Such books are so numerous it will be impossible to do more than call attention in this chapter to some of the best and to list a slightly wider selection in the bibliography.

American Historical Fiction

ELIZABETH GEORGE SPEARE

The Witch of Blackbird Pond

The Witch of Blackbird Pond, winner of the 1959 Newbery Medal, is beyond the level of most elementary-school children but is well worth while for mature readers of the sixth and seventh grades. It deals with that grim time in our history when witch hunting had reached the point where carefree Kit Tyler could be imprisoned and tried for guilt by association.

Orphaned Kit, luxuriously raised in tropical Barbados, comes to live with her Puritan relatives in Connecticut. These cousins try to be kind but they disagree with Kit about almost everything. Her silk dresses and befeathered bonnets scandalize the whole community, and Kit willfully flouts local customs in many ways, most seriously by making friends with an old Quaker woman, Hannah Tupper, the suspected witch of Blackbird Pond. Kit's recklessness climaxes in her arrest, imprisonment, and trial for witchcraft. This terrifying experience brings Kit to realize that no one of us can live to himself alone. Her stern old uncle defends her even at considerable danger to himself and his family. A forlorn waif Kit had befriended stands by her, and her disapproving, seafaring beau Nat finally manages to extricate Kit. The strength of this book lies in its theme and its well-drawn characters. They are neither wholly good nor wholly bad but a very human mixture of heroism and bigotry, frailty and courage, rebellious recklessness and generous loyalty.

RACHEL FIELD

Calico Bush

One of the finest books Rachel Field (p. 152) ever wrote is *Calico Bush* (1931), the story of Marguerite Ledoux, a French bound-out girl of thirteen, who travels to the state of Maine with a Massachusetts family in 1743. On the long sail from Marblehead to Mount Desert, Marguerite comes to know the Sargent family and proves to them her grit and resourcefulness. She remains, nevertheless, a servant and an alien in their midst. When the Sargents finally reach Maine, they find their land, but the house has been burned down by the Indians. What is more, they are told that the Indians want no settlers on that particular property. Joel Sargent builds his house there anyway. In this new country Marguerite makes a fast friend of a remarkable old woman, Aunt Hepsa. There are brief days of joy in the new settlement, but there are tragic and frightening days, too—the Sargent baby is burned to death, and an Indian raid is diverted only by Marguerite's courage and ingenuity. At the end of the story, the Sargents gratefully offer Marguerite her freedom, but she will not leave them. She has shared their joy and their sorrows; they are her family, and she knows, besides, that she will never find anyone else so wise as Aunt Hepsa.

This book may well serve as a model of sound historical fiction. The picture of the times and the people is not only authentic but unusually well balanced. The hardships, the monotony, and the perils of pioneer life are there, unvarnished and frightening. The compensatory rewards may seem slight to modern readers, but there can be no doubt in their minds about the sturdy, undismayed character of these early settlers.

Although many people consider *Calico Bush* Rachel Field's finest book, *Hitty* (p. 359), her story of a doll, won the Newbery Medal. It is primarily a tale of the doll's adventures, but it gives a good picture of a century of American life and so might be included among the books of historical fiction.

CORNELIA MEIGS

Clearing Weather
Master Simon's Garden

Cornelia Meigs was born in Illinois and grew up in the Midwest, but since she came from New England stock on both sides of her family, ships and the sea were in her blood. Perhaps this heritage explains why many of her books are about the sea and why most of them are historical.

She has written well over twenty books for children, from a good train story for the youngest, *The Wonderful Locomotive,* to such fine tales for youth as *Clearing Weather* and *Vanished Island.* In between lies the bulk of her books, written for children from nine to twelve or fourteen years of age. She is an able and versatile writer of children's books but not overwhelmingly popular.

Cornelia Meigs is interested not only in our historical past but also in the beginnings of ideas and their development. Her stories sometimes start in the Old World, England or Ireland; they include such historical events as colonial settlements in New England, the explorations of Zebulon Pike in the West, and pioneering in the Mississippi country. But her stories are always something more than historical fiction. Each one carries a theme which, regardless of the setting or time, continues to be a sound idea for any generation. Indeed, Cornelia Meigs manages frequently, in these stories of the past, to illuminate certain problems of the present.

For example, *Clearing Weather* (1928) deals with Nicholas Drury's struggles to keep alive his uncle's shipbuilding business in the discouraging days following the American Revolution. Only through the cooperation of the whole community is the little town able to reëstablish itself. The successful voyage of their beautiful new ship, the *Jocasta,* built and given a cargo by their own efforts and sacrifice, brings clearing weather for both Nicholas and the town. The theme of community cooperation is a good one today.

Master Simon's Garden (1929) carries a still more striking theme. In the little Puritan New England settlement called Hopewell, where everything is done for utility and thrift, Master Simon develops his beautiful garden —a riot of colorful flowers and sweet herbs. It is an expression of his philosophy of tolerance and love in complete contrast to the intolerance and suspicion of some of his neighbors. This ideal is followed through three generations, and at the end of the story, Master Simon's great-grandson Stephen, in the period of the American Revolution, is still fighting intolerance and the whispering campaigns which foster it.

But these are not propaganda stories, and Cornelia Meigs is not writing with a message always in mind. Every one of her books has action aplenty and plots that are absorbing and often exciting. However, the plots are stronger because of their genesis in a strong theme. It is the theme which gives unity to the action and significance to the conclusion.

Analyzing Cornelia Meigs' books, you realize that it is the idea of the story that remains in your mind rather than the characters. There are a few exceptions. Master Simon, for example, is a memorable figure. But the characters are frequently less clearly drawn than the events in which they play their parts. The girls in Cornelia Meigs' stories are particularly indistinguishable but never the parts they play.

This inability to create memorable characters may help explain why Miss Meigs' books are not so popular as they might be. The dominance of ideas rather than vivid, individual characters means that these stories are more intellectual than those most children are used to. Certainly the books should be discussed if children are to grasp their implications and enjoy fully the exciting action with which most of the stories culminate. *Willow Whistle, Wind in the Chimney,* and *The Covered Bridge* are for children eight to ten years old. *Master Simon's Garden, Swift Rivers,* and *Clearing Weather* are liked by the more serious readers from eleven to fourteen.

ELIZABETH COATSWORTH

Away Goes Sally
Five Bushel Farm

The Newbery Medal was given to Elizabeth Coatsworth's *The Cat Who Went to Heaven,* a fanciful tale, exquisite and sad, involving a poor artist, a humble cat, and a Buddhist miracle. But the children like her historical fiction much better, particularly *Away Goes Sally* (1934), *Five Bushel Farm* (1939), and *The Fair American* (1940). Her writing has an easy flow and establishes unerringly the mood and temper of the tale. Take the opening page of *The Fair American:*

The first thing that Pierre saw as he wakened was the moonlight that lay across the darkness of his room like the blade of some great sword. Jean, the old valet, was beside him, or at least the boy thought so; but since the man, whoever he was, carried no light, he could not be certain until he heard Jean's voice low and urgent:

"Get up, Master Pierre, quickly. They are coming back, I think."

Pierre slipped out of bed in silence. It was May, and the polished floor felt cold to his bare feet. He could smell the odor of damp earth and blossoming bushes from the overgrown gardens that surrounded the drafty old château in which he had always lived. He stood for a moment listening; but nothing stirred except something small in the ivy outside his window, and near at hand the quick dry breathing of the servant.

"I hear nothing," said the boy.

"Hush." Again there came the whisper. "Here are your clothes. Hurry."[1]

Here is suspense, something hushed and fearful in every line, and that one phrase, "like the blade of some great sword," strikes the note of terror that is to recur throughout

1. From *The Fair American.* The Macmillan Company, 1940. Reprinted by permission.

the book. The story has to do with a boy of the French aristocracy, escaping from the terrorists after the French Revolution. This beginning establishes the atmosphere and the suspense. Contrast it with the first page of *Away Goes Sally*. There the chatter of the aunts sounds the prevailing feminine note.

Away Goes Sally has to do with the migration of Sally's whole family of uncles and aunts from Massachusetts to Maine not long after the American Revolution. The family travels in a little house on sledges pulled by six yoke of oxen, and the story moves along as leisurely as the little house. *Five Bushel Farm* sees the family established on their new farm. Andy joins Sally's circle of friends and introduces a desirable masculine note into their activities. In *The Fair American,* the French boy, Pierre, ships on an American sailing vessel. Sally's resourcefulness saves Pierre's life when a French officer boards the ship to look for refugees. Again, as in the books of Cornelia Meigs, the past throws fresh light on some of the poignant problems of the present, and the *Fair American,* bearing to our shores the stricken refugee child, is a moving symbol. These three books about the early nineteenth century appeal to children of ten or eleven. The exquisite poems dividing the chapters (p. 176) add to their unusual value and charm.

WALTER D. EDMONDS

The Matchlock Gun
Tom Whipple

Walter D. Edmonds is the author of the popular adult book *Drums Along the Mohawk.* His first book for children, *The Matchlock Gun,* was given the Newbery Medal in 1942. A mother, alone with her baby and young son, suddenly discovers that the Indians are near. Her little boy, who has been trained to fire an old matchlock gun at her signal, stays on guard in the house while she watches outside until the Indians discover her. As the Indians start for her, she gives the signal, the gun goes off on schedule, but she falls unconscious with a tomahawk through her shoulder. The suspense in this story is almost unbearable, and the terrifying climax is heightened by lurid pictures. The story is well written, and the preliminary glimpse of happy family relationships balances somewhat the harrowing quality of the story. Boys of nine and ten enjoy this story.

Mr. Edmonds' next book, *Tom Whipple* (1942), also historically authentic, is the amusing story of a country boy who ships aboard a sailing vessel for the express purpose of paying a visit to the Czar of all the Russias. How he achieves his exotic purpose and remains, throughout the story, Tom Whipple, upstate New York farm boy, is an amazing yarn.

These two books remind us that historical fiction for children must be more than authentic. It must seem as probable and possible as life today. The extraordinary may enter in, as it does in modern life, but it should not constitute the whole story. Life for most people has only its occasional moments of terror or rapture or triumph. Focusing a whole story upon such moments not only leans toward sensationalism but puts an undue strain on the reader's credulity. Mr. Edmonds barely skirts these pitfalls.

REBECCA CAUDILL

Tree of Freedom

Tree of Freedom (1954), a story about the Revolutionary War period, is sounder historical fiction because of its vivid characterizations and homely details of everyday living, which make the past understandable and natural. Each child of a family moving to Kentucky may take one prized possession. Stephanie carries an apple seed, because that is what her grandmother brought from France. When Noel, the eldest son, wants to take his dulcimer, it starts anew the feud between father and son. But the mother intervenes, " 'Twon't hurt him any. An' a little music won't hurt Kentucky, either. . . . He's got his rifle, ain't he, as well as his dulcimore? He'll use it like a man. See if he don't." And he does, but the quarrel is not resolved until the end of the war.

In the stockade, where the family takes

refuge from the Indians, the mother is horrified by the smells, the flies, the bad water, and the crowding. After they are on their own land, the father, Jonathan, and Noel go to war, and the backbreaking care of the crops falls to the mother, Rob, and Stephanie. There are anxieties, too, big and little ones. But always Stephanie tends her little sprout of an apple tree, "tree of freedom," she calls it. This is the theme of the story, and it speaks to us today, because in every generation the tree of freedom must be nurtured if it is to survive.

ESTHER FORBES

Johnny Tremain

Esther Forbes received the 1942 Pulitzer Prize for her adult biography *Paul Revere and the World He Lived In.* Her *Johnny Tremain,* which was an outgrowth of the research expended on *Paul Revere,* received the 1944 Newbery Medal. In her Newbery acceptance speech, she explained that while she was working on the adult biography she had to stifle any tendency toward fiction. But she was continually teased by the story possibilities of Boston's apprentices, who were always getting into scrapes of one kind or another. To illustrate her point, she related the hilarious doings of one of these apprentices who precipitated the Boston Massacre, and she concluded:

> *In this way an apprentice of whom we know nothing except that he was "greasy and diminutive" played his minute part in our history and disappears forever. I'd like to know more of him.*[2]

So she promised herself that as soon as possible she would write some fiction about the apprentices. The resulting book, *Johnny Tremain,* represents a high point in American historical fiction for children and young people. It is a great book for children to read at twelve or fourteen and to reread with added appreciation in college. In fact, like all of the greatest juveniles, it is a book as much for adults as for children.

Johnny Tremain tells the story of a silversmith's apprentice who lived in the exciting days that marked the beginning of the American Revolution. Johnny's master is second only to the famous Paul Revere as a silversmith, but Johnny knows that he himself is unrivaled among all apprentices. Competent and cocky, a humble artist but an unbearably conceited boy, Johnny is harsh and overbearing with his fellow apprentices and ambitious for himself. Just as he achieves a notable design, the apprentices decide to play a joke on

The theme of this picture is dramatically suggested by the exaggerated size of Johnny's erect figure set against the distant buildings and the tiny figures of the armed men. It tells as plainly as James Otis' words, "We give all we have . . . that a man can stand up." Illustration by Lynd Ward. From Johnny Tremain *by Esther Forbes. Copyright, 1943, by Esther Forbes Hoskins. Reprinted by permission of the publishers, Houghton Mifflin Company. (Original with color, book 5¼ x 8)*

2. Esther Forbes, "The Newbery Medal Acceptance," *The Horn Book,* July-August, 1944, p. 264.

him. The results are far worse than they intended. Not only is Johnny's design lost but he is left with a burned hand, maimed for life. His career as a silversmith is over even before it is well begun. Out of work and embittered, he still must stand on his own feet or go under. He stands.

This is the beginning of a story that carries Johnny and his friend Rab into the thick of Boston's pre-Revolutionary activities. These two friends come in contact with such men as John Hancock, Samuel Adams, and Paul Revere. The boys turn into men, as boys have a way of doing in stirring times. Johnny hates and loves and gets over both. He is fascinated with the rich and glamorous but is disillusioned with them before he gets through. He is devoted to his friend Rab and realizes his worth even when he falls out with him. Indeed, his inarticulate love for Rab intensifies the tragedy of that scene when he finds Rab dying from wounds received in the first little skirmish of the Revolution. In that fight men and boys lined up in the square—some to die. But they knew what they were dying for, Miss Forbes assures us, and they believed it "was worth more than their own lives." "We are still," she adds, "fighting for simple things 'that a man may stand up.' "

So Johnny Tremain from the past illumines the present. The book has so many values they are difficult to summarize. To children carrying any physical handicaps, Johnny's bitterness over his maimed hand is understandable. When, at the end, Dr. Warren tells Johnny that his hand could have been healed so that it would have been usable, Johnny's indifference shows how far he has traveled since those first days when he vowed he'd "get" Dove for his part in the tragedy. *Johnny Tremain* gives no one-sided account of pre-Revolutionary days. The book makes the colonists and Red Coats alive as the histories never seem to. The British, especially, are amazingly human in their forbearance, while the confusion and uncertainty of the colonists are frighteningly real. All the details of the everyday life of the period are drawn from the full stores of Miss Forbes' long research; but they are casually and expertly woven into the story, never dragged in for themselves.

In 1946 Miss Forbes made a second book from *Paul Revere and the World He Lived In*—a juvenile biography called *America's Paul Revere*. This book has an extremely solid text and a sound one. The illustrations by Lynd Ward are so startling in their beauty and drama that many young readers who enjoy *Johnny Tremain* will also wish to read *America's Paul Revere*.

WILLIAM O. STEELE

Winter Danger and other stories

There is no writer for children today who can re-create wilderness life more vividly and movingly than William Steele. Children eight to twelve read his books for themselves, but the books will also command the respectful interest of fourteen-year-olds. The stories are well written in the vernacular of the times, with good dialogue and plenty of suspense and action. This writer creates flesh-and-blood characters —grownups who struggle and survive in a tough pioneer world and expect their children to do the same; frontier boys, ignorant, prejudiced, or wrong-headed, but resourceful and enduring. The significant thing about William Steele's boys is that life changes and develops them, so that the reader sees them grow. The breath and beauty of the wilderness, as well as the very human yearning for security, are in these stories.

The Buffalo Knife (1952) follows the vicissitudes of two families who travel down the Tennessee River. The character development of the boys is an important part of the story.

In *Tomahawks and Trouble* (1955) two boys and "a mite of a girl" are taken captive by hostile Indians. Janie's biting the leg of her captor, who is trying to throw away her cornhusk dolly, wins the children their deadliest enemy. Their escape and survival in the wilderness require the killing of old "Tater Nose," as Janie calls him. This story is not for young or overly sensitive children, though Janie, "the bravest, addle-pated little girl in creation," comes through safely with her doll. The two boys learn the hard way that anyone can make a mistake but no one can afford to hold a grudge.

Winter Danger (1954) is the moving story of a conflict between a "woodsy" father, who knows no trade and cannot farm, and his son Caje, who has rarely had a roof over his head. Signs of hostile Indians and a bitter winter force the father to leave his son with farmer relatives. Poor, dirty, half-starved little Caje loves the cleanliness, good food, and gentle ways of his kinsfolk, but he learns that the only security to be had in this world we must make for ourselves. He also learns compassion for his lonely, intrepid father, and a great deal about sharing.

Wilderness Journey (1953) has unique values, too. Children are likely to think of all pioneers as hardy, and a wilderness journey as a kind of prolonged Boy Scout hike. But poor, measly, ten-year-old Flan can't hold an ax or shoot an animal or even skin it. His big brothers scorn him, and when quinsy lays him low the family travels on without him. How he makes the journey later with Chapman Green, a "Long Hunter," is an exciting study in wilderness ways and skills. It is also the story of a pindling boy who develops into a resourceful lad.

The Far Frontier (1959) shows another strong-willed boy who is outraged when he finds himself bound out to an absent-minded scientist from Philadelphia. But before their long, danger-beset journey through the Tennessee wilderness is over, Tobe has acquired a deep respect for his brave, eccentric companion. Best of all, the boy survives with a lasting hunger for learning and is well on his way with both reading and figuring. Tobe and the naturalist, Mr. Twistletree, are a memorable pair. The steadily growing social perceptiveness of the characters makes William Steele's books significant as well as entertaining.

EVELYN SIBLEY LAMPMAN

Tree Wagon

Another outstanding book that re-creates a particular historical period and movement is *Tree Wagon* (1953), the story of an enormous wagon train that traveled from Iowa to Oregon in 1847. The story is unique because Mr. Luelling was a nurseryman, and his wagon carried seven hundred tree shoots for the new country. When his wagon slowed up the rate of travel, the big train decided to go

Paul Galdone can be relied on for historically accurate details. Here in these two pictures he reveals the heedless ignorance of the savages in contrast to the sorrow of the man of science whose book they have destroyed. Illustration by Paul Galdone. Reproduced from The Far Frontier, *© 1959, by William O. Steele, by permission of Harcourt, Brace & World, Inc. (Book 5¼ x 8)*

to his chest, and the blows rained down over him. His spectacles fell off, and the Indian left off hitting him and picked up the eyeglasses. He looked at them carefully, felt the glass between his thumb and finger, squinted through them, and then stuck them on his nose. The others ran up to see.

Mr. Twistletree stayed with head bowed, right where he'd been left and never made a murmur.

134

Even when he was lying beside Tobe later, tied up tight and with the red men all about him, he didn't seem to see or hear them or notice where he was. He was still mourning his book, Tobe knew. It was gone for sure now, most of it used to get the wood burning.

The braves moved around their campfire, talk-

135

on without him. One other family remained with the tree wagon, and the little group moved into hostile Indian country on its own. When yelling Indians in war paint swooped down on them, an amazing thing happened which guaranteed their safety. Sure enough, the two families got through to Oregon with half the trees living, as well as Seenie's special gooseberry bush for which she had long ago sacrificed her extra petticoat to serve as a sunshade. The author vouches for the authenticity of this fine story.

HAROLD KEITH

Rifles for Watie

Rifles for Watie, winner of the 1958 Newbery Medal, is the most substantial historical fiction for children we have had in this country since *Johnny Tremain.* The hero of the book is young Jefferson Davis Bussey, who despite his name is a Kansas farm boy and a rabid Unionist. Once in the army, Jeff's name and his stubborn forthrightness get him into trouble with a brutal officer, who persecutes him endlessly. Finally, Jeff is sent as a spy behind the Rebel lines to try to discover where Confederate Stand Watie, full-blooded Cherokee Indian, is getting the new rifles issued for the Union armies. Jeff is captured by the Rebels, but his name, together with a plausible story, allays suspicions. Jeff lives, works, and fights with this Indian regiment for fourteen months. When he finally gets his information and escapes to the Northern side, he leaves his Confederate friends with real regret. He leaves them also with the disturbing realization that heroic, well-intentioned men are fighting and dying on both sides in this horrifying struggle.

Among the unforgettable characters is Jimmy Lear, the fourteen-year-old drummer boy, too young to carry a gun but old enough to die gallantly. There is big-eared, ugly Heifer, the cook, who is like a father to Jeff, and Lucy, the beautiful Confederate half-breed, and finally, Watie himself, much like a gentle old farmer but in action a ruthless raider and fighter. All the hunger, dirt, and weariness of war are in this book to balance the heroism of men and boys on both sides. This is a magnificent story to use along with the biographies of Lincoln and Lee.

CAROL RYRIE BRINK

Caddie Woodlawn

In addition to the great historical stories about our country, there is another kind of book which, although its scenes may be laid in the colonial or Revolutionary period, does not seem to qualify as historical fiction because interest is centered in the *story,* and not the story of a *period. Little Women* is such a book; its setting is the Civil War period, but it is predominantly a story of family life. Carol Brink's *Caddie Woodlawn,* one of the children's great favorites today, is like *Little Women* in this respect.

Like *Little Women, Caddie Woodlawn* (1935) belongs to the Civil War period, but the war plays no part in the story. Caddie and her family lived in Wisconsin when Indians were still a menace, but life on the whole was fairly comfortable. Red-headed Caddie, the tomboy, and her two brothers extracted every possible bit of fun and adventure the frontier settlement could yield. Caddie's long friendship with the Indians and her courageous personal appeal to them helped prevent a threatened uprising. Even so, this book is far less of a frontier story—settlers versus Indians—than it is the entertaining evolution of a tomboy. The fun Caddie gets out of life suggests the usefulness of this book in the historical group in counteracting the overseriousness of most historical fiction. One little girl said, "I just hate pioneer stories. All the people do is struggle and struggle and struggle!" To such a child we may well give *Caddie Woodlawn,* if only to prove that the children of the frontier had their fun, too.

LAURA INGALLS WILDER

Little House in the Big Woods and other stories

Children's sense of the past is a confused one at best. Gas burners are more incredible to them than candlelight, and horse-and-buggy travel quite as odd as a trip by canal boat. Indeed, it may be easier for them to understand and enter into the colonial period of American history than into the more immediate past. The pioneering and settling of the Midwest have fewer picturesque details than has the dramatic first colonization. Frontier life has more of the humdrum "struggle" the little girl complained of, less romantic adventure. Until Laura Ingalls Wilder undertook the writing of her family's experiences in settling the Midwest, there were no books of this period which really held children's interest.

In 1953 Mrs. Wilder's publisher reissued the books with new illustrations by Garth Williams (see Ch. 21), and the Children's Library Association presented a special and long overdue award to Mrs. Wilder for her "substantial and lasting contribution to children's literature." Children love all eight books and grow up with the Ingalls girls and the Wilder boys, from *Little House in the Big Woods* to the romantic *Happy Golden Years* when Laura Ingalls and Almanzo Wilder are married. In the process they have seen the sod houses in the Midwest giving place to wood, and claims growing into towns. Best of all, the maturity of these books grows with the children. The first book appeals to children of eight or nine; the last is written for the almost-grown-up girl, who by this time feels that Laura is her oldest and her dearest friend. Few other books give children this sense of continuity and progress.

The following passage from *On the Banks of Plum Creek* could well serve as the keynote to all the books about the Ingalls family:

> *The wind was screaming fiercer and louder outside. Snow whirled swish-swishing against the windows. But Pa's fiddle sang in the warm, lamp-lighted house.*

Here are the family's bulwarks against all misfortunes—the warm, lighted house made beautiful by Ma, their own love and sense of security, and Pa's courageous music-making in the face of every difficulty.

The saga begins with the Ingalls family in their log cabin in the Wisconsin forests, *Little House in the Big Woods*. The children are all girls. The oldest is Mary (who later goes blind) then the active Laura, and baby Carrie. Grace eventually displaces Carrie as the baby. In this first book we become acquainted with Ma's skill in cooking wonderful, triumphant meals out of limited resources, and especially we know her good bread, baked every Saturday. It fills the small cabin with its delicious fragrance and nourishes the girls' growing bodies even as Pa's gay songs and fiddle music nourish their spirits. Here, too, we first see the little china woman which Ma is to carry with her through all their journeys. She puts it over the fireplace only when the dwelling is worthy, a real house and home. All these things give the children a sense of comfort and security.

> *But Laura lay awake a little while, listening to Pa's fiddle softly playing and to the lonely sound of the wind in the Big Woods. She looked at Pa sitting on the bench by the hearth, the firelight gleaming on his brown hair and beard and glistening on the honey-brown fiddle. She looked at Ma, gently rocking and knitting.*
>
> *She thought to herself, "This is now."*
>
> *She was glad that the cosy house, and Pa and Ma and the firelight and the music, were now. They could not be forgotten, she thought, because now is now. It can never be a long time ago.*

So every child thinks, but soon for Laura the Big Woods *are* long ago. The family moves out to the wild Kansas country and begins the adventures described in the *Little House on the Prairie. On the Banks of Plum Creek* finds the Ingalls family in Minnesota; *By the Shores of Silver Lake* carries them to the Dakota Territory, where they remain either on their lake or in town.

Meanwhile *Farmer Boy* begins the account of the Wilder family of boys on their prosperous New York farm, where everything is abundant and the meals they eat make our mouths water. We follow Almanzo Wilder from his first day at school to the proud moment when he is given his own colt to break and train. In this book the modern child is given incidentally a sense of money values in terms of human labor. Almanzo knows fifty cents as so many hours of backbreaking toil over the family potato crop. Fine horses, good food, and prosperity give the Wilder boys an easier but no happier start in life than the Ingalls girls have.

The Long Winter finds the Ingalls family living in town. Of the whole series, this book is one no modern child should miss. One blizzard follows another until the railroads cease to run and the little town is cut off from supplies for months. Fuel gives out, and they have to twist straw into sticks to burn. Ma devises a button lamp to save oil. All day the sound of their little hand mill is heard as different members of the family take turns grinding wheat, their last stand against hunger. Finally the wheat begins to give out, and the whole community faces starvation. Then it is Almanzo Wilder, not Pa Ingalls, who rides out into the trackless, snow-driven prairie to buy wheat from a farmer who has it. He succeeds, and the conclusion of the book is happy and humorous. Once more the Ingalls family has survived, but, alas, Pa, the ever resourceful hero of all the earlier books, is here supplanted by the youthful Almanzo. The last two books —*Little Town on the Prairie* and *These Happy Golden Years*—carry Laura into teaching and then into marriage with Almanzo.

Here is a splendid cycle of time and events, chronicled with a simplicity and humor that children heartily enjoy. There are plenty of hard struggles in these books—struggles with droughts, grasshopper plagues, blizzards, food shortages, floods, and fire. But there is fun, too—heavenly days on the sun-soaked prairies, triumphs of ingenuity in cookery or sewing or carpentry, a real glass window achieved unexpectedly, a guest arriving out of nowhere, spirited horses to ride behind, and Pa's old songs and gay tunes to lift the heart. These books are never lugubrious but are filled instead with heart-warming courage and high spirits. In the last book, *These Happy Golden Years*, a title which speaks for the whole series, Laura Ingalls Wilder wrote in her daughter's copy:

And so farewell to childhood days,
Their joys, and hopes and fears.

"Pa Prepares for Winter," "An Evening of Music," and "Hauling Wood" are the captions given by the young Cleveland artists to their illustrations for On the Banks of Plum Creek *and* By the Shores of Silver Lake. *Robert Fulton School, sixth grade; principal, Mrs. Edna Skelly; teacher, Miss Ophelia Smith.*

But Father's voice and his fiddle's song
Go echoing down the years.[3]

A sixth-grade teacher, Miss Ophelia Smith of the Cleveland Robert Fulton School, made these Wilder books the center of a valuable unit of work. For their English, the children (a major work group[4]) read the whole series; each child reported in detail on one particular book; and the group evaluated them all at the conclusion of the reports. They noted the geographical setting of each story, the growth and development of the characters, the problems, difficulties, and joys the family shared. They wrote about or discussed such items as the author's powers of characterization, her ability to rouse sympathy and hold interest, her descriptions, humor, and general style. In science they studied the flora and fauna of the tales and also noted every implement or mechanical device employed by Ma, Pa, or their neighbors in subduing the wilderness and making life more comfortable. They looked up the historical aspects of the books, particularly the homestead laws and the Indian problem. A visit to the Historical Museum clarified and enriched their ideas of clothing, transportation, household equipment, farm implements, even the games of the times. In music they learned Pa's songs and many others, as well as the dances of the times. Their art work centered on the animals or favorite scenes from the different books, and finally they made a mural summarizing the whole series. The synthesis of all these activities was a spirited assembly program for the whole school, with reports, exhibits, and discussions of the Wilder books. This unit occupied almost two months, but the children's interest never flagged.

ALICE DALGLIESH

The Courage of Sarah Noble
Thanksgiving Story

A young mother who was taking her eight-year-old to visit her home town was rudely jolted when he remarked, "Gee! Mom, it will be fun to learn about the long, long ago when you were a little girl." This is fairly typical of a young child's time sense. His excursions into the past must be made gradually by means of unusual episodes that give him momentary glimpses of other days and ways.

Alice Dalgliesh is especially successful in this field. *The Bears on Hemlock Mountain* (1952) can be read to five-year-olds and read by the eights. At first the story seems almost contemporary—a little boy is sent to his aunt's to borrow a kettle. But the kettle is a huge iron one, and Jonathan must go up and over a mountain—and there could be bears up there. His mother says that's all nonsense, that there are no bears on Hemlock Mountain. But there *are,* and Jonathan meets two big ones. What he does to save himself is surprising. For young children this story is not only a thriller, it is a chiller, and they love quick-thinking Jonathan of long ago.

The Courage of Sarah Noble (1954) is more richly historical and, according to Miss Dalgliesh, a real episode as well. Little eight-year-old Sarah is sent into the wilderness to cook and care for her father because her mother cannot leave or move a sick baby. But before Sarah and her father set off, her mother wraps the little girl in a cloak as warm as her love and says, "Keep up your courage, Sarah Noble." Little Sarah travels to her mother's marching words, and when wolves threaten them in the forest, or they sleep in strange cabins with unfriendly folk, or Sarah is left alone with an Indian family, she wraps her mother's cloak and her words warmly about her and keeps up her courage. When this story was read to a particularly timid urban youngster just Sarah's age, her teacher asked, "Pat, do you think you could do what Sarah did?" Pat, big-eyed and grave, said slowly, "Well, I'd be awful scared but I'd try. Yes, I could do it, I know I could." That is one of the wonderful results of historical stories—they give youngsters new vistas and stretch their young spirits. (See illustration, p. 22.)

Thanksgiving Story (1954) is a fictional account of the voyage of the *Mayflower* and the first year at Plymouth, culminating in the thanksgiving feast with the Indians. It is

3. Irene Smith, "Laura Ingalls Wilder and the Little House Books," *The Horn Book,* September-October, 1943, p. 306. Delightful account of Mrs. Wilder, with family photographs of Ma, Pa, the four girls, and Almanzo.
4. Able children with an enriched curriculum.

centered in the experiences of the Hopkins family, especially the children, and is a remarkably moving little story considering how difficult it must have been to avoid the stereotyped episodes. Helen Sewell's clear, bright pictures reinforce the colorful narrative which young children thoroughly enjoy.

The Fourth of July Story (1956) must have been even more difficult to do, with its large gallery of leading characters and the complex theme of independence and restoration of good relationships with England. But again Miss Dalgliesh has selected her people and episodes so carefully that the story is dramatic and not too complicated for the understanding and enjoyment of children six to eight.

The Columbus Story, a good beginning biography, will be considered later (p. 529). With these simple, colorful stories Miss Dalgliesh has set a new pattern for developing in young children a feeling for the moving drama of history. It is a significant contribution.

Stories About the Ancient World

Stories of the Old World begin with primitive man and touch almost every major country and period. They are too numerous to permit more than a cursory review of a few outstanding books and periods most frequently used in schools and enjoyed by children in general.

HARRY BEHN

The Faraway Lurs

The introduction to *The Faraway Lurs* (1963) is so fascinating that no reader should miss it. Harry Behn went back to Denmark to learn the story of his mother's childhood, but instead he found another story about another girl who had lived and had been buried in this same place some three thousand years ago. She was found, still beautiful, with her blond hair in a pony tail, her fingernails neatly manicured, and wearing a crudely made bronze bracelet and earring that did not belong to her tribe of peace-loving Forest People. So it was her story Harry Behn chose to tell.

The poet calls her Heather. She is the daughter of the chief, betrothed to bear-like Blue Wing, the most skilled archer in the tribe. She hears the compelling music of the faraway lurs—great bronze trumpets—of the warlike Sun People. She sees their shining Sun chariot near the lake, close to her well-hidden village. Then, near the tree she has climbed a young man from the Sun People suddenly appears and sees her. Their growing romance cannot survive the conflict of their tribes. The Sun People are determined to find and destroy the Sacred Tree of the Forest People, and the latter have only archers against the swordsmen of the enemy. There are evil ones in both camps, and this Bronze Age Romeo and Juliet come to a sorrowful and heroic end, their dream unfulfilled.

When a poet tells a story, poetry often results. Harry Behn has given mature readers of twelve and over a story of the past that is sheer magic.

ELIZABETH GEORGE SPEARE

The Bronze Bow

The title of the 1962 Newbery Medal winner comes from II Samuel 22:35—"He trains my hands for war, so that my arms can bend a bow of bronze." This verse fascinates young Daniel, who, along with many Israelites, is looking for the Deliverer who will drive the cruel Romans out of their land. Daniel had seen his mother and father wantonly slain by these conquerors. So, thinking Rosh is perhaps such a deliverer, Daniel deserts his grandmother and sister to join Rosh's band. Daniel's loyal friends try to tell him that Rosh is no more than a greedy bandit. They tell Daniel also about another Deliverer called

Jesus, a gentle teacher who preaches love and says that he who wields the sword will perish by the sword. But Daniel consumed with bitterness believes violence is the only way. Blinded by his hatred, Daniel kills his sister's hope of love, thereby driving her into mental darkness. Not until he has seen his mute but devoted follower killed and has almost lost his love Thacia, does Daniel come face to face with the healing love of Jesus. Then at last he understands that it is not hatred and violence, but only love that is strong enough to bend the bow of bronze.

This action-packed story makes absorbing reading in spite of the subtle and difficult theme which develops slowly. The characters are powerfully drawn—Thacia and Leah, two contrasted girls, Joel the scholar, Simon, a selfless older man, and Samson, the slave who dies for Daniel. This memorable theme can speak to each generation.

LUCILE MORRISON

The Lost Queen of Egypt

For the superior reader, the child who at twelve or thirteen can read anything he wishes to, Lucile Morrison's *The Lost Queen of Egypt* (1937) is a thrilling story. The author presents an intimate picture of the family life of one of the Pharaohs and makes understandable their peculiar devotion to each other and to the dynasty. The heroine is Ankhsenpaaten, the Pharaoh's third daughter, a lively, mischievous five-year-old at the beginning of the story. Through her eyes, the reader sees the court ceremonies, the dress, the foods, and the customs of this ancient Egyptian kingdom.

The story begins about 1580 B.C. in the royal nurseries of Akhenaten, Pharaoh of Egypt, and Nefertiti, his queen. Their six little daughters are being arrayed for the arrival of the Great Royal Mother. Ankhsenpaaten, or "Small Bird" as she is called, is more than ordinarily intelligent. Already she has begun to sense the disquieting overtones in the apparently serene life of the royal family. She knows that their grandmother's visit is for a purpose. Enemies threaten the kingdom of the idealistic Pharaoh; the old queen knows there must be sons immediately to stabilize the dynasty and hold the enemy at bay. The Royal Mother decides that three of the little girls must be betrothed at once to guarantee the succession, and she attends to the betrothals promptly.

Ankhsenpaaten is relieved when the soldierly Tutankhaten is chosen for her, since he alone of the royal blood has shown a reckless courage and vitality equal to her own. At the time of their betrothal, it seems unlikely that they will ever have to reign, for they are third in the line of succession. Nevertheless, their education for ruling begins at once under the loving eye of the frail king. The royal children are also guided and encouraged by a young artist, Kenofer, who loves them both.

When a series of deaths calls this popular young pair to the throne, they become Tutankhamon and Ankhsenamon and seem destined to happiness and a long reign. Instead, they find themselves the victims of one intrigue after another. Kenofer is able to protect them for a while. Meanwhile, he discovers how deeply he loves the queen, but he never swerves for an instant in his devotion

The King and Queen Hunting

The artist has illustrated this book beautifully in the ancient Egyptian manner—stylized figures, plants, and animals. Notice how elegantly the sitting King hunts while the Queen delicately supplies the arrows. Illustration by Winifred Brunton. From The Lost Queen of Egypt *by Lucile Morrison. Copyrighted 1937 by J. B. Lippincott Company. Reprinted by permission of the publishers. (Book 5⅜ x 8)*

to them both as rulers of Egypt. Even Kenofer's vigilance and the queen's watchfulness are unequal to the machinations of Ay, the court villain. When the young king dies by poisoning, the queen is trapped in the palace to be forced either to marry the traitorous Ay or to die herself. How Kenofer rescues her; how, in disguise, they turn to the river and live on their boat like hundreds of humble river people; and how the tragic young queen learns at last that she can find happiness only by ceasing to be a queen make a satisfying end to a fine story.

ELOISE JARVIS McGRAW

Mara, Daughter of the Nile

Another novel of ancient Egypt is *Mara* (1953), which parents will probably read along with their twelve-year-olds. It is a hair-raising tale of royal intrigue, spies, and true love, in the days when a feminine Pharaoh, Hatshepsut, has usurped the throne from the rightful king. Mara is a slave who vaguely remembers better days and is determined to escape. She is bought by a mysterious man who offers her luxury if she will serve at court as a spy for the queen. She accepts, and also sells her services to a young nobleman, Lord Sheftu, as a spy for the king. Eventually, her love for Sheftu and a deep pity for the wronged king change her from a liar and a cheat to a selfless heroine who endures torture rather than betray her new loyalties. The action is terrifying. Detailed pictures emerge of the daily life of different classes—shopkeepers, rivermen, soldiers, slaves, and royalty.

A second book about ancient Egypt by this writer is a boys' story, *The Golden Goblet*. While it is not quite so powerful a tale as *Mara*, it, too, affords a detailed picture of the times, with a vigorous plot and convincing characters.

OLIVIA E. COOLIDGE

Egyptian Adventures

Although the stories in *Egyptian Adventures* (1954) are at junior high school reading level, many of them may be read aloud to elementary-school children who are having their first look at the ancient world. Olivia E. Coolidge is a scholar, and in the course of these entertaining tales she gives children lively pictures of the Egyptians' superstitions and magic, harvests and hunts, festivals and funerals. The characters emerge fully drawn and colorfully alive. These twelve well-written stories will do much to develop children's feeling for the people and adventures of a far-distant past.

ISABELLE LAWRENCE

The Gift of the Golden Cup

The time of ancient Greece and Rome is another period in history at which children in elementary school look briefly, but it is so remote from anything they know that it is generally a dull abstraction. There are only a few stories about this period, and only a few authors who can build an authentic background for the tales. Isabelle Lawrence's stories pile action upon action and intrigue upon intrigue, but her characters are exuberantly alive and entertaining. Young readers follow their adventures and emerge breathless and doubtless a bit confused, but right at home in Rome, Pompeii, or Athens.

In *The Gift of the Golden Cup* (1946) twelve-year-old Atia and her seven-year-old brother, Gaius, are children of the famous Roman family of Julians, with Julius Caesar for an uncle. While their parents are away from home, there is a well-organized revolt of the slaves, a terrifying experience for the children. They find themselves, after a series of misadventures, on a pirate ship, slaves of the captain. Fortunately, their captor is kind to them, and young Gaius takes to the pirates' life enthusiastically. However, both children now learn the bitterness their own slaves, some of them of noble birth, must feel. The adventures of the young Julians include sea battles, the sinking of a ship, rescue, and a long journey home with a young Roman and two slaves. Once home, the children persuade their father to free the two Greek slaves who helped them. Later the mother of the former slaves invites Atia and Gaius to visit the family in Athens. This visit provides an interesting chance to contrast Roman and Greek life. It also supplies more action and a mystery which continues in the second book, *The Theft of the Golden Ring,* an equally complex and exciting story. Athenian life is vividly recreated in *Niko, Sculptor's Apprentice.*

Were it not for Isabelle Lawrence's ability to bring her characters vividly to life, from the irrepressible Gaius to Caesar himself, these books might be merely action-packed thrillers of small value. But besides an impressive gallery of well-drawn characters, the stories provide unforgettable pictures of Greek and Roman houses, cities, ships, clothes, food, slave conditions, patrician luxuries and obligations, schools for the boys, and the duties of girls and women. These will remain in memory when some of the action is forgotten.

HENRY WINTERFELD

Detectives in Togas

Although *Detectives in Togas* (1956) is frankly a juvenile "whodunit," very funny and full of suspense, it also gives an excellent picture of ancient Rome. Trouble starts in the school for patrician boys when Rufus writes on his wax tablet, "Caius is a dumbbell." Zantippus, the schoolmaster, punishes Rufus, but the next day the same legend, "Caius is a dumbbell," is found scrawled on the walls of the Temple in Rufus' own script. Rufus convinces his friends that he did not desecrate the Temple—but who did? The boys, aided by Zantippus, set out to unravel the mystery and save Rufus. Politics and politicians are involved, and there are hairbreadth escapes, some grim and some farcical. By the time young readers finish this intriguing story they feel right at home in the ancient city and can approach their high school Latin with amusing memories. With the sleuthing boys the reader sees the crowded streets, the shops, the famous Temple, the Baths of Diana, the Forum, and the school.

Henry Winterfeld tells us that some excavations revealed a childish scrawl on the walls of a temple, "Caius asinus est." This was the inspiration for the lively story of *Detectives in Togas.*

Except for the togas, these boys might be friends of Henry Huggins or Little Eddie. Convincing realism and a cartoon-like humor make these pictures as amusing as the text of this "whodunit" in ancient Rome. Illustration by Charlotte Kleinert. Reproduced from Detectives in Togas, *© 1956, by Henry Winterfeld, by permission of Harcourt, Brace & World, Inc. (Book 5¼ x 8, picture 4 x 4½)*

European Historical Fiction

ROSEMARY SUTCLIFF

The Lantern Bearers
Dawn Wind

Most critics would say that at the present time the greatest writer of historical fiction for children and youth is unquestionably Rosemary Sutcliff. Her books are superior not only because they are authentic records of England's earliest history with its bloody raids and its continuous wars for occupation by Norsemen, Romans, Normans, and Saxons, but also because every one of her memorable books is built around a great theme. Her characters live and die for principles they value and that men today still value. The action of the stories takes place against the haunting beauty of the land these people love, and through these books the reader comes to know "the heart of heroes."

The theme of all her stories, as Margaret Meek[5] points out, is "the light and the dark. The light is what is valued, what is to be saved beyond one's own lifetime. The dark is the threatening destruction that works against it." In *The Lantern Bearers*[6] (1959), the blackness of despair is concentrated in the heart of Aquila, a Roman officer who, when a Saxon raid sweeps down on his father's farm, sees his father slain, and his sister Flavia carried off by the raiders. He himself is left tied to a tree for the wolves and later made a slave by another band. Years later,

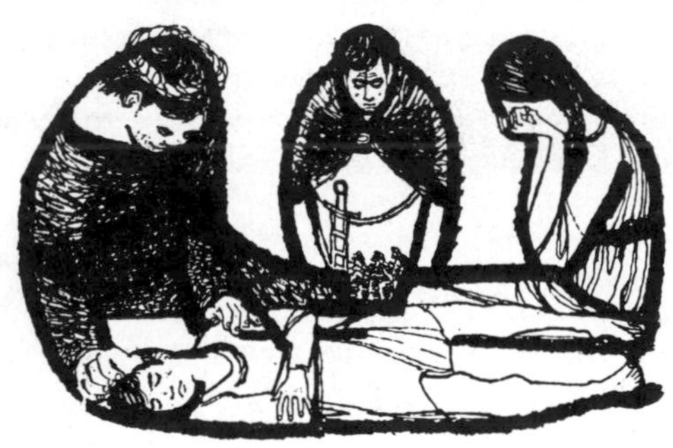

Charles Keeping has made somber, powerful illustrations for this book and for Dawn Wind. *Here tension is created by the use of black outlines to contrast white patterns. The symmetrical composition and the bent figures make this a dignified scene of sorrow for the injured boy.*
Illustration by Charles Keeping. From The Lantern Bearers *by Rosemary Sutcliff. © 1959 by Rosemary Sutcliff. Reprinted by permission of the publishers, Henry Z. Walck, Inc. (Book 5½ x 8½, picture 3¼ x 2)*

after he has escaped his thralldom and has given his allegiance to a Prince of Britain (the Romans are gone), through loyal service, the love of his wife Ness, gentle Brother Ninnias, and finally his son, Aquila learns to love again and to believe in the future. An old friend says to him:

> *It may be that the night will close over us in the end, but I believe that morning will come again. . . . We are the Lantern Bearers, my friend; for us to keep something burning, to carry what light we can forward into the darkness and the wind.*

No briefing of these stories can give any conception of their scope and power, and when young people read them they live with nobility. The sooner our children can begin to read these Sutcliff books the better, as they will help to build intellectual maturity. Nevertheless, these are difficult books, not because of vocabulary problems, but because of the complexities of the plots in which many peoples are fighting for dominance in England. Sometimes it is merely a raid by some neighboring tribe, sometimes it is a battle for occupation. Aquila's family become more British than Roman after three generations, and their allegiance shifts. Even adult readers have difficulty in following these complexities. In England, where the children have some background of their own history, these books are recommended for the elevens to sixteens. Most of our eleven-year-olds would find them hard going.

Fortunately, *Dawn Wind* (1962), one of the finest of the books, is also the least complex. Chronologically it follows *The Lantern Bearers,* but it is complete in itself and will undoubtedly send some readers back to the trilogy.

For the fourteen-year-old hero Owain, the light of the world seems to have been extinguished. He finds himself the sole survivor of a bloody battle between the Saxons and the Britains in which his people, the Britains,

5. *Rosemary Sutcliff.* A Walck Monograph, Walck, 1962.
6. *The Lantern Bearers* is the third book in a trilogy which also includes *The Eagle of the Ninth* and *The Silver Branch.*

were completely destroyed. Although he is badly wounded, he starts traveling and is joined by a half-starved, frightened dog. An old man and woman take them in when Owain collapses on their doorstep.

Once healed of his wounds, Owain and Dog set out once more to find his people. But in the gutted remains of the city from which he had come, the only life the boy finds is a pitiable waif of a girl, lost and half-starved. At first Owain, Dog, and Regina are bound together in mutual misery, but eventually they are united in respect and affection. So when Regina is sick and dying, Owain carries her to a Saxon settlement, even though he knows what will happen to him. The Saxons care for the girl but sell Owain into slavery. He and Dog are carried away. Like Aquila, Owain can do nothing less than serve his master with all his skill and strength. This proud, competent youth is loved and trusted by his master and his family. If sometimes despair almost overcomes Owain, his work, in which there is both conflict and triumph, absorbs him. After eleven years, he is freed and sets out at once to find his people and Regina, who has never doubted he would come for her.

> *"Are we still going to Gaul?" Regina asked carefully, after a few moments.*
>
> *"No. That was for the dark; now, there's a dawn wind stirring.... We are going south-west into the hills. There was an old man and an old woman there; I do not think I ever told you about them, but they were kind to me once...."*
>
> *"And if they are not still there?"*
>
> *"Then we'll build a turf hut and light a fire in it, and in-take a patch of hillside, and I'll find a sheep to go with your little brown hen," Owain said.*

So life is not snuffed out by the night. A dawn wind blows and two people start all over again with those basic qualities that have always made for survival. Whether it is her great trilogy or *The Shield Ring* or *The Outcast* or *Warrior Scarlet,* Rosemary Sutcliff gives children and youth historical fiction that builds courage and faith that life will go on and is well worth the struggle.

ERIK CHRISTIAN HAUGAARD

Hakon of Rogen's Saga

Hakon of Rogen's Saga (1963) is not a traditional saga but a realistic story taking place in the last days of the Vikings. The rocky, mountainous island of Rogen, where Hakon was born, has been handed down in his family from father to son for generations. To Hakon, Rogen Island and his powerful father seem indestructible and their home the best of all places to live, especially after Thora, his gentle stepmother, comes bringing love both to the boy and his father. But Thora was a kidnapped bride, and so when spring comes her father sends three ships and many men to bring her back. When the bloody battles are over, Hakon is an orphan at the mercy of his treacherous uncle, who wants Rogen for his own. How Hakon suffers enslavement and brutal treatment, bides his time, finds a hide-out in the mountain caves, mobilizes his few loyal men, and eventually takes Rogen again reads much like an old Norse saga. The author, a Dane steeped in Icelandic sagas, says at the beginning:

> *"Your dog, your horse, your friend, and you yourself: all shall die. Eternally live only your deeds and man's judgment over them," this was the credo of the Vikings.*

Throughout the book their philosophy of living and dying is stated or chanted and at the end of the book when Hakon has won Rogen and rescued Helga, with whom he had been raised, he says to her:

> *That is everyone's birthright, his freedom, and the gods have only one message for us, that we must live.*

In this book the Vikings are of heroic stature and the author clothes their story with nobility.

HOWARD PYLE

Otto of the Silver Hand
Men of Iron

Howard Pyle was steeped in the traditions and customs of the Middle Ages. He not only

Fine composition, elegant drawing and details. Tension is introduced by use of diagonal lines cutting the verticals.
From Otto of the Silver Hand *by Howard Pyle. Copyright, 1916, by Anne Poole Pyle. Reprinted by permission of the publisher, Charles Scribner's Sons.*
(Book 5½ x 7¾)

wrote fascinating stories about them, but provided powerful illustrations for his own books from a storehouse of detailed and seemingly inexhaustible information. The convincing dialogue in his tales, while not of course reproducing exactly the speech of the period, suggests it. Old speech forms and difficult words make hard reading in places but add to the flavor of the tale. His running narrative is always clear, direct, and vigorous, and how he loves fights! These range from terrible to farcical, but each story has a liberal sprinkling of them. His books are excellent to read aloud and are exciting materials on which the good readers may try their mettle.

Otto of the Silver Hand is a horrifying tale of the robber barons of Germany. One of these had plundered ruthlessly. For revenge, his enemies struck off the hand of his only son, the delicate Otto. Later, because of the silver substitute, the boy was known as Otto of the Silver Hand. The story presents two phases of the life of the period: the turbulent life within the castle strongholds of the robber barons and the peaceful, scholarly pursuits of the monks within their great monasteries. The mutilation of the boy is gently handled. There are no details, only the infinite pathos of a child in the power of cruel men. Children read the book without harm, and Otto is always remembered.

Pyle's *Men of Iron* is tremendously popular with boys from twelve to fourteen. The sixteen-year-old Myles Falworth is sent to be a squire to a powerful earl. There he learns that his own father is practically an outlaw, suspected of being one of the plotters against the king's life. In the earl's great castle, Myles is trained in all the intricate feats of knighthood and in the code of chivalry and is eventually knighted. He frees his father from suspicion and wins the earl's daughter for his wife. Myles has to battle with his own impulsiveness and his too-quick temper as well as with his enemies. The friendship between Myles and a fellow squire, Gascoyne, is an example of fine loyalty on both sides. This is one of the outstanding books about medieval England.

ELIZABETH JANET GRAY

Adam of the Road
I Will Adventure

Another book about the medieval period which children should not miss is the Newbery Medal winner for 1943, Elizabeth Janet Gray's *Adam of the Road*. Elizabeth Gray has also written a distinguished series of American historical fiction and some excellent biographies (see Bibliography, Chapter 17).

Elizabeth Gray is a born storyteller, although paradoxically she is weak in plot construction. Her books develop little excitement; the conflicts are mild; no breathtaking suspense leads to a smashing climax. Her stories move quietly, as life moves for most of us, full of simple pleasures—dogs, books, the out-of-door world, and, above all, people. She is a careful historian, and her tales have all the authentic minutiae of everyday life long ago which make history convincing. But chiefly she is concerned with people.

Children from twelve to fourteen years old will find that Adam is a boy much like themselves. It just happened that he lived in the thirteenth century instead of today. Adam's two loves are his golden cocker spaniel and his minstrel father, but he loses them both for a time. How he seeks the two of them up and down the roads of old England gives children a glimpse into every variety of medieval life—that of jugglers, minstrels, plowmen, and nobles, as real as the people today. Adam's adventures are varied and often amusing; the plot concerns his search for dog and father, and their reunion is tremendously satisfying.

The hero of *I Will Adventure* (1962) is Andrew Talbot, a most beguiling young imp, who takes to himself a line from Shakespeare's *Romeo and Juliet,* "I will adventure." Andrew is journeying to London to be a page to his uncle Sir John Talbot when he has the good luck to hear this play and by way of a fight with one of the boy players, meets Master Burbage and Shakespeare himself. Andrew is all for signing up with the players, but they won't take him, though Shakespeare, grieving for his own boy Hamnet, lets Andrew ride with him for a day's journey. Eventually Andrew reaches his uncle's house, but being a page is not what he had hoped. His jolly uncle is away a good part of the time, his aunt neglects him, and the steward really persecutes him, not without some provocation. Andrew is continually in trouble and consumed with homesickness which no one senses or does anything about. Through Andrew's eyes the reader comes to know intimately many facets of London life in 1596, especially the theater, the plays, and the audiences. Andrew's problems are happily solved, thanks to Shakespeare and a sympathetic uncle.

In spite of all the fascinating historical details in the background of this picture, interest centers on the two boys, squaring off for a fight like two young bantams.
Illustration by Corydon Bell. From I Will Adventure *by Elizabeth Janet Gray.*
 (Book 6 x 9)

MARGUERITE DE ANGELI

The Door in the Wall

Marguerite de Angeli has grown steadily in her work, both as artist and writer. From the pictures for her first little *Ted and Nina* books to the prodigal overflow of beauty in her *Mother Goose,* and from those same slight stories to her Newbery Medal book, *The Door in the Wall,* is enormous progress for one busy lifetime. And amiable, charming Mrs. de Angeli must have been busy indeed with all her books and five children. Her son's account of how the children interrupted her work is amusingly related in *Newbery Medal Books.*

The Door in the Wall (1949) is her first book of historical fiction. Robin's noble father is off to the wars and his mother is with the Queen when the plague strikes. Robin falls ill, unable to move his legs, and is deserted by the servants. Brother Luke finds the boy, takes him to the hospice, and cares for him. To the despairing Robin he says "Always remember . . . thou hast only to follow the wall far enough and there will be a door in it." The monks teach the boy to use his hands and his head, "For reading is another door in the wall. . . ."

Robin learns to swim and to get around swiftly on his crutches, but his bent back never straightens. However, his spirit is strong, and he plays so heroic a part in saving a beleaguered city that the king honors him, and his parents are moved with joy and pride. This heart-warming story is beautifully illustrated in the author's most colorful style. The characters are less convincing than the situations, but the book is of great interest to all children, and brings special comfort to the handicapped.

MARCHETTE CHUTE

The Wonderful Winter
The Innocent Wayfaring

Marchette Chute, the author of *Shakespeare of London* and similar studies of Chaucer and Ben Jonson for adult readers, has also written some delightful stories for young people. *The Wonderful Winter* (1954) carries young readers straight into Shakespeare's theater with young Robin, Sir Robert Wakefield, who has escaped from an intolerable home situation. London seems to spell starvation for him until he is befriended by some actors and is taken into the home of the famous John Heminges. Through the warmth and affection of this crowded household, young Robin learns to give and accept love and gaiety. Meanwhile he works and plays small parts in the theater, knows the great Shakespeare, and falls in love with *Romeo and Juliet.* When Robin returns to his castle and his duties, he is happy and confident as a result of his wonderful winter.

The Innocent Wayfaring (1955) is fourteenth-century England brought vividly and authentically to life. Anne is so averse to learning the arts of housewifery that she runs away from her convent school with the prioress' pet monkey for company. The monkey is responsible for her meeting Nick, a poet and a most resourceful young man. He tries to get away from her, but Anne sticks like a bur. Their adventures provide a view of fourteenth-century life, from seamy inns to manor houses. After three days Nick takes Anne back to her family with the agreement that when she has learned housewifery and he his father's business, Nick will come for her. Meanwhile, they have the memory of three enchanting days which led them back to home and responsibility.

Both books are beautifully written by a scholar who can paint a glowing background for her charming stories.

Some Criteria for Historical Fiction

These examples of historical fiction have certain qualities which may serve as standards by which to scrutinize other books in this field. First, they are historically accurate, not merely in the major events but also in the small details of everyday living which make the past understandable. Second, these stories so re-create the past that people, places, and problems seem almost as real to us as those we know today. Third, they tell a good story regardless of the period—a story so absorbing that the historical background and details fall into a properly secondary place and do not seem an end in themselves. Fourth, in these books the problems and difficulties of the past throw a helpful and sometimes reassuring light upon our problems today.

Looking at the past through the pages of these substantial historical stories, we discover that human nature and human aspirations remain much the same. The boy in *Adam of the Road* encountered thieves, but he also tasted the kindness of many sorts of people. Little

Sarah Noble and puny young Flan endured the perils of the wilderness because it was expected of them. And the boys and girls of today would do the same. Master Simon, in the book by that title, made a garden that was an oasis of peace in a disordered world. Intolerance comes and goes; gardens remain. Johnny Tremain fought and won a personal battle against his physical handicap, but he and his friends fought also for bigger things, outside themselves, so "that a man can stand up." In the American saga of a pioneer family, the Ingalls girls learned that love and fortitude can make homes blossom even in the wilderness. So, in good historical fiction, the past may give us inspiration and courage and insight for dealing with the present.

Early Books About Children of Other Lands

Hans Brinker and *Heidi,* like *Tom Sawyer* and *Little Women,* not only are among the first of the realistic books for older children but are still popular. The stories of Dutch Hans and Swiss Heidi give American children authentic and exciting accounts of life in foreign lands and acquaint them with children who seem as real as the children next door.

MARY MAPES DODGE

Hans Brinker, or the Silver Skates

Mary Mapes Dodge is notable not only as the author of *Hans Brinker* but also as the first editor of the famous old magazine for children, *St. Nicholas* (1873). This magazine, numbering among its contributors such names as Alcott, Longfellow, Burnett, Kipling, and Whittier, is said to have marked the beginning of the Children's Age,[7] but Mrs. Dodge's own famous novel for children and young people certainly contributed to its propitious start. *Hans Brinker* (1865) was immediately successful. It was translated into many languages, and the Dutch people accepted it as the best picture of childhood in Holland that had ever been written up until that time.[8]

In this country *Hans Brinker* has remained on most book lists, as a good story and a picture of Dutch life, though some librarians say its popularity is beginning to wane. Mrs. Dodge had become deeply interested in the history of the Dutch republic and had saturated herself with the best references she could find on the subject. When she began to write her book she had a twofold purpose: to tell a story about the children of Holland and to weave into that story as much of the history and customs of the people as she could. It is this burden of information that bogs it down here and there, or even interrupts the story entirely. For instance, the book begins with a chapter which introduces Hans and his little sister Gretel, with something of their problems. The second chapter abandons the story to give a brief history of the country. Later, the boys go on a forty-mile skating trip, and we are given many facts about the towns they pass through, their art collections, their legends, and their heroes. Some of these digressions are interesting in themselves; others are less so; but all of them disrupt the unity of the exciting plot which Mrs. Dodge develops so successfully. If these digressions were deleted, the story might go right on being as popular as ever because it is exciting, with a competition for the wonderful silver skates and two fascinating mysteries to be solved.

Mrs. Dodge's powers of characterization are exceptional. There are eight boys and girls to be kept track of besides Hans and his sister, yet we know each one of them, his virtues and his petty or downright odious characteristics. The plot is complex, too. There is a main plot concerned with the restoring of

7. Mahony and Whitney, *Realms of Gold,* p. 611.
8. *Ibid.,* p. 610.

Raff Brinker's memory and with finding both the lost money and the secret of the watch. Then there are the secondary threads of interest in the old doctor and his missing son, and finally in the competition for the skates. Mrs. Dodge vouches for the authenticity of the Raff story. Some of the other episodes seem melodramatic, like the one about the thief in the night, but not too incredible considering the date of the narrative. It is, on the whole, still a lively and satisfying tale, with mysteries and suspense aplenty. This substantial old book has provided generations of American children with an exciting story as well as a gracious introduction to the people and customs of Holland.

JOHANNA SPYRI

Heidi

Heidi was written in German by Mrs. Johanna Spyri, a Swiss, and translated into English (1884) soon after its publication. This book continued the fine tradition of *Hans Brinker* by introducing American children to children of other lands through a delightful story.

Throughout the years the popularity of *Heidi* has never diminished, though some translations of it are difficult to understand. It is a long book, too, with pages of solid reading. Still, children read it, and many college students say it is one of the books they reread in childhood.

Heidi uses the most popular of all themes —a variation of Cinderella, the unwanted neglected child who comes into her own— but there is a convincing quality about *Heidi* which many of the modern Cinderellas lack. The child is full of the joy of living. She skips and leaps and she falls in love with an apparently grouchy old grandfather, the goats, and the mountains, all with equal vehemence and loyalty.

Later on, when she is torn away from them by force and deception and sent to live in town as a companion to the invalid child, Clara, she suffers acutely. Still she manages to make friends, to secure kittens and a turtle for Clara, and to send out shy tendrils of affection in many directions. In the town she learns to read and gets her first religious instruction. This is of a kind that will offend no religious group today, since it is built on a faith in God and on the ability to draw strength and wisdom from communion with God, in prayer and thanksgiving. This is a deeply religious book, yet children read it all. Probably because the emphasis is reassuring, it gives both faith and hope. Homesickness for her mountains and her loved ones almost destroys Heidi, and not until she is restored to them does she recover. From the security of her life in the mountains she is able to reach out to the town friends and help them, too. Clara is brought to the mountains, and there the good milk from the goats, the clear, fresh air, Grandfather, and Heidi cure her. The little invalid walks for the first time in her life, and Heidi keeps her mountains and her town friends, too.

No child who has read and loved *Heidi* will ever enter Switzerland without a feeling of coming home. The incredible, rosy fire of the Alpine sunset he will see through Heidi's eyes. In every old man he will see Heidi's grandfather; in every village, Heidi's Dorfli. This is what books about other lands should do for children—leave them feeling forever a part of that country, forever well disposed toward the people. In such stories of other people, they have no sense of oddity, no feeling of irreconcilable differences, but a desire to know these people so like themselves.

To accomplish this, a book about other lands must be completely authentic and sincere. *Heidi* has both these virtues because of the experiences and character of the author, Johanna Spyri. She was a doctor's daughter, greatly moved by the ill health of her father's patients. She, too, went to the mountains in the summer and lived on goat's milk, black bread, cheese, and the good, fresh butter. She, too, knew the bounding health of this free life under sunny skies, amid the great mountain peaks, and she breathed the crystal-clear air. Nothing in the book is labored or superficial. Heidi is as wholesome and real as her mountains. Every child reading this book will wish for a bed of straw just like Heidi's, up in the loft, looking out on the mountain peaks under their glittering crown of stars.

Recent Trends in Books About Other Lands

The nineteen twenties, which marked the growing emphasis upon the social studies as the core of the curriculum, saw also the beginning of a great influx of books about other lands. Today an avid correlator of social studies and English can dash into any sizable library and find children's stories about almost any region, from Albania to the Congo, from Russia to the South American jungle. A few years ago a student who was planning a unit on United States territories and possessions found stories for every one of them except the Virgin Islands. Today the Virgin Islands are also represented. The coverage of foreign countries by juvenile fiction is so comprehensive that it somehow suggests hasty editorial conferences devoted to such themes as: What are the new emphases in the social-studies curriculums going to be for the next year or so—Our Neighbors North and South, or East and West Forever?

Great stories, however, do not seem to roll off the assembly line according to specifications. For example, during a drive on good neighboring, over two hundred juvenile books about South America appeared in a space of two or three years. While many of these are fair, there is not among them all one great and memorable book of the caliber of *Heidi* or *The Good Master* or *Young Fu of the Upper Yangtze*. Of course, great and memorable books are rare at best. And, of course, some of these books about other lands are up to date and authentic, but many others are superficial and do not portray foreign countries fairly or adequately.

The early books in this field had a tendency to present the picturesque at the expense of the usual. They gave us the China of bound feet, the Holland of wooden shoes and lace caps, South America by way of some primitive tribe of Indians about as typical of modern South America as Navahos would be of the United States. Some of these faults are still to be found in our most recent books. We must be careful to check the stories they tell with what we know to be true of the present everyday life of average people.

Outstanding Books About Foreign Lands

FOR THE YOUNGEST

Time was when the curriculum experts used to say that children are not ready for books about foreign lands before the third or was it the fourth grade? Now kindergarten children are hearing picture-stories about France, Japan, Italy, Greece, or any other foreign land you can think of. Bettina's Italian *Pantaloni* (1957) goes on a desperate search for his lost dog, and Italian streets are no more confusing than our own would be for such a search. Evaline Ness' Haitian *Josefina February* (1963) is beset with problems. She must find a birthday present for her grandfather and the owner of a baby burro which she wants to keep for herself. What a day! Whether in Nova Scotia or Hindustan, such problems are understandable to most children, and youngsters take pictures and stories about other countries in their stride if the themes are universal.

LUDWIG BEMELMANS

Madeline

Like Little Tim, Madeline is a rugged individualist who takes matters in her own hands and manages them with great competence. The other little girls in the French boarding school walk in two straight lines, but Madeline falls off the bridge, finds the lost dog, and has a grand case of appendicitis which wins her so much attention that the other little girls weep enviously. Madeline

The use of wide spaces and few details adds meaningful drama to this illustration. Notice how the two children walking chummily under one umbrella point up the loneliness of the queer, solitary figure of Crow Boy.
From Crow Boy *by Taro Yashima. Copyright 1955 by Mitsu and Taro Yashima. By permission of The Viking Press, Inc. (Original in color, book 5⅜ x 8, picture 5 x 5½)*

tames the horrid little boy next door, has an adventure with the gypsies, and explores London. Each adventure is a separate book, and the children love them all. Ludwig Bemelmans has given little girls an up-and-doing heroine, and through his superb pictures for these books has made the landmarks of Paris and London completely familiar to the young devotees of *Madeline*. (See illustration 19 in color section.)

ELEANOR FRANCES LATTIMORE

Little Pear

The author and illustrator of *Little Pear* (1931), Eleanor Frances Lattimore, has lived a good share of her life in China. In telling about the everyday ups and downs of the well-meaning but mischievous Little Pear, Miss Lattimore lets us observe an average Chinese family going about its regular duties with only an occasional festival to break the ordinary routine of life. Little Pear's antics provide some extra excitement now and then, but they are not any more sensational than those of any American child on any pleasant suburban street. That is the charm of the *Pear* books. Houses, clothes, and foods may differ from ours, but everyday living is so usual it might be our own. One little girl said, "You know, all the time I was reading *Little Pear* I kept thinking of my little brother. He is just as mischievous as Little Pear." These stories, with an escapade to each chapter, are completely satisfying to young children. They are easy to read, and they are also delightful to read aloud.

TARO YASHIMA

Crow Boy

Also for the youngest children are Taro Yashima's striking picture-stories of his native Japan. His first book, *The Village Tree* (1953), was the sensitively recorded play of children on and under a big tree that leaned over the water. *Plenty to Watch* (1954) by Taro and Mitsu Yashima tells of the shops and workers that Japanese children stop to watch as they walk home from school. The stores and the workers may differ from ours, but the children's insatiable curiosity about both is universal.

Crow Boy (1955), Taro Yashima's third book, was a runner-up for the Caldecott Medal and won the Child Study Award. It has unusual social values as well as great pictorial beauty. Crow Boy is a small, silent child who walks to school alone, sits alone, and does not talk. The children call him derisively "Chibi"—tiny boy. But a new schoolmaster discovers that the small outcast walks in from a great distance. He knows where wild potatoes and wild grapes grow, and he knows every call the crows make and can imitate them perfectly. When he does this for the children they call him "Crow Boy" with respect, and he is one of them at last. Not since Eleanor Estes' *The Hundred Dresses* has this theme of the outsider been so sensitively handled.

The chairs having passed, the boys again fell into step

Kurt Wiese is a remarkably versatile artist. Whether he is illustrating a "tall tale" or a story of twentieth-century China, he suits his pictures to the mood of the story and to the age of the children for whom the book is intended.
Illustration by Kurt Wiese. From Young Fu of the Upper Yangtze *by Elizabeth Foreman Lewis. Copyright 1932, copyright renewed © 1960 by Holt, Rinehart and Winston, Inc. Reproduced by permission of Holt, Rinehart and Winston, Inc. (Book 5 x 7½)*

ESTHER WOOD

Silk and Satin Lane

An outstanding Chinese story for the eight to tens is Esther Wood's *Silk and Satin Lane* (1939), a great favorite with girls. Ching-ling, an orphan, is an unwanted Chinese girl. Her brother is placed with a bachelor uncle who most decidedly does not want a girl child. Ching-ling promises to be useful and to be no bother whatever, and she is finally allowed to stay with the uncle. But she is in trouble most of the time, always through her well-meaning efforts to be helpful. She washes clothes in the canal and loses most of them. She lovingly takes the babies out of an orphanage and deposits them on various door-sills with surprising results. The uncle is to be married, and Ching-ling delivers his gifts to the wrong bride. Fortunately, the bride is an understanding girl. She makes Ching-ling her first real dress; she helps her and loves her; and Ching-ling knows at last what it is to be wanted, to have a secure place in a family. This modest little book, a real contribution to the gallery of lovable heroines, gives young readers a sympathetic insight into Chinese life.

ELIZABETH FOREMAN LEWIS

Young Fu of the Upper Yangtze
To Beat a Tiger

For the oldest children there are the fine books of Elizabeth Lewis, who lived long in China. *Young Fu of the Upper Yangtze* (1932), which won the Newbery Medal, is the exciting story of a thirteen-year-old Chinese country boy who is brought to the rich city of Chungking and apprenticed to a skillful coppersmith. In time, Young Fu becomes a fine craftsman, but neither easily nor quickly. Meanwhile, he explores the great modern city and finds everywhere the conflict of old and new ideas—bound feet still to be seen but somewhat disapproved of, old superstitions and prejudices, frightful poverty the lot of most of the Chungking people, and the country involved in a civil war. Fu's adventures carry him into the thick of everything. He sees a poor coolie shot down by looting Chinese soldiers; he assists in detecting opium smugglers; he helps a foreign woman whose house is on fire and wins her friendship. Best of all, he becomes the humble student of a great scholar who teaches him wisdom along with the classics. Fu is no idealized hero but exhibits the usual contradictory human traits. He is brave and honest, yet he wastes his master's time and gets into trouble. He works hard, grows skillful, and then gets unbearably cocky. He is frugal one moment and wasteful the next. The book is full of Confucian proverbs used by adults to point out to Fu the error of his ways:

Laziness never filled a rice bowl.
A scholar is a treasure under any rooftree.
There is no merit worthy of boasting!
If a man's affairs are to prosper, it is simply a matter of purpose!
He who rides on a tiger cannot dismount when he pleases.
The shallow teapot does the most spouting, and boils dry the quickest.

Mrs. Lewis has a later book, *To Beat a Tiger* (1956), for teen-agers and young adults. It is the grim story of sixteen Chinese boys living by their wits on the outskirts of Shanghai. They all know the proverb, "To beat a tiger, one needs a brother's help." Their tiger is starvation and death, and so they lie, steal, and cheat, but share their wretched scraps of food, their hut, filthy rags, and scanty heat. Death strikes one of the gang, and the chance to rise by sheer villainy claims another. Nationalists and Communists are not named, but the two factions are there and the boys are involved. It is a complex story, but once the large gallery of characters is identified, the plot gains momentum and suspense is high. Although the picture of a country torn with civil strife is a sad one, the book ends on a hopeful note for at least three of the boys.

MARGOT BENARY-ISBERT

The Ark
Rowan Farm

The Ark and *Rowan Farm* are not so grim as Mrs. Lewis' picture of civil war in China. Still, these books give children an impressive account of the aftereffects of war on the people, cities, and countryside of Germany, where these stories were very popular.

In *The Ark* (1953) the Lechow family, a mother and four children, are trying to reestablish something approaching a normal life in a bombed-out city. The doctor father may be dead or a prisoner of war. Even so, they waste little time lamenting the past and are grateful to obtain three unheated attic rooms from a reluctant landlady. The frail mother has a gift for homemaking, even in a freezing attic. Matthias, the fifteen-year-old boy, is a born scholar but knows he cannot go to school any more; so he works and studies at night as best he can. Margret, the next oldest, is at loose ends grieving over the death of her twin brother, a war casualty. Joey and Andrea, seven and ten, return to school reluctantly. They furnish the comedy in both books, Andrea all dramatics and Joey thoroughly enjoying his daily diggings in the rubble of the city. The family circle expands, too, to include friends and acquaintances of all the children.

The story centers on Margret, who obtains a job as kennel maid to Mrs. Almut, who has brought her farm and famous breed of Great Danes through the war with the minimum care and the maximum grit. Margret loves and nurses the dogs back into condition, serves as midwife to the stock on the farm, and even helps to restore an old railroad car, which becomes "The Ark" to shelter the whole Lechow family.

In *Rowan Farm* (1954) the father has returned, new characters are introduced, and Margret suffers the pangs of first love and jealousy. These stories are chiefly focused on the gallant struggles of one family to reëstablish normal life, not only for themselves but for others more lost than they. Both are superlative stories, and through the eyes of these vividly drawn characters young readers see the rubble of bombed-out cities and the wastelands of what were once beautiful farms. They feel the miseries of food deprivations, bitter cold, and, above all, the dislocation of hopes and plans. Yet these stories are filled with minor triumphs—a birthday cake, very dry but miraculously sweet to the last unbelievable crumb, and music, which feeds the spirit and is a glorious link with the past. And every reader will understand Mrs. Lechow's courageous attempts to keep alive the precious traditions of Christmas and will rejoice when, out of cold and deprivation, she succeeds in making not merely a merry Christmas but a blessed one for her family and all those people who have come into the circle of the Lechows' energy and courage.

Mrs. Benary tells us that most of the episodes in these two books are true of someone she knew during the postwar period in Germany. In her youth novel, *Castle on the Border* (1956), which was written in her new home in the United States, she tells a story about a hard-working group of young actors whose lives she shared for a year in postwar Germany. Whether biographical or fictional, these books reflect Mrs. Benary's own overflowing warmth and kindness.

ARMSTRONG SPERRY

Call It Courage

Call It Courage (1940), a Newbery Medal book, is an exciting story about Mafatu, the son of a Polynesian chief, rejected by his people for his cowardice and marooned on a desert island. This island proves to be the sinister shrine of man-eaters. Mafatu maintains life, develops all the necessary arts and skills, makes his own weapons and his own canoe, finally escapes the man-eaters and returns home a hero. This book about the conquest of fear will give young readers many a spinal chill and subsequent shiver of relief. The illustrations are beautiful.

KATE SEREDY

The Good Master

The Good Master (1935), written and beautifully illustrated by Kate Seredy, was an instantaneous favorite with children. If they were to be consulted, they would give this book the Newbery Medal rather than Miss Seredy's *White Stag*. *The Good Master* is the story of a Hungarian tomboy, Kate—a regular brat of a child. She is sent by her father to stay on her uncle's ranch. Her young cousin Jancsi imagines she will be a frail, dainty girl, and so he is horrified by the wild, impish Kate. She causes a runaway of horses; she climbs the rafters and there eats sausage until she is sick; she knows how to do nothing useful and is a general pest. The gentling of Kate makes a charming story. "The Good Master" is the understanding uncle. The aunt is just as patient with Kate, and Jancsi takes a hand, too, in the girl's reformation. But it is Kate's growing love of the horses and riding, as well as her affection for her newly found relatives, that helps her learn gentler ways. Hungarian festivals and legends, the household crafts, the work of the ranch, the good food, and the warm family life add color and charm to a delightful story. The sequel to *The*

The author's illustrations, in strong blues and white, add much to the interest of this exciting story. Here the swirling water, the suggestion of ocean bed, the lines of the great fish, the downward plunge of the figures give this battle with the shark a terrifying reality. From Call It Courage *by Armstrong Sperry. Copyright 1940, The Macmillan Company. Reprinted by permission of the publishers. (Book 6¼ x 8¾)*

In this breezy sketch, the head and the book, being most important, are drawn with careful details. Raman is reading at the bookseller's stall, completely oblivious to what is happening in the street beyond. Illustration by Hans Guggenheim. From "What Then, Raman?" *by Shirley L. Arora. © 1960 by Shirley L. Arora. Follett Publishing Company. (Book 6½ x 9)*

Good Master is *The Singing Tree,* which sees Kate and Jancsi into their teens and the father gone to World War I. Anti-Semitism arises, but, in this story, it is happily banished. It comes perhaps too close to the didactic to be a popular story, but it is well worth reading and timely, too.

MONICA SHANNON

Dobry

One of the greatest children's books about people of other countries is Monica Shannon's *Dobry,* Newbery Medal winner for 1935. Because this book is not immediately popular with children, it needs some help from adults in promoting it. Read it aloud, discuss and savor the colorful episodes. The Bulgarian Christmas celebration, climaxing in Dobry's fine snow carving of the Nativity, makes a beautiful excerpt to read aloud for Christmas.

Dobry is a Bulgarian peasant boy whose family has been at work on the land for generations and who finds himself longing both to stay at home and to go away to become a sculptor. His mother is frightened and disappointed that he should think of anything but the land. The old grandfather, a remarkable character, believes that there lives in every human being "a spark of God" and only when that burns clear does life have any value. Even the mother comes to see, at last, that Dobry's "Spark of God" belongs not to the land but to the creation of another kind of beauty.

Here is a picture of Bulgarian peasants, living close to the earth and never forgetting to enjoy the flavor of their juicy tomatoes, brown crusty loaves of bread, little sourdough cakes with cheese melting richly in the center, good buttermilk, and special treats of Turkish coffee, black and flavorous. The coming of the gypsies with their massaging bear, the snow-melting contest which lusty old Grandfather wins, the diving into the icy river for the crucifix on a cold St. John the Baptist Day, and the everyday work make this story of a boy's choice of his life's work a picture of rich living. Help children to discover this book, children twelve to sixteen. Not all of them will like it, but many will. We who guide children should remember Grandfather's philosophy:

> . . . *Everything is different, each leaf if you really look. There is no leaf exactly like that one in the whole world. Every stone is different. No other stone exactly like it. That is it, Dobry. God loves variety. . . . He makes a beautiful thing and nothing else in the whole world is exactly like it. . . . In odd days like these . . . people study how to be all alike instead of how to be as different as they really are.*

JAMES RAMSEY ULLMAN

Banner in the Sky

Banner in the Sky (1954) is a book about Switzerland by the author of the adult novel *The White Tower*. It gives children a dramatic story of self-discipline and the stern code of ethics that governs the famous guides of the Alps. Rudi is the son of the greatest of these guides. His father, Josef Matt, gave his life for the men in his care in their unsuccessful attempt to scale the Citadel. Since then, the guides of Kurtal have decided the mountain cannot be climbed. But brash young Rudi is determined that someday he is going to conquer the great peak and put his father's red shirt at the top of it. The story tells of Rudi's training, his mistakes, discouragement, and stubborn determination. When a party finally sets off, young Rudi is along, a sternly disciplined climber, well aware of his obligations. The suspense grows with the inclusion in the party of a treacherous guide from another village. In the end, Rudi is called upon to make the greatest sacrifice to duty that a guide can. He yields his chance of success to save a life. But in spite of this, his father's red shirt flies from the peak of the Citadel at last.

For young outdoor enthusiasts, this combination of meticulous discipline and thrilling action provides a wonderful story.

SHIRLEY ARORA

"What Then, Raman?"

A young Indian woman studying in this country protested that children's books about India are generally more exotic than authentic. However, she cited *"What Then, Raman?"* (1960) as a happy exception. It is the story of a shy, earnest Indian boy who has learned to read, the only person in his village with this accomplishment. His ambition is to become a scholar and possess a beautiful black and gold copy of the *Ramayana*, the great Indian classic. But his learning sets him apart. The village boys avoid or taunt him, and Raman feels no special responsibility for them or for the needs of his family. To earn money for the book, he works for an American teacher. Slowly she brings him to the realization that the privilege of learning carries with it responsibility for teaching and helping others. Raman begins with his little sister, teaching her to read, then the boys in the village, and presently he finds himself not only accepted but deeply involved in their longings and needs. When he finally has the money for his precious book, somehow he can't buy it; his family comes first. Still Raman keeps his dreams. Someday he will be a scholar and own the book. This is not so moralistic as it sounds but is sensitively written with a deep perception of the boy's conflict and a thorough knowledge of India today.

MEINDERT DeJONG

The Wheel on the School

The Wheel on the School (1954), a tenderly told story which won the Newbery Medal, gives a remarkably detailed picture of life in a Dutch fishing village and also has unusual social values. The story begins in the tiny village school, when Lina, the only girl, asks, "Do you know about storks?" This leads to more questions, "Why are there no storks in Shora?" and "How can we bring them

Lina and the boys hear the old invalid. Illustration by Maurice Sendak. From The Wheel on the School *by Meindert DeJong. Copyright, 1954, by Meindert DeJong. Reprinted by permission of Harper & Row, Publishers. (Book 5 x 7¾, picture 3¾ x 2⅛)*

The pictures for The Family Under the Bridge *are simple and realistic with interesting details. The artist uses a variety of gray tones with black and white contrast employed delicately.*
Illustration by Garth Williams. From The Family Under the Bridge, *copyright © 1958 by Natalie Savage Carlson. Pictures copyright © 1958 by Garth Williams. Reprinted by permission of Harper & Row, publishers. (Book 6½ x 8¾)*

back?" These two questions launch a series of activities that begin with the six children and the schoolmaster but presently draw into the circle every person in the village, including the fishermen fathers and a good many people from other villages. The boys perform miracles of hard work and persuasion. Plucky little Lina nearly loses her life but never her courage. Everything is ready when a terrible storm kills or drives off course hundreds of the birds. But at last the storks do settle in Shora again.

Although the book is too long for its story, it reads aloud wonderfully and will promote many discussions about the people, the lonely land of sea and sky that is Holland, and the wonder of those great birds that fly home all the way from Africa. Meindert DeJong has the gift of wonder and delight. Read his Newbery acceptance speech and know something of the rich inner life of this man who approaches children so reverently. His *Dirk's Dog, Bello* is a fine story of a Dutch boy's love for his dog. *Smoke above the Lane* is the gentle, humorous story of a tramp and a little skunk. Whatever the outward action of Mr. DeJong's tales may be, it is the inner grace of his children and animals that moves every reader, young or old.

NATALIE SAVAGE CARLSON

The Family Under the Bridge
The Happy Orpheline

Some of the gayest stories about Paris are Natalie Carlson's *The Family Under the Bridge* (1958) and her series about the Orphelines. *The Family Under the Bridge* has to do with that postwar period in Paris when housing was at a premium. The hero is an elderly, jaunty hobo named Armand, completely averse to work, family life, and especially "starlings," as he calls children. Armand has found himself a snug corner under an old bridge. So imagine his horror to return there one night and find it occupied by three children. "Starlings!" he cried. "A nest full of them!" What's more when he ordered them out, the girl Suzy defied him ". . . because we're a family, and families have to stick together! That's what mama says." This is the beginning of the end for carefree, soft-hearted Armand. His series of adventures with the starlings are sometimes very funny and sometimes sad, but in the end he finds himself shaved, cleaned up, regularly employed, and the adopted grandfather of a family. More gallant, undepressed poor never appeared in a child's book. No pathos here, just a determined struggle for a stable, decent way of life.

The books about the Orphelines reverse the usual pattern of sad, sad orphans hoping to be adopted. These French orphans love Mme. Flattot, Genevive, and their home to the point where their one fear is adoption. When in *The Happy Orpheline* (1957), poor

Brigitte is about to be adopted, she knows she must perform a very wicked deed of some kind to prove she isn't fit for adoption. What she does is hilarious and makes a fitting if confused climax to the adventures of the twenty orphelines who are still twenty strong at the end. *A Brother for the Orphelines* (1959) finds them happily confronted with a foundling but alas! the baby is the wrong sex for a girls' orphanage. Their loving care of this little brother and their struggles to keep him make a tender and amusing story, one of the most appealing of the series. *A Pet for the Orphelines* (1962) is fun, too, and follows the pattern of the others. Each chapter is a complete adventure in the course of which young readers see French life from a child's-eye-view.

This sampling of stories about peoples of other lands demonstrates certain criteria for such books. First, children should be able to identify themselves wholeheartedly with the hero or heroine. Certainly any little girl would like to be Atia or Mara or Kate or Lina. And every boy will, as he reads, suffer the ups and downs of Chinese Fu or Swiss Rudi or Hungarian Jancsi and share his successes with pride. These books show the everyday life of work and responsibility that is the lot of most people everywhere—celebrations are only occasional. And finally, although these books induct the reader into the unique character of the national life, they show people more like us than different, with similar needs, strengths, and weaknesses.

Because books about other lands and historical fiction may so obviously enrich social studies in the schools, there may be a tendency to use them with too heavy an emphasis on their social implications. *The Wheel on the School* pictures village-wide cooperation finally, but it is also the story of children with a wonderful idea continually frustrated just because they are children. *The Gift of the Golden Cup* contrasts Greek and Roman life and demonstrates the evils of slavery. But it is primarily a rousing adventure story of revolt, pirates, and mystery. So these books, rich with historical and modern social values, are entertaining stories, as well as good literature.

SUGGESTED READING, PROBLEMS, AND PROJECTS

Suggested reading: Every student of children's books should have read *Heidi* or *Hans Brinker, Caddie Woodlawn,* and at least two of the Wilder *Little House* books.

Kindergarten-primary: Read one of the Dalgliesh books, two of the *Madeline* series, *Little Pear, Crow Boy, Family Under the Bridge,* one of the *Orpheline* series.

Middle and upper grades: Read one of William Steele's books, one of the Sutcliff books, one book from any historical period you are particularly interested in. Or read any two of these books about Shakespeare's period and plays: *Master Skylark, Wonderful Winter, I Will Adventure.*

1. As a child did you read any of the books discussed in this chapter? If so, what do you remember about them? How does your appraisal of them then compare with your appraisal now?

2. List criteria for evaluating sound historical fiction. With these in mind evaluate a particular book, such as *Johnny Tremain* or *The Tree of Freedom* or *Hakon of Rogen's Saga,* for example.

3. Why do you think *Caddie Woodlawn* has remained so continuously popular with children? What values does it have for children?

4. Give examples not discussed in the text of ways in which the *Little House* books minister to a child's need for security, belonging, competence, love, change, and esthetic satisfaction.

5. State your criteria for stories about other lands. What are some of the books you have read in this field and how do they measure up to these standards? How much action, suspense, humor, and vivid characterization do you find in these books? What are the themes? Where would you place the books for interest and reading levels?

6. Compare *Henry Huggins* or *The Moffats* with *Little Pear* or the *Orphelines;* or compare a William Steele book with either of the Elizabeth Gray or Rosemary Sutcliff books. Is the vernacular of the Steele books a problem?

7. Outline briefly how a unit of work might grow out of any one of the books or series of books in this chapter.

AMERICAN HISTORICAL FICTION

Note: Other American historical fiction titles may be found in the bibliographies for Chapters 15 and 17.

BALL, ZACHARY [pseud.]. *North to Abilene*. Holiday, 1960. The thousand-mile cattle drive from Texas to Abilene challenges the resourcefulness of orphaned Seth in this fine tale of the early cattle industry. 12-15

BELL, MARGARET. *Daughter of Wolf House*. Morrow, 1957. The coming of the white trader and his sons to the Alaskan salmon country changes the lives of the Indian villagers and brings romance to Nakatla, granddaughter of the chief. 12-15

BERRY, ERICK [pseud. for Allena Best]. *Hay-Foot, Straw-Foot*, ill. by author. Viking, 1954. Tale of a little drummer boy in the French and Indian War who inspired the tune of "Yankee Doodle." 9-12

BRINK, CAROL RYRIE. *Caddie Woodlawn*, ill. by Kate Seredy. Macmillan, 1935.

______. *Magical Melons; More Stories about Caddie Woodlawn*, ill. by Marguerite Davis. Macmillan, 1944. 9-12

BRONSON, LYNN [pseud.]. *The Runaway*. Lippincott, 1953. A runaway farm boy in the Oregon Territory joins the soldiers at Fort Columbia. His contact with kindly Captain Ulysses Grant and other men who have become historical figures makes this an unusual and distinctive tale set in the gold rush days. 12-16

BULLA, CLYDE ROBERT. *Down the Mississippi*, ill. by Peter Burchard. Crowell, 1954. Erik leaves his Minnesota farm to go down the great river on a log raft as a cook's helper. Storms and an Indian raid add plenty of excitement.

______. *Riding the Pony Express*, ill. by Grace Paull. Crowell, 1948. An easy-to-read but never commonplace story of a boy who carried the mail in an emergency.

______. *The Secret Valley*, ill. by Grace Paull. Crowell, 1949. A Missouri family goes to California in search of gold but finds other treasures instead. Mr. Bulla with his easy texts manages always a unique and pleasing style. 8-10

BURCHARD, PETER. *Jed*, ill. by author. Coward, 1960. Teen-age Jed's integrity and compassion prove stronger than his consciousness of being a Yankee soldier when he gives needed help to a Rebel family during the Civil War. 10-13

______. *North by Night*, ill. by author. Coward, 1962. Swift moving escape tale of two Yankee soldiers from a South Carolina Confederate prison. 12-

BUTLER, BEVERLY. *The Fur Lodge*, ill. by Herb Mott. Dodd, 1959. In a story of early fur trading with the Yankton Sioux Indians, the courage of young Jules is cruelly tested as, alone in the wilderness, he guards an isolated fur lodge. 12-15

CATTON, BRUCE. *Banners at Shenandoah*. Doubleday, 1955. Bruce Catton, Pulitzer Prize winner, writes absorbingly of Civil War days in this story of young Bob Hayden, flag bearer for General Sheridan. 12-16

CAUDILL, REBECCA. *Tree of Freedom*, ill. by Dorothy Bayley Morse. Viking, 1949. 12-14

COATSWORTH, ELIZABETH. *Away Goes Sally*, ill. by Helen Sewell. Macmillan, 1934.

______. *The Fair American*, ill. by Helen Sewell. Macmillan, 1940.

______. *Five Bushel Farm*, ill. by Helen Sewell. Macmillan, 1939.

______. *The Golden Horseshoe*, ill. by Robert Lawson. Macmillan, 1935. The daughter of an Indian princess and a Virginia officer finally wins the respect and affection of her English half-brother. 10-12

CRAWFORD, PHYLLIS. *"Hello, the Boat,"* ill. by Edward Laning. Holt, 1938. A resourceful family journeys from Pittsburgh to Cincinnati in 1816 aboard a steamboat fitted out as a store. 9-11

DALGLIESH, ALICE. *America Travels*, rev. ed., ill. by Hildegard Woodward. Macmillan, 1961. Short stories about each phase of transportation from the stagecoach to the space age. 9-11

______. *The Bears on Hemlock Mountain*, ill. by Helen Sewell. Scribner, 1952.

______. *The Courage of Sarah Noble*, ill. by Leonard Weisgard. Scribner, 1954.

______. *The 4th of July Story*, ill. by Marie Nonnast. Scribner, 1956.

______. *The Thanksgiving Story*, ill. by Helen Sewell. Scribner, 1954. 7-10

DAVIS, VERNE T. *The Time of the Wolves*, ill. by Ezra Jack Keats. Morrow, 1962. An engrossing tale of two young Michigan pioneers winter-trapped at a remote feeding place with their father's cattle, and endangered by wolves. 9-11

DOUGLAS, EMILY. *Appleseed Farm*, ill. by Anne Vaughan. Abingdon, 1948. Ten-year-old Penny hears about a visit Johnny Appleseed once made to her family's Indiana farm. 8-10

EDMONDS, WALTER D. *The Matchlock Gun*, ill. by Paul Lantz. Dodd, 1941. Newbery Medal.

______. *Tom Whipple*, ill. by Paul Lantz. Dodd, 1942. 10-12

ERSKINE, DOROTHY WARD. *Big Ride*, ill. by Hubert Buel. Crowell, 1958. The story of Captain De Anza's colonizing expedition from Mexico to California and the dangers encountered on the long and perilous journey. 10-14

FIELD, ELSIE KIMMELL. *Prairie Winter,* ill. by Bernard Case. Lothrop, 1959. Heartwarming pioneer story of the Kimmell family's year on the Dakota prairie, highlighted by a blizzard, a runaway cow, and a menacing rattlesnake. 10-13

FIELD, RACHEL. *Calico Bush,* ill. by Allen Lewis. Macmillan, 1931. 10-14

FLEISCHMAN, SID. *Mr. Mysterious & Company,* ill. by Eric von Schmidt. Little, 1962. Traveling under their intriguing stage name, the delightful Hackett family give magic shows in small pioneer towns as they work their way west from Texas to a San Diego ranch. A very different and appealing story of the early West. 10-12

FORBES, ESTHER. *Johnny Tremain,* ill. by Lynd Ward. Houghton, 1943. Newbery Medal. 12-14

FRAZIER, NETA LOHNES. *One Long Picnic,* ill. by Don Lambo. McKay, 1962. For the grown-up Gales, the wagon train journey from Wisconsin to Oregon was arduous and danger filled. To undersized dreamy David it was one grand lark with vast possibilities for heroic action if the chance ever came. 10-12

FRITZ, JEAN. *Brady,* ill. by Lynd Ward. Coward, 1960. Indiscreet young Brady at last learns there is a time for silence in this fine tale of the Underground Railroad in the 1830's. 10-13

______. *The Cabin Faced West,* ill. by Feodor Rojankovsky. Coward, 1958. A warm and moving story of a lonesome little pioneer girl of western Pennsylvania has its basis in the author's family history. 8-10

GENDRON, VAL. *The Fork in the Trail,* ill. by Sidney Quinn. McKay, 1952. Teen-age Wint Hanners starts up a cattle trading post on the route to the West during the gold rush days. 11-14

HOFF, CAROL. *Johnny Texas,* ill. by Bob Meyers. Follett, 1950.

______. *Johnny Texas on the San Antonio Road,* ill. by Earl Sherwan. Follett, 1953. These two stories follow the fortunes of a German immigrant family in Texas during the 1830's. 9-12

JOHNSON, ANNABEL and EDGAR. *Torrie.* Harper, 1960. It took the grim realities of a covered-wagon journey to California to jolt rebellious fourteen-year-old Torrie from her self-centered ways. Family relationships are well depicted in this pioneer story of the 1840's. 13-15

KEITH, HAROLD. *Rifles for Watie.* Crowell, 1957. Newbery Medal. 12-16

LAMPMAN, EVELYN. *Tree Wagon,* ill. by Robert Frankenberg. Doubleday, 1953. 10-13

LATHAM, JEAN. *This Dear-Bought Land,* ill. by Jacob Landau. Harper, 1957. An outstanding story of Captain John Smith and the settlement of Jamestown. 11-14

LAURITZEN, JONREED. *The Legend of Billy Bluesage,* ill. by Edward Chavez. Little, 1961. The author creates a legendary figure in Billy Bluesage, a lone boy rider of the old Southwest, whose appearance on the scene saves wagon trains from danger. 12-15

LENSKI, LOIS. *Puritan Adventure,* ill. by author. Lippincott, 1944. Massachusetts is the background of this vivid tale of colonial times. A lighthearted young aunt from England visits a strict Puritan family, bringing gaiety and laughter with her. 11-14

LEVY, MIMI COOPER. *Corrie and the Yankee,* ill. by Ernest Crichlow. Viking, 1959. Corrie, a little Negro girl on a South Carolina plantation, rescues a wounded Yankee soldier and helps him to safety. 10-13

MC MEEKIN, ISABEL. *Journey Cake,* ill. by Nicholas Panesis. Messner, 1942. Six motherless children, in the care of an intrepid old free Negro woman, journey through the wilderness to join their father in Boone's Kentucky. 10-12

MASON, MIRIAM. *Caroline and Her Kettle Named Maud,* ill. by Kathleen Voute. Macmillan, 1951.

______. *Little Jonathan,* ill. by George and Doris Hauman. Macmillan, 1944.

______. *The Middle Sister,* ill. by Grace Paull. Macmillan, 1947.

______. *Susannah, the Pioneer Cow,* ill. by Maud and Miska Petersham. Macmillan, 1941.

Easy-to-read pioneer stories full of humor and action. 8-10

MEADER, STEPHEN W. *Boy with a Pack,* ill. by Edward Shenton. Harcourt, 1939. An exciting story of a young Yankee peddler.

______. *River of the Wolves,* ill. by Edward Shenton. Harcourt, 1948. This story of boys held captive by Indians gives an unusually detailed picture of Indian life and individual Indians. 11-14

MEADOWCROFT, ENID. *By Secret Railway,* ill. by Henry C. Pitz. Crowell, 1948. The story of a white boy's rescue of a freed Negro who had been carried to the South again illegally. 11-14

MEIGS, CORNELIA. *Clearing Weather,* ill. by Frank Dobias. Little, 1928. 11-14

______. *The Covered Bridge,* ill. by Marguerite de Angeli. Macmillan, 1936. 8-10

______. *Master Simon's Garden,* new ed., ill. by John Rae. Macmillan, 1929. 11-14

______. *Swift Rivers,* ill. by Peter Hurd. Little, 1937. 11-14

______. *The Willow Whistle,* ill. by E. B. Smith. Macmillan, 1931. 8-10

______. *Wind in the Chimney,* ill. by Louise Mansfield. Macmillan, 1934. 8-10

Well-written historical tales less used today.

POPE, ELIZABETH MARIE. *The Sherwood Ring,* ill. by Evaline Ness. Houghton, 1958. Beautifully told romances of Revolutionary times and of today are skillfully interwoven in a story rich in suspense and mystery. 12-16

SPEARE, ELIZABETH GEORGE. *Calico Captive,* ill. by W. T. Mars. Houghton, 1957. Stirring junior novel of Miriam Willard, a young Indian captive taken to Canada during the French and Indian Wars. 11-15

______. *The Witch of Blackbird Pond.* Houghton, 1958. Newbery Medal. 12-16

STEELE, WILLIAM O. *The Buffalo Knife,* ill. by Paul Galdone. Harcourt, 1952.

______. *Far Frontier,* ill. by Paul Galdone. Harcourt, 1959.

______. *Flaming Arrows,* ill. by Paul Galdone. Harcourt, 1957.

______. *Tomahawks and Trouble,* ill. by Paul Galdone. Harcourt, 1955.

______. *Wilderness Journey,* ill. by Paul Galdone. Harcourt, 1953.

______. *Winter Danger,* ill. by Paul Galdone. Harcourt, 1954. 9-12

SWIFT, HILDEGARDE H. *Railroad to Freedom,* ill. by James Daugherty. Harcourt, 1932. A true story of a Negro slave who helped her people to freedom during the Civil War. 10-14

WIBBERLEY, LEONARD. *John Treegate's Musket.* Farrar, 1959. First in an outstanding series which tells of one family's experiences from before the American Revolution until the surrender at Yorktown. The vividly told series gives coverage to leading figures and events of the time. Other titles are: *Peter Treegate's War* (1960), *Sea Captain from Salem* (1961), *Treegate's Raiders,* (1962). 12-15

WILDER, LAURA INGALLS. *Little House in the Big Woods,* ill. by Garth Williams. Harper, 1953. Other titles in the series are: *Little House on the Prairie, On the Banks of Plum Creek, By the Shores of Silver Lake, The Long Winter, Little Town on the Prairie, These Happy Golden Years, Farmer Boy.* 9-14

WILLIAMSON, JOANNE S. *The Glorious Conspiracy.* Knopf, 1961. Ben Brown was a half-starved child laborer in the Manchester cotton mills when he escaped to America. In New York City he found a richer future and a chance to work for the Federal Party's democratic ideals. 12 16

WILSON, HAZEL. *His Indian Brother,* ill. by Robert Henneberger. Abingdon, 1955. Based on a true incident of the 1800's is this story of Brad Porter, left alone in a Maine pioneer cabin and rescued from starvation by an Indian chief and his son. 10-14

______. *Tall Ships,* ill. by John O'Hara Cosgrave II. Little, 1958. Through young Ben Wingate's adventures as an impressed British seaman, the period before the War of 1812 is vividly portrayed. 11-14

WRISTON, HILDRETH. *Susan's Secret,* ill. by W. T. Mars. Farrar, 1957. Suspense-filled story of a little Vermont girl who undertook her absent family's task of guiding fugitive slaves to the next Underground station. 9-12

THE ANCIENT WORLD

BEHN, HARRY. *The Faraway Lurs.* World, 1963. 12-15

COE, FREDERICK. *Graven with Flint,* ill. by Robert Hallock. Crowell, 1950. Adventures of Hia and Ag, two Cro-Magnon boys, in their struggle for survival. 11-14

COOLIDGE, OLIVIA. *Egyptian Adventures,* ill. by Joseph Low. Houghton, 1954. 12-16

______. *Roman People,* ill. by Lino Lipinsky. Houghton, 1959. The Rome of Augustus comes alive in ten stories, each of which portrays a different social or economic level. *Men of Athens* (1962) portrays Athens' Golden Age. 12-15

HAYS, WILMA PITCHFORD. *The Story of Valentine,* ill. by Leonard Weisgard. Coward, 1956. A vivid story of a Christian priest who, when imprisoned, achieved a miracle of faith. 9-12

JONES, RUTH FOSDICK. *Boy of the Pyramids; a Mystery of Ancient Egypt,* ill. by Dorothy Bayley Morse. Random, 1952. Ten-year-old Kaffee helps capture a thief who was stealing from a Pharaoh's tomb. An exciting story, set in the days of the building of pyramids. 10-12

LAWRENCE, ISABELLE. *The Gift of the Golden Cup,* ill. by Charles V. John. Bobbs, 1946. 11-14

______. *Niko, Sculptor's Apprentice,* ill. by Artur Marokvia. Viking, 1956. Athenian life in the days when the Parthenon was being built is vividly re-created in this story of the boy Niko, his noble slave Peron, and a lively family. 9-12

______. *The Theft of the Golden Ring,* ill. by Charles V. John. Bobbs, 1948. 11-14

MC GRAW, ELOISE JARVIS. *The Golden Goblet.* Coward, 1961. This is a suspense-filled tale of ancient Egypt and of a young apprentice who traps tomb robbers and wins royal favor. Historical background is excellent. 11-15

______. *Mara, Daughter of the Nile.* Coward, 1953. 11-15

MORRISON, LUCILE. *The Lost Queen of Egypt,* ill. by Franz Geritz and Winifred Brunton. Lippincott, 1937. 12-14

SNEDEKER, CAROLINE DALE. *The Forgotten Daughter,* ill. by Dorothy Lathrop. Doubleday, 1933. A good tale and a thorough study of Roman life. 10-14

______. *Theras and His Town,* ill. by Dimitris Davis. Doubleday, 1961. Life in Sparta and Athens is sharply contrasted as young Theras is forced to live under the Spartan regime. First published almost 40 years ago. 9-11

______. *A Triumph for Flavius,* ill. by Cedric Rogers. Lothrop, 1955. The story of a young Roman boy who, in compassion for his Greek slave and teacher, works to secure his freedom. Interesting background of ancient Rome and early Christian days and dangers. 8-11

______. *The White Isle,* ill. by Fritz Kredel. Doubleday, 1940. An interesting picture of the stormy beginnings of the Christian era in Rome. 10-14

SPEARE, ELIZABETH G. *The Bronze Bow.* Houghton, 1961. 12-

WINTERFELD, HENRY. *Detectives in Togas,* tr. by Richard and Clara Winston, ill. by Charlotte Kleinert. Harcourt, 1956. 10-13

EUROPEAN HISTORICAL FICTION

BENNETT, JOHN. *Master Skylark,* ill. by Reginald Birch. Grosset, 1924 (first pub. in 1897). One of the outstanding tales of Shakespeare's day. 12-14

BUFF, MARY. *The Apple and the Arrow,* ill. by Conrad Buff. Houghton, 1951. The stirring story of William Tell and his son Walter, with many dramatic illustrations by Swiss-born Conrad Buff. 9-12

BULLA, CLYDE. *The Sword in the Tree,* ill. by Paul Galdone. Crowell, 1956. King Arthur administers justice at the plea of young Shan, whose uncle has cast his father into prison and seized the castle. 8-10

CHUTE, MARCHETTE. *The Innocent Wayfaring,* ill. by author. Dutton, 1955.

______. *The Wonderful Winter,* ill. by Grace Golden. Dutton, 1954. 11-14

COBLENTZ, CATHERINE CATE. *The Beggars' Penny,* ill. by Hilda van Stockum. McKay, 1943. A fine historical story of the siege of Leyden by the Spanish. 12-14

DE ANGELI, MARGUERITE. *The Door in the Wall,* ill. by author. Doubleday, 1949. 8-11

GIBSON, KATHARINE. *Oak Tree House,* ill. by Vera Bock. McKay, 1936. An old couple build a tree house in the middle of the King's Highway, save the King's messenger, and receive the tree legally for life from the King. 10-12

GRAY, ELIZABETH JANET. *Adam of the Road,* ill. by Robert Lawson. Viking, 1942. Newbery Medal. 12-14

______. *I Will Adventure,* ill. by Corydon Bell. Viking, 1962. 11-14

HARNETT, CYNTHIA. *Caxton's Challenge,* ill. by author. World, 1960. As an apprentice, young Bendy shares the problems and perils of the great fifteenth-century printer. 12-16

______. *Nicholas and the Wool-Pack,* ill. by author. Putnam, 1953. Young Nicholas Fetterlock solves the mysterious wool thefts which were bringing disgrace to his father. A colorful story of the medieval wool industry. 11-15

HAUGAARD, ERIK CHRISTIAN. *Hakon of Rogen's Saga,* ill. by Leo and Diane Dillon. Houghton, 1963. 11-14

HAWES, CHARLES B. *Dark Frigate.* Little, 1924. An exciting sea tale in the days of the Stuarts. Newbery Medal. 12-14

HODGES, C. WALTER. *Columbus Sails,* ill. by author. Coward, 1950. This well-liked story of Columbus and his voyages is fiction based on facts and is tremendously moving. 11-14

KELLY, ERIC P. *The Trumpeter of Krakow,* ill. by Angela Pruszynska. Macmillan, 1928. Difficult to read but an absorbing story. Newbery Medal. 12-14

KENT, LOUISE ANDREWS. *He Went with Magellan,* ill. by Paul Quinn. Houghton, 1943.

______. *He Went with Marco Polo,* ill. by C. L. Baldwin and Paul Quinn. Houghton, 1935.

______. *He Went with Vasco da Gama,* ill. by Paul Quinn. Houghton, 1938.

Fun and adventures, with enough background to make the books good historical fiction. 10-14

KYLE, ELISABETH [pseud.]. *The Story of Grizel.* Nelson, 1961. Colorful fictionalized biography of young Grizel Hume, seventeenth-century Scotch patriot, who waged her own war for religious freedom and found romance as well. 12-15

LEWIS, HILDA. *The Gentle Falcon.* Criterion, 1957. A poignant and moving story of little Princess Isabella of France, who was married to Richard II of England when she was seven. Romantic in vein and rich in historical detail. 12-

MAGOON, MARIAN AUSTIN. *Little Dusty Foot,* ill. by Christine Price. Longmans, 1948. Absorbing story of the far-traveled merchants of Charlemagne's reign, and of young Rauf, who shared their adventures. 10-14

OLIVER, JANE [pseud.]. *Faraway Princess,* ill. by Jane Paton. St. Martin's Press, 1962. Princess Margaret, in flight from England after the Norman Conquest, finds sanctuary in Scotland and later a throne. Excellent historical fiction. 10-13

PARKER, RICHARD. *The Sword of Ganelon,* ill. by William Ferguson. McKay, 1958. Young Binna, the Jute, discovers the lost sword of Ganelon in a sea-destroyed burial mound and carries it to King Alfred. A stirring tale of ninth-century England invaded by the Danes. 11-16

POLLAND, MADELEINE. *Children of the Red King,* ill. by Annette Macarthur-Onslow. Holt, 1961. Grania and Fergus, children of Ireland's embattled king, are sent as captives to their father's enemy. The events leading to reunion with their father offer a vivid story of the Norman Conquest. 11-13

PYLE, HOWARD. *Men of Iron,* ill. by author. Harper, 1891.

———. *Otto of the Silver Hand,* ill. by author. Scribner, 1888. 10-14

ROBBINS, RUTH. *The Emperor and the Drummer Boy,* ill. by Nicolas Sidjakov. Parnassus, 1962. The seas at Boulogne were stormy when Napoleon insisted on naval maneuvers which doomed many ships and men. This true incident centers about two young drummer boys. Distinguished in illustrations and format. 9-12

SUTCLIFF, ROSEMARY. *Dawn Wind,* ill. by Charles Keeping. Walck, 1962.

———. *The Eagle of the Ninth,* ill. by C. Walter Hodges. Walck, 1954. The story of a lost legion in Roman Britain of the second century.

———. *The Lantern Bearers,* ill. by Charles Keeping. Walck, 1959.

———. *The Outcast,* ill. by Richard Kennedy. Walck, 1955. Unwanted by either Briton tribesmen or the Romans, orphaned Beric is forced to build a new life. Service as a galley slave is an unforgettable part of the story.

———. *The Shield Ring,* ill. by C. Walter Hodges. Walck, 1957. Eleventh-century England is the background for this tale of Norsemen against Norman invaders, and of the advance of two young people in the war-torn land.

———. *The Silver Branch.* Walck, 1958. Two young Romans, involved in the bitter intrigue between the ruler of Roman Britain and his rival, play a heroic part in bringing an assassin to justice.

———. *Warrior Scarlet,* ill. by Charles Keeping. Walck, 1958. In a unique tale of Bronze Age England, Drem kills his wolf and regains his tribal status despite a crippled arm. 12-16

TREECE, HENRY. *Viking's Dawn,* ill. by Christine Price. Criterion, 1956. First in an absorbing trilogy of eighth-century Viking life, in which youthful Harald Sigurdson accompanies his father on his first dangerous sea journey. In *The Road to Miklagard* (1957) his voyages are interrupted when he becomes a Moorish slave. In *Viking's Sunset* (1961) Harald, now a chieftain, sails his longboat to the shores of Lake Superior, and death intervenes on this last voyage. Harald's life saga conveys the vast scope of early Viking travels. 11-14

VARBLE, RACHEL M. *Pepys' Boy,* ill. by Kurt Werth. Doubleday, 1955. The England of the Restoration and of Samuel Pepys' diary is portrayed in all its splendor and misery in this story of Toby, who works as a page boy for Pepys. 12-14

———. *Three Against London.* Doubleday, 1962. Told against the background of seventeenth-century London and the Great Fire, slum-bred Kip Skeet faces imprisonment as a falsely accused arsonist, until Samuel Pepys comes to his aid. Excellent as a junior novel and a period piece. 12-16

WILLIAMS, URSULA MORAY. *The Earl's Falconer,* ill. by Charles Geer. Morrow, 1961. Training falcons was not the privilege of peasant boys, but young Dickson's rare talent earned him the Earl's favor. A colorful tale of medieval England. 11-14

OTHER COUNTRIES: HISTORICAL FICTION

BAUMANN, HANS. *Sons of the Steppe.* Walck, 1958. A gripping story of Genghis Khan's two grandsons, whose views on brutal warfare conflict. 12-16

GUILLOT, RENÉ. *The Elephants of Sargabal,* tr. by Gwen Marsh, ill. by Felix Hoffmann. Criterion, 1957. A tale of old India, and of two young orphan boys who thwart plans to destroy their princess. 11-14

RITCHIE, RITA. *The Golden Hawks of Genghis Khan,* ill. by Lorence F. Bjorklund. Dutton, 1958.

———. *Secret Beyond the Mountains.* Dutton, 1960.

———. *The Year of the Horse,* ill. by Lorence F. Bjorklund. Dutton, 1957.

These are outstanding tales of the years of Mongol supremacy. 12-15

STORIES ABOUT MODERN CHILDREN OF OTHER LANDS

Forerunners

DODGE, MARY MAPES. *Hans Brinker: or the Silver Skates,* ill. by George Wharton Edwards. Scribner, 1915. 10-12

SPYRI, JOHANNA. *Heidi,* ill. by Agnes Tait. Lippincott, 1948. 10-12

Africa

CLAIR, ANDREE. *Bemba,* tr. from the French by Marie Ponsot, ill. by Harper Johnson. Harcourt, 1962. The integrity of a French archaeologist finally overcomes the distrust of young Bemba and his Congolese tribesmen in this fine tale of modern Africa. 10-12

DAVIS, NORMAN. *Picken's Treasure Hunt,* ill. by Winslade. Walck, 1955. Exciting tale of a Gambian chief's son sent to search for a golden throne which has been mysteriously concealed. 8-11

HUBBARD, MARGARET C. *Boss Chombale,* ill. by Peter Spier. Crowell, 1957. Accompanying their surveyor father to Northern Rhodesia, a young American family absorb its beauty and mystery. 10-13

MIRSKY, REBA. *Seven Grandmothers,* ill. by W. T. Mars. Follett, 1955.

______. *Thirty-One Brothers and Sisters,* ill. by W. T. Mars. Follett, 1952. Stories of the African veld which give an unusually vivid picture of family life. In *Thirty-One Brothers and Sisters,* Nomusa, the daughter of a Zulu chief, reluctantly abandons her tomboy role for more womanly duties. In the sequel, Nomusa decides to train for professional nursing so she can help her people most effectively. 9-12

STINETORF, LOUISE A. *Musa, the Shoemaker,* ill. by Harper Johnson. Lippincott, 1959. Lame Musa had little future in his North African village of trained acrobats. His resigned acceptance of a shoemaker's apprenticeship leads to an even more promising career. 10-13

China and Japan

BRO, MARGUERITE. *Su-Mei's Golden Year,* ill. by Kurt Wiese. Doubleday, 1950. It is Su-Mei and her friends of the younger generation who save their Chinese village from famine when the wheat crop is endangered. 11-14

BUCK, PEARL. *The Big Wave,* ill. by Hiroshige and Hokusai. Day, 1948. Jiya leaves the coast after a tidal wave destroys his home and the entire fishing village. When he is grown, he courageously returns to his traditional occupation. There is a heroic quality in the telling which makes this Japanese story a memorable one. 9-13

GALLANT, KATHRYN. *The Flute Player of Beppu,* ill. by Kurt Wiese. Coward, 1960. Music-loving Sato-San resists the temptation to keep the lost flute of a traveling musician and is rewarded with lessons. 7-9

HANDFORTH, THOMAS. *Mei Li,* ill. by author. Doubleday, 1938. The pleasant adventures of a little Chinese girl at the Fair. Caldecott Medal. 5-8

HUGGINS, ALICE M., and HUGH ROBINSON. *Wan-Fu, Ten Thousand Happinesses,* ill. by Roberta Moynihan. McKay, 1957. Rescued by missionaries, a crippled Chinese beggar girl finds a brighter future. 11-14

LATTIMORE, ELEANOR. *Little Pear,* ill. by author. Harcourt, 1931. Followed by *Little Pear and His Friends* (1934) and *Little Pear and the Rabbits* (1956). 6-10

LEWIS, ELIZABETH. *To Beat a Tiger, One Needs a Brother's Help,* ill. by John Heuhnergarth. Holt, 1956. 12-16

______. *Young Fu of the Upper Yangtze,* ill. by Kurt Wiese. Holt, 1932. Newbery Medal. 10-14

MARTIN, PATRICIA. *The Pointed Brush,* ill. by Roger Duvoisin. Lothrop, 1959. In a family crisis, small Chung Kee proves the value of the schooling he gained because his father thought him too young to work in the rice fields with his bigger brothers. 7-10

MATSUNO, MASAKO. *A Pair of Red Clogs,* ill. by Kazue Mizumura. World, 1960. A little Japanese girl chooses beautiful but impractical new red clogs and soon rues her choice. Beautifully illustrated in color, with a universal theme. 5-8

MUHLENWEG, FRITZ. *Big Tiger and Christian,* ill. by Rafaello Busoni. Pantheon, 1952. An English and a Chinese boy cross the Gobi Desert on a dangerous mission for a Chinese general. Here are nearly six hundred pages packed with adventure, people, and strange places. A rare treat for the superior reader. 12-

REISS, MALCOLM. *China Boat Boy,* ill. by Jeanyee Wong. Lippincott, 1954. The possession of a rare cormorant used in fishing, a father absent and injured in war, and the mother and children victimized by a ruthless moneylender add up to an exciting tale of a Chinese river boat family during World War II. 10-14

TREFFINGER, CAROLYN. *Li Lun, Lad of Courage,* ill. by Kurt Wiese. Abingdon, 1947. Story of a Chinese boy who compensates for his fear of the sea by growing rice on a lonely mountaintop. He learns of a new way of life for himself and his people. 9-12

WOOD, ESTHER. *Silk and Satin Lane,* ill. by Kurt Wiese. McKay, 1939. 9-12

YASHIMA, TARO [pseud. for Jun Iwamatsu]. *Crow Boy,* ill. by author. Viking, 1955.

______. *The Village Tree,* ill. by author. Viking, 1953. 6-9

YASHIMA, TARO and MITSU [pseuds. for Jun and Tomoe Iwamatsu]. *Plenty to Watch,* ill. by Taro Yashima. Viking, 1954. 6-9

France

BEMELMANS, LUDWIG. *Madeline,* ill. by author. Viking, 1939. Other titles in the series include *Madeline's Rescue* (1953), *Madeline and the Bad Hat* (1957), *Madeline and the Gypsies* (1959). 5-8

BISHOP, CLAIRE HUCHET. *All Alone,* ill. by Feodor

Rojankovsky. Viking, 1953. Villagers in the French Alps learn to work together when two children, herding in the mountains, are isolated by an avalanche. 9-11

——. *Pancakes-Paris,* ill. by Georges Schreiber. Viking, 1947. A half-starved postwar French child receives a miraculous package of American pancake mix. How he meets two American soldiers and gets the recipe makes a heart-warming tale. 8-12

——. *Toto's Triumph,* ill. by Claude Ponsot. Viking, 1957. A small Parisian boy outwits a harsh landlord opposed to babies in the house. 10-12

CARLSON, NATALIE SAVAGE. *A Brother for the Orphelines,* ill. by Garth Williams. Harper, 1959.

——. *The Family Under the Bridge,* ill. by Garth Williams. Harper, 1958.

——. *The Happy Orpheline,* ill. by Garth Williams. Harper, 1957.

——. *A Pet for the Orphelines,* ill. by Fermin Rocker. Harper, 1962. 9-12

Holland

DEJONG, MEINDERT. *Dirk's Dog, Bello,* ill. by Kurt Wiese. Harper, 1939. 10-12

——. *Shadrach,* ill. by Maurice Sendak. Harper, 1953. The story of a Dutch boy's devotion to his small black rabbit.

——. *Smoke above the Lane,* ill. by Girard Goodenow. Harper, 1951.

——. *The Wheel on the School,* ill. by Maurice Sendak. Harper, 1954. 9-12

DODGE, MARY MAPES. *Hans Brinker; or the Silver Skates* (see Forerunners).

VAN STOCKUM, HILDA. *The Winged Watchman,* ill. by author. Farrar, 1962. The Verhagen family, in constant danger from an informer, conceal a British pilot during the occupation. 10-12

India

ARORA, SHIRLEY. *"What Then, Raman?"* ill. by Hans Guggenheim. Follett, 1960. 10-12

BATCHELOR, JULIE. *A Cap for Mul Chand,* ill. by Corinne V. Dillon. Harcourt, 1950. In spite of interference from the village bully, eleven-year-old Mul Chand finally earns the money for his longed-for cap. 8-10

BOTHWELL, JEAN. *The Little Flute Player,* ill. by Margaret Ayer. Morrow, 1949. Minor disasters stalk Teka, the little village flute player, and grow into tragedy when famine comes. The ten-year-old boy takes his father's place and saves his family from starvation. 9-12

RANKIN, LOUISE. *Daughter of the Mountains,* ill. by Kurt Wiese. Viking, 1948. Tells of the journey of a little Tibetan village girl to far-off Calcutta in search of her stolen puppy. 10-13

SINGH, REGINALD LAL, and ELOISE LOWNSBERY. *Gift of the Forest,* ill. by Anne Vaughan. McKay, 1942 and 1958. In this distinguished story of rural India, Young Bim, a Hindu boy, finds a tiger cub and cares for it until he is forced to return it to the jungle. 11-14

Italy

ANGELO, VALENTI. *The Marble Fountain,* ill. by author. Viking, 1951.

——. *Nino,* ill. by author. Viking, 1938. Both these stories offer a background of Italian village life written with rare feeling. *Nino* is the story of a little boy's happy time before the family immigrates to America at the turn of the century. In *Marble Fountain,* the postwar recovery of a bombed village is aided when the children recover the lost statue of Saint Francis. 11-14

BETTINA (pseud. for Bettina Ehrlich). *Pantaloni,* ill. by author. Harper, 1957. Colorfully illustrated, this is a warm story of Italian village life and of a little boy's search for his lost dog. 5-8

FLETCHER, DAVID. *Confetti for Cortorelli,* ill. by George Thompson. Pantheon, 1957. To be in the Children's Fancy Dress Parade, Angelo, an orphan of Sicily, needed a costume. How he earned it and gained a home as well makes an original and distinctive story. 6-8

Mexico and South America

BEHN, HARRY. *The Two Uncles of Pablo,* ill. by Mel Silverman. Harcourt, 1959. Small Pablo copes with two antagonistic uncles as well as his own problem of trying to gain an education. An appealing story of Mexico written by a poet very popular with children. 9-11

BUFF, MARY and CONRAD. *Magic Maize* (see Bibliography, Chapter 15).

BULLA, CLYDE. *Benito,* ill. by Valenti Angelo. Crowell, 1961. The encouragement of a successful artist helps orphaned Benito assert his need for time from the endless farm drudgery at Uncle Pedro's to develop his talent. 8-10

DESMOND, ALICE CURTIS. *The Lucky Llama,* ill. by Wilfrid Bronson. Macmillan, 1939. A charming picture of boy and llamas. 10-12

ETS, MARIE HALL, and AURORA LABASTIDA. *Nine Days to Christmas,* ill. by Marie Hall Ets. Viking, 1959. Ceci, a little girl of Mexico, discovers the fun of Christmas with her first piñata. Caldecott Medal. 5-8

GARRETT, HELEN. *Angelo the Naughty One,* ill. by Leo Politi. Viking, 1944. The amusing reform of a small Mexican boy who did not like to take baths. 6-9

HADER, BERTA and ELMER. *Story of Pancho and the Bull with the Crooked Tail,* ill. by authors. Macmillan, 1942. A very funny story of a little Mexican boy's accidental capture of a ferocious bull. Pictures in brilliant colors. 6-9

MORROW, ELIZABETH. *The Painted Pig,* ill. by René d'Harnoncourt. Knopf, 1930. A slight but pleasant story with good pictures. 7-10

PARISH, HELEN RAND. *At the Palace Gates,* ill. by Leo Politi. Viking, 1949. Appealing adventure story of a small Peruvian boy living on his own in Lima. His fortunate overhearing of a plot against the governor is rewarded by a chance to gratify his greatest ambition. 9-11

RHOADS, DOROTHY M. *The Corn Grows Ripe,* ill. by Jean Charlot. Viking, 1956. Twelve-year-old Tigre, spoiled and lazy, grows up suddenly when his father is injured. Background of the story is Yucatan, among the Mayan Indians. 9-12

SAWYER, RUTH. *The Least One,* ill. by Leo Politi. Viking, 1941. A touching tale of a boy and his donkey. 8-10

TARSHIS, ELIZABETH K. *The Village That Learned to Read,* ill. by Harold Haydon. Houghton, 1941. A robust story of an unwilling scholar. 10-12

Sweden

ANCKARSVARD, KARIN. *Aunt Vinnie's Invasion,* tr. by Annabelle MacMillan, ill. by William M. Hutchinson. Harcourt, 1962. The six Hallsenius children live with Aunt Vinnie for a year. This is an amusing story of modern Sweden. 10-13

LINDGREN, ASTRID. *Rasmus and the Vagabond,* tr. by Gerry Bothmer, ill. by Eric Palmquist. Viking, 1960. Written in a more serious vein than the author's *Pippi Longstocking* series, this is an appealing story of a runaway orphan and the part-time tramp who befriended him. 9-12

UNNERSTAD, EDITH. *The Saucepan Journey,* ill. by Louis Slobodkin. Macmillan, 1951. The Larrson children, all seven of them, spend a wonderful summer in the traveling caravan, helping father sell his saucepans through Sweden. 9-12

______. *The Spettecake Holiday,* tr. by Inger Boye, ill. by Iben Clante. Macmillan, 1959. A lonely little boy, pining for his sick mother, finds both hope and contentment on his grandmother's farm. 9-11

Switzerland

BUFF, MARY and CONRAD. *Kobi: a Boy of Switzerland,* ill. by Conrad Buff. Viking, 1939. A quiet story of a Swiss boy's everyday work and play, marked by one thrilling episode in which the boy leads his herd through a storm. 8-12

CHONZ, SELINA. *A Bell for Ursli,* ill. by Alois Carigiet. Walck, 1953. One of the most beautiful picture-stories to come out of Europe, this is also the exciting story of a small Swiss boy determined to have the largest bell to ring in the spring procession. 6-9

KAROLYI, ERNA M. *A Summer to Remember,* ill. by author. McGraw, 1949. Margitka, a little Hungarian girl, frail after years of war, regains her health as the guest of a kindly Swiss family. 10-12

RUTGERS VAN DER LOEFF-BASENAU, ANNA. *Avalanche!* tr. by Dora Round, ill. by Gustav Schrotter. Morrow, 1958. Holland's prize-winning children's book for 1955 tells the dramatic story of an avalanche that struck the tiny Swiss village of Urteli and how it affected three young boys. 11-13

SPYRI, JOHANNA. *Heidi* (see Forerunners).

ULLMAN, JAMES RAMSEY. *Banner in the Sky.* Lippincott, 1954. 12-16

Other countries

ARASON, STEINGRIMUR. *Smoky Bay,* ill. by Gertrude Howe. Macmillan, 1942. The story of an Iceland boy whose wish to visit America finally comes true. An interesting story in an unusual setting. 10-14

AYER, JACQUELINE. *Nu Dang and His Kite,* ill. by author. Harcourt, 1959. A colorful introduction to Siamese life is provided by this story of a small boy's search along the river banks for his lost kite. *The Paper Flower Tree* (1962) is the story of a little girl of Thailand who at last finds her longed for ornamental tree. 6-8

BENARY-ISBERT, MARGOT. *The Ark,* tr. by Richard and Clara Winston. Harcourt, 1953. 12-15

______. *Castle on the Border,* tr. by Richard and Clara Winston. Harcourt, 1956. 14-16

______. *Rowan Farm,* tr. by Richard and Clara Winston. Harcourt, 1954. 12-15

BONZON, PAUL-JACQUES. *The Orphans of Simitra,* tr. from the French by Thelma Niklaus, ill. by Simon Jeruchim. Criterion, 1962. Orphaned by an earthquake in Greece, Porphyras and his little sister find a new home in Holland. The homesick Marina disappears and Porphyras works his way to Paris in search of her. Sensitively written and rich in background of people and places. 11-14

CHAUNCY, NAN. *Devil's Hill,* ill. by Geraldine Spence. Watts, 1960. An outstanding tale of family life in the Tasmanian bush country climaxed by an exciting journey into the wilds in search of a lost heifer. 10-12

COATSWORTH, ELIZABETH. *Lonely Maria,* ill. by Evaline Ness. Pantheon, 1960. Maria was never again lonely on her West Indies island after she discovered the fun and activity her own imagination could provide. Color illustrations. 7-9

FREUCHEN, PETER. *Whaling Boy,* ill. by Leonard Everett Fisher. Putnam, 1958. Per List, not quite twelve, finds life aboard a Danish whaling ship a rugged and adventurous experience. A powerfully written and moving story. 10-13

LINDQUIST, WILLIS. *Burma Boy,* ill. by Nicolas Mordvinoff. McGraw, 1953. Suspense and atmosphere combine to make this an absorbing story of a boy's search for a lost elephant. 9-11

LIPKIND, WILLIAM. *Boy with a Harpoon,* ill. by Nicolas Mordvinoff. Harcourt, 1952. Little Seal, an Alaskan Eskimo boy, earns the right to accompany the men on a hunting expedition. 8-11

MERRILL, JEAN. *Shan's Lucky Knife,* ill. by Ronni Solbert. W. R. Scott, 1960. Young Shan outwits the tricky boatman who has taken all his possessions. An excellent read-aloud with a Burmese background and folktale flavor. 7-10

NAN KIVELL, JOICE M. *Tales of Christophilos,* ill. by Panos Ghikas. Houghton, 1954. Christophilos, the young goatherd, lives near Mount Athos in Greece. His adventures, told with humor, give a fine picture of the life and people. 10-14

NESS, EVALINE. *Josefina February,* ill. by author. Scribner, 1963. 6-8

PHIPSON, JOAN. *The Boundary Riders,* ill. by Margaret Horder. Harcourt, 1963. The suspense-filled journey to safety of three Australian children and their dog. 10-13

RASP-NURI, GRACE. *Yusuf: Boy of Cyprus,* tr. from the German by J. Maxwell Brownjohn. Criterion, 1958. Taken by thieves and harshly trained to steal, orphaned Yusuf warns his prospective victims and gains a happier future. Fine background. 11-13

SEREDY, KATE. *The Good Master,* ill. by author. Viking, 1935. 10-14

———. *The Singing Tree,* ill. by author. Viking, 1939. 10-14

SERRAILLIER, IAN. *The Silver Sword,* ill. by C. Walter Hodges. Criterion, 1959. The unforgettable journey of four children who make their way from Warsaw to Switzerland and safety during World War II. 11-14

SEUBERLICH, HERTHA. *Annuzza: A Girl of Romania,* tr. by Stella Humphries, ill. by Gerhard Pallasch. Rand, 1962. A poignant story of rural pre-war Rumania tells of a gifted peasant girl who wins a scholarship and for a time loses her perspective on home and family. 12-15

SHANNON, MONICA. *Dobry,* ill. by Atanas Katchamakoff. Viking, 1934. 11-14

SOMMERFELT, AIMEE. *Miriam,* tr. by Pat Shaw Iversen. Criterion, 1963. A provocative and penetrating story of the ordeal of a teen-age Jewish girl in Nazi-occupied Norway. 12-15

SPERRY, ARMSTRONG. *Call It Courage,* ill. by author. Macmillan, 1940. Newbery Medal. 10-12

TUNIS, JOHN R. *Silence over Dunkerque.* Morrow, 1962. The evacuation of Dunkirk is the dramatic background for the story of British Sergeant Williams stranded in enemy-occupied France. A powerful story. 12-15

VON GEBHARDT, HERTHA. *The Girl from Nowhere,* tr. by James Kirkup, ill. by Helen Brun. Criterion, 1959. No one believes her father will return, but a little German girl's faith surmounts mockery and pity and is happily rewarded. 10-13

WATSON, SALLY. *To Build a Land,* ill. by Lili Cassel. Holt, 1957. War-orphaned Leo and his small sister, rescued from the streets of Naples, find a new life in a children's camp in Israel. 11-14

WILHELMSON, CARL. *Speed of the Reindeer,* ill. by Rafaello Busoni. Viking, 1954. An unusual tale of life among the Lapps of the Arctic Circle, heightened by suspense. When the most beautiful deer in the herd disappears, young Mikko sets out to solve the mystery. 10-14

WUORIO, EVA LIS. *The Island of Fish in the Trees,* ill. by Edward Ardizzone. World, 1962. The daylong adventure of two little sisters who trail the doctor around the island to get him to mend their broken doll. The setting is the Balearic Islands, and both story and pictures are exceptionally appealing. 7-9

chapter 17

Biography

For a long time it was difficult to find any biographies for children that were not stereotyped, stuffy, and unpopular. Then in the nineteen thirties some excellent biographies appeared in the juvenile field, and by the next decade biography had become an important and popular branch of children's literature. Now it is flooding the market and threatening to capture young readers so completely that they will have no time or taste for any other kind of reading. This is a remarkable phenomenon, due in part to the rise of exceptionally successful biography series. The series in turn seem to have grown out of our deep feeling and jealous concern for our democratic way of life. Adults see it threatened by hostile ideologies, and they want their children to know what democracy is and what it cost our early settlers. Above all, they want children to know just how courageous, troubled, and far-sighted the founding fathers were when they molded a bewildered young nation into its present form. The biography series record these men and their successors. Children in the United States are learning their history in terms of the men who made it.

Best of all, the children are enthusiastic about biography. In one small city there is a boys' club named for its favorite series of biographies. In another, the children bring in a publisher's list of new titles and harry the librarian for the latest books. Decidedly, these are books adults should know about.

The problem is to keep up with them. A librarian or a book reviewer used to receive a single biography to consider, but she now receives a box of twenty or more from one publisher. One series becomes well established and four more spring up. The multiplicity of biographies is so overwhelming that one suspects they cannot all be excellent. Some may even be slipping back into the old stereotypes. At any rate, it behooves the adults who guide children's reading to know what constitutes sound biography, so that they can pick out the best examples from the numerous books in this important field of children's reading.

What Is Biography?

The heroes of recent biographies, for adults as well as children, are different from those of a few decades ago. Readers want and find in many of these new books an honest reporting of a man's life. In this age of science, we believe not only in biological evolution but also in the evolution of human character, for better or for worse. We are accustomed to see goodness, wisdom, and strength growing slowly out of a muddle of weaknesses and confusions, some of which are never eradicated. Or we are not surprised to see, sometimes, weakness growing weaker in spite of fine, lovable qualities, and folly degenerating into vice. The course of a man's life depends, we realize, both upon his inherent capacities and upon his surroundings. Today we are interested in this combination of heredity and environment and in its influence on a man's tendencies and drives and on his will to discipline and forge himself into a certain pattern.

One reason for the improvement of biography is that in the last several decades there have been some systematic and critical appraisals of the field. Intelligent criticism helps to formulate standards and to inspire and direct creative enterprise. Modern biography owes much not only to some of the great models of the past but to such evaluations as Harold Nicolson's *The Development of English Biography* (1928) and André Maurois' *Aspects of Biography* (1929). The book by Mr. Nicolson is an exceptionally sound appraisal of biography, and Mr. Maurois' book adds the French point of view, which is important also.

The *Oxford English Dictionary* defines biography as "the history of the lives of individual men as a branch of literature." Here, as Mr. Nicolson points out, are the three points of emphasis: *history,* that is, facts authentic and verifiable; an *individual,* not a paragon or a type; *literature,* that is, a conscious work of art. This description with some amplifications not only defines biography, but suggests the standards by which we should judge it.

Biography As History

AUTHENTICITY

If a biography is the history of a person's life, it should be as accurate and authentic as research can make it. The biographer must read the complete literary works of his hero and study everything he has created—music, paintings, or sculpture. He must examine any letters or diaries or journals left by the man. He must in turn compare the man's personal papers with the comments of his contemporaries as recorded in their books or letters or diaries. If these seem contradictory, the biographer must discover what the attitude of the contemporary was—friendly, worshipful, or definitely antagonistic. This may involve consulting the available writings of still other contemporaries who knew both men and who in turn left records of their relationships. The mass of personal papers and documents which a conscientious modern biographer goes through in order to be even reasonably certain of the authenticity of his material is staggering. Esther Forbes in her meticulous research for her *Paul Revere and the World He Lived In* gathered enough information about the lively antics of Boston's apprentices to give body to a second book, *Johnny Tremain* (p. 481). The limitations of biography had prevented her from using her imagination or guessing at some of the things that happened in the life of Paul Revere; so *Johnny* was the fictional outlet for all her wonderings about those busy apprentices.

OBJECTIVITY

Esther Forbes' experience in writing the life of Paul Revere suggests another test for biography as history. A biographer is not free to give his own opinions or to present an interpretation for which he has no evidence. His hero's deeds should speak for themselves. If they seem ambiguous, the author may speculate about the contradictory evidence, but he may not take sides or tell the reader what to think. Was Sam Houston completely honest and disinterested in his dealings with the Indians and with his Cherokee foster father? Marquis James in *The Raven,* a biography of Sam Houston, never tells us how he regards Houston's actions. He presents the evidence and lets the reader draw his own conclusions. And readers of *The Raven* differ in their judgment of Sam, just as Sam's contemporaries themselves differed. James, then, is objective in presenting Houston's life. He scrupulously refrains from imposing his judgments on the reader.

It also follows that the biographer may report only those words and thoughts which the hero has recorded or is known to have spoken. Some biographers have got around this strict limitation by saying, "Perhaps he thought...." or "Perhaps he meant what he said, who knows?" Lytton Strachey uses this device repeatedly in his *Queen Victoria.* When the gouty old king whom she was to succeed asked the young Victoria for her favorite tune, she replied without a moment's hesitation, "God Save the King." This, Strachey tells us, "has been praised as an early example of a tact which was afterwards famous." Then he adds cryptically, "But she was a very truthful child, and perhaps it was her genuine opinion." He closes his book with a dramatic use of this device. Describing the dying queen, old, blind, and silent, he suggests that she *may perhaps* have recalled her past. Then, as if Victoria were thinking aloud, he briefly and tenderly reviews her life, going back to the little girl in "sprigged muslin, and the trees and the grass at Kensington." Maurois uses this same device differently but just as dramatically in relating the possible "dreams" of the old and ailing Disraeli. So Jeanette Eaton also uses it in her account of the dying Washington in *Leader by Destiny.* It is a legitimate device, but when it is overused it may become a not too subtle method of influencing the opinions of the reader.

SOURCES

For many people, one of the most important tests of a good biography is the accuracy and thoroughness of its documentation. Mr. Nicolson in *The Development of English Biography* insists that a biography should be as scrupulously documented as history. Strachey's *Queen Victoria* is a model in this respect, for every incident and every description is conscientiously documented in the footnotes.

Juvenile biographies are usually not documented. Although children may never read footnotes, nevertheless, careful documentation is a guarantee to adults of the authenticity of the material, and it could serve a similar purpose for older children and young people. A respect for objective, verifiable reporting can be started with any child old enough to read substantial biographies. Perhaps if children were taught this respect for truth and accuracy, as adults they would be more critical of prejudiced or fictionalized biographies. A careful acknowledgment of sources is a guarantee to the reader of the historical accuracy and the objectivity of a biography.

Biography As the Individual

TYPED CHARACTERS UNACCEPTABLE

All of us are familiar with the older biographies which presented a man as a type —Washington the ever truthful, Lincoln the sad, and Benjamin Franklin the thrifty. Franklin seems to have been cast in the role of the *thrifty* merely because he wrote a number of wise saws on the desirability of this virtue. As a matter of fact, he sent home from England a continual stream of handsome and extravagant presents, such as silver-handled knives, fine china, a whole box of table glass, flowered dress goods "at nine guineas," silk blankets "of a new kind," silver candlesticks, carpets, even a harpsichord for Sally.[1] These gifts would indicate a happy spender to whom cost was of small moment. Later, in France, his bills for his wine cellar were lavish, and he finally remarked plaintively that frugality was "a virtue I never could acquire in myself."[2] So "perhaps," as the biographers say, his adages on thrift were reminders for his unthrifty self, as well as for the rest of the world.

Franklin is indeed a good example of a figure almost spoiled for young people because he has been typed as a paragon. Today in the new biographies young people and even children may catch a glimpse of the real Franklin—witty, worldly, urbane, adored by the ladies and adoring them in turn, equally at home in the wilderness and in the court, a scientist, a man of letters, a diplomat, an amateur musician, lazy and prodigiously industrious, in short, a composite of strength and weakness on a grand scale, with a tremendous brain directing the whole. To have made Franklin, of all men, into the image of a stuffy prig was a crime. To rediscover the whole man and reveal him to this generation, as Carl Van Doren has done, is a crowning achievement of modern biography.

THE WHOLE MAN

Carl Van Doren's *Benjamin Franklin* is an example of the way in which modern historical research, in the hands of skillful writers, is destroying the typed hero of the past and portraying the whole man. The book that is generally considered the greatest biography in the English language, James Boswell's *Life of Samuel Johnson* (1791), is as modern in this respect as Strachey's *Queen Victoria* (1924). But despite Boswell's early demonstration of what a good biography should be, the typed life somehow or other became firmly established in the years before Strachey and as such was thoroughly disliked by youngsters.

But, it is objected, while it may be all right to give adults the whole truth about a man—his vices, the tragedies in his life, his failures—still children cannot and should not have the complete account. This may be true. The younger children are, the less they are able to understand or to accept the ultimate tragedy of a life. A child's life of Mozart[3] terminates with his first adult triumphs, and a biography of Shelley[4] for the teen age concludes before the tragedies and the scandals begin. Neither record is falsified; it just does not continue long enough to catch up with sorrow. *The Raven,* Marquis James' adult biography of Sam Houston, tells about Sam's taking an Indian mate and abandoning her when it was convenient. *Six Feet Six,* the Bessie and Marquis James' version of this biography for children, omits such episodes. This certainly is not presenting the whole man. But while adults are entitled to a complete picture, children are not always ready for it. Juvenile biographies should be true as far as they go, with no falsifications, but the whole adult truth may not be within the children's range of comprehension and judgment.

VIVID DETAILS

Boswell remains the greatest of all biographers, partly because of his tremendous gusto for details. We know how Samuel Johnson dressed, how he went through a door—it had to be with one particular foot or he backed up and tried it again. We know what prayers he said; how desperately he feared death and how he loved the company of men; how he sneaked out at night so that the servants would not know about his buying oysters for Hodge, his cat; what he thought about taverns and second marriages; how he regarded David Garrick. In fact, we scarcely know anyone else so well as we know Samuel Johnson when we have finished reading Boswell. In the same way, Katherine Drinker Bowen brings *John Adams and the American Revolution* to life, and Van Doren portrays the real *Benjamin Franklin*—not through large generalizations but through a multitude of rich and arresting details.

1. Carl Van Doren, *Benjamin Franklin,* pp. 276-277.
2. *Ibid.,* p. 637.
3. Opal Wheeler and Sybil Deucher, *Mozart, the Wonder Boy.*
4. Laura Benét, *The Boy Shelley.*

In the past, biographies written for young people failed at precisely this point. They told children about the large affairs in which their heroes played a part but neglected to give any account of the individual man with his amusing idiosyncrasies, peculiar bents, and special talents which made him unique among other men. Children delight in Franklin's account of himself as a boy floating in a pond on his back propelled by a kite;[5] or in the story of Davy Crockett crossing an icy river in December, sometimes in and sometimes out of the water, but managing to keep dry his keg of gunpowder, a bundle, and his gun, "Betsey";[6] or of Haydn cutting off the pigtail of a fellow chorister;[7] or of Lewis and Clark, the intrepid explorers, feeling uncomfortable when the Indians at a ceremonial feast served a stewed dog, reminding them of their own Spot;[8] or of Lincoln holding a child upside down to make tracks on the ceiling as a joke on the stepmother he dearly loved, a joke he righted with a fresh coat of whitewash.[9] Such escapades are intelligible to children.

To be told that Penn dressed in sober clothes is dull enough. To learn that even after he turned Quaker he still loved good apparel and went to meet the velvet-clad Lord Baltimore in sober brown but cut by the best London tailor from the finest materials—ah, that is more human.[10] To read that Penn was tried for holding a meeting with other Quakers is dreary, but young people warm immediately to the picture of Penn on trial, shut up in a cage at the back of the courtroom, shouting out his own defense so effectively that he won the jury to his side and later won the right of the jury to have its decisions upheld in the English courts.[11] Little incidents and big ones which reveal the spirited human being who will not be downed and who travels his own unique way bring the individual to life for the reader. Revealing details are the very essence of good biography.

5. Carl Van Doren, *Benjamin Franklin,* p. 17.
6. Constance Rourke, *Davy Crockett,* pp. 94-97.
7. Opal Wheeler and Sybil Deucher, *Joseph Haydn: The Merry Little Peasant,* p. 45.
8. Julia Davis, *No Other White Men,* p. 71.
9. Ingri and Edgar d'Aulaire, *Abraham Lincoln* (unpaged).
10. Elizabeth Janet Gray, *Penn,* p. 206.
11. *Ibid.,* Chapter 15.

Biography As Literature

If biography is a branch of literature, then it, like any other work of art, should be a consciously planned composition. It has a subject, a theme, unity attained through that theme, style, a pattern of the whole, and a pattern of the parts. These may not be evident to the casual reader, but if the life is written with any skill, they are there.

THEME AND UNITY

Biography like history is based on documented facts. No liberties may be taken with these facts; no flights of fancy are permissible. The biographer begins by assembling all the documents and examining all the evidence. But the modern biographer feels that he should not give his accumulated research to the reader in its endless and often trivial details. He must choose those which he thinks will most truly reveal the man as the author has come to know him. It is in this matter of selection and organization that the biography ceases to be purely history and becomes a work of art. For the author, through his reading of all the sources and his weighing of all the evidence, gradually develops a theme. Around this theme he organizes the facts so that they not only reveal the man as he has come to see him but give unity to that life and to the book. If he selects his theme before he examines the evidence, he will write a biased, subjective biography. If he sees no theme emerging out of the chaos of events, he will write a chronological record which may lack wholeness and charm. This is the modern point of view, influenced especially by the French. André Maurois, for example, in *Aspects of Biography,* compares the writing of a biography to painting:

The biographer, like the portrait painter and the landscape painter, must pick out the essential qualities in the whole subject which he is contemplating. By such a choice, if he can make the choice without weakening the whole, he is very precisely performing the artist's function. (p. 50)

Maurois speaks too of the symmetry of certain lives and remarks that even Byron's life, with all its incidents, "must also have its hidden unity; the problem is to find it." So the author of a biography must first saturate himself with facts; then he must synthesize these facts until the hero begins to emerge as an integrated human being in spite of contradictions, with purposes and a direction of energies that give wholeness and significance to the life. In this unity of a life the author finds his theme, and around the theme composes his book.

Carl Van Doren, in his *Benjamin Franklin,* states his theme clearly in his last paragraph. Franklin, says the author, "seems to have been more than any single man: a harmonious human multitude." There it is, the core of the man's life—his remarkable diversity, all the interests and powers of the man in balance, "a harmonious human multitude."

Turning to children's or young people's biographies, we often find the theme in the title—*Carry On, Mr. Bowditch* (Nathaniel Bowditch), *He Heard America Sing* (Stephen Foster), *Invincible Louisa* (Louisa M. Alcott).

In *Leader by Destiny,* the life of George Washington, Jeanette Eaton shows how over and over again circumstances and the times interfered with Washington's life and called him to other ways of living. He might have been a homespun frontiersman, playing a gallant part no doubt, but his brother's death gave him Mount Vernon and turned him into a country gentleman. This role was forwarded by his neighbor's wife, the lovely Sally Fairfax (destiny again), who taught him the manners and ways of gentlemen. Then the country squire was called upon for soldiery and more soldiery, and finally he was made the head of the Continental Army. Seven long years of campaigning followed, with his whole heart yearning for the gracious life of Mount Vernon. Then came peace and a chance to realize his desires, but destiny called him once more, this time to the Presidency, the gravest responsibility an American had ever faced. Washington played a great part in every role he undertook, but it would seem that these roles were not of his own choosing. He would have been a leader in any situation, but destiny called him to national greatness.

Not all biographies adhere so closely and obviously to theme and unity as those just cited, certainly not the early examples of biography. But modern biographies, including those for young people, seem to follow this pattern and are organized around a central theme which gives a dramatic unity to the book.

STYLE AND PATTERN

If biography is to be judged as literature, it must also have a pleasing style. As one authority has said, style is "the auditory effect of prose." The prose must be good to read and it must be appropriate to the subject matter and to the mood of the story. Read aloud this excerpt from James Daugherty's *Daniel Boone:*

When Daniel came back to the Boones' farm in the Yadkin valley, he up and married his Irish sweetheart, Rebecca Bryan, whose family had settled in the valley near them. There was a hilarious shindig with the Carolina fiddles shaking down the moon. When the logs were all cut for the house-raising, the neighbors for miles around took a hand. By sundown they stuck a pine tree on the ridgepole of a brand new cabin in the clearing and ate and danced till morning. (p. 21)

Or read this brief account of the old man:

He roused himself and went to the fire where he was roasting a venison steak on the ramrod of his gun. Some friends were coming and he rose to greet them. "Mr. Harding, the painter, has come all the way from St. Louis to take your likeness," they explained. He didn't quite know what it was all about. The next day the young man came and asked him to sit very still while he painted his picture on oil-cloth. So he sat and talked of old memo-

ries and answered the young man's foolish questions. Had he ever been lost? He, Daniel Boone, lost! He thought back a while, shook his head, and said very slowly: "No, but I was bewildered once for three days." (pp. 94-95)

And the conclusion:

So they took a day off for remembrance about humble, great-hearted men whose lives were a strong invisible substance for enduring cornerstones for these United States of America. (p. 95)

Notice the strong swing and rhythm of this prose. Notice, too, the homespun quality of the words—pioneer talk, not recorded in tiresome detail, but richly suggested. Daugherty's opening chant on Pioneer Babies is a gem and so is his preliminary letter to Colonel Boone, ending with:

This "hilarious shindig" is typical of the way Daugherty's pictures parallel the swinging rhythm of his writing. The angles of the bent arms and legs, the curving lines of the flying skirts and coattails, feminine grace and masculine vigor make a picture of earthy action—a frontier bacchanal!
From Daniel Boone *by James Daugherty, with original lithographs in color by the author. Copyright 1939 by James Daugherty. Reprinted by permission of The Viking Press, Inc. (Book 8¼ x 10¾)*

"Rise up, you lanky sons of democracy. . . .
That you may have the enduring courage to
cut a clean straight path for a free people
through the wilderness against oppression
and aggression,
For generations marching on to higher freedoms
Riding towards the sun
Singing in the canebrakes
Singing in the tough spots
Chanting: Democracy, here we come.
Millions of cantankerous laughing sons and
strong daughters
Shouting to the bullies, the tyrannies, the
hosts of Darkness
Shouting with a seven-times-mighty shout of
Jericho:
NO SURRENDER."
And so, Daniel Boone, I wish you a hearty
Tennessee
Howdy and So Long. (p. 7)

This book, deservedly a Newbery Award, is one of the finest modern biographies ever written for young people and serves as an example of the way in which style may reflect the subject matter and mood of the narrative. James Daugherty's illustrations for this book have the same sweep and swing of his verbal style. Fat babies "wrassling" with wildcats and coasting "down the Cumberlands in three cornered pants," North Carolinian youth dancing the moon down, big husky women cradling their babies tenderly or defending themselves against the painted savages—these pictures have an epic flow and a stirring sense of movement which rightly picture the tale.

The excerpts quoted from *Daniel Boone* demonstrate not only prose style but different patterns—a pervading pattern of the whole with subtle changes in the patterns of the individual parts. Another fine example of style and pattern in biography is Carl Sandburg's *Abe Lincoln Grows Up,* adapted from the first twenty-seven chapters of his book for adults, *The Prairie Years.* Picking the book up anywhere, you discover that it reads aloud so easily and naturally you just keep reading. Of Tom Lincoln, the father, Sandburg writes:

He wasn't exactly lazy; he was sort of independent, and liked to be where he wasn't in-

terfered with. . . . He was a wild buck at fighting, when men didn't let him alone. A man talked about a woman once in a way Tom Lincoln didn't like. And in the fight that came, Tom bit a piece of the man's nose off. . . . Though he was short spoken, he knew yarns, could crack jokes, and had a reputation as a story-teller when he got started. (pp. 12-13)

Of Nancy Hanks, Sandburg writes differently:

The Lincolns had a cabin of their own to live in. It stood among wild crab-apple trees.

And the smell of wild crab-apple blossoms . . . came keen that summer to the nostrils of Nancy Hanks.

The summer stars that year shook out pain and warning, strange laughters, for Nancy Hanks. (p. 30)

Then, when she dies of the milk sickness he says:

So the woman, Nancy Hanks, died, thirty-six years old, a pioneer sacrifice, with memories of monotonous, endless everyday chores of mystic Bible verses read over and over for their promises, and with memories of blue wistful hills and a summer when the crab-apple blossoms flamed white and she carried a boy-child into the world. (p. 87)

The wild crab-apple blossoms mark the completion of the pattern.

A different use of pattern is well illustrated by the opening chapter of Elizabeth Janet Gray's *Penn.* She describes Penn's father, young Captain Penn, already rising in the English navy, in which eventually he becomes admiral; his wife with her Irish estates; the king with his two sons, James and Charles; a shoemaker named George Fox; an eight-month-old heiress, Gulielma Springett; and the lusty baby, William Penn.

And all these scattered lives were to play their part in the life of the baby who slept and cried and ate and slept again in sight of the steep walls of the old, grim Tower, into which had gone, down the centuries, many prisoners, young and old, frightened and defiant; and from which fewer had come out. The Tower too had its part. (p. 7)

Here, we are told, are all the threads of the story, all the important elements in the life of the baby, who grew to be the man of whom it was said later, "the world has not yet caught up with William Penn." There in that first chapter are the small patterns which will make up the large pattern.

These examples show how biography, although as scrupulously documented as history, may become in the act of composition a branch of literature. Yet good adult biographies are as sound sources for facts as histories. This may also be true of biographies for children and young people but with certain differences.

Biographical Types for Children

As we have already seen, juvenile biographies differ from adult biographies in several important respects. First, biographies for children are usually not documented. Second, these biographies may not be complete accounts of the men—particularly if the men's lives include objectionable incidents or many unrelieved tragedies.

In the third place, biographers for the young usually feel that it is legitimate to cast known facts about an episode into actual dialogue and to interpret the thoughts of their characters. In other words, they put sentences into their heroes' mouths and thoughts into their heads for which there is no actual documentary evidence. Their excuse, and it is a legitimate one, is that this makes the narrative more dramatic. They contend that anyone who starts to relate a hero tale to a child invariably begins to tell what the people thought or said. It is true that the moment we start some episodes about George Washington or Abraham Lincoln we find ourselves saying, "So George thought to himself. . . ." or "When Sarah Bush saw her new stepson, Abe, she liked the boy at once, and said to him. . . ." Of course such methods bring the scene more vividly to life for a child. Furthermore, the author of such fictionalized conversations would justify them by saying that while they are not to be found in so many words in any record, they have basis in known facts. Certainly whether fictionalized dialogue is justified or not, we find a great deal of this sort of thing in most biographies written for the young, and since the authors give no sources the casual reader cannot tell whether or not there is a sound reason for such free interpretation.

If these biographies for children carried footnotes and source references, we could tell which authors had done a scholarly piece of work in a partially fictionalized vein, and which ones had simply used the hero as a basis for a creative story. There are two hybrids in this field: First, there is *fictionalized biography,* in which the facts are documented and only a few liberties are taken, such as occasional dialogue for which there is no actual record. Second, there is *biographical fiction,* which takes a historical character as a basis for a story semihistorical in nature.

FICTIONALIZED BIOGRAPHY

Most of the biographies for children are fictionalized. That is, they are based on careful research, but known facts are often presented in dramatic episodes complete with conversation. For instance, Elizabeth Janet Gray in relating the moving quarrel between Admiral Penn and his young son lately turned Quaker begins the account with the old Admiral exploding wrathfully, ". . . three people you may *not* thee and thou—the King, the Duke of York, and myself." This speech is much more exciting than the plain statement, "The Admiral objected to his son's Quaker use of thee and thou." The quarrel continues the next day, climaxing in the Admiral's terrible threat:

"I am going to kneel down and pray to God that you may not be a Quaker, nor go ever again to any more of their meetings."

and in William's frenzied reply:

"Before I will hear thee pray after any such manner," he cried, "I'll leap out of the window."

It was a high window, too, and, according to Elizabeth Gray, William was saved only by the interruption of one of his father's most elegant friends come to call. Since Elizabeth Gray is a scrupulous research scholar, she probably had some sort of documentary evidence for this quarrel. She does, for instance, give the Admiral's actual letters to William summoning him home for this grim conference. Assuming then that there is a historical basis for the scene, we accept the dialogue, which certainly heightens the drama, the words fairly crackling with suppressed emotion.

Perhaps fictionalized biography is the best pattern of biography for young people and children. We find it again in the biographies written by Clara Judson, James Daugherty, Sidney Rosen, Jean Latham, and Carl Sandburg. There is no doubt that dialogue based on facts, written by a scholar and an artist, brings history to life and re-creates living, breathing heroes, who make a deep impression on children.

BIOGRAPHICAL FICTION

It is sometimes difficult to decide what should be classified as biographical fiction. But *Columbus Sails* by C. Walter Hodges is a distinguished and clear-cut example of biographical fiction at its best. The great admiral's story is told in four parts, each from the standpoint of a supposed eyewitness. A monk at La Rabida tells of the events leading up to the sailing of the *Pinta,* the *Nina,* and the *Santa Maria.* A vagabond sailor relates the harrowing details of the voyage and also the settlement at La Navidad. And one of the Indian converts, brought back to Spain by Columbus, describes the closing tragedy. This is a beautifully written and dramatic story; it makes Columbus live. No adult would mistake it for biography, but young readers take it much as they take the historically accurate account in Armstrong Sperry's *The Voyages of Christopher Columbus.* Young readers accept the books in the Childhood of Famous Americans series as true biographies, though libraries rightly classify them as fiction. Each is predominantly an imaginative re-creation of a childhood, written to fit a theme.

Jean Lee Latham's Newbery Medal book, *Carry On, Mr. Bowditch,* is also sometimes catalogued as fiction, but the reason is not so clear. In her acceptance speech the author describes her book as fictionalized biography. She probably makes no more use of imaginary dialogue than does Elizabeth Janet Gray in *Penn,* which is listed as biography. *Mr. Bowditch* does include around a dozen imaginary characters, such as members of ships' crews, but the author adds that "there are about four dozen historical characters . . . handled with accuracy as to time, place, and personality."[12] Certainly this book, based on all the historical documents available, is a magnificent record of a little-known genius. In purpose and in effect on the reader it is biography.

These distinctions among different types of historical literature are not greatly important to the children's use of the books. When young people read biographical fiction, they might be warned, "This is the way it may have happened, but history does not tell us for sure." And when they read biography or even fictionalized biography, they might be told, "In so far as the author can find historical records, this is the way it *did* happen."

Briefly, the chief distinctions between good biographies for adults and those for children are that, in the latter, sources are rarely stated, unsavory episodes are usually omitted, and recorded events are more likely to be enlivened with imaginary dialogue. On the whole, however, modern biographies for children represent scholarly research and conscientious retelling of events in a dramatic style. Such characteristics make these books one of the finest modern contributions to children's literature.

12. *Horn Book,* August 1956.

Biographies for Young Children

It has been generally assumed that there is little interest in biography before adolescence, but, as a matter of fact, when the small child says, "Daddy, tell me about when you were a little boy," he is asking for biography. It is true that young children are not interested in certain kinds of biographies. When the small boy asks for a story about his father's boyhood, he wants to hear what he *did,* not how he conquered his bad temper or became interested in science and finally decided to make it his lifework. For the young child is not ready for career stories unless they are strictly careers of action. Nor is he concerned with character development—why a man behaves as he does or how he grows gradually in self-discipline, unselfishness, and nobility. Least of all is the child able to appreciate or even follow an account of a man's pursuit of an abstract idea or of an ideal. Biographies of such heroes are not for young children. Penn, with his deep concern for Quakerism and social ideals, is a hero for the older children. It is difficult to make Jefferson come to life for children because he was so predominantly a man of ideas. It is for these reasons that biography, which has so often been concerned with the saints and the reformers, the emancipators and the idealists, has been rather generally allocated to older children and adults.

However, the preadolescent child yearns to know everything there is to know about his special heroes, the doers—from explorers to his favorite baseball stars. Moreover, through fairy tales and stories of everyday action, he has been arriving gradually at a few broad standards of right and wrong. He may not understand self-abnegation or altruism, but he knows all about fair play, honesty, justice, bravery, and kindness. These simple ethics of action he respects and will uphold stoutly. Furthermore, he admires men who embody these virtues. In the beginning he may not always distinguish between real and imaginary heroes. Jack the Giant Killer and Columbus, Mollie Whuppie and Joan of Arc may be much alike in his mind, but the stories about these people are laying a necessary foundation for his understanding of behavior and for his standards of morality.

Biography for children, then, begins simply with heroes of action. Mothers and Sunday school teachers have long known this and have told children some of the rousing biographies from the Old Testament—Moses, Abraham, Jacob, David, and, above all, Joseph. These are great biographies with all the dramatic appeal of a story. Such men the child can understand because they are men of deeds.

Teachers in the elementary schools, even those working with the five-year-olds, launch a few biographies also. When the older children celebrate Washington's or Lincoln's birthday, the small children are sure to ask, "Who was Washington?" or "Who was Lincoln?" and the experienced teacher obliges with an episode or two from those lives or a brief summary of the whole life.

A few years back, many teachers would tell such stories as the cherry-tree incident. Poor Washington is all too often fixed in the children's minds with that incredible myth concerning the cherry tree, sponsored by Parson Weems. This priggish tale has probably done more than anything else to damn Washington in the minds of normal children or at least to remove him from reality. Children who have encountered some deviousness, not to say bald untruth, in the adults with whom they live are not to be deceived by this impossible Georgie, not for a minute. They suspect, if he ever said such a thing ("Father, I cannot tell a lie"), that he was just putting up a front of some kind. Maybe he belonged to one of those odd families who don't spank children for their misdeeds if they "come clean." In which case Georgie was just taking an easy way out of the first-class spanking he so obviously deserved. Anyway you look at that old tale, so villainously cut out of whole cloth by the pedantic parson, it is no way to introduce George Washington—the best wrestler, the highest jumper, the hardest riding youngster in his district. Children deserve a better start with the founding fathers than such myths.

INGRI AND EDGAR PARIN D'AULAIRE

George Washington
Benjamin Franklin
Abraham Lincoln
Columbus

It is something of a shock to discover in the d'Aulaires' fine picture-book life of *George Washington* (1936) for the youngest children this repellent phrase, "He learned to be good and honest and never tell a lie." Fortunately, the d'Aulaires give other and more winning pictures of Washington. The children will probably forgive the authors this absurdity and remember George racing his horse to school with his hard-riding playmates. There is the mature George in the making, a glimpse of the future squire and tireless general.

The picture-book biographies of Ingri and Edgar d'Aulaire are a real contribution to the youngest. They are large books, eight by eleven inches, copiously illustrated with full-page lithographs in deep, glowing colors on alternate pages, and with black and whites and innumerable small pictures in between. These small pictures fulfill a definite purpose in each book, sometimes adding droll touches to the interpretation of the hero's character, sometimes showing something of his work or progress. In *Benjamin Franklin* (1950), for instance, the decorative borders throughout the book carry a series of Franklin's wise sayings. These are fun for children to discover and read, and they make *Poor Richard's Almanac* more real. Throughout the series, the illustrations are somewhat stylized and occasionally stiff. But this is a minor criticism of pictures alive with action and full of humor. Study the details of the pictures in *Abraham Lincoln* (1939). No need to talk about the doorless dwellings—in one picture a horse has stuck his head into the single room of the cabin and seems to be taking a neighborly interest in the new baby. Notice the little boys' single galluses upon which hang all the responsibility for holding up their scanty pants. Look at that three-sided shelter of the Lincolns, so hard to describe but so completely re-created with all its pitiable details. You see for yourself the dangers of sand bars and fallen trees in the river. Abe's tallness is amusingly revealed over and over without the necessity for verbal descriptions. No need to say that Mary Todd was something of a termagant, nor that she had a few problems to contend with in Abe. That picture of the wildly disordered parlor, with Abe on the floor in stocking feet, and with Mary, arms akimbo, reflected in the elegant mirror, is a demonstration of their fundamental unlikeness. The book is full of just the sort of sly humor that characterized Abe.

In the early books of this series, the texts were simple and the life stories were incomplete. But with *Benjamin Franklin, Buffalo Bill,* and *Columbus,* the content has grown richer, with more details. In the case of *Columbus,* the man's whole life is related, even those tragic last voyages. While these books may be read to or by third-grade children, older boys and girls respect their content and enjoy reading the stories themselves.

This picture leads the eye from the center of interest—the new baby—back and up to the fireplace and the clock. Patches of light and dark are evenly distributed on each side. Homely details of frontier life are evident, and the old horse looking in at the baby is a humorous touch.
From Abraham Lincoln *by Ingri and Edgar Parin d'Aulaire. Copyright 1939 by Doubleday & Company, Inc. Reprinted by permission of the publisher. (Original in color, book 7¾ x 11⅞)*

ALICE DALGLIESH

The Columbus Story

The text, less than thirty pages long, of *The Columbus Story* is vividly alive and recreates with simple dignity the boyhood of Columbus. Leo Politi's brilliantly colored illustrations are some of the finest he has produced. Since the book carries Columbus only through his triumphant first voyage, with none of the tragedy of the later years, it can be read aloud to children as young as five or six. Third-graders can read it for themselves. With Miss Dalgliesh's gift for making the past alive for young children (see Chapter 16), it is logical that she should also succeed in writing biography for the young children.

CLYDE ROBERT BULLA

Squanto, Friend of the White Men

Squanto, the Indian friend of the Pilgrims, is an almost mythical figure to most Americans. Children will be thrilled by his amazing life. He was taken to England in 1605 and lived there for eight years. Then he returned to this country with John Smith only to be captured and sold to Spain by slave hunters. In Spain he was rescued by the friars and returned once more to his native land. This is an incredible tale beautifully told by Clyde Bulla, who has a gift for writing easy-to-read books that are never commonplace. His historical tales have a pleasant lilt and swing and substantial content. *Squanto* (1954) has the same virtues, and a fascinating hero as well. He appears again in *John Billington, Friend of Squanto,* the story of a spirited boy who got the Pilgrims and himself into considerable trouble.

OPAL WHEELER AND SYBIL DEUCHER

Biographies of musicians

The happy collaboration and later the individual work of Opal Wheeler and Sybil Deucher have resulted in a series of biographies of musicians for younger children, about seven to ten, which have proved unusually popular. The books follow a similar pattern—family, birth, amusing or extraordinary episodes of childhood, hardships (but never tragedies), artistic achievements and triumphs. With Mozart the story terminates before the tragedies begin. The title indicates the theme—*Mozart, the Wonder Boy*.

Knowing the tragedies in the lives of many of these musicians, the biting poverty and the humiliations, you may wonder if the tone of these books is not a shade too merry and light-hearted. The description of the Bachs copying music for their choir at night after a day's work does not suggest enslavement to the task but just another happy evening. There is no hint in the *Mozart* or the *Schubert* of the neglect, the pitiable poverty, and the tragedies that continually haunted these two men. Perhaps this treatment is legitimate, since the books are directed to an audience under eleven. Some teachers and parents, on the other hand, feel that young children should not be protected from all harsh realities, that they should know of the ultimate tragedy in Mozart's life, of Beethoven's deafness, and Schubert's poverty. Then, knowing the deprivations of their lives, children may listen with even greater appreciation to the music of these great men.

The fact remains, however, that for young children the Wheeler-Deucher formula is extremely popular. Certainly, children love the episodes these authors have chosen for them—the little Mozart enchanting the Austrian court and announcing that he will marry Marie Antoinette when he grows up, or Bach copying by moonlight the music locked away from him, or Haydn's *Surprise Symphony,* which made all the comfortably napping old dowagers jump. These and dozens of other little episodes recorded in the biographies make the lives of the musicians memorable and delightful to young children.

The books have a similar format and narrative treatment and they all include black-and-white illustrations and excerpts from the music. They are easy and popular introductions to musicians and to biography. In addition to Haydn, Mozart, Schubert, Bach, Beethoven, and Grieg, the books include two American composers—Edward MacDowell and Stephen Foster. In every case, the authors have chosen musicians whose music is enjoyed by young children.

MARGUERITE HENRY

Benjamin West
and His Cat Grimalkin

One of the most enchanting story biographies for young children is Mrs. Henry's *Benjamin West and His Cat Grimalkin* (1947). She introduces America's first artist as a child in the midst of the affectionate Quaker family that ran Door-Latch Inn. Grimalkin, the cat, was beloved by every member of the family, and he in turn loved them all. But young Benjamin was his favorite. Everyone said the cat and boy talked to each other, Grimalkin meowing louder and louder until he was sure Benjamin understood. Then the boy began to draw, which was a problem in a Quaker family. Father feared it was a worldly sin, but he capitulated to the charm of his son's pictures.

Indians helped Benjamin to his colors, and Benjamin, alas, helped himself to Grimalkin's fur for his brushes. Not knowing the cause of the poor cat's mangy appearance, Father prayed over Grimalkin, and the whole Quaker community prayed over what to do with Benjamin and his passion for painting. The results were wonderful for cat and boy. Grimalkin got his fur back and America got her first artist. No briefing of this book can even suggest its humor and tender understanding, both of the cat and of all the people involved.

THE CHILDHOOD OF FAMOUS AMERICANS

There are comparatively few good biographies for young readers. That is one of the reasons for the popularity of the series of some one hundred books known as The Childhood of Famous Americans. These books are listed for children seven years old and over. Libraries classify them not as biography, but as fiction or literature or easy reading or remedial reading, or group some of the books with social studies or science or language arts. The titles indicate the themes to which the life stories are fitted—*John Quincy Adams: Boy Patriot* or *Pocahontas: Brave Girl* or *Ben Franklin: Printer's Boy*. The authors are numerous and include such able writers as Augusta Stevenson, Marguerite Henry, William Steele, Ann Weil, Helen Albee Monsell, and Miriam Mason.

When, in 1932, Augusta Stevenson wrote the first little book in the series, *Abe Lincoln: Frontier Boy,* probably neither she nor her publishers knew what she was starting. From the beginning these books were enormously popular with children and teachers, and they still are. Indeed, one state lists the series as "High Interest—Low Vocabulary Books." And that is what they are. Her formula, which all the other authors have followed, is worth examining. In easy-to-read vocabulary, with plenty of conversation, she tells an enthralling story that makes her hero or heroine as real to the children as their schoolmates are. The heroes talk, plan their lives, perform deeds that point definitely to the great men they are about to become, and reveal their thoughts and feelings. These are not biographies, but young readers like the stories, and they have started many a reluctant reader on his way to better reading.

Yet this series has definite limitations which adults who guide children's reading should be aware of. The pattern is too rigid and the atmosphere is too completely merry and gay. Too many of the stories are fairy tales of success. Mistakes are few and success is easy. The young heroes hew to the line too continually to be real.

This is close to the old stereotyped biography of the Parson Weems variety—George Washington the ever truthful. Once the children start reading this series, they are likely to read too many of the books. Then the good or superior reader may be reading far below his capacities. Direct those able readers to books that are genuine biographies, with rich details and full accounts of their heroes—their confusions and mistakes as well as their persistence and success. For that is life.

The Series Multiply

The Bobbs-Merrill Childhood books seem to have launched the biography fever with both children and publishers. As a result, not only is the numerical impact of these books staggering, but the duplication of biographies has reached the point where it is a

Wesley Dennis draws boys as understandingly as he draws horses. And here you see he has given lively Benjamin a convincing cat. Illustration by Wesley Dennis. From Benjamin West and His Cat Grimalkin, *by Marguerite Henry. Copyright, 1947, by Bobbs-Merrill Company. Reprinted by permission of the publisher. (Book 6½ x 9⅛, picture 4¼ x 3¼)*

major feat of memory to recall which George Washington is whose and whose Abraham Lincoln is which.

It would be convenient to be able to make a judgment of each series as a whole, but this is impossible, because within one set of books some are thin or pedestrian and others are of major importance. Although it is difficult to select from a list, it is wasteful for schools or homes or libraries to order every one of any series. It is best to watch for authoritative reviews of individual books. Many of the books discussed in this chapter are from one or another of the series. However, since each series is designed to perform a definite function in the child's reading program, several of them are considered below.

INITIAL BIOGRAPHIES

Scribner has issued a series of Initial Biographies by Genevieve Foster, author of the admirable *George Washington's World, Abraham Lincoln's World,* and *Augustus Caesar's World.* Brief as the *George Washington* or *Theodore Roosevelt* biography is, it covers the man's whole life and provides children from ten to teen age with a summary of the man's childhood, youthful struggles, and mature contributions. Because these books are brief, they add little that is new to our knowledge of their heroes, and they lack the rich tapestry of details that makes history live for children. *Andrew Jackson* and *Theodore Roosevelt* provide the liveliest reading. Like all of Genevieve Foster's books, the Initial Biographies combine excellent literary style with charming illustrations by the author.

SIGNATURE BOOKS

Grosset and Dunlap call their Signature Books "life stories," which is correct. They are biographical fiction for children eight to twelve years old, with a strong appeal for slow readers at high school level. The publishers insist that close attention is paid to the historical accuracy of the books, but to compare Iris Vinton's *The Story of John Paul Jones* with Armstrong Sperry's life of Jones is to wonder if you are reading about the same man. That is the trouble with biographical fiction. How can anyone except historians tell where truth ends and fiction begins?

These stories are told with the maximum conversation and action. Most of them cover all or a large part of the man's life, but some end on a triumphant note in early maturity, when there is still tragedy ahead. The books of Hazel Wilson, Margaret Leighton, Iris Vinton, Nina Brown Baker, and Enid Meadowcroft (the editor of the series) are particularly good, and all are written in a lively, fast-moving style children enjoy.

LANDMARK BOOKS

In 1950, Random House launched the now famous Landmark Books. The name of the series indicates its approach to history. The books present the men, movements, or moments in history which have been turning points or landmarks in our national life. A series of World Landmark Books is now appearing as well. Sometimes the events are more important than the men, and sometimes it is a man who makes history. The titles show this varied emphasis—for example, *The Voyages of Christopher Columbus, The Louisiana Purchase, Daniel Boone, Robert E. Lee and the Road of Honor,* and *The F.B.I.* Obviously, some of these are biographies and some are not. Such notable writers as Dorothy Canfield Fisher, Quentin Reynolds, John Mason Brown, Samuel Hopkins Adams, Frank Dobie, Bob Considine, Stewart Holbrook, and MacKinlay Kantor have given these books a literary quality not to be found in any other series.

The publishers mark the books R for reading level by grades and I for interest level, also by grades. Many teachers feel that the publishers are a little too optimistic about children's reading ability. Certainly only a few of these books can be read by a nine-year-old. There are many for the twelves and more for the junior and even senior high school boys and girls. On the whole, they are most enjoyed by the good and superior readers of the upper elementary grades. But these books, more than any other series or single books, have made historical narratives and biographies enormously popular with children. And the fact that more and more outstanding authors of adult books are writing for this series is evidence of their quality.

CLARA INGRAM JUDSON

There is another historical series, written by a single author and prepared with such meticulous research that the books deserve special mention. They are the biographies of presidents of the United States by Clara Ingram Judson. In uniform format, with handsome illustrations, these books are a fine addition to school libraries or to a child's personal library.

Mrs. Judson began writing biography in 1939 with a modest little book about Frances Willard called *Pioneer Girl.* That was followed by *Boat Builder: The Story of Robert Fulton* (1940) and others. In 1950, when her *Abraham Lincoln, Friend of the People* appeared, it was evident that this writer, competent in so many fields, had attained new stature as a biographer. It was also evident that Mrs. Judson's research into source materials was to yield a fresh slant on the man. Her careful studies convinced her, for example, that Abe's childhood was no more "poverty stricken" than that of most of the neighbors. She also brought out the warm family love and loyalty of the Lincoln tribe, and Abe himself emerges as a real person.

Mrs. Judson believes that the only justification for new biographies of such well-known national figures as George Washington, Thomas Jefferson, Andrew Jackson, and Theodore Roosevelt is that they throw fresh light on, and give children new facts or a new point of view about, the man. Before she writes a biography, she reads the letters, journals, or papers of her hero, searches contemporary magazines and newspapers, and studies the life of the times. As a result, she has rescued Washington from the stereotypes that had nearly obliterated him. She even makes Jefferson, the man of ideas, intelligible to children. Mrs. Judson's writing is sometimes stilted, but somehow her deep love of family, her respect for all kinds of people, and her sense of the struggles through which these men came to greatness communicate themselves to children. They like her books, and they know a man when they finish one of her biographies.

Although new biography series are still springing up, these examples will suffice to show types, ranges, and limitations. The fact remains that some of the finest biographies for children and youth are still to be found outside any series.

Biographies for Older Children: Exploration and Settlement

The tens to twelves still demand action, but the teen-age group moves toward the men of ideals and ideas as well as of deeds. For children from ten years on, there are excellent biographies and a variety of heroes. In fact there are so many books for this age group that the long bibliography listed on pages 554-562 is still inadequate. The following discussion can only suggest some groupings and some ways of using biography which may help in guiding the reading of both individual children and classes studying a particular area in time (as periods in United States history) or fields of endeavor (as music or literature).

RONALD SYME

Columbus, Finder of the New World

Ronald Syme, like Mrs. Judson, is also responsible for a series. His biographies of the explorers began as an easy-to-read series for the middle and upper grades—Columbus, Cortés, Champlain, Balboa, Magellan, and

Columbus laughs at the doubting questions of the townspeople of Palos, from where he set sail. Strong light on Columbus' face, in contrast to the shadowed faces of the townspeople, makes a dramatic composition. Illustration by William Stobbs. From Columbus, Finder of the New World *by Ronald Syme. Copyright 1952 by William Morrow and Company, Inc. Reprinted by the permission of the publishers. (Book 6½ x 7¾)*

others. They now include the more detailed biographies of La Salle, John Smith, and Henry Hudson, which command the interest of the twelves to fourteens whether they are good or poor readers. All of the stories are augmented by the dramatic and virile illustrations of William Stobbs.

Mr. Syme's *Columbus, Finder of the New World* (1952) is typical of the style and approach of all of the books. Christopher Columbus is a difficult character to present to children. The drama of his life rises grandly to the successful conclusion of the first voyage. After that, failure and tragedy stalk his path. He diminishes in heroic stature to a sorrowful ignominy, which is hard for children to accept because it violates their sense of justice. It is greatly to Mr. Syme's credit that he presents the gloom as well as the glory. In this brief, well-written biography, the Admiral of the Ocean Sea goes down to his death apparently defeated, but his name and his achievements live after him.

So Mr. Syme's books, more than most other biographies for children, reveal pictures of the dark as well as the bright side of the hero's character or experiences. They are authentic biographies, written with a directness children like, and his heroes are never stereotyped.

Along with Mr. Syme's *Columbus,* some children in a class should read Armstrong Sperry's fine *Voyages of Christopher Columbus* (Landmark) and then, for another slant on the Admiral, Nina Brown Baker's *Amerigo Vespucci.* This is a biography of the man for whom our continent was named, a modest, scholarly scientist, more interested in stars, navigation, and maps than in position or money. But why was the continent named for him and not for Columbus? Mrs. Baker explains the relationship between the two explorers and their voyages, and the picture she gives of Columbus helps to explain the nature of his downfall. Like all the biographies by this author, the book is good reading, written in easy style with the dialogue characteristic of fictionalized biography.

ESTHER AVERILL

Cartier Sails the St. Lawrence

Cartier Sails the St. Lawrence is a book of rare distinction in both text and illustrations. First published in 1937, the new edition of this book includes a few additional pictures by Feodor Rojankovsky. The author said she "leaned heavily upon [the illustrations] for dramatic interest."[13] They are indeed among the finest Mr. Rojankovsky has made, for they illustrate in the true sense of the word. That is, they pick up the essence of the text and make it brilliantly visible to the reader. Such pictures are both an interpretation and an amplification of the text, which is the true function of pictures in a book. *Cartier Sails*

13. *Horn Book,* August 1956, p. 265.

the St. Lawrence needed such pictures because it is not fictionalized.

Miss Averill's factual account of the three voyages makes fascinating reading, even so. After all, when a man sets off to discover the Northwest Passage to China and finds himself sailing up a river as magnificent and extensive as the St. Lawrence, the adventure can hardly be called dull. The book is less biography than history, but still belongs to the children's gallery of explorers.

Colonial and Revolutionary Periods

The colonial and Revolutionary periods in the United States are so crowded with great men that it is impossible to use biographies of all of them. This chapter can give only samplings. (See the Bibliography for other examples.)

ELIZABETH JANET GRAY

Penn

Penn's day in the New World ended before the Revolution began, but many of his ideas lived after him. Elizabeth Janet Gray (Mrs. Vining), like Penn a Quaker, has written a magnificent biography of William Penn. It brings life and color to this generally nebulous national figure. So many references to detailed episodes in this book have already been made earlier in this chapter that it is mentioned here only as a reminder of its distinction and values. It is a full-length portrait of the man who brought to America ideas of religious and racial tolerance and judicial standards and who lived in such concord with his Indian neighbors that when there were massacres in Pennsylvania, no Quaker was ever harmed. Because of the rich and vivid details of this narrative William Penn lives for young readers as a very real and human man.

JEANETTE EATON

Leader by Destiny
Young Lafayette

Washington is undoubtedly one of the most difficult figures to bring alive for children, both because he has been belittled by the trivial anecdotes told about him and because he has the subtle, intangible qualities of a highly civilized human being. Self-discipline and restraint are not easy for children to un-

When Cartier established a winter fort on the banks of the St. Charles River, his men found Indians able to withstand freezing weather and sharp winds without clothing. Notice the faces in this picture—the Indian child happy and oblivious to the cold, the soldier bundled up and miserable. Illustration by Feodor Rojankovsky. From Cartier Sails the St. Lawrence *by Esther Averill. Copyright 1937, 1956 by Esther Averill. Reprinted by permission of the publisher, Harper & Row. (Book 7 x 9¾)*

derstand or to appreciate, and for this reason in particular Washington is a better character for adolescents than for children.

The best juvenile biography of Washington, Jeanette Eaton's *Leader by Destiny* (1938), is for the teen age, but it is such an extraordinary book that adults could also profit by reading it. You catch in it, for instance, Washington's lifelong regret for his inadequate education, dating back, perhaps, to that humiliating treaty with the French, when he signed a shameful and erroneous admission because he could not read French and his staff interpreter was little better. This incident made Washington the laughingstock of the young blades of Williamsburg. A lesser man might never have recovered from the humiliation, but Washington did. You find in this book Washington's single indiscretion, in his relations to his friend's wife, the beautiful Sally Fairfax. He wrote her one letter declaring his love. This letter Sally kept secret until the day of her death, and it remained secret for a hundred years after. In this book you see Washington's affectionate relations with his wife's children, and you see Martha herself as a charming and devoted helpmate to Washington, who came to appreciate her more and more. This book will help young people and adults know Washington as a very human, often bewildered man with a strange gift for inspiring confidence in other men.

For less able or less mature readers, Jeanette Eaton has written *Washington, the Nation's First Hero*. Her two biographies of Washington may be supplemented with those by Clara Judson and Genevieve Foster. Girls will enjoy the charmingly written *Martha, Daughter of Virginia* by Marguerite Vance. And from these books some children will turn to biographies of Lafayette. Jeanette Eaton has written one of the finest, *Young Lafayette,* in the mature style of *Leader by Destiny*.

Young Lafayette (1932) gives a picture of the young French idealist, and again throws an interesting light on Washington. In Lafayette's almost awed reverence for his hero, we see the strange power of Washington over the men who surrounded him. He never lost his stature as a hero to them in spite of his very human weaknesses. This biography of Lafayette, which carries him through the French Revolution, is both authentic and finely written, as are all the biographies by Jeanette Eaton.

HAZEL WILSON

The Story of Lafayette
The Story of Mad Anthony Wayne

In spite of the fact that *The Story of Lafayette* and *The Story of Mad Anthony Wayne* (both Signature biographies) read as conversationally as fiction, Hazel Wilson is too conscientious a research student not to base her episodes on documented facts. *The Story of Lafayette* (1952), gives children a full-length portrait of a man whose life is more romantic than any novel. Mrs. Wilson shows glimpses of Lafayette's happy childhood, his introduction to court life which, far from turning his head, confirmed his idealism and love of liberty. His marriage at sixteen was a happy one —only from recent research have we learned how happy.

Lafayette's coming to the aid of our struggling colonies was inevitable, but the wonder lies in his immediate recognition of Washington's greatness. This helped him to forget the Congress which received him so miserably, half starved and half paid his men, and gave Washington himself inadequate and delayed support. The author holds children's interest not only through this familiar story but also through her account of the French Revolution and Lafayette's long imprisonment. Mrs. Wilson finishes her full-length portrait of the man with Lafayette, full of years and honors, making a triumphal tour of this country and receiving a tardy but generous recognition of his services from another Congress. A coincidence which will delight children is the fact that the first man on our shores to receive Lafayette cordially into his home had a little boy who, when he had grown up, attempted a gallant rescue of Lafayette from the French prison. The attempt failed, but Lafayette's heart must have warmed when he knew his would-be rescuer's identity. Here is wonderful material for a play!

So in Mrs. Wilson's biography of Mad Anthony Wayne lively details and the full cycle of his life make this appealing Revolutionary hero real to children. There are delightful flashes of humor in these stories, but the bite of tragedy is not always so convincing. These are, nevertheless, good introductory accounts of both men.

JAMES DAUGHERTY

Poor Richard

For superior readers with mature interests, James Daugherty's *Poor Richard* has unusual distinction. This book covers Franklin's whole life, his manifold activities, and his amazing talent for friendship among people of all varieties and ages. The chapter called "An American in Paris" opens in this way:

> *One man alone captured a city. An American had taken Paris single-handed.*
>
> *All the king's horses and all the king's men could not do what the friendly seventy-year-old journeyman printer was doing in spite of himself. He was surprised and pleased to find himself a hero. He was ready to act the part, knowing all that it might mean for America.*

The chapter includes a visit with John Paul Jones, "a one-man navy," and a little later we are treated to the scandalized Abigail Adams' report of a dinner where Mme. Helvétius sat with one arm around Franklin's shoulder and the other on the chair of Abigail's own John. "After dinner," wrote the outraged Mrs. Adams, "she threw herself on a settee where she showed more than her feet." Here, obviously, is a somewhat mature interpretation of the times, written and illustrated with Daugherty's usual gusto and swing. For children who can enjoy it, it is a fine book to read and to own, but for the most part, it belongs to the teen-age group.

NARDI REEDER CAMPION

Patrick Henry, Firebrand of the Revolution

Patrick Henry was one of the leaders of the American Revolution, and yet his character and achievements have always been open to question. In her book *Patrick Henry* (1961), Mrs. Campion shows why. She never glosses over the weaknesses of her hero. As a boy, growing up in a cultured home where education was highly valued, he was lazy and irresponsible and soon discovered that he could talk himself out of most scrapes. He developed a fine speaking voice and a feeling for words and the cadence of language that were to be his greatest assets as long as he lived. Amiable and talented, he married when he was still penniless, failed twice at storekeeping, but, with three children to support, decided to become a lawyer. For once he studied intensively, if briefly, and became a close friend of the scholarly Jefferson. Once admitted to the bar, he won an unpopular case against the clergy and the king that rocked the State and made him famous. This was the beginning. Caught up in the rising tide of pre-Revolutionary activity, Patrick Henry in the Virginia House of Burgesses became the spellbinding voice of the Revolutionists. It was said that without the fiery oratory of Patrick Henry there would have been no successful break with England. And somehow, that dream of freedom from tyranny and a union of the colonists so possessed the man that it forged him into a finer, stronger person than he had been. Yet after years of devoted friendship, Jefferson broke with him completely and denounced him venomously. Mrs. Campion records his words and accusations but concludes that there were no valid stains on Henry's honor. On July 5, 1776, he was overwhelmingly elected first governor of Virginia, an office which he administered wisely and well in five different terms. Jefferson was wrong, this author concludes, and this strange, passionate "Son of Thunder" died gently and courageously, well loved by his family and his State. This is a fascinating and well documented biography, well adapted to elementary school children but enjoyed at high school level also.

GENE LISITZKY

Thomas Jefferson

Gene Lisitzky's account of *Thomas Jefferson* (1933) is as satisfactory a biography as any single volume that has been written about the man. Jefferson is almost as complicated and diverse a human being as Franklin, and he is far more difficult to bring to life for children. For Jefferson was an intellectual, and he dealt continually with abstract ideas as easily as his neighbors dealt with their crops. Even for adults, the biographers have tended to simplify their task by giving only one special slant on the man—his youth, or his statecraft, or his life in Virginia.

Gene Lisitzky, in one book, has given us glimpses of many phases of the whole man, from boyhood through his active and complex maturity. We see Jefferson never too concerned with world affairs to enjoy a ride on a fine horse or an hour with his violin; never too busy to write long letters to his motherless little girls and to await anxiously their all too brief replies (the actual letters are given); never too important to remember his native state and to send from Europe flowers, vegetables, trees, and shrubs to be cultivated in Virginia's rich soil. Gene Lisitzky shows all the aspects of this man, who was the founder of a university and one of the builders of a new nation. Here is a great biography for any child who can read it, a biography worth owning. If the twelves cannot take it all, and they probably can't because it is a big canvas, then give them references to parts of it.

For less mature children and less able readers, there is the Jefferson biography by Clara Judson, and for girls, there is Marguerite

The solitary figure of Nathaniel Bowditch looks tiny in this vast ship chandlery with all its sailing necessities drawn in realistic detail.
Illustration by John O'Hara Cosgrave II. From Carry On, Mr. Bowditch *by Jean Lee Latham. Copyright, 1955 by Jean Lee Latham and John O'Hara Cosgrave II. Reproduced by permission of the Houghton Mifflin Company. (Book 5½ x 8¼)*

Vance's delightful *Patsy Jefferson of Monticello.*

PARALLEL BIOGRAPHIES

Considering only three of these mighty molders of a nation—Franklin, Jefferson, and Washington—it is evident that biographies are available for children of any reading or maturity level. And so prodigal of greatness was the colonial period and so diligent are our biographers that for quite a range of other heroes a choice of books is available. There is a fine biography of Paul Revere by Esther Forbes and another by Dorothy Canfield Fisher (Landmark). There is a book about Ethan Allen by Stewart Holbrook and another by Slater Brown (Landmark). And there are the Iris Vinton and Armstrong Sperry books about John Paul Jones.

Some teachers are convinced that for less intellectual children the best approach to history is through a series of biographies of the men of a period. If you try such an experiment for the colonial period, certainly you will wish to read for yourself Esther Forbes' *Paul Revere and the World He Lived In,* Carl Van Doren's *Benjamin Franklin,* Rupert Hughes' *George Washington,* Catherine Drinker Bowen's *John Adams and the American Revolution,* and one of the Jefferson biographies for adults, perhaps *Jefferson: The Road to Glory* by Marie Kimball. With a background of such books you could give rich details and deeper meaning to the children's necessarily simplified pictures of these men and their times.

JEAN LEE LATHAM

Carry On, Mr. Bowditch

Between the great leaders in the American Revolution and the sturdy frontiersmen of the push westward is the unique figure of Nathaniel Bowditch. Born in Salem, Massachusetts, in 1773, he never had a day's schooling after he was ten years old. Yet he became an outstanding astronomer, mathematician, and author of *The New American Practical Navigator,* published in 1802 and still considered the bible of modern navigation.

When Nathaniel was twelve, his father bound him out for nine years to a ship's chandlery. The boy was near despair, when an old fellow told him, "Only a weakling gives up when he is becalmed! A strong man sails by ash breeze!" That is, he "sails" his boat with ash oars. So Nat sailed. His story is one of continuous toil in the chandlery by day and with books at night. Then came the end of his indenture, and a knowledgeable young man set off on the first of his five adventurous voyages. There is romance in Nat's story, and some tragic as well as some extremely humorous episodes. The climax came when Harvard, to which he had yearned to go, bestowed upon this unschooled but brilliant scientist an honorary degree. It is a thrilling story of New England fortitude and love of learning. Mrs. Latham has told it splendidly, and strong illustrations add to the distinction of this Newbery Medal book.

Westward Ho!

One of the most important moves in Jefferson's Presidency was the launching of the Lewis and Clark expedition to explore the West. Jefferson's vision of the significance of the Louisiana Purchase and the opening of the West, like his vision of abolishing slavery, was ahead of his day. Meriwether Lewis had been Jefferson's private secretary when the President called upon him to head this important exploration. Lewis immediately chose his boyhood friend, Lieutenant William Clark, to accompany him and divide the command.

JULIA DAVIS

No Other White Men

Julia Davis in her *No Other White Men* (1937) has given children an unforgettable account, not merely of the exploration but of an enduring friendship between two fine men. The narrative tells little of their youth and ends with the successful completion of their journey to the Pacific and back, but the portraits of these two men for the period of their two-year adventure together (1804-1806) are unexcelled. We see Lewis, the dignified gentleman with his curled hair, who kept lengthy reports of the journey in his delicate handwriting; and we see Clark, big, bluff, hearty, redheaded, and practical, keeping a diary, too, with spelling "as free and joyous as his nature." Both men were completely loyal to their cause and to each other, and no trace of jealousy or competition for fame ever sullied their relationship. Miss Davis uses both journals as sources and frequently quotes Clark for the pleasure of his original spelling. Needless to say, it delights the children. "A butiful promising child," he writes of the Bird Woman's baby.

There are many funny episodes in this narrative; the action is often exciting, with considerable suspense; the discipline of the men is impressive in its prompt severity; and Sacajawea's meeting with her Shoshone brother is as dramatic as any scene in fiction. This book has been a continuous favorite with eleven- and twelve-year-old children.

JAMES DAUGHERTY

Of Courage Undaunted

Of Courage Undaunted (1951) also makes good use of the explorers' journals. There is a stirring quality about this narrative that highlights the dangers and drama of the expedition and makes a strong appeal to young readers. James Daugherty makes not only Lewis and Clark but other members of the group distinct personalities. His powerful illustrations, as always, give a feeling of vigorous action which enhances the text.

FRANCES JOYCE FARNSWORTH

Winged Moccasins: The Story of Sacajawea

Another biography that should be used with those of Lewis and Clark is the life of Sacajawea. Children have always asked, "What happened to the Bird Woman and her son?" Here is the answer, based on authentic and comparatively recent research. It follows this adventurous daughter of a Shoshone Indian chief from childhood through her ninety years, and no novel ever made more compelling reading. Lewis and Clark recognized the remarkable character of this young woman, whose greatness is proved by the facts of her life. It is good to know that she escaped from Charbonneau's brutality, made her way west once more, and lived out her long life in comparative peace and happiness.

Old Hickory and His Colleagues

The Jacksonian period bristles with great names and is a source of several good juvenile biographies. Old Hickory himself and all of his colleagues are cut after the child's own pattern of a hero—fighters, explorers, woodsmen! The group begins with Daniel Boone and includes, besides Jackson, such colorful figures as Crazy Horse, Davy Crockett, and Sam Houston.

Genevieve Foster's Initial Biography makes a good introduction to Andrew Jackson, and Clara Judson's *Andrew Jackson, Frontier Statesman* is a notable contribution which children like and should not miss. Most of the children's books about Andrew Jackson have played down the scandal which dogged his life, and yet the cruel injustice of that scandal points up the man's deep feelings and loyalty. For that reason the biography by Mrs. Vance is important.

MARGUERITE VANCE

The Jacksons of Tennessee

Despite the title, *The Jacksons of Tennessee* (1953) is somewhat more the story of

Rachel Jackson than it is of her husband, Andrew Jackson. Beautiful and kindly Rachel Donelson had made a tragic first marriage. In the days when news traveled slowly, she had every reason to believe her divorce was complete when she married Jackson. Mrs. Vance presents the details of this tragic misunderstanding (for such it was) which almost wrecked Jackson's career. The gentle beauty of Rachel, their all too brief moments of fun and triumph, their love of the children they gathered around them—nothing could ameliorate the shadow of that bitter story. In the end it killed Rachel. This is a mature and complex social problem, compassionately handled. It brings out what youth should know—the often disastrous effect of malicious gossip—and it tells a moving story of two high-spirited and devoted people.

JAMES DAUGHERTY

Daniel Boone

James Daugherty's superb *Daniel Boone* (1939) (p. 523) is one of the finest bits of Americana we have for children. The old woodsman was a contemporary of Jackson; Audubon knew him, and so perhaps did Davy Crockett; and it was over his "Wilderness Road" through the Cumberland Gap that Lucy Hanks carried her baby Nancy. So Daniel Boone seems to be a link which pulls together different men and periods.

For a fuller biography of the man at a more mature level, some children should read John Mason Brown's *Daniel Boone* (Landmark).

SHANNON GARST

Crazy Horse

Toward the end of this period of westward expansion came the terrible struggles between the advancing hordes of white men and the Indians. Several fine biographies of Indian leaders of this period will give children the other side of the picture. *Crazy Horse* (1950) is one of the best of these. It begins with his training as a boy, shows his bitter experiences with the bad faith and cruelties of the white men and his growing determination to stop their invasion at all costs. The end is sheer tragedy. Crazy Horse is defeated, his people scattered or herded into a reservation, and Crazy Horse, rather than submit, fights to his death. No child who reads this moving record will ever believe the cruelties were all on one side.

CONSTANCE ROURKE

Davy Crockett

Constance Rourke has never written a better biography than her *Davy Crockett* (1934). In spite of the confused legends about him, she has done her best to hold to the facts and has used his own famous "Narrative," original spelling and all, as one of her chief sources. Children will be amused to discover that the eight-year-old Davy was given a gun and taught to shoot and if he missed his game he got no supper. Davy was "bound out" several times, once to a drover who practically enslaved him and once to a kindly Quaker who made him go to school for one winter (his only schooling). The Quaker is supposed to have said, "Thee's bound to be a rolling stone, I fear, for all that thee can bend thy back and work hard."

Davy married and set up as a farmer at eighteen, but farming was not for him. Tales of his skill as a hunter were soon circulating. He served under Jackson in the War of 1812, and at that time seems to have admired Jackson greatly. After the war was over, he was elected magistrate, though he could barely write his name. He served in the legislature and was elected congressman; during this service as "the coon-skin congressman," he broke with Jackson over Jackson's treatment of the Indians. But another young man who had also fought under Old Hickory stood by and helped the President in the matter of dislodging the Cherokees and four other tribes from their lands given them by treaty. That man was Sam Houston. Davy always was loyal to his friends, the Indians, and never trusted either Jackson or Houston again. Years later old Davy, disappointed in politics, went out to Texas just in time to catch up with the fighting. He placed himself under

Travis' command rather than serve under Sam Houston, and there he perished gallantly during the siege of the Alamo. The twelve- to fourteen-year-olds find in this well-written story of Davy Crockett a hero after their own hearts.

MARQUIS AND BESSIE JAMES

Six Feet Six

The Landmark series can supply books about numerous colorful figures of this period. But for a swashbuckling hero none can compare with Sam Houston, and so far there is no book about him comparable to Marquis and Bessie James' *Six Feet Six: The Heroic Story of Sam Houston* (1931). This is the book Bessie James cut and adapted for children from her husband's authoritative adult biography, *The Raven,* which won the Pulitzer Prize.

In *Six Feet Six,* we see Sam, the handsome, dark boy who hated farming and who ran away to live with the Indians. Sam was adopted by Oo-loo-te-ka, the Cherokee chief. Throughout his life we see how Sam, when things got too much for him, would invariably go back to his Indian friend and foster father, Oo-loo-te-ka. In the war with the Indians, Houston attracted the attention of Jackson. After the War of 1812, Jackson sent Sam to try to talk the Cherokees and the other tribes into a new treaty, one which would force them to give up their lands in Tennessee and move west of the Mississippi.

Houston persuaded the Indians that they would be better off in the West—perhaps he believed it—and the Cherokees and Osages agreed to go. Later they sent a half-breed playmate of Sam's to tell him that they had been swindled again. They were hungry, harassed, and cheated by agents. The old chief begged for his foster son's aid, but Sam was advancing politically at that time and did nothing about this appeal. Perhaps there was nothing he could do. He was the popular governor of Tennessee with a dozen irons in the fire. He was even being talked of as the next President. But suddenly, for some unsolved reason, he left the wife he had just married, resigned as governor, and fled to his old haven, the lodge of Oo-loo-te-ka.

Then Houston seems to have done all he could to help his Indian friends, and he managed to rid them of the thieving government agents who had been harassing them. In Washington again, the protégé of President Jackson, Sam continued to help the Indians. This is one of his most picturesque periods. Having spanked a senator, he pleaded his own case before the House of Representatives so wittily that he became a national hero. He finally left Washington to organize the war that was to take Texas from Mexico. The last and noblest part of Sam's life in Texas is too well known to need reviewing here. He left the imprint of his colorful personality, his selfless love for the state he had brought into being, and his unswerving devotion to the Union, not only upon Texas but upon our whole country. Sam, grandiloquent, handsome, witty, a fighter from away back, did enough in his life for two heroes, and the children like every inch of his "six feet six." This is a book most twelve to fourteens will read and reread.

Civil War Period

The Lincoln period as well as the Washington and the Jackson periods is well represented by many fine juvenile biographies of great men. Children can saturate themselves in these periods by reading several of the biographies. Or a whole group of biographies can be covered in class reports by individual children. Through familiarity with the lives of these men, children often get a vivid and lasting impression of historical eras.

CARL SANDBURG

Abe Lincoln Grows Up

There are almost as many fascinating biographies of Lincoln for children as there are for adults. The outstanding favorite is Carl

Sandburg's *Abe Lincoln Grows Up* (1928) (p. 524), adapted from his adult *The Prairie Years.* The fourteens and the superior readers among the twelves can read this for themselves, but even the poorest readers in the upper grades should not miss it entirely. Read aloud to them excerpts from this book. They will be encouraged and entertained by the language Abe talked in his childhood (Chapter V). They will enjoy the chapters titled "Pleasant Superstitions" (Chapter XVII) and " 'Peculiarsome' Abe" (Chapter XVIII), and these chapters will help them see how long a road Abe had to travel to the literacy of his adult years, the moving beauty of his prose, and the strength of his maturity.

JAMES DAUGHERTY

Abraham Lincoln

The teen-age child can swing from this Sandburg story of Lincoln's youth, with its lively illustrations by James Daugherty, to Mr. Daugherty's own *Abraham Lincoln* (1943), which covers Lincoln's whole life. This book is as unhackneyed as Sandburg's. It avoids the usual anecdotes found in most of the other juveniles, and with remarkable clarity and power tells the story of Lincoln in relation to the stormy war years. A reviewer summarizing Mr. Daugherty's contribution in his three biographies writes:

> *. . . "Daniel Boone," "Poor Richard" and now "Abraham Lincoln"—are linked together in unity of spirit, an appreciation, in the true sense, of the restless, surging, visionary America which, with all its faults, has borne Titans.*[14]

There is something in the spirit which animates Mr. Daugherty's pen and brush that seems particularly adapted to the interpretation of titans. His *Abraham Lincoln* illustrations show all the rowdy vigor of his earlier drawings, but predominant in the book is the brooding melancholy of the strangest and perhaps loneliest of our great men. *Abraham Lincoln* is the most serious of Mr. Daugherty's three biographies, as we should expect, and is a magnificently clear if tragic picture of this great man.

CLARA INGRAM JUDSON

Abraham Lincoln, Friend of the People

Many think *Abraham Lincoln, Friend of the People* is the finest book in Mrs. Judson's biography series. Certainly it can take its place with the Sandburg and Daugherty Lincolns. The illustrations are unique also. In addition to the pen-and-ink drawings, there are colored photographs of the Lincoln dioramas from the Chicago Historical Society. These pictures are eye-catching and curiously alive.

BERNADINE BAILEY

Abe Lincoln's Other Mother

Bernadine Bailey's *Abe Lincoln's Other Mother* (1941) is an interesting book about Lincoln's early days. It is fiction founded on facts and concerns the warm, affectionate relationship that existed between Abe and his stepmother, Sarah Bush, during the years they were together in Tom Lincoln's household. The story is tenderly told, and those last visits from the boy who had grown into the great man Sarah had somehow expected him to be are less well known than some of the earlier episodes. They are very moving. Girls will like the detailed pictures of the housekeeping of those days and the descriptions of the difficult tasks which the girls were supposed to assume. Sarah Bush emerges from this picture a very real woman and a loving mother to all her brood. She is a fine rebuke to the old concept of the stepmother.

HENRY STEELE COMMAGER

America's Robert E. Lee

America's Robert E. Lee (1951) is significant, emphasizing as it does the fact that Robert E. Lee is a hero all America is proud of. Northern children should certainly read a

14. Ellen Lewis Buell, "The Story of Honest Abe," a review of Mr. Daugherty's *Abraham Lincoln* in *The New York Times Book Review,* December 19, 1943.

good biography of this man, who was held in such high regard, both as a strategist and as a man, by his contemporaries on both sides of the tragic struggle. The authenticity of the text is guaranteed by Mr. Commager's eminence as a historian. Lee's career progressed so smoothly that it is probably difficult to make him as colorful or dramatic a figure as some of our other national heroes. This biography sketches in briefly the distinguished family background of the Lees, follows Robert through his youth, his remarkable record at West Point, and his marriage. The war years are there, too, climaxing in that epoch-making day at Appomattox. Children will close this quiet biography with a deeper understanding for that sorrowful war, so gallantly maintained by the losing side. Some of the finest pictures Lynd Ward has ever made illustrate this biography. Boys pore over the battle scenes, which have the dramatic quality the text sometimes lacks.

For the story of the Lees' family life, children can read Marguerite Vance's *The Lees of Arlington: The Story of Mary and Robert E. Lee.*

DOUGLAS SOUTHALL FREEMAN

Lee of Virginia

Douglas Southall Freeman, like Mr. Commager, is an eminent historian, and his *Lee of Virginia* (1958) is absorbing reading. He brings out strongly the self-sacrifice Lee made when he returned to the South and espoused the Southern cause. The narrative shows his calm acceptance of the early triumphs and his sorrow when the tide turned, and carries him through those bitter days concluding with the surrender. After that came the quiet obscurity of his work in a small college. Lee's selfless nobility shines through everything he did. Here is a man, like Lincoln, with "the heart of heroes," and children should know him.

MACKINLAY KANTOR

Lee and Grant at Appomattox

The author of the Pulitzer Prize novel *Andersonville* has written one of the most thrilling books in the whole Landmark series. *Lee and Grant at Appomattox* (1950) is the day-by-day account of the last weeks of the war, climaxing in the surrender. The armies were encamped three miles apart. Both generals knew the end was inevitable, and both were heartsick over the loss of life. General Lee was so proud of his men that it broke his heart to have to surrender. In flashbacks the author fills in the backgrounds of both generals. For Lee there had been a lifetime of aristocratic distinction, an unblemished record of high honors. Grant's shabby past had included a forced resignation from an army commission, then a slow rehabilitation and a remarkable rise to be Commander of the Union Army. Now the two men faced each other.

A boy who had been racing through this intensely dramatic and moving narrative kept challenging his family with questions. At dinner he would burst forth with, "Did you know that on those last days Grant got the most terrible headache, so he couldn't eat or sleep, but when the note of surrender came, he said he was cured in a minute? And did you know that Grant sent food to Lee's men, right off? And what do you think? When the Union troops started celebrating, Grant stopped them. He said, 'The war is over, the Rebels are our fellow countrymen again.' And what's more, he let the Southern men keep their horses, 'cause they had furnished their own horses and now it was time for the spring planting!" And when his family admitted ignorance of these details, the boy said impatiently, "Well, gosh! You'd better read this book and you'll know something about these men!"

Biographies Which Meet Special Interests

Each important era in United States history had a remarkable group of heroes, many of whose lives are admirably recorded in biographies suitable for children or young people.

As has been suggested, these books may be used in groups to supplement or even, in some cases, to take the place of the usual history textbook. So you can build a group study around notable women or musicians or writers or around a group in almost any field of human endeavor.

HEROINES

Sometimes girls complain that biographies are always about men, but actually there are many fine biographies of women. Jeanette Eaton's magnificent *Jeanne d'Arc, the Warrior Saint,* Albert Bigelow Paine's *Girl in White Armor,* and Elizabeth Meigs' *Candle in the Sky* are all about the same girl and are all fine books. Not to have wept over the Warrior Maid is to have missed one of the poignant thrills of youthful reading. And coming to the battles of later days, girls enjoy Margaret Leighton's *The Story of Florence Nightingale.* It is a sympathetic account of her struggles against family opposition and public indifference.

The American counterpart of Florence Nightingale, Clara Barton, belongs to the Lincoln period. A biography of her by Mildred Pace shows the girl who became a great nurse and the organizer of the Civil War service to the wounded.

Louisa M. Alcott is another Civil War heroine who also nursed the wounded and tried to clean the unsanitary hospitals of the day, but we tend to forget all this, identifying her with her own creation—Jo in *Little Women.* Cornelia Meigs has given us a remarkable biography of this energetic, gifted woman in her *Invincible Louisa,* Newbery Medal winner for 1934.

There are several good collections of brief biographies of women. E. M. Sickels' *In Calico and Crinoline* tells of heroines from colonial through Civil War days. Sonia Daugherty's *Ten Brave Women* gives well-written accounts of women who have made history, from Mary Lyon, the founder of Mount Holyoke College, to Eleanor Roosevelt. Jane and Burt McConnell give diverting accounts of our *First Ladies.* A fine recent book, *Women Who Made America Great* by Harry Gersh, tells the stories of ten completely dissimilar women, from Maria Mitchell "astronomeress," as they called her at first, to "Babe" Didrikson, Margaret Bourke-White, and Lillian Wald. Every one of the ten dared to be different, not to achieve notoriety, but to accomplish what she apparently felt a compulsion to accomplish, in science, sports, photography, or in the struggle for freedom of the press. Their stories are well told and will open girls' eyes to the variety of women's work and the opposition and hardships involved.

Royalty is well represented by Marguerite Vance's *Elizabeth Tudor, Sovereign Lady,* Marian King's excellent life of *Young Mary Stuart,* and two fine biographies of Marie Antoinette, one by Mrs. Vance and one by Bernardine Kielty. In these books girls will see pictures of royalty triumphant and tragic.

Clara Judson's *City Neighbor, The Story of Jane Addams* brings us to modern women. Adolescent girls are often idealists, and this fine record of a dedicated life appeals to them.

For the children interested in ballet, *Dancing Star: The Story of Anna Pavlova* by Gladys Malvern presents not only the story of a great ballerina but a fascinating picture of ballet training. This array of heroines should convince girls that biography records the lives of a variety of important women.

NEGROES

Not until Elizabeth Yates' *Amos Fortune, Free Man* (1950) won the Newbery Medal had most of the world heard of this man. Born an African prince, sold in Boston, well treated by a series of masters, Amos learned the tanner's trade and eventually earned his freedom. After that, this humble, mighty soul devoted everything he earned to buying freedom for other slaves. Freedom and education were the greatest things in his life. He died a respected member of the little New Hampshire town of Jaffrey, where he had lived so long. When Miss Yates saw the tombstones of Amos and Violet, she tells us, she knew she must write his biography. It is written with the same warmth and human compassion that mark her stories *Mountain Born* and *A Place for Peter.* Since most books about slavery deal with the South, it is good to have this picture of slave running and sales in the North. The details are grim, but Amos Fortune carried suffering lightly because his eyes were on the freedom of the future.

Ann Petry, the Negro novelist, has told a well-documented story of another famous slave, *Harriet Tubman: Conductor on the Underground Railroad* (1955). The subtitle indicates the exciting action that fills a good part of the book. But the writer also gives a detailed picture of Harriet's childhood and youth on the plantation, the training and influences that made her what she was. She led three hundred slaves to freedom, and her exploits are a record of courage and uncanny skills that make an incredibly thrilling story.

No American child should come out of our high schools without having read that unexcelled autobiography—Booker T. Washington's *Up from Slavery* (1928). The title is also its theme. This is the focus of the whole book—the struggle up from slavery. The struggle for education, a smaller pattern of the central idea, is repeated over and over: first an education for himself, then for his brother, then for the Indians, then for more and more of his own people. Here, indeed, was a life with a great theme, a life which attained the symmetry, the wholeness of a work of art. There is also a fine biography of Booker T. Washington by Shirley Graham.

George Washington Carver's contributions to science are little short of miraculous. For adults and mature young people, his life has been well written by Rackham Holt (Mrs. Margaret Van Vechter Holt) in her book *George Washington Carver: An American Biography*. *The Story of George Washington Carver* by Arna Bontemps is a substantial study of the man for the middle grades. A much more mature biography for children twelve to fourteen is *Dr. George Washington Carver, Scientist* by Shirley Graham and George Dewey Lipscomb.

ARTISTS, MUSICIANS, AND WRITERS

Most biographies of artists, musicians, and writers are for the older or the teen-age group. But children with strong interests in any one of these special fields will find a few books within their reach. *Paderewski* is one.

Charlotte Kellogg's *Paderewski* (1956) is the biography of a great man whose gifts were many and whose life was as complex as it was distinguished. Musically gifted from early childhood, the boy Ignace was determined to be a pianist and despite every discouragement he became a concert pianist. From Vienna to Paris to London to the United States, his tours were one continuous triumph. This man with the beautiful face and spectacular aureole of red-gold hair, playing as no one had played before, captured the United States from coast to coast. He came to love it as his second country. Then World War I intervened, with Poland caught between Russia and Germany, and Paderewski poured his private fortune into relief. Later he was Poland's Premiere and then President, and his life as a musician seemed to be over. But when this new life came to an end also, he found himself bereft of son and wife and faced with the immediate need to recoup the fortune he had given away. To return to his long neglected piano required a grueling practice that would have killed a lesser man, but his triumphs in the concert hall were again spectacular. His burial with military honors in Arlington, an honor accorded only once before to someone not a native son, serves to underscore what Justice Harlan Stone said of him while he was still alive, "Paderewski is the world's greatest pianist . . . and perhaps the greatest living man."

Elizabeth Ripley is writing a splendid series of books about artists. Each is illustrated with black-and-white reproductions of the artist's pictures, showing something of his scope and style. Her texts follow a similar pattern throughout the series. She sketches the childhood and youth of the artist briefly. Then with the beginning of his productivity she tells about his life as it relates to his major works. For instance, she shows Michelangelo as almost the victim of his two gifts—for painting and for sculpture. Painting with its vision of endless details seemed to enslave him, while sculpture freed his energies and let his creative spirit soar. He agonized four years painting the ceiling of the Sistine Chapel; it left him crippled and almost blind. But he carved his David and the superb tombs with ease. Children, young people, and the whole family will enjoy these fine books.

In his *Rainbow Book of Art,* Thomas Craven, the distinguished art critic, has written a lively history of artists and art from cave drawings to modern painting on both sides of the Atlantic. Within this one big volume he has managed to give some exceedingly sharp vignettes of the artists. When, for instance, he tells about Michelangelo, lying flat on the scaffold at work on that endless Sistine ceiling and bitterly denouncing young Raphael's proclivity for copying his betters, he tells something about both men. This is one of the most readable texts on the development of art and artists to be found anywhere. Illustrated with black-and-white and glorious color reproductions, it is a treasure for any school or family to own.

Lives of the musicians above the level of the Wheeler and Deucher series are for mature readers. Claire Lee Purdy's *He Heard America Sing: The Story of Stephen Foster* is perhaps the simplest. It is also a well-balanced picture of an overindulged child who was allowed to stay away from school and who, all of his life, continued to run away from difficulties and discipline. Even in his beloved music he never forced himself to master harmony. Yet the man's lovable qualities, his talent, his songs, and his sorrows make him an appealing figure.

Madeleine Goss writes at youth level of such master musicians as Beethoven and Bach. Her sound musicianship and feeling for her subjects make these books worth while for the more mature child with a special interest in the field.

Jenny Lind Sang Here (1959) by Bernardine Kielty might easily have followed the rags to riches stereotype. Instead it is the human story of an unwanted child with a God-given gift that brought her phenomenal success and also loneliness and hard work as part of the price for that success. Her pure, lovely voice made her a star at eighteen and the darling of the music world. Her tours of America under the flamboyant banner of P. T. Barnum would have killed a less sturdy woman, and Miss Kielty's descriptions of our cities, hotels, and transportation are both amusing and horrifying. Jenny's success was fabulous and her romances were as numerous as her honors until she married Otto Goldschmidt, who gave her the love and security she had always longed for. This is both a career story and a Cinderella tale to charm readers of almost any age.

Note the interesting details of the costumes, the candles around the mirror in the star's dressing room, and the contrast in the two figures—Barnum, heavy, authoritative, and amusing; Jenny, happy and amiable. Illustration by Douglas Gorsline. From Jenny Lind Sang Here *by Bernardine Kielty. Copyright © 1959 by Bernardine Kielty. Reprinted by permission of the publishers, Houghton Mifflin Company. (Book 5 x 8⅛)*

Among the biographies of writers, one of the finest for children and young people is *Young Walter Scott* by Elizabeth Janet Gray. It is real biography based on careful research, and carries the novelist from early childhood to his romance. The boy's courage in overcoming his lameness, his gaiety, his fights—despite the lameness—and his early passion for the ballads which were to become a lifelong interest make him a boys' hero. The story of his life is superlative reading.

River Boy, Isabel Proudfit's life of Mark Twain, will also be liked by twelve-year-old boys. This biography often adds to the enjoyment of Twain's own *Tom Sawyer.*

On the other hand, Lincoln Steffens' *Boy on Horseback,* an adaptation of this newspaperman's adult autobiography, is always extremely popular with boys. Twelves can read it, and the fourteen-year-olds thoroughly enjoy it. As one boy said to his mother, "Now there's a kid *on his own,* but he learned how to take care of himself, and that's what we've all got to do." The mother was a little startled, but upon reading the book herself decided the boy was right.

Boys also delight in *On Safari,* Theodore Waldeck's account of his first adventure in the jungle where as a cub explorer he did everything wrong and was thoroughly disciplined.

Here is Bombastus, indeed! Dr. Paracelsus, as a student, throws the works of Avicenna into the fire to dramatize his intention of changing medicine. The sketch catches his violence and the horrified reactions of his peers. Illustration by Rafaello Busoni. From Doctor Paracelsus *by Sidney Rosen. Copyright, © 1959, by Sidney Rosen. Reprinted with the permission of Little, Brown and Company. (Book 5½ x 8¼, picture 4½ x 3)*

The fact that he not only survived but succeeded as an explorer and as a writer is a great comfort to young readers.

SCIENTISTS

Sidney Rosen's *Doctor Paracelsus* and *Galileo* and Hildegarde Hoyt Swift's *From the Eagle's Wing* would have special appeal for any young person interested in science.

Doctor Paracelsus (1959) was a runner-up for the Newbery Medal. In this book Mr. Rosen tells the story of Theophrastus Bombastus von Hohenheim, the son of an honest and dedicated Swiss doctor in a day of quacks. The boy studied with an alchemist, not to make gold out of dross but to learn ways of refining metals. From this experience came his lifelong passion for experimenting and for turning to nature to discover her secrets. Thoroughly grounded in Latin and Greek and such science as his father could teach him, Theophrastus set off for a university to study medicine. But when he discovered that the professors only read notes copied from ancient Greek and Roman doctors, he was disgusted and moved on from university to university. In the course of his career he took the name of Paracelsus to indicate his own superiority to Celsus, an ancient authority on remedies. This was so typical of the man's cocksureness that the name Bombastus became, even in his lifetime, a synonym for brash, blustering conceit. Yet here was a bold, original mind unafraid to challenge the superstitions of the day or to try new methods. Despite quarrels and continual moves from place to place, Paracelsus made important contributions to medical research. From the Tartars he derived the sedative he named Laudes or, as we know it today, laudanum. He introduced mercury in diluted form as a medicine, and many other tinctures. He tried to simplify treatments and always turned to nature for clues. Reading this fascinating account of a contradictory personality, young people will catch a glimpse of early medical research and gain some understanding of the stubborn heroism it takes to stand out against the beliefs and practices of the times.

This sort of heroism is even more evident

in Mr. Rosen's *Galileo and the Magic Numbers* (1958). Like Paracelsus, Galileo began with the study of medicine, but he was so fascinated with mathematics and physics that he transferred his studies to those fields. In nontechnical language, this biography manages to give young readers absorbing accounts of Galileo's discovery of many important mathematical, physical, and astronomical truths and his invention of the thermometer and the telescope. The latter enabled him to be the first to see the moons of Jupiter and this, in turn, confirmed his belief in the Copernican theory of the solar system. This theory was contrary to the theology of the times, and as his experiments and writings continued he attracted the displeasure of the Church, and the Inquisition followed. The trial and his recanting are so adroitly handled that they give no offense to any group. Galileo emerges from his ordeals a great scientist to whom nothing mattered save the search for truth at all costs. Banishment, seclusion, and blindness handicapped this search but never stopped him.

A fascinating biography for budding naturalists is Hildegarde Hoyt Swift's story of John Muir's life, *From the Eagle's Wing* (1962). Born in a little Scotch town, the Muir boys found the ruins of an old castle a wonderful spot for what they called their "daring scootchers." That was where blue-eyed, red-haired John learned to climb like a cat and haul the others to safety when they got in a tight spot. Once the family was settled on a farm in Wisconsin the father enslaved all his children and even his wife. Neighbors protested, but the drudgery went on. John slept only four or five hours at night in order to have time to study or to invent strange gadgets. One of these—a clock that waked the sleeper and rolled him out of bed—won John a prize and the lifelong friendship of Mrs. Carr and her professor husband. How this overworked, half-starved boy ever got to college and stayed there is a miracle. Geology fascinated him, and he longed to prove the Agassiz theory that "from the universal ice sheet has come the shape of the land." Once through with his study, John struck out for the wilderness, which few men have ever loved so deeply. He proved his glacial theory against bitter opposition. He was an explorer, a brilliant writer, and a happily married man, thanks to Mrs. Carr, who introduced him not only to his future wife, a remarkable woman, but to distinguished men of his time—Emerson, Burroughs, Theodore Roosevelt, and many others. Of all his writings the story of his incredible escape with his dog Stickeen from death on a glacier by means of a rope of ice is the most thrilling. But it is also important to remember that he was the father of conservation and that he established the great national parks of the West.

This scene pictures, with strong black and white forms, John Muir, the wilderness lover, who would climb a giant spruce and hang on for hours to experience the movement of wind through the trees.
Illustration by Lynd Ward. From the Eagle's Wing: A Biography of John Muir *by Hildegarde Hoyt Swift. Copyright, © 1962, by Hildegarde Hoyt Swift. Reprinted with the permission of the publisher, William Morrow and Company, Inc. (Book 6 x 9)*

ADVENTURERS

Waldeck's *On Safari* was mentioned earlier in this chapter, but it also belongs in the group of biographies which stress adventure. Commander Byrd's *Alone,* one of the best of this group, has been a favorite with young people ever since it appeared. The suspense in the chapter in which he tells how he was unable to find the opening to his underground dwelling and was shut out in the unbelievable cold leaves the reader fairly panting with vicarious exertion. Indeed, suspense is the key to the fascination of the whole narrative, and boys revel in it. Osa Johnson's *I Married Adventure* is equally popular with girls.

A different type of adventure is to be found in the life of *Raymond L. Ditmars* by Laura W. Wood. Ditmars, author of several authoritative books on snakes, had enough adventures in the process of mastering his curious profession to satisfy the most avid thirst for the unusual. Here is a scientist and an author who began the serious study of snakes in his boyhood with little encouragement or guidance from any direction until he was in his teens. Some of his boyhood troubles with his odd pets are really very funny, and it is surprising that his apartment-dwelling family indulged his troublesome interest as much as they did. This is an entertaining, well-written biography that rouses fresh respect for the difficult way of the scientist. These biographies of men of action have a tremendous appeal and stir emulation in young minds as fiction rarely does.

Using Biography with Children

In this sampling of available biographies for children and youth it is clear that for important periods in history and for many notable men biographies are available at almost any reading level. Take the period of the American Revolution and such men as Washington and Franklin, for example. There are the picture biographies of the d'Aulaires, the simplified stories of the heroes' boyhoods in the Bobbs-Merrill series, the Initial Biogra-

Sixth-grade students present an effective dramatization as a culmination of their study of early manuscripts. Franklin School, History of Records Unit. Santa Barbara City Schools.

phies of Genevieve Foster, or Enid Meadowcroft's easy-to-read books, and, finally, the mature and detailed records of the men by James Daugherty, Clara Ingram Judson, and Jeanette Eaton. This means that in class discussions the most retarded readers will have books from which they can obtain facts, anecdotes, and a respectable overall picture of the man and his contribution to the building of our nation. And the superior readers will have detailed records of the man.

Throughout the chapter, pairs of biographies about the same man have been suggested, and also biographies of notable contemporaries. The bibliography for this chapter adds to these suggestions.

CORRELATION WITH SCHOOL SUBJECTS

One student teacher used *Young Walter Scott* with a sixth-grade class which was reading some of Scott's poems. These poems, together with the biography, led back to the old English ballads which Scott collected.

The courtroom scene in *Penn* (p. 522) dramatizes well and is particularly important because upon that trial hung the right of jurors to have their verdicts sustained by the court. The Washington and Lafayette biographies suggest endless scenes for dramatization and, with the addition of the stories about Patrick Henry, Thomas Jefferson, Benjamin Franklin, Paul Revere, and others, a whole pageant of colonial days leading up to the Revolution can be developed. Surely *Johnny Tremain* would be found in the thick of it, too.

There are scenes from Lincoln's boyhood which may be dramatized effectively—the "blab" school, the coming of the new stepmother, Lincoln with his rain-soaked *Life of Washington,* his farewell to his father and stepmother, and that great farewell to his fellow townsmen in Springfield with the speech that forecast the ever-growing greatness of the man. In all such plays and pageants, costume design, stage settings, and scenery would occupy the artists of the school and stimulate profitable art work for everyone.

The three notable books about the Lewis and Clark expedition—James Daugherty's *Of Courage Undaunted,* Julia Davis' *No Other White Men,* and Frances Farnsworth's *Winged Moccasins*—suggest a whole series of scenes for either a play or a pageant: the gathering of the men and the start of the expedition; a scene with one of the Indian tribes—arrival, gift giving, feast, games, and dancing afterwards; winter quarters; the encounter with the bear; Charbonneau and Sacajawea hired as guides. Sacajawea may tell her story of capture. There is the dramatic meeting with the Shoshones when Sacajawea finds her brother, and then the Pacific at last. For the final scene there could be the parting with Sacajawea and her little son as the men return to the East. These and other scenes could be portrayed by children in a wonderful series of paintings or crayon pictures to be brought together in a mural.

DISCUSSION

Reading biography opens up some excellent opportunities for airing honest differences of opinion about the acts and policies of some of these men. Why was Jefferson's clause abolishing slavery struck out of the Declaration? Was Franklin conciliatory to the English too long? Who was right in his view of Jackson's Indian policy—Davy Crockett or Sam Houston? If Sam Houston had been nominated for the Presidency on the Democratic ticket, he might have been elected instead of Lincoln. Would Houston's election have prevented the Civil War? What was Lincoln's real stand on slavery at the outset of his Presidency? These are all good subjects for speculation and debate, and the children can find in these biographies different kinds of evidence justifying various and conflicting answers.

COMPOSITION

Robert Lawson's *They Were Strong and Good* may serve as a stimulus for writing. To start youngsters collecting and recording the unique stories about their own families is not only good motivation for writing but a good habit to grow up with. Amateur historians are contributing much lively information to our pictures of the past, and twelve-year-olds are not too young to begin a little local research. Mr. Lawson's sketches are brief, and yet each one is a dramatic unit. Such a pattern is easier for children to comprehend and try than a long biography. Even so, biography reading is almost certain to inspire some child to embark on an autobiography. Some of these family sketches and personal reminiscences illustrated with kodak pictures or old photographs have given great pleasure to the children and have inspired some amazingly good writing.

Encouraging the Reading of Biography

Biographies written with authenticity and a high regard for the lively human qualities of great men and women are among the newest and most important developments in children's books. To know and use them in our classrooms and to help children discover them for their individual reading is to utilize one of the richest book offerings available.

Sometimes fiction will send children to biography. An amusing example of this was in a classroom where the teacher was reading Robert Lawson's *Ben and Me* to her children. They found it hilarious, but one day she stopped her reading and remarked, "It just occurred to me that here we are laughing over this funny story about Benjamin Franklin, but how much do we know about his real life?" Precious little, they soon discovered, and the teacher, too, admitted frankly that she had forgotten a good deal of what she had once known. "So—" said she, "I am not going to finish reading *Ben and Me* until you and I among us can piece together the main events of his whole life." The children rallied enthusiastically. One group took Franklin's childhood and youth, another his life through the Revolution, another his years in France and his death in this country. The local librarian could not imagine what had happened when the whole mob descended upon her demanding everything available about Benjamin Franklin. In a week's time they had their material. Every child reported some facts, and together the children covered the story of Franklin's whole life, supplemented by significant episodes from the teacher, who assured them that she, too, had been working. After that, the reading of *Ben and Me* was resumed, and the children agreed that it seemed funnier now that they knew the real facts.

Another teacher, whose children were sure they "just hated biography," used the anecdote to illumine her history periods. These anecdotes she chose from various juvenile books of biography. In the English period they discussed the anecdote and its power to reveal a man's character or attitude. The children were then to find anecdotes by themselves which would show something important about a man. They went to their school library, chose a biography that looked readable, and went to work. Sometimes the librarian guided their choices or even gave chapter references. The children enjoyed relating their anecdotes and presently were making reports of whole books. These reports led readily into the use of some of the newer biographies in connection with their history, and presently one child after another was saying with surprise, "Why, I liked that book and it was a biography!" or "I thought biography was dull, but this one was exciting." The anecdote had turned the tide.

Why should we make this effort to steer children into reading which they might not otherwise discover? Why should not biography wait until adolescence and maturity, when it is a natural interest? First, because it is also a natural interest in childhood. Children have always liked to hear about the lives of their heroes provided the stories were not too ponderous. Second, because we now have appealing, authentic biographies of men of action, soundly and beautifully written for children. To omit them would be to miss one of the best recent contributions to children's reading. Hero worship begins young. Baseball idols are all right, but a child may also begin to thrill over explorers, both of the globe and of science, founding fathers, great men and women who have helped to build this country. A college professor, looking over some of these new biographies for children and young people, was astonished at their use of recent research findings and at the charm of their style. He said, "Why, if our children could be raised on such books as these, they would have a background for United States, and, indeed, for world history which would carry them far in college. For those who never go to college it would give a warmer appreciation of our national life than anything else. Here, in these biographies, they can see democracy in the making."

His use of the word *warm* is apt because these *are* warm books, these new biographies. From their pages human beings emerge, confused and bewildered like ourselves, struggling blindly toward goals they are not always sure of, growing through their mistakes and failures, developing clearer purposes, picking themselves up grimly after a fall and plodding on again, pausing for an act of kindness, a breathing space for laughter, a little frolic and fun between chores.

Reading about these men and women, we find out about ourselves. They were afraid sometimes even as we are afraid, but they took no "council of their fears." They had bad tempers, but they learned to hold them in leash; maybe we can do so, too. They grew desperately tired, but still they kept at their tasks; well, after all, so can we. They were sometimes impatient and "bombastic," but they kept working. No other reading can ever quite approach the effective moral implications of a good biography. Emulation, encouragement, faith in human nature, and faith in ourselves are some of the by-products of reading these stirring accounts. As James C. Johnson says in his *Biography: The Literature of Personality:*

> *Many successes in life give testimony, indeed, to the statement that biography, more than any other form of literature, has been known to inspire a youth with faith in himself and to give him a determination to make the most of his life.* (p. 97)

Whether in the idyllic mood of "Beulah Land" or the relaxed Little Georgie or the world of fairy or the broadly comic as in this picture of Ben evolving the first stove, Robert Lawson's style is invariably sharp and clear. Illustration by Robert Lawson. From Ben and Me *by Robert Lawson. Copyright 1939 by Robert Lawson. Reprinted with the permission of Little, Brown and Company. (Book 6 x 8)*

SUGGESTED READING, PROBLEMS, AND PROJECTS

Suggested Reading: Read *Penn,* at least one of the Daugherty biographies, and one biography from a special field—for example, musicians.

Kindergarten-primary: Read two books of the d'Aulaires, one by Bulla, Dalgliesh, Henry, Wheeler and Deucher, and one of the Childhood of Famous Americans series.

Middle and upper grades: If you plan to teach these grades, group your readings around a period or a special interest (scientists, musicians, explorers, writers). In your selected group, you should read carefully and analyze at least one of the long biographies and skim four or five of the briefer and easier ones in order to gauge their values for slow readers.

1. Appraise a biography for older children according to the standards for good biography outlined in this chapter. Do not use a book which is analyzed in this text.

2. Find examples other than those given in this chapter of flowing rhythm in both the text and pictures of Daugherty's biographies. How can you help children to understand and appreciate his unusual pictures?

3. Familiarize yourself with several books in the major biography series. Then appraise each series for such things as age level, factual correctness, style of writing, format and illustrations, and range of subjects. Suggest situations in which the books of each series might be most useful. Be sure to consider the differences within each series, too.

4. What notable qualities do you find in Sandburg's *Abe Lincoln Grows Up?* Compare it with the usual history-book account of Abe's boyhood.

5. Skim a juvenile or adult biography for unusual and interesting anecdotes to tell children on the birthdays of our great men. Present these to the class.

6. Take one biography and outline a possible plan for using it as a basis for the correlation of such activities as English (reading historical fiction that adds life to the period, reports, discussions, written or oral composition, book reviews, dramatization, puppetry, pageantry); art (illustration, murals, scenery, costumes, book design, bookmaking); music (singing, music appreciation, dances); integration of such subjects as geography, science, history, arithmetic, and physical education—where such integration is natural. Plan a culmination of your unit.

COLLECTIONS OF BIOGRAPHICAL SKETCHES FOR CHILDREN

BAKELESS, KATHERINE. *Story-Lives of American Composers.* Lippincott, 1953.

______. *Story-Lives of Great Composers.* Lippincott, 1953.

For each collection, nineteen composers have been selected. 12-15

BEARD, CHARLES AUSTIN. *The Presidents in American History.* Messner, 1961. Offers good historical background for each Presidential career. 12-16

BENÉT, LAURA. *Famous American Poets,* ill. with photographs. Dodd, 1950. Over twenty poets both recent and past are introduced in brief biographies. 11-14

DAUGHERTY, SONIA. *Ten Brave Men,* ill. by James Daugherty. Lippincott, 1951. Good accounts of such national heroes as Roger Williams, Patrick Henry, Thomas Jefferson, and Andrew Jackson.

______. *Ten Brave Women,* ill. by James Daugherty. Lippincott, 1953. 11-15

FANNING, LEONARD M. *Fathers of Industries.* Lippincott, 1962. Emphasis is on men who from industrial revolution days to the present have contributed significantly to inventions having social and economic significance. 12-

GERSH, HARRY. *Women Who Made America Great,* ill. by Mel Silverman. Lippincott, 1962. 11-14

KAUFMAN, HELEN L. *History's 100 Greatest Composers,* ill. by Samuel Nisenson. Grosset, 1957. Music critics selected the composers who achieved eminence from the sixteenth century to the present. 11-

KELSEY, VERA. *Young Men So Daring.* Bobbs, 1956. Entertaining brief biographies of fur traders who helped develop the western frontier; includes Peter Pond, Manuel Lisa, John Jacob Astor, and Jim Bridger. 11-15

KUNITZ, STANLEY, and HOWARD HAYCRAFT, eds. *The Junior Book of Authors* (see Bibliography, Chapter 2).

MC CONNELL, JANE and BURT. *Our First Ladies,* ill. by Isabel Dawson. Crowell, 1961. 12-

MC NEER, MAY, and LYND WARD. *Armed with Courage,* ill. by Lynd Ward. Abingdon, 1957. Brief, entertaining biographies of seven dedicated men and women: Florence Nightingale, Father Damien, George W. Carver, Jane Addams, Wilfred Grenfell, Gandhi, and Albert Schweitzer. 9-12

MEYER, EDITH PATTERSON. *Champions of Peace,* ill. by Eric von Schmidt. Little, 1959. Timely sketches of fourteen Nobel Peace Prize winners, followed by a complete listing of all the award winners up to 1959, Nobel's will, and the rules for the award. 11-

MONTGOMERY, ELIZABETH RIDER. *The Story Behind Great Books,* ill. by Friedebald Dzubas. Dodd, 1946.

______. *The Story Behind Great Stories,* ill. by Elinore Blaisdell. Dodd, 1947.

______. *The Story Behind Modern Books.* Dodd, 1949. Short sketches about authors and illustrators of children's books, both classic and recent. 11-

RICHARDSON, BEN. *Great American Negroes,* rev. by William A. Fahey, ill. by Robert Hallock. Crowell, 1956. Vivid accounts of twenty Negroes who have overcome obstacles and who have contributed to American culture in many fields. 12-16

SICKELS, ELEANOR. *In Calico and Crinoline, True Stories of American Women, 1608-1865,* ill. by Ilse Bischoff. Viking, 1935. 11-16

SIMON, CHARLIE MAY. *Art in the New Land.* Dutton, 1945. Stories of famous American artists from Benjamin West to Grant Wood, with illustrations and descriptions of their work. 12-14

SULLIVAN, NAVIN. *Pioneer Germ Fighters.* Atheneum, 1962. The discoveries of a dozen scientists, ranging from Leeuwenhoek to Salk. 10-12

BIOGRAPHIES OF FIGURES IN AMERICAN HISTORY

See also Collections of biographical sketches and Bibliography for Chapter 16.
F stands for historical fiction.

ALDERMAN, CLIFFORD LINDSEY. *Samuel Adams, Son of Liberty.* Holt, 1961. Distinguished writing and an outstanding evaluation of one of the American Revolution's most controversial figures. 12-16

AVERILL, ESTHER. *Cartier Sails the St. Lawrence,* ill. by Feodor Rojankovsky. Harper, 1956. 10-14

BAILEY, BERNADINE. *Abe Lincoln's Other Mother: The Story of Sarah Bush Lincoln,* ill. by Howard Simon. Messner, 1941. *F* 10-12

BAKER, NINA BROWN. *Amerigo Vespucci,* ill. by Paul Valentino. Knopf, 1956. 9-12

______. *Pike of Pike's Peak,* ill. by Richard Powers. Harcourt, 1953. Well-paced, entertaining biography of a famous soldier and explorer. 11-14

______. *Texas Yankee: The Story of Gail Borden,* ill. by Alan Moyler. Harcourt, 1955. The harsh experiences of his own pioneer days led Gail Borden to experiment with condensed foods and later with milk, which proved of tremendous value in Civil War days. 11-14

BELL, MARGARET E. *Kit Carson, Mountain Man,* ill. by Harry Daugherty. Morrow, 1952. A short dramatic biography with large print and many illustrations. 8-11

BROWN, JOHN MASON. *Daniel Boone: The Opening of the Wilderness,* ill. by Lee J. Ames. Random, 1952 (Landmark Book). Fine characterization adds distinction to this biography of the Kentucky pioneer. 12-15

BROWN, SLATER. *Ethan Allen and the Green Mountain Boys,* ill. by William Moyers. Random, 1956 (Landmark Book). The character of the Vermont hero emerges as a courageous one; Ethan Allen is not crushed by imprisonment or personal disappointments. 11-15

BULLA, CLYDE. *John Billington, Friend of Squanto,* ill. by Peter Burchard. Crowell, 1956. A small boy's troubles win Squanto's friendship, and his help for the Pilgrims. *F* 7-10

______. *Squanto, Friend of the White Men,* ill. by Peter Burchard, Crowell, 1954. *F* 8-10

BURNETT, CONSTANCE BUEL. *Captain John Ericsson: Father of the "Monitor."* Vanguard, 1961. Failure as well as success marked the life of the Swedish-born genius. 12-16

CAMPION, NARDI REEDER. *Patrick Henry: Firebrand of the Revolution,* ill. by Victor Mays. Little, 1961. 12-

COMMAGER, HENRY STEELE. *America's Robert E. Lee,* ill. by Lynd Ward. Houghton, 1951 (America's Series). 11-15

CROUSE, ANNA ERSKINE and RUSSEL. *Alexander Hamilton and Aaron Burr: Their Lives, Their Times, Their Duel,* ill. by Walter Buehr. Random, 1958. (Landmark Book). Skillfully interwoven biographies and a well-drawn historical background. 11-15

DALGLIESH, ALICE. *The Columbus Story,* ill. by Leo Politi. Scribner, 1955. 8-11

DAUGHERTY, JAMES. *Abraham Lincoln,* ill. by author. Viking, 1943.

______. *Daniel Boone,* ill. by author. Viking, 1939.

______. *Poor Richard,* ill. by author. Viking, 1941.

______. *Marcus and Narcissa Whitman: Pioneers of Oregon,* ill. by author. Viking, 1953. A heroic story of the life and tragic death of two brave doctor-missionaries to the Indians. 12-15

______. *Of Courage Undaunted: Across the Continent with Lewis and Clark,* ill. by author. Viking, 1951. 11-15

D'AULAIRE, INGRI and EDGAR. *Abraham Lincoln,* ill. by authors. Doubleday, 1939. Other titles include *Benjamin Franklin* (1950), *Buffalo Bill* (1952), *Columbus* (1955), *George Washington* (1936), *Leif the Lucky* (1951), *Pocahontas* (1946). 6-10

DAVIS, JULIA. *No Other White Men.* Dutton, 1937. 12-14

DAVIS, RUSSELL, and BRENT ASHABRANNER. *Chief Joseph, War Chief of the Nez Percé.* McGraw, 1962. The tragic story of a peace-loving chief forced into war as his people opposed the westward movement. 12-16

EATON, JEANETTE. *Leader by Destiny,* ill. by Jack Manley Rosé. Harcourt, 1938.

______. *Lone Journey: The Life of Roger Williams,* ill. by Woodi Ishmael. Harcourt, 1944. Story of the courageous Puritan who left the Massachusetts colony and helped establish Rhode Island. 12-16

______. *Narcissa Whitman: Pioneer of Oregon,* ill. by Woodi Ishmael. Harcourt, 1941. This inspiring life of a great pioneer woman is based on early letters and memoirs. 12-16

———. *That Lively Man, Ben Franklin,* ill. by Henry C. Pitz. Morrow, 1948. Franklin's many-sided career, from printer to ambassador. 11-14

———. *Young Lafayette,* ill. by David Hendrickson. Houghton, 1932. 12-16

FARNSWORTH, FRANCES JOYCE. *Winged Moccasins: The Story of Sacajawea,* ill. by Lorence Bjorklund. Messner, 1954. 12-15

FISHER, AILEEN. *My Cousin Abe,* ill. by Leonard Vosburgh. Nelson, 1962. Dennis Hanks was ten when Lincoln was born, and he tells the story of his younger relative with the warmth and tenderness inspired by the close family relationship. Although introducing a narrator, the author faithfully follows the details of Lincoln's life. *F* 11-15

FISHER, DOROTHY CANFIELD. *Paul Revere and the Minute Men,* ill. by Norman Price. Random, 1950 (Landmark Book). 10-13

FORBES, ESTHER. *America's Paul Revere,* ill. by Lynd Ward. Houghton, 1946. Vigorous prose and superb illustrations do much to illumine the history of the Revolutionary period. 11-15

FOSTER, GENEVIEVE. *Abraham Lincoln: An Initial Biography,* ill. by author. Scribner, 1950. Other Initial Biographies include *Andrew Jackson* (1951), *George Washington* (1949), and *Theodore Roosevelt* (1954). 9-12

FREEMAN, DOUGLAS SOUTHALL. *Lee of Virginia.* Scribner, 1958. 12-

GALT, TOM. *Peter Zenger: Fighter for Freedom,* ill. by Ralph Ray. Crowell, 1951. Biography of a famous pre-Revolutionary War printer, who faced trial and prison rather than yield the right of freedom of the press. 12-15

GARST, DORIS SHANNON. *Chief Joseph of the Nez Percés,* ill. by Douglas Gorsline. Messner, 1953.

———. *Crazy Horse, Great Warrior of the Sioux,* ill. by William Moyers. Houghton, 1950.
Both these biographies give good perspective on why the Indians so bitterly opposed the white men. 12-15

GOWDY, GEORGE [pseud. for J. H. Gage]. *Young Buffalo Bill,* ill. by Howard Simon. Lothrop, 1955. Emphasis is on the young boy forced to assume responsibility for the family at his father's death. A well-told story. *F* 11-14

GRAY, ELIZABETH JANET. *Penn,* ill. by George Gillett Whitney. Viking, 1938. 12-16

GURKO, LEO. *Tom Paine, Freedom's Apostle,* ill. by Fritz Kredel. Crowell, 1957. Outstanding characterization and historical substance. 12-

HODGES, C. WALTER. *Columbus Sails* (see Bibliography, Chapter 16).

HOLBROOK, STEWART. *America's Ethan Allen,* ill. by Lynd Ward. Houghton, 1949. Spirited illustrations in color add to the dramatic story of the "Green Mountain Boys" and their fighting leader. 11-15

HUNT, MABEL LEIGH. *Better Known As Johnny Appleseed,* ill. by James Daugherty. Lippincott, 1950. The life of John Chapman, "American pioneer, missionary, and apple lover," based on old legends and reminiscences gathered by the author. 12-16

JAMES, BESSIE and MARQUIS. *Six Feet Six: The Heroic Story of Sam Houston,* ill. by Lowell Balcom. Bobbs, 1931. 12-16

JOHNSON, ENID. *Cochise: Great Apache Chief,* ill. by Lorence F. Bjorklund. Messner, 1953. A tragic story of a great leader's trust and disillusionment. 11-15

JUDSON, CLARA INGRAM. *Abraham Lincoln, Friend of the People,* ill. by Robert Frankenberg. Includes photographs. Follett, 1950.

———. *Andrew Jackson, Frontier Statesman,* ill. by Lorence F. Bjorklund. Follett, 1954.

———. *Benjamin Franklin,* ill. by Robert Frankenberg. Follett, 1957. 11-15

———. *City Neighbor, The Story of Jane Addams,* ill. by Ralph Ray. Scribner, 1951. 10-13

———. *George Washington, Leader of the People,* ill. by Robert Frankenberg. Follett, 1951.

———. *Theodore Roosevelt, Fighting Patriot,* ill. by Lorence F. Bjorklund. Follett, 1953.

———. *Thomas Jefferson, Champion of the People,* ill. by Robert Frankenberg. Follett, 1952. 11-15

KANTOR, MACKINLAY. *Lee and Grant at Appomattox,* ill. by Donald McKay. Random, 1950 (Landmark Book). 10-14

LATHAM, JEAN LEE. *Carry On, Mr. Bowditch,* ill. by John O'Hara Cosgrave II. Houghton, 1955. Newbery Medal. *F* 11-15

———. *Trail Blazer of the Seas,* ill. by Victor Mays. Houghton, 1956. Absorbing story of the scientific U.S. Naval Lieutenant Matthew Fontaine Maury, who studied winds and currents to reduce ships' sailing time. *F* 11-15

———. *Young Man in a Hurry: The Story of Cyrus Field,* ill. by Victor Mays. Harper, 1958. An account of the laying of the Atlantic cable and of the unconquerable Cyrus Field. 12-

LE SUEUR, MERIDEL. *Chanticleer of Wilderness Road: A Story of Davy Crockett,* ill. by Aldren Watson. Knopf, 1951. Young readers not yet ready for the more difficult Rourke biography of Davy Crockett will find this one completely satisfying. 10-13

LISITZKY, GENE. *Thomas Jefferson,* ill. by Harrie Wood. Viking, 1933. 12-16

MC GEE, DOROTHY HORTON. *Herbert Hoover: Engineer, Humanitarian, Statesman,* ill. with photographs. Dodd, 1959. An exceptionally well-presented biography. 12-

MC KOWN, ROBIN. *Thomas Paine.* Putnam, 1962. A more detailed life of Paine than Leo Gurko's biography, this equally fine book provides a deeply sympathetic picture of the man. 12-16

MARRIOTT, ALICE. *Sequoyah: Leader of the Cherokees,* ill. by Bob Riger. Random, 1956 (Landmark Book). Story of the scholarly Indian who made a syllabary of the Cherokee language so that his people could learn to read and write. 10-14

MEADOWCROFT, ENID. *The Story of Crazy Horse,* ill. by William Reusswig. Grosset, 1954 (Signature Book). Biography of the Oglala chief who opposed Custer and who died escaping imprisonment. 9-12

MILL, LOIS. *Three Together: The Story of the Wright Brothers and Their Sister,* ill. by William Moyers. Follett, 1955. A biography rich in human values and persistence in the face of many failures. 9-13

NORTH, STERLING. *Abe Lincoln: Log Cabin to White House,* ill. by Lee Ames. Random, 1956 (Landmark Book). A stimulating, well-rounded biography based on careful research. 11-15

———. *George Washington, Frontier Colonel,* ill. by Lee Ames. Random, 1957 (Landmark Book). A vivid picture of young Washington which highlights his adventurous years as a surveyor and frontier fighter and leader. 11-15

———. *Young Thomas Edison,* ill. by William Barss. Houghton, 1958 (North Star Book). Outstanding biography of Edison both as a man and as an inventive genius. 11-15

PACE, MILDRED. *Clara Barton,* ill. by Robert Ball. Scribner, 1941. 10-12

PEARE, CATHERINE OWENS. *The FDR Story,* ill. Crowell, 1962. A remarkably perceptive biography of Roosevelt as an individual and as a political figure. 12-15

PETRY, ANN. *Harriet Tubman: Conductor on the Underground Railroad.* Crowell, 1955. 12-16

RANDALL, RUTH PAINTER. *I Mary,* ill. with photographs. Little, 1959. A sincere and honest biography of Mary Todd Lincoln which helps to dispel some of the unhappy legends associated with her life. 12-16

ROGERS, FRANCES, and ALICE BEARD. *Paul Revere, Patriot on Horseback,* ill. by Frances Rogers. Lippincott, 1943. Offers a good background of the American Revolution. 11-14

ROURKE, CONSTANCE. *Davy Crockett,* ill. by James MacDonald. Harcourt, 1934. 12-16

SANDBURG, CARL. *Abe Lincoln Grows Up,* ill. by James Daugherty. Harcourt, 1928. 11-16

SHIPPEN, KATHERINE. *Leif Eriksson; First Voyager to America.* Harper, 1951. Well-written, exciting biography of the explorer of Vinland. 11-13

———. *Mr. Bell Invents the Telephone,* ill. by Richard Floethe. Random, 1952 (Landmark Book). Alexander Graham Bell's achievement is doubly satisfying because of the disheartening failure that preceded his successful invention. 10-13

SPERRY, ARMSTRONG. *John Paul Jones: Fighting Sailor,* ill. by author. Random, 1953 (Landmark Book). The life of the naval hero who suffered ingratitude and injustice throughout his career. 10-13

STEELE, WILLIAM O. *John Sevier: Pioneer Boy,* ill. by Sandra James. Bobbs, 1953 (Childhood of Famous Americans Series). F 8-10

STEVENSON, AUGUSTA. *Abe Lincoln: Frontier Boy,* ill. by Clotilde Embree. Bobbs, 1932.

———. *Ben Franklin: Printer's Boy,* ill. by Paul Laune. Bobbs, 1941. F 8-10

SYME, RONALD. *Balboa, Finder of the Pacific,* ill. by William Stobbs. Morrow, 1956. Other explorer biographies include *Champlain of the St. Lawrence* (1952), *Columbus, Finder of the New World* (1952), *Henry Hudson* (1955), *John Smith of Virginia* (1954), *La Salle of the Mississippi* (1953), *Magellan, First Around the World* (1953). 10-12

VANCE, MARGUERITE. *The Jacksons of Tennessee,* ill. by Nedda Walker. Dutton, 1953.

———. *The Lees of Arlington: The Story of Mary and Robert E. Lee,* ill. by Nedda Walker. Dutton, 1949.

———. *Martha, Daughter of Virginia: The Story of Martha Washington,* ill. by Nedda Walker. Dutton, 1947.

———. *Patsy Jefferson of Monticello,* ill. by Nedda Walker. Dutton, 1948. 11-14

WIBBERLEY, LEONARD. *Wes Powell, Conqueror of the Grand Canyon.* Farrar, 1958. One of America's little-known heroes is Wes Powell, who explored the Colorado River and Grand Canyon and foresaw the importance of irrigation for arid western lands. 11-16

WILSON, HAZEL. *The Story of Mad Anthony Wayne,* ill. by Lawrence Beall Smith. Grosset, 1953 (Signature Book). 10-13

WYATT, EDGAR. *Cochise: Apache Warrior and Statesman,* ill. by Allan Houser. Whittlesey (McGraw), 1953.

———. *Geronimo, the Last Apache War Chief,* ill. by Allan Houser. Whittlesey (McGraw), 1952. Stories of two great Indian heroes. 11-14

YATES, ELIZABETH. *Amos Fortune, Free Man,* ill. by Nora S. Unwin. Dutton, 1950. Newbery Medal. 10-13

OTHER HISTORICAL FIGURES

See also Collections of biographical sketches.

BAKER, NINA BROWN. *He Wouldn't Be King: The*

Story of Simón Bolivar, ill. by Camilio Egas. Vanguard, 1941.

______. *Robert Bruce: King of Scots.* Vanguard, 1948.

______. *Sir Walter Raleigh.* Harcourt, 1950. This author can be depended upon to write an exciting biography, somewhat fictionalized but authentic in the main and exceedingly readable. 12-14

BLACKSTOCK, JOSEPHINE. *Songs for Sixpence: A Story About John Newbery,* ill. by Maurice Bower. Follett, 1955. The story of one of the earliest publishers of books for children. *F* 9-12

BRAYMER, MARJORIE. *The Walls of Windy Troy.* Harcourt, 1960. Distinguished biography of Henry Schliemann, who achieved his dream of archaeological research on the site of ancient Troy. 12-16

BULLA, CLYDE. *Song of St. Francis,* ill. by Valenti Angelo. Crowell, 1952. The appealing story of St. Francis of Assisi presented in simple fashion for younger readers. 8-10

CARBONNIER, JEANNE. *Congo Explorer: Pierre Savorgnan de Brazza.* Scribner, 1960. Through peace and friendship rather than conquest, a daring explorer opened the French Congo to colonization. 12-16

COOLIDGE, OLIVIA. *Winston Churchill and the Story of Two World Wars,* ill. with photographs. Houghton, 1960. The twentieth century becomes vividly alive and significant in this story of the great British statesman. 13-16

DE GERING, ETTA. *Seeing Fingers,* ill. by Emil Weiss. McKay, 1962. Beautifully told story of Louis Braille, who was blinded at three, and of his development of the raised alphabet. 11-13

EATON, JEANETTE. *David Livingstone, Foe of Darkness,* ill. by Ralph Ray. Morrow, 1947. As a missionary and explorer, David Livingstone played an important part in the history of Africa.

______. *Gandhi: Fighter Without a Sword,* ill. by Ralph Ray. Morrow, 1950. This is a fine biography of the Hindu nationalist who worked for the political independence of his people. 12-15

______. *Jeanne d'Arc, the Warrior Saint,* ill. by Harve Stein. Harper, 1931. 10-12

GOTTSCHALK, FRUMA. *The Youngest General: A Story of Lafayette,* ill. by Rafaello Busoni. Knopf, 1949. The author had access to unusual original sources in writing this life of Lafayette. 10-14

HALL, ANNA GERTRUDE. *Nansen,* ill. by Boris Artzybasheff. Viking, 1940. Stirring biography of the famous Arctic explorer and Nobel Peace Prize winner. 12-16

KIELTY, BERNARDINE. *Marie Antoinette,* ill. by Douglas Gorsline. Random, 1955 (World Landmark Book). A well-written biography which gives an excellent background of the causes of the French Revolution. 11-14

KING, MARIAN. *Young Mary Stuart, Queen of Scots.* Lippincott, 1954. A moving tale of the young queen which places emphasis on her childhood and the years in France. 11-14

LEIGHTON, MARGARET. *The Story of Florence Nightingale,* ill. by Corinne Dillon. Grosset, 1952 (Signature Book). 9-12

MEIGS, ELIZABETH B. *Candle in the Sky,* ill. by Dorothy Bayley Morse. Dutton, 1953. 11-14

MERCER, CHARLES. *Alexander the Great,* ill. American Heritage, 1963 (Horizon Caravel Book). The stirring account of Alexander's conquests, colorfully illustrated. 13-

MILLS, LOIS. *So Young a Queen.* Lothrop, 1961. Story of the lovely Jadwiga, fourteenth-century queen of Poland. 12-15

NOLAN, JEANNETTE COVERT. *Florence Nightingale,* ill. by George Avison. Messner, 1946. Florence Nightingale's life story stresses her work rather than her personal life. 11-14

PAINE, ALBERT BIGELOW. *Girl in White Armor, the True Story of Joan of Arc.* Macmillan, 1927. This is a fine authentic biography based on careful research. Abridged from the author's adult biography. 12-15

ROOS, ANN. *Man of Molokai: The Life of Father Damien,* ill. by Raymond Lufkin. Lippincott, 1943. Moving story of a great modern saint who spent his life in the service of lepers. 11-14

ROSEN, SIDNEY. *Galileo and the Magic Numbers,* ill. by Harve Stein. Little, 1958. 12-

______. *Doctor Paracelsus,* ill. by Rafaello Busoni. Little, 1959. 12-16

SHIRER, WILLIAM L. *The Rise and Fall of Adolf Hitler,* ill. with photographs. Random, 1961. In this biography of the Nazi dictator, emphasis is on political events, stirringly recorded for younger readers. **11-14**

SYME, RONALD. *Captain Cook: Pacific Explorer,* ill. by William Stobbs. Morrow, 1960. The English navigator's eighteenth-century explorations of the South Pacific climax a fast-paced, fully illustrated biography. 10-13

______. *Cortés of Mexico,* ill. by William Stobbs. Morrow, 1951. An introductory story of Cortés' exploration and conquest. 10-14

______. *The Man Who Discovered the Amazon,* ill. by William Stobbs. Morrow, 1958. Francisco de Orellana's danger-ridden eighteen months' journey of exploration across South America offers a superb tale of human courage and endurance. 10-14

THOMAS, M. Z. (pseud.). *Alexander von Humboldt,* tr. by Elizabeth Brommer, ill. by Ulrik Schramm. Pantheon, 1960. Von Humboldt's adventures in the South American jungles are vivid and unforgettable in this life story of the explorer-naturalist. 11-15

VANCE, MARGUERITE. *Elizabeth Tudor, Sovereign Lady,* ill. by Nedda Walker. Dutton, 1954.

———. *Lady Jane Grey, Reluctant Queen,* ill. by Nedda Walker. Dutton, 1952.

———. *Marie Antoinette, Daughter of an Empress,* ill. by Nedda Walker. Dutton, 1950.

These three stories of young queens are sympathetically and dramatically told and are a stimulus to further historical reading. 12-15

WIBBERLEY, LEONARD. *The Life of Winston Churchill.* Farrar, 1956. An account of the life of one of England's greatest notables, from his mischievous childhood to retirement as Prime Minister. Told with humor and dignity. 12-16

WILSON, HAZEL. *The Little Marquise: Madame Lafayette,* ill. by Paul A. Sagsoorian. Knopf, 1957. Lafayette's aristocratic wife emerges as a figure of unforgettable courage as she shares his imprisonment and fights for his freedom. 12-15

———. *The Story of Lafayette,* ill. by Edy Legrand. Grosset, 1952 (Signature Book). 10-12

ARTISTS

See also Collections of biographical sketches.

CRAVEN, THOMAS. *The Rainbow Book of Art* (see Bibliography, Chapter 19).

FISHER, CLYDE. *The Life of Audubon,* ill. by John James Audubon. Harper, 1949. Written by a former staff member of the American Museum of Natural History, this biography is enhanced with reproductions of Audubon's own paintings in black and white and full color. 10-14

HENRY, MARGUERITE, and WESLEY DENNIS. *Benjamin West and His Cat Grimalkin,* ill. by Wesley Dennis. Bobbs, 1947. *F* 9-12

LANE, MARGARET. *The Tale of Beatrix Potter: A Biography,* ill. by Beatrix Potter. Warne, 1946. Delightful story of the Victorian artist whose Peter Rabbit tales have delighted young children. 13-16

NEWCOMB, COVELLE. *The Secret Door: The Story of Kate Greenaway,* ill. by Addison Burbank. Dodd, 1946. Entertaining fictional biography about one of the popular early illustrators for children. 12-15

RIPLEY, ELIZABETH. *Botticelli,* ill. with reproductions. Lippincott, 1960. Other biographies in this series include *Dürer* (Lippincott, 1958), *Goya* (Walck, 1956), *Leonardo da Vinci* (Walck, 1952), *Winslow Homer* (Walck, 1963), *Michelangelo* (Walck, 1953), *Picasso* (Lippincott, 1959), *Raphael* (Lippincott, 1961), *Rembrandt* (Walck, 1955), *Rubens* (Walck, 1957), *Titian* (Lippincott, 1962), and *Vincent van Gogh* (Walck, 1954).

MUSICIANS

See also Collections of biographical sketches.

ARNOLD, ELLIOTT. *Finlandia: The Story of Sibelius,* ill. by Lolita Granahan. Holt, 1950 (Holt Musical Biography Series). Biography of the great Finnish composer who through his music interpreted the spirit of his people. 12-15

BENÉT, LAURA. *Enchanting Jenny Lind,* ill. by George G. Whitney. Dodd, 1939. 12-14

DEUCHER, SYBIL. *Edvard Grieg, Boy of the Northland,* ill. by Mary Greenwalt. Dutton, 1946. 9-10

EWEN, DAVID. *Leonard Bernstein: A Biography for Young People.* Chilton, 1960. Story of the notable American composer and conductor. 13-

———. *The Story of George Gershwin,* ill. by Graham Bernbach. Holt, 1943 (Holt Musical Biography Series). Memories of an American composer of popular music by a personal friend. 12-16

———. *Tales from the Vienna Woods: The Story of Johann Strauss,* ill. by Edgard Cirlin. Holt, 1944. The composer of some of the best-loved dance music is presented against a background of romantic nineteenth-century Vienna. 12-14

GOSS, MADELEINE. *Beethoven: Master Musician,* ill. by Carl Schultheiss. Holt, 1946 (Holt Musical Biography Series).

———. *Deep Flowing Brook: The Story of Johann Sebastian Bach,* ill. by Elinore Blaisdell. Holt, 1938. Mrs. Goss writes unusually perceptive and comprehensive studies of musicians and their works. Her books are highly recommended. 12-16

KELLOGG, CHARLOTTE. *Paderewski.* Viking, 1956. 13-

KIELTY, BERNARDINE. *Jenny Lind Sang Here.* Houghton, 1959. 10-13

KOMROFF, MANUEL. *Mozart,* ill. by Warren Chappell and with photographs. Knopf, 1956. Written to commemorate the two-hundredth anniversary of Mozart's birth, this is an outstanding biography. 11-15

LINGS, ANN M. *John Philip Sousa.* Holt, 1954. Entertaining biography of the composer and conductor who was known as the "March King." 12-15

PURDY, CLAIRE. *Antonin Dvorák: Composer from Bohemia.* Messner, 1950. A warm and sympathetic story of a great musician. 13-

———. *He Heard America Sing: The Story of Stephen Foster,* ill. by Dorothea Cooke. Messner, 1940. 12-14

WHEELER, OPAL. *Ludwig Beethoven, and the Chiming Tower Bells,* ill. by Mary Greenwalt. Dutton, 1942. 9-10

WHEELER, OPAL, and SYBIL DEUCHER. *Franz Schubert and His Merry Friends,* ill. by Mary Greenwalt. Dutton, 1939.

———. *Joseph Haydn: The Merry Little Peasant,* ill. by Mary Greenwalt. Dutton, 1936.

———. *Mozart, the Wonder Boy,* ill. by Mary Greenwalt. Dutton, 1934.

———. *Sebastian Bach: the Boy from Thuringia,* ill. by Mary Greenwalt. Dutton, 1937. 9-10

WYMER, NORMAN. *Gilbert and Sullivan.* Dutton, 1962, 1963. A distinguished and authoritative biography of England's famous composers of light opera. 12-

WRITERS

See also Collections of biographical sketches and Bibliography, Chapters 6-8, Biographies of Poets.

BECKER, MAY L. *Presenting Miss Jane Austen,* ill. by Edward Price. Dodd, 1952. This picture of the life and times of Jane Austen, written by an Austen enthusiast, is a good introduction to the novels. 14-16

BENÉT, LAURA. *The Boy Shelley,* ill. by James MacDonald. Dodd, 1937. Well written, a tragic record of a school's changing the whole temper of a boy. 13-16

———. *Young Edgar Allan Poe,* ill. by George G. Whitney. Dodd, 1941. Sympathetic portrayal of a gifted, ill-fated writer. 13-16

COLLIN, HEDVIG. *Young Hans Christian Andersen,* ill. by author. Viking, 1955. Sensitively told story of the Danish writer from his childhood years to his first literary recognition. 11-14

DEUTSCH, BABETTE. *Walt Whitman: Builder for America,* ill. by Rafaello Busoni. Messner, 1941. A sensitive study of the man, illustrated with copious selections from his poems. 14-16

EATON, JEANETTE. *America's Own Mark Twain,* ill. by Leonard Everett Fisher. Morrow, 1958. Mississippi riverboat days and life in the West are absorbing highlights of this well-rounded story of one of America's most colorful authors. 12-16

FRANCHERE, RUTH. *Jack London: The Pursuit of a Dream.* Crowell, 1962. The author has skillfully conveyed the poverty, the rough adventurous life, and the taste of glory achieved by London in his brief forty years, without emphasizing the details more suited to an adult biography. 12-

———. *Willa,* ill. by Leonard Weisgard. Crowell, 1958. Willa Cather's pioneer childhood in Nebraska is vividly portrayed, and younger readers unfamiliar with her novels will enjoy the biography as a good story. 11-14

GITTINGS, ROBERT, and JO MANTON. *The Story of John Keats,* ill. by Susan Einzig. Dutton, 1963. An outstanding and objectively written story of the young English poet who in his short life created lyrics of rare loveliness. 14-

GRAY, ELIZABETH JANET. *Young Walter Scott,* ill. by Kate Seredy. Viking, 1935. 12-14

GURKO, MIRIAM. *Restless Spirit: The Life of Edna St. Vincent Millay.* Crowell, 1962. With rare skill, the biographer has achieved a rounded picture of the life and creative output of this gifted American poet and has related her as well to her talented contemporaries. 14-

HARLOW, ALVIN F. *Joel Chandler Harris: Plantation Story Teller,* ill. by W. C. Nims. Messner, 1941. A fine account of the lovable creator of Uncle Remus. 12-15

JACKSON, PHYLLIS WYNN. *Victorian Cinderella,* ill. by Elliott Means. Holiday, 1947. Good picture of the life and times of Harriet Beecher Stowe. F 12-15

JARDEN, MARY LOUISE. *The Young Brontës: Charlotte and Emily, Branwell and Anne,* ill. by Helen Sewell. Viking, 1938. An exceedingly well-written biography for girls who are interested in the Brontës. 14-16

MC NEER, MAY. *America's Mark Twain,* ill. by Lynd Ward. Houghton, 1962. Colorful illustrations and a lively text make this biography attractive to a wide range of readers. 10-14

MEIGS, CORNELIA. *Invincible Louisa,* ill. with photographs. Little, 1933. Newbery Medal. 12-16

PAINE, ALBERT BIGELOW. *Boys' Life of Mark Twain: The Story of a Man Who Made the World Laugh and Love Him.* Harper, 1916. This book captures the spirit and individuality of the great humorist. 14-16

PROUDFIT, ISABEL. *River Boy: The Story of Mark Twain,* ill. by W. C. Nims. Messner, 1940. An excellent life of the author of *Tom Sawyer* for older boys and girls. 12-14

———. *The Treasure Hunter, the Story of Robert Louis Stevenson,* ill. by Hardie Gramatky. Messner, 1939. A full-length biography of a favorite children's author. 10-14

WAITE, HELEN. *How Do I Love Thee? The Story of Elizabeth Barrett Browning.* Macrae, 1953. An absorbing story of the Victorian poetess, climaxed by her romance with Robert Browning. 12-16

WILDER, LAURA INGALLS. *On the Way Home,* ill. with photographs. Harper, 1962. Rose Wilder Lane has supplemented her mother's recently found diary of the journey from South Dakota to their permanent home in Mansfield, Missouri, in 1894. It will be welcomed by countless enthusiasts of the *Little House* series. 10-

MISCELLANEOUS

BONTEMPS, ARNA. *The Story of George Washington Carver,* ill. by Harper Johnson. Grossett, 1954 (Signature Book). 11-15

BURT, OLIVE. *Luther Burbank: Boy Wizard,* ill. by

Clotilde Embree Funk. Bobbs, 1948 (Childhood of Famous Americans Series). *F* 9-10

BYRD, RICHARD E. *Alone.* Putnam, 1938. 14-

CLAPESATTLE, HELEN. *The Mayo Brothers.* Houghton, 1962. Lively and warmly human story of the two great doctors whose professional careers paralleled times of great progress in medicine. 12-15

DALGLIESH, ALICE. *Ride on the Wind,* ill. by Georges Schreiber. Scribner, 1956. Miss Dalgliesh has skillfully retold the boyhood and famous flight of Charles Lindbergh for children too young to read *The Spirit of St. Louis.* 6-10

DESMOND, ALICE CURTIS. *Bewitching Betsy Bonaparte,* ill. with photographs. Dodd, 1958. A romantic biography tells the story of Baltimore belle Betsy Patterson and her ill-fated marriage to Napoleon's younger brother Jerome. 14-

DOOLEY, THOMAS A. *Doctor Tom Dooley: My Story,* rev. ed. Farrar, 1962. This personal account of a heroic young doctor's medical work in the Far East is adapted for younger readers from his earlier books. 11-15

FABER, DORIS. *Printer's Devil to Publisher; Adolph S. Ochs of the New York Times.* Messner, 1963. A vital and absorbing biography of one of the world's greatest newspaper men, who gave renewed life to the failing *New York Times* through his high standards and original thinking. 12-15

FOSDICK, HARRY EMERSON. *Martin Luther,* ill. by Steele Savage. Random, 1956 (World Landmark Book). Written by one of the best-known Protestant ministers, this is a thoughtful biography of the great reformer. 12-16

GRAHAM, SHIRLEY. *Booker T. Washington: Educator of Hand, Head, and Heart.* Messner, 1955.

———. *The Story of Phyllis Wheatley,* ill. by Robert Burns. Messner, 1949.

GRAHAM, SHIRLEY, and GEORGE LIPSCOMB. *Dr. George Washington Carver: Scientist,* ill. by Elton C. Fax. Messner, 1944.

A trio of biographies about famous Negroes who made contributions in the fields of literature, education, and science. 11-15

GUTHRIE, ANNE. *Madame Ambassador: The Life of Vijaya Lakshmi Pandit,* ill. with photographs. Harcourt, 1962. Both an absorbing personal story of India's great stateswoman and a unique picture of India's changing history. 13-16

HERRON, EDWARD A. *First Scientist of Alaska.* Messner, 1958. The story of William Healey Dall, who as a dedicated naturalist explored the wild Alaska territory in post-Civil War days. 12-

———. *Wings over Alaska.* Messner, 1959. In his brief adventurous life which ended in a plane crash in Siberia, Carl Ben Eielson made Alaskan flight history as an explorer and a commercial and air-mail pilot. 12-15

HOLT, RACKHAM [pseud. for Margaret V. Holt]. *George Washington Carver.* Doubleday, 1942. 14-

JOHNSON, OSA. *I Married Adventure.* Lippincott, 1940. 12-

LATHAM, JEAN LEE. *On Stage, Mr. Jefferson,* ill. by Edward Shenton. Harper, 1958. The story of a great actor from his early stage-struck years until his great dramatic achievement as Rip Van Winkle. 12-

LAVINE, SIGMUND. *Steinmetz: Maker of Lightning,* ill. with photographs. Dodd, 1955. This biography of the crippled German immigrant is a happy combination of good characterization and scientific information. 13-

LAWSON, ROBERT. *They Were Strong and Good,* ill. by author. Viking, 1940. *F* 8-12

MC CONNELL, JANE, *Cornelia.* Crowell, 1959. Youthful Cornelia Hancock literally had to fight her way into serving as a Civil War nurse in a period when only mature women were considered adequate. 12-15

MAC GREGOR-HASTIE, ROY. *Pope John XXIII,* ill. with photographs. Criterion, 1962. There is humor, vitality, and reverence in this fine biography of the "Pope of Peace." 11-

MAC LEAN, ALISTAIR. *Lawrence of Arabia.* Random, 1962. The absorbingly told life story of the great military leader in the Arab-Turkish revolt. 11-14

MC NEER, MAY. *John Wesley,* ill. by Lynd Ward. Abingdon, 1951.

———. *Martin Luther,* ill. by Lynd Ward. Abingdon, 1953.

Rousing biographies of two great religious leaders. Methodist John Wesley is easier for children to understand. The fighting spirit of Martin Luther makes his complex life both difficult and thrilling. Superb illustrations add distinction to these books. 12-14

MALVERN, GLADYS. *Dancing Star: The Story of Anna Pavlova,* ill. by Susanne Suba. Messner, 1942. 13-

MANTON, JO. *The Story of Albert Schweitzer,* ill. by Astrid Walford. Abelard, 1955. Beautifully written biography of the famous musician and missionary to Africa. 12-16

MURCHIE, GUY, JR. *The World Aloft,* ill. by author. Houghton, 1960. An abridgment of the author's *Song of the Sky,* this is an outstanding portrayal of the flier's world. Technical knowledge and love of nature are enriched with personal anecdotes. 13-

POWER-WATERS, ALMA. *The Story of Young Edwin Booth,* ill. with photographs. Dutton, 1955. Ill-fated young Edwin Booth finally rose above the blows of fate that were crowned with his brother's assassination of Lincoln. Written with distinction and penetration. 12-16

STEFFENS, LINCOLN. *Boy on Horseback,* ill. by Sanford Tousey. Harcourt, 1935. The boyhood of Lincoln Steffens taken from his adult autobiography. 12-16

STERNE, EMMA GELDERS. *Mary McLeod Bethune,* ill. by Raymond Lufkin. Knopf, 1957. A substantial biography about the child of a slave-born mother who did so much to advance the education of her people. 12-16

STOUTENBURG, ADRIEN, and LAURA N. BAKER. *Snowshoe Thompson,* ill. by Victor De Pauw. Scribner, 1957. In the early mining days of the West, Norwegian-born Jack Thompson made skis to carry mail in the Sierras. His story is a saga of unselfish service, heroic rescues, and dangers from wild animals. 12-

SWIFT, HILDEGARDE. *From the Eagle's Wing: A Biography of John Muir,* ill. by Lynd Ward. Morrow, 1962. 12-

SYME, RONALD. *African Traveler,* ill. by Jacqueline Tomes. Morrow, 1962. A British woman exploring West Africa alone was unprecedented in the 1890's but Mary Kingsley did just that. A colorful biography with a blending of heroism and humor. 11-15

WALDECK, THEODORE J. *On Safari* (see Bibliography, Chapter 14).

WASHINGTON, BOOKER T. *Up from Slavery.* Houghton, 1917. 12-

WELLS, HELEN. *Barnum, Showman of America,* ill. by Leonard Vosburgh. McKay, 1957. Barnum's life spanned a dramatic era in American history, and the author gives an outstanding and highly entertaining picture of the man and his times. 12-

WONG, JADE SNOW. *Fifth Chinese Daughter,* ill. by Kathryn Uhl. Harper, 1950. Fine writing distinguishes this autobiography of a young girl raised in an American Chinatown, with the usual conflict between old and new ways. 12-

WOOD, LAURA. *Raymond L. Ditmars: His Exciting Career with Reptiles, Animals and Insects,* ill. with photographs. Messner, 1944. The early struggles of a young scientist to obtain and study the snakes that became his life work will interest young animal-lovers. 10-14

Reading Follows Many Paths

part five

18. Reading for Information

19. Reading and Creative Expression

20. Reading and the Mass Media

21. Reading in the Family

chapter 18

Reading for Information

As the name implies, informational books, in contrast to books of fiction, are primarily concerned with facts. The distinction between these two types is somewhat nebulous in the books for younger children. For example, Elsa Beskow's *Pelle's New Suit,* like a book of fiction, tells an interesting story, but, like the informational books, is based on facts—explanation of the various steps that go into the making of a suit. In books for older children, the distinction is usually more marked. Their informational books ordinarily have no obvious story framework, though the authors usually try to present facts interestingly.

One glance at a well-stocked library for children reveals an astonishing variety of fine informational books. For the social studies there have never been such varied and delightful books, some focused on geography, some on history, some on the better understanding of other peoples, and some designed to correlate with popular school units. There are also innumerable science books which not only are good reference books but are a stimulus to new science interests. In this chapter we will discuss informational books in these two main categories—social studies and science.

There are so many informational books available today and so many new ones appearing each year that it would be impossible to review even the most important of such books in one chapter. However, this chapter will set up the criteria for judging these books, discuss how these books can be used, and consider a few noteworthy examples of informational books in the general categories in which they might be organized.

Criteria for Informational Books

The first chapter of this book speaks about man's hungry curiosity which through the centuries has kept him searching for more accurate information in more and more fields.

Shepherds of long ago wondered about the stars and kept records of them. They were the first astronomers, and star lore and mathematics were early studies in man's search for exact knowledge. Each succeeding generation has advanced the total information of the race along many lines. Children today are born into a world which has assembled and systematized that information in numberless books which are usually called by the names of their subjects: geography, astronomy, physics, ornithology, or history. But children's books carry no such ponderous titles. Their informational books are called variously *Big Tree; Men, Microscopes, and Living Things; Paddle-to-the-Sea; The World in Space*. The books as well as their titles are often designed to attract children to subjects they might otherwise pass by. But are these books reliable? Can a child use them and depend upon them? Do they give adequate and not oversimplified information? These are some of the questions adults should ask about the factual books they are examining for children, and these are some of the tests the books should pass before we recommend them to children.

ACCURACY

Accuracy is the most important criterion for judging any informational book. There has never been a greater need for accurate information in many fields than there is today to help counteract the widely disseminated misinformation to which children and adults are continually subjected. Through discussions with children, you can discover their gullibilities and encourage them to check so-called facts in reliable sources. This is one way of arming children against overcredulity and teaching them to weigh arguments, question sources, and search for facts.

But if we supply children with factual information which is out of date or superficial, we only add to their confusion. Suppose, for instance, we give children purportedly modern books about the Holland of picturesque costumes and quaint, old-fashioned customs or about the old China of rickshaws and queues or about the South America of primitive Indian villages only. Meanwhile, newspapers, magazines, and television newscasts show them pictures of progressive Holland today, China in a state of revolution, and large South American cities. Discerning children can only conclude that their books are less reliable references than other sources. Furthermore, they are not able to check the accuracy of many of their materials and they are prone to accept what "the book says." So it is imperative that every statement and the implications of every statement in such books be as sound as recent information can guarantee.

At the same time we must recognize that accuracy is necessarily qualified to some extent as we simplify scientific information for young readers. For example, in a description of our solar system for young students, certain points would be omitted and so we could not call this account scrupulously accurate. Actually in judging children's informational books, we must also consider how useful, meaningful, and interesting they are. And what is useful, meaningful, and interesting information differs at each age level.

CONVENIENT PRESENTATION

When we are searching for information, we want the material presented in such a way that we can find what we are looking for quickly and easily. This is equally true of children. The three-year-old wants an airplane book with pictures so clear that he can see everything he wants to know about. The eight-year-old needs bird books in which he can identify his specimen by colors and size. He does not know species yet—that will come later—and the only clues he is sure of are color and size. Older children and adults look for detailed indexing, perhaps from several points of view, pronouncing guides, and headings as keys to the organization of the text. To present materials conveniently, authors must consider the age and the needs of the readers and must provide the kind of clues they can use most readily.

CLARITY

The information we are seeking must be so clearly stated that we come away from our reading satisfied that we have some grasp of the subject. If an eight-year-old turns to books for information about electricity but cannot comprehend the material, he is not likely to repeat the process. Clarity for one age may be befuddlement for another. Children need informational books they can read and understand. But books need not be babyish or talk down to children in order to be comprehensible. Youngsters sense patronage instantly and resent it. Information for any age level should be written directly and sensibly, with obvious respect for the reader's intelligence.

ADEQUATE TREATMENT

When we are in search of facts, we want to be supplied with sufficient details to leave us reasonably certain about at least a small area of information. The amount of detail to give children is always a ticklish question. Too many details confuse them; too few make for an oversimplification that may be misleading. We have to weigh factual books for children with their ages and experiences in mind. Irrelevant details that clutter up the important ideas and obscure the facts children are seeking are especially bad. In this respect some of the early science books for children which used personification in story form were poor. The child who asks how all the trees got into the forest does not want to hear about old Mother South Wind and little Sara Seedling, who grew up into a great big tree; he wants his facts, clear, straight, and amplified sufficiently so that he gets a fair picture of the process of foresting. Certainly enough significant information must be given for children to form a realistic and balanced picture.

STYLE

If, in addition to measuring up to these utilitarian standards, informational books are well and interestingly written, so much the better. The child who finds his geography or his history text full of lively facts is more apt to return to the text with a hopeful heart. If it is not interesting, he may still use it if it answers some of his questions, but he will not cherish it as he might a better composed narrative. A lively, well-written book is an invaluable aid to learning.

These are the qualities we look for in all informational books for both adults and children —accuracy (first and above all), convenient presentation, clarity, adequate treatment, and an interesting style. For children's books we'll add pictures—pictures so colorful and appealing that they will make readers and even specialists of the children.

Books for the Social Studies

Through television, class trips, and personal experiences, children have a variety of interests in the area of the social studies. To meet this variety of interests, there is an equal variety of books. By furnishing additional details and interesting information, these books complement the necessarily brief and survey-type treatment of the textbook.

FOR YOUNGER CHILDREN

For the very youngest there are picture books charmingly illustrated which give information while acquainting children with the pleasures of extracting knowledge from between the covers of a book. Tasha Tudor's *Around the Year* has a simple rhymed text for the months of the year an easy way to become acquainted with months and seasons. Other aspects of the abstract concept of time are dealt with in picture books like *The True Book of Time* by Feenie Ziner and Elizabeth Thompson. Children learn that time is measured in many ways other than by watches and clocks. Miriam Schlein's *It's About Time* gives children interesting answers to their questions on this subject and the puzzling relationships implied in "long time, short time," and so on.

Other picture books give young children ideas of the work of people in their communities. They learn about city helpers in *The True Book of Policemen and Firemen* by Irene Miner, and in *The First Book of Firemen* by Benjamin Brewster. Children who have some reading skills as well as those who can "read" only pictures will find especially thrilling *The Big Book of Real Fire Engines, The Big Book of Real Trains,* and *The Big Book of Real Building and Wrecking Machines,* all by George Zaffo. *The Big Book of Real Fire Engines,* for example, through its brief text describes fire equipment in use today, while its colored pictures on every page provide information about such things as common fire hazards, the mechanics of the fire alarm system, and a night with a fireman on duty.

Many of the informational books for the youngest are more fictional than factual. This may be seen in the inclusion of characters like the readers themselves with whom the latter can identify, and in the interweaving of small plots and activities. Such books fill a need for children up to the time when they ask their inevitable "Is it true?" "Is it real?" When they want facts, whether in science or social studies, informational books are required. Not too many well-written books are yet available, however, in the area of nonfiction for children of picture-reading age.

Once he has mastered the art of reading on his own, the young child finds worlds of enchantment open to him. He no longer needs to wait until some busy adult finds time to answer his questions. He can have the satisfaction of immediate answers, of "finding it myself." Among the easier informational books available to inquisitive young readers today are *Let's Take a Trip to a Fire House* and *Let's Go to the Library* by Naomi Buchheimer. These books would be good to read either before or after such trips.

The trend toward illustrating informational books with photographs to clarify social-studies concepts is exemplified in a picture-story produced by the Encyclopaedia Britannica, *We Learn About Other Children.*

FOR OLDER CHILDREN

The incomparable thrill of discovery is not reserved for world explorers and daring scientists. The young reader whose curiosity has led him to pages which dramatically portray conquests, pioneering in the wilderness, or the building of skyscrapers can also experience the excitement of discovery.

Several authors have presented a survey of mankind's development to the current stage of civilization. Hendrik Willem Van Loon's

Types of clothing

This collection of clothing demonstrates that man's dress reflects the conditions of his environment. Illustration by W. T. Mars and Jan Fairservis. From People and Places *by Margaret Mead. Illustrations copyright © 1959 by The World Publishing Company. Reprinted by permission of the publisher. (Book 8¼ x 11, picture 7 x 4½)*

The artist's use of bold contrasts and misty details seems especially appropriate for this book about the beginnings of our world. Illustration by Leonard Weisgard. From First Days of the World *by Gerald Ames and Rose Wyler. Pictures copyright © 1958 by Leonard Weisgard. Reprinted by permission of Harper & Row, Publishers. (Original in color, book 7½ x 9¾, picture 5½ x 3¼)*

The Story of Mankind, which received the first Newbery Medal, is the history of man's origin and evolution. The author traces man from his beginnings through all the major stages of historical development; for example, the wanderings of the Jews, Caesar's western conquests, the rise of towns, the period of explorations and discoveries, the rise of factories and machinery. There are brief glimpses of the development of the arts, and the whole panorama is illumined with Van Loon's inimitable sketches. Writing about *The Story of Mankind* in the *Horn Book,* Frances Clarke Sayers said:

> *Van Loon gave a whole generation of writers in the field of nonfiction the courage to be learned and gay at one and the same time. After* The Story of Mankind, *the death knell was rung for any book which did not communicate to children the excitement which should be inherent in all processes of learning.*[1]

Because of its detailed and comprehensive content this book may be designated for the more sophisticated readers in the upper grades and junior high school.

Another survey of world history is provided by the illustrated book *The Golden History of the World* by Jane Watson, written for children in the intermediate grades. Geographic concepts are explained in simple text and with good pictures in Elsa Werner's *Golden Geography* and in V. M. Hillyer's *A Child's Geography of the World,* revised in 1951 by Edward Huey. These books are useful in the classroom or home as supplementary reading when children want more information than is supplied by their textbooks. Munro Leaf's *Geography Can Be Fun* is a good beginning geography written with the author's usual humor.

Many of the recent books for children have been written with the objective of making the story of man's past and present a "real experience" rather than a superficial one. One stimulating volume to which older children can be guided is *People and Places* by Margaret Mead. The book is richly informative, springing out of Miss Mead's expert knowledge of people and countries. She begins her first chapter, "Man's Discovery of Man," by stating that human beings are curious about each other and even the most primitive peoples in the world today wonder about those unlike themselves. Next she progresses to a discussion of "How Some Peoples Live," giving a fascinating picture of the Eskimos, the Indians of the Plains, the Balinese, and others. She concludes her book with discussions about "Man Asks About Man," in which she talks about similarities and differences among peoples of the world. She also offers suggestions as to what steps must be taken to solve man's problems so that all may live in a more orderly world. All in all, Margaret Mead's book challenges its readers to a deeper understanding not only of themselves but also of other people and places.

Why We Live Where We Live by Eva Knox Evans helps children develop an understanding of the interdependence of people and the limitations of geographic conditions upon the choice of homes. The author has included a personal touch in her final chapter, entitled "Your Own Home Town," in which she suggests that the reader do some research on his own town. In *The Growing Human Family* by Minocheher Masani, chil-

1. *The Horn Book,* May-June 1944, p. 157.

dren learn concepts of social organizations, from the family unit to the plans for world government proposed for the future.

Books About Man's Past

PREHISTORIC AND ANCIENT TIMES

What was it like long ago? What did cave men eat and wear? What kinds of weapons did medieval people have? Children raise questions like these and countless more as they begin to delve into the past. In answer to such questions, many excellent books have appeared recently by authors who have documented their accounts with research findings. In many cases, the writers were actually on the scene themselves as they collected data. In other cases, they reported examining diaries and other written records upon which they based their writings. Through books, children can become armchair archaeologists and discover facts and legends about the past.

Children *do* learn about the past from books of historical fiction, where the narrative enlivens the "bones of history." Such books play an important role in interesting children in the past. However, readable factual books are becoming more accessible than formerly to the young and inquisitive student.

First Days of the World and *The First People in the World* by Gerald Ames and Rose Wyler describe the formation of the earth, the evolution of animals, and man's development through the years. The text of these books for middle-graders is clarified by Leonard Weisgard's excellent pictures.

When children develop an interest in the past, they often ask, "How did we find out about times so long ago?" Anne Terry White has provided one answer by describing archaeologists as detectives whose discoveries have helped men piece together the story of past civilizations. Her *All About Archaeology, The First Men in the World,* and *Prehistoric America* describe modern discoveries which have led to a better understanding of prehistoric times.

Another answer to the question of how we learn about the past is given by Victor von Hagen in *Maya, Land of the Turkey and the Deer.* He includes a section in which he tells the reader that his account is based upon documents known and used by scholars.

Most children will understand ancient times better if they can relate those events to some contemporary matters. In Estelle Friedman's *Digging into Yesterday* the author bridges the time-span by stating:

> *The Cretans, 4,000 years ago, played a game like checkers, had circus performances and ate in cafeterias. The Greeks played hockey 2,500 years ago.*[2]

Simple, clear line drawings give an accurate view of details of dress, customs, and rituals of the Mayans. The artist, by giving weight to his line, has evoked the style of Mayan art, chiseled into stone, somewhat stylized yet skillfully delicate.
Illustration by Alberto Beltrán. From Maya, Land of the Turkey and the Deer *by Victor W. von Hagen. Copyright © 1960 by Victor W. von Hagen. Reprinted by permission of The World Publishing Company. (Book 6½ x 9¼, picture 3½ x 2¾)*

2. Estelle Friedman, *Digging into Yesterday,* Putnam, 1958, p. 11.

A brief yet helpful account of the civilization of ancient Egypt is found in *The First Book of Ancient Egypt* by Charles A. Robinson, Jr. One of the *First Book* series, it may be useful as an initial exposure to the impressive kingdom of tombs and temples. The significance of the river Nile with its effect on religion, culture, and agriculture is but one concept presented in the book. The straightforward style of writing helps pupils grasp the somewhat difficult concepts of this period. In contrast to this survey of Egypt is Leonard Cottrell's *Land of the Pharaohs,* a richly detailed history of ancient Egypt. While the text deals mainly with the country during Tutankhamen's reign, it begins and ends with descriptions of the investigations which have clarified our knowledge of the period. The handsome black and white illustrations by Richard Powers are based on ornamentation found in the Pharaoh's tomb.

Generally speaking, books on specific subjects at each level of reading interest and ability are scarce. Therefore, one dealing with an important single subject of ancient Egypt is especially welcome. *The Art of Ancient Egypt* by Shirley Glubok provides a short but delightful introduction to the painting, sculpture, and everyday objects of early Egyptian culture. It appeals to students interested in art, but anyone who enjoys any aspect of Egyptian life will find it satisfying. Reproductions of hieroglyphics are shown and all pictures and color reproductions are accompanied by interpretive texts.

This drawing of the Chinese philosopher Lao-Tzu shows details of dress and one mode of travel in China during the days of Augustus Caesar.
From Augustus Caesar's World *by Genevieve Foster. Copyright, 1947, by Genevieve Foster. Reprinted by permission of Charles Scribner's Sons. (Book 7 x 9¾, picture 4¼ x 3½)*

Charles A. Robinson, Jr., has given us a valuable book about another ancient civilization—*The First Book of Ancient Mesopotamia and Persia.* The author tells us:

> *Whenever it began, we know that a highly developed civilization was flourishing in Mesopotamia as long ago as 3000* B.C. *For centuries it lay buried under the drifting sands of a desert waste.*[3]

The book is clearly organized and has helpful photographs. Its wide range of subjects, including a discussion of the first form of writing, invented by Sumerians (cuneiform), and a discussion of the alphabet that we now use, can introduce children to this area of ancient civilization. Professor Robinson is a member of the Commission for Excavation of the Athenian Agora; has taught in America, Rome, and Athens; and has also written *The First Book of Ancient Greece* and *The First Book of Ancient Rome.*

Turning to Greece, we have *Everyday Things in Ancient Greece* by Marjorie and C. H. B. Quennell. In it children can discover what daily living in ancient Greece was like. The book is full of descriptions of the conditions, both common and unique, under which the Greeks lived. Boys and girls will find that this book stirs curiosity, especially if they compare their own experiences with those of the early Greeks.

Chronicles of more recent times tell children of life in other ancient countries that bordered the Mediterranean Sea. *Everyday Life in Ancient Rome* by F. R. Cowell is useful to the student of ancient Roman history and Latin. A comprehensive history of the customs, religions, and economy of these ancient peoples is found in C. B. Falls' *The First 3000 Years,* in which a distinguished

3. Charles Alexander Robinson, Jr., *The First Book of Ancient Mesopotamia and Persia,* Watts, 1962, p. 1.

artist has shown the rise of early civilizations with numerous maps and drawings.

Genevieve Foster describes the culture of China, India, and the Mayans at the time of such historical figures as Augustus Caesar, Cicero, Virgil, and Cleopatra in *Augustus Caesar's World.* In *Birthdays of Freedom, I* she presents a picture of the background of freedom from the discovery of fire to the fall of Rome in 476 A.D. The account is continued to the signing of the Declaration of Independence in *Birthdays of Freedom, II.* After older students have acquired a good knowledge of world history, they can use these books as supplementary reading to tie together people and events of the times. Recognition of Genevieve Foster's *World* books has been on an international scale. They have been widely translated because of their interpretation of our country and their contribution to better world understanding. They take a horizontal view of life around the world at the different periods of each man's life: birth, childhood, youth, maturity, and death. The idea grew, she tells us, when in the course of the usual vertical study of history she was always wondering what was happening in other parts of the world at the same time. In this world's-eye view of various periods, children see trends develop and then disappear, history-making men emerge and vanish, leaving behind them ruin or a better world. The effect is curiously impressive. These fascinating books provide children with a rounded sense of a period, seldom to be found in a textbook. Mrs. Foster makes great leaders in other countries alive and memorable. Only an author-artist with a remarkable sense of design could integrate her text and illustrations as Mrs. Foster does.

All the illustrations in this book give details characteristic of medieval life. Here we have information about the structure and interior of a castle, the clothing, the eating customs, and some typical forms of entertainment.
From Knights and Castles and Feudal Life *by Walter Buehr. © 1957 by Walter Buehr. Reprinted by permission of the publisher, G. P. Putnam's Sons. (Book 6¼ x 8)*

THE MIDDLE AGES (476-1500 A.D.)

The fall of Rome led to the so-called Middle or Dark Ages and to a whole new set of concepts and beliefs. This period of conflict and of varied ways of life was marked by the rise of the Christian Church, the conquests of the Mohammedans, the Crusades, feudalism, and the Hundred Years' War. For children, this era can be made exciting, inspiring, and not unlike their own in some ways. Just as Christians strove for freedom and progress, so people today strive to preserve and widen these same ideals.

The Crusaders by Walter Buehr gives a vivid picture of the medieval period. He tells us:

In autumn of the year 1095, in south central France, a crowd of nearly two thousand stood in silence to hear the words of one of the greatest men of the day. . . . The Christians of Europe were about to begin an in-

credible series of journeys to the holy city of Jerusalem to try to free it from the hands of the Turks.[4]

This book has a pageantry that holds readers spellbound right up to the last page where the results of the Crusades are revealed, Europe climbing up from the depths of the Dark Ages into a new period of creativity. Unusual in information and tone, the book makes the reader feel that he has actually taken part in one of the important movements in history.

The First Book of Medieval Man by Donald Sobol is a factual account of life in the Middle Ages during the time of Richard the Lion-Hearted. Technical terms are defined for upper-grade readers. In Christine Price's *Made in the Middle Ages* excellent illustrations accompany the account of the craftsmen and their work in making armor, jewelry, and other items used in the castles and cathedrals. Further information about life in medieval castles is furnished in *Knights and Castles and Feudal Life* by Walter Buehr. Aided by his illustrations, the reader will gain a clear understanding of the medieval castle—its construction, peacetime castle life, and the training of knights. Boys will be interested in the description of various weapons used in sieges of early castles. This book has been followed by the author's well-illustrated *Chivalry and the Mailed Knight.*

This sketch of the "Lost Colony" of Virginia shows a typical early settlement with several buildings within the protection of the fort and a few close by.
Illustration by Lois Maloy. From America Begins *by Alice Dalgliesh. Copyright, 1938, © 1958 by Charles Scribner's Sons. Reprinted by permission of the publishers.*
(Book 8 x 8, picture 6 x 2½)

DISCOVERIES IN THE NEW WORLD (1492-1600)

There are several outstanding books that tell about the men who braved the seas to discover the New World. With this period, children become a bit more adept at understanding because the discoveries concern their own country and continent.

The editors of *American Heritage* have written *Discoverers of the New World,* one of a series about American history. Children are intrigued by this book from the moment they turn to the first page and read that America was once the biggest secret on earth. Children today, whose minds are primarily focused "out of this world," may find this puzzling at first, but they soon discover its meaning in this fine book. Illustrated with outstanding paintings in color and in black and white and chronicled in immensely interesting fashion, this is an impressive book for older readers. The text, unlike that in some factual books, offers helpful transitions, and the whole book reads smoothly. From the account of the geographers of the fifteenth century, who believed there was only a scattering of islands in the ocean from Spain to China, to the true story of Sir Francis Drake, who docked in Plymouth, England, in 1580 to tell of his world adventure to the delighted Queen Elizabeth I, this book holds the reader's interest.

Other books which give children a factual account of the early history of America, its discovery, and settlement include Alice Dalgliesh's *America Begins* and Louise Rich's *The First Book of New World Explorers.* And for a record of our country's history from 1492 to the present, we have *The First Book of American History* by the noted historian Henry Steele Commager.

Enid Meadowcroft's *The Land of the Free* reflects the careful study, shown in her bibliography, which preceded the writing of the book. It is a brief history, but it weaves together the straws of events that form America's history from 1492 to the end of the Second World War. Reading like fiction, *The Land of the Free* points out America's failures as well as her triumphs and so places our country's character in true perspective.

4. Walter Buehr, *The Crusaders,* Putnam, 1959, p. 7.

Children will also find much interesting material concerning early discoveries in the biographies which have appeared in recent years. (See Bibliography, Chapter 17.)

COLONIAL AMERICA (1600-1775)

Less than a hundred years after Columbus discovered America, people from the Old World managed to make their way to the New World. Their ideas of courage, the hardships they experienced, and their anticipation of a good future are expressed in books about colonial America. These concepts were not necessarily new to mankind, but the setting in which they were expressed and the circumstances of the history make them important to young American readers.

The Pilgrims and Plymouth Colony, published by American Heritage, affords much interesting supplementary material for older children who have already studied the beginnings of our nation. They will find a map of Plymouth Harbor, drawn by Samuel de Champlain and included in a book printed in 1613. On another page there is a reproduction of a seventeenth-century print of Southhampton Harbor, from which the *Mayflower* sailed.

In *America Is Born: A History for Peter,* Gerald W. Johnson has furnished detailed information concerning the times between 1492 and 1787 along with his interpretation of the ideas and ideals of the era. The author is well known for his historical books for adult readers. Now, in his first volume of a three-part history of the United States for young people, Mr. Johnson presents vividly the emergence of a new nation from the scattered colonies along the Atlantic Coast, showing objectively the roles of the European powers. This latter feature is somewhat unique in historical writings for elementary-school children.

Edwin Tunis has contributed two excellent source books to the period. His *Colonial Living* gives details of life in colonial America, including directions children can follow for making such items as candles, soap, and furniture. This book was awarded the Thomas Alva Edison Foundation Children's Book Award for 1958 for special excellence in portraying America's past. *Indians* is another of Tunis' very readable and profusely illustrated books and is an excellent reference for study of the Indians of the United States. Some of the groups include The Buffalo Hunters, The Desert Townsmen, The Southern Farmers. For each group, the author discusses such aspects of Indian life as food, clothing, dwellings, crafts, communication, weapons, and social customs. To show children the care with which some social-studies books are being prepared today, teachers will want to call attention to the page of acknowledgments, where the author mentions his gratitude for help from the Enoch Pratt Free Library; the Johns Hopkins University Library; the Peabody Institute Library; the Museum of the Modern Indian, Haye Foundation; and the Museum of Natural History.

Using scratchboard technique, that is, scratching black pigment off a white pulp board, Leonard Everett Fisher has re-created a dramatic Revolutionary War battle scene. Illustration by Leonard Everett Fisher. From America Is Born *by Gerald W. Johnson. Copyright © 1959 by Gerald W. Johnson. Reprinted by permission of William Morrow and Company, Inc.*
(Book 6 x 9⅛, picture 5¾ x 5)

Sonia Bleeker has written a number of books about individual tribes in the Western Hemisphere. Among her most recent ones are interesting accounts of the culture and daily life of the Mayas, Aztecs, and Incas. Robert

Hofsinde (Gray-Wolf) has told about Indian customs and traditions, traps and weapons, sign language, and picture writing, in recent books which he illustrated for children. His *Indian Sign Language* shows children how the Indian made a sign for a word. *Indian Picture Writing* gives 248 symbols, with sections on exploit markings, some sample letters in picture writing, and an illustration of the Cree alphabet.

AMERICAN GROWTH AND DEVELOPMENT (1775-1945)

Our colorful history from 1775 to 1945 began with George Washington's struggle for independence and victory in the Revolutionary War and ended with America struggling for world peace in the Second World War.

The American Revolution and the Declaration of Independence are events of special significance for our youngsters. Fortunately, we have a number of good books to offer them about this period of revolution and confederation. *The First Book of the American Revolution* by Richard B. Morris and *The Fourth of July Story* by Alice Dalgliesh will help younger readers understand what these events meant then and what they mean today. Both books are effectively illustrated in color. At the junior-high level *The Golden Book of the American Revolution,* adapted by Fred Cook from the *American Heritage Book of the Revolution,* provides an excellent summary of events leading to the war and covers the tactics of battles on land and sea, the development of our armed forces, the contributions of our allies, and the final victory. Prominent men of the newly formed government are well drawn in *The Great Declaration* by Henry Steele Commager. The author uses excerpts from official documents, letters, and diaries in weaving together the story of the Declaration of Independence.

To help young people better understand this country's early position in world affairs, we can turn to Genevieve Foster's *George Washington's World,* written in the pattern of her other *World* books (see p. 571).

Along with books which tell about the people who were active in this period of America's growth and development are several factual books which give authentic accounts of the whole period. A good example is *America Grows Up: A History for Peter,* the second in Gerald Johnson's trilogy written for his grandson Peter. It describes vividly the influence of people and events on the growth of America from the Revolutionary War to the beginning of World War I.

A stirring and delightful introduction to the history of the United States is Frances Cavanah's *Our Country's Story.* For children eight to ten it gives brief glimpses of Pilgrims and Dutch settlers; of such leaders as Paul Revere, Washington, Boone, and Lincoln; of such events as the Revolution and the Civil War; of such movements as Westward Expansion; of such inventions as trains and airplanes; and it climaxes with the idea of people learning to live together. The text is vigorous and authentic and the pictures are appealing. The ideals of our democracy are shown growing slowly and steadily through people's movements and the national struggle for survival.

The excitement of the gold rush can be enjoyed vicariously by children who pick up *The Alaska Gold Rush* and *The California Gold Rush,* both by May McNeer.

The Hudson River is a chronicle of the river and its Indians and white explorers through the nineteenth century, written by Carl Carmer, an outstanding contributor to authentic literature for children.

THE CIVIL WAR (1861-1865)

Benjamin Franklin once said that there never was a good war or a bad peace. When children read about our Civil War period, they will gain insight into the conflict of ideas that divide men, into the personal sacrifices that men make under war conditions, into the responsibilities undertaken by armies, and into the causes and aftereffects of war. Grim and sad as these events are, the study of the American Civil War may help readers develop the kind of understanding which may prevent future wars.

The Fight for Union by Margaret Coit is excellent for upper-graders who seek more information about the background of that war. Miss Coit, a Pulitzer Prize winner for her biography *John C. Calhoun: American Patriot,* now shares her talent with children in this account of the forty years preceding the Civil War, when men tried, in vain, to keep the Union together. The Missouri Compromise, the Great Debate, and the Texas controversy gain in perspective through her careful appraisal.

A number of books for older boys and girls deal with the actual campaigns and battles on land and water. *The Story of the Civil War* by Red Reeder is the result of his lifetime interest in and study of the Civil War from the point of view of a career army officer. His objective handling of a great mass of detail enables the reader to look with understanding and sympathy upon the strengths and weaknesses of the generals on both sides.

Henry Steele Commager provides added insight into this critical period of our history. In *The Great Proclamation: A Book for Young Americans,* he gives a vivid account, woven from the words of Lincoln, his cabinet, and other citizens, and excerpts from letters and journals, of the thinking and events which led to the Emancipation Proclamation and the Thirteenth Amendment to the Constitution.

Books About Man's Present

NORTH AMERICA

The Picture Map Geography of the United States by Vernon Quinn supplies up-to-date information concerning each state of the Union and its people, together with a pictorial map. *America Moves Forward* by Gerald Johnson is the third in his series for Peter; it shows the history of the United States from 1917 to the present.

Books on American cities have appeared recently. Colorful illustrations in *This is New York* by Miroslav Sasek take the reader on a tour of New York City—its buildings, stores, ferries, Statue of Liberty, and other famous attractions. *Young Folks' New York* by Susanne Szasz and Susan Lyman includes nearly one hundred fifty photographs of children viewing places of interest in the big city. Sam and Beryl Epstein describe the development of Washington and its buildings in *The First Book of Washington, D.C.,* illustrated with photographs. *This is San Francisco* by Miroslav Sasek gives colorful impressions of famous landmarks in and around that historic city, with a brief accompanying text.

Contemporary books with a history and present-day account of the forty-ninth state include *Getting to Know Alaska* by Jim Breetveld and *Alaska: The Forty-Ninth State* by Willis Lindquist. Evelyn Stefansson, wife of the famous Arctic explorer, has written a detailed study in contrasts, an account of both Eskimo family life and contemporary Alaska, in the revised Statehood edition of *Here Is Alaska.* Changing customs and occupations are described and illustrated with photographs in *Alaska: The Land and the People* by Evelyn Butler and George Dale, who wrote out of their own experiences in the Alaska Native Service.

The fiftieth state is represented by a number of well-illustrated small books which capture the attention of young readers. Teachers in intermediate grades will want to have copies of Erna Fergusson's *Hawaii,* Oscar Lewis' *Hawaii: Gem of the Pacific,* and Hester O'Neill's *The Picture Story of Hawaii.* Another book for the room library is *The Islands of Hawaii* by Bradford Smith, illustrated with photographs and including descriptions of Oahu, Kauai, Maui, and Hawaii.

Several books provide information about Canada, our neighbor to the north. Regina Tor, in *Getting to Know Canada,* describes the people of the various provinces, their government, customs, and industries. Lithographs by Lynd Ward help to make May McNeer's *Canadian Story* an exciting account of the history of Canada from the time of the Vikings to the opening of the St. Lawrence Seaway.

Realistic drawings and photographs in *First*

Many of the recent children's books about other lands are illustrated with photographs. Here we see an Eskimo wearing snow goggles fashioned from animal bone—an ingenious solution to the problem of sun glare on snow. Photograph by Richard Harrington. From Here Is the Far North *by Evelyn Stefansson. Charles Scribner's Sons, 1957. Reproduced by permission of the publisher and photographer. (Book 6 x 9, photograph 6 x 7¾)*

Under the North Pole by Commander William Anderson show the atomic submarine *Nautilus* in dry dock before the 1958 cruise, and under way at sea. Navy life and polar explorations are pictured by the skipper of the ship in a scintillating account for young readers. In *Here Is the Far North* Evelyn Stefansson describes her flight from Los Angeles to Copenhagen and provides photographs of Greenland, Iceland, and the Soviet sector. John Euller's *Arctic World,* also with photographs, provides an excellent survey or review of the numerous Arctic explorations. Another authentic account is given by Sergeant F. S. Farrar, RCMP, the first man to circumnavigate the North American continent, as he describes the voyage from notes taken while he was first mate of the little *St. Roch,* in *Arctic Assignment.* Older children interested in life at the poles, experimental work there, and the possibilities for colonization and research will find *The Poles* by Willy Ley and the editors of *Life* an informative account of the Arctic and Antarctic.

Transportation by land and water has a natural setting in the geography and history of a country. Two beautiful books produced by Holling C. Holling illustrate this fact. They constitute a unique contribution to geography, history, and science for children. Because of his painstaking research, the author took three or four years to produce each book. That he should be an artist as well as a scientist is sheer good luck for children. *Paddle-to-the-Sea* is an unusual and excellent book to use with geography. It tells the story of a small canoe made by an Indian boy far to the north, in the Nipigon country. In the tiny canoe the boy placed the kneeling figure of an Indian, carved with his paddle in his hand. On the underside of the canoe the boy wrote: "Please put me back in water. I am Paddle-to-the-Sea." Then he set the Paddle Person afloat in the spring freshets. The Paddle Person traveled far and was often grounded, but someone or some force always set him afloat again and he journeyed all the way to France and back. *Tree in the Trail,* excellent for use in studying our westward movement, is a favorite of many children. It tells the story of what happened under and around one tree that stood on the trail westward. Anthropology, history, geography, and lively imagination make this a notable book. The large colored illustrations of each book are strikingly dramatic, and the marginal drawings by Lucille Holling, the author's wife, carry a wealth of detailed information which adds greatly to the value of these books.

LATIN AMERICA

Several books are useful reference works on the countries and islands of Latin America. Vernon Quinn's *Picture Map Geography of Mexico, Central America and the West Indies* gives a brief description of each country and its products. A history and description of each of the islands can be found in *The First Book of the West Indies* by Langston Hughes. Children of Puerto Rico at work and at play are presented in text with photographs in *Young Puerto Rico* by Jack Manning.

The First Book of South America by William Carter gives an account of the folklore, religions, and history of the continent. Recent books on Brazil include John Caldwell's *Let's Visit Brazil* and Sally Sheppard's *The First Book of Brazil.* Both were written for upper-grade children and are illustrated with photographs. Caldwell has also given us *Let's Visit Argentina,* a general introduction to that country. Sam Olden in *Getting to Know Argentina* takes the reader on a trip from the northern jungle land to the southern tip of the country.

OTHER CITIES AND COUNTRIES

So numerous are the children's books about countries in Europe, Asia, Africa, and other far-flung places, that only a few of the most recent ones can be examined here. Miroslav Sasek has written and illustrated several charming books which show the landmarks and the people of foreign cities. *This is Paris, This is Munich, This is Rome,* and *This is Venice* are a few of the titles. *This is Rome,* for example, is as informative as an Italian travel book and as gay as a Roman holiday. Through his stylized paintings of characteristic scenes of Rome, with photographs of Roman statuary embedded in some of them, and his accompanying text, Sasek does a superb job of presenting the Eternal City as it might appear to a young tourist—as a kaleidoscopic array of strange and fascinating sights with its gaily garbed theological students, whizzing Vespas, imposing relics of antiquity, all of the things which make Rome like no other city in the world. Each of Sasek's books is a distinct contribution to children's knowledge and understanding of people and places.

Children can obtain a realistic view of life in such distant places as England, Holland, Italy, Africa, Ceylon, and Cambodia through studying the photographs as they read *The Land of the English People* by Alicia Street, *Battle Against the Sea* by Patricia Lauber, *The Key to Rome* by Monroe Stearns, *The New Africa* by Ellen and Attilio Gatti, *Ceylon* by Christine Weston, and *Cambodia: Land of Contrasts* by Ruth Tooze—to name a few. Photographs give students the feeling of being eyewitnesses to history and of being "on the scene" in distant lands, even while they sit quietly at home or in school.

Older children will find that they can better understand the current conflicts in Africa after reading John Gunther's books *Meet North Africa, Meet South Africa,* and *Meet the Congo.* These give the geographical, historical, and sociological information which helps to show clearly what are the present-day problems of the people on that continent.

Armstrong Sperry, who has contributed some fine books to children's literature, has produced two informational volumes which reflect his talents as writer and artist: *Pacific Islands Speaking* and *All About the Arctic and Antarctic.*

Books About Man's Work

Today, students of social studies in primary as well as in upper grades will find a good supply of books to satisfy their curiosity about the multiplicity of tasks with which men occupy themselves. The books answer their "how" questions—how we get our water, food, clothing, metals and oil, homes and other buildings; how men solve the problems of communication, transportation, and government. They answer the "what" questions as they describe what types of work men do in various parts of our country and the world; what types of communication, transportation, and government have been developed through the years.

Many recent books give children an understanding of the contemporary scene, while pointing out relationships to the past and future. Among books which give older students a broad overview of their world and its work are Katherine Shippen's *Miracle in Motion: The Story of America's Industry,* Donald Cooke's *Marvels of American Industry,* and Charles Joy's *Race Between Food and People: The Challenge of a Hungry World.*

Henry Lent has written a series of books which describe "Men at Work" in various parts of our country—New England, the South, and the Great Lakes states, among others. Curious middle-graders will enjoy such well-illustrated volumes as *Let's Take a Trip to a Skyscraper* by Sarah Riedman, *Let's Look Under the City* by Herman and Nina Schneider, and *A World Full of Homes* by William Burns.

Boys fascinated by machines will find much to interest them in *Machines at Work* by Mary Elting, *The Tractor Book* by Margaret and Stuart Otto, *Machines That Built America* by Roger Burlingame, and *Engineers Did It!* by Duane Bradley.

Modes of transportation through the years may be explored by the younger children in Anne Alexander's *ABC of Cars and Trucks;* Jeanne Bendick's "First Books" of airplanes, automobiles, and ships; Henry Lent's *Here Come the Trucks;* and Laura Sootin's *Let's Go to an Airport.* Older children will enjoy Walter Buehr's *Railroads Today and Yesterday* and *Trucks and Trucking,* David Cooke's *Dirigibles That Made History,* Beman Lord's

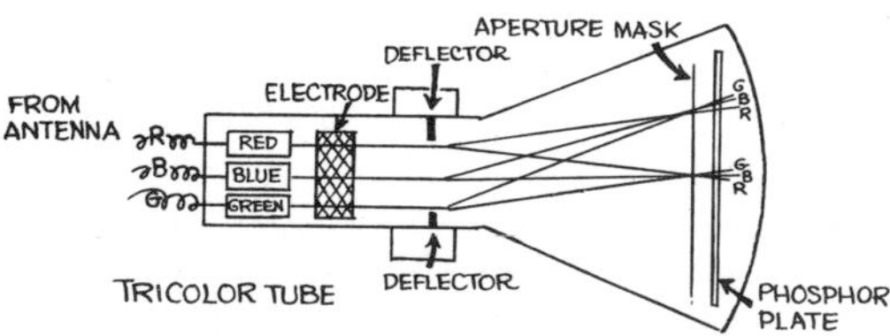

This diagram of a color television tube is a good example of another way to illustrate informational books.
From Television Works Like This *by Jeanne and Robert Bendick. Copyright © 1959 by the McGraw-Hill Book Company, Inc. Reprinted by permission of the publisher. (Book 6½ x 9⅝, picture 6 x 2)*

Look at Cars, and Edwin Hoyt's *From the Turtle to the Nautilus.*

How man has communicated with others through the years and how he has speeded up the process in modern times have been the themes of several well-written books for children. A good overview is given in Julie Batchelor's *Communication: From Cave Writing to Television,* which can be read by middle-graders. Sam and Beryl Epstein have written *The First Book of Words, The First Book of Codes and Ciphers,* and *The First Book of Printing,* all of which help interest the middle-grade student in the romance of our language as a form of communication. Among the books which explain the telephone and television in terms that elementary-school pupils can understand are *Let's Go to the Telephone Company* by Naomi Buchheimer and *Television Works Like This* by Jeanne Bendick.

For their units on government, older children will find several books that clarify the workings of the local, state, and federal government. A background of the history of the constitution is laid in *The First Book of the Constitution* by Richard Morris and *The Great Constitution* by Henry S. Commager. A simplified explanation is presented in *You and the Constitution of the United States* by Paul Witty and Julilly Kohler.

Useful reference sources are Patricia Acheson's *Our Federal Government* and George Ross' *Know Your Government.* Both are clearly written with many details. Gerald Johnson has made a welcome contribution to this area in his recent books, *The Congress, The Presidency,* and *The Supreme Court.* All are well illustrated and are interesting to children in the upper elementary grades.

Excellent photographs in *United Nations* by Dorothy Sterling help children understand the organization of that body and make it a good first book to read on the subject. Another comprehensive overview is provided by Edna Epstein in her revised edition of *The First Book of the United Nations.* Children in the primary grades can read about the United Nations in *A Garden We Planted Together,* a publication of the United Nations Department of Public Information. These concepts of living together and of international cooperation are presented so that even very young children can begin to develop an appreciation of the rights and needs of people throughout the world.

Science Books for Today's Children

One often hears the comment today that children seem to know more about science than many adults, and indeed this sometimes appears to be true. Parents can sympathize with the mother and father who had never heard of the ionosphere or troposphere until their fourth-grader asked them which one was nearer the earth. Teachers could report numerous situations similar to the one in which a fifth-grader was able to give his class an impromptu lecture in answer to another child's question on how a rocket works. Where, we ask, are children getting this information?

The science books for children certainly are one of the most important sources of this information. Partly because of the nationwide concern for more science in the schools, the list of these books continues to grow in length as each year publishers rush more and more of them to press. The list, however, has also grown in breadth of subject. No longer are the science books concerned primarily with familiar plants and animals—today they cover almost every area of scientific knowledge from the tiny atom to outer space. No longer are sciences like physics, chemistry, and archaeology reserved for the high-school and college student—today even the primary child is given an opportunity to learn about these exciting fields of knowledge.

Parents and teachers who are embarrassed by their lack of scientific background would find themselves infinitely better informed if they would delve into this gold mine of information. They need not fear that it will be too elementary, for children's science books have abandoned the pseudo-scientific stories and watered-down terminology of a decade or so ago and have adopted instead a kind of seriousness that children and adults alike can appreciate. It is not unusual in children's books to come across words like *acoustics, electronics, meteorology,* and *molecule.* Titles such as *The World in Space, Understanding Time, America Before Man,* and *Exploring the Weather* are indicative of this new respect for the child's intelligence. Children's science books have indeed grown up.

This gradual maturing, of course, did not occur without doubts and criticism. There were, and probably still are, many adults who felt that exposing the child to "advanced" ideas and vocabulary could only confuse and frustrate him. Yet reports from teachers show that today children are exhibiting more interest and acquiring more knowledge in science than ever before. Surveys and reports from librarians reveal that science rates highest in both the types of questions children ask and the kinds of books children request. Reports such as these are indicative of the enthusiastic response with which children are greeting the new maturity of their science literature.

The secret of this success, of course, lies in the writing. Properly presented, almost any area of scientific knowledge can be made both comprehensible and fascinating to children. It is important that we consider the characteristics which accomplish this, not only because we wish our children to receive more of the kind of literature they want and need, but because science books have grown so in number that schools and libraries, not to mention bewildered parents, find it increasingly difficult to choose among them.

The criteria for informational books discussed earlier in this chapter (see p. 564)—accuracy, convenient presentation, clarity, adequate treatment, and interesting style—of course are applicable in evaluating science books. In addition we should consider some of the special characteristics that distinguish good scientific writing for children. Perhaps the most important characteristic is one that is essential for all children's books, namely, that the author write from the child's point of view. Authors of books in other areas have long recognized the importance of writing from the child's point of view, but until recently it was

This excellent drawing of several fungi in a typical environment is rich in varied textures and also has a strong sense of form. Illustration by Rudolf Freund. From The Rainbow Book of Nature *by Donald Culross Peattie. Copyright © 1957 by Donald Culross Peattie. Reprinted by permission of The World Publishing Company. (Book 7¾ x 10¾)*

seldom observed by the authors of science books. Authors tended to write down to children so that science was often disguised by insipid stories of personified raindrops and stars. It is debatable whether much of this was truly science.

Fortunately many of today's authors have recognized that children are capable of understanding science in its true and natural form. Children do not want science sugar-coated or diluted in strength—they simply ask that it be prescribed specifically for them. In other words, they ask that it be presented within the bounds of their limited experiences, that it begin with what is known to *them* before proceeding to the unknown. Whether we lead children inward toward an understanding of the atoms of which they are made or outward toward an exploration of space, we must first begin with the children themselves and their small world of familiar things.

This kind of approach is essential to emotional as well as intellectual growth, for the questioning child is more than just curious—he is also trying to determine his place in relation to all the things around him. The struggle to orient himself is particularly true of the very young child. In *How Big Is Big?* Herman and Nina Schneider have tried to help him by showing that "bigness" and "smallness" are entirely a matter of relationships. The child is led to realize that compared with an elephant, a tree, a skyscraper, a mountain, the moon, or the sun, he himself is "small"; but compared with a puppy, a mouse, a flea, a mite, protozoa, algae, or an atom, he himself is "big." Notice how wisely these authors relate everything to the size of the child, how cleverly they lead the child up and down a scale from things he can measure directly with his eye to things whose true size must be inferred, like an atom or the sun.

This, then, is what is meant by writing from the child's point of view. The author must be able to begin within the framework of the child's limited world. He must expand that world *step by step* at a pace which the child can follow—if he leaps, he may leave the child behind. Leading, though, is not enough, for the child will choose to stay behind if the journey becomes uninteresting. What, therefore, is necessary to maintain interest?

Naturally clarity and good organization are of primary importance if we wish the child to follow our thoughts. Yet no matter how carefully and logically an author develops his material, if it sounds like an article for an encyclopedia, the child will often lose interest. Unfortunately many adults look upon science as a cold collection of facts. To them it is void of emotion, entirely unrelated to imaginative writing. To the child, however, science is quite different. The child, we must remember, is seeking to find his way out of a dark world of ignorance. For him finding out is full of excitement, fascination, joy, and reassurance that the great bewildering world around him *can* be understood.

Authors are now recognizing the need for these qualities in science books. Consider the effect of this introduction to Donald Peattie's *Rainbow Book of Nature:*

> *Did you ever wake up early and slip out into a world fresh with a new day? The familiar scene sparkles with beauty and wonder and the sense of possible adventure. The air smells, perhaps, of pine needles and wood smoke and a secret, earthy odor like mushrooms. The grass is alight with dewdrops darting tiny rainbow fires. There may be squirrels playing tag in the trees, tweaking each other's tails, behaving as if life were one long frolic. Or crows are telegraphing in their ragged code all the gossip of the sunburnt clearings, the far-off groves. The ants in their dusty hill at your feet are toiling, the workers slavishly hurrying to and fro, the soldiers patrolling stiffly. On a branch a black and yellow spider works out in glittering silk the perfect geometry of her web. And through the aspens runs a panic of whispering, as if the trees leaned together to tell old tales of Indian scares and forest dangers.*
>
> *How did it all come to be here, this shining, quivering, intensely alive world of Nature?...*[5]

How exciting the world of nature sounds when science is imbued wtih imagination.

Good illustrations are important in all children's literature, but they are particularly necessary in science books. Here they must never be merely decorative. Their purpose must be evident, their meaning clear. Moreover, they must correspond with the text in both detail and placement, for the child has no patience with discrepancies between text and illustrations or with unnecessary page turning.

One point should be given special emphasis in considering children's science books—that is, they must be accurate in their presentation of fact. When the facts are not known, the child deserves to be told. We should appreciate and demand of all authors of science books the kind of approach taken by Gerald Ames and Rose Wyler in *First Days of the World.* They say:

> *Parts of the story are surely true, but other parts are filled in with guesses. We can never know everything that happened millions and millions of years ago.*[6]

This kind of honesty not only gives the child greater confidence in the author, but may also stimulate in him a desire to seek the unknown or verify the tentative answers himself someday.

Certainly children's science books would benefit if more scientists would concern themselves with these books. Interestingly enough, it is often the scientist writing for children who is best able to convey the kind of enthusiasm for finding out that children feel. Today, a number of authors of children's science books are scientists—Franklyn Branley, Carroll Fenton, Ira Freeman, Roy Chapman Andrews, Isaac Asimov, George Gamow, William Scheele, and Glenn Seaborg, to cite a few. Others, like Glenn Blough, are authorities in science education. And still others have their manuscripts checked by science authorities prior to publication.

Because today's science books cover material that is often largely unfamiliar to parents, teachers, librarians, and reviewers, this trend must be encouraged. The child may reject the book that is unappealing in format, that lacks his kind of enthusiasm, that is poorly organized, or that does not seem to be written especially for him, but he rarely has the experience to reject it on the basis of incompetence.

5. Donald C. Peattie, *Rainbow Book of Nature,* World, 1957, pp. 11-12.
6. Gerald Ames and Rose Wyler, *First Days of the World,* Harper, 1958, p. 4.

General Science Books

There are a number of excellent science books on the market today which cannot be assigned to a specific scientific category because the nature of their subject matter is either too general or too broad. Some of these are introductory books for preschool and primary-grade children. They might be called "getting-acquainted-with-science" books, for they concentrate less on conveying factual information and more on developing an awareness of the scientific world through direct observation.

Jeanne Bendick has written two books which aim to encourage children's natural curiosity and enthusiasm for finding out. Her first, entitled *All Around You,* is subtitled "a first look at the world." It encourages the child to observe the many wonders that can be found right at his feet or over his head, and its simple prose conveys the kind of excitement the young child feels upon discovering these things for himself. The second book, *What Could You See?* begins by inviting the child to imagine what he might see on certain exciting adventures—blazing a trail through an uncharted forest or rushing through space toward the moon. Then in each case the child is led to realize that many of the fascinating things he imagines can be found right in his own backyard.

An awareness of everyday reflections, vibrations, shadows, weather, and other natural phenomena is developed in *Now I Know* by Julius Schwartz, while *I Know a Magic House* by the same author and *Things Around the House* by Herbert S. Zim develop an appreciation for some of the many wonders that can be found inside the average home. Samuel Exler's *Growing and Changing* points out the numerous changes that are constantly taking place during every moment of life. The book does not explain these changes—it simply brings them to the child's attention. When the child begins to ask "how" and "why," then we know that he is ready to explore further in the world of science. It is the primary purpose of all of these books to encourage this desire to know more.

There is a second group of science books which cover such a wide range of topics that it would be misleading to assign them to a specific category. They are comprehensive books which offer the child a sweeping view of large areas of scientific study. An example is Bertha Morris Parker's *Golden Book of Science.* Beautifully illustrated in color, it is primarily designed to introduce the child to the many-faceted world of science and to encourage him thereafter to explore one or more of these facets in detail. Animals, plants, air, weather, rocks, fossils, prehistoric life, volcanoes, glaciers, stars, magnets, light, sound, machines, atoms, fire, and numerous other subjects are all covered in this fast but exciting tour. It is a panoramic view of the surface, not of the depths, for it would be impossible to present more than the most basic concepts when such a broad coverage is undertaken at the nine- to twelve-year-old level, for which this book was written. In a sense, therefore, its use is limited, for it will not satisfy the child who is ready to explore the depths and is looking for more detailed information. Nevertheless, it has a definite value in helping the child see relationships which are often lost when small segments of science are studied apart from the total picture.

When written for older children, the same type of book can successfully introduce more detail about each of its subjects without detracting from the overall view. Jane Werner Watson's adaptation of *The World We Live In,* a lavishly illustrated, full-color book which was originally written for adults by Lincoln Barnett and the editorial staff of *Life* magazine, is an excellent example. It, too, covers a broad scope, but at the same time offers a wealth of information about each subject. Books such as this provide valuable reference sources as well as fascinating reading and are often enjoyed as much by adults as by children.

Bertha Morris Parker's *Golden Treasury of Natural History* is a colorful book which covers the world of living things or biology—one of the larger subdivisions of science—but it also contains information on geology, astronomy, and paleontology. A number of very interesting charts are included at the end which illustrate such things as the pull of gravity on various planets, the differences in the speeds of planets, the eras in which certain types of plants and animals predominated, and the size of a giant dinosaur compared with a whale and a man. A fascinating account of the physical sciences can be found in the revised edition of William H. Crouse's *Understanding Science,* which was written in an effort to supply "an understanding of our modern world of science and the inventions that have come out of it." Atomic energy, steam engines, electricity, transistors, rockets, and many other topics are presented with imagination and clarity. Moreover, every page is filled with Jeanne Bendick's pen and ink drawings which clarify the presentation.

The series books introduced in recent years are intended to supply a comprehensive study of one area of science or social studies. Some of the best informational books available today are found within these series, although not all series books meet the same high standards.

Golden Press has been particularly active in developing these series. Their *Golden Nature Guides,* a series sponsored by the Wildlife Management Institute, are probably the most usable guides on the market today. Specialists in science, authorities in science education, and first-rate nature artists have all contributed their knowledge and talents to the production of these excellent books. Available both in paperback and in hard-cover form, they include enough information to make them valuable to adults and at the same time are so organized and developed that they can be understood and appreciated by children. The same staff, under the editorial supervision of Dr. Herbert S. Zim, has also produced Golden Press' *Golden Library of Knowledge,* which includes many science books as well as books in other fields.

Other excellent series are the *First Books* (Franklin Watts), the *All About* books (Random House), the *True Books* (Childrens Press), and the *Wonderful World* books (Garden City). The *First* and *All About* books are intended for middle and upper elementary-school children and, although planned as introductory books, usually include enough information on each subject to satisfy all but the more advanced students at those age levels. Many of these books have been written either by well-known children's authors or by scientists themselves, and in some cases they have been checked by authorities in the particular field. The *True Book* series, which is intended for primary-grade children, generally offers very basic information and simple explanations, while the handsomely illustrated volumes which comprise the *Wonderful World* series usually contain enough advanced and detailed material to make them mainly suitable for upper elementary, junior high, and sometimes even high school students. There are also numerous other smaller series, and the trend in this direction seems to be continuing.

Finally, there is the comprehensive "doing" book, which presents information about a variety of scientific topics through suggested activities and experiments. An example is Elizabeth K. Cooper's *Science in Your Own Back Yard.* Here again, careful observation is encouraged. In fact, all of the senses are employed, for the reader is led to feel, hear, smell, and even taste many of the things which can be found in the immediate environment of most children. Interest is stimulated through numerous simple experiments and exciting projects—ant villages, weather instruments, spider web collections, a backyard "laboratory"—which can be developed by individual children or an entire classroom. Although the explorations never go beyond the average backyard and although the experiments and projects utilize materials which generally can be found around the average home, the child is led to uncover an amazing amount of information about such things as plants, animals, geology, fossils, weather, and stars.

The experiment book has a definite value in that it guides the child toward direct participation in the discovery of knowledge, and since so many experiences must be gained vicariously, first-hand discovery should be encouraged whenever possible. But experiment books also have a more subtle value. We realize today that education must do more than impart knowledge—it must also teach the child how to *use* that knowledge in the solution of problems. Glenn Blough once stated:

> *If pupils are to grow in ability to solve problems they must grow in ability to think of appropriate things to do to discover solutions.*[7]

Teaching the child how to set up sound experiments and how to interpret the results of these experiments is one way of training him to "think of appropriate things to do."

Today there are general experiment books

7. Glenn O. Blough, "Quality Is What Counts!" *Instructor,* September 1958, p. 6.

for every age level, from Nancy Larrick's *See For Yourself,* which describes easy experiments on air, water, and heat for the primary child, to Alfred P. Morgan's *Boys' Book of Science and Construction,* which not only describes more advanced experiments but also includes instructions for making such things as steam turbines, pinhole cameras, and weather vanes. The numerous other books of experiments which are confined to a specific scientific subject will be discussed later.

Good experiment books, for obvious reasons, will suggest only those activities which are safe and those which can be performed with readily available and inexpensive materials. At the same time, however, it is important that children learn about the more sophisticated tools of science, even though they may never actually practice science beyond the use of a simple magnifying glass or a high-school biology class microscope. The most comprehensive treatment of this subject appears in *The Tools of Science: From Yardstick to Cyclotron* by Irving Adler. The child who has at least a reading knowledge of the cyclotron, for example, will have a far better understanding of atomic energy than the child who has never heard of this instrument.

Likewise, it is important that children realize the essential role that mathematics plays in the advancement of scientific research and in the training of future scientists. The fascinating story of numbers comes to life when told by Lancelot Hogben in *The Wonderful World of Mathematics,* which traces the history of mathematics from its earliest beginnings to its application in today's industrial world. Squares, octagons, and other geometric figures frequently appear in the dynamic drawings of Anthony Ravielli's *An Adventure in Geometry,* which poetically describes and shows how everything in the universe conforms to certain geometrical principles which have guided man and enabled him to build shapes of his own. Suggestions for actual practice in drawing geometrical figures and in putting geometrical principles to use can be found in *Fun with Figures* by Mae and Ira Freeman.

Clocks, calendars, and other tools for measuring time are also essential to the work of scientists. As with the history of mathematics, the development of man's concept of time and his efforts to measure it can be a fascinating story. When told by Harry Zarchy in *Wheel of Time* or by Beulah Tannenbaum and Myra Stillman in *Understanding Time: the Science of Clocks and Calendars,* it is just that. Not only do these books describe every type of time device from the simplest sundial to the atomic clock, but they also show how such devices have been and are being used in science and navigation as well as in our daily lives.

Under the leafy layer, there is a rich spongy soil in which there are not so many animals. Here, between the roots of trees and other plants, are tunnels dug by earthworms, moles, chipmunks, and woodchucks.
The tiny tunnels are those of earthworms. They swallow the soil and pass it through their long bodies as they wriggle through the ground. That little animal with a wedge-shaped head and strong front claws is a mole. It is scooping out a new side tunnel and looking for earthworms to eat. The ever-hungry shrew is chasing a mouse in an underground passage made by a chipmunk. The woodchuck is taking a nap in his burrow.

This imaginary section through the forest floor is made especially clear by the artist's use of different tones for the animal life, the earth, and the plant life. Illustration by Winifred Lubell. From See Through the Forest *by Millicent Selsam. Copyright © 1956 by Harper & Row, Publishers. Reprinted by permission of the publishers. (Original in color, book 6¼ x 8½, 2-page spread 12½ x 8½)*

There is drama in these books—the drama of struggle and achievement. They can be exciting and inspiring, particularly for the young mind that is likewise engaged in a struggle for knowledge. And they can call forth a new appreciation for scientific knowledge which otherwise might be taken for granted. But they must never end on a note of finality, for much remains to be learned.

The World of Living Things

LIFE IN VARIOUS ENVIRONMENTS

Every living thing in the forest is linked to the others around it. What happens to one member of the forest community may touch the lives of all the other plants and animals in it.[8]

This is the final statement in Millicent E. Selsam's *See Through the Forest,* but the same may be said of the living things in any environment. A good book about a particular community of plants and animals will never fail to reveal this interdependence of all living things, for only in view of this broad underlying principle can the individual way of life and the unique construction of each member of the community be understood.

Margaret Waring Buck has contributed three books—*In Yards and Gardens, In Woods and Fields,* and *In Ponds and Streams*—which explore the relationships between living things that can be found in areas accessible to most children. Color, particularly in the illustrations of birds and flowers, might have been a desirable addition, but the black and white drawings by the author are excellent and depict their subjects with scientific accuracy.

A less familiar environment is presented in *Walt Disney's Living Desert* by Jane Werner and the staff of the Walt Disney Studio. The title here is particularly appropriate. The desert, which is so often thought of as dull and lifeless, emerges as a place of luxuriant color, a place that is teeming with all kinds of life. An even stranger environment is revealed in Delia Goetz' *Tropical Rain Forests,* which describes the products and people as well as the plant and animal life of the tropics and is enhanced by numerous soft-green illustrations by Louis Darling.

Exploring such strange and exotic environments—indeed, exploring the familiar backyard and woodland—can be exciting and profitable. With the current interest in rockets and satellites, we may be in danger of forgetting this fact. It is *at least* as important that children gain an understanding of the living things of which they are a part and of the world in which they live as it is that they explore space and the more abstract physical sciences.

PLANT LIFE

Some of the books just mentioned emphasize an important fact—that although many animals eat only meat, all living things depend finally on plants. In *Grass: Our Greatest Crop,* Sarah R. Riedman makes this fact have real meaning for the child's own life. Without grass, she points out, we would have no wool nor milk, for without grass there would be no sheep nor cattle. Neither would we have grain for such things as breads or cereals, for many grains are part of the grass family. Our lawns would be mud or dust, and everywhere soil would erode and wash away without the roots of grass to hold it in place. How many *adults* have stopped to consider what life would be like without the simple grass plant? Learning to appreciate the valuable role that every plant plays in the world of living things should be as much a part of our study as learning to identify the plants or learning how they live and survive.

A good way to begin the study of plants is to start with their source. Clear and simple

8. Millicent E. Selsam, *See Through the Forest,* Harper, 1956, unpaged.

explanations of seeds, spores, roots, and bulbs can be found at the primary level in Irma E. Webber's *Bits That Grow Big: Where Plants Come From* and *Travelers All: The Story of How Plants Go Places.* Alfred Stefferud, a member of the U.S. Department of Agriculture, has written about this subject for older children in a book entitled *The Wonders of Seeds.* Here the author not only offers excellent information on how seeds grow, how to buy and plant them, and how to care for them after they are planted, but he also relates some interesting stories from botanical history, such as the recent discovery of lotus seeds that were still viable after lying in the ground for over a thousand years. By conveying the excitement with which botanists greet discoveries like this and by helping the reader realize their importance, the author has written a book that captures the reader's interest from beginning to end.

Turning from the seed to the plant itself, we find some excellent identification books in two of the Golden Nature Guides–*Flowers; a Guide to Familiar American Wildflowers* and *Trees; a Guide to Familiar American Trees,* both of which have been written by Herbert S. Zim and Alexander C. Martin. Full-color illustrations by Rudolf Freund (*Flowers*) and by Dorothea and Sy Barlowe (*Trees*) accurately picture each plant on a separate page, with the pertinent facts about that plant beneath the illustration. The guides are pocketsize so that they may be conveniently carried on nature walks, and their arrangement, accompanied by an excellent index, makes them handy for quick reference. These guides appeal to all ages. Sometimes, however, the very young child finds more satisfaction in a guide that he can read himself. Illa Podendorf has provided two such books–*The True Book of Weeds and Wild Flowers* and *The True Book of Trees.* Both contain colorful illustrations and large print and make good introductory books for primary-grade children.

Identification is only one phase of plant study, however. In *The First Book of Plants* by Alice Dickinson, children can find facts about how plants grow, how they make their food, how they reproduce themselves, and other essential information, as well as descriptions of many kinds of plants, including bacteria, fungi, algae, and mosses. Some exceptionally good books about the growth of trees are M. B. Cormack's *First Book of Trees* and Dorothy Sterling's *Trees and Their Story,* while an interesting and well-written account of more unusual plants can be found in *The Story of Mosses, Ferns and Mushrooms,* also by Miss Sterling, and *The Wonders of Algae* by Lucy Kavaler. These last three books contain some excellent photographs, many of them close-ups which give the child a good picture of small sections of a tree or plant.

One more book must be mentioned before we turn to the animal kingdom. Entitled *Big Tree,* it is another of Mary and Conrad Buff's outstanding contributions to children's books. Imaginative writing, enhanced by the soft, misty beauty of distinctive illustrations, tells the story of Wawona, a famous giant redwood tree. The story begins in the days before man when Wawona was a tiny seed. We are shown its size when the Egyptians were building their pyramids, when Moses led his people out of Egypt, when Christ was born, when the gold rush began in California, and finally when a park was created to preserve these oldest of all living things. *Big Tree* tells us many exciting tales of fights between forest animals, of storms and forest fires. We learn a great deal about the forest in which Wawona lives, but mainly it is the story of Wawona itself.

THE ANIMAL KINGDOM

In *The Rainbow Book of Nature,* Donald C. Peattie points out that there are over 700,000 species of animals, each of them fascinating and waiting to be studied. It sometimes seems as though there are equally as many books about animals, many of them fascinating and worth exploring.

To begin with, there are many good books which serve as introductions to animals for very young children. One is Glenn O. Blough's *Who Lives in This House?* Through the medium of an enjoyable story about the animal families which live in an old deserted house, simple information is given about the habits and behavior of robins, mud-dauber wasps, squirrels, skunks, spiders, bees, and other animals. The book ends by pointing out how all of these different families need and help one another. An unusual book by Millicent E. Selsam called *A Time for Sleep* introduces the subject of hibernation and also describes the everyday sleeping habits of many types of animals, some of which are quite amusing.

Hibernation becomes the subject for an older child's book in *Winter-Sleeping Wildlife* by Will Barker. Here we find a wealth of information about the numerous animals that disappear in the fall to emerge in the spring. Carl Burger's illustrations are both delightful and accurate. The author is honest with his readers—he tells how little scientists really know about this strange biological process. But he also explains how eager they are to learn more about it, for it is thought that the secrets of hibernation might be useful to the medical profession in such procedures as "deep-freezing" the body for heart operations.

The zoo is an exciting and interesting place, and the more one knows about it, the more meaningful a visit to it becomes. *When You Go to the Zoo* by Glenn O. Blough and Marjorie H. Campbell offers a great deal of information about both the animals and the zoo itself. Interesting facts, such as how much zoo animals cost, are included throughout, and at the end there is a directory of some of the more famous animals with explanations of why they are famous. William Bridges has also written a number of excellent zoo books, two of which are *Zoo Babies* and *Zoo Doctor*. Both contain delightful true stories which come from the author's experiences as curator of publications for the New York Zoological Park. All of these books are illustrated with excellent, and often amusing, photographs, and all of them help to assure the child that a zoo *can* be a comfortable place for animals when the proper treatment and conditions are provided.

From books about the whole animal kingdom, we turn to those which explore specific categories. Beginning with birds, we find another Golden Nature Guide to help us learn the numerous species which can be found in our own country—*Birds; A Guide to the Most Familiar American Birds* by Herbert S. Zim and Ira N. Gabrielson. Identifying birds can be exciting fun for people of all ages, but as with plants, a study should not be limited to this kind of activity. In Margaret Williamson's *First Book of Birds* more general information is given, such as the structures of birds and what enables them to fly. *Birds and Their Nests,* written and illustrated by Olive L. Earle, contains information about forty-two varieties of birds that were chosen because of the unusual types of homes they build. The author did not limit her choices to American species, and consequently some very strange and fascinating birds appear in this study, such as the hoatzin and the oropendola.

The world of insects is one that children love to explore, and, perhaps to the annoyance of some parents, there are excellent books which not only encourage them to do so but also describe in detail the best ways of collecting and studying them. One of the best books on this subject for children is Su Zan N. Swain's *Insects in Their World.* The author not only is a trained biologist who has studied insects but is an accomplished artist who has filled her book with exquisite and scientifically accurate color illustrations. Other highly recommended insect books which have been written from a more specific point of view are Ross E. Hutchins' *Insect Hunters and Trappers* and Dorothy Sterling's *Insects and the Homes They Build* and *Caterpillars.* These latter books have been illustrated with clear and exciting black and white photographs.

We move on in our study of living creatures to the animals which first established themselves on land—the reptiles and amphibians. Extensive information for older children can be found in Clifford Hillhouse Pope's *Reptiles Round the World* and in Percy A. Morris' *Boys' Book of Frogs, Toads, and Salamanders,* which offers a comprehensive scientific study of some of the amphibians found in the United States. For younger children there are delightful books on individual animals, such as Herbert S. Zim's *Frogs and Toads* and Robert McClung's *Bufo: The Story of a Toad,* which manage to present simple but accurate and interesting information about life cycles, homes, and habits.

We find that many books study plant and animal fresh-water life together and that many of these books include animals that live near the water as well as those that live in it. Harriet E. Huntington's *Let's Go to the Brook,* which follows a brook on its way to a river, is designed for primary-grade children. The sentences are short and simple, and they read along in a loose rhythm that nicely conveys the feeling of tumbling water. Along the way we encounter many forms of plant and animal life that live near or in this brook, and excellent full-page photographs picture them for us. Albro Gaul's *The Pond Book,* also illustrated with photographs but written for an older child, describes a typical pond's plants and animals in all of the four seasons and points out the interrelationships between these forms of life.

Then, at last, we come to the sea—the birthplace of all living things. Wonderful books have been written about the sea, for it is a fascinating place of beauty and terror, of poetry, mystery, and adventure. In Rachel Carson's *The Sea Around Us,* which has been adapted for junior high and older children by Anne Terry White, it is all of these things and more. Imaginative prose tells of the origin of the sea, the life within it, and the record of past life that can be found in the sediment that has drifted to the bottom since the sea began. We learn about man's efforts to understand and conquer its many mysteries and dangers, and the glorious color of its plentiful life is shown in numerous photographs. *The Wonderful World of the Sea* by James Fisher is a similar book that can be read by upper elementary-school children. There are books for younger children, too. Examples are Marie Neurath's *The Deep Sea* and another of Millicent Selsam's excellent environmental studies, this one having been written with Betty Morrow, *See Through the Sea.* Both books describe and picture many of the forms of sea life, some of them very strange to behold. *See Through the Sea* does a particularly good job, as do all of the books in this series, of showing how the different environments at different levels cause changes in the type of life which inhabits these levels.

Thus we see that there are books for children about almost every animal in existence today. Important, too, are the "pet" books which teach the child to give proper care and respect to the animals he chooses to keep. A comprehensive treatment of this subject is presented in Frances N. Chrystie's *Pets* and in Alfred P. Morgan's *Pet Book for Boys and Girls,* both of which cover the care of a variety of possible pets from the usual dog or cat to the more unusual skunk or alligator. For children who wish to start an aquarium, Alfred P. Morgan's *Aquarium Book for Boys and Girls* is an excellent source. Helpful information can also be found in Gertrude Pels' *The Care of Water Pets* and in Margaret Waring Buck's *Pets from the Pond.*

By emphasizing the responsibility involved in owning a pet, these books serve an important purpose. Too frequently the burden of pet care falls on the shoulders of parents, with the result that parents often refuse to allow pets in the home. When this happens, it is indeed unfortunate, for pets can contribute a great deal to the emotional life of a child. They may provide him with a sense of security—surely we have all seen at least one small child pour out his heart to a friendly dog. But what is more important, pets can teach a child to love. The dependent child may be used to *receiving* love, but he rarely experiences the tenderness of *giving* love until something depends on him for its care.

THE HUMAN BODY

Herbert S. Zim's *What's Inside of Me?* is very popular with children—understandably so, for if a child is curious about the world around him, it is natural for him to be curious about his ever-present self. Sometimes this curiosity has been a problem to parents, for one of the first things children want to know is how they are born. For a while the young child may be content with a book like Millicent Selsam's *All About Eggs and How They Change into Animals,* but the day will come when he will want a book that is "just about himself."

Fortunately, two excellent ones will be waiting for him. *The Wonderful Story of How You Were Born* by Sidonie M. Gruenberg is a well-written account that has been approved by educators, psychologists, and religious leaders. The second book, *A Baby Is Born,* is also approved by the clergy and is well recommended, having been written by a pediatrician, Milton I. Levine, and a nurse, Jean H. Seligmann. Both of these books should be helpful to parents who would like guidance in answering their child's questions about birth.

The child's curiosity does not end here, however. He is told that the beat he hears is his heart, that his food goes to his stomach, that fresh air is good for his lungs, and naturally he is going to wonder what these parts look like and how they work. The primary-grade child will enjoy the Zim book mentioned above. For every page of easy-to-read information in large type, there is a page of additional, more detailed explanations which parents or older children can use. The diagrammatic illustrations are in color and are simple enough to be easily understood by younger children. A good book for the middle and upper elementary-school child is Herman and Nina Schneider's *How Your Body Works,* which is filled with lively pictures of children engaged in typical childhood activities and with good explanations of how the body must operate in order to allow them to do these things. But the most outstanding presentation has been written for older children by Anthony Ravielli and is entitled *Wonders of the Human Body.* The text is excellent, and the drawings by the author are some of the best that have appeared in children's science books.

These books describe the body as it should work, but of course all children are curious about what causes the body to fail to operate properly. In *The First Book of Microbes* by Lucia Z. Lewis and in *The Story of Microbes* by Albert Schatz and Sarah R. Riedman, children are given an opportunity to learn about the tiny microbes which contribute both to disease and to health. The authors of both of these books are competent authorities in this field, and they include simple experiments and suggestions for growing microbes at home or in school. But the story of disease and its cure receives the most comprehensive treatment in a book by Ritchie Calder, *The Wonderful World of Medicine.* Parts of the text may be too difficult for the elementary-school

The author's illustrations for this book present detailed views of the bones, muscles, organs, and systems of the body. Here the muscles of the face are depicted along with a variety of facial expressions, which are controlled by these muscles.
From Wonders of the Human Body *by Anthony Ravielli. Copyright 1954 by Anthony Ravielli. Reprinted by permission of The Viking Press, Inc. (Original with two colors, book 5¼ x 8)*

child to read, but the full-color illustrations, some depicting medical history and others revealing the great complexity of such things as the human heart and the highly developed brain, tell much of the story.

What a vast distance life on earth has traveled! Today there are books for children which describe almost every step in the ladder of life from the single cell to the complex system of machine-like parts that make up man's body. But Anthony Ravielli tells the child:

You are not quite finished yet. This is just the machinery. . . . We are more than just machines, *because we love and want to be loved . . . and have pity . . . and know why . . . and dream . . . and have ideals and faith.*[9]

It is *these*—the "gifts of the spirit"—that "set man above all other creatures." Let us not end this lesson in science without this understanding!

The Earth and the Universe

It has been pointed out that science is, and always has been, "imagination's other place." Actually, it should not be necessary to argue that science and imagination go together, for anyone who thinks about it should realize that without man's imagination science would never have originated, nor would it advance today. This is particularly apparent in a study of the earth and the universe. Here we explore periods of existence that man has never directly experienced, depths of the earth that man has never entered, regions of space where life has never existed. Science fiction may have machines that take man back to the earliest times or catapult him into the farthest regions of space, but until these fictional machines become actualities, our only way of escaping the natural boundaries of time and space is through the unique gift of the imagination.

It is exciting to stretch our imaginations like this, and it is particularly exciting for children who have never before realized the vastness of time and space. It is not easy, however—even adults find it difficult to imagine billions of years or billions of miles. These are understandings which will grow as the child grows, but we must never make the mistake of thinking that because he cannot fully perceive the concepts of time and space, he should not be exposed to sciences which explore them. If the child is not required to exercise his imagination, it will, like his body, fail to grow to its full potential.

THE EARTH'S BEGINNING YEARS

Let us begin with books that stretch the imagination back into time to the days when the earth was first created. It is wise to begin at the beginning with children. If we step into the time line elsewhere—say, at the age of reptiles or at the beginning of man—we run the risk of causing confusion about the chronology of developments. If we start at the beginning, however, we can build the world anew in the order that science tells us it happened. The child may not realize the lengths of time which elapsed between these steps of development, but at least he can perceive the order and continuity in the evolution of life as we know it today.

Gerald Ames and Rose Wyler have written an excellent book to begin this study. Appropriately entitled *First Days of the World,* it simply but clearly offers some of the facts and theories which science has now developed regarding the earth's beginning and the evolution of life. It is not, however, merely a collection of facts. It is a story—a scientific story of genesis—told with a touch of the beauty and awe that children and adults alike feel upon realizing the wonder of this mighty creation.

Alice Dickinson's *First Book of Prehistoric Animals* also covers the period from the beginning of the earth to the time of man's appearance, but its main emphasis, as the title indicates, is on the evolution of life. Its outstanding feature is the way in which it simply but clearly explains the process of evolution. The author also emphasizes the causes of evolution by showing how changes in the earth during millions of years forced life to adopt new ways of living and how an animal's intelligence helped or prevented its adaptation. It is this same approach which makes Marie Bloch's *Dinosaurs* an excellent book,

9. Anthony Ravielli, *Wonders of the Human Body,* Viking, 1954, pp. 120-123.

for even though the author's text never rises above the primary level, it clearly reveals the causes for the rise and fall of these giant reptiles as well as facts about their appearance and habits. Children must be provided with this kind of information—otherwise they will have no insight into why life continually changed its forms, and the concept of evolution will be meaningless to them.

Naturally one of the first questions children will ask when reading about prehistoric life is "How do we know that all this is true?" Many of the books about prehistoric times include some account of the work of the archaeologist in order to provide answers to this question. In *All About Dinosaurs,* Roy Chapman Andrews describes some of his own experiences as an archaeologist and also manages to convey the excitement and sense of achievement that he and his coworkers experienced during their expeditions. There are also a few books which are entirely devoted to explaining archaeology, one of the best and most thorough being *The Wonderful World of Archaeology* by Ronald Jessup. An excellent feature of this book is the way in which it indicates the interrelationship between the various sciences by showing how physics, biology, botany, geology, chemistry, and engineering all contribute to the work of the archaeologist.

In our study of early man, we find that some of the most valuable clues to his existence have been found in caves which he once inhabited. Since several of the most important cave discoveries have been made by children, the stories of these discoveries are particularly interesting and inspirational to young readers. In *The Caves of the Great Hunters,* which was originally written in German by Hans Baumann and has been translated into English by Isabel and Florence McHugh, there is a novel-like but scientifically accurate account of three such discoveries. This book has been entirely illustrated with reproductions of paintings and sculpture found in these ancient caves, and the explanations that stem from studying this art tell a great deal about the life of early man.

A more complete history of early man, however, has been written by Anne Terry White in *The First Men in the World.* Here again we have a scientific account which is not a book of facts but an exciting and highly dramatic story. It is often hard to make children realize the importance of such things as the invention of speech, of weapons such as the bow and arrow, of the discovery of ways to make and use fire. The modern child has difficulty comprehending why such a fuss is made about inventions which seem so absurdly simple today. Miss White, however, has managed to convey the greatness of early man's achievements as she traces his development through the various stages known as Java man, Peking man, Neanderthal man, Cro-Magnon man, and upward until he reaches the stage of planned agriculture, the Mother of Civilization. "Finally came agriculture," says the

This painting pictures the reconstruction of Stonehenge, which was based on facts uncovered by archaeologists. Illustration from The Wonderful World of Archaeology *by Ronald Jessup. Published by Rathbone Books, Ltd. Reprinted by permission of Doubleday & Company, Inc. (Original in color, book 9½ x 12½, picture 5½ x 2¾)*

author as she ends her book. "And agriculture was the great beginning."

GEOLOGY

Naturally not many children have an opportunity to go "spelunking" in caves or on dinosaur hunts in the desert, but when it comes to geology, almost any child can directly participate by collecting rocks and minerals. Properly guided, such a hobby can result in some valuable learning about geology and perhaps even about prehistoric life.

Numerous books have been written to guide the young (or adult) "rockhound." *Rocks and Minerals,* by Herbert S. Zim and Paul R. Shaffer, another of the Golden Nature pocket guides, helps in the identification of more than 400 rocks, minerals, and gems, all of which have been beautifully illustrated in color by Raymond Perlman. In addition, it offers some basic geological information with explanations of the uses and economic importance of many of the materials described. Another excellent guide is Dorothy E. Shuttlesworth's *Story of Rocks,* which is illustrated in color by Su Zan N. Swain and offers very helpful suggestions for recording, displaying, and studying rocks and minerals as well as for collecting and identifying them.

There are other books which introduce children to the science of geology as a whole. For very young children there is Herbert S. Zim's *What's Inside the Earth?* which again combines an easy-to-read text in large print with more advanced information in small print. Very simple explanations and diagrams reveal the inside of a mine, a cave, a well, a volcano, and a mountain as well as the entire earth. In *The First Book of the Earth* by O. Irene Sevrey, older children will find more detailed information about these geological formations and a simple explanation of how the earth was formed and of its relationship to the sun.

Finally there are books which primarily emphasize man's efforts and success at procuring and using the earth's contents. In *Underground Riches,* written and illustrated by Walter Buehr, the earth's minerals and how they originated are briefly explained, but the major portion of the book is devoted to early and modern methods for obtaining these minerals, with special emphasis on the mining of gold, coal, and iron. An exciting account of one of the earth's most valued treasures can be found in *The Story of Gold* by Ruth Brindze, which dramatically shows how man's search for and procurement of gold have shaped the history of our world. Famous discoveries beginning with those of ancient Egyptian times, methods of mining gold, and ways in which man has used it for decorative and economic purposes are interestingly described and brilliantly illustrated by Robert Bruce's color drawings.

THE ATMOSPHERE AND WEATHER

Once children have studied about our own planet and the life upon it from its beginning days to the present, they are ready to head outward from the earth to explore the rest of the universe. Unless we help children realize that the atmosphere is only a narrow ring which encircles the earth, they will indeed be confused when they try to understand, for example, the problems involved in space flight. Therefore, a study of the atmosphere and its weather should be prerequisite to a study of space and man's efforts to conquer it.

One of the most comprehensive books on this subject is Roy Gallant's *Exploring the Weather,* which has been handsomely illustrated in color and in black and white by Lowell Hess. It explores the "ocean" of air first, then goes on to wind, water, vapor, clouds, forms of precipitation, and various types of storms, and finally examines the work of the weatherman or meteorologist through discussions of warm and cold fronts, weather map reading, "cloud seeding," and weather instruments. Similar information is offered in Herman Schneider's *Everyday Weather and How It Works* and, on a slightly more advanced level, in *Weathercraft* by meteorologist Athelstan F. Spilhaus. These latter books also include suggestions and diagrams for performing experiments and for building weather instruments with inexpensive, readily available materials. Thus they provide invaluable help for teachers, as well as children, who desire guidance of this sort for classroom use.

In addition to these more comprehensive studies of weather, there are books which limit their subject matter to a specific type of phenomenon of weather. One example is *Snow* by Thelma Harrington Bell. A surprising amount of interesting information about snow and its "cousins"—frost, rime, glaze, sleet, and hail—is offered in this book, and the soft blue and white drawings by Corydon Bell continually remind the child of the beauty of snow as he reads the scientific explanation.

Books about water conservation often contain information about the weather, and since an understanding of the importance of water helps the child to appreciate the weather which brings this water, it is good to study the two together. In *Water for America,* by Edward H. Graham and William R. Van Dersal, the sources of water, ways of controlling, storing, and purifying it, and ways in which it can be useful (and sometimes harmful) to industry, farm, and home are thoroughly described and pictured in excellent photographs that fill half the book. For younger children there are books which do not discuss conservation directly but which serve as an introduction to this subject by indicating water's great value. An example is *The River's Journey* by Anne Marie Jauss. While it points out the many ways in which all living creatures depend on water and on its control, it is basically a story of the rain cycle.

SPACE

Ask children today what area of science they want to study, and more often than not they will answer "space." But if the enthusiastic teacher rounds up books and prepares a unit on astronomy, she may discover that this is not what the children meant at all. In the minds of today's children, studying space often means studying rockets and satellites, not the sun and moon. Their disappointment may cause them to complain that study of the sun and moon is "old and boring" or that they already "know it all," and the enthusiastic teacher finds her well-planned unit getting off to a most discouraging start!

We must excuse this attitude in today's children, for when man has already accomplished the feat of entering space for the first time, even the youngest children want and deserve

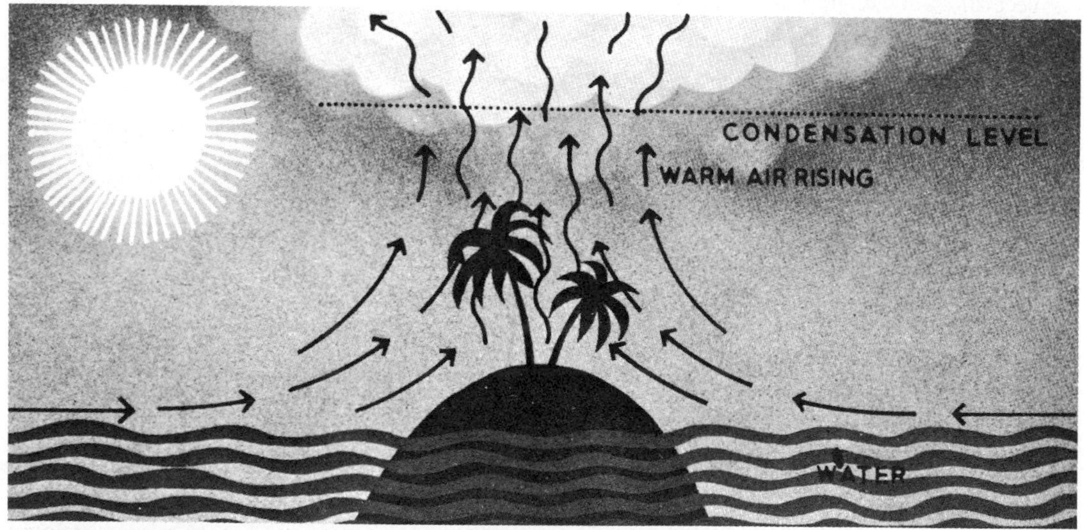

This picture diagram showing how clouds form over land masses is not only informative but also beautiful because of the stylized symbols for each factor.
Illustration by Lowell Hess. From Exploring the Weather *by Roy A. Gallant. Copyright © 1957 by Roy A. Gallant. Reprinted by permission of Doubleday & Company, Inc. (Book 8½ x 12, picture 6 x 2¾)*

an opportunity to participate in the excitement. At the same time, however, we cannot allow their high enthusiasm to cause us to ignore the fact that the goals and problems of space flight will be meaningless unless children first understand such things as the environmental conditions on the moon, the effect of the sun's rays, the distances between the bodies of the solar system, and other important relationships. Perhaps if we launch an imaginary rocket or two, we can divert their interest to a study of what can be "seen" from the rocket, for once the minds of children get orbiting in space, they are truly fascinated by such mundane things as the sun and moon and stars.

There are wonderful books available for building enthusiasm in children for the teachings of astronomy. If we glance through the pages of *The Golden Book of Astronomy* by Rose Wyler and Gerald Ames, for example, we find inviting large print and exciting color illustrations by John Polgreen which make it difficult to turn away without reading the text. This book covers a wide introductory scope, from the atmosphere and seasons and phases of the moon, to the members of our solar system and the billions of far-flung stars, and finally to man's hopes and plans for continuous exploration of space. Mr. Polgreen is also responsible for the magnificent illustrations which appear in Roy Gallant's *Exploring the Planets,* while equally good art work by Lowell Hess adds to the interest of Mr. Gallant's *Exploring the Universe, Exploring Mars,* and *Exploring the Moon.* When considered together, Mr. Gallant's books cover a very wide scope, but since each individual book is limited to a specific phase of astronomy, they are able to offer extensive information. Another excellent book is Franklyn M. Branley's *The Nine Planets,* which has been illustrated by Helmut K. Wimmer with exceptionally fine air-brush drawings that often achieve a three-dimensional effect. The author, who is an associate astronomer at the Hayden Planetarium in New York, presents his material in an adult, authoritative manner that will appeal to older children, but at the same time the text never sacrifices simplicity and clarity.

There are also some unusual books, such as *Find the Constellations* by H. A. Rey. The conventional pictures of constellations are often confusing to children, for they elaborate so on the natural outline of the stars that it often requires an adult imagination to transfer these pictures from the pages of a book to the sky itself. H. A. Rey, however, has simplified these drawings to the point where only the true outline of the stars is revealed. Naturally the pictures are not realistic, but the clever illustrations are well labeled to point out difficult-to-recognize constellations, such as Orion's sword or the Great Bear's paws.

Another clever approach, designed for beginners, can be found in *You, Among the Stars* by Herman and Nina Schneider. As in other books by these same authors, the emphasis is on orienting the young child. Through the theme of an envelope address, the child moves from his own home outward into space step by step until his familiar street address becomes greatly elaborated.

Robert and Lucy Taylor
46 Elm Street
Central City
Illinois
U.S.A.
The Earth
The Solar System
The Milky Way
The Universe[10]

Finally, there are two books for older children by Irving Adler which are outstanding because of their emphasis on proof. In the words of the author:

> *To see the difference between fact and fancy, we have to follow the* thinking *of the scientist, and see what* proof *he has for the things he asks us to believe.*[11]

Both of these books—*The Stars: Steppingstones into Space* and *The Sun and Its Family*—offer excellent information about *how* scientists have found out facts about the universe and also *why* they know that these facts are true. As astronomy professor Lloyd Motz

10. Herman and Nina Schneider, *You, Among the Stars,* W. R. Scott, 1951, unpaged.
11. Irving Adler, *The Stars: Steppingstones into Space,* Day, 1956, p. 14.

has pointed out in his preface to the first of these books, it is often difficult to explain these hows and whys to children who lack knowledge of advanced mathematics and astronomy. Mr. Adler, however, has managed to offer clear scientific proof in simple terms of such things as the roundness of the earth or the fact that it turns.

Whether we explore the earth from its beginning days or explore space and all its wonders, we are constantly reminded of the fact that much still remains for man to learn. Therefore, as we introduce children to these exciting realms of science, we must do so with the same hope that is expressed by Professor Bart J. Bok in his introduction to *The Golden Book of Astronomy.* He says,

> *I welcome you to the wonders of the heavens, and I hope this first glimpse of the vast unknown may whet your appetite for more.*[12]

Matter and Energy

So far, our discussion has dealt with sciences which mainly examine those aspects of existence which man has had little or no part in creating or ordering. When we come to physics and chemistry, however, we are entering realms of science which have increasingly enabled man to reorder natural existence to suit his particular wants or needs. While we want our children to appreciate fully these achievements of applied science, they must also be helped to recognize its limitations if they are to gain a realistic picture of the world in which they live. In this atomic age, it is perhaps more apparent than ever before that science alone can bring great good *or* harm, depending on how man puts it to use.

CHEMISTRY

The science of chemistry can be traced back to early man. Roy A. Gallant's *Exploring Chemistry,* for example, begins with the discovery of fire and thereafter tells the absorbing history of man's efforts to understand and change matter. Ira M. Freeman elaborates upon this story for older children in *All About the Wonders of Chemistry,* describing at greater length such things as molecular structure, the elements, chemical change, and the many ways in which chemistry has contributed to medicine, farming, and industry, for the benefit of modern life. Older children will also enjoy a book entitled *Elements of the Universe,* by Glenn T. Seaborg and Evans G. Valens, which contains dramatic accounts of some of chemistry's greatest discoveries, written by men who have directly participated in the thrill of such achievements.

Chemistry, of course, offers boundless opportunities for the young experimenter, but it can also involve many dangers. For this reason, we appreciate the efforts of those authors who have carefully planned books that introduce worth-while experiments that are advanced enough to capture the interest of the budding young chemist, but at the same time are safe enough to be performed by him alone. *The First Chemistry Book for Boys and Girls* by Alfred P. Morgan and *Experiments in Chemistry* by Nelson F. Beeler and Franklyn M. Branley are two excellent examples of such books, both having been written for middle- and upper-grade children.

PHYSICS

In the purest sense, chemistry is the study of matter only—its composition, its nature, and the changes it constantly undergoes—while physics is the study of matter and energy and the relationship between them. Even this simple definition makes it apparent that the two sciences are interrelated. In elementary-school science we generally stay within the classical categories that have long characterized basic introductions to chemistry and physics—chemistry is the study of elements and compounds, while physics involves mechanics, heat, light, sound, magnetism, and electricity. But even at the elementary-school level, more and more books are appearing that

12. Rose Wyler and Gerald Ames, *The Golden Book of Astronomy,* Golden Press, 1959, p. 4.

cross boundary lines and reveal the strong interrelationship between these sciences. For example, there are now several books which borrow learnings from chemistry regarding atoms and molecular structure and then go on to apply these learnings to the recent developments in physics regarding atomic energy and its many uses.

An excellent example for younger children is John Lewellen's *The Mighty Atom,* which very simply, with the aid of familiar analogies and Ida Scheib's clever illustrations, moves from a discussion of the atom with its neutrons, protons, and electrons, to molecular structure and the basic elements, and finally to atomic power, the construction and operation of atomic furnaces and engines, and the uses of atomic energy in both war and peace. Older children will find similar but more advanced information on this subject in Isaac Asimov's *Inside the Atom,* while Raymond F. Yates' *Atomic Experiments for Boys* provides numerous suggestions for helpful projects which will aid in clarifying the principles of atomics.

Mechanics, an area of great interest to children, paves the way for a study of transportation and, unlike chemistry and atomics, offers even the young child a chance to participate in interesting experiments. *Now Try This* by Herman and Nina Schneider, for example, suggests many experiments which introduce primary children to friction, levers, inclined planes, and wheels, show how they work, and indicate how they can be applied in laborsaving devices. Another interesting book for this level is *The True Book of Toys at Work* by John Lewellen, which describes the mechanical principles involved in such things as whistles, electric trains, and balloons. Hy Ruchlis' *Orbit: A Picture Story of Force and Motion* successfully explains Newton's law of universal gravitation plus his three laws of motion in terms that can be understood by most children above the fourth grade. Action-packed photographs of such things as "flying" cars, acrobatic stunts, and daredevil sports, plus excellent diagrams by Alice Hirsch, help to illustrate these scientific laws, all of which contribute a great deal toward an adequate understanding of transportation vehicles and particularly of space flight.

Naturally the machines which man has built on the principles of mechanics would have limited use indeed without the harnessing of some type of energy other than man power to run them. One of the most comprehensive books on this subject, excitingly illustrated in color by John Teppich, is Lancelot Hogben's *Wonderful World of Energy.* This book constantly reminds the child that, of all the many sources of energy, the greatest is the one which has mastered the others—man's own will and drive to go forward. We learn how man has gradually harnessed and put to work energy from wind, water, steam, fire, electricity, and now the atom and the sun. This last source of energy, vast and unlimited, still requires a great deal of study. Its history, present status, and future possibilities have been extensively discussed by Franklyn M. Branley in a book entitled *Solar Energy.*

Of all the forms of energy, however, the one with which the child has had the most direct experience is usually electricity. This is not an easy subject for children, and yet it plays such an important role in their everyday lives that we should help them gain at least an appreciation of its great value and some understanding of how it operates. One of the clearest and simplest explanations of this complex subject can be found in *The First Book of Electricity* by Sam and Beryl Epstein. Since this book is designed for the beginner with no previous knowledge of electricity, new concepts have been fully explained and are further clarified by Robin King's delightful cartoon-like illustrations, which often add humor to a subject which might otherwise become tedious to younger children. In addition, there are pages of easy-to-follow instructions for experiments. For older children who already have a basic knowledge of this subject, the greater complexities of electricity are explained in detail in such books as Alfred P. Morgan's *First Electrical Book for Boys,* which is particularly valuable for the numerous excellent experiments it suggests, and in Ira M. Freeman's *All About Electricity,* which introduces a good deal of the history of the development of electrical power and contains whole chapters on various uses of electricity, such as the telephone, radio, motion pictures, and television.

Actually the science concerned with the communication devices just mentioned is no longer spoken of as "electricity," but rather a branch of electricity now known as "electronics." In *Understanding Electronics,* John Lewellen writes:

> *. . . electronics now brings us radio and television, opens supermarket doors for us, guides airliners safely through cloudy skies at night, warns us with radar signals if an enemy approaches our borders, makes possible long-distance telephone calls, automatically turns down our automobile headlights as we approach another car, helps light our homes, solves incredibly complex problems in seconds, runs factories automatically, warns us of thunderstorms, tornadoes, and hurricanes, and does a thousand and one other things. . . .*
>
> *Science is even now toying with the idea that some day it may be possible to build an electronically controlled machine that can "grow" new parts for itself when a part becomes worn or damaged. Or even a machine that can make new machines like itself. . . .*[13]

Exciting? Perhaps you feel, as many do, that it is all rather frightening. Nevertheless, the inventions which have derived from the study of electronics already play such an important role in our daily lives that there is a definite need for this kind of writing for children.

Today as never before we find the shelves of the public libraries spilling over with informational books for children. This situation is a reflection of the times, of course, for parents want their children to be conversant with world happenings, past and present, and with subjects scientific.

Children may learn important facts from their reading, but they should grow also in interest in and appreciation for the world in which they live. Through satisfying their curiosity and discovering answers to their questions, their understanding should increase; as understanding grows, so should wonder. Many adults believe, however, that practical knowledge is needed more than wonder to meet the demands of modern life—that we should concentrate more on science, mathematics, and the like. But we need wonder in our lives! Indeed, teachers have a far greater responsibility than just to impart *learning.* If we are to have leaders with imagination, vision, and sensitivity, we will do well to encourage the beginnings of *wisdom.* Good books do not automatically endow children with wisdom, but they do plant seeds for its growth. For wisdom comes from understandings of life and self.

Many of the informational books for children are outstanding. They present accurate information in a clear, lively style and in an attractive format. Sometimes they are even artistic and literary, as *Snow* by Thelma Bell and the books created by the Buffs. The books of Herman Schneider, Bertha Parker, Anthony Ravielli, Herbert Zim, Gerald Johnson, Edwin Tunis, Miroslav Sasek, Roy A. Gallant, and the Hollings have set high standards for the science and social-studies collections. With these well-written, authentic, and beautifully illustrated books teachers can enliven and enrich the textbooks, and parents will find they can enjoy and respect their children's reading.

13. John Lewellen, *Understanding Electronics,* Crowell, 1957, pp. 4-5.

SUGGESTED READING, PROBLEMS, AND PROJECTS

Suggested Reading: Read a fair sampling of the following:

Kindergarten-primary: Jeanne Bendick, *What Could You See?;* Glenn O. Blough, *Who Lives in This Meadow?;* Franklyn Branley, *A Book of Satellites for You;* Benjamin Brewster, *The First Book of Firemen;* Mary and Conrad Buff, *Elf Owl;* Clyde Robert Bulla, *A Tree Is a Plant;* Samuel Exler, *Growing and Changing;* Louise Floethe, *The Farmer and His Cows;* Alice Goudey, *Here Come the Beavers!* or *Here Come the Squirrels!* or *Houses from the Sea;* Sidonie Gruenberg, *The Wonderful Story of How You Were Born;* Miriam Schlein, *It's About Time;* Laura Sootin, *Let's Go to a Zoo;* Tasha Tudor, *Around the Year.*

Middle and upper grades: Gerald Ames and Rose Wyler, *The First People in the World;* Hans Baumann, *The Caves of the Great Hunters;* Nelson Beeler and Franklyn Branley, *Experiments with a Microscope;* Margaret Buck, *Pets from the Pond;* C. B. Falls, *The First 3000 Years;* Genevieve Foster, *George Washington's World;* Roy A. Gallant, *Ex-*

ploring the Planets; Gerald W. Johnson, *America Is Born: A History for Peter;* Robert McClung, *Buzztail: The Story of a Rattlesnake* or *Whitefoot: The Story of a Wood Mouse;* Margaret Mead, *People and Places;* Alfred Morgan, *Aquarium Book for Boys and Girls;* Illa Podendorf, *101 Science Experiments;* Anthony Ravielli, *Wonders of the Human Body;* Miroslav Sasek, *This is Israel;* William Scheele, *Prehistoric Animals;* Herman Schneider, *Everyday Weather and How It Works;* Su Zan N. Swain, *Insects in Their World;* Herbert S. Zim, *Comets* or *Insects: A Guide to Familiar American Insects.*

1. List the criteria by which you would evaluate science and social-studies books for primary-grade children. Select and evaluate two books for the youngest in each category.

2. By what criteria would you evaluate upper elementary-school science and social-studies books? Evaluate Anne Terry White's adaptation of Rachel Carson's *The Sea Around Us* and Genevieve Foster's *The World of Captain John Smith.* Indicate how each of these meets the standards for good informational books.

3. Compile an annotated bibliography of children's books written about your state or region (New England area, Great Lakes region, or others). Begin with the informational books that tell about the geography, history, customs, products, people. Expand your bibliography to include poetry, biography, and fiction (stories with your state or region as a setting).

4. Evaluate the illustrations in several social-studies or science books on a single topic such as Brazil, trains, plant life, the atmosphere and weather, or colonial America. Rank the books according to your criteria for pictures. Show the books to several children and ask them to name and explain their preferences.

5. How can science books lead to interesting hobbies for individual children and to exciting projects for groups of children? Suggest specific books which might initiate such activities.

6. Show how a science unit might be built around a topic such as life in various environments, the animal kingdom, or space. What factors should govern your selection of books for these units?

7. Read part or all of Hendrik Van Loon's *Story of Mankind.* Could you use any part of it with the age level you are interested in? What influence did this book have upon writers of biographies and social-studies books?

REFERENCES

The numbers of informational books now in print and the numbers appearing each year are staggering. Furthermore, the books in this area tend to date more rapidly than those in any other area. For these reasons, it is impossible to provide a comprehensive, up-to-date bibliography of informational books for this textbook. Instead, it is suggested that the student familiarize himself with the specialized bibliographies in this area, keep up with the review of informational books in the various current magazines, journals, and newspapers, and, of course, consult the local librarian.

For the student's convenience, complete bibliographical data are provided here for all the books discussed or mentioned in this chapter. For a listing of dictionaries and encyclopedias, see Bibliography, Chapter 21.

BOOKS FOR THE SOCIAL STUDIES

ACHESON, PATRICIA C. *Our Federal Government: How It Works. An Introduction to the United States Government,* ill. by Everett Raymond Kinstler. Dodd, 1958. 12-14

ALEXANDER, ANNE. *ABC of Cars and Trucks,* ill. by Ninon. Doubleday, 1956. 5-6

AMERICAN HERITAGE. *Discoverers of the New World,* narrative by Josef Berger in consultation with Lawrence C. Wroth, ill. American Heritage, 1960. 10-14

_____. *The Golden Book of the American Revolution,* adapted by Fred Cook from *The American Heritage Book of the Revolution* by the editors of American Heritage, ill. Golden Press, 1959. 12-14

_____. *The Pilgrims and Plymouth Colony,* narrative by Feenie Ziner, in consultation with George F. Willison. American Heritage, 1961. 9-13

AMES, GERALD, and ROSE WYLER. *First Days of the World,* ill. by Leonard Weisgard. Harper, 1958. 8-10

_____. *The First People in the World,* ill. by Leonard Weisgard. Harper, 1958. 8-10

ANDERSON, WILLIAM R. *First Under the North Pole: The Voyage of the Nautilus,* ill. with photographs and drawings. World, 1959. 9-13

BATCHELOR, JULIE F. *Communication: From Cave Writing to Television,* ill. by C. D. Batchelor. Harcourt, 1953. 8-11

BENDICK, JEANNE. *The First Book of Airplanes,* ill. by author. Watts, 1958. 7-10

_____. *The First Book of Automobiles,* ill. by author. Watts, 1955. 8-10

———. *The First Book of Ships,* ill. by author. Watts, 1959. 8-11

BENDICK, JEANNE and ROBERT. *Television Works Like This,* ill. by Jeanne Bendick. Whittlesey, 1959. 11-13

BLEEKER, SONIA. *Indians of the Longhouse: Story of the Iroquois.* Morrow, 1950. The first book in a continuing series on American Indian tribes. 9-12

BRADLEY, DUANE. *Engineers Did It!,* ill. by Anne M. Jauss. Lippincott, 1958. 10-12

BREETVELD, JIM. *Getting to Know Alaska,* ill. by Don Lambo. Coward, 1958. 8-10

BREWSTER, BENJAMIN. *The First Book of Firemen,* ill. by Jeanne Bendick. Watts, 1951. 6-9

BUCHHEIMER, NAOMI. *Let's Go to the Library,* ill. by Vee Guthrie. Putnam, 1957. 6-9

———. *Let's Go to the Telephone Company,* ill. by Barbara Corrigan. Putnam, 1958. 8-10

BUEHR, WALTER. *Chivalry and the Mailed Knight,* ill. by author. Putnam, 1963. 9-12

———. *The Crusaders,* ill. by author. Putnam, 1959. 10-12

———. *Knights and Castles and Feudal Life,* ill. by author. Putnam, 1957. 9-12

———. *Railroads Today and Yesterday,* ill. by author. Putnam, 1958. 9-11

———. *Trucks and Trucking,* ill. by author. Putnam, 1956. 9-11

BURLINGAME, ROGER. *Machines That Built America,* Harcourt, 1953. 12-14

BURNS, WILLIAM A. *A World Full of Homes,* ill. by Paula Hutchison. Whittlesey, 1953. 8-11

BUTLER, EVELYN, and GEORGE A. DALE. *Alaska: The Land and the People,* ill. with photographs. Viking, 1957. 10-12

CALDWELL, JOHN C. *Let's Visit Argentina,* ill. with photographs and maps. Day, 1961. 9-11

———. *Let's Visit Brazil,* ill. with photographs and maps. Day, 1961. 10-12

CARMER, CARL. *The Hudson River,* ill. by Rafaelo Busoni. Holt, 1962. 9-13

CARTER, WILLIAM E. *The First Book of South America.* Watts, 1961. 9-12

CAVANAH, FRANCES. *Our Country's Story,* rev. ed., ill. by Julia Keats. Rand McNally, 1962. 7-10

COIT, MARGARET L. *The Fight for Union.* Houghton, 1961. 11-13

COMMAGER, HENRY STEELE. *The First Book of American History,* ill. by Leonard E. Fisher. Watts, 1957. 10-12

———. *The Great Constitution: A Book for Young Americans.* Bobbs, 1961. 12-14

———. *The Great Declaration: A Book for Young Americans,* ill. by Donald Bolognese. Bobbs, 1958. 12-14

———. *The Great Proclamation: A Book for Young Americans.* Bobbs, 1960. 11-14

COOKE, DAVID COXE. *Dirigibles That Made History,* ill. with photographs. Putnam, 1962. 11-13

COOKE, DONALD. *Marvels of American Industry.* Hammond, 1962. 11-14

COTTRELL, LEONARD. *Land of the Pharaohs,* ill. by Richard M. Powers. World, 1960. 11-13

COWELL, F. R. *Everyday Life in Ancient Rome,* ill. by D. Stredder Bist. Putnam, 1961. 12-14

DALGLIESH, ALICE. *America Begins: The Story of the Finding of the New World,* rev. ed., ill. by Lois Maloy. Scribner, 1958. 8-11

———. *The Fourth of July Story,* ill. by Marie Nonnast. Scribner, 1956. 8-11

ELTING, MARY. *Machines at Work,* ill. by Lászlo Roth. Harvey, 1962. 8-10

EPSTEIN, EDNA. *The First Book of the United Nations,* rev. ed., ill. with photographs. Watts, 1961. 9-12

EPSTEIN, SAM and BERYL. *The First Book of Codes and Ciphers,* ill. by Lászlo Roth. Watts, 1956. 9-12

———. *The First Book of Printing,* ill. by Lászlo Roth. Watts, 1955. 9-12

———. *The First Book of Washington, D.C.,* ill. with photographs. Watts, 1961. 9-12

———. *The First Book of Words,* ill. by Lászlo Roth. Watts, 1954. 10-13

EULLER, JOHN. *Arctic World,* ill. with photographs and maps. Abelard, 1958. 10-13

EVANS, EVA KNOX. *Why We Live Where We Live,* ill. by Ursula Koering. Little, 1953. 9-12

FALLS, C. B. *The First 3000 Years: Ancient Civilizations of the Tigris, Euphrates, and Nile River Valleys and the Mediterranean Sea,* ill. by author. Viking, 1960. 11-14

FARRAR, SERGEANT F. S., RCMP. *Arctic Assignment: The Story of the St. Roch,* ill. by Vernon Mould. Macmillan, 1955. 11-13

FERGUSSON, ERNA. *Hawaii.* Fideler, 1962. 10-12

FLOETHE, LOUISE. *The Farmer and His Cows,* ill. by Richard Floethe. Scribner, 1957. 5-8

FOSTER, GENEVIEVE. *Augustus Caesar's World: A Story of Ideas and Events from B.C. 44 to 14 A.D.,* ill by author. Scribner, 1947. 12-14

———. *Birthdays of Freedom, I: America's Heritage from the Ancient World,* ill. by author. Scribner, 1952. 12-14

———. *Birthdays of Freedom, II: From the Fall of Rome to July 4, 1776.* Scribner, 1957. 12-14

———. *George Washington's World,* ill. by author. Scribner, 1941. 11-14

FRIEDMAN, ESTELLE. *Digging into Yesterday,* ill. by Leonard E. Fisher. Putnam, 1958. 10-13

A Garden We Planted Together. United Nations Department of Public Information. Whittlesey, 1952. 5-8

GATTI, ELLEN and ATTILIO. *The New Africa,* ill.

with photographs, maps by Rafael Palacios. Scribner, 1960. 11-14

GLUBOK, SHIRLEY. *The Art of Ancient Egypt,* designed by Gerard Nook. Atheneum, 1962. 10-13

GUNTHER, JOHN. *Meet the Congo and Its Neighbors,* ill. by Grisha (pseud.). Harper, 1959. 12-14

GUNTHER, JOHN, with SAM and BERYL EPSTEIN. *Meet North Africa,* ill. by Grisha. Harper, 1957. 10-12

_____. *Meet South Africa,* ill. by Grisha. Harper, 1958. 10-12

HILLYER, V. M. *A Child's Geography of the World,* rev. ed. by Edward Huey, ill. by Mary Sherwood and Wright Jones. Appleton, 1951. 10-12

HOFSINDE, ROBERT (GRAY-WOLF). *Indian Picture Writing,* ill. by author. Morrow, 1959. 10-12

_____. *Indian Sign Language,* ill. by author. Morrow, 1956. 9-13

HOLLING, HOLLING C. *Paddle-to-the-Sea,* ill. by author. Houghton, 1941. 9-11

_____. *Tree in the Trail,* ill. by author. Houghton, 1942. 9-11

HOYT, EDWIN P. *From the Turtle to the Nautilus: The Story of Submarines,* ill. by Charles Geer. Little, 1963. 9-12

HUGHES, LANGSTON. *The First Book of the West Indies,* ill. by Robert Bruce. Watts, 1956. 9-11

JOHNSON, GERALD W. *America Grows Up: A History for Peter,* ill. by Leonard E. Fisher. Morrow, 1960. 10-13

_____. *America Is Born: A History for Peter,* ill. by Leonard E. Fisher. Morrow, 1959. 10-13

_____. *America Moves Forward: A History for Peter,* ill. by Leonard E. Fisher. Morrow, 1960. 10-13

_____. *The Congress,* ill. by Leonard E. Fisher. Morrow, 1963. 9-12

_____. *The Presidency,* ill. by Leonard E. Fisher. Morrow, 1962. 9-12

_____. *The Supreme Court,* ill. by Leonard E. Fisher. Morrow, 1962. 9-12

JOY, CHARLES R. *Race Between Food and People: The Challenge of a Hungry World.* Coward, 1961. 9-11

LAUBER, PATRICIA. *Battle Against the Sea; How the Dutch Made Holland,* ill. with photographs. Coward, 1956. 10-14

LEAF, MUNRO. *Geography Can Be Fun,* rev. ed., ill. by author. Lippincott, 1962. 8-9

LENT, HENRY B. *Here Come the Trucks,* ill. by Renee George. Macmillan, 1954. 8-10

LEWIS, OSCAR. *Hawaii: Gem of the Pacific,* ill. by Stephen Medvey. Random, 1954. 10-13

LEY, WILLY, and editors of *Life. The Poles,* ill. with photographs. Time, 1962. 13-

LINDQUIST, WILLIS. *Alaska: The Forty-Ninth State,* ill. by P. A. Hutchinson. Whittlesey, 1959. 12-14

LORD, BEMAN. *Look at Cars,* ill. with photographs. Walck, 1962. 10-13

MC NEER, MAY. *The Alaska Gold Rush,* ill. by Lynd Ward. Random, 1960. 10-13

_____. *The California Gold Rush,* ill. by Lynd Ward. Random, 1950. 9-11

_____. *The Canadian Story,* ill. by Lynd Ward. Ariel, 1958. 11-13

MANNING, JACK. *Young Puerto Rico,* ill. by author. Dodd, 1962. 9-12

MASANI, MINOCHEHER. *The Growing Human Family,* ill. by C. G. H. Morehouse. Walck, 1951. 12-14

MEAD, MARGARET. *People and Places,* ill. by W. T. Mars and Jan Fairservis and with photographs. World, 1959. 12-14

MEADOWCROFT, ENID LA MONTE. *The Land of the Free,* ill. by Lee J. Ames. Crowell, 1961. 8-10

MINER, IRENE. *The True Book of Policemen and Firemen,* ill. by Irene Miner and Mary Salem. Childrens Press, 1954. 6-8

MORRIS, RICHARD B. *The First Book of the American Revolution,* ill. by Leonard E. Fisher. Watts, 1956. 9-13

_____. *The First Book of the Constitution,* ill. by Leonard E. Fisher. Watts, 1958. 10-12

OLDEN, SAM. *Getting to Know Argentina,* ill. by Haris Petie. Coward, 1961. 9-11

O'NEILL, HESTER. *The Picture Story of Hawaii,* ill. by Ursula Koering. McKay, 1950. 9-11

OTTO, MARGARET F. and STUART. *The Tractor Book,* ill. with photographs. Morrow, 1953. 8-11

PRICE, CHRISTINE. *Made in the Middle Ages,* ill. by author. Dutton, 1961. 10-13

QUENNELL, MARJORIE and C. H. B. *Everyday Things in Ancient Greece,* 2nd ed., rev. by Kathleen Freeman. Putnam, 1954. 12-14

QUINN, VERNON. *Picture Map Geography of Mexico, Central America and the West Indies,* rev. ed., ill. with maps and drawings by Da Osimo. Lippincott, 1963. 10-12

_____. *Picture Map Geography of the United States,* rev. ed., ill. with picture maps by P. S. Johst. Lippincott, 1959. 10-13

REEDER, RED. *The Story of the Civil War,* ill. by Frederick Chapman. Duell, 1958. 12-14

RIEDMAN, SARAH R. *Let's Take a Trip to a Skyscraper,* ill. by John Teppich and with photographs. Abelard, 1955. 8-10

RICH, LOUISE DICKINSON. *The First Book of New World Explorers,* ill. by Cary Dickinson. Watts, 1960. 9-11

ROBINSON, CHARLES A., JR. *The First Book of Ancient Egypt,* ill. by Lili Réthi. Watts, 1961. 9-12

_____. *The First Book of Ancient Greece,* ill. by Lili Réthi. Watts, 1960. 9-12

_____. *The First Book of Ancient Mesopotamia*

and Persia, ill. with maps and photographs. Watts, 1962. 10-13

———. *The First Book of Ancient Rome,* ill. by John Mackey. Watts, 1959. 9-12

ROSS, GEORGE E. *Know Your Government,* ill. by Seymour Fleishman. Rand McNally, 1959. 10-13

SASEK, MIROSLAV. *This is Israel,* ill. by author. Macmillan, 1962. 8-11

———. *This is Munich,* ill. by author. Macmillan, 1961. 8-11

———. *This is New York,* ill. by author. Macmillan, 1960. 8-11

———. *This is Paris,* ill. by author. Macmillan, 1959. 8-11

———. *This is Rome,* ill. by author. Macmillan, 1960. 9-11

———. *This is San Francisco,* ill. by author. Macmillan, 1962. 8-11

———. *This is Venice,* ill. by author. Macmillan, 1961. 9-11

SCHLEIN, MIRIAM. *It's About Time,* ill. by Leonard Kessler. W. R. Scott, 1955. 6-8

SCHNEIDER, HERMAN and NINA. *Let's Look Under the City.* W. R. Scott, 1954. 8-10

SHEPPARD, SALLY. *The First Book of Brazil,* ill. with photographs. Watts, 1962. 9-11

SHIPPEN, KATHERINE B. *Miracle in Motion: The Story of America's Industry.* Harper, 1955. 11-14

SMITH, BRADFORD. *The Islands of Hawaii,* ill. with photographs. Lippincott, 1957. 11-13

SOBOL, DONALD J. *The First Book of Medieval Man,* ill. by Lili Réthi. Watts, 1959. 10-12

SOLEM, ELIZABETH. *We Learn About Other Children, Encyclopaedia Britannica Picture Stories,* text by Elizabeth Solem, under editorial direction of the staff of Britannica Junior. Encyclopaedia Britannica, Inc., 1954. 7-11

SOOTIN, LAURA. *Let's Go to an Airport,* ill. by George Wilde. Putnam, 1958. 7-9

———. *Let's Go to a Zoo,* ill. Putnam, 1959. 7-9

SPERRY, ARMSTRONG. *All About the Arctic and Antarctic,* ill. by author. Random, 1957. 9-11

———. *Pacific Islands Speaking,* maps and drawings by author. Macmillan, 1955. 11-13

STEARNS, MONROE. *The Key to Rome,* ill. with photographs. Lippincott, 1961. 9-11

STEFANSSON, EVELYN. *Here Is Alaska,* rev. Statehood ed., ill. with photographs. Scribner, 1959. 10-13

———. *Here Is the Far North,* ill. with photographs; map by Richard E. Harrison. Scribner, 1957. 10-13

STERLING, DOROTHY. *United Nations,* rev. ed., photographs by Myron Ehrenberg. Doubleday, 1961. 12-14

STREET, ALICIA. *The Land of the English People,* rev. ed., ill. with photographs. Lippincott, 1953. 11-13

SZASZ, SUSANNE, and SUSAN LYMAN. *Young Folks' New York,* ill. with photographs. Crown, 1960. 9-11

TOOZE, RUTH. *Cambodia: Land of Contrasts,* ill. with photographs. Viking, 1962. 9-12

TOR, REGINA. *Getting to Know Canada,* ill. by author. Coward, 1956. 9-11

TUDOR, TASHA. *Around the Year,* ill. by author. Walck, 1957. 5-8

TUNIS, EDWIN. *Colonial Living,* ill. by author. World, 1957. 10-12

———. *Indians,* ill. by author. World, 1959. 12-14

VAN LOON, HENDRIK WILLEM. *The Story of Mankind,* rev. ed. Liveright, 1951. 12-14

VON HAGEN, VICTOR W. *Maya, Land of the Turkey and the Deer,* ill. by Alberto Beltrán. World, 1960. 11-14

WATSON, JANE W. *The Golden History of the World,* ill. by Cornelius DeWitt. Golden Press, 1955. 9-11

WERNER, ELSA JANE. *The Golden Geography,* ill. by Cornelius DeWitt. Golden Press, 1952. 9-11

WESTON, CHRISTINE. *Ceylon,* ill. with photographs. Scribner, 1960. 12-14

WHITE, ANNE TERRY. *All About Archaeology,* ill. by Tom O'Sullivan, with photographs. Random, 1959. 10-13

———. *The First Men in the World,* ill. by Aldren Watson. Random, 1953. 10-13

———. *Prehistoric America,* ill. by Aldren Watson. Random, 1951. 9-11

WITTY, PAUL, and JULILLY KOHLER. *You and the Constitution of the United States,* ill. by Lois Fisher. Childrens Press, 1948. 10-14

ZAFFO, GEORGE J. *The Big Book of Real Building and Wrecking Machines,* ill by author. Grosset, 1951. 7-10

———. *The Big Book of Real Fire Engines,* ill. by author. Grosset, 1950. 5-9

———. *The Big Book of Real Trains,* ill. by author. Grosset, 1949. 7-10

ZINER, FEENIE, and ELIZABETH THOMPSON. *The True Book of Time,* ill. by Katherine Evans. Childrens Press, 1956. 6-8

SCIENCE BOOKS

ADLER, IRVING. *The Stars: Steppingstones into Space,* ill. by Ruth Adler. Day, 1956. 12-14

———. *The Sun and Its Family,* ill. by Ruth Adler. Day, 1958. 12-14

———. *The Tools of Science: From Yardstick to Cyclotron,* ill. by Ruth Adler. Day, 1958. 12-14

AMES, GERALD, and ROSE WYLER. *First Days of the World,* ill. by Leonard Weisgard. Harper, 1958. 9-11

ANDREWS, ROY CHAPMAN. *All About Dinosaurs,* ill. by Thomas W. Voter. Random, 1953. 9-12

ASIMOV, ISAAC. *Inside the Atom,* rev. ed., ill. by John Bradford. Abelard, 1958. 12-14

BARKER, WILL. *Winter-Sleeping Wildlife,* ill. by Carl Burger. Harper, 1958. 10-14

BAUMANN, HANS. *The Caves of the Great Hunters,* rev. ed., tr. by Isabel and Florence McHugh. Pantheon, 1962. 11-14

BEELER, NELSON F., and FRANKLYN M. BRANLEY. *Experiments in Chemistry,* ill. by A. W. Revell. Crowell, 1952. 10-13

______. *Experiments with a Microscope,* ill. by Anne Marie Jauss. Crowell, 1957. 10-13

BELL, THELMA HARRINGTON. *Snow,* ill. by Corydon Bell. Viking, 1954. 8-12

BENDICK, JEANNE. *All Around You: A First Look at the World,* ill. by author. Whittlesey, 1951. 6-8

______. *What Could You See?,* ill. by author. Whittlesey, 1957. 6-9

BLOCH, MARIE HALUN. *Dinosaurs,* ill. by Mason. Coward, 1955. 8-11

BLOUGH, GLENN O. *Who Lives in This House?,* ill. by Jeanne Bendick. McGraw, 1957. 6-9

______. *Who Lives in This Meadow?,* ill. by Jeanne Bendick. Whittlesey, 1961. 6-9

BLOUGH, GLENN O., and MARJORIE H. CAMPBELL. *When You Go to the Zoo,* ill. with photographs. Whittlesey, 1955. 9-13

BRANLEY, FRANKLYN M. *A Book of Satellites for You,* ill. by Leonard Kessler. Crowell, 1958. 6-9

______. *The Nine Planets,* ill. by Helmut K. Wimmer. Crowell, 1958. 10-

______. *Solar Energy,* ill. by John Teppich. Crowell, 1957. 11-14

BRIDGES, WILLIAM. *Zoo Babies,* ill. with photographs. Morrow, 1953. 6-10

______. *Zoo Doctor,* ill. with photographs. Morrow, 1957. 9-11

BRINDZE, RUTH. *The Story of Gold,* ill. by Robert Bruce. Vanguard, 1955. 9-11

BUCK, MARGARET WARING. *In Ponds and Streams,* ill. by author. Abingdon, 1955. 9-12

______. *In Woods and Fields,* ill. by author. Abingdon, 1950. 9-12

______. *In Yards and Gardens,* ill. by author. Abingdon, 1952. 9-12

______. *Pets from the Pond,* ill. by author. Abingdon, 1958. 9-13

BUEHR, WALTER. *Underground Riches; the Story of Mining,* ill. by author. Morrow, 1958. 10-13

BUFF, MARY and CONRAD. *Big Tree,* ill. by authors. Viking, 1946. 9-14

______. *Elf Owl,* ill. by authors. Viking, 1958. 6-9

BULLA, CLYDE R. *A Tree Is a Plant,* ill. Crowell, 1960. 5-8

CALDER, RITCHIE. *The Wonderful World of Medicine,* diagrams by Isotype Institute, art by A. Bailey and others. Garden City, 1958. 10-14

CARSON, RACHEL. *The Sea Around Us,* adapted by Anne Terry White and ill. with photographs, maps, and drawings. Golden Press, 1958. 11-14

CHRYSTIE, FRANCES N. *Pets,* ill. by G. G. Griffin. Little, 1953. 10-14

COOPER, ELIZABETH K. *Science in Your Own Back Yard,* ill. by author. Harcourt, 1958. 10-13

CORMACK, M. B. *The First Book of Trees,* ill. by Helene Carter. Watts, 1951. 9-12

CROUSE, WILLIAM H. *Understanding Science,* rev. ed., ill. by Jeanne Bendick. Whittlesey, 1956. 10-14

DICKINSON, ALICE. *The First Book of Plants,* ill. by Paul Wenck. Watts, 1953. 9-12

______. *The First Book of Prehistoric Animals,* ill. by Helene Carter. Watts, 1954. 9-13

EARLE, OLIVE L. *Birds and Their Nests,* ill. by author. Morrow, 1952. 9-11

EPSTEIN, SAM and BERYL. *The First Book of Electricity,* ill. by Robin King. Watts, 1953. 9-12

EXLER, SAMUEL. *Growing and Changing,* ill. by Florence Exler. Lothrop, 1957. 6-9

FISHER, JAMES. *The Wonderful World of the Sea,* ill. by Eileen Aplin and others. Garden City, 1957. 10-14

FREEMAN, IRA M. *All About Electricity,* ill. by Evelyn Urbanowich. Random, 1957. 10-13

______. *All About the Wonders of Chemistry,* ill. by George Wilde. Random, 1954. 10-13

FREEMAN, MAE and IRA. *Fun with Figures,* ill. with photographs and diagrams. Random, 1946. 9-12

GALLANT, ROY A. *Exploring Chemistry,* ill. by Lee Ames. Garden City, 1958. 9-13

______. *Exploring Mars,* ill. by Lowell Hess. Garden City, 1956. 9-12

______. *Exploring the Moon,* ill. by Lowell Hess. Garden City, 1955. 9-12

______. *Exploring the Planets,* ill. by John Polgreen. Garden City, 1958. 9-13

______. *Exploring the Universe,* ill. by Lowell Hess. Garden City, 1956. 9-13

______. *Exploring the Weather,* ill. by Lowell Hess. Garden City, 1957. 10-13

GAUL, ALBRO. *The Pond Book,* ill. with photographs by the author. Coward, 1955. **9-13**

GOETZ, DELIA. *Tropical Rain Forests,* ill. by Louis Darling. Morrow, 1957. 8-11

GOUDEY, ALICE E. *Here Come the Beavers!,* ill. by Garry MacKenzie. Scribner, 1957. 7-9

______. *Here Come the Squirrels!,* ill. by Garry MacKenzie. Scribner, 1962. 7-9

______. *Houses from the Sea,* ill. by Adrienne Adams. Scribner, 1959. 5-8

GRAHAM, EDWARD, and WILLIAM R. VAN DERSAL. *Water for America: The Story of Water Conservation,* ill. with photographs. Walck, 1956. 10-14

GRUENBERG, SIDONIE M. *The Wonderful Story of How You Were Born,* rev. ed., ill. by Hildegard Woodward. Garden City, 1959. 6-9

HOGBEN, LANCELOT. *The Wonderful World of Energy,* ill. by Eileen Aplin and others. Garden City, 1957. 11-14

———. *The Wonderful World of Mathematics,* ill. by Andre, Charles Keeping, Kenneth Symonds; maps by Marjorie Saynor. Garden City, 1955. 10-14

HUNTINGTON, HARRIET E. *Let's Go to the Brook,* ill. with photographs by the author. Doubleday, 1952. 6-8

HUTCHINS, ROSS E. *Insects, Hunters and Trappers,* ill. with photographs by the author. Rand McNally, 1957. 10-14

JAUSS, ANNE MARIE. *The River's Journey,* ill. by author. Lippincott, 1957. 8-10

JESSUP, RONALD. *The Wonderful World of Archaeology,* ill. by Norman Battershill and Kenneth Symonds; diagrams by Isotype Institute. Garden City, 1956. 10-14

KAVALER, LUCY. *The Wonders of Algae,* photographs and drawings by Barbara Amlick and Richard Ott. Day, 1961. 11-14

LARRICK, NANCY. *See For Yourself,* ill. by Frank Jupo. American Book, 1952. 6-8

LEVINE, MILTON I., and JEAN H. SELIGMANN. *A Baby Is Born,* ill. by Eloise Wilkin. Golden Press, 1949. 9-11

LEWELLEN, JOHN. *The Mighty Atom,* ill. by Ida Scheib. Knopf, 1955. 8-11

———. *The True Book of Toys at Work,* ill. by Karl Murr. Childrens Press, 1953. 6-8

———. *Understanding Electronics,* ill. by Ida Scheib. Crowell, 1957. 12-14

LEWIS, LUCIA ZYLAK. *The First Book of Microbes,* ill. by Marguerite Scott. Watts, 1955. 9-12

MC CLUNG, ROBERT. *Bufo: The Story of a Toad,* ill. by author. Morrow, 1954. 5-8

———. *Buzztail: The Story of a Rattlesnake,* ill. by author. Morrow, 1958. 8-11

———. *Whitefoot: The Story of a Wood Mouse,* ill. by author. Morrow, 1961. 7-10

MORGAN, ALFRED POWELL. *Aquarium Book for Boys and Girls,* rev. ed., ill. by author and photographs. Scribner, 1959. 10-14

———. *Boys' Book of Science and Construction,* rev. ed., ill. with plates and diagrams. Lothrop, 1959. 11-14

———. *The First Chemistry Book for Boys and Girls,* ill. by Bradford Babbitt and Terry Smith. Scribner, 1950. 11-14

———. *A First Electrical Book for Boys,* 3rd ed., ill. by author. Scribner, 1951. 11-13

———. *A Pet Book for Boys and Girls,* ill. by author and Ruth King. Scribner, 1949. 9-13

MORRIS, PERCY A. *Boy's Book of Frogs, Toads, and Salamanders,* ill. with photographs. Ronald Press, 1957. 11-14

NEURATH, MARIE. *The Deep Sea,* ill. by author. Sterling, 1958. 5-8

PARKER, BERTHA MORRIS. *The Golden Book of Science,* ill. by Harry McNaught. Golden Press, 1956. 8-10

———. *The Golden Treasury of Natural History.* Golden Press, 1952. 8-14

PEATTIE, DONALD CULROSS. *Rainbow Book of Nature,* ill. by Rudolf Freund. World, 1957. 10-14

PELS, GERTRUDE. *The Care of Water Pets,* ill. by Ava Morgan. Crowell, 1955. 9-12

PODENDORF, ILLA. *101 Science Experiments,* ill. by Robert Boria. Childrens Press, 1960. 9-12

———. *The True Book of Trees,* ill. by Richard Gates. Childrens Press, 1954. 6-8

———. *The True Book of Weeds and Wild Flowers,* ill. by Mary Gehr. Childrens Press, 1955. 6-8

POPE, CLIFFORD HILLHOUSE. *Reptiles Round the World,* ill. by Helen Damrosch Tee-Van. Knopf, 1957. 11-14

RAVIELLI, ANTHONY. *An Adventure in Geometry,* ill. by author. Viking, 1957. 12-14

———. *Wonders of the Human Body,* ill. by author. Viking, 1954. 9-13

REY, H. A. *Find the Constellations,* ill. by author. Houghton, 1954. 9-13

RIEDMAN, SARAH R. *Grass: Our Greatest Crop,* ill. by Glen Rounds. Nelson, 1952. 10-14

RUCHLIS, HY. *Orbit: A Picture Story of Force and Motion,* ill. by Alice Hirsch. Harper, 1958. 10-

SCHATZ, ALBERT, and SARAH R. RIEDMAN. *The Story of Microbes,* ill. by Ida Scheib. Harper, 1952. 9-14

SCHEELE, WILLIAM E. *Prehistoric Animals,* ill. by author. World, 1954. 11-14

SCHNEIDER, HERMAN. *Everyday Weather and How It Works,* rev. ed., ill. by Jeanne Bendick. McGraw, 1961. 9-13

SCHNEIDER, HERMAN and NINA. *How Big Is Big?,* ill. by Symeon Shimin. W. R. Scott, 1950. 8-11

———. *How Your Body Works,* ill. by Barbara Ivins. W. R. Scott, 1949. 9-12

———. *Now Try This,* ill. by Bill Ballantine. W. R. Scott, 1947. 8-10

———. *You, Among the Stars,* ill. by Symeon Shimin. W. R. Scott, 1951. 8-10

SCHWARTZ, JULIUS. *Now I Know,* ill. by Marc Simont. McGraw, 1955. 6-8

———. *I Know a Magic House,* ill. by Marc Simont. Whittlesey, 1956. 5-7

SEABORG, GLENN T., and EVANS G. VALENS. *Elements of the Universe,* ill. with photographs, charts, and diagrams. Dutton, 1958. 12-

SELSAM, MILLICENT E. *All About Eggs and How*

They Change into Animals, ill. by Helen Ludwig. W. R. Scott, 1952. 5-8

———. *See Through the Forest,* ill. by Winifred Lubell. Harper, 1956. 8-11

———. *A Time for Sleep: How the Animals Rest,* ill. by Helen Ludwig. W. R. Scott, 1953. 5-9

SELSAM, MILLICENT E., and BETTY MORROW. *See Through the Sea,* ill. by Winifred Lubell. Harper, 1955. 8-11

SEVREY, O. IRENE. *The First Book of the Earth,* ill. by Mildred Waltrip. Watts, 1958. 9-13

SHUTTLESWORTH, DOROTHY E. *The Story of Rocks,* ill. by Su Zan N. Swain. Garden City, 1956. 10-13

SPILHAUS, ATHELSTAN F. *Weathercraft,* ill. with photographs and charts. Viking, 1951. 11-14

STEFFERUD, ALFRED. *The Wonders of Seeds,* ill. by Shirley Briggs. Harcourt, 1956. 10-13

STERLING, DOROTHY. *Caterpillars,* ill. by Winifred Lubell. Doubleday, 1961. 9-12

———. *Insects and the Homes They Build,* photographs by Myron Ehrenberg. Doubleday, 1954. 10-13

———. *The Story of Mosses, Ferns and Mushrooms,* photographs by Myron Ehrenberg. Doubleday, 1955. 10-14

———. *Trees and Their Story,* photographs by Myron Ehrenberg. Doubleday, 1953. 10-13

SWAIN, SU ZAN N. *Insects in Their World,* ill. by author. Garden City, 1955. 9-11

TANNENBAUM, BEULAH, and MYRA STILLMAN. *Understanding Time: The Science of Clocks and Calendars,* ill. by William D. Hayes. McGraw, 1958. 10-13

WEBBER, IRMA E. *Bits That Grow Big: Where Plants Come From,* ill. by author. W. R. Scott, 1949. 7-9

———. *Travelers All: The Story of How Plants Go Places,* ill. by author. W. R. Scott, 1944. 7-9

WERNER, JANE, and the staff of the Walt Disney Studio. *Walt Disney's Living Desert,* ill. by Kodachromes by Walt Disney Studio. Golden Press, 1954. 10-14

WHITE, ANNE TERRY. *The First Men in the World,* ill. by Aldren Watson. Random, 1953. 10-14

WILLIAMSON, MARGARET. *The First Book of Birds,* ill. by author. Watts, 1951. 9-12

The World We Live In, by the editorial staff of *Life* and Lincoln Barnett, text adapted by Jane Werner Watson, ill. Golden Press, 1956. 10-14

WYLER, ROSE, and GERALD AMES. *The Golden Book of Astronomy,* rev. ed., ill. by John Polgreen. Golden Press, 1959. 10-14

YATES, RAYMOND F. *Atomic Experiments for Boys,* ill. with drawings and photographs by author. Harper, 1952. 12-14

ZARCHY, HARRY. *Wheel of Time,* ill. by Rene Martin. Crowell, 1957. 11-13

ZIM, HERBERT S. *Comets,* ill. by Gustav Schrotter. Morrow, 1957. 9-12

———. *Frogs and Toads,* ill. by Joy Buba. Morrow, 1950. 8-11

———. *Things Around the House,* ill. by Raymond Perlman. Morrow, 1954. 7-11

———. *What's Inside of Me?,* ill. by Herschel Wartik. Morrow, 1952. 7-10

———. *What's Inside the Earth?,* ill. by Raymond Perlman. Morrow, 1953. 8-10

ZIM, HERBERT S., and CLARENCE COTTAM. *Insects: A Guide to Familiar American Insects,* rev. ed., ill. by James Gordon Irving. Golden Press, 1961. 10-14

ZIM, HERBERT S., and IRA N. GABRIELSON. *Birds: A Guide to the Most Familiar American Birds,* ill. by James Gordon Irving. Golden Press, 1956. 10-14

ZIM, HERBERT S., and ALEXANDER C. MARTIN. *Flowers: A Guide to Familiar American Wildflowers,* ill. by Rudolf Freund. Golden Press, 1950. 10-14

———. *Trees: A Guide to Familiar American Trees,* ill. by Dorothea and Sy Barlowe. Golden Press, 1952. 10-14

ZIM, HERBERT S., and PAUL R. SHAFFER. *Rocks and Minerals: A Guide to Familiar Minerals, Gems, Ores, and Rocks,* ill. by Raymond Perlman. Golden Press, 1957. 10-14

chapter 19

Reading and Creative Expression

Over and over again we discover that reading sparks creative expression. Children who are enjoying a saturation with poetry suddenly begin to write poems themselves. A dramatic story or an episode in a biography will inspire a dramatization. Historical fiction may launch a pageant, and fairy tales have given rise to almost every sort of creative expression—puppetry, the dance, murals, plays, and music. A college student who was particularly gifted in composition used to say that when she had something to write she would first read a story or a poem completely unrelated to her assignment and then, her mind cleared of the clutter of her personal concerns, she could settle down to work. Perhaps this is the clue. Literature or any of the arts in which we become temporarily absorbed can free us of the self, and so freed and caught up in wonder and pity or wonder and delight, we in turn feel the need for a creative outlet.

What is a creative act? Isn't it an act that is unique and individual, that takes tangible form in words, paints, clay, music, or dance, in response to an idea, an emotion, a sensory experience, people, or circumstances? This is a dull definition for an exciting personal experience. Certainly the essence of creativity is uniqueness and for fulfillment it must take tangible form so that others may see, hear, touch, and sometimes judge it.

No definition can say all there is to say about creativity. For instance, a creator in any field knows the sudden surge of joy that accompanies the successful culmination of his struggles. Creativity sharpens or restores a sense of joy, heals hurt spirits, and gives an abiding sense of life's goodness and gladness.

This is why adults who guide children's first tentative experiments with paints or words or any other media must walk warily between overpraise and not enough, between too much guidance and none at all. There is probably creative power of one kind or another in every child, but young spirits step forth timidly, and the courage to create is easily snuffed out by brusqueness, impatience, belittling, or, worst of all, sarcasm. But in a home or a classroom where there is warm friendliness, patience, and a genuine respect for each child as an individual, in such an atmosphere children will begin to think, speak, and act for themselves, and creativity will grow.

Adults must also remember that not every child will create verbally. Throughout this book, examples have been given of children's experiences with literature carrying over into clay modeling, or drawing, or skipping to the jingles of *Mother Goose*. Adults must accept the fact that some children are much less verbal than others. For one child, to create a poem would be as difficult or unnatural as for another child to express himself in a dance. The perceptive parent or teacher will welcome and encourage any form of creative expression.

Intelligence and Creativity

When Hughes Mearns' *Creative Youth*[1] appeared in 1925, it made a deep impression on teachers everywhere. In it Mearns recorded his methods of guiding children's creativity into writing poetry, and the book included an anthology of the children's original poems, which were astonishingly good. His methods were simple enough—a preliminary and continuous saturation with poetry read aloud, encouragement to try writing it themselves, *no adverse criticism* either from the teacher or the group, praise when possible, encouragement always. The impact of this book was so great that for a long time creative expression was thought of only in terms of writing poetry. But when teachers tried these methods and their results fell short of Mearns' examples, they consoled themselves by saying, "Oh well, he was working with children with high IQ's, not the kind that fill our classrooms."

Since Mearns' book there has been considerable research in the field of creativity, and for the teacher of average children the findings are encouraging. For one thing, high IQ's are not the essential element in creativity. Quite the contrary would seem to be true. In fact, Elliot W. Eisner said that "if scores of tests of intelligence were used to identify creative youngsters, approximately 70 per cent of the most highly creative would be overlooked."[2] This conclusion is based on Jacob Getzels' and Philip Jackson's study[3] and others which further suggest that high IQ's and creativity are almost incompatible. To this Eisner takes exception on the grounds that this conclusion is due to our limited conception of intelligence as the tests score it. After all, any child who formulates a new idea with words or paints, or an old idea in a fresh form is using a special kind of intelligence of a high order whether the tests record it or not. And a child with a high IQ who lacks the initiative to make use of what he knows in a fresh and original synthesis lacks something important that the other child has.

So if we are seeking and encouraging creativity, let's not worry about IQ's high or low, but rather let's worry about ourselves. Can we detect and not be irritated by the nonconformist in the group, the child who thinks for himself and is willing to stand out against the group for what he believes? Have we enough wisdom and tact to guide such a child without restricting him, to challenge him without demanding the result *we* thought of, to lead him to discipline himself for the sake of his work? If we can do these things, we are ready to guide those free, creative thinkers and doers that occur every so often.

Creative Expression in the Early Years

Children have always expressed themselves as exuberantly as life and their elders will permit, but the youngest children can't write, and for the sevens and even eights,

1. Hughes Mearns, *Creative Youth; How a School Set Free the Creative Spirit,* Doubleday, 1925.
2. Elliot W. Eisner, "Research in Creativity," *Childhood Education,* April 1963.
3. Jacob Getzels and Philip Jackson, *Creativity and Intelligence: Explorations with Gifted Students,* Wiley, 1962.

writing is a laborious task. So, in these early years, children's creativity may find expression chiefly in drawing and painting or dramatics. Of course, young children, while not able to write a poem or a story, nevertheless may express their ideas verbally with freshness, humor, and wisdom that are unique and sometimes poetic.

On a nursery school playground a child suddenly called out to his teacher, "Look, it's snowing crooked today! Why is it snowing crooked?"

Wisely, the teacher turned the question back to the child. "Why do you think it's snowing crooked?" she asked.

He thought a moment and then came back triumphantly, "The wind's blowing it. That's why it's snowing crooked!"[4]

Here is an example of the fresh expression of a new experience, made more accurate by a teacher's casual question.

A little girl, playing with her newly discovered shadow and enchanted with the miracle, cried out,

Look!
When the sun shines there are two of me.
One of me is big, one of me is little.
Both of me is me.[5]

And here is another observation turned into words as fresh and gay as the prancing child, posturing with her shadow. Incidentally, this child had heard Robert Stevenson's "My Shadow," so it is more than likely the poem had made her shadow-conscious.

Sometimes children are moved to deep feeling by the advent of a new baby in the family. This happened to a five-year-old child of a displaced family.[6] In kindergarten she scooped her clay into the shape of a cradle, so the teacher said, "Wanda, tell us what you have made." The child held up the clay cradle and spoke slowly and shyly,

Came the dawn.
Came the sun.
Creeping to the cradle,
Waking the little baby.

She spoke it like poetry which it certainly was, tender and touching. Wanda had heard poetry in two languages read aloud for sheer enjoyment. Had it influenced her cadenced speech?

In quite a different mood, a small third-grader, looking out at an April day of sleet, slush, and grayness, wrote his discouragement:

Snow is here,
Snow is here,
But spring is
Spost to be here!

Did the teacher say, "Henry, that word is *supposed,* not *spost*"? She did nothing of the sort. She said, "Henry, that's just the way I feel about this weather. I don't know why, but your poem makes me think of another spring poem that is just the opposite of yours." And she said for him the verse of Browning's poem beginning

Such a starved bank of moss
Till that May morn
Blue ran the flash across—
Violets were born.

No one can say how much this poem meant to Henry, but he certainly had a strong feeling that he and the teacher had a lot in common—a dismal spring day with better days just around the corner, violets for her maybe and marbles for him![7]

A first-grade teacher had started a weather record, but it had become a deadly routine. The children declared, "It's raining," or "It's sunny today." It occurred to her that the children might make a little more of a picture in words and still be accurate. Even though they could read only three- or four-word phrases, they *talked* in compound sentences with fluency and variety. Why not utilize their oral powers and stimulate their observation? First, she read the children some poems about weather. She chose Langston Hughes' "April Rain Song," John Drinkwater's "The Sun," Melville Cane's "Snow Toward Evening," and

4. Overheard by Miss Amy Hostler, Mills College.
5. Fernway School, Shaker Heights, Ohio; teacher, Mrs. Corinne Fox.
6. Superior School, East Cleveland, Ohio; reported by Wilda Bayes.
7. Wade Park School, Cleveland, Ohio; reported by Helen Burchfield.

many others. Poets seemed to enjoy writing about all kinds of weather, the children thought. Presently, she was getting from the children such descriptions as

The sun shines.
There are soft, white clouds
with blue sky between.

It is raining today.
The whole sky is gray with rain.

Snow fell today
from heavy clouds.
But it was not very cold,
so the little snowflakes
melted when they fell.

These were certainly improvements on the daily stereotypes—"It is raining," "It is snowing."

Factual and imaginative observations crowd together into a child's speech. Imaginative expression is apparently fostered when the teacher is imaginative, too, and has a sensitivity to children's creative imagery. In a second grade the children were doing some beautiful finger painting.[8] They had worked with only one color, but one day the teacher turned them loose with many colors, and the results were startlingly beautiful and sometimes weird. Studying them, the teacher said, "When I look at your finger paintings I begin to see pictures just the way I sometimes do when I look into the flames in my fireplace. You look at your own picture and see if you see something in it that suggests a name. Perhaps you can give your picture a name. You know they do name pictures." Then she held the pictures up one at a time and let the children look. The child who had painted it had the first chance to name it and usually succeeded, but occasionally a literal-minded child was stumped and the others named it for him. Some of the titles came quickly, some thoughtfully and slowly. One child said, "Mine looks something like a bridge in winter with icicles hanging down." So they named his picture "Bridge in winter with icicles." Others were "Sun shining on a garden," "Flowers and flames," "Rivers and mountains," "Snakes in the road," and "A Chinese house with flowers." Notice that these titles are as imaginative as the pictures. Children who have created and verbalized imaginatively in this way are more ready to accept imaginative literature, the fairy tales and modern fantasy. "A Chinese house with flowers" might lead to almost anything.

When art work, which furnishes an emotional release for a child, carries over into verbal expression, that expression is likely to

8. Superior School, East Cleveland, Ohio; teacher, Miss Marjorie Jamison.

Real experiences and book experiences provide young artists with subjects for illustration. The first crayon drawing gives a vivid impression of an Amish farm; the second is convincing proof that the young artist has understood and enjoyed his reading about westward expansion. Superior School, East Cleveland, Ohio; principal, Miss Wilda Bayes.

be less inhibited and more imaginative than his usual classroom talk. In a Cleveland third grade the children had been reading about cities and studying their own city in particular.[9] They had read poems about city life—"Taxis," "B's the Bus," "City Streets and Country Roads," "E is the Escalator," "City Rain," and others—but when they settled down to paint a large mural of their own Cleveland, their thinking and expression at first were definitely realistic. In the foreground the children painted all the different workers they had encountered—policemen, firemen, builders, nurses, teachers, even the neighborhood priest. As they discussed the background of the mural, the children agreed that there must be Lake Erie with its freighters and pleasure boats, and skyscrapers, churches, schools, houses, and stores. Then, a little girl, catching fire as the picture of their city grew in her mind, suddenly stretched up her arms and exclaimed, "And over the city and running through the city the singing wires of the telephones and telegraph going everywhere, all over the world!" This the teacher recorded to be used later in their script of "The City," an original narrative about Cleveland that was used with the mural for an assembly program.

An early book by Eva Knox Evans called *All About Us* dealt with the different peoples in different parts of the world. The children were fascinated with the idea of darker skin color as related to tropical sun, or the red or yellow pigmentation of other peoples. They made pictures of Chinese, East Indians, North American Indians, Eskimos, Negroes, Japanese, and Mexicans. One child summed up their exhibition of pictures neatly, "There are people of many colors all over the earth, and the right color for each people everywhere."[10]

Creative Writing

Creative writing may seem a pretentious name for the original prose and poetry children are assigned or inspired to write. But from third grade, it increases in quantity and is apt to be closely related to the literature the children are enjoying.

For example, a group of children who had been studying roads in their social studies[11] listened to Rachel Field's "Roads" beginning, "A road might lead to anywhere" and Nancy Byrd Turner's "The Little Road"—"travel stained and shabby," and decided that they might write some poems about roads. Admittedly, most of their first efforts were doggerel:

Some roads are humpy
Some roads are lumpy
Some roads are bumpy.

But from one of the boys came these surprising lines:

I'm a great big plot of grass,
But I might be a road some day.

And another boy, inspired perhaps by the personification in "The Little Road," produced a charming personification of his own:

Robert Road and Peter Path

Oh, Robert Road goes up, up, up,
Then down, down, down,
On his way to town.

But Peter Path has flowers
And the windy breeze
As he ambles on.

If you look at the Turner poem, you will see how little the boy's poem resembles it. His is a fresh use of personification.

Another example of creative writing inspired by literature comes from Lakewood, Ohio. The children, a group of third-graders, were deeply moved by Felix Salten's *Bambi*, which the teacher read aloud to them. They wrote poems about different parts of it and of them all, this has the uniqueness of deep feeling expressed with a fresh and inventive use of pattern:

9. Robert Fulton School, Cleveland, Ohio; teacher, Miss Sara Ronis.
10. *Ibid.*
11. Onaway School, Shaker Heights, Ohio; teacher, Miss Mabel Everett.

Winter

Rain, rain, rain,
Wet to the skin.
Snow, snow, snow,
And ice that is thin.
Food, food, food,
There is none to be found.
Bambi suffers hunger
Though he digs in the ground.
Poor deer!

Recently a wave of writing in some sort of approach to the Japanese haiku has been sweeping over the country. One modern poet feels that this is a mistake because the haiku is actually an extremely sophisticated form of poetry, exact, subtle, with overtones of meaning that go well beyond what the words actually say. Be that as it may, teachers have evidently been reading to their children some of the easier examples, translated from the Japanese, and letting the children try a looser form of haiku. Here are two examples from the Japanese:

Eaten by the cat!
Perhaps the cricket's widow
may be bewailing that!

This road:
with no man travelling on it,
autumn darkness falls.

This third example is by Onitsura, one of Japan's finest poets, who wrote these curiously perceptive three lines in 1668, when he was eight years old:

Although I say,
"Come here! Come here!" the fireflies
keep flying away![12]

In *Elementary English,* June 1961, Elizabeth Scofield gave a delightful account of what resulted from her reading haiku to the children and letting them try to write in this form. The children made their own rules which permitted considerable leeway:

1. Write the poem in three lines.
2. Tell what the subject is.
3. Tell where the subject is.
4. Tell when the action is taking place.

Miss Scofield added, "the most important rule came out in our discussion, although it was not verbalized as such. The poem must be something expressed from one's heart." These rules ignored syllable counts and said nothing about double meanings although such meanings do occur in the poems—for example,

The deer!
Look how gaily he bounds—
then goes.

Did this fourth grade boy have any consciousness that his verse is a moving expression of the evanescence of life? Or did the eight-year-old Japanese boy, three hundred years ago, think of his elusive fireflies as symbolizing the fleeting character of bright pleasures? Probably not, but perhaps from reading and hearing this particular type of verse, they were conscious of overtones of feeling beyond explanation. Who knows?

This subtle form of poetry requires extreme condensation, gives vent to feeling, and, finally, as Miss Scofield suggests, the three lines require clear thinking and free the writer from the burden of many words—"leaving a picture of beauty etched in fine clear lines." One of her boys wrote:

Petals on the ground—
beautiful, so beautiful!
birds singing in the starlight.

Here are sight and sound expressed simply with no extraneous decorations.

The teachers in the Randolph Elementary School, Lincoln, Nebraska, encouraged by their principal, Mrs. Ethel Baskins, have done a great deal with creative writing in the classroom. Here are a few of the haiku done by their pupils in 1963:

The tender flower in spring
Lightly, quietly,
Drops its golden petals.
Mike Morris, Grade 4

12. From *An Introduction to Haiku* by Harold G. Henderson. Copyright © 1958 by Harold G. Henderson. Reprinted by permission of Doubleday & Company, Inc.

Tender 'neath my feet
Sweet grass
Blows in the wind.
Vicki Pulos, Grade 4

The cranes
In midnight flight
Called over the mountains.
Chris Johnson, Grade 6

A twisted pine
Alone on the crag;
Mist over the rock-bound coast.
Bob Dzerk, Grade 6

Scrutinizing these diverse examples of children's use of haiku, we discover certain outstanding qualities. The idea or picture is fresh and unhackneyed and is expressed with the utmost economy. These examples may not be exact haiku, but in their poems, the youngsters catch a more subtle sense of secondary meanings than is usual with children. If through attempting to write haiku, children learn disciplined economy in the use of words, teachers will probably find the form well worth trying with children.

Saturation with poetry or with a particular subject is often enough to set children to writing. One year, in February, around the time of the patriotic festivals, a teacher read the Benéts' "Nancy Hanks" on the Cleveland school broadcasting station. Of all the ten thousand children listening, one group happened, at that particular time, to be steeped in Lincoln lore. They were studying the period and reading Sandburg's *Abe Lincoln Grows Up,* and they had been helped with the understanding of the poem by an artist-teacher. When they heard "Nancy Hanks," which is always deeply moving, one child said to the teacher, "Why don't we write answers to Nancy Hanks' questions, 'What's happened to Abe? What's he done?' " So they did. All thirty-five or -six answers were sincere attempts to reassure the wistful ghost of Nancy Hanks. They were not all masterpieces, but they were honest efforts.[13]

Sometimes children become so obsessed with rhyming that anything that rhymes is automatically a good poem to them, even if it is as bad as the roads—humpy, lumpy, and bumpy! When this happens, read them Hilda Conkling's poems and ask them why they think people call these unrhymed verses poems. This proved a poser when tried with a group of children. It took time and listening over and over to some of the verses (see pp. 178-180) before they arrived at these conclusions:

1. She says a lot in a few words.
2. She says things that no one has ever said before.
3. What she says about weather "is my wonder/About the kind of morning/ Hidden behind the hills of sky" surprises you.
4. It's like seeing something you never saw before, like the snail's shell being "his umbrella."

The children always came back to the poet's unique, surprising, new way of looking at and saying things. Freed of the burden of rhyme, children can write more naturally. The upper grades can handle rhyme with more ease than the lower grades, but over and over, when they are deeply moved, or sometimes when they need to clarify an idea, the older children, too, will use free verse.

Here, for instance, is a somber reflection of a deep emotion, written by a fifth-grade girl living in a depressed area of a big city. It was a dark, gloomy day with a steady downpour of rain. She stared out of a third floor window in her school, looking down on the wet city streets full of hurrying people. Soberly she walked back to her seat and wrote the following lines:

When raindrops fall,
It seems as if they were tears of God,
God weeping over the people of the streets.
But the people put umbrellas over their heads.[14]

Here was a precocious sensitivity expressed in strong, simple words, unrhymed but beautifully cadenced and climactic.

13. Two of them were so completely satisfying that they are included in *Time for Poetry* following the Benét poem.
14. Jennie Ross, fifth grade, William Brett School, Cleveland, Ohio.

Dramatization

M*other Goose,* folk tales, poetry, all may inspire dramatization. These dramas, formless in the beginning, usually manage to get to the heart of the idea that the rhyme or story embodies, even in the nursery school where these crude dramas begin. "The Three Billy-Goats Gruff" is a favorite. Some children were riding their bikes. Suddenly one called out belligerently, "I'm goin' to gobble you up."

Immediately the challenge was answered, not according to the letter of Dasent's text but true to the spirit.

"No you won't. You just wait for my big brother. He's bigger. He's lots bigger."

"All right, be off."

Again the challenge and a giggling answer from another bicyclist, until finally the third challenge brought a loud reply.

"O.K., you just come on. I've got horns, I have. Come on."

Two bicycles clashed—rather mildly—and the ferocious troll and the billy goat roared with laughter.

"Now you gotta fall down dead," prompted the goat.

So the self-appointed troll obliged by falling off his bike, and everyone laughed again. One of the children said hastily, while the troll was still down and unable to protest, "Now, I'll be the troll," and it started all over.

These were four-year-olds; this was their drama. It was crude and spotty with no attempt to reproduce the scene or the correct action, yet these children had selected the very heart of the drama—the conflict which makes this and most of the other folk tales essentially dramatic and fascinating to children of all ages.

The kindergartners also enjoy playing "The Three Billy-Goats Gruff" and "The Three Bears." The first- and second-graders like "The Bremen Town-Musicians," "The Sleeping Beauty," and "Hänsel and Gretel." These early dramatizations should be the children's own, not fussed up by adults into something finished and correctly dramatic. Polished performances are all right for an assembly or for a P.T.A. meeting, provided they are only occasional. Then costuming these little dramas and carrying them through in some detail may be justifiable and desirable. For everyday fun, trust young children to mangle the text a bit but to come out with the essence of the conflict every time. As a matter of fact, children soon develop a sense of form and dramatic sequence by themselves if we don't press our adult standards upon them prematurely.

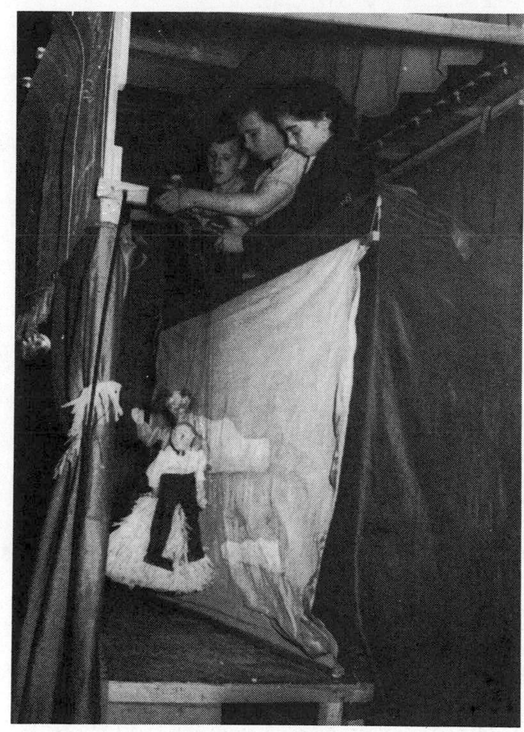

Marionette plays provide an opportunity for organizing, interpreting, and supplementing reading experiences. They are particularly valuable in the middle grades, where children are interested in costumes, stage properties, and planned dialogue.
Madison Public Schools, Madison, Wisconsin.

Don't try to have the children dramatize every story. There is nothing deadlier than a perfunctory, routine dramatization every day. Once or twice a week will probably be the limit. When dramatic stories cry out to be played, let the children try them. One of these will come to life so gaily and completely that nothing will do but an assembly or a sortie upon the grade next door for the satisfaction of sharing the story with an audience.

From the fourth grade up, dramatizations diminish as factual studies increase. But still the children love them and should have a fling at them three or four times a year. The group composition of a play—outlining acts, scenes, and action—is a fine English experience for upper grades. The dialogue usually remains fluid, chiefly because children cannot endure the mechanical bother of much writing, but occasionally an especially able group may even write down its dialogue.

WITH PUPPETS

Self-consciousness begins to trouble older children, and, worse still, the eleven- or twelve-year-old girls have a way of turning into young Amazons, leaving the boys their age embarrassingly smaller. So for the upper grades, puppets or marionettes are likely to be more popular than straight dramatization. Stick puppets are the easiest and the crudest; hand puppets are next easiest and have a great range of possibilities; marionettes are the most difficult. Shadow plays are also charming. They are all ideal media for the beauty and fantasy of fairy tales. "Hänsel and Gretel," "Cinderella," "Sadko," and "Rumpelstiltskin" can be remarkably beautiful when given as puppet shows.

Scenery, properties, and puppets are fun to make and fun to work with. The dreamlike quality and magic of the fairy tales can be more exquisitely suggested with these small creatures than they can be by human beings. And the tiny properties only enhance the magic—Rumpelstiltskin's pile of straw turned to gold, the Czar of the Sea's coral palace, the old witch and her gingerbread cottage, and Cinderella's pumpkin transformed into a splendid coach are especially convincing in the small. The puppets or marionettes are fascinating to manipulate and offer the protection of anonymity to the children who play the parts. In fact, children often become so attached to their particular puppets that they will ask if they can take the puppets home with them. These glorified dolls, with personalities, movement, and speech, have interested adults through many centuries and make a delightful hobby for children.

WITH SOCIAL STUDIES

Although social studies are factual and fairy tales quite the reverse, they may supplement each other. If, for instance, a class is studying colonial life in Nieuw Amsterdam, the work may be enlivened and research motivated by dramatizing "The Gift of St. Nicholas."[15] After the children have heard the story, they might work it into this form.

Act I: A gay street in Nieuw Amsterdam on Christmas Eve, with a background of shop windows painted by the children. People with bundles hurry by with cheery Christmas greetings. Children skip along, talking of Christmas goodies, sometimes stopping for a Dutch ring dance. Three ragged children peer wistfully into a toy shop window. Old Roeloffsen the burgomaster points them out gloatingly—"The children of Claas the cobbler with hardly a shoe to their feet. Anitje will be sorry she didn't marry me now."

Act II: A bare, dreary room, dimly lighted, with the children huddled around the feeble coals. Claas and Anitje are talking over their misfortunes when the stranger knocks. The story supplies the dialogue and action for this scene. The magical appearance of the birch logs on the fire and the feast in the oven is accomplished by having the stranger command the family to "Shut your eyes and look again. Maybe you'll see better." In the moment of darkness the scene is changed. The act ends with the feast, a thanksgiving hymn, and a gay dance led by the stranger.

Act III: Same room, richly furnished, with the chest full of money in a conspicuous place. The burgomaster pounds on the door, startling the sleeping Claas by accusing him of being a wizard. The dialogue and action are found in the story, as Roeloffsen opens the chest and is forced to beat a hasty retreat from the "unseen paddlers"—who may be St. Nicholas himself. The play ends with Claas

15. From Anne Malcomson's *Yankee Doodle's Cousins;* also found in *Time for Fairy Tales.*

and Anitje inviting the neighbors to a feast and merrymaking.

Such a play involves research to discover what clothing the people of that period wore; what the stores, furniture, music, and dances were like; and what the various Dutch legends of St. Nicholas were. In addition, it stimulates original composition, art work, and music.

In the same way, one class climaxed an Indian unit by performing "Little Burnt-Face." Before their play, the children explained to the audience that the story was a nature myth of the Southwest. "Little Burnt-Face" was the parched desert burned with the sun, and the invisible chief was the spring rain that brought beauty once again to the desert.[16]

Pecos Bill was the English center of a Westward Expansion unit. It might easily have turned into a puppet play. Instead, after the children had read the whole book and retold it at home, they developed their own tall tales. The boys were at their best as they chewed straws, tipped their hats down over their eyes, or, with legs crossed, sprawled in chairs and told yarn after yarn in the manner of old Pecos Bill himself.[17]

Since fairy tales have been collected from most of the countries the children are likely to study, and since such tales are often easier for children to dramatize than the more realistic stories, they supplement the social studies program admirably.

Both historical fiction and biography are fertile fields for creative expression. Can you think of more thrilling scenes for dramatization than the argument in the tower room between William Penn and Admiral Penn on the question of his Quakerism, or the great court scenes with Penn caged at the back of the room, pleading and winning his own case?[18] The great scene of surrender with Lee and Grant at Appomattox[19] is another thriller, or the scene in the House of Burgesses with Patrick Henry pleading the cause of freedom[20] is a natural for dramatization.

In Chapter 16 there is an account of the way one teacher made Laura Ingalls Wilder's Little House books the unifying factor for the study of almost every subject in the curriculum. This sort of living in a period can be accomplished with other periods and other books.

The Caledonia School, East Cleveland, backs up to a heavily wooded ravine. This setting, together with an intensive study of the Westward movement in our history, inspired the children to an outdoor dramatization that was eventually made into an amateur movie. This will probably remain one of the major thrills of the children's school days. The actual drama remained fluid and changed and grew from day to day. The pioneers marched and suffered everything from sickness to wild attacks from hostile Indians. The women carried their babies, the men made campfires and kept guard. There were Sabbath services of thanksgiving, even funeral services in the deep woods for a fallen comrade. Friendly Indians sometimes aided them, but the children greatly preferred the attacks. Episodes from many books were woven into this ever growing drama, and the great difficulty was getting the children to bring it to a close. They lived and loved the period, and could hardly bear to bring those long suffering pioneers triumphantly to their destination because it meant the end of their drama.[21]

Illustration

Many stories are fun to illustrate, especially fairy tales where one person's interpretation may be as valid as anyone else's. (See the illustrations on p. 286.) But poems are often so highly pictorial that they are especially good subjects for paints, crayons, or even clay—"Susan Blue" and her friend talking over a garden gate, "plump Bess" clapping her platter to call the chickens,

16. Ethical Culture School, New York City.
17. Caledonia School, East Cleveland; teacher, Miss Ethel Hunter.
18. Elizabeth Janet Gray, *Penn,* Viking, 1938.
19. MacKinlay Kantor, *Lee and Grant at Appomattox,* Random, 1950.
20. Nardi Campion, *Patrick Henry: Firebrand of the Revolution,* Little, 1961.
21. Miss Muriel Schoen, student teacher, under whom this project was conducted.

Using a special technique, sixth-graders made bright, bold pictures of various birds. Here are five pictures from the collection entitled "Birds of a Feather."
Taylor Elementary School, Cleveland Heights City School District, Ohio; teacher, Mr. Merrill Grodin; principal, Mr. Morris Sorin. Used with permission.

"Shadow Dance," "Puppy and I," "Until We Built a Cabin," "Hoppity," "April Rain Song," "Windy Wash Day," "The Kite," "Stopping by Woods on a Snowy Evening," and dozens of others. (See the illustrations on pages 109, 199, and 241.)

One classroom that had enjoyed a long exposure to poetry decided to illustrate their favorite poems.[22] Each child chose a poem and when his picture was finished, the teacher had the poem typed and ready to put down in one corner of the mat the picture was mounted on. Then they had an "at home" for another grade. They spoke the poems that went with the pictures and exhibited the other pictures for which there had been no space. Room and pictures were beautiful, and the children's unself-conscious speaking of the poems made a relaxed and pleasant occasion.

A Rich Experience with Art and Literature

Sometimes art or music or the dance will lead into literature. For instance, in one class, listening to the record of Stravinsky's *Fire Bird* led to the folk tale and that in turn suggested a dramatization using puppets. So dance-pantomime might well lead to the myths. The following account gives a striking example of an art project enormously expanded and enriched with music, myth, poetry, and stories.

"Birds of a Feather" was the title the children in the sixth grade gave to their pictures of birds, produced by a new technique their teacher had seen and liked.[23] The bird was drawn, then individual feathers of different colored construction papers were snipped, bent, and pasted to the body of the bird. The results were astonishingly beautiful. Incidentally, what interested the adults was that each of these bird portraits somehow suggested the child who had made it. When the portraits were completed, teacher and children were so proud of the results that they offered the collection to the school librarian for exhibition in the spacious library. The librarian, a creative and gifted person, saw at once the far-reaching possibilities of those handsome birds and accepted them with enthusiasm. Once mounted and hung, they brought color and drama into the room. All classes use this library, both in groups and as individuals, so the librarian began assembling related books.

For the kindergarten-primary groups, picture-stories were displayed, and since the pictured birds were both fanciful and realistic, the literature included both. For example, *Petunia* and *Jemima Puddle-Duck* were lined up side by side with *Fly High, Fly Low* and *Come Again, Pelican* by Don Freeman.

Another exhibit contained the factual books —how to identify birds, how to build bird houses, feeding stations, and the like. Because these informational books are so handsomely illustrated, this exhibit vied with literature in appeal.

For the middle and upper grades there were such books as Mukerji's *Gay-Neck,* Meindert De Jong's *Wheel on the School,* and Jean George's *Summer of the Falcon.*

Folk and fanciful tales ranged from Hans Andersen's "The Emperor and the Nightingale" to bird myths, bird folk tales, and *Summer Birds* by Penelope Farmer.

Poetry was plentiful. The librarian listed anthologies containing groups of bird poems, for example, Walter de la Mare's *Peacock Pie* and James Reeves' *Blackbird in the Lilacs.* Favorite poems were typed and placed on the bulletin board or attached to the mount of one of the birds. For example, Tennyson's "Eagle" appeared with that fine swooping bird; "The North wind doth blow" with one of the robins, and "What Robin Told" with the other one; and of course, "There Once Was a Puffin" accompanied that fanciful bird.

As each class came to the library to see the birds for the first time, the librarian talked to the children, introducing the pictures

22. Taylor Road School, Cleveland Heights, Ohio; teacher, Miss Verna Lewis.

23. Taylor Elementary School, Cleveland Heights, Ohio; teacher, Mr. Merrill Grodin; librarian, Mrs. Winifred Machan; and principal, Mr. Morris Sorin.

and the books. On later days she told bird stories and myths, had them listen to records of actual bird songs, and then included the music gradually. For the youngest children she began with simple folk songs and carols about birds, and for the older children with Stravinsky's *Fire Bird,* Rimsky-Korsakov's *Le Coq d'Or,* Tchaikovsky's *Swan Lake,* the garden section of Respighi's *Pines of Rome,* and Wagner's "Forest Birds" from *Siegfried.*

Such an outline can barely suggest the richness of this experience. The children read, painted, listened, and were thrilled. They found stories and poems on their own. They brought their parents to see the pictures and the books. And later in the year, when the pictures had been taken down and new books were displayed, the children still harked back to the birds. Such a rich experience with related arts cannot take place without genuinely creative adults to show the way. In this case a deeply interested principal, a creative teacher, and an equally creative librarian worked together to encourage and develop this continuously expanding project.

The Atmosphere for Creativity

These challenging examples of creative expression bring the practical question, "But how can I get such results with *my* children?"

First of all, we need to remember that *being able to talk and to be listened to* is basic to growth in verbal expression. It is a frightening fact that in the child's first years of school when language is developing more rapidly than it ever will again, the sheer numbers of children in our classrooms require a damming up of speech for a good part of the school day. A mother asked her five-year-old if he had told the teacher and children about their new baby, and he replied, "No, it wasn't my turn to talk today." At home if there are several children, the battle for the floor may be equally keen. One small boy with three big brothers developed a stutter during his early years of struggling for a hearing. So, if young children are to develop verbal fluency, let there be time to talk and someone to listen. Turning a question back to a child, or helping him to verify statements or observations can help, too, when done casually without pressure.

Times of solitude or quiet are also essential and difficult to provide. Today the child with a room of his own is fast becoming an exception. In the crowded areas of big cities, children take to the streets to find elbow room. How then can the schools be expected to provide space and quiet? It can be done if the need is recognized. Even in crowded classrooms teachers can plan for a period of quiet in every day, when children can read or paint or write on their own, or listen to music if they choose, or go to the library to browse. Visits to the children's room in the public library and to the various museums of a great city will equip children with sources of quiet and of wonder which will stay with them all their days. It was Dr. Alexis Carrel who said, "A work of art has never been produced by a committee of artists. . . ."[24] Togetherness has its place, but genuinely creative work is done in solitude or by a single mind. Children as well as adults need quiet and solitude in order that dreams may grow and ideas take root.

Appreciation rather than negative criticism was a universally accepted dictum by the teachers reported in this chapter. Whether the child's creative expression bursts forth in paints, the dance, words, or clay modeling, carping negative criticism either from the teacher or from the children kills the urge to originate. The child who timidly holds up his picture to show the group only to have it picked to pieces dies a thousand deaths of the spirit. Suppose that a book report or an original poem or story is subjected to this kind of baiting: "I think John spoke real clearly but . . . ." When the *but's* are over, John is done in and won't risk anything more than the usual stereotypes ever after. Children's ideas are entitled to respect and the child to

24. Alexis C. Carrel, *Man, the Unknown,* Harper, 1935, p. 47.

what Elliot Eisner calls "psychological safety." Over three decades before Carl Rogers' paper "Toward a Theory of Creativity"[25] stated this conclusion, Hughes Mearns was also avoiding negative criticism when working with children's creative efforts. He wrote: "I so manage the controls that the highest praise goes solely to the work that bears the mark of original invention." His method is still sound.

Children are unconsciously imitative, as indeed we all are. But children do not recognize their borrowings nor their clichés and must be helped to the disciplines their art requires. This means that you will bear with flagrant imitations with little or no comment. When a five-year-old announces that he is going to tell a story about a Little *Black* Hen, you let him have the language practice this effort involves and say only, "Henry told his story well." When another child tells a wild and woolly tale out of the blue, you say, "I liked that story because it was your very own. I don't believe anyone ever made up a story like that before." For older children there may be such comments as, "Nancy, that is your best writing. No unnecessary adjectives make your lines stronger." "Jennie, I don't believe I will ever again see people in the streets with umbrellas over their heads without thinking of your poem. That was a new and different idea." "John, without saying 'It was summer,' the description of yourself made me much more aware of heat than that statement could have done. I felt warm just reading it." In short, specific, honest appreciation makes a child aware of his progress and of his goals.

One teacher who had unusual success with composition tried to make sure first that a child was really fired with some idea and then she let him write fast and furiously with no niggling corrections of grammar, sentence structure, or spelling. She kept the child's attempts focused on clarity and strength of expression. In another period she would drill on the collective mistakes found in many papers. An exercise in being more specific or stating an ordinary idea more effectively would go something like this: "Let's take an ordinary statement such as 'He went away' and see how many different ways you can say that so it tells the reader something about the person or the situation."

He went away	He crawled away
He slunk away	He slouched away
He limped away	He dashed away
He stalked away	He hurried away

Such exercises can be amusing, but they also call the child's attention to the disciplines of writing. For the dancer, the disciplines are bodily control, exact and, to the beginner, formidable; for the artist, basic skill in drawing and knowledge of colors in all their combinations and subtleties. Stephen Foster never developed his capacities as a composer because he would not subject himself to studying harmony, one of the basic disciplines of music. Once a child has tasted the heady delights of invention, of creativity in his favorite art, then he should he helped to a consciousness of the peculiar disciplines that this art demands. Dr. Miriam E. Wilt once said,

> *Extrinsic control means death to creative thinking . . . . the most highly developed discipline in the world is required for genuine creative endeavor, intrinsically conceived and internally applied. Far more rigid rules are applied by the creator than any external force can ever apply.*[26]

But this means that sometime the creative child must be guided to the sources of his strength and to the disciplines he needs to develop further. Then once he knows what to work for and feels power growing, he will work.

In conclusion, let's remember that in all forms of creativity, whether it is the dance, painting, poetry, storytelling, or dramatization, the child's secret self steps forth shyly. A perceptive adult can learn from such creative expression something about the child's inner life, his confusions, anxieties, conflicts, fears, and strengths. But in this realm of the spirit, an adult must move gently and unobtrusively. Among all the banal or raucous or commonplace or superficial expressions she receives as the general rule (and for these she must brace

25. Harold Anderson, ed., *Creativity and Its Cultivation*, Harper, 1959.
26. Miriam E. Wilt, "Shall We Let Them Create?" *Elementary English*, April 1963, p. 357.

herself and pray for patience), she will glimpse every now and then revelations of beauty and precocious insight that will leave her humble. After all, eight-year-old Hilda Conkling knew that

Loveliness that dies when I forget
Comes alive when I remember.

SUGGESTED READING, PROBLEMS, AND PROJECTS

1. What other art besides literature might inspire creative expression? Give an example.

2. From the examples of children's creative expression scattered throughout the chapter, cite an example that seems to grow out of or give rise to a strong sensory impression (visual, auditory, tactile, etc.), a mood or emotion, an idea.

3. How can teachers or parents provide children with varied and interesting experiences that stimulate creativity?

4. Find examples from newspapers or other sources that show boredom, dullness, drabness as the enemies of creativity and breeders of destructiveness.

5. Give an example of what you would call a genuinely creative self-initiated activity on the part of children.

6. Try writing a haiku. Describe the experience and your result.

7. Find a proverb you think children might develop into a story.

8. In the discussion of "Birds of a Feather" only a few of the many available children's books are cited. Add some others at each age level—primary, middle, and upper grades. Add also specific myths, folk tales, and poems. Try to think of another topic that might grow and expand as richly as this one did.

9. What is meant by "psychological safety" in a classroom?

10. Why is it important to help children feel free and competent in creative expression of one kind or another? Do you remember any such experiences in your school days? If so, describe them in detail and evaluate them.

REFERENCES

ANDERSON, HAROLD, ed. *Creativity and Its Cultivation.* Harper, 1959. A compilation of outstanding research papers in the field of creativity. Carl Rogers' paper entitled "Toward a Theory of Creativity" presents his findings on psychological safety, which he considers essential to creative thinking.

ARNSTEIN, FLORA J. *Adventure Into Poetry.* Stanford Univ. Press, 1951. Since Mearns this was the first well-recorded account of a creative use of poetry with elementary children. It is good reading, and both teachers and parents will profit by her discussions of qualities that mark authentic poetry.

EISNER, ELLIOT W. "A Typology of Creativity in the Visual Arts." *Studies in Art Education,* 4, Fall 1962. "Research in Creativity and Intelligence: Some Findings and Conceptions." *Childhood Education,* April 1963. In both of these papers, an assistant professor of education, University of Chicago, summarizes some recent research findings in the field of creativity and takes issue with some of them.

GETZELS, JACOB, and PHILIP JACKSON. *Creativity and Intelligence: Explorations with Gifted Pupils.* Wiley, 1962.

READ, HERBERT. *This Way, Delight.* Pantheon, 1956. An excellent anthology, mentioned here because of its unusual introduction in which the author defines poetry and gives practical suggestions for writing it.

SANDBURG, CARL. *Early Moon.* Harcourt, 1930. Almost any child in or beyond third grade would enjoy the author's comments on poetry. Sandburg's advice both on the enjoyment and on the writing of poetry is good.

TORRANCE, E. PAUL. *Education and the Creative Potential.* Univ. of Minn. Press, 1963.

ART AND MUSIC BOOKS

Also see references for artists and musicians in Chapter 17, Biography.

BAUER, MARION, and ETHEL PEYSER. *How Music Grew,* rev. ed. Putnam, 1939. A brief history of the growth of music from primitive beginnings. 11-

BRITTEN, BENJAMIN, and IMOGEN HOLST. *The Wonderful World of Music.* Doubleday, 1958. An introduction to the history of music, composers, and performers, illustrated with superb reproductions chiefly in color. 11-16

BULLA, CLYDE R. *The Ring and the Fire,* ill. by Clare and John Ross. Crowell, 1962. Richard

Wagner's operas based on the German epic of the Nibelung are dramatically related for a wider audience than opera students. Casts of characters and musical themes are included. 12-

CARMER, CARL. *America Sings; Stories and Songs of Our Country's Growing,* ill. by Elizabeth Carmer. Knopf, 1942. Some thirty folk songs arranged according to locale. 10-

CHAPPELL, WARREN. *The Nutcracker.* Knopf, 1958. Warren Chappell's colorful pictures and brief musical themes from Tchaikovsky add luster to the old fantasy of the *Nutcracker and the Mouse King.* 8-12

CHASE, ALICE. *Famous Paintings, an Introduction to Art for Young People.* Platt, 1951, 1962. Five thousand years of art, with numerous color reproductions and brief, challenging text. 10-

COMMINS, DOROTHY BERLINER. *All About the Symphony Orchestra and What It Plays,* ill. by Warren Chappell, and with photographs. Random, 1961. A useful supplement for the student with some musical background. 12-15

CRAVEN, THOMAS. *The Rainbow Book of Art.* World, 1956. A history of world art from primitive times to the present. Lavishly illustrated with almost 400 pictures of which 32 are in color. 12-

FREUND, MIRIAM. *Jewels for a Crown: The Story of the Chagall Windows,* ill. McGraw, 1963. 10-

GLUBOK, SHIRLEY. *The Art of Ancient Egypt,* ill. Atheneum, 1962. Fine photographic reproductions of toys, mummies, household goods, statues, and bowls, together with brief text, give insight into how Egyptians lived from sometime before 3100 B.C. until Roman times. 9-12

GOMBRICH, E. H. *Story of Art,* ill. Phaidon, 1954. A historical summary of sculpture, painting, and architecture. 14-

HASKELL, ARNOLD. *The Wonderful World of Dance,* ill. Doubleday, 1960. Outstandingly illustrated history of the evolution of the dance from primitive to modern times. 12-16

HILLYER, VIRGIL M., and EDWARD G. HUEY. *A Child's History of Art.* Appleton, 1951. 10-14

HUNTINGTON, HARRIET. *Tune Up,* ill. with photographs. Doubleday, 1942. The seating plan of an orchestra is included in this excellent introduction to orchestral instruments. 9-12

JANSON, H. W., and D. J. JANSON. *The Story of Painting for Young People.* Abrams, 1962. Termed a textbook edition, this is a beautiful reduced-size edition of an outstanding survey of painting, artists, and significant periods and trends. Fine color reproductions. 12-

MONTGOMERY, ELIZABETH RIDER. *The Story Behind Musical Instruments.* Dodd, 1953. Absorbing accounts of instruments and the men who developed them. 11-15

POSELL, ELSA. *This Is an Orchestra,* ill. with photographs. Houghton, 1950. An introduction to each kind of orchestral instrument. 8-12

PRICE, CHRISTINE. *Made in the Middle Ages,* ill. by author. Dutton, 1961. Fascinating information on medieval arts and crafts. Followed by *Made in the Renaissance* (1963). 11-

SAMACHSON, DOROTHY and JOSEPH. *The Fabulous World of Opera,* ill. with photographs. Rand McNally, 1962. Combines a brief history with a behind-the-scenes account of the workers and artists who contribute to opera. 14-

SLOBODKIN, LOUIS. *The First Book of Drawing,* ill. by author. Watts, 1958. Constructive drawing guidance for amateurs. 8-13

SPENCER, CORNELIA. *How Art and Music Speak to Us,* ill. with photographs. Day, 1963. An approach to communication through the arts. 11-14

WALDEN, DANIEL. *The Nutcracker,* ill. by Harold Berson. The story is adapted from the ballet by Lev Ivanov and Peter Ilych Tchaikovsky. Lippincott, 1959. Colorful, imaginative drawings and a sparkling text offer a fine introduction to the classic Nutcracker ballet. 6-11

WEISS, HARVEY. *Pencil, Pen and Brush,* ill. by author. W. R. Scott, 1961. Valuable basic drawing techniques for beginners. 10-14

PUPPETS

ACKLEY, EDITH F. *Marionettes: Easy to Make! Fun to Use!* ill. by Marjorie Flack. Lippincott, 1929. An excellent book on the making of cloth marionettes, with many aids to play production. Full-size paper patterns are included. 10-14

FICKLEN, BESSIE. *Handbook of Fist Puppets.* Lippincott, 1935. Detailed instructions for making hand puppets and their theater are given along with three plays. 12-

JAGENDORF, MORITZ. *First Book of Puppets,* ill. by Jean Michener. Watts, 1952. An aid to the making of different types of puppets and marionettes, and technical guidance in play production. 8-12

LEWIS, ROGER [pseud. for Harry Zarchy]. *Puppets and Marionettes,* ill. by author. Knopf, 1952. Some adult guidance is needed to help the child follow these instructions. 9-12

LEWIS, SHARI. *The Shari Lewis Puppet Book.* Citadel, 1958. Even preschool children can make and use puppets with assistance, in this attractively illustrated guide for many ages. 8-12

PELS, GERTRUDE. *Easy Puppets.* Crowell, 1951. A unique handbook on how to make puppets of almost anything from potatoes to papier mâché. The book also includes directions for making stages, scenery, curtains, and props. 7-12

chapter 20

Reading and the Mass Media

When the critics suggest that our Johnnies and our Janeys can't read, it is time for someone to reply firmly, "But they can read and they do read—more books than any generation of children ever read before." Children's librarians can produce the statistics on book withdrawals to prove the point, reading research specialists can vouch for children's reading skills (not just word reading, but reading for understanding and enjoyment), book publishers can quote enormous figures in sales of children's books, teachers can boast about many of their students who habitually read a book a week, and parents can tell about their children's enthusiasm for pleasure reading at home. What then of the rivals—the comics, television, radio, motion pictures, recordings, magazines, and newspapers—which are supposed to have competed so successfully for the child's time that he couldn't possibly read a book even if he wanted to?

There they are—the lively arts of the mass media—and the child patronizes all of them. And why shouldn't he? They are a part of his world, and some of them are among the wonders of our age. Moreover, many of them require of their young patrons little more than an unlimited ability to sit. But there are the books, too—books which he has withdrawn from the public or the school library, or which fond relatives have bought for him, or which he has purchased for himself with his allowance—books which he reads and rereads with continued affection. As one little girl said, "I've read *Brighty* five times, and I'll probably read it again." She was not a particularly bookish child, and all the entertainment mass media were available to her.

For children, it is not a matter of television *or* reading. It is, happily, reading plus, for over and over again television, radio, or motion pictures will send a child to the book source to find out more about the program or movie he has enjoyed or to savor it again in the more thoughtful process of reading.

Adults need not be too fearful of the usurpation of all book reading time by these media. But it is essential to know what the child is reading, seeing, and hearing. While it is true that comics can be grim, television and radio stories banal, movies suggestive, and newspapers and magazines sensational, books also can be trite and offensive. Part of the process of growing up is to learn to discriminate—in every field. Just as there are great books available in the juvenile field, there are great entertainment and enlightenment to be found on radio and television and in motion pictures. Whether there has ever been a masterpiece in the field of the comics may be debatable, but at least some comics are satirical and innocent bits of entertainment. In all leisure-time activities for children, careful parents and teachers are or should be keeping their eyes on the young consumer and aiding him in finding wholesome sources for enjoyment and information.

Television and Radio

Every age has its chief whipping boys. When grandfather as a boy read penny paperbacks and dime novels, adults were positive he would lose his eyesight and his morals; when our mothers and fathers as youngsters watched movies, adults were just as positive that their eyesight and virtue would be ruined. And now the question is, what is the effect of radio and, in particular, television on the current generation?

Television, which offers an opportunity for both a visual and an auditory response, seems to occupy a more important position than radio in the lives of today's children. In *Changing Times,*[1] Professors Wilbur Schramm, Jack Lyle, and Edwin B. Parker reported from their studies of 6000 children that since the advent of television, comic-book reading has declined 50 percent, movie attendance has declined 67 percent, and radio listening has decreased 50 percent. They also reported that heaviest television viewing is in early adolescence (ages 11 and 12) and that teen-agers listen to the radio chiefly as background for other activities.

Since radio and television have much in common and can be evaluated by many of the same criteria, we shall discuss them together. The programs of both media range from superb to good to poor. In both areas, the problem is largely one of developing children's tastes, skills, and appreciation, just as it is in their reading.

EVALUATION OF TELEVISION AND RADIO

In terms of physical effects, television and radio seem to have caused no appreciable damage to eyesight or hearing, although parents are told to leave a light on in the room with the television and to encourage children to sit at least six feet from the screen. On the other hand, teachers say that children who watch television programs far into the night come to school hollow-eyed, unable to concentrate on the day's activities.

However, the question which most concerns adults is undoubtedly the moral effect upon children of radio and television programs. Speaking generally, newscasts and informational programs are morally sound; situation comedies and programs where games are played are usually devoid of provocative ideas and morally insignificant; shows of violence usually point out that "crime doesn't pay," at least during the last few minutes; and dramas usually develop fairly obvious universal truths and are therefore morally instructive to a degree.

A popular belief is that television and radio are causes of juvenile delinquency. However, juvenile delinquency characteristics are far too broad and complex for one to lay the blame on mass media alone. As one person has said, "Juvenile delinquency has been with us a long, long time. Television is very recent." Of course, there is hardly an adult who hasn't witnessed children playing Indians and cowboys and calling each other their favorite "western" names. So there is involved, to some degree, imitation of what children watch or hear. However, most often this imitation is done with naïveté, and if children otherwise have a wholesome balance of ideas in their home, community, and school life, the imitation is probably harmless.

For the most part, normal children aren't

1. July 1961, pp. 23-24.

being turned into delinquents through the mass media, but values and tastes can be distorted by too much television and radio. Young girls, for instance, who continually watch television's so-called soap operas may feel that life is one unsolvable problem after another. Or children's views of normal family relationships could be warped by a steady diet of situation comedies in which parents—and father in particular—are usually slow-witted and children are uncommonly clever and unchildlike. And, too, children's tastes may never develop beyond the level of slapstick television programs or round-the-clock programs of popular music if they are not subtly guided on to other things. While we adults may feel fairly confident that radio and television are not damaging most children's ethical code, we should not feel so sanguine about the effect of unlimited and unguided viewing or listening upon their tastes and values. While these two media may not be *causing* delinquency, they may not be reinforcing desirable ideas and ethical standards or encouraging a high level of taste.

This situation might be improved by two means. First, as we have suggested above, children should have guidance from adults in their use of radio and, in particular, television. This guidance should be in the form of regulations set up by the parents and discussion of programs at home and in the classroom. Second, the radio and television industry should continually work for self-improvement.

Teachers and parents can help children by talking over programs and, in the case of the soap operas, for example, bringing the children to see their unrealistic approach to life. It is wise to attempt evaluation of programs from a child's point of view as well as from an adult's. Children very often do not interpret as do adults, and what may seem absurd or terrifying to the latter may affect youngsters differently, and vice versa.

Parents have the responsibility of making reasonable regulations and then enforcing them. If the children in the family are old enough, they may be consulted and in this way be brought to evaluate their favorite programs. But both the rules and the enforcement are ultimately the responsibility of the parents.

Here are some questions that might be asked in determining whether or not a program is suitable for children: 1. Are the interests of the program and the children compatible? 2. Is the emotional tone of the program wholesome? Or is there a preponderance of violence and brutality? 3. Is the humor original, kindly? 4. Does the drama have convincing characters? 5. Is there enough plot for a good story? 6. Is the theme logical and worth while? 7. Is news objectively reported? 8. Are there harmful propaganda techniques? 9. Are news reports distinguished from news commentaries? 10. Does advertising detract in both time and presentation? 11. Is the advertising honest and appropriate for children? Through discussion, children should be encouraged to use these evaluation techniques also. Not only their ability to select programs but also their skills in viewing and listening would improve.

Approved programs will probably differ for each family. Ideally, the rules will take into consideration the interests of each member of the family and will also try to achieve some balance between types of programs—between entertainment and informational programs, for example. Before bluntly banning all programs of a certain sort, try to find good substitutes.

One of the most important points to consider in setting up rules for television and radio is the question of time. How much time are children to spend listening and viewing?

Television viewing for children and adults occupies many hours. If watching television results in healthy entertainment and informative sessions, some of that time may not be wasted. If, on the other hand, a child spends an excessive amount of time in aimless, passive preoccupation with television, it may be a symptom of something wrong. What is he running away from? What is he finding in these programs that he does not find in the active world of children's play and creative activities? The answer may be nothing more serious than that he is temporarily finding life boring. Or there may be a more significant cause. He may be running away from his social failures or inadequacies. Whatever the cause, adults should be giving guidance and understanding, rather than simply blaming television. All television viewers need activities that provide mental challenges as well as physical exercise.

Like reading, radio and television are no substitute for living. It is wonderful for a child to hear an orchestra and watch a great conductor on television, but it is better for him to attend a concert with his schoolmates or his family—and it is still better for him to learn to play some instrument at home or in a group at school. It is good for a child to watch a televised travel program, but it is better for him to take a day's trip with his family to an interesting landmark. There is no reason, however, why he should not do both. Regulations for television viewing may be essential; they should be humanly flexible also.

Generally speaking, the effect of television and radio on children and adults alike will depend on what is brought to those media. Skills and standards are developed through guidance in the home primarily but also in the schools and churches. Adults play a vital role in determining which standards and abilities are taken to television and radio, and in deciding which standards and thoughts are ultimately taken away.

It does seem fair also to ask the industry to take some responsibility for maintaining high standards. While there is still much room for improvement, television programing for children has gained in quality, and some programs such as Leonard Bernstein's *Young People's Concerts* present rare opportunities for children all over the country to enlarge their experiences. Parents and teachers should voice their opinions pro and con (in writing if possible) about programs both to the sponsors and to the local stations and national networks.

CHILDREN'S PROGRAM CHOICES

Favorite programs change with the age of the child and the year's offering. One thing is certain—specific programs popular today will be gone tomorrow and in a year or two will be as forgotten as a dream. There is a curious evanescence about them that is not characteristic of children's favorite books. Not only do certain programs disappear, but they go out of favor with inexplicable suddenness. *Howdy Doody,* which in 1950 was a national favorite, had by 1953 dropped to one of the programs most disliked.[2] The same shift in popularity overtakes individual performers, too. Children are not faithful to these programs or performers as they are to favorite books and authors.

The stirring cry of the Lone Ranger, "Hi-yo, Silver, away!" and the heartbreak of John's love for Mary in Monday morning's soap opera have been replaced by a radio program schedule that includes opera and jazz, sportscasting and newscasting, scientific programs and weather reports. Presidential press conferences and Shakespearean festivals, personal interviews and on-the-spot coverage of important current events, and prize fights and poetry programs. AM and FM radio today offer a wide selection of programing, often sophisticated in nature, yet varied enough for the tastes of most youngsters. Children, through the urging of parents and teachers, listen to many of these programs and, on their own, often listen to programs of music as a background to other activities—including homework.

A radio program that is heard in many cities and that has been very successful with older children is Ruth Harshaw's distinguished *Carnival of Books.* Each week she introduces a book and its author. The book is vividly described, or an excerpt from it is read. Then the author is introduced to a panel of children who question him to their hearts' content with Mrs. Harshaw serving as a competent moderator. A similar program on television is called *The Reading Room.* The show often has a general theme. In one instance it was the coming of spring, and the book discussed was *Out of Doors in Spring,* by Clarence Hylander.

Children enjoy the variety that television offers, including science, adventure, comedies, science fiction, puppet shows, programs about peers, variety shows, specials, and so forth. Westerns rate high with children, now as always, but are not always to be recommended. Animal programs, especially dog or horse sagas, rival the westerns with children

2. Paul Witty, "Research about Children and Television," *Children and TV, Making the Most of It,* 1953-1954 (Bulletin No. 93). Association for Childhood Education.

of all ages. Whether it is Flicka or Fury, Lassie or the great-grandson of Rin Tin Tin, these animal heroes, like the cowboys, have character traits which children greatly admire. The heroes are continually misunderstood, but they suffer in silence. They perform heroic feats with nonchalance, and they are loyal to pals or mate or master with no romantic nonsense to spoil the program.

It has been said that Walt Disney's television programs are commercials for his motion pictures or Disneyland, but see what they have provided. Most members of the family have shared the children's enthusiasm for Disney's *African Lion, Living Desert, Vanishing Prairie,* and *Beaver Valley.* His true-life nature series on *Walt Disney's Wonderful World of Color* is outstanding television entertainment.

You Are There has taught history in a memorable way to children and adults, *The Twentieth Century* has given insight into public affairs, and *What's My Line?* is often popular with children as well as adults. Older children, following current events at school, are as thrilled as their parents with political conventions, meetings of the United Nations, Presidential press conferences, and such momentous events as the inauguration of a President of the United States, the coronation of a Queen or King, or the thrilling moments of a championship event in the Olympics. Such programs as *Winston Churchill—The Valiant Years,* Bob Hope's comedy shows, and the better dramas are a means of bringing the whole family together to share the same enjoyment. This is significant and by itself would justify television as a desirable part of family life, if, in fact, families share other activities.

EDUCATIONAL TELEVISION AND RADIO

Up to this point we have been discussing commercial radio and television, which include local and network affiliated stations whose financial support comes from advertising. Let us now examine educational radio and television, which are of particular importance to the schools.

In *Goals for Americans,* the President's commission on national goals reports that television holds great promise for use in education. The commission believes that one of the challenges of the 1960's is to learn to use television well because, while television has great potential for good, it can be used to foolish ends. Further, it is suggested that by 1970 every school in the nation should be equipped for instruction by television, and the advantages and limitations of educational television should be universally understood. In its best form, television could present, for example, outstanding lectures to every school child—resources that schools couldn't otherwise afford and that children might not otherwise be exposed to.[3]

Educational channels are noncommercial and devoted to producing programs of an educational nature for schools and communities. Financial support varies and constitutes educational television's major problem. In 1963, educational television stations numbered 75, the largest number since noncommercial video began in the early 1950's.[4] Nearly a third of these stations are financed by state and local governments, another third receive support from university affiliation, and the remaining stations from philanthropic grants and from local viewers and industry. Programs on educational television include college instruction, in-school instruction, cultural programs, live broadcasts of poets and others, information programs, and some entertainment with an educational overtone. Filmed programs are sometimes sent from one city to another. The quality of educational television is in constant danger of falling far below commercial television unless it is well financed. It must be remembered that a child usually has a choice of television channels when at home, and if the educational channel is not stimulating, he can easily switch to a commercial one that is more interesting.

A second type of educational television is referred to as closed-circuit television. This kind is not viewed by the general public, but rather it is offered to special audiences, particularly school audiences. Closed-circuit tele-

3. Commission on National Goals, *Goals for Americans,* Prentice-Hall, 1960, p. 98.
4. New York *Times,* April 9, 1963, p. 35.

vision is growing in popularity throughout the country as teachers make use of its programs in their curriculums and teaching procedures. Since this is a growing field and one that promises much for the future of education, let us examine its strengths and weaknesses.

First of all, this kind of television makes it possible for children to view a variety of visual materials. In addition, each pupil has a prime seat and can see for himself the examples used by the studio teacher, which is not the case with most teaching tools. It provides the teacher with another motivating device. The studio teacher (that is to say, the teacher who gives the television lesson) also has an advantage: she is able to devote full time to lesson preparation. It gives the classroom teacher additional time to concentrate on individual student problems and progress. Too, this type of television makes good use of the team approach to material presentation. In closed-circuit teaching usually more can be taught in a single lesson in a given period of time than in a regularly scheduled class period. Also, from the administrative point of view, quality closed-circuit television provides a means for in-service training: teachers can watch first-hand examples of well-planned lessons. These are some of the good points in favor of closed-circuit television.

What about the limitations? First of all, there is no communication between studio teacher and pupils, except when letters are written or phone calls are made to the teacher after the lesson. Second, closed-circuit television provides no opportunity for on-the-spot class discussion and individual clarification. Third, the lesson cannot be repeated unless it is put on video tape. In addition, face-to-face contact is missing, and unless the television teacher achieves a sufficient degree of intimacy, pupils may not develop necessary confidence in her. In spite of its limitations, closed-circuit television appears to have a definite future in the classroom. Furthermore, it may help to improve the quality of television programing in general by conditioning students to view and therefore demand excellent programs. And if viewers' skills are improved, their viewing may become active rather than passive.

Throughout the country, boards of education have taken over their own radio broadcasting, not merely for lessons in arithmetic or music or language but for entertainment as well. Many boards have now added televised programs, and undoubtedly more will follow.

Wherever educational groups have assumed responsibility for such broadcasting, children's literature has been given a tremendous impetus. Stories are told, poetry is read, verse choirs of children perform, dramatizations of children's stories are given by children—and these programs are enthusiastically received by the youngsters. Librarians say there is an immediate rush for the books containing the stories broadcast. Teachers record the children's lively discussions and their requests for "more stories like that."

TELEVISION, RADIO, BOOKS, AND CHILDREN

Can television, radio, children, and reading be compatible? Of course there are many variables, but, generally, the four can get along quite well, especially with teacher and parent guidance and continued program improvement.

In children's literature there are far more possibilities than the producers of television and radio have realized. Even when the "good guy" is winning against incredible odds, no western would be a substitute for a well-televised version of Meindert DeJong's *Wheel on the School* or Carol Brink's *Caddie Woodlawn* or Esther Forbes' *Johnny Tremain* or Elizabeth Speare's *The Witch of Blackbird Pond.* Poorly televised books are another thing—there was a version of *Heidi* so awful that its slight resemblance to the original was merely an irritant. On the other hand, Maurice Evans' production of *Alice's Adventures in Wonderland* was so perfect in text and pictures that one mother made a dash for her old copy of the book with the Tenniel illustrations. As the program developed, she showed these illustrations to the children, and when they saw how marvelous the reproductions on the screen were, they became fascinated with each new character as it appeared. That night the mother read aloud snatches from the book, although up to that time the children had never cared much about it. The following week some of them read the whole book with new interest and enjoyment.

Schools, too, can prepare for and enrich a program with surprising results. One high school teacher mentioned casually the Olivier production of *Richard III* and advised the teen-agers to watch it on television. Not one student sat through it, although the class was superior in social backgrounds and better than average in intelligence. In another neighborhood of much lower socio-economic status, the teacher devoted two periods to preparing pupils for this most complex and involved text. She listed characters, outlined relationships, and sketched the story of Crookback's villainies. Not only did her students sit through that three-hour drama, but they enjoyed it and offered to read the play as one of their outside assignments. Radio, motion pictures, and television may lead to books, and the school in turn can prepare children for the enjoyment of programs which may be unusual or difficult or complex. Mary Martin's annual production of *Peter Pan* needs no briefing ahead of time, but the children who watch the show are often eager to read the book.

A teacher will want to keep her eyes open for excellent programs and recommend them to students for watching at home. If television does not promote a quantity of reading at certain ages, it can certainly result in an enriched background for reading in many fields. In the social sciences, the teacher can suggest programs that will, for instance, take children vicariously to foreign countries, to the past, to the present to look at actual social conditions, and to the homes and offices of famous people. Teachers and librarians can guide students to these programs by some imaginative means—announcements on prominent bulletin boards, previews of programs in class, creative displays, and student committees appointed to select a list of "programs for the week." For example, when one of Leonard Bernstein's children's concerts is scheduled, a bulletin board display could be devoted to Mr. Bernstein. His interest in jazz might lead children to read more about jazz, his interest in musicals to the writing of essays on the history of musical comedy; artists might want to sketch costumes from his musicals; collectors might wish to bring appropriate album covers or book jackets; and musicians might give a recital of Mr. Bernstein's music. Suggestions of this sort can be fun for children and also enlightening as preparation for viewing worthwhile programs. If a class is particularly enthusiastic about television and radio, it may wish to study about them, visit local stations, write to outstanding people in the field, give a discussion panel on mass media, produce its own mock television show, and read books about these media. Among the books for children which deal with television and radio (either in part or in total) are: Ruth Harnden's *Golly and the Gulls,* Lucy M. Boston's *Stranger at Green Knowe,* Jeanne and Robert Bendick's *Television Works Like This,* Carol Kendall's *The Big Splash,* Lee Kingman's *The Saturday Gang,* Naomi Buchheimer's *Let's Go to a Television Station,* and Jerome S. Meyer's *Picture Book of Radio and Television.*

In addition to suggesting programs for children to watch at home, teachers may use television, radio, and reading in various combinations. For example, after a child has read the book *It's Fun to Know Why: Experiments with Things Around Us* by Julius Schwartz, a teacher or librarian might suggest he watch *Coal: recent experiments* on the following Saturday's *Exploring* program. Or if a child tells his teacher how much he enjoyed the *Wild Kingdom* program about attack defense of animals, his teacher might suggest that he read Ross Elliott Hutchins' *Wild Ways: A Book of Animal Habits,* which goes into such subjects as the protective devices of insects. Another idea is to provide the books of plays that are presented on television. The younger set enjoys reading the stories after they have been presented, for instance, on *Captain Kangaroo.* One librarian said, "I can't keep enough of these stories on the shelf to supply the demand!" Another follow-up technique is to provide appropriate magazines for children to read. For instance, the *National Geographic School Bulletin* would be good to have at home or in school after children have watched *Discovery,* which visits places all over the world. After viewing, children might be encouraged to start hobbies based on their favorite programs. Shari Lewis and her puppets often stimulate interest in puppetry, and Mr.

Wizard's program often stimulates interest in science. Playing games at home after watching them on television is fun for children—*Password* and *College Bowl* offer patterns for educational games, both in class and at home. Local and national television programs should be encouraged to mention children's books over television and radio. *Captain Kangaroo* does a good job in this respect. At home, reference books—dictionary, atlas, encyclopedia, almanac—should be kept near the television set so that children may look up answers to questions that arise from their viewing. In addition, children can be helped to organize their week to include a good balance in viewing, playing, and reading, to get a coordination between their programs and their books and interests in general. When children are studying a unit at school, parents can watch for programs that would fit in. For example, if boys and girls are studying Western history, they could watch a western in order to evaluate it for its contribution to knowledge about the West and its authenticity in costumes, language, story, and setting. At home, also, parents can make sure that their younger children are not spending too much time in viewing television, and that they are being read to, taken to local points of interest, and provided with materials to build and create with their hands. In choosing television for the very young, we should remember that children need vicarious experiences as well as real ones in order to bring interest and knowledge to their reading—and, in this respect, a child's experience can be enriched by television and radio.

We should also remember that all these entertainment mass media may stimulate creative activities or lifelong interests. Many older girls have become deeply interested in cooking or sewing by way of televised demonstrations. Ballet programs have pushed little girls into dancing lessons. They may not become prima ballerinas, but they still will grow up more graceful and poised young women. The science programs launch boys' interests in exploration or marine life or perhaps in the wonderful camera work of the men behind the science or the news pictures. These may become lifelong hobbies or even careers. What radio and television do to help or harm children depends in part upon how they are used by the young people and what guidance is given by interested adults, at home and in school. It takes ingenuity, wit, and wisdom to help children develop discriminating judgment and taste in their program choices and to capitalize on the best of what they see and hear.

Motion Pictures

About the time television really got under way in this country, motion pictures seemed to have reached an all-time low in quality. But with the stiff competition of the new medium of entertainment, they improved their offerings to the point where they were discussed seriously by laymen, and critics were appointed to review them for our leading newspapers and such magazines as *The New Yorker, Time,* and *The Saturday Review.* Along with improved offerings, the motion pictures introduced better color techniques and the wide screen, which greatly enhanced their pictorial impressiveness.

Motion pictures can achieve the heights of great dramatic action better than any other medium except live theater. The color, the sense of reality, and the scope of the finest motion pictures, their greatly improved dramatic offering, and the distinguished actors and actresses who appear in some of them make the best pictures formidable rivals of both the theater and books.

COMMERCIAL FILMS

Motion pictures may be classified as either commercial or educational. Commercial films are produced within the motion picture industry and are viewed by the public at the cost of theater tickets. Today, commercial pictures designed strictly for children's viewing are infrequent. Also, there are very few child stars on the screen such as Jackie Coogan and Shirley Temple were many years ago. Walt Disney, however, consistently produces acceptable family entertainment such as his movies *Old Yeller, The Absent-Minded Professor, The Lady and the Tramp,* and *The Incredible Journey.* One producer in particular is concerned with the juvenile market—Robert Radnitz. In two of his films, *Dog of Flanders* and *Misty,* he showed skill in letting the pictures tell the story, since children respond more directly to images than to conversation. *Misty,* based on Marguerite Henry's book *Misty of Chincoteague,* is an enchanting movie, full of the simplicity of childhood.

Still, there are the third-rate gangster movies, the screaming vampire shows, horror pictures, the pounding and never-ending spectaculars, and the erotic pictures "for adults only." Most adults feel that movies of this sort are likely to build prejudices, give people overseas a regrettable picture of American life, glorify crime and undesirable people, suggest that a lawless life is an exciting one and that physical pulchritude is a guarantee of a luxurious life, and finally lead to juvenile delinquency. Research has not reported conclusively, thus far, just how influential sadistic movies are on young people's behavior.[5] This does not mean, however, that adults should wait for studies to tell them if their children should be exposed to such violent fare. Many states and local theaters are now classifying films. One theater owner puts a sign in his theater stating, "No children under the age of 16, whether or not accompanied by adults, can be admitted to this theater for any part of the program." Other groups are taking action to improve films. For instance, the Motion Picture Council of Greater Cleveland and the Motion Picture Preview Group of Philadelphia are interested in the general idea of upgrading films. And, in a less formal manner, the Mothers' Clubs of Norwalk, Ohio, and Healdsburg, California, supply rated film lists for families and schools.

Frances Ilg and Louise Ames have supplied us with worth-while information about a child's behavior pattern in terms of motion pictures.[6] They point out that movies are not a problem generally in the first ten years of a child's life. By kindergarten, he usually has gone to some children's movies and possibly has looked at home movies. By first grade, children enjoy home movies but are still restless in the movie theater, go out frequently to get drinks of water, and generally do not enjoy themselves. By second grade, some children do attend movies on Saturday afternoons. At this point, the children enjoy musicals, animal pictures, and cartoons. Nearly all object to love stories and some are not sure about adventure stories. When children arrive in third grade, many attend Saturday movies as a matter of ritual. Boys are keen about action, westerns, baseball, and war movies, while girls are interested in musicals. Both enjoy animal and adventure stories, and movies about their peers. They still do not favor love stories. By now, most of them know which movies or parts of movies are too much for them and protect themselves by closing their eyes, hiding their heads, or leaving their seats for a drink of water. By fourth grade, enthusiasm varies. Some attend weekly, others attend less often. Some want to see certain movies over; most feel more strongly about the bad parts of movies; most behave reasonably well in the theater as long as they don't get tired. Their taste in movies is about the same. All enjoy the Saturday afternoon contests and prizes offered by local theaters! Fifth graders become more choosey. They want to see a "good" movie with friends of their own sex and will sometimes go with their parents in the evening. On the whole, they attend less frequently than before. They like westerns, comedies, cartoons, horse movies, historical shows, and adventure shows. At this age, some children say movies give them a headache and bad dreams. Most of them will accept their parents' ban on certain movies or ruling on the number of times they can attend.[7]

EDUCATIONAL FILMS

The so-called educational films raise such questions as these: Which films, if any, encourage learning? Can we use films in teach-

5. Anna W. M. Wolfe, "TV, Movies, Comics—Boon or Bane to Children," *Parents Magazine,* April 1961, p. 47.
6. Frances L. Ilg and Louise Bates Ames, *The Gesell Institute's Child Behavior,* Harper, 1962.
7. Ibid, pp. 265-266.

Various forms of marine life, all in a dramatic struggle for survival, are shown in this eleven-minute color film Marine Life. *In the frames reproduced here, a hermit crab has just won possession of his only form of shelter, an empty sea shell.*
Stills from Marine Life, *courtesy of Encyclopaedia Britannica Films Inc.*

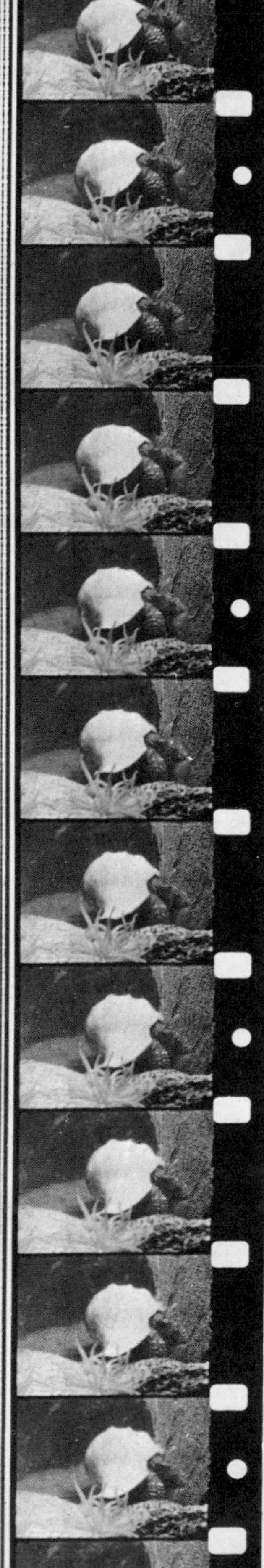

ing to enhance usual classroom techniques? Where can we find films children will enjoy?

First, a film suitable for classroom use should respect the intelligence of children and be in good taste. It should have an underlying mood that children are eager to share and for which the film script provides the stimulation. Further, the film should stir their imaginations and senses and leave them with a better understanding about some aspect of their world. Too, a film should be a film. That is, it should not be a lecture, but rather material presented dramatically with professional skill and care. A good film also should have style and a clear point of view. If treated properly, even such subjects as murder, childbirth, and death (subjects often frowned upon by adults) can be handled wisely for the purpose of instruction.

At one large city public library, the storytelling hour admittedly is not so popular as the movie hour among children; but often they want to read a book after watching the movie based on it. As one teacher put it, "Movies are the best method for stirring interest!" Why and how films are used is an individual matter for the most part. One teacher may wish to stress a specific point in the study of ocean habitation and will decide to show "Marine Life" (Encyclopaedia Britannica Films—11 minutes, in color) that gives a colorful account of underwater creatures at Marineland in Florida. Another teacher may wish to stimulate reading interests and will show "Andy and the Lion" (Weston Woods Studios —10 minutes, in color), James Daugherty's famous story of a boy, a book, and a lion. For whatever purpose, teachers will find that educational, entertaining, and enlightening movies have been made as a result of competition, skill, and growing demand.

Educational films can be found in several

places. Public libraries, for example, often house collections of films that can be borrowed like books. These films are usually excellent because the film librarian has chosen them carefully from the thousands available. Often libraries join in a trade system whereby a film requested, but not housed, in one library may be borrowed from another. In addition, many state universities have film libraries. Films can be rented inexpensively by schools within the state. Also, governmental agencies at local, state, and federal levels have collections of films that are available on loan. These films cover such subjects as agriculture, commerce, and conservation. Interestingly enough, Joseph Krumgold's Newbery Medal-winning book *. . . and now Miguel* was first a documentary movie for the State Department. It is now available for schools and is almost as fine as the book. Likewise, industry and business offer free films. Many are interesting and informative, but, as with all films, careful selection is called for. A catalog of free films is usually available at the public library.

How surprised she was to find a handsome little prince, no larger than herself! They immediately fell in love, and the prince put his crown on Thumbelina's head. From every flower came other little people, each bearing a gift for Thumbelina.
BUT . . .
. . . the swallow flew back to Denmark, where the man lived who could tell fairy tales. And that's where the whole story comes from.
NOW . . .
. . . let's tell the story ourselves while we look at the pictures.

FILM SELECTION AND EVALUATION

Techniques for evaluation and selection are important in choosing educational as well as commercial films. Films used for particular in-class units need, ideally, to be chosen, ordered, previewed, presented, and discussed. Teachers should guide students in their viewing and evaluating techniques. Such techniques should be an essential part of going to the movies for young people. Students should become familiar with the names of producers, directors, and actors, because their participation in the making of a film may

This color filmstrip of the story Thumbelina *was made by photographing a series of fabric collages. In this filmstrip, the illustrations are preceded by a synopsis and followed by discussion questions. In the filmstrip on the opposite page, each still is accompanied by a story caption.*
Filmstrip from Thumbelina, *courtesy of Encyclopaedia Britannica Films Inc.*

The wonderful episode in Chapter 2 of Tom Sawyer *is retold in this color filmstrip. Tom arranges matters so that his friends pay him with their dearest treasures for the privilege of doing his work. Filmstrip from* Tom Sawyer Whitewashes the Fence, *courtesy of Encyclopaedia Britannica Films Inc.*

mean exceptionally good entertainment. Students should learn to use the reviews of films in newspapers and in quality magazines, noting what the reviewer says about the acting, the photography, the use of sound and color, the sets, the costumes, and the theme. Of course, the reviewer's reactions should be analyzed to see whether or not he himself had been objective in his remarks. After attending the movies—in school or outside—students should form the habit of talking about the films with their parents, teachers, and peers.

They might tell how the movie affected them and others; what mood they were in after looking at the film; what moods were created by the characters and events; whether the picture glorified crime and corruption; whether the movie was well cast. If the movie was humorous, they might tell whether they laughed at or with the characters. Again they might indicate whether the movie seemed to be giving a slice of real life or left them thinking about a worth-while idea, or whether it seemed commercial and geared only to mass appeal.

Other Audio-Visual Aids

FILMSTRIPS

A filmstrip is a strip of film bearing a sequence of frames of still pictures with explanatory text and captions. Attractive, interesting, and informative filmstrips have been produced for every imaginable subject, many of them geared to curriculum needs, and an alert teacher can use them to supplement the children's regular classroom work. Often they include questions and suggestions for effective follow-up activities.

Filmstrips are particularly helpful to teachers in working with a large class, but they are also helpful with individuals and small groups. Pupils can turn to them as they do to books and so be provided with another rich resource for learning. Individuals can look at a frame, scan it for details, and form their evaluations before proceeding to the next frame. Beware of filmstrips that are too long for young children to sit through, those that are labored in their presentation, and those whose captions are unsuitable for the group. Filmstrips can be used for both reading and viewing. For instance, pupils can be given time first to enjoy the picture, and then to read the captions or listen to the recording script. After finishing with the frames, the teacher can lead a discussion of what has been seen and read (or heard, in the case of the sound filmstrip), and so learn a great deal about her pupils' viewing, reading, and listening abilities.

Combining filmstrips with reading can prove interesting and profitable for the children. For study, the teacher could choose filmstrips in the *Famous American Stories* series, which includes *Tom Sawyer Whitewashes the Fence* and *Man Without a Country;* for adventure, a *Walt Disney Adventure* series, including the *Adventures of Pecos Bill,* the *Legend of Sleepy Hollow,* and others. For enjoyment and enrichment, there is the *Hans Christian Andersen Stories* series with *The Tinder Box, The Little Mermaid,* and *Thumbelina;* and scores of others are available. Whether used for study or entertainment, filmstrips should send pupils to the library to read the stories.

RECORDINGS AND TAPES

Recordings make it possible for students to be exposed at home or in school to the most talented actors, musicians, and speakers; to the most exciting plays, operas, and holiday programs; to the most significant speeches, conferences, and discussions. Records, like books, can be repeated, and the repetition can help us gain understanding; also they can easily be stopped to give periods for discussion. Too often recordings are thought of only in connection with music. Recording companies, however, are reproducing the voices of authors, statesmen, and other famous people, as well as providing educational material for use in various parts of the curriculum.

Recordings can play an important part in stimulating creative thinking. Motion pictures, filmstrips, and television, all require of the student his eyes and ears. But recordings, like books, call on the student to make mental images. Good readers "see pictures" as they read of action, characters, setting; they are, in effect, thinking creatively. Likewise, the student who listens to recordings with skill and imagination "sees pictures" through creative listening. Recordings, then, can be thought of as an important audio-visual tool.

Language recordings form a large portion of the library of spoken records. Publishers are bringing out more and more of these valuable educational and cultural materials, among which talking books are relatively new. If used to supplement, review, and evaluate books, they can become practical teaching and learning devices. Some of the talking books available are *Abraham Lincoln,* his writings and speeches as read by Raymond Massey; *Arabian Nights* read by Marian Carr; *Gulliver's Travels* read by Michael Redgrave; *Just So Stories* read by Boris Karloff. Many of these, as is true for the poetry recordings, include the actual printed word for the teacher's use. Among the numerous recordings in the area of drama are Gilbert and Sullivan's *The Pirates of Penzance* and *Peter Pan,* as interpreted by Mary Martin and Cyril Ritchard.

Tapes, like recordings, offer a large variety of materials for classroom use. Two interesting innovations are worthy of attention. First, there is a national repository of over 5000 tapes located at the University of Colorado. These can be re-recorded for any individual, group, or institution that desires them. In one year alone, over 500 sets of language tapes in each of five different languages were duplicated by the service.[8] Second, there is a plan

8. Donald W. Johnson, "National Tape Repository," *Educational Screen and Audiovisual Guide,* April 1963, p. 204.

called Tape Adventurers, by which tapes are exchanged by school children. For example, suppose a class in Boston was studying the geography of Wisconsin and wanted answers to questions that occurred to them. The inquiring group would record these questions on tape and send the tape to a school in Wisconsin with which arrangements had been made. The students in the Wisconsin school would put their answers on the same tape and send it back to the Boston classroom. This tape exchange program has met with enthusiastic response from participants and may lead to an international exchange program. Certainly this is an imaginative way of extending the listening experiences of students and of exploring areas for up-to-date material that cannot be found in reference books.

AUDIO-VISUAL AIDS AND READING

Obviously the audio-visual aids can offer much in the teaching of reading. Television and radio can further reading interests by capturing the viewing and listening interests of the child; films and filmstrips can motivate readers; and recordings and tapes can present literature for enjoyment and study. Following are three examples of ways in which audio-visual aids may be combined with books for enriched pleasure and understanding:

Charlotte's Web by E. B. White
Recordings: "Animal Song Parade" (Harmony Records) and "The Reluctant Dragon" (Caedmon Records); Filmstrips: "Animals—Helpful and Harmful" (Jam Handy); Films: "Buckshot Goes to the Fair" (free film: Texaco, Inc.).

How Baseball Began in Brooklyn by LeGrand
Recording: "Who Built America" (Folkways Records); Filmstrip: "True Book of Indians" (Childrens Press); Films: "Twenty Years of World Series Thrills" (free film: American and National Leagues of Professional Baseball Clubs).

Secret of the Andes by Ann Nolan Clark
Recording: "Music of Peru" (Capitol); Filmstrips: "The Incas" (Life Filmstrips); "Peru" (Stillfilm, Inc.); and "Market Day at Cusco" (Young America).

Comics

Comics appear to interest almost everyone—the rich, the poor, the city dweller, the country dweller, young, old, the educated, the uneducated. There are dozens and dozens of different comics to appeal to everyone. One Harvard professor admittedly buys a local newspaper just to read "Li'l Abner."

Comics in one form or another are a regular household fixture. Characters and episodes are as familiar as neighbors and have been since 1890. Today, some comics are still devoted only to humor, but many deal seriously with today's living and today's foibles, frequently in the manner of television and radio's soap operas. In fact, the comics have been marked by a lack of comedy in recent years. In the popular comic strip "Peanuts," however, the creator, Charles Schulz, is consistently humorous and, at the same time, through little children typifies all humanity with its failures and successes, its joys and its disappointments, its sadness and its laughter.

Like many hobbies and interests of children, comic reading starts out slowly, grows with great enthusiasm, gradually fails to hold interest until the children go on to discover a new interest.

A preschooler often reads comic-strip pictures on Sundays, listens to comics over the radio, or sits in his father's lap while the latter reads to him. These children are not interested in reading the words of comics or in reading comic books, but they will sit and look at the pictures and listen to others read to them. By first grade, a youngster can sometimes manage to read some of the words of the comics. Certainly his interest has been developed, and he likes a variety of subjects. By second grade, a child usually has the comic habit. He not only reads comics and looks at pictures, but he buys them with his allowance money, trades them with friends, collects them like precious jewels, and spends hours of solitude in their company. Favorites at this age are comics about peers, daily adventure, adventure of the superman variety, and those with some violence. These youngsters need guidance from and control by parents to limit the number and kinds purchased. A third-grader is still a comic-book enthusiast, now preferring bold adventure and bloody plots. In fourth grade, most children have reached the peak in comics interest. Many now treat their comics like a big business—they classify them, arrange them, count them, take inventory, and sell them. If at this time comic-book reading seems to come before or to exclude other types of recreation and reading, parents and teachers need to exert firm and consistent restraint. Fifth-graders will still hoard great numbers of comics, but they will admit that the comics are somewhat childish. Generally until this age children will like to read *Bugs Bunny, Superman, Little Orphan Annie,* and others. At the fifth-grade level, children enjoy crime and detective comics, but since they do not read comics as frequently as before, this choice is not too serious. In sixth grade, children will turn more and more from comics to books and other forms of recreation; and in seventh grade, while they may read comics casually, they are growing away from their earlier habits. At this point, only a handful of children are still in the comics stage.[9]

Comics in recent years have shown some improvement. The Comics Magazine Association of America has adopted a self-regulatory program: the Comics Code Authority places a seal on approved comics. This apparently has been so successful that in the fall of 1960 the National Office for Decent Literature declared they could find no comics "objectionable for youth."

This comment is quite different from the public opposition to comic books in the 1950's. In 1954, disapproval of some comics was so strong that nearly all of the comic publishers joined in a self-enforcing program aimed at the welfare of young people. The results were not perfect, but marked improvement resulted. Today, comics of violence are at a minimum, crime stories center on detectives rather than on gangsters, and comics about monsters have given way to adventures in space. In some cases, community groups have been successful in persuading newsstand dealers to discontinue the sale of suggestive and sensational materials and in their place to display those of a wholesome and appealing nature. The adults who have been active in this work are not interested so much in censorship *per se* as in the quality of reading available for their own children.

What are we to do about comics? This question was once a desperate one. Now, because comics have improved and because we realize that comics are simply a phase for most children, we ask the question with less apprehension. Still, parents and teachers want to know what to do about comics during the period

9. Frances L. Ilg and Louise Bates Ames, pp. 260-264.

Robert McCloskey can turn a drugstore scene into something irresistibly funny. Here he spoofs the comics with satirical gusto. From Homer Price *by Robert McCloskey. Copyright 1943 by Robert McCloskey. Reprinted by permission of The Viking Press, Inc. (Book 6 x 8¾)*

when they seem to overshadow every other interest. It would seem wise, for one thing, for parents and teachers not to try to ban them completely. Such action would result only in tempting the child to read his comics "behind the barn." Rules and regulations can and should be made by parents in terms of money for comics, numbers to be bought, kinds to be read, amount of time spent reading, and space to store them. Also, both teachers and parents can discuss the content of comics with their children, thus helping them to develop judgment and evaluation in all reading matter. Rather than censoring all comics, adults should attempt to show that comics are picture reading rather than real reading. Get children to compare for themselves a comic book of adventure with a fictional book of adventure—Armstrong Sperry's *Call It Courage,* for example—as to content, pictures, printing, and language. If then a child stubbornly sticks exclusively to the comics, we should look for something wrong in his reading skills, outlets for vicarious adventure, personal adventure experiences, and so forth. If it is found that reading skills are the problem, lead him to pleasure reading of high interest and easier vocabulary.

When a child is going through his comic craze, parents and teachers should provide other reading matter that competes with the adventure, humor, fun, ease, nonsense, danger, and heroes of comic books. For instance, Robert McCloskey's *Homer Price* is an excellent substitute to offer Dick who can't be torn away from his humorous comics; Beverly Cleary's *Henry Huggins* books are good competitors for Joe's everyday adventure comics; and Alice Hazeltine's *Hero Tales from Many Lands* is a fine book to offset Steve's hero comics. After the peak in comic interest has been reached, other reading matter still needs to be provided to keep children from returning to their first loves for lack of something better to read. Unfortunately, there will always be some youngsters whose tastes never mature and who never outgrow the comic habit. At nearly every Army base or bus depot, grown men can be seen deeply involved in the latest edition of their favorites, reading them as though they were classics and worthy of memorizing.

Paperback Books

Radio, television, comics, movies—all these may compete with books for a child's time and interest. The printed mass media—paperback books and magazines and newspapers—are not competitors, however. They also are reading, although sometimes they require reading skills of a different sort than those required for a book of poems or a story. Paperback books may not be considered technically part of the mass media, but such a variety of material is being published today in paperbacks that they defy classification in any of our other chapters. Furthermore, they do require some attention in any discussion of children's reading because of their great popularity with children and young people.

A new era in education was born with the introduction of paperback books. Flexibility, wide choice, economy, and informality are but four reasons for the great impact of this new medium in our schools and colleges.

Perhaps one reason for their success with young people is their enormous popularity among adults. In one twelve-month period more than 4500 new titles were published, increasing the total number to 19,500.[10] All but a handful of publishers are now issuing paperbacks. But the biggest breakthrough in recent years has been in the children's field. A few years ago, some adults complained that one of the few areas that soft-cover books had yet to penetrate was the world of literature for young people. The few exceptions were books such as *Lost Horizon, Jane Eyre,* and *Treasure Island.* Currently, however, some of the largest publishing houses are entering this field and distributing books.

Too, schools with paperback bookstores on the premises have increased from a dozen to

10. Raymond Walters, Inc., "It's Been a Time of New Heights, New Hopes, and Upsets," New York *Times Book Review,* paperback books supplement, April 7, 1963, p. 2.

over 1000. Some schools have only racks; others provide elaborate rooms with student volunteers selling books. In one elementary school, an enterprising young man organized his own sales staff for paperbacks, sent his orders to a large publishing firm, and distributed the books when they were shipped to the school. These efforts toward paperback reading and buying seem to have much in common: acceptance, enthusiasm, and interest in reading by students, teachers, librarians, and administrators. One teacher said, "I can hardly believe my eyes when I now see students who never previously read books for pleasure walk into class with paperbacks tucked under their arms—and they don't stay under their arms long because children read them before school, at lunchtime, and after school. Paperbacks are a reading revolution!"

Paperback books have not always held such popularity. At one time they were thought of as sensational literature. Another objection out of the past was that paperbacks would have as little value as comic books and as little appeal to children as yesterday's newspaper. For the most part this has not been found to be true. For instance, in one midwestern city, a reading consultant used a set of paperbacks in a junior high school developmental reading program. After the program, the children were so enthusiastic that 120 of them purchased over three hundred dollars worth of paperbacks the first semester and twice as many the next. She said, "The children not only enjoyed the titles that were offered, but they also enjoyed owning their own books—and buying them with their own savings!"[11] Then, too, teachers who experimented with paperbacks in classroom situations found that paperbacks encouraged students' reading; they especially tantalized formerly unenthusiastic readers; and they served as exciting teaching tools to supplement textbooks. Paperbacks are also useful in introducing children to outstanding works of contemporary writing. With the low-priced editions, teachers can tailor their courses to suit the tastes and intellectual abilities of the class members. As one teacher put it, "The value of having students read the same book, discuss it, and then go on to another, can't be overlooked."

The availability of paperbacks is worthy of mention. The R. R. Bowker Publishing Company provides a very helpful list of those in print. For a long time, Scholastic Book Services was the only distributor of paperbacks for elementary and junior and senior high students, and it is an excellent and efficient source of information. Through their clubs, such as their Lucky Book Club, Arrow Book Club, and Teen Age Book Club, they offer paperback books for different age levels. In addition, for science enthusiasts, the Science World Book Club offers paperbacks about earth science, life science, physical science, and mathematics. The Reader's Choice, a division of Scholastic Book Services, is a catalog service featuring over 500 selected paperbacks for schools and libraries, grades 2-12. It offers the convenience of ordering books of many publishers from one source.

As with other media, selectivity and discretion are required in choosing paperbacks for children. Letting the distributor or publisher stock your bookshelves is not good enough. Teachers will want to order books with specific purposes in mind, just as they order films. Children may, though, be given an opportunity to order their own paperbacks for pleasure reading. Here, too, both parents and teachers can guide the students' selections after becoming familiar with their interests and reading capabilities.

While some libraries are purchasing paperback books, others are not. The life of a paperback is usually not long, especially if it is widely circulated. Librarians who use paperbacks claim that they are worth while by virtue of their low cost and the elimination of waiting lists for popular books. One librarian remarked, "Paperbacks are a blessing for us because we can provide copies of books that children enjoy and sometimes never get to read because they are always checked out. With our urging, children take rather good care of paperbacks and in fact project this good care to hardback books. Paperbacks mean to us that another method has been provided to help children enjoy reading for information and pleasure."

Some school centers for developmental and remedial reading provide paperbacks almost

11. Mrs. Barbara Ann Kyle, Fairview Park Schools, Cleveland, Ohio.

exclusively. Reading consultants believe that paperbacks can be used informally with children who may think that books are formidable. Many young readers like the adult feeling they get when carrying and reading a paperback. Too, these youngsters seem to make their books a part of themselves because they can underline important words and passages and make marginal notes, something that rarely is done in hardback books. Students like the "handlability" of paperbacks.

Thus, whether for individual use or group situations, the paperback book has become an additional tool of learning.

Magazines and Newspapers

Magazines and newspapers for most adults are an essential part of everyday life. But what about magazines and newspapers for young readers? Because these media become an established habit with most adults and a great necessity in many cases, and because they are important influences on attitudes and opinions, it is wise to expose young people to them early so that they can begin to gain information and entertainment from them; to develop skills necessary for efficient reading of the media; and to discriminate between good and poor examples, fair and biased news.

If, then, it is desirable for students to be exposed to magazines and newspapers, should adult items be used or should children's magazines and newspapers be the chief sources for instruction? The answer probably should be, a combination. While most adult newspapers and magazines are too difficult for pupils below the seventh grade, they can serve as examples when, for instance, the teacher wishes to point out characteristics of editorials, features, news stories, and so forth. Also, adult fare can be read aloud to children for both information and interest.

On the other hand, children, by reading young people's magazines and newspapers, can discover their variety—the editorials, the columns, the features, the entertainment sections, the news, the sports, the pictures. Primarily they will be informed by this reading, but hopefully they will also be on the road to habits that will make smooth the transition from young people's magazines and newspapers to adult media.

Numerous magazines and newspapers are available for young people. Some of them may be purchased through subscription for the home, school, or library; others are offered exclusively for schools and libraries. Few are offered on the newsstand.

The three major newspaper and magazine publishers in the field of current affairs education are Scholastic, American Education Publications, and the Civic Education Service. Leading metropolitan papers such as the New York *Times,* St. Louis *Post-Dispatch,* and Cleveland *Plain Dealer* also have school service departments that prepare special material for current affairs education. The *Scholastic* magazines are examples of school subscription magazines, offered weekly at every age level through twelfth grade. Each magazine attempts at a given grade level to appeal to the audience through interest and readability. For example, the third-grade *News Trails* offers more news and science than does the second-grade *News Ranger.* This magazine provides training in the use of charts and graphs and in map reading as well as including fiction and poetry as regular features. Most of the accompanying teacher guides include some sections with study skill exercises. *My Weekly Reader* is an example of a newspaper that attempts to gear its publication to current affairs mainly but also includes feature articles about people and places, maps, crossword puzzles, jokes, and cartoons. A "How to Study" article gives students an opportunity to learn the skill of news reading while absorbing current affairs.

Other children's magazines include *Plays* (a drama magazine for young people that prints short plays with production notes); *Children's Digest* (stories, riddles, jokes, and picture-stories that have for the most part been published in other periodicals or books);

Jack and Jill (read-aloud stories, songs, holiday features, activities); *Highlights* (stories and activities planned for reading preparation, easy reading, advanced reading, health and safety); *Child Life* (organized in content around story time, feature time, and play time). Many of these magazines preview parts from books that will soon be published.

What criteria should be used in selecting magazines and newspapers? First, they might be judged by the criteria which we apply to adult journalism. These are—truthfulness: a magazine and newspaper should report only what actually happens and what has actually been said; completeness: magazines and newspapers should include essential details; fairness: they should not confuse opinion with facts, and should present both sides of an issue.

Second, in ordering magazine and newspapers, a teacher or parent should have in mind a specific aim. If, for instance, a newspaper is purchased in order to keep students informed of current affairs, it should serve that purpose. If a magazine is chosen for children's entertainment, that aim should be fulfilled. Subscribing to magazines just to give children busy work is not justifiable.

Third, the magazine and newspaper should be suitable for the age level and interest level of the children for whom they are intended. They should not talk down to students nor should they be so advanced that only the pictures are enjoyed and understood.

Fourth, these media should be attractive in format, printing, photography, and artwork. Many magazines such as the *National Geographic School Bulletin* include excellent photography. "Children are becoming increasingly picture minded," said one teacher. Children as well as adults enjoy reading if the printed matter is pleasantly presented.

Fifth, magazines and newspapers should be selected to bridge the gaps believed to exist between young people's reading and adult reading. If, for instance, the media stress over and over the study aspect without including a variety of other material, children are apt to get the false notion that magazines and newspapers are only for study.

Sixth, the magazines and newspapers should so appeal to the students that their arrival is looked forward to.

Seventh, the cost, of course, should be considered. The magazine or newspaper should be worth the money paid for it.

Magazines and newspapers demand reading skills. In many ways, they call for techniques different from those required in reading books. For instance, children need to understand the technique of reading a newspaper news story with its inverted-pyramid style paragraph. Many skills, on the other hand, are essentially the same: critical skills, comprehension, and varied rate of reading. Picture reading is another essential technique and one that should be given consideration.

Magazines and newspapers can supplement standard classroom materials. They can complement the study of particular units, can provide various opinions on subjects, and can engender enthusiasm for certain topics. But they, like other classroom materials, need to be carefully selected, and children need to be provided with techniques for reading them appropriately. Many children gain their initial reading enthusiasm from magazines and newspapers, which can, therefore, act as springboards to other reading.

The relation of children to the mass media can be a controversial subject. "Too much time spent away from books," "lack of mental stimulation," "wasted effort," "unhealthy subjects," "morally degrading," and "sadism" are words and phrases often heard in discussions of the mass media to which children are exposed. On the other hand, such words and phrases as these are also heard: "supplement knowledge," "stimulate imagination," "send children to books," "provide vicarious experiences," "entertain," and "provoke reading."

What, then, will the future be in terms of the relationship of mass media and children's reading? Will television and motion pictures completely eliminate a child's interest in books? Or will the mass media be a positive addition to the field of children's reading? Most interested people believe that there is a time and a place for mass media as well as reading, and that the two can have a friendly relationship. For example, through guidance it is perfectly possible for children to find time for abundant reading both in and out of school, for a family to attend an excellent movie or to watch an outstanding television program together; for paperback books, magazines, and newspapers to be used as teaching tools and enjoyed as leisure reading. Then, in addition, it is possible that television, recordings, motion pictures, radio, and other media will realize their great potential and contribute to children's reading by dramatizing, discussing, and recommending really fine literature for young people. Newspapers and magazines can also contribute to children's reading by including articles about authors and reviews of new books. Children's literature is an exciting field and makes readable copy!

In order to achieve this ideal—a close yet separate relationship between mass media and children's reading—effort must be expended in the right direction by the right people. Irving Gitlin, a television producer, said at a White House Conference:

> *. . . we as parents and citizens are quite capable of deciding the values we stand for, the values we wish our children to follow. We do not want censorship or pressure tactics; but democracy calls no less for leadership and noble action . . .*[12]

Certainly, it is not reasonable to expect children to set up their own television viewing schedules; balance this activity with hobbies, sports, and reading; avoid listening to ridiculous programs; write to a director about a harmful movie; or keep up with the latest research about the implications of mass media. Adults must assume this leadership. Those people who feel strongly about the kinds of materials available should make their feelings known to the sponsors and distributors of such materials.

Newton N. Minow, former chairman of the Federal Communication Commission, made a statement about television that can be appropriately applied to the future of mass media in general:

> *. . . television is . . . an educational "fourth force" to be ranked along with home, school, and church as one of the powerful influences that help shape our children's hopes, fears, tastes, ambitions—in short, their hearts and minds.*

He concluded that we need to encourage

> *. . . children to enjoy the good and reject the poor—in television just as we do in books, movies, food, clothes, and all other aspects of life.*[13]

Finally, if books are going to meet the competition of television, motion pictures, radio serials, and comics, we must find many that are easy to read, with clear-cut themes and plenty of exciting action. We must find books which help the child understand his own world today, and sometimes books that help him escape from today by going back to times that were simpler and more understandable. We must find stories as realistic and homey as a loaf of bread, and others as fantastic as a mirage. Above all, to balance the speed and confusions of our modern world, we need to find books which build strength and steadfastness in the child, books which develop his faith in the essential decency and nobility of life, books which give him a feeling for the wonder and the goodness of the universe.

SUGGESTED READING, PROBLEMS, AND PROJECTS

1. Divide the class so that each member will be able to watch several children's television programs and so that all the important programs are covered by some member of the class. If possible, watch some of the programs in the company of children. Each person or group of people should then report to the class on the programs watched. How did the children like them? What things appealed to the children? What things weren't they interested in? Evaluate the programs from an adult standpoint.

2. What educational television and radio programs are available in your locality? How are the schools using them? Can you see any way to improve their use?

3. Analyze a recent motion picture you have seen. What ideals and attitudes did it seem to present? How desirable do you think this movie would

12. Anna W. M. Wolfe, "TV, Movies, Comics—Boon or Bane to Children," *Parents Magazine,* April 1961, p. 78.
13. Newton N. Minow, "Is TV Cheating Our Children?" *Parents Magazine,* February 1962, pp. 116-117.

be for children? How can you help promote critical judgment of movies among children?

4. Which addicts of comic books, television, and movies do you need to be concerned about? Prepare a list of children's books that you think would be good bait for these nonreaders. Become acquainted with, and take steps to keep up to date with, published lists of easy-to-read books that would hold the interest of average readers.

5. Analyze three or four popular comic books for type, plot, characters, language, satisfaction of needs, format. What possible good or bad effects could they have on children?

6. Survey the children's magazines available at a public library. To what age groups and interests do they appeal? Examine the content of several magazines to determine the kinds of materials included. In what ways could children's magazines be used in the classroom?

7. Suggest some ways in which teachers can make use of the mass media to interest or stimulate children to read better literature or to supplement schoolwork.

REFERENCES

BARNOUW, ERIK. *Mass Communication: Television, Radio, Film and Press.* Holt, 1956. The history, psychology, media, and sponsors of mass communication are treated interestingly and authoritatively by Professor Barnouw of Columbia University, editor of the Center for Mass Communication.

BLUM, ELEANOR. *Reference Books in the Mass Media.* Univ. of Ill. Press, 1962. An annotated, selective booklist covering book publishing, broadcasting, films, newspapers, magazines, and advertising. The bibliography is intended to provide sources for facts and figures, names, addresses, and other biographical information, and to suggest starting points for research.

BOUTWELL, WILLIAM D., ed. *Using Mass Media in the Schools.* National Council of Teachers of English, 1962. Mr. Boutwell and his committee discuss the nature of mass media and what teachers are doing to help students evaluate and select from them. An excellent source of critical appraisals of the role of mass communication in today's culture.

BROWN, JAMES W. *AV Instruction: Materials and Methods.* McGraw, 1959. A textbook for teacher training courses in audio-visual instruction with emphasis on interrelatedness of all teaching aids and the role of the instructor in the presentation of such material.

CASSIRER, HENRY R. *Television Teaching Today.* UNESCO, 1960. Although the discussion is limited to present practices in the use of television for teaching purposes by educational institutions in the United States and a number of other countries, the author develops general principles to guide future action.

ELLIOT, WILLIAM Y., ed. *Television's Impact on American Culture.* Mich. State Univ. Press, 1956. For perhaps the first time, television is placed in a setting that shows how it fits into the culture which created it. An impressive group of authors examine its true nature and impact, exploring its possibilities for the future. The sections on educational television will be of particular interest to teachers and parents.

EMERY, EDWIN, PHILLIP AULT, and WARREN AGEE. *Introduction to Mass Communications.* Dodd, 1960. An overview of newspapers, magazines, radio, television, book publishing, and films, including a brief history and analysis of the function of each. Chapters on advertising, public relations, and mass communications are also presented. Education for mass communications is covered in a separate section.

HARRIS, DALE B. *Children and Television: An Annotated Bibliography.* National Asso. of Educational Broadcasters, 1959. Abstracts of articles listed under the following headings: Surveys and Studies: General Approaches; Surveys and Studies: Educational and Character Effects of TV; Educational Outcomes of TV for Children; Discussions for Parents; General Comments and Opinions on Children's TV Programs, Reviews, etc.; and Principles and Recommendations Concerning Programs for Children.

HESS, ROBERT D., and HARRIET GOLDMAN. "Parents' Views of the Effects of Television on Their Children," *Child Development,* June 1962, 411-426. Interviews with 99 mothers in metropolitan Chicago provide data for this study of the image that parents hold of TV's influence upon their children and the effect the image has upon the tendency to supervise their child's viewing.

IRVING, JOHN A., ed. *Mass Media in Canada.* Ryerson Press, 1962. Written by Canadian specialists and published in Canada, this book deals systematically with the nature and function of mass media in that country—the press, books, films, radio, TV, and advertising. It lends both historical perspective and immediate urgency to the study of diverse technologies of communication.

LACY, DAN. *Freedom and Communication.* Univ. of Ill. Press, 1961. An overview of the progress of the mass media in society, documented by the results of relevant studies. Lacy skillfully describes the problems of the American communication system brought about by the current explosion in learning.

"Mass Media—Their Impact on Children and Family Life in our Culture," *Child Study,* Summer 1960, 2-38. The entire summer issue is devoted to conference addresses and discussions of the mass media. Among the questions are: Are the mass media meeting the wishes and needs of people? How much is known about the effects on children of "good" or "bad" books, movies, and TV programs? What is the parents' role in helping children make choices and develop values out of what they read, see, and hear? What is being done, and what more could be done, to utilize the rich resources of the mass media for the greatest benefit to children?

Radio and Television; a Selected Bibliography, prepared by Patricia Beall Hamill. Government Printing Office, 1960. Published by the Office of Education, this bibliography includes materials which report findings of research and experimentation, teaching with television, and production skills.

SCHRAMM, WILBUR, JACK LYLE, and EDWIN B. PARKER. *Television in the Lives of Our Children.* Stanford Univ. Press, 1961. Based on information obtained from a study of over 6000 children and from 2300 parents, teachers, and school officials, this report analyzes the effects of television on children. Data in the appendix include those related to children's use of other mass media.

SCHRAMM, WILBUR, JACK LYLE, and ITHIEL DE SOLA POOL. *The People Look at Educational Television.* Stanford Univ. Press, 1963. A comprehensive picture of the present status and problems of educational television in America, based on nine representative stations.

STEINER, GARY A. *The People Look at Television: A Study of Audience Attitudes.* Knopf, 1963. A comprehensive study of how the American viewer feels about the medium and how he uses it.

THOMAS, R. MURRAY, and SHERWIN G. SWARTOUT. *Integrated Teaching Materials,* rev. ed. McKay, 1963. Designed to help teachers improve their skills in choosing, creating, and using audio-visual teaching materials, including reading sources, this book also presents specific classroom illustrations—both verbal and photographic—which add to its practicality.

WITTY, PAUL A., PAUL KINSELLA, and ANNE COOMER. "A Summary of Yearly Studies of Televiewing, 1949-1963," *Elementary English,* October 1963, 590-597. Presents and discusses findings of studies of TV; lists favorite TV and radio programs and movies; points out programs which pupils feel aid in school work. The parents' role in viewing and listening is explored also.

FILM COMPANIES

Churchill Films, Educational Film Sales Dept., Suite 1520, 6671 Sunset Blvd., Los Angeles 28, Calif.

Contemporary Films, 267 W. 25th St., New York 1, N.Y.

Coronet Instructional Films, Sales Dept., 65 E. South Water St., Chicago 1, Ill.

Encyclopaedia Britannica Films Inc., 1150 Wilmette Ave., Wilmette, Ill.

Film Associates of California, 11014 Santa Monica Blvd., Los Angeles 26, Calif.

McGraw-Hill Book Co., Text-Film Dept., 330 W. 42nd St., New York 36, N.Y.

National Film Board of Canada, 680 Fifth Ave., New York 19, N.Y.

Sterling Educational Films, 6 E. 39th St., New York 16, N.Y.

United Nations, Film and Visual Information, New York, N.Y.

United World Films, 1445 Park Ave., New York 29, N.Y.

Univ. of Southern California, Dept. of Cinema, Los Angeles 7, Calif.

Walt Disney Productions, Educational Film Division, 2400 W. Alameda Ave., Burbank, Calif.

Wayne State Univ., A-V Materials Consultation Bureau, Detroit 2, Mich.

Weston Woods Studios, Inc., Weston, Conn.

Sy Wexler Film Productions, 801 Seward, Los Angeles 28, Calif.

Young America Films (see McGraw-Hill Book Co.).

FILMSTRIP COMPANIES

Curriculum Filmstrips, 1319 Vine, Philadelphia 7, Pa.

Eye Gate House, 146-01 Archer Ave., Jamaica 35, N.Y.

Encyclopaedia Britannica Films Inc., Filmstrip Catalog, 1150 Wilmette Ave., Wilmette, Ill.

Filmstrip House, 432 Park Ave., South, New York 16, N.Y.

Life Magazine Filmstrips, Rockefeller Plaza, New York, N.Y.

McGraw-Hill Filmstrips, 330 W. 42nd St., New York 36, N.Y.

Society for Visual Education, 1345 Diversey Parkway, Chicago 14, Ill.

Jam Handy Organization, 2821 E. Grand Blvd., Detroit 11, Mich.

United States Publishers Association, Inc., 386 Park Ave., New York 16, N.Y.

chapter 21

Reading in the Family

A gentleman who received a book for a birthday gift held it up with mock surprise. "It's a book!" he chuckled. "Do people still read?" And what with television, radio, golf, and bridge, new houses and apartments with built-in stoves and television sets but never a shelf for books, you begin to wonder if his question isn't justified—"Do people still read?"

Happily, librarians, backed by withdrawal statistics, can answer with a strong affirmative, "Yes, people *do* read, both children and adults, more books than ever before." And teachers report children's intense delight in a bright new allotment of books for the school library or a fresh selection of books for the classroom. The format of the new books is alluring, with gay, handsome jackets and the publishers' enticing leads into the books just inside the flaps of the jackets. And don't think the canny children have not learned to use those summaries in book selection. Paper and print are better than ever, and the illustrations are so beautiful they break down the resistance of the most determined nonreader. Finally, the content of the new books is so varied and well written, there is a book to meet almost any interest at almost every stage of life.

Home Environment for Reading

When parents say, "My children just don't seem to have time for reading—they aren't much interested in books," it usually means that neither are the parents. Generally, children who like to read come from families where reading is taken for granted and books are all about the house, not according to an interior decorator's plan, but according to use and convenience. There are overflowing book shelves with space for the children's books, and there are also books in every room. The kitchen, in addition to the cookbooks, has the novel mother is currently reading and a book or two of poetry for those odd moments when she must wait for the pot to boil. In the living room beside father's easy chair there is a table for his newspaper and the book or books he is reading. Books are found on bedside tables, on window sills, and even occasionally on chairs where the interrupted reader has left his book hoping for a speedy return. An atlas is near the television set to look up the strange country involved in the latest conflict. In short, this is the bookish house of a reading family. Eleanor Farjeon describes such a home:

In the home of my childhood there was a room we called 'The Little Bookroom.' True, every room in the house could have been called a bookroom. Our nurseries upstairs were full of books. Downstairs my father's study was full of them. They lined the dining-room walls, and overflowed into my mother's sitting room, and up into the bedrooms. It would have been more natural to live without clothes than without books. As unnatural not to read as not to eat.[1]

In this wonderful pen-and-ink sketch sunlight falls on a profusion of books and highlights a small, deeply absorbed reader. Illustration by Edward Ardizonne. From The Little Bookroom *by Eleanor Farjeon. ©Eleanor Farjeon, 1955. Reprinted by permission of Henry Z. Walck, Inc., Publishers. (Book 5½ x 8½, picture 4¼ x 3¾)*

In the modern house, television and radio sets occupy prominent positions, but there is no reason why they and books cannot enjoy a peaceful coexistence. Most of the time, reading is a solitary activity, whereas a fine television program can bring the whole family together in pleasant relaxation. Often the radio or television program may send the family right back to its books—because they need to look up a word for pronunciation or meaning or because the program has launched a new interest that demands more information, available only in books.

In such homes, a book is a prized possession. Birthdays and Christmas are made doubly important by such acquisitions. In one home, a child gradually acquired a complete set of the Little House books for her very own. A boy collected a good basic group of science books. In another home, where family councils are the rule, the members chose an encyclopedia rather than barbecue equipment on the somewhat utilitarian grounds that, after all, the barbecue could only be used part of the year, while the encyclopedia was practically a necessity the year round. Even the die-hards for the barbecue rejoiced when that encyclopedia, in all its glory, was unpacked and placed on a handy shelf. Everyone had something to look up, and mother had the inspiration to look up *cats* with the four-year-old cat-lover. They looked at the pictures together, and mother read enough to satisfy the youngest of the worth of this imposing set of books. This, by the way, is precisely the proper start for the reference habit with prereaders and limited readers. Use the reference books with them, read the information to them if necessary, explain how you found the information, so that the child will know how to use such books when he is on his own in reading. And what better investment for a growing family than a fine encyclopedia which will go with them from kindergarten through college and through life.

1. Eleanor Farjeon, *The Little Bookroom,* Walck, 1955, p. vii.

Reading Aloud in the Family

Good television programs are not the only means of bringing the family together for shared enjoyment. Lucky is the family with the accepted habit of reading aloud now and then. Not every night, or perhaps not even every week, because hungry readers like to fly over the pages of a chosen book with the speed that only silent reading permits. But when the outstanding book comes along—so well written or beautiful or humorous or all round compelling that the entranced reader can't bear to have the other members of the family miss it—then, that is the book to read aloud. It doesn't matter whether the content is for the oldest or the youngest just so it is first-rate reading with depth and significance.

A party in the old style with the very young and the very old enjoying the fun equally is shown with gay spirit by Garth Williams. Illustration by Garth Williams. From Little House in the Big Woods *by Laura Ingalls Wilder. Copyright, 1953, as to pictures, by Garth Williams. Reprinted by permission of Harper & Row, Publishers. (Book 5⅜ x 7¾)*

Kon-Tiki has held many a family enthralled, and the young children who listened to it read aloud when it was first published were old enough to read *Aku-Aku* for themselves when it appeared several years later. Ruth Gagliardo, in her delightful introduction to *Let's Read Aloud,* writes that

> *When* Mr. Popper's Penguins *first appeared the children's father missed not a word. "Don't read* Mr. Popper *without me," he would warn as he set off in the morning for The Hill.*[2]

And surely other fathers said the same about *Charlotte's Web,* if that was being read aloud in the family.

A child came home from the public library with *Island of the Blue Dolphins* and announced gravely, "I won't even start this because the librarian said it is a wonderful read-aloud book." Then she added the librarian's bait to reading, a briefing of the book; she said, "It's the true story of a twelve-year-old Indian girl who got left behind on a barren island with a pack of ferocious wild dogs, and she lived there all alone for eighteen years before she was rescued!" That sold the book, and the expectant family audience was not disappointed. *The Incredible Journey* holds all ages, with the younger ones begging each night for just one more chapter or else the promise that nothing more will be read after they go to bed.

Of course, the prereaders in the family have special privileges beyond the communal reading-aloud sessions. Going to bed is made bearable by the stories that accompany it. In one family, Great-Aunt Mary always told her stories, Mother read hers, and Father's deep, rumbly voice sometimes intoned made-up stories about a little girl called Melissa Melinda, who was remarkably like the recumbent child listening to familiar adventures. There were also other times with Father that were special for the youngest. After supper, with Mother and the girls still polishing off the

2. Ruth Gagliardo, *Let's Read Aloud,* Lippincott, 1962, p. 9.

dishes, Father would settle in his easy chair with his youngest child on his lap, and together they would look at the latest favorite in the picture-story group, stopping now and then to study the illustrations appreciatively. Father liked books about dinosaurs or rockets which made a pleasant variation from Mother's daytime choices of *The Storm Book* or *Snow Party* or maybe *Winnie-the-Pooh.* This last book was for the private hearing of the youngest because the older children had already heard it many times. Even so, they occasionally dropped in to listen when a favorite section was underway.

This induction of the prereading child into the magical variety of books should, of course, continue after he is six. For such a child, who has already known the heady delights of books, that first year of learning to read may come as something of a shock. He generally thinks he will be reading by the end of the first day, and great is his amazement at the slowness of the process. Here the home can help the school by providing the child with book experiences that keep him wanting to read for himself. Also it may occur to him that something the adults and the older children do so easily, he too will be able to do if he keeps at it.

If families realized half the power of reading aloud in the home, more families would try it. Glance at *That Eager Zest,* an anthology compiled by Frances Walsh of "First Discoveries in the Magic World of Books."[3] Here men and women, now writers themselves, have recorded some of their childhood experiences with books. Here are a few excerpts. The poet Robert P. Tristram Coffin wrote,

Peter's father had said Shakespeare to him long before he knew what half the words were about. Peter knew from the first, though, that they were about something fine. . . . They came up from something deep. (p. 99)

Lionel Trilling, speaking of *The Jungle Books,* said,

. . . it was not until I read the stories aloud that I fully understood how wonderful they are. (p. 60)

Robert Lawson wrote about a teacher who used to read aloud to her children,

. . . although I have not the faintest recollection of what she looked like, I can still remember her low, mellow voice as she read to us. (p. 61)

And Elizabeth Enright, describing the good, stout fare read aloud to them by their cook, quotes excerpts from those stories:

"Gretel gave a push which sent the wicked witch right in, and then she banged the oven door and bolted it. The witch howled horribly but Gretel ran away and left her to perish in misery."

. . . I often think of that rich bedtime fare when I am reading to my youngest son. Opening whatever book he chooses, I find myself declaring something like this: "Jimmy had a red express wagon. His little sister Janie had one, too." (p. 155)

Don't these few excerpts suggest what listening to good reading aloud can do for children? And Mrs. Enright's caustic selections of contrasting styles should remind adults not to read aloud what is not worth reading in the first place. When a child listens to an adult reading aloud, not only does the selection take on the prestige of adult approval, but the child hears the story or the poems plus the reader's interpretation and enjoyment. That is why later, as an adult, he remembers such selections so vividly, and the whole occasion of the reading, the room, the family circle, the light falling on loved faces becomes a cherished memory for life. Isn't such companionship with a child worth cultivating?

Certainly reading aloud is the way of ways to introduce children to exceptional books that they might not choose for themselves or might not enjoy without this added lift of family enjoyment and the reader's enthusiasm. *The Wind in the Willows, The Children of Green Knowe, A Stranger at Green Knowe, The Gammage Cup, Rifles for Watie,* perhaps even *Smoky* because of the vernacular—these are

3. Frances Walsh, *That Eager Zest,* Lippincott, 1961.

just a sampling of the choice books that need such a lift. And besides, to read any one of these aloud is to discover inestimable values, both literary and social, that neither the adult reader nor the juvenile listeners would have felt as strongly from silent reading.

How wonderful to have someone in the family read aloud with gusto such old favorites as *Tom Sawyer* and *Huckleberry Finn.* Those are generally the choices of the man in the house, and there is many an adult today who cannot read either one of those books without recalling the father's voice as he read aloud, and remembering how he stopped now and then, his eyes crinkled up with laughter over some favorite episode. To hear *Penn* or *Johnny Tremain* (which are beautifully written) beautifully read is a literary treat; and to read *Winnie-the-Pooh* silently, in solitude, isn't one half the fun as to read it aloud or to listen to it read aloud. And, by the way, every family needs an excursion into sheer hilarity now and then, whether by way of *Pippi Longstocking* (the first book in the series) or *Henry Reed, Inc.* To laugh together is to relax and to blow not only the cobwebs away, but anxieties and the doldrums as well.

So much has already been said about the necessity of reading poetry aloud for its own sake as well as the children's that little more need be added. This is a field admittedly where there are fewer volunteers for reading aloud. Half the adult population is self-conscious about its ability to read poetry well. That is probably a superlative understatement. It is to be hoped that many, many children heard the late Frederic Melcher read Milne's "The King's Breakfast." They would have loved it as did all the librarians and their friends when he read it each year at the Newbery dinner. Most mothers manage to read to their children *Mother Goose,* Stevenson, and A. A. Milne, and rarely go further. But one young mother, who was born in a foreign country and spoke English with a heavy accent, fell in love with the poetry available for children in this country and began to read it aloud when her children were mere toddlers. She and her brood literally wore out one anthology, replaced it, and bought others. Those children of hers are going to remember their poetry with a loved accent, but by the time they reach high school, they are going to know a range of fine lyric poetry such as few American children know. If that young woman can so love and so read our poetry, other parents who are not handicapped by a strange language can do so, too. Children may start with an ear for only doggerel. But by hearing better poetry intelligently read, they will gradually develop an ear for our language and an enjoyment of poetry richer both in content and lyric quality.

The Reluctant Reader

It does happen that in the midst of a bookish family there appears a cheerful extrovert who is determinedly anti-reading. There are so many things to do he can't possibly settle down indoors to reading. The family read-aloud sessions he admits are "Okay," but reading by himself—"Haven't time!" says he and dashes off, ball and bat in hand. Then, somewhere along third or fourth grade his sins of omission begin to catch up with him. He can't read with the other children either in or out of the daily reading sessions. Is he a retarded reader? If so, perhaps his reading disabilities explain his aversion to books. Somewhere along the line the basic reading skills were not established and he is running away from his failures and chagrin.

This is, of course, a school problem that calls for diagnostic tests and expert help to establish those basic skills and bring his reading up to the point where it is genuinely fluent and therefore an enjoyable activity.

Suppose, on the other hand, your nonreader is competent enough in the basic reading skills, but just averse to books. Then perhaps the problem is in the home. Perhaps he is going through a period of temporary rebellion against home pressures of one kind or another. If he is in conflict with some member of the family, his defiance may take the form of rejecting books. Or his problem may be intensely and painfully personal—a sudden consciousness of being too fat or too tall or being the youngest in the family and always being told to "Shush!" or "You're too young to do this" or "Too little to do that!" And suddenly life is repressive and frustrating. Then the child has one of two ways out—aggressive, rebellious behavior or discouraged withdrawal, a won't-try kind of behavior. In either case, the cause should be discovered and life made easier and happier for the child. Once he is comfortable and confident, he'll learn to live and to read with satisfaction.

Another cause of rebellion from the bookish pattern of a family is a too continuous emphasis on the importance of reading as if it were the most worth-while activity in the world. Nonsense! Books are indeed sources of ideas, information, and entertainment, but the outgoing extroverts who love people, get on well with them, and give warm, continuous service both to their friends and to the community are worth their weight in books. Reading can add to the richness of life, but for the vast majority of people it is not a way of life, and it may, on occasion, be invested with disproportionate importance.

Perhaps for this reason, every bookish family should have one little rebel to keep things in balance. High-pressure salesmanship on reading in general or one book in particular is almost certain to bring to the surface that streak of contrariness that lurks in most of us. When a friend says in a burst of superlatives, "It's the very *best* book I *ever* read in my *whole* life. You just *must* read it," what happens? Unconsciously, your resistance stiffens, and you don't read that book, no matter what. So when you say to a child, "This is a perfectly wonderful book. You *must* read it," and three days later you add, "My goodness, haven't you started that book yet?" you really know the answer. Of course, he hasn't started it, and what's more he's never going to start that book if he can help it.

Go easy on your book enthusiasms with any age child. Recommend gently. Leave books around, so that they are visible and tempting. Speak about them casually, "I read a review of this book that sounded good. If you read it let me know what you think of it." Or if you happen to know a book, use the librarians' bait to reading, a brief lead into the book as—"*A Stranger at Green Knowe* is an unusual story about a friendship that sprang up between a young gorilla in a zoo and a little boy from a refugee camp. Both escaped and met in a deep woods. What happened to them is strange indeed." Or you say, "Here is another book by William Steele, *Tomahawks and Trouble*. It's about three children captured by Indians in a raid. There are two boys and a little eight-year-old girl. She bites her Indian captor in the leg when he starts to throw her dolly away. The other Indians laugh at him and the two captive boys know they have made a deadly enemy. Their escape, since they are pursued by old 'Tater-Nose,' is a terrible ordeal."

Alluring as you may make these samples, it is always well to remember that some children are more readily attracted to reading through informational books than through fiction. Fortunately, they are available in every field of science, social studies, travel, and space exploration. Just name the child's interest and there are books to meet it. When a father came home one night with a bright new copy of Bertha Parker's big *Golden Book of Science,* everyone in the family took turns poring over its lavish and colorful illustrations and getting the feel of its scope and usefulness. William Reed's *The Stars for Sam* and a star map set the family scanning the heavens for one whole summer.

These are just a few ways of bringing the reluctant reader and books together. Of course, people, sports, and the outdoor world are wonderful, too, and no bookworm should be allowed to miss them. But when rock hunting or bird watching are temporarily out, when games are over and friends gone home, then there are books to satisfy the need for change and to furnish new ideas, new leads into new activities, and maybe new dreams besides. According to Ruth Gagliardo, her geologist son once said:

"Without imagination all the scientific training in the world will make only technicians."

When asked if he was saying that The Wind in the Willows *made scientists, he replied in utter seriousness, "Exactly. Washburne's* Story of Earth and Sky *plunged me into science at eight but it was* Winnie the Pooh *and old Toad that kept me there quite as much as the factual books I pored over.*"[4]

Religious Books for Children

Since there can no longer be any exposure to religious literature in the public schools, such books become the exclusive responsibility of churches and homes.

The wide religious diversity in this country must be understood and accepted by adults and children if we are to live realistically, and let us hope tolerantly, in our modern world. This religious diversity should be reflected in children's books, and happily it is. For instance, here is a sampling of lively stories, each written against a particular religious background and presenting that religious group sympathetically and warmly:

Thee, Hannah! by Marguerite de Angeli is the story of a rebellious little Quaker girl who comes to a sudden respect for her sect.

Henner's Lydia by Marguerite de Angeli and *Plain Girl* by Virginia Sorenson are delightful stories about the children of Pennsylvania Amish.

All-of-a-Kind Family by Sidney Taylor, together with the other books in this series, presents the everyday adventures of a city family with an orthodox Jewish background appealingly described.

In My Mother's House by Ann Nolan Clark affords a glimpse of Navaho Indian customs, and *Waterless Mountain* by Laura Armer concerns the childhood of a Navaho boy who expects to become a medicine man. Their religious concepts are impressive.

Juanita by Leo Politi for the youngest, *Dobry* by Monica Shannon, *...and Now Miguel* by Joseph Krumgold, are all rich in Catholic customs and beliefs.

Wee Joseph by William MacKeller is a Scotch Protestant story of a "wee" miracle for a boy and his dog. The Little House books by Laura Ingalls Wilder are Protestant in background, but not as markedly so as you might expect.

Daughter of the Mountains by Louise Rankin is the story of a little Tibetan Buddhist girl's search for her dog, a dangerous journey which she successfully accomplishes with the help of her deep religious faith.

Young Fu of the Upper Yangtze by Elizabeth Lewis is China in conflict, with Young Fu raised on the Confucian ethic.

If young readers encounter these religious diversities in books, all sympathetically presented, they should develop not merely tolerance but a warm respect for good people who are earnestly practicing the religion of their choice. And biographies of such divergent religious leaders and heroes as St. Francis of Assisi, John Wesley, Father Damien, Sir Wilfred Grenfell, Dr. Tom Dooley, George Washington Carver, and Albert Schweitzer cannot fail to expand their understanding of the fact that a sense of security, rising from a belief in prayer and communion with God, may be an impelling force and source of strength in the lives of men and women everywhere.

Time was when there was daily Bible reading in homes, a time set aside and known as "family prayers." Now, it is said, there is considerable evidence of a revival of interest in family worship in many homes—briefer, more informal, but equally reverent, and with every member of the family taking his turn, even the youngest. This is desirable so long as adults set the tone and carry the bulk of the responsibility. Needless to say, each home will choose and interpret according to its own ideology books for religious education and family worship. This discussion can only suggest the types of books now available.

BOOKS OF PRAYERS

There are a number of prayer books for children, and they range from mediocre to excellent. The illustrations for these books often seem to have an overliteralness and oversweetness that reduce their imaginative

4. Gagliardo, op. cit., pp. 10-11.

appeal. Even for very small children "Give us this day our daily bread" need not be limited to the tight literalness of a fat loaf of white bread, and praying children need not be so plumply cute or ethereally sweet as some of the illustrators have made them. As a matter of fact, the illustrations for prayers often seem to be adult reminiscences of childhood, *about* but not *for* children. Several books of prayers, though, can be recommended both for their selections and their pictures.

Tasha Tudor has created some of her loveliest water colors for her *First Prayers*. The collection includes well-known prayers and some less familiar. The twenty-third Psalm is there, as are the words of several hymns, all designed to give a child a reassuring sense of God's nearness and care. Small as the book is, the pictures have a breath-taking loveliness and dignity that lift the spirit.

One particularly fine book is called *A Little Book of Prayers*. The text was prepared by Emilie E. Johnson, and the illustrations were done by Maud and Miska Petersham. The rhymed prayers in the first part are mediocre, but the second part of the book with its selections from the Bible contains as perfect a group of prayer verses as you could find for a three- or four-year-old. The pages, bordered in blue and decorated by the Petershams, are beautiful and suggestive rather than literal. A decoration of flowers carries beneath it:

Whatsoever things are true,
Whatsoever things are honest,
Whatsoever things are just,
Whatsoever things are pure,
Whatsoever things are lovely,
Whatsoever things are of good report;
If there be any virtue,
And if there be any praise,
I will think on these things.

Such selections give both guidance and reassurance.

For use with children of all ages is *Bless This Day*, compiled by Elfrida Vipont and illustrated with great beauty and strength by Harold Jones. This is really a book for the whole family. It contains prayers for different age levels, Bible verses, and the words of some of the great devotional hymns that can be read without the music. This book has more range and more depth than any of the others. Indeed it would be hard to find a more inspirational book to read at the bedtime hour.

Elizabeth Orton Jones' pictures for *Small Rain* are more childlike and illuminating than her pictures for *Prayer for a Child*, a Caldecott winner. *Small Rain* contains a well-selected group of Bible verses. It is illustrated with pictures of children's activities which interpret the verses in terms of the child's understanding without being too tightly literal. A small pajama-clad boy gazing at myriads of stars is the illustration for

The Heavens declare the glory of God;
And the firmament sheweth his handywork.

There is no escaping the implications of the large picture which portrays children of different races and colors playing together, an illustration interpreted by the single line:

All of you are children of the most High.

Engaging twins, pigtailed and bespectacled, run through the pictures, playing as hard and having as much fun as the other children. Individual as well as racial differences are unobtrusively and cheerfully suggested. Poring over the illustrations, children will learn the verses which will be theirs in happy association with the appealing pictures.

Elizabeth Orton Jones has also made some exquisite pictures for Eleanor Farjeon's *A Prayer for Little Things*. Pictures of fledglings, drops of rain, colts, and children make this a beautiful book which expands rather than limits the imagination.

The same imaginative beauty is found in her interpretation of St. Francis' *Canticle of the Sun*. A small boy wanders through the pictures, and the little birds, beasts, and flowers she has woven into her decorations are in themselves a hymn of praise.

THE BIBLE

The Bible as a book for children offers certain obvious problems which we worry over, perhaps unnecessarily. Our real worry should

By isolating David's body from the top and the bottom of the picture, the artist powerfully depicts David's aloneness as he faces Goliath. Illustration by Harvey Schmidt.
From The Mighty Ones *by Meindert De Jong. Copyright © 1959 by Meindert De Jong. Reprinted by permission of Harper & Row, Publishers (Book 6¼ x 9¼)*

be over modern children's and young people's ignorance of Bible literature. Today, large numbers of college students are not sure who Moses was or what he did, know Joseph only as a modern novel (if at all), and have encountered Paul chiefly as a popular name for churches. It is surely time for us to stop worrying about the implications of some of the Bible stories and to try to make Bible readers of our children once more.

The Bible is a book to grow on and rediscover at different stages of our lives for different reasons, partly because it contains the most civilized code of morals in existence, couched in memorable words. The Old Testament tales, the Book of Psalms, and the dramatic sequence of the New Testament not only are great literature but have the power to widen our vision and renew our strength. Believe or reject whatever you wish theologically, the Bible will continue to be a source of strength and wisdom, if children know it well enough to turn back to it and search its richness.

RELIGIOUS INSTRUCTION

Mary Alice Jones has done a long series of books of religious instruction for young children, beginning with *Tell Me about God* and *Tell Me about Jesus.* Some parents like these books and use them gratefully. Others feel that the primer-like language completely destroys the majesty of the ideas, and that if the ideas are too difficult for a young child, they should not be introduced until the child is old enough to understand them. A pedestrian text will induce neither wonder nor reverence. Bright, large pictures have made these books exceedingly popular. You must decide for yourself whether or not you wish to use them.

Jewish and Christian children share alike that rich heritage of Old Testament hero tales, unsurpassed in variety and interest. Whether the story is about David and Goliath or Joseph and his brothers or Samuel or Samson or Solomon, these heroes have one characteristic which differentiates them from all others. They carry with them a deep sense of their relationship to God and a resultant consciousness of good and evil. When they sin, it is because they have broken God's laws. When they undertake impossible tasks, it is because they are strong in the strength of the Lord. There is violence in these tales, but there are also fortitude and faith and moral implications. You may tell or read these stories to children from the Biblical text or you may use that well-written but controversial book by Meindert De Jong, *The Mighty Ones.* Each story is introduced with an excerpt from the Bible. Then Mr. De Jong takes over and gives his elaboration and interpretation of the story in modern language. The book reads beautifully, but not everyone will agree with his interpretations. Look it over and decide for yourself. The questions of interpretation of the Bible stories themselves and of the use of the fiction that has grown about and around these Bible times and figures will have to rest with the individual. Florence Mary Fitch in *One God: The Ways We Worship Him* provides children with a feeling for the beauty and likeness in dissimilar religious practices. This book has been approved by each of the three great religious bodies. Appealing photographs and a clear forthright text bring "The Jewish Way," "The Catholic Way," and "The Protestant Way" to children's attention. This clear, sympathetic interpretation of different religious beliefs can do much to give children respect for their neighbor's pattern of worship.

We seem at last to be upon a wave of fine and varied books for children of different ages —books imparting religious concepts without dogma, editing or retelling Bible literature, and illuminated by authentic and memorable illustrations. The spirit of these books emphasizes the points of agreement in all religion. Regardless of what faith or form of orthodoxy or unorthodoxy you may belong to, you should know these religious books. Teachers should acquaint themselves with this new literature, and parents not only should examine it but should use it with their children. Choose from among these books those with which a child can begin exploring religious ideas. Teach him some of the great hymns whose words will stand the test of our modern search for meaning. Give him simple, honest little prayers and verses of supplication, building toward the great prayers gradually. Tell him stories of the Old Testament heroes who grew slowly in their knowledge of God and in the practice of His laws. Tell the child stories of the Saints or episodes from the New Testament until he can read them for himself. Say over with him verses from the Psalms or whole Psalms which he can understand and learn with you. Thanksgiving is above all times the natural occasion for introducing the Psalms. These interpret, as no other literature in the world has done, man's heartfelt gratitude to God for the blessings of life and the eternal yearnings of the human spirit for goodness. Give a child the Psalms for spiritual reinforcement, because they will steady him when he needs to be steadied, comfort him when he needs comfort, and they will bring him a renewal and refreshment of life through communion with God.

Using the Public Library

Whether a home is spacious and equipped with many books or small and cramped, with no books at all, children should discover early the resources of our wonderful public libraries. It is a tremendous experience for a small child to walk into a big library and see the stacks and stacks of books. Do you remember in *The Human Comedy,* Lionel and Ulysses, neither of whom can read, exploring the public library?

> *. . . they entered an area of profound and almost frightening silence. . . . Lionel not only whispered, he moved on tiptoe. Lionel whispered because he was under the impression that it was out of respect for books, not consideration for readers. . . . "These," he said. "And those over there. And these. All books, Ulysses." He stopped a moment to think. "I wonder what they say in all these books.". . .*
>
> *A little frightened at what he was doing, Lionel lifted the book out of the shelf, held it in his hands a moment and then opened it. "There, Ulysses!" he said. "A book! There it is! See?" . . . He looked at the print of the book with a kind of reverence, whispering to himself as if he were trying to read. Then he shook his head. "You can't know what a book says, Ulysses, unless you can read, and I can't read," he said.*[5]

But wouldn't you be ready to wager Lionel was eager when his chance came to learn to read?

5. William Saroyan, *The Human Comedy,* Harcourt, 1943, pp. 200-203.

Now that the dark, fortress-like type of library architecture is giving way to sunny or brightly illuminated buildings gay with color, the public library has become one of the most inviting spots in our towns and cities. Even in old buildings, the children's rooms are invariably warm and appealing places. Sometimes there are fireplaces with real fires to add glamor to the story hour. More often there are plants, pictures, little storybook figurines, easy chairs, even rocking chairs, and everywhere enticing displays of books for all ages. These are unique features of children's rooms, but all secondary to the books themselves. What a pity Lionel and Ulysses did not discover such a room, with a friendly librarian ready to steer them over to the picture books, just right for them to "read."

As space in our big cities grows more expensive and harder to come by, there are going to be fewer books in the home. Hence the importance of establishing the library habit early with children, even with the prereaders. If parents begin taking children to the library as young as three and help them select their books, this aid will seem the natural thing and will prevent the deadly reading ruts some children fall into when left to their own selection—all fairy tales or none whatever, all horse stories or mysteries or sports or army or doll stories! If the mother or the father who has the child in tow says casually, "Try this book along with your others," she does not seem to be casting any reflection on his choice, merely offering a dividend. Then if the mother knows her books or the librarian helps her to choose, she will select a charmer that the child can't resist, and so will make a first step away from his narrow field of interest. To be sure there are some books children want and need again and again, as did the little boy in Julia Sauer's story, who called the library "Mike's House." That was where he always found his favorite book *Mike Mulligan and His Steam Shovel*. He really needed to own that book if possible, but if not, what a blessing to have discovered "Mike's House." Adolescents may not need to own Maureen Daly's *Seventeenth Summer*, but they certainly need to read it when the problems common to teen-age girls begin to bother them. So there are many books that command a temporary but, while it lasts, a strong interest, and these interests are better satisfied by library withdrawal than by ownership.

One tremendous service a library can render both homes and schools is to supply quantities of those books which bridge the gap between reading ability and reading skill. That lag can by third and fourth grade assume discouraging proportions for some children. For instance, a child may be reading at first or second grade level but be capable of comprehending and enjoying books which he can't possibly read for himself at fifth, sixth, or even seventh grade level. Then the experts, among other recommendations, advise that the child be given a lot of practice reading and that he be provided with easy-to-read books in order to acquire the confidence that comes from a sense of comfortable fluency. But unfortunately for the bright child who is a retarded reader, many of these easy-to-read books bore or disgust him with their childishness. At this point the books of Clyde Bulla are invaluable. They are written with unaffected simplicity but with satisfying style, and they have characters and subject matter that command the respect of the oldest children.[6] There are several lists of these easy-to-read books available, but the books should be checked for maturity of content as well as for reading level. Librarians can help adults make intelligent selections from these lists and can provide a good supply of the books.

Buying Books for Children

Advice on how to build a child's library may sound unrealistic today and a little pretentious, but it is encouraging when a grandmother turns up at a lecture on "Signifi-

6. For instance, Clyde Bulla's *The Ring and the Fire* (1962), *Valentine Cat* (1959), *The Sword in the Tree* (1956), and *Down the Mississippi* (1954). All are subjects for older children, but appealing and easy to read.

cant Values in Children's Books," and explains, "I have ten grandchildren and I am one relative who always gives them books for Christmas and on their birthdays, so I have to keep up with what is new and worth while. Fortunately, they like to read." For the encouragement of others like her, it may be added that in a family of nonreaders, the girls, now with children of their own, insist that their best remembered Christmas presents came from an aunt who always sent them books. She had supposed they were wasted, but not only were they read, somehow or other, but remembered; and some of those books miraculously survived to be shared with the girls' own children. So you never can tell. Better to waste a book or two than to leave a child bookless. The problem is—what to buy and when.

There are several pitfalls waiting for the unwary purchaser of children's books, and the first is common to all book buying—impulse buying. In the children's field, this generally results in acquiring novelty or toy books with popups, or fur covers, or something to cut out or color—toys, not books, temporary entertainment with no substance! Buying on the recommendation of total strangers can be almost as bad. People who know nothing about a child can be of small help in choosing books for him.

The eye-appeal of books may be another pitfall. Bright colors and "cute" or "sweet" pictures may sell a mediocre book. If possible, read a child's book before you buy, and evaluate the illustrations by respectable art criteria. Think of the illustrations as a part of the total stream of art, as the text should be evaluated as a part of the total stream of literature.

Some criteria for your guidance in buying books for children are, first, *know your child*[7]—his special interests, his reading ability, what books he owns, what he wants, and what he needs. Then, if you haven't time to read a lot of children's books, consult a children's librarian for your choice books, books worth buying and owning over the years. Sometimes a book store will include one person who really knows and loves children's books. The late Veronica Hutchinson was such a person. Not only did she know the books, but she knew every child for whom books were purchased in her department: his age, likes and dislikes, and what he needed to get him out of a reading rut or on a more mature reading level. She was not only a trained librarian but a rarely perceptive person. If your book shop includes no such guide to the best, take the advice of the children's librarian before you buy.

The child's age is not always a safe guide. He may be reading far under or far beyond his chronological age, and this is an important consideration. *Choose books he can read, enjoy, and respect,* regardless of age. Parents sometimes say about the picture-stories, "Oh, they outgrow them so fast, they are not worth buying." That is true of many of them, but when a child wants a book over and over and over again, that book holds something special for him at that particular time. For each age there are such books and the child should have them to own, if possible. You don't want the child forever dressed in clothes too big for him or his mind forever ill-fitted with books.

This means that in your choice of books for each child you will *pick a book in the area of his special interests* at the time. Little girls are apt to go through a fairy tale stage, "not too fairy" as Phyllis Fenner's child said, but at least fantasy. So when that spell is upon her, find for her a few standard collections, such as Grimm, Hans Andersen, and perhaps one of the newer collections such as *Thistle and Thyme,* and of course one of the newer fantasies—*The Borrowers* or *The Witch and the Wardrobe*. The latter will start her on the Narnia series. If the boy is all for facts, give him what he wants in the best of the science books—*Prehistoric Animals, The Stars for Sam, First Book of Stones, Snakes, Paddle-to-the-Sea* or any of a dozen other magnificent informational books. Help the teen-ager into adult books with such choices as *To Kill a Mockingbird* or *Greengage Summer* or maybe one of their own choices—*Catcher in the Rye* or *Lord of the Flies*. Rough on aunties but "the real thing" to adolescents!

Help children to mature in their reading. Adults should be more conscious of this. For

7. Review Chapters 1 and 2 for a discussion of the child's needs and for criteria for judging books.

instance, can you carry the fairy-tale addict into myth and epics? Can you get the science-minded boy beyond his pictorial introductions to science to the meatier reference books in the same field? Are you letting a good reader take his Lincoln and Washington biographies at the easy-reading level instead of giving him Sandburg, Daugherty, Jeannette Eaton, and Clara Ingram Judson? Have the oldest children progressed from William Steele to Rosemary Sutcliff? Are you teaching them how to use and enjoy reference books and encyclopedias? And are your good readers beginning to browse among the adult book shelves? If so, you have been encouraging them properly, without undue pressure but with the lure of more substantial books.

Finally, *choose a decently balanced literary offering* for the child's own library. Children are very sure of what they like, but they don't begin to know all the kinds of books they might like if they ever encountered them. Fortunately, adults in the family also have strong preferences and these will be reflected in their book buying for the children and the home.

Dictionaries and Encyclopedias

As soon as the child can read, he should have reference books of his own. Then when questions come up you can say to him, "You look that up in your book and I'll look it up in mine and we'll see if they agree." Checking one reference against another is a good habit. If the child's text agrees with the adult text, adult prestige is added to the child's book. Certainly juvenile dictionaries and encyclopedias are good to use in this way and are a fine investment for children. Their definitions and information are suited to the child's understanding, and their print is adapted to young eyes.

The child who owns his own personal dictionary should discover early the fun of words—not just the words of the spelling lesson but all the strange and glorious words floating around in print and on the air. A great many adults have acquired a strange self-consciousness about "the twenty-five dollar word"—as if it were a crime to use one of the good old Latin derivatives if there is a one-syllable Anglo-Saxon substitute. After all *guts* may not always be the happiest description of *stamina*. Perhaps writers and orators in the past did use words pompously, but that should not mean that this generation must do penance for their sins by never venturing out of the small-word class. The infinite range of the English language was developed by the infiltration of words from many peoples—words which can express fine shades of meaning with precision and discrimination. Different sorts of words are needed when we wish to exult or lament or exhort or voice our praise. And when we do speak in praise of noble men, we need such words as *courage, fortitude, stamina, endurance,* and *fidelity* rather than the Anglo-Saxon monosyllable.

Incidentally, children can be introduced to dictionary arrangement by way of alphabet books. There are many excellent ones for this purpose, for example, any of Edward Lear's alphabet verses and, of course, Wanda Gág's *ABC Bunny*. Children are amused and fascinated by these books, learn their alphabet by way of them, and often enjoy making alphabet books of their own. These activities give them a pleasant start toward understanding the dictionary's alphabetical arrangement.

Most adults believe children should have their own dictionaries, but they are not so sure that youngsters need their own encyclopedias. In homes where books must be carefully budgeted, many families feel that the adult encyclopedia is the better investment. When children are young, parents can help them with it. Then by the time they are ten or eleven, the good readers will be using it by themselves. The best adult encyclopedias last for a lifetime; they may become dated in a few respects, but the bulk of the material will carry a child through high school, college, and adult life. If a choice must be made between a juvenile and adult encyclopedia, then decidedly the adult set should be purchased because of its greater richness and long-range value. But when a family can afford both, the child should have his own set.

There are several good children's encyclopedias today,[8] and families which have purchased one of them for their children praise the investment. Certainly a well-worn encyclopedia on a child's bookshelf is a cheerful sight. It seems to guarantee a human being who is going to enjoy ideas, all of the things his mind can explore.

Against the brilliant yellow background of this window are shown a blue eagle and a muted-red deer resting under a jeweled, green and blue tree. The color plates of this book vividly reproduce the jewel colors of the Jerusalem Windows designed by Marc Chagall for the synagogue of Hebrew University Medical Center.
From Jewels for a Crown *by Miriam Freund. Illustrations © 1962, André Sauret. Reprinted by permission of McGraw-Hill Book Co., Inc. (Original in color, book 6½ x 9¾)*

The Reading Family

In the reading family, father generally likes facts; so he buys the family encyclopedia and the big dictionary, and he helps the children use them. He sees that there is a reliable dictionary for the children at their level, and when they go off to college, it is father who sees that every child is equipped with his own standard dictionary. Father also loves biography; so he is delighted to find the superlative quality of biography and historical fiction available for children and youth today. He liked *Penn* and *Patrick Henry, Firebrand of the Revolution* so much that he not only bought them for the boys but could not resist reading them aloud to the family. Bird books, star books, books on travel, and other interesting fields, father and the children examine at the library before they buy, making sure the book is just what they want. So for science books, information and reference books of all kinds, father can be counted on to see that these are adequately represented by the best available.

Mother likes poetry, stories, and art. It is she who chose the big, fat, gloriously illustrated edition of *Mother Goose* that has been worn to shreds by three athletic book-loving babies. Mother reads poetry aloud so compellingly that she and the children have worn out one anthology, replaced it, and are careening happily through two new ones. But mother also keeps the children and herself familiar with individual poets. Of course, they own *A Child's Garden of Verses* and *When We Were Very Young,* but also De la Mare's *Peacock Pie,* Harry Behn's *Little Hill,* and David McCord's *Far and Few.* "When there isn't time to read a story," says mother, "you can always slip in a few poems." And then she adds thoughtfully, "Maybe we had better get acquainted with John Ciardi and we do need Frost's *Come With Me.*"

It is mother who brings home from the library the big handsome art books and shares them with her children so that they learn

8. See bibliography for this chapter.

how to look at pictures—not flipping through the pages but looking long and intensively and seeing more and more. For instance, in 1963, mother was so entranced with the Chagall stained-glass windows that she added to the family library *Jewels for a Crown,* the story of the windows by Dr. Miriam Freund. She read "Reuben, thou art my first born, my might, . . . unstable as water," and the children saw how the blues of Reuben's window flowed and swirled "awash with fish." With the youngest, they found together the little crooked houses Chagall remembered from his youth. They picked out the birds and beasts, the flowers and the glorious colors. With the older children, she read the text and with its help they studied the symbolism, the color, and the meaning of each window. In short, with this, as with other art books, the children learned almost unconsciously what it means to see a picture.

It is mother who keeps the stories in balance. She doesn't say, "Too many fairy tales, Nancy!" Instead she begins to read *The Jungle Books* aloud and she moves from those stories to realistic animal stories. If the boy in the family is so fact-minded that he is in danger of falling into a too tight literalness, she gives him *Henry Reed, Inc.,* hoping he'll see the joke, and he does. And oddly enough, he is so captivated by the archaeological background of *The Faraway Lurs* that he reads it and then rereads it and says to his mother, "Well, maybe it didn't happen that way, but the author certainly convinces you. Wow, what an ending!" Mother watches the fiction and poetry building up on the children's book shelves to see that if horse stories predominate for a spell, historical fiction and biography make their appearance. Fantasy is kept in balance. There are a few "funny books" and a few classics such as *Wind in the Willows, Tom Sawyer, The Odyssey,* and *Robin Hood,* but in each category there are choice selections. As mother looks at her children's book shelves, she can smile to herself at the special interests and maturity levels they represent, but she can also take pride in what the range of books means. For when the readers have grown from Wanda Gág's *Millions of Cats* to Rosemary Sutcliff's *Warrior Scarlet,* they have grown and grown well.

When those children go off to college, an amusing thing happens. They take along a dog-eared book or two from those shelves. They think they are going to reread them. Usually they don't, but that favorite book sitting on the book shelf of a strange room in a far away college dormitory, speaks to them warmly of home. "Mother read that book aloud or father and I picked out that book together or Pete and I read and reread that book I don't know how many times." The book is their symbol of home, family, and good times together. They'll keep that book for their own children. It is all tied up with their sense of family happiness which they in turn mean to create. Isn't this reward enough for family reading, for buying books and sharing them in read-aloud sessions? Families which send their children out of the home knowing good books of many kinds, honest, dependable books, sensibly written and absorbing, written with imagination and beauty, have given their children a lifelong source of strength and enjoyment.

SUGGESTED READING, PROBLEMS, AND PROJECTS

1. Suggest three or four ways in which you might use this chapter with your parent groups.

2. What parts of the chapter might lend themselves especially to discussion?

3. Prepare for parents' use a bibliography of Holiday Book Gifts for Children or Vacation Reading for the Family. First, plan your categories of books and then list some eight or ten outstanding examples under each. Be sure to list the age range for each book. And annotate each book from the standpoint of its usefulness for reading aloud, easy reading, special interest appeal. In short, make your list useful for parents.

4. Make a list of not more than twenty books which you consider essential for a school or child's library. Compare this list with the one you made at the beginning of the course. See page 27, problem 6.

REFERENCES

In connection with this chapter, many of the books listed in the bibliographies for Chapters 1, 2, 4, and 19 will be useful to parents.

ALMY, MILLIE. *Ways of Studying Children.* Bureau of Publications, Teachers College, Columbia University. Chapter 5 relates to the use of literature in studying children.

ARBUTHNOT, MAY HILL. "Books–a Family Bond." *National Parent-Teacher,* Nov. 1960. An article on family reading.

———. "Recreational Activities–Reading." *Childhood Education,* April 1959. How books can unlock new worlds for children and keep them growing.

BURTON, DWIGHT L., and NANCY LARRICK. "Literature for Children and Youth," in *Development in and Through Reading.* The Sixtieth Yearbook of the National Society for the Study of Education, Part I, Univ. of Chicago Press, 1961. One paper from a compendium by specialists in this field.

TINKER, MILES A., and CONSTANCE M. MC CULLOUGH. *Teaching Elementary Reading,* 2nd ed. Appleton, 1962. This is a teachers' textbook on reading methods, but Chapter 2, "The Reading Teacher as a Reader"; Chapter 14, "Interests and Tastes"; and Chapter 18, "Parents as Partners in the Reading Program" are excellent for parents.

WHITE, DOROTHY MARY NEAL. *About Books for Children.* Oxford, 1947. Although the author selects predominantly British children's books, she also represents many American publications.

RELIGIOUS BOOKS

Prayers and Stories

FARJEON, ELEANOR. *A Prayer for Little Things,* ill. by Elizabeth Orton Jones. Houghton, 1945. 3-8

FIELD, RACHEL. *Prayer for a Child,* ill. by Elizabeth Orton Jones. Macmillan, 1944. A charming prayer written by a poet for her own little girl. Caldecott Medal. 4-7

FRANCIS OF ASSISI, SAINT. *Song of the Sun,* from *The Canticle of the Sun,* ill. by Elizabeth Orton Jones. Macmillan, 1952. 6-9

JONES, JESSIE ORTON, comp. *Small Rain,* ill. by Elizabeth Orton Jones. Viking, 1943. 4-8

———. *This Is the Way,* ill. by Elizabeth Orton Jones. Viking, 1951. "Prayers and precepts from the world's religions," illustrated with children growing together in peace and harmony. 6-9

LINES, KATHLEEN. *Once in Royal David's City,* ill. by Harold Jones. Watts, 1956. This exquisite picture-book of the Nativity tells the story simply, with a line or two for each picture and the Biblical verses at the end of the book. 4-8

MAURY, JEAN, comp. *A First Bible,* ill. by Helen Sewell. Walck, 1934. Contains the main episodes in the life of Jesus and a selection of the important Old Testament stories. 8-12

POLITI, LEO. *St. Francis and the Animals,* ill. by author. Scribner, 1959. A happy combination of legend and biography illustrated with Leo Politi's color-filled drawings. 7-11

TUDOR, TASHA, ill. *First Prayers,* Cath. and Prot. eds. Walck, 1952. 4-7

VIPONT, ELFRIDA. *Bless This Day,* ill. by Harold Jones. Harcourt, 1958. All ages

YATES, ELIZABETH, comp. *Your Prayers and Mine,* ill. by Nora Unwin. Houghton, 1954. Moving prayers from the Bible and other sources are assembled in a beautiful book with pages that have the appearance of an old manuscript. 11-15

Religious Stories and Instruction

BARNHART, NANCY, ed. *The Lord Is My Shepherd,* ill. by editor. Scribner, 1949. A book beautiful in text and format which tells the Bible stories briefly but with considerable use of Biblical language. 10-14

BOWIE, WALTER RUSSELL. *The Bible Story for Boys and Girls–New Testament,* ill. by Stephani and Edward Godwin. Abingdon, 1951.

———. *The Bible Story for Boys and Girls–Old Testament,* ill. by Stephani and Edward Godwin. Abingdon, 1952.

Companion volumes illustrated in color and black and white. 9-14

BUNYAN, JOHN. *Pilgrim's Progress* (see Bibliography, Chapter 3).

DE JONG, MEINDERT. *The Mighty Ones: Great Men and Women of Early Bible Days,* ill. by Harvey Schmidt. Harper, 1959. 11-

EVERS, ALF. *The Three Kings of Saba,* ill. by Helen Sewell. Lippincott, 1955. Three angry kings journey to Bethlehem to find out from a new prophet which of them should be the sole ruler. Before the Child and His mother, they learn humility and love. 8-14

FARJEON, ELEANOR. *Ten Saints,* Prot. and Cath. eds., ill. by Helen Sewell. Walck, 1936. Stories of St. Francis, St. Christopher, and others, beautifully told by a distinguished writer. 8-12

FITCH, FLORENCE MARY. *One God–The Ways We Worship Him,* ill. with photographs chosen by Beatrice Creighton. Lothrop, 1944. 8-12

GALDONE, PAUL, ill. *The First Seven Days; The Story of Creation from Genesis.* Crowell, 1962. Handsome picture-book format. 5-8

GOODSPEED, EDGAR, ed. *The Junior Bible,* ill. by Frank Dobias. Macmillan, 1936. Large, clear type; modern sentence and paragraph structure. 9-13

The Great Story, from the Authorized King James Version of the Bible. Harcourt, 1938.

The Great Story, from the Douay Version of the Bible, Harcourt, 1938.
The life of Jesus in Bible language with modern sentence and paragraph structure. Illustrated with color reproductions from fifteen famous paintings. 8-12

GWYNNE, JOHN HAROLD. *The Rainbow Book of Bible Stories,* ill. by Steele Savage. World, 1956. This text, by a scholarly clergyman, covers the favorite stories of the Old and New Testaments. The illustrations are superb. 10-

HARTMAN, GERTRUDE. *In Bible Days,* ill. by Kathleen Voute. Macmillan, 1948. Stories from the Old and New Testaments in which considerable geographical and historical information is incorporated. 12-16

JEWETT, SOPHIE. *God's Troubadour; the Story of Saint Francis of Assisi,* rev. ed., ill. with reproductions of frescoes by Giotto. Crowell, 1957. 9-12

JONES, MARY ALICE. *Tell Me about God,* ill. by Pelagie Doane. Rand McNally, 1943.

______. *Tell Me about the Bible,* ill. by Pelagie Doane. Rand McNally, 1945. 4-9

KING, MARIAN. *Coat of Many Colors; the Story of Joseph,* ill. by Steele Savage. Lippincott, 1950. A good biography which retains the spirit of the Bible in language and incident. 12-15

LATHROP, DOROTHY, ill. *Animals of the Bible,* with text from the King James Version. Lippincott, 1937. A beautiful picture book, by a distinguished illustrator, of Bible stories in which animals have a part. Caldecott Medal. 6-9

MALCOLMSON, ANNE. *Miracle Plays,* ill. by Pauline Baynes. Houghton, 1959. Seven miracle plays of Noah, Abraham and Isaac, the Nativity, and Saint Nicholas are adapted from medieval sources. A valuable supplement to study of the Middle Ages. 11-14

MENOTTI, GIAN-CARLO. *Amahl and the Night Visitors,* adapted by Frances Frost, ill. by Roger Duvoisin. McGraw, 1952. In this beautifully and reverently told Christmas story of the Wise Men, a little crippled shepherd boy is healed after he sends his most treasured possession to the Christ Child. 10-

PETERSHAM, MAUD. *The Shepherd Psalm: Psalm XXIII from The Book of Psalms.* Macmillan, 1962. The author-illustrator has created a charming picture book of the psalm, with a story-like introduction about King David's inspiration in composing its rich phrases. 5-10

PETERSHAM, MAUD and MISKA, ill. *The Christ Child; As Told by Matthew and Luke.* Doubleday, 1931. 4-9

______. *David.* Macmillan, 1958. 7-12

______. *Jesus' Story,* Bible text from King James Version. Macmillan, 1942. 6-10

______. *Joseph and His Brothers.* Macmillan, 1958. 7-12

______. *Moses.* Macmillan, 1958. 7-12

______. *Ruth.* Macmillan, 1958. 7-12

______. *The Story of Jesus,* Bible text from the Confraternity of Christian Doctrine Edition. Macmillan, 1944. 6-10
The Petershams' books, illustrated with painstaking authenticity, have a moving beauty and a childlike grace.

SHIPPEN, KATHERINE. *Moses.* Harper, 1949. The story of a great leader's sense of dedication to his people and to God. 12-15

SMITH, RUTH, ed. *The Tree of Life* (see Bibliography, Chapter 11).

SMITHER, ETHEL. *A Picture Book of Palestine,* ill. by Ruth King. Abingdon, 1947. Pictures and text describe how people lived and worked in Bible times. 8-11

TERRIEN, SAMUEL. *The Golden Bible Atlas,* ill. by William Bolin. Golden, 1957. A handsome color-illustrated guide and history of the Bible lands. 9-14

WERNER, ELSA J., ed. *The Golden Bible; from the King James version of The Old Testament,* ill. by Feodor Rojankovsky. Golden, 1946. 6-12

______, ed. *The Golden Bible; The New Testament,* ill. by Alice and Martin Provensen. Golden, 1953. Large, profusely color-illustrated books which offer simple retellings of the Bible stories. Both Catholic and Protestant editions. 6-12

Hymns and Carols

DE ANGELI, MARGUERITE, ill. *Marguerite de Angeli's Book of Favorite Hymns.* Doubleday, 1963. Colorful illustrations and the words and music for fifty well-loved hymns make this a book popular with the entire family.

SEEGER, RUTH, comp. *American Folk Songs for Christmas,* ill. by Barbara Cooney. Doubleday, 1953. A book beautiful in format which contains over fifty holiday songs.

SIMON, HENRY, ed. *A Treasury of Christmas Songs and Carols,* ill. by Rafaello Busoni. Houghton, 1955. A comprehensive collection from many lands, with historical notes for each song. Colorfully illustrated.

WASNER, FRANZ, ed. *The Trapp-Family Book of Christmas Songs,* ill. by Agathe Trapp. Pantheon, 1950. Songs from many lands, with foreign language songs appearing in the native language and English.

WHEELER, OPAL, comp. *Sing for Christmas,* ill. by Gustaf Tenggren. Dutton, 1943. Twenty-nine carols, with the stories of their origins and an attractive full page color illustration for each.

DICTIONARIES AND ENCYCLOPEDIAS

Check with libraries or publishers for latest editions of reference materials, since they are frequently revised.

Basic Dictionary of American English. Holt. Numerous very clear illustrations, large print. Comprehensive information on how to use the dictionary. 9-14

Britannica Junior; the Boys' and Girls' Encyclopaedia, prepared under the supervision of the editors of the Encyclopaedia Britannica. Encyclopaedia Britannica, 15 vols. Content is directed to children of elementary and junior high grades. Articles are well illustrated and authentic. 9-14

Compton's Pictured Encyclopedia and Fact-Index. F. E. Compton, a division of Encyclopaedia Britannica, 15 vols. A survey of the whole field of knowledge with good illustrations, convenient indexing, and reliable articles. 9-16

Funk and Wagnalls Standard Junior Dictionary, Funk and Wagnalls. Useful for inclusion of names and maps. 10-14

Information Please Almanac, Simon & Schuster.

World Almanac and Book of Facts. New York World-Telegram and Sun.

Published each year, these are invaluable, inexpensive sources for up-to-date information on countries of the world, statistics, government officials, etc. 10-

MONROE, MARION, and W. CABELL GREET. *My Little Pictionary,* rev. ed. Scott, 1964. Pictures with labels representing words that children often want to spell and write are grouped in meaning categories. There are 1341 entries and 265 four-color pictures. Includes an index. 6-7

______. *My Second Pictionary*. Scott, 1964. To solve a word problem, children may turn to "words and pictures," where 3600 words are grouped and illustrated much as they are in *My Little Pictionary;* or they may consult "words and meanings," where the same list of words is arranged alphabetically, with definitions and illustrative sentences at the second-grade level. 7-8

Thorndike-Barnhart Beginning Dictionary. Scott. 8-10

Thorndike-Barnhart Junior Dictionary. Scott. 9-12

Thorndike-Barnhart Advanced Junior Dictionary. Scott. 11-14

Definitions that are easy to comprehend, an abundance of illustrative material, and a simple pronunciation system distinguish all of these.

Webster's Elementary Dictionary. Merriam. Clear large print; many illustrations. 10-12

Webster's New World Dictionary; Elementary Edition; World. Includes brief information on many countries, people, and classic names. 11-14

Winston Dictionary for Schools. Holt. Useful and well illustrated. 10-14

World Book Encyclopedia. Field Enterprises, 20 vols. Authentic, comprehensive articles. May be used as a popular reference by adults as well as children. Well illustrated and bound. 9-

World Book Encyclopedia Dictionary, ed. by Clarence Barnhart and others. Field Enterprises, 2 vols. Planned to supplement its encyclopedia, this dictionary of 180,000 words serves upper elementary grades to adults. 10-

WRIGHT, WENDELL W., assisted by Helene Laird. *The Rainbow Dictionary,* rev. ed., ill. by Joseph Low. World, 1959. A fresh, imaginative dictionary containing more than 1000 pictures in color and definitions for 2100 words. 6-8

Publishers and publishers' addresses 664

Guide to pronunciation 666

Subject index 669

Index to authors, illustrators, and titles 673

PUBLISHERS AND PUBLISHERS' ADDRESSES

ABELARD. Abelard-Schuman, 6 W. 57th St., New York 19.

ABINGDON. Abingdon Press, 201 Eighth Ave. S., Nashville 3, Tenn.

ABRAMS. Harry N. Abrams, 6 W. 57th St., New York 19.

ALADDIN. (Discontinued Publications. Some available from Dutton or Follett.)

AMERICAN BK., 55 Fifth Ave., New York 3.

AMERICAN COUNCIL ON EDUCATION. 1785 Massachusetts Ave., N.W., Washington 6, D.C.

AMERICAN HERITAGE. American Heritage Publishing Co., 551 Fifth Ave., New York 17.

AMERICAN LIBRARY ASSOCIATION. 50 E. Huron, Chicago 11.

APPLETON. Appleton-Century-Crofts, 440 Park Ave. S., New York 6.

ARIEL. See Farrar, Straus.

ATHENEUM. Atheneum Publishers, 162 E. 38th St., New York 16.

BARNES. Barnes & Noble, 105 Fifth Ave., New York 3.

BEECHHURST PRESS, INC. 11 E. 36th St., New York 16.

BELL. George Bell & Sons, Ltd., York House, 6 Portugal St., W.C. 2, London.

BENTLEY. Robert Bentley, 993 Massachusetts Ave., Cambridge 38, Mass.

BOBBS. The Bobbs-Merrill Co., 4300 W. 62nd St., Indianapolis 6, Ind.

CAMBRIDGE. Cambridge Univ. Press, 32 E. 57th St., New York 22.

CENTURY. Century House, Watkins Glen, N.Y.

CHATTO. Chatto & Windus, 40-42 William IV St., W.C. 2, London.

CHILDRENS PRESS. Jackson Blvd. & Racine Ave., Chicago 7.

CHILTON. Chilton Books, 525 Locust St., Philadelphia 6.

CITADEL. Citadel Press, 222 Park Ave. S., New York 3.

CLARENDON. See Oxford.

CLOWES. William Clowes & Sons, Ltd., Little New St., E.C. 4, London.

COMPTON. F. E. Compton & Co., 1000 N. Dearborn, Chicago 10.

COWARD. Coward-McCann, 200 Madison Ave., New York 16.

CRITERION. Criterion Books, 6 W. 57th St., New York 19.

CROWELL. Thos. Y. Crowell, 201 Park Ave. S., New York 3.

CROWN. Crown Publishers, 419 Park Ave. S., New York 16.

DAY. John Day Co., 62 W. 45th St., New York 36.

DIAL. Dial Press, 461 Park Ave. S., New York 16.

DODD. Dodd, Mead & Co., 432 Park Ave. S., New York 16.

DOUBLEDAY. 575 Madison Ave., New York 22.

DOVER. Dover Publications, 180 Varick St., New York 14.

DUCKWORTH. Gerald Duckworth & Co., Ltd., 3 Henrietta St., W.C. 2, London.

DUELL. Duell, Sloan & Pearce, 60 E. 42nd St., New York 17.

DUTTON. E. P. Dutton & Co., 201 Park Ave. S., New York 3.

ENCYCLOPAEDIA BRITANNICA. 425 N. Michigan Ave., Chicago 11.

EXPRESSION. The Expression Co., Magnolia, Mass.

FABER. Faber & Faber, Ltd., 24 Russell Sq., W.C. 1, London.

FARRAR, STRAUS. Farrar, Straus & Co., 19 Union Sq. W., New York 3.

FAXON. F. W. Faxon Co., 83 Francis St., Boston 15.

FIDELER. The Fideler Co., 31 Ottawa Ave. N.W., Grand Rapids, Mich.

FIELD ENTERPRISES Educational Corp., 510 Merchandise Mart Plaza, Chicago 54.

FOLLETT. 1010 W. Washington Blvd., Chicago 7.

GARDEN CITY BOOKS. See Doubleday.

GINN. Ginn & Co., Statler Bldg., Back Bay P.O. 191, Boston 17.

GOLDEN. Golden Press, 850 Third Ave., New York 22.

GROSSET. Grosset & Dunlap, 1107 Broadway, New York 10.

HALE. E. M. Hale & Co., 1201 S. Hastings Way, Eau Claire, Wis.

HAMMOND. C. S. Hammond & Co., Maplewood, N.J.

HARCOURT. Harcourt, Brace & World, 757 Third Ave., New York 17.

HARPER. Harper & Row, 49 E. 33rd St., New York 16.

HASTINGS HOUSE. Hastings House, Publishers, 151 E. 50th St., New York 22.

HEATH. D. C. Heath & Co., 285 Columbus Ave., Boston 16.

HERITAGE. See Macy.

HILL AND WANG. 141 Fifth Ave., New York 10.

HOLIDAY. Holiday House, 8 W. 13th St., New York 11.

HOLT. Holt, Rinehart & Winston, 383 Madison Ave., New York 17.

HORN BOOK. Horn Book, Inc., 585 Boylston, Boston 16.

HOUGHTON. Houghton Mifflin Co., 2 Park St., Boston 7.

KNOPF. Alfred A. Knopf, 501 Madison Ave., New York 22.

LIBRARY JOURNAL. Published by R. R. Bowker Co., 1180 Ave. of the Americas, New York 36.
LIPPINCOTT. J. B. Lippincott Co., E. Washington Sq., Philadelphia 5.
LITTLE. Little, Brown & Co., 34 Beacon St., Boston 6.
LIVERIGHT. Liveright Publishing Corp., 386 Park Ave. S., New York 16.
LONGMANS. See McKay.
LOTHROP. Lothrop, Lee & Shepard Co., 419 Park Ave. S., New York 16.
MCBRIDE. McBride Books, 60 Laight St., New York 13.
MCGRAW. McGraw-Hill Book Co., 330 W. 42nd St., New York 36.
MCKAY. David McKay Co., 119 W. 40th St., New York 18.
MACMILLAN. 60 Fifth Ave., New York 11.
MACRAE SMITH. 225 S. 15th St., Philadelphia 2.
MACY. The George Macy Co., 595 Madison Ave., New York 22.
MESSNER. Julian Messner, 8 W. 40th St., New York 18.
MODERN LIBRARY. 457 Madison Ave., New York 22.
MORROW. William Morrow, 425 Park Ave. S., New York 16.
NATIONAL COUNCIL OF TEACHERS OF ENGLISH. 508 S. Sixth St., Champaign, Ill.
NELSON. Thomas Nelson & Sons, 18 E. 41st St., New York 17.
NOVELLO. 160 Wardour St., W. 1, London.
NUTT. David Nutt, 41 Colebrooke Row, N. 1, London.
OXFORD. Oxford Univ. Press, 417 Fifth Ave., New York 16.
PAGE. See Farrar, Straus.
PANTHEON. Pantheon Books, 22 E. 51st St., New York 22.
PARNASSUS. Parnassus Press, 33 Parnassus Rd., Berkeley 8. Calif.
PELLEGRINI. See Farrar, Straus.
PETER PAUPER. Peter Pauper Press, 629 McQueston Parkway, Mount Vernon, N.Y.
PHAIDON. Phaidon Publishers, 95 E. Putnam Ave., Greenwich, Conn.
PLATT. The Platt & Munk Co., 200 Fifth Ave., New York 10.
PRAEGER. Frederick A. Praeger, 64 University Pl., New York 3.
PRENTICE-HALL. Prentice-Hall, Englewood Cliffs, N.J.
PUTNAM. G. P. Putnam's Sons, 200 Madison Ave., New York 16.
RAND MCNALLY. P.O. Box 7600, Chicago 80.
RANDOM. Random House, 457 Madison Ave., New York 22.
RINEHART. See Holt.
RONALD. Ronald Press Co., 15 E. 26th St., New York 10.
ROW. See Harper & Row.
ROY. Roy Publishers, 30 E. 74th St., New York 21.
ST. MARTIN'S PRESS. 175 Fifth Ave., New York 10.
W. R. SCOTT. 8 W. 13th St., New York 11.
SCOTT. Scott, Foresman & Co., 433 E. Erie, Chicago 11.
SCRIBNER. Charles Scribner's Sons, 597 Fifth Ave., New York 17.
SHEED. Sheed & Ward, 64 University Pl., New York 3.
SIMON & SCHUSTER. 630 Fifth Ave., New York 20.
STERLING. Sterling Publishing Co., 419 Park Ave. S., New York 16.
STOKES. See Lippincott.
STUDIO. Studio Publications, 625 Madison Ave., New York 22.
ALAN SWALLOW. 2679 S. York, Denver 10, Colo.
TIME. Time Inc., Book Division, Time & Life Bldg., Rockefeller Center, New York 20.
TUTTLE. Charles E. Tuttle Co., 28 S. Main St., Rutland, Vt.
VANGUARD. Vanguard Press, 424 Madison Ave., New York 17.
VIKING. 625 Madison Ave., New York 22.
WAKE-BROOK HOUSE. Box 1286, Coral Gables 34, Fla.
WALCK. Henry Z. Walck, 19 Union Sq. W., New York 3.
E. WARD. Edmund Ward, 194-200 Bishopsgate, E.C. 2, London.
WARNE. Frederick Warne, 101 Fifth Ave., New York 3.
WASHBURN. Ives Washburn, 119 W. 40th St., New York 18.
WATSON-GUPTILL. Watson-Guptill Publications, 1564 Broadway, New York 36.
WATTS. Franklin Watts, 575 Lexington Ave., New York 22.
WELLS. Wells Gardner, Darton Co., Ltd., 49 Brighton Rd., Redhill, Surrey.
WESTMINSTER PRESS. Witherspoon Bldg., Philadelphia 7.
A. WHITMAN. 560 W. Lake St., Chicago 6.
WHITMAN. Whitman Publishing Co., 1220 Mound Ave., Racine, Wis.
WHITTLESEY HOUSE. See McGraw.
WILCOX & FOLLETT. See Follett.
WILEY. John Wiley & Sons, 605 Third Ave., New York 16.
WILSON. H. W. Wilson, 950 Univ. Ave., New York 52.
WINSTON. See Holt.
WORLD BK. See Harcourt.
WORLD. The World Publishing Co., 2231 W. 110th St., Cleveland 2, Ohio.

GUIDE TO PRONUNCIATION

The following list contains names of authors and illustrators, titles of books, characters, and a few miscellaneous items. Words which can be found in a standard college dictionary, those which are spelled phonetically, and those with which students are likely to be familiar from other fields are not included. Symbols used are as follows: a as in hat; ā as in age; ã as in care; ä as in father; e as in let; ē as in see; ėr as in term; H as in the German *ach;* i as in pin; ī as in five; o as in hot; ō as in go; ô as in order, all; ou as in house; u as in cup; u̇ as in full; ü as in rule; ū as in use; zh as in measure; ə represents the a in about, e in taken, i in pencil, o in lemon, u in circus; Y, as in the French du, is pronounced by speaking ē while the lips are rounded for ü; as in the French bon, is not pronounced, but the vowel before it is nasal. All other consonants have their phonetic pronunciations.

Afanasiev ä fä nä′syif
Aiken-drum ā′kən drum
Akhenaten ä ke na tən
Aldis ôl′dis
Amlak äm lak′
Analdas ə näl′dəs
Anansi ə nan′si
Anitje ə nich′ə
Ankhsenpaaten anH′sen pät′en
Ardizzone är di zō′ni
Arora ə ro′rə
Artzybasheff är tsi ba′shif
Asbjörnsen äs′byėrn sen
Asimov a si′mov
Aucassin ō ka saN′
Averill ā′və ril
Aymé e mā′
Baba Yaga bä′bə yä gä′
Babar bä′bär
Barbauld bär′bōld
Barchilon, Jacques bär shē yoN′, zhäk
Baudouy, Michel-Aimé bô dü ē′, mē shel-e mā′
Behn bān
Beim bīm
Benary-Isbert, Margot ben ãr′ē is′bėrt, mär′gō
Benét be nā′
Beowulf bā′ə wu̇lf
Berquin, Armand bėr kaN′, ar mäN′
Beskow bes′kō
Bevis bē′vis
Bewick bū′ik
Bidpai bid′pī
Binnorie bin′ə rē or bin′ô rē
Blegvad bleg′vad
Blough blou
Bontemps, Arna bôN tôN′, är nə
Brigitte brē zhēt′
Brindze brin′zē
Bubo bū′bō
Buchheimer bu̇k′hī mėr
Budulinek bu dū′lin ek
Buehr būr
Bulla bu̇l′ə
Carabas kar′ə bas
Cares kãr′ēz
Caudill kô′dl
Cavanna kə van′ə
Chappell chap′el
Charlot, Jean shär lō′, zhôN
Chincoteague ching′kə tēg
Chute, Marchette chüt, mär shet′
Chwast kwäst
Ciardi chär′dē
Cinderlad, Per, Paal, Espen
sin′dər läd, pãr, pôl, es′pən
Claas kläs
Colum, Padraic kol′um, pô′drig
Comenius kə mē′ni us
Contes de Ma Mère l'Oye kôNt də mä mãr lwä
Cottrell kot′rəl
Cowper kü′pėr
Credle crā′dəl
Cuchulain kü chü′lin
D'Armancour där môN kür′
Dasent dā′sənt
D'Aulaire dō lãr′
D'Aulnoy dōl nwä′
De Angeli də an′jel ē
De Beaumont, Madame Leprince
də bō môN′, ma dam′ lə praNs′
De Brunhoff, Jean də brün′ôf, zhôN
De Genlis, Madame də zhôN lē′, ma dam′
DeJong, Meindert də yung′, min′dėrt
De Regniers də rãn′yā
Deucher dü shā′
Dobry dō′brē
Dodge, Mary Mapes māps
Dolbier dôl′bēr
Druon drü äN′
Du Bois, William Pène dY bwä, pen
Duvoisin dY vwä zaN′
Eckenstein, Lina ek′en stīn, lē′nä
Edda ed′ə
Eichenberg ī′ken bėrg
Epaminondas i pam i non′dəs
Euller ū′lėr
Eumêlus ū mē′ləs
Farjeon fär′jun
Farquharson fär′kwėr sən
Fjeld fē′el or ′fyel
Flattot fla tō′
Freund froind

Fyleman fīl′man
Gaer gār
Gág gäg
Galland, Antoine gə läN′, äN twôn′
Gallant gä lant
Gatti, Attilio gat′ē, a tēl′ē ō
Gekiere ge′ki ā (r)
Glubok glü′bok
Gramatky gra mat′kē
Galdone gal dōn′
Goss gäs
Gudbrand gủd′bränd
Guiterman git′ėr mən
Gummere gum′ėr ē
Gylfi gYl′fə
Haas häs
Hader hā′dėr
Hakon hô′kən
Hamm häm
Hatshepsut hat shep′süt
Haugaard hou′gärd
Hazard a zär′
Heinlein hīn′līn
Heminges hem′ing gāz
Heyerdahl hā′ėr däl
Hind Etin hīnd et′ən
Hitopadesa hi tō pa dā′sha
Hofsinde hof′sin də
Holle hôl′lə
Jancsi yan′sē
Jataka jä′tä kə
Jeanne-Marie zhan′ mä rē′
Josian jō sī′ən
Kaa kä
Kahl käl
Karana kä rä′nä
Kavaler ka′vủl ėr
Kenofer ken′o fėr
Kepes kep′esh
Kielty kēl′tē
Kinder- und Hausmärchen
kin′dėr ủnd hous′ mār′Hən
Krush crush
Kjelgaard Kel′gärd
La Fontaine, Jean de lä fon ten′, zhôN də
Latham lā′thum
Lathrop lā′thrəp
Le Hibou et la Poussiquette
lē bü′ e lä pü si ket′
Leodhas, Sorche Nic ly ō′us, sôr′ä nic
Liam lē′am
Liddell lid′əl
Liers lirs
Lipkind lip′kind
Lisitzky li sit′skē
Llyn-Y-Fan Hlin′ə van′
Lurs lürz

Mafatu ma fa tu
Mara mä′rə
Mārchen mār′Hən
Mary-Rousselière, Guy mä rē′-rü se li ā, gē
Masani mä sä′nē
Mearns mėrnz
Mei Li mā lē
Melendy mə lən′dē
Milne miln
Minarik min′ə rik
Moe mō′ə
Monvel, Boutet de môN vel′, bü tā′də
Mordvinoff mord′vin of
Mowgli mou′glē
Mukerji mủ kėr′jē
Munari, Bruno mü nä′rē, brü′nō
Nefertiti ne fėr tē′ti
Neurath nū′rath
Nibelungs nē′bə lủngz
Nicolette nē kô let′
Niko nē′ko
Nino nē′nyō
Okada, Rokuo ō ka da, rō kủ ō
Orphelines ôr fel ēnz′
Padre Porko pä′thre pôrk′ō
Palazzo pa lat′zō
Panchatantra pän chə tän′trə
Pantaloni pan tə lō′nē
Paracelsus par ə sel′səs
Peattie pe′ti
Pecos pā kəs
Pelle pel′lē
Perrault pe rō′
Petrides, Heidrun pə trē′dēz, hīd′drun
Petry pē′tri
Pettit pe tē′
Pibroch of Donnel Dhu pē′broH, don′nel dū
Picard, Barbara Leonie pi′käd, lā′ō nē
Piet pēt
Planudes plə nū′dēz
Plouhinec plü′i nek
Podendorf, Illa pō′den dorf, ī′lə
Polgreen pol′grēn
Politi pō lē′tē
Procyon prō′si on
Pwyll and Pryderi pü′il, pru dā′rē
Quennell kwe nel′
Raman rä′mən
Ramayana rä mä′yə nə
Rasmussen, Knud räs′mus ən, nủd
Rey rā
Ripopet-Barabas rē′pō pā-bä′rä bä
Rojankovsky rō jan kôf′skē
Ruchlis ruk′lis
Rugh rü
Saba sā′bə
Sacajawea sak′ə jə wē′ə

Sadko säd′kô
Saemundr sā′mu̇n dėr
Sarett sä ret′
Schatz shatz
Schlein shlīn
Seignobosc, Françoise sāngn′yō bosk, fräN swäz′
Selsam sel′səm
Seredy shār′ə dē
Serraillier sə räl′yā
Seuss süs
Severy sev′er ē
Sheftu shef′tü
Sidjakov sij′ə kof
Sita sē′tä
Slobodkin slō bod′kin
Smolicheck smol′i chek
Snegourka snye gür′kä
Sojo, Toba sō jō, to bä
Solbert sol′bėrt
Soupault sü pō′
Spilhaus, Athelstan spil′hous, a′thəl stan
Stefferud stef′fėr ud
Stolz stōlts
Strachey strā′chi
Sture-Vasa stu̇r-vä sä
Spyri, Johanna shpē′rē, yō hän′ä
Sturluson, Snorri stür′le sôn, snôr′ā
Suba sü′bə
Szasz säz

Thacia thā′shä
Thorne-Thomsen, Gudrun thôrn-tom′sen, gü′drun
Tistou tē stü′
Tresselt tre selt
Tutankhaten tüt änH ä′tən
Tymnes tim′nēz
Udry ū′dri
Ullman u̇l′män
Urashima Taro ü rä shē mä tä rô
Valkyr val kir′ or val′kir
Viehmann vē′män
Vipont vī′pont
Volsung vol′su̇ng
Vulpes vul′pēz
Watie wā′tē
Wawona wə wō′nə
Weisgard wīs′gärd
Whippety Stourie wip′ə tē stür′ē/stu̇r′ē
Whuppie wu̇p′ē
Wier wēr
Wiese vē′zə
Wild, Dortchen vilt, dôrt′shən
Yashima, Taro yä′shi ma, tä′rō
Yonie Wondernose yō nē wun′dər nōz
Zantippus zan tēp′pus
Zhenya zhā′nyə
Ziner, Feenie zī′nėr, fē′nē
Zolotow zol′ə tou

Subject Index

Note: "(listing)" indicates bibliographical listings on the subject.

ABC books, 90, (listing) 113-114
Adventure tales, beginning of, 38-40
Adventurers, biographies of, 550
Africa,
—folk tales of (listing), 289-290
—modern historical fiction of (listing), 512-513
Alaska, books for children, 575
Allegory, 307-308
Ancient world,
—historical fiction of, 488-491, (listing) 510-511
—informational books of, 569-571
Animal stories, 22, 347-357, 399-419
—animals as animals, talking, 400-403
—animals seen objectively, 403-418
—criteria for judging, 418-419
—for readers eight to eleven (listing), 421-423
—for readers twelve and older (listing), 423-424
—picture-stories of (listing), 420-421
—talking beasts, 398-400
Animals, informational books, 586-688
Arabia, folk tales of, (listing) 290
Art books for children, (listing) 620-621
Artists, biographies of, 546-548; (listing) 559
Atmosphere and weather, informational books, 592-593
Awareness school of writing, 427-428

Ballads and story-poems, 94-107
—characteristics of popular ballads, 99-102
—folk ballads in the United States, 105-107
—use of with children, 106-107
—(listing), 114-115
—origins of popular ballads, 94-97
—printed sources of popular ballads, 97-98
—traditional ballads, use of with children, 102-105
Battledores, 31
Biography, 22, 48, 518-553
—as history, 519-520
—as literature, 522-525
—as the study of an individual, 520-522
—biographical fiction, definition of, 526
—Civil War Period, 542-544
—Colonial and Revolutionary periods, 535-539
—definition of, 518
—encouraging reading of, 552-553
—fictionalized biography, definition of, 526
—for older children (exploration and settlement), 533-535, (listing) 554-555
—for special interests, 544-550
—for young children, 527-531
—Jacksonian period, 540-542
—Presidents of United States, 533
—series, 531-533
—use of with children, 550-552
Birth, books on, 588
Book selection, aids for, 26-27

Caldecott Medal, 45, 48, list of winners, 57
Canada, folk tales (listing), 290
Carols for children (listing), 660
Chapbooks, 31-33
Chemistry, books for children, 595
China,
—folk tales (listing), 290
—modern historical fiction (listing), 513
Choral speaking. *See* Verse choirs
Civil War,
—biographies of period, 542-544
—informational books, 574-575
Classics in development of children's books (listing), 46-47
Color printing, 56
Comics for children, 635-637
Creative expression and reading, 606-621
—atmosphere for creativity, 618-620
—creative expression in the early years, 607-610
—creative writing, 610-612
—dramatization, 613-615
—illustration, 615-616
—intelligence and creativity, 607
Czechoslovakia,
—folk tales, 264, (listing), 290

Dame Goose,
—of England, 78
—of Boston, 77-78
Denmark, folk tales (listing), 290-291
Dictionaries for children, 656-657, (listing) 661
Didacticism,
—in eighteenth and nineteenth century France and England, 41-43
—in 19th century America, 43
Dramatics, children's uses of, 613-615
Drolls, 270-271

Earth, books for children, 590-595
Egypt,
—historical fiction of, 489-490
—informational books on, 570
Encyclopedias for children, 656-657, (listing) 661
Energy, books for children, 595-597
England,
—epics of (listing), 232
—folk tales of, 261-263, (listing) 291
—modern fantasy, 333-344
—realistic fiction of, 436-438, (listing) 468-469
Epics, 314-319
—characteristics of, 314
—King Arthur, 317-318
—*Odyssey*, 315-316
—*Ramayana*, 318
—*Robin Hood*, 316-317
—*Sigurd the Volsung*, 316
Eskimos,
—folk tales (listing), 291
—poems of, 180
Europe, historical fiction, 491-497, (listing) 511-512
Experiment books, 583-584

Fables, 298-305
—collections of, 300-303

—Aesop, 300-301
—*Jatakas,* 301-303
—La Fontaine, 303
—*Panchatantra, The,* 301
—of the modern day (listing), 321
—use of, 303-305
Fairies and magic makers, 272-275
Fairy tales. *See* folk tales
Family life, stories of, 20-21
Fanciful tales for children, 326-367, (listing) 369-375
Fantasy in the late nineteenth and early twentieth centuries, 337-347
Filmstrips for children, 633-634
Finland, folk tales, 264, (listing) 291
Folk tales, 20, 44, 252-287
—anthologies of (listing), 297
—collections of, 257-269
—*Arabian Nights,* 263-264
—British, 261-262
—Czechoslovakian, 264
—Finnish, 264
—French, 257-258
—German, 258-260
—Norwegian, 260-261
—Russian, 264
—Spanish, 264-265
—United States, 265-269
—diffusion of, 256-257
—elements of, 275-281
—modern adaptations of, 332-333
—misuses of, 283-284
—origin of, 252-255
—dreams and the unconscious, 254-255
—polygenesis, 253-254
—remnants of myth and ritual, 252-253
—sources of, 255-256
—types of, 269-272
—uses of, 281-283, 284-287
Format, 24-25
France,
—fables of (listing), 320-321
—fairy tales of, 36-37
—folk tales of, 257-258
—modern realistic fiction (listing), 513-514

Geology, books for children, 592
Germany, folk tales of, 258-260, (listing) 292
Greek myths, 308-309, (listing) 321-322
Guiding children through books, 10-13

Haiku, children's use of, 610-612
Hawaii, books for children, 575
Here and now stories. *See* Realistic fiction
Historical fiction, 21-22, 476-507
—American, 477-488
—criteria for, 496-497
—European, 491-497
—of the ancient world, 488-491
History of children's literature,
—beginnings, 30-43
—emergence of modern books, 43-46
—recent trends, 47-48
Holland, modern realistic fiction (listing), 514
Hornbooks, 31
Human body, books on, 588-590
Humorous books for children, 363-367
Hymns for children (listing), 660

Illustrators, 52-71
—of the nineteenth century, 56-60
—of the twentieth century, 60-71
India,
—fables of (listing), 321
—folk tales of, 255-256, (listing) 292-293
—modern realistic fiction (listing), 514
Indians (North American),
—folk tales of, 267, (listing) 295-296
—realistic fiction of, 450-454, (listing) 470-471
Informational books, 5, 48, 564-597. See also Social studies and Science.
—criteria for, 564-566
Ireland,
—folk tales of, 256, (listing) 293
—realistic fiction of, (listing) 468-469
Italy, folk tales (listing), 293

Jacksonian Period, biographies of, 540-542
Japan,
—folk tales of, (listing) 293-294
—modern realistic fiction (listing), 513

Korea, folk tales of, (listing) 294

Library,
—home library, 654-657
—public library, use of, 653-654
—school library, 25-26
Limericks, of Lear, 121

Magazines for children, 639-641
Mass media and reading, 622-641
—comics, 635-637
—filmstrips, 633-634
—magazines and newspapers, 639-641
—motion pictures, 629-633
—paperbacks, 637-639
—recordings and tapes, 634-635
—television and radio, 623-629
Matter, books on for children, 595-597
Mexico,
—folk tales of, (listing) 294
—modern realistic fiction, (listing) 514-515
Middle Ages,
—historical fiction of, 493-496
—informational books on, 571-572
Minority groups, realistic fiction, 7, 8, 446-458, (listing) 469-472
—American Indians, 450-454
—Negroes, 446-450
—Regional and religious minorities, 454-458
Minstrels, 94-96
Mother Goose, 77-94
—children's editions of, 113
—early editions of, 78-79
—identity of, 77-78

—modern illustrated editions, 86-89
—uses of, 90-94
—verse origins, 79-81
Motion pictures for children, 629-633
Music books for children (listing), 620-621
Musicians, biographies of, 546-548, (listing) 559-560
Mystery stories, 459-463, (listing) 472-473
Myths, 305-314
—evolution of, 305-307
—nineteenth-century adaptations, 45
—sources of, 308-310
—Greek, 308-309
—Norse, 309-310
—Roman, 309
—types of, 307-310
—uses of, 312-314

Needs, children's, 3-10
Negroes,
—American folk tales, 266, (listing) 296
—biographies of, 545-546
—realistic fiction of, 446-450, (listing) 469-470
Newbery Medal, list of winners, 50-51
Newspapers for children, 639-641
Nonsense verse, 116-126
Norse myths, 309-310, (listing) 323
North America, informational books on, 575-576
Norway, folk tales of, 260-261, (listing) 294

Pakistan, folk tales, (listing) 292-293
Paperbacks for children, 637-639
Parable, definition of, 299-300
Personification, 357-363
—of machinery, 360-363
—of toys, 357-360
Pets, books about care of, 588
Philippines, folk tales of, (listing) 291
Physics, books for children, 595-597
Picture-biography, origin of, 67
Picture books, 48, definition of, 52
Picture-stories, 20, definition of, 52
Plant life, books, 585-586
Poetry,
—anthologies of, criteria for selection, 200-201
—beginning poetry with children, 40-41
—definition of, 192-193
—difficulties for children, 195-197
—elements of good poetry, 193-195
—how to instill children's love of, 197-205
—humorous poetry, 126-138
—lyric poetry, 166-175
—modern narrative poetry, 107-111
—for children 5-9, 107-109
—for children up to 14, 109-111
—nonsense verse, 116-126
—value of, 116-117
—of fairyland, 180-186
—of manners and morals, 138-141
—of nature, 175-180
—of the child's world, 141-162
—reading aloud, 198-219
—uses in the schoolroom, 210-213
Poets,
—biographies of, (listing) 218
—lyric, 166-174
—of fairyland, 180-186
—of manners and morals, 138-141
—of nature, 175-180
—of the child's world, 141-158
Poland, folk tales of, (listing) 294
Prehistoric times, informational books, 569, 590-592
Proverbs, 299
Puppets, children's uses of, 614, (listing) 621
Puritan influence on literature, in England, 33-34, in New World, 34-36

Radio for children, 623-629
Reading aloud, the art of, 394-395
Reading in the family, 644-658
Realistic fiction, 426-464
—birth of, 45-46
—classics about foreign lands,
—early, 497-498
—recent, 499-507
—classics of the late nineteenth century, 434-436
—criteria for judging, 464
—for older children (listing), 467
—for young children, 427-434
—mystery tales, 459-463
—of Indians (North American), 450-454
—of modern America and Great Britain, 436-446
—of Negroes, 446-450
—of regional and religious minorities, 454-458
—recent trends in books about other lands, 499
—romance, 463-464
Recordings for children, 634-635
Regional books. See Minority groups.
Religious ballads, 96-97
Religious books for children, 650-653, (listing) 659-660
Revolutionary War, biographies of period, 535-539
Romance, stories of, 6, 7, 463-464, (listing) 473-474
Roman myths, 309, (listing) 321-322
Rome, historical fiction, 490-491
Russia, folk tales of, 264, (listing) 294-295

Science books, 579-585, (listing) 601-604
—animal kingdom, 586-588
—atmosphere and weather, 592-593
—chemistry, 595
—earth's beginnings, 590-592
—experiment books, 583-584
—general science books, 581-585
—geology, 592
—human body, 588-590
—physics, 595-597
—plant life, 585-586
—series, 583
—space, 593-595
Science fiction. *See* Space fantasy
Scientists, biographies of, 548-549
Scotland, folk tales of, (listing) 291

Series books,
—biography, 531-533
—science and social studies, 583
Social studies, books for,
—communication, 578
—discoveries in the New World, 572-573
—government, 578-579
—Latin America, 576-577
—man's work, 578
—Middle Ages, 571-572
—North America, 575-576
—other cities and countries, 577
—prehistoric and ancient times, 569-571
—transportation, 578
—United States history, 573-575
South America,
—folk tales of, (listing) 294
—informational books on, 576-577
—modern realistic fiction (listing) 514-515
Space, informational books, 593-595, fantasy, 346-347
Spain,
—folk tales, 264-265, (listing) 295
Storytelling, the art of, 376-395
—learning and telling a story, 389-392
—requirements for performance, 380-389
—when to read, when to tell, 377-380
Sweden, modern realistic fiction, (listing) 515
Switzerland,
—folk tales of, (listing) 295
—modern realistic fiction of, (listing) 515

Tall tales, 268-269
Tapes for children, 634-635
Television for children, 623-629
"Toy books," 58

United States,
—biographies of historical figures, 527-544, (listing) 555-557
—Civil War, informational books, 574-575
—colonial times, informational books, 573
—folk ballads of, 105-107
—folk tales of, 265-269, (listing) 295-297
—historical fiction of, 477-488, (listing) 508-510
—modern realistic fiction, 438-446, (listing) 468-469
—Presidents, biographies of, 533

Verse choirs, 220-245
—casting a poem, 227-239
—dialogue, 230-232
—group work, 234-238
—line-a-child, 232-234
—refrains or choruses, 229-230
—solo voices, 234
—unison speech, 238-239
—criteria for choosing poems, 240-241
—dangers of, 241-243
—definition of, 220
—history of, 221-222
—leader of, 239
—poems for elementary school use, (listing) 246-249
—public performance, 239-240
—standards of judgment for, 243-245

Wales, folk tales of, (listing) 291
Weather, books for children, 592-593
Westward expansion, biographies of period, 539-540
Women, biographies of, 545
Writers, biographies of, 546-548, (listing) 560
Writing, children's creative, 610-612

Index to Authors, Illustrators, and Titles

Note: Selections within the text are preceded by a bullet (•). Page references listed after "ill.," indicate that an illustration has been reproduced within the text. The "color section" appears between pages 66-67.

A Apple Pie, 90
A for the Ark, 90; ill., 92
"A was once an apple-pie," •121
Abbott, Jacob, 43
ABC (Bruno Munari), 52, 90; ill., 93
ABC Bunny, 63, 90; ill., 92
Abe Lincoln Grows Up, 524, •525, 542-543
Abe Lincoln's Other Mother, 543
Abraham Lincoln (d'Aulaire), 67, 528-529, 543; ill., 529
Abraham Lincoln (Daugherty), 543
Abraham Lincoln, Friend of the People, 533, 543
Adam of the Road, 65, 494-495
Adams, Adrienne, 48, 70, 160; ill., color section, 359
Addison, Joseph, 78, 97
Adler, Irving, 594
Adventure in Geometry, An, 584
Adventures of Huckleberry Finn, The, 47, 435
Adventures of Pinocchio, The, 357-358
Adventures of Rama, The, 318; ill., 318
Adventures of Tom Sawyer, The, see also Tom Sawyer.
Acsop, 300-301
Aesop's Fables, 46, 54 55, •298-299, 300-301; ill., 31
Afanasiev, A. M., 264
"Against Idleness and Mischief," •138-139
"Alas, Alack!," •132
Alcott, Louisa May, 45-46, 435
Aldis, Dorothy, 91, 154
Alice's Adventures in Wonderland, 44, 46, 57, 69, •122, 338-341, •339; ill., color section; 57, 156
All About books, 583
All About Dinosaurs, 591
All About Electricity, 596
All About the Wonders of Chemistry, 595
All-American, 450
All Around the Town, 90; ill., 92
All Around You, 582
Alligators All Around, 367
Allingham, William, 108, 181-182
All-of-a-Kind Family, 7, 455
Almanacs of Kate Greenaway, 140
Alone, 550
Amahl and the Night Visitors, 66; ill., color section
America Begins, ill., 572
America Grows Up: A History for Peter, 574
America Is Born: A History for Peter, 204, 573; ill., 573
America's Robert E. Lee, 543-544
American Ballads and Songs, 107
American-English Folk Songs, 105
American Heritage Book of the Revolution, 574
American Mother Goose, The, 85, 89
Ames, Gerald, 568, 569, 581, 590, 594
Amigo, Circus Horse, 410
Amos Fortune, Free Man, 545
Anatole and the Cat, 356
Andersen, Hans Christian, 44, 46, 64, 70, 327-333
Anderson, C. W., 406-407
Anderson, William (Commander), 576
. . . and now Miguel, 7, 17, 444-445
Andrews, Roy Chapman, 591
And to Think That I Saw It on Mulberry Street, 365-366
Andy and the Lion, 63, 64; ill., 65
Anecdotes and Adventures of Fifteen Gentlemen, 118
Angelo, Valenti, 458
Anglund, Joan Walsh, 428-429
Angus and the Ducks, 405
Animal Frolic, The, 53-54, 399-400; ill., 53
Animals of the Bible, 65
Ape in a Cape, 90; ill., 92
"April Rain Song," •206
Arabian Nights, The, 263-264; ill., 264
Arbuthnot Anthology, The, 238
Ardizzone, Edward, 66, 431; ill., color section, 645
Ark, The, 17, 21, 502
Armer, Laura, 7, 452
Arora, Shirley, 505
Art of Ancient Egypt, The, 570
Artzybasheff, Boris, ill., 186, 300
Asbjörnsen, Peter Christian, 260-261
Ashton, John, 32
Ask Mr. Bear, 356-357
Aspects of Biography, 519, •522-523
Asquith, Herbert, 235
As You Like It, •166
At the Back of the North Wind, 57, 341
Atwater, Richard and Florence, 366
Auden, W. H., 281-282
Augustus Caesar's World, 571; ill., 570
Austin, Mary, 151
Authentic Mother Goose, Fairy Tales and Nursery Rhymes, The, 38, 78
Autobiography of A. A. Milne, •126, 127
Averill, Esther, 52, 534-535
Away Goes Sally, 176, •177, •178, 480
Aymé, Marcel, 69

"B" Is for Betsy, 433
Babar and Father Christmas, 356
Babbitt, Ellen C., 302
Baboushka and the Three Kings, 70
Baby's Bouquet, 58; ill., color section
Baby's Opera, 58
Baby's Own Alphabet, 90
Bacon, Peggy, 406; ill., 407
Bailey, Bernadine, 543
Bailey, Carolyn Sherwin, 344-345
Bailey, Flora, 7
"Ball," •139-140
"Ballad of the Harp-Weaver, The," 109
Ballet Shoes, 437-438

Bambi, 62, 402
Bambi's Children, 402
"Bandog, The," •184
Banner in the Sky, 505
Bannerman, Helen, 47, 336
"Barbara Frietchie," 110
"Barber's The," •184
Barchilon, Jacques, 38, 78, 254-255
Barker, Will, 587
Barlowe, Dorothea and Sy, 586
Barney of the North, 407
Barrie, Sir James, 341-342
Barry, Florence, 33
Baruch, Dorothy, 196, 427
Bate, Norman, 362-363
Battershill, Norman, ill., 591
"Battle of Harlaw, The," 102
"Battle of Otterburn, The," 102
"Baucis and Philemon," 307-308
Baudouy, Michel-Aimé, 415-416
Baumann, Hans, 591
Baynes, Pauline, ill., 342
Beanie, 456; ill., 456
Bear Party, 345
Bears on Hemlock Mountain, The, 487
Beatinest Boy, The, 456
Beaumont, Mme. Leprince de, 327
"Beauty and the Beast," 37, 327
Bedford, F. D., ill., 134
"Bed in Summer," •142
"Beggar's Rhyme," •212
Behn, Harry, 154-155, 158, 488; ill., 155
Beim, Lorraine and Jerrold, 447
Bell, Corydon, 593; ill., 495
Bell, Thelma Harrington, 593
"Bellerophon and Pegasus," 308, •386-387
Bells and Grass, 183
Bells of Bleecker Street, The, 458
Beltrán, Alberto, ill., 569
Bemelmans, Ludwig, 65-66, 499-500; ill., color section
Ben and Me, 65, 353; ill., 553
Benary-Isbert, Margot, 21, 502-503
Bendick, Jeanne and Robert, 578, 582, 583
Benét, Rosemary Carr and Stephen Vincent, 109, 110, 111, 131-132
Benét, William Rose, 193
Benjamin Franklin, 67, 521, 523
Benjamin West and His Cat Grimalkin, 530; ill., 531
Bennett, Richard, 337
Bennett, Rowena, 230
Beowulf, 319
Beskow, Elsa, 429, 430
Bettina (Ehrlich), 71
"Between Two Hills," •145
Bewick, John, 55, 87
Bewick, Thomas, 55, 87
Bewick's Select Fables of Aesop and Others, 55; ill., 55
Beyond the High Hills, •180
Bianco, Margery Williams, 358
Bible, The, •211, •236, 651-652
Big Book of Real Fire Engines, The, 567
Biggest Bear, The, 48, 67, 405-406; ill., 406
Big Golden Animal ABC, 90
Big Red, 414-415
Big Snow, The, 62; ill., 64
Big Tree, 63, 586
Bill Bergson stories, 461
Billy and Blaze, 407
Binns, Archie, 443
Biography: The Literature of Personality, 553
Birch, Reginald, 59; ill., 61
Birthday Book, 140
Black Beauty, 46, 401
Blake, William, 40, 46, 55-56, 118, 166-171, 197, 229, 241; ill., color section; 168, 169, 170
Bleeker, Sonia, 573
Blegvad, Erik, 71, 161; ill., 329
Bless This Day, 657
Blind Colt, The, 407
Bloch, Marie, 590
Blough, Glenn O., 586-587
"Blow wind, blow, and go mill, go," •224
Blueberries for Sal, 68, 431-432
Blue Canyon Horse, 453
Blue Fairy Book, The, 47
Blue Willow, 457; ill., 21
Bock, Vera, ill., 264
"Bonny Barbara Allan," •99, 100, •101, 102, 105
"Bonny Earl of Murray, The," 102
Bontemps, Arna, 449
Book of American Rhymes and Jingles, A, 89
Book of Americans, A, 110, •131; ill., 111
Book of Greek Myths, The, 67, 312, 394
Book of Martyrs, 33-34
Book of Myths, 65
Book of Nonsense, 44, 46, 117-118, 119
Book of Nursery and Mother Goose Rhymes, 87
Books, Children and Men, 16, 36, 332, 340
Boom Town Boy, 457
Borrowers, The, 52, 71, 342-343; ill., 343
Boston, Lucy Maria, 6, 344, 418
Boston, Peter, ill., 6
Boswell, James, 521
Box with Red Wheels, The, 64
Boy Blue's Book of Beasts, 136
Boy on Horseback, 548
Branley, Franklyn M., 594
Brewton, John, 201
Brian Wildsmith's ABC, 90
Bridges, William, 587
Bright April, 449; ill., 448
Brighty of the Grand Canyon, 408
Brindze, Ruth, 592
Brink, Carol Ryrie, 5, 484
Brock, Charles E., 40
Bronze Bow, The, 22, 488-489
Bronzeville Boys and Girls, •158-159; ill., 156
Brooke, Leslie, 47, 60, 87, 125-126; ill., color section; 84, 120
Brooke, Rupert, 183
Brooks, Gwendolyn, 156, 158-159
Brother for the Orphelines, A, 507; ill., color section
Brown, Marcia, 333; ill., color section
Brown, Margaret Wise, 69, 303, 356, 427-428

Brownie series, 24
Brownies: Their Book, The, 59; ill., 58
Browning, Robert, 107-108, 110, 111, 206
Bruce, Robert, 592
Brunton, Winifred, ill., 489
Bryant, William Cullen, 196
"Bubbles," •145
Bubo, the Great Horned Owl, 416
Buck, Margaret Waring, 585
"Buckingham Palace," 129
Buehr, Walter, 571-572, 592
Buff, Conrad, 63, 404, 452, 586; ill., color section; 405
Buff, Mary, color section; 63, 404, 452, 586
Buffalo Bill, 67
Bulfinch, Thomas, 385-386
Bulla, Clyde Robert, 335, 529-530, 654
Bulletin of the Center for Children's Books, 26
"Bunches of Grapes," •184-185
Bunyan, John, 33-34
Burger, Carl, 587; ill., 417
Burnett, Frances Hodgson, 47, 61, 435-436, 437
Burnford, Sheila, 417
Burton, Virginia, 68, 360-362, 449; ill., color section; 99, 361
Busoni, Rafaello, ill., 548
"Butterbean Tent, The," •149
Butterfly's Ball, 41, 46, 56; ill., 56
Buttons, 406; ill., 407
Byrd, Commander, 550

"Cabin in the Clearing, A," 205, •231
Caddie Woodlawn, 5, 484; ill., 5
Caldecott, Randolph, 45, 46; ill., color section; 110
Calder, Ritchie, 589
Calico Bush, 152, 478
Call It Courage, 12, 503; ill., 503
Call Me Charley, 449
Campbell, Marjorie H., 587
Campion, Nardi Reeder, 537
Canterbury Tales, 69
Captain January, 123
Carey, Ernestine Gilbreth, 13
Carlson, Natalie Savage, color section; 68, 506-507
"Carnal and the Crane, The," 96
Carnan, T., 78
Carroll, Lewis, color section; 44, 46, 122-123, 156, 338-341
Carroll, Ruth and Latrobe, ill., 456
Carry on, Mr. Bowditch, 3, 527, 539; ill., 539
Carson, Rachel, 588
Cartier Sails the St. Lawrence, 534-535; ill., 535
Castle on the Border, 503
Cat Came Fiddling, A, 70
"Cat Heard the Cat-Bird, The," •137
Cat Who Went to Heaven, The, 176, 479
Caudill, Rebecca, 480-481
Cavanah, Frances, 574
Caves of the Great Hunters, The, 591
Caxton, William, 31, 46, 54; ill., 31
Century of Children's Books, A, 33
Chaga, 68
Changing Times, 623
Chanticleer and the Fox, 69; ill., color section
Chapbooks of the Eighteenth Century, 32
Charley Starts from Scratch, 449
Charlotte's Web, 47, 68, 355-356, 394; ill., 395
Chase, Richard, 267-268, 393-394
Chaucer, 69
Cheaper by the Dozen, 13
"Cherry Tree Carol, The," •96-97
Chicago Poems, •145
"Chicken-Licken," •390
Chicken Soup with Rice, 367
Chicken World, 60, 404
Child, Charles, ill., 111
Child, Francis James, 96, 98
Children of Green Knowe, The, 344
Children's Bells, The, 47
Children's Books in England, 31-32
Children's Books Too Good to Miss, 27
Children's Catalog, 26, 263
Children Sing in the Far West, The, •151
Child's Garden of Verses, A, 47, 60, 141, •142, •143, •144; ill., 62, 156
Choo Choo, 361
Christ Child, The, 64; ill., color section
Christmas Carol, A, 46
Chute, Marchette, 496
Chwast, Jacqueline, 161; ill., 157
Ciardi, John, 136-137
"Cinderella," 69
Circus Shoes, 438
"City Rain," 153, •154
Clark, Ann Nolan, 8, 452-453
Clark, Margery, 429
Clearing Weather, 478-479
Cleary, Beverly, 8, 12, 441-442
Clemens, Samuel L. *See* Mark Twain.
"Clever Elsie," •270
"Clever Manka," 277-278
Coatsworth, Elizabeth, 176-178, 202, 479-480
Cocola, 71
Coit, Margaret, 574-575
Cole, William, 138
Coleridge, Samuel, 165
Collected Poems of T. S. Eliot, •207
Collected Poems of Walter de la Mare, •132, •184-185
Collection of German Popular Stories, 57
Collier, Mary, J., 3
Collodi, Carlo. See Lorenzi, Carlo.
Colonial Living, 573-574
Colum, Padraic, 312, 376
Columbus, 67
Columbus, Finder of the New World, 534; ill., 534
Columbus Sails, 526-527
Columbus Story, The, 529
Come Christmas, 212
Come Hither, 207
"Come In," •203-204
Comenius, 46, 53-54; ill., 54
Commager, Henry Steele, 543-544, 574, 575
Comparative Studies in Nursery Rhymes, 78, 81
Complete Nonsense Book, The, •121; ill., 135
Conkling, Hilda, 178-180

Contes de ma Mère l'Oye, 36, 46, 78
Continuation of the Comic Adventures of Old Mother Hubbard and Her Dog, A, 56; ill., color section
"Conversation Between Mr. and Mrs. Santa Claus," •230
Coolidge, Olivia E., 490
Cooney, Barbara, 69, 119; ill., color section; 120
Cooper, Elizabeth K., 583
Cooper, Page, 410
Corsine, Douglas, ill., 547
Cosgrave, John O'Hara, II, ill., 538
Cottage at Bantry Bay, The, 438
Cotton, John, 35, 46
Cotton in My Sack, 25, 457; ill., 457
Cottrell, Leonard, 570
Courage of Sarah Noble, The, 487; ill., 22
Cowper, William, 58
Cox, Palmer, 24, 59; ill., 58
Country Bunny and the Little Gold Shoes, The, 357
"Cradle Hymn," 40, •139
"Crafty Farmer, The," 100, 102
Crane, Lucy, 280
Crane, Walter, 46, 57-58, 90; ill., color section
Craven, Thomas, 547
Crazy Horse, 541
Creative Youth, 607
Credle, Ellis, 455-456
"Crescent Moon," •149
Crew, Fleming, 402-403
Crouse, William H., 582-583
"Crow and the Pitcher, The," •298
Crow Boy, 500-501; ill., 500
"Cruel Brother, The," •99, •101-102, 111
Cruikshank, George, 57, 283-284; ill., 44
Cruikshank Fairy-Book, The, 283-284
Crusaders, The, •571-572
Crystal Mountain, 461; ill., 461
"Cup," •133
"Cupboard, The," 242
Curious George, 356
"Cynthia in the Snow," •158-159

"Daemon Lover, The," •100-101, 102
"Daffodil," •173
Dalgliesh, Alice, 22, 487-488, 529, 572
Daly, Maureen, 6
Dancing Cloud, 452
Daniel Boone, 64, 110, •523-524, 541; ill., 524
Darling, Louis, ill., 442
d'Armancour, Pierre Perrault, 36
Darton, F. J. H., 31
Dasent, Sir George Webbe, 253, 260-261
Dash and Dart, 63, 404
Daugherty, James, 63-64, 523-524, 537, 540, 541, 543; ill., 65, 524
Daughter of the Mountains, 7
d'Aulaire, Ingri and Edgar Parin, 22, 67, 312; ill., color section; 261, 529
D'Aulnoy, Mme., 37
Davis, Julia, 539-540
Davis, Marguerite, ill., 134
Davis, Robert, 265
Davy Crockett, 541-542
Dawn Wind, 492, •493
Day, Thomas, 42
de Angeli, Marguerite, 48, 63, 87, 449, 454-455, 495-496; ill., color section; 449
"Death of a Hired Man, The," 188
de Beaumont, Mme., 37
de Brunhoff, Jean, 71
de Brunhoff, Laurent, 356
Deer Mountain Hideaway, 460-461
Deer River Raft, 461
"Defense of the Alamo, The," 110
Defence of Poesie, 97
Defoe, Daniel, 38-39, 46
DeJong, Meindert, 70, 505-506, 652-653
de la Mare, Walter, 64, 109, 165, 180-181, 182-186, 207, 242, 352
Dennis, Wesley, 409; ill., 408, 531
de Regniers, Beatrice Schenk, 69, 70, 159, 162
"Desperado, The," •107
Detectives in Togas, 491; ill., 491
Deucher, Sybil, 530
Development of English Biography, The, 519
"A diamond or a coal," •174
Dickens, Charles, 46
Dickinson, Alice, 586, 590
Dickinson, Emily, 193
Dick Whittington and His Cat, 69
"Differences," 182
Digging into Yesterday, •569
Dinosaurs, 590-591
Discoveries of the New World, 572
Disney, Walt, 333, 626
Diverting History of John Gilpin, The, 46, 58-59
Divine and Moral Songs for Children, 40, 46, •138, 139
Divine Emblems, 34
Dobry, •504
Dr. Paracelus, 548; ill., 548
Dodge, Mary Mapes, 46, 497-498
Dodgson, Charles Lutwidge. *See* Lewis Carroll.
"Dogs and Weather," 209-210
Doll's House, The, 360
Door in the Wall, The, 3, 9, 63, 495-496
Doré, Gustave, ill., 257
Down Down the Mountain, 455-456
"Drake's Drum," •110-111
Dream Keeper, The, •206
"Drumlin Woodchuck, A," •188
Druon, Maurice, 344
du Bois, William Pène, 119, 345; ill., 120
Duchess Bakes a Cake, The, ill., 18
"Duck and the Kangaroo, The," •119-120
"Duel, The," 108, 132
"Dunkirk," •111
"Dust of Snow," 238-239
Dutton, Maude Barrows, 301
Duvoisin, Roger, 66, 90, 357, 431; ill., color section; 92, 355

Eastman, Mary Huse, 263
East o' the Sun and West o' the Moon, 47, 260; ill., 261

Eastwick, Ivy O., 232
Eaton, Jeanette, 523, 535-536
Eckenstein, Lina, 78, 81
Edey, Marion, 238
Edgeworth, Maria, 42-43
Edmonds, Walter D., 480
"Edward," •95-96, 99, 100, 102
Egyptian Adventures, 490
Eichenberg, Fritz, 40, 90; ill., 92, 265
Elements of the Universe, 595
"Elephant's Child, The," 364
"Eletelephony," •124
Elf Owl, 404; ill., 405
Eliot, T. S., 207, 236
Elsie Dinsmore series, 43
Émile, 41
Emperor and the Drummer Boy, The, 70; ill., color section
"Endymion," •208
Eness, ill., 11
English and Scottish Popular Ballads, Student's Cambridge Edition, 98
English Children's Books, 1600-1900, 37, 57
English Fables and Fairy Stories, 262; ill., 273
English Fairy Tales, ill., color section
English Folk Songs from the Southern Appalachians, 105
Enright, Elizabeth, 11, 19, 440-441
Epstein, Sam and Beryl, 596
Erskine, John, 199
Estes, Eleanor, 438-439
Ets, Marie Hall, 48, 62, 353, 447
Evans, Edmund, 57-58
Evans, Eva Knox, 568
Evers, Alf, 65
Everyday Things in Ancient Greece, 570
Exler, Samuel, 582
Exploring Chemistry, 595
Exploring the Weather, 592; ill., 593

Fables of India, The, ill., 302
Fables of La Fontaine, The, •303
Fair American, The, 176, 177, •178, •479, 480
"Fairies, The," •181-182
Fairies and Suchlike, •232
Fairservis, Jan, ill., 567
Fairstar, Mrs. *See* Horne, Richard Henry.
Fairy Shoemaker and Other Fairy Poems, The, 108; ill., 186
Fairy Tales of Hans Christian Andersen, 44, 46, 327-333
"Falling Star, The," •176
Family Under the Bridge, The, 506; ill., 506
Far and Few: Rhymes of the Never Was and Always Is, 132, •133; ill., 194
Faraway Lurs, The, 488
Far Frontier, The, 483; ill., 483
Farjeon, Eleanor, 145-147, 192, 212, 232, 645
Farmer Boy, 485-486
"farmer went trotting, A," •228
Farnsworth, Frances Joyce, 540
Farquharson, Martha, 43
"Father William," •122-123
Fatio, Louise, 47, 66, 356
Fava, Rita, ill., 157
Fenner, Carol, 345-346
Field, Eugene, 108, 132, 212
Field, Rachel, 152-154, 206, 359, 478
Fight for Union, The, 574-575
Fillmore, Parker, 264
Finders Keepers, 68
Find the Constellations, 594
Finley, Martha. *See* Martha Farquharson.
"Firefly," •149
First Bible, The, 65
First Book of Ancient Egypt, The, 570
First Book of Ancient Mesopotamia and Persia, •570
First Book of Electricity, The, 596
First Book of Plants, The, 586
First Book of Prehistoric Animals, 590
First Book of the Earth, The, 592
First books, 583
First Days of the World, 569, •581, 590; ill., 568
First Men in the World, The, 591
First Prayers, 651
First Under the North Pole, 576
Fischer, Hans, ill., 277
Fisher, Aileen, 70, 159-160, 235
Fisher, Leonard, ill., 573
"Fisherman and his Wife, The," •390
Fish in the Air, 62; ill., color section
Fitch, Florence Mary, 653
Five Bushel Farm, 176, •177, 480
500 Hats of Bartholomew Cubbins, The, 366
Flack, Marjorie, 62, 356, 404-405, 430-431
Flowers; a Guide to Familiar American Wildflowers, 586
"Flowers, The," 142
Fog Magic, 345
Forbes, Esther, 481-482
Forest Folk, 63, 404
"For Going A-hunting," •151
Foster, Genevieve, 532, 570, 571; ill., 570
"Four Little Foxes," •237
Fourth of July Story, The, 488
Foxe, John, 33-34
Francie on the Run, 438
Françoise (Seignobosc), 71
Freeman, Douglas Southall, 544
Freeman, Ira and Mae, 584, 595, 596
French Fairy Tales, ill., 257
French Legends, Tales and Fairy Stories, 258
Freund, Rudolf, 586; ill., 580
Friedman, Estelle, 569
Friendly Beasts, The, 70
Friskey, Margaret, 356
Frog Went a-Courtin', 64, 88; ill., color section
"From a Railway Carriage," •143-144
From the Eagle's Wing, 549; ill., 549
Frost, Arthur, 59; ill., 59
Frost, Frances, color section; 158, 232
Frost, Robert, 186-189, 193, 199, 202-205, 206, 231, 238-239
Funk, Tom, 109
Funny Thing, 63

Fun With Figures, 584
Fyleman, Rose, 127, 129-130, 182, 224, 228, 235

Gaer, Joseph, 302, 318
Gág, Wanda, 62-63, 90, 336-337, 378; ill., 92, 336
Gaier, Eugene L., 3
Gaily We Parade, ill., 201
Galdone, Paul, 71, 356; ill., 385, 483
Galileo and the Magic Numbers, 549
Gall, Alice Crew, 402-403
Galland, Antoine, 263-264
Gallant, Roy, 592, 593, 595
"Gardens," •155, 158
Garrick, David, 97
Garst, Shannon, 541
Gates, Doris, 21, 457
Gaul, Albro, 588
Gay, Zhenya, 135, 160; ill., 135
Geisel, Theodor Seuss. *See* Seuss, Dr.
George, Jean, 416-417, 445-446; ill., 416, 445
George, John, 416-417
George Washington, 67
"Gest of Robyn Hode, A," 102
"Get Up and Bar the Door," 100, 101, 102
Giant, The, 345
Gift of the Golden Cup, The, 490-491
"Gift Outright, The," •204
Gilbert and Sullivan, 123
Gilbreth, Frank B., 13
"Girls' Names," •232
Glubok, Shirley, 570
"Gnome, The," •155
Goals for Americans, 626
"Goblin, The," •228
Goblin Market and Other Poems, 172
Godden, Rumer, 359-360
"Godfrey Gordon Gustavus Gore," 109
Going Barefoot, 70, •159-160
Golden Book of Astronomy, The, 594
Golden Book of Science, 582
Golden Egg Book, The, 69
Golden Name Day, 68
Golden Nature Guides (series), 583
Golden Touch, The, ill., 385
Golden Treasury of Natural History, 582
Goldsmith, Oliver, 38, 79, 97
Gone-Away Lake, 19, 440
Good-bye, My Lady, 443
Good Master, The, 12, 13, 17, 503-504
"Good Night," •238
"Good Play, A," •143
Goodrich, Samuel G. *See* Peter Parley
"Good Samaritan, The," •236
"Goody Gainst the Stream," •390
Goody Two Shoes, 38, 46, 55
"Goose-Girl, The," •280
Gorgon's Head, The, 312; ill., 384
Gorsline, Douglas, ill., 547
Goss, Madeleine, 547
Goudey, Alice, 70
"Graciosa and Percinet," 37
Graham, Edward H., 593
Grahame, Kenneth, 47, 61, 348-351
Gramatky, Hardie, 362; ill., 362
"The Grand Old Duke of York," •224
Grass: Our Greatest Crop, 585
Gray, Elizabeth Janet, 494-495, 525, 526, 535-536, 547-548
Great Declaration, The, 574
Great Proclamation: A Book for Young Americans, The, 575
Greenaway, Kate, 46, 58, 85, 88, 90, 140-141, 195, 232; ill., color section
Green Grass of Wyoming, 413
"Green Hill Neighbors," •158; ill., 233
Grider, Dorothy, 238
Grimm, Jacob Ludwig, and Wilhelm Carl, 44, 57, 70, 258-260, 277, 281
Grimm's Fairy Tales, 60, 63, 65, 259-260, •390; ill., 66
Grimm's Popular Stories, 44; ill., 44, 46
Growing and Changing, 582
"Gudbrand on the Hill-side," •271, •279
Guggenheim, Hans, ill., 504
Guiterman, Arthur, 110
Gullan, Marjorie, 221-222
Gulliver's Travels, 40; ill., 41, 46
Gummere, Francis B., 97, 100
Gunther, John, 577
Gypsy and Ginger, •147
"Gypsy Laddie, The." *See* "Raggle Taggle Gypsies."

Haas, Irene, 70, 159; ill., 70
Hader, Berta and Elmer, 62; ill., 64
Hah-Nee, 452; ill., color section
Hailstones and Halibut Bones, •161
Hakon of Rogen's Saga, 493
Hale, Edward Everett, 79
Hale, Lucretia, 46, 363-364
"Halfway Down," •129
Hamm, Agnes Curren, 222
Handbook to Literature, A, 19
Handforth, Thomas, 62, 63
Hans and Peter, 433; ill., 433
Hans Brinker, or the Silver Skates, 46, 497-498
Hansi, 66
Happy Lion, The, 66, 356; ill., 355
Happy Orpheline, The, 506-507
Happy Prince and Other Fairy Tales, The, 335
"Hard from the southeast blows the wind," •177
Hargis, Ed, 89; ill., 85
Harriet Tubman: Conductor on the Underground Railroad, 546
Harris, Joel Chandler, 47, 59, 266
Harris, John, 56
Harrison, Richard E., photograph, 576
Hassall, Joan, 87
Haugaard, Erik Christian, 493
Hawthorne, Nathaniel, 45-46, 58, 310-311, 333, 385-386
Haywood, Carolyn, 433-434
Hazard, Paul, 16, 36, 332, 340
Heather and Broom, 262-263
He Heard America Sing: The Story of Stephen Foster, 547
Heidi, 498
Heinlein, Robert, 346
Hello and Goodbye, 160

Hemans, Felicia Dorothea, 109
Henner's Lydia, 63
Henry, Marguerite, 408-409, 530
Henry and Beezus, 442
"Henry VIII," •146
Henry Huggins, 8, 12, 441-442; ill., 442
Henry Reed, Inc., 446; ill., 23
Hercules, 362
"Herding the King's Hares," 274-275
Here and Now Story Book, 427
Here is the Far North, 576; ill., 576
Heroes, The, 312, •313-314
"Hero in the Preferred Childhood Stories of College Men, The," 3
Hesiod, 308-309
Hess, Lowell, 592; ill., 593
"He who has never known hunger," •178
Hey Diddle and Baby Bunting, ill., color section
Heyward, Du Bose, 357
Hibbard, Addison, 19
Hibou et la Poussiquette, Le, 119; ill., 120
Hide and Go Seek, 65, 404
"Hiding," 154
"Hie Away," •234
"Highwayman, The," 109
Hildegarde books, 123
"Hind Etin," 102
Hirsch, Alice, 596
Histoires ou contes du temps passé avec des moralités, 36, 78
History of Little Goody Two Shoes, The, 38, 46, 55
History of Sanford and Merton, The, 42
History of the House That Jack Built, The, ill., color section
"History of Valentine and Orson, The," 32
Hitty, Her First Hundred Years, 152, 359
H.M.S. Pinafore, •123
Hoberman, Mary Ann, 160
Hodges, C. Walter, 526-527
Hoffman, Felix, 71; ill., 281
Hofsinde, Robert, 573-574
Hogben, Lancelot, 584, 596
Hole Is to Dig, A, 69, 428
Holling, Holling C., 576
Holling, Lucille, 576
Holmes, C. Hugh, 19
Homer, 315-316
Homer Price, •441; ill., 636
Honk the Moose, 62, 410; ill., 411
"Hoppity," 129
Horn Book Magazine, The, 26
Horne, Richard Henry, 357
"Horse," •150
"Horseman, The," •165
House at Pooh Corner, The, 61, 358-359; ill., 63
Household Stories from the Collection of the Brothers Grimm, ill., 280
House Next Door, The, 458
Houses from the Sea, 70
House That Jack Built, The, 46
How Big Is Big?, 580
"How gray the rain," •177
How Your Body Works, 589
Hudson, W. L., 64
Hughes, Arthur, 57; ill., 173
Hughes, Langston, 206
Hugo, Victor, 238
Human Comedy, The, •653
Humorous Poetry for Children, 138
Hunt, Mabel Leigh, 449
"Hunting of the Cheviot, The," 102
Huntington, Harriet E., 588
Hurd, Clement, 356
Hurry, Skurry, and Flurry, 404
"Huski Hi," •130, 224

Ice to India, 462
"I do not know much about gods," 236-237
"If You Find a Little Feather," •159
I Go A-Traveling, 148
Iliad, The, 315-316
Iliad and the Odyssey, The, ill., 315
I Live in a City, 147, •148
Imagination's Other Place, 207; ill., 207
I Met a Man, •137
I'm Hiding, 160
Impunity Jane, 360; ill., 359
"Incident of the French Camp," 110
Incredible Journey, The, 417; ill., 417
Index to Fairy Tales, Myths and Legends, 263
Indians, 573
"Infant Joy," •197
Initial Biographies, 532
In My Mother's House, •453
Innocent Wayfaring, The, 496
"Inter-Diabolus et Virgo," 96
In the Clearing, 187, •202, •231
In the Middle of the Trees, •160
"Into My Own," •204
"Introduction," 241
"Introduction to Parents and all who are concerned in the Education of Children," •139
Irish Red, Son of Big Red, 415
Irving, Washington, 58
"Is John Smith within?" •230
Island of the Blue Dolphins, 22, 452; ill., 11
"It Is Raining," 230
I Will Adventure, 495; ill., 495

"Jabberwocky," •122
Jackson, Jesse, 449
Jacksons of Tennessee, The, 540-541
Jack Tales, The, 47, 267-268
Jacobs, Joseph, 261-262
James, Bessie, 542
James, Marquis, 520, 542
James, Philip, 56
James, Will, 410-412
Janeway, James, 33
Japanese Proverbs, •299
Jatakas, 301-302
Jauss, Anne Marie, 593
Jeanne-Marie Counts Her Sheep, 71
Jenny Lind Sang Here, 547; ill., 547
Jessup, Ronald, 591
Jewels for a Crown, 658; ill., 657

Jingle Jangle, 160; ill., 135
"Joe," •133
"Jog on, jog on, the footpath way," •224
Johansen, Margaret A., 462
"John Gilpin's Ride," 109; ill., 110
John J. Plenty and Fiddler Dan, 304-305
Johnny Appleseed, •130
Johnny Crow books, 60, 125-126
Johnny Crow's Garden, 47, 125-126
Johnny Crow's New Garden, 126
Johnny Crow's Party, 126
Johnny Tremain, 22, 481-482; ill., 481
Johnson, Emilie E., 657
Johnson, Gerald W., 204, 573, 574
Johnson, Helen and Margaret, 407
Johnson, James C., 553
Johnson, Samuel, 193
Jones, Elizabeth Orton, 657
Jones, Gwyn, 262
Jones, Harold, 48, 71, 88, 657; ill., color section; 171
Jones, Mary Alice, 652
Jones, V. S. Vernon, 298
Jonson, Ben, 97
Juanita, 7, 67, 431
"Judas," 96
Judson, Clara Ingram, 458, 533, 543
"Jumblies, The," 117, 119
Jungle Book, The, 47, 62, 401-402
Junior, a Colored Boy of Charleston, 448
Junior Book of Authors, The, 152
Junket, 399; ill., 399
Justin Morgan Had a Horse, 408
Just So Stories, •364

"Kaa's Hunting," 402
Kahl, Virginia, 18
Kakuyu. *See* Sojo, Toba.
Kane, Henry B., ill., 157, 194
Kantor, Mackinlay, 544
Kapp, Paul, 70
Katy and the Big Snow, 361
Keats, Ezra Jack, 71, 447; ill., color section
Keats, John, 208
"Keep a poem in your pocket," •192
Keeping, Charles, ill., 492
Keith, Harold, 484
Kellogg, Charlotte, 546
Kenny's Window, 70
Kent, Rockwell, ill., 268
Kepes, Juliet, ill., 135
Ker, John Bellenden, 80
Kiddell-Monroe, Joan, ill., 273
Kielty, Bernardine, 547
Kildee House, 69
Kinds of Poetry, The, 199
King, Robin, 596
King Arthur legends, 317-318
"King John and the Abbot of Canterbury," 100, 102
Kingman, Lee, 69
King of the Golden River, The, 334; ill., 334
King of the Wind, 408-409; ill., 408
Kings and Queens, •146
"King's Breakfast, The," 128
Kingsley, Charles, 45, 312, 313, 338
Kintu, 11-12
Kipling, Rudyard, 47, 62, 364, 401-402
Kittredge, George Lyman, 98
Kjelgaard, James Arthur, 414-415
Kleinert, Charlotte, ill., 491
Knights and Castles and Feudal Life, 572; ill., 571
Kon-Tiki, 4
Krauss, Ruth, 69, 428
Kredel, Fritz, ill., 334
Krumgold, Joseph, 7, 444-445
Krush, Beth and Joe, 52, 71; ill., 343, 440
"Kubla Khan," •165
Kuskin, Karla, 160

Ladycake Farm, 449
La Fontaine, Jean de, 303
"Lamb, The," •229
Lampman, Evelyn Sibley, 453-454, 483-484
"Landing of the Pilgrim Fathers, The," 109
Landmark Books, 532-533
Land of the Free, The, 572
Land of the Pharaohs, 570
"The lands around my dwelling, •180
Lang, Andrew, 47, 78, 253-254
Langstaff, John, color section; 64, 88
Lansing, Elizabeth, 460-461
Lantern Bearers, The, •492; ill., 492
Lantz, Paul, ill., 8, 21, 453
"Last Word of a Bluebird, The," 206-207
Latham, Jean Lee, 3, 527, 539
Lathrop, Dorothy, 64-65, 175, 359; ill., 176, 352, 403-404
Latrobe, John, 56
Lattimore, Eleanor Frances, 448, 500
Laughing Time, •136; ill., 135
Lavender's Blue, 48, 71, 88; ill., color section
Lawrence, Isabelle, 462, 490-491
Lawson, Robert, 65, 353-354, 400; ill., 201, 553
"Lazy Jack," 270
Leader by Destiny, 523, 535-536
Leaf, Munro, 400
Lear, Edward, 44, 46, 47, 90, 117-123; ill., 135
Lee and Grant at Appomattox, 544
Lee of Virginia, 544
Leif the Lucky, 67; ill., color section
Leighton, Clare, ill., 207
Lemon and a Star, A, 442-443
L'Engle, Madeleine, 12, 346-347, 445
Lenski, Lois, 7, 10, 430, 457-458
Lentil, 68, 441
Leodhas, Sorche Nic, 262-263
Let's Build a Railroad, 109
Let's Go to the Brook, 588
Lewellen, John, 596, 597
Lewis, C. S., 342
Lewis, Elizabeth Foreman, 7, 62, 501-502
Lide, Alice, 462
Liers, Emil E., 417
Life of Samuel Johnson, 521
Light at Tern Rock, The, •13
Lindgren, Astrid, 273, 366-367, 461

Lindquist, Jennie, 68
Lindsay, Vachel, 109, 130
Lines, Kathleen, 88
Lion, the Witch, and the Wardrobe, The, 342; ill., 342
Lipkind, William, color section; 19, 68, 432
Lippincott, Joseph Wharton, 409-410
Lisitzky, Gene, 537-538
Little Auto, The, 430
Little Bear's Friend, ill., 20
Little Bear stories, •400
Little Black Sambo, 47, 336
Little Book of Prayers, A, •657
Little Bookroom, The, •645; ill., 645
"Little Boy Found, The," •170
"Little Boy Lost, The," 64, •169
Little Eddie, 433-434
"Little Fox, The," •238
Little Hill, The, •155, •158
Little History of the Horn-Book, A, ill., 32
Little House, The, 68, 361-362; ill., 361
Little House in the Big Woods, •19, 47, •485; ill., 646
Little House of Your Own, A, 70; ill., 70
Little Island, 69
"Little John Bottlejohn," 108, •124
Little Juggler, 69
Little Leo, 67, 431
Little Lord Fauntleroy, 47, 59, 435-436; ill., 61
Little Lost Lamb, The, 427
"Little Mermaid, The," 330
Little Naturalist, The, •158, •233; ill., 233
Little Navajo Bluebird, 453; ill., 8
"Little Orphant Annie," 108
Little Pear, 500
Little Plum, 360
Little Pretty Pocket-Book, A, •37, 46
Little Red Lighthouse and the Great Gray Bridge, The, 67
"Little Red Riding Hood," 36, 253
Little Silver House, 68
Little Tim and the Brave Sea Captain, 66, 431; ill., color section
Little Toot, 362; ill., 362
Little Whistler, The, 158
"Little wind, blow on the hill-top," •232
Little Women, 45-46, 435
Livingston, Myra Cohn, 157, 160-161
"Lizie Lindsay," 99, 100, 102
Lofting, Hugh, 351
Lomax, John and Alan, 106
Loner, The, 446
Longfellow, Henry Wadsworth, 109, 110
Long Winter, The, 486
Loopy, 362
"Lord Randal," 99, 100, 102, 105
Lorenzini, Carlo, 357-358
Lost Queen of Egypt, The, 489-490; ill., 489
"Lost Shoe, The," 109
Love Is a Special Way of Feeling, 428
Love Letters of Phyllis McGinley, The, 138
Lubell, Winifred, ill., 584
Lucas, Fielding, 56
McCloskey, Robert, 24, 52, 431-432, 441; ill., 23, color section; 399, 432, 636
McCord, David, 132-133, 157, 194
MacDonald, George, 57, 341
MacDonald, Golden, *See* Brown, Margaret Wise.
McGinley, Phyllis, 90, 92, 138
McGraw, Eloise Jarvis, 451, 490
McHugh, Isabel and Florence, 591
Madeline, 66, 499-500
Madeline's Rescue, ill., color section
Magic Maize, 452
Mahony, Bertha, 23
Main Street, 68
Make Way for Ducklings, 24, 53, 68, 431; ill., 432
Malcolmson, Anne, 99
Maloy, Lois, ill., 572
"Maltese Dog, A," •206
Ma Mère l'Oye, 78
Man Who Sang the Sillies, The, •137
Mara, Daughter of the Nile, 490
Marigold Garden, 140, •195-196
"Marine Life," ill., 631
Mars, W. T., ill., 567
"Marsh King's Daughter, The," 330
Martin, Alexander C., 586
"Mary Hamilton," 98
Mary Jane, 450
Mary Poppins, 364-365; ill., 365
Mary Poppins Comes Back, 364-365
Mary-Rousselière, Father Guy, 180
Masefield, John, 222
Masked Prowler: The Story of a Raccoon, 416; ill., 416
"Master I Have," •225
Master Simon's Garden, 479
Matchlock Gun, The, 480
Maurois, André, 519, 522-523
Maya: Land of the Turkey and the Deer, 569; ill., 569
Mead, Margaret, 567, 568
Meader, Stephen, 462-463
Meadowcroft, Enid, 572
Mearns, Hugh, 607
Meet the Austins, 9, 12, 445
Meigs, Cornelia, 478-479
Meigs, Mildred Plew, 108
Mei Li, 62, 63
Melcher, Frederic G., 38, 45, 648
Memoirs of a London Doll, 357
Memoirs of a Midget, 183
Memoirs of Martinus Scriblerus, 40
Men of Iron, 59, 494
Meph, the Pet Skunk, 416-417
Merry Adventures of Robin Hood, 47; ill., 316
Metamorphoses of Ovid, The, 309, •311
"Mice," 235
Middle Moffat, The, ill., 439
Mighty Atom, The, 596
Mighty Ones, The, 652-653; ill., 652
Mike Mulligan and His Steam Shovel, 17, 68, 360-361; ill., color section
Milk for Babes, Drawn out of the Breasts of Both Testaments, Chiefly for the Spirituall Nourish-

ment of Boston Babes in either England, but may be of like Use for any Children, •35, 46
"Milkmaid and Her Pail, The," •299
Millay, Edna St. Vincent, 109
Miller, Joaquin, 110
Millions of Cats, 62-63, 336-337; ill., 336
Milne, A. A., 47, 63, 91, 126-129, 135, 358-359
Minarik, Else H., 400
Miss Happiness and Miss Flower, 360
Miss Hickory, 344
Mister Penny, 62, 353
Misty of Chincoteague, 408-409
Mitchell, Lucy Sprague, 230, 427
"Mix a pancake," •172-173
Moccasin Trail, 451
Moe, Jörgen E., 260-261
Moffat stories, 438-439
Monk, Randy, ill., 302, 318
"Monkeys and the Crocodile, The," 108
Monro, Harold, 240
Montgomery, Rutherford, 69
"Moon," 136
Moon Jumpers, 70
"Moon Song," •179
Moore, Clement Clarke, 44, 46, 107-108
Mordvinoff, Nicolas, 19, 47, 48, 65, 68, 432; ill., color section
More Nonsense, •118
Morrison, Lillian, 89
Morrison, Lucile, 489-490
Mother Goose, 24, 46, 76-94, •77, •81, •82, •83, •86, 111, 140, 199, •224, •225, •228, •230; ill., 84, 85
Mother Goose; or, The Old Nursery Rhymes, 88
Mother Goose Quarto, or Melodies Complete, 79
Mother Goose's Melody; or Sonnets for the Cradle, 39, 46, 78; ill., 46
"Motivation Reconsidered: The Concept of Competence," 3
Moy Moy, 67; ill., color section
Mr. Popper's Penguins, 65, 366
Mr. Rabbit and the Lovely Present, 70; ill., color section
Mr. Revere and I, 65, 353
"Mr. Wells," •150
"Mrs. Peck-Pigeon," •147
"Mrs. Snipkin and Mrs. Wobblechin," •125
Muir, Percy, 37, 57
Mulready, William, 41, 56-57; ill., 56
Munari, Bruno, 52, 71, 90; ill., 93
Munroe and Francis, 79
"My Cat," •159
My Dog Rinty, 447
"My Donkey," 229
My Friend Flicka, 412
"My Last Duchess," 111
My Side of the Mountain, 445-446; ill., 445
Mystery of Burnt Hill, The, 462
Mystery of the Mahteb, 462
My Weekly Reader, 639

"Nancy Hanks," 110
Nash, Ogden, 138
Nason, Thomas W., ill., 187
Nathan, Robert, 111
Navaho Sister, 454; ill., 453
Nesbit, E., 47
Ness, Evaline, ill., 11, 263
Newberry, Clare Turlay, 406
Newbery, Elizabeth, 56
Newbery, John, 37-38, 78-79
Newbery Medal Books, 26
Newbolt, Henry, 110
New England Primer; or An Easy and Pleasant Guide to the Art of Reading, •35, 46; ill., 36
Nicolson, Harold, 519
"Night," •175
Night Before Christmas, The, 44, 46, 107-108
"Night Will Never Stay, The," •147
Nights with Uncle Remus, 47, 59
Nine Days to Christmas, 62
Nine Planets, The, 594
Ninna Nanna, 172
Nino, 458
Nonsense Songs and Stories, 119; ill., 120
No Other White Men, 539-540
Norton, Mary, 342-343
Nothing at All, 63
"Notice," •133
Now Try This, 596
Now We Are Six, 61, 127
Noyes, Alfred, 109
Nursery and Household Tales. See Grimms' Fairy Tales
Nursery Rhymes of London Town, 146
Nursery Songs from the Appalachian Mountains, 105
Nutshell Library, 70, 367; photo of, 366

O'Dell, Scott, 11, 452
Odyssey, 4, 61, 315-316, 387
Of Courage Undaunted, 540
O'Hara, Mary, 412-413
Okada, Rokuo, 299
Old Christmas, 58
Old Man Is Always Right, The, 64
Old One-Toe, 415-416
Old Peter's Russian Tales, 264
O'Moran, M., 451
Once a Mouse, 69; ill., color section
One God: The Ways We Worship Him, 653
O'Neill, Mary, 161
One Morning in Maine, 432
One Was Johnny, 367
Onion John, 444-445
Onitsura, 611
Only True Mother Goose Melodies, The, •77, 79; ill., 77
On Safari, 413, 548
On the Banks of Plum Creek, 485
Open the Door, •238
Opie, Iona and Peter, 80-81, 87
Orbis Pictus, 46, 54-55; ill., 54
Orbit: A Picture Story of Force and Motion, 596
"Oregon Trail, The," 110
Original Mother Goose's Melody, The, 79; ill., 39, 80

Original Poems for Infant Minds: By Several Young Persons, 40, 46
"Others," •155
"Otter Creek," •158
Otter's Story, An, 417
Otto of the Silver Hand, 59, 494; ill., 494
Our Country's Story, 574
Outlaw Red, 415
"Overheard on a Saltmarsh," 240
Over the Garden Wall, •147, •232
Ovid, 309
"O Wind," •173
"Owl and the Pussy-Cat, The," •119; ill., 120
Oxford Dictionary of Nursery Rhymes, The, 81, 87

Paddle-to-the-Sea, 106, 576
Paderewski, 546
Padre Porko, 265; ill., 265
Palazzo, Tony, 417
"Pancake, The," •269
Panchatantra, The, •301
Pantaloni, 71
Paradise Valley, 458
Parker, Bertha Morris, 582
Parker, Elinor, 207
"Park, The," •148
Parley, Peter, 43
Path Above the Pines, The, 461
Patrick Henry, Firebrand of the Revolution, 537
Paul Bunyan, 47; ill., 268
"Paul Revere's Ride," 110
Peacock Pie, 183, •184
Pearce, A. Philippa, 344
Pease, Howard, 463
Peattie, Donald Culross, 580, 581, 586
Pecos Bill, 107
Pegeen, 438
Pelle's New Suit, 429; ill., 430
Penn, •525, 526, 535
"People" (William Jay Smith), •136
"People, The" (Elizabeth Madox Roberts), •150
People and Places, 568; ill., 567
Pepper, 69
Pepper and Salt, 334-335
Pepys, Samuel, 97
Percy, Bishop, 95, 98
Percy, Polly, and Pete, 406
Perkins and Marvin, 35
Perlman, Raymond, 592
Perrault, Charles, 36, 46, 78, 257-258
Perrault's Popular Tales, 78
Peterkin Papers, The, 46, 363-364
Peter Pan, 341-342
Peter Rabbit, Tale of, 20, 47, 60, 347-348; ill., color section
Petersham, Maud and Miska, 64, 89, 657; ill., color section; 429
Peter's Long Walk, 69
Petrides, Heidrun, 433
Petry, Ann, 546
Pettit, Henry, 38, 78, 254-255
Petunia books, 66
Phantom Deer, 410
Picard, Barbara Leonie, 258
Picture Book Number One, ill., 110
Picture Rhymes from Foreign Lands, 130, •228
"Pied Piper of Hamelin, The," 107-108, •206
Pierre, 367
Pilgrims and Plymouth Colony, 573
"Pilgrims and Puritans," •131
Pilgrim's Progress, 33, •34, 65
Pillicock Pie, •235
Pinocchio, 47
Pippi Longstocking, 366-367
"Pirate Don Durk of Dowdee, The," 108; ill., 109
Place for Peter, A, 444; ill., 444
Plain Girl, 455
"The plant cut down to the root," •178
Play with Me, 48, 62
Plenty to Watch, 71, 500
Plotz, Helen, 207
Pocahontas, 67
Poems (Rachel Field), 153
Poems by a Little Girl, •179
Poetic Edda (Elder), 309
Poetic Origins and the Ballad, 96
"Poetry" (Eleanor Farjeon), •192
Pointed People, The, 152
Polgreen, John, 594
Politi, Leo, 7, 67, 431, 529; ill., color section
Pond Book, The, 588
Poor Richard, 64, •537
Pope, Alexander, 40
Poppy Seed Cakes, The, 429; ill., 429
Poppy Seeds, The, 335
Popular Ballad, The, 97
Popular Rhymes and Nursery Tales, •390
Popular Tales from the Norse, 260-261
Portrait of a Family, 146
"Potatoes' Dance, The," 109, •130
Potter, Beatrix, 60, 347-348, ill., color section
Potter, Charles Francis, 89, 91
Pound, Louise, 96, 107
Powers, Richard, 570
Prairie Years, The, 145
Pretty Book of Pictures For Little Masters and Misses or Tommy Trip's History of Beasts and Birds, A, 55
Price, Laurence, 34
"Primer Lesson," •145
Princess and the Goblin, The, 57
"Princess and the Vagabone, The," •390
Prishvin, Mikhail, 64
Prose Edda (Younger), 309-310
Proudfit, Isabel, 548
Provenson, Alice and Martin, ill., 156, 315
Psalm 103, •236
"Puppy and I," 129
Purdy, Claire Lee, 547
"Purple Jar, The," 42, •43
Puss in Boots, 69
Pyle, Howard, 47, 59-61, 333, 334-335, 493-494; ill., 316, 494

Queen Victoria, 520
Quennell, Marjorie and C. H. B., 570

"Questioning Faces," •202

Rabbit Hill, 65, 353-354; ill., 354
Rabbits' Revenge, 62
Rackham, Arthur, 40, 60, 88; ill., color section; 84
"Raggedy Man, The," 108
"Raggle, Taggle Gypsies, The," 99, 101, 102, 230
"Railroad and Work Gangs," 106
"Rain," •144
Rainbow Book of Art, 547
Rainbow Book of Nature, The, •581-586; ill., 580
Ramayana, 318
Ramsay, Allan, 97
Rands, William Brighty, 109
Rankin, Louise, 7
Ransome, Arthur, 264, 436-437
Rapunzel, 71
Rasmussen, Knud, 180
Raven, The, 520
Ravielli, Anthony, 584; ill., 589
Rawlings, Marjorie Kinnan, 413-414
Raymond L. Ditmars, 550
Real Mother Goose, The, 87; ill., 84
Real Personages of Mother Goose, The, 80
Red Horse Hill, 463
Reeder, Red, 575
Reeves, James, 262, 273, 301
Reid, Forest, 185
Reliques of Ancient English Poetry, 97-98
Remember Me When This You See, 89
Return to Gone-Away, 440; ill., 440
Rey, H. A., 594
Reynolds, Barbara, 69
Rhead, Louis, ill., 41
Rhymes and Verses, 183, •185
Richards, Laura, 108, 117, 123-125, 134
Riedman, Sarah R., 585
Rifles for Watie, 484
Riley, Henry T., 311
Riley, James Whitcomb, 108, 132
Ring o' Roses, 60, 87; ill., color section; 84
Ripley, Elizabeth, 546-547
River Boy, 548
River's Journey, The, 593
"Road not taken," ill., 187
Robbins, Ruth, color section
Roberts, Elizabeth Madox, 134, 148-151
Robertson, Keith, 446, 461-462
Robin Hood, 59, 61, 316-317
Robin Hood and His Merry Outlaws, ill., 377
"Robin Hood and Little John," •99
Robin Redbreast, •181-182
Robinson, Charles, Jr., 570
Robinson, Tom, 406
Robinson Crusoe, 38-39, 41, 46, 61
Rocket in My Pocket, A, 89; ill., 88
Rocket Ship Galileo, 346
Rocks and Minerals, 592
Rockwell, Norman, ill., 46
Rojankovsky, Feodor, 64, 87-88, 535; ill., color section; 84, 535
Rooster Crows, The, 64, 89
Roscoe, William, 41, 46, 56
Rosen, Sidney, 548-549
Rossetti, Christina, 46, 57, 171-175
Rounds, Glen, 407
Rourke, Constance, 541-542
Rousseau, Jean-Jacques, 41
Rowan Farm, 502-503
Ruchlis, Hy, 596
Rugh, Belle Dorman, 461
"Rumpelstiltskin," 262
Runaway Bunny, The, •356, 427
Runny Days, Sunny Days, •159
Ruskin, John, 334
Russet and the Two Reds, 68, 432; ill., color section

Sad-Faced Boy, 449
Salten, Felix, 62, 402
Samber, R., 37
Sandburg, Carl, 106, 144-145, 524-525, 542-543
Santiago, 453
Sara Crewe, 435-436
Sarett, Lew, 237
Sasek, Miroslav, 577
Saturdays, The, 440
Sauer, Julia, 13, 345
Sawyer, Ruth, 382-383, 392
Sayers, Frances Clarke, 568
Scheib, Ida, 596
Schmidt, Harvey; ill., 652
Schneider, Herman and Nina, 580, 589, 594, 596
Scholastic Magazine, 639
Science in Your Own Back Yard, 583
Scott, Sir Walter, 79, 95, 98, 109, 234
Scottish Folk Tales and Legends, 262
Scrappy the Pup, 137
"Scroll of Animals," 53-54
Sea Around Us, The, 588
Seaborg, Glenn T., 595
"The sea gull curves his wings," 202
Sea Pup, 443
Secret Cargo, 463
Secret Garden, The, 436; ill., 437
Secret of the Andes, 453
Seeger, Ruth Crawford, 109
See Through the Forest, •585; ill., 584
See What I Found, 160
"Selfish Giant, The," •335
Selsam, Millicent E., 584, 585
Sendak, Maurice, 69-70, 428; ill., 20, color section; 505
Seredy, Kate, 503-504; ill., 5
Serraillier, Ian, 21, 384
Seuss, Dr., 47, 66, 67, 365-366
Seven Diving Ducks, 356
"Seven Little Tigers and the Aged Cook, The," 124, 125
Seventeenth Summer, 6
Sevrey, O. Irene, 592
Sewell, Anna, 46, 401
Sewell, Helen, 65, 488; ill., 66
Shadow in the Pines, 463
"Shadow March," 143
Shaffer, Paul R., 592
Shakespeare, William, 166, 224

Shannon, Monica, 504
Sharp, Cecil J., 105
Sharpe, Stella Gentry, 447-448
Sharps and Flats, •212
Shawneen and the Gander, 337
Shedlock, Marie, 379, 392
Shenton, Edward, ill., 415
Shepard, Ernest H., 61, 129, 359; ill., 63, 134, 349, 461
Shephard, Esther, 268
Shepard, Mary, ill., 365
Shepherd's Nosegay, The, 264
Shoemaker and the Elves, 70
Shoes of the Wind, 179
Shuttlesworth, Dorothy E., 592
Sidjakov, Nicolas, 48, 65, 70-71; ill., color section
Sidney, Sir Philip, 97
Signature Books, 532
Sigurd the Volsung, 316, 388
"Silas Pie," •162
Silk and Satin Lane, 501
Silver Sword, The, 21
Sing a Song of Sixpence, and other Toy Books, 46
Sing for your Supper, •192
"Singing," •144
Singing and the Gold, The, 207
Singing Tree, The, 504
Sing Song, 46, 57, 171-175, •172-174; ill., 173
"Sing-song of Old Man Kangeroo, The,"•364
"Sir Bevis of Southampton," 32
"Sir Patrick Spens," 96, 98, 101, 102, •103
Six Feet Six: The Heroic Story of Sam Houston, 542
"Skating," •235, 236
Skippack School, 63
Skipping Along Alone, 152
Sleep Book, ill., 67
Sleeping Beauty, 71; ill., 281
"Sleepyhead," 185, •186; ill., 186
Slobodkin, Louis, 439-440; ill., 377, 439
Slow Smoke, •237
Small Rain, 657
Smith, E. Boyd, 60, 404; ill., 301
Smith, Jessie Willcox, 60, 63; ill., 62
Smith, William Jay, 135, 136
Smoky, 47, 410-412, •412
"Snare, The," 202
Snippy and Snappy, 63
Snow, 593
Snow Dog, 415
"Snow Queen, The," 330, •331
Snowy Day, The, 447; ill., color section
Sojo, Toba, 53, 399-400
Solbert, Ronnie, ill., 156
Something Special, •159, •192
"Something Told the Wild Geese," 206-207
"Song," •212
"Song of Greatness, A," •151
Song of Robin Hood, 68; ill., 99
Songs of Childhood, 182
Songs of Experience, 40
Songs of Innocence, 40, 46, 55, 166-171; ill., 170, 171
Songs of Innocence and Experience, ill., color section
Sorenson, Virginia, 455, 458
Southey, Robert, 109, 334
Speaking of Cows, •161-162; ill., 157
Speare, Elizabeth George, 477-478, 488-489
Spectator, The, 97
Spectator Papers, 78
Sperry, Armstrong, 12, 503, 513, 577
"Spring" (William Blake), •169
"Spring" (Karla Kuskin), •160
Spy in Williamsburg, A, 462
Spykman, E. C., 442-443
Spyri, Johanna, 47, 498
Squanto, Friend of the White Men, 529-530
Starbird, Kaye, 157, 161
"Stars," •175-176
Stars Tonight, 64, 175-176, •175; ill., 176
Steadfast Tin Soldier, The, 69
Steegmuller, Francis, 119, 120
Steele, Richard, 32
Steele, William O., 22, 482-483
Stefansson, Evelyn, 576
Steffens, Lincoln, 548
Stefferud, Alfred, 586
Stephens, James, 202
Stepping Westward, •123
Sterling, Dorothy, 450
Stevenson, Augusta, 531
Stevenson, Robert Louis, color section; 47, 60, 62, 141-144, 156, 228, 241-242, 459-460
St. Nicholas, 497
Stobbs, William, ill., 384, 534
Stokes, Ray Wood, 85
Stone, Helen, 71, 90; ill., 92
Stone Soup, 69
Stong, Philip Duffield, 62, 410
"Stopping by Woods on a Snowy Evening," •203, 203-204
Story About Ping, The, 62, 405
Story of Babar, The, 71, 356
Story of Dr. Dolittle, The, 351
Story of Ferdinand, The, 65, 400
Story of Gold, The, 592
Story of Lafayette, The, 536
Story of Mankind, 47-48; ill., 568
Story of Pocahontas and Captain John Smith, The, 60
Story of Rocks, 592
Story of the Civil War, The, 575
Story of the Treasure Seekers, The, 47
Strachey, Lytton, 520
Stranger at Green Knowe, A, 418; ill., 6
"Strange Tree," •151
Strange Victory, 175
Strawberry Girl, 7, 457
Streatfeild, Noel, 437-438
Street, James, 443
Stuart, Jesse, 456
Stuart Little, 68
Suba, Susanne, 89; ill., 88
Summer at Yellow Singer's, 7
"Summer Song," •137
"Susan Blue," •195-196, 197
Sutcliff, Rosemary, 491-493

Swain, Su Zan N., 587, 592
Swallows and Amazons, 436-437
Swamp Cat, 415; ill., 415
Swift, Hildegarde, 67, 549
Swift, Jonathan, 40-41, 46
"Swift things are beautiful," •177, 202
Swineherd, The, ill., 329
Syme, Ronald, 533-534
Symonds, Kenneth, ill., 591

Tail books, 402-403
Take Sky: More Rhymes of the Never Was and Always Is, •133, ill.; 157
"Taking Off," 234
Tale of Peter Rabbit, The, 20, 47, 60, 347-348; ill., color section
Tales from the Fjeld, 260-261, •269, •390
Tall Book of Mother Goose, The, 87-88; ill., 84
"Tam Lin," 102
Tanglewood Tales for Girls and Boys, 45, 333
Tarry, Ellen, 447
Tatler, The, 32
"Taxis," •153
Taxis and Toadstools, 152
Taylor, Ann and Jane, 40, 46, 118, 139-140
Taylor, Edgar, 44
Taylor, Sydney, 7, 455
"Tea Party," •154
Teasdale, Sara, 64, 175-178
Television Works Like This, ill., 578
Tempest, The, •208
Temporal Things Spiritualized, 34
Tenniel, Sir John, 44, 340-341; ill., 57, 156
Teppich, John, 596
Thanksgiving Story, 487-488
Thayer, Ernest L., 109
Thee, Hannah! 7, 63, 454
Theogony, 309
Thimble Summer, 440-441
"This Is My Rock,"•133
This Is Rome, 577
Thistle and Thyme, 262-263; ill., 263
Thomas, Isaiah, Jr., 39, 46, 79
Thomas, Katherine Elwes, 80, 81
Thomas Jefferson, 537-538
Thorne-Thomsen, Gudrun, 392-394
Thrall, William Flint, 19
"Three Bears, The," 334
"Three Billy Goats Gruff, The," •276
Three Kings of Saba, The, 65
"Three Little Pigs, The," •18, 277
Three Royal Monkeys, The, 183, 352; ill., 352
Three Stuffed Owls, 461-462
Through the Looking Glass, 44, 57, •122-123, •339-340
Thumbelina, 70; ill., color section; 632
Thunderhead, 412-413
Tigers in the Cellar, 345-346
"Tillie," •185
Tim All Alone, 66
Time for Poetry, 238
Time of Wonder, 68, 432; ill., color section
Tippett, James S., 147-148
"Tired Tim," •184; ill., 199
Tirra Lirra; Rhymes Old and New, •124-125; ill., 134
Tistou of the Green Thumbs, 344
"Toaster, The," •136
"To a Waterfowl," •196-197
Tobe, 447-448
To Beat A Tiger, 502
Token For Children, A, 33
Told Under the Stars and Stripes, 458
Tomahawks and Trouble, 482
"Tom Hickathrift," •32
Tom Sawyer, 45, 47, 434-435; ill., 46, 633
Tom's Midnight Garden, 344
"Tom Thumb His Life and Death," 32; ill., 35
Tom Whipple, 480
Tongue Tanglers, •89; ill., 91
Tortoise and the Geese and Other Fables of Bidpai, The, ill., 301
Tortoises, Terrapins and Turtles, 118
Totem, The, 273
Tough Winter, The, 65, 354
Trail of the Little Paiute, 451
Traveling Musicians, The, ill., 277
Travels into Several Remote Nations of the World, 40
Travers, P. L., 364-365
Treasure Island, 47, 61, 142, 459, •460; ill., color section
Treasure Mountain, 454
Treasure Trove of the Sun, 64
"Tree at My Window," •204
Tree in the Trail, 576
Tree of Freedom, 480-481
Tree of Life, The, 312
Trees: a Guide to Familiar American Trees, 586
"Tree Toad," •179
Tree Wagon, 483-484
Tresselt, Alvin, 66, 431
Troyer, Johannes, ill., 212, 280
True Book of Toys at Work, The, 596
True books, 583
Tudor, Tasha, 48, 71, 89, 651; ill., 85, 437
Tunis, Edwin, 573-574
Tunis, John R., 8, 450
"Turtle Who Couldn't Stop Talking, The," •302
Twain, Mark, 45-46, 47, 434-435
"Twa Sisters, The," 102
Twenty-One Balloons, 345
"Twinkle, twinkle, little star," 40
Two Is a Team, 447
Two Reds, The, •19, 68, 432
Tymnes, 206

Udry, Janice, 70
"Ugly Duckling, The," 330-331, 401
Ullman, James Ramsey, 505
Umbrella, 71; ill., color section
"Umbrella Brigade, The," •125
Uncle Remus and His Friends, ill., 59
Uncle Remus Tales, 47, 266
Underground Riches, 592
Understanding Electronics, •597

Understanding Science, 582-583
"Under the Greenwood Tree," •166
Under the Tree, •148, •149, •150, •151
Under the Window, 46, 58, •140, •232; ill., color section
Untermeyer, Louis, 257
"Until We Build a Cabin," 235
Unwin, Nora S., 71; ill., 444
Up from Slavery, 546
Up the Hill, 63, 454-455

Valens, Evans G., 595
Vance, Marguerite, 540-541
Van Dersal, William R., 593
Van Doren, Carl, 521, 523
Van Loon, Hendrik Willem, 47, 567-568
Van Stockum, Hilda, 438
Varner, Velma, 53
Velveteen Rabbit, The, 358
"Vern," •159
Very Special House, A, 428
Village Tree, The, 500
Vipont, Elfrida, 657
"Visit from St. Nicholas, A," 44, 46, 107-108
Von Hagen, Victor, 569
Vulpes, the Red Fox, 416

"Wagtail," 402-403
Wahoo Bobcat, 409-410
Wait for William, 430
Waldeck, Theodore J., 413, 548
"Walrus and the Carpenter, The," •339-340
Walt Disney's Living Desert, 585
Ward, Lynd, 48, 67, 405-406, 481, 544; ill., 406, 481, 549
War Years, The, 145
Washington, Booker T., 546
Water-Babies, The, 45, 338
Water for America, 593
Waterless Mountain, 7, 452
Watson, Jane Werner, 315, 582
Watts, Isaac, 40, 46, 118, 138-139
Way of the Storyteller, The, •390
Webber, Irma E., 586
Weekes, Blanche, 196
"Wee Wee Man," 100, 102
Weisgard, Leonard, 69, 161, 427, 569; ill., 22; color section; 568
Welles, Winifred, 151-152, 209-210
"Well of the World's End, The," •280
Welsh Legends and Folk Tales, 262
Werner, Jane, 585
Werth, Kurt, ill., 233
What Can You Do with a Shoe?, 69
What Could You See?, 582
"What Is Black?," •161
"What Is Pink?," •174
"What Is White?," •161
"What the Good-Man Does Is Sure to Be Right!," •328
What's Inside of Me?, 588-589
What's Inside the Earth?, 592
"*What Then, Raman?,*" 505; ill., 504
Wheel on the School, The, 70, 505-506; ill., 505
Wheeler, Opal, 530
When We Were Very Young, 47, 61, 127, •129; ill., 135
When You Go to the Zoo, 587
Where Does Everyone Go?, 70, 160
"Where Go the Boats?," 142, •144
"Where's Mary?," •232
"Whippety Stourie," •279
"Whispers," •161
Whispers and Other Poems, •161
"Whistle, Whistle," •117
White, Anne H., 399
White, Anne Terry, 569, 591
White, E. B., 68, 355-356, 395
White, Robert, W., 3
White Panther, The, 413
White Snow, Bright Snow, 66, 431
Whitmore, W. H., 79
Who Built the Bridge?, 362
Who Built the Highway?, 362
Who Goes There?, 65, 403-404; ill., 404
Who Lives in This House?, 586-587
Who Rides in the Dark?, 463
Why We Live Where We Live, 568
"Wide Awake," •161
Wide Awake and Other Poems, •161; ill., 157
Wier, Ester, 446
Wiese, Kurt, 61-62, 405, 410; ill., color section; 411, 501
Wiesner, William, ill., 91
"Wife of Usher's Well, The," •101, 102
"Wife Wrapt in Wether's Skin, The," 99, •100
Wilde, Oscar, 335
Wilder, Laura Ingalls, 7, 19, 68, 484-487, 646
Wilderness Champion, 409
Will and Nicolas. *See* Lipkind, William *and* Mordvinoff, Nicolas.
Williams, Garth, 68, 90, 485; ill., color section; 395, 506, 646
Wilson, Barbara Ker, 262
Wilson, Hazel, 536-537
Wimmer, Helmut K., 594
"Wind, The," •227, 241-242
"Wind has such a rainy sound, The," •173
Wind in the Willows, The, 61, 348-351, •349-350, 399; ill., 349
Wind Song, •145
Windy Morning, •154
"Windy Nights," •143
Winged Moccasins: The Story of Sacajawea, 540
Winnie-the-Pooh, 47, 61, 358-359
Winter Danger, 483
Winterfeld, Henry, 491
Winter-Sleeping Wildlife, 587
Witch of Blackbird Pond, The, 477-478
Withers, Carl, 88
Wizard in the Well, The, •155
Wonder-Book for Girls and Boys, A, 45-46, 58
Wonder Clock, 333
Wonderful Farm, The, 69
Wonderful Winter, The, 496
Wonderful World of Archaeology, 591; ill., 591

Wonderful World of Energy, 596
Wonderful World of Mathematics, The, 584
Wonderful World of Medicine, The, 589
Wonderful World series, 583
Wonders of Seeds, The, 586
Wonders of the Human Body, 589, ill., 589
Wood, Esther, 501
Wood, Laura W., 550
Wood, Ray, 89
Wooden Locket, The, 462
Works and Days, 309
World books of Genevieve Foster, 570
World of Pooh, The, 61
"The world turns and the world changes," •207
World We Live In, The, 582
"Worm, The," •148-149
Wright, Blanche Fisher, 87; ill., 84
Wrinkle in Time, A, 346-347
"Write Me a Verse," 133
Wyeth, Newell, 61, 414; ill., color section; 413
Wyler, Rose, 568, 569, 581, 590, 594

Yashima, Taro, 71, 500-501; ill., color section; 500
Yates, Elizabeth, 444, 545
Yearling, The, 61, 413, •414; ill., 413
Yeats, William Butler, 199
"Yellow Dwarf, The," 37
"Yesterday in Oxford Street," 182
Yonie Wondernose, 63, 454; ill., color section
You, Among the Stars, 594
You Come Too, Favorite Poems for Young Readers, 188; ill., 187
Young Fu of the Upper Yangtze, 7, 62, 501-502; ill., 501
Young Lafayette, 536
"Young Lochinvar," 109
Young Walter Scott, 547-548
You Read to Me, I'll Read to You, 137
Yours Till Niagara Falls, 89

Zaffo, George, 567
Zim, Herbert S., 586, 588-589, 592
Zolotow, Charlotte, color section; 70

4 5 6 7 8 9 10 11 12 13 14 15 16 17 18 19 20 21 22 23 24 25 RM 70 69 68 67 66